PSYCHOLOGY

THIRD EDITION

Ludy T. Benjamin, Jr.
TEXAS A&M UNIVERSITY

J. Roy Hopkins
ST. MARY'S COLLEGE OF MARYLAND

Jack R. Nation
TEXAS A&M UNIVERSITY

MACMILLAN COLLEGE PUBLISHING COMPANY
New York

MAXWELL MACMILLAN CANADA
Toronto

MAXWELL MACMILLAN INTERNATIONAL
New York Oxford Singapore Sydney

Editor: Christine Cardone
Development Editor: Madalyn Stone
Production Supervisor: Katherine Evancie
Production Manager: Su Levine
Art Director: Pat Smythe
Text Designer: Pat Smythe
Cover Designer: Leslie Baker
Photo Researchers: Diane Austin and Chris Migdol
Electronic Text Management: Ben Ko and Marilyn Wilson Phelps
Illustrations prepared by Cecile Duray-Bito and Jane Lopez
Cover illustration: *La condition humaine*, by René Magritte (Belgian 1898–1967),
1933, oil on canvas; National Gallery of Art, Washington; Gift of the Collectors
Committee

This book was set in Dutch 823 by Macmillan College Publishing Company and
was printed and bound by R. R. Donnelley and Sons, Inc.
The cover was printed by Lehigh Press, Inc.

Macmillan Publishing Company
113 Sylvan Avenue, Englewood Cliffs, NJ 07632

Library of Congress Cataloging-in-Publication Data
Benjamin, Ludy T.
      Psychology / Ludy T. Benjamin, Jr., J. Roy Hopkins,
Jack R. Nation.—3rd ed.
        p. cm.
  Includes bibliographical references and indexes.
  ISBN 0-02-308290-9
  1. Psychology.   I. Hopkins, J. Roy.   II. Nation, Jack R.
III. Title.
BF121.B397 1994
150—dc20   93-5036
                                            CIP

Printing: 2 3 4   Year: 4 5 6 7

This book is dedicated to those most special to us

Priscilla, Melissa, and Melanie

Janis, Karl, Carol, John, and Keven

Patricia, Derek, Shannon, and Jamie

Preface

French novelist Anatole France has written that the art of teaching involves the awakening and subsequent satisfaction of an individual's curiosity. Our reasons for writing this textbook are closely connected to our commitment to the art of teaching. We wanted to share with others our excitement about the field of psychology. We hope this book will engage its readers in the sense of discovery and wonder that comes from an increased awareness of the world. In essence, this is a book about behavior appreciation.

Psychology deals with the total spectrum of behavior, behavior of all people and animals in our world. Thus, loving, thinking, hating, fearing, conforming, worrying, enjoying, dreaming, eating, learning, developing, creating, working, remembering, and playing are just a few of the forms of behavior that psychologists write about. In short, psychology is about people who are like us, and about people who are not like us at all.

We firmly believe that the relevance of psychology can be established with academic integrity. Throughout this book we have portrayed psychology as a field that seeks to explain behavior and the workings of mental processes.

DISTINGUISHING FEATURES

Our major goal has been to create a book that is engaging, informative, and relevant to the personal lives of students. The introductory course is often the only psychology course that college students take, and it is our hope that in this book we can bring the excitement of psychology to their world. We have worked closely with Macmillan College Publishing Company to ensure that the final product achieves these aims.

Applications

Throughout the book we have emphasized *critical thinking skills*. We pose questions for our readers. We ask them to reflect on the course content as it relates to events in their lives, and, in the *Thinking Ahead* essays at the end of most chapters, we consider the impact that developments in psychology may have on their lives in the future. There are special application sections entitled *Thinking About Psychology, Applying Psychology*, and *Spotlight on Research*. These sections bring to life some of the recent events in psychology that are relevant to people in their everyday lives. Although these sections deal with applications of psychological research, they also challenge the reader to go beyond the simple description of the phenomena and consider the implications of psychological principles in a broader context. Additional examples and applications appear throughout the book, providing lively coverage of topics that affect all of us.

Scientific Basis

The information in this book is drawn from the many books and journal articles comprising the literature of psychology. Throughout the text of each chapter are parenthetical citations. Many of these references are from the 1990s and reflect the most current findings in the literature. These references are listed in full at the end of the book. Much of this literature can be found in college or university libraries, and we encourage readers to pursue those books and articles that seem especially interesting. For those of you who wish to read further, we have also provided a *Suggested Reading* list at the end of each chapter. These lists contain sources that should be accessible to most college students, in terms of both availability and comprehensibility.

What's New in the Third Edition

Each of the chapters in the third edition has been extensively revised to reflect the most recent changes in psychology. In addition to updating the theoretical and empirical coverage of psychological research, we have added a new chapter on the changing focus of psychology. **Chapter 13, "Social Development,"** covers the effects of the social environment on human behavior across different age ranges, and in this sense we have added to our previous coverage of developmental psychology and social psychology.

The new material in other chapters is equally exciting. A partial list of new topics includes the following:

the neurochemical workings of drugs such as cocaine (Chapter 2)

the controversy of fetal tissue transplants (Chapter 2)

recent findings that result from advances in brain imaging techniques (Chapter 2)

cultural factors in pain control and experience (Chapter 3)

the role of learning in infantile autism (Chapter 6)

the molecular basis of classical conditioning (Chapter 6)

the role of memory in cross-racial identification (Chapter 7)

explicit and implicit memory (Chapter 7)

recent developments in cognitive neuroscience, including neural network models (Chapter 8)

obesity, dieting, and the role of short-term and long-term cues in eating (Chapter 9)

cross-cultural personality research (Chapter 10)

the latest in psychological testing (Chapter 11)

material on physical and cognitive development, and the relevance of this information to parenting and child growth and development (Chapter 12)

the effects of divorce on children (Chapter 13)

methods of coping across diverse cultures and ethnic groups (Chapter 15)

new sections on family and marital therapy (Chapter 17)

This is only a partial list of the many new topics that have been added to the third edition of *Psychology*. Together they present the vitality and richness of the field. We have made deliberate decisions about which topics to include, and we believe that you will find the coverage interesting, current, and accurate.

RECOGNIZING DIVERSITY

From the partial list of new materials previously cited, you will notice that there are several cases where information on cultural diversity has been added. This reflects our decision to integrate more research on ethnic and cultural differences into each chapter. In addition, new chapter-opening vignettes introduce most chapters with a cross-cultural or multicultural example of human behavior. Psychology is for all people everywhere on Earth, and the numerous references to cultural differences throughout this book make this clear.

Cultural diversity is perhaps the most rapidly expanding dimension of psychology in the 1990s. In truth, there have been investigators in this important area for many years, but it has only been in the past few years that psychologists have awakened to the significance of culturally diverse profiles. Psychologists are no longer willing to make general statements that are intended to apply to everyone. Rather, it is acknowledged that the same events may have decidedly different effects on people of different cultural and ethnic orientations.

In recognizing cultural diversity in this book, we feel that the book has been made more current and relevant to the human condition of the modern world. We hope you agree with us that through understanding comes appreciation and mutual enlightenment.

PEDAGOGICAL ELEMENTS

In addition to our applications, examples, and research citations throughout the book, we have systematically employed devices to promote and reinforce learning in every chapter. They are distinguished typographically.

Chapter Outlines. A chapter outline with major headings and subheadings appears on the first page of each chapter to help the student preview and organize what he or she is about to read. These listings also include the titles of the application sections.

Graphs, Illustrations, Tables. Graphic presentation of concepts contributes to comprehension and learning new ideas. Throughout the book we use charts, graphs, and photographs extensively. Color and descriptive captions add to the effectiveness of the illustrations. Summary tables are also included throughout the book to compare and review major concepts such as personality theories.

Key Terms. Part of learning about psychology is learning psychological terms and how these terms are used. Throughout the text, we introduce key terms in **boldface** print. At the end of each chapter, these key terms are listed for quick reference, with page numbers indicating where the term is introduced and defined. You will also find these key terms and their definitions in the margins and in the **Glossary** at the back of the book. Additional terms in the vocabulary of psychology are emphasized with *italics* in the text.

Summaries. At the end of each chapter, summaries are provided as a review of the chapter contents; they are a way to check your memory and understanding of what you have read. For easy reference these summaries are organized point by point and grouped under the major headings that appear in the chapter.

Ancillary Program

The third edition of *Psychology* is accompanied by a complete learning and teaching program to reinforce the strengths of the text. Individually as well as collectively these items help to increase the effectiveness of learning and teaching psychology.

Study Guide. A *Study Guide* to accompany this text was written by Barbara Nodine, a distinguished educator in psychology whose honors include election as President of the American Psychological Association's Division on the Teaching of Psychology. She is the co-author of a book on writing skills and a former section editor of the journal *Teaching Psychology*. The *Study Guide* she has written increases understanding of the textbook and thus improves student performance on examination material based on the textbook. The *Study Guide* contains review exercises (fill-in and matching) and practice exams (multiple choice and essay), as well as conceptual devices (diagraming, tabular, and graphing exercises) to aid comprehension of the textbook. It also contains a useful chapter on *study skills*, written by Ludy T. Benjamin, Jr., and Melissa Benjamin.

Instructor's Manual. The *Instructor's Manual* was written by George Diekhoff, whose research focuses on the cognitive dimensions of teaching and learning. Although it was written especially to assist the beginning instructor in introductory psychology, the *Instructor's Manual* contains much information that should be helpful to more experienced instructors as well. It includes a section on teaching the introductory psychology course as well as outlines, learning objectives, biographical sketches of key figures in the history of psychology, additional lecture topics, controversial issues, student misconceptions, and recommended audiovisual materials for each chapter.

Activities Handbook. Dr. Diekhoff has also compiled a separate book with an average of seven classroom demonstrations and activities for every chapter. Background information for each activity includes a statement of purpose, procedures, and results as well as materials required and references to relevant research.

Test Bank and Computerized Test Bank. An important resource for teachers of introductory psychology (especially large sections) is a reliable and expansive bank of objective test items. Michael Toglia and Melvin King, of the State University of New York at Cortland, have written a completely new *Test Bank* for the third edition of *Psychology*. It includes approximately 2,000 multiple-choice items with a mixture of factual and applied/conceptual questions. The *Test Bank* is also available on computer disk (for IBM and Macintosh computers). Instructors can choose different configurations of questions or add original questions.

Computer Simulations. David Pittenger and Jay Allen created fifteen interactive programs which simulate experiments and demonstrations that reinforce common areas taught in introductory psychology. They are available on computer disk for IBM or Macintosh computers.

Transparencies and Slides. One hundred full-color illustrations are available as overhead transparencies or slides. Some provide enlarged projections of illustrations from the text; approximately one-third of the total are original teaching transparencies or slides.

Videos and Laser Disc. To supplement lectures, videos are also available from the publisher.

Acknowledgments

One does not undertake lightly a writing project as daunting and massive as an introductory psychology textbook. This book reflects the intellectual efforts of numerous friends and colleagues.

Four of our colleagues were especially helpful in the revision of this book. James Grau made many helpful suggestions on Chapters 3 and 4; Steven Smith helped with Chapters 7 and 8, Jeff Simpson assisted with Chapter 14; and John Knight provided input on Chapter 15. Because each of these psychologists is a specialist in the area relevant to his contribution, the book has benefited substantially from their ideas and suggestions.

The book has also been improved by the efforts of many other people who offered their suggestions. Much credit is due these individuals who read parts or all of the manuscript, sometimes reading multiple drafts of the book. We gratefully acknowledge the assistance of the following individuals.

Thomas R. Alley	Clemson University
Sharon Lee Armstrong	Central College
James Baerwaldt	University of Texas at Arlington
William A. Barnard	University of Northern Colorado
Robert Batsell	Southern Methodist University
Amy D. Bertelson	Washington University in St. Louis
Deborah L. Best	Wake Forest University
James F. Calhoun	University of Georgia
Steven G. Cole	Texas Christian University
Stanley Coren	University of British Columbia
Florence L. Denmark	Pace University
Anne E. Fowler	Bryn Mawr College
Grace Galliano	Kennesaw State College
Ajaipal S. Gill	Anne Arundel Community College
Richard Gist	Johnson County Community College
William J. Gnagey	Illinois State University
Gilbert R. Gredler	University of South Carolina at Aiken
David K. Hogberg	Albion College
James J. Johnson	Illinois State University
James M. Jones	University of Delaware
Michael Kernis	University of Georgia
Harold O. Kiess	Framingham State College
Melvyn B. King	State University of New York, Cortland
Randy J. Larsen	University of Michigan
Richard Leavy	Ohio Wesleyan University
Frederick Leong	Ohio State University
Joanne Lindoerfer	Lamar University
Walter J. Lonner	Western Washington University
Benjamin Newbury	Kent State University
Nancy Eliot Parker	Embry Riddle Aeronautical University
Janet D. Proctor	Purdue University

Dennis T. Regan	Cornell University
Sherry Rise	South Suburban College
Mark P. Rittman	Baldwin Wallace College
W. Scott Terry	University of North Carolina at Charlotte
D. Rene Verry	Milliken University
Bradley Waite	Central Connecticut State University
Maxine A. Warnath	Western Oregon State College
Wilse Webb	University of Florida, Gainesville
Edmond E. Willis	Central College

This book bears the imprint of the Macmillan College Publishing Company. Since we began working on the first edition in 1983, and continuing through the third edition, we have come to know this company as much more than a corporate giant in the publishing industry. We have come to know it as a company composed of enormously talented people who pride themselves on the quality of their books. We cannot list all of the individuals who have contributed their technical expertise to the three editions of this book, but we would like to acknowledge a few of them, whose assistance was especially important. James D. Anker, a former senior editor at Macmillan, is responsible for bringing this team of authors together. He recognized in us a common philosophy in the teaching of psychology and urged us to undertake the first edition of this book.

Madalyn Stone served as the principal Development Editor on this book. Madalyn has worked closely with us in the first and third editions and has been extraordinarily helpful as we have gone through the multiple drafts that such a book demands. She has also been a colleague skilled in providing encouragement and support and gentle reminders about deadlines. We thank her for the greater clarity that has resulted from her efforts. Christine Cardone, the Executive Editor of psychology at Macmillan, has been the persistent shepherd of this project in all three editions, in the first edition as the marketing manager and in the second and third editions as editor. Her marketing and editorial insights have helped to make each edition better. We thank her for her endurance and support through this project. We also greatly appreciate the special support of Editor-in-Chief D. Anthony English, who has demonstrated an unwavering commitment to this project. Others who have worked on the book include Katherine Evancie, who coordinated its production, including its vast illustration program; Diane Austin and Chris Migdol, whose helpful suggestions and diligent searches contributed to the visual appeal of the book's photographs; and Pat Smythe, whose creative labors produced the attractive interior design as well as the cover.

Finally, we are indebted to our many students, who over the years have participated with us in the learning environment that makes the college setting such a stimulating place to spend one's life. We have learned much from them about how to teach psychology, and we are sure their collective influence is evident in the pages of this book. For us, in a very personal sense, this book is a reflection of our commitment to psychology and the importance it has for each of us.

Ludy T. Benjamin, Jr.
J. Roy Hopkins
Jack R. Nation

Author Biographies

Ludy T. Benjamin, Jr., received his PhD in experimental psychology from Texas Christian University in 1971. He has taught a class in introductory psychology every year since that time, except for a two-year period he spent in Washington, DC, as Director of the American Psychological Association's Educational Affairs Office. His interests in psychology are wide-ranging, having published articles on topics as diverse as visual perception, children's ideas about Santa Claus, the benefits of napping, and the fear of death. But most of his research has focused on the history of psychology. His thirteen books include four on the teaching of psychology, among them the *Activities Handbook for the Teaching of Psychology* (1981) and *Handbook for the Teaching of Introductory Psychology* (1985). He was a member of the faculty of Nebraska Wesleyan University before going to Washington, and is now Professor of Psychology and Director of Undergraduate Studies at Texas A&M University. Elected a Fellow of the American Psychological Association in 1981, he has also served as President of two of APA's divisions: Division on the History of Psychology and Division on the Teaching of Psychology. In 1984 he received a Distinguished Teaching Award from Texas A&M University, and in 1986 the prestigious Distinguished Teaching Award from the American Psychological Foundation.

J. Roy Hopkins received his PhD in 1974 from Harvard University, with training in developmental, social, and personality psychology. He began teaching part-time at Harvard while doing graduate work and has been teaching full-time for 20 years, first at Vassar College and now as Professor of Psychology at St. Mary's College of Maryland. He has taught introductory psychology in a variety of settings, from small honors seminars to large lecture classes. His early research focused on infant cognitive development and perception. More recently he has specialized in adolescence and early adulthood psychology and is currently studying cognitive and social development longitudinally during the college years. Professor Hopkins is the author of a number of papers on infancy and adolescence, with articles appearing in such journals as *Cognition, Child Development*, and *The Journal of Social Issues*. He has also written a successful textbook, *Adolescence: The Transitional Years*, and is currently North American book review editor for the *Journal of Adolescence*. Professor Hopkins heads the Division of Human Development at St. Mary's College of Maryland, which was the host institution for the American Psychological Association's 1991 National Conference on Enhancing Undergraduate Education in Psychology, for which he served as site coordinator.

Jack R. Nation is Professor of Psychology at Texas A&M University. He received his PhD in psychology from the University of Oklahoma in 1974. In 1987 he was invited by the People's Republic of China to give a series of lectures at Peking University. At Texas A&M University, he has taught both honors and regular classes in introductory psychology for more than a decade. In addition to the teaching of psychology, his interests are in the areas of learning, animal behavior, and neurotoxicology. He has written more than 70 papers on such varied topics as student motivation in nontraditional and introductory psychology courses, learning models of depression, goal-directed responding in humans and animals, and the behavioral effects of environmental exposure to toxic chemicals. His articles since 1990 include reports in *Behavioral Neuroscience, Neurotoxicology*, and *Alcoholism: Clinical and Experimental Research*. He is a recent recipient of a grant from the National Institute on Alcohol Abuse and Alcoholism (NIAAA), which supports his research on the effects of environmental contaminants on alcohol-related changes in behavior. In 1984 Professor Nation received a Distinguished Teaching Award from Texas A&M University.

Brief Contents

Detailed Contents

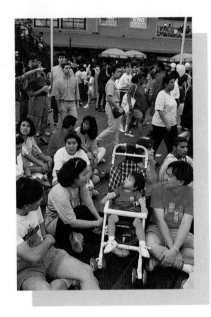

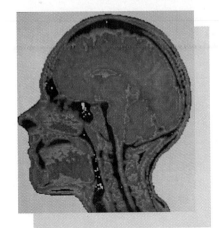

Applications

PSYCHOLOGY

CHAPTER 1
Introduction to Psychology

Psychology is an essential part of the fabric of life. The subject matter of this discipline affects your very existence more so than for virtually any other course you will take in your college career. The importance of psychological issues in your world is measured not on a daily basis, but moment to moment. Whether you are awake, asleep, active, or reflective, psychological events define the quality of your experience and the direction of your growth.

In some cases, events relevant to psychology are obvious. The devastating 1992 riots in Los Angeles sparked by police officers' treatment of Rodney King had many psychological overtones. Prejudice, intergroup conflict, aggression, fear, revenge, mistrust, and other psychological causes are clearly a part of any such hostile demonstration. But psychology involves more than high-profile displays. It is pervasive in the world about us. Randomly turn to any page of the newspaper and see if psychology is represented there in one form or another. We did just this as we began writing this book, and here are a few of the things we found. The national news from the United States reported that consumer spending dropped sharply last month, as did belief in the honesty of public officials. In other stories, a female corporate executive accused her superior of sexual harassment, and the Federal Aviation Administration agreed to review a policy that would permit airline pilots to take midflight naps.

In the local news, census figures maintained by the Chamber of Commerce indicated that the county courts had tried fewer divorce cases

◀ Some of the questions psychologists might ask after looking at this picture are: What motivated these people to gather together? How do they feel about each other? The subject of psychology relates to your life probably more than any other discipline you will study.

1

than the state average but more than the average number of civil litigation cases. Another story described an adult/student mentor program, in which members of the police force volunteer to visit elementary campuses to eat lunch and play with the children. Still another article described the effectiveness of an American Telephone & Telegraph program that permits employees to evaluate their supervisors and to let their supervisors know that praise for doing a job well done would improve productivity.

In the sports section, a college coach actually recommended that his star basketball player forego his final year of eligibility and turn pro, because flagrant fouls designed to put the individual out of the game were placing the player at risk. From the comics, we see that Snoopy is forlorn because his owner, Charlie Brown, is absent, but that this condition is easily reversed by the introduction of a bowl of food. Once again, Rodney of "The Wizard of Id" lands in the dungeon for unintentionally disclosing that he thinks the king is short, and a guilt-ridden Billy from "The Family Circus," after a talk with his father, realizes that his carelessly discarded candy wrapper can contribute to environmental decline.

In each of these newspaper pieces, we see psychology at work. Psychologists are concerned with variables that improve performance efficiency in the workplace. Whether it be supervisor attitudes or employee fatigue, the study of psychology can structure a more gratifying and successful career. Psychology is an important part of close relationships, and it surely affects the way we treat other people. In short, psychology relates to almost everything we do, think, and say. It is because of the universal presence of psychological phenomena that psychology as a topic has enjoyed such popularity. We welcome you to this most stimulating and exciting study.

WHAT IS PSYCHOLOGY?

We begin by defining psychology in terms of what it does. Then we describe the kind of education and training that psychologists receive, and illustrate psychology's diversity with some examples of the psychologists who function in different ways within our society.

A Definition of Psychology

psychology is the systematic study of behavior and mental processes. In defining psychology, we have not limited it to the study of humans; it is intended to include other animals as well as the rationale for animal study.

We define **psychology** as the systematic study of behavior and mental processes. Note that in defining psychology we have not limited psychology to the study of humans. Our definition is intended to include animals other than humans; we will discuss the rationale for animal study in a later section of this chapter.

scientific method a procedure for conducting research that states that a testable hypothesis should be verifiable and the results repeatable

Psychology's systematic approach typically means that psychological study proceeds according to the rules of science. No discipline is inherently scientific. Science refers to a specific methodology, a way of doing things. Insofar as a researcher adheres to the rules of science, that investigator's work can be labeled "scientific." For example, the **scientific method** requires that hypotheses be testable and that results be repeatable and thus verifiable by others. Science also requires considerable rigor in the precision of measurements used and in the effective control of relevant variables. We will discuss these issues in a later section of this chapter dealing with the experimental method. Psychologists make substantial use of the scientific method; many believe that it offers the best strategy for unlocking the secrets of behavior. But valuable information comes from other methods, such as the intensive study of individuals, a technique known as the *case study* method.

We have defined the subject matter of psychology as behavior and mental processes. Behavior is directly observable and includes such things as laughing, running, operating a computer, writing, and eating. But many events of interest to psychologists cannot be directly observed; for example, thinking, dreaming, and changes in physiological events such as heart rate or blood pressure. Physiological events can be studied with a variety of recording instruments, and thinking and dreaming can be studied through self-reports. Thus, in psychology, behaviors and mental processes are interwoven. To understand eating it is important to know something about hunger. Although hunger cannot be directly observed, it can be studied in terms of changes in physiological processes, such as blood sugar levels, and in terms of its manifestations in mental processes, such as the thoughts and feelings people experience when they are hungry. Similarly, to understand laughter we must know something about additional mental processes—the emotion or emotions that underlie laughter. Another way to define psychology is to describe the diversity of subfields that make up the profession of psychology.

Freda Rebelsky is a developmental psychologist at Boston University, where she teaches and conducts research. She is a recipient of the American Psychological Foundation's award for Distinguished Teaching in Psychology.

The Diversity of Psychology

If you meet a photographer, you have a good idea about what that person does for a living. The same is true for many other occupations such as nurse, accountant, farmer, and newspaper reporter. Yet the image of what a psychologist does for a living is often unclear and very often wrong. Psychologists are a diverse group who have trained in different subfields of the discipline and who are employed in a multitude of settings (see Table 1–1). For most people, the title "psychologist" evokes an image of a grave professional, pen and note pad in hand, listening to a patient reclining on a couch. For most psychologists, this image is totally inaccurate (Wood, Jones, & Benjamin, 1986). As reflected in Table 1–1, in the 1990s psychologists perform in many different settings and under different conditions. In the following paragraphs we discuss some of the major subfields that make up psychology.

Clinical Psychology. The field of **clinical psychology** represents the largest group of practitioners. Some clinical psychologists do research, and others work in university psychology departments or medical schools. Most, however, are involved in the diagnosis and treatment of psychological disorders in settings such as hospitals, community mental health centers, crisis counseling services, drug rehabilitation centers, and their own private offices. Clinical psychologists work with people with serious disorders such as schizophrenia, but they also deal with more common problems such as the anxieties associated with adjustment during adolescence. Clinical psychologists deal with the same sets of problems that psychiatrists treat. The approaches of these two professionals to treatment often differ, however, partly because of differences in their training: clinical psychologists are trained in psychology and hold a doctoral degree, typically the doctor of philosophy (PhD); psychiatrists are trained in medicine and hold a doctor of medicine (MD). As physicians, psychiatrists can prescribe medications; psychologists cannot. We discuss the work of clinical psychologists more fully in Chapters 16 and 17, which deal with psychological disorders and their treatment.

clinical psychology a field of psychology that focuses on diagnosis and treatment of psychological disorders

Counseling Psychology. Training in **counseling psychology** is rather similar to that in clinical psychology. Whereas counseling psychologists are often found in a variety of work settings such as hospitals and clinics, many work in educational settings, usually colleges or universities.

counseling psychology a field of psychology that provides services to moderately disturbed patients

TABLE 1-1
Major Fields of American Psychological Association Members in 1993

	Total			Total	
	N	**%**		**N**	**%**
N=	73,268	100	Computer science	59	.1
Provider Psychology Fields			Counseling	892	1.2
Child clinical	721	1.0	Counselor education	135	.2
Clinical	31,629	43.2	Criminolgy, criminal justice	43	.1
Counseling psychology	7,206	9.8	Economics	2	.0
Geropsychology	88	.1	Education, teaching	261	.4
Health	637	.9	Engineering	27	.0
School	2,926	4.0	Epidemiology	7	.0
Subtotal	43,205	59.0	Industrial relations	32	.0
			Information science	4	.0
Research and Other Psychology			Law	72	.1
Cognitive	451	.6	Linguistics	5	.0
Community	668	.9	Medicine	36	.0
Comparative	55	.1	Nursing	39	.1
Developmental	2,081	2.8	Organizational behavior	101	.1
Educational	1,778	2.4	Political science	6	.0
Environmental	62	.1	Psychiatry	70	.1
Experimental	1,316	1.8	Public administration	109	.1
General/methods and systems	986	1.3	Public health	40	.1
Industrial/organizational	2,806	3.8	Rehabilitation	450	.6
Neurosciences	135	.2	Social work	67	.1
Personality	437	.6	Sociology	35	.0
Physiological, psychobiology	408	.6	Statistics	41	.1
Psychopharmacology	152	.2	Student personnel	10	.0
Quantitative/mathematical, psychometrics, statistics	401	.5	Social/behavioral sciences	79	.1
			Speech and hearing	53	.1
Social	1,794	2.4	Special education	114	.2
Subtotal	13,530	18.5	Theology/religion	55	.1
			Other	5,271	7.2
Other Fields			Subtotal	8,735	11.9
Anthropology	4	.0			
Behavioral medicine	224	.3	Not specified	7,798	10.6
Business or management	323	.4			
Cognitive science	11	.0			
Communication–journalism	58	.1			

Source: 1993 APA Directory Survey. Comiled by Office of Demographic, Employment, and Educational Research, APA Education Directorate.

Although there are exceptions, most counseling psychologists work with people who exhibit moderate difficulties in their day-to-day functioning. These problems may include extreme anxiety about taking tests, the stress experienced in a broken love relationship, low morale in a job situation, or uncertainty about career choices.

School Psychology. As the title implies, **school psychology** is practiced typically in elementary or secondary schools. School psychologists are concerned with school children in terms of their intellectual, social, and emotional development. They work not only with children who have problems in these areas, but with parents and teachers as well. School psychologists may advise teachers on ways to improve class discipline or talk with parents about changes in the home environment that could help their children's performance in school. The school psychologist may test children for special programs and do research to evaluate the success of those programs. Many school psychologists are also certified as elementary or sec-

school psychology a field of psychology that provides services in a school setting

Psychology is important to all people, all over the world. Shown here is a client talking to her therapist Diana Castelliano (on right) at the Roberto Clemente Guidance Center in New York City.

ondary school teachers. School psychologists should not be confused with counselors found in most high schools. These school counselors usually have taught school for several years and possess a master's degree in counseling from an education department, rather than a psychology department.

Industrial–Organizational Psychology.   The field of **industrial–organizational psychology** focuses on issues in business and industry. "I/O psychologists" may conduct research, develop and evaluate programs, and try to improve productivity and the quality of work life. They deal with such issues as worker morale, employee–management relations, absenteeism, job boredom, and job stress. They may develop programs for selecting employees or for choosing candidates with high managerial potential, and training programs for providing workers with the skills needed by the company.

industrial–organizational psychology a field of psychology that focuses on issues in business and industry

Sports psychologists such as Dr. Richard Suinn of Colorado State University work with athletes and athletic teams to increase performance by increasing motivation and minimizing the psychological effects of injuries.

I/O psychologists are also involved in advertising and marketing strategies and studies of consumer behavior. Some are employed in the design of equipment (such as computers, automobiles, and telephones) that involves interaction between humans and machines, a subfield called *human factors psychology*. At times I/O psychologists may recommend a new organizational structure to facilitate the aims of a particular organization. The nature of this field is discussed more fully in a special appendix to this book (see Appendix B).

experimental psychology a field of psychology that typically involves laboratory research in basic areas of the discipline

Experimental Psychology. The person trained in **experimental psychology** does research primarily in a specific area such as perception, learning, memory, language, thinking, motivation, physiological psychology, or animal behavior. Typically, experimentalists do their research in a laboratory setting. They may examine how humans learn by imitation or investigate that kind of learning in various other animal species. Those interested in memory may investigate the capacity of memory and those factors that produce forgetting. Others who specialize in the relationship between the brain and behavior may do research into the control exerted by the nervous system over behaviors such as sleep, eating, and aggression. Most of these psychologists work in universities and colleges where they combine

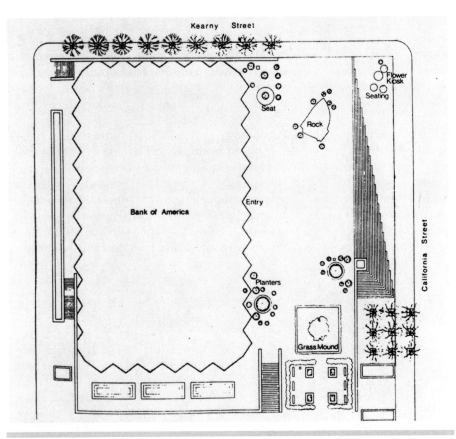

FIGURE 1-1
Environmental psychologists, who typically have training in social and industrial/organizational psychology, worked on the design of Giannini Plaza in San Francisco. The grouping of benches, the diversity of seating options, the arrangement of planters, and the location of fountains were designed to facilitate human needs such as eating, relaxing, people watching, sunbathing, and escaping from city/work life. Thus, by working with architects, psychologists can use their knowledge of human behavior to design environmental spaces that encourage desired human interactions.

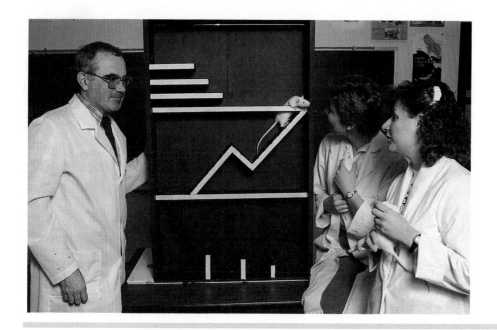

Dr. Stephen F. Davis, an experimental psychologist at Emporia State University in Kansas, demonstrates the operation of a vertical rat maze to some of his students.

their research interests with teaching. Other experimental psychologists work in settings such as industry or government. We cover the very broad area that is experimental psychology in Chapters 2 through 9.

Social Psychology.   Behavior often occurs in a social situation, which involves two or more persons. People in **social psychology**, who are also experimental psychologists, study how these social conditions affect the behavior of individuals. They investigate such matters as intergroup conflict, stereotyping, prejudice, why people generally conform and why some do not, what kinds of leadership styles are most effective in various situations, and what variables determine whether people will be attracted to one another. Like other experimental psychologists, most social psychologists are affiliated with universities and colleges, but some work in other research settings. This area of psychology is the focus of Chapters 13 and 14.

social psychology a field of psychology that is concerned with how social conditions affect the individual

Developmental Psychology.   As the name implies, workers in the field of **developmental psychology**, who are also experimental psychologists, are interested in the changes in behavior that occur as a result of developmental processes such as maturation and experience. Some developmental psychologists focus their research on infants, studying early motor and perceptual processes. Others study the opposite end of the developmental continuum— the psychology of aging. Some are interested in a particular human attribute, such as a sense of humor, and study the changes that occur in that attribute over the life span. Prominent research topics in developmental psychology include language, social skills, sexuality, intellectual abilities, emotion, and personality. This area of psychology is presented in Chapters 12 and 13.

developmental psychology a field of psychology that examines the impact of maturational processes and experience on behavior

Psychometric Psychology.   Psychologists in the area of **psychometric psychology**, often called "psychometrists," specialize in the measurement of various behaviors. They are involved in the design and construction of assessment devices, typically referred to as "psychological tests." These tests may be used to measure such things as intelligence, aptitude for a particular job, ability to handle various kinds of stress, vocational interests, and personality. Psychometrists are especially skilled in using statistical

psychometric psychology a field of psychology that specializes in the measurement of specific behaviors

Curtis Banks, shown explaining an experimental apparatus for the delivery of rewards and punishments, is Professor of Psychology at Howard University, where he conducts research on personality and social behavior. Stanley Sue is Director of the National Research Center on Asian American Mental Health located at UCLA. He is shown here lecturing at Zhongshan University in China.

procedures to develop tests that, with repeated use, produce consistent results. These assessment instruments are continually being refined to ensure that they measure what they are supposed to measure, which means that psychometrists work to improve the "validity" of tests. This topic is covered more fully in Chapter 11.

Because behavioral questions pervade most aspects of life, it is not surprising that psychologists are employed throughout the work force. They can be found working for NASA in the space program, at General Motors, at American Telephone & Telegraph, at hospitals, in museums, in rehabilitation centers, in all the military services, in schools and colleges, at all levels of government, in prisons, in law firms, and just about anywhere you look.

A BRIEF HISTORY OF PSYCHOLOGY

The subfields of psychology evolved, for the most part, after World War II. Thus, they are somewhat recent events in the history of psychology. However, many issues within these various subfields have their roots in philosophy, the discipline from which psychology emerged. Issues concerning individual differences, motivation, memory, personality, and mental illness can be traced from the ideas of Plato (c. 428–347 B.C.), who argued that human potential was determined largely at birth, to the empiricist philosophers of the eighteenth and nineteenth centuries, who stressed the importance of experience in determining a person's capability.

The Greeks and the Age of Rationalism

Plato's emphasis on individual differences is evidenced in his belief that humans differ in the powers they possess. Some, he said, are notable for their intellectual and reasoning abilities, others for their courage, and others for their motivation. Plato, who as an aristocrat devoted his life to the study of ideas, argued that reason is the highest of human powers and that individuals so possessed should be the leaders of society. On the other hand, those possessed of great courage should be called on to serve as warriors. In his

Plato, like his teacher Socrates, did not trust information gained directly from the senses because they are subject to illusions. Instead, he advocated using the powers of reason and common sense to arrive at truth, a philosophy known as *rationalism*.

version of an ideal world, which he called the Republic, individual capacities would determine the role a person plays in society. This recognition of individual differences has been at the core of psychological thinking for the past 2,000 years.

For Plato, the source of those individual differences is the human soul, whose makeup is determined at birth. Galen (c. 129–199 A.D.), a Greek physician, was also interested in the differences among humans. Borrowing from some of the work of the physician Hippocrates, Galen proposed four types of temperament that he assumed were caused by an abundance of a particular kind of bodily fluid. He decided that depressed people have too much "black bile," whereas apathetic and dull people possess too much "phlegm." These pronouncements about human behavior and ability were not the result of experimental investigations, nor were they derived by any kind of systematic observations. They were arrived at by the use of reason, logic, and common sense, a philosophical approach to knowledge known as **rationalism**.

Galen's views persisted until the sixteenth century. Although ultimately discredited, his theory is of historical importance because it illustrates a recognition of psychological differences among people, and it explains those differences in terms of natural, rather than supernatural, causes.

rationalism a philosophical approach that argues that human behavior can be best understood by the application of reason, logic, and common sense

The Renaissance and the Rise of Mechanism

The Renaissance began in Italy in the fourteenth century and spread to the rest of Europe. Lasting through the sixteenth century, it represented a revival of interest in, and new approaches to, art, literature, and knowledge, including science. It was the era of Michelangelo and da Vinci, of Shakespeare and

Chaucer, and of Copernicus and Galileo. For science the Renaissance generated alternative views to rationalism regarding the acquisition of knowledge. Gradually replacing the philosophy of Plato was a belief that knowledge should be acquired through observation and experimentation, a philosophy that marked the beginning of the scientific method. Psychology, as an experimental science, grew from both the post-Renaissance developments in philosophy and the development of physiological studies of the nervous system and sensory mechanisms (Benjamin, 1988).

mechanism a view of the world as a machine

A new world view emerged from the Renaissance, initially due to the work of Galileo (1564–1642). Galileo saw the universe as composed of matter in motion; atoms of one object would come into contact with atoms of another object, causing movement or a change in the second object. This view of the world was known as **mechanism**, and it meant that by conceiving of the universe as a giant machine, lawful explanations of the universe would be possible. According to this view, the universe, like any machine, must operate in an orderly way. Thus, its operation can be understood by discovering the laws that govern it. This order and lawfulness meant that actions in the universe could be predicted by understanding the causal relationships within the world. Such a view was a very important advance for science.

Prescientific Psychology

Because humans are part of the universe, could they also be viewed as machines? Yes, according to French philosopher and mathematician René Descartes (1596–1650), who extended the mechanistic view to human behavior. Descartes viewed both the body and part of the mind as machines, capable of interacting with—and influencing—one another. This idea, radical at the time, provided an excellent explanation for both involuntary (reflexive) and voluntary behavior. In adding human actions to the mechanistic world view, Descartes was arguing that human behavior is lawful and that its causes can be understood.

empiricism a philosophical approach that argues for study through observation

Descartes was interested in the nature of the human mind and proposed that it consisted of two kinds of ideas: *innate ideas*, such as "self" and "God," and *derived ideas*, which are acquired through experience in the world and reflection. A viewpoint that opposed Descartes' doctrine of innate ideas was emerging in Great Britain in the philosophy of **empiricism**, which held that knowledge should be acquired by careful observation. The British empiricists were a group of philosophers who spanned a period of approximately 200 years, beginning with John Locke (1632–1704). Locke rejected the notion of innate ideas and argued forcefully that all ideas are derived from experience. Resurrecting the ancient Greek philosopher Aristotle's notion of the mind as a *tabula rasa*, or "blank slate," Locke described how experience would write on this slate, filling the mind with its ideas. Thus, according to Locke and the other empiricists, all knowledge is learned. Their work involved study of the sensory mechanisms, such as the processes of vision, and the nature of associations, the building blocks of learning. Although not experimental in nature, their work dealt with many of the basic questions in human perception, learning, and thinking, questions that are very much a part of contemporary psychology and are discussed in later chapters.

Concurrent with the work in philosophy, advances in physiology unlocked some of the mysteries of brain function and the ways in which the nervous system transmits information. Researchers discovered that specific regions of the brain have particular functions. For example, French physician Paul Broca (1824–1880) used the clinical autopsy method to examine the brains of individuals who had lost the ability to speak during their lifetime. In the brains Broca found localized damage (lesions) in the area of the third convolution of the frontal lobes, an area that he believed was responsible for the production of speech. Today, neuroscientists refer to that area of the brain as Broca's area (discussed further in Chapter 2). Later in the nineteenth century, researchers demonstrated that certain motor and perceptual responses could be reliably produced from mild electrical stimulation of particular areas of animal brains.

By the latter part of the nineteenth century, the philosophical and physiological advances had progressed to the point that an experimental science of the mind was possible. Drawing on the techniques of the physiologists, scientific psychology sought to understand the processes of sensation and association, those two primary emphases of the British empiricists.

Founding of Scientific Psychology

Historians of psychology usually honor Wilhelm Wundt (1832–1920) as the founder of scientific psychology. A German, trained in physiology, Wundt wrote his first book on psychology, a treatise on sensory perception, in 1862. Yet his special significance for psychology was established 17 years later when he founded the first research laboratory in psychology at the University of Leipzig (see Figure 1–2).

Wundt realized that he was developing a new science, and he actively promoted this new field through his research and writing. His new laboratory began to attract attention in Europe and North America. Students who were interested in the questions of human behavior soon learned that a university in Germany was devoted to the experimental study of those questions. Consequently, many students, including a number from the United States and Canada, journeyed to Leipzig to train in the new field (Sokal, 1980). They returned to North America to become the shapers of psychology on this side of the Atlantic Ocean.

For Wundt, the initial goal of psychology was to understand the nature of human consciousness. Toward this end, he trained his students in the method of **introspection**, a technique of self-observation in which a person experiences something and then describes the personal nature of that experience. As used by Wundt, the technique was quite rigorous, and students were very carefully trained in the introspective method. Stimulus presentations were rigidly controlled, so that introspective accounts could

René Descartes is important to the history of psychology for many reasons. In particular, he localized the functions of the mind in the brain, whereas some earlier views had assigned certain mental processes, such as emotions, to organs like the liver and heart.

introspection a technique of self-observation

John Locke distinguished between primary and secondary sensory qualities. *Primary qualities* are sensory qualities that exist in an object, such as the thorny shape of a rose stem or the whiteness of a feather. *Secondary qualities* exist in the experiencing individual and are not part of the object itself, for example, the pain experienced from the rose thorn or the tickle from the feather. Instead, these qualities of sensory experience are a part of the individual. This distinction by Locke was especially important for the science of psychology because it recognized experience that was independent of the physical objects of the world. In essence, these secondary qualities were products of the mind, and as such were the very basis of psychological study.

FIGURE 1–2
Silver medals struck in 1979 to commemorate the 100th anniversary of the first psychology laboratory—Wilhelm Wundt's laboratory founded at the University of Leipzig, Germany, in 1879.

be compared from one experience to another. Replication of these results was an important part of Wundt's experimental methodology. These researchers reported their experiences in terms of specific sensations and feelings, which were judged to be the building blocks of consciousness. The task of Wundtian psychology was first to specify these elements of consciousness, and then to discover how they combined in more complex mental processes. This atomistic approach to the study of consciousness, which reduces consciousness to its most basic elements, was characteristic of much of Wundt's psychology.

Most of the research in Wundt's lab involved studies of sensation and perception, investigating such topics as color vision, touch, and the perception of time, although research was also done on emotion, attention, and reaction time. The purpose of the reaction time studies was to assess the speed of mental processes. For example, in a simple reaction time task, the time it took for an individual to press a button after a light appeared was measured and recorded. That task was repeated until an individual's average reaction time was established. Then the person was given a so-called choice reaction time task that required the individual to press one of two buttons that corresponded to the color of a light that appeared. Thus, if the light was green, the subject had to press the button on the left; if the light was red, the correct response was to press the button on the right. This task, which involved a more complex decision-making process, also yielded a measure of average reaction time. In the first task, the subject had only to perceive a light and then respond by pushing a button. In the second task, however, the subject had to detect the light, decide on its color, and then decide on the correct button to press. By comparing the differences in reaction time on these two tasks, Wundt believed it was possible to measure the speed of mental processes of varying complexity (see Figure 1–3).

Other psychology laboratories emerged in Germany, some started by Wundt's students and others by his contemporaries. One of this latter group was Hermann Ebbinghaus (1850–1909), whose classic studies on memory are still cited today (see Chapter 7). These other laboratories challenged Wundt's psychology, criticizing its overreliance on introspection and its insistence that consciousness could be explained by a description of its elemental parts.

A branch of German psychology that vehemently opposed Wundt's views was **Gestalt psychology**. This theoretical view of psychology originated with Max Wertheimer (1880–1943) and two colleagues, Kurt Koffka

Gestalt psychology a view of psychology that claimed that the whole is different from the sum of its parts

FIGURE 1–3
Wilhelm Wundt in 1912 at the age of 80 with some of his Leipzig colleagues and former students in a reaction time demonstration.

(1886–1941) and Wolfgang Köhler (1887–1967). These investigators disagreed with the atomistic approach and argued that aspects of consciousness exist that cannot be explained just by analyzing its elements. They claimed that the whole is different from the sum of its parts. For example, a melody played at opposite ends of a piano keyboard is still clearly recognized as the same melody, even though the actual elements (the sound frequencies) are completely different in the two versions. Thus, there are qualitative aspects of consciousness that transcend the combination of its elemental components.

Gestalt psychology reached considerable prominence in Germany by the 1920s and made substantial contributions to psychology in the areas of perception and learning. When the Nazis came to power in Germany in the mid-1930s, most of the Gestalt psychologists emigrated to the United States. Their ideas influenced the development of psychology in America, but Gestalt psychology never became part of the mainstream. Some of the Gestaltists' work is now being rediscovered because it relates to the cognitive approach to psychology, one of the important approaches in contemporary psychology, as we discuss throughout this book.

Beginnings of American Psychology

The atomistic portion of Wundt's psychology was best represented in America by his British student E. B. Titchener (1867–1927), who came to Cornell University in Ithaca, New York, in 1893. Titchener's psychology became known as **structuralism** because—like Wundt's—it emphasized studying the elemental structures of consciousness. Whereas Wundt sought to explain consciousness by invoking hypothetical mental processes, Titchener sought to avoid mentalism by focusing his efforts on a purely descriptive science. His books on experimental psychology (Titchener, 1901–1905) were very influential in the training of an entire generation of the "new" psychologists in America.

Other Americans had trained with Wundt but were not as committed to the structural view or the method of introspection. Many of these American psychologists were influenced by ideas from England, most notably by the work of Charles Darwin (1809–1882). American psychologists found Darwin's research on variation (individual differences) within

structuralism a psychological approach that emphasized studying the elemental structures of consciousness

species of special interest. His theory of evolution linked humans with the rest of the animal kingdom, a fact that was crucial to the beginning of the field of comparative psychology. If humans and other animals shared a common ancestry, then one could study the behavior of animals in an effort to understand human behavior. (We have more to say about that a little later.) Yet Darwin's most important contribution to American psychology was his emphasis on evolution, especially in terms of the selection of those characteristics that were of greatest adaptive value. Psychologists reasoned that consciousness must have adaptive significance as well.

James and Functionalism.   Influenced by Darwin, many American psychologists turned from the structure of consciousness to its functions; that is, how it aids the organism. One American psychologist who believed in the adaptive significance of consciousness was William James (1842–1910). James was greatly influenced by the theories of Charles Darwin, and he believed that mental processes had evolved like other processes. For James, the goal of psychology was to understand the role consciousness played in helping the organism adapt to its environment. James's ideas are presented in a two-volume work entitled *The Principles of Psychology* (1890), a book that required 12 years to write. This work is recognized as one of the most important in the history of psychology (Evans, 1981). Its clarity of expression, elegance of style, and promise of psychology's potential attracted many students to this new field. James's emphasis on the functions of consciousness, as opposed to its structure, led to the founding of a new system of psychology known as **functionalism**, a largely American system of psychology. This viewpoint fostered a great deal of applied work, as psychology sought to use its new knowledge to address concerns in education, business, and other matters of everyday life.

Watson and Behaviorism.   A third variety of psychology soon emerged that took issue with both structuralism and functionalism. Known as **behaviorism**, this system of psychology was revolutionary in that it called for vast changes in the content of psychological studies as well as in the acceptable methodologies. The leader of this movement was John B. Watson (1878–1958), who described his view of psychology in a 1913 article entitled "Psychology as the Behaviorist Views It." He wrote, "I do not wish unduly to criticize psychology. It has failed signally, I believe, during the fifty-odd years of its existence as an experimental discipline to make its place in the world as an undisputed natural science. . . . The time seems to have come when psychology must discard all reference to consciousness; when it need no longer delude itself into thinking that it is making mental states the object of observation" (pp. 158–159).

Watson believed that psychology's embrace of science had been half-hearted, and he called for radical changes within the discipline. In his view, psychology should become the study of behavior, not consciousness. Because the latter was not directly observable, it was difficult to measure, and Watson felt that it had no place in the domain of science. Thus, he viewed both structuralism and functionalism as failures. Behavior, on the other hand, represented those actions that were subject to direct observation. The task of psychology was to discover the causes of behavior, accomplished by investigating the lawful relations connecting stimuli with responses (the term "S–R psychology" is sometimes used to denote this position).

Watson minimized the role of heredity in human behavior, arguing that behavior is determined principally by experiences within the environment. As an ardent environmentalist, he denied the existence of instincts or inherited traits. This view led him to propose that a person's achieve-

functionalism an approach to studying psychology that emphasized the functions of consciousness

behaviorism an approach to studying psychology that argued that actual behavior was the only event worthy of analysis

ments are limited only by the restrictions that the environment places on the person's ability. He saw in psychology a means to better the human condition in particular and society in general. These views made him quite popular with the American public of the 1920s.

Watson's objective, scientific psychology, did not permit use of a method so imprecise as introspection. Instead, he wanted psychology to rely on such techniques as

1. Experimental observation, using instruments that increased the precision of observations
2. Objective testing, using test results as sample behaviors
3. The conditioned reflex method, a technique developed by the Russian physiologist Ivan Pavlov (see Chapter 6).

The introduction of these ideas caused quite a stir in the psychological community. Acceptance of Watson's behaviorism meant abandoning much of what was sacred to structuralism and functionalism, such as studies of emotion and thinking. But many younger psychologists and students of psychology were enthusiastic about this new approach; they agreed with Watson that it was necessary if psychology ever hoped to discover the laws governing behavior.

Eventually the various systems of psychology disappeared, and behaviorism—actually, several varieties of behaviorism—emerged as the dominant theme in American psychology. Other European influences also had an impact on the development of American psychology, such as Sigmund Freud's psychoanalytic theory (see Chapter 10). However, these alternate views of psychology did not enjoy the dominance of behaviorism. Behaviorism has enjoyed supremacy among American psychological views, although since the 1960s its position has been challenged by cognitive psychology. In this next section we describe the nature of behaviorism, cognitive psychology, and other major approaches in contemporary psychology.

CONTEMPORARY APPROACHES TO PSYCHOLOGY

At the beginning of this chapter we defined the subject matter of psychology as behavior and mental processes. Contemporary psychologists differ in their emphases; some focus on overt behaviors, others stress knowledge of mental processes. Further, the methods they use in their investigations and the explanations they give for what they discover differ markedly. We will briefly define six approaches that dominate contemporary psychology.

The Behaviorist Approach

We have already discussed behaviorism; in its contemporary form it resembles quite closely the principles John Watson first described more than 80 years ago. Adherents to the **behaviorist approach** emphasize the importance of environmental determinants in shaping behavior. They do not deny the role of heredity, but they argue that whereas one cannot do much about manipulating heredity, the environment can be altered to change behavior. They emphasize the study of learning and the conditions that govern whether learning will occur. Changing environments by changing stimuli or the consequences that follow behavior can profoundly change an organism's behavior.

The functionalism of William James (*top*) and the behaviorism of John B. Watson were two of the early systems of American psychology.

behaviorist approach an orientation in psychology that emphasizes the importance of environmental determinants of behavior

Behaviorists stress the importance of dealing with behaviors that are directly observable. They argue that behavior can be completely explained by understanding the effects of the presence or absence of external stimuli. In other words, external events dictate the occurrence of behavior. The most prominent advocates of this approach in modern psychology have been the followers of B. F. Skinner (1904–1990), who stress that behavior is determined by its consequences. That is, responding is *determined* by what events follow a particular response. Skinner's views are discussed in detail in Chapter 6.

The Biological Approach

biological approach an approach to understanding psychology in terms of physiological and molecular mechanisms

Some psychologists seek to understand overt behavior by describing it in terms of its underlying neurological, biochemical, and neuromuscular causes. This **biological approach** is reductionistic in the sense that it reduces explanations of observable behaviors to physiological responses. For example, destroying a small segment of the hypothalamus leads rats to increase their food intake and become fat. Destroying tissue in another area of the hypothalamus causes animals to stop eating. Other brain lesions produce animals that mate, will not mate, sleep, cross their eyes, behave docilely, behave aggressively, and so forth. Electrical stimulation of the human brain produces a variety of effects, including motor behaviors, memories, sights, and sounds. Injecting female sex hormones into male rats induces them to build nests. Injecting chemicals into the brain also produces a wide array of behavioral changes.

Obviously, the nervous system, the endocrine glands, and the body's musculature have a lot to do with behavior. But do these events tell the whole story of behavior? To ask the question a different way, is behavior totally determined by biological processes? If the answer is yes, then psychology is not really a separate field; instead, it represents a different level of physiology. At the moment, our state of knowledge does not permit us to answer this question. Perhaps in the future, all behaviors, including your reason for taking a course in psychology and your choice of a particular college, will be interpretable in terms of physiological events. We do not believe that to be the case, but some psychologists do. Understanding of these underlying events increases almost daily, due to the rapid technological advances in this area. The bulk of this physiological knowledge is discussed in Chapters 2 and 3; however, you will note its presence in all chapters of this book.

The Cognitive Approach

cognitive approach an approach to studying psychology that emphasizes mental processes

As a major force in psychology, the **cognitive approach** is relatively recent, yet it has ties to earlier periods of psychology, including the work of William James, E. B. Titchener, and Gestalt psychology. The cognitive psychologist is interested in concepts such as consciousness, feeling, image, and meaning, which, under the domination of behaviorism, had not received much study.

The cognitive approach has been bolstered in recent years by several factors. One has been a realization that behavioristic accounts have had trouble explaining some aspects of human behavior. Cognitive psychologists are studying the mental processes that intervene between stimulus inputs and response outputs, and they believe that an understanding of these processes is necessary to provide a complete picture of behavior.

Second, cognitive psychologists have improved our methods of studying mental processes; their techniques are more scientific than those used earlier. These methods are discussed in Chapter 7 on memory and in Chapter 8 on language and thought, areas in which the cognitive approach has made significant contributions. Cognitive views have also been applied to the understanding of psychological disorders and to their treatment, and these contributions are also discussed in later chapters.

One result of the influence of the cognitive approach is the study of varieties of consciousness and a recognition of the differences in levels of awareness. Consciousness has returned as a concept in contemporary psychology, and Chapter 5 discusses the recent research on this topic. Chapters on states of consciousness are commonplace in present-day introductory psychology books, whereas 20 years ago they did not exist.

The Psychoanalytic Approach

As mentioned briefly before, the **psychoanalytic approach** comes from the writings of Sigmund Freud (1856–1939) and his followers. Freud, trained as a physician, developed a therapeutic procedure for use with people who were mentally ill and a theory to explain behavior, including the causes of mental illness.

Freud viewed unconscious processes as being the primary determinants of human behavior. According to his position, humans are born with instincts for personal gratification that may be contrary to the mores of society. Society seeks to suppress these innate tendencies, and part of the individual's normal development means successful mastery of these impulses. Yet these suppressed impulses can be powerful influences on behavior; they can cause people to speak or act without being aware of the real causes of their actions. According to Freud, these suppressed impulses can be expressed through everyday behavior as well as by dreams and mental illness.

Freud's views emerged about the same time that behaviorism was dominating the scene in American psychology, and a psychology dominated by behaviorism was quite opposed to the psychoanalytic approach. Two factors that worked against the widespread acceptance of psychoanalytic theory by American psychology were (*a*) the fact that Freud's theory was based on case histories rather than on experimental evidence and (*b*) the fact that many aspects of Freud's theory could not be tested by the methods of science.

Still, Freud's views have influenced American psychology, for example, in recognizing the importance of early experience as a determinant of later behavior patterns and in discovering such coping processes as rationalization and repression. These concepts and others derived from psychoanalytic theory are discussed in Chapters 10 and 17.

The Humanistic Approach

The cognitive approach was not the only viewpoint of psychology to develop in the 1960s. Another approach was taking shape under the influence of Carl Rogers (1902–1987) and Abraham Maslow (1908–1970), who opposed the dominant views guiding research, explanation, and treatment in psychology. Both behaviorism and psychoanalysis had proposed that human behavior is determined; according to the former, by environmental conditions including rewards and punishers, and to the latter, by unconscious processes. The **humanistic approach** opposed determinism, arguing instead that human behavior is largely the result of free will. This viewpoint opposed the rat psychology of the behaviorists, claiming too much of human psychology had been derived inappropriately from the study of non-

psychoanalytic approach a view of human behavior that focuses on the unconscious mind as a determinant of responding; began with Sigmund Freud

humanistic approach an approach to understanding human behavior that emphasizes free will and the basic goodness of people

human animals. And they railed against the pessimistic view of human nature offered by the psychoanalysts, arguing instead for the basic goodness of human beings and their innate motivations to achieve their full potential.

Although this approach has made important contributions to the study of personality and psychological treatments, it has provided very little to the science of psychology. It has offered valid critiques of some methods in psychological science but has not developed alternative methods of its own. Its impact on psychology is discussed more fully in Chapters 10 and 17.

The Multicultural Approach

multicultural approach the study of psychological phenomena across diverse cultures, populations, and groups

The **multicultural approach** in psychology refers not to a particular theoretical persuasion or view on the determinants of behavior, but rather to the study of psychology within the context of cultural diversity. Multicultural studies have been conducted for many years, but only in recent years has interest in the topic spread throughout the discipline.

Included as topics in this area are such traditional cross-cultural issues as child rearing that are examined by researchers across several distinctive cultures. However, other concerns are the effects of societal prejudice on gay and lesbian populations, the plight of the disabled, and the stereotyping of ethnic groups (Bronstein & Quina, 1991). Multicultural studies are relevant throughout psychology, as this book illustrates. Race, gender, and cultural heritage are as much a part of modern psychology as any other influential variable. Indeed, at several points in our coverage we will show that such factors are the dominant forces in behavior.

RESEARCH METHODS IN PSYCHOLOGY

hypothesis a clearly stated, testable idea about how something works or why it happens

Research usually begins with a **hypothesis**, an idea about how something works or why things happen the way they do. In science, a hypothesis must be clearly stated; it must be testable. Such notions are the starting point for scientific research. The assertions that one hears in ordinary conversation can provide sources for hypotheses. For example, people frequently assert the following: athletics builds character; exposure to pornography leads to sex crimes; listening to music while studying interferes with learning; changing answers on an exam usually results in a wrong answer; kids today are more knowledgeable (or less so) than earlier generations because of exposure to television; and alcohol interferes with judgment. All of these statements imply cause and effect relationships; that is, they say that one event is caused by another. These statements may or may not be accurate. Merely saying something is so does not make it so, no matter how much such statements seem in agreement with common sense. For the scientist, hearsay evidence and common sense are not sufficient justification. Instead, the scientist seeks to test such assertions by forming them into testable hypotheses and then using appropriate research methods to gather evidence that supports or refutes the hypotheses.

theory an organized framework that guides research and permits certain predictions to be made

Scientific **theory** is an important source for hypotheses. A theory in science is constructed to explain a set of facts that were previously unrelated. For example, Darwin's theory of evolution was developed to explain the myriad observations he made about variation in animal species. As explanatory devices, theories also allow predictions to be made about the relationships among certain variables. These predictions can be stated in the form of testable hypotheses that can be the basis for an experiment. Thus, the role of theory in science is not only to offer explanation but also to guide future research. The knowledge gained from testing hypotheses generated by a theory will cause the theory to be accepted or discarded. Throughout this book—for example, see the chapters on learning, motivation, and personality—you will see evidence of the importance of theory, both as an explanatory device and as a tool for guiding new research.

The Nature of Proof

In testing a hypothesis, it is possible to find not only evidence that is consistent with the hypothesis but also evidence that disproves the hypothesis; however, it is not possible to prove a hypothesis. Proof exists only in formal systems such as mathematics and logic, but it does not exist in the other sciences. Even when the results of 20 or more experiments support a particular hypothesis, that hypothesis is not *proven*. The following exercise should help to explain this concept.

Consider the following sequence of three numbers:

$$2 \quad 4 \quad 6$$

We have generated these numbers according to a particular rule that we have in mind. However, you do not know what that rule is. Your job is to discover the rule, and you can try to do that by generating other sets of three numbers. In each case we will tell you if your numbers are consistent with our rule.

Perhaps you began with the hypothesis that the rule is "any set of numbers that increases by 2." So you generate the numbers 8, 10, and 12, and are told that your numbers do fit the rule. You decide to try 12, 14, and 16, and again you are told that the numbers are okay. Encouraged, you try 18, 20, and 22, and are told those numbers also fit the rule. At this point, you may assume that your hypothesis is correct; in fact, you have not established that. To do so, you need to generate a set of numbers that does *not* increase by 2. So, suppose you propose 8, 14, and 24; you are told that those numbers are consistent with the rule. Now you know that the rule does not require that the numbers increase by 2; you have disproved that hypothesis.

Perhaps the rule is that all the numbers have to be even numbers; to test this new hypothesis, you propose 3, 5, and 11. Once again you are told that the sequence of numbers is consistent with the rule. Now you have disproved your hypothesis about a requirement for even numbers. Maybe the rule is that the numbers have to be either all odd or all even, so you try 1, 6, and 8, which has one odd and two even numbers. That hypothesis is disproved when you are told that those numbers are also consistent with the rule. So you generate another hypothesis: it does not matter whether the numbers are odd or even, and the size of the interval between the numbers is not important; what is important is that the numbers have to be in an ascending series. To test this hypothesis you propose 33, 15, and 4, and are told that this set of numbers is not consistent with the rule. Have you discovered the rule? That is, have you proved your hypothesis? The answer is no. You can never say for certain just what the rule is, unless we tell you the rule. But you can prove what the rule is not. Such is the nature of scientific inquiry. The scientist proposes a hypothesis and then seeks to collect evidence that will disprove the hypothesis. In the case of behavioral science, by showing what is *not* the cause, we get closer and closer to knowing what *is* the cause.

Returning to our rule for the numbers, you could continue to test your hypothesis about ascending numbers with another set of numbers such as 15, 11, and 4. Our response to that set would be yes, because our rule was that any set of numbers was acceptable as long as no number exceeded 25.

Dr. Patricia Cowings (facing the camera) is an experimental psychologist working at NASA's Ames Laboratory in California. She is shown with a subject who is strapped into a machine that produces motion similar to that which astronauts experience during their space flights. Dr. Cowings has trained a number of shuttle astronauts to use biofeedback (see Chapter 15) to minimize or prevent the occurrence of motion sickness.

Even if you guessed the correct rule, you could never be certain that you were right because you would never be sure that you had tested all of the possible alternative rules (Wason & Johnson-Laird, 1972).

The Experiment

Of the scientific methods available in psychology, the **experiment** is the most popular and the most useful. The reason for this is that the experiment is the only scientific method that allows the researcher to draw definite conclusions about cause and effect. Because of that, it is the most powerful of many research methods.

In an experiment, the experimenter manipulates a certain variable (the **independent variable**) to determine its effect (if any) on another variable (the **dependent variable**). Recall the statement made earlier about alcohol affecting judgment. In an experiment, the experimenter might manipulate the level of alcohol in a number of subjects, to determine the drug's effects on judgment. The alcohol would be the independent variable, whereas the dependent variable would be some measure of judgment. In this case, it would be hypothesized that changes in judgment are dependent on varying amounts of alcohol consumption; thus the names of the variables.

To begin our experiment, we need a testable hypothesis in which the crucial terms are well defined: "Blood alcohol levels exceeding .10% will produce lowered performance on a managerial decision test." Here we have defined precisely what we mean by alcohol consumption, and we have selected a measure, the decision test, for use as our dependent variable.

In conducting this experiment, we could manipulate our independent variable by simply giving three alcoholic drinks to each of our subjects. The problem with this procedure is that people vary in terms of how their bodies metabolize alcohol, and they also vary in terms of tolerance to the

experiment a research procedure in which variables are systematically manipulated in an effort to determine their importance for the phenomena under investigation

independent variable a variable that the experimenter manipulates or changes

dependent variable a variable that the experimenter actually measures or records for later analysis

drug (based, in part, on experience). Thus, giving each of several people the same number of drinks produces subjects with varying degrees of intoxication. This extraneous variability destroys the power of the study, so efforts must be taken to eliminate it. Having subjects drink until they reach the desired blood alcohol level gets rid of that unwanted variability.

Control Groups in Experimentation. Usually one can choose from a number of possible experimental designs. One way to pursue our hypothesis about the effect of blood alcohol level on performance would be to select a group of 50 subjects and randomly assign 25 of them to one group and the other 25 to a second group. One group, the **experimental group**, would be required to drink until they had a .10% level of alcohol in their bloodstream. The other group, referred to as the **control group**, would not drink anything. The control group serves two purposes: it provides a basis for the comparison of results with the experimental group, and it offers a means of eliminating alternative explanations (hypotheses) of the results. If we conducted the study as described and found that the subjects in the experimental group performed more poorly on the managerial decision test than did the control group, what would we know? We might assume that our hypothesis was correct, that alcohol impairs judgment. But perhaps what we showed was that increased bladder pressure affected judgment. Although not likely, such an explanation could account for the results. The case could also be made that subjects in the experimental group knew they were drinking alcohol, and that they were expected to perform more poorly on the test, and proceeded to act in accordance with those expectations.

One way to counteract these alternative hypotheses is to add several other control groups to the study or change the existing control group. If a second control group drank a nonalcoholic liquid, of the same quantity as the alcohol consumed by the experimental group, and if the taste qualities of both drinks were disguised in such a way that neither group knew what they were drinking, then the two alternative hypotheses we have mentioned could be rejected. When subjects are given a substance that is not supposed to affect them physiologically, it is called a **placebo** control. Most studies using drugs require such a control group. Table 1–2 shows the experimental designs just described.

When subjects in various groups are not aware of the groups to which they are assigned, a **single blind** control technique is being used. If an experimenter's knowledge of a subject's group assignment might bias the

experimental group the group in the experiment in which the independent variable is changed to see what effect a new value will have

control group a group in the experiment in which the independent variable is neutral or unchanged

placebo a control technique in which an inactive substance is administered to the subjects in the group

single blind a control method in which group membership is unknown to the subject

---

TABLE 1-2
Two Experimental Designs for Studying the
Effects of Alcohol on Task Performance

Experimental Design 1

Group Designation	Condition
Experimental group	Drinks alcohol
Control group	Drinks nothing

Experimental Design 2 (with Placebo)

Group Designation	Condition
Experimental group	Drinks alcohol
Placebo control group	Drinks nonalcoholic drink
Control group	Drinks nothing

double blind a control method in which group membership is unknown to the subject and the experimenter

results of the experiment, the study should be conducted in such a way that the experimenter does not have that information. In experiments where both the experimenter and the subjects are unaware of subjects' group assignments, a **double blind** control technique is being used. Our proposed study on alcohol and judgment could benefit from a double blind control technique. It would mean that subjects' expectations about what they were drinking would be minimized, and that the experimenter would not bias, even inadvertently, the assessment of the subjects' performance on the decision task.

Using Subjects as Their Own Control Group. Another way to conduct this experiment is to use only one group of subjects. We could test the subjects on half of the managerial decision test when they were totally sober, and test them on the other half of the decision test when they had attained the required blood alcohol level. In this case, the subjects would serve as their own controls. Even so, some of the same problems discussed previously would have to be solved. We could test all the subjects when they were sober in a placebo control on one day, and then test them again on the second day after they had consumed the requisite amount of alcohol. However, a problem with that design is that by the second day of the study, the subjects would have some experience with the managerial decision test and might do better because of the practice they have had on the test. One way to deal with that problem is to split the group so that half of them take the test sober and later under the influence of alcohol, while the other half take it in reverse order (see this design in Table 1–3). This kind of control technique, called **counterbalancing**, is important to use when the experimenter feels that the order of conditions may bias the results. Counterbalancing is typically used in experiments in which two or more conditions or treatments are administered to the same group of subjects. Like all control procedures, it is employed to eliminate alternative explanations, in this case, the effects of different orders.

counterbalancing a procedure that is used to take out the bias that results from test position in the testing sequence

Control of Confounding Variables. By now you may have realized that control is the hallmark of good science. If an experimenter does not use adequate controls, the results are open to many different interpretations. In any experiment, a number of variables must be considered as possible influences on the dependent variable. Variables that could possibly influence the experiment are called **confounding variables**, and they must be controlled. The only variation an experimenter wants to introduce into an experiment is that produced by the independent variable. Other confounding variables must be controlled. Possible confounding variables might be subjects' sex, age, educational level, athletic ability, religious persuasion, number of siblings, eating habits, musical tastes, and so forth. If one or more of these variables is likely to affect the study, and if the experimenter does not want

confounding variables variables not being directly considered that may affect the results of an experiment and must be controlled

TABLE 1-3
A Counterbalanced Experimental Design
in Which Subjects Serve as Their Own Controls

Experimental Design 3 (with Counterbalancing)		
Group	First Day	Second Day
Group 1	Drinks alcohol	Drinks nonalcoholic drink
Group 2	Drinks nonalcoholic drink	Drinks alcohol

that to happen, one of two procedures can be followed: (*a*) one can eliminate the variable in the study, or (*b*) one can see that the groups in the study are matched in terms of the variable of concern. For example, in the experiment using alcohol as an independent variable, experience with drinking alcoholic beverages is a variable that could easily affect the results of the experiment. The experimenter could select only those subjects who had never drunk alcoholic beverages (eliminating that confounding variable), or assign subjects to the various groups in the experiment so that the average drinking experience was comparable across all groups (control through **group matching**). Then if group differences occur on the dependent variable, the experimenter could make a stronger case for that result being due to the independent variable.

Another way to have the confounding variables evenly distributed across groups, assuming the groups are not too small, is to randomly assign subjects to groups. This procedure is known as **randomization**. For example, if an experimenter planned to use 100 people in a two-group design, one way to assign the subjects to groups is to write the 100 names on slips of paper and then draw them out of a hat one at a time, assigning the first name selected to Group 1, the second name to Group 2, and so forth. Such a procedure tends to minimize the preexperimental differences that might exist between the two groups if some other assignment procedure were used. Consider a situation in which an experimenter invites 100 subjects to appear at a particular place and time for testing. When the first 50 people appear, they are assigned to Group 1; the next 50 are assigned to Group 2. Such a procedure can cause problems. These first 50 people may differ from the second 50 in some important ways: they may tend to be prompt; they may be more affluent, because they live in the high-priced neighborhood near the psychology lab; they may be less interested in sports, inasmuch as the other 50 people were late because they were watching a football game; and so forth. If an experimental design uses different groups, then it is important that the groups not differ on variables other than the independent variable. Use of randomization can usually eliminate that problem.

Sampling for Experiments. Besides control, there are other important issues to consider in designing a good experiment. One immediate concern is the **sample**, the group of subjects selected for the experiment. For many studies, experimenters seek out subjects with certain characteristics. In a study of language learning ability, the experimenter might want to use only those subjects who do not know a second language. In selecting a sample it is important to get an appropriate set of subjects. That decision is dictated partly by what the experimenter wants to investigate in the study, and partly by how the results are to be used. If one purpose of the study is to generalize the findings to a larger population, the sample used must be representative of that population. An experiment on humor using children as the subjects is not likely to be generalizable to adults. Doing an experiment with subjects selected from rural South Carolina can provide some interesting results about rural South Carolinians, but it may not be appropriate to generalize those findings to rural people in other states or even to people from urban areas of South Carolina. This raises an issue about the relevance of many psychological experiments for different cultural groups. Most experiments have used white college students as subjects. Are the findings generalizable to Africans, Asians, the elderly, and other populations? We really cannot say until we collect the data and determine the extent of overlap across diverse groups. We will discuss sampling issues again in Appendix A.

group matching purposely arranging or creating two or more groups that have the same characteristics

randomization a procedure in which every subject is randomly assigned to a particular group

sample a subset of subjects drawn from a larger population

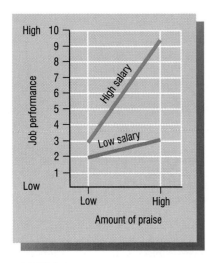

FIGURE 1–4
The figure illustrates an interaction effect of two independent variables: level of salary and amount of praise.

interaction the combined effect of two or more independent variables on a dependent variable

inferential statistics testing for differences in samples (groups) using tests that determine if a difference is real or due to chance

ex post facto method when subject characteristics are used to determine group assignment, based on preexisting conditions

Interaction Effects.   Behaviors are rarely the result of a single cause, and psychological studies recognize that reality. Consequently, experiments are designed using multiple independent variables and multiple dependent variables. Complex statistical procedures allow the researcher to separate the variables in these studies so that cause and effect relationships can be discovered. Such designs have the added advantage that they permit the study of the **interaction** of independent variables, showing how their combined influence affects a particular dependent variable.

As an example of an interaction effect, consider a study of job performance based on various work incentives. One part of the study might look at the effects of salary on job performance; another might investigate how that performance is affected by the amount of praise workers receive. A third portion of the study might combine both independent variables, salary and praise, looking at how the two together affect job performance. Figure 1–4 provides some hypothetical data from such a study. Note that when salary is low, job performance is relatively low, whether the worker receives a little or a lot of praise. But when the salary level is high, praise has a big effect, greatly increasing job performance. This interaction effect is produced by the joint action of the two independent variables and cannot be predicted from studies looking at each of the independent variables separately.

Regardless of the number of variables, experiments are designed to show differences, either between or among groups of subjects, or within the same subjects when they are exposed to different conditions. When differences occur, how does the experimenter know if the difference is a real one, and not just due to some chance variation? Such a determination is crucial in science. Suppose the alcohol group averaged 75% on the managerial decision test, whereas the nonalcohol control group averaged 80%. Is the difference in performance between those two groups significant? That question, which is ultimately the most important in any experiment, is a statistical question and can be answered only by using a test involving **inferential statistics**. These tests tell the experimenter how likely it is that such a difference could have occurred by chance. Only when the difference is statistically significant do we accept the results as indicating a real difference. In psychology, the consensus procedure is that a difference must be likely to occur by chance fewer than 5 times in 100 if the difference is to be considered significant. Inferential statistics, as well as other statistical techniques important in behavioral science, are explained in Appendix A in this book.

The Ex Post Facto Method

Some very interesting questions in psychology cannot be answered using the experimental method. Sometimes this situation is due to ethical concerns, other times to the artificiality of experimental studies. One solution to these difficulties is to use the **ex post facto method**, which selects subjects on the basis of a preexisting set of conditions. In this kind of study, the independent variables have already been manipulated by nature or some other force beyond the experimenter's control.

Suppose a psychologist was interested in how various home environments affect the personality development of children, for example, homes with two parents versus homes with one parent. In an experiment, a psychologist could find 50 couples with newborn babies. Twenty-five couples would be allowed to remain together, while the other 25 would be required to divorce. Years later, the children from the two groups could be given personality tests and the results compared. Obviously, because of ethical concerns, no one is going to do such a study. But the question can be pursued by finding and comparing children who have been raised in those two kinds of home environments. In this case, the experimenter is selecting the subjects according to a variable that has already been manipulated, then testing them on the dependent variable; this is an example of the ex post facto (literally, "after the fact") method.

Because the "independent" variable in an ex post facto study has already been determined and is not actually manipulated by the experimenter, it is not a true independent variable. Consequently, it is not possible to claim cause and effect relationships from the results of these experiments. Still, they offer the only research alternatives in certain situations, and their outcomes, although not conclusive in causal terms, are often suggestive.

Naturalistic Observation

We have devoted considerable attention to the experimental method because of its explanatory power; however, there are a number of other useful methods that we wish to describe briefly. In **naturalistic observation**, the researcher attempts to observe behavior in its natural setting, but without altering or interfering with the behavior of the subjects being studied. Of course, most organisms, whether they are pigeons or people, do behave differently when they are aware of being observed. So researchers in this situation must take steps to eliminate this problem. For example, someone studying play behavior in preschool children might seek concealment behind a one-way mirror. Or, an observer of chimpanzees in the wild might spend sufficient time with the chimps so that they would become accustomed to the observer's presence. This is what Jane Goodall does in her studies of chimpanzees in the Gombe Stream National Park in Tanzania, Africa (Goodall, 1971).

In using the naturalistic observation method, you do not have the control that you would have in an experiment, but you can gain insights from these studies that you could not possibly achieve in an experimental situa-

naturalistic observation when behavior is observed in a natural setting, as opposed to a laboratory environment

The one-way mirror can be used in research or in the training of psychologists. Here a psychologist observes, through the mirror, a psychological testing session in progress.

unobtrusive measures measures that are taken without the knowledge or awareness of the subject

tion. And often the naturalistic studies provide observations of behavior that lead to experimentally testable hypotheses. Thus, the two methods are complementary in the science of psychology.

One of the techniques of naturalistic observation is the collection of data by **unobtrusive measures**, meaning measures that can be taken without the cooperation (and knowledge) of the subject and without interfering with the behavior being studied. For example, one way to discover the relative popularity of various exhibits in museums is to observe whether the floor is worn around them. Using this method, the Museum of Science and Industry in Chicago discovered its most popular display was its hatching chicks, because the floor tiles in front of that exhibit had to be replaced every 6 weeks due to excessive wear. Such information can help museums in planning other displays and in enhancing access to the more popular ones. Another example involves an automobile dealer's desire to know the most popular radio stations. To discover what they were, the dealer had his mechanics record the position of the radio dial on all cars they serviced. Then he used that information to focus his radio advertising (Webb et al., 1966). The advantages of such methods should be obvious. Use of unobtrusive measures does not bother those being observed, and the data collected are based on what people do, rather than on what they say they do.

The Correlation Method

correlation a statistical technique that establishes the extent to which two variables vary together

Some psychological topics, such as violence, racial prejudice, and child abuse, are difficult to investigate using any of the methods we have discussed thus far. It would not be ethical to select randomly two groups of children and instruct the parents of one of those groups to engage in daily abuse of their children. Further, assuming an agency has ascertained that certain children are abused, those children obviously are not going to remain in that setting so that a psychologist can observe that abuse. How, then, can child abuse be studied? There are several ways, including the method of **correlation**. Correlation is actually a statistical technique that measures the strength of a relationship between two variables, that is, the degree to which they covary.

Using correlation requires that both variables be quantified, so that scores on one variable can be statistically compared with scores on another variable. In using correlation to learn about child abuse, a psychologist might select several variables to study, such as the employment history or educational level of the abusing parent. Agencies, through case records, often have data of that nature that can help clarify some of the variables associated with abused children or abusing parents.

One study of child abuse using the correlation method found that abused children tended to have lower intelligence quotients (IQs) than nonabused children (Reidy et al., 1980). What interpretation can you make of these data? Does child abuse cause lower intelligence, or are children with lower IQs more likely to be abused? Actually, correlational findings do not allow either conclusion, because merely establishing a relationship between two variables does not mean that the relationship is a causal one. It may be that either of the interpretations just offered is correct, but the experimental method would have to be used to show that one variable caused another. Correlation tells us when two variables are related and how much they are related, but it does not, by itself, establish cause and effect. For example, there is a correlation between getting married and having children. It is easy to see that these variables are related, but the relationship is not a causal one. Getting married does not cause a person to have a child, nor does having a child necessarily cause someone to get married. Although correlations do not establish causation, neither do they deny it. Correlation is simply neutral with respect to the issue of causation.

Although correlation cannot be used to establish cause and effect relationships, discovering relationships between variables can guide research by pointing to probable causes, which can be transformed into testable hypotheses. Further, correlations allow psychologists to make predictions. If the relationship between two variables is known, then knowing the value of one variable allows the prediction (within limits) of the other variable. For a more complete discussion of the correlation method, see Appendix A.

The Survey Method

Surveys exist in a variety of forms. Some are short, some long, some written, some oral, some structured, and some unstructured. The **survey method** includes questionnaires, interviews, and opinion polls. Whatever the form, surveys are intended to measure people's attitudes, opinions, emotions, motives, and actions. Because the responses to surveys are necessarily a person's self-report, some care must be taken in interpreting survey results. Survey respondents sometimes answer questions the way they think the questioner desires, or in such a way as to make themselves appear in a favorable light. The concept underlying this latter response tendency is known as *social desirability*.

Other concerns in survey research center around the sample. One such concern is the *response rate*. For example, suppose a university polls all of its 36,000 students in a questionnaire asking about the adequacy of the university library. A total of 275 students reply; 231 of those say they think the library is adequate, but the other 44 respondents say it is inadequate. What can be said about such a survey? Because the response rate is less than 1% of the student body, it is best not to draw any conclusions—except that for some reasons, more than 99% of the student body did not reply. When questionnaires are returned (for example, in a mail survey), it is often safe to assume that there are some significant differences of opinion between those who responded and those who did not. For that reason, the best survey techniques are those that select an appropriate group and then obtain responses from a random sample of that group. A small return rate virtually assures that the sample is *not* random (see Figure 1–5).

Survey results are reported to the public daily in newspaper stories, political newsletters, and television advertisements. Because these surveys differ markedly in their degree of sophistication, it is to your benefit to recognize surveys that have questionable findings due to some methodological errors. When survey techniques are used appropriately, they can provide a wealth of useful and interesting information. We can learn what school teachers think are the most serious problems in education today, and how their views compare with parents' views. We can learn about the frequency of napping behavior in college students, and about the content of their dreams. In short, survey methods are useful tools in psychological research.

PSYCHOLOGICAL RESEARCH WITH ANIMALS

Earlier we indicated that psychology involves the study of both humans and animals. When people think of psychology, they typically think of it only in human terms, and most of the research in psychology does involve humans. According to the American Psychological Association (APA), ani-

survey method a method of collecting data that includes questionnaires, interviews, and opinion polls

FIGURE 1–5
Currently, surveys on television invite viewers to register their opinions on a particular issue by typically calling one of two telephone numbers. Such surveys are scientifically worthless. Even if the survey question was phrased well, which it usually is not, the lack of a random sample and the absence of any information about the nature of the return rate make the results uninterpretable. Scientific surveys are carried out with considerable rigor and precision. Consumers need to distinguish between surveys that have validity and those that do not.

mals are used in only about 7% to 8% of the current experiments in psychology. Of the more than 73,000 psychologists who are members of the APA only a small percentage are involved in animal research. Some investigators use primates, such as chimpanzees or monkeys, but more than 90% of the animals are rodents or birds, typically rats, mice, gerbils, and pigeons that are specifically bred for laboratory research (APA, 1993). Despite their small numbers, these animal researchers have made important contributions to the field of psychology, many of which have resulted in improvements for human life (Miller, 1985).

The APA has strict ethical guidelines for the conduct of animal research, and APA members are sworn to adhere to those standards in their research. Serious sanctions can be imposed on researchers who violate that ethical code. Although pain and stress are used in some animal studies, the actual number of such studies is relatively small.

Why Psychologists Study Animal Behavior

Psychologists study animals for many reasons. First, psychologists are interested in their behavior. Thus, a psychologist might study the learning capacity of a cockroach, the mating habits of a fly, or the social structure of a colony of baboons. The purpose of these studies need be no more than the advancement of knowledge or the satisfaction of curiosity about animal behavior. Sometimes this knowledge can be put to some practical use; consider, for example, the case of the screw worm fly. The female screw worm fly lays her eggs in open sores on cattle. The eggs hatch and the larva feed off the host animals, making the animal sick and sometimes killing it. This particular pest caused trouble in the cattle industry in the American Southwest for a number of years. Then someone discovered a possible solution. Behavioral research on the fly had found that females mate only once in their lives. Using that knowledge, scientists created a vast number of sterile male screw worm flies, which they released in areas of heavy infestation. The procedure worked, and the screw worm fly problem has been substantially reduced (Baumhover, 1966).

Dr. Terry Maple, a comparative psychologist, is currently the head of the Atlanta Zoo. He is pictured here (on left) with Heini Hediger, who was one of the first people to study animal behavior and to apply it to the care and management of captive animals.

Basic Research.   Research that is undertaken to add to the storehouse of knowledge and that has no immediate application is usually called **basic research**. Such research is vital to the progress of science and technology. A good example is the laser, which was developed as a result of basic research. At the time of its discovery, it is likely that no one realized the immense benefits the laser would have. A great deal of behavioral research with animals has had immediate application, for example, in agriculture, zoos, forest management, and medicine (Miller, 1985). However, such applications are not required as justification for the conduct of research. For some researchers, merely understanding how a fly is capable of landing on a ceiling (Dethier, 1962) or how a bee is able to communicate to other bees about a newly discovered source of nectar (von Frisch, 1962) or how gorilla infants learn from their elders (Fossey, 1979) is reason and reward enough.

basic research research for which the findings have no apparent or immediate application

Using Animals to Understand Human Behavior.   Psychologists also study animals such as rats or pigeons in order to improve their understanding of human behavior. But if they are interested in human behavior, why do they use animals? One reason is that these lower animals are less complex than people. Certain systems in these animals are quite similar to those in humans, but the added complexity in a human system may make it difficult to discover the way it works. Knowledge derived from animal studies of systems such as perception and learning is then applied to human research. In essence, this animal research has pointed the way for human studies by helping psychologists know where to look for the answers to their questions (APA, 1993).

Animals are also used because of their accelerated life span. Studying aging effects in people can be impractical, because a study might require 70 to 80 years. Similar studies can be conducted in animals whose life spans are much shorter. For example, rats live about 2 years, reaching adulthood at about 4 months old. The female rat is in estrus (sexually receptive) every 4 days. After conception, the gestation period is about 21 days. You can see the advantages from a research point of view of using such an animal. With rats, it is possible to study a number of successive generations in a relatively short time span. As an illustration of the kinds of research questions pursued, consider the effects of crowding on behavior and how physiological and psychological changes might occur over generations as a result of crowding. With humans, that kind of research is virtually impossible. Rats, however, can be placed in a precisely controlled, crowded environment, and their behavior (and physiology) can be studied through several generations. Under such conditions, a psychologist can investigate the parental care of young, the frequency of mating behavior, feeding patterns, displays of aggression, blood pressure, activity levels, learning ability, and so forth. Such findings may provide useful clues to the effects of crowding on human behavior and an understanding of what humans might do to minimize the negative effects of living in a crowded environment.

Animals are also used in psychological experiments when the risks for humans are too great. Consider the work of psychologist James Devine of the University of Texas at El Paso. Devine is interested in the problem of memory loss as a function of age, particularly the problems elderly people have in remembering recent events. Devine is experimenting with several drugs that appear to reduce these memory deficits, but at this stage his work involves only elderly monkeys. At some point these drugs may be tried on people. Such psychological research with animals has contributed to the rehabilitation of persons recovering from strokes; aided in learning communication with severely retarded children; helped in the treatment of alcoholism and drug addiction; developed procedures to reduce blood pressure and the risk of heart attack; and led to the development of instructional programs in industry and education (APA, 1993).

Finally, psychologists experiment on animals because they can maintain greater precision. In using animals, it is possible to control the confounding variables, such as the animal's diet, day–night cycle, and experience with other animals. Such control in experimentation is extremely important, as you have seen in the previous sections of this chapter. With humans that kind of control is simply not possible.

EVALUATING PSYCHOLOGICAL RESEARCH

We have reviewed many of the techniques that are designed to render reliable, robust, and most important, believable findings. With this arsenal available to psychology investigators, it would seem scientific data could be collected and presented in such a fashion that controversy could be avoided, or at least minimized. But, as with research in the rest of the scientific community, this is not the case for psychological research. Media accounts of sensational issues such as eyewitness credibility or a legal defense based on an instance of multiple personality are all too familiar. The more basic (and sometimes less publicized) scientific findings, however, are also questioned, such as the debate over statistics reported for low-level lead toxicity in young children (Needleman, 1992) or the role of genetics in the determination of sexual orientation (LeVay, 1992). What is a person to believe? How is an unsophisticated reader of psychological research supposed to evaluate a study when specialists in the area seemingly cannot even agree?

There are no clear guidelines for determining what to believe. However, a few recommendations about trusting a scientific report have been made (Cohen, 1992). We offer this amended list only as a general framework for evaluating the trustworthiness of psychological findings:

1. Were people studied, or only animals? We have noted that animal research is invaluable. But sometimes events that hold for animals fail to translate to humans.
2. How good are the numbers? Generally speaking, the more subjects used in a study, the more authoritative its findings will be.
3. Who paid? When a pharmaceutical research branch of a drug corporation confirms the effectiveness of a diet product that promises to make the corporation millions, be careful. This is not to say that the information is fraudulent, but corroboration from independent laboratories is a good idea.
4. How were the subjects chosen? Some studies may be marred by volunteer subjects who have a vested interest in the success of the project.
5. What do the bulk of the reports say? Except in rare cases, findings from different laboratories will vary to some extent. But some findings will overlap from study to study and it is a relatively safe bet that these results are genuine.
6. Is it an isolated finding? If strong assertions are being made on the basis of a single study, accept the information cautiously and await further evidence.
7. Is it a finding relevant to all cultural groups? Do the results hold for diverse populations?

Sensible approaches to deciphering research findings in any area are essential, because they help us better understand the meaning and relevance of the data. For psychological research, this orientation is especially important because the subject matter pertains to so much of our daily lives.

ETHICAL ISSUES IN RESEARCH

Research in psychology involves living creatures who think and feel. Using people and other animals as subjects in psychological experiments requires that basic rights be respected. To ensure that psychological research is conducted in ways that respect those rights, a number of safeguards have been instituted at various levels. For example, most research in psychology is conducted on university campuses, often using students. Psychology departments typically have a review panel to screen all proposals for research using human and animal subjects. These proposals must conform to the APA Ethics Code (1993) and to the standards of other agencies who have published guidelines for the proper conduct of such research. Other agencies that fund human and animal research, such as the National Science Foundation (NSF) and the National Institute of Mental Health (NIMH), have their own review panels and ethical guidelines, all based on federal guidelines issued by the U.S. Department of Health and Human Services.

Issues of Risk

In research with people, the guidelines require that the subject not be put at risk, physically or psychologically, except in circumstances in which there is no other way to conduct the research and when the results of the research offer a promise of advancement of knowledge that can justify the risk. There is great controversy surrounding the issue of risk, yet very few psychological studies impose such a risk. Approval for such studies is extremely difficult to achieve. When they are approved, the risks must be completely explained to prospective subjects who must then sign a consent form. Obviously, there can be no coercion to recruit subjects for such studies. Even when people have signed agreements to participate in a study, they can choose to withdraw from it at any time.

The Right to Privacy

Other issues involve a subject's right to privacy, so studies are conducted in a way that ensures confidentiality. Individuals' names are omitted from the data of these studies, and in most cases, data are reported in group form rather than as responses from individuals. If there is no need to know a person's name, the participant may be anonymous. Experimenters often work with data sheets using coded numbers so that it is difficult to identify a particular subject.

Deception

Another concern in research is the issue of deception. In some studies, it is not possible to tell the whole truth about the study. To do so would likely bias the subjects and destroy the integrity of the study, making it difficult, if not impossible, to interpret the results. For example, in an experiment to investigate how people deal with perceived failure, the subjects might be given a problem that cannot be solved but be told that most people solve the problem in 5 minutes or less. Deception can involve risk, usually to a person's self-esteem, and because of that, studies using deception are carefully scrutinized under the same guidelines as other studies that impose potential risks to subjects.

Debriefing

debriefing following a study, participants are informed about the nature and purpose of the research

One requirement of all psychological research with people is that subjects should be fully informed about the nature and purposes of the research immediately following participation or as soon as possible thereafter. Psychologists call this phase of the study **debriefing**, and it is an important step. Subjects should be told about the purpose of the research, the hypotheses being tested, the nature of the results or anticipated results, and the implications of those results for the science of psychology. This debriefing serves a valuable educational function for the subjects and answers important questions they may have about their participation.

Rights and Responsibilities of the Research Participant

To this point we have mostly described ethical issues in research with human subjects in terms of the responsibilities of the researcher, largely borrowed from the APA guidelines. But some alternative views are more subject oriented than researcher oriented. Whereas the APA guidelines consider deception an acceptable practice in research, as we described earlier, some psychologists argue that deception is never justified because it does not allow informed consent (see Korn, 1987). Students in introductory psychology classes are often used as research participants and need to be aware of both their rights and their responsibilities in that regard. A list of those, written by James Korn, a psychologist at Saint Louis University, appears in Table 1–4. Korn (1988) has based his list on the ethical principle of autonomy, the notion that research participants should make their own decisions about benefit or harm.

Issues in Animal Research

In animal research, the concern focuses on the care of the animals and the risks imposed on them. The guidelines specify the proper care and maintenance of animals, including the adequacy of space requirements, maintenance of good health, and supervision by qualified personnel. Researchers are required to make every effort to minimize the pain and discomfort of animal subjects and to seek alternative methods for their research, if possible.

Animal care guidelines exist to establish minimally acceptable standards for the treatment of animal subjects in experiments. Unfortunately, some researchers regularly violate the ethical principles of animal research, despite the efforts of funding agencies, universities, and research labs to eliminate these transgressions. Those individuals are guilty of unethical, if not unlawful, practices. Such violators should be identified and punished for their disregard of professional standards for the conduct of good research.

In recent years, increased public awareness of abuses in animal research has caused greater compliance with ethical standards in this work. Still, problems exist. Isolated animals may become depressed; some are confined in small cages that allow very limited movement, and some have no

TABLE 1-4
Rights and Responsibilities of Research Participants

Rights

1. Participants should know the general purpose of the study and what they will be expected to do. Beyond this, they should be told everything a reasonable person would want to know in order to decide whether to participate.

2. Participants have the right to withdraw from a study at any time after beginning participation in the research. A participant who chooses to withdraw has the right to receive whatever benefits were promised.

3. Participants should expect to receive benefits from participation which outweigh the costs or risks involved. To achieve the educational benefit, participants have the right to ask questions and to receive clear, honest answers. When participants do not receive what was promised, they have the right to remove their data from the study.

4. Participants have the right to expect that anything done or said during their participation in a study will remain anonymous and confidential, unless they specifically agree to give up this right.

5. Participants have the right to decline to participate in any study and may not be coerced into research. When learning about research is a course requirement, an equivalent alternative to participation should be available.

6. Participants have a right to know when they have been deceived in a study and why the deception was used. If the deception seems unreasonable, participants have the right to withhold their data.

7. When any of these rights are violated or participants object to anything about a study, they have the right and the responsibility to inform the appropriate university officials, including the chairpersons of the psychology department and the institutional review board.

Responsibilities

1. Participants have the responsibility to listen carefully to the investigator and ask questions in order to understand the research.

2. Participants have the responsibility to be on time for the research appointment.

3. Participants should take the research seriously and cooperate with the investigator.

4. When the study has been completed, participants share the responsibility for understanding what happened.

5. Participants have the responsibility for honoring an investigator's request that they not discuss the study with anyone else who might be a participant.

Source: From Korn, 1988.

stimulation (see Goodall, 1987). Researchers defend these practices as necessary for proper control in their experiments, and that position is often defensible. However, an alternate view argues that treatment that produces physical or psychological harm to animals is never justified. An extreme view is that *no* animal research is ever justified, regardless of the potential human benefits that might be derived from that research. Those views are also quite defensible. Investigations of methods of care and experimentation in animal research laboratories show that the majority of animal researchers recognize their subjects as feeling creatures and treat them accordingly. Sometimes that fact is overlooked because of the negative publicity that surrounds the violators.

Whether one is talking about animals or humans, research ethics are a part of good science, and researchers must attend to good ethical practices in the same way that they attend to good methodological practices.

OVERVIEW OF THE BOOK

In this opening chapter, we have provided a definition of psychology, described its major subfields, presented a brief history of psychology, discussed its principal contemporary approaches, discussed its research methods, detailed the rationale for conducting animal research, provided guidelines for evaluating psychological research reports, and discussed ethical procedures in psychological research. In so doing, we have attempted to prepare you for the comprehensive coverage that is to follow. The breadth of psychology presents a challenge to the new reader, but the relevance of the content makes it a worthy study.

The coverage in introductory psychology texts is constrained to some extent by subject areas, classical experiments, and so on. But books do differ in organization and style. Our focus will be on the scientific rather than artistic nature of psychological phenomena. Collectively speaking, after more than a half-century of teaching the introductory course, we have selected an organizational approach that should make this initial encounter with the study of psychology a positive one. We begin our coverage in Chapter 2 with the biological bases of behavior, focusing on the nervous system and endocrine function. Chapters 3 and 4 describe the sensory mechanisms and the higher-order processes of perception. Because all behavior to some degree depends on biology and perception, it would seem logical to start with this information.

Chapter 5 treats the various states of consciousness, with an emphasis on sleep and dreaming, activities that are closely tied to physiological regulation. Chapters 6, 7, and 8 are concerned with learning—how learned material is remembered and how learned information is used in higher-order processes such as language, thinking, and problem solving.

Chapters 9 through 11 are concerned with the reasons for responding and the product of behavior. Chapter 9 addresses the mechanisms underlying motivation and emotion, and in this sense tells us about the purpose and direction of behavior. Chapter 10 on personality surveys classical and recent models of individual behavior, and explores the impact of many psychological factors discussed earlier in the text. Chapter 11 describes the procedures and tests involved in the assessment of personality and intelligence.

Chapters 12 and 13 deal with developmental issues as they relate to individual and group processes. Chapter 12 covers the topic of human development, examining both physical and cognitive dimensions of growth and maturation. Chapter 13 looks at parallel phenomena in terms of social development.

Chapter 14 provides more detailed coverage of social behavior, and examines the interactive relation between the individual and the social environment.

Finally, the last section of the book emphasizes the health service areas of psychology. Chapter 15 deals with health psychology, including the impact of stress and the ways people cope with it in modern society. Chapter 16 offers a careful review of the many categories of psychological disorders, and Chapter 17 tells us how disorders may be treated.

The book also has three appendices. The first appendix discusses statistical techniques that are commonly used by psychologists as they conduct their research. A second appendix on industrial–organizational psychology provides coverage of psychology in the workplace. The third appendix is included to help students learn about resources in psychology that can be used when writing research papers.

Applications: A World View

As the geopolitical mosaic changes, and as nationalities assume more interdependent economic and cultural postures, global awareness becomes even more essential. It is in this spirit that we introduce most chapters with a multicultural illustration of how psychology touches all people everywhere. These vignettes, and others placed throughout the text, are intended to enhance appreciation of how psychology is applied in the real world.

The book uses many other examples to bring psychology to life. Applied sections dealing with issues relevant to each of us appear in every chapter, and when a topic has gained a special status because of controversy, potential impact, or interest, that topic is distinguished by special treatment. In almost all cases, the applications draw on basic research, and it is this balance that we hope to convey in this text.

Thinking About Psychology

A careful and deliberate study of any discipline necessarily requires the assimilation of basic facts. It is impossible to grapple with loftier issues if the fundamental scholastic structure is incomplete or otherwise compromised. But once the key concepts are firmly in place, we can advance only by considering alternatives; otherwise, our study will reduce to a simple restatement of existing ideas.

It is in this context that we ask that you spend some time thinking critically about selected topics or issues. Our invitation for further reflection and analysis is presented in several ways. Throughout the book we raise questions about the subject matter that are provocative, and in many instances these questions do not have clear-cut answers. It is an immensely enriching experience to think through these issues on your own, and we hope that you will accept the challenge of critical thinking. We have also included some special features that focus on research and applications of psychology. These features are referred to as "Spotlight on Research" and "Applying Psychology" and appear throughout the text.

Another vehicle for engaging in more in-depth thought about psychology is the "Thinking Ahead" section that closes each chapter. These sections are designed to stimulate imaginative applications of the chapter content in novel ways. What lies before us? Where do we go from here? We hope that the awesome potential of psychology will recruit you to follow this fascinating study for a lifetime.

Summary

What Is Psychology?

1. Psychology is defined as the systematic study of behavior and mental processes.
2. Psychology is made up of a number of subfields, including clinical, counseling, school, industrial–organizational, experimental, social, developmental, and psychometric psychology.

A Brief History of Psychology

3. Psychological questions date to the time of ancient Greece, but scientific psychology began to emerge after the Renaissance with the development of the philosophies of mechanism and empiricism, and the discoveries related to the physiology of the nervous system.
4. Wilhelm Wundt is credited with founding scientific psychology in 1879 when he began a research laboratory in Leipzig. Wundt's psychology involved an elemental analysis of consciousness, focusing on sensations, feelings, and images. His chief research method was introspection.
5. The first American system of psychology was known as functionalism and was influenced heavily by William James, who was interested in the functions of consciousness rather than its structure. In 1913, John Watson initiated a radical new system of psychology that he labeled "behaviorism." It called for an end to mentalistic terms in psychology, such as "consciousness," and a strict adherence to objective methods of study.

Contemporary Approaches to Psychology

6. The behaviorist approach has dominated psychology for the past 70 years and has only recently been challenged by an alternative view, the cognitive approach, which stresses the study of mental processes through scientific methods. Four other approaches in contemporary psychology are the biological approach, which emphasizes the biological and biochemical bases of behavior; the psychoanalytic approach, which stresses the role of unconscious processes in behavior; the humanistic approach, which views human behavior as the result of free will and an innate striving to achieve one's full potential; and the multicultural approach, which examines psychological processes across diverse populations.

Research Methods in Psychology

7. Research begins with a hypothesis, a prediction about the way things happen and why they happen that way. Proof does not exist in science, except in math and logic. In testing hypotheses, the strategy followed in all sciences is to try to gather evidence in an attempt to disprove the hypothesis.
8. The preferred research method in psychology is the experiment because it is the one method that can determine cause and effect relationships. In this method, the experimenter manipulates one variable (the independent variable), and studies how that variable affects some other variable (the dependent variable).
9. Control groups are used in experiments to eliminate alternative hypotheses that might be used to explain the results. When drugs are used as an independent variable in a study, a placebo control group is usually necessary. Other control techniques include single blind and double blind experiments, counterbalancing, group matching, and randomization.
10. Psychologists recognize that behavior is the result of multiple causes, so experiments often involve the simultaneous investigation of a number of dependent and independent variables. Whether differences are significant or not is a determination made by inferential statistics.
11. In the ex post facto method, subjects are selected on the basis of a preexisting set of conditions. The "independent" variables have already been manipulated by some force other than the experimenter.
12. In naturalistic observation, behaviors are observed in their natural setting with attempts made not to interfere with the behavior.
13. The correlation method is used to investigate the relationship between two variables.
14. Another popular research method in psychology is the survey method.

Psychological Research with Animals

15. Psychologists study the behavior of animals for a variety of practical reasons. In some cases they are interested in the behavior of nonhuman animals; in other cases they seek to generalize the results to human behavior.

Evaluating Psychological Research

16. Several guidelines are provided for evaluating the meaning of experimental findings. Some results may be relevant only to specific populations.

Ethical Issues in Research

17. Ethical considerations are an important part of any research project, with humans or animals.

Key Terms

psychology (2)
scientific method (2)
clinical psychology (3)
counseling psychology (3)
school psychology (4)
industrial–organizational psychology (5)
experimental psychology (6)
social psychology (7)
developmental psychology (7)
psychometric psychology (7)
rationalism (9)

mechanism (10)
empiricism (10)
introspection (11)
Gestalt psychology (12)
structuralism (13)
functionalism (14)
behaviorism (14)
behaviorist approach (15)
biological approach (16)
cognitive approach (16)
psychoanalytic approach (17)
humanistic approach (17)

multicultural approach (18)
hypothesis (18)
theory (18)
experiment (20)
independent variable (20)
dependent variable (20)
experimental group (21)
control group (21)
placebo (21)
single blind (21)
double blind (22)
counterbalancing (22)

confounding variables (22)
group matching (23)
randomization (23)
sample (23)
interaction (24)
inferential statistics (24)
ex post facto method (24)
naturalistic observation (25)
unobtrusive measures (26)
correlation (26)
survey method (27)
basic research (29)
debriefing (32)

Suggested Reading

American Psychological Association. (1986). *Careers in psychology*. Washington, DC: American Psychological Association. A booklet available free upon request from the APA (750 First St., N.E., Washington, DC 20002–4242). It describes a number of careers in psychology in teaching, research, professional practice, and public service.

Danziger, K. (1990). *Constructing the subject: Historical origins of psychological research*. New York: Cambridge University Press. This in-depth look at the development of psychological research from the beginning of the nineteenth century to present time provides a comprehensive account of the social and scientific factors that have contributed to the experimental approach in psychology. Excellent discussion of the evolution of "laboratory psychology."

Dethier, V. G. (1962). *To know a fly*. San Francisco: Holden-Day. A 119-page book that is perhaps the most delightful and insightful account of behavioral science ever written. We warn you in advance that many readers become so captivated with its message that they change their career goals to pursue a life of science.

Schultz, D., & Schultz, S. E. (1992). *A history of modern psychology* (5th ed.). Fort Worth, TX: Harcourt Brace Jovanovich. A history of psychology from approximately 1850. The major systems of American psychology (e.g., functionalism, behaviorism) receive the bulk of the coverage.

Woods, P. (Ed.). (1986). *Is the psychology major for you*? Washington, DC: American Psychological Association. A collection of articles related to employment with a bachelor's degree in psychology.

CHAPTER 2
Biological Bases of Behavior

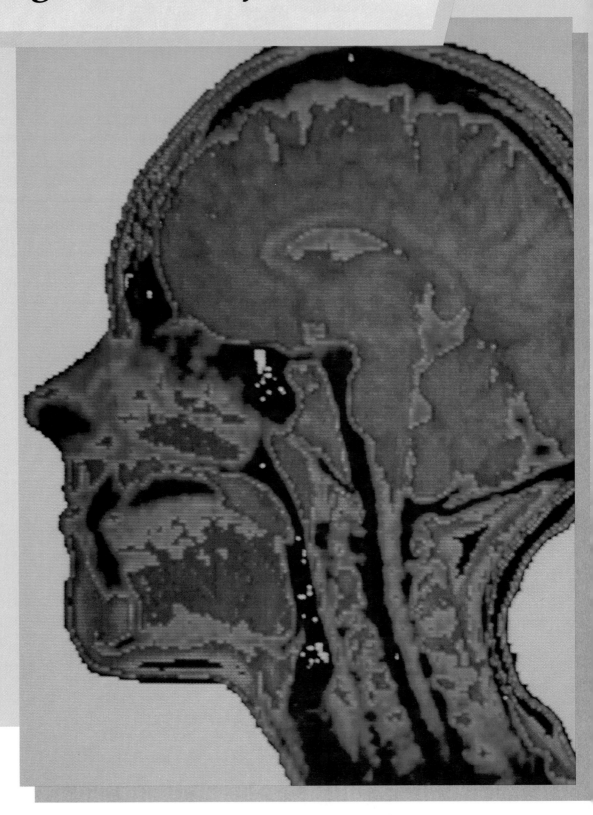

As a participant in the study abroad program at her university, Kitra Krystinik was given an opportunity to study for a semester at Fudan University in the People's Republic of China. The intelligence of the Chinese students and faculty was apparent from the beginning, and Kitra found the discussion of the ancient technique of acupuncture fascinating.

"With the insertion of the acupuncture needle into selected body locations, mechanical stimulation causes the release of naturally occurring opiates called endorphins," remarked Kitra's Chinese lecturer. "We know that the opiate pathways are responsible for acupuncture effects because when we block these pathways with a chemical known as naloxone, acupuncture treatments do not work. That is, when the activity of the body's endorphins is chemically restricted, acupuncture procedures do not decrease pain."

As this discussion continued, foreign and native Chinese students alike talked about how scientific explanations had begun to replace a more traditional, cultural perspective on the workings of acupuncture. Everyone agreed that sometimes even the most mysterious of events can be reduced to basic biological changes.

Although the unknown is appealing, discovering underlying causes for events such as acupuncture that previously have eluded explanation is equally intriguing. Discovery is the byword of the rapidly expanding discipline of **neuroscience,** which is concerned with the workings of the nervous system. Each day witnesses the identification of new chemicals and structures in the brain and spinal cord that are linked to human behavior. As we increase our understanding of the anatomical components of the nervous system (structure) and the manner by which these components alter our responses (function), we sharpen our ability to predict and control the events that define our existence.

neuroscience scientific study of the nervous system

◀ Techniques such as magnetic resonance imaging (MRI) have aided psychologists in their study of the biological bases of behavior.

THE NERVOUS SYSTEM: STRUCTURE AND FUNCTION

The nervous system is part of the body that carries messages from one location to another. It is a complex network of billions of **neurons**, or individual nerve cells, that communicate either directly or indirectly to produce integrated response patterns. The nervous system is like a complex telephone system in which the installer forgot to connect all the phones with each other. Some calls can be made locally and some by long distance, but others simply will not get through. When this happens, signals must be passed along alternate routes until the information reaches the proper destination. It is the neural chain that determines precisely which route the signal will follow in the nervous system. And it is the neural chain that is of particular interest for psychology, for it constitutes the most elementary behavioral system.

The Neural Network: The Wiring of the Nervous System

The neural chain of events that is set in motion by an environmental stimulus makes up an arc that ends in some form of response (see Figure 2–1). Specialized cells, called **receptors**, are activated when a sufficiently intense stimulus is present in the environment. Subsequently, the receptors send a signal to the brain or spinal cord along **afferent**, or sensory, neurons. Information arriving at the brain or spinal cord from afferent neurons is then transmitted by way of *interneurons* that carry the signal to other interneurons or to efferent neurons. **Efferent**, or motor, neurons send the signal away from the brain and spinal cord to **effectors**, which respond to produce changes in either the internal or the external environment. Effectors are either glands (secretory cells) or muscles.

The neural chain is now complete. Environmental energy stimulates the receptors, and in turn afferent and efferent neurons interact to provoke specific behavioral reactions. When you step on a tack, for instance, pain receptors react by firing signals along afferent neurons to connecting interneurons. At this point other interneurons are excited, and eventually your misfortune is registered in higher brain areas—so you won't forget! At the same time, still other interneurons stimulate efferent fibers, forming a reflex arc that engages the appropriate muscle groups (effectors) and thereby prompting you to lift your foot off the tack. What appears to be a gross bodily reaction, then, may be viewed at a more molecular level as a series of simpler changes. The wiring of this intricate network that controls our behavior is, unfortunately, not always well understood. What is known is that the nervous system is made up of cells of particular sizes and shapes, with specific structural characteristics. Let's take a closer look.

The Hardware of the Nervous System

As with other cells in the body, the neuron contains an outer membrane, a cell nucleus, and various other subcellular structures. But the neuron is different from other cells in that it sends messages to neighboring cells and tells them what to do. As Figure 2–2 shows, the four parts or regions of a neuron are the

1. Cell body, or soma
2. Dendrites
3. Axon
4. Terminal buttons.

neurons individual nerve cells

receptors specialized cells that receive information from the environment

afferent neurons that transmit a signal to the brain or spinal cord

efferent neurons that send a signal away from the brain or spinal cord

effectors glands or muscles that change the internal or external environment

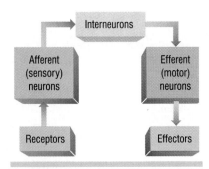

FIGURE 2–1
In the neural chain, information is transmitted only in one direction from receptor cells to effectors. Afferent neurons, interneurons, and efferent neurons complete the arc.

Neural transmission (the movement of a signal from one point to another) typically begins in the cell at the **dendrites**, which are branchlike structures that reach out to neurons or receptors in order to gather information. Once the information, or signal, is picked up by the dendrites, it is passed to the soma of the cell. The **soma**, which contains the nucleus, is concerned with the regulatory functions of the cell. From here, the message continues down a long cylindrical fiber that looks like a cable. This cable is the **axon** of the cell, and it is often the largest component of the neuron. Axons vary greatly in length; they may be shorter than the span of a red blood cell or as long as a person's leg. As the axon comes to an end, it sprouts a number of fingerlike projections that terminate in microscopic knobs. These are the **terminal buttons**.

It is important to note that the axons of many neurons fork to form collaterals, or additional neural pathways, as shown in Figure 2–3 on page 42. This separation of the axon permits the simultaneous stimulation of multiple locations in the nervous system. Thus, exciting a single neuron sometimes results in messages being delivered to different areas within the body.

In addition to being in contact with each other, the neurons that are responsible for receiving, integrating, and transmitting information are also in contact with other cells known as **neuroglia**. Coined from a Greek word meaning "nerve glue," nonexcitable neuroglia cells exist along with neurons in such great abundance that they make up as much as half the weight of the brain (Kimelberg, 1988). The most significant type of neuroglia are the *astrocytes*, named for their starry shape (see Figure 2–4 on page 42). For decades, neuroanatomy textbooks have presented astrocytes as little more than passive support elements. Although it is true that astrocytes are important in insulating neurons against harmful physical and chemical injury, in the 1990s it has become clear that astrocytes also have key roles in helping neurons communicate. Recently, it has been shown that astrocytes provide the raw materials that neurons need to communicate with other neurons (Kimelberg & Norenberg, 1989). When astrocytes die off, as they do with certain diseases, the neurons they supply fail to function, and the result is a dramatic change in behavior. Once considered relatively uninteresting maintenance cells, astrocytes are now recognized as equal partners with neurons. Both are required for the normal transmittal of neural messages, and ultimately for everything from a handshake to the recall of the Pythagorean theorem.

Other types of neuroglia cells help neurons complete their tasks by laying down a wrapping of white, fatty tissue around the axon. This covering is called the **myelin sheath** (refer to Figure 2–2). The purpose of the myelin sheath is to increase the rate of transmission of information along the length of the axon. Considering the extraordinary length of some axons, this can save a lot of time. An additional feature of the myelin sheath is that it is segmented or broken by gaps. These gaps, called **nodes of Ranvier**, further assist in speeding the message along the axon by permitting the neural signal to skip down the nerve cell fiber.

The Synapse and Neurotransmitters: Getting the Message Across

The point at which two or more neurons interconnect is called a **synapse**. It may come as a surprise to you to discover that the neurons in your body do not actually come in physical contact with each other. Rather, there is a space between neurons called the *synaptic cleft*. The synaptic cleft is defined

dendrites branchlike structures at the beginning of neurons

soma the cell body of a neuron that contains the cell nucleus

axon the long cablelike part of the neuron

terminal buttons projections at the end of the axon

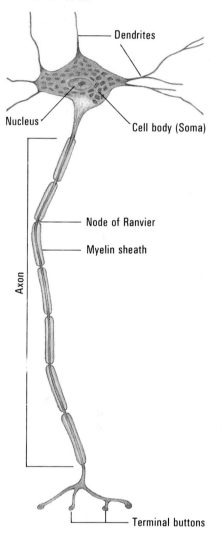

FIGURE 2–2
A drawing of a neuron with its basic structural components detailed.

neuroglia nonexcitable support cells that aid neural transmission

myelin sheath an envelope of white, fatty tissue that surrounds some axons and aids the rate of neural transmission

nodes of Ranvier gaps in the myelin sheath

synapse a connecting point between two neurons

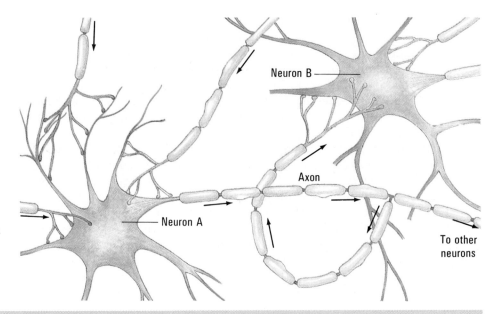

FIGURE 2–3
Overview of the branching action of axons. Neural messages from neuron A travel along the axon to neuron B and to other locations at the same time. Thus, information can be sent simultaneously to different parts of the body.

Neuron B

Neuron A

Axon

To other neurons

neurotransmitters chemicals that carry a signal from one neuron to the next

as the area between the terminal buttons of one neuron and the dendritic ends of another (see Figure 2–5 on page 43). Signals are transmitted from one neuron to the next across the synaptic cleft by chemicals called **neurotransmitters**.

Neurotransmitters are housed inside the terminal buttons of the presynaptic neuron, which is the neuron sending the signal (for a detailed discussion see Trimble, Linial, & Scheller, 1991). When the neural signal arrives at the axon terminals, a change in the internal state of the cell causes the neurotransmitters to move to the outer cell membrane. Then the

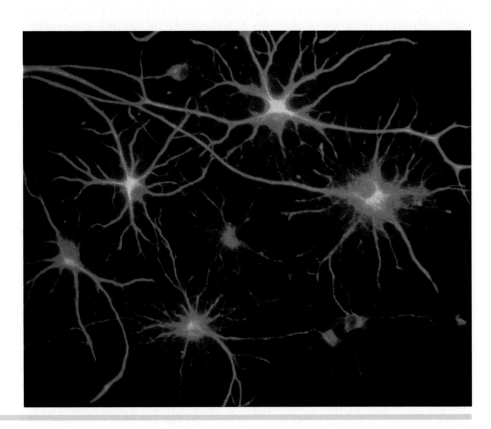

FIGURE 2–4
Astrocytes, as shown here, are believed to assist neurons in transmitting information by functioning as a storehouse for raw materials.

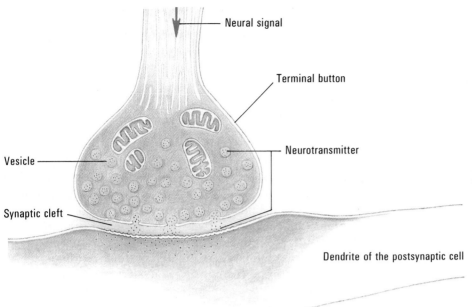

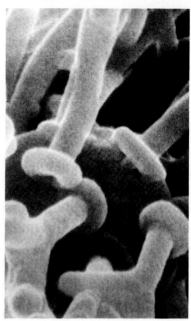

FIGURE 2–5
The synapse. *Right:* Electron micrograph of terminal buttons magnified 11,250 times (Lewis, Everhart, & Zeevi, 1969). *Left:* Schematic outline of synaptic transmission. Neurotransmitters stored in the terminal buttons move across the synaptic cleft and stimulate sensitive sites of the dendrite of the postsynaptic cell.

neurotransmitters are dumped into the synaptic cleft. These chemicals diffuse (spread out) across the synapse and accumulate in higher and higher concentrations on the dendritic ends of the postsynaptic neuron (the receiving neuron). Depending on the type of neurotransmitter and the properties of the postsynaptic cell, sufficient buildup of the transmitter substance either *excites* or *inhibits* firing of the postsynaptic neuron. In the case of excitation, the signal continues in the postsynaptic neuron, thereby forming a chain within the nervous system. Conversely, with inhibition, the signal dies at the point of the synapse.

Actually, in the human nervous system, there may be literally thousands of excitatory synapses on the dendrites of a single neuron, and also thousands of inhibitory synapses. Because of this, the combined effect of excitatory and inhibitory chemical transmission must be considered. Chemicals coming from one set of presynaptic neurons can cancel out or override the effects of chemicals coming from another set of presynaptic neurons.

The number of substances known or suspected to be transmitters continues to increase each year. Table 2–1 lists some of the more common ones, with their characteristic location and excitatory or inhibitory effects. No one can explain why there are so many different neurotransmitters, but it is clear that all must be present for a person to behave normally; that is, when neurotransmitters do not exist in their usual amounts, psychological changes can result. One example of such a behavioral change happens with cocaine use.

THINKING ABOUT
Cocaine Use and Abuse

Cocaine use and abuse in North American society have become major concerns for governmental officials and health professionals. Although the response to cocaine, or any drug, varies from person to person, the "euphoric" feeling sometimes described by users can hook someone after a single encounter (Horger et al., 1991). Most people are aware of the psychological changes that are ascribed to cocaine use: increased awareness, heightened feelings of well-being, and so on. But have you ever thought about what this illicit drug actually does to your body? What is really happening to cause these psychological changes?

It is generally accepted that cocaine works by inhibiting the reabsorption of the neurotransmitter dopamine in discrete brain regions (Cooper, Bloom, & Roth, 1990). Normally, when transmitters such as dopamine are released into the synaptic cleft, they are broken down by enzymes. The smaller parts of the compound are taken back inside the presynaptic neuron, and the transmitter is manufactured once again from its fundamental components. But when cocaine is in the system, dopamine remains in the synaptic cleft. As a result, signals on the postsynaptic neuron are more likely to occur. The behavioral result is an increase in behavioral activity and a feeling of euphoria.

Recent evidence indicates that other chemicals alter the effects of cocaine, perhaps by changing the levels of the dopamine transmitter, which is the ultimate target of the drug. For instance, nicotine has been shown to increase the reward value of cocaine in animals (Horger, Giles, & Schenk, 1993). Long-term exposure to the toxic metal cadmium, which also is in high concentrations in cigarette smoke, has been shown to weaken the impact of the behavioral effects of cocaine (Nation et al., 1991). What these events mean in terms of drug use is unknown. But it is clear that the effect cocaine has on people may be changed by our chemical environment.

Why do you think this is important? Can we do something about it?

Along with the effects of drugs, certain psychological disorders are linked to the disruption in the normal patterns of neural transmission. All of us from time to time experience anxiety, but in some persons the level of

TABLE 2-1
Major Neurotransmitters, Their Locations, and Effects

Neurotransmitter Substance	Location	Hypothesized Effect
Acetylcholine (ACh)	Brain, spinal cord, autonomic ganglia, target organs of the parasympathetic nervous system	Excitation in brain and autonomic ganglia, excitation or inhibition in target organs
Norepinephrine (NE)	Brain, spinal cord, target organs of sympathetic nervous system	Inhibition in brain, excitation or inhibition in target organs
Dopamine (DA)	Brain	Inhibition
Serotonin (5-hydroxy-tryptamine, or 5-HT)	Brain, spinal cord	Inhibition
Gamma-aminobutyric acid (GABA)	Brain (especially cerebral and cerebellar cortex), spinal cord	Inhibition
Glycine	Spinal cord interneurons	Inhibition
Glutamic acid	Brain, spinal sensory neurons	Excitation
Substance P	Brain, spinal sensory neurons (pain)	Excitation

anxious discomfort swells to a point at which life becomes maddening. In this type of clinical anxiety attack, it is now clear that the primary inhibitory transmitter in the brain, gamma-aminobutyric acid (GABA), falls to very low levels (R. B. Graham, 1990). Without the inhibitory control provided by GABA, brain activity is so accelerated that the person senses an anxiety overload. Unhappily, anxiety often moves people to take other drugs such as alcohol that increase GABA activity and diminish fear and suffering (Pohorecky, 1991). A preferred method for handling anxiety, which, neurochemically speaking, accomplishes the same effect as drinking alcohol, is to have a physician prescribe such GABA agonists (chemicals that strengthen the effects of a neurotransmitter) as Xanax and Valium.

In all the cases we have mentioned, behavioral disturbances occur when neurotransmitter levels stray from the normal ranges. In the next section we see that even when the usual amounts of a neurotransmitter are present, a changing internal chemical environment can dictate whether or not a neural signal actually gets through.

Neuromodulators

In addition to neurotransmitters, scientists have identified a second class of chemicals that influence neuronal activity. Because it is believed that these chemicals alter the sensitivity of neurons in the brain and elsewhere, they are sometimes referred to as **neuromodulators** (Kow & Pfaff, 1988). Unlike conventional neurotransmitters, which are released at presynaptic terminals, neuromodulators may be dispatched from remote sites in the brain, as well as from other places within the body. Therefore, whereas neurotransmitter chemicals operate on a specific point-to-point (axon-to-dendrite) basis across a synaptic gap, neuromodulators behave in a more general way by floating into broader regions containing numerous synapses. Table 2–2 lists some of the more common neuromodulators.

neuromodulators chemicals that affect the excitability of neurons

The Opioid Peptides. Of the many neuromodulators that have been isolated to date, perhaps the most exciting are the **opioid peptides** that are formed from short chains of amino acids. This general class of naturally occurring (endogenous) painkillers consists of three distinct families of chemicals: the enkephalins, the beta-endorphins, and the dynorphins (A. P. Smith & Lee, 1988). Molecular biology experiments had found natural brain receptor sites for opiate drugs (drugs derived from the opium poppy). Because it was unlikely that nature put these opiate receptors in human bodies just to accommodate the pharmacists of the world, it seemed reasonable to explore the possibility that the body might manufacture its own chemical that would normally occupy these opiate receptor sites. In 1975, John Hughes and Hans Kosterlitz of the University of Aberdeen, Scotland, discovered two naturally occurring brain peptides that would lock onto opiate receptors. Indeed, these chemicals were observed to bind even more tightly to the receptors than the powerful painkiller morphine. The names given these chemicals were leu-enkephalin and met-enkephalin. Discovery of the remaining morphinelike peptides would soon follow (D. A. Lewis & Bloom, 1987).

opioid peptides amino acids that function as natural pain regulators

We are only now beginning to understand how we can make opiates work for us. For example, we can increase the release of opioid peptides directly by stimulating the brain, as the following case history shows.

One day in 1976, as navy veteran Dennis Hough was working at a hospital's psychiatric unit, a disturbed patient snapped Hough's back and ruptured three of his vertebral discs. Five years later, after two failed back operations, Hough was bedridden with constant shooting pains in his legs, back, and shoulders

TABLE 2-2
Some Common
Neuromodulators

Adrenocorticotropin
Angiotensin II (AII)
Cholecystokinin (CCK)
Corticotropin releasing factor (CRF)
Insulin
Neurotensin (NT)
Opioids
Source: Kow & Pfaff, 1988.

and was depressed to the point of suicide. Doctors were just then pioneering a technique of implanting platinum electrodes in the brain region called the peri-aqueductal gray, and Hough soon underwent the skull drilling and emplacement. He remembers it as "the most barbaric thing I've experienced, including my tour of duty in Vietnam," but the results were worth the ordeal: for the past several years, Hough has been able to stimulate his brain's own endorphins four times a day by producing a radio signal from a transmitter on his belt. The procedure is delicate—too much current and his eyes flutter, too little and the pain returns in less than 6 hours. But it works dependably, and Hough not only holds down an office job now but is engaged to be married.

Substance P. Although it is not yet clear how endogenous opiates function as painkillers, there is widespread belief that these chemicals block a pain transmitter called **substance P** (Aronin, Coslovsky, & Leeman, 1986). Substance P was discovered over 50 years ago but has only recently been accorded transmitter status. Much of the evidence favoring substance P as a critical pain transmitter comes from studies that show that the substance is abundant in sensory pathways associated with pain, such as those that originate in the pulp of teeth. Apparently, the opioid peptides produce their painkilling effects by inhibiting the release of substance P into the synaptic cleft. In this regard, these neuropeptides work like gatekeepers (see Figure 2–6). In their absence, pain information is readily passed from neuron to neuron; but when they are present, the pain gates close and the level of reported discomfort diminishes.

Acupuncture. We opened this chapter with an account of the mutual fascination of Kitra and the Chinese students with the role played by opiates (endorphins) in the control of pain. Although everyone agrees that neuropeptides are involved in the regulation of pain, in the nonscientific community there has been some resistance to the idea that opiates are respon-

substance P the neurotransmitter associated with pain

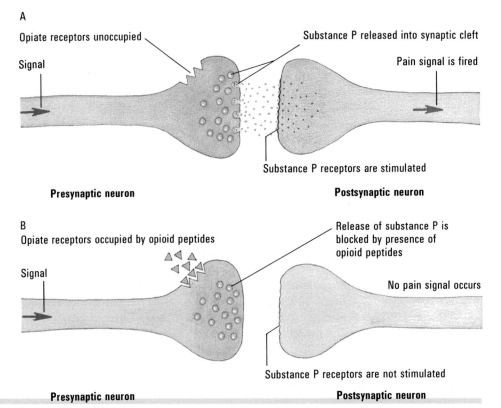

FIGURE 2–6
The gatekeeping action of opioid peptides. (*A*) In the absence of opioid peptides, a pain transmitter known as substance P is released at the synapse when a presynaptic signal occurs. (*B*) The presence of opioid peptides in receptor sites blocks the release of substance P that otherwise occurs in response to a presynaptic signal.

sible for such heretofore mysterious events as acupuncture. This ancient Chinese technique is designed to control pain through the insertion of needles into various parts of the body. Even though it may not be a popular interpretation in nonscientific quarters, neuroscientists are united in their opinion that acupuncture works by releasing beta-endorphins (see Hopson, 1988). As we have seen, these opiates disrupt pain signals, so when they are released by the mechanical stimulation of the needles, pain levels should decrease. As mentioned in the chapter opening, a chemical called *naloxone*, which counters the effects of beta-endorphins (McKim, 1991), will block the effects of acupuncture treatment when it is present in the body (Kroening & Oleson, 1985). This finding confirms that the opiate mediation of pain is the basis for acupuncture treatment. Does this make you wonder how many other, apparently unscientific or folk medical treatments around the world actually have legitimate biochemical underpinnings? Perhaps some of the so-called voodoo approaches to treating illness are more credible than we think. But until we really understand how they work, these procedures remain potentially dangerous and harmful.

Placebos. It is also possible to reduce pain in some patients by administering an inactive substance called a placebo. As noted in Chapter 1, usually this takes the form of a sugar pill or capsule that really is not intended to do anything in a medical sense. But until recently, no one has really understood why placebo treatments work. It is now clear that the suppression of pain by placebos is a physiological phenomenon involving endogenous opiate release. Somehow, when a person merely thinks he or she has taken medication to relieve pain, beta-endorphins are released into the system. Documentation of this astonishing example of the mind healing the body is available from reports that show that the placebo effect does not occur when patients take naloxone (Fields & Levine, 1984). That is, when beta-endorphins are chemically inactivated, placebo treatments will not decrease the levels of reported pain.

For further evidence that beta-endorphins are involved in placebo effects, Lipmann, Cross, & Young (1990) looked at endorphin levels in the cerebrospinal fluid of both responders and nonresponders to placebo treatments. For the responders (chronic pain patients who verbally reported complete pain relief after an injection of a placebo agent), the levels of beta-endorphin were two to three times the levels that were measured before the placebo was administered. Conversely, for the nonresponders (patients with chronic pain who verbally reported no change in their level of pain following the injection of the placebo agent), the beta-endorphin levels either did not increase or actually dropped after the placebo was administered. These findings indicate that if placebo changes occur at all, they are due to increased levels of opiates.

Of course, in placebo effects the person is unaware of any mental involvement in pain control. But even in cases where people are aware of the involvement of their minds in controlling their pain, the ability to alleviate pain by mentally blocking it out seems to be affected by opiates. For instance, some people can reduce the perceived pain of an earache just by concentrating and telling themselves, "The pain is going away. My ear is no longer hurting." However, when those people are administered naloxone, their attempts to control pain often fail (Bandura et al., 1987). Evidently, thinking through pain does work, but only when opiate channels are free to operate.

It should be mentioned that the release of opiates does not always produce benefits. Indeed, under some conditions, the presence of endogenous opioid peptides may place your life at risk.

Have you ever heard that stress can kill you? Is it possible that people can really die from grief? If you worry about a malignant tumor, is it likely to grow more rapidly? These questions and others concerning the interaction between psychological variables and the immune system have received increased attention over the last few years. The area of **psychoimmunology** examines the relationships among the brain, behavior, and immune system reactions (R. Adler, Felten, & Cohen, 1990). Of special interest to scientists in this field is the effect of stress on the body's immunity. Several early studies showed that stress can decrease the ability of the human body to fight infectious diseases (Sklar & Anisman, 1981). More recently, it has been shown that marital separation and divorce (Kiecolt-Glaser & Glaser, 1986), as well as the death of a family member (Mor, McHorney, & Sherwood, 1986), can diminish resistance and increase a person's vulnerability to illness and death. Perhaps this research explains why the death of a spouse is often followed closely by the death of the partner. Bereavement and death may quite literally claim the life of a loving companion.

A chief candidate for explaining the effects of stress on the immune system is the opiate pathway. It is now obvious that opiates such as beta-endorphins are released in humans under stressful circumstances, and, as we just observed, these chemicals bind to receptor sites that are involved in regulating pain. Unfortunately, the opiates also bind to natural killer (NK) cells. *NK cells* are components of the immune system that are essential in defending the human body against disease. Normally, these cells proliferate when a foreign agent enters the body; they attack the invader, destroy it, and dispatch it to points outside the body. But when opiates such as the endorphins attach to the NK cell, the cell fails to respond to a foreign challenge, and the NK cell may die. The result is that when opiates are present at high levels, as they are when a person is experiencing a great deal of stress, the body's natural defense system is neutralized. Consequently, death and disease are more likely.

Cancer is one instance in which the release of opiates in response to stress clearly threatens survival. Shavit et al. (1984) have shown that cancer cells spread more rapidly when the organism is repeatedly faced with a stressful situation. Yet, when the opiate system is blocked, stress does not seem to accelerate tumor growth as much. Given this apparent connection, why don't we administer medicines that block the effects of opiates? The reason is there is a trade-off between pain and immunosuppression. If we block the effects of opiates to prevent suppression of the immune system under conditions of stress, we also limit the ability of these peptides to control pain. For cancer patients, pain control is essential, so an opiate blockade is not really an option.

Finally, bear in mind that even less severe life stresses can change the function of the immune system. As long ago as 1938, Farris found that suppression of the immune system occurred in football players in response to an impending football game. Even fans were affected! More recently, it has been shown that medical students suffer from faulty immune reactions immediately before examinations (Kiecolt-Glaser & Glaser, 1986). Clearly, stress is hard on your body, and although it cannot be avoided, there may be ways to control it.

What do you do to control stress? Are you doing enough?

psychoimmunology the study of the interrelation of the brain, behavior, and the immune system

The Neural Impulse: What Is the Message?

Up to this point, we have purposely avoided referring to what happens neurochemically to the neuron when it is stimulated. The informational unit, which we have continually called a signal or message, obviously is not passed down the axon in the form of a handwritten memo or by a miniature pony express system. So how does information get transmitted? The answer has to do with changes in the electrical activity across the neural cell membrane.

With modern technology, it is possible to insert a tiny electrical probe (microelectrode) inside an axon and record its electrical potential. Electrical potentials are set up in biological systems when there are more charged particles (ions) on one side of a membrane than the other. In neurons, electrical potentials of varying amounts are created by a disequilibrium of negatively charged proteins and sodium (Na^+), potassium (K^+), and chloride (Cl^-) ions (see Figure 2–7). When the neuron is inactive, our microelectrode readings will show an estimate of its **resting potential**. During this resting state, the potential is negative (usually around –70 millivolts) inside the cell relative to the outside. This is a situation brought about due to the semipermeable status of the cell membrane. In this case, it means that the membrane allows some sodium ions to pass outside, but once outside the cell membrane these ions cannot get back inside. Typically, this produces a higher concentration of positively charged sodium particles outside the cell, resulting in the negative electrical charge inside the cell.

Batteries Are Included. Because a neuron is "charged up" in a resting state, it resembles a battery. As with any battery, both positive and negative electrical poles exist. Thus, it is appropriate to say that the membrane is polarized when the neuron is not being stimulated. But when the neuron is stimulated by either receptors or transmitters from presynaptic fibers, then **depolarization** occurs. It is this depolarization of the neuron that defines the neural **impulse**. What happens is that when a sufficient volume of an excitatory chemical transmitter collects on the dendrites of the postsynaptic cell (reaching the so-called threshold), part of the axonal membrane suddenly becomes permeable to sodium. Consequently, sodium rushes inside the cell, making it less negative, and eventually the membrane is depolarized. In fact, the inside of the cell is briefly positive compared with the outside until the internal machinery of the cell begins to force sodium back out, at which time the cell resumes its semipermeable (resting) status. Figure 2–8 shows the pattern of changes in electrical potential produced by a stimulus of sufficient strength to evoke an impulse. The sequence of changing electrical shifts are collectively referred to as the **action potential**. The entire process lasts only for a millisecond or two.

Down Time: The Refractory Period. It should be apparent from Figure 2–8 that there is a short time period following the onset of the action potential during which a second action potential cannot begin. This period, called the **refractory period**, is caused by the decreased excitability of the membrane that occurs due to the depolarization of the cell. Without a difference in the electrical charge across the membrane, an impulse is not possible. Therefore, if two equally intense stimuli are presented back-to-back at close time intervals, only the first one is likely to have any effect.

Rules of Travel. When an impulse does occur, it travels in a wave. The wave begins at the axon hillock where the axon connects to the soma and then travels down the full length of the axon (Nauta & Feirtag, 1986). It is at the end of the axon (terminal buttons) that the change in membrane

Axon

Resting state

FIGURE 2–7
The concentrations of the ions in the diagram are represented by the sizes of the symbols. The inside of the cell has high concentrations of negatively charged protein (A^-) and positively charged potassium (K^+). The outside of the cell has a high concentration of chloride (Cl^-) particles and an unusually high concentration of sodium (Na^+) ions.

resting potential electrical potential that occurs across a neural membrane when the neuron is not being fired

depolarization occurs when a polarized membrane becomes permeable to ions such as sodium and the electrical potential across the membrane drops

impulse the depolarization of a neuron that causes a signal to be sent from one point to another

action potential a sequence of changes in electrical potential during the activation of a neuron

refractory period period after the onset of the action potential during which the neuron cannot be reactivated

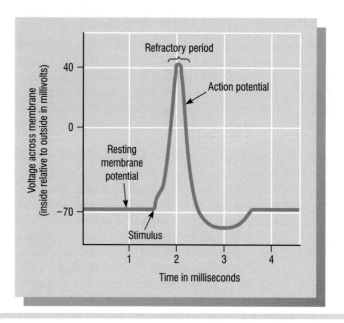

FIGURE 2–8
The pattern of changes in electrical potential during the neural impulse.

all-or-none law a biological law that states an action potential occurs either at full strength or not at all

potential forces a release of the neurotransmitter, and once threshold values are reached on neighboring dendrites, the process starts again in different neurons. So, the impulse can travel in only one direction, and it must travel from one axonal region to the next, much as a bullet goes down a rifle barrel.

Of all the rules that govern neural transmission, possibly the most dramatic is the **all-or-none law**. This law states that with a given level of stimulation, you either get an action potential on an individual neuron or you do not. It is not the case that weak stimuli evoke weak neuronal responses, and stronger stimuli evoke stronger ones. We may use our example of the rifle again. The bullet does not travel at a speed parallel to the vigor of the trigger pull. Rather, once a particular point (threshold) is reached, the bullet is fired and is on its way at a speed predetermined by other factors. Neuronal impulses behave similarly.

The preceding paragraphs focus on how excitatory synapses work. But what about inhibitory synapses? Basically, inhibitory neurotransmitters produce changes in the membranes of dendrites that make it more difficult for depolarization to occur. Returning to our rifle analogy, it is rather like putting the safety catch on. You lock the triggering device; consequently, events that normally produce a reaction (a trigger pull/the accumulation of an excitatory neurotransmitter) are without effect.

ORGANIZATION OF THE NERVOUS SYSTEM

Now that we have discussed the basic terminology of physiological psychology, we are ready to examine the nervous system within a broader framework. It is customary to divide the nervous system into subsystems. This is done partly for convenience, because the nervous system is so massive and complex. But more than that, the classification system that has been adopted in recent years represents a logical distinction between and among structures on the basis of where they are, how they look, and what they do. Figure 2–9 presents a summary chart of the major components of the nervous system. We urge you to refer to this chart often as you read on.

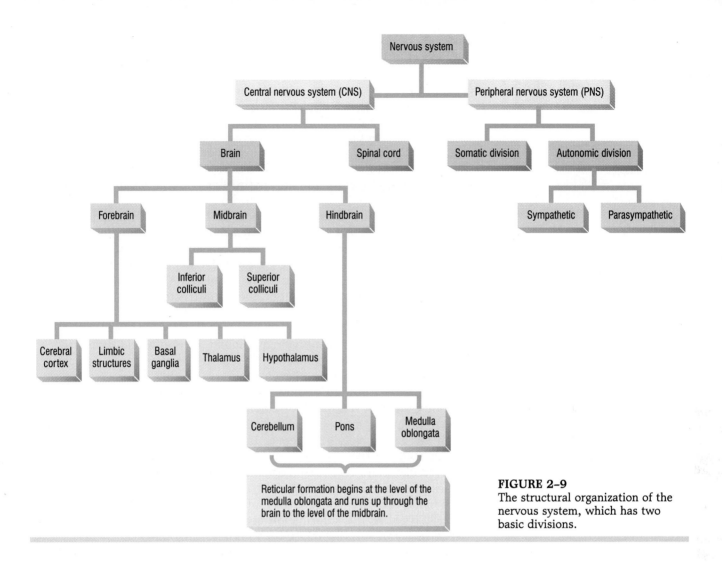

FIGURE 2–9
The structural organization of the nervous system, which has two basic divisions.

The Peripheral Nervous System

The **peripheral nervous system (PNS)** is one of the two major subdivisions of the nervous system; the other is the **central nervous system (CNS)**. The CNS consists of the brain and spinal cord, and we will discuss it later. The PNS consists of everything else in the nervous system; it is largely through the PNS network that we communicate with the rest of the world. With only a few exceptions (such as with visual information), new inputs must travel along sensory (afferent) neurons of the PNS. Once the incoming information has been appropriately processed, messages flowing along motor (efferent) fibers of the PNS tell the effectors that it's time to make a move. Therefore, much of what we sense and all that we express are made possible by the PNS.

The PNS is further subdivided into two parts: the **somatic nervous system** and the **autonomic nervous system**. The somatic division of the PNS is made up of both sensory and motor neurons that are involved in the control of voluntary muscle groups. When you place a coin in a vending machine, you are using the motor channels of the somatic division of the PNS. The autonomic division of the PNS is primarily concerned with the internal working of the body, and as a rule it operates on an involuntary basis. Effectors controlled by the autonomic division of the PNS include smooth muscle (e.g., in blood vessels, urinary bladder), heart muscle, and glands (both digestive and endocrine).

peripheral nervous system (PNS) the nervous system other than the brain and spinal cord

central nervous system (CNS) the parts of the nervous system consisting of the brain and spinal cord

somatic nervous system the division of the PNS involved with voluntary muscle movement

autonomic nervous system division of the PNS that works involuntarily to control the internal environment

Divisions of the Autonomic Nervous System.   The autonomic division of
the PNS is further subdivided into two anatomically separate systems, the
sympathetic and **parasympathetic nervous systems**. Look at Figure 2–10.
Notice how fibers from the sympathetic and parasympathetic divisions go
into the same organs and glands. This happens because the two divisions
are antagonists; that is, they battle for dominance. In effect, one system is
an internal check on the other. The sympathetic division is the alarm system. Stimulation of these neurons produces increased blood flow to the
skeletal muscles that line the long bones of the body. At the same time, *epinephrine* (another word for adrenalin) from the adrenal glands is also
released to provide more energy for the body.

A true story that illustrates the potential impact of sympathetic excitement comes to mind. A West Texas farmer was out plowing, accompanied
only by his 11-year-old son. When the youngster took his turn on the tractor, he had a tragic accident. On one of the slopes at the far end of the
field, the tractor tipped, pinning the boy beneath. Alone with no time to get
help, the father miraculously lifted the 2-ton tractor off his son, breaking
his own back in the process. Clearly, this was an emergency situation, and
if the father's sympathetic system had not responded and thereby provided
the needed supernormal energy requirement, his son would have died.

In contrast to the mobilization of reserves brought on by sympathetic
stimulation, parasympathetic activity conserves bodily resources. Heart rate
decreases, as does the blood flow to the extremities, but digestive processes
increase. Although a number of different and unrelated sensory events can
activate the parasympathetic system, as likely as not the system springs into
action due to sympathetic excesses. In the preceding story about the father
and his son, the father's body could not have survived indefinitely in that
extended high state of arousal. Fortunately, there are internal sensors located
at various places throughout the body. They tell the parasympathetic system
when blood pressure, epinephrine levels, and other alarm elements are dangerously high. As this information becomes available, the parasympathetic
system reacts by relaxing the smooth muscle lining the blood vessels, reducing the amount of epinephrine released from the adrenals, and so forth.
Bodily functions are thus brought back to normal. Of course, should the
parasympathetic effects become too pronounced, be assured that the sympathetic system again can go into action to restore stability. As you can see, the
body functions as a beautifully, internally balanced piece of machinery.

The Central Nervous System

Technically, the central nervous system is the neural tissue that lies inside
the protective housing provided by the skull and the vertebral column. In
humans, this translates into the brain and spinal cord. Although the brain
may be the ultimate ruler of the body, the spinal cord is the principal
instrument of body governance. It is appropriate that the most majestic
structure in nature sits atop so noble a foundation.

The Spinal Cord.   The spinal cord is a tubelike structure that begins at the
base of the brain as a cylindrical swelling about the size of a small broom handle and tapers off in size as it descends to the lower back region. It is called

FIGURE 2–10
The autonomic division of the peripheral nervous system (PNS). Note the antagonistic effects produced by the two subdivisions of the autonomic system (parasympathetic and sympathetic systems) on a given gland or body part.

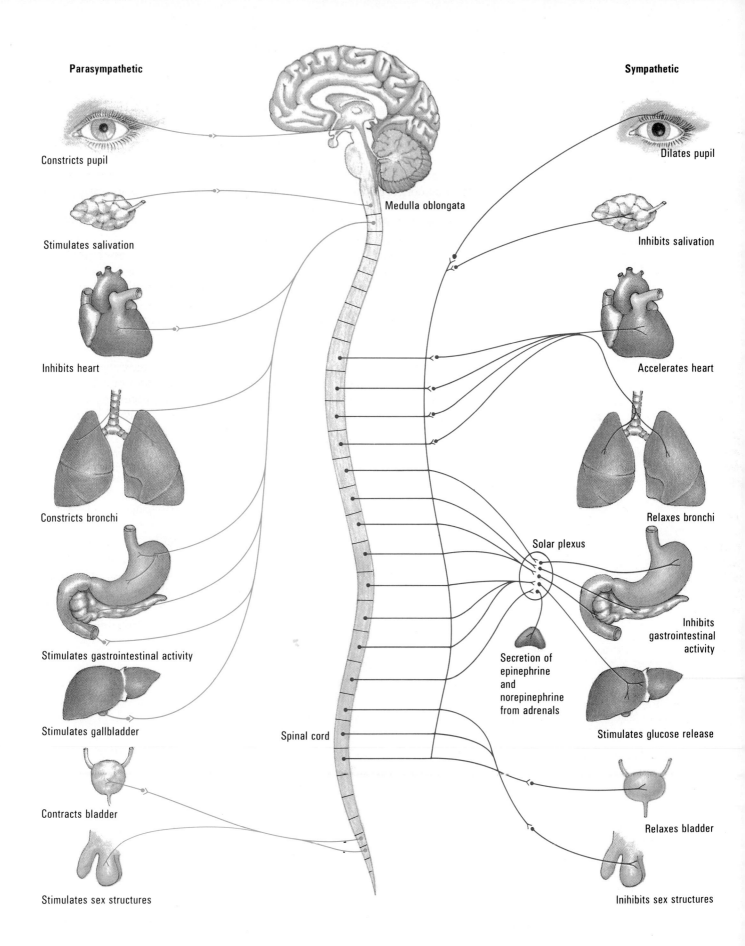

Parasympathetic

Constricts pupil

Stimulates salivation

Inhibits heart

Constricts bronchi

Stimulates gastrointestinal activity

Stimulates gallbladder

Contracts bladder

Stimulates sex structures

Sympathetic

Dilates pupil

Inhibits salivation

Accelerates heart

Relaxes bronchi

Inhibits gastrointestinal activity

Stimulates glucose release

Relaxes bladder

Inihibits sex structures

Medulla oblongata

Solar plexus

Secretion of epinephrine and norepinephrine from adrenals

Spinal cord

"the final common pathway of the nervous system," and it works both independently and in conjunction with the brain.

Figure 2–11, which illustrates the familiar knee-jerk reflex, shows how sensory information may come in at the level of the spinal cord and be quickly redistributed to muscle effectors. This process completely bypasses the circuitry of the brain.

From the cross section of the spinal cord shown in Figure 2–11, you can see that small bundles of neural tissue emerge from the spinal cord to form the dorsal and ventral roots. There are 31 paired root sets in the body, and each pair converges to form a spinal nerve. Incoming sensory information enters the spinal cord over the fibers of the dorsal root; motor impulses leave the spinal cord along ventral root fibers. *Dorsal* means "back side" and *ventral* means "front side"; sensory information is registered first in the back part of the spinal cord, and motor outputs originate in the front section of the spinal cord. Accordingly, damage to the very back of the spine that may result, for example, from an athletic injury, might impair sensations of touch, but movement would still be possible. Damage to the entire spinal cord (front and back) would result in paralysis, however. Now our discussion moves to the other part of the central nervous system, the brain.

Brain Images. The human brain is an exceedingly complex structure consisting of over 180 billion cells (Kolb & Whishaw, 1990). Of those 180 billion cells, 50 billion neurons are actively involved in thought processing, and each of these may have synapses with 15,000 neighboring neurons. Curiously,

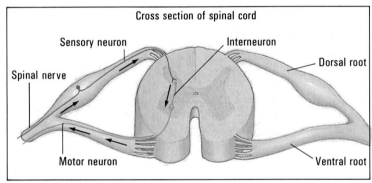

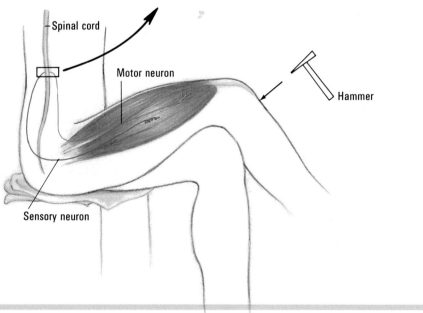

FIGURE 2–11
Many neurologists use the knee-jerk reflex as a test of spinal cord functioning. Normally, when the tendons below the knee are tapped with a hammer or other instrument, the thigh muscle is stretched. This stretching causes sensory neurons going to the spinal cord to fire. When these impulses arrive at the spinal cord, connecting interneurons immediately send messages back out along motor neurons to the thigh muscle, causing it to contract. As the muscle contracts, the lower part of the leg (calf and foot) jerks upward. In the person whose spinal cord functions normally, this reflexive behavior takes place automatically without any command from higher central nervous system (CNS) centers.

brain size has very little to do with intelligence, at least when comparing one human to another. The brains of people of extraordinary ability are no different in size from those of ordinary ability, with brain weights for both gifted and nongifted adults ranging between 1,100 and 2,000 grams (gm).

Due to the complexity of the human brain, for many years researchers in neuroscience have been hesitant to take on the difficult task of explaining its intricacies. However, this situation is changing rapidly because of recent advances in imaging technology, especially as it relates to computerized body-scanning systems.

Special attention has been given to research issues in **clinical neuropsychology**, which is a branch of psychology associated with identifying and interpreting various brain disorders. The early detection of neurological disorders has always been difficult. Often, by the time the first symptoms are noticeable, the problem has progressed so far that nothing can be done. But now a new breed of instruments is providing computer-generated displays of malfunctioning brain regions, nerve cell death, and cerebral hemorrhage. Such pictures greatly assist scientists in the difficult task of identifying the biological bases of disordered behavior. Among the most sophisticated detection systems, **computerized axial tomography (CAT)**, **positron emission tomography (PET)**, **magnetic resonance imaging (MRI)**, and **electroencephalograph (EEG) computerized classification schemes** are perhaps of most interest for psychology and medicine. These techniques, which were originally designed for diagnosing medical problems, have provided us with a better understanding of normal brain phenomena.

Computerized Axial Tomography (CAT). Originally developed in Great Britain in 1972 (Sochurek, 1987), CAT scanners convert information from X-ray pictures into a digital code that a computer can read. The computer presents a high-resolution video image based on the X-ray data and reassembles the picture as a three-dimensional array. One advantage of this technique is that it can "slice" the brain from many different angles and reconstitute the different views in a single video image. This makes it less likely that small but abnormal tissue features can be visually blocked by other structures. Figure 2–12 shows a CAT scan of a tumor embedded in the brain of a 37-year-old woman.

clinical neuropsychology branch of psychology associated with the study of brain disorders

computerized axial tomography (CAT) an imaging technique that creates a picture by converting X-ray data to a digital code

positron emission tomography (PET) imaging technique in which sugar (glucose) metabolism is used to provide color codes of brain activity

magnetic resonance imaging (MRI) technique in which an image is created by displacing hydrogen atoms using a magnetic field

electroencephalograph (EEG) computerized classification scheme a technique in which brain wave patterns are converted to pictures or brain maps

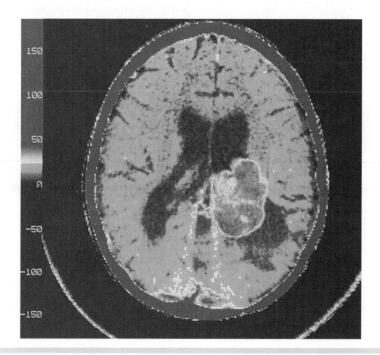

FIGURE 2–12
Computerized axial tomography (CAT) scans are images that a computer generates from X-ray data. This scan shows a tumor (*in red*) in a young woman's brain.

Positron Emission Tomography (PET). For a PET scan, the individual is injected with a radioactive sugar that is metabolized by the brain. The scan determines brain activity (metabolism) in various brain regions and converts the information to color codes. Certain darker colors correspond to low sugar use, and other brighter colors indicate that sugar is being used at very high rates. Color maps then can be created to provide details about how special populations compare to normal individuals. As an example of how this imaging procedure assists our understanding of human behavior, a recent study conducted by scientists from the NIMH used PET scans to study adults who have been identified as having **attention deficit hyperactivity disorder (ADHD)**. Typically diagnosed during childhood, ADHD is characterized by impulsiveness and an inability to sit still. Later in life, these children are more likely to become juvenile delinquents. In an extensive study of 25 ADHD adults (who also had children with the same disorder), it was discovered that brain activity was lower than it was in the normal adult control group (Zametkin et al., 1990); see Figure 2–13. Why decreased brain-activity would lead to hyperactivity is still under investigation. But considering that many people diagnosed as having ADHD respond favorably to stimulants such as methylphenidate (Ritalin), the relation does seem to exist (McNamara, Davidson, & Schenk, 1993). In any event, in this instance a technological advancement in brain imaging has helped us better understand a complex psychological phenomenon.

PET scans also can be used to tell us more about how people process information. Slow readers, for example, light up brain regions that indicate that the person first speaks the word silently and then attaches meaning to it. On the other hand, these operations occur at the same time in fast readers; that is, parallel processing occurs (Peterson et al., 1988). Perhaps this is why slow readers are more likely to move their lips when they read; they are saying the words to themselves before they attempt to understand them.

Magnetic Resonance Imaging (MRI). This truly extraordinary technique relies on the principle that hydrogen atoms, when exposed to a magnetic field, are arrayed in straight lines like so many tiny soldiers. When a radio signal is aimed at these soldiers, they disperse, but then regroup when the signal is turned off. As the hydrogen atoms return to their original position, they give off small electrical signals that can be evaluated by a computer. Because the human body is composed primarily of hydrogen, the color-enhanced images produced by MRI are incredibly detailed (Figure 2–14).

attention deficit hyperactivity disorder (ADHD) disorder associated with decreased brain activity during which there is actually an increase in behavioral activity

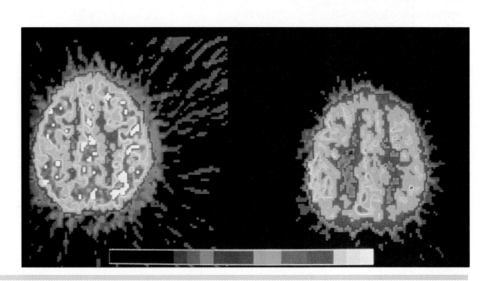

FIGURE 2–13
The PET scan of the brain on the left is from a normal person. The scan on the right is from an adult patient diagnosed with Attention Deficit Hyperactivity Disorder (ADHD). The colors white, red, and orange correspond to high brain activity (metabolism), whereas blue, green, and purple correspond to low brain activity. Notice how much less activity is shown in the scan of the ADHD patient.

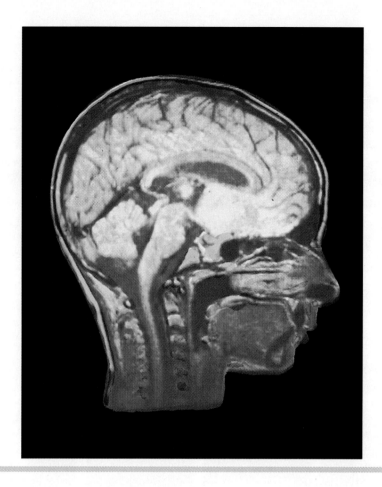

Electroencephalograph (EEG) Computerized Classification Scheme. This
procedure (John et al., 1988) proposes that departures from the usual electrophysiological readings can be used to diagnose subtle brain dysfunctions. For instance, the brain wave (EEG) patterns of some patients with
psychological disorders are known to be different from normal patterns.
Using computer-assisted techniques, the degree of difference can be determined and converted to a color code. Thus, different-colored brain maps
indicate differences from normal. Figure 2–15 shows computer-generated
colored brain maps for a normal individual, and for individuals with
depression, alcoholism, and schizophrenia. Note that the EEG patterns,
and consequently the map colors, vary for each classification within a
given brain region. In addition to helping diagnose existing disorders, this
technique promises to help identify so-called trait markers of vulnerability.
This means that it may be possible to spot a person with schizophrenia
before the individual is fully in the throes of the disorder, and thus its
development might be slowed or halted.

The Brain and Behavior. Even with such impressive picture-taking techniques as those we have just mentioned, investigating even the most basic
operations of the brain can be pretty tricky business. Fortunately, the brain
is put together in such a way that it permits us to study it in subdivisions.
The hindbrain, midbrain, and forebrain constitute the major subdivisions,
and these are further divided according to structure and function.

Hindbrain. Figure 2–16 depicts part of the human brain stem, as well as
the spinal cord, cerebellum, and remaining brain regions. The spinal cord

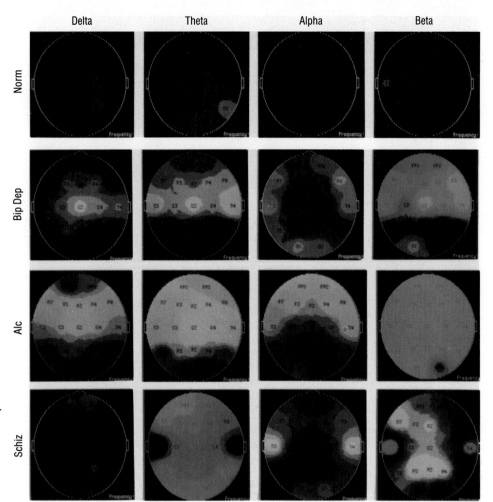

FIGURE 2–15
These computer-generated color maps were created by converting brain wave patterns (delta, theta, alpha, and beta waves) to color codes. Using this electroencephalograph (EEG) computerized classification scheme, it is evident that the brain wave patterns of patients suffering from bipolar depression (Bip Dep), alcoholism (Alc), and schizophrenia (Schiz), are different from normal (Norm).

brain stem part of the brain that includes the medulla oblongata, pons, and cerebellum

connects to the brain at the **brain stem**, which includes the *medulla oblongata* and the *pons*. The latter two structures, with the *cerebellum*, constitute virtually the entire hindbrain, which is the oldest and most primitive part of our brain. In fact, the hindbrain is the only brain that some lower organisms possess.

The medulla oblongata is the first structure that we encounter, moving up from the spinal cord into the brain. Despite this structure's small size, it has extremely large responsibilities. The medulla oblongata contains clusters of neurons that are involved in the control of such vital activities as breathing, swallowing, blood circulation, and skeletal muscle contraction and coordination. In addition, the medulla oblongata is known to influence levels of consciousness and alertness and even waking and sleeping. Continuing our ascent, we notice the pons, on the brain's ventral surface. The pons is quite literally a bridge that connects higher and lower brain regions. It contains numerous brain nuclei (clusters of nerve cell bodies inside the central nervous system) that are important in the formation of facial expressions. Off to the back of the pons sits a discrete structure that appears to have been tacked to the rest of the brain. This is the cerebellum, and it is essential for standing, walking, and coordinated movements of all sorts. The cerebellum functions to smooth and integrate muscular events, so as to produce a blended ensemble of behaviors. An injury to this structure produces discordant, spasmodic movements that are noticeably awkward.

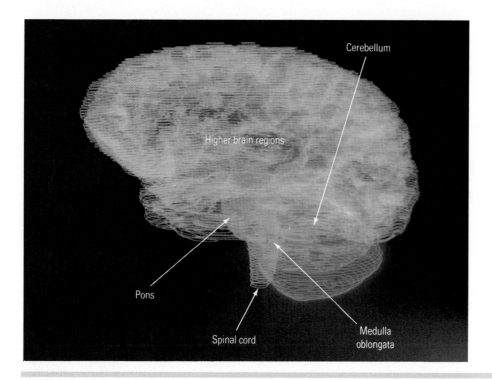

FIGURE 2-16
The human brain stem, which includes the medulla oblongata and the pons, connects to the spinal cord, cerebellum, and higher brain regions.

Midbrain.   Still higher on the brain stem is the midbrain. At the back of the midbrain are large relay nuclei involved in hearing. These are called inferior colliculi (the singular form, *colliculus*, means "little hill"). Just above the inferior colliculi another cluster of nerve cells form bumps at the top of the brain stem. These are the superior colliculi, and they have an important role in coordinating whole-body movements in response to visual stimuli.

A more interesting part of the midbrain anatomy is a complex network of fibers located in the very core of the brain stem. This complicated system of branching neurons is known as the **reticular formation**. Impulses travel throughout the reticular formation along ascending tracts to higher brain centers and then back along descending pathways to lower brain stem areas. The ascending component of this complex highway system plays a critical role in controlling levels of human arousal. It is as if the reticular formation operates as a listening post that alerts the rest of the brain to incoming signals. If the listening post were wiped out, incoming messages might get through to the rest of the brain, but an interpretation would never be made. It would be like dialing someone's phone number and having the phone ring but with no one home to pick up the receiver. Chemical or surgical destruction of the reticular formation has long been known to produce sleep, or even a coma.

Certain types of neurological disorders result from changes in midbrain neurochemistry. **Parkinson's disease** is one such disorder. Named after London physician James Parkinson, this disease is associated with the degeneration of an area in the midbrain known as the *substantia nigra*. The substantia nigra is a brain region rich in dopamine neurons. When the disease claims the neurons in this area, the resulting drop in the availability of dopamine triggers four major symptoms: tremors, rigidity of posture, slowness of movement, and disturbances in posture (Kolb & Whishaw, 1990). In an effort to restore the proper levels of dopamine, the drug *L-dopa*, which is converted to dopamine in the brain, is administered to

reticular formation a diffuse network of ascending and descending pathways in the midbrain, believed to be associated with arousal

Parkinson's disease a disorder associated with degeneration of the substantia nigra that progressively leads to movement problems, including difficulties with walking and fine-motor skills

Parkinsonian patients. This form of drug therapy can produce significant benefits, but prolonged treatment can cause unpleasant side effects such as rapid breathing and behavioral tics. We will address the problems associated with chronic drug therapy more fully in Chapter 17.

Some have argued that rather than attempting to resuscitate existing neurons in Parkinson's patients, these patients should be given replacements. Why attempt to rebuild when you can go with a new model? This issue relates to the controversy of fetal tissue transplants.

> ### THINKING ABOUT
> ## Fetal Tissue Transplants

Over the last two decades, basic scientific research efforts have focused on the possibility that tissue from the brain, or chromaffin cells from the adrenal gland, could be taken from an unborn vertebrate animal (a fetus) and be transplanted into specific brain regions of living adults. There, the transplanted cells have been observed to thrive and take over the function of similar neurons that were surgically destroyed. Recently, numerous attempts have been made to use this type of neural transplantation in Parkinson's patients (Yurek & Sladek, 1990). Solid tissue chunks of healthy nerve cells have been placed in the substantia nigra region of the brains of Parkinson's patients, with the hope of restoring dopamine transmission (Sladek & Shoulson, 1988). However, the results have not always been good. The recovery of function is brief, the grafts do not survive well, and the patients must continue on their medication for a very long time before benefits are realized (D. I. Peterson et al., 1988).

Despite such problems, continued experimental work with different donor/recipient combinations has been promising. Human fetal tissue taken after elective abortions has been transplanted with positive results (see Yurek & Sladek, 1990). Still, not much is known about the long-term effects of such transplants. Will the transplants hold up in the elderly? What options are there when the graft fails?

Regardless of the ultimate success of fetal tissue transplants, the technique may never be used extensively. Opponents of the procedure warn of the development of labs that culture replacement parts from living tissue. The entire issue is a moral outrage for some people for whom it ties in with all the emotion that surrounds abortion issues. Proponents point squarely to the health benefits; a life may be reclaimed. These people argue that if there is a moral issue, it's that we have a moral obligation to help those we can. In the final analysis, each of us must decide this question for ourselves. But we should not decide without deliberation.

What is your position on the matter? How did you come to this point? Most important, are you willing to review your position, and if necessary, change your view?

Forebrain. The most important part of the human brain, at least for psychology, is the forebrain. Although the forebrain is composed of many substructures, we will discuss only the thalamus, hypothalamus, basal ganglia, limbic system, and cerebral cortex. Figure 2–17 shows a detailed schematic of the forebrain and its components. Note that the forebrain substructures discussed in the following sections are located on both sides of the brain.

Thalamus. The **thalamus** is a relatively large anatomical structure located near the center of the brain (see Figure 2–17). It is often considered "the great relay station of the brain," for it is through here that all auditory, visual, taste, and touch sensory signals must pass. The thalamus receives messages from the ears, eyes, and spinal cord and then projects those signals to the appropriate areas in the cortex (see the discussion of cortical brain areas later in this chapter). In this sense, the thalamus works like a central switch panel where interconnections are made to ensure that sensory inputs do not get lost in traffic. In addition, the thalamus functions as a clearing-house for motor impulses that need direction. When brain commands are sent to the various regions of the body, it is the thalamus that sends them along the proper channels.

thalamus the great relay station of the brain

Hypothalamus. The **hypothalamus** is a tiny neural mass that is located between the thalamus and the pituitary gland (see Figure 2–17). The hypothalamus is important to behavioral scientists because it is involved in regulating emotions and food intake. Regarding emotional behavior, the hypothalamus interacts with the pituitary to affect the way we feel. As we shall see, the pituitary is the master controller of the endocrine system, and it is part neural and part glandular. Because the endocrine system is prominently associated with emotional events related to fighting and fleeing (see Chapter 9), it makes sense that the hypothalamus—which affects the pituitary, and thereby other endocrine components—also influences emotions.

hypothalamus the part of the brain that interacts with the pituitary gland to affect the endocrine system

Because behaviors relating to the intake of food are strongly influenced by motivational variables, discussion of the link between the hypothalamus and hunger is reserved for Chapter 9. For now, we note that it is a complex issue that has received a great deal of research attention.

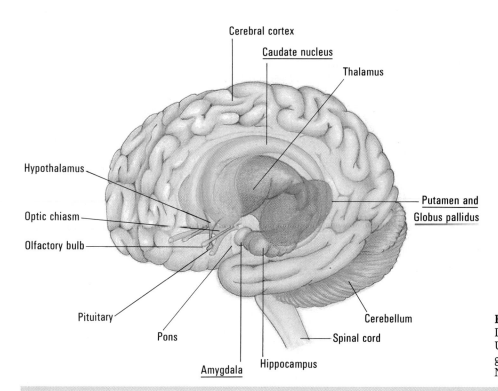

FIGURE 2–17
Detailed schematic of the forebrain. Underlined labels indicate basal ganglia structures. (Adapted from Nauta & Feirtag, 1979.)

basal ganglia a set of brain structures located between the thalamus and outside shell of the brain

Basal Ganglia. The term **basal ganglia** refers to a set of structures that are scattered between the thalamus and the outer shell of the brain: the amygdala, caudate nucleus, putamen, and globus pallidus (see Figure 2–17). The amygdala has attracted a great deal of attention from neuroscience investigators recently. Because of its role in the expression of emotions such as rage, fear, and happiness, the amygdala has lately been referred to as "emotion central." For years, the scientific position has been that the amygdala receives information from higher brain centers about emotional events and then communicates back to these higher centers, confirming that the expression of a particular emotion is appropriate. But recently, scientists have argued that incoming emotional transmissions come through the amygdala before that information ever makes its way to higher brain areas. It seems that the amygdala determines whether new information is emotionally relevant. For example, when a hunter is walking along and suddenly hears a loud noise that cracks the silence of the woods, that information goes directly to the amygdala. At this level the determination is made that this particular noise came from a falling tree branch. Once the amygdala catalogs the event as nonthreatening (it is not a gun shot, it is not an animal), the appropriate message is registered with higher brain centers. So, rather than being a secondary feature in the development and formation of emotional behavior, it is now believed that the amygdala is a primary agent of emotional control.

Along other lines, it has been shown that disruption of the neurochemistry of the basal ganglia leads to disturbances in motor behaviors, such as walking or drawing a picture. The problem seems to be one of integrating the different signals that are sent to the same muscle groups. When the basal ganglia are not working, the brain fires inconsistent signals to the limbs; thus, delicate movements are difficult to execute. This is precisely what happens with the hereditary disease known as **Huntington's chorea**. This disease is a degenerative disorder that begins around 40 or 50 years of age. It results when the cells of the basal ganglia begin to deteriorate. Because Huntington's is a genetically transmitted disease in which at least one parent must also have the affliction, neuropsychologists have attempted to control the incidence of the disorder through genetic counseling. Recent advances have been made in identifying psychological markers for it (Kolb & Whishaw, 1990). When these markers (memory impairment, low word fluency) indicate that a person who is at risk for Huntington's likely has the disease, that person and her or his spouse can be educated about the potential problems inherent in having children (for Huntington's patients, the chances are 50–50 that their children will also have the disease). It goes without saying that there are some sensitive moral challenges involved in genetic counseling, but many people would like to know what the chances are of transmitting the disorder to their children. Why? Because the disease involves severe disabling symptoms, such as delusions, uncontrollable jerking, and severe changes in personality.

Huntington's chorea a disorder resulting from degeneration of the basal ganglia, often associated with uncontrollable jerking and spasms

Limbic System. The limbic system is a collection of a number of structures, including the *septum, cingulate gyrus,* and *hippocampus.* In 1937, Papaz suggested that the limbic system was the anatomical location of emotion. We now know that while limbic structures may contribute partly to emotions, the real control of emotional responding lies elsewhere. Still, the limbic system has immense responsibilities. Consider the hippocampus as one example.

The hippocampus, named for its shape (sea horse), likely has received more attention from neuropsychologists than any other part of the limbic system. Unlike most other parts of the brain, the hippocampus can be completely removed with virtually no impairment of motor or sensory processes.

However, destruction of this brain region does affect memory events (see Chapter 7 for more details). Curiously, when the hippocampus is damaged, new memories cannot be formed, but old memories are left intact. Even more astonishing is the fact that the correlation between a dysfunctional hippocampus and memory problems is peculiar to certain types of forgetting.

Using modern brain imaging techniques such as the MRI procedure discussed earlier, it has become possible to relate memory difficulties to neuropathology in living patients (Press et al., 1989). By visualizing brain structures, it may be possible to classify patients according to the specific anatomical region that shows signs of cell death, deterioration, or physical abnormality. This is precisely what Larry Squire and his colleagues at the University of California at San Diego have recently accomplished.

Using a high-resolution MRI protocol, Squire, Amaral, and Press (1990) mapped the brains of four normal control subjects, four amnesia patients with *Korsakoff's syndrome*, and four amnesia patients not suffering from Korsakoff's syndrome. Korsakoff's syndrome results from excessive alcohol consumption over an extended period of one's life. Representative brain scans of a control patient, a Korsakoff's patient, and a non-Korsakoff's patient are shown in Figure 2–18. Close inspection of these pictures shows that the size of the hippocampus has shrunk for the non-Korsakoff's amnesia patient, but the hippocampus of the Korsakoff's syndrome patient is essentially the same size as that of the control subject. This pattern was evident across all other comparisons. Although not shown here, it was further observed that among the Korsakoff's syndrome patients, the brain region containing structures known as the *mammillary nuclei* was abnormally small compared to controls and non-Korsakoff's amnesia patients.

Such findings that point to the selective anatomical differences associated with contrasting types of neurological disturbance are truly exciting. Think of the advantages that such precision techniques may afford in terms of diagnosis. Whenever a particular neurological problem is difficult to identify, it might be possible to help classify and treat a patient through brain mapping. Scientists and medical professionals will always be needed to render human judgment, of course, but it is possible that more of the diagnostic load in medical evaluations will be computerized in the future.

Cerebral Cortex. Because *cortex* means "bark," this part of the human brain is appropriately named. The **cerebral cortex** covers the rest of the

cerebral cortex thick outer covering of the brain

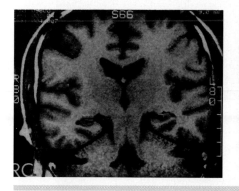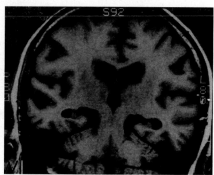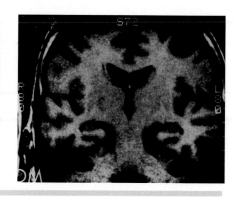

FIGURE 2–18
Modern neuroimaging techniques have greatly assisted in the classification of patients according to specific physical abnormalities. In this series of MRI scans, the anatomy of the hippocampus (shaded areas) is studied in control (*left*), non-Korsakoff's amnesiatic (*center*), and Korsakoff's (*right*) patients. Note that the size of the hippocampus of the non-Korsakoff's amnesiatic patient is smaller than either of the other two.

brain, and it has the same rough, wrinkled appearance as the bark of a tree. The cortex increases in size as we ascend the phylogenetic scale, and in humans, the cortex makes up over two thirds the weight of the entire nervous system. More than anything else in the human body, it is the cerebral cortex that distinguishes us from lower organisms. The ability to reason and think analytically is a talent unique to humans, and it is our superior cortical development that makes us more versatile and intelligent than our nonhuman counterparts. But recent technological advances have quite literally shed new light on the notion that increased cortical activity is associated with a more proficient brain. Let's have a closer look.

THINKING ABOUT
The Human Brain

Many aspects of human behavior present themselves so conspicuously that they really do not seem to require scientific examination. We all know, for example, that smarter people with lively intellects have more skillful minds than less intelligent individuals. You see it in their use of the language, in their ability to handle routine decisions, and even in their ability to grasp the injustices of nature—such as some people being blessed with better brains than others. Smart people just have more animated brains than those who are, let us say, less smart. So why bother to compare brain activity in intelligent and not-so-intelligent individuals? We have the answers already, and we do not need another scientist to restate the obvious.

Perhaps not, but science does have a way of debunking conventional wisdom. In one of the latest assaults on common sense, scientific research has challenged the old prejudice that less intelligent brains are lazy brains. Richard Haier, a psychiatrist conducting research at the University of California at Irvine, measured cortical activity of eight volunteers who varied considerably in terms of intelligence (Haier et al., 1988). While each of

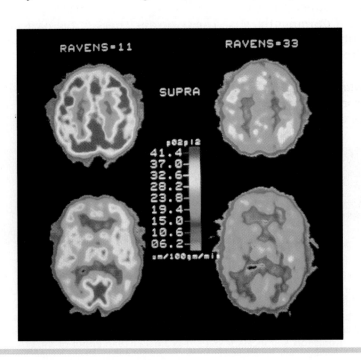

FIGURE 2–19
PET scans of less intelligent (*left*) and more intelligent (*right*) brains during a test of abstract reasoning.

the eight persons worked a series of problems that required abstract reasoning, PET scans were made. Recall from our previous discussion on imaging techniques that PET traces sugar metabolism and presents a color-coded map of neural activation in different brain regions. As Figure 2–19 shows, Haier discovered that more intelligent brains produced lackluster PET scans. By contrast, less intelligent brains generated colorful scans that would rival a Matisse painting because of splashes of red, green, and other bright colors, all of which are indicative of cell excitement. In an outrageous contradiction, this means that slow brains run fast, and fast brains run slow.

What accounts for the increased activity in the less intelligent brain? One possibility rests with the circuitry of the brain. Maybe smarter people have brains that are wired so elegantly that information is processed effortlessly; consequently, problems are solved quickly without inefficient expenditures of energy. By comparison, people with less intelligent brains may be "trying to solve the problem everywhere in the brain." Therefore, neural information may be transmitted pell-mell so that nothing much gets accomplished despite a lot of effort.

Whatever the explanation, such neurobiological findings underscore the need to investigate apparent relationships. Just because something seems that it should be a certain way, or just because we have always viewed it that way, does not mean that it *is* that way.

Can you think of another example of some conventional wisdom that has been discredited scientifically? How commonly does this occur?

Although fast and slow brains work differently on the inside, on the outside they are apt to look pretty much the same. Figure 2–20 shows some major landmarks that exist on the outer surface of the cortex. When looking down on the top of the brain (see three-quarter view), one sees a deep canyon that runs the full length of the brain (back to front). Such canyons are called **fissures**; this one, known as the longitudinal fissure, divides the brain into two symmetrical **hemispheres**. Two other smaller fissures are the central fissure and the lateral fissure (see side view). These help distinguish between the front (anterior) and back (posterior) sections of the brain. Conveniently, the boundaries created by these fissures partially identify the four major lobes that occur in each hemisphere of the brain: the frontal, parietal, occipital, and temporal lobes (see Table 2–3).

Frontal Lobes. The **frontal lobes** are located above the lateral fissure and in front of the central fissure (see Figure 2–20). The area of the frontal lobes closest to the central fissure is called the *motor cortex.* This band of

fissures deep canyonlike crevices in the brain's surface

hemispheres the two halves of the brain (left and right)

frontal lobes areas of the brain above the lateral fissure and in front of the central fissure

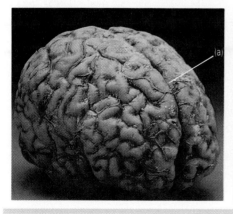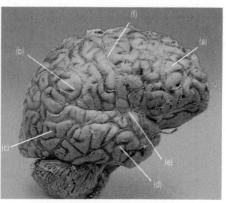

FIGURE 2–20
The human brain. *Left*: The longitudinal fissure (*a*) shown in three-quarter view from front. *Right*: Side view of right cerebral hemisphere, showing (*a*) frontal lobe, (*b*) parietal lobe, (*c*) occipital lobe, (*d*) temporal lobe, (*e*) lateral fissure, and (*f*) central fissure.

TABLE 2-3
Lobes of the Human Brain

Lobe	Location	Components	Functions
Frontal	Above lateral fissure, in front of central fissure	Motor cortex	Controls body movements
		Premotor cortex	Controls delicate motions
		Prefrontal cortex	Decision making
Parietal	Behind central fissure	Somatosensory cortex	Sensory processing
Occipital	Very back (posterior) section of brain	Primary visual cortex	Visual processing
Temporal	Below lateral fissure, in front of occipital lobe	Sensory and motor connections	Audition, memory, sexual behavior

cells is responsible for controlling movements in different parts of the body. Amazingly, it seems that specialized subsections of the motor cortex correspond to very specific body parts, such as the elbow, the knee, and the leg. Figure 2–21 presents a "motor homunculus," or graphic portrayal of the body as it is represented in different parts of the motor cortex. A number of experiments have been performed that show that electrical stimulation of discrete regions of the motor cortex evoke specific reactions like the turning of the head (see Kolb & Whishaw, 1990). It is not surpris-

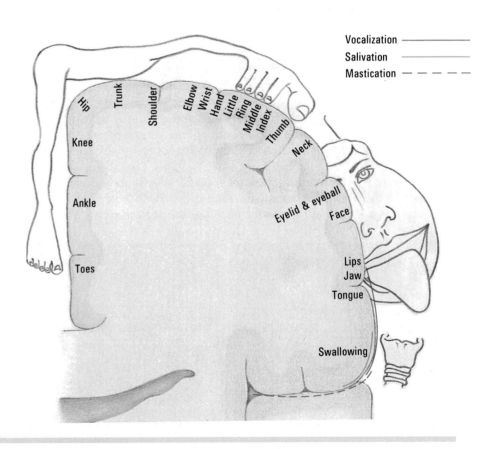

FIGURE 2–21
This "motor homunculus" reflects various regions of the motor cortex and the body parts they are believed to control. The drawing represents a cross section of the brain just in front of the central fissure.

ing, therefore, that when the motor cortex is damaged, paralysis often results. You may know of some child who has fallen from a swing or of an auto accident victim who has suffered the loss of movement of some part of the body. Barring a spinal cord injury, there is a good chance that the area affected by the accident was the motor cortex.

Near the forehead in the frontal region is the *premotor cortex*, which has the colossal chore of controlling our most delicate motions, such as threading a needle or performing triple-bypass heart surgery. But even more interesting is the large *prefrontal cortex* at the very front of the brain. This area is what most scientists have in mind when they speak about the frontal lobes. Although the prefrontal cortex barely exists in such standard laboratory animals as the rat, in humans it accounts for almost one third the entire weight of the cerebral cortex. The functional properties of the prefrontal cortex apparently include the ability to make judgments and to map out plans for solving problems. Working with rhesus monkeys, psychologist Patricia Goldman-Rakic of Yale University has shown that metabolic activity in the prefrontal cortical area changes when the animal has to make a decision. In fact, she has isolated individual neurons that are excited only when the monkey plans on making a certain response (Kojima & Goldman-Rakic, 1984).

Damage to the prefrontal cortex produces an assortment of behavior changes that include reduced abilities in visual scanning and problems with learning new concepts. Soviet psychologist Alexander Luria recorded the eye movements of patients with frontal-lobe damage as they examined the photograph reproduced in Figure 2–22. Notice the different ways a normal person and a patient scanned the picture. It is evident from the records of eye movement patterns that the patient's eye movements were chaotic and lacked organization or focus. By contrast, the patterns of the normal individuals showed concentrated attention to the important details (Luria, 1980).

Parietal Lobes. The **parietal lobes** of the cerebral cortex are in the region immediately behind the central fissure (refer to Figure 2–20). The front part of each parietal lobe is known as the *somatosensory cortex*. This section of the brain is the main part of the cortex that deals with sensations of touch, pressure, pain, temperature, itch, vibration, and even muscle tension. Over the years, studies have shown conclusively that specific locations on the somatosensory cortex correspond with sensory regions in some part of the body (Figure 2–23 represents this relation with a "sensory homunculus"). For example, pain coming from a sore thumb would be registered in a different place on the cortex than pain coming from abdominal cramps. Generally speaking, the amount of cortex devoted to a particular body region is directly proportional to the sensitivity of that region. Thus, the more sensitive hands and face should have greater representation than less sensitive body areas like the lower back, and indications are that this is the case.

It is important to note that the neural sensory fibers that go into the region of the somatosensory cortex actually deliver messages from the opposite side of the body. This means that if you fall and scrape your left knee, the damage report is sent to somatosensory cells in the right hemisphere. The evolutionary advantage of this crossover effect is unclear, but it seems to occur consistently in higher organisms, and it is true for both motor and sensory neurons.

Occipital Lobes. The **occipital lobes** of the cortex are found at the very back of the head and contain the *primary visual cortex*. The cells in this

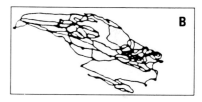

FIGURE 2–22
Eye movement records of subjects examining the above painting. (*A*) The normal person concentrates on important details, such as faces. (*B*) The eye movements of the patient, whose frontal lobes have been damaged, lack focus. (From Luria, 1980.)

parietal lobes areas of the cortex behind the central fissure

occipital lobes areas of the brain at the very back of the head

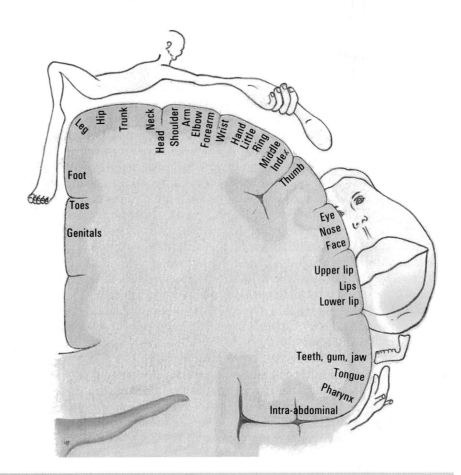

FIGURE 2-23
A "sensory homunculus" expressing the relation between various regions of the somatosensory cortex and the body parts they monitor. The drawing represents a cross section of the brain just in back of the central fissure.

reconstruct visual images coming from the eye so that selected features can be recognized. To get to the visual cortex, an impulse must begin at the receptor level in the eye (these receptors, located in the retina, are discussed in detail in Chapter 3). Light energy hitting the receptor provokes a neural signal that travels along the optic nerve to a major visual relay center in the thalamus. This center, known as the *lateral geniculate nucleus*, works to sharpen the contrast of the image and to organize certain visual features before they are reassembled in the cortex. When the visual information finally arrives at the visual cortex in the occipital region, specialized cells respond to specific stimulus features. For example, some cells will react to patterns that appear in the form of concentric rings, whereas others will detect only information about color.

When damage to the occipital lobe occurs, a *visual agnosia* may result. This term refers to an inability to combine individual visual impressions into complete patterns (Brown, 1988). Thus, a person shown an object might see only elements of the whole and therefore be unable to recognize it, demonstrate what to do with it, or even remember it as being familiar. Hécaen and Albert (1978) describe a case of visual object agnosia in a patient who had apparent damage to the left occipital lobe. The patient was shown a bicycle and described it as "a pole with two wheels, one in front, one in back." Without an intact visual cortex, the person evidently was unable to integrate the information obtained from the environment.

Temporal Lobes. The **temporal lobes** (refer to Figure 2–20) constitute the part of the cortex below the lateral fissure and bounded in the rear by the occipital region. The temporal lobes, which are rich in both sensory and

temporal lobes areas of the brain on the side of the head (below the lateral fissure)

motor connections to other brain regions, have many functions. Some of the operations that take place here are events related to the recording and interpreting of auditory sensations, memory processing, and the formation of personality traits. Even sexual behavior seems to be partly regulated by the temporal lobes.

Brain Differences

The notion that the hemispheres of the brain may look and perform differently—that is, are *asymmetrical*—has long been a matter for speculation among scientists and nonscientists alike. Scientists ask whether each hemisphere is a duplicate of the other, and if so, how much variation in appearance there is from person to person. Laypeople often make casual references to individuals as "left brain" or "right brain" dominant, and such remarks implicitly affirm the belief that one part of the brain is subordinate to another. Left brain people are thought to be more logical and verbal because they rely on language centers in the left hemisphere to solve problems. By comparison, right brain people supposedly cannot express themselves with words very well, but they are insightful and grasp the big picture quickly.

As intriguing as these ideas are, the evidence on anatomical and functional asymmetry in the brain is sometimes ambiguous and misleading. In the following sections we examine these provocative issues.

Anatomical Asymmetry: Different Looks.   Brain researchers who are concerned with differences in the anatomical organization of the brain have focused their attention on two variables: handedness and gender.

Witelson (1985) reviewed the available literature regarding the anatomical differences in the cerebral hemispheres of left- and right-handed persons, and concluded that in comparison to right-handers, left-handers are less likely to show asymmetry. This means that, anatomically speaking, the halves of the brain are more alike for left-handed people than for right-handed ones. Why is this true? Reasoning that the greater symmetry across hemispheres among lefties might be correlated with increased information exchange, and more shared responsibilities between the two hemispheres, Witelson measured the size of the corpus callosum in the postmortem brains of left- and right-handed people. Indeed, this connecting pathway between the hemispheres was found to be larger for the left-handers. Perhaps because of differences in early brain development, the lines of communication between the two hemispheres may become restricted for some people (right-handers); and as cognitive demands provoke changes in tissue formation, structural differences appear on one side but not the other. The greater communication permitted between hemispheres by the larger callosum in left-handers, however, would be associated with dual development in the hemispheres, and therefore greater symmetry between them.

This makes for a nice and clean, if somewhat speculative, picture of the relationship between handedness and anatomical asymmetry. This picture gets murky, however, when more recent evidence is considered. With the advantage of the sophisticated MRI technique, discussed earlier in this chapter, Kertesz, Polk, Howell, & Black (1987) were unable to see differences in the size of the corpus callosum for left-handers and right-handers. Although these disparate findings may derive from legitimate differences, they also may have something to do with the level of exactness that the measurement techniques entail. In any event, it would be reckless at this point to argue forcefully that handedness and anatomical asymmetry are meaningfully related.

Another controversial issue involving anatomical asymmetry of the brain concerns gender differences. At one time it was argued that the size and shape of the corpus callosum and hippocampus were different for males and females (Lacoste-Utamsing & Holloway, 1982). However, this argument was based on crude measurements of brains that were taken from corpses. More sophisticated brain imaging tests on persons still alive have failed to indicate that the brains of men and women are different (Kertesz et al., 1987). At this point, we can say that if anatomical asymmetry does vary according to sex, the difference is extremely slight and probably insignificant.

Functional Asymmetry: Different Work Loads. The idea that the left and right cerebral hemispheres may have different responsibilities and perform different tasks is referred to as *asymmetry of function* (Hellige, 1990). Over 100 years ago, Broca (1861) and Wernicke (1874) described the relationship between injuries to specific brain regions and behavioral changes. This work has been continued by Roger Sperry, Michael Gazzaniga, and others, and today represents one of the most fascinating studies in neuroscience. Findings in this area have shown that everything from hyperactivity to schizophrenia may be correlated with peculiar hemispheric patterns (Hynd et al., 1991). But of all the exciting discoveries in this area, perhaps none have proved more noteworthy than those dealing with language.

Language. Early work on language focused on the notion that speech is localized in the frontal lobe of the left hemisphere. In the 1800s Paul Broca identified a section of the left frontal lobe (**Broca's area**) that seemed to relate to expressive language. Damage to cells in this region (see Figure 2–24) produces a condition known as **expressive aphasia**, wherein the patient has difficulty speaking, although he or she continues to understand speech. The importance of specific brain regions for language events became even more apparent when an area in the left temporal–parietal cortex known as **Wernicke's area** was discovered to be the center for understanding language (see Figure 2–24). Lesions (any damage to the nervous system) in this part of the brain that occur because of disease or accidents produce a disorder known as **receptive aphasia**, which consists of an inability to grasp the meaning of words. The person hears the word correctly but

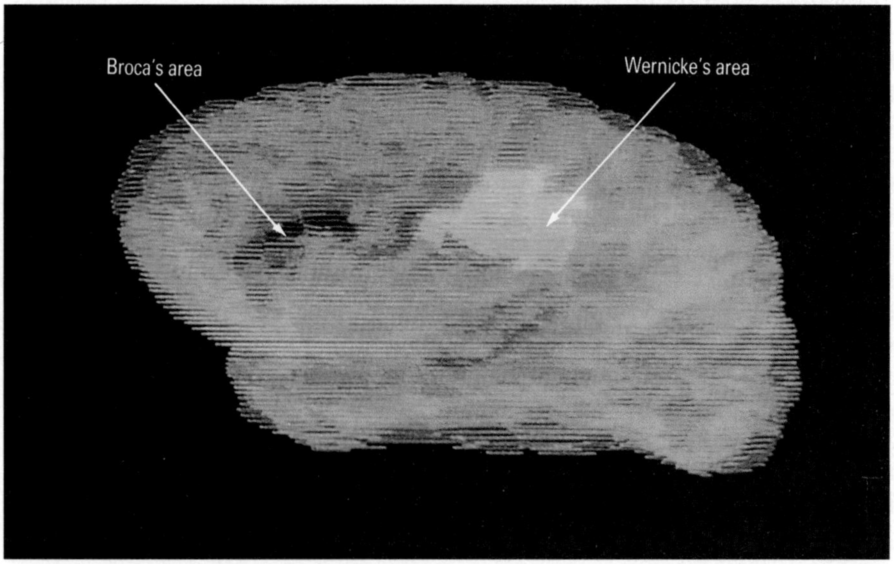

Broca's area the left frontal lobe region, associated with expressive language

expressive aphasia a condition in which the patient has difficulty speaking

Wernicke's area the left temporal–parietal lobe region, associated with receptive language

receptive aphasia a condition in which the patient has difficulty understanding language

FIGURE 2–24
The language areas of the left cerebral hemisphere. Broca's area is shown in red; Wernicke's area is shown in blue.

finds it difficult to interpret. In some cases a patient may act as if words are being spoken in a foreign language and may ask to hear them again. Other receptive aphasics confuse the grammatical arrangement of words. For example, the phrase "the boy's brown belt" may be understood as "the brown boy's belt," in which case the original intent of the statement is lost.

Although it is true that the bulk of language events take place in the left hemisphere, it should be understood that verbal processing is not the exclusive province of the left brain. Although the right brain does not normally have much to do with speech production, it may assist Wernicke's area in the recognition of words (Kitterle, 1989). Indeed, as indicated from the following case history reported by E. Sherman (1987), all language operations may be assumed by the right side of the brain in extreme instances. The story began on a lazy summer night in Denver, Colorado. Terry Francisco suddenly heard a clamor coming from her 18-month-old daughter Maranda's room. She raced into the bedroom. Maranda was having a massive seizure, and she was convulsing so violently that it appeared that her tiny body would break apart. Terry went to the kitchen and dialed 911. An ambulance arrived in moments.

After an hour, doctors finally were able to stop the wild twitching, and the seizure gave way to sleep. But Maranda suffered an even greater seizure within 2 weeks, and medication proved to be less effective. Diagnosed as epilepsy, Maranda's problem only grew worse. Seizures started coming once or twice a week, then once or twice a day. Soon Maranda was having more than 100 seizures a day—they were virtually nonstop.

Two and one half years after her initial seizure, Maranda was almost paralyzed on the right side of her body, and the right side of her lip drooped so much she couldn't even smile. All Maranda would say was, "Please, no more seizures, Mommy." Then, a physician at the epilepsy center at the Children's Hospital in Denver made a startling discovery. Brain scans showed that Maranda was suffering not from epilepsy but from *Rasmussen's encephalitis*, a progressive brain disorder. A bad situation became even worse. If something was not done, Maranda would soon be incapacitated for life.

Following a referral to the Johns Hopkins Medical Center in Baltimore, a dramatic decision was made. The entire diseased left half of Maranda's brain would have to be removed. Because the left hemisphere controls speech, it was likely that Maranda would lose her ability to speak, and possibly all movement on the right side of her body, assuming she survived at all. In an act of desperation, the parents approved this extreme effort. Following the 10-hour surgery, Terry looked down on Maranda as she lay on her hospital bed during recovery.

"She was so puffy. I couldn't see her eyes. Her lip was five times its normal size and drooped terribly over the left side of her face," Terry recalls. "Yet she looked beautiful to me, because she was alive."

Terry leaned over, gave her daughter a kiss and said, "I love you, Maranda." And then, something wonderful happened. Maranda unexpectedly kissed her mother back and whispered, "I love you, Mommy and Daddy." (E. Sherman, 1987)

The fact that Maranda was able to speak at all, let alone so soon, has been cause for neuroscientists to reevaluate the ability of the brain to transfer responsibilities of given brain regions to other areas, and even to a different hemisphere. Today, Maranda tests above grade level in vocabulary, and her motor development on the right side of her body continues to show marked improvement.

Case histories such as Maranda's, along with numerous laboratory experiments, have sparked an interest in studying right brain functions in greater detail. Although left brain functions attract considerably more attention because of the language centers located in this hemisphere, some aspects of the right hemisphere are proving to be equally exciting.

Spatial Reasoning. One of the most important discoveries made to date concerning the specialized abilities of the right hemisphere has to do with spatial reasoning. Patients suffering from damage to the right hemisphere perform consistently more poorly on standard psychological tests that require the patient to distinguish among several visual stimuli. The puzzling thing is that these people have quite good verbal ability, but when the task requires them to manipulate geometric figures, complete missing parts of a puzzle, or recognize pictures, their performance is substantially impaired. In some cases, it is difficult for patients with a damaged right hemisphere to recognize faces, and they may not recognize once familiar friends and relatives at all (de Schonen & Mathivet, 1989).

Studies of left-handedness provide additional evidence that the right half of the brain is involved with spatial reasoning. Consistent with the notion that a given hemisphere controls the opposite side of the body, it has been shown that left-handers are three times more likely to be right brain dominant than their right-handed counterparts (Hellige, 1990). It follows that activities linked to the special abilities of the right brain should be easier to accomplish for left-handers. Mathematics, for example, should be easier for left-handed persons because of their increased spatial reasoning ability. In support of this rationale, Benbow and Stanley (1983) report that 20% of the students scoring high (above 700) on the math section of the Scholastic Aptitude Test (SAT) were left-handed. This figure on the incidence of left-handedness among talented math students is double that of the general population. But many psychologists question the validity of Benbow and Stanley's interpretation. For one thing, males are more likely than females to be left-handed and to enroll in math classes. Consequently, the increased representation of left-handers among the mathematically gifted may merely reflect differences in interests and experiences.

This brings us to a major controversy in psychology today. Are males and females biologically predisposed to perform differently on spatial reasoning and language usage tasks? Although uninformed prejudices have undoubtedly contributed to a widely held belief that females have better verbal ability and that males have better quantitative ability, the real catalyst in this debate was a pioneering scientific review of the literature presented by Maccoby and Jacklin (1974). According to these researchers, evidence indeed suggests that girls tend to perform better in English classes, and boys tend to do better in math classes. Many people have assumed that these performance differences reflect native differences in underlying cognitive abilities. But an update on this topic questions the validity of such an assumption. In a comprehensive, cross-sectional study of cognitive differences between the sexes, psychologist Alan Feingold of Yale University found that even if differences between females and males did exist in earlier generations, they are disappearing rapidly. In an examination of test scores in the Differential Aptitude Tests (DAT) and the SAT from 1960 until 1983, Feingold found substantial verbal and quantitative differences between the sexes in 1960. However, by the 1980s these differences had either disappeared or lessened by half (Feingold, 1988).

The fact that the verbal and quantitative test scores of males and females have been converging over the past few decades does not completely resolve the controversy, however. Scientists favoring the idea that biology dictates cognitive differences between women and men quickly point out that some performance differences remain, as does the question of gender-related differences in brain anatomy. In contrast, those who oppose the deterministic biological position focus on childhood training and attitudes as an explanation for cognitive gender differences. As they note, our society still promotes stereotypes of males as good engineers and females as good English teachers. Although clear conclusions about gender differences cannot be made yet, one point is clear: the average score—and not the range of scores—differs for males and females. In other words, some females have math ability as good as the best males, and some males are as eloquent and fluent as the most verbal females. Therefore, on an individual basis, no one should feel handicapped in a particular quantitative or verbal situation.

The Split Brain

Ordinarily, there is a perpetual flow of neural messages back and forth between hemispheres along a major nerve-fiber pathway known as the **corpus callosum**. As detailed in Figure 2–25, this bundle of connecting neu-

corpus callosum the pathway connecting left and right cerebral hemispheres

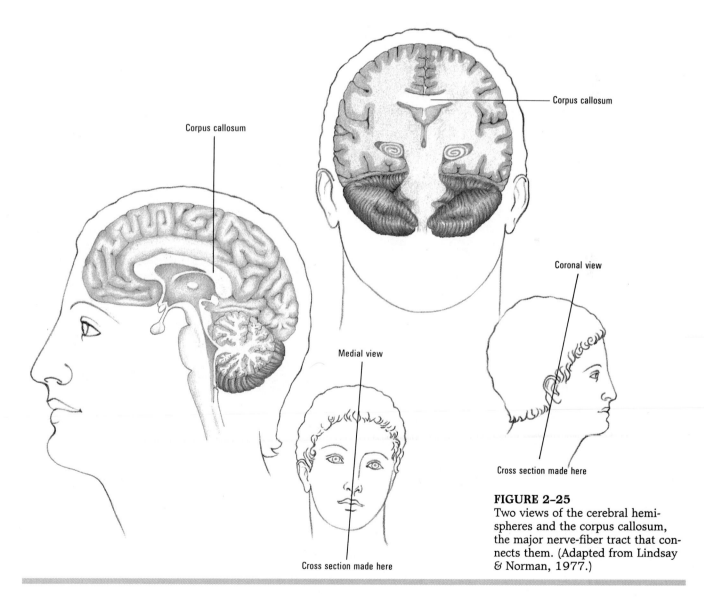

Corpus callosum

Corpus callosum

Coronal view

Medial view

Cross section made here

Cross section made here

FIGURE 2–25
Two views of the cerebral hemispheres and the corpus callosum, the major nerve-fiber tract that connects them. (Adapted from Lindsay & Norman, 1977.)

rons is positioned immediately below the large longitudinal fissure that separates the brain hemispheres. This anatomical arrangement is particularly convenient for surgery because the callosum can be cut without affecting other brain regions.

The opportunity to study the psychological and behavioral effects of splitting the human brain (cutting the corpus callosum) came when Roger Sperry and his co-workers were given access to hospital patients who already had split brains due to prior surgeries performed in an effort to control seizures (Sperry, 1974). Using a creative testing methodology (as follows), the researchers demonstrated that sensory information sent to only one side of the patient's brain was not transferred to the other side.

Understanding human split-brain research requires some basic grasp of the way that visual processing takes place. The diagram of the visual pathways to each hemisphere in Figure 2–26 shows how visual cues from the right visual field are registered only in the left hemisphere, and how visual cues from the left visual field are registered only in the right hemisphere. To ensure that stimuli are present in only one of the two visual

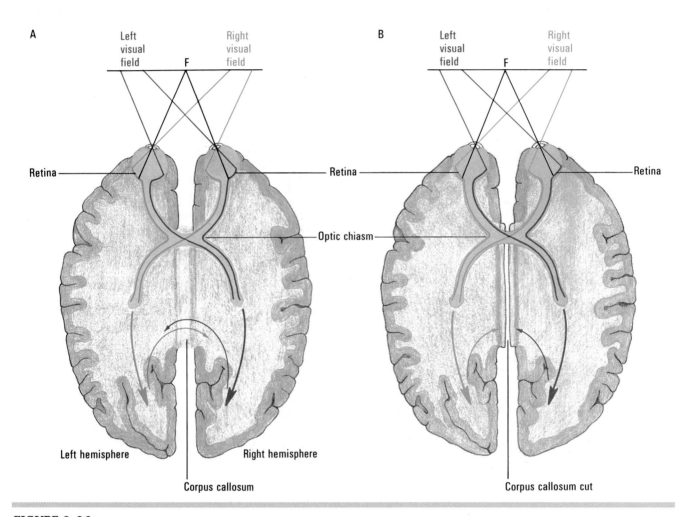

FIGURE 2-26
Visual pathways to the left and right hemispheres. When focusing on point F, each eye sees both visual fields, but information about a specific field is sent only to the opposite hemisphere. Normally, (A), this information is shared across hemispheres. When the corpus callosum is cut, however, (B), communication from one hemisphere to the other is not possible. In such a case, each hemisphere can see only half the total visual array.

FIGURE 2–27
The basic apparatus used in testing
split-brain patients.

fields, the person is instructed to fixate on an object in the center of the overall field. This effectively freezes the entire visual array. It also guarantees that objects to the right of the fixation point will be represented only in the left occipital cortex, whereas those on the left will be seen only by the right side of the brain. Normally, the visual world is fully represented in both hemispheres because of the communication through the corpus callosum. But in split-brain patients, the usual sort of communication does not occur (Figure 2–26B). Therefore, it is possible to inform one side of the brain about something without the other side finding out about it.

Preliminary split-brain studies were conducted using equipment similar to that shown in Figure 2–27. Patients were seated at a table in front of a screen that had a small black dot projected onto its center. With the patient focusing on the dot (and thus freezing the visual array, as just discussed), a picture of a spoon, for example, was projected to the right of the dot. When the patient was asked at this point what had been seen, he or she accurately reported that a spoon had been presented. The patient was again asked to focus on the dot, but this time the visual cue, say a cup, was presented to the left of the dot. When asked what he or she had seen, the patient was unable to verbally report seeing anything. But the patient had seen the cup, because when asked to reach under the screen and, with the left hand, to feel for the object that had been presented, the patient had no difficulty in selecting the cup from among several objects that were available.

Here is apparently what happened in this astonishing illustration of split-brain behavioral disturbance. When the spoon was presented in the right visual field, the information was sent to the left hemisphere. Because the left hemisphere contains the major language centers, the patient had no problem providing a verbal report of what had been seen. But when the visual stimulus was sent from the left visual field to the right hemisphere and confined there by virtue of the dysfunctional corpus callosum, a verbal description of the cue was not possible. In other words, because the right hemisphere is not usually involved in speech, a word could not be used to communicate what had been seen. But the left hand, which is controlled by the right side of the brain, could be used to show what was seen, as these motor operations were intact and centered on the side of the brain that received the message.

Split-brain studies have been used to evaluate the functional capacity of each hemisphere regarding the control of such behaviors as reading, writing, memory storage and retrieval, and even reasoning. For example, it has been shown that split-brain patients do almost as well at solving abstract problems using the right hemisphere as they do when using the left hemisphere (Cronin-Golomb, 1986). This tells us that such learning is not necessarily tied to the language processes that occur predominately in the left hemisphere. Even more ambitious studies should help us better understand the complex interactions between the halves of the brain.

THE ENDOCRINE SYSTEM

It is unlikely that any present-day psychologist would argue against the idea that the nervous system is the most important biological feature underlying human behavior. But the chances are equally remote that any psychologist would argue that the nervous system is the only determinant of human conduct. In this section we discuss another body system that plays a significant role in controlling our actions. This system is a complicated but elegantly regulated internal feedback network known as the **endocrine system**.

The endocrine system is composed of glands that secrete (empty) their chemical products into the bloodstream (see Figure 2–28). These secreted products, called **hormones**, circulate with the blood to influence parts of the body that are distantly located from the site of the endocrine gland. This pattern of action is to be distinguished from that of exocrine glands (e.g. salivary glands), which dump their products into local body cavities.

If you had the opportunity to undertake a serious, in-depth study of the endocrine system, you would very likely be stunned, first by the complexity of the biochemical machinery and then by the splendor of it all. The spectrum of behavior influenced by hormone balances or imbalances is enormous, yet in every case there is a monitoring station that makes sure nothing goes wrong. One event is checked by another, which in turn is checked by yet another, and this process continues in a state of suspended harmony. Or, at least this is true until some outside force excites the system and challenges its tranquility. Not surprisingly, this aggravation often comes from the nervous system.

The nervous system exerts its influence on the endocrine system through the pituitary gland. The **pituitary**, which has been called the master gland of the body, is a pea-sized structure located beneath the hypothalamus. The posterior part of the gland is made up of neural tissue, and it is this part of the gland that receives direct input from the brain. This input leads to the release of hormones that affect internal water balance (vasopressin) and the production of breast milk (oxytocin). The anterior portion of the pituitary, on the other hand, receives input indirectly from the brain

endocrine system an internal feedback network that maintains hormonal balance

hormones chemicals released from endocrine glands

pituitary master gland that provides brain and hormonal control of endocrine functions

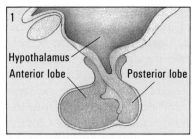

Posterior lobe of pituitary: controls internal water balance, production of breast milk.
Anterior lobe of pituitary: hormones influence secretions of the thyroid, pancreas, adrenal cortex and gonads (ovaries, testes). Also secretes growth hormones.

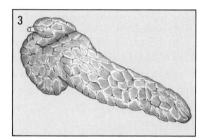

Pancreas: insulin and glucagon control glucose metabolism

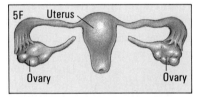

Ovaries: produce hormones that affect bodily development and that maintain reproductive organs in adult female.

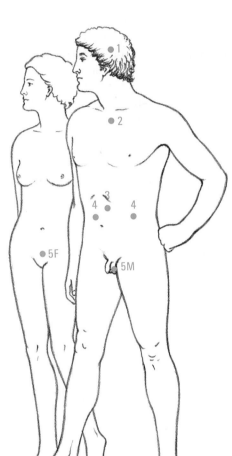

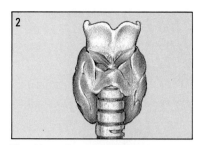

Thyroid: regulates metabolic processes.

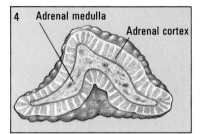

Adrenal medulla: secretion of epinephrine and norepinephrine.
Adrenal cortex: glucocorticoids control glucose metabolism.

Testes: produce hormones that affect bodily development and that maintain reproductive organs in adult male.

FIGURE 2–28
Locations and functions of some major endocrine glands.

by way of "releasing hormones" that the brain dumps into the blood-stream. These releasing hormones cause the anterior pituitary to secrete a variety of other hormones. Chief among these hormones are growth hormone (somatotropin), adrenocorticotropic hormone (ACTH), and thyroid-stimulating hormone (TSH).

In addition to the pituitary gland, the adrenal gland should be considered one of the endocrine structures that is most essential to psychological functioning. There is an adrenal gland located next to each kidney. One group of hormones released by the adrenals is called glucocorticoids, so named because they produce dramatic changes in glucose (sugar) metabolism. In addition to their healing actions on damaged bodily tissue, these hormones extensively modify the properties of muscle tissue, increasing strength and endurance under conditions of stress. It is these latter effects that prompt both amateur and professional athletes to supplement the body's natural supply of these hormones. The adrenal glands also secrete epinephrine and norepinephrine. These hormones double as neurotransmitters, and both are very much involved in emergency reactions. When you are frightened, angry, or otherwise aroused, the autonomic nervous system stimulates the release of epinephrine and norepinephrine from the adrenals. The resulting increase in these hormones aids the body's effort to respond to environmental demands by increasing blood flow, heart rate, blood sugar levels, and so forth.

We see that in addition to the nervous system, the endocrine system has been a focus for psychologists. Still another concern is the genetic makeup of the individual.

GENETICS AND BEHAVIOR

To understand fully why people behave as they do, you must have some knowledge of their biological predispositions to respond in certain ways. Each of us has been provided with a hereditary makeup that distinguishes us from everyone else, and in that sense we are special. It is because we are special that psychological principles must be applied cautiously and with an awareness that the mechanism responsible for one person's behavior may exist in diminished form or not even be present in another person. The field of psychology that undertakes the awesome task of clarifying the role played by our inheritance in behavioral development is called **behavioral genetics**.

As you read this section, understand that all psychologists subscribe to the basic idea that both our genetic endowment and our environmental experiences influence behavior. The real issue is where to draw the line; that is, which contributes more, nature or nurture (see Chapter 12)? The tendency in the past has been to favor nurture (environment), but recently there has been a gravitation toward nature, or the genetic side. Our discussion of inherited abilities begins with an examination of the most basic mechanisms of heredity and behavior.

Chromosomes and Genes

Inside the nucleus of each cell in the human body are structures known as **chromosomes**. Chromosomes appear in the cell as visible strands of material that are aligned in pairs. There are a total of 46 chromosomes dispersed in the cell as 23 separate pairs. At the moment of conception, the sperm from the father and the egg from the mother each contribute 23 chromosomes, in order to make up 23 matched pairs. It is pairing number 23 that determines the sex of the offspring, and for this reason the chromosomes comprising the 23rd pair have been labeled the sex chromosomes. Chromosomes serve as carriers of **genes**, which are the basic building blocks of life.

Chromosomal Abnormalities

Chromosomal abnormalities are actually quite common, but in most cases the genetic prescription is so badly out of line that spontaneous abortion occurs. Nevertheless, about 1 in 200 babies is born with some abnormality in chromosomal makeup (Gorlin, 1977). Because our intellectual and cog-

behavioral genetics study of the effects of genetics on behavior

chromosomes strands of material inside a cell nucleus that contain genes

genes basic building blocks of life

nitive abilities are believed to be controlled by so many different genes, it is not surprising that in most cases reports of chromosomal abnormality include some evidence of behavioral disturbance as well. We will concentrate on a few of the more dramatic versions that involve entire additional or deleted chromosomes.

Down Syndrome. In 1959, it was discovered that a certain type of mental deficiency was associated with having a 47th chromosome. This condition, called **Down syndrome**, results from an extra chromosome on the 21st pair. This disorder is relatively common, occurring once in every 700 births. Formerly known as mongolism, the most obvious physical characteristics of Down syndrome are obliquely slanted eyes, small folds of skin over the inner corners of the eyes, a round face and head, and short, stubby fingers and toes. Along with the mental retardation of Down syndrome comes a delightful disposition characterized by cheerfulness and affection. Although the life expectancy for someone who has Down was only a few years ago little more than 20 years, recent advances in modern medicine are extending the chances for longer survival.

Down syndrome a type of mental retardation resulting from an extra chromosome on the 21st pair

Abnormal Sex Chromosomes. We noted previously that the 23rd pair of chromosomes determines the sex of the offspring. Close inspection of this pair reveals that females possess two chromosomes that are the same size and shape. It is principally because of their shape that they are called X chromosomes. Males, on the other hand, have one X chromosome in pair 23 and one chromosome called a Y chromosome that is of a different shape and size. It follows that at fertilization, the mother contributes an X chromosome (the only type she has to offer), and the father contributes either an X or a Y chromosome. XX pairs create females, and XY pairs produce males. Thus, it is really the father who determines the sex of the child. What an irony it is that Henry VIII, King of England, cast off several wives for failure to provide him with a male heir. If there was a culprit, it was Henry, and not the wives he abandoned.

Sometimes the offspring does not get the full sex chromosomal complement, or, by contrast, extra sex chromosomes may appear. When only a single X chromosome is present, and nothing else, **Turner's syndrome** is the result. People with this disorder have only limited secondary sexual development, short stature, and a webbed neck, but there is no associated mental retardation. When a phenotypic male receives an extra X chromosome (XXY), **Klinefelter's syndrome** occurs. In this condition, the person has the outward appearance (phenotype) of a male who has only minimal sexual development, and personality disturbances such as passiveness and reclusiveness are common clinical symptoms. Because the disorder can occur in varying degrees, it is often difficult to diagnose. Consequently, it is not unusual to discover that people who are diagnosed originally as suffering from depression, eating disorders, and so forth, actually have an extra X chromosome (Hindler & Norris, 1986).

Turner's syndrome a condition that results when a single X chromosome is present

Klinefelter's syndrome a condition that results when there is an extra X chromosome in a phenotypic male

Genetics and Crime

There has been a long history associated with attempting to link violent criminal behavior to a particular genetic profile. Dating back to the middle of the nineteenth century, Sir Francis Galton launched a scientific initiative that he called *eugenics*. Eugenics was designed to uncover the genetic basis for a variety of human behaviors, including aggression. Later, in 1876, Cesare Lombroso published *L' Uomo Delinquente*, stating that criminals were the products of heredity and could be recognized by features such as small restless eyes (thieves) or cracked voices (sex criminals). Then, as recently as the 1970s, a study that was later discredited was published that argued that violence and crime were more likely among XYY males (males with an extra Y sex chromosome).

Despite the fact that none of the theories on crime as an inherited trait have been substantiated, many continue to argue for the idea that genetics is an important determinant of criminal behavior (Goleman, 1992). An international conference on "Genetic Factors in Crime" was scheduled for October 1992 at the University of Maryland, and the National Institutes of Health (NIH) initially indicated the agency would cover the costs of the meeting. Funds were later withdrawn, however, because of the limited scientific information on the subject. So, although the idea of a genetic basis to criminal behavior has advocates even today, there is meager empirical support for this position.

Twin Studies

An ideal method for studying the effects of genetics on behavior is to sample two different people having the same genotype (genetic makeup) and place them in different environments. Similarities in behavior between such people could then be attributed to biologically determined factors, such as a built-in genetic program.

Twin studies have been used in the past to get at some of these very issues. Typical comparisons involve identical, or monozygotic, twins and fraternal, or dizygotic, twins. Because monozygotic twins come from a single zygote (fertilized egg), they have exactly the same genes. This is not true for dizygotic twins, who develop from separate zygotes. Dizygotic twins are no more alike genetically than ordinary siblings. The research in this area is fairly consistent in showing that general physical and psychological traits are more highly correlated among monozygotic than dizygotic twins (also see Chapter 12). Much of what we know along these lines has come from the Minnesota Study of Twins Reared Apart, which began in 1979. Psychologist Thomas Bouchard and his colleagues collected data from more than 100 twins who were separated early in life and reared in different homes (Bouchard et al., 1990). Only the fourth such data set compiled in history, this Minnesota group has reported evidence favoring a genetic basis for behavior. For example, intelligence has been found to be much more alike for identical twins than for fraternal twins.

Additional research from the Bouchard group has shown more directly that it really does not make that much difference if monozygotic twins grow up in the same environment or a different one; they turn out much the same (Bouchard et al., 1990). For instance, as shown in Table 2–4, physical characteristics, IQ, personality, and even interests were highly correlated for identical twins, regardless of whether they were reared together. This implies that genetic factors play a strong role in the formation of behavior and that environmental experiences have a limited impact in determining everything from our temperament to the way we spend our leisure time. Of course, these data have not gone unchallenged. Dudley (1991) has argued that many of the twins in the Minnesota data set were in fact reared in the same community, went to the same schools, and so on. Were their environments really that different? Besides, the mere fact that identical twins have the same physical appearance may cause people to react to them similarly (Beckwith, Geller, & Sarkar, 1991). The *effective psychological environment* in such cases might not be dramatically different.

TABLE 2-4
The correlations on several physical and psychological measures for
monozygotic (identical) twins reared apart or together. The higher the
correlation statistic (r), the greater the similarities.

Variables (reference)	Identical twins living apart		Identical twins living together	
	Correlation r	Pairs (no.)	Correlation r	Pairs (no.)
Anthropometric variables				
Fingerprint ridge count	0.97	54	0.96	274
Height	0.86	56	0.93	274
Weight	0.73	56	0.83	274
Psychophysiologic variables				
Systolic blood pressure	0.64	56	0.70	34
Heart rate	0.49	49	0.54	160
Mental ability—general factor				
WAIS IQ–full scale	0.69	48	0.88	40
WAIS IQ–verbal	0.64	48	0.88	40
WAIS IQ–performance	0.71	48	0.79	40
Raven, Mill-Hill composite	0.78	42	0.76	37
Personality variables				
Mean of 11 Multidimensional Personality Questionnaire (MPQ) scales	0.50	44	0.49	217
Mean of 18 California Psychological Inventory (CPI) scales	0.48	38	0.49	99
Psychological interests				
Mean of 23 Strong Campbell Interest Inventory (SCII) scales	0.39	52	0.48	116
Mean of 17 Minnesota Occupational Interest scales	0.40	40	0.49	376

Source: Adapted from Bouchard et al., 1990.

With such warnings about interpreting twin data, it is easy to see why
psychologists are cautious about making strong statements about genetics
and behavior. Still, the opportunity to study identical and fraternal twins
who have lived apart provides a fascinating experiment of nature, and the
model will continue to be used.

THINKING AHEAD . . .

In this chapter, we have seen that there is a profound link between biology and behavior. Really, we should not be surprised by the scientific interest in looking for physiological explanations of behavior. Historically speaking, this connection has been a rich one. Even the magnificent frescoes on the ceiling of the Vatican's Sistine Chapel, painted between 1508 and 1512 by the brilliant Italian Renaissance artist Michelangelo, may have been inspired by the anatomy of the human brain (see Figure 2–29). In addition, more than three centuries ago the French philosopher René Descartes maintained that human behavior was the end product of machinelike changes inside the body. Walking, speaking, writing, sailing, laughing, expressing anger, and indeed everything we do was viewed as an elaborate combination of changes in relays, pulleys, and switches. Fundamentally, the neuroscientists of the 1990s have not shifted from this early frame of reference. The general belief is that, ultimately, ordinary and extraordinary behavioral events can be reduced to molecular and biochemical operations. Although the characterization of the shape, size, and form of Descartes' machine parts has been modified appreciably, the basic contention that psychology should address the mechanisms of behavior remains.

At present, much of the incredible human machinery eludes description. While the advances in imaging and recording techniques have contributed substantially to the information base in neuroscience, most of the nervous system is a still unanswered riddle. While we understand that certain types of neurological diseases such as Parkinson's disease and Huntington's disease are correlated with disturbances in specific nerve pathways, we cannot grasp the true complexity of a disordered brain. What happens to the millions of synapses that are affected by deteriorating neurons? Because of the compensatory capability of the human brain, what biochemical rescue attempts are launched by remote brain regions, and why aren't they more successful? Elsewhere, inasmuch as the endorphins were detected only about 20 years ago, what other endogenous chemicals await discovery? Neuroscientists are very much aware of the fact that there is a naturally occurring chemical inside our body that regulates GABA-mediated changes in anxiety and fear, but we have yet to isolate this anxiety correlate. What happens when we do? Will there be a new raft of drugs designed to control this negative emotional state? There probably will be. Beyond that, what is the fate of this relentless pattern of search, characterize, exploit, and change?

Along these lines, what does the future hold? Because the future belongs to each of you, the answers must come from your private thoughts and points of reflection. Think about the world you will be shaping. If it becomes within your power to chemically control behavior (and someday this may happen), what will you do with this immense power? Will you render all people happy and free of pathology? What limits will you impose with respect to making all people alike? Think carefully here and be deliberate as you muse—the consequences may devastate or exalt.

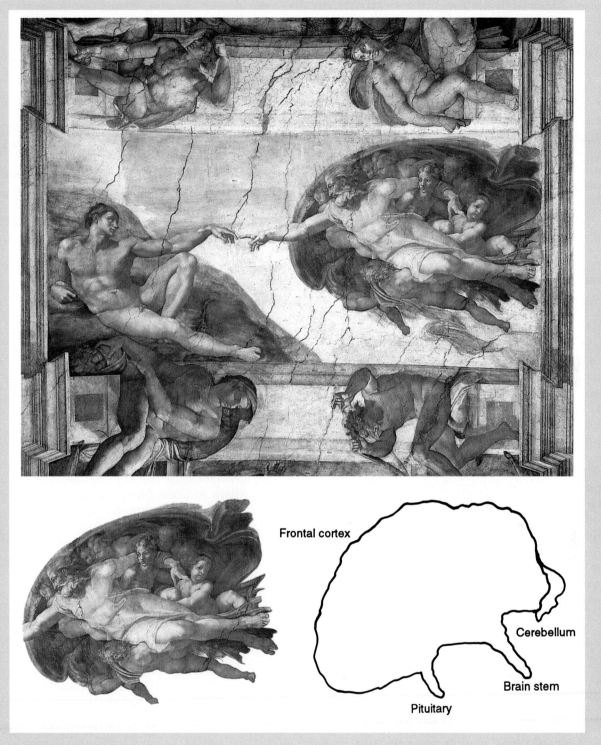

FIGURE 2–29
The top photo is a picture of Michelangelo's *Creation of Adam*, painted on the ceiling of the Vatican's Sistine Chapel. Below, you can see that the image that surrounds God and the angels has the shape of a human brain. (From Meshberger, 1990.)

The Nervous System: Structure and Function

1. The neural chain consists of (a) specialized cells called receptors that pick up information from the environment, (b) afferent (sensory) neurons that carry the neural message toward the central nervous system, (c) interneurons that serve to transmit the signal from one location to another within the central nervous system, (d) efferent (motor) neurons that send the neural message away from the central nervous system, and (e) effectors, which are muscles and glands that operate back on the environment.

2. The four basic regions of a neuron are (a) dendrites, (b) soma or cell body, (c) axon, and (d) terminal buttons.

3. The point where two neurons interconnect is called the synapse. The synaptic cleft is the space between the terminal buttons of the neuron sending the signal and the dendrites of the neuron receiving the signal. Chemicals called neurotransmitters cross the synaptic cleft and in this way allow the neural signal to pass from one neuron to the next. Some drugs such as cocaine have their effect by altering the way that neurotransmitters work. Neurotransmitters may be either excitatory or inhibitory. Imbalances in neurotransmitter levels are associated with many behavior disorders, including schizophrenia, anxiety, and hyperkinesis.

4. Neuromodulators are a newly discovered class of chemicals that affect neuronal activity. Unlike neurotransmitters that operate on a point-to-point basis, neuromodulators come from remote body regions to affect the excitability of neurons. The opioid peptides (enkephalins, beta-endorphins, dynorphins) are examples of neuromodulators that seem to play an important role in pain transmission.

5. Prolonged or intense stress can cause the immune system to be impaired, leading to an increase in disease, and even death.

6. The neural signal, or impulse, involves the depolarization of the neural membrane. The change in electrical potential that accompanies the ion exchange is the key feature of the impulse.

Organization of the Nervous System

7. The nervous system is subdivided into the central nervous system (CNS) and the peripheral nervous system (PNS). The CNS is further broken down into the brain and spinal cord, and the PNS is comprised of the somatic and autonomic subsystems. Within the autonomic classification, a further distinction is made between the sympathetic and parasympathetic divisions.

8. New imaging techniques help us better understand the brain. Such techniques include computerized axial tomography (CAT), positron emission tomography (PET), magnetic resonance imaging (MRI), and electroencephalograph (EEG) computerized classification schemes.

9. The brain is a complicated anatomical structure that is divided into forebrain, midbrain, and hindbrain sections according to structure and functions. The hindbrain and midbrain are concerned with movement, alertness, and vital bodily activities such as breathing and swallowing. One disorder that occurs when the midbrain neurochemistry is disturbed is Parkinson's disease. Fetal tissue transplants represent one possible, although controversial, treatment for this disorder. The forebrain is really the thinking part of the brain. Of the various forebrain substructures, the massive cerebral cortex is by far the most important to humans. Although contrary to expectation, it seems that cortical activity in less intelligent brains is greater than in more intelligent brains.

10. Large crevasses in the cortex called fissures form four discrete lobes in the brain; they are the frontal, parietal, occipital, and temporal lobes. The longitudinal fissure that runs the full length of the brain (back to front) further divides the brain into the left and right cerebral hemispheres.

11. Brain differences may occur as structural differences in the cerebral hemispheres. Although there is some evidence of anatomical differences according to handedness and gender, the differences are not compelling.

12. Functional differences exist to the extent that the left and right hemispheres control different processes. For example, there is now evidence to indicate that the left hemisphere possesses the control centers for language, whereas the right hemisphere's specialty is spatial reasoning.

13. Split-brain patients are those persons who have had the corpus callosum cut. The corpus callosum is the bundle of fibers that connects the left and right cerebral hemispheres. Split-brain research by Roger Sperry and his associates has revealed that the hemispheres are capable of working independently of one another.

The Endocrine System

14. The endocrine system controls the balance of hormones in our body, primarily through the involve-

ment of the pituitary gland. Hormonal effects on behavior include changes in arousal level, sexual habits, and amount of reported stress.

Genetics and Behavior

15. The field of psychology that attempts to clarify the role played by our inheritance in behavioral development is called behavioral genetics. Physical and mental features are passed from parent to offspring by way of genes that are located on chromosomes in each human cell. Chromosomal abnormalities often produce pronounced behavioral and emotional disturbances. However, at this point there are no reliable data to indicate that violent behavior is caused by genetics. Twin studies have been especially useful in providing clues about the relationship between genetics and behavior.

Key Terms

neuroscience (39)
neurons (40)
receptors (40)
afferent (40)
efferent (40)
effectors (40)
dendrites (41)
soma (41)
axon (41)
terminal buttons (41)
neuroglia (41)
myelin sheath (41)
nodes of Ranvier (41)
synapse (41)
neurotransmitters (42)
neuromodulators (45)
opioid peptides (45)
substance P (46)
psychoimmunology (48)
resting potential (49)
depolarization (49)

impulse (49)
action potential (49)
refractory period (49)
all-or-none law (50)
peripheral nervous system (51)
central nervous system (51)
somatic nervous system (51)
autonomic nervous system (51)
sympathetic nervous system (52)
parasympathetic nervous system (52)
clinical neuropsychology (55)
computerized axial tomography (CAT) (55)

positron emission tomography (PET) (55)
magnetic resonance imaging (MRI) (55)
electroencephalograph (EEG) (55)
attention deficit hyperactivity disorder (ADHD) (56)
brain stem (58)
reticular formation (59)
Parkinson's disease (59)
thalamus (61)
hypothalamus (61)
basal ganglia (62)
Huntington's chorea (62)
cerebral cortex (63)
fissures (65)
hemispheres (65)

frontal lobes (65)
parietal lobes (67)
occipital lobes (67)
temporal lobes (68)
Broca's area (70)
expressive aphasia (70)
Wernicke's area (70)
receptive aphasia (70)
corpus callosum (73)
endocrine system (76)
hormones (76)
pituitary (76)
behavioral genetics (78)
chromosomes (78)
genes (78)
Down syndrome (79)
Turner's syndrome (79)
Klinefelter's syndrome (79)

Suggested Reading

Bloom, F. E., Lazerson, A., & Hofstadter, L. (1985). *Brain, mind and behavior*. New York: Freeman. A recent in-depth account of the latest advances in brain science, enhanced by color illustrations. The interaction between the machinery of the brain and behavior is discussed.

Delgado, J. M. R. (1969). *Physical control of the mind: Toward a psychocivilized society*. New York: Harper & Row. A thought-provoking discussion of the possible behavioral implications of brain control. Classic experiments on electrical stimulation of the brain are presented.

Graham, R. B. (1990). *Physiological psychology*. Belmont, CA: Wadsworth. This textbook on basic biological processes as they relate to behavior offers an in-depth review of the role of physiology in the expression of psychological phenomena. Of particular interest is the coverage of the neurobiology of learning and memory.

Rodolfo, R. (1988). *The biology of the brain: From neurons to networks*. New York: Freeman. This series of readings provides expert statements on a variety of neuroscience topics including discussions of invertebrate systems, vision, neuropeptides, and secondary messengers in the brain.

Watson, J. D. (1968). *The double helix*. New York: Signet. A classic work written by the Nobel Prize winner who, along with Francis Crick, discovered the molecular composition of DNA. The search for the double helix and the implications of this important genetic discovery are reviewed.

CHAPTER 3
Sensory Processes

Imagine that two large hooks are embedded in your back and that you are hanging from them, suspended in air. This might sound like an odd form of torture that would surely cause excruciating pain. However, in India, it was part of an ancient ritual that was practiced until recently, and may still be practiced in some remote regions. According to Kosambi (1967), a "celebrant" is chosen to bless the children and the crops in the neighboring villages. After two large hooks are inserted under the skin and muscles of his back, the celebrant is suspended from a pole by a rope attached to the hooks. In this fashion, the celebrant is carried from village to village. As he is moved about, he hangs onto the ropes. But at the climax of the ceremony, the celebrant lets go of the ropes and hangs freely from the hooks embedded in his back. What is remarkable about this ritual is that the celebrant never appears to experience any pain. Instead, as he swings from the hooks, the celebrant appears to be in a "state of exaltation." It seems the culture in which he was raised leads the celebrant to perceive the experience as pleasurable rather than painful (Melzack & Wall, 1988).

Such differences in how an event is perceived are not limited to the Indian culture (Melzack & Wall, 1988). For example, the level of pain reported by women during childbirth varies considerably across cultures. Even within our own culture, people's responses to a certain painful stimulus appear, at least in part, to be determined by the ethnic group to which they belong. Why are these differences observed? Is it the case that people in some cultures are simply insensitive to pain? Evidence suggests this is not the case. The ability to *sense* aversive or painful stimuli varies little across different cultures or ethnic groups. Instead, what appears to vary is the way this sensory information is processed and interpreted by the *perceptual* mechanisms that give meaning to the sensory input.

◀ At any given moment, each person exists in a sensory world typically filled with an abundance of available stimulation. Within that sensory system we experience sights, sounds, smells, and many other stimuli.

sensory system neural network for processing information in a single modality; examples include systems that report on pain, hearing, smelling, and touching

Your ability to sense that a pinprick is painful is mediated by a **sensory system**, a network of receptors, neural pathways, and brain areas that process information about a class of physical events (e.g., damage to the body). In addition to sensory systems that alert you to pain, you also have sensory systems that allow you to see, hear, smell, and feel your environment. In this chapter, we explore the various sensory systems and the environmental stimuli to which those systems respond. In the next chapter we will consider the perceptual mechanisms that are used to interpret this sensory information.

SENSORY PROCESSES—AN OVERVIEW

At any given moment, each person exists in a sensory world typically filled with an abundance of available stimulation. Within that sensory world are sights, sounds, smells, and many other stimuli that may or may not be perceived by organisms in that environment. Each sensory system is composed of specialized cells known as *receptors*. These cells are sensitive to environmental stimuli, such as light and sound. Our sensory systems function as an important part of a complex process called **perception**, a process that selectively extracts information from the environment and then interprets that information.

perception involves the extraction and interpretation of sensory information; the basis for interpreting our environment

Perception occurs when we recognize a friend in a crowded room, judge the speed of an oncoming car while we drive, decide to add more oregano to the spaghetti sauce after tasting it, select a shirt to match a pair of pants, work a jigsaw puzzle, listen to music, and take an exam. Our sensory systems are such an integral part of the process of perception that separating them from perception is actually somewhat arbitrary. However, for purposes of clarity, we have chosen to make this separation in this book. This chapter focuses on the sensory systems themselves, detailing the physiological bases of sensation, describing the stimuli that activate the sensory receptors, and discussing the theories that have been proposed to explain sensory functioning. The chapter that follows focuses on the higher-order processes of perception: attention, depth perception, perceptual learning, and the recognition of shapes and patterns.

Animals differ in the nature of their sensory systems and the extent to which they rely on those systems. Humans are basically visual creatures. They also make considerable use of their hearing but, ordinarily, somewhat less use of other sensory processes, such as smell or taste. Rats, on the other hand, are night creatures and operate in a perceptual environment where there is little light. Thus, it is not surprising to find that rats rely heavily on senses other than vision—most notably smell. This chapter reflects the human bias, because much of it is devoted to the processes of vision and hearing. The fact that most sensory research in psychology has been done on these two senses is understandable, inasmuch as human beings might be expected to investigate those sensory systems most important to their own behavior. If rats could write a psychology book, they would likely devote most of their chapter on sensory processes to smell, with very little attention to vision. Similarly, dolphins, bats, and great gray owls would emphasize hearing (see Figure 3–1).

Before we begin our discussion of the specific sensory systems, let us discuss two concepts that relate to all of those systems: threshold and receptor. An understanding of these concepts will give you a better appreciation of the functioning of the various sensory systems.

FIGURE 3–1
The fruit bat uses its extremely acute sense of hearing to capture its prey in the dim illumination of the forest.

Threshold

Imagine that you were studying in your room and you saw something pass by your open door. It looked like a person, but you were not able to recognize the individual. In fact, you may not even be sure that it was a person; you are certain only of the fact that you saw "something" move by your door. That perceptual judgment is far simpler than the perception of identifying the "something" as a person, in fact, as the dorm counselor, or perhaps even noticing that he had not shaved that day. The perceptual judgments you could make are listed below from the least to the most complex:

1. Something moved past the door.
2. A person moved past the door.
3. Robert, the dorm counselor, moved past the door.
4. Robert, the dorm counselor, moved past the door; and by the stubble on his face, it appears that he did not shave today.

It is possible that you could have all these perceptions, almost simultaneously, if you were given enough time to identify the stimulus (Sagi & Julesz, 1985). In the first instance, you detected something; in the second instance, you were able to recognize that something as a person. In the third instance, you not only recognized it as a person but were actually able to identify the person. And in the fourth instance, you not only identified the person but were able to note particular features of his appearance. One explanation for the differences in these perceptions can be found in the concept of threshold.

Technically, threshold is defined as a boundary; thus, it acts to separate things. In the preceding case, it might separate detection (a person moved) from recognition (it was Robert). As a perceptual concept, threshold can be used in different ways, most notably to define minimal values of stimulation. In that way it answers such questions as, "How loud must a tone be for a person to be able to hear it?" or, "How bright must a light be for a person to be able to see it?" Thresholds define other kinds of boundaries in perception, but we will start with stimulus values.

Absolute Threshold. Suppose you are taking a hearing test. How intense must a sound be for you to be able to detect its presence, that is, to hear it? You may be given a number of trials in which the person doing the testing may say, "I am going to play a tone for you, and I want you to tell me when you can no longer hear that tone." Typically, the results of those trials will be averaged to determine the **absolute threshold**, that is, the stimulus value above which the stimulus can be detected and below which it cannot be detected. This threshold is not really absolute; it is a statistically determined concept that specifies the probability that the stimulus will be detected on any given trial. In the example just given, a 50% criterion would mean the minimal sound intensity that could be detected 50% of the time, whereas a higher sound intensity would be required if the sound was to be detected on 75% of the trials. Because "absolute threshold" is really a misnomer, some psychologists prefer to use the label "detection threshold."

absolute threshold a statistically determined value that refers to a point at which a stimulus is detected 50% of the time

Difference Threshold. Another type of threshold is the **difference threshold**, which defines the minimal *change* in stimulation that can be reliably detected. That change is measured with respect to some existing condition of stimulation. For example, if you are observing a light, the investigator will attempt to discover how much greater the intensity of that light must be before you can say that it is brighter. The answer to that question is the value

difference threshold minimum change in stimulation required for a change in detection to be noticed

of the difference threshold. Stimulus values can change, but if the magnitude of the change is not sufficient, then the change will not be perceived.

Weber's Law.   The magnitude of the required change in stimulation is obviously dependent on the existing level of stimulation: lights that are dim require small increases in intensity to be perceived as brighter, whereas very bright lights need much larger increases in intensity before observers notice that they are brighter. In the first half of the nineteenth century, this fact was known to the physiologist Ernst Weber (1795–1878). Weber described the relationship between existing stimulation and changes in that stimulation in what historians of psychology have called the "first quantitative law of psychology" (Schultz & Schultz, 1992). **Weber's law** can be written as follows:

$$\frac{\Delta S}{S} = K$$

This law states that the ratio of the change in stimulation (ΔS) to the stimulation (S) is equal to a constant value (K) for each sensory quality. Thus, if K = .1 for the perception of relative weights, it means that a 100-gm weight is perceived as heavier if increased by 10 gm (that is, one tenth of its existing weight). Yet adding 10 gm to a 1,000-gm weight is not a large enough change to produce a perceptual judgment of "heavier." However, by using the constant of .1, you know that to produce a weight that is noticeably heavier (or lighter) than 1,000 gm you must add (or subtract) one tenth of that amount, or 100 gm. In other words, a 1,100- (or 900-) gm weight is easily distinguished from a 1,000-gm weight. But subjects would have difficulty distinguishing between weights of 1,000 and 1,050 gm (or between 1,000 and 950 gm) because the change does not exceed the difference threshold, or what is also called the *just noticeable difference (jnd)*.

Studies in the early part of the twentieth century demonstrated limitations in Weber's law. Research indicated that the constant values derived for various stimuli (e.g., sound intensity, saltiness of a solution, brightness of a light) worked only in the midrange of most stimulus values and not at the endpoints of the stimulus range. Thus, for weights, the value K = .1 predicts difference thresholds for a substantial portion of the range of weights but not for weights under 50 or over 8,000 gm.

Signal Detection Theory.   Research has shown that stimulus values or changes in those values are not the only important determinants of thresholds. Also of critical importance are such variables as the characteristics of the organism being tested and the condition of the environment in which the testing takes place. You would expect to obtain very different values for the absolute threshold when it is measured in a quiet testing chamber and when it is measured in a testing booth situated in a busy shopping mall. Further, a host of variables associated with the organism, such as fatigue and receptor sensitivity, affect the measurement of threshold.

An approach to measuring thresholds that is more sensitive to these concerns is called **signal detection theory**, which measures the subject's ability to detect a stimulus against the background of noise produced by changes in the environment and variability within the nervous system (Green & Birdsall, 1978; Swets, Tanner, & Birdsall, 1961). This approach views the detection of a stimulus as a process in which the perceiver is faced with the task of distinguishing the stimulus from the rest of the perceptual world of which it is a part. The stimulus to be detected is called the signal, and the rest of the existing stimulation is called noise. Some level of noise is always present in our environment; even in the quietest of settings our bodies generate their own "noise" in terms of biochemical, muscular, and neural events.

Weber's law called the first quantitative law of psychology; relates changes in perception to stimulus magnitude

signal detection theory view that is based on the subject's ability to detect a stimulus against an environmental background of noise

Thus, some background stimulation always exists. In signal detection experiments, noise is present in each trial, but the signal occurs randomly. Thus, the subject must decide whether the signal is present or absent in each trial. The presence of noise often leads subjects to think they heard the signal and to report its presence when in fact it did not occur.

This situation is very similar to the task we face in making many of the perceptual judgments of our world. For example, suppose you are listening to the radio in your room when you hear a knock at the door. Much to your surprise, when you answer the door, no one is there. In fact, no one is even near your door. In this case, the sounds in the room (such as the radio) provide the noise, and the signal is the knock on the door, which apparently did not occur. In signal detection theory such a response would be called a *false alarm*. These responses might not be common, but their likelihood of occurring can be increased. Again suppose you are in your room listening to the radio and you are anxiously waiting for your blind date to arrive. Under these circumstances you might be particularly likely to experience false alarms, thinking you hear a knock on the door when in fact no one is there. Therefore, detecting a signal is dependent not only on the perceptual sensitivity of the individual, but also on certain decision factors that affect thresholds. Called **receiver operating characteristics**, they are part of the perceiver.

If you are a sonar operator and it is important that you not miss reporting a signal that could indicate the presence of a potential enemy ship, you are likely to report all kinds of signals, including those that turn out to be whales. But false alarms will be tolerated in a sonar operator, because to miss a signal could be disastrous. These factors obviously influence perceptual reports and are part of the individual's operating characteristics.

In a detection task in which a signal occurs in some trials but not in others, one subject might want to be sure to detect every signal that is presented (like the sonar operator). To do so, the person will have to say the signal is present on a number of trials when it does not occur. We would call this a liberal strategy for detection. Another person might want to be absolutely certain that a signal is present before making such a judgment, which is a conservative strategy for detection. The liberal observer will produce many false alarms but will have a high hit rate; the conservative observer will have a lower hit rate but also a lower false alarm rate (see Figure 3–2). Such differing response strategies are further examples of receiver operating characteristics. These kinds of behavior can obviously disrupt the measurement of thresholds. Therefore, special steps must be

receiver operating characteristics
individual decisional factors that affect thresholds

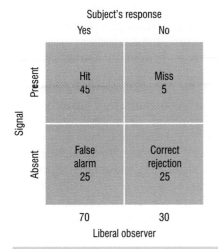

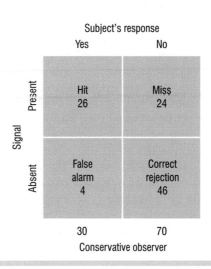

FIGURE 3–2
Comparison of a liberal and conservative observer in a signal detection task of 100 trials. In 50 trials the signal was present, and in 50 it was absent. Correct responses (hits + correct rejections) are essentially the same for the two observers: 70 for the liberal observer and 72 for the conservative observer. If we paid attention to the hits only, we might assume that the liberal observer had a lower threshold. But looking at the pattern of responses suggests that we have subjects with very different response criteria.

	To counter conservative responding	Neutral	To counter liberal responding
Hit	Win $5	Win $1	Win $1
Correct rejection	Win $1	Win $1	Win $5
False alarm	Lose $1	Lose $1	Lose $1
Miss	Lose $1	Lose $1	Lose $1

FIGURE 3–3

Three payoff matrixes used in a signal detection task. For observers whose tendency is to say yes (a liberal approach), the payoff system in the right-hand column can be used to increase their likelihood of saying no by providing a large incentive for correct rejections. Similarly, conservative observers can be made to become less conservative (say yes more often) by giving them a larger reward for hits, using the payoff schedule in the left-hand column. By manipulating subject responses in this way, different success ratios (comparing hits to false alarms) can be obtained. These ratios are plotted to define a response curve, called the *receiver operating curve* (ROC). Using this technique, it is possible to compare subjects in terms of their sensory thresholds. Subjects whose hit/false alarm ratios fall on the same ROC have equal sensory thresholds, even though their response tendencies may differ.

subliminal perception perception that occurs below some threshold point where the stimulus events are not obvious

taken to see that the threshold measure is primarily a function of the sensory capabilities of the individual, and not heavily influenced by decision characteristics. In reality, these decision characteristics cannot be eliminated, but their effects on detection tasks can be reduced. One way to accomplish this is to use a payoff matrix that rewards hits and correct rejections (saying no when no signal is present), and punishes misses and false alarms (see Figure 3–3). Measuring thresholds in this manner increases confidence in the measure in two ways. It controls for differences in reporting strategies, and it assesses the detection of signals in a realistic background of noise, similar to what a person might encounter in ordinary circumstances.

In summary, thresholds are perceptual judgments and, as such, are subject to all of the problems inherent in any judgmental process. The advantage of signal detection theory is that it provides a way to measure sensitivity to some stimulus relatively independent of receiver operating characteristics.

Subliminal Perception. Before we leave the concept of threshold, we should discuss **subliminal perception**. (*Limen* is another name for "threshold"; thus *subliminal* means "below threshold.") The controversy over subliminal perception has existed in psychology for some time as researchers have debated whether people can perceive stimulus presentations that are below their threshold. The argument continues, but the scientific literature does contain a number of well-designed studies indicating that stimuli presented below threshold levels can affect behavior in small ways (Moore, 1982).

By now you should understand that a threshold is not a fixed point above which a stimulus can be perceived and below which it cannot be perceived. Thresholds vary across individuals, at different times of the day, in different sensory environments, and so forth. For subliminal perception to be proven, the researcher must demonstrate that the stimulus presentations are indeed below threshold for that person in that situation. The subject must not be able to report the presence of the stimulus, and there must be evidence that the undetected stimulus affects behavior. Only a few studies have supported the existence of subliminal perception, e.g., Bevan, 1964.

Many psychologists accept the results of such studies as evidence that stimuli that are below threshold can affect behavior. They are cautious, however, about characterizing the reliability or magnitude of that effect. One controversial application began in the field of advertising in 1957. A movie theater announced that it had greatly increased its sales of popcorn by superimposing the words *buy popcorn* at a subliminal level on the movie screen during the showing of a film. Similar practices continue today; for example, a department store includes subliminal messages warning against shoplifting in the music program it broadcasts throughout the store. How effective are such techniques? In reviewing these studies, Moore (1982, 1985, 1988), Saegert (1987), and Vokey and Read (1985) say there is no scientific evidence to support the claim that subliminal messages used in advertising or marketing can affect behavior. The research literature on stimulation is rather clear, showing that the greater the intensity of the stimulus, the greater is its effect on behavior. "To propose that people can be affected in important ways by stimuli so weak that their mere presence is undetectable is an extraordinary claim that should not be accepted without clear, well-replicated evidence. So far, none exists" (Moore, 1985). Nevertheless, many people still choose to believe ridiculous claims (see Figure 3–4).

Receptors

Information (stimuli) in our environment exists in a variety of forms—as air vibrations, electromagnetic waves, gases, chemicals, and tactile pressures. You will recall from the previous chapter that to receive these various stimulus forms, the body possesses specialized cells called **receptors**. Functioning as transducers, the receptors convert one form of energy into another. In the case of vision, it is the rods and cones that convert light energy into the electrochemical impulses that can be transmitted in the nervous system. Similarly, taste buds located on the tongue convert chemical signals to a pattern of electrical activity that will be sent to the brain regions involved in taste perception.

Earlier we mentioned that animals differ in their reliance on various sensory systems. Animals also differ with regard to the receptors they possess, although members of the same species are usually similarly endowed. Some animals, such as homing pigeons, seem capable of responding to magnetic fields. Other animals can respond to electrical fields. However, apparently no such responses occur in humans, presumably because of a lack of appropriate receptors. Some animals have receptor capabilities beyond those of humans. Bats and dogs are two of a number of animals that can hear sound frequencies far above the range of human hearing (see Figure 3–5). And many birds have color vision abilities generally superior to those of humans.

Within the human species there are receptor differences across individuals. Some people have greater sensitivity to taste, some have difficulty hearing sounds at particular frequencies, and some have problems distinguishing among different colors. Some of the changes in receptor sensitivity are related to developmental processes. Even within the same person, receptor sensitivity differs from time to time. For example, suppose you attend a rock concert in which the music is very loud. Immediately after the concert, you may have trouble hearing what your friends are saying and have to increase the volume of your radio for the sound level to seem normal.

There is another way in which receptor sensitivity can change. Perhaps you have had the experience of moving to a new place where you find that the water has a bad taste because it contains certain minerals or chemicals. Yet after a short time you no longer notice the bad taste. Or you might perceive a horrible smell as you enter a friend's house yet find that, after a short stay, the smell seems to disappear. These examples describe a process known as **sensory adaptation**, a loss of sensitivity that usually occurs at the receptor level in all sensory systems when stimuli are unchanging. Thus, you can easily fall asleep despite the noisy fan in your room because you have become used to it, but your neighbor's record of great drum solos can keep you awake, even if the fan is louder. Thus, sensory adaptation is generally a useful process, and we are often grateful that our senses act in this way. Nevertheless, when adapted, our receptors can be less sensitive to certain stimuli, so that we might not be able to hear sounds or taste certain foods that we could perceive when our receptors were in a more normal state of operation. Responsivity may also decrease at the neural level due to repeated stimulation. This related process is called **habituation**. It differs from adaptation in that responsiveness can suddenly reappear if the stimulation level is increased or decreased (Groves & Thompson, 1970).

In some cases, sensory adaptation actually increases sensitivity. Most people have had the experience of entering a dark movie theater from a bright, sunny street and groping in the dark trying to find a seat, preferably one that is not occupied. After 10 minutes or so, vision is much improved. This phenomenon is called dark adaptation, and it occurs because of chemi-

FIGURE 3–4
Related to claims for subliminal auditory messages are claims of the influence of satanic messages that are recorded backward in rock music. These backward messages can allegedly be found in certain recordings of groups such as the Beatles, Styx, and the Electric Light Orchestra. The once-popular song "Stairway to Heaven" by Led Zeppelin (*above*) purportedly has many backward phrases, including one that sounds something like "So here's to my sweet Satan." Although there are undoubtedly some individuals who view these messages as subliminal enticements to Satan worship, there is no scientific evidence that they can affect behavior (Moore, 1988). Most of these messages seem to be products of imaginations working overtime. However, it seems very likely that publicity about them affects consumer behavior—that is, increases record sales.

receptors cells that detect different forms of energy and convert it into the electrochemical signals used by the nervous system

sensory adaptation decline in receptor activity elicited by an unchanging stimulus that results in a loss of sensitivity

habituation decline in the response elicited by repeated stimulation, not due simply to adaptation

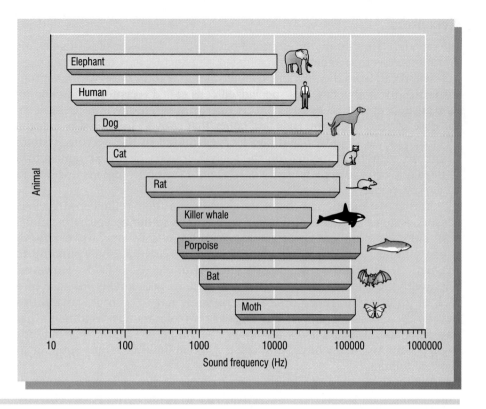

FIGURE 3–5
The auditory ranges for selected species.

cal changes within the visual receptors. This process is discussed in a later section of this chapter.

In summary, species differ in the kinds of receptors they possess and in the stimulus ranges to which those receptors are sensitive. Receptor functioning also differs within members of the same species, and even in the same organism on a day-to-day basis. Because the initial stage of the perceptual process is the organism's ability to pick up information from the environment, the nature of the organism's receptors is also of crucial importance to an understanding of perception, our topic in Chapter 4.

SEEING

Of all the human sensory systems, vision is the most important in everyday perceptual functioning. Indeed, we rely so much on vision that most of us never realize how much unused potential we have in our other sensory systems. That we are capable of better using our other sensory systems is illustrated when a person loses the sense of sight. Soon that person becomes quite efficient at using smell, touch, and hearing to make more accurate perceptual judgments.

We rely so heavily on vision for many reasons. Quite simply, it has some important advantages over other senses (except in the dark). Animals that rely primarily on touch must make actual contact with objects to experience them. Animals that rely on smell cannot always accurately locate the source of the odor, nor can they perceive objects that emit no odors. Reliance on sound similarly requires that objects make noises to be heard; inanimate objects will not be perceived. But with vision, objects, both animate and inanimate, can be perceived, their distances estimated, their features recognized, and so forth. Light, the stimulus for vision, is exceptionally rich in information, perhaps accounting for the fact that so many members of the animal kingdom have at least some visual ability.

Visible Spectrum

Vision begins with light entering the eye. Light, as the visual stimulus, represents a narrow range of the electromagnetic energy in our world. Electromagnetic waves include radio waves, infrared waves, the ultraviolet waves of the sun, and a very narrow band of energy we call the **visible spectrum** (see Figure 3–6) that ranges from violet (390 nanometers, or nm) to red (760 nm). (One *nanometer* equals one billionth of a meter.) The photoreceptors within the human eye are sensitive to energy only within that wavelength range. Electromagnetic waves above or below that range simply will not be perceived visually.

visible spectrum band of electromagnetic radiation we see, ranging between 390 and 760 nm

The Eye

Study the drawing of the human eye in Figure 3–7 before returning to this part of the text. The most important features are labeled for you. In vision, light enters the eye through the transparent **cornea**, a structure that helps the eye focus. The cornea is a specialized portion of the outer protective

cornea clear membrane that lies in front of the lens

FIGURE 3–6
Left: The visible spectrum. *Below:* The visible spectrum as a part of the entire spectrum of electromagnetic energy.

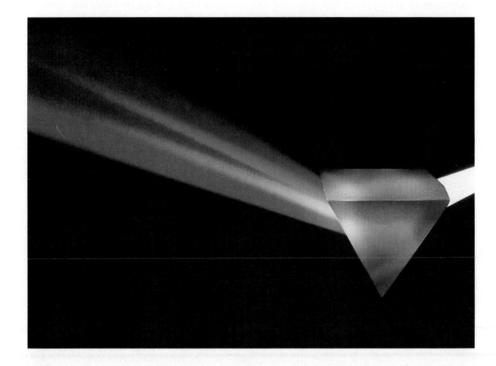

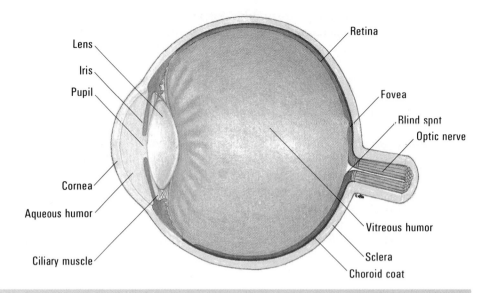

FIGURE 3–7
The structure of the human eye.

coating of the eye known as the sclera. The opaque portion of the sclera constitutes the "white" of the eye. Under the sclera is another layer of tissue called the choroid coat, a darkly pigmented layer that serves to keep extraneous light from filtering into the eye. The amount of light entering the eye is controlled by the opening in the **iris**, the pigmented portion of the eye that gives us our eye color. Acting like a diaphragm—in fact, like the shutter of a camera—the iris contracts and expands according to the amount of light

iris colored part of the eye that controls the amount of light reaching the retina by expanding or contracting in size

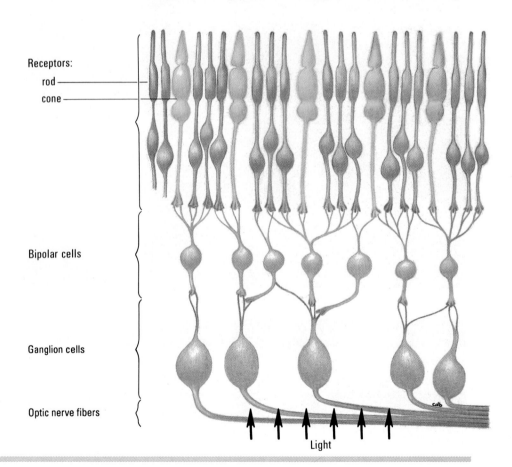

FIGURE 3–8
Layers of the retina. Light entering the eye passes through the ganglion and bipolar cells to strike the receptors (rods and cones) at the back of the eye. Once activated, these receptors relay their visual messages to the brain via the bipolar and ganglion cells.

that is present, changing the size of its opening, which is called the **pupil**. Behind the pupil is the **lens**, a transparent body that can change its shape to focus the image on the photoreceptive portion of the eye known as the **retina**. The lens is held in place by the ciliary muscles that tense and relax to change the shape of the lens, a process known as **accommodation** (Millodot, 1982). Accommodation is particularly important for viewing objects that are nearby. We describe this process in more detail in our coverage of the perception of depth in the next chapter.

Another process important for vision is **convergence**. In this process, the eyeballs are rotated in their sockets in order to keep the same visual image on the fovea (see next section) of each eye. Convergence is accomplished by the three pairs of extrinsic eye muscles that can move each eye in virtually any direction. The processes of accommodation and convergence, both present at birth, are not terribly efficient at first. As the human infant matures, these abilities increase, due at least partly to the role of experience.

The Retina

The retina is a multilayered circular region of tissue along the back of the eye that is particularly important because it contains the photoreceptors for vision (see Figure 3–8). It is in the retina that light is changed to neural energy in the specialized cells known as **rods** and **cones**, so named because of their shapes (see Figure 3–9). Each human eye contains approximately 6 million cones and 120 million rods. The cones are located primarily in the central portion of the retina, and the rods are more prevalent in the periphery. These two types of receptors play very different roles in vision, as we shall see in a moment.

In addition to the layer of rods and cones, two other retinal layers are important to our discussion. **Bipolar cells** are specialized nerve cells that provide the synaptic connections for the rods and cones. In turn, the bipolar cells connect with cells in a third layer called **ganglion cells** (see Figure 3–8). It is the axons of these ganglion cells that actually form the **optic nerve**. The optic nerve exits the back of the eye, forming what is known as

pupil opening in the center of the iris

lens translucent structure that lies behind the pupil and changes shape to focus an image

retina tissue that lines the back of the eye and contains the photoreceptors

accommodation change in the lens used to maintain a focused image, particularly when the image is presented close up

convergence moving the eyes inward to look at a nearby object

rods photoreceptors used for colorless vision in dim light

cones photoreceptors used for color vision under well-lit conditions

bipolar cells specialized cells that connect rods and cones to ganglion cells

ganglion cells carry the visual information from the bipolar cells to the brain

optic nerve cranial nerve exiting from the back of the eye that is formed from the axons of the ganglion cells

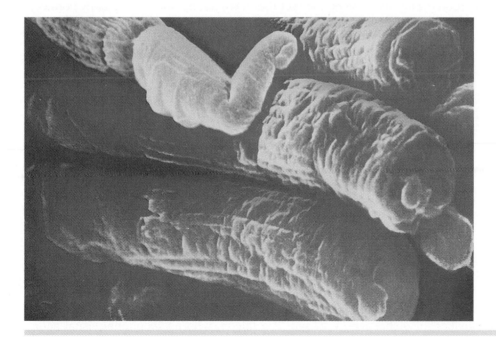

FIGURE 3–9
Enlarged picture of rod and cones in the eye. The light blue structure is a cone.

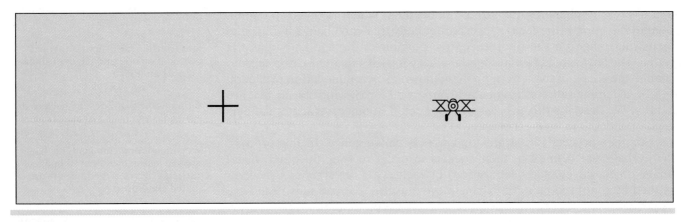

FIGURE 3–10
To demonstrate the blind spot in your retina, hold this page about 18 in. from your eyes. Close your left eye and stare at the cross with your right eye. Keep looking at the cross and slowly bring the book toward your eyes. You will notice that you can see the airplane in the periphery of your vision, but at a distance of about 10 in. it should disappear. The disappearance is caused when the image of the airplane falls on the blind spot. Continue moving the book closer and the airplane will reappear.

blind spot region of the retina that has no receptors where the optic nerve exits the eye

summation occurs when a single ganglion cell connects with many bipolar cells, resulting in a smaller optic nerve

visual acuity ability to make fine visual discriminations between and among objects in the visual environment

fovea small, cone-rich area of the retina that supports high acuity

the **blind spot**, an area of the retina that is not sensitive to light. Follow the instructions in Figure 3–10 to demonstrate the absence of vision in your own blind spot.

Interestingly, the three retinal layers just described are arranged in an order opposite to what you might expect. The rods and cones are at the very back of the eye, with the bipolar cell layer in front of them and the ganglion cell layer closest to the lens. Thus, light entering the eye must first pass through the ganglion and bipolar layers before reaching the light-sensitive photoreceptors (rods and cones). This arrangement of retinal cells is common in vertebrates and is called an *inverted retina* (Bruce & Green, 1985). The reason for this arrangement is not exactly understood. Some psychologists propose that it is important to have the photoreceptors in close contact with the epithelium at the back of the eye for nutritional purposes.

We mentioned that there are approximately 126 million rods and cones in each retina. If each of those cells were connected in a one-to-one ratio with the retinal secondary cells, the diameter of the optic nerve would be larger than a silver dollar, and you can imagine the vision problems that would be caused by the resulting size of the blind spot. Such vision problems are avoided by the fact that a single bipolar cell typically connects with many rods and cones, and a single ganglion cell connects with many bipolar cells. This process, which is called **summation**, permits the optic nerve to be smaller, but it also produces some decreased visual abilities, particularly visual acuity (Barlow, 1982; Cohn & Lasley, 1986).

Visual Acuity.   **Visual acuity** refers to the keenness of our vision, that is, our ability to make fine visual discriminations among objects in our visual field. When people say they have 20/20 vision, they are referring to a standard measure of acuity and are indicating that they have normal vision (see Figure 3–11). Visual acuity differs across various regions of the retina (Riggs, 1965). It is best in the area of the retina known as the **fovea**, a small region (about one square millimeter) consisting entirely of cones. Figure 3–12 shows the relative visual acuity in various regions of the retina, illustrating the dramatic loss of acuity that occurs as the visual image is displaced to either side of the fovea, toward the periphery of the retina.

Why is acuity so much better in the fovea than anywhere else? For two reasons: First, the cones in the center of the fovea are very densely packed together. This increased density makes for much better visual resolution in the eye in the same way a denser dot matrix on a television picture tube makes for a sharper TV image. The falcon, whose exceptional visual acuity

three times as close together as those in the human eye (Fox, Lehmkuhle, & Westendorff, 1976). Second, acuity is greatest in the fovea because the cones in that region are connected in a one-to-one relationship with the bipolar and ganglion cells. In other words, there is no *summation* in the fovea, and thus visual information that would ordinarily be lost through the process of summation is retained in foveal vision.

Although not directly affecting visual acuity, eye movements certainly assist it. In attempting to see well, we often move our eyes in a series of jerky, rapid movements, called *saccadic eye movements*, to focus the object of interest on our fovea. When objects move, or we move in relation to them, *pursuit eye movements* serve to keep objects fixated on the fovea. Should the distance of the objects that we are viewing change, *convergence eye movements* help keep them fixated in the foveas of both eyes. At any moment the human visual field consists of a small part in focus and a much larger part that is rather blurred. Eye movements allow the perceiver to shift the high-resolution part of the visual field around (Bruce & Green, 1985).

Rods and Cones.   Rods and cones are both sensitive to light, but that sensitivity differs in some important ways. During normal daylight we see largely as a result of the functioning of our cones. Our night vision, however, is a function of the rods, which are more sensitive than cones and thus respond to lower levels of illumination. Recalling the discussion of thresholds earlier in this chapter, we would say that the absolute threshold for vision in rods is lower than that for cones.

Retinas that contain both rods and cones are called *duplex* retinas. Although a number of animals possess both kinds of photoreceptors, the ratio of one to the other varies greatly. Rats are said to have a nocturnal retina, having a rod-to-cone ratio of 4,000:1. By contrast, the diurnal (day and night) retina of humans has a rod-to-cone ratio of 20:1. Some animals, such as fish

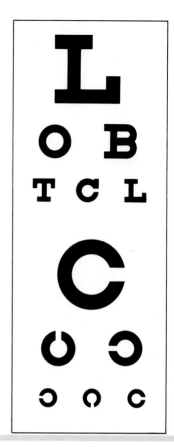

FIGURE 3–11
There are many different ways to measure visual acuity. *Top*: Snellen letters, used to measure recognition acuity. *Bottom*: Landolt rings, used to measure resolution acuity. In an actual test, there are many rows of letters or rings, each row printed smaller than the one above it. These stimuli are presented at a standard distance from the subject (usually 20 ft), and the person is asked to observe a particular row. Subjects must identify Snellen letters or indicate the location of the gap in a ring (e.g., top, bottom, right, or left). A person with 20/20, or normal, vision can correctly perceive, at 20 ft, a row of letters or rings that the average person can see at 20 ft. An acuity score of 20/200, however, means that the individual perceives at 20 ft what people with normal vision can perceive at 200 ft. Thus, the larger the second number, the poorer is a person's visual acuity. (Adapted from Riggs, 1965.)

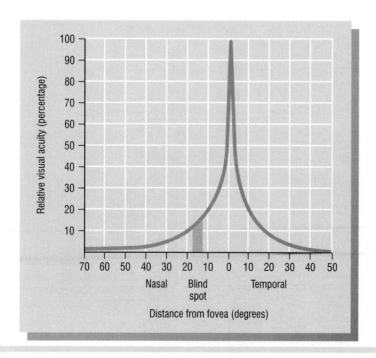

FIGURE 3–12
The graph shows visual acuity when images fall on different locations on the retina. The fovea is indicated by 0°. The shape of the curve shows how dramatically acuity is reduced when the visual image is located only a few degrees on either side of the fovea.

whose habitat is deep water, have retinas composed only of rods, yet no animals have been found to have retinas composed only of cones, although some lizards and birds of prey come close (Fein & Szuts, 1982).

Rods and cones respond to different wavelengths of light. Both kinds of photoreceptors are selectively tuned to a small segment of the light spectrum, but the cones play the dominant role in color vision. Color vision is best in the central portion of the retina, where the cones are more dense, and gets progressively worse as it moves to the periphery of the retina (Gordon & Abramov, 1977). Although some of the mysteries of color vision have yet to be solved, research in psychology and physiology has provided us with a reasonably clear understanding of this important facet of human perception.

Color Vision

Recall that the stimulus for sight is light within the visible spectrum (wavelengths of 390 to 760 nm). Wavelength is a physical characteristic of light that corresponds to the perceptual term **hue**. When most people think of *color* they may use *hue* as a synonymous term, yet color is more than just hue. Light has characteristics other than wavelength, namely, intensity and complexity. Intensity is a physical dimension of light, and psychologists refer to the perception of intensity as **brightness**. The complexity of light refers to the mixture of wavelengths present. A pure light is composed of light of a single wavelength, but most lights we experience are not pure, meaning that the light is composed of two or more wavelengths. This purity or complexity of light is called **saturation**.

Although hue is the principal determinant of what we mean by color, it is important to recognize that color perception is the result of hue, brightness, and saturation (see Boynton, 1971). As an illustration of this point, look at the colored squares in Figure 3–13. The dominant hue is the same

hue psychological dimension of color related to wavelength; different hues correspond to different colors

brightness psychological dimension of color related to amplitude

saturation psychological dimension of color related to the complexity of the waveform, or how many wavelengths are in a given light source

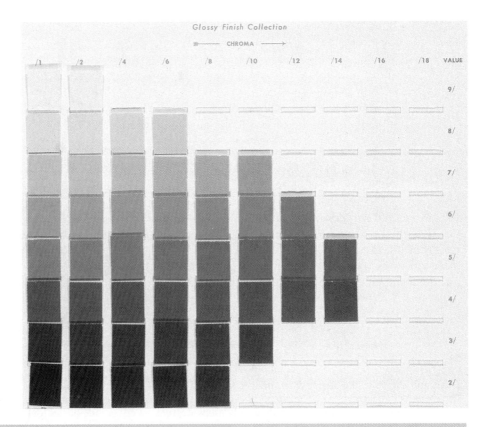

FIGURE 3–13
This page from the *Munsell Book of Color* illustrates how color is influenced by brightness and saturation when the dominant hue is held constant.

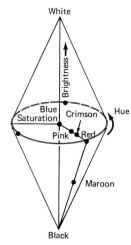

FIGURE 3–14
The color solid is a model illustrating the three dimensions of color. Brightness is shown by points on the vertical axis, hue by points around the outside of the solid, and saturation by distance from the vertical axis of the solid. The farther a color lies from the vertical axis, the more saturated it is. Brighter colors can be found near the top of the solid, and darker colors are toward the bottom of the solid.

for each of these squares; however, they will appear to be of different colors because they differ in brightness and saturation. To conceptualize how hue, brightness, and saturation combine to produce different color experiences, study the color solid shown in Figure 3–14. The color solid is a model that demonstrates the interrelationships of the factors determining color. It should be added that color perception is often a relative process, meaning that we judge the colors of objects in relation to the reflection of light from other objects in the visual field. Thus, we may see some objects as darker, brighter, greener, and so forth, depending on how they compare with nearby objects and surfaces (Brou et al., 1986).

Young–Helmholtz Color Theory. There are two major theories of color vision, the oldest of which was proposed initially by Thomas Young (1773–1829) at the beginning of the nineteenth century and modified by the German physiologist Hermann von Helmholtz (1821–1894) in 1857. Although there are recent modifications of the **Young–Helmholtz color theory**, which is also known as the **trichromatic theory**, the basic premise has remained unchanged: there are three types of cones that are differentially sensitive to red, blue, or green lights. Although each type of cone is maximally sensitive to light of a particular wavelength, each also responds more broadly to receive other adjacent wavelengths as well. These spectral sensitivities are shown in Figure 3–15. Support for this theory comes from the fact that lights corresponding to the hues of red, blue, and green can be combined in various amounts to produce any color in the visible spectrum (color television sets work on this principle). For example, a red light and a green light can be combined to produce a yellow light in the process known as **additive color** mixture.

You may not believe that statement, based on your own childhood experience of mixing paint colors. Mixing paints produces a **subtractive color**

Young–Helmholtz color theory/trichromatic theory proposes color is determined by the relative activity in red-, blue-, or green-sensitive cones

additive color color mixture based on the addition of wavelengths

subtractive color color mixture based on the subtraction of wavelengths

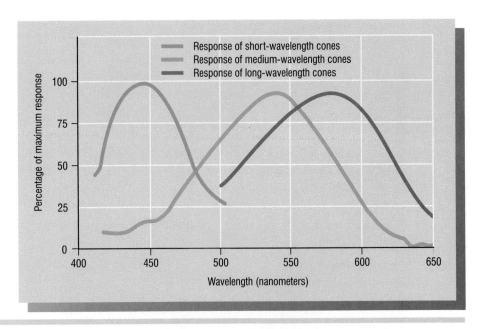

FIGURE 3-15

Response profiles of the three types of cones to different wavelengths of light.

mixture. For example, you know that if you mix blue paint with yellow paint the resulting paint color is green. The reason for the green color is as follows. Paint color is determined, like any surface color, by the light waves that are reflected back to our eye. White light striking the painted surface contains many, and perhaps all, of the wavelengths that correspond to the colors we see. Most of those will be absorbed, but some will be reflected, and the dominant reflected wavelength will determine the color of the paint. Blue paint looks blue because it absorbs all other wavelengths except blue, which it reflects back to the eye. But it also reflects back a little of the green light, a wavelength adjacent to that of blue. Yellow paint absorbs all wavelengths except yellow, but it too reflects a little of the green light that is adjacent to the yellow. When blue and yellow paint are mixed, the blue paint absorbs all of the yellow light, and the yellow paint absorbs all of the blue light. But neither is capable of absorbing all the green light, some of which is reflected back to the eye. Since green is the only color reflected from the two mixed paints, the paint appears green. When colors are absorbed, they are subtracted from the color mixture, which is how this type of color mixture gets its name.

When mixing lights, all wavelengths represented in each of the lights reach the eye. Recall that the three types of cones are differentially sensitive to various wavelengths. When we superimpose a red light (long wavelength) and a green light (medium wavelength) on a screen, the combined wavelengths that reach the eye activate both the medium- and long-wavelength cones. Activating both types of cones leads you to see a color that lies between green and red. For example, consider the point at which the curves for the medium- and long-wavelength cones intersect in Figure 3–15. In this case, both types of cones are equally activated and you would perceive the color yellow.

Both color mixture processes offer support for the trichromatic theory. Combining red, green, and blue lights (additive mixture) will produce white light, because all wavelengths are reflected. Mixing red, yellow, and blue paints will produce black paint, because all wavelengths are absorbed (subtractive mixture). These mixtures are shown in Figure 3–16.

Further support for the Young–Helmholtz theory comes from the discovery of three different chemical substances (pigments) that have been

French neo-impressionist painter Georges Seurat (1859–1891) is famous for his pointillist technique employing thousands of dots of paint on canvas. He was well read in the color theory of Helmholtz and selected his paint hues according to the tenets of that theory. For example, he would place dots of white paint next to other hues to enhance their intensity when seen at a distance. For Seurat, the canvas was to be a mass of points of light that would be mixed in the eye. Thus, the colors of the images were in the eyes and brains of the observers, not on the canvas itself. Shown here are his *Sunday Afternoon on the Island of La Grande Jatte* and a detail from the upper right showing the pointillist technique.

found in different cones (Rushton, 1962). The difference in sensitivity of these visual pigments matches the curves shown in Figure 3–15. Yet some color phenomena, such as color blindness and negative color afterimages, are not easily explained by this theory. These issues are better accounted for by opponent-process theory.

Opponent-Process Color Theory.   To understand some of the basic observations that gave rise to the opponent-process theory of color vision, you should try the demonstration illustrated in Figure 3–17. After staring at the green, black, and yellow flag and then shifting your gaze to the blank surface at the right, you should see a red, white, and blue version. By staring at the green and yellow flag you adapted your visual system to these colors.

FIGURE 3–16
Left: The overlapping circles illustrate the results of additive color mixture (all wavelengths combined produce white). *Right:* the rectangles show subtractive color mixture (all wavelengths combine to produce black). Note the difference in primary colors in the two systems: red, green, and blue for additive color; red, blue, and yellow for subtractive color.

When you then shifted your focus to the white region, you perceived blue where yellow had been and red in the regions that were green. If you had stared at a blue and red flag, exactly the opposite would have occurred; adaptation to blue would have produced a yellow afterimage and adaptation to red would have produced a green afterimage. This phenomenon is

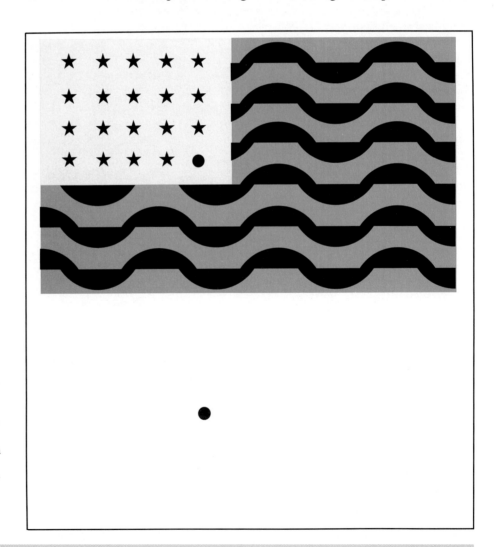

FIGURE 3–17
To illustrate the appearance of a negative color afterimage, stare at the dot in the star field of the flag for about 20 seconds (sec). Then quickly shift your gaze to the blank surface below. You should see another flag in colors complementary to those of the flag shown in this figure. In the afterimage flag, the star field should appear blue and the stripes red and white. Phenomena like this support an opponent-process view of color.

known as *negative color afterimages* and is one of the observations that gave rise to the **opponent-process color theory**.

opponent-process color theory proposes that color information is organized into three antagonistic pairs

Another important observation was originally made by Ewald Hering (1834–1918). He observed that certain color combinations never occurred; for example, green and red, or blue and yellow. You can picture a bluish-green (turquoise), bluish-red (purple), reddish-yellow (orange), and so forth, but a greenish-red or bluish-yellow seems unimaginable. Given these observations, Hering, and more recently Leo Hurvich and Dorothea Jameson (1957, 1974), suggested that the colors of red, green, blue, yellow, black, and white do not exist as independent processes. Instead, they appear to be organized in three pairs: red–green, blue–yellow, and black–white. Within each pair, the colors appear to have an opponent-process, or antagonistic, relationship to each other. Thus, from this perspective, the visual system takes the information provided by the three types of cones and organizes it into three opponent-process pairs. A diagram as to how this might be accomplished is provided in Figure 3–18. Because red and green are coupled in an antagonistic fashion, you cannot perceive a color that is reddish-green. Instead, a single neural output determines which color you see; at one extreme you see red, at the other you see green, and in between the output would be achromatic (without color). A similar relation holds for the colors of blue and yellow.

Hurvich and Jameson proposed the modern version of opponent-process theory on the basis of perceptual observations. Subsequently, neurophysiological studies revealed that color-sensitive neurons within the visual system are organized in an opponent fashion. For example, DeValois (1960) showed that some cells within the monkey's lateral geniculate nucleus of the thalamus (a relay station in the neural pathway for vision) are excited by wavelengths in the region of the spectrum we see as blue and are inhibited by wavelengths in the region we see as yellow (B+ Y-). Other cells respond in exactly the opposite fashion (B- Y+). Yet other cells appear to function as red-green opponents.

It is important to realize that acceptance of the opponent-process theory does not imply that researchers have rejected the Young–Helmholtz theory. Instead, contemporary researchers generally assume that the Young–Helmholtz theory accurately describes the relationship between activity in the three types of cones and our perception of color. It is then assumed that opponent-process theory explains how the information from these three

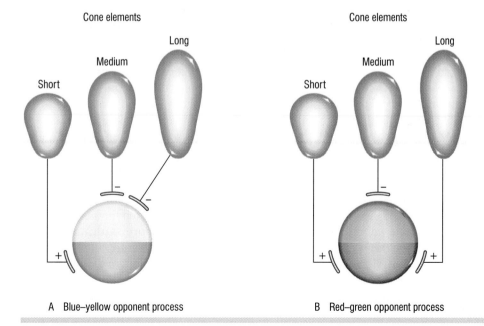

A   Blue–yellow opponent process

B   Red–green opponent process

FIGURE 3–18
This figure represents how opponent-process cells could be generated from the output of the three types of cones (short, medium, and long wavelength). A ganglion cell that was excited (+) by short-wavelength cones and inhibited (–) by the other two would function as a B+ Y- opponent cell. Similarly, a ganglion cell that was excited by both short- and long-wavelength cones but inhibited by medium-wavelength cones would function as a R+ G- opponent cell.

types of receptors is processed in the ganglion cells of the retina and at higher levels of the visual pathway (Goldstein, 1989; Hurvich, 1981; Matlin & Foley, 1992).

What Do Color-Blind People See?

Consider for a moment what opponent-process theory predicts should occur if a person is color blind to red. You would expect that the individual would also be color blind to green. Similarly, if a person was color blind to blue, you would expect that person also to be color blind to yellow. These predictions are in fact true, and they provide yet another piece of evidence for the opponent-process theory.

Most forms of color blindness are hereditary and sex linked. They are usually caused by cone types that are missing or have deficient pigment. Color blindness is more common in males (about 8% in males of European descent) than females (about 1%) (Matlin & Foley, 1992). There are a number of different types of color blindness that can be distinguished on the basis of which cone system(s) is dysfunctional. The extreme situation involves individuals who totally lack functioning cones. Luckily, this condition, known as **monochromacy** (*mono* meaning one and *chroma* meaning color), is extremely rare, having an incidence of only about one in a million. People with this affliction see what you see on a black-and-white television set; their world is composed totally of blacks, whites, and grays.

Dichromacy (meaning two colors), another kind of color blindness, is much more common. Although dichromats experience some colors, they do not perceive the full range of colors a person with normal vision sees (see Figure 3–19). There are three basic types of dichromats: *protanopia*, *deuteranopia*, and *tritanopia*, each of which is linked to a deficiency in one type of cone (the long-wavelength, medium-wavelength, and short-wavelength cones, respectively). The majority of dichromats are either protanopes or deuteranopes; tritanopia is quite rare, occurring in only about 1 in 20,000 people (Matlin & Foley, 1992).

What is the perceptual world of dichromats like? What do they see when they look at a rainbow? Only people who are color blind in one eye but have normal vision in the other eye could answer this question. These individuals could look at a color with the dichromatic eye and tell us the color to which it corresponds when they look at the world through the normal eye. Although extremely rare, such people do exist and have been tested by psychologists (Goldstein, 1989; Graham, Sperling, Hsia, & Coulson, 1961; Sloan & Wollach, 1948). The results from these studies are summarized in Figure 3–20. Individuals with the two most common forms of color blindness, protanopia and deuteranopia, perceive just two colors: blue and yellow. Thus, they are color blind to red and green. At one end of the spectrum, they perceive blue, which becomes less and less saturated as they approach the blue/yellow border. At this border, called the neutral point, they see gray. After the neutral point, they perceive yellow, which becomes progressively more saturated as they approach the other end of the spectrum. Individuals with tritanopia perceive a colored world of green and red and are color blind to blue and yellow. These individuals see green at one end of the spectrum, which becomes less saturated as the neutral point is approached. After the neutral point, they see red, which increases in saturation as the other end of the spectrum is approached.

monochromacy condition that results when people have absolutely no color vision; they see only black and white

dichromacy condition that results when a person has some color vision but cannot see red and green, or blue and yellow

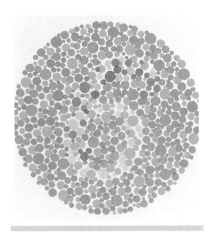

FIGURE 3–19
Patterns similar to this one are used to test for color blindness. Do you see a number? If not, then you have trouble with red–green vision. Stimulus materials like this are used because they present different hues that are equal in brightness. (The number is 6.)

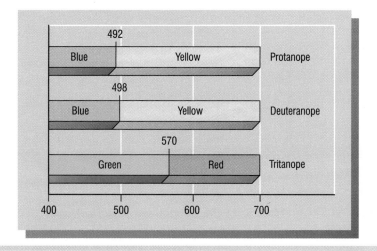

FIGURE 3–20
The colors perceived by the three types of dichromats. The center line in each rectangle represents the neutral point, which is perceived as gray. On either side of the neutral point, saturation increases as the edge of the visible spectrum is approached. (Adapted from Goldstein, 1988.)

What about animals? Are they color blind? Evidence suggests that humans and some other primates are the only mammals known to possess complete color vision (see Figure 3–21). Dogs, rats, and other mammals can learn, for example, to find food behind a red door as opposed to a green door, but their "color" discriminations are based on brightness differences, not on hue. Many birds, on the other hand, have excellent color vision and are often able to perform better than people on color tasks.

Dark and Light Adaptation

Before we leave this section on the eye, we should discuss one other visual process. Earlier in the chapter we discussed the topic of sensory adaptation, and we now want to talk about a special form of visual adaptation known as **dark adaptation** and the reverse process of **light adaptation** (see MacLeod, 1978). The human visual system functions across a range of light intensities that is greater than a billionfold. It is hard to imagine a sensory system that could handle such a vast range of stimulation, but our eyes have that remarkable capability.

One way the visual system adapts to changes in the level of illumination is by controlling the amount of light that reaches the rods and cones. The primary mechanism adjusts the size of the pupil. Through this mechanism, your eyes can bring about a 16-fold change in the amount of light that reaches the rods and cones. Animals with slit-shaped pupils (e.g., cats) can make even greater adjustments. These pupil adjustments are almost instant when the organism goes from bright to dim light or vice versa.

It is clear, however, that this cannot be the sole mechanism of adaptation. For one, a change in pupil size occurs almost immediately after you move from a light to dark environment. Yet, when you enter a dark environment such as a movie theater, it takes 10 minutes (min) or more to adapt. Moreover, after you have adapted to the dark, you may be up to 100,000 times more sensitive to light. But a change in pupil size can bring about only a 16-fold change in the amount of light that enters the eye. These observations suggest that other mechanisms must contribute to adaptation. The most important one is a change in the photopigments of the rods and cones (Matlin & Foley, 1992). When you are in a very brightly lit environment, much of the photopigment is broken down and insensitive to light. If you move to an area

FIGURE 3–21
Although inconclusive at present, recent neurophysiological evidence suggests that cats and squirrels may be dichromats and thus possess some limited color vision.

dark adaptation increased visual sensitivity that occurs in a dark environment

light adaptation reduction in visual sensitivity that occurs when you enter a light environment

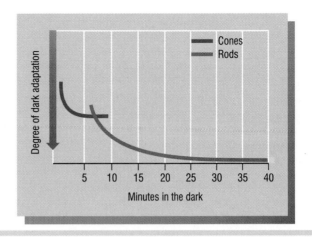

FIGURE 3-22
Total dark adaptation requires about 30 to 40 min. The cones adapt first, requiring between 5 and 10 min; the rods adapt much more slowly. In this figure, the blue curve shows cone adaptation; the purple curve represents rod adaptation.

that is dark, the photopigments in the rods and cones begin to regenerate, moving back to their light-sensitive active state. This process takes about 10 min for the pigments in the cones and 30–40 min for the pigments in the rods (see Figure 3–22). As the photopigments regenerate, you slowly become more sensitive to light. If you then return to a light environment, much of the photopigment will be rapidly broken down by the onslaught of electromagnetic radiation. This process occurs much more rapidly, so that within about a minute you may be fully light adapted and able to see normally.

Light adaptation is much faster than dark adaptation, yet the reasons for that difference are not clear. Perhaps it is because we encounter such a variety of light levels during the day. We face problems with dark and light adaptation frequently, for example, going from a bright street into a darkened theater, experiencing the lights being turned on in a classroom after viewing slides, and driving at night and having your companion turn on the interior lights to read a road map. In this last example, you, the driver, have dark adapted and thus have good night vision. Turning on the interior light causes you to light adapt, and thus you cannot see well into the dark outside.

Visual Pathways to the Brain

It is important to recognize that vision does not end with the reception and processing of light within the eye. Figure 3–23 shows the visual pathways leading from the eye to that portion of the occipital lobe of the brain known as the **visual cortex**. The optic nerves come together at the **optic chiasm**, where certain neurons will cross over and project to the opposite side of the brain. We can divide each retina into two regions: that portion toward the nose is called the nasal retina; the other half, closer to the side of the head, is called the temporal retina. Visual information from the temporal retinas will project to the same side of the brain, whereas information from the nasal retinas will cross over to the other hemisphere (Willmer, 1982). Figure 3–23 shows that this pathway arrangement means that images in the right side of the visual field will project to the left visual cortex, and vice versa.

Just how the visual cortex functions is not completely understood. However, recent advances in neuroscience, particularly in the technique of single-cell recording, have given us some important and fascinating insights into the process. This research has led to a better understanding of the relationships among rods and cones and the cells that make up the visual cortex. We now know that cortical cells in vision respond to very specific stimuli.

In most of this research, electrodes have been implanted in various regions of the neural pathways for vision. Some studies have recorded the activity of a single neuron; others have looked at specific groups of neurons.

visual cortex the part of the occipital lobe located at the back of the brain that receives visual information

optic chiasm point at which the optic nerves from each eye join, cross over, and project to the opposite side of the brain

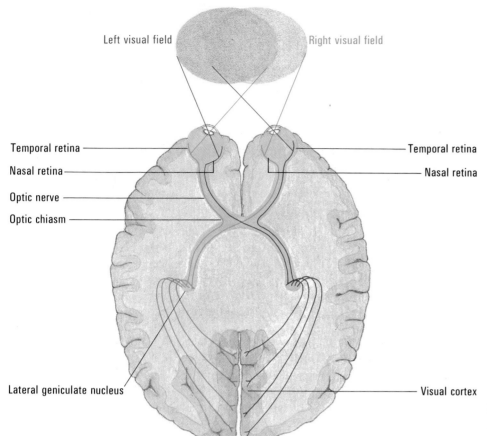

Left visual field　　Right visual field

Temporal retina

Nasal retina

Optic nerve

Optic chiasm

Temporal retina

Nasal retina

Lateral geniculate nucleus

Visual cortex

FIGURE 3-23
The visual pathways, showing the crossover of some retinal information to opposite sides of the brain.

Some studies have simultaneously recorded the activity of the rods and cones, retinal ganglion cells, neurons in the lateral geniculate nucleus of the thalamus, and neurons within the visual cortex. Much of this research is new, but these kinds of studies began in 1938 when H. Keffer Hartline recorded the activity of single optic nerve fibers (the axons of the ganglion cells) in frogs. The stimulus Hartline used was a small spot of light that was shone into the frog's eye. Hartline discovered three different types of optic nerve fibers: "on" fibers that responded (changed their rate of firing) when the stimulus light was turned on; "off" fibers that responded when the light was turned off; and "on–off" fibers that responded when the light was turned on or off, but not while the light was continuously illuminated.

Hartline noted that each optic nerve fiber represented the activity of a number of receptor cells (on the average, more than 125). The specific receptors that were tied to a particular optic nerve fiber formed the **receptive field** of that optic nerve fiber. Hartline's research showed that an optic nerve fiber responded only when a sufficient portion of its receptive field had been stimulated (this concept provides a physiological definition of threshold).

Research in the 1950s showed that optic nerve response patterns were not as specific as Hartline had thought. Using cats, Kuffler (1953) found that the response of optic nerve fibers resulted from the stimulation of a particular portion of the receptive field. Receptive fields were found to be generally circular in shape. In the center of each receptive field was a region that responded to light with either an increase ("on" center) or decrease ("off" center) in neural activity. This central region was surrounded by a doughnut-shaped area that responded in the opposite fashion (see Figure 3–24). Thus, if

receptive field the region of the retina that, when stimulated, affects the cell

Receptive field
("on" center;
"off" surround)

A ||||||||||| B |||||||||||||||| C | | | | | | | D | | | | |

FIGURE 3–24
The receptive field shown has an "on" center and an "off" surround. Shining a spot of light on the center (A) produces a pattern of neural impulses. That neural rate of firing is increased when the entire center is covered by a stimulus light (B). But if the light spot is larger than the center, so that some of the surround is stimulated as well, then both excitatory and inhibitory processes will be initiated, reducing the firing rate (C). When more of the surround is stimulated (D), the firing rate will be further reduced. (From Goldstein, 1988.)

simple cells cortical cells in the visual cortex that respond to a line of light presented in a particular orientation, or to a small spot of light

complex cells cortical cells in the visual cortex that react to a bar moving in a particular direction

hypercomplex cells cortical cells in the visual cortex that respond to a moving bar of a particular length

feature detectors cortical cells in the visual cortex that respond to specific stimulus patterns

the cell had an "on" center, it would have an "off" surround. Conversely, cells with an "off" center had an "on" surround.

In the 1960s, research on receptive fields moved higher in the visual system, investigating the neurons in the lateral geniculate nucleus (LGN) and the visual cortex. Much of the early work in these regions was done by David Hubel and Torsten Wiesel (1962, 1963, 1965), whose efforts won them the Nobel Prize in 1981. Their work confirmed the on–off arrangement in LGN and cortical cells, as well as the fact that these higher visual neurons were tied to specific receptive fields at the retinal level.

But Hubel and Wiesel's most important discovery was of the increasing specificity of response that occurred as the information reached higher levels of the visual system, particularly the visual cortex. Using cats, with electrodes implanted in many locations in the visual cortex, these investigators attempted to "map" the visual cortex in terms of its responsivity to various visual stimuli. Cats saw small spots of light, larger spots of light, and lines of light that were presented in various orientations (vertical, horizontal, or oblique). Sometimes the spots or lines of light were moved across the visual field, sometimes left to right, sometimes right to left, top to bottom, and bottom to top. By knowing the retinal areas stimulated (the receptive fields) and comparing those with responses in the various cortical cells, the researchers discovered that specific cells in the visual cortex respond only to specific kinds of stimuli. **Simple cells** respond best to a line of light presented in a particular orientation. They also respond to a small spot of light. **Complex cells**, which have larger receptive fields, do not respond to a small light spot; rather, they react to a moving line of light oriented in a particular direction. **Hypercomplex cells** react only to moving lines of light of a specific length. They also respond to corners and angles, again, when they are moving and presented in a particular orientation.

Such specialized cells that react so selectively to stimulation have been called **feature detectors**. They indicate the nature of information processing that occurs within the visual system. As such, they play an important role in all visual processes, but particularly in pattern recognition, shape perception, and movement perception. The importance of the visual system for reading, a skill that requires feature detection, is described in the next section on dyslexia.

APPLYING PSYCHOLOGY
Dyslexia

Sensory processes are obviously important in education, for learning is based on information gathered through the use of the senses. A number of learning disabilities are related to perceptual problems of one kind or another. One of these, **dyslexia**, occurs because the brain, specifically the visual cortex, seems unable to interpret correctly the information coming from the eyes. Dyslexia is defined as a learning disorder characterized by a "difficulty in learning to read, write, or spell despite conventional instruction, adequate intelligence, and socio-cultural opportunity" (Redington, 1987). Reading symptoms that seemingly are related to vision include reversing letters in words, skipping words, and the inability to recognize printed words. But visual problems occur no more often in dyslexic children than in other children. Researchers studying dyslexic children usually report that they have normal scores for visual acuity, thresholds for vision, and color vision (Ysseldyke et al., 1982).

Typically, dyslexia is diagnosed once the child reaches school, especially as the cognitive demands of reading increase. The diagnosis of dyslexia is usually made when the child is 2 or more years behind in reading ability but is working on his or her grade level in other subjects such as arithmetic. Children with dyslexia find that they cannot keep up in some of the learning assignments. Not surprisingly, they become frustrated and often direct this frustration inward, labeling themselves as "stupid" because they cannot seem to learn at the rate of many of their classmates. Some of these children may become withdrawn, whereas others behave aggressively or demonstrate other emotional problems. The frustration they experience with their schoolwork may cause them to lose interest in their studies.

Treating these children involves teaching directed at those perceptual systems that seem to function normally, for example, teaching to the child's capacities for hearing and touch, when visual perception is the problem. The standard teaching strategies for dyslexic children are labeled *multisensory* because they present material to be learned in two or more sensory systems. For example, children might be asked to sound out letters they see as they trace the letter shape in the air, using their finger as a kind of "skywriter." Children with dyslexia have trouble with tasks that require the integration of sensory information, and these multisensory approaches help them overcome that problem (Horn & O'Donnell, 1984). Many of these children will overcome their learning difficulties by not only relying more heavily on nonvisual sensory systems but also using these other senses to generate learned cues to help them interpret visual information. But for others, dyslexia remains a lifelong problem.

dyslexia impairment in the visual cortex that leads to difficulty in learning to read, write, or spell

HEARING

Next to sight, humans rely most heavily on their hearing (audition). An appreciation of much of our perceptual environment would not be possible without the ability to hear. Not only would we be unable to listen to the speech of others, but we could not enjoy such auditory wonders as the sounds of an ocean surf, the laughter of a small child, or the incredible complexity and beauty of music. For each of these auditory marvels, the source of the stimulation is sound, the stimulus for hearing.

Sound

Sound is a form of mechanical energy, typically caused by vibrating objects such as vocal cords, strings on a guitar, the reed of a clarinet, or the paper cone inside a stereo speaker. These sources of vibration produce changes in the air molecules surrounding them; that is, the molecules are alternately

FIGURE 3-25

Striking a tuning fork produces regular changes in air pressure that can be represented by a simple waveform. The magnitude of these fluctuations is represented by the amplitude of the waveform. A tuning fork that has a higher pitch would produce more rapid changes in air pressure, which would be represented as a decrease in the wavelength. The wavelength determines the frequency of a sound. Counting the number of peaks in a waveform that occur in 1 second (s) would tell you its frequency. Because the waveform illustrated on the right would oscillate less during a second, it has a lower frequency.

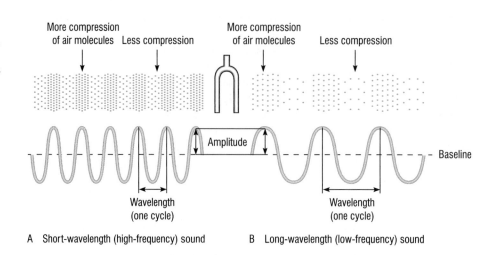

A Short-wavelength (high-frequency) sound   B Long-wavelength (low-frequency) sound

sound waves changes in air pressure that produce sound

frequency rate at which the waveform expands and contracts; measured in hertz (Hz)

pitch psychological dimension of sound related primarily to frequency

loudness psychological dimension of sound tied to amplitude but also affected by frequency

timbre psychological dimension of sound related to the complexity of the waveform

harmonics sounds that are multiples of the fundamental frequency

expanded and compressed (see Figure 3–25). This pattern of compression and expansion is called **sound waves**, and the rate at which the air is expanded and contracted defines the **frequency** of each wave. A wave that compresses 1,000 times in a second is a sound of 1,000 cycles per second (cps); it is also called a tone of 1000 hertz (Hz). The range of human hearing is usually defined as 20 to 20000 Hz. People with exceptional hearing can perceive the entire range; however, the extremes of that range (the very high sounds and the very low sounds) are rarely heard unless their amplitudes are very high. Remember that many sounds exist outside the range of human hearing. You know, for example, that dogs can be called with a whistle that the dog owner cannot hear. If sounds cannot be heard by humans, are they really sounds? If a tree falls in the forest and there is no animal present to hear it, does it make a sound? These questions can be answered either yes or no depending on your point of reference. If you define sound as reception by an auditory mechanism (that is, an ear), then sound occurs only when an organism is there to hear it. However, most psychologists and others who work in the field of audition (hearing) define sound in terms of its initiation rather than its reception. From that perspective, the tree falling in the forest makes a sound, whether or not anyone is around to hear it.

Like light, sound is a complex stimulus consisting of *frequency, amplitude,* and *complexity.* Whereas these terms describe the physical characteristics of sound, psychologists use other terms to refer to their psychological counterparts: **pitch, loudness,** and **timbre.** (The analogous terms for light are *hue, brightness,* and *saturation*). Striking middle C on the piano produces a note that has a fundamental frequency of 256 Hz. Thus, when we talk about particular musical notes, we are speaking of pitch. Another characteristic of that note is its loudness, a characteristic that can be altered by the force a person uses in striking the key on the piano. In essence, pitch is determined by the frequency of the sound and loudness by its amplitude. However, perceived loudness also depends on the frequency of the waveform, and for simple waveforms like those illustrated in Figure 3–25, the psychological quality of pitch depends a bit on amplitude.

When middle C is played on the piano, other sounds besides 256 Hz are produced. If you listen carefully to a note played on any musical instrument, you will hear higher notes as well. These are called **harmonics,** or overtones. Playing middle C also causes other strings to vibrate, such as the one tuned to 512 Hz that is C, an octave above middle C. (An octave refers to the distance between two tones, with one tone double the frequency of the other.) Nearly every sound you will ever hear has harmonics. The particular combination of frequencies defines the complexity of a sound, or in psychological terms, its timbre. Listen to yourself whistle and you can hear the harmonics you are generating. Pure tones (sounds composed of a single frequency) are rare. Even when such tones are generated, your own auditory mechanism may, through reverberation, add its own harmonics to the incoming tone (Yost & Nielsen, 1985).

The Ear

Figure 3–26 shows a cross section of the human ear. When we use the word *ear*, we are usually talking about the external flap of skin and cartilage called the *pinna*. In some animals, the pinna is large and can be used to funnel sounds into the auditory canal. In humans it plays a small role in localizing sound. (Of course, it also provides a means for securing eyeglasses and a display area for jewelry.)

Sound reaching the ear travels down the auditory canal (in what is called the outer ear) to the **tympanic membrane**, or eardrum. This elliptically shaped, translucent membrane divides the outer ear from the middle ear; the latter contains three small bones collectively called the **ossicles**. The first of these bones (the *hammer*) is attached to the eardrum. Sound waves reaching the eardrum cause it to vibrate, which, in turn, causes the hammer to vibrate. At this point, the method of conducting the sound changes from air to bone. The sound is transmitted from the hammer to the next of the ossicles (the *anvil*), and finally to the third bone (the *stirrup*), which is attached to a membrane of the **cochlea** (from the Latin word for "snail") known as the oval window. The vibration of the oval window causes the fluid in the cochlea to vibrate, which means that the sound is now conducted by fluid.

It is within the inner ear, more specifically in the cochlea, that the complexities of hearing occur (see Figure 3–27). Pressure changes within the cochlear fluid cause movement in the **basilar membrane**. This membrane

tympanic membrane membrane of the ear that detects changes in air pressure; commonly referred to as the eardrum

ossicles bones of the middle ear that transmit vibrations from the eardrum to the cochlea

cochlea fluid-filled coil that contains the hair cells

basilar membrane membrane of the cochlea that supports the hair cells

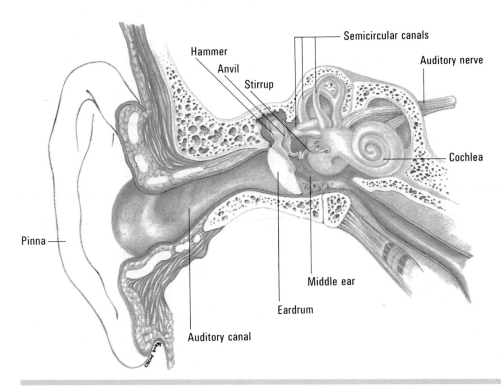

FIGURE 3–26
The structure of the human ear.

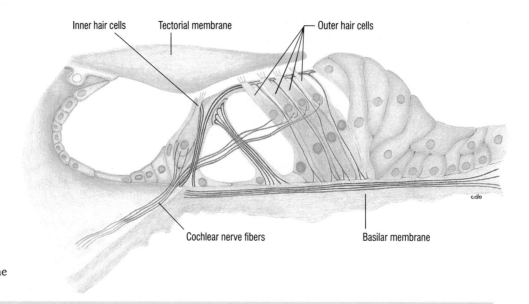

Inner hair cells — Tectorial membrane — Outer hair cells

Cochlear nerve fibers — Basilar membrane

FIGURE 3–27
A cross section of a portion of the cochlea.

hair cells receptors for hearing

tectorial membrane membrane that lies over the hair cells

auditory nerve cranial nerve that carries auditory information from the hair cells to the cortex in the brain

auditory cortex region of the temporal lobe of the brain that receives auditory (hearing) information

place theory relates perceived pitch to the region or place along the basilar membrane that is activated by a particular auditory stimulus

holds the Organ of Corti, which in turn contains the **hair cells** that are the actual receptors for hearing. The hair cells sit atop the basilar membrane in two groups. In each ear, the *inner hair cells* number about 3,500 and occupy a single row. The *outer hair cells* number about 12,000 and are arranged in three to four rows. Atop the hair cells is the **tectorial membrane**, whose shearing action, produced by a different motion than that in the basilar membrane, alters the electrical charge of the hair cells (Gelfand, 1981; Yost & Nielsen, 1985). Surrounding the hair cells are auditory neurons that convert these changes in electrical potential to neural impulses. These impulses are carried via the **auditory nerve** to a portion of the temporal lobe of the brain known as the **auditory cortex**. Like the visual system, the auditory nerves from the ears branch, sending information to both hemispheres of the brain. Thus, if the auditory cortex on one side of the brain were destroyed, a person would not be totally deaf in either ear.

Theories of Hearing.   Although the mechanisms for hearing are understood, some of the functional details remain open to question. The sound waves reaching the ear are of specified frequency and amplitude. How is this information relayed to the auditory cortex? The question concerning loudness has become easier to answer since research has demonstrated that louder sounds produce greater movement in the eardrum, ossicles, and cochlear fluid, causing the auditory nerve cells to fire at more rapid rates and perhaps in greater numbers. For pitch, the answer is not so straightforward. There are two classical, competing views; one is called place theory, the other is called frequency theory.

Place Theory.   In 1863, Hermann von Helmholtz (we discussed his trichromatic theory of color vision earlier) proposed the original version of **place theory**. Helmholtz's theory of pitch perception was based, in part, on his knowledge of the shape of the basilar membrane, which is wide at one end (near the narrow end of the spiraled cochlea at the point called the helicotrema) and narrow at the other end (closest to the oval window). Helmholtz noticed the similarity between the shape of the basilar membrane and the arrangement of strings in a piano. Given this difference in thickness, he suggested that different frequencies would have their maximum impacts at different places along the basilar membrane. If this were true, the brain could infer the pitch of a waveform from the region of the basilar membrane activated—thus the name "place" theory.

Helmholtz thought that the basilar membrane was composed of independent transverse (crosswise) fibers, each tuned to a particular frequency. Subsequent research revealed that the membrane is not constructed in this fashion. However, pitch could still be coded by the place on the membrane that was activated the most. This was shown by Georg von Békésy (1899–1972) in the 1920s. Békésy was especially interested in the action of the basilar membrane, but the techniques of his time did not permit the study of the membrane in a hearing situation. Therefore, using what he knew about the shape of the membrane and its placement within the cochlea, Békésy built a model that he hoped would function similarly. Presenting sounds of differing frequencies, one at a time, he discovered what he called a *traveling wave* (see Figure 3–28). Although this wave, which was produced in his model membrane, stimulated many parts of the membrane, it had the most effect at one particular location on the membrane. Békésy saw this discovery as support for a kind of place theory (although not the version proposed by Helmholtz). Later research by Békésy and others using a microscopic study of a human basilar membrane confirmed the wave action Békésy had observed in his model. Békésy's research not only showed how frequency was handled in the cochlea, but led to his observation that more intense sounds caused the wave to have higher peaks, which would lead to increased stimulation of the adjacent hair cells.

In 1961 Békésy won the Nobel Prize for his work on hearing (see Békésy, 1960). **Békésy's theory** of the traveling wave in the basilar membrane is one of the dominant theories of present-day pitch perception. However, although this theory is useful in explaining some aspects of hearing and in guiding research, it has some limitations. In particular, waveforms below about 150 Hz produce traveling waves that are nearly identical. Yet, people can readily discriminate frequencies that lie below 150 Hz. This means that the brain must use another cue to infer the pitch of low-frequency sounds.

Békésy's theory version of place theory that ties pitch to the form of a traveling wave

Frequency Theory.   A solution to this problem is provided by a theory suggested by Ernest Rutherford (1861–1937) in 1886. This theory, known as **frequency theory**, proposes a matching between the frequency of the incoming sound waves and the frequency of the firing of the impulses of the auditory nerve. According to Rutherford, a tone with a frequency of 100 Hz causes the basilar membrane to vibrate at a rate of 100 times each second, which in turn produces a train of impulses of 100 per second in the auditory nerve. Each dif-

frequency theory relates perceived pitch to the frequency of incoming sound waves and the frequency of firing in the auditory nerve

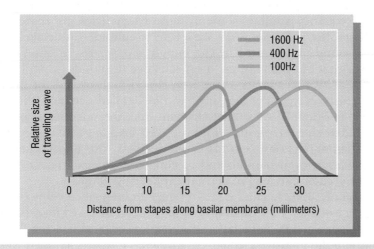

FIGURE 3–28
The relationship between frequency of the waveform and the degree to which the basilar membrane is displaced. Notice how the place of maximum displacement changes as a function of frequency.

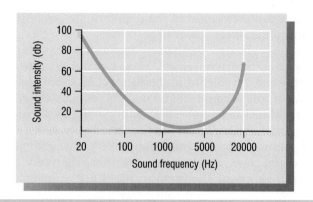

FIGURE 3-29
The auditory sensitivity curve shown is for normal human hearing across the frequency range of 20 Hz to 20000 Hz. Sounds around 1000 Hz need only be a few decibels (db) in intensity to be heard. However, sounds at either extreme of the auditory range must be very intense to be heard.

ferent frequency is matched in this way; that is, the vibratory rate in the basilar membrane and the neural firing rate in the auditory nerve are the same. Although this theory offers a simple and straightforward explanation of pitch perception, it encounters a major stumbling block from findings in neurophysiology. Specifically, all neurons are limited in their firing rates by a refractory period during which they are incapable of firing, regardless of the strength of the stimulation (recall the discussion of the refractory period in Chapter 2). It is known that the maximum firing rate of any neuron is less than 1,000 times per second. Frequency theory cannot account for pitch perception above 1000 Hz; therefore, it cannot explain most of the range of human hearing.

Recognizing that problem, Wever and Bray (1937) offered what they termed the **volley principle**. According to this notion, auditory neurons alternate in their firing, producing a volley of responses that are capable of matching the sound frequencies reaching the ear. In this way, a sound of 4000 Hz could be produced by a group of 40 auditory neurons that fired sequentially at a rate of 100 times per second. This pattern of neural activity could be the way sound frequency is matched in the auditory nerve. Research on auditory nerve fibers has indicated that patterns of the type proposed by the volley principle do occur, but that even with the volley capability, frequency matching is reliable only up to a maximum of 4000 Hz. Consequently, above this cutoff, pitch must be encoded by the place on the basilar membrane that is activated the most. Conversely, below about 150 Hz, the frequency of neural firing is presumably used to code pitch. Between 150 and 4000 Hz, the brain may rely on both cues (Matlin & Foley, 1992).

volley principle a cluster of neurons may share in the coding of higher frequencies

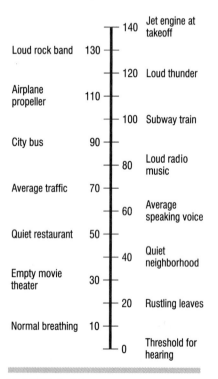

FIGURE 3-30
Loudness of various sounds, expressed in decibels (db). (Adapted from Goldstein, 1988; Matlin, 1988; Sekuler & Blake, 1985.)

Thresholds for Hearing. Earlier you read that the range of human hearing is around 20 to 20000 Hz. Yet, in terms of the amplitude required to make the frequency audible, some of those frequencies are more difficult to hear than others. Figure 3-29 shows the amplitude (in decibels) necessary for a sound to be heard by the human ear across its audible range. You can see that our ears are the most sensitive to sounds around 1000 Hz and least sensitive to sounds at the lowest and highest ends of the range. Sound intensity is typically measured in units called decibels (the unit *bel* was named in honor of Alexander Graham Bell, the scientist whose inventions included the telephone). Figure 3-30 displays various sounds in terms of their intensities. Sounds of 90 decibels (db) and higher can be quite unpleasant, even painful, and prolonged exposure to sounds of that intensity or greater can lead to permanent hearing damage.

A sound of 1000 Hz can be heard when its intensity level is only a few decibels, yet a sound of 35 Hz may have to be at an intensity level of 90 db to be heard. One practical application of the knowledge of hearing thresholds can be seen in the improved technology in stereo music systems. If you listen to your stereo system at a low volume, meaning that the sound intensity is low, some of the high frequencies and some of the low frequencies will be inaudible to you. To be able to hear all of the frequencies in the recorded music you are playing, you will have to turn up the volume to a very high level, which your neighbors may not appreciate. To counteract this problem, stereo manufacturers have installed a "loudness" switch on many models. When activated, this control increases the amplification of the low and high frequencies without affecting those in the middle range. As a result, you can listen to your stereo at a reasonable volume level and still be able to hear all the frequencies, because the lows and highs have been boosted (in amplitude) so that they are now above your threshold for hearing.

Deafness.   *Deafness* refers to a total or partial loss of hearing ability. It can result from a great variety of causes, including some congenital conditions. Diagnosing hearing losses in infants and young children is not always easy, but failing to do so can cause significant learning problems, including language learning. Not surprisingly, these hearing problems can cause social problems for children as well.

There are two major categories of deafness. In **conductive deafness**, the conductive properties of the ear are hindered. This condition may result from obstruction in the auditory canal (such as an excessive buildup of ear wax), a damaged eardrum, or problems in the middle ear that prevent the ossicles from operating normally. **Perceptive deafness**, also called nerve deafness, results from damage to the hair cells, auditory nerve, and higher subcortical and cortical areas in the auditory system, including the auditory cortex itself. There are many causes of this type of deafness, including tumors, skull injuries, poisons, birth trauma, and loud noise. Pregnant women who contract rubella and other viral diseases during the first trimester of their pregnancy run a greater risk of delivering a baby with perceptive deafness.

> **conductive deafness** loss of hearing due to a problem in conducting air vibrations to the cochlea

> **perceptive deafness** hearing loss caused by a problem in the hair cells, auditory nerve, or cortical neurons

OTHER SENSES

Although sight and hearing are the most important senses for human beings, we do rely on our other senses as well. Eating would provide little if any enjoyment without our senses of taste and smell. A rose is beautiful to see, but it is perhaps best appreciated by a sniff that allows us to experience its distinctive fragrance. By using our sense of touch, we can perceive the varying textures of different fabrics, feel the smoothness of a piece of furniture, know when we have been injured because of the pain we experience, and enjoy that feeling we get when we are touched by a person special to us. Much of the richness of our perceptual world is produced through these senses, so even though psychologists may label them "other senses" because of their secondary role for humans, we need to be aware that they are indeed quite valuable.

Taste

The receptors for taste are located in clusters called **taste buds** (see Figure 3–31). Most of the taste buds are situated on the sides and back of the tongue, but some are also located on the tip of the tongue and in parts of the throat and in the soft palate. The mouth contains thousands of taste buds, and each bud contains approximately 20 **taste cells**, which are the actual taste receptors (Bartoshuk, 1978).

For some time psychologists have known that there are four basic taste qualities: sweet, salt, sour, and bitter. Initially, researchers argued that certain

> **taste buds** clusters of receptors located on the tongue that determine different tastes, such as sweet and sour

> **taste cells** individual taste receptors located on taste buds

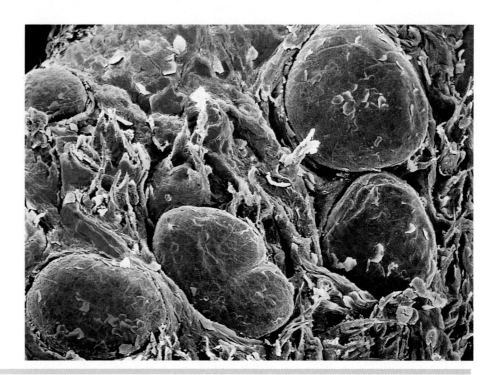

FIGURE 3–31
This picture is an enhanced scan of the surface of the tongue. The taste buds are the obvious, larger round and red structures.

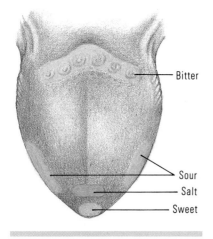

Bitter

Sour
Salt
Sweet

FIGURE 3–32
Areas of the human tongue that are maximally sensitive to the four basic tastes.

taste cells responded only to certain tastes, so that one could classify some taste cells as sweet receptors and others as sour receptors, and so forth. Yet recent research has demonstrated that taste cells are capable of responding to all four basic tastes. Still, specialization does exist, because these cells show different thresholds for one of the four basic tastes. In other words, a particular cell will react to any of the four tastes, but it will react more quickly (perceive lower concentrations) to one particular taste quality. Further, there is some orderliness to the distribution of these cells within the tongue (Collings, 1974); sweetness is most often perceived in the tip of the tongue, but bitterness is typically detected at the back of the tongue (see Figure 3–32).

As in sight and hearing, continued exposure to a particular taste can cause adaptation to that taste. For example, repeatedly tasting a salty solution will decrease your sensitivity to salt. You may have actually demonstrated this to yourself in the process of cooking. Suppose you are seasoning a soup, slowly adding a pinch of salt and tasting the soup until the desired level of saltiness has been attained. But when you try the soup an hour later, it seems much too salty. The reason is that you adapted to the saltiness of the soup while you were attempting to season it. Because you were much less sensitive to the taste of salt, you had to add much more than normal to perceive the appropriate level of saltiness. Similarly, many a chili has been ruined by cooks slowly adding chili powder until the desired "hotness" was attained, only later to discover they had created a fiery monster that was so hot it was nearly inedible.

The phenomenon of adaptation provides some support for the notion that taste is coded by the four qualities of sweet, salt, sour, and bitter, for adaptation to one taste quality does not lessen sensitivity to the other three. In fact, the opposite phenomenon, enhancement, is often observed. For example, adaptation to a sweet sticky bun enhances the sourness of orange juice.

Technically, the term *taste* should be restricted to the perceptual experience arising from the taste cells, yet taste is actually determined, in part, by other sensory systems as well. Smell plays a very important role; what we believe to be the taste of certain foods is actually their smell. When you have

118   Chapter 3

a head cold, you cannot smell as well; as a result, you may perceive your dinner as tasteless. Taste is also influenced by touch, in terms of the textures of foods, and some food qualities can induce pain, such as foods that are particularly spicy. Temperature also provides touch perceptions that affect taste. Some people like the taste of hot coffee but do not like iced coffee. The basic taste qualities are the same in both instances, but the overall perception of the coffee's "taste" is quite different.

Our sense of taste is operational at birth and may even function in utero. It is certainly important for babies, because they sample so much of their environment by putting objects in their mouths. Research has indicated that, unlike smell, the sensitivity of taste buds undergoes little change during your lifetime (Cowart, 1981).

Smell

Only about 5% of the human cerebral cortex is devoted to the sense of smell. As mentioned previously, smell is very important to other animals, such as rats. For most fish, smell is the dominant sense, and their cortex is chiefly devoted to this sense. In dogs, who use smell more than humans but less than fish, one third of the cerebral cortex is devoted to this sense. Many animals use special odors to communicate with other members of their species (Shorey, 1977). These conspecific (meaning same-species) odors are called **pheromones** and are a form of chemical communication among members of the same species. Researchers have found pheromone use by many animals, including insects, mammals, and birds. These odors may signal a receptivity to sex, a path to food, or an animals' territorial boundaries (Rogel, 1978).

pheromones odors used for communication by animals

It is less clear whether humans use pheromones, but there has been increasing evidence that humans also communicate chemically. For example, psychologists have noted that

1. Special glands exist in humans with no known function other than the production of odors
2. These glands produce powerful odors
3. Human smell has greater sensitivity and discriminative powers than previously thought
4. Behavioral evidence exists that humans can respond to other human odors (Van Toller, Dodd, & Billing, 1985).

For example, individuals have been found to be quite good at recognizing the body odor (from garments) of relatives compared to nonrelatives, even when they have been separated from those relatives for nearly 3 years. Researchers have speculated that these family-specific odors may be biologically determined by our genes (Porter et al., 1986).

Other research on human pheromones has established differences in perspiration and breath odors between men and women. In one study, subjects were able to discriminate perspiration differences in more than 80% of the trials (Wallace, 1977). Females were found to be more accurate in their judgments than males. In the breath odor studies, subjects placed their noses into plastic funnels connected by tubes to donor breathers on the other side of a partition. These donors exhaled into the tubes and the subjects tried to identify the sex of the breather. Again, females performed better than males; however, the performance for both sexes was significantly above what you would expect to occur by chance (Doty et al., 1982). Although these studies show that humans have gender-related odors and that they can successfully discriminate between them, it is not clear what role these odors play in governing human behavior.

olfactory cells receptor cells located in the olfactory epithelium that are responsible for smell

The receptors for smell in humans are located on the *olfactory epithelium*, a thin membrane present in the upper nasal cavity in both nostrils. The **olfactory cells** located in this membrane are stimulated by gases that are dissolved in the fluid covering the membrane. For a stimulus to be smelled it must be volatile—that is, in a gaseous state—and it must be soluble in water. However, there is no guarantee that a substance that meets these two conditions will be smelled. Some stimuli that reach the olfactory epithelium do not activate the cells there, and in many cases researchers are unable to explain why. These substances are labeled "odorless." Traditionally, there has been agreement that molecular structure is an important determinant for odors, and one popular theory of smell proposes a kind of lock-and-key mechanism where certain odors fit with certain olfactory cells (receptors) based on their molecular configuration (Amoore, 1970). Yet chemicals with very similar molecular structures often produce very different smells, or one will have a strong odor while the other is odorless. More recent research, particularly the work of psychologist Susan Schiffman, does not support a lock-and-key interpretation of smell. She has investigated such chemical characteristics as molecular structure, molecular weight, and solubility in water, and none of those allows the prediction of odor (Schiffman, Reynolds, & Young, 1981).

trigeminal sense chemoreceptor system in the nose that is responsive to certain food flavors

A second chemoreceptor system that exists in the nose is called the **trigeminal sense**. Trigeminal fibers in the olfactory epithelium are extensions of the trigeminal nerve, one of the 12 cranial nerves (the olfactory nerve is a separate cranial nerve). Research has shown that the trigeminal sense responds to a number of common odors, and that it is especially important for the flavor of some foods as well as the flavor of cigarettes (Van Toller et al., 1985). At this point, not much is known about this sense and its role in relation to the sense of smell.

Losing the Sense of Smell. As with the other senses, smell is an ability that differs among people. Typically these are threshold differences, meaning that the concentrations of the odors have to be much higher for some people to smell them. But some people cannot smell at all. This total lack of a sense of smell is called **anosmia**, and occurs rarely. Usually it is a congenital condition, but it also can result from brain tumors and other causes. In fact, about 1 of every 15 people who suffer a head injury will lose the ability to smell.

anosmia inability to detect odors

On a rainy October night in Chicago 11 years ago, 33-year-old mathematician David Griffin (not his real name) stepped off a curb and into the path of a Dodge van. He was on his usual after-dinner walk. . . . Griffin considered himself something of an epicure, with an ability to taste and smell that was the functional equivalent of perfect pitch. Impressed once, for instance, by some broiled fish he had eaten in a restaurant in Pisa, he divined the secret recipe and re-created the dish, down to the basting of lime juice, rosemary, and mustard.

The van was moving about five miles an hour when it hit him. He cracked his head on the pavement. His recovery was good, and during the eight days he spent in the hospital he did not have any remarkable symptoms. True, he noticed that the hospital food was terribly bland and yet very salty, but that was clearly just a sign of his good taste. It appeared he would suffer no deep or lasting injury. The day after returning home he poured his father a snifter of pear brandy—sweet, ethereal, redolent of fruit ripening in a sun-washed orchard— and discovered he could smell absolutely nothing. "I was devastated," he says.

The doctors said that if he still couldn't smell anything after six months to a year, he probably never would. The blow, they explained, apparently tore nerves connecting his brain and nose. Griffin's taste buds worked fine, so at least he sensed the salty, bitter, sour, and sweet ingredients in food. . . . But in the absence of the ability to smell, foods lost their rich flavor. These days he has resigned himself to an odorless existence. But Griffin says he [feels] deprived now of the memory that an odor can let loose, he feels cut off from his past. "Think about rotting leaves or a campfire or a roast or a Christmas tree—I enjoyed those smells so much. I miss not being able to experience them again and be reminded of other times. A dimension of my life is missing, I feel empty, in a sort of limbo." (Monmaney, 1987)

The loss of our ability to smell also occurs as a result of the aging process. Smell sensitivity seems best in the 20- to 50-year age range but decreases after that. Of people between the ages of 65 and 80, 25% probably are anosmic, and half of those older than 80 show no evidence of being able to smell (Doty et al., 1984). What seems to occur is that thresholds undergo considerable change. Appetites wane because foods begin to have little flavor. Consequently, many elderly persons may suffer serious malnutrition from poor eating habits. Some researchers have proposed adding flavor enhancers to food, increasing its aromatic qualities. Special foods are sold for infants, why not for senior citizens? The technology exists to improve the quality of life and restore the pleasures of eating for older people (Van Toller et al., 1985).

The Skin Senses

Sensations from the skin, such as cold or pain, as well as the perception of our body position, are aspects of what is called **somesthetic perception**. Receptors from this system are diverse in function and, unlike receptors for the other sensory systems we have discussed so far, are located over your entire body.

somesthetic perception perception of the skin senses such as cold or pain, and also body position

The Receptive Surface. Skin is composed of three layers (see Figure 3–33). The outer layer is composed of dead cells and is known as the **epidermis**. Under the epidermis is a layer of living cells called the **dermis**. This layer contains a variety of sensory receptors and manufactures the cells that form the epidermis. Beneath the dermis is **subcutaneous tissue**, which contains connective tissue and fat globules (Matlin & Foley, 1992).

epidermis outermost of the three layers of skin, composed of dead cells

dermis middle layer of the three layers of skin, composed of living cells

The dermis contains many different types of receptors. Some receptor endings, such as the *Pacinian corpuscles*, have small bulblike capsules on their endings. Such receptors are said to have *encapsulated endings*. In contrast, *free nerve endings* lack a covering, and instead may simply branch out or wrap around the base of hair. From the skin, nerve fibers travel to the spinal cord, where they connect with neurons that carry the sensory information to the somatosensory cortex (see Chapter 2).

subcutaneous tissue inner layer of the three layers of skin

Neural Code. Stimuli applied to the skin can elicit a variety of sensations, including cold, warmth, touch, and pain. Given this, and the diversity of receptors that exist in the dermis, researchers were naturally led to think that a simple relation might exist between the type of receptor stimulated and the psychological quality experienced. For example, stimulating a free nerve ending might inevitably produce the experience of pain, whereas activating an encapsulated receptor might produce the perception of being touched. This simple idea is known as **specificity theory** and was originally proposed by Johannes Muller in 1842.

specificity theory each sensation is coded by the activity in a particular kind of receptor

There is a simple, but painful, way to test this theory. In areas of your skin, such as your arms and back, there are relatively few receptors. In fact, there are regions where the receptors are so sparsely distributed that small areas can be found where only one type of sensation can be elicited (e.g., touch). According to specificity theory, such a sensory spot for touch should always contain the same type of receptor. The same should be true of regions that respond only to cold, warmth, and so forth. To test this notion, researchers identified sensory spots on the skin, peeled the skin away, and identified the type of receptor that existed within each sensory spot. Contrary

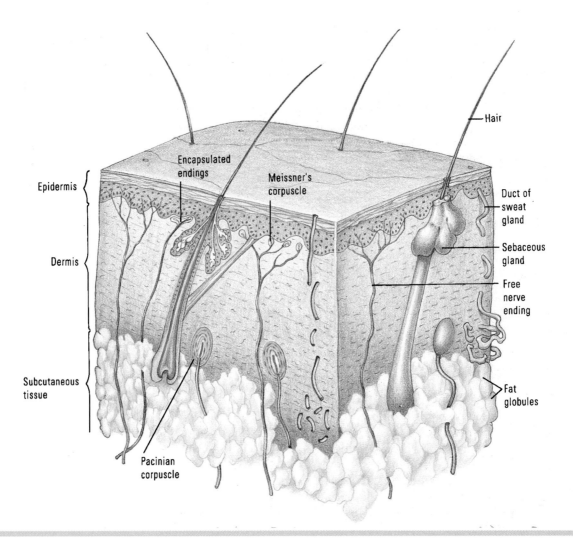

FIGURE 3-33
A cross section of skin. Notice how the skin is composed of three layers and the different types of receptor endings found in the dermis.

pattern theory sensations are coded by the pattern of activity in a group of receptors

to specificity theory, these researchers failed to find a simple correlation between receptor type and the sensory experience. To further complicate matters, other researchers demonstrated that stimulating a single type of receptor, such as free nerve endings, can give rise to a variety of psychological qualities, including touch, warmth, and pain (Goldstein, 1989). Given these findings, researchers such as Melzack and Wall (1965) have argued that we must reject specificity theory. In its place, they advocate a **pattern theory** that assumes psychological qualities are coded by the pattern of neural activity observed across a group of neurons.

APPLYING PSYCHOLOGY
The Development of Artificial Visual Systems

For many of us, most skin sensations receive little attention. For example, although you surely notice a pinprick, the heat of the sun, or icy cold water, you probably seldom attend to the sensations caused by your clothing or the pressure of your back against the chair. In contrast, people who have lost their vision often come to rely heavily on their skin senses. For example, we are all familiar with the Braille alphabet blind people use to read. Recent advances in technology may allow blind people to "see" much more of the world through their skin. For example, researchers at the Smith–Kettlewell Institute of Visual Sciences in San Francisco have developed what they call a **visual substitution system (VSS)**. The system consists of a television camera controlled by the perceiver and connected to a matrix of vibrating pins located on the perceiver's back. In essence, the visual field of the camera is a matrix of points that corresponds exactly to the matrix of points placed on the skin of the person's back. The camera picks up the image in terms of points of brightness, and those brightnesses are translated to the back by a system that matches them with varying degrees of vibration (Scadden, 1969). When a point in the camera matrix is dark, the corresponding vibrator point on the back does not vibrate. The brighter the point in the visual field, the greater the frequency of vibration. In this way the person is able to use the skin of the back to "see."

visual substitution system (VSS) a matrix of vibrating pins used to convey visual information to the skin

The researchers found that blind subjects could perform well after only a few hours' experience with the VSS. They could successfully identify the arrangement of objects in their environment and could even judge the relative distances and sizes of objects. Further, they could identify distinctive characteristics of people, such as hair length and body posture.

Initially, subjects had to sit in a chair equipped with the special vibrators and turn several cranks to manipulate the camera. Refinements of the system have continued, and now it is completely portable. The camera is mounted on a special pair of eyeglasses so that the person scans the visual field with head movements. The vibrator matrix is built into a kind of vest with the vibrators using the skin of the abdomen rather than the back (Bach-Y-Rita, 1982). Subjects using the newer system are able to develop what could be called eye–hand coordination, picking up small objects in the visual field. They can learn to perceive perspective cues as objects change in their orientation, and subjects even report experiencing objects as "out there." In other words, the perceptual experience is not just on their skin, but the objects seem as if they are actually in their spatial locations. A combination of technological advances as well as improvements in perceptual training, resulting in an even better perception of the vibrations, may place a system like this in many blind persons' future. Although many years away, it is hoped that technological advances will allow the development of artificial visual systems that allow the blind to "feel" the world as clearly as most of us see it. Interestingly, because such a system could be built to detect physical energy that our senses cannot (e.g., ultraviolet or infrared radiation), the development of VSSs could allow blind people access to physical information to which the rest of us are "blind."

Pain.   Pain is a sensory quality that seems fundamentally different from the other senses we have discussed. For example, consider vision and hearing. Our experience in these domains seems to be of objects that are "out there" and, at best, only weakly tied to our emotional experience (Matlin & Foley, 1992). In contrast, pain is an experience that seems within, not outside, of us. In addition, pain seems more closely tied to emotional experience than any other sensory dimension.

Another unusual aspect of pain is that the same stimulus may produce very different levels of pain, depending on both the individual and the situation. Examples of this were provided earlier in our chapter opening story, in which we discussed how culture can help to determine whether you perceive an event as intolerably painful or only mildly unpleasant. Even within a single culture, tremendous variability is observed. For example, Beecher (1959) reported that only one out of three men wounded in battle complained of enough pain to require morphine. This was observed in men who did not appear to be in a state of shock. Moreover, these same men would complain normally about an inept vein puncture. It would appear that the pain from their wounds was somehow being selectively blocked (Melzack & Wall, 1988).

To account for these and other observations, Melzack & Wall (1965) proposed a **gate control theory** of pain. According to this theory, there is a neural gate within the spinal cord that controls whether information about tissue damage is allowed to travel on to the brain. The researchers argued that this gate could be closed by activating other receptors in the region of the wound, which is why rubbing an area that hurts can help to alleviate the pain. More important, it was proposed that the brain, through a descending mechanism, could control whether the gate was open.

Over the last 25 years, researchers have made a great deal of progress in identifying the physiological mechanisms that control the level of pain you experience. This research revealed that our bodies manufacture opiate-like peptides (the endorphins) that eliminate pain (discussed in Chapter 2). Interestingly, some of these opiate peptides are manufactured in the spinal cord, where they could effectively close the gate to incoming pain signals. Other physiological studies have confirmed the notion that neural systems within the brain can, through descending tracts, inhibit the flow of pain within the spinal cord. By activating these systems artificially through a stimulating electrode, surgeons have been able to treat effectively people who suffer from chronic pain. It is hoped that future research will yield even more effective and less intrusive methods to control pain, methods that take advantage of the body's own pain inhibitory systems.

gate control theory proposes pain is modulated by a spinal gate that determines whether a pain signal is allowed to go on to the brain

◄ THINKING ABOUT
Pain ►

Pain is an experience that you might believe you would be better off without. But consider what this would mean. In the absence of pain, you wouldn't be bothered by being sunburned, biting your tongue, touching a hot burner, or stepping on a nail. Consequently, you would not be motivated to avoid such stimuli, which could have very grave results, as is illustrated by people who are, due to a genetic defect, congenitally insensitive to pain (see Melzack & Wall, 1988).

A particularly well-documented case of this condition is provided by a woman known as "Miss C." (Baxter & Olszewski, 1960; Melzack & Wall, 1988). Miss C. seemed normal in all regards and possessed an above average intelligence. It seemed her only peculiarity was that she never felt pain. Sunburn, headaches, earaches, and toothaches never caused her any discomfort. On several occasions her extremities were frostbitten during the winter months, but this too never elicited any pain.

In the absence of pain, Miss C. slowly destroyed her body. As a young child, she bit her tongue so hard that it was permanently deformed. At the age of 3, she crawled up and onto a hot radiator during the winter to watch the children playing outside. As she watched, she sustained a third-degree burn to her legs. As she grew older, she became aware of her strange condition and learned to inspect her body for injuries. But this could not prevent the bodily damage that led to her death. Normally, if you stand in one position for a long period, you slowly begin to feel uncomfortable, and this discomfort motivates you to change positions. Similarly, if you injure a joint, you feel pain in that joint that causes you to favor the injured limb. Because Miss C. did not feel any pain, she did not adjust her position normally or favor an injured limb. Instead, she continued using the limb, causing further damage. By the age of 29, Miss C. was badly deformed and suffered from a condition known as Charcot joints. She died that year from massive infections brought on by this condition.

Do you still believe that you would be better off if you never felt pain?

Position and Balance

If you were asked to name your sensory systems, the system that rules awareness of body movement, location, balance, and position would probably be absent from your list, yet it is very important to your everyday functioning. We are able to know our body position at any time. We know when we are standing, when we are sitting, when our left arm is extended to the side, and when our right arm is held above our head. We are capable of knowing our body's orientation with the gravitational pull of the earth. We take this knowledge for granted and never even give it a thought, yet damage in this sensory system can produce disorientation that makes functioning very difficult.

This sensory system, sometimes called the basic orienting system, is actually two systems, whose information is coordinated in the brain. The **kinesthetic system**, which is composed of receptors found in the joints and ligaments, serves to communicate information about the movement and location of various parts of our bodies. You probably have had the experience of sleeping on your arm and waking to find that you had little or no control over that arm. The arm seems to flop about as if it belonged to someone else. Such experiences allow you to see, on a temporary basis, what would happen if you lost your kinesthetic capabilities.

The **vestibular system**, also called the equilibratory system, is composed of the semicircular canals and the vestibular sacs, both of which are located in the inner ear (Benson, 1982). The vestibular system is concerned with the sense of balance and knowledge of body position. There are three semicircular canals, each located in a plane that is essentially perpendicular to the other two. When the head moves or changes its rate of movement, fluid within these canals shifts, stimulating hair cells that are similar to those in the cochlea. In this way, information about the motion of the body is communicated to the brain via the vestibular nerve. That nerve also carries information from the vestibular sacs which, like the semicircular canals, are fluid filled and contain hair cells as receptors. This part of the system communicates body position when the body is stationary (Geldard, 1972). Disturbances within the vestibular system cause problems with maintaining body equilibrium. The space careers of several U.S. astronauts were ended early when it was found that they had vestibular system problems.

kinesthetic system the system that tells us about the movements of our body

vestibular system the system in the inner ear that is concerned with controlling balance

THINKING AHEAD . . .

John Locke argued that basic sensations provide the building blocks out of which complex perceptions are created. Thus, the sensations correspond to the most elementary events of conscious experience and, as such, may be the most amenable to scientific study. Much is now known about the biological processes that produce our basic sensations. We understand how our sense of color is related to the activity in three types of cones and how subsequent neural interactions modify the output from the cones. We have learned that changes in our sensitivity to light are, to a large extent, due to a modification of the photopigments contained in the rods and cones. Research has shown how pitch must be coded by the frequency of neural firing for low-frequency stimuli and must be coded by location of maximum activation for high-frequency stimuli. We even know how our body can change the level of pain we experience.

But much remains a mystery. In fact, perhaps the most important questions have yet to be answered. How does neural activity generate a sensation that we *consciously* experience? How is this transformation brought about? How does a pattern of neural activity produce the experience of red? Why does one profile of activity from receptors in the skin produce a light touch while another produces heat or pain? Could we build a machine, a supercomputer, that experiences sensations in the same way we do? Could people blind from birth ever image the sensation of red? How could we know if they did? For that matter, how do you know whether your best friend, who has normal vision, experiences the same thing you experience when you see the color red? These questions have perplexed psychologists and philosophers for many years and will surely continue to baffle us for many years to come.

Summary

Sensory Processes—An Overview

1. A sensory system is a network of receptors, neural pathways, and brain areas that process information in a single sensory modality. Examples include vision, audition, smell, taste, and touch.
2. The absolute threshold is the stimulus value above which the stimulus can be detected and below which it cannot be detected. The difference threshold, also called the just noticeable difference, defines the minimal change in stimulation that can be detected.
3. Signal detection theory allows for a more accurate determination of sensory thresholds by taking into account the response biases of the observer.
4. The specialized cells that convert the various forms of sensory stimuli into electrical impulses for the nervous system are called receptors. Sensory adaptation occurs in receptors when stimulus conditions are unchanging.

Seeing

5. Light is the stimulus for vision that activates the receptors in the retina known as rods and cones. Cones are responsible for color vision and daytime vision. Rods are more sensitive in very low levels of illumination.
6. Visual acuity is best in the area of the retina known as the fovea, where the cones are densely packed and connected on a one-to-one basis with the secondary cells.
7. Modern color theory proposes that the Young–Helmholtz theory accurately expresses color vision at the receptor level, but that opponent-process theory better describes color vision in the ganglion cells and higher portions of the visual system.
8. Dark adaptation increases the sensitivity of the eye, whereas light adaptation decreases it. Pigment changes in the rods and cones are principally responsible for these changes. Dark adaptation is much slower than light adaptation. In the former, the cones require about 10 min to adapt, but the rods need about 35 min to adapt fully.
9. Receptive fields exist in a circular form within the retina and are composed of a center and surround with opposite functions. These fields are tied to neurons higher in the visual system, including neurons in the visual cortex that respond selectively to stimuli of varying sizes, orientations, and movement patterns.

Hearing

10. The stimulus for hearing is sound that is conducted within the ear to the cochlea that houses the hearing receptors known as hair cells. Békésy's theory of pitch perception proposes that sound stimuli generate a traveling wave along the basilar membrane that causes a maximal response in a particular membrane location, maximally stimulating the hair cells in that region.
11. The range for human hearing is 20 Hz to 20000 Hz, yet sensitivity changes across that range. The ear is maximally sensitive to sounds around 1000 Hz, but very low and very high frequency sounds must be much more intense to be heard.

Other Senses

12. Taste and smell are related sensory systems that depend on chemical stimulation of the relevant receptors—taste cells located in the taste buds, and olfactory cells located in the olfactory epithelium.
13. The total inability to smell is called anosmia. This condition is often the result of a head injury. Smell sensitivity, unlike taste sensitivity, declines over the life span.
14. The skin sensations include cold, warmth, pressure, and pain. These sensations are not linked in a simple way to specific receptors. Rather, it appears the pattern of neural activity determines the quality of the sensory experience.
15. Our bodies control the level of pain we experience by gating sensory input at the level of the spinal cord. The release of endorphins may act to close this gate. People who cannot feel pain often inadvertently damage their bodies.
16. The kinesthetic and vestibular systems are used to monitor the position of your body parts and maintain balance.

Key Terms

sensory system (88)
perception (88)
absolute threshold (89)
difference threshold (89)
Weber's law (90)
signal detection theory (90)
receiver operating characteristics (91)
subliminal perception (92)
receptors (93)
sensory adaptation (93)
habituation (93)
visible spectrum (95)
cornea (95)
iris (96)
pupil (97)
lens (97)
retina (97)
accommodation (97)
convergence (97)
rods (97)
cones (97)

bipolar cells (97)
ganglion cells (97)
optic nerve (97)
blind spot (98)
summation (98)
visual acuity (98)
fovea (98)
hue (100)
brightness (100)
saturation (100)
Young–Helmholtz color theory (101)
additive color (101)
subtractive color (101)
opponent-process color theory (105)
monochromacy (106)
dichromacy (106)
dark adaptation (107)
light adaptation (107)
visual cortex (108)
optic chiasm (108)
receptive field (109)
simple cells (110)
complex cells (110)

hypercomplex cells (110)
feature detectors (110)
dyslexia (111)
sound waves (112)
frequency (112)
pitch (112)
loudness (112)
timbre (112)
harmonics (112)
tympanic membrane (113)
ossicles (113)
cochlea (113)
basilar membrane (113)
hair cells (114)
tectorial membrane (114)
auditory nerve (114)
auditory cortex (114)
place theory (114)
Békésy's theory (115)
frequency theory (115)
volley principle (116)

conductive deafness (117)
perceptive deafness (117)
taste buds (117)
taste cells (117)
pheromones (119)
olfactory cells (120)
trigeminal sense (120)
anosmia (120)
somesthetic perception (121)
epidermis (121)
dermis (121)
subcutaneous tissue (121)
specificity theory (121)
pattern theory (122)
visual substitution system (VSS) (123)
gate control theory (124)
kinesthetic system (125)
vestibular system (125)

Suggested Reading

Békésy, G. von. (1960). *Experiments in hearing*. New York: McGraw-Hill. A description of Bekesy's classic work on hearing, spanning four decades. An excellent first-hand account of the research that earned Bekesy the Nobel Prize in 1961.

Corso, J. F. (1981). *Aging sensory systems and perception*. New York: Praeger. An account of the changes that take place in the various sensory systems during the life span.

Hurvich, L. M. (1981). *Color vision*. Sunderland, MA: Sinauer. A thorough coverage of modern theory of color vision.

Matlin, A., & Foley, M. A. (1992). *Sensation and perception*. Needham Heights, MA: Allyn and Bacon. Provides a broad overview of all of the sensory systems.

Melzack, R., & Wall, P. D. (1988). *The challenge of pain*. New York: Penguin. An intriguing, and very readable, paperback describing the puzzle of pain and recent theories.

Randi, J. (1980). *Flim-flam: The truth about unicorns, parapsychology, and other delusions*. New York: Lippincott & Crowell. A book by a well-known magician, who describes how tricks of extrasensory perception (ESP) are accomplished.

CHAPTER 4
Perception

Looking out your window in winter, you watch it snow. You may be struck by the beauty of the snow, but beyond this observation you notice little about how these flakes are very different from those of the last storm. In the English language, we have but a single word for snow, and for most of us, a single word is all that we need. Eskimos, in contrast, have many words for snow. They have a word for blowing snow, for drifting snow, and snow you can make igloos from. An Eskimo watching the storm could tell you what kind of snow it was and how these flakes differed from those of the last storm.

It seems the diversity of experience that accompanies growing up in a different culture can profoundly affect the way you look at the world and label the events you perceive. As an American, you learn to identify rice, yet you may not be able to recognize a rice plant. By contrast, the Hanuos of the Philippine Islands have 92 names for the different kinds and states of rice. Because their lives depend on the cultivation of rice, the Hanuos have learned how to perceive subtle differences in rice that most Americans would never notice.

You too may have recently engaged in such perceptual learning. In biology class, the first time you looked through a microscope at a cell, it was probably hard to perceive any recognizable parts. But with experience, you learned what to attend to and how to identify the nucleus, mitochondria, and so forth. Similarly, students in a geology class find it hard at first to discriminate different types of rocks. But with practice, they learn what to observe and how to recognize whether the rock is, for example, basalt or obsidian.

Consider for a moment what your brain must do to accomplish these feats. First, it must organize the sensory information into coherent objects and separate those objects from the background. To recognize the object, your mind must then relate this sensory information to an existing knowledge of structures. Finally, to make fine discriminations within a class of objects, you need to learn what features of the object you must attend to. These feats are accomplished by the processes of **perception**, processes that are used to organize, interpret, and selectively extract sensory information.

perception the process of organizing, interpreting, and selectively extracting sensory information

◀ The manner in which objects and events in our lives are perceived affects the quality of our lives.

In this chapter we first discuss the mechanisms that organize sensory information. We will then consider the processes that are used to recognize and attend to objects in the environment. Many of these processes appear to be functioning at birth, which suggests that they are **innate**. However, as we saw previously, the way they are applied depends on experience. This issue is addressed in the last section, where we discuss how perceptual learning can affect what you perceive.

innate features or traits that exist from birth

PERCEIVING AN ORGANIZED WORLD

Take a moment to look at the objects around you. What you perceive is a world made up of independent objects that are readily distinguished from background stimuli. How does your perceptual system decide which sensations belong together? How does it determine how far away an object is, how large it is, and whether the object is moving? In this section we will consider the tricks your perceptual system uses to create the well-organized world you perceive.

Perceptual Organization

Perceptual organization occurs when we group the basic elements of our sensory world into the coherent objects that we perceive. The ability to organize the perceptual world makes our perception more efficient; that is, perceptual judgments can be made accurately in a short period of time. Perceptual organization allows us to make sense of the complex stimuli that comprise our perceptual world. Further, it is the basis for many special perceptual abilities such as reading a road map, identifying the melody in an unfamiliar piano piece, recognizing the face of a friend, and seeing various animal shapes in the clouds.

perceptual organization processes used to group sensory elements together

There are two basic principles of perceptual organization. One involves perceiving the world in terms of a figure embedded in some perceptual background. The other asserts that organization tends toward simplicity. We will discuss both of these principles shortly.

Much of the actual research on perceptual organization is recent, but the ideas germinated in the soil of Gestalt psychology, beginning with Wertheimer's writing in 1912 (see Chapter 1). The Gestalt psychologists argued that people are born with organizing tendencies in perception. These psychologists did not deny that learning played a role in perception, but they did believe that organization of the perceptual world is the same for everyone, and that these innate tendencies add structure to perception. Modern perceptual research has generally been supportive of many of the organizing tendencies originally proposed by Wertheimer and his colleagues, yet many questions about perceptual organization remain.

Figure–Ground Perception.   Organizing the perceptual world generally means identifying a part of the world as the target of perception and viewing that target image in relation to its surrounding stimuli. The target stimulus is called the *figure*, whereas the surrounding stimulus elements make up the *ground*, or background. This tendency to differentiate the perceptual world is called **figure–ground perception**. The top half of Figure 4–1 is a version of a classic figure–ground stimulus that has been part of psychology for more than 70 years. What do you see? If you see the white as figure and the blue as ground, then the perception is that of a vase or drinking goblet. On the other hand, if you see the blue as figure and the white as ground, then your perception is of two profiled heads, facing each other.

figure–ground perception tendency to differentiate target stimuli from background stimuli

This figure is constructed intentionally to be ambiguous. Observers typically see it both ways, although in this version there is a tendency to see the vase first, partly because the blue area totally encloses the white area, and partly because of the symmetry of the vase. The ambiguity of this figure and the tendency to organize the perceptual world into figure and ground has been demonstrated through perceptual work in other cultures (Carpenter, 1980), thus providing some support for the Gestalt claims that organizing tendencies are innate.

Figure 4–2 is another example of figure–ground perception. Again, like Figure 4–1, the picture is totally in two colors, but in this case the black and white are scattered throughout, rather than clustered into well-defined portions of the picture. Have you identified the object in Figure 4–2 yet? We will provide the answer a little later in our discussion.

What determines what will be perceived as figure and what will be perceived as background? We can best answer this question by focusing on the figure, as it is the figure that is "lifted" from the rest of the perceptual array. In fact, in perception we give most of our attention to the figure. Studies of the way people view pictures have shown that most attention is given to the figure and little is reserved for the ground. This difference has been determined by recording the eye movement patterns of individuals while they look at pictures. These studies not only show the direction and order of the eye movements, but also reveal the amount of time spent looking at each part of the picture (Loftus & Mackworth, 1978).

One feature that helps to identify the figure is size; smaller areas are more likely to be seen as figure than larger areas. Familiarity is also important, meaning that familiar shapes and forms are more often perceived as figures. Figures are more likely to exist in either a horizontal or vertical orientation than in some other orientation. Objects that are symmetrical, as we noted earlier, are more often seen as figures. Some research has shown that

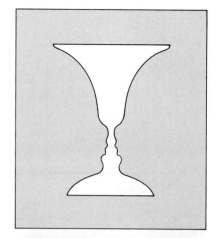

FIGURE 4–1
At the top is an ambiguous figure–ground drawing. At the bottom is a vase created by Kaiser Porcelain for Queen Elizabeth's Silver Jubilee in 1977. The vase is intentionally nonsymmetrical, showing the two famous royal profiles.

FIGURE 4–2
What do you see as the figure in this picture?

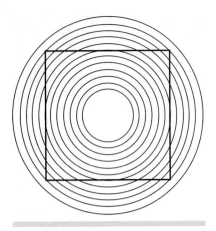

FIGURE 4-3
This figure consists of a square superimposed on a background of concentric circles. Because the square is smaller, it is usually seen as the figure. Yet notice that the sides of the square do not appear straight; they look bowed. It is the background that produces this illusion (the figure is a true square). Take away the circles and the square will look normal. We call this a *background-mediated* illusion because the ground produces the distortion in the figure. The fact that this illusion occurs is evidence of the role ground plays in figure–ground perception.

law of Prägnanz the tendency to perceive the simplest form possible; certain stimulus elements just seem to belong together

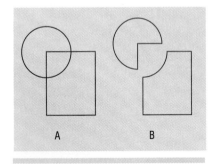

FIGURE 4-4
An illustration of the law of Prägnanz, which states that perception will follow the simplest form possible.

figures are typically brighter than the ground (Coren, 1969), whereas other studies note the importance of movement of the figure relative to background stimuli.

This ability to organize our perceptual world into figures and grounds is important because it adds considerable stability to the perceptual environment. It also increases our perceptual skills, making our judgments more valid. You should realize that perception does involve attention to both figure and ground; it is just that most of our attention is focused on the figure. But both interact in determining perception, which is to say that figure influences ground and vice versa (see Figure 4–3).

Organization by Minimum Tendency. There is general agreement within psychology that perception is an economical process. Perceptual economy is expressed in two ways: first, we tend to perceive the world in the simplest way possible; second, we tend to make perceptual judgments based on a small number of the most obvious cues. Both of these tendencies emphasize the simplicity of perception, what researchers have referred to as perception by minimum principle or minimum tendency (Hatfield & Epstein, 1985). We will discuss the second of the tendencies a little later and focus on the first one at this time.

Law of Prägnanz. The Gestalt psychologists proposed the **law of Prägnanz**, also called the *law of simplicity*, which stated that we have a tendency to see things in the simplest form possible. Certain perceptual elements are seen as belonging together because they provide better continuity of the stimulus. If we were to ask subjects to look at Part A of Figure 4–4 and describe what they saw, they would most likely answer, "a circle and a square"; they might even report that the two shapes overlapped. If we asked subjects to draw the two shapes they saw separately on two pieces of paper, virtually everyone would draw a circle and a square. We would expect no one to draw the two shapes pictured in Part B of that figure, for that drawing violates the principle of simplicity with respect to form. The circle and the square are quite simple shapes, but the forms pictured in Part B are irregular. If indeed people saw the two shapes in Part B, perceptually it would mean adding two straight lines to a portion of the circle and adding a curved line to two sides of our square. According to Gestalt theory, such a perception violates the principle of good continuation, which states that lines are perceived as continuing in direction or form. That continuation is simplest in perceptual terms. If you trace the circle or the square in Part A, at some point you come to a choice point where the two shapes join, but you have no trouble deciding which way to move: you continue the curved line with the circle and the straight line with the square. For another example of good continuation, see Figure 4–5. Most people looking at Part A will see two continuous lines; in fact, they will see the two lines shown separately in Part C. But what about the two lines shown in Part B? Combined, they would also produce the arrangement shown in Part A. In this case we do not have the differences of curving versus straight lines, because all of the lines in this figure are straight. Instead, we see the two lines shown in Part C because that particular perception is consistent with the continuing direction of the lines. Perception of this kind is amazingly uniform, even in studies using nonsense shapes or forms that are intended to be unfamiliar. It also appears that this kind of perceptual organization may be innate, because it can be demonstrated in the testing of very young children and even in infants (Strauss & Curtis, 1983). But studies comparing the performances of infants, children, and adults do illustrate some improvement in perceptual organization abilities with age, especially for complex shapes and patterns.

Closure. Another principle involved in organization by minimum tendency is called **closure**. Closure refers to the tendency to fill in information that is missing from the perceptual array by closing in gaps. In looking at Figure 4–6, your initial tendency might be to see a triangle, even though most of that image is missing. Closure leads you to fill in the sides. This does not mean that you actually see a triangle; if you asked an observer to report the form shown in Figure 4–6 by drawing it, typically, the person would produce an accurate drawing. But the tendency to fill in the gaps among the three angles is quite strong. In fact, it is so strong that it can produce *subjective contours,* contours that are perceived even though they do not physically exist (see Figure 4–7).

Laws of Grouping. A third organizing tendency in perception refers to the ways in which perceptual elements are grouped, sometimes referred to as **laws of grouping**. Two such laws are *similarity* and *proximity*. As these labels imply, we tend to group things on the basis of how similar they are to one another and on how near (in terms of physical location) they are to one another. Figure 4–8 depicts three arrangements of stimuli. In looking at each part of the figure, ask yourself to judge whether you see the stimuli arranged in rows or columns. In Part *A*, all elements are the same, and the distance between any two adjacent elements in the array is the same. In this case, similarity and proximity are of no use, for the elements do not differ on these dimensions; as a result, we are equally likely to see the dots arranged in rows or columns. In Part *B*, the tendency is to organize the stimuli in columns, based on similarity, whereas in Part *C*, the dots are seen in rows, because of proximity.

Now look back at Figure 4–2. You are likely able to see the Dalmatian pictured there, even though much of the perceptual array is missing. The dog becomes the figure you view against a rather ambiguous ground. Closure helps to fill in some of the missing information. Laws of grouping, particularly similarity, may also play a role, for the dots on the dog's body tend to be round, unlike the shapes of the black areas in other parts of the picture.

Organization Throughout the Senses. Thus far we have described the principles of perceptual organization as though they existed solely for the visual sense. This emphasis is partly due to the ease of using visual examples for the printed page. However, these organizing principles exist for all senses. Figure–ground principles can be seen in the way people perceive music; they listen to the melody as distinct from its harmonies. At times an instrument or voice dominates the others in an orchestra or chorus, thus becoming the figure, while the remaining voices or instruments serve as ground. In taste, certain substances may stand out from the other components of a particular taste, while the more subtle components of the taste

closure the tendency to fill in missing information from a perceptual array; to fill in the gaps

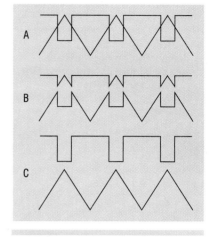

FIGURE 4–5
Because of the principle of good continuation, Part *A* is seen as being composed of the two lines in Part *C* but not of the lines in Part *B*. Yet either *B* or *C* could comprise *A*.

laws of grouping the tendency to perceive similar or proximal stimuli as belonging together

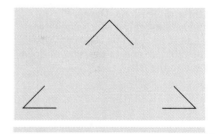

FIGURE 4–6
Closure causes this incomplete figure to be seen as a triangle.

FIGURE 4–7
The orientation of the three "Pac man"-like figures leads you to see a white border-less triangle lying on top of another triangle outlined in blue. When the white triangle is seen as the figure, people generally claim it looks lighter and is set off from the background by a clear contour. These contours are an illusion, for they do not exist in the physical stimulus. You can convince yourself of this by covering the three pac man figures with small pieces of paper. When these cues are removed, the subjective contours disappear. (From Matlin & Foley, 1992.)

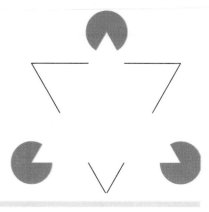

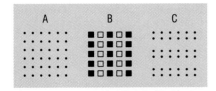

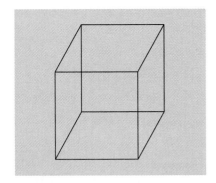

FIGURE 4–8
A demonstration of two laws of grouping: similarity and proximity (see text for explanation).

FIGURE 4–9
The image on the retina is essentially a two-dimensional picture of our visual world. The interpretive processes of the brain convert that image to a three-dimensional one. Although the figure drawn here is two dimensional, it can be seen as a cube in three dimensions. Depending on which face of the cube you see as closest to you, this cube can be seen as tilted up and to the right or down and to the left.

binocular disparity depth cue based on difference in images as the image reaches each of the two eyes

convergence depth cue based on the tension of the muscles that control eye movement

stereopsis comparison of retinal disparity by overlaying images in each eye

serve as ground. Laws of grouping and other examples of perception in the simplest manner have been illustrated in a number of studies on hearing (Vicario, 1982). Series of impulses will be grouped according to the principles of similarity (pitch or loudness) or proximity.

Depth Perception

The ability to perceive depth is a function of the arrangement of objects in the perceptual environment, the capacities of the eyes, and the interpretive processes of the brain (see Figure 4–9), which include the use of memory stores. We perceive depth by using a number of cues, a few of which we can use at birth, but most of which we have to learn how to use. One important facilitator of depth perception is the fact that we have two eyes that see the world from different perspectives (Foley, 1985). Yet two eyes are not required for depth perception. This has been demonstrated by a number of people who have sight in only one eye, including a professional football player who made his living catching passes, which is impossible to do without the ability to perceive depth. Depth cues that require two eyes are called binocular cues, whereas those needing only one eye are termed monocular cues. Although we rely heavily on binocular cues to perceive depth, monocular cues are also very important; for example, they are needed by artists who wish to create depth in a two-dimensional surface and by viewers of artwork who wish to appreciate that depth experience.

Binocular Cues. There are two depth cues that require both eyes: **binocular disparity** and **convergence**. The former is an effective cue for considerable distances, perhaps as far as 1,000 ft; the latter can be used only for objects within about 80 ft of the observer.

Binocular Disparity. Because your eyes are separated by a space, each retina receives a slightly different view of the world. There is a simple way to demonstrate this to yourself. Close your right eye and hold your left thumb about 6 in. in front of your left eye. Then position your right thumb behind your left thumb so that it is hidden from view. If you now look at your fingers with your other eye, you should be able to see both thumbs. This difference in the images received by the two eyes is known as binocular disparity. The disparate images are compared in the brain through a process known as **stereopsis**. In a sense, the brain compares the information from the two eyes by overlaying the retinal images. The greater the disagreement between the two retinal patterns, the closer the object. Stereoscopes, popular in the early part of this century (and a modern version of the stereoscope, known as the Viewmaster), use the cue of binocular disparity to create impressions of depth in the pictures one views in them.

Convergence. Convergence does not depend on the retinal images in the two eyes, but on the muscle tension that results from the external eye muscles that control eye movement. When you look at objects up close, your eyes converge and the tension in the eye muscles is noticeable. You can demonstrate this by extending your arm straight out in front of you and holding up your thumb. Then, while staring at your thumb with both of your eyes, slowly bring your thumb in toward your nose, watching your thumb all the time. As your thumb approaches your nose you will begin to notice the tension in your eyes. Indeed, your eyes may even hurt a little as your thumb gets very close to your nose. By monitoring the tension of the eye muscles, the brain is provided with a measure of convergence that can be used to make judgments about the distance of objects.

Objective motion

FIGURE 4-10
As the observer moves through the environment, objects flow by at different rates. As indicated by the size of the arrows, the closer the object, the faster it appears to move. This difference in the rate of movement provides a cue for depth known as motion parallax.

Monocular Cues.   There are only two binocular cues, but there are many cues that can be provided by only one eye. We discuss some of the major ones in this section.

Motion Parallax.   When your head is moved, the images produced by objects in the environment move across the retina. The relative rate of this movement will vary as a function of distance, providing a cue for depth known as **motion parallax**. It is particularly easy to see this when you are traveling in a vehicle. For example, consider looking out of the window of a moving train (see Figure 4–10). Nearby objects will appear to move by rapidly while objects that are farther away will appear to move more slowly.

motion parallax depth cue based on the rate objects move when our head moves

Elevation.   The **elevation** of objects above the horizon in our visual field is an important cue to their depth. Typically, objects located higher in the field are farther away. This is one of many depth cues important to artists in simulating depth in their paintings. Indeed, young children learn to create some depth in their pictures by drawing objects that are supposed to be farther away higher in the picture (see Figure 4–11).

elevation depth cue based on height in the visual field; typically, objects higher in the field are interpreted as farther away

Interposition.   Objects in our environment often overlap, with nearer objects obscuring parts of distant objects. This depth cue is known as **interposition** or superposition (see Figure 4–12).

interposition nearby objects obscure or block parts of faraway objects

Linear Perspective.   As parallel lines recede in the distance, the lines appear to come closer and closer together. Standing on a railroad track and looking down the rails, or driving down a straight stretch of highway and observing the road ahead, are good ways to demonstrate the monocular cue of **linear perspective**. Studies of children's art have shown the cue of linear perspective to be another early cue used by children to simulate depth in their drawings (see Figure 4–11).

linear perspective parallel lines appear to converge as they move farther away

Aerial Perspective.   Another depth cue comes from the changes in coloration of distant objects. Objects that are farther away appear to be more bluish. This color change is primarily a function of atmospheric haze, but it also depends on the level of illumination. The cue of **aerial perspective** is

aerial perspective atmospheric haze causes distant objects to appear bluish

FIGURE 4-11
This scene by a 7-year-old child uses the monocular cues of elevation and linear perspective to create the impression of depth.

FIGURE 4-12
Boating was painted by Gabriele Münter in 1910. It makes substantial use of the cue of *interposition* to establish the different distances of the people in the boat as well as the placement of the boat in the foreground.

operative outdoors and at considerable distances. It is not one you can use in your living room. It is also not very effective in the dry air of the desert, where distances are usually underestimated.

Relative Brightness.   Brightness is a cue we use to judge depth. If two objects are the same size and exist at the same distance from us but differ in brightness, we will perceive the dimmer object as being farther away. This depth judgment (an error in judgment, in this case) is due to **relative brightness**, a cue we have learned to depend on because brighter objects are typically closer to us.

Texture Gradient.   The mystery behind depth perception is how the brain takes the two-dimensional information it is provided and reconstructs the third dimension. One way might be calculating the magnitude of binocular disparity, or convergence, and using this information in conjunction with monocular cues to infer the distance of each object in your environment. Of course, it is assumed that these inferences are not consciously computed. Thus, you do not consciously think about the perceived magnitude of disparity and then use this information to compute the depth of each object. Instead, an object's depth appears to be automatically presented to you without your expending any mental effort. Similarly, it is assumed that the computation of size–distance invariance involves such an *unconscious inference.*

James J. Gibson (1966, 1979) has argued that in our everyday world, the perception of size and depth may not require these complex calculations. Instead, *higher-order information* produced by the relative position and movement of objects may allow you to perceive depth and size directly and to do so without performing any complex computations. For example, we have seen that the relative motion of objects provides information about their depth. Another important cue for depth is provided by the natural environment in which objects occur. For example, consider the rock-covered beach depicted in Figure 4–13. The rocks in this picture provide what Gibson calls a **texture gradient**, a surface of regular-sized objects. Similarly, the grass in a field or the waves on an ocean can provide a texture to your environment. In each case, the objects that make up the texture gradient tend to be about the same size. Consequently, their change in retinal size provides you with a cue for depth. According to Gibson, this allows you to infer the depth of most objects directly in the natural environment by simply noting their location on the texture gradient.

Because Gibson's theory emphasizes how we see in the natural world, it is called an **ecological theory of perception**. Of course, Gibson would admit that under artificial conditions such as those used in the laboratory, texture gradients may provide little or no information about depth. Under these conditions, you can show that other cues, such as binocular disparity, can be used to infer depth. However, Gibson would argue that under natural conditions, such computations are not necessary.

Depth Perception: Innate or Learned?   So far, we have described a number of cues for perceiving depth; most require one eye, but a few require both eyes. Is the ability to use these cues innate or learned? Research has demonstrated that it is both. At birth, the binocular cues are of little use, because the infant cannot coordinate its eye movements and will not be able to do so reliably until it is approximately 3 months of age (Aslin, 1977). And even then infants are not capable of interpreting the disparate images from the eyes in terms of depth, because the ability to use the cue of binocular disparity does not emerge until some time between the ages of 3.5 and 6 months (Fox et al., 1980). This acquisition of binocular skills may be the result of learning or simply due to maturation. Research on the development of perception in humans has shown that use of the monocular and binocular cues is primarily the result of learning but that some capability, probably monocular in nature, exists at birth.

Researchers have also looked at whether depth perception is innate or learned in animals (Walk & Gibson, 1961). One way this issue can be addressed is by placing subjects on a glass-covered table. In the region where the subjects are placed, the floor is directly under the glass (see Figure 4–14). Adjoining this area is a *visual cliff* where the floor drops away a few feet. When a young kid or lamb that has just learned to walk is placed on the shallow side, it avoids venturing over the cliff. Similarly, chicks less than a day old avoid the area where the floor is recessed. Other studies have shown that even animals raised in impoverished environments that lack normal depth cues avoid the deep side of the visual cliff.

Testing human infants on the visual cliff is not as easy, because it would be unethical to rear a human in a perceptually restricted environment. Infants must be capable of crawling before they can be tested, and by that time they are typically 6 months old or older. During that time they have had many experiences that could have contributed to the learning of depth perception. Studies on the cliff show that human infants, like other animals, prefer the shallow side and rarely venture onto the deep side (Gibson & Walk, 1960). But because normal babies have had the opportunity for learning, these studies could not establish that depth perception is innate in humans. This response difficulty was resolved when researchers chose a different dependent variable. Using newborn infants, they suspended them in a sling above either the shallow or deep sides of the cliff and found a difference in the infants' heart rate when the infants viewed the deep versus the shallow side (Campos, Langer, & Krowitz, 1970). This difference did not necessarily indicate that the infants were afraid of the deep side; it may have meant sim-

relative brightness nearby objects tend to be seen as brighter, even when objects farther away are the same size

texture gradient depth cue based on the texture gradient provided by regularly sized objects in the environment

ecological theory of perception Gibson's theory emphasizing information in the external (distal) stimulus

FIGURE 4–13
The depth in this photograph does not come from the separate rocks that are located at various distances from one another. Instead, higher-order information is provided by the gradient of texture that gives the picture its perceived slant and depth. James Gibson's ecological theory of perception says that information inherent in the environment can provide a complete account of perceptual responses.

FIGURE 4–14
A kitten peers over the edge of a visual cliff. A variety of cues, including motion parallax, linear perspective, and texture gradients, can be used to determine that the floor drops away.

auditory localization ability to locate direction and distance of a sound source; usually a result of sound waves reaching each ear at different times

ply that the infants were showing a greater interest in one side than the other. But it did show that newborn infants could perceive some elements of depth.

Depth Perception and Sound.   To this point we have discussed depth perception as a visual phenomenon, the location of different objects at different distances in our visual environment. Yet a somewhat similar process exists for the sense of hearing and is usually labeled **auditory localization**, the ability to locate the direction and distance of sounds. Unlike vision, with its abundance of monocular depth cues, audition depends largely on two ears (binaural) for sound localization. Sounds can be localized using only one ear (monaural), but that is a difficult and often inaccurate process.

Sound localization is important for many animals and especially critical for some. The great gray owl you saw in the previous chapter uses its auditory localization ability to find food. Bats use it to avoid obstacles in their environment (as do blind humans), frogs use it to locate a mate, and many young animals use it to find their parents and vice versa. Humans use this auditory ability daily: college professors use it to locate the person asking a question in class, drivers use it to avoid an accident in traffic, and choir directors use it to find the person singing off key.

Sounds are localized in binaural listening by two important cues: *time differences* and *intensity differences*. A sound located to your left will reach your left ear slightly ahead of its arrival at your right ear. Similarly, it will reach your left ear with slightly greater sound intensity. Understand that these interaural time and intensity differences are very small, but they provide a cue that is sufficient for the brain to use in judging the distance and direction of the sound source. Time differences are particularly important for localizing low sounds (below 1500 Hz). Intensity differences are most useful for higher frequencies, especially those above 6000 Hz (Gelfand, 1981). But what about sounds that come from the median plane, for example, a spot directly in front of or in back of us? Those sounds will reach the ears with equal intensity and at the same time. The solution to that problem is to move your head, which will then create the interaural differences needed to localize the sound successfully. Whereas head movements are very effective for such sounds, it is possible to localize sounds in the median plane without moving the head. Recall from Chapter 3 that a piece of skin and cartilage called the pinna is attached to each side of your head. These structures weaken the incoming sound (more so for sounds coming from behind the person), and the fact that the pinnae differ slightly in shape and size means that each affects the sound a little differently. Apparently, this difference provides a monaural cue for sound localization (Warren, 1982; Yost & Nielsen, 1985).

Perceptual Constancy

The appearance of objects in our perceptual world is always changing. Sometimes objects move. Sometimes we move, thus changing the angle at which we view objects. Sometimes changes in perception occur because of differences in lighting. It is important to understand that these changes are in appearance and typically do not represent changes in the object itself. For example, when one of the authors of this book was a young boy, he went to a pier in Norfolk, Virginia, to await the arrival of an aircraft carrier that was bringing his father home from Korea. He remembers his mother telling him that the ship carried several thousand men. Yet when he saw the carrier approaching in the distance, he was amazed at how small it was. In fact, it looked no bigger than the toy boats in his bathtub at home. How could it possibly carry his father, much less thousands of other people? But as he watched it approach, it grew larger and larger, until it was massive.

This kind of experience is common among children of preschool age and indicates that they are not governed by the principle of **size constancy**, which holds that objects stay the same size, even though the size of the retinal image changes as the distance of the object varies. As an adult, this same author was able to witness a size constancy failure in his own children. He had taken them to a July 4th concert by the Beach Boys on the lawn in front of the Washington Monument in Washington, DC. The crowd was huge, in excess of 400,000, and he, his wife, and their daughters were several hundred yards from the stage. Later, one of his daughters told a young friend about seeing the Beach Boys. Holding her thumb and index finger about two inches apart, she said, "Did you know the Beach Boys are only this big?"

You, or any other reader of this text, would not make that mistake because size constancy exists for you. Perceptual constancy is a most useful perceptual ability in our everyday functioning. There are many changes in the perceptual world, and we need to respond only to those that are most meaningful. If we reacted to every change in our perceptual environment, we would often be confused and our perceptual processes would be far from maximally efficient. For example, the visual system is interested in properties of objects and not in the accidental properties of light reflected from those objects. Thus, we want to see the same color of an object even if the light source changes from the sun to a light bulb. We want to see a square as a square even if it is viewed from an oblique angle. And we want to detect the motion of the object, not the motion of our eyes.

Perceptual constancies provide us with a way of creating some stability in a world of constant flux. The examples we have given so far illustrate size constancy, but perceptual constancy operates with respect to shape and lightness as well. We briefly describe research on each of these three constancies.

Size Constancy. Objects that exist in the real world and as images on our retina represent two kinds of stimuli. The stimulus of the object as it actually exists is called the **distal stimulus**, whereas the retinal image of that object is called the **proximal stimulus** (see Figure 4–15). When we move away from objects, or when they move away from us, the distal stimulus remains the same, but the proximal stimulus changes in size. Once size constancy has been learned, the perceiver correctly learns to interpret changes in the retinal image size as a cue to changes in distance. Research has shown that infants, even in their first year, can demonstrate some minimal size constancy. However, their performance on size constancy tasks does not equal adult performance until about age 6 (Cohen, DeLoache, & Strauss, 1979).

Initially, researchers believed that size constancy existed only for familiar objects. Because experience is so important in the development of size constancy, this notion would seem to make sense. And, in fact, size constancy has been found to be better for familiar objects. Nevertheless, studies with nonsense shapes (which are, by definition, unfamiliar) show that size constancy holds for these objects as well (Matlin, 1988).

An important variable in size constancy is *distance*. In fact, when there are few distance cues (we talk about these cues later in this chapter), it becomes difficult to judge size. Imagine viewing an airplane against a cloudless blue sky. You might perceive it to be an actual airplane flying at an altitude of 30,000 ft, yet it could be a model airplane whose altitude was only several hundred feet. Against a uniform sky, there are almost no cues for distance, so it becomes difficult to judge the size of the plane accurately, based solely on its retinal image size. This important relationship between size and distance was first described by Helmholtz (whose color and pitch theories you learned about in the preceding chapter) and has become known as the **size–distance invariance hypothesis**. The hypothesis holds that

size constancy perceived size remains constant despite a change in retinal size, so changes in the distance of an object do not alter how large or small we think it is

distal stimulus the stimulus of an object as it actually exists in the real world

proximal stimulus the image of a distal stimulus on the retina

size–distance invariance hypothesis says that size judgments are made by comparing the size of the retinal image with perceived distance

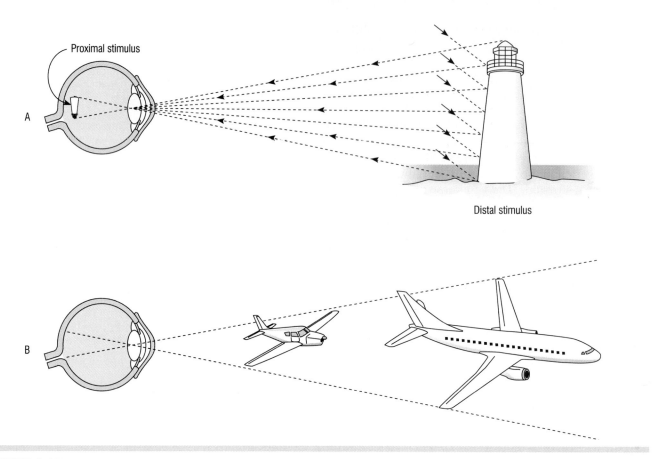

FIGURE 4-15

(*A*) Light rays are reflected from objects in the environment, the distal stimuli, and enter the eye to form images on the retina. The size of the retinal image, or proximal stimulus, will vary, depending on both the size of the distal stimulus and its distance. (*B*) Consequently, a small plane that is close could produce a proximal stimulus having the same size as a much larger jet farther away. (Adapted from Goldstein, 1989).

perceivers make judgments of the actual size of objects by comparing the size of the retinal image with their perception of the object's distance.

The size–distance invariance hypothesis may help us understand a common illusion. You have surely noticed that when the moon is on the horizon (see Figure 4–16), it appears much larger than when it is overhead (a zenith moon). Research has shown that the horizon moon is judged to be 30% larger than a zenith moon (Baird & Wagner, 1982; Rock & Kaufman, 1962). It sometimes has been argued that this effect is due to refraction of the light rays as they pass through the atmosphere. You can prove this theory wrong by taking pictures of the horizon and zenith moons, cutting the images out, and comparing their sizes. If you did this, you would find they are identical. Thus, our perception that the horizon moon is larger is an illusion, a misperception of size, because the proximal stimulus does not change. Why then does the illusion occur? Although a variety of explanations have been presented (Plug & Ross, 1989), they all tend to relate the illusion to differences in perceived distance. The basic idea is that your perceptual system infers that the horizon moon is farther away than the zenith moon. One reason this might occur is that you can compare the horizon moon to objects on the terrain with which you are familiar. Because you know these objects are far away, and the moon is behind them, your perceptual system concludes that the horizon moon must be very far away. According to the size–distance invariance hypothesis, perceived size depends on both the retinal size of the image and its perceived distance. If the object is judged to be farther away, its perceived size is inflated.

On the face of it, this explanation of the moon illusion would appear to run counter to a basic observation: not only does the horizon moon look larger, but it also looks closer than the zenith moon. How can this be? Our

FIGURE 4–16
The moon illusion. Notice how the disk near the horizon appears larger. This is an illusion. If you measure the two disks, you will find that they are identical in size.

application of the size–distance invariance hypothesis assumed that the horizon moon was judged to be farther away. To make sense of this discrepancy, you need to bear in mind that you may have little or no conscious access to the mechanisms that produce size–distance invariance. All that you consciously experience is the output from this perceptual mechanism, which leads you to "see" the horizon moon as large. Because you consciously perceive the moon as larger, you are tempted to claim that it looks closer.

One other important factor in size constancy is *relative size*. We often make judgments about the size of objects in comparison to other objects located nearby. Suppose that you have set the table for dinner. When you stand near the table, the retinal images of the plates, knives, and spoons are much larger than they will be when you look at the table from a distance of 10 ft. But all of those retinal images are changing in size together, which provides an added cue to the task of judging the actual size of any one object.

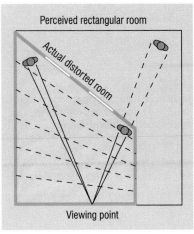

If you assume that the room is regularly shaped, you misperceive this image. The child appears larger than he really is because of a viewing point unique to the trapezoidal shape of the room.

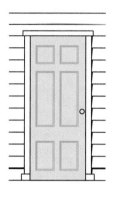

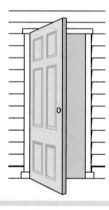

shape constancy we see shapes as remaining the same despite changes that occur at the retina

FIGURE 4–17
The door still looks rectangular, even when it is opened and its shape is objectively that of a trapezoid. This is an example of shape constancy.

lightness constancy perceived lightness stays the same despite changes in the level of illumination

albedo the proportion of light reaching a surface that is reflected back to the eye

Shape Constancy. The fact that the shape of an object, such as a door, does not change, even though the retinal image changes, is an example of perceptual constancy known as **shape constancy**. If you look at an ordinary door, closed in front of you, the image produced on your retina is that of a rectangle. Yet if the door is partially opened, the retinal image changes to that of a trapezoid (see Figure 4–17). However, if you ask the perceiver if the door is seen as trapezoidal, the answer will be no.

Shape constancy is not as easily explained as size constancy. It appears, though, that some of the same factors are involved. For example, changes in shapes of nearby objects provide cues about the shape of the target object (relative shape). Familiarity is also important for shape constancy, even more so than for size constancy. Further, the size–distance invariance hypothesis has been changed to the *shape–slant invariance hypothesis.* This hypothesis proposes that shape constancy is the result of a comparison of the shape of the retinal image and the perceived slant (orientation) of the object. But researchers question this hypothesis, for people have little success in estimating retinal image shape (Lappin & Preble, 1975).

In Figure 4–17, the shape of the door changes, whereas the wall surrounding the door remains unchanged. Yet shape constancy is maintained for the door. Shape constancy is also maintained when we view a scene at a slant, in which all components of the scene change their shapes. Consider, for example, watching a movie from a seat in the front row of a theater, all the way toward one of the side walls. The images on the movie screen are considerably distorted in terms of retinal image shapes. Still, shape constancy is reasonably good (Cutting, 1987a). One explanation for why constancy is maintained in this situation is what Irvin Rock (1984) has called the *taking-into-account theory.* In the example of the movie screen, the perceptual system picks up information regarding the slant of the screen; that is, this unusual viewing condition is taken into account. This perception causes an adjustment in the geometry used to interpret the visual images so that the distorted images are not seen as distorted. These adjustments in the perceptual system occur rapidly and without awareness. As a result, perceptual order is maintained instead of the perceptual chaos that might otherwise result.

Lightness Constancy. When sunlight shines through the window onto a floor, the amount of light reflected from that portion of the floor changes. Yet, that part of the floor is not seen as lighter. A black piece of construction paper in bright sunlight reflects more light than a white piece of paper exposed to very dim light. But still we do not see the black paper as lighter. The fact that object lightness tends to be perceived as unchanging, despite changes in the amount of light striking the surface of an object, is called **lightness constancy**. Unlike size and shape constancy, which seem to develop mainly through experience, lightness constancy appears to exist from birth (Forgus & Melamed, 1976).

Lightness is determined essentially by the percentage of light reflected from an object's surface, a quality that is called **albedo** (defined as the proportion of light reaching a surface that is reflected back to the eye). The albedo is a constant property of any object. Although the light illuminating the object may increase, the light reflected will be a constant proportion of that increase. Lightness constancy occurs because objects and their surround are typically illuminated by the same illumination source. When the illumination increases, it increases proportionately for both object (figure) and surround (ground), maintaining a constant ratio between the two (Wallach, 1963). As long as the ratio remains unchanged, the activated ganglion cells will send the same neural message to the visual cortex, which is why the brain interprets the lightness of the object (and surround) as being unchanged. But if illumination of the object changes without changing the illumination of the surround (something that can be made to happen in a laboratory but rarely happens in everyday experience), then lightness constancy breaks down (Sekuler & Blake, 1985). As in the case of size and shape constancy, lightness constancy adds stability to our perceptual experience.

Movement Perception

How do we see movement? That question is simple and straightforward, and we wish we could give you a comparable answer. But as you will see, the question is made rather difficult by the conditions under which we see movement and those in which no movement is seen. One of the oldest and most popular explanations is that motion perception occurs when an image moves across the retina. Imagine yourself sitting on the beach, staring at the surf, when a seagull flies across your field of vision from left to right. In doing so, its image successively stimulates different areas of your retinas. The information about that displacement is transmitted to the visual cortex, where the interpretation of movement is made.

Recall from Chapter 3 that specialized cells exist in the visual cortex that respond only to a stimulus moving across the retina in a particular direction. These specialized cells have been called *motion detectors*. But what if you track the seagull with your eyes, moving your eyes and head to follow its flight? In that case you keep the image of the bird roughly on the same area of the retina, and thus there is almost no displacement. Yet you can still clearly perceive that the bird is moving. So displacement of an image across the retina does not seem to be a necessary condition for the perception of movement.

Realize too that when you move your eyes, objects that are stationary in the visual field will appear as displaced images across your retinas. If you visually scan a room from left to right, all of the objects in that room will move across your retinas in an opposite direction, yet you will not see them as moving. So displacement of an image across the retina does not seem to be a sufficient condition for the perception of movement.

As confusing as these facts may seem, it is possible to provide an account that is consistent with each condition. The accepted view of movement perception argues that the brain "knows" whether or not the eyes and/or head are in motion. When the eyes are stationary, the displacement of the image of an object signals a moving object. Conversely, when the eyes are moving, objects whose images are stationary on the retina are moving in the same direction and with a comparable velocity to the eye movements. Objects whose images move across the retina in an opposite direction and at the same velocity are stationary objects, whereas image displacements across the retina in any direction that are faster or slower than the velocity of the eye movements are seen as moving objects. Thus, the brain takes into account whether the eyes are moving as a basis for assessing the displacement or nondisplacement of the images of objects across the retina. This interpretation allows for an accurate assessment of motion in the conditions described.

Sometimes movement occurs that we cannot see. The critical determinant in this situation is *velocity*, the distance traveled by the moving object in a specified time span. Movement can be perceived within a wide range of velocity, but if the velocity of the moving object is too slow or too fast, movement will not be seen. We know that all the hands on a clock move. Seeing the movement of the second hand is no problem, but we are unable to actually see the hour hand move, and under most circumstances we are not able to see the minute hand move. Both move too slowly for the displaced retinal image to be recognized as signaling movement.

On the other hand, if the velocity is too fast, it will exceed the tracking capacity of the eye movements and the moving object will not be seen (Becklen, Wallach, & Nitzberg, 1984). Consider the speed of a professional athlete's baseball pitch (95 miles per hour, or mph) or tennis serve (110 mph). In either sport, the approaching velocity of the ball is such that it cannot be visually tracked in the last 6 to 8 ft of travel. In baseball, the ball is traveling at an angular velocity of more than 500°/sec as it passes the batter. The maximum angular velocity that humans can track is approximately 70°/sec, which means that as the ball nears home plate it is impossible for the batter to track the pitch. Thus, the batter must anticipate the position of the ball as it crosses the plate. Obviously, batters can hit the ball even though they cannot see it in those last few moments (Bahill & LaRitz, 1984).

We have described conditions in which we are unable to see movement in objects that are moving. However, we often perceive movement where no movement occurs. These illusions of movement are collectively referred to as *apparent movement*. One example of this kind of movement, the **autokinetic effect**, is produced by shining a point of light in an otherwise black room. After watching the light for a brief interval, subjects will begin to see it move. The apparent movement pattern differs greatly from person to person. Yet if the subjects are watching the light together and are allowed to comment aloud about the "movement" of the light, their perceptions of its movement will begin to resemble one another. This demonstration shows how suggestibility can influence other perceivers (Sherif, 1935). Although suggestibility is a factor in the autokinetic effect, the perceived movement is due largely to slow eye movements that occur in the cueless dark environment. Measurement of these movements shows them to correlate with the perceived motion of a stationary light (Pola & Matin, 1977). You can observe the autokinetic effect in real life by watching a single star in an otherwise black sky.

Another kind of apparent movement in which nothing moves is called **stroboscopic movement**, familiar to people as motion pictures. Although the reality of movement in motion pictures seems undeniable, the stimulus for that perceived movement is nothing more than the successive presentation of a series of still pictures, projected on the screen at a speed of 24 frames per second. This projection speed was not randomly determined. It represents the optimal rate, given what is known about processing in the visual system, for movement to be perceived. Psychologists have studied this form of movement for more than 75 years since Max Wertheimer did his pioneering experiments on a form of stroboscopic motion that he called the **phi phenomenon** (see Figure 4–18). Wertheimer found that two points of light could be successively illuminated so that subjects saw only one light, moving

autokinetic effect illusory movement of a point of light in a dark environment; a single point of light appears to move

stroboscopic movement illusory movement produced by the successive presentation of still images; motion pictures are produced through this phenomenon

phi phenomenon when two successively presented lights are seen as a single moving light

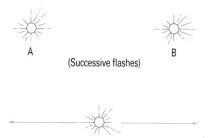

FIGURE 4–18
Left: When lights *A* and *B* flash successively, the observer perceives one light moving back and forth. This is a demonstration of a type of stroboscopic movement known as the phi phenomenon. *Right:* The phi phenomenon used as a traffic signal.

back and forth, rather than two discrete lights blinking on and off in succession. That phenomenon is used today in some advertising signs designed to create the illusion of movement.

For the perceiver, these forms of apparent movement create a reality of movement perception as real as that of actual movement. Consequently, perception psychologists have sought to explain both kinds of movement because of this phenomenal equality. Many forms of apparent movement are believed to simulate a pattern of information to the brain that closely resembles that of real movement (Algom & Cohen-Raz, 1987; Ramachandran & Antis, 1986).

So what is required for movement perception to occur? You have read that displacement of an image across the retina is sometimes important but at other times is not, that velocity is a key variable and must be within a certain range, and that sometimes we see movement when no movement exists. Each of these phenomena can be explained in terms of our knowledge of the visual system. And growing evidence points to movement perception, both real and apparent, being the result of specialized cells at the cortical and subcortical levels that detect and integrate information relevant to judgments about movement (Braddick, 1986; Burr & Ross, 1986).

THINKING ABOUT
Motion Perception

Suppose you could not perceive movement. What would your perceptual world be like? An answer to this question can be gleaned from case reports of people who have experienced a brain lesion that selectively disrupted their ability to perceive visual movement. A particularly well-documented case was described by Zihl, von Cramon, and Mai (1983).

> The visual disorder complained of by the patient was a loss of movement vision in all three dimensions. She had difficulty, for example, in pouring tea or coffee into a cup because the fluid appeared to be frozen, like a glacier. In addition, she could not stop pouring at the right time since she was unable to perceive the movement in the cup (or a pot) when the fluid rose. Furthermore the patient complained of difficulties in following dialogue because she could not see the movements of the face and, especially, the mouth of the speaker. In a room where more than two other people were walking she felt very insecure and unwell, and usually left the room immediately, "because people were suddenly here or there but I have not seen them moving." The patient experienced the same problem but to an even more marked extent in crowded streets or places, which she therefore avoided as much as possible. She could not cross the street because of her inability to judge the speed of a car, but she could identify the car itself without difficulty. "When I'm looking at the car first, it seems far away. But then, when I want to cross the road, suddenly the car is very near." She gradually learned to "estimate" the distance of moving vehicles by means of sound becoming louder.

A brain scan revealed that the woman had a lesion of the cerebral cortex along the border of the occipital and temporal lobes (Goldstein, 1989). Psychophysical testing revealed that her perception of movement in senses other than vision was normal. For example, she had no difficulty detecting a stick moving across her arm or when the source of a sound was moved. Moreover, other aspects of her vision, such as her ability to perceive color and depth, were unaffected, and she had no trouble recognizing stationary objects and reading words. Her only apparent deficit was an inability to perceive visual movement. Interestingly, the perception of illusory movement was also eliminated. Thus, unlike normal individuals, two lights blinking in succession did not produce the illusion of a single light moving back and forth (the phi phenomenon). Instead, she continued to see two separate lights.

Now try to imagine for yourself what your visual world would be like if you could not perceive movement. Would you be able to enjoy the movies?

RECOGNITION AND SELECTION

We began the previous section by discussing the perceptual rules your brain uses to organize and integrate sensory information, and to determine the depth of objects. We then looked at a number of mechanisms that help you perceive objects as having a constant size, shape, and lightness over a wide range of distances, orientations, and levels of illumination. Finally, we considered how the brain infers whether an object is moving. These processes allow your perceptual system to create an image of a well-organized world of objects laid out in three dimensions.

The perceptual system, however, has to do much more. To see this, consider playing a game of basketball. Seeing that there is a round orange object in front of you at a particular distance is not, in itself, particularly helpful. To use this information effectively, you have to *recognize* what the object is. This requires that you relate the perceptual information to what you know about the object: that this round orange object is a basketball. Next consider all of the objects you would probably be able to recognize in your environment. You might see your father or mother in the bleachers, the coach on the sidelines, the beams forming the roof, the garbage can at the end of the court, and so forth. Your perceptual systems provide you with much more information than you can possibly process. To play the game effectively, you would need to ignore most of the objects in your environment and attend to only those objects that are critical to the task at hand. Thinking back about how your performance on the court has improved, you might remember how you used to have a hard time ignoring all of these irrelevant stimuli. After a great deal of practice, you *learned* what to attend to.

In this section of the chapter we consider the processes that help you recognize and attend to objects in your environment and how these processes have been shaped by learning.

Pattern Perception

pattern perception recognition of familiar forms such as faces, pictures, and objects

You are practicing **pattern perception**, or form perception, when you recognize and identify shapes, faces, melodies, words, pictures, objects, and so forth. Babies learn the facial characteristics of their parents and react pleasantly to those faces, perhaps crying at the sight of unfamiliar faces. Children learn to make important facial discriminations that allow them to know when their mothers are happy or angry. Adults can read diverse samples of handwriting even though the stimulus elements in each may be quite different. Rats, pigeons, pigs, and many other animals can easily learn the differences among shapes such as triangles, squares, and circles when those stimuli are paired with certain rewards. Each of these cases illustrates the recognition of a set of stimuli that are arranged in such a way that we would say they constitute a form or pattern. Thus, we define a pattern as a collection of stimuli arranged in a reasonably specific way.

The neural equipment in the visual system that is required for pattern perception seems to exist in humans at birth. Fantz (1961) and others have demonstrated that newborn babies can reliably discriminate among different patterns and that they show clear pattern preferences. For example, when newborns are given the opportunity to look at two drawings of a humanlike face—one a normal face with the features (eyes, nose, mouth) appropriately placed, and another with jumbled features—they spend significantly more time looking at the normal face. Although some ability to perceive patterns exists at birth, most pattern recognition is learned. Recall from the previous chapter our discussion of the variety of cells in the visual cortex that respond to specific stimuli. Thus, a newborn human has the feature detectors necessary to recognize lines in various orientations, such as the lines of the letter *R* or the letter *K*. But the ability to discriminate between these two letters comes later, and the ability to recognize letter combinations as words develops even later than that. The changes are believed to be due to learning rather than the maturing of the visual system.

Theories of Pattern Recognition.   Pattern perception is important for every sense. You recognize the words a friend has spoken, a familiar face, and the smell of freshly brewed coffee. In discussing this topic we will focus on just one sense-vision. Keep in mind, however, that similar principles could be applied to pattern perception for the other senses as well.

In order to recognize a word or an object, the visual system has to compare the sensory input to information stored in long-term memory. This raises a number of basic issues. How is the comparison performed? What is stored in memory? In the next section we consider some theories that attempt to answer these questions. We will then look at how what you know affects what you perceive.

Template-Matching Theory.   When you look at this page and see the letter *B*, how is it that you recognize this stimulus as the second letter of the alphabet? To do so, the visual system must somehow take the sensory input and compare it to information stored in long-term memory. How is this accomplished? A simple theory is that you have stored little copies, or *templates*, to represent each letter of the alphabet. When a letter is detected, the recognition system then quickly compares the sensory information to each of the stored templates. When a match is detected, recognition occurs. But now consider Figure 4–19, which depicts a small sample of all the ways in which the letter *B* might be written. How could a template be used to recognize all of these variations? It would seem that you would need a template for every possible variation. The same would be true for every other letter of the alphabet and all of the other objects in the world you can recognize. This means that our simple theory has a basic shortcoming—to allow for variation, you need to assume a nearly infinite number of templates have been stored in memory. Because this seems implausible, psychologists have come to reject the template-matching theory.

Prototype-Matching Theory.   Many psychologists now believe that, instead of storing an exact copy of an object, you store the object's average characteristics (see Figure 4–20). For example, birds tend to be small in size, to be feathered, to fly, and to sing. These and other characteristics could be stored in memory and used to recognize whether the sensory input corresponded to a bird. From this perspective, being a bird would not require having all of the essential characteristics. Thus, a perfect match would not be required. Instead, all that would be needed is a critical sum of evidence; if the sensory input shared enough characteristics with your representa-

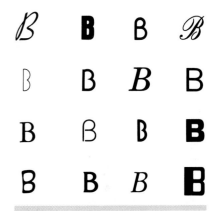

FIGURE 4–19
Some of the many possible ways we might encounter the letter *B*.

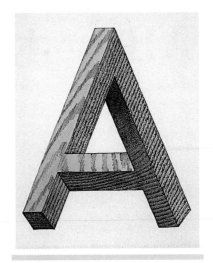

FIGURE 4–20
At first glance you might decide that you are looking at the letter *A*, but closer inspection shows you that the pattern above could not in fact exist. Psychologists call this an impossible figure. It might fit with your prototype for the letter *A*, but it is most unlikely that you have a template for this pattern. (Letter *A* from Anno, 1975.)

tion, you would recognize the object as a bird. If this theory is valid, there should be quite a bit of variability in how long it takes you to recognize something as a bird. For example, a bird such as a robin has many characteristics common to all birds, and can be thought of as a **prototype** of the category. In contrast, for a typical North American college student, an ostrich seems to be a poorer example of a bird, for it has far fewer of the characteristic qualities. Given this, **prototype-matching theory** predicts that it should take longer to judge that an ostrich is a bird. As predicted, the closer the pattern is to the prototype, the faster and more accurately the stimulus is recognized (Franks & Bransford, 1971; Solso, 1991).

According to the prototype-matching theory, recognizing an object involves comparing the sensory input to information about the object's average characteristics. To accomplish this, the sensory input must be broken down into some basic characteristics, which are then compared to the prototype patterns stored in memory. What is the nature of these characteristics? Put slightly differently, how does the visual system break down the sensory input?

Feature Analysis Theory.   A variety of suggestions have been made to account for the issue just discussed, many of which are not mutually exclusive. One common proposal is that stimuli are represented by sets of features. For example, consider the letter T. It is composed of two line segments, the vertical one being slightly longer than the horizontal one. In addition, the horizontal line is bisected by its placement atop the vertical line. This arrangement produces two right angles. According to **feature-analysis theory**, we would identify the features of the letter T as the following four:

A feature-analysis approach to pattern perception would propose that the resultant perception of the pattern (in this case, the letter T) depends on detecting and recognizing the relevant features. According to a popular version of this theory (see Lindsay & Norman, 1977; Selfridge, 1959), pattern perception by feature analysis proceeds through four ordered stages: (*a*) detection, (*b*) pattern dissection, (*c*) feature comparison in memory, and (*d*) recognition.

Figure 4–21 describes these steps in terms of recognizing the letter R. The initial stage involves detecting the pattern of stimulation, a job accomplished by the visual receptors, in this case. In the second stage, the pattern is dissected into its individual features (a job that may be accomplished by the specialized feature detectors in the visual cortex). The third stage involves comparing these features with information already stored in visual memory to see which letters might contain some or all of the features. On a neural basis this third stage could depend on the degree of excitation, meaning that the more relevant features present, the greater would be the excitation. Finally, in the fourth stage, a decision is made to identify the correct letter. Note that the letter R shares features in common with the letters T and P (and others not shown in this figure). But in the decision stage, the letter R would be correctly identified, because that cortical region received the greatest excitation.

Feature-analysis theory is an attractive explanation because of the discoveries about the physiology of the visual cortex, but also because a number of studies have shown features to be an important part of the way people recognize patterns. For example, Eleanor Gibson's work on reading has shown that it is the distinctive features of letters that people use in discriminating between pairs of letters (Gibson & Levin, 1975).

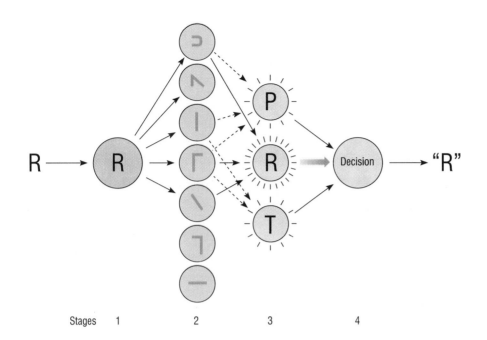

Stages   1   2   3   4

FIGURE 4–21
A feature analysis approach to recognizing the letter *R*. Stage 1 involves detecting the pattern of stimulation; in this case the visual receptors accomplish the task. In Stage 2, the pattern is dissected into its individual features (the specialized feature detectors in the visual cortex may accomplish this). In Stage 3, those features are compared with information already stored in visual memory to see which letters might contain some or all of the features. This third stage may operate on the basis of neural excitation; thus, the more relevant features present, the greater the excitation. Stage 4 involves the decision process, seeking to identify the letter correctly. This model of pattern recognition proposes that the letter *R* is correctly identified (as opposed to *P* or *T*) because the neural activity is greatest in the cortical region associated with that pattern. (Adapted from Goldstein, 1988.)

Recognition by Components.   Although it is easy to understand how simple features could be used to represent letters, it is difficult to see how these primitive features could be used to represent complex objects. For example, how could you represent an object as complex as a horse? Are thousands of feature detectors somehow linked together? Irving Biederman (1987) has suggested a simpler alternative. According to his theory of **recognition by components**, complex objects can be represented by a relatively small set of simple shapes he calls *geons* (short for geometrical ions). He estimates that the average individual may be familiar with as many as 30,000 objects, and that recognizing those objects easily could be handled by no more than 36 geons (see Figure 4–22). According to Biederman, object perception begins by the perceiver segmenting the object, usually at regions where edges join or where curves markedly change. These segmented components are then compared against the geons to determine a best match. This theory is also of interest to perception psychologists because it provides considerable support for several of the Gestalt principles of perceptual organization, particularly simplicity and good continuation. Apparently those principles apply quite readily to the components of objects, although not necessarily to the objects themselves.

recognition by components this theory of pattern perception claims that patterns are represented by a relatively small set of simple shapes

Fourier Analysis.   There is another way of thinking about how visual information might be represented. Consider the two sine waves depicted on the bottom of Figure 4–23. By adding these two waveforms together, one obtains the complex waveform illustrated at the top of the figure. This is actually how a music synthesizer works. It contains a set of sine wave generators, the output of which is combined to produce the notes you hear. By varying the relative amplitude, period, and starting point (phase) of the sine wave components, the synthesizer is able to emulate the waveforms produced by most musical instruments. This process is known as *Fourier synthesis* after the mathematician Jean Baptiste Joseph Fourier (1768–1830). Fourier was able to show that any complex pattern can be represented by a set of sine waves. Given this, psychologists have suggested that our sensory systems might per-

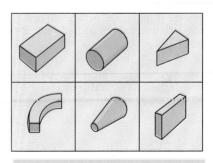

FIGURE 4–22
Some geons that could be used by the perceiver in object perception according to Biederman's theory of recognition by components. (From Biederman, 1987.) See text for explanation.

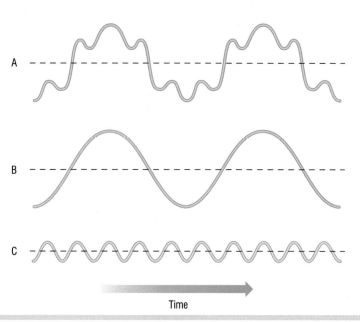

Time

FIGURE 4-23
Fourier demonstrated that any complex waveform can be generated by adding together sine waves of the appropriate amplitude, period, and phase relation. For example, the complex waveform illustrated here (A) can be generated by simply adding two sine waves together (B) and (C). (Adapted from Brown & Deffenbacher, 1979.)

Fourier analysis analysis of a stimulus into its component sine waves

form a **Fourier analysis**, using sine waves to represent the objects and textures of our environment. For such a system to work in the domain of vision, one would have to assume that our visual system can break a scene down into its sine wave components. This would require a series of channels, each of which is designed to detect a narrow range of spatial frequencies. Interestingly, researchers have found cells in the visual cortex that are tuned to particular frequencies. Indeed, it has been suggested that complex cells (see Chapter 3) may function as *spatial frequency channels* rather than edge detectors.

Bottom-Up and Top-Down Processing. Up to now we have discussed pattern perception as a process that begins with detecting information in the environment, continues with interpreting that information, and results in recognizing the pattern. This kind of information processing is labeled **bottom-up processing**, because it begins at the level of the receptors and works its way up to the higher brain centers. But researchers in pattern perception recognize that this process can go in reverse order, when the higher perceptual centers give directions to the lower centers about information to be extracted. This **top-down processing** is illustrated by the concept of perceptual set. By **set** we mean that the perceiver has some kind of perceptual readiness, or expectancy; that is, the observer is "set" to perceive something. Read the handwritten message depicted in Figure 4–24. Now go back to the message and compare the "is" written in the first line to the fourth and fifth numbers of the phone number. Notice that they are identical. Yet, you naturally read the first as *is* and the second as *15*. Similarly, the *h* in phone and *b* in the

bottom-up processing information processing from receptors (bottom) to higher centers in the brain

top-down processing information processing from higher perceptual centers to lower centers such as receptor sites

set an expectancy, preconceived idea, or orientation that influences how a stimulus is processed

FIGURE 4-24
An example of how the context in which a stimulus occurs can influence how it is perceived. (From Coren & Ward, 1989.)

My phone number is area code 604, 876-1569. Please call!

152   Chapter 4

word *number* are also identical, as are the *d* in code and *l* in please. In each case, how you perceived the ambiguous stimulus was determined by the context in which it occurred. You interpreted the sensory information in a way that made sense, given the context in which the stimulus was presented.

We possess a lot of information about the way our world is, information that we have gathered in our years of perceptual experience. This information directs our perception, as Biederman (1981) found in his pattern recognition research. Biederman showed subjects scenes in which they were to identify familiar objects, such as fire hydrants. When the objects were in a typical location (fire hydrant on the sidewalk) rather than an atypical one (fire hydrant on top of a mailbox), recognition time was faster. Observers can be expected to look where they believe objects should be, again showing perception as top-down processing (see Figure 4–25).

The existence of top-down processing explains the speed at which most human pattern perception takes place. Bottom-up approaches by themselves would be a real hindrance to perception. But top-down processing means that some perceptual decisions, made in advance, dictate the particular bottom-up approaches used. This means that the hypotheses that direct top-down processing cause the perceiver to search for certain features or to select certain prototypes that test the hypotheses. In turn, the information reaching the higher perceptual centers in the bottom-up mode either confirms the existing hypotheses or causes new ones to be generated. This two-way flow of information greatly enhances the efficiency of pattern perception.

Attention

There are so many stimuli in our perceptual environment at any time that we surely cannot attend to them all—or can we? Picture yourself sitting in the stands watching a football game. You are watching the action on the field, particularly the play of a defensive back who is a friend of yours. Your roommate is sitting next to you, and the two of you are carrying on a conversation. Other conversations are taking place around you, and occasionally you eavesdrop on some of these. You are also aware when the band is playing. Because you are thirsty, you are keeping an eye out for one of the people selling soft drinks in the stands. A little boy sitting directly behind you enjoys swinging his feet and has kicked you repeatedly throughout the game. The aroma of popcorn reaches you and smells so good you decide you are hungry and search the crowd, successfully, for a popcorn seller. You occasionally check the time on the scoreboard, eat your popcorn, wave to a friend you spotted several rows in front of you, join in the cheers for your team's successful play, and hand the program to your roommate when asked. All of these actions reflect **attention**, a mechanism used to select which stimuli and events will be processed and consciously perceived.

attention a cluster of integrated events and processes that determine which stimuli receive further processing

In vision, focusing one's attention on a particular object or event is often a simple task. All you need to do is direct your gaze toward the stimulus in question. However, such a peripheral mechanism cannot account for all examples of stimulus selection. For example, consider a phenomenon known as the *cocktail party effect* (Cherry, 1953). Imagine that you are talking in small groups, so that the room contains a half-dozen conversations, all of which may be about equally audible. Yet you have no trouble focusing attention on the conversation of your group. Moreover, you can easily listen in on a conversation of another group. In this case, what you are attending to is not determined by a simple peripheral mechanism (e.g., which conversation is louder). Instead, central mechanisms are being used to determine which sensory information receives further processing.

FIGURE 4–25
Subjects were asked to search for a familiar object, a bicycle, in the two photographs shown on the opposite page. Because of experience in our visual world, we have expectancies about where to look for familiar objects. But the photograph on the bottom shows a jumbled visual world, and subjects require more time to find the bicycle compared with the photograph on the top. (From Treisman, 1986.)

Let's consider this example in a bit more detail. While you are intently listening to a friend at a party, you might notice that your name comes up in another conversation. It appears that even when you focus your attention on a single source, *preattentive processes* continue to analyze some of the content of the conversations you are not listening to. When an important word is mentioned, such as your name, these processes alert you to the fact that there is another conversation you may want to attend to. At this point, you may try to divide your attention between the two sources, trying your best to follow what your friend is saying while you listen in on the other conversation. In the sections that follow, we consider both the selection, division, and determinants of attention in more detail.

Selective Attention.   **Selective attention** refers to the different processing of coexisting perceptual events, meaning that the perceiver has the ability to focus on one stimulus while ignoring other stimuli that are present. Such a process has obvious advantages, because it allows the perceiver to maximize the information that is picked up from one particular source while reducing the potential sensory interference from another source. According to one early view, *Broadbent's filter theory*, selective attention is possible because interfering messages are eliminated at the level of the senses, before the information becomes a part of perceptual processing (Broadbent, 1957). Such is not the case, however, as you will soon see.

In studying selective attention, psychologists have made use of a technique known as **dichotic listening**. In this technique, a subject wearing earphones simultaneously receives two different auditory messages, one in each ear. The subject is told to pay attention to the message in one ear (the attended message) and to ignore the message in the other ear (unattended message). To ensure that the subjects are attending, researchers typically ask them to repeat aloud the words they hear in the attended message. This technique is called *shadowing*, because the subjects' verbalizations are, in effect, a shadowed version of the attended message. At the end of the session, subjects are asked various questions about both the attended and the unattended messages.

The results of these studies reveal the power of selective attention. They have shown that when the unattended message is switched to a foreign language, such as German, or when the words are spoken backward, the subjects usually are unable to report these changes (Cherry, 1953). Indeed, subjects are able to recall little, if any, of the unattended message. When the content of the messages is very similar, the subjects' attention wanders between the two so that neither message is accurately perceived (Bartley, 1972).

Neisser and Becklen (1975) used a visual version of the dichotic listening task. Subjects were required to watch a television screen that contained superimposed images from two films. The films depicted two games, one a hand-slapping game played by two contestants and the other a game of catch played among three men. The subjects were instructed to watch one of the two games and to press a switch each time a particular action occurred. For the hand game, subjects were to press the switch when one contestant

selective attention the ability to focus consciousness on a single event in the environment while ignoring other stimuli

dichotic listening concurrent presentation of two auditory messages

FIGURE 4-26
Pictured is a line drawing of the television screen watched by the subjects in the experiment on attention by Neisser and Becklen (1975). See text for explanation.

stimulus variables characteristics of the objects themselves, such as intensity, that can affect attention

organismic variables processing characteristics of the organism or perceiver that determine which stimuli gain attention

divided attention ability to monitor two events presented simultaneously

successfully slapped the hands of the other. For the game of catch, the subjects were to respond every time the ball was thrown. Neisser and Becklen found that when asked to attend to one of the games, the subjects' reports were quite accurate. However, when subjects were asked to watch both games at once, pressing a switch in the left hand for one game and the right hand for the other, their performance deteriorated immediately. In fact, the number of errors in the latter condition was eight times greater than when subjects were required to attend to only one game (see Figure 4–26).

Experiments such as these have shown that people can focus attention rather exclusively on a single stimulus, but some conditions can reduce their selective attention capability. Although **stimulus variables** (e.g., intensity) can elicit attention, attention is usually directed by processes within the perceiver (e.g., memories, motivation, or interests) (Hoffman, 1987). These **organismic variables** predispose, or bias, the perceiver toward attending to certain stimuli or searching for stimuli in certain locations (look back to Figure 4–25).

Divided Attention.   Although dichotic listening studies support the existence of selective attention, they also provide evidence that attention can be divided. In one experiment, the unattended message informed the subjects that "you may stop now." Yet subjects ignored that message and continued to shadow the attended message. But when the unattended message included the person's name, for example, "Beth Davis, you may stop now," the subjects were much more likely to hear that message and stop their shadowing (Moray, 1969). Obviously, some monitoring of the unattended message was taking place. Our earlier description of the cocktail party effect provides support for the existence of **divided attention**. The fact that you heard your name in another conversation suggests that at some level you were listening to more than one conversation, but you would probably fail in any attempt to recall the content of the different auditory messages. Divided attention is generally quite difficult to achieve; however, there are some situations that are conducive to its occurrence.

One way to make the occurrence of divided attention more likely is to use two tasks that involve different senses, such as vision and hearing. Thus, you can watch a movie and still listen to what your roommate is saying. Research has shown that subjects can easily read a book aloud (ignoring the meaning) while listening to a conversation (McBurney & Collings, 1984). In this situation, the subjects are attending to the printed text enough to read the words, but not enough to recall what was read. In other words, it is not possible to attend to the meaning of the book and the conversation, even though it is possible to divide attention, at some level, between these two sensory events.

A second way to improve the capacity to divide attention is through practice. A number of studies have used intensive training procedures to help people learn to accomplish several tasks at the same time (Shaffer, 1975; Spelke, Hirst, & Neisser, 1976). One study (Hirst et al., 1980) trained subjects to read a story and take dictation at the same time. At first subjects were unable to do the two tasks simultaneously, but after much training they were capable of reading at a normal rate, showing normal comprehension for what they read, and taking dictation at a rate of approximately 30 words per minute. The work of Schneider and Shiffrin (1977) has helped to explain how practice can affect attention. When there is consistency in a task, that is, when the stimuli occur in highly predictable ways, with practice the appropriate responses can be made automatically, through **automatic processing**, thus allowing us to attend to several tasks at once. **Controlled processing** refers to those situations in which the connections between stimuli and responses vary enough from time to time to require focused attention. For example, you can drive your car from work to home with little attention to driving or to navigating the familiar route (automatic processing), while at the same time conversing with a fellow worker about marketing strategies for your company's products (controlled processing).

Although divided attention is an ability that can be improved with practice, it can also be lost over time. Researchers have studied this ability across the life span and have found that older adults show significant decrements in divided attention for complex tasks but not for simple ones or ones that principally involve automatic processing (McDowd & Craik, 1988).

automatic processing processing that does not require conscious attention

controlled processing processing that requires conscious attention

Determinants of Attention. Many stimuli exist in our perceptual world. It is through the process of attention that we select certain stimuli from others in the perceptual array. We might search for a friend we have temporarily lost in a crowded department store or scan our cluttered workbench looking for a pair of pliers. But sometimes stimuli seem to seek us out; there is something about a particular stimulus that draws our attention to it. What are these stimulus characteristics that grab our attention? To a great extent the answer to this question is different for everyone, since individual interests, feelings, motives, and so forth, are principal determinants of attention. Nevertheless, there are some universally shared stimulus characteristics that are attention-getting (Wilding, 1983). Context is important, meaning that stimuli that are different or unusual are likely to get our attention. You might ignore a cow in a pasture along the road as you drive in the country, but you most certainly will notice one wandering among the aisles of your grocery store.

Color is another important variable in attracting attention, as are movement and size. Advertisers clearly recognize what stimulus qualities attract attention and capitalize on that information in selling their products. Repetition is another way to maximize attention. When the instructor says the same thing several times in a lecture, the students are more likely to think it is important and will attend more closely to it (see Norman, 1976). Intensity is also an important variable. The loudest speaker in a group is likely to attract your attention.

In short, perception directs attention and attention directs perception. This focusing of perception to a limited portion of our sensory world means (in most cases) that our perceptual capability is enhanced (Moran &

Desimone, 1985). Although our perception is enhanced, it is not maximized. Research shows that attention induces selection of the *minimum* information necessary to accomplish the required perceptual task (Broadbent, 1987). That produces economy of perception, but at a price. It means that important information may go ignored, which can have fatal consequences.

◀ ▶ THINKING ABOUT
Attention

The potential dangers of focusing on a single event are known to nearly all of us. You see a young child run into the road thinking only of retrieving her ball. While you are tuning the radio, you nearly run a stop sign. As you talk intently to a friend, you fail to notice that you have been driving on empty.

human factors psychology area of psychology that focuses on the human–machine interface and studies ways to make it easier for women and men to work with machines

The area of **human factors psychology** is concerned with how we can improve the interface between humans and machines to make it safer to operate cars, planes, and other machinery. Our cars must have horns that we can use to get a child's attention. Before a dangerous intersection, bumps on the road may alert you of the impending stop sign. A warning light tells you that your car's gas tank is empty.

Although such warning devices have helped make it much safer to operate machinery, these devices should not be thought of as foolproof. An example is provided by what happened on Eastern Airlines flight 401 in 1972. The plane was approaching Miami airport at night when a warning light came on indicating that the nosegear may have malfunctioned. After aborting the approach, the crew was cleared to fly west over the Everglades at 2,000 ft while they checked out the problem. After the autopilot was turned on, a flight engineer and mechanic headed below to inspect the gear visually. Meanwhile, the captain and first officer began to disassemble the warning light to check whether it was malfunctioning. During all of this activity, somehow the setting on the autopilot was moved. The stress of the situation helped to narrow the crew's attention to solving the problem at hand. As they worked, the air controller noticed that the plane seemed to be descending, which prompted an inquiry. Visual and auditory cues within the cockpit provided further warning of impending danger. All of these cues were effectively ignored while the captain and first officer continued to work on the problem with the landing gear. Seconds later, the plane crashed in the Florida Everglades (Weiner, 1977).

A variety of factors contributed to this accident. One problem concerned the warning devices that signaled a deviation in altitude. Because they came on fairly frequently, the crew had gotten used to them. Consequently, they went unnoticed as the crew worked on fixing the nosegear. For warning devices to be effective, they need to be novel so that they can capture the user's attention. Another major problem concerned the interaction between the controller and the pilot. The controller on the ground knew from a warning device on his radar screen that the plane had descended to within 1,000 ft of the ground, which prompted the following inquiry: "Eastern 401, how are things comin' along out there?" Again, a warning stimulus was present but it was not effectively used. Why didn't the controller direct the pilot's attention to his altitude? The primary reason probably lies in the social psychology of the role relationship between pilot and controller (Weiner, 1977). Controllers have a lower-status, lower-paid position than pilots. As a result, many believe that they are not in a position to challenge a pilot, and when they do so, often find that their remarks are answered with sarcasm. Thus, psychologists have worked to improve not only the way warning information is presented by machines, but also the way this information is conveyed by people. Their work has helped to prevent the recurrence of this type of accident.

Can you think of a situation in your life in which you missed an important warning signal because your attention was focused on another stimulus? How could we prevent others from making the same mistake?

Perceptual Learning

In several sections of this chapter we have raised the question of the role of learning in perception. You might say that all learning is perceptual learning, inasmuch as learning comes by way of the senses. But this is not what is meant by the term **perceptual learning**. Rather, the term refers to an increase in a person's ability to extract information from the environment. In essence, it means that the person learns to be a better perceiver.

Perceptual abilities differ among individuals for a variety of reasons, but most often because of differences in the functioning of their sensory systems. Some people have greatly enhanced sensory skills in such areas as visual acuity, color vision, hearing range, tactile sensitivity, and so forth, because of the physiological nature of their sensory systems. But perceptual learning does not refer to differences produced by physiological advantage. Instead, perceptual learning is a label reserved for those cases where perceptual ability has been increased due to learning.

Earlier in this chapter we noted that the perceptual environment is filled with many stimuli that are never extracted in the process of perception. Some of these stimuli would be most useful if we knew how to attend to them; part of perceptual learning is just that, learning how to extract more useful information from the environment. And many individuals have learned to draw on the wealth of stimulation around them. For example, some persons are so expert at judging the quality of flour that by feeling its texture they can tell if it was made from wheat grown in Iowa or Texas. Sonar operators learn to interpret the auditory signals (echoes) they receive with such precision that they can distinguish schools of fish and whales from submarines. Dog breeders who raise show dogs learn to identify the subtle characteristics that judges value. These additional perceptual skills are most important for people in their hobbies, their jobs, and in everyday living. Some perceptual learning is by choice, such as becoming an expert wine taster. Some occurs out of necessity, such as learning to improve the use of hearing and smell when sight is lost.

Eleanor Gibson (1969) and her colleagues identified a number of changes that occur when perceptual abilities are significantly improved. Obviously, much of perceptual learning is simply learning to extract information from the environment that was not being extracted before. However, perceptual learning is not just the extraction of larger quantities of information— you can probably see why that strategy would have diminishing returns after awhile—but also has to do with how that information is extracted.

Gibson says that there is an increase in the *economy* of information extraction: the time required to make decisions is reduced, and one learns to make finer discriminations. Further, there is an equal decrease in stimulus generalizations. Attention is maximized, so that irrelevant stimuli are ignored and one focuses on the most relevant stimuli. If the task is a visual one, new eye movement strategies may be learned. One learns distinctive features that are usually overlooked by perceivers who see them only as part of a whole.

perceptual learning improvement in the ability of a person to extract information from the environment and make use of it

But the perceptual learner picks out those distinctive features and uses them as a basis for more accurate perceptual judgments (see Walk, 1978).

> ## THINKING ABOUT
> # Reading

Many of the difficulties children encounter when they are first learning to read can be traced to problems in perceptual learning. Obviously, to read a child must be able to recognize the various letters used in the language to construct words. Some letters are more troublesome than others, for example, *b* and *d* or *p* and *q*, letters that are mirror images of one another. Research shows that these particular letters are confusing for children because they perceive the orientation of the vertical part of the letter but ignore the orientation of the curved portion. The latter dimension just does not seem as important to them. Because they do not attend to it, they make many errors (Braine, 1978). Most children eventually learn to use the other dimension, but some do not, and they carry that misperception into adulthood. Many reading disabilities reflect perceptual errors of this kind (Layton, 1979). Research has been directed toward teaching relevant stimulus dimensions to beginning readers (Vogel, 1980).

Another aspect of the relationship between vision and reading is eye movement (Just & Carpenter, 1980). Eye movements during reading are composed of fixations, brief periods (typically less than 1 sec) when the eye is focused and not moving, and saccades, which are the rapid eye movements made in shifting the gaze from one point to another. Not surprisingly, good readers make fewer and briefer fixations. Further, good readers do not regress in their fixations, which means they do not repeatedly back up to earlier fixations (Massaro et al., 1980). Speed-reading strategies involve teaching the reader to make fewer fixations, perhaps training the reader to fixate only one point on each line. Despite personal testimonials to the contrary, research on various speed-reading techniques has shown them to be ineffective (Carver, 1981). The ultimate test of speed reading lies in measures of comprehension, and current methods simply do not appreciably increase comprehension. If speed reading is to be effective, designers of those courses will need to pay more attention to the psychological literature on reading. Research indicates that eye movements are only one part of the complex ability of reading (see Kolers, 1972) and they play only a minor role in pattern perception (Schlingensiepen et al., 1986).

What factors help you remember what you have read? Does thinking about the material you are reading help you remember it?

THINKING AHEAD . . .

Humans are endowed with some very remarkable perceptual mechanisms. From the chaos of sensations our receptor systems detect, these mechanisms are able to create a stable image of a well-organized world. Although a great deal is known, much still remains a mystery. For example, consider the principles of perceptual organization. Psychologists have been able to describe the principles that govern how we perceive the world. Having identified the principles, we need to understand the mechanisms that underlie them. As we saw in the section on pattern recognition, researchers are beginning to develop formal theories about how these mechanisms work. In the years to come, this work should provide fundamental insights into how our minds operate.

As we obtain a greater understanding of how our perceptual processes work, our ability to build machines that emulate these processes also increases. At present, this technology is being used for everything from helping to guide missiles to sorting mail for the post office. In the not-too-distant future, your home computer will probably have a voice recognition system as well as a keyboard. Similarly, instead of pressing buttons, you may soon find yourself talking to a variety of mechanical devices, including such things as elevators and microwaves.

But what about building the ultimate machine, a robot that has humanlike mental abilities? We already have the technology needed to translate environmental stimuli into electrical signals. However, a computer with sophisticated problem-solving and reasoning abilities would find this input nearly useless; it would soon be overwhelmed with bits of information. The solution to this problem would be to give the robot the ability to organize the input into simple objects and textures. In short, the robot would need to be endowed with some perceptual abilities. Research on this topic is progressing at a rapid rate. It seems likely that simple robots with limited pattern recognition abilities will be performing mundane chores, such as vacuuming, early in the next century. Down the road, more sophisticated machines will surely follow, for the idea of building a machine that has abilities to rival our own, and that could possibly transcend our own mortality, has always intrigued people. Years ago it was Frankenstein. Today we have Lieutenant Commander Data (Star Trek: The Next Generation) and the Terminator. Yet many of the issues raised by the creation of such a system remain the same. Could the system "feel" pain and emotion in the same way we do? When would it be ethical to end the machine's "mental life"? Would these systems be destined forever to be our "slaves"? Would they stand for this?

Summary

Perceiving an Organized World

1. Perceptual organization groups the smaller units of the perceptual world into larger ones. The principal organizing tendency is to perceive the world as figure and ground. Other organizing tendencies include the law of Prägnanz (law of simplicity); good continuation; closure; and laws of grouping, such as proximity and similarity.

2. The perception of depth depends on several cues, two requiring the use of both eyes (binocular cues) and a number requiring only one eye (monocular cues). Binocular disparity, the fact that the two retinal images differ due to the distance between the eyes, is an especially important cue. At least some ability to perceive depth is innate, but experience also plays an important role. Location of the distance and direction of sound is called auditory localization, an ability derived from interaural time and intensity differences.

3. Perceptual constancy refers to the fact that the perception of invariant object properties (distal stimuli) remains constant despite changes in proximal stimulation. Lightness constancy appears to be innate, whereas size and shape constancy are largely influenced by experience.

4. Movement perception results from the brain's assessment of eye movements and the displacement or nondisplacement of images across the retina. Velocity is a key variable determining whether movement can be tracked by the eyes. Apparent movement seems due to a simulation of neural information normally associated with real movement.

Recognition and Selection

5. A pattern is a collection of stimuli arranged in a reasonably specific way. Prototype-matching theory proposes that patterns are recognized by comparing incoming sensory information to a representation stored in memory that contains information about the object's average characteristics. Objects may be represented by sets of features, geons, or a series of sine waves.

6. Bottom-up and top-down processing approaches recognize the fact that perception can begin with the receptors relaying information to higher perceptual centers, or with the higher perceptual centers giving directions to the receptors about what features of the perceptual environment to extract.

7. Attention is a perceptual process in which we focus our consciousness on a particular stimulus or event. Selective attention focuses on one stimulus while ignoring all others; divided attention means that two or more sources of information are being monitored simultaneously. Novelty, color, movement, size, and repetition are all determinants of attention.

8. Perceptual learning refers to an increase in the ability to extract information from the environment. Perceptual learners make use of higher-order information, reduce their stimulus generalizations, reduce discrimination time, maximize attention, and learn to recognize distinctive features.

9. Perception is typically a process of minimum effort, which is economical and efficient. Perception misses the richness of the perceptual world by focusing on a limited array of stimulation.

Key Terms

perception (131)
innate (132)
perceptual organization (132)
figure–ground perception (132)
law of Prägnanz (134)
closure (135)
laws of grouping (135)
binocular disparity (136)
convergence (136)
stereopsis (136)
motion parallax (137)
elevation (137)
interposition (137)
linear perspective (137)

aerial perspective (137)
relative brightness (138)
texture gradient (139)
ecological theory of perception (139)
auditory localization (140)
size constancy (141)
distal stimulus (141)
proximal stimulus (141)
size–distance invariance hypothesis (141)
shape constancy (144)
lightness constancy (144)
albedo (144)

autokinetic effect (146)
stroboscopic movement (146)
phi phenomenon (146)
pattern perception (148)
prototype (150)
prototype-matching theory (150)
feature-analysis theory (150)
recognition by components (151)
Fourier analysis (152)
bottom-up processing (152)
top-down processing (152)

set (152)
attention (153)
selective attention (155)
dichotic listening (155)
stimulus variables (156)
organismic variables (156)
divided attention (156)
automatic processing (157)
controlled processing (157)
human factors psychology (158)
perceptual learning (159)

Suggested Reading

Bartley, S. H. (1972). *Perception in everyday life*. New York: Harper & Row. A practical guide to perceptual phenomena in everyday experiences.

Coren, S., & Girgus, J. S. (1978). *Seeing is deceiving: The psychology of visual illusions*. Hillsdale, NJ: Lawrence Erlbaum. Comprehensive coverage of the psychological research on visual illusions. Includes excellent treatments of perceptual theory as it relates to illusions.

Gibson, E. J. (1969). *Principles of perceptual learning and development*. New York: Appleton-Century-Crofts. Although a little dated, this book is still the most important work in the field of perceptual learning. A most interesting account of the theory and research in this field, it is an intellectual history of a research area.

Goldstein, E. B. (1989). *Sensation and perception*. Belmont, CA: Wadsworth. A comprehensive and extremely lucid account of the research and theory in the field of perception.

Matlin, M. & Foley, M. A. (1992). *Sensation and perception*. Needham Heights, MA: Allyn and Bacon. A broad overview of the field of perception. It is very well written, and each chapter contains demonstrations that can be conducted by the reader.

Power, R. P., Hausfield, S., & Gorta, A. (1981). *Workshops in perception*. London: Routledge & Kegan Paul. A collection, from all areas of perception, of 30 demonstrations and experiments to be performed by the reader.

Rock, I. (1990). *The perceptual world: Readings from Scientific American*. New York: W. H. Freeman. Selected readings from many of the top researchers in the field of perception.

Shepard, R. N. (1990). *Mind sights*. New York: W. H. Freeman. Visual illusions, ambiguous figures, and depictions of impossible objects drawn by the perceptual psychologist Roger Shepard.

CHAPTER 5
States of Consciousness

Although the encroachment of civilization and the continuing harvest of the forests in northern central South America have disrupted the habitat and lives of many of the native tribe members in the region, in very remote areas the vestiges of some primitive cultures remain. For the Jivaro—once a nomadic group of warriors who were labeled heathen, and even headhunters, by others from the outside—the life-style was one of constant vigilance. There was always the possibility of an aggressive attack by an enemy tribe, so understandably the Jivaro would not spend a great deal of time in slumber. Indeed, the average amount of sleep for this tribal group was around 4 hr out of every twenty-four. When you consider that logs and fallen tree limbs provided the beds for these people, it seems even more incredible that they could get by on so little sleep.

In stark contrast, when the Europeans first made contact with the Society Islands in the South Pacific, they discovered that the Islanders, on the average, slept more than 15 hr each day. This is understandable, when you consider the climate and economic demands in the region posed minimal work requirements. Food sources were readily available in the form of fish from the sea, fruit was simple to pick from a tree, and so on. In the absence of pressure to fight for survival, sleep and relaxation were encouraged.

Such contrasts in sleep patterns are evident throughout the world even today. In Greece, many people actually cut their days in half. A person often goes to work in the morning, works until just after noon, goes home and naps for a few hours, and returns to complete the day in late afternoon and evening. In North America, the pattern is much different. Although there are some exceptions, on the whole people rise early in the morning, work all day, return home at night, and sleep all night.

◀ Psychologists have studied changes in consciousness, including sleep, for many years.

Obviously, sleep is influenced by cultural factors as well as other factors. But have you ever wondered why we sleep at all? What is sleep, and what purpose does it serve? Are there other states such as sleep that are important in our daily lives yet equally mysterious? Yes, there are many different states of consciousness, and it is this topic that forms the basis of this chapter. Historically, shifts in consciousness have been a fascination for artists and literary figures, inspiring productions such as the painting *The Nightmare* shown in Figure 5–1. Of course, any discussion of *changes* in consciousness first requires us to define what consciousness is. That is how we begin this chapter.

CONSCIOUSNESS: AN OVERVIEW

Consciousness is an old term in psychology, dating to the very beginnings of experimental psychology, a little more than a century ago. Indeed, at that time psychology was defined as the study of consciousness, not as the study of behavior. However, with the emergence of behaviorism (see Chapter 1) as the dominant approach to psychology, the study of consciousness was abandoned as being too mentalistic. The term disappeared from mainstream psychology for many years, but in the last part of this century it has made a comeback, largely due to the growth of the cognitive approach in contemporary psychology. Today, most textbooks of introductory psychology, like this one, include a separate chapter devoted to research on various states of consciousness (Webb, 1992).

Initially, those who studied consciousness investigated the processes of perception, emotion, and thinking, all normal activities in an awake individual. These processes are still considered part of consciousness. Yet in today's usage, the term *consciousness* includes not only the various waking states,

FIGURE 5–1
The Nightmare, an eighteenth-century painting by Swiss artist John Henry Fuseli, shows an incubus seated atop a dreaming woman, while the "night" mare looks on from the background. Demonic possession as a source of nightmares was a common belief in medieval times.

but also altered states of consciousness such as sleep, dreaming, drug-induced states, hypnosis, and meditation.

At any moment in time, a person may be experiencing particular perceptions, thoughts, and emotions that can be the result either of current experience or of the recollection of past experiences. Implicit in consciousness is awareness. An individual's awareness may be of what is going on in the environment or of what is taking place within the body. Consciousness may even be an awareness of mental events. Knowledge of ourselves is part of consciousness and is often referred to as self-awareness. Thus, we can think of **consciousness** as the state of awareness of our world and ourselves. In an **altered state of consciousness**, awareness has been changed in some way from normal waking consciousness. Of course, by these definitions, consciousness is a mental process and something that is difficult to study using scientific methods (see Natsoulas, 1981, 1983).

Research on states of consciousness usually investigates two very different kinds of response variables: the *physiological activity* that accompanies a particular state of consciousness, and a person's *subjective report* of what is experienced in that particular state. Needless to say, subjective reports are less precise than scientists prefer. For example, consider people who meditate daily. In studying meditation, a researcher could monitor a person's physiological activity during the meditative state, recording such activities as heart rate, respiration, blood pressure, brain waves, muscle tension, and so forth. But an analysis of these body conditions provides only *some* of what the researcher wants to know about the meditative experience. The researcher also needs knowledge about that state of consciousness from the people who are meditating. What are they feeling, thinking, and perceiving? What benefits do they feel they derive from the meditation? The answers to these questions, although subjective, provide data that are important to an understanding of the nature of consciousness. In short, consciousness is difficult to define and difficult to study; nevertheless, it is a very important concept in psychology and one that is related closely to every other chapter in this text. Our examination of states of consciousness, although not exhaustive, includes sleep and dreaming, hypnosis, and drug effects.

consciousness state of our awareness of our world and ourselves

altered state of consciousness shift in our awareness from the normal waking state

SLEEP

Death and taxes are not the only certainties in life; sleep must be included as well. If you live to be 75, you will likely have slept for 25 years, a period that surpasses even the long sleep of the legendary Rip van Winkle. Everyone sleeps, although the patterning of that sleep and its average duration differ from person to person, as noted in the opening section of this chapter. Some people are long sleepers, some are short sleepers, some take naps, and some sleep during the day rather than at night. Although sleep is a prominent part of our everyday life, most people know amazingly little about even its most basic facts. From a scientific standpoint, a great deal has been learned about sleep over the past couple of decades, but many phenomena remain a mystery. What we do know has come largely from only a few sleep laboratories, which we will describe next.

The Sleep Laboratory

The typical sleep lab makes use of volunteers who are willing to come to the laboratory on successive nights, or even over a period of weeks, and sleep in a specially designed bedroom. The sleepers are connected to assorted gadgetry (see Figure 5–2) to produce an electroencephalograph (EEG), which as we

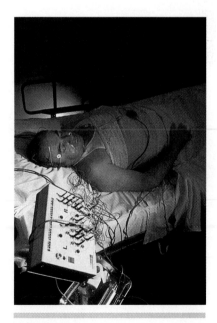

FIGURE 5–2
This person is in a sleep laboratory that provides information on several different responses while the person sleeps.

electromyograph (EMG) recording device that monitors muscle movement and muscle tension

electro-oculograph (EOG) recording device used to measure eye movements in various sleep stages

electrocardiograph (EKG) recording device that monitors heart rate

noted in Chapter 2, is a report from a machine that measures electrical activity in the brain. Standard electrode placements, referred to as the International 10–20 System, used by all sleep labs, make it easier to compare sleep research findings (Jasper, 1958). In addition to the EEG, an **electromyograph (EMG)** records selected muscle tension levels and movement. An **electro-oculograph (EOG)** is a recording of eye movements during various stages of sleep, and an **electrocardiograph (EKG)** comes from monitoring heart rate and other heart activity. Attached to these and other machines that measure breathing, body temperature, and so forth, the sleeper would look more like an astronaut than someone about to enter a night's sleep. But usually the subject does surprisingly well, drifting off in sleep as observers watch through a window; records are made unobtrusively in an adjacent room.

It takes a few nights for the patterns produced during sleep to stabilize, but once they do, the investigator is in a position to manipulate the duration (length of the sleep), fatigue, deprivation, drugs, and other variables that might affect sleep. Carefully evaluating changes in sleep patterns that result from changes in routine help researchers understand the mechanisms underlying sleep (we will have more to say about this later in this chapter). What the charts, graphs, and other records cannot tell us is why we sleep at all. We may be good at characterizing an important phenomenon without knowing why the phenomenon is important. But we can make some informed guesses about the functions of sleep.

Functions of Sleep

Sleep is not a simple process, as shown by the approximately 1,500 studies that are published on this topic each year. Therefore, it is not likely that any single theory can account for sleep. Another way to state this point is to say that sleep has not one function, but many.

The literature of the past harbors most of the contemporary notions of why we sleep: sleep is a useless habit that can be discarded if only we try hard enough; sleep is due to a severe reduction in sensory stimulation; sleep allows for dreaming, which gives us time to solve the problems of our day; and sleep replenishes the processes of our mind and body that are depleted during the course of everyday life (Webb, 1981b). The last of these theories of sleep function is a very popular one and is commonly known as the **restorative theory** of sleep. Ask the average person why sleep occurs, and it is the answer you are most likely to hear. Even William Shakespeare's Macbeth espoused the restorative theory in suggesting that sleep "knits up the ravelled sleeve of care."

restorative theory theory of sleep that states that we sleep in order to replenish essential body processes

The Restorative Theory. The restorative theory implies that during the day, waking activities deplete the body of important substances or build up fatigue products (perhaps in the muscle tissues, the blood, or the cerebrospinal fluid) that must be disposed of during sleep. Support for this theory comes from both common observation—lots of tired people go to sleep every night and wake up refreshed—and from scientific studies. For example, increases in slow wave sleep (which is discussed later) are correlated with increases in physical exertion. Also, it is during slow wave sleep that the secretion of growth hormone peaks.

In another kind of sleep, called rapid eye movement (REM) sleep (also discussed later), proteins and other cellular components are restored so the system will function smoothly the next day. When people are deprived of REM sleep or when they suffer from a neurological disorder that impairs REM function, the result is a disturbance in thinking and mood (Kolb & Whishaw, 1990). It seems, then, that when critical sleep periods are missed, and the body is deprived of the opportunity to rebuild and prepare for the next day, behavioral problems are likely.

Although such findings argue in favor of the restorative functions of sleep, other facts are inconsistent with this rationale (Shapiro, 1982). For instance, people's sleepiness often disappears even when they have not slept. You probably have experienced this, for example, when you felt you were too sleepy to study but resisted the need for sleep and found that 30 min later you were wide awake. This "second wind" phenomenon, which is common, is inconsistent with a restorative theory. Studies comparing napping with just resting in bed have shown that both are equally capable of improving mood, showing again that restorative effects can occur without sleep (Daiss, Bertelson, & Benjamin, 1986). Other problematic evidence comes from studies of the biochemistry and physiology of sleep. Researchers have discovered that a number of activities go on in the brain and body that are clearly not restorative in nature. During sleep, blood flow in the cerebral arteries is elevated, gastric secretions may occur, heart rate and respiration become irregular, and neural activity in some brain areas is greatly enhanced. These findings do not indicate that the restorative theory is invalid, but they do suggest that sleep includes functions other than just restoration.

The Adaptive Nonresponding Theory.   One method of studying sleep function has taken a comparative approach, looking at the sleep of animals other than humans. Researchers have found many differences, including differences in the duration of sleep. Deer, for example, sleep an average of 2 hr each day, whereas gorillas average about 14 hr. Why are there such great differences? The answer is related to an animal's placement in the environment as predator or prey. Animals that are more vulnerable to attack need to be ever vigilant (see Figure 5–3). Food needs are also important; animals that must spend a lot of time acquiring food will necessarily have less time for sleep.

Psychologist Wilse Webb has proposed the **adaptive nonresponding theory**, an evolutionary theory that accounts for these sleep differences. According to Webb, sleep is an adaptive response. "Sleep developed, in the particular forms and patterns it took in each species, as a behavior that increased the likelihood of that species' survival" (Webb, 1975). For humans,

adaptive nonresponding theory theory of sleep that suggests that sleep and inactivity at night have survival value

FIGURE 5–3
Domestic animals that are cared for by their owners have much time to lie around and sleep. If the animal lived in a more threatening environment, it would likely sleep less.

FIGURE 5–4
Wilse B. Webb has been one of the leading researchers in sleep for more than 30 years. His more than 200 publications include research on free running rhythms, napping, dream recall, sleep changes in the aging process, EEG patterning in sleep, and personality characteristics of short and long sleepers. He is perhaps best known for his adaptive nonresponding theory of sleep.

this adaptive response was "nonresponding." Webb believes that sleep evolved as a behavior that had adaptive significance for the human species. He asserts that in prehistoric times, cave dwellers who did not sleep wandered about at night, falling in pits and being eaten by animals better suited to the dark. Those who slept in caves at night were safe. They were thus more likely to pass their genes to future generations. For Webb (see Figure 5–4), sleep may be a product of evolution that has outlived its usefulness. This view is supported by surveys in the twentieth century showing a decline in total sleep time in successive generations (Webb, 1974). Of course, this decline may represent increased work demands in modern society, or the growth of options for work or leisure during the nighttime hours. Thus, the amount of sleep people get is diminished, but the need for sleep may remain the same. Although this theory is interesting and accounts for some of the facts of sleep, there are many sleep questions it cannot answer, such as the existence of different stages of sleep.

More recently, Webb (1988) has proposed a theory of sleep that combines some of the best explanatory features of the restorative and adaptive nonresponding theories. This new theory explains sleep as a function of *sleep demand* (based on the time of wakefulness preceding sleep), *circadian tendencies* (which are discussed in the next section), and *behaviors* that facilitate or inhibit sleep (such as body position, noise, or worrying). In addition, several variables play a determining role, for example, species differences and developmental stages. Future research will determine the adequacy of this theory in accounting for the facts of sleep.

You can see that we have raised more questions than we have answered in this section. Although we cannot provide a good answer for the question of why we sleep, we can fill in some parts of the puzzle. We begin with a discussion of the biological clocks that are part of sleep and wakefulness.

Biological Rhythms and Alertness

Like any clocks, our biological clocks allow us to keep time in a world that changes constantly with respect to the temperature of our environment and the length of our days and nights. They offer some stability of functioning in what might otherwise be a chaotic situation. Among these time markers are a number of **circadian rhythms**, meaning rhythms whose cycle corresponds to approximately 24 hr. These circadian rhythms include endocrine activity, metabolic function, and body temperature. Daily fluctuations in body temperature are closely related to sleep and wakefulness and to alertness (see Figure 5–5). An understanding of these relationships can prove crucial in human performance, as the following episode illustrates:

> At 1:50 a.m., Burlington Northern freight train Number 7843 pulled out of Eagle Butte Coal Mine in Gillette, Wyoming. The engineer and head brakeman operated the 115-car train from the lead locomotive; the conductor and rear brakeman were in the caboose. At 4:18 a.m. Number 7843 was moving east on the single main track at the restricted speed of 35 mph. Flashing yellow signals indicated that several trains were on the same main track, about twenty miles ahead at Pedro, Wyoming, but the engineer and head brakeman had nodded off and missed them. At Y. T. Hill, a steep downgrade a few miles from Pedro, the train's rapid acceleration alarmed the conductor in the caboose. He radioed the engineer in the lead locomotive. The engineer woke up and saw the speedometer registering 62 mph. His application of the air brake startled the head brakeman, who awoke to see the engineer in a state of panic. The engineer asked the brakeman if he had seen the last signal. No. He too had been asleep. . . . They saw two other freight trains dead ahead at Pedro. The engineer shouted over the radio, "Get off your way car," and sounded the whistle repeatedly. Crew members on the nearest of the two trains at Pedro heard a garbled message but were unaware of an oncoming train. Five hundred feet before Pedro, the engineer and head brakeman jumped off Number 7843, by now speeding out of control at 45 mph. At 4:45 a.m., Number 7843 struck Number 8112. Two crew members in the caboose of 8112 were immediately killed. (Coleman, 1986)

This collision marked the second disaster for Burlington Northern in less than 2 weeks; 9 days earlier, two of its trains had collided, killing five crew members. The time of that collision was 3:55 a.m. Figure 5–5 suggests a probable cause for these events; the curve shows that body temperature closely parallels that of alertness. Note that alertness is lowest during the hours from midnight to 6:00 a.m., corresponding to the time when most people are

circadian rhythms internal biological rhythms that are tied to our 24-hr day

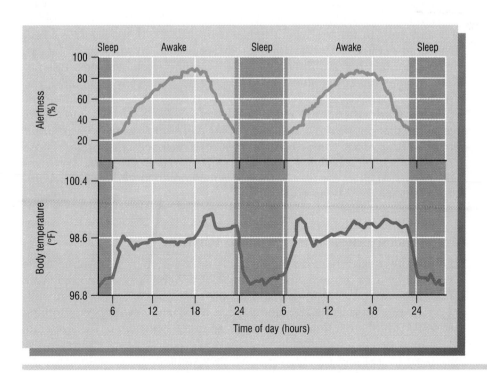

FIGURE 5–5
Body temperature, a circadian rhythm, is lowest during sleep, dropping nearly two degrees. Note that body temperature and alertness are very closely correlated. (Adapted from Coleman, 1986.)

asleep, or at least not working. Both train collisions occurred in that time frame. Indeed, many accidents that result from a loss of human alertness occur in the early morning hours: the explosion at the Union Carbide Plant in Bhopal, India, that killed thousands of people, and the nuclear power plant accidents at Three Mile Island in the United States and Chernobyl in what was formerly the Soviet Union (Coleman, 1986; Lauber & Kayten, 1988).

Internal Clocks and Shift Work. The 9-to-5 job is accepted as the standard in the United States, and although most of the work force may be at work during this traditional period, many people work a much more irregular schedule. In fact, over 25% of all women and men endure shift work in which on alternate weeks they work days, evenings, and nights. As Stanford University psychologist Richard Coleman notes, when internal and external clocks get out of synchrony, the result is often disastrous (Coleman, 1986).

People who work nights experience more frequent health problems and more marital problems and difficulties in their home life, besides being more prone to psychological distress. The situation is even worse for employees who are rotating from one shift to another. Everything is made more difficult. It is harder for them to fall asleep, and when they finally do, the quality of their sleep decreases. Enjoying family activities is less likely because many of them occur during "normal" time periods. Even when the worker is on an occasional daytime shift, scheduling must be done far in advance for the person to enjoy things that are routinely available to those with 9-to-5 jobs.

Because shift life is unavoidable in some industries such as hospitals, municipal services, and mining operations, attention has been devoted to exploring ways to alleviate the stress inherent to "clocks in collision." It has been suggested that shift workers would make the transition across day, evening, and night shifts if the shifts were rotated after several weeks instead of each week. This would permit more time for internal clocks to adjust and match external clocks, and it would make the employee's personal schedule more predictable and easier to manage. Czeisler, Moore-Ede, and Coleman (1982) have confirmed that a 21-day shift rotation results in greater worker satisfaction than a 1-week shift rotation. More recent attempts at improving the health of shift workers and their job production have focused on limiting their exposure to intense bright light during the daytime (Czeisler et al., 1989), and using exercise techniques to accelerate the shift in biological rhythms, so that they are in line with the changing work demands. It is not likely that the stresses of shift work will ever be completely eliminated, but conditions can improve.

What kinds of changes might you suggest? First put yourself in the role of the worker, and ask yourself "What can I do to make the situation better?" Then, place yourself in the role of a member of a family whose activities must be scheduled around a shift worker's schedule. Are there some events, such as meals, the time of which could be changed to accommodate the worker? What else?

Sleep–Wakefulness as a Circadian Rhythm

Traditionally, researchers have assumed that the human sleep–wake cycle was timed by a 24-hr clock, that is, until Wilse Webb (1975) reported some startling research. Webb tested subjects individually in an environment without time cues. Subjects had no clock, radio, television, newspapers—nothing that could give them a time clue. They lived in the bedroom of the sleep lab, where their meals were brought to them upon request. These subjects were told to go to bed and get up whenever they wanted. They controlled their own day–night cycle. Webb found that without time cues, most subjects went

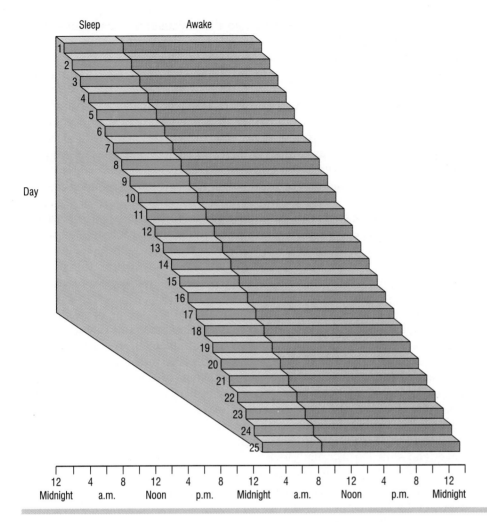

Sleep   Awake

Day

12   4   8   12   4   8   12   4   8   12   4   8   12
Midnight a.m.   Noon   p.m.   Midnight a.m.   Noon   p.m.   Midnight

FIGURE 5–6
A hypothetical record of free running activity. On Day 1 the subject goes to sleep at midnight. On each successive night, sleep onset is an hour later, so that by Day 13 the subject is going to sleep at noon. This 25-hr rhythm is the natural sleep–wake rhythm for most humans when placed in an environment without time cues. (From Coleman, 1986.)

to bed a little later each night until they were actually sleeping during the day and staying awake at night. He called these natural sleep–wake rhythms **free running rhythms** and noted that the cycle for most people was not 24 hr, but was closer to 25 hr (see Figure 5–6).

Why such a natural cycle exists for beings that live on a 24-hr planet is a mystery. Fortunately, we are able to adjust to the discrepancy by readjusting our own internal clocks every day. At least that is true for most of us. But if the deviation from 24 hr is more than 2 hr (some people have free running rhythms that are closer to 28 hr), the daily readjustment does not work. People with these abnormally long free running rhythms make up a small part of the population of chronic insomniacs. The concept of free running rhythms also has helped us understand problems of jet lag.

free running rhythms the natural rhythms that occur in the absence of time cues; typically running about 25 hr in humans

◄►► THINKING ABOUT
Jet Lag ◄◄►

Jet lag is produced when individuals travel rapidly across time zones, which results in their internal biological clocks colliding with the new external clock. With shorter flights eastward when the day is shortened, travelers, not yet ready for bed, must force themselves to go to sleep early.

jet lag internal biological clocks collide with external clocks as a result of moving quickly across several time zones

Most people cannot fall asleep early, so they awaken the next day having had too little sleep. By comparison, people traveling westward over several time zones usually have less of a problem. In this case the day is being extended beyond 24 hr, which is more in line with the body's natural free running rhythm.

Jet lag becomes a major problem when travel occurs across several time zones; direction doesn't seem to matter. In some instances the internal and external clocks may be so out of phase that serious problems with alertness develop. This can be disastrous in an industry such as aviation, where pilot fatigue can result in overshooting the runway (Wegmann, Conrad, & Klein, 1983). International diplomats, heads of state (see Figure 5–7), and corporate executives often travel halfway around the world and are expected to function at their best. Yet there is insufficient time to adapt to the acute changes in temporal conditions. Imagine the difficulties a Russian neurosurgeon from St. Petersburg has when she is brought in as a specialist on a high-risk case in Lima, Peru. There is no time to wait, yet the surgery requires extreme precision, which the surgeon may not be able to offer, at least for a few days.

Jet lag is a serious issue. However, gains in treating or preventing jet lag are being made, especially with recent developments in simulation environments where jet lag can be induced and studied in laboratory settings (Monk, Moline, & Graeber, 1988). Charles Czeisler and Richard Kronauer of Harvard Medical School have designed one of the most illuminating approaches to cure jet lag. These sleep researchers have shown that internal biological clocks can be set backward or forward by being briefly exposed to bright light at strategic points in the internal rhythm (Czeisler et al., 1989). For instance, being exposed to sunlight for 6 to 8 hr on the first day after travel can shift the internal clock by 12 hr! With both laboratory subjects and actual jet lag victims, this dramatic change seems to result from light crushing the peak of the existing internal rhythm and thereby permitting a new rhythm to be established almost immediately. Consider the differences this bright light system can make. Suppose you fly from Toronto, Canada, to Beijing, China, which places you 13 hr ahead. If you go to work immediately and are exposed to normal room lighting, your clock will reset only by about 1 hr each day. It will take 10 days to recover fully from the trip.

FIGURE 5–7
International diplomats and leaders often must travel halfway around the world. The resulting jet lag can be a problem in making key decisions immediately upon returning from such trips, but researchers are finding new ways to minimize the impact of this phenomenon.

However, if you stay out in the bright sunlight for 6 hr on the first day after you arrive in China, your internal circadian pacemaker will be in synchrony with local time by the second day.

If you are planning to travel abroad soon, what might you do to avoid jet lag? Would you arrive early and spend some time on the beach? What else?

Stages of Sleep

In the late 1930s, EEG studies showed that sleep was not a uniform activity but one that produced a variety of different brain waves throughout the night. This was an important discovery, but the major breakthrough came in 1953 when Eugene Aserinsky and Nathaniel Kleitman noticed periodic bursts of eye movements during sleep. As a result of their research, we now recognize two radically different types of sleep that are regulated by different brain systems and different neurotransmitters. They also are characterized by a multitude of physiological, biochemical, and psychological differences. One type of sleep is called **rapid eye movement (REM) sleep;** the other is **non–rapid eye movement (NREM) sleep** (see Figure 5-8).

Obviously, rapid eye movements occur during REM sleep and not during NREM sleep. Yet this difference is only one of many between the two kinds of sleep and may not even be the most important difference. Research in the 1950s and 1960s led to a standardization of the method of scoring individual sleep records according to the various stages (Rechtschaffen &

rapid eye movement (REM) sleep stage of sleep characterized by frequent eye movements, suppression of the muscles, and usually associated with dreaming

non–rapid eye movement (NREM) sleep all sleep that occurs outside REM periods

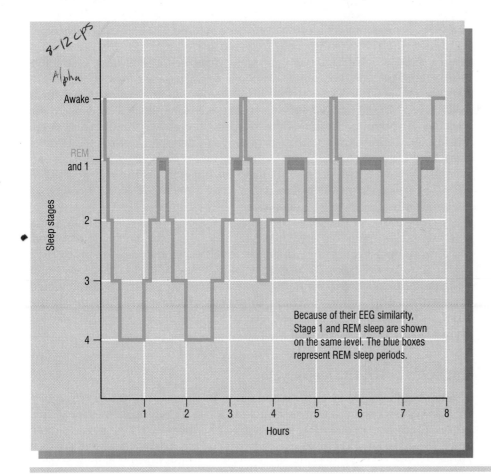

Because of their EEG similarity, Stage 1 and REM sleep are shown on the same level. The blue boxes represent REM sleep periods.

FIGURE 5–8
The NREM-REM periodicity of a "typical night's sleep." Note that most slow wave sleep (stages 3 and 4) occurs in the first half of the night, whereas most REM sleep occupies the second half. REM periods usually occur at 90-min intervals, and the duration of each REM sleep period typically lengthens throughout the night.

Kales, 1968). Today, we recognize the existence of five distinct stages of sleep that cycle throughout the night. Four of these five stages are part of NREM sleep and are simply numbered 1, 2, 3, and 4. The fifth stage of sleep is REM sleep.

Using the records from the EEG, EMG, and other instruments discussed earlier, researchers are able to differentiate the various stages of sleep. Although there are a few exceptions, usually sleep follows an orderly cycle (see Figure 5–8). Typically we begin in stage 1 and serially move through stages 2–4 before the pattern reverses (1–2–3–4–3–2). At this point the first REM period occurs.

Each stage has a distinctively different character. Stage 1 follows a period of drowsiness in which **alpha waves** (8–12 cps) appear in the EEG (see Figure 5–9). As the sleeper enters stage 1, the alpha waves are replaced with **theta waves** (3–7 cps), and breathing and heart rate slow down as muscles relax and body temperature falls. After about 5 or 10 min, a slightly deeper sleep occurs in stage 2, during which mixed EEG activity is present along with special brain waves called *sleep spindles*. Spindles occur throughout stage 2 in mammals; precisely why, we do not know (Ferri et al., 1989). Stages 3 and 4 are the deepest form of NREM sleep, at least as defined in terms of arousal to external stimuli. We enter stage 3 when 20% of the overall EEG activity includes **delta waves** (.5–2 cps), and stage 4 when the record shows 50% or more delta waves. Collectively, stages 3 and 4 are called **slow wave sleep (SWS)**, or **delta sleep.** As Figure 5–9 shows, delta waves are lower in frequency but higher in voltage than either alpha or theta waves.

The forward transition from stages 1–4, and the return trip, do not involve an abrupt shift from one stage to the next. Indeed, it is often difficult to tell when you have come out of one stage and moved into the next. But when you move from NREM to REM brain wave activity changes suddenly, and there is no doubt which stage you have entered. On an electrophysiological basis, the patterns are characterized as low-voltage, high-frequency brain waves, much like stage 1 or even wakefulness. The most distinctive change, and the one that names this stage of sleep, is the onset of rapid lateral eye movements. These twitches are so obvious that you can see them easily when you watch someone sleep (try this sometime). You can see the eyes darting about beneath the closed lids as the person continues to sleep. During REM sleep, muscle tone is greatly suppressed. Indeed, the body is incredibly relaxed, virtually totally limp. For example, cats, which like all mammals, have REM sleep, remain in an upright posture during NREM sleep but roll over on their sides when they enter REM sleep (see Figure 5–10) because they have lost most of their muscle tone.

Research shows that REM sleep is a deep form of sleep, and that intensive external stimulation is required to wake a person during this period. The intriguing aspect of this finding is that the brain doesn't seem to have "very far to move" from REM sleep to wakefulness. That is, because brain wave patterns of REM sleep and wide-awake periods are so similar, it would appear that a person is nearly awake during REM already. Yet, clearly the REM period is one of our deepest sleeps. For this reason, the REM stage is often referred to as **paradoxical sleep**.

The NREM-REM Sleep Cycle

Throughout the night we cycle in and out of REM and NREM sleep in a fairly reliable 90-min cycle (60 min for human infants). This cycle defines the period between the onset of one REM sleep period and the onset of the next (Carman et al., 1984). In a typical night of sleep a person has between four and six such cycles. The 90-min period remains relatively constant; the distribution of REM

---

alpha waves brain wave patterns that are characteristically high frequency–low voltage (8–12 cps)

theta waves brain wave patterns of about 3–7 cps

delta waves very low frequency–high voltage brain wave patterns that are evident in deep sleep (.5–2 cps)

slow wave sleep (SWS)(delta sleep) the component of sleep that is defined by the inclusion of stages 3 and 4

paradoxical sleep the very deep period of REM sleep in which, paradoxically, brain activity is high yet extensive external stimulation is required to move the person to a state of wakefulness

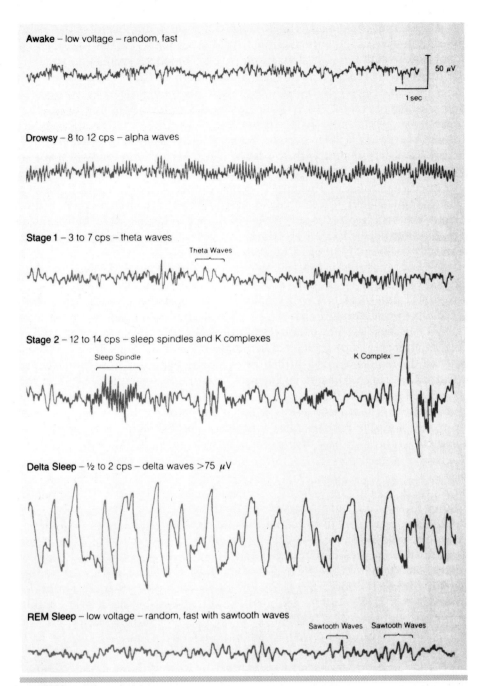

Awake – low voltage – random, fast

50 µV

1 sec

Drowsy – 8 to 12 cps – alpha waves

Stage 1 – 3 to 7 cps – theta waves

Theta Waves

Stage 2 – 12 to 14 cps – sleep spindles and K complexes

Sleep Spindle

K Complex

Delta Sleep – ½ to 2 cps – delta waves >75 µV

REM Sleep – low voltage – random, fast with sawtooth waves

Sawtooth Waves   Sawtooth Waves

FIGURE 5–9
Brain wave patterns (EEG) associated with the stages of human sleep. (From Hauri, 1982.)

and NREM sleep within each cycle, however, changes over the night (see Figure 5–8). Most slow wave sleep occurs early in the night, typically within the first four hours of sleep, whereas most of the REM sleep occurs in the second half of the sleep night. You will note that REM sleep periods lengthen throughout the night. On average, a person who sleeps 8 hr spends the following percentages in each sleep stage: stage 1, 5%; stage 2, 50%; stages 3 and 4, 20%, and REM sleep, 25%. Typically, about 2 hr each night is spent in REM sleep, and this amount of time is usually spread across four or five REM periods. Because we know that REM sleep is highly correlated with dreaming, the average sleeper probably spends 2 hr dreaming each night.

NREM

REM

FIGURE 5–10
During REM sleep, the muscles become very relaxed. The cat on the top is in NREM sleep and maintains a semierect posture. But when it goes into REM (*bottom*), it loses its muscle tone and falls over on its side. (Adapted from Jouvet, 1967.)

States of Consciousness   **177**

Recall that REM and NREM sleep differ on a number of dimensions other than eye movements. During NREM sleep, heart rate is lowered and regular, respiration is also slower and regular, blood pressure is down, body temperature decreases, and oxygen consumption in the brain is lower. For REM sleep, the opposite conditions prevail; that is, the heart rate increases and is irregular, blood pressure increases, and so forth. Another interesting occurrence during REM sleep is penile erections. These erections occur during each of the REM sleep periods. Males often awaken in the morning with an erection, associated with the REM sleep period immediately prior to awakening. No one knows why these erections occur. Also, there is some evidence that there is increased vaginal blood flow during REM sleep (Fisher et al., 1980). These changes are not related to dream content; they occur whether dream content is sexual or not. Like the other biochemical and physiological changes, erections and vaginal blood flow changes are a naturally occurring part of REM sleep.

Finally, in examining the differences in NREM and REM sleep discussed in this section, you might think of REM sleep as active sleep and NREM sleep as quiet sleep. There is ample evidence to support this position. There is a great amount of literature that shows REM sleep is associated with long-term memory processing. For example, Smith and Lapp (1991) followed college seniors after they took their final semester exams and found that the actual number of REMs increased during the examination period. Apparently, active REM periods are produced by intensive learning sessions, indicative of the prominent role that REM functions play in storing new information. Yet, despite such evidence that points to the active nature of REM sleep, the label does not always fit. Perhaps most conspicuous in this regard is the previously mentioned dramatic suppression of muscle tone during REM sleep.

Need for Sleep

One of the most frequently asked questions concerning sleep is, how much sleep does a person need? Like the question on the function of sleep, researchers do not have a definite answer for this one either. We do know that some sleep is required for everyone. There is no well-documented case of any human who does not sleep. Yet sleep among adults varies greatly; some sleep as little as 4 hours per day, and others sleep more than 10 hours per day. One way to answer the question about the need for sleep is to say that your body will tell you. For example, if you are not getting enough sleep, you will be sleepy during the day.

In essence, we do not know what determines why some people seem to need a lot of sleep whereas others can get by on very little. This difference may be genetically determined, a function of diet, the result of some hormonal or neurological condition, related to certain kinds of personality, or due to the demands of life. Maybe it is all of these factors. We do know that most people sleep an average of 7.5 hr, and that only 1 out of 10 adults qualifies as a short or long sleeper (Hartmann et al., 1971).

Are there harmful effects from being either a long or short sleeper? A study by Kripke and his colleagues (1979) found that life expectancies for short and long sleepers were less, by a few years, than for average sleepers. Those data are correlational and should not be interpreted in a causal way. Too much or too little sleep may not shorten your life, but those sleep styles are likely related to other variables, unknown at present, that may be responsible for reducing life expectancy. In other words, changing the length of time you sleep is not likely to affect your longevity.

Most of us probably get less sleep than we need. Some sleep researchers have gone so far as to argue that we are a nation of chronically sleep deprived people (Webb & Agnew, 1975), and the data strongly support that conclusion. Daytime sleepiness is a common problem for many people, and they deal with it by struggling through those groggy periods. Recent research on adolescents and young adults shows that both groups report daytime sleepiness as a frequent problem, and both groups wish they could sleep more (Levine et al., 1988b). So why don't they? It is not because they are unable to get more sleep. Daiss, Bertelson, and Benjamin (1986) found that people who never or rarely took naps could nap quite readily when given the opportunity to do so. The subjects in that study, college students, like most people find that the demands of living—work and social life—require more waking hours than they have. The only way to add to our waking hours is to subtract from the sleeping ones. And within limits we can do that without dire consequences, as you will see in the next section on sleep deprivation.

Sleep Deprivation

One way to look at the function of sleep is to investigate what happens to people when they are not allowed to sleep or when their sleep time is reduced. Studies that eliminate sleep or reduce it are called **sleep deprivation** studies. Some studies have tried to deprive persons totally of sleep by keeping them awake 24 hr a day. Most of these investigations have lasted only a few days, but some have kept persons awake for as long as 11 days. Technically, total sleep deprivation is something of a misnomer. After 2 to 3 days of such deprivation, the person engages in **microsleeps**, brief 2- to 5-sec bursts of sleep that intrude into wakefulness. The incidence of these microsleeps increases as the deprivation continues. Other researchers have wanted to deprive sleepers of certain kinds of sleep, while leaving other kinds of sleep intact. These *selective sleep deprivation* studies usually involve the deprivation of REM sleep (see Figure 5–11).

Sleep deprivation studies have been going on for about 90 years now, and the results have been disappointing to researchers. Surely if you deprive someone of several days of sleep, the effects must be devastating—they should suffer motor and speech problems, have perceptual difficulties, experience memory and thinking problems, and undergo some personality changes. Although certain studies have found all of these changes to occur, the reliability of the findings is very poor, and in fact the results are often a result of the testing procedure (Johnson, 1969).

In college, periods of sleep deprivation are almost unavoidable. Examination schedules, social commitments, and the numerous other activities that are inherent to college life, ensure occasional sleep loss. Have you wondered what happens to your ability to function after staying up all night? Realistically, should you expect to perform at your best intellectual and physical levels? In terms of difficult tasks that require focused concentration over long periods, such as polishing a draft of a term paper, losing a night's sleep likely will have a harmful effect, and in a few cases prolonged sleep loss can produce more serious problems (Webb, 1992). But for most of us, problems associated with sleep loss are easily compensated, and temporary. After an "all-nighter" just be sure to get back into a routine and you will be fine.

The Rebound Effect. One of the reasons that you recover so quickly from sleep deprivation relates to **REM rebound**. When you are deprived of REM sleep, your body tends to make up for the loss by increasing the REM sleep during periods of sleep following the period of deprivation. For example, if you are a participant in a sleep research project in which the experimenter wakes you every time you start into REM but allows you to sleep the usual number of hours, you will find that your level of functioning drops off. This is

sleep deprivation experimental operations force an individual to remain awake, in an effort to determine the impact of sleep loss on a variety of physical and psychological functions

microsleeps brief 2- to 5-sec bursts of sleep that intrude on wakefulness, often triggered by sleep deprivation

FIGURE 5–11
Monitoring of EEG records is typically used to selectively deprive humans of REM sleep, but for rats the "inverted flowerpot" technique works just as well. As long as the rat is in NREM sleep, it has sufficient muscle tone to stay on the flowerpot. When it goes into REM sleep, however, it loses muscle tone and falls into the water, where it is awakened and thus prevented from having any REM sleep.

REM rebound the body makes up for deprivation of REM sleep by increasing the relative amount of REM sleep during subsequent sleep periods because you need a certain amount of REM sleep. When the experimenter permits you to sleep without interruption, you will exhibit more REM sleep than normal. That is, your body will catch up and reclaim the REM sleep it needs.

This same rebound effect will occur when REM sleep is suppressed by drugs such as alcohol. Eventually, the body will restore itself and normal sleep activity will return.

Sleep Changes with Age

The NREM-REM cycle changes from infancy to adulthood, as sleep changes from a polyphasic pattern (sleeping in many periods) to a monophasic one (sleeping in one period). Many other age-related changes in sleep are believed to be biologically determined (see Figure 5–12). Recall that human newborns sleep an average of 16 hours per day. Unlike adults, newborns spend 50% of their sleep time in REM sleep. It is believed that REM sleep in infancy is related to maturation of the nervous system, a process that is not complete at birth. The gradual reduction of REM sleep as a percentage of total sleep time is closely related to the decline in neurological maturation; the adult level of 25% REM sleep is reached at about age 11. REM sleep remains at that level until it declines again to about 15% around age 60. Over the life span there is also a major change in SWS. This type of sleep diminishes in percentage throughout the aging process and may not exist in some elderly adults. What this loss of SWS means for older individuals is not clear. Research to date has not found any correspondence between declines in SWS and any physiological or psychological condition in the elderly (Spiegel, Koberle, & Allen, 1986).

Total sleep time also declines. In early adulthood it stabilizes at the 7.5-hr average already mentioned and remains there for most of our adult life. However, at about age 60, sleep duration diminishes. One of the persistent myths about older people is that they need a lot of sleep. Although there are clearly individual differences, many people in their 60s or 70s need no more than 6 to 7 hr of sleep. Yet many of these people spend a lot of time in bed awake, trying to get the extra sleep they feel they need.

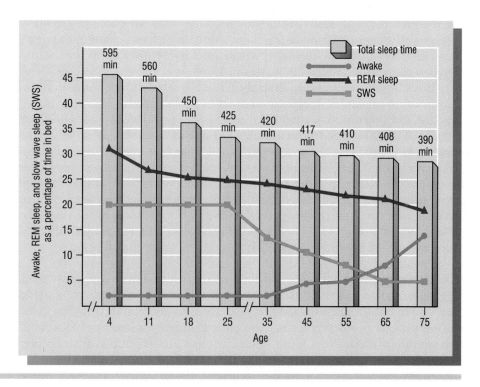

FIGURE 5–12
More than any other variable, age is associated with changes in sleep patterns. Note the dramatic changes with respect to REM sleep, slow wave sleep, and time spent in bed awake. (Based on data from Williams, Karacan, & Hursch, 1974.)

Some other age-related changes in sleep can be quite bothersome. As we get older we are more easily awakened during the night, have more difficulty getting back to sleep, and are more bothered by deprivation of sleep (Webb, 1985). Our *sleep latency* may also increase, meaning it takes us longer to fall asleep.

Sleep Disorders

As we noted earlier, no one can be sure of why we must sleep. But sleep we must. In this regard, sleep disorders are of interest because of the health threats they pose. When you cannot sleep, or sleep too much, your quality of life is at risk. Indeed, with some sleep disorders, life per se is at risk. Here, we discuss several sleep disorders, including insomnia, narcolepsy, sudden infant death syndrome, sleep apnea, sleepwalking, and sleeptalking.

Insomnia. The most common sleep disorder is **insomnia**, a condition that may affect a third of the population at some time in their lives (Borkovec, 1982). Insomnia is characterized by difficulty in falling asleep and/or in staying asleep that has persisted beyond one or two nights. Some people have insomnia for several weeks or even years. A physician will often treat an insomnia complaint by prescribing one of the sleeping pills known as **hypnotics** (Hartmann, 1978). These medications can be very effective in helping someone get to sleep, but their effectiveness lasts only for a short period of time, usually no longer than 2 weeks. After that time, the person develops a tolerance for the drug. *Tolerance* describes the body's resistance to the effects of the drug. As tolerance develops, a dosage must be increased if the drug is to remain effective. This cycle can escalate until, just to get a few hours of sleep, the insomniac is taking massive quantities of sleeping pills. A condition described as *drug dependency insomnia* may then develop. The person's insomnia is now largely due to the medication. In order to recover, the sleeping pills must be gradually withdrawn and the individual usually must undergo some form of behavioral or pharmacological therapy (Institute of Medicine, 1979).

One form of insomnia is called *learned* or *conditioned insomnia*. Individuals with this kind of insomnia are different from other insomniacs in that they usually show no signs of any psychological problems that might have produced the insomnia. Instead, their insomnia has been acquired from their own bad sleeping habits (Hauri & Fisher, 1986; Van Egeren et al., 1983). Therapists who treat insomnia warn against reading or eating in bed, for both activities can become associated with the bed and thus cause difficulty in falling asleep. The standard advice to a person who is having trouble falling asleep is to get out of bed, go to another room, and do something like read a dull book until sleepiness occurs (Lacks et al., 1983). Such people are also advised to avoid motor arousal at bedtime, as vigorous exercise before bedtime is not conducive to sleep (Bunnell, Bevier, & Horvath, 1983; Horne, 1981). Cognitive arousal can also be problematic. Many people lie in bed thinking either about the problems they had that day or about problems they may face tomorrow. Understandably, this kind of arousal increases sleep-onset latencies.

We mentioned earlier that many elderly people think they need more sleep than they actually do. Consequently, they attempt to force themselves to sleep. Because so many elderly people lie in bed awake, it is understandable that the number of complaints about insomnia increases with age. It is estimated that more than half of all individuals over 65 years of age suffer from insomnia (Anch et al., 1988). The result is that many of these people take some form of sleeping medication, which often is expensive. In addi-

insomnia the most common of all sleep disorders, in which a person has difficulty falling asleep or staying asleep

hypnotics sleeping pills that may be prescribed by a physician and are intended to promote sleep

tion, because many elderly people are already taking other medicines, they may suffer from adverse drug interactions. In order to avoid such problems, many practitioners are suggesting the use of *stimulus control therapy*. In this therapy, the person is conditioned to associate bed and bedroom with only one event—sleep. Everything else that occurs in that person's life takes place somewhere else. Thus, when the person goes to bed, the dominant response of sleep is the most probable behavior to be evoked by the "bed stimulus." Other behavioral techniques for treating insomnia include restricting a person's time in bed, with the aim of improving sleep efficiency (called *sleep restriction therapy*), and psychotherapy (Bertelson and Walsh, 1987).

Narcolepsy. Unlike insomnia, in which the individual has trouble falling asleep, a person with **narcolepsy** (narco = numbness; lepsy = seizure) has inappropriate sleep attacks (Kolb and Whishaw, 1990). The term *narcolepsy* was first used by Jean Baptiste Gelineau in 1880 to describe a condition wherein, at any time of day, a person may collapse into sleep. Often the uncontrollable entrance into sleep occurs in embarrassing and inappropriate moments, such as during a conversation with someone or preparing to give an important address at a key business meeting. Narcolepsy is surprisingly common, affecting between two and five persons out of every thousand. The onset of narcolepsy is generally first witnessed between the ages of 10 and 20, and once the sleep disturbances begin, they continue throughout life.

Narcolepsy has four characteristic features: (1) sleep attacks; (2) cataplexy; (3) sleep paralysis; and (4) auditory, visual, or tactile hallucinations that occur just as the person drifts into sleep. The sleep attacks are usually brief, lasting only 15 min or so, but they may occur in the middle of physical activities such as sexual intercourse or chasing down a fly ball in center field. As a rule, once the individual has an attack, she or he is resistant to a second attack for several hours. Cataplexy is a sudden loss of muscle tone that is often triggered by intense emotions such as anger or laughter. The danger for people suffering from narcolepsy is that their legs may buckle and they may fall and hurt themselves during the attack. In sleep paralysis the person cannot move during the transition period between wakefulness and sleeping, which make victims afraid. Most hallucinations are frightening anyway, but the inability to move accentuates the terror during the attack.

Over the years, many questions have been raised about the causes of narcolepsy. Is it genetically based? Why do people with narcolepsy sleep so much? What role does the internal biological clock play in the expression of the disorder? Although research findings have placed us in a position to better address these important questions, we do not have a full understanding of the origins and development of narcolepsy (Webb, 1992). It does seem to be somewhat more prevalent in certain families, yet no genetic basis for the disorder has been identified. Regarding the issue of total sleep time, it has been determined that people with narcolepsy have the same amount of total sleep time as normal individuals, they just need to go to sleep more often (Pollack, 1989). This may be the result of flattened circadian rhythms in which the day and night patterns look very much the same (Broughton, 1989).

Various drugs have been used in the treatment of narcolepsy but with only limited success. Some chemicals are more effective at alleviating one symptom; others more effectively control another. Until more help is forthcoming, people suffering from narcolepsy must live in an uncertain world.

Think about how disquieting it is not to know when another attack will come. Would you feel safe driving a car? What about working around machinery? What sort of behavioral interventions can you think of that might assist the control of this disorder?

narcolepsy inappropriate sleep attacks in which a person involuntarily falls asleep during the middle of a waking episode

Sudden Infant Death Syndrome. Perhaps the sleep disorder that receives the most public attention is **sudden infant death syndrome (SIDS)**. *SIDS* refers to the sudden unexplained death of an apparently healthy infant during the first year of life (Anch et al., 1988). Just knowing that such a phenomenon occurs, however infrequently, is enough to frighten parents to the point of losing sleep. To think that your baby, although completely healthy, may not survive the night is tormenting. A great amount of literature offers only a meager understanding of this important but complex syndrome.

The suggestion has been made that SIDS may result from the infant's inability to wake up from a deep sleep. During the night, it is typical for the airway to become obstructed momentarily, but the normal reaction is that the infant wakes, clears the throat, and returns to sleep without gaining full consciousness. It may be that the SIDS victim never makes the switch from sleep to waking, thus the airway is not cleared and death results. Some support for this idea is available from studies that show that the siblings of SIDS victims exhibit longer intervals between REM sleep, or abnormal NREM-REM-awake sequences (Webb, 1992). Still, this hypothesis remains largely speculative.

Other attempts to understand SIDS point to the possibility that the development of identifiable sleep stages may be delayed in SIDS victims. Specifically, it has been proposed that the coordination between heart rate and various respiration measures present at birth in most newborns is not evident in SIDS victims. Confirming this idea, Schechtman et al. (1990) have shown that heart rate and breathing in infants who died from SIDS were uncorrelated, unlike the correlated patterns of control babies who did not develop SIDS. Most important, this disrupted pattern was apparent in the first 2 weeks of life. Because the vast majority of SIDS deaths occur between 2 and 4 months of age, such an early warning device might be able to predict SIDS. Yet, because the research in this area is barely underway, firm conclusions are not possible at this time. Obviously, this is an area of sleep research that begs for more work to be completed.

What can be done? Some parents have resorted to devices that monitor the breathing of their baby and are designed to trigger an alarm in the parent's bedroom when the infant quits breathing. Numerous commercial models of these monitors are available, but unfortunately there is no solid evidence, at least at this time, that such hardware will actually prevent SIDS. In the final analysis, not much can be done at present in terms of controlling this deadly and heartbreaking sleep dysfunction.

Sleep Apnea. The term **sleep apnea** refers to a rare disorder that occurs during sleep when a person stops breathing for no apparent reason. Technically, sleep apnea is defined as the condition that occurs when a person ceases to breathe for as long as 10 sec after falling asleep. Research on sleep apnea has a history of little more than a decade, and not much is known about what causes it. Originally, a person was diagnosed as suffering from sleep apnea only if he or she stopped breathing at least five times during the night (Webb, 1992). However, now the clinical diagnosis of the disorder is based more on an overall pattern of symptoms than specific criteria.

Included in the list of behaviors that characterize sleep apnea are daytime sleepiness, fatigue, loss of memory, and recurring morning headaches. During sleep, the person often snores loudly before stopping breathing and may exhibit many unusual spasmodic movements during the sleep period. Although the disorder may be evident in most anyone, typically the person is male, is excessively overweight, and may have high blood pressure.

One of the greatest characteristics of patients who exhibit sleep apnea is fear. A colleague of the authors who suffers from the disorder reported that

sudden infant death syndrome (SIDS) during sleep, a sudden inexplicable death of an infant who has been in perfectly good health

sleep apnea a rare sleeping disorder in which the person stops breathing momentarily

he was afraid to fall asleep because he might die while sleeping. On occasion, he would awaken when he wasn't breathing and feel he was suffocating. The chances of actually dying are virtually nil, but the disorder can cause considerable anxiety and sleep loss, ultimately leading to the daytime fatigue mentioned previously. Professional help is available for sleep apnea, and family members should encourage spouses and other relatives who show symptoms of the disorder to seek treatment.

Sleepwalking.   Have you ever known a person who gets up in the middle of the night and walks about the apartment or house, opens doors, moves a lamp from one location to another, returns to bed, and has no recollection of any of this activity in the morning when she or he awakes? This form of sleepwalking is called **somnambulism**; at one time it was believed to be a result of neurotic dreaming that was symptomatic of some underlying psychological problem. We now know that this is not true. Sleepwalking is not a dream state at all; it occurs during slow wave sleep (stage 4) and not during the REM state that is commonly associated with dreaming.

As a rule, sleepwalking is restricted to simple repetitive movements such as getting out of bed and getting dressed, undressed, and dressed again. The length of the sleepwalking episode may be as short as a few minutes or as long as a half-hour or more (Anch et al., 1988). The person doesn't remember anything that happens during the sleepwalk.

Sleepwalking may occur as infrequently as once in a lifetime or as often as several times a week. The disorder tends to peak during early adolescence, and then the frequency seems to gradually decrease with age. Only about 5% of the population of students are likely to be true sleepwalkers. Of course, there is always the possibility that a sleepwalker may get hurt during a sleepwalking episode, but this is not as much an issue for older persons as it is for younger children. Parents who have children who sleepwalk must be very careful to keep doors latched and to protect them from falling down stairs, into swimming pools, and so on.

No one knows what causes sleepwalking. The various explanations offered over the years have not been supported empirically. At present, the best advice is probably not to worry about the condition, be sure the person is not harmed during the episode, and gently guide him or her back to bed. More often than not, the situation will pass.

Sleeptalking.   Life as a college student often means that you live with a roommate in relatively tight quarters, studying together, sleeping in the same room, and so on. Accordingly, if a student is going to talk in his or her sleep, there likely will be someone who will be available to file a full report at a later time. It goes without saying that such reports have added appreciably to the college experience.

Not much in the way of scientific information is available on the dynamics of sleeptalking. What evidence that does exist seems to indicate that sleeptalking is most likely during stage 1, and clearly during NREM, so it has little if anything to do with dreaming. Because sleeptalking is apparently associated with stage 1 sleep, which occurs immediately after one "drifts off," some sleep researchers suggest that sleeptalking occurs during a period when the individual is "half asleep, half awake." This may be why it is sometimes easy to carry on an actual conversation with the sleeptalker.

There are no reliable data to indicate that sleeptalking is correlated with stress, emotional fatigue, or any other psychological variables. If you wake the person, more than likely the individual will just return to sleep and have no memory of what was said. This approach may result in a more restful night for *both* the talker and the uninterested listener.

somnambulism sleepwalking that typically involves repetitive acts performed while asleep that are not recalled once the person wakes

DREAMING

For most people, dreaming represents a venture into another world over which they have little control. Some dreams are famous as visions, foretelling years of famine and years of plenty. Others have provided poetic inspiration, such as Coleridge's tale of Kubla Khan, and still others have illuminated scientific development, such as Kekule's discovery of the structure of benzene (see Figure 5–13). Some dreams bring great pleasure; others cause concern. Until the discovery of REM sleep, researchers had no way of telling when someone was dreaming. In studies prior to that time, subjects were randomly awakened in the hope of catching a dream or asked to keep dream diaries for analysis.

There is still only one way to know if someone is dreaming, and that is to wake the person and ask for a dream report. It is true that REM sleep is highly correlated with dreaming, but in about 15% of REM awakenings, people fail to report dreaming. Further, about 20% of the time, people report dreaming in NREM sleep. Some researchers discount the NREM dream accounts because they lack the vividness of imagery and detail of content seen in REM reports. These differences in imagery and content are meaningful. Nevertheless, after being awakened from NREM sleep, people have given verbal reports that, using even the most stringent requirements, would qualify as dreams (Antrobus, 1983).

EEG studies of infants in the sleep lab tell us that babies spend a lot of their time in REM sleep. But are they dreaming? No one can answer this question because infants cannot provide verbal reports. One question that is often raised about infant dreaming has to do with the possible content of their dreams. What might they dream about? Their experiences in life are very limited. The psychological experts in this field speculate that dreaming does not exist in newborns, but probably begins sometime in the second or third year of life.

All mammals experience REM sleep, and there is some evidence that REM sleep occurs in birds as well (Bon, Benassi, & Morigi, 1983). Do these animals dream? Dog fanciers often relate their observations of Fido chasing cats while asleep, usually citing small twitches of the paws to support their speculation. Although many people are convinced that their pets dream, there is no evidence to substantiate these claims because we cannot ask animals to tell us their dreams.

FIGURE 5–13
Belgian postage stamp commemorating the discovery of benzene in 1865 by chemist Frederich August Kekule. He is said to have discovered the molecular structure of benzene when he dreamed about a chain of snakes that formed a ring in which each snake was biting the tail of another.

Dream Recall

All sleep researchers know people who say they do not dream. Yet when tested in the sleep laboratory and awakened during a REM sleep period, a large percentage of these "nondreamers" do recall a dream. This finding has led to the conclusion that there are few nondreamers in the world (if any), and that people who say they do not dream are in fact nonrecallers. Why is it that some people can recall their dreams so easily whereas others can never seem to remember a dream?

We have said that the average sleeper has about four or five REM sleep periods each night. The first one, which usually onsets about 90 min after the beginning of sleep, is brief—typically, it lasts 5 min or so. As the night goes on, REM periods increase in length so that the last one may be as long as 45 min or more. In some dream research studies, subjects who were awakened at each of the nightly REM periods generally produced a dream report (in about 85% of the cases). This means that the average sleeper has four dreams per night. But, how many of these dreams are usually recalled during the day? On average, slightly less than one dream is recalled. People who recall as many as two or three dreams each day are extremely rare. At the other end of the dream-recall spectrum are those people who may recall one dream every 4 to 6 months (Koulack & Goodenough, 1976).

Some dream researchers have subjected the differences between good dream recallers and poor dream recallers to intensive investigation. A logical assumption that guided initial research was that because dream recall is basically a memory task, people with better memories should be better dream recallers. However, that hypothesis proved to be wrong. Then in 1975, researchers tested subjects using several different kinds of memory measures, including visual memory. Subjects were shown a picture containing an array of items. They were allowed only a brief look at the picture and then were asked to recall as many of the items as they could. Subjects who recalled more of the items from the picture, a visual memory task, proved to be better dream recallers as well. This finding makes a lot of sense intuitively, because dreams consist largely of visual imagery (Cory et al., 1975).

Why do we forget so many of our dreams? One of the popular answers to this question involves the **repression hypothesis**. This hypothesis, which states that forgetting dreams is a defensive act to keep the person from experiencing troublesome dream content, is developed principally from the theories of Sigmund Freud (see Figure 5–14). In *The Interpretation of Dreams* (1900/1955), Freud proposed that dreams are essentially the fulfillment of wishes, some of which would be taboo in the waking world. When the person is awake, a simple way to deal with these potentially threatening dreams is not to remember them, to repress them. Freud noted that even when dreams were recalled, the real meaning of the dream was often hidden. He called this hidden meaning the **latent content** of the dream, which was represented only symbolically in the version of the dream as recalled by the dreamer. Freud named the dream content that the dreamer actually recalled the **manifest content**.

repression hypothesis a Freudian hypothesis that our inability to recall the content of dreams derives from the threatening nature of the dream; forgetting protects us from unpleasant dream material

latent content the hidden part of the dream that is obscured by various dream processes

manifest content that part of the dream that is available for report

FIGURE 5–14
This photograph shows a small portion of Sigmund Freud's collection of Greek, Roman, and Egyptian antiquities. His intense interest in ancient cultures provided him with some of the symbolism described in one of his classic books, *The Interpretation of Dreams*.

Another explanation of differences in dream recall is the **salience hypothesis**, which argues that emotionally arousing dreams are more easily recalled than others. The salience effect is thought to occur because the emotional impact of the dream is likely to increase the awareness of the dreamer of that particular dream (Reinsel, Wollman, & Antrobus, 1984). A third explanation of the problem of recalling dreams is the **interference hypothesis**. Proponents of this view argue that people forget dreams because of interfering events that occur at the time they awake or throughout the day following the dream. For example, research on this hypothesis has noted that people recall dreams better when they are awakened suddenly than when they are awakened gradually.

At this time there are insufficient data to say which of these hypotheses may better account for our forgetting of dreams. There is better experimental support for the salience and interference hypotheses, but all three probably play some role in dream recall (Cohen, 1970, 1974). They are clearly not opposing views.

salience hypothesis the idea that highly emotional dreams are more likely to be remembered because of increased awareness of the dream content

interference hypothesis an account of dreaming that states that our inability to recall dreams is due to the interfering effects of events that occur after the dream takes place

Dream Content

One way to study dreams is to study their content. This can be done by laboratory studies in which sleepers are awakened during REM sleep and their dream reports are tape recorded. Subjects can also keep a dream diary in which they write all they can remember about their dreams. These different methods have revealed some interesting facts about the nature of dream content.

What causes you to dream the things you dream? That question cannot be answered as yet (see Rados & Cartwright, 1982). Research can point to individual cases where the dream content is obviously related to immediate events in a person's life, but the reason why a lot of dreams occur is something of a mystery. One explanation of dream content proposes that during REM sleep specific brain neurons are activated, such as those involved in running or laughing or hearing. In an attempt to make sense of this specific neural activation, the brain produces a dream based on a synthesis of the stimulation present. Called the **activation-synthesis hypothesis** of dreaming, this view does account for the seemingly random dream content that often occurs, and it is consistent with the neurological changes known to accompany REM sleep (Hobson & McCarley, 1977). However, it does not explain the coherence, detail, and purposefulness common to many dreams. Studies of dream content must now recognize that dreamers may alter their content while they are actually dreaming.

activation-synthesis hypothesis the idea that dreams represent a blending of thoughts that are produced by spontaneous neural activation during the REM period

---

THINKING ABOUT
Lucid Dreaming

For most people, the content of their dreams is beyond their control. How often have you gone to bed wishing you could dream about a particular someone, or afraid you might dream about an especially distressing subject? Sometimes in dreaming we think to ourselves that "this is a dream." Yet in the morning if we remember the dream and recall thinking that we knew it was a dream at the time, we find that we still accepted the content as plausible, even if events in the dream would be unlikely or impossible in real life. Some people are able to carry this awareness during dreaming a step fur-

lucid dreaming dreaming in which a person is aware of dreaming

ther: they claim the ability to know when they are dreaming and to actually control some or all of the content of their dreams. This phenomenon is known as **lucid dreaming**. In the past such claims have attracted little interest from dream researchers because there seemed no way to test these assertions. However, working with the sleep research lab at Stanford University, Stephen LaBerge, a lucid dreamer, was able to demonstrate his special ability. LaBerge told the researchers that during dreams he would suddenly become aware that he was dreaming and that he could signal the researchers of this awareness by a prearranged pattern of eye movements. They agreed on a mixture of horizontal and vertical eye movements that he would use when he knew he was dreaming. The probability that the particular eye movement pattern would appear by chance was infinitesimally small. During the night the researchers watched the EEG records, and in one of the REM sleep periods, to their excitement and delight, they saw the coded eye movement pattern (LaBerge et al., 1981). Other lucid dreamers have since been identified and are being studied.

It is not known how many people have the ability for lucid dreaming. Surveys based on self-report provide estimates of between 15 and 28%. Laboratory studies of lucid dreaming usually begin by asking people if they frequently are aware of their dreams while dreaming. Those who say that they have that ability are tested in the sleep laboratory, and most are able to demonstrate their lucid dreaming ability using some prearranged signal (typically an eye movement code, sometimes a respiration pattern). These studies have found that lucid dreamers are not lucid in all of their dreams; in fact, the majority of their dreams are nonlucid. Many subjects can become aware of their dreaming, but few can manipulate their dream content. Still, some studies have been successful in giving instructions about specific dream content to lucid dreamers and having them dream about those subjects. When lucid dreams occur, they are more likely to be in the longer REM sleep periods toward morning. Further, physiological activation (e.g., heart rate, respiration rate) is significantly higher during lucid dreams (LaBerge, Greenleaf, & Kedzierski, 1983; LaBerge, Levitan, & Dement, 1986).

Researchers hope to discover how lucid dreaming is possible because the phenomenon has some interesting implications for our understanding of consciousness. For in essence, the lucid dreamer is partly in one state of consciousness, the dream, and partly in a totally different state of consciousness, the awareness of the dream. A practical application of this research might be an understanding of the process so that many dreamers could learn how to control their dream content (Galvin, 1982).

Have you ever had a lucid dream in which you felt you were part awake and part asleep? How often does it occur? What do you think your last dream really meant?

Dream Interpretation

The interpretation or analysis of dreams remains one of the most controversial topics in psychology. A number of disparate views on this subject exist, ranging from the notion that all dreams are interpretable in a psychoanalytic framework (Freud, Carl Jung) to the idea that dream content is essentially randomly generated from the memory stores of the brain and thus meaningless (activation-synthesis hypothesis). We adopt a position somewhere in the middle of this controversy, believing that dreams probably have meaning for the dreamer and may be accurately interpreted by the dreamer or by someone who knows the dreamer well.

The psychology shelves in bookstores typically contain numerous books on how to interpret your dreams (see Figure 5–15). These books are of very questionable value because they all assume some universal symbolism in dreams. Does dreaming of reaching for an apple mean the dreamer is reaching for something that is forbidden? Perhaps. It might also mean that the dreamer is hungry, that the dreamer has a job picking apples, that the dreamer hopes to buy a computer, that the dreamer is considering accepting a job in New York City, and so forth. Again, the dreamer may be in a good position to know the best answer as would a good friend of the dreamer or the dreamer's therapist. But a book interpreting dreams is likely to be no more useful than one on astrology in terms of its accuracy.

Dream interpretation is a critical element of Freudian theory, and it is an essential treatment tool for the analyst. In addition to the Freudian focus on the symbolic nature of dream processes, some believe that dreams accurately portray the way we really feel and think. Freud once recounted an episode following a lecture he gave on the notion that dreams fulfill unconscious desires that cannot be acted on at a conscious level.

> She [a woman protesting Freud's assertion] reported that a few years previously, her oldest nephew had died. Since she was unmarried and lived in her brother's house, the loss of the nephew was like the loss of a son, and it left the household with only one child, a younger nephew. She then reported a recurring dream in which she is standing in front of the younger nephew's casket, accompanied by a military officer friend of her brother. The woman exclaimed, "Certainly you [Freud] cannot mean that this dream represents my wish for the death of my only remaining nephew!" After questioning the woman briefly, Freud discovered that the officer in the dream was unmarried and attractive to her, and that she had not seen him in waking life since the funeral of the older nephew. Freud concluded that the unconscious wish underlying this dream was to once again be standing near the officer, and with the death of the younger nephew, this could be accomplished. The dream image, therefore, more accurately reflects the true self than the waking image, and provides some satisfaction for lustful ambitions (adapted from Rainville, 1988).

Which is the real us? Is the dream state a more genuine description of what we are all about, or are our conscious deliberations, which are free of distorting symbolism and hidden meanings, really better indicators of who and what we are? Probably, both viewpoints have something to offer; they represent two different perspectives on the way we see ourselves. But the idea that the unconscious dream world is accurate and the waking world inaccurate is not accepted by most present-day psychologists.

In any event, it is fun to think about our own dreams and explore their contents. What dreams have you had lately? Are they recurring?

Some people have little interest in their dreams. They make no great effort to recall them, and they do not try to discover the meaning of those they do recall. Real dream aficionados are aghast at this lack of interest. For them, not exploring your dreams is like not bothering to look at photo albums of your life. You have to decide for yourself whether you wish to spend some of your time thinking about your dream life. As we said earlier, most dreams, if not all, have meaning for the dreamer (see Figure 5–16). You need not assume that the meaning of the dream is hidden and requires interpretation. Instead, you can examine the dream as you recall it. If you are a serious observer of your dreams, you may want to keep a dream diary. That allows you to look at a large series of dreams instead of just a single dream, and the series will likely be more revealing to you than will any one dream. Remember the principle of simplicity in exploring your dreams— that is, do not accept a complicated or improbable interpretation if a simpler and more believable one exists.

FIGURE 5–15
The book pictured here is the English translation (1644) of the five-volume *The Interpretation of Dreams*, originally written by the Greek philosopher Artemidorus in the second century, A.D. Portions of this book foreshadow more modern ideas, for example, his belief that some dreams represent wish fulfillments.

FIGURE 5-16
Dreams have special significance in the history of American Indians, who often viewed them as visions of the future. Black Elk, a Sioux holy man and cousin of the legendary warrior Crazy Horse, was 9 years old when spirits took him to another world where he was given a great vision about the rebirth of his people. That dream governed his entire life. When he was quite old, he told the story of the vision to historian/poet John Neihardt, who published *Black Elk Speaks* in 1932. The painting shown here is by Standing Bear and shows Black Elk in the flaming rainbow teepee with the "six grandfathers" (the powers of the earth and sky). This book had a profound influence on the dream theory of Carl Gustav Jung (discussed in Chapter 10).

night terror class of nightmare that usually occurs during stage 4 sleep

REM nightmare bad dream common in late childhood

Nightmares and Night Terrors

As indicated at the beginning of this chapter, nightmares have been the source of inspiration for a considerable amount of literature and art. These troublesome dreams occur across all ages, but they are most common in children. One especially terrifying class of nightmares is more correctly called a **night terror**, and its peak occurrence is in children of preschool age. In night terrors the child awakens screaming. Obvious signs of fear are present: increased heart rate, rapid breathing, and dilated pupils. These children are usually disoriented; they do not seem aware of where they are or who has come to help them. This disorientation may last for 5 min or more. Children recall very little, if any, dream content associated with the night terror, and in the morning they are unable to remember the awakening episode at all. One other fact that makes this kind of nightmare different from others is that it occurs when the sleeper is in stage 4 sleep. Is the person then dreaming? No one knows if the night terror arises from dream content or not, but clearly fright is experienced. Although this condition is distressing for the parents, the usual recommendation is to wait and see if the night terrors disappear on their own. If they persist, therapy may be indicated (Hauri, 1982).

Most people experience nightmares as a part of REM sleep (called **REM nightmares**) and can recall the disturbing content of the dream quite completely. The peak age for these nightmares is between the ages of 7 and 10, although they are still common during the adolescent years. Adults have nightmares infrequently, and they are usually associated with times of stress, such as studying for the Certified Public Accountant's exam, going through a divorce, or adjusting to a new job. Research shows that nightmares are more common in the longer REM sleep periods, and that nightmares are rare if the REM period is less than 20 min, indicating that REM nightmares occur later in the night (Hartmann, 1970, 1981).

College students have a higher incidence of nightmares than other people their age, probably because of the many stresses associated with college life. Surveys of the content of nightmares among college students have revealed an interesting finding: the most commonly recurrent nightmare theme is about missing an exam or an entire course! (See Robbins & Houshi, 1983.)

Functions of Dreams

As we conclude our discussion of dreaming, the major question still remains: Why do we dream? A multitude of theories have been offered to answer that question, yet few have earned much scientific support. We mention only a few of those theories here. Remember that dreaming is highly correlated with REM sleep; thus, in speculating about dream function it is often impossible to separate the two.

As previously discussed, Freud believed the purpose of dreaming was wish fulfillment, to enable the dreamer to achieve at a fantasy level goals that would not be allowed in waking life because of social taboos. Another psychoanalyst, Carl Jung, proposed that dreams are used to process important experiences that have been repressed during the day. In the dream the person is able to work through these experiences and perhaps be better adjusted by that process. Thus, the dominant theme for a psychoanalytic theory of dream function is that of problem solving and psychological adjustment.

Biological theories of dream function have emphasized changes in the central nervous system, particularly in the forebrain. More specifically, it has been suggested that dreaming (and REM sleep) may be involved in the repair of neurons through increased levels of protein synthesis (Cohen, 1979).

Cognitive theories have stressed the benefits of dreaming for information processing and for the consolidation of memories (see Chapter 7). Dream deprivation studies (which are REM deprivation studies) have shown deficits in thinking and memory. Nobel laureate Francis Crick (codiscoverer of the structure of DNA) has proposed that the purpose of dreaming is ridding the memory of useless or nonsensical information (Crick & Mitchison, 1983). An interesting addition to the theories in this category is the view of dreaming as important for information processing within the right hemisphere of the brain. Proponents of this view argue that waking activity provides ample stimulation for the left hemisphere but not for the right one. Thus, dreaming is a compensatory activity that maintains the right hemisphere so that it is capable of carrying out its functions (see Chapter 2). Of course, dreaming may do all of these things. Or dreams may exist to provide us with entertainment during the night. The shows are free, and rarely do we have to endure reruns.

HYPNOSIS

Hypnosis is an altered state of consciousness that a person enters voluntarily with the aid of another person (the hypnotist). Experienced subjects can hypnotize themselves (self-hypnosis), but commonly someone is present to induce the hypnotic state in someone else (see Figure 5–17). Hypnosis has been called sleeplike, but it is clearly not a state of sleep; at least, the brain wave patterns in hypnosis do not resemble sleep. The person in hypnosis is usually quite relaxed and the eyes may be closed, but there the similarities with sleep end. In hypnosis the person is quite alert, although attention may be very focused, for example, attending only to the voice of the hypnotist. The person may even become quite emotional or physically active at the hypnotist's suggestion.

Much of our understanding of hypnosis comes from scientific investigations over the past 30 years, stemming partly from the use of hypnosis as an anesthetic for surgical procedures. However, for much of this century, hypnosis has been used in psychotherapy. Modern research on hypnosis has helped us understand a number of interesting facts about this mysterious state of consciousness. Scientists today are less likely to argue whether or

hypnosis sleeplike state that a person enters with the aid of another person

FIGURE 5–17
The beginnings of hypnosis can be traced to the Austrian physician Franz Mesmer (1734–1815), who practiced what he called "animal magnetism" as a means of treating his patients. Mesmer's methods were so controversial that King Louis XVI of France formed a commission to investigate the phenomenon. The commission concluded that animal magnetism was without validity, and the topic remained in ill repute for much of the nineteenth century. The name "hypnosis" was coined by James Braid (1795–1860), whose research gave some measure of respectability to hypnosis as a legitimate phenomenon.

posthypnotic suggestions responses to suggestions given under hypnosis after emerging from the hypnotic state

not hypnosis works; rather, they focus on *how* hypnosis works, and for the most part, that question remains unanswered.

Hypnotic Susceptibility

Some sources claim that all people can be hypnotized to at least some degree (Wallace, 1979). Clearly, however, people differ with regard to hypnotic susceptibility, and researchers have developed tests to identify subjects who are highly susceptible to hypnotic suggestion. Psychologists Andre Weitzenhoffer and Ernest Hilgard developed one such susceptibility scale. They found that like many psychological variables, hypnotizability is normally distributed, meaning that most people are moderately susceptible, whereas about 5 to 10% of all people are either very highly susceptible or not susceptible at all. Susceptibility tests are frequently used to select subjects for use in hypnosis research (Hilgard, 1965). Hypnotic susceptibility reaches its peak around 9 to 11 years of age and declines throughout adolescence. However, it is a relatively stable trait in adulthood. Retesting of adults after 10 years shows stability of susceptibility scores similar to the stability obtained in intelligence testing (Spiegel, 1987).

What determines a person's susceptibility is not clear. Heredity plays some role, as demonstrated by studies on fraternal and identical twins, which show more susceptibility for identical twins (Morgan, 1973). But environment also plays a role, and research indicates that experiences during childhood, such as having parents with vivid imaginations, are linked to the development of hypnotic susceptibility.

Hypnotic Phenomena

A number of claims are made for hypnosis, and some of these have not been substantiated. In the following discussion, we describe the phenomena of hypnosis that have some scientific standing.

Increased Suggestibility. Under hypnosis, individuals are quite suggestible, even when the level of hypnosis is very light. Of course, they must be suggestible to be hypnotized in the first place. Subjects may be made to experience any number of emotions, including the physiological changes that normally accompany particular emotions. They can be made to appear blind, deaf, and insensitive to pain. They can be told that their arms are steel bars and cannot bend, and indeed they are unable to bend them. These dramatic effects cannot be induced in all subjects, but under hypnosis the subject is ready to accept suggestions and generally does.

Can subjects under hypnosis be made to engage in actions that would go against their moral beliefs? Most experts in the field of hypnosis don't think so, but they add that people can be made to go against their own values if the hypnotist can structure the suggestion in a particular way. For example, a man who would never undress in front of strangers might be made to do so if he believed that his clothes were covered with biting ants. In general, however, people who are hypnotized are not mindless robots that can be totally manipulated by the hypnotist; hypnotized subjects maintain considerable control over their behavior and often refuse to comply with the suggestions given them.

Posthypnotic Suggestions. Under hypnosis, subjects can be given a suggestion to be carried out later when they are no longer hypnotized. These **posthypnotic suggestions** are usually linked to a particular stimulus. For instance, the subject under hypnosis might be told by the hypnotist, "When I cough, you are to take off your glasses." After the hypnotic session is concluded and the subject and hypnotist are talking, the hypnotist can test the posthypnotic suggestion by coughing. Typically, the subject removes the glasses as instructed. Interestingly, when questioned, the subject does not give the suggestion as a reason for taking off the glasses. Instead, the subject gives reasons like "My eyes were watering" or "I saw a spot on one of my lenses."

Posthypnotic Amnesia.   Another of the posthypnotic phenomena that is easily demonstrated is that of causing the subject, by suggestion, to forget what was said and done during either the entire hypnotic session or for only a portion of it. The subject can even be induced to forget material that was not a part of the session. Hypnosis researcher Martin Orne (1966) told subjects to forget the number 3. After the hypnosis was ended, Orne had subjects count, and typically they would say "1, 2, 4, 5, . . . 21, 22, 24," and so forth. Not surprisingly, some of these subjects felt quite incompetent.

Subjects differ widely in their response to the suggestions for posthypnotic amnesia (Cooper, 1979); some subjects will comply with the suggestion and others will not. In most studies involving posthypnotic amnesia, researchers arrange a signal in hypnosis that will restore the subjects' memory in the posthypnotic state. Thus, for those subjects who show the forgetting, recall of the material can be restored by a snap of the fingers or some other prearranged cue. The fact that the subjects can recall the forgotten material indicates that the forgetting in posthypnotic amnesia represents a retrieval problem, not a problem of encoding or storing the learned material.

The Hidden Observer.   While performing a demonstration on hypnosis for one of his classes in the 1970s, Ernest Hilgard (see Figure 5–18) made a most amazing discovery. Using a blind subject, Hilgard induced deafness under hypnosis. He told the subject he would not be able to hear, except when Hilgard placed his hand on the subject's shoulder. The subject indeed seemed deaf; oblivious to the sounds around him and bored with the lack of stimulation, he began to think about a problem in statistics. Someone in the class wondered if he really could not hear. Hilgard asked the subject, "If there is some part of you that can hear, then raise your index finger." To the surprise of the class, Hilgard, and the subject, the finger was raised.

Then Hilgard asked for a report from "that part of you that listened to me before and made your finger rise" (Hebb, 1982). At the same time, Hilgard instructed the subject that he would not be able to hear what he himself was saying. It became obvious that there was a part of the subject's consciousness that had heard everything that was going on in the room and could report on it. Yet the rest of the subject's consciousness was unaware of the auditory events in the room and the existence of the "hearing" part of his consciousness. Hilgard named this phenomenon the **hidden observer**, using that term as a metaphor for a concealed form of consciousness existing during hypnosis.

Experiments on the hidden observer in hypnosis have now been performed by a number of researchers. Although the studies are not without criticism, the hidden observer phenomenon is accepted as a reliable hypnotic event. However, it does not occur in a number of subjects, a fact that is being investigated. Hilgard (1977) has described his work on the hidden observer in a book that offers a new theory of hypnosis, viewing it as a form of divided consciousness. One part of consciousness responds to the suggestions of the hypnotist while the other observes the situation. A subject's arm can be placed in very cold water while in hypnosis, and the subject may be told that there is no feeling in the arm. When questioned, the subject will

FIGURE 5–18
Ernest R. Hilgard, professor of psychology at Stanford University, has been one of the most important researchers contributing to our knowledge about hypnosis. His discovery of the "hidden observer" has dramatically influenced the modern study of consciousness.

hidden observer during hypnosis, a part of consciousness is unaffected by the hypnosis procedure and appears to monitor unconscious operations

report no pain; however, the hidden observer can be called upon to describe the pain that was experienced.

This discovery is extremely important because it provides a totally new way to view hypnosis, in which one part of consciousness is altered and one part is not. Hilgard's discovery calls into question the very notion of the existence of an unconscious. Memories that cannot be recalled may be, rather than part of an unconscious, part of another stream of consciousness that can be reported when the stimulus conditions are right for revealing that information (Hebb, 1980b).

Uses of Hypnosis

As research helps us to understand hypnosis more fully, the usefulness of this process will increase as a therapy technique and as an adjunct to therapy. For some time, psychologists have used hypnosis with little understanding of how it works or of why it works for some people and not for others. For example, sports psychologists have used it with certain athletes to enhance performance. In its clinical usage, hypnosis often serves as an aid to another therapeutic procedure, such as *cognitive restructuring*, in which patients are taught new ways of thinking about their problems. Hypnosis is also used as an adjunct in various forms of psychotherapy to extract information that is helpful to the psychologist or psychiatrist (Frankel, 1976).

But the greatest success of hypnosis has been in the control of pain, either by substantially reducing it or eliminating it. Children, because of their increased hypnotic susceptibility, are particularly good candidates for pain control. One study of children with leukemia found they were able to substantially reduce the pain they experienced from a bone marrow transplant procedure. The discovery of endorphins led many to assume that hypnosis acts like a placebo in causing the body to release these natural painkillers.

But more recent studies using naloxone (recall from Chapter 2 that this drug blocks the activity of endorphins) have shown that the pain-reduction effects occur even in the absence of endorphin activity. Spiegel (1987) rejects the biological theories and argues for a cognitive one. He proposes that hypnosis works in pain control by focusing the patient's attention on something other than the pain, often a sensation in another part of the person's body, or by having the patient imagine the painful area has been deadened with an anesthetic such as novocaine. Although the mechanism is still under debate, the effectiveness of hypnosis in pain control is not. Hypnosis works for many pain sufferers on acute pain as well as chronic pain, without the negative side effects of addictive drugs—our next topic.

DRUGS AND THEIR EFFECTS ON CONSCIOUSNESS

Psychologists have long been interested in drugs because these substances often produce dramatic behavioral changes. Most drugs that affect behavior act through the nervous system, including the biochemical aspects of that system (for example, neurotransmitters), or less commonly, through the endocrine system.

Drugs are a common feature of most cultures and have been used for centuries as a means of altering states of consciousness. There are many kinds of drugs, but we restrict our discussion in this chapter to those that produce changes in consciousness, including perception and mood. **Psychoactive drugs** are ones that produce these kinds of changes. The use of particular drugs varies from culture to culture. In North America, the three most widely

psychoactive drugs drugs that produce changes in perception and mood

used psychoactive drugs are *caffeine* (found in coffee and many soft drinks), *nicotine* (in tobacco products), and *alcohol*. These drugs may be obtained legally, although most localities impose age restrictions, and some communities actually prohibit the sale of alcoholic beverages. One way to classify drugs is by using the labels "licit" and "illicit," meaning legal and illegal, respectively. These labels largely reflect the acceptance of drugs by a particular society and are not necessarily related to the potential harm drugs can cause. For example, cigarette smoking persists as an acceptable, even government-subsidized, form of drug use in the face of overwhelming evidence of its role in heart disease, cancer, and respiratory disorders.

Reasons for using drugs are quite varied. Some people use them as a way of feeling better, perhaps by achieving a measure of euphoria or by enabling themselves to forget troubles and reduce anxiety. Some people use drugs to get to sleep, and others use them to reduce pain. Many people take drugs to relax, for example before a job interview or before flying. Others take drugs to increase their alertness, as when studying for an exam or working a night shift. Many people use drugs in social situations because of the acceptance provided within the group. And some individuals use drugs because of the greatly enhanced perceptual experiences that are induced; for example, some drugs produce visual hallucinations.

Table 5–1 lists the most common psychoactive drugs, as well as the source of the drug, how the drug is taken, the duration of its effect, its medical uses (if any), and its addictive potential. The drugs in this table are grouped in four categories: narcotics, depressants, stimulants, and hallucinogens.

Narcotics

An *opiate* drug is any drug that either occurs naturally or is produced synthetically and has properties similar to opium. Examples of such drugs are morphine, heroin, and codeine. The term **narcotic** is often used to refer to this family of drugs. Narcotics have traditionally been used in medicine to alleviate pain and suffering, but heroin has also served as the major opiate of drug abusers. Because of the risk of abuse in this class of drugs, the word *narcotic* has come to mean "a habit-forming drug," and it often is associated with sleazy and degenerate life-styles. In truth, narcotics are extremely valuable tools for health professionals.

narcotic family of drugs, derived from the opium poppy, that are effective in controlling pain

The use of opium and its derivatives has a long history, dating back to a 4000 B.C. Sumerian translation that refers to the opium poppy as the "joy plant." The Greeks and Romans advocated the use of opium, and it was also used in Imperial China. Although many people were addicted to opium, it was not until the nineteenth century that attempts to regulate its use were introduced. Morphine, which makes up 10% of the weight of opium, has long been used primarily by physicians as a painkiller. But when morphine was synthesized into heroin in 1898, problems began. Ten times more potent than morphine, heroin quickly evolved into a drug of abuse. Many users equate the "rush" they experience when taking the drug with the pleasure of sexual orgasm. Heroin abuse continues to present significant problems for contemporary society.

Drug Addiction. The addictive properties of narcotics are twofold. **Physiological addiction** occurs when bodily changes require the continued use of the drug. When a person faces prolonged pain, such as in recovery from surgery, the body's natural painkillers (endorphins) may become depleted. To help control the pain, opiate drugs such as morphine can be administered. In short-term usage morphine causes no problems, but when its use is prolonged, physiological addiction may occur. This addiction occurs

physiological addiction after repeated use of a drug, the body comes to require the drug

TABLE 5-1
Psychoactive Drugs: Sources, Uses, Degree of Dependence

Drugs	Source	Methods of Administration	Duration of Effects (hours)	Medical Uses	Dependence	
					Physiological	Psychological
Narcotics						
Morphine	Opium poppy	Oral, injected, smoked	3–6	Painkiller, cough suppressant	High	High
Heroin	Morphine	Injected, smoked	3–6	Under investigation	High	High
Codeine	Opium poppy	Oral, injected	3–6	Painkiller, cough suppressant	Moderate	Moderate
Depressants						
Barbiturates (e.g., Seconal, phenobarbital)	Synthetically derived	Oral, injected	1–16	Sedative, sleeping pill, anesthetic, anticonvulsant	High to moderate	High to moderate
Benzodiazepines ("Minor" tranquilizers such as Valium & Librium)	Synthetically derived	Oral, injected	4–8	Antianxiety, sedative, sleeping pill, anticonvulsant	Low	Low
Alcohol	Fermenting sugar & yeast	Oral	1–5	Antiseptic	Moderate	Moderate
Stimulants						
Cocaine	Coca plant	Sniffed, injected	1–2	Local anesthetic	Possible	High
Amphetamines	Synthetically derived	Oral, injected	2–4	Hyperkinesis, narcolepsy, weight control	Possible	High
Hallucinogens						
LSD	Ergot fungus	Oral	8–12	None	None	Unknown
Phencyclidine (PCP)	Synthetically derived	Oral, smoked	Variable	Veterinary anesthetic	Unknown	High
Peyote	Peyote cactus	Oral, injected	8–12	None	None	Unknown
MDMA (Ecstacy)	Synthetically derived	Oral	Variable	None	Unknown	Unknown
Marijuana	Cannabis sativa plant	Oral, smoked	2–4	Under investigation	Unknown	Moderate

Source: Adapted from Tompkins, 1981.

withdrawal the physical and psychological discomfort that an addict experiences once chronic drug use is discontinued

psychological addiction feeling a need for a drug in order to function, in the absence of a physical need for it

because the brain recognizes the opiate levels in the body and reduces the body's own production of endorphins, thus creating the physiological need for the drug. Persons addicted to narcotics such as morphine have to experience **withdrawal** if they are to be free of their need for the drug. Withdrawal is the physical and psychological distress experienced by the addict when drug use ceases. Its symptoms include chills, sweating, cramps, and nausea. **Psychological addiction**, which presumably has no physiological basis, defines a drug dependency that exists because of the pleasure experienced or because of a desire to avoid pain. These two kinds of addiction are not so easily separated; indeed, the distinction forces a kind of mind–body separation that some researchers are unwilling to accept.

Heroin use often begins as a search for a new experience, a search that unfortunately may lead to a life of misery and/or death. As addiction develops, use increases in frequency and often in dosage. Because the body develops a tolerance to most drugs, increasingly greater amounts are required in order to experience the drug's effects. The pleasure heroin users once derived is gone, except for the initial rush they experience immediately after taking the drug. Now they must take the drug just to feel normal. To be without the drug means to undergo withdrawal, which is an agonizing experience that may last for several days or even weeks. To avoid withdrawal, the addict must continue using the drug, and the habit may cost as much as $60,000 a year. But many heroin users will do whatever is required to support their habit. They steal, engage in prostitution, and even commit murder to obtain the necessary money.

In addition to the social and behavioral problems produced by heroin addiction, prolonged use can cause physiological disturbances. Endocrine processes, chromosome structures, and reproductive function are all damaged by long-term heroin use (McKim, 1991).

Depressants

The most widely used drug in the depressant class is alcohol. You may be surprised to see *alcohol* listed as a depressant because you probably have heard someone say that "a few beers loosen me up and make me have a good time." **Depressants** are drugs that have a general sedative effect on the central nervous system, and alcohol clearly has that effect. Initially, alcohol reduces a person's inhibitions through action on the brain stem. Continued drinking, however, affects higher brain centers in the cortex and leads to reduced alertness, impaired motor functioning, and slowed reaction times. Higher doses can produce unconsciousness and even death. Table 5–2 shows the behavioral effects of various amounts of alcohol in the bloodstream.

depressants drugs such as alcohol that have a sedative effect on the CNS

Alcohol abuse is a major problem for society, costing billions of dollars annually in medical care, insurance costs, job loss, tax loss, and welfare costs, as well as the loss of priceless human life and other human miseries it produces. For example, one half of fatal automobile accidents involve a driver who is intoxicated (World Health Organization, 1981).

Alcohol is addictive, and abusers will experience withdrawal once alcohol use is terminated. Withdrawal from alcohol is characterized by **delirium tremens**, "the DTs," which include such symptoms as visual hallucinations, hyperactivity, irritability, headaches, fever, and nausea. Alcohol abuse also

delirium tremens hallucinations, nausea, and other disturbances that occur during a period of withdrawal from alcohol

---

TABLE 5-2
Blood Alcohol Levels and Behavioral Effects for People
with Moderate Drinking Experience

Level of Alcohol in the Blood (%)	Behavioral Effects
0.05	Lowered alertness; person usually "feels good"
0.10	Reaction time is slowed; less caution is exercised
0.15	Reaction time is greatly slowed
0.20	Marked suppression of sensory-motor abilities
0.25	Severe motor disturbances, such as staggering; perception is greatly impaired
0.30	Semistupor
0.35	Level for surgical anesthesia; death is possible
0.40	Death is likely (usually because of respiratory failure)

Source: Adapted from Ray & Ksir, 1993.

has a number of physical consequences, including liver damage, heart disease, and neurological damage.

Other depressants include prescription drugs such as **barbiturates**. These drugs, popularly called *sedatives*, are strong CNS depressants used to reduce anxiety or irritability. Hypnotics, also a member of this class of drugs, are used in the short-term treatment of insomnia. In increased dosages these drugs can produce a state of intoxication similar to that produced by alcohol. Still larger dosages may lead to death.

Causes of Alcoholism. Alcohol researchers sometimes disagree about the reasons people drink. Some contend that people drink to feel better; others argue that people drink in order not to feel so bad (Pohorecky, 1991). Regarding the latter, one of the authors is reminded of a comment from a close friend, "I drink to avoid the mental acuity that comes with extended periods of sobriety." Regardless of the reasons for drinking, tolerance to alcohol does occur, and it is easy to progress from use to abuse. Dependency on the drug is known as **alcoholism**, a condition that affects as many as 20 million Americans.

For the last several years, there has been a spirited controversy surrounding the causes for alcoholism. One position is that psychological processes such as learning, motivation, and modeling determine consumption patterns. In this context, excessive alcohol use is believed to be regulated by sociocultural factors such as stress, crowding, economic privation, and so forth. An alternative account argues that there is a biological predisposition toward alcoholism. Along these lines, the contention that "an alcoholism gene" has been isolated on chromosome 11 has inflamed the most recent debate. Noble and Blum (1992) have conducted postmortem biochemical analyses of numerous brains from people who died from alcoholism. These scientists have discovered that the alcoholic individuals had impaired dopamine (see Chapter 2) binding sites in brain regions associated with reward. Because a specific gene from chromosome 11 controls the development of these dopamine neurons, it is possible that a disturbance in the expression of the gene could provoke increased alcohol consumption in an attempt to gain compensation. Perhaps, but critics correctly point to the evidence showing that the environment is the real determining force in the development of alcoholism (Bower, 1992). Likely both psychological and physiological factors are involved, and future research should clarify the role of each.

Stimulants

The class of drugs known as **stimulants** includes a variety of substances whose principal effect is to increase arousal by facilitating CNS release of neurotransmitters such as norepinephrine (discussed in Chapter 2). The two principal stimulants are amphetamines and cocaine.

Amphetamines. Actually a subclass of stimulants, these drugs include Dexedrine, Benzedrine, and others. Known as "speed" or "uppers," amphetamines are used to increase arousal, stay awake, suppress appetite, relieve depression, and provide a sense of well-being. The high that is produced may last for 2 to 4 hr. Then the drug must be taken again to renew the high. Eventually, tolerance develops and the high becomes difficult to establish. Some negative side effects, such as muscular aches, develop at this time. These effects increase with further drug use. After prolonged use, the person usually "crashes," sleeping perhaps for several days. Upon awakening, the person is usually depressed, apathetic, and fatigued. For the abuser, the cycle begins again in the pursuit of the high. Chronic users run the risk of brain damage, thought disturbances, hallucinations, high fever, convulsions, and

barbiturates prescription medication that is designed to alleviate stress and anxiety; often called sedatives

alcoholism a disorder in which a person becomes dependent on alcohol

stimulants chemicals such as amphetamines and cocaine that increase central nervous system activity

even death, usually from cardiovascular failure. Some heavy users exhibit what is called *amphetamine psychosis*, the symptoms of which are virtually identical to those of schizophrenia.

How Amphetamines Work. How do amphetamines work? What kind of neurochemical changes are produced by stimulants such as Dexedrine? As graphically depicted in Figure 5–19, amphetamines affect serotonin and cat-

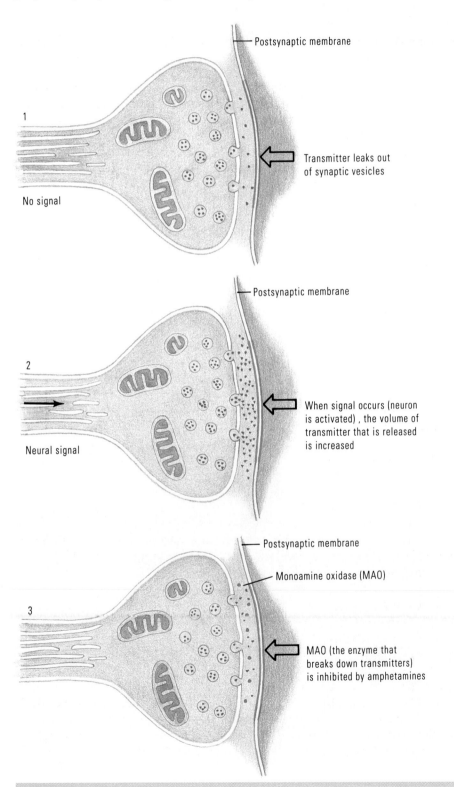

FIGURE 5–19
Three effects of amphetamines on neurotransmitter activity.

echolamines (epinephrine, norepinephrine, and dopamine) three ways. First, amphetamines mimic the action of the transmitter by causing the transmitter to leak out the synaptic vesicles into the synaptic cleft (see Chapter 2). Second, when a neuron is activated, the amount of the transmitter released by the change in electrical potential is increased in volume. So, when a presynaptic signal comes down the axon, more of the transmitter becomes available postsynaptically. Third, amphetamines deactivate *monoamine oxidase*, the enzyme that breaks down catecholamines. The result is that the transmitter stays in the cleft longer (reuptake is blocked), causing neural activation and behavioral stimulation.

Cocaine. Use of cocaine dates back at least 4,500 years (see Figure 5–20). Its popularity in the United States began around the turn of the twentieth century but diminished greatly in the 1920s. However, beginning in the 1970s, it has once again become popular, at least among those who have the money to afford what is called the champagne of drugs. Costs for this illegal drug range between $150 and $300 per gram. It is estimated that 6% of adults in the United States are regular users, and among young adults (ages 18–25), 28% say they have used cocaine at least once (Miller et al., 1982).

How Cocaine Works. As a stimulant, cocaine produces many of the same mood changes as amphetamines, but the mechanism of action differs. Unlike amphetamines, which produce multiple effects on neurotransmitters, cocaine works principally by blocking the reuptake of dopamine (see our earlier discussion of this phenomenon in Chapter 2). Another major difference is that the stimulatory effects of cocaine last a shorter time than those of amphetamines, usually 1 or 2 hr at most. What are likely consequences of the short life of cocaine?

Ordinarily cocaine is sniffed into the olfactory epithelium of the nasal passages, and peak blood levels are reached within 10 to 20 min (Javid et al., 1983). Most of the cocaine sold in the United States is in the form of cocaine hydrochloride (cocaine HCL), and, as a rule, this is how it is absorbed. However, there have been no shortage of inventive techniques

FIGURE 5–20
The coca plant grows in abundance in South America, where as early as 2500 B.C. natives chewed the leaves as a stimulant for prolonged strength. When the Spanish conquistadors arrived there in the sixteenth century, they banned native use of the leaves. However, when they discovered their slave laborers could work longer hours using the leaves, they rescinded the ban. Today South America is the major exporter of cocaine, principally from Peru, Bolivia, and Colombia. (From Erickson et al., 1987.)

designed to increase the psychoactive properties of the drug. When the cocaine is separated from the HCL, the free base can be burned and the vapor produces a much stronger than normal effect. This procedure, called *freebasing*, became extremely popular in the 1980s. Freebasing, using ether to remove the HCL, almost killed comedian Richard Pryor when the highly flammable gas burst into flames during a "tooting" session. Another comedian, John Belushi, died from an overdose by mixing cocaine and heroin, a procedure called *speedballing*.

A more recent method of using cocaine involves converting the drug into *crack*. Crack is formed by mixing cocaine HCL with a solution of common baking soda, and then simply letting the water evaporate. What remains is in the form of tiny crystalline chunks or "rocks" that may be heated in pipes and the vapors inhaled. Crack produces reactions that are difficult to control, and it is even more dangerous than many of the other procedures designed to enhance the rush associated with cocaine use. But, because crack is generally sold in smaller, cheaper quantities, it has become enormously popular on the street.

So with all of the obvious dangers, why is cocaine use gaining popularity? Many users see it as the "in" thing to do. Users often say they began because of the high status of the drug. According to one study, many cocaine users had previously used marijuana, so they did not see barriers to illegal drug use as an issue. Also, most had enjoyed marijuana use either for the pleasure of the drug or for the social context in which it was used (Murray, 1984). Like marijuana, cocaine is considered a social-recreational drug. Users say that it makes them more relaxed in social situations, gives them extra confidence, energizes them, sharpens their perceptions, and facilitates communication. On the down side, frequent users report that they sometimes experience insomnia, inability to relax, nervousness, increased heart rate, dry mouth and throat, and a congested nose (Erickson et al., 1987). Other research shows that cocaine users are at high risk for cardiac failure and that regular use produces significant brain damage, affecting memory, thinking, and emotion (Tompkins, 1981).

Unlike the narcotics and depressants, where both physiological and psychological addiction occur, physiological addiction has not been substantiated for most stimulants. However, psychological addiction is very strong and makes it extremely difficult for many users to quit. The result is substantial human misery for users, their friends, families, and co-workers.

Caffeine and Nicotine.   Two other stimulants deserve mention, more for their frequency of use than for their power as stimulants. They are *caffeine* and *nicotine*. Their power in altering consciousness is typically slight, although effects vary among individuals.

For the American consumer, caffeine is consumed as part of coffee (85 mg/5 oz), tea (40 mg/5 oz), and cola soft drinks (15 mg/5 oz). Most of the caffeine intake is from coffee, which accounts for 75% of caffeine consumption in the United States and 60% in Canada (Barone & Roberts, 1984). Coffee consumption is high (450 million cups daily in the United States alone), but statistics indicate that the number of coffee drinkers has been dropping steadily since 1961. Of course, a number of current coffee drinkers have switched to decaffeinated coffee (Goulart, 1984). Caffeine has been suggested as a factor in a number of health problems, including heart rate irregularities, pancreatic and bladder cancer, spontaneous abortion in pregnant women, high blood pressure, and diabetes. Its behavioral effects are not well documented, partly because dosages for most consumers are small (Dews, 1984). But among heavy coffee drinkers (perhaps as many as 20% of the coffee-drinking population) increased anxiety can be a serious problem.

This anxiety may be resistant to forms of psychotherapy, yet be eliminated when caffeine consumption is reduced or eliminated.

There is even some debate about caffeine's action as a CNS stimulant. This uncertainty is caused by results relating caffeine to prolonged wakefulness. For many coffee drinkers the drug is used to maintain alertness. Yet for others, coffee drinking has no such effect.

Nicotine is another of the legal stimulants used frequently in our society, consumed essentially through cigarette smoking by an estimated 25% of the adult population. That percentage has dropped over the past decade as the scientific evidence for the dangers of smoking has been accumulating, but among smokers, the number of cigarettes used daily has increased. Further, social pressure from nonsmokers (e.g., demanding cleaner air in restaurants and other public places) has also contributed to the decline in the number of smokers (Mangan & Golding, 1984).

Smokers indicate a number of motives for their use of tobacco, but most prevalent are the pleasure derived from smoking (partly taste variables) and the alleged calming effects smokers feel it produces (Schalling & Waller, 1980). Despite the positive motives, the majority of smokers would like to quit smoking, and most have tried either to reduce or eliminate their smoking.

Nicotine is just one of the many substances in tobacco smoke and probably is not the most harmful one (that distinction is held by tar). But evidently nicotine produces an addiction that is both psychological and physiological. Smokers who give up their habit show withdrawal symptoms of increased irritability, lack of concentration, tremors, and heart palpitations (Stepney, 1984). Interestingly, the withdrawal symptoms are the same for both heavy and light smokers. However, some heavy smokers stop smoking and show no withdrawal symptoms whatsoever. These findings have led psychologists to question whether nicotine addiction is actually the same as other drug addictions.

True to its classification as a stimulant, nicotine does have some behavioral effects due, perhaps, to heightened arousal. The drug has been shown to aid performance in boring tasks and to increase the speed and accuracy of information-processing tasks. These results can be achieved by smoking as well as ingestion of nicotine tablets (Wesnes & Warburton, 1984). Because of these effects, students often use stimulants with the goal of improving their studying.

THINKING ABOUT
Drugs and Alertness

Although some stimulants such as cocaine and caffeine have been used for a long time, amphetamine use has gained popularity only recently. In the 1930s, Benzedrine was introduced as a drug for asthma sufferers (McKim, 1991). However, college students were quick to discover the mood-enhancing properties of the drug, and it soon became a campus favorite among students pulling all-nighters before exams. The drug became available in pill form, popularly known as "bennies." Since then, other amphetamines, such as Dexedrine, have been produced but are available only by prescription. Even without a prescription, college students who want amphetamines can get them easily.

Earlier we mentioned the problems of mild sleep deprivation. College life places considerable demands on the average student, and sleep is one of the activities that often gets slighted. Under mild sleep deprivation, students can function well most of the time, but regular periods of lowered alertness occur. A majority of students will try to increase their alertness through the use of caffeine, typically by consuming coffee, cola drinks, or over-the-counter (OTC) drugs, such as No-Doz. For some people caffeine is an effective short-term stimulant. But it is not an effective long-term strategy for coping with lowered alertness due to sleep loss. (Sleep is the recommended prescription here.)

Students who adopt a caffeine strategy need to know the facts. The recommended maximum dosage from the Federal Drug Administration (FDA) is 100 to 200 mg of caffeine every 3 or more hours. A full cup of brewed coffee contains 100 to 150 mg, a 12-oz cola drink about 36 mg. Also, if you buy OTC drugs, you are buying caffeine. For example, one No-Doz tablet contains 100 mg of caffeine and no other active ingredient. Double-E Alertness capsules contain 180 mg of caffeine and a vitamin that has no stimulant properties. Vivarin tablets contain 200 mg of caffeine and an almost equal amount of dextrose, a sugar. The advantage of using the liquid varieties (coffee and cola) is that it is harder to overdose. With the tablets, students are too easily tempted to take multiple tablets when they do not become as alert as they want to be. The unfortunate results can be anxiety, irritability, irregularities in heartbeat, headache, and nausea, and a generally bad feeling (Zimmerman, 1983).

Some students, frustrated by the fact that caffeine cannot deliver the needed alertness, turn to prescription amphetamines—"speed," "pep pills," "wake-ups," as they are known. These drugs are prescribed for narcolepsy, hyperactivity, and, occasionally, weight control, but not to help someone stay awake (although the U.S. military used them in Vietnam for that purpose). Amphetamines do increase arousal and give the impression of increased alertness. Blood pressure increases, as do heart rate and respiration. As in caffeine use, students often ignore dosage rates, but with more serious consequences. Withdrawal from amphetamines can produce moderate depression—the crash. To avoid these effects, some users continue to use them, creating tolerance and a vicious cycle of increasing dosages. Long-term users may suffer serious physical and psychological consequences. Suicide is common.

Clearly, all college students occasionally face a need for increased alertness in the face of fatigue. They should address those situations with intelligence rather than desperation.

So think about what you are doing. Are you using anything to force yourself to stay awake? How frequently do you resort to it? Are you concerned it may become a habit that persists after college? Be careful.

Hallucinogens

Substances that radically distort the perception of reality, usually producing vivid hallucinations, are called **hallucinogens**. Another general term for these drugs is *psychedelic*. When psychologists and others think of mind-altering drugs, they are usually thinking about this category of drugs, which includes LSD (lysergic acid diethylamide); MDMA (methylenedioxymethamphetamine, also called Ecstacy); PCP (phencyclidine, also called Angel Dust); and to a lesser extent, marijuana. The action of these drugs is not entirely understood, but there is some evidence that they interfere with the neurotransmitter serotonin (Jacobs, 1987). These drugs alter mood, generally producing euphoria, although some users become severely depressed.

hallucinogens psychedelic drugs such as LSD that alter perception to the point where vivid hallucinations are produced

Time becomes distorted, colors increase in vividness, sounds take on new dimensions of space and tonal qualities, contours and shapes change, and distance perception is altered. Under the effect of the hallucinogens, some individuals report cross-sensory experiences such as seeing sounds or hearing colors. This latter type of sensory experience is known as *synesthesia* (Lemley, 1984).

Continued use of hallucinogenic drugs leads to tolerance. As dosages are increased to maintain the effects, the situation becomes more dangerous, and the predictability of the effects—not high to begin with—decreases.

Problems with LSD. Illicit use of *LSD* began in the 1940s and reached its greatest popularity among drug users in the 1960s. Its use has declined since, but some reports suggest it may be increasing again (Watson, 1991). LSD, or "acid," is extremely dangerous, primarily because of its unpredictability. A number of deaths have been attributed to its use when users have jumped off buildings thinking they could fly or set themselves on fire "to kill the millions of bugs eating their bodies." Some LSD users report experiences that are spiritual in nature, whereas others may report little or no effects at all. Some people experience terrifying hallucinations and may suffer depression and other psychological disturbances long after the effects of the drug have worn off. Another problem with LSD is that long after drug use has stopped, the hallucinations may return. These experiences are termed *flashbacks*, and they continue to haunt some former users.

MDMA. An example of a "designer drug" that was invented by a major drug house instead of being synthesized in some illegal, back-street lab is *MDMA*, or Ecstacy. MDMA was originally made by the Merck drug company in 1914, but did not come on the drug scene until the 1960s. In the beginning, psychiatrists gave the drug to their patients because it increased intimacy and helped facilitate therapy. Patients reported feeling more at ease and expressed a sense of warmth and well-being. But MDMA was later found to produce toxic side effects, and even death. As a result, the drug was banned. This did not stop the illegal use of MDMA, however. Ecstacy continues to be a popular drug among young people, and in that sense it is unique. Most designer drugs enjoyed brief popularity, and have been unceremoniously dropped from the list of popular hallucinogens.

PCP. Another common synthetic drug, *PCP*, was developed in the 1950s. PCP was used as an anesthetic for humans. However, undesirable side effects, most notably hallucinations and disorientation, ended its medical use. Then, in the 1960s, veterinarians began to use PCP as an anesthetic for animals. Since that time it has been used in the drug culture as a psychedelic drug. The most common symptom experienced in moderate doses is **depersonalization**. The person feels estranged from others and from the environment. Reactions are usually quite pronounced. Some users experience feelings of impending doom; others report feelings of unlimited power and invulnerability. Violent behavior is not uncommon even among people who are not otherwise violent. The high number of deaths attributed to PCP use has caused considerable concern, resulting in decreased use of the drug. Chronic users suffer memory loss and intelligence scores drop. Anxiety and depression are common, and because PCP produces permanent brain damage, these symptoms may persist long after use of the drug has stopped.

Marijuana. Without a doubt the most popular hallucinogen is *marijuana*, which is known by a multitude of other names including, "pot," "grass," and

depersonalization a reaction that often occurs following repeated use of psychedelic drugs, in which persons feel totally isolated from other people and their surrounding conditions

"weed." Experimentation with and use of this drug have increased markedly during the past 25 years. A survey conducted in 1962 found that 4% of the American population had used marijuana. By 1980 that figure was 68% (Tompkins, 1981).

Marijuana comes from the plant *Cannabis sativa*, which grows in most parts of the world. Although this plant contains many chemicals, the psychoactive ingredient is delta-9-tetrahydrocannabinol, also known as THC. The potency of this chemical is indicated by the fact that the average street sample of marijuana contains less than .5% THC. Some samples are considerably higher in THC content; thus, effects from the drug vary according to its quality, meaning its THC content.

Most people use marijuana for the altered states it produces. These states are a little easier to control than those produced by other hallucinogenic drugs, unless the dosage is very high. At low to moderate dosages, hallucinations are not present. Instead, the person typically reports feelings of calmness, increased sensory awareness, changes in space and time, and increased appetite, often with a craving for sweets. At higher dosages the person may experience thought disturbances, rapid emotional changes, a loss of attention, and a sense of panic.

Marijuana has been one of the most researched drugs in the history of pharmacology, and there is still considerable disagreement about its short-term and long-term effects (Abel, 1980). It was made an illicit drug in the United States in 1937, and many states have established harsh penalties for those convicted of possession of even small amounts. In recent years there has been a move toward decriminalization of marijuana. Although this policy would not legalize the drug, it would establish more appropriate punishments, for example, fines instead of imprisonment for possession of small amounts for personal use (Cohen, 1981a).

The growing consensus of research on marijuana would suggest that it is not a safe drug. Indeed, it is doubtful whether any drug taken frequently by choice is advisable. Marijuana does not appear to be addictive, at least not in a physical sense, and few users seem to have any real psychological dependence on the drug. Many researchers have concluded that smoking marijuana is no more dangerous, and perhaps even less so, than smoking cigarettes or using alcohol. The issue, though, is frequency of use. The literature on chronic users of marijuana—that is, people who use it a lot and over a long period of time—suggests rather strongly that there are serious deficits in some cognitive abilities such as memory. In addition, heavier users experience some undesirable personality changes, problems with sleep, deficits in psychomotor abilities such as driving, and changes in motivational levels that produce apathy and a lack of striving for achievement.

Finally, there are a number of factors that influence the effect of a particular drug. There are factors associated with the drug, including its purity and the method of its administration. Subject variables that are important include body weight, metabolic rate, whether or not the person has eaten, general state of health, and previous experience with the drug. In trying to predict how any one person will react to a drug, these factors, and many others, must be taken into account. But there is another important variable that plays a major role in drug reactions, and too often its effects are overlooked. That variable is the user's *expectation* of the drug's effect. Research has shown that the experience many drug users will have is not just a result of the physiological and biochemical changes produced by the drug, but also depends on how they think they are supposed to respond, or how they see others around them responding. These factors must be also be considered when evaluating the reasons for altered states of consciousness through drug use.

THINKING AHEAD . . .

Throughout history, disturbances in consciousness have been the subject of intense interest. Cultural beliefs, rituals, and spiritual posture have been fashioned by dreams and visions, and drug-induced hallucinations have inspired hunts, relocation, war, or perhaps the development of a new religious dogma. Fundamental to civilization is the belief that altered states of awareness reflect an essential element of existence, an element that transcends the routine and pursues a dimension of life that is uniquely human.

In this chapter, we have seen that sleep is a much more complicated phenomenon than anyone ever realized. What Shakespeare characterized as a "false death" is far from being a quiescent state of inactivity and dormancy. Rather, sleep is a period of animation in which bursts of activity are cloaked in a deceptive paralysis. Dreaming is an even more enigmatic process. Each of us will likely have more than 100,000 dreams during our lifetime, and on the whole, we will be clueless about what they mean or what subtle purpose they may serve. Through hypnosis and drugs we are able to achieve states of consciousness that at once frighten us and implore us to do it all again. One is left to muse over the curious need that we all have to depart consciousness, to willfully forfeit rational thought and install images that are on occasion bizarre, outrageous, and even threatening. What selective advantage could there be in assuming a mental state in which we cheat reality? What is there about the human condition that demands we drift episodically in and out of awareness? Is it not a logical inconsistency that unawareness and enhanced awareness could be equally attractive alternatives, even for the same person, and at the same time?

At the moment such questions take on a rhetorical character; we simply don't have the answers. But as this chapter shows, we have made a solid start at unraveling the mystery of consciousness. Consider how much we have learned about EEG patterns during sleep, just in the last two decades. How long will it take us to complete our understanding of the factors that determine sleep quality? Will it be possible to artificially control sleep processes and dictate a more efficient, and less time-consuming, sleep strategy? What psychoactive chemicals await discovery, and will we be able to offer assurances about their safe use? Might it not make more sense to make consciousness more desirable than to expend our energies on structuring a more inviting alternative? These are matters of the mind—a frontier that although unfamiliar is navigable.

Consciousness: An Overview

1. Consciousness is the state of awareness of what is going on in the environment or within our own body. An altered state of consciousness is one in which the state of awareness has been changed from normal waking consciousness.
2. Consciousness is altered by sleep, dreams, hypnosis, and drugs.

Sleep

3. Fully equipped modern sleep labs are telling us a great deal more about the nature of sleep.
4. The primary function of sleep is not known. It may have a number of functions, one of which may be to eliminate the physiological changes produced by fatigue, a function that is the heart of restorative theory.
5. Circadian rhythms, like the body's temperature cycle, are approximately 24 hr in length. But the sleep–wakefulness cycle in humans, when free running, is 25 hr. The body temperature cycle and alertness are closely correlated.
6. Shift workers rarely get the amount of sleep they want, and they suffer a number of physical and psychological problems because of the frequent changes in their sleep–wake schedules. Jet lag can also cause disruption in sleep patterns.
7. Sleep in mammals is composed of five distinct stages. Four stages comprise NREM sleep, and the other stage is called REM sleep because of the rapid eye movements present.
8. Sleep begins with NREM sleep. The first REM sleep period begins after 90 min, and subsequent REM periods occur at regular intervals thereafter on a 90-min basis. This periodicity is called the NREM-REM cycle. REM periods lengthen throughout the night so that most of the REM sleep occurs in the second half of the night. An important kind of NREM sleep, called slow wave sleep (stages 3 and 4), is contained largely in the first half of the sleep night. In infancy, the amount of REM sleep declines markedly, as does total sleep time. Slow wave sleep declines later in life.
9. Short-term sleep deprivation studies have produced surprisingly little effects on behavior other than making the subject sleepy. Motivation to perform appears to be a critical variable.
10. Insomnia is the most common sleep disorder, and it is usually treated by the use of sleeping pills (hypnotics). Many insomniacs' problems result from bad sleep habits. Other sleep disorders include narcolepsy, SIDS, sleep apnea, sleepwalking, and sleeptalking.

Dreaming

11. Although REM sleep exists in nonhuman mammals and in human infants, we cannot be sure they dream. The only way to know if dreaming is occurring is to obtain a verbal report of the dream. Most people are poor dream recallers, remembering less than one dream per night on the average. People with good visual memory skills tend to be better dream recallers. The stimuli for dream content are not generally known. Dreams during the night are typically unrelated in terms of their theme.
12. People who become aware that they are dreaming and are capable of altering their dream content while dreaming are called lucid dreamers.
13. Although the psychoanalytic model of dream interpretation is well known, few psychologists endorse it. Dreams are probably meaningful, but their interpretation depends on considerable knowledge about the dreamer.
14. Nightmares occur in NREM sleep and REM sleep. The former are very frightening, but little or nothing of the dream content can be recalled. REM nightmares can be remembered, often in great detail.
15. Dreams are thought to serve a number of functions that aid neurological processing, thinking and problem solving, and psychological adjustment.

Hypnosis

16. Hypnosis is an altered state of consciousness in which the person is extremely suggestible. People differ markedly in terms of their hypnotic susceptibility.
17. Instructions given in hypnosis to be carried out after hypnosis is over are called posthypnotic suggestions. During hypnosis subjects can be instructed to forget things following hypnosis, a phenomenon known as posthypnotic amnesia.
18. The hidden observer refers to a part of the person's consciousness that monitors the environment when the person is hypnotized. It suggests two separate streams of consciousness.
19. Hypnosis is as an adjunct to psychotherapy, but its greatest utility has been in the reduction of pain.

Drugs and Their Effects on Consciousness

20. Drugs that produce changes in consciousness by altering mood and/or perception are called psychoactive drugs.

21. Narcotics are especially addictive drugs derived from the opium poppy. Use of these substances, which include heroin, produces an immediate and pleasant high.
22. Depressants are drugs that act to sedate the central nervous system. Alcohol is the major drug in this class, which also includes barbiturates and hypnotics.
23. Drugs whose principal effect is to increase arousal are called stimulants. The two major stimulants are amphetamines and cocaine. Addiction to these drugs appears largely psychological. Caffeine and nicotine, two commonly used drugs (especially among students), are also classified as stimulants. Stimulants are not effective in maintaining alertness for long periods of time.
24. Drugs that radically distort the perception of reality, usually producing vivid hallucinations, are hallucinogens. Included in this class are LSD, MDMA (Ecstacy), PCP, and marijuana.

Key Terms

consciousness (167)
altered state of consciousness (167)
electromyograph (EMG) (168)
electro-oculograph (EOG) (168)
electrocardiograph (EKG) (168)
restorative theory (168)
adaptive nonresponding theory (169)
circadian rhythms (171)
free running rhythms (173)
jet lag (173)

rapid eye movement (REM) sleep (175)
non–rapid eye movement (NREM) sleep (175)
alpha waves (176)
theta waves (176)
delta waves (176)
slow wave sleep (SWS) (delta sleep) (176)
paradoxical sleep (176)
sleep deprivation (179)
microsleeps (179)
REM rebound (179)
insomnia (181)
hypnotics (181)
narcolepsy (182)

sudden infant death syndrome (SIDS) (183)
sleep apnea (183)
somnambulism (184)
repression hypothesis (186)
latent content (186)
manifest content (186)
salience hypothesis (187)
interference hypothesis (187)
activation-synthesis hypothesis (187)
lucid dreaming (188)
night terror (190)
REM nightmare (190)
hypnosis (191)

posthypnotic suggestions (192)
hidden observer (193)
psychoactive drugs (194)
narcotic (195)
physiological addiction (195)
withdrawal (196)
psychological addiction (196)
depressants (197)
delirium tremens (197)
barbiturates (198)
alcoholism (198)
stimulants (198)
hallucinogens (203)
depersonalization (204)

Suggested Reading

Anch, A., Browman, C. P., Mitler, M. M., & Walsh, J. K. (1988). *Sleep: A scientific perspective*. Englewood Cliffs, NJ: Prentice-Hall. This book provides extensive research into various sleep phenomena, including the neuroanatomical and neurochemical basis for sleep. The coverage of sleep disorders is especially strong.

Cohen, D. B. (1979). *Sleep and dreaming: Origins, nature, and functions*. Elmsford, NY: Pergamon. A scholarly treatment of the research on sleep and dreaming by one of the leading researchers in this field. REM sleep and dreaming are emphasized.

Coleman, R. M. (1986). *Wide awake at 3:00 a.m. By choice or by chance?* New York: Freeman. A very readable account of the important work on biological clocks as they relate to sleep and to events such as shift work and jet travel.

Hilgard, E. R. (1977). *Divided consciousness: Multiple controls in human thought and action*. New York: Wiley. A discussion of much of the research on hypnosis, particularly the work on the hidden observer phenomenon, an important discovery made by this author.

Webb, W. B. (1992). *Sleep: The gentle tyrant*. (2nd ed.). Bolton, MA: Anker. This introduction to sleep covers the range of sleep phenomena in a relatively nonacademic, preliminary manner that is ideally suited for the unsophisticated reader.

CHAPTER 6
Learning

For Jon and Lorissa, the time of anticipation was over. The joyous moment of the delivery of their first child had come, and now in the wake of receptions, visits, and a steady flow of uninvited advice, there was the very serious task of caring for an infant. That this very special life was entirely dependent on them was a challenge that the loving parents accepted readily. Nothing would be overlooked, and all the child's physical and psychological needs would be satisfied.

For the first four months, events unfolded pretty much as expected. As with most babies in North America, Jon and Lorissa's child was sleeping through the night, at least most of the time. If the scene had been Kipsigi, Kenya, in Africa, the story would have been different because in this culture babies typically do not sleep through the night until they are well over 1 year old. In any case, at about 5 months problems began for Jon and Lorissa. For no apparent reason, their baby began throwing tantrums in the middle of the night. The child would wake up and cry until one or the other parent came to the bedroom. These tantrums became more frequent over the next couple of weeks, translating into a total absence of rest for the beleaguered parents.

Desperate for sleep, Jon and Lorissa agreed that they would ignore the tantrum crying. On the first night, the crying persisted for more than a half hour without interruption. Finally, the parents gave in and went into the bedroom to quiet the child, which their presence did, and the child was asleep in minutes. Reenactments of this ordeal occurred the next night and for several more nights in succession, and it seemed that the crying episodes were getting worse. At a loss to control the situation, and on the advice of a friend, Jon and Lorissa turned to the community family counseling center.

◀ Through learning and experience, we master our world, as have these stilt fishermen from Sri Lanka.

After listening to a common problem, the psychologist explained that it was they, Jon and Lorissa, who were perpetuating the irregular sleeping pattern and crying episodes. "When your child cries at night, and you attend to her, you are rewarding her for crying," remarked the counselor. "When you make an attempt to let the child cry herself back to sleep, but eventually go to her out of desperation, in reality you are teaching your child to cry harder. She learns that she must cry longer and louder to get what she needs. Now, this behavior is not self-sustaining, it will go away when it does not lead to some sort of reward. So, just let her cry. She will be alright, and you will be too."

Committed to changing their child's sleeping pattern, Jon and Lorissa were up all night that night, as was their baby. It was a horrific experience for everyone. There were blood-curdling screams for almost 2 hr, but the parents stayed away. The second night was much better, with the crying lasting less than 1 hr. The length of the crying episodes systematically diminished over the course of the next several days, and soon the child was sleeping through the night. Jon and Lorissa had learned an important lesson about behavioral principles.

When a behavior leads to a reward, or as psychologists call it, a reinforcer, it gains strength. This process is called *acquisition*. When a behavior no longer produces a reward, it loses strength, which is known as *extinction*. Acquisition and extinction are two principles that illustrate how the environment contributes to behavior. The interaction of the environment and behavior is the focus of the psychology of learning.

WHAT IS LEARNING?

learning a relatively permanent change in behavior or knowledge that occurs as a result of experience

We shall define **learning** as a relatively permanent change in behavior or knowledge that occurs as a result of experience. Because we cannot see learning occurring directly, we estimate it by measuring performance. The distinction between learning and performance, no doubt, will be made clear to you again and again during your college career. If it has not already happened, at some point in your education you will take an exam and get a poor grade, even though you legitimately know 90% of the material presented in the course. The problem is that, by chance, some exam is going to have questions on only the small amount of material you do not understand. Although the professor will infer that you have learned virtually nothing about the subject matter, this is an invalid inference because it is based on the assumption that learning and performance are identical, overlapping events. Although you can argue your case, in the final analysis not much is likely to change because the professor has no evidence other than your performance. No one can look at the effects of experience and see actual changes in learning. So, we record performance (behavior) and make inferences about the learning processes that are believed to underlie it.

Despite the problems inherent in studying a process that cannot be measured directly, an understanding of learning concepts is possible and indeed necessary for a discussion of later topics, such as psychotherapy, where behavior change is the goal of treatment. Our discussion will involve three basic types of learning operations. The first two types of learning that we discuss are classical conditioning and instrumental learning. Both of these approaches assume that associations, or connections, form between events when sufficient training takes place. These associative perspectives are contrasted with the more mentalistic cognitive learning approach discussed later in the chapter.

CLASSICAL CONDITIONING

Traditionally, **classical conditioning** has come to mean that learning takes place when two or more events are associated because they occur together. In this manner, as shown in the passage from Lope de Vega's 4-century-old play *El Capellon de la Virgen* ("The Chaplain of the Virgin"), a cat may learn to fear a noise (cough) when that noise is paired with an aversive (painful) event (thrashing). In each example, temporal contiguity (closeness in time and space) is the basis for learning. Once bonded by contiguity, the reinstatement of one event brings forth the other.

Scientific references to classical conditioning are commonly associated with Ivan P. Pavlov (1849–1936), the Russian physiologist who was awarded a Nobel Prize in 1904 for his research on digestive functioning. Pavlov's disdain for studying fragments of physiology disposed him to examine the whole organism. While he was investigating digestive processes, he noticed that, given food in dishes, dogs would, after several presentations, show salivation reactions to the dish itself, whether or not food was present. Pavlov proceeded to explore the range of circumstances that could produce effects such as these, and eventually a standard experimental procedure emerged. Using the apparatus shown in Figure 6–1, experiments were conducted with two stimuli, the conditioned stimulus and the unconditioned stimulus. An **unconditioned stimulus (US)** is an event that reflexively (automatically) produces a response called an **unconditioned response (UR)**, even when there has been no previous training. A **conditioned stimulus (CS)** is originally a neutral cue that, when paired with the US, comes to elicit a **conditioned response (CR)**, which often resembles the original UR. For example, some of Pavlov's early work on conditioned salivation automatically recorded the amount of saliva (UR) secreted by the parotid gland when meat powder (US) was presented on a food pan in a soundproof chamber. It was discovered that when a metronome (a device that marks exact time by emitting a sound at regular intervals) was presented as a sound CS immediately before presenting the meat powder, after a few pairings the animal salivated (CR) to the sound of the metronome alone, apparently in anticipation of forthcoming food. The relations among these events in classical conditioning are shown in Figure 6–2.

In terms of preliminary experimental work on classical conditioning in humans, emotional development was an early topic of interest. Along these lines, the famous American behaviorist John B. Watson, in collaboration with Rosalie Rayner, conducted what may well be the most celebrated experiment in the history of psychology. In a report published in 1920, Watson and Rayner presented detailed accounts of a project designed to show the conditioning of a fear reaction in a 9-month-old infant, Albert B. Because classical conditioning was believed to underlie the acquisition of fear in humans, a CS and US were selected as critical conditioning elements in this ambitious study. The US was a loud noise produced by striking a hammer on a 4-ft-long suspended steel bar. This loud noise (US) produced sudden disturbances in breathing patterns, crying, a change in skin resistance, and increased blood pressure (URs).

Two months after this first experience with the US, little Albert was given a harmless white rat as a potential playmate. When Albert reached for the rat, a steel bar was once again struck immediately behind his head (US), causing him to jump violently and fall forward and begin to whimper (UR). To test the notion that the CS (the white rat) would acquire control over the conditioned fear response (CR), Albert was presented with the rat precisely 1 week later, but this time no loud sound was introduced. The instant Albert saw the rat, he began to cry and tried to crawl rapidly away.

classical conditioning learning that occurs when two or more events are paired in time

> Saint Ildefonso used to scold me and punish me lots of times. He would sit me on the bare floor and make me eat with the cats of the monastery. These cats were such rascals that they took advantage of my penitence. They drove me mad stealing my choicest morsels. It did no good to chase them away. But I found a way of coping with the beasts in order to enjoy my meals when I was being punished. I put them all in a sack, and on a pitch black night I took them out under an arch. First I would cough and then immediately whale the daylights out of the cats. They whined and shrieked like an infernal pipe organ. I would pause for a while and repeat the operation—first a cough, and then a thrashing. I finally noticed that even without beating them, the beasts moaned and yelped like the very devil whenever I coughed. I then let them loose. Thereafter, whenever I had to eat off the floor, I would cast a look around. If an animal approached my food, all I had to do was to cough, and how that cat did scat!

A passage from Lope de Vega's 4-century-old play *El Capellon de la Virgen* ("The Chaplin of the Virgin").

unconditioned stimulus (US) stimulus event that reflexively produces a response

unconditioned response (UR) unlearned reaction to a US

conditioned stimulus (CS) neutral event that, when paired with a US, acquires the ability to elicit a CR

conditioned response (CR) learned response to the CS, resembling the UR

FIGURE 6–1
A drawing of the type of appartus used by Ivan Pavlov in his work on classical conditioning. During training, the dog was restrained in the harness, and the amount of salivation was recorded automatically from the tube inserted into the salivary (parotid) gland. (Adapted from Yerkes & Morgulis, 1909.)

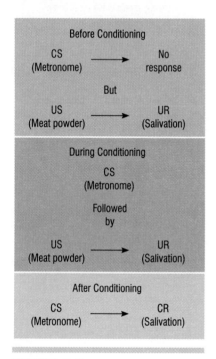

FIGURE 6–2
The relations among the various events involved in classical conditioning.

asymptote highest level of performance during acquisition for a specific set of training conditions

The assertion made by Watson and Rayner was that conditioned emotional reactions of the sort described in their investigation make up the majority of human emotions, including not only behaviors common to fear, but rage and love as well. In effect, the argument was made that people express different emotional reactions to the environment because of their different experiences.

In addition to the laboratory demonstrations of classical conditioning by Pavlov and Watson, we have many nonlaboratory examples of the phenomenon as well. A song associated with a happy period in your life may make you feel good when you hear it, even though you may not be able to make the connection at a conscious level. Also, how about your reaction to the persuasive influence of a commercial because a product has been associated with an attractive setting? Isn't this a form of classical conditioning? Or, more like Pavlov's dogs, perhaps you begin to salivate as the waiter starts to serve your meal at a restaurant. In each of these cases, neutral events have been associated with situational stimuli which cause certain reactions to occur. The resulting learned responses to the previously neutral stimuli thus are understandable within the framework of classical conditioning.

In the sections that follow, we discuss some of the more important phenomena associated with classical conditioning. As we note, some of these events have forced us to reexamine our position on what classical conditioning really is.

Acquisition

Acquisition training in classical conditioning involves repeated pairings (trials) of the CS and US. Learning curves associated with response acquisition usually look like the curve shown in the left panel of Figure 6–3. Gradual increases in the magnitude of the CR occur over trials until performance levels off for the remainder of training. This leveling off, or plateau, is called the **asymptote** of acquisition. It means that for the given set of experimental conditions, maximum learning has taken place.

Variables Affecting Acquisition. When conducting an experiment on classical conditioning, the selection of CSs and USs may have a major impact on the acquisition of the CR. As a rule, *US strength* affects the amount of conditioning that is possible. A strong US will produce better conditioning than a weak one. Thus, it is not surprising that an experience involving a vicious

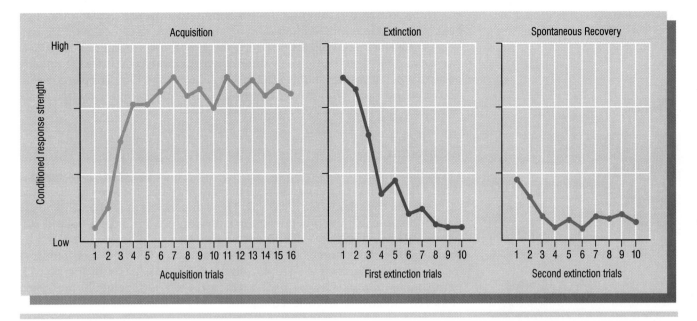

FIGURE 6–3
Acquisition, extinction, and spontaneous recovery curves in a typical
study of classical conditioning.
(Adapted from Pavlov, 1927.)

attack by a pit bulldog will promote greater fear and terror of animals than a
moderately unpleasant encounter with the neighbor's collie. Also, *CS
saliency* is an important factor in determining the rate of acquisition of the
CR. The more salient (noticeable) the CS, the more rapid the acquisition of
the CR (Schwartz & Reisberg, 1991). Perhaps, in the previously mentioned
little Albert experiment, CS saliency is the reason the rat was so readily associated with the fear induced by the loud noise (the US). The rat, compared to
fixtures in the room, other persons, and so forth, was more unusual and thus
more conspicuously associated with the aversive event.

The time at which the CS and US are presented is also an important
factor in acquiring a CR. As shown in Figure 6–4, five basic procedures, or
paradigms, have been considered. Of the five, the four most common are
simultaneous conditioning, delayed conditioning, trace conditioning, and
the special case of temporal conditioning. Procedural efforts have also
included backward conditioning.

In **simultaneous conditioning** the CS and the US begin at the same
time. Despite the intuitive attractiveness of this method, it produces minimal
conditioning (Hall, 1989), and in fact it is sometimes used as a control condition. A preferred technique is **delayed conditioning**, in which the CS starts
prior to the onset of the US yet continues at least until the US begins. This
procedure probably produces the most effective conditioning. A similar procedure is available in the form of **trace conditioning**, in which the onset of
the CS occurs prior to the onset of the US. Here, however, the CS stops
before the US actually is presented; thus the label "trace." As a rule, the
longer the interval between the ending of the CS and the beginning of the
US, the less effective the conditioning is likely to be.

Temporal conditioning is unique, in that there is no identifiable CS;
rather, the US is presented alone at discrete time intervals, such as every 30
sec. Eventually, the amount of time that has elapsed since the last stimulus
presentation becomes a signal for a forthcoming delivery of the US. So, time
becomes a CS, such that conditioned responses occur to a time period
immediately prior to the beginning of the US. Perhaps this is why many people begin having food-related thoughts as noontime approaches. Hungry or
not, the noon hour is associated with lunch, and people produce anticipatory
eating behaviors accordingly.

simultaneous conditioning classical
conditioning procedure in which the
CS and the US are presented at the
same time

delayed conditioning classical conditioning procedure in which the CS is
presented before the US, but the two
events overlap

trace conditioning classical conditioning procedure in which the CS is
presented and offsets before the US
presentation

temporal conditioning classical conditioning procedure in which time
functions as the CS

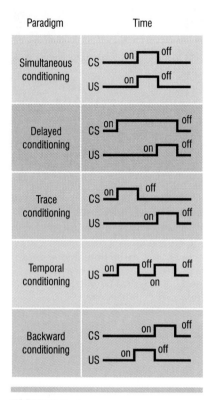

Paradigm	Time
Simultaneous conditioning	CS ___on__⌐_off__ US ___on__⌐_off__
Delayed conditioning	CS _on__⌐‾‾‾‾‾‾_off US ___on__⌐_off
Trace conditioning	CS _on__⌐_off US ___on__⌐_off
Temporal conditioning	US _on_⌐_off__⌐_off on
Backward conditioning	CS ___on__⌐_off US _on_⌐_off

FIGURE 6–4
Basic paradigms of classical conditioning (see text for explanation).

In **backward conditioning** the US is presented before the CS. Although backward conditioning is often difficult to obtain, it does occur under certain circumstances (Williams & Overmier, 1988). For example, if the US is intense and presented only a few times, then backward conditioning reliably occurs. When a young child is attacked by a large dog, for example, associations may be made with events that occur immediately following the attack as well as with those that precede it.

Extinction

Extinction involves repeatedly presenting the CS in the absence of the US. When the pairings of the two stimuli are discontinued for several trials, the CS loses the capacity to elicit the CR. This happens because the CS is really a neutral stimulus, and when training stops, the CS resumes a neutral status. For Pavlov's original experiment, extinction would be accomplished by sounding the metronome, or some other auditory CS, and then omitting food deliveries. As depicted graphically in the middle panel of Figure 6–3, performance diminishes over trials when the CS is repeatedly presented alone. Eventually the CR is lost altogether.

Extinction is of practical interest as well as a laboratory concern, because we often want to get rid of an undesirable classically conditioned response in the treatment of mental disorders or even in social settings. As noted in Chapter 17, phobic reactions, or irrational fears, are often successfully treated by extinction. For example, someone who has acquired a fear of elevators may be asked to think about standing in an elevator with the doors open. Relatively speaking, this is not a very frightening thought, and in conditioning terms it is like presenting the CS (elevator) without the US (falling). Along other lines, a person might eliminate the hypertension associated with public speaking by practicing a speech over and over in front of a friendly audience. The objective is to present the CS (the public-speaking situation) in such a fashion that pairings with aversive circumstances (US) are not likely to occur. Eventually the message comes across, the previously disturbing event is no longer viewed as troublesome, and extinction is complete.

It is in this area of applying the basic laboratory principles of classical conditioning to a treatment setting that two other phenomena related to extinction take on added meaning. Of special concern is how permanent the conditioned effect is. Is it possible that a CR, having been extinguished to the point where detectable responses no longer occur to CS presentations, may suddenly reappear even though there has been no reconditioning with the US? Indeed it is possible, even likely, when there is no activity occurring during the rest interval between the end of extinction and the reinstatement of the CS. This phenomenon, graphically portrayed in the right panel of Figure 6–3, was first observed and reported by Pavlov, and it is known as **spontaneous recovery**. It is probably the least well understood and, mysteriously, the most ignored research topic of all the major phenomena bequeathed by Pavlov. Its importance for clinical psychology is evident from reported case histories that tell of phobic patients who, by virtue of extinction treatment, lose their fears of harmless objects only to have them resurface after their therapy is completed, and for no apparent reason.

It should be understood that most of the conditioning principles that we have discussed so far were presented decades ago. Acquisition and extinction phenomena in classical conditioning have been thoroughly explored. Yet, the relevance for these events for the world we live in continues to unfold, and new applications remain to be discovered. Along these lines, exciting uses of classical conditioning principles have emerged in the medical sciences.

Drug Tolerance

Drug tolerance is one of the greatest problems facing chronically ill patients who require recurrent drug treatments. When a patient becomes tolerant to a drug due to repeated use, the patient requires higher and higher doses of the drug to get the same benefits. The problem is that eventually the dose the patient needs is so high that toxic side effects result. If patients did not become tolerant to chemotherapy, the drugs could be given for much longer times. The result would be that treatment could be extended.

drug tolerance the decreasing impact of drug administrations that occurs with repeated drug exposures

Several years ago, Canadian psychologist Shepard Siegel established that classical conditioning was involved in the development of drug tolerance. As it turns out, when drugs are administered repeatedly there is a natural biological reaction that offsets the active effects of the drug. This offsetting reaction is conditionable (Siegel, Krank, & Hinson, 1987); that is, an internal response that is naturally opposite to a given drug (the tolerance reaction) can be connected to external stimuli. When these external CSs are present in the future, tolerance (the CR) is more likely.

What does this mean for a hospital setting? It could mean that nurses, the hospital bed, the sounds made in the halls by support staff—virtually every aspect of the treatment environment—actually promotes tolerance, and therein compromises the patient's care. In effect, the context of the drug administrations limits what the drug can do because the contextual stimuli elicit a tolerance reaction.

Reasoning that the hospital context might corrupt treatment, psychologist Dennis Dyck and his Canadian colleagues examined the possibility that extinction of the contextual cues that control the tolerance response to the drug might buy some time for patients (Dyck, Greenberg, & Osachuk, 1986). Using an animal model, it was determined that when CSs were paired with saline (a neutral solution) *between* pairings with an immunostimulatory drug (the US), tolerance was less likely to occur. In essence, the contextual stimuli (the syringe and needle, the injection, and so on) were placed on an extinction schedule when they were paired with saline but not the drug. Accordingly, the conditioned tolerance response (the CR) to these cues, which would otherwise develop as a result of pairings with a medicinal drug, was weakened. Extinction training simply made it more difficult to connect the tolerance reaction to the context in which the drug was given.

What are the implications of this research for long-term chemotherapy? Perhaps the medical intervention program should interchange bogus treatments with true drug administrations. Under these conditions, all the events surrounding treatment should be less likely to facilitate tolerance. Longer treatments could be conducted; patients could be given chemotherapy for longer periods with fewer toxic effects. Through the judicious application of classical conditioning principles, the practice of medicine may be enhanced.

Generalization

When we discussed the conditioning of the infant, Albert, who was trained to fear the white rat, we really only reported a part of that study. Investigating an issue related to the main point of the research, the researchers tested Albert with a variety of objects that differed with respect to how well they

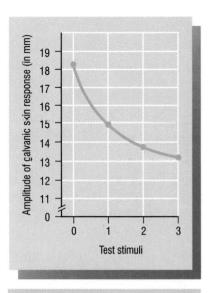

FIGURE 6–5

In Hovland's 1937 investigation of generalization, a mild electric shock was used as the US to elicit a galvanic skin response (GSR). The GSR is a change in the electrical conductivity of the skin that is thought to fluctuate with changing emotions. A tone was used as the CS that was paired with shock. Following 16 such pairings, each subject was presented with the original tone CS (Test Stimulus 0) as well as three additional test tones (Test Stimuli 1, 2, and 3) selected for their increasing distance from the original CS along the dimension of tonal frequency. Hovland found that GSR strength (CR strength) diminished with increasing differences between the original CS and the test tones. Note that none of the added test tones had ever been paired with the US.

generalization when a CR occurs to stimuli that are rather like the original training CS, even though these events have never been paired with the US

discrimination learning to respond to a narrow range of stimuli that vary along some dimension of the CS

approximated the form, texture, and color of the original CS (the rat). Included among these stimuli were a rabbit, a dog, a sealskin coat, a package of white cotton, and a bearded Santa Claus mask, all of which produced a fear reaction similar to that produced by the rat. The fact that Albert was afraid of objects that had not actually been paired with the US (the loud noise) but that were physically rather like the original CS that was paired with the US is evidence of a principle called **generalization**. This principle states that when a CS is paired with a US and comes to elicit a response, other stimuli that vary along the same dimension as the CS may also evoke that conditioned response. In addition, the more the new stimuli are like the original CS, the greater should be the strength of the conditioned response. Much of the early experimental work done in the United States on stimulus generalization was performed by Carl Hovland (see Figure 6–5).

The practical significance of the concept of generalization is apparent from a story one of our students told us recently. As an infant, she had a lengthy illness that required extensive medical attention including numerous, painful injections of an antibiotic. Eventually, the mere presence of the nurse in the white laboratory coat was sufficient to frighten the child and cause her to begin crying. Curiously, she reacted the same way to her father when he came home from work and tried to play with her or hold her in his lap. The girl's father, it seems, was an ensign in the U.S. Navy and wore dress whites. Evidently, the white uniform of her father was enough like the white laboratory coat of the needle-brandishing nurse to evoke a generalized conditioned fear response. In this case, the problem was easily resolved by the father changing into casual clothing before playtime.

Generalization is at work in a variety of other settings. It is usually beneficial that social behaviors learned in one context transfer to other situations, as it is similarly beneficial that a healthy respect for the potential dangers of hot stoves extends to many different types of stoves. Through the process of generalization we associate responses with different stimuli without having actually to experience each and every stimulus event.

Discrimination

A principle related to generalization is **discrimination**. Whereas generalization is concerned with the extent to which newly acquired behaviors transfer across similar stimuli, discrimination involves the organism's ability to detect differences among stimuli and respond to only one or a few such stimuli, to the exclusion of all others. In effect, you teach the animal or person *not* to generalize.

Suppose we were interested in discrimination training in a salivation study. A typical laboratory experiment would involve something like the following. A subject, say a dog, is placed in a harness, and the amount of salivation (in drops) is continually noted. The animal might then be given 50 training trials consisting of 25 trials with a 1000-Hz tone and 25 trials with an 800-Hz tone, administered in a random order. On trials where the 1000-Hz CS is present, food is delivered following the termination of the tone. No such food deliveries follow the presentation of the 800-Hz tone. In the early part of the training, the animal is likely to experience some difficulty in distinguishing between the two sounds, and therefore conditioned salivation is expected to occur after both cues. But with continued training, the dog eventually learns that the 1000-Hz tone is always followed by food and that the 800-Hz tone is never followed by food. Accordingly, the conditioned salivation response is restricted to the 1000-Hz stimulus. Figure 6–6 shows how the results from a laboratory discrimination study might look.

In addition to laboratory demonstrations of discrimination training, we can point to many examples in which discrimination effects are apparent in our real lives. Just think about when you were a child and heard your mother call your name for dinner. Now, think about her calling your name again, this time in the context of being caught red-handed in the cookie jar. The voice volume and inflection in each instance were likely so different that you could predict with great certainty the events that were about to unfold. Your previous experiences (discrimination training) signaled the behavioral course appropriate to the circumstance, in precisely the same way that the previously mentioned tones signaled the presence or absence of food.

Second-Order Conditioning

An immensely important consideration for classical conditioning is the effect the CS is likely to have on other neutral cues with which it is paired. Once a CR has been firmly established, the CS that elicits it may function in a manner similar to a US and thereby serve to strengthen responses to novel stimuli. In their early experiments, Pavlov and his associates took their observations of this effect as evidence of **second-order conditioning** (also called higher-order conditioning). For instance, in Pavlov's conditioned salivation studies a metronome (CS_1) was first paired with food, enabling it to evoke salivation (the CR). After sufficient training with this first-order arrangement, a second neutral stimulus, a black square (CS_2) was repeatedly followed by CS_1 but was never actually paired with food. Nonetheless, the presentation of the black square (CS_2) came to evoke a CR as if in fact CS_2-US training trials had been administered. It seems that CS_1 became a functional US for CS_2, thus establishing second-order conditioning (see Figure 6–7).

The significance of second-order effects is that the range of behavior for which classical conditioning might be responsible is extended. To limit learning only to the association of neutral events (CSs) and naturally important events (USs) decreases how much of an impact classical conditioning can have on human behavior. But if one event builds on another, elaborate linkages are possible.

For example, consider an incident observed by one of the authors of this textbook. At the halftime of a basketball game, former great players

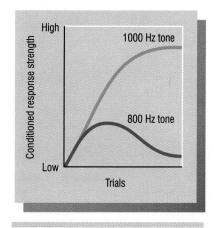

FIGURE 6–6
Typical performances in a discrimination study where a 1000-Hz tone is paired with food and an 800-Hz tone is paired with the absence of food.

second-order conditioning occurs when a CR responds to a second CS that has been paired with a first-order CS

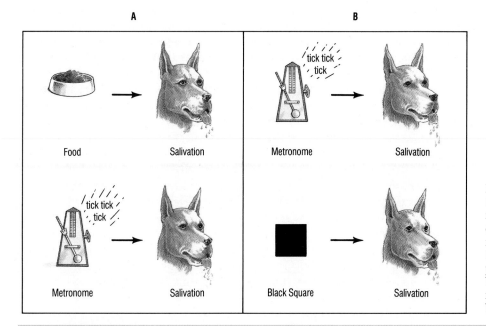

FIGURE 6–7
Second-order conditioning. (*A*) A metronome is paired with food, causing a salivation response to the metronome to occur. (*B*) Subsequently, a black square is paired with the metronome, and the black square produces a salivation response, even though it has not been directly paired with food.

from the home team were being presented to the crowd. One such person was introduced as a distinguished vice-president of a major telecommunications corporation. However, because the corporation was mired in a price-fixing scandal, the introduction met with a chorus of boos! Why? From the standpoint of second-order conditioning, the interpretation is clear. The corporate label (CS_1) was associated with a conspiracy (US) that evoked negative feelings (UR). Because the former athlete (CS_2) was associated with the corporation (CS_1), the crowd's antipathy was transferred to him, even though he had absolutely nothing to do with the much publicized scandal. So, through second-order conditioning, we can experience complex, even unfair, situations.

Classical Conditioning Today

contiguity model model of classical conditioning that states learning occurs when two events are paired in time

The preceding sections on classical conditioning record the impact that Pavlov's simple notion about learning has had on psychology. For over 75 years, the **contiguity model**, which states that conditioning occurs when two events are presented closely in time, has been a widely accepted principle. Indeed, the Pavlovian (contiguity) account of classical conditioning is so entrenched in the thinking of some psychologists that it is likely to be embraced for years to come—even though it may not be accurate!

Contiguity or Contingency?   Leading the opposition to the simple contiguity model of Pavlov is psychologist Robert Rescorla of the University of Pennsylvania. In response to the question of what is wrong with the conventional Pavlovian interpretation of conditioning, Rescorla remarked "almost everything" (Rescorla, 1988). Research during the last 25 years has produced numerous findings that contradict the view that contiguity between events is sufficient to produce conditioning.

One line of research that challenges Pavlov's contiguity position compares laboratory treatments where the numbers of CS and US pairings are the same, but the informational value of the CS differs. Such a relation is schematically represented in Figure 6–8. To illustrate this procedure, consider that each day one group of rats receives a 2-min-long tone CS that signals a mild electric foot shock US, and that this pattern recurs five times. In addition, other shock US applications are randomly interspersed between tone-shock presentations (top panel). Now, further consider a second group of rats that receives the same pattern of five daily pairings of the tone CS and the shock US, with no added shock exposures (bottom panel). How much conditioning should occur for each group? What does the Pavlovian model predict about such treatments that share identical contiguity experiences?

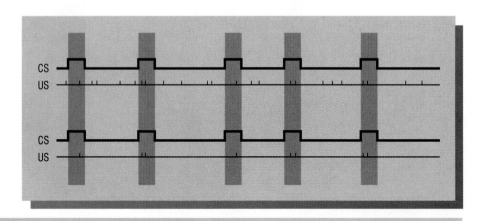

FIGURE 6–8
Schematic of two CS-US relations that share the same contiguity but differ in the information the CS gives about the US.

The answer is that Pavlov's theory predicts equal conditioning for both groups, because the same CS and US have been used on both occasions, and they have been paired an equal number of times. But the actual results (Rescorla, 1988) consistently show that less conditioning will occur in the group that receives the added shock exposures (top panel). It is as if the additional shock US presentations render the tone CS experiences meaningless; the CSs do not reliably signal anything, so the rat ignores them.

Rescorla's findings have led many psychologists to think in terms of a **contingency model** of classical conditioning. In such a model, conditioning only occurs when one event reliably predicts another. For instance, when you see lightning you expect to hear thunder, so you may cringe a bit. Or, if you have an allergic reaction to cat hair, you can fully anticipate that you will be sneezing momentarily when someone brings a cat into the room. The point is that one circumstance is perceived to be dependent on the other. It is not just that the events occurred together; rather, one event forecasts the other, and so the connection is made.

contingency model model of classical conditioning that states learning occurs when one event reliably predicts another

The Blocking Phenomenon.   In addition to Rescorla's experiments on contingency, another phenomenon that has proven especially problematic for the contiguity position is blocking. **Blocking** occurs when prior experience with one stimulus prevents later conditioning to a second stimulus (see Figure 6–9). The literature on blocking began in 1969 with a series of experiments reported by Princeton psychologist Leon Kamin. In the basic experiment, rats were pretrained for 16 trials in which a tone CS was followed by an electric shock US on each trial. Subsequently, the subjects were given 8 trials in which the same tone and a novel light were presented together as a compound CS and followed by the shock US on each trial. The interesting finding was that conditioning occurred to the tone CS but not the light CS. Because conditioning did occur to the light CS in a control group where the light–tone CS compound was paired with the same shock US at the very beginning of the experiment, it was not simply a case of a stronger stimulus overpowering a weaker stimulus. Rather, it seems that experience with the tone CS blocked conditioning to the light CS that normally would have developed. A contiguity model such as Pavlov's would predict that conditioning to the light should have occurred regardless of pretraining conditions. After all, in all cases the light was paired with the US for a sufficient number of training trials for learning to take place.

blocking when conditioning to a CS is prevented due to prior training with another CS

Blocking				
	Pretraining	Training	Test	Result
Group 1	Pair tone (CS$_1$) with shock (US)	Pair tone and light (CS$_1$ and CS$_2$) with shock (US)	Present tone (CS$_1$) alone	Conditioning to tone occurs
Group 2	Pair tone (CS$_1$) with shock (US)	Pair tone and light (CS$_1$ and CS$_2$) with shock (US)	Present light (CS$_2$) alone	No conditioning to light occurs **(Blocking)**
Group 3	No pretraining	Pair tone and light (CS$_1$ and CS$_2$) with shock (US)	Present tone (CS$_1$) alone	Conditioning to tone occurs
Group 4	No pretraining	Pair tone and light (CS$_1$ and CS$_2$) with shock (US)	Present light (CS$_2$) alone	Conditioning to light occurs

FIGURE 6–9
Procedure for obtaining blocking in classical conditioning.

Contemporary theories of classical conditioning offer different accounts of why blocking occurs. Rescorla and Wagner (1972), for example, favor the idea that only a certain amount of conditioning can be sustained by a given US. Thus, when a specific CS is presented with the US before subsequent pairings, it may prevent (block) later conditioning simply because some limit has already been reached. For example, the second CS in Kamin's study (the light) was presented after all the available conditioning had been committed to the first CS (the tone). Alternatively, attentional accounts of classical conditioning propose that the organism learns first to attend to CS_1, and when the second CS is presented, it is ignored as redundant information (Mackintosh, 1975). Whatever the mechanism, blocking has called into question the role played by contiguity in learning.

Pavlov as a Foundation. So we see that Pavlov's early model falls short as a comprehensive theoretical account of classical conditioning. Perhaps Rescorla's contention that "almost everything" is wrong with the traditional Pavlovian perspective seems excessively harsh, but it may take such extreme statements to cause many psychologists to rethink a position they have taken for granted. It is now clear that different amounts of conditioning occur, even when the contiguity features are the same. Although future theoretical developments may incorporate some aspects of Pavlovian conditioning theory, perhaps the time has come to lay to rest the simple idea that conditioning occurs when two events are presented at the same time. Pavlov provided us with an intellectual beginning, not an irreversible, complete theoretical scheme.

The Biochemistry of Classical Conditioning. Apart from theoretical issues, many scientists have focused on the biological foundations of classical conditioning. As we close in on the biochemistry of the CR, we increase our appreciation of how molecular processes may affect complex behaviors.

Research associated with the biological bases of learning has received a big assist from the blue and yellow sea snail. When this organism is placed on an electronic shaker table, a sudden shake of the table floor (the US) causes the snail to anchor itself reflexively by extending a muscular "foot" (the UR). When a light (CS) is paired with the shake, the light elicits a foot extension (the CR) that it did not elicit previously. It now appears that the molecule responsible for this learned connection is *protein kinase C (PKC)*. When PKC is activated internally in neural cells of the snail it has the effect of changing the structure of the cell so that it may branch out and make contact with neighboring cells (Ezzell, 1991). This branching action may be the basis for the learned response. When the shaking and light occur together, PKC activity increases and a "hard-wire" connection is made in the nervous system. This newly formed connection is excited by future presentations of the light (Alkon et al., 1990). Furthermore, when PKC activity is chemically blocked, the classical conditioning of the snail's foot extension to the light is prevented. Although research must be conducted with other organisms, the snail research gives hope of discovering a biochemical link between an external stimulus and the CR.

Elsewhere, it has been shown that persons suffering from Alzheimer's disease have only about half as much PKC in their brain cells as people who don't have the condition (Saitoh et al., 1990). Because Alzheimer's patients have profound learning and memory difficulties, some researchers have argued rather forcefully that PKC is the Holy Grail of learning. But this is highly unlikely; the complete answer will likely be very complex.

INSTRUMENTAL LEARNING

We introduced this chapter with an illustration of the importance of parental attention in the control and maintenance of irregular sleep patterns in a newborn. The consequence of responding is the most important element in **instrumental learning**. In this type of learning, the behavior is instrumental in producing a change in the environment, and that environmental change in turn affects the probability of the behavior that produced it. In the following sections, we review and evaluate historical developments as well as the current status of instrumental learning.

instrumental learning learning that occurs when a response is strengthened or weakened by its consequences

Thorndike on Outcomes

Serious experimental inquiry into the nature of instrumental processes began with Edward L. Thorndike (1874–1949). Thorndike secured the title of father of instrumental conditioning with the publication of his classic *Animal Intelligence*, which was also his 1898 doctoral dissertation at Columbia University. This monograph was to set the tone for learning theory research for the next 50 years.

Thorndike began his task of documenting the role of behavioral consequences in learning by conducting the now-famous "cat in the puzzle box" experiments. In these studies, a cat was deprived of food and placed in a small box with a latched gate (see Figure 6–10). Depending on the contingencies imposed by Thorndike, the cat pulled a string or pressed a treadle-like lever that released the latch and permitted it to go out through the gate and eat from a dish of food placed outside the box. Naive animals, of course, did not immediately move to the string and pull it. But eventually their spontaneous behavior produced the intended result, and they discovered the relation between responding and reward. As reflected in Figure 6–11 the amount of time taken to execute the required behavior decreased systematically with subsequent placements (trials) in the apparatus. According to Thorndike's casual observations, inappropriate emotional responses aimed at escaping (such as howling and clawing) gave way to solution-oriented responses that produced reward.

In order to account for his findings, Thorndike theorized that it is the connection between a stimulus (S) and a response (R) that determines

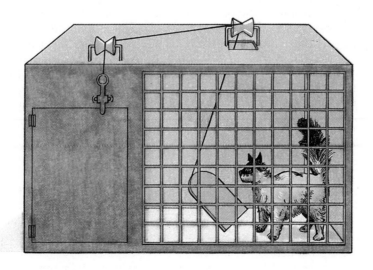

FIGURE 6–10
Puzzle box similar to the one Edward L. Thorndike used in his research on instrumental conditioning.

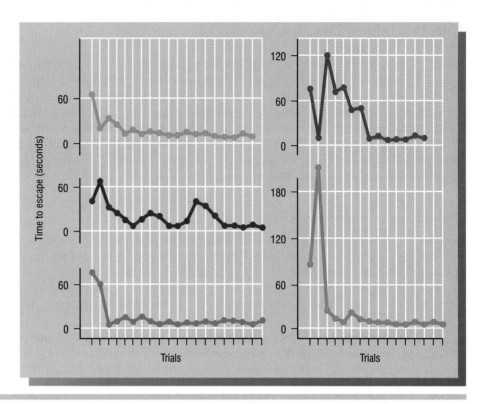

FIGURE 6–11
Individual performance records for five animals learning to solve Thorndike's puzzle box. (From Thorndike, 1898.)

law of effect Thorndike's principle of reward and punishment that encourages and discourages responding, respectively

behavioral probability. This S-R connection was believed to form automatically and slowly, without the animal being aware of it. Graphs of individual performance show that neither insight nor sudden grasp of the solution was the basis for the animal's intelligent response. Thorndike's animals showed no signs of dramatic performance shifts that would suggest a sudden avalanche of "ideas" appropriate to the solution of the problem. Thus, the cats evidently did not figure out the solution; rather, the habit of performing the correct response just became stronger through experience.

But what was the precise mechanism for habit growth? The answer from Thorndike was contained in his best-known principle, the **law of effect**. This principle states that it is the effect of a response on the environment that determines whether or not the S-R connection will form. If the effect of the response is pleasant and occasions "satisfaction," then the S-R connection will strengthen and behavior will become likely under the conditions that prompted it. Alternatively, if the effect of the response is unpleasant and occasions "annoyance," then the S-R connection will weaken and the behavior will be less likely to be evoked when similar circumstances recur. In current terminology, the law of effect corresponds to positive reinforcement (reward) and punishment.

Skinner and Operant Conditioning

Although Thorndike was the first to recognize the importance of instrumental concepts, the legacy of B. F. Skinner has had a more lasting impact in the area. Skinner's version of instrumental conditioning, called **operant conditioning**, provided a technologically based model that continues to generate a great deal of research.

operant conditioning Skinner's account of instrumental learning that involves environmental control of responses

Because it is easier to control learning environments for animals than for humans, operant conditioning researchers have often used rats and pigeons as subjects. Should you ever enter an operant conditioning labora-

FIGURE 6–12
Developed by B. F. Skinner, the operant chamber automatically records lever responses. Under certain conditions, such as when a light comes on, lever responses deliver a reinforcer (food) to a feed trough protruding into the chamber.

tory, you may well see a rat in a chamber called a Skinner box (operant chamber), similar to the one shown in Figure 6–12. Inside the chamber you might see a feed trough, a lever, a light display, a tone generator, and perhaps some other objects, depending on the design of the experiment in progress. For purposes of illustration, let us suppose that we are observing a rat that has learned to depress a lever when a light comes on in the chamber. When the light goes off, the animal loses interest in the lever, but as soon as the light is turned on again the rat rushes over and presses the lever. How did the rat learn to do this?

From the point of view of operant conditioning, the answer to this question rests with what has happened in the past when the rat has pressed the lever in the presence of the light. A program has been implemented that delivers food to the chamber when the lever is pressed, but this is true only when the light is illuminated. When the light is off, lever pressing has no effect—the rat gets no food. In operant terms, the food is a *reinforcer*, and it increases the rate of those responses that produce it. Thus, the positive outcome (reinforcement) associated with pressing the lever under certain conditions increases the likelihood that lever presses will occur under just those conditions. In this regard, the light is viewed as a **discriminative stimulus (S^D)** because it serves as a cue to indicate the particular conditions under which responses will be reinforced. Reinforcement, then, controls responding by selectively strengthening behaviors (called operants) that act on the environment to produce change. Consider, for example, that the way we dress may be determined by the reactions we get from others when we wear a particular garment. Even our attitudes or beliefs about certain things may be determined by the agreement, or lack of it, that follows our expression of an opinion. The key is that the outcome of responding determines the future probability of behavior.

Reinforcement manipulations seem easy to carry out, but this is often a deception. The best conditioning occurs when reinforcers are given immediately so that the proper associations are formed. Otherwise, you may unintentionally strengthen the wrong responses. Take the case of Marvin, a 9-year-old boy. Marvin is irrefutably mean, a heedless little brat justifiably

discriminative stimulus (S^D) stimulus that sets the occasion for a response that leads to reinforcement

disliked by his friends, brother and sister, parents, and the family dog. One afternoon after school, Marvin comes home and is tempted by the tulips his mother has painstakingly attended for several months. Giving in somewhat lyrically to his darker side, Marvin proceeds to pluck every flower from the bed, using them to spell out some vulgarity on the front porch. Immediately he goes inside the house, only to realize what is going to happen when his mother finds out about the tulips. As a result, he is inspired to clean his room, to make up for his misdeed. Meanwhile, Marvin's mother discovers that her tulips have been ravaged, and knowing that he is the culprit, she administers a severe thrashing that gets even Marvin's attention. The resulting hostility and aggression felt by Marvin lead him to go out back and abuse the perfectly innocent dog. Meanwhile, Mom finds that Marvin has cleaned his room. She wants to encourage this sort of behavior, so she asks her "reformed" son to come in for milk and cookies. In operant terms, this is what has taken place. Marvin, in this bizarre sequence of errors, has been *punished* for cleaning his room and *rewarded* for assaulting the dog.

Along the same lines, one is reminded of a true story that involved the leader of one of the world's superpower countries. Fond of dogs, the leader kept his pet with him in his office. But a problem soon developed. The animal began to chew the carpet in the office. To distract the dog from the undesirable behavior, this nation's most powerful person would simply toss the animal a doggie biscuit, which would cause the dog to stop, at least for a while. In a short time, however, the animal was back at it, and the cycle repeated itself. Finally, an observant cabinet member who had been a witness to this scene several times explained to the dog's owner that he was reinforcing the chewing of the carpet. "You are teaching the dog to chew the carpet in order that he may receive the biscuit," was the studied comment. The leader just couldn't make the connection. "No, the dog stops chewing the carpet when I give him the biscuit," was the reply. In this case, deference to authority ruled, and the dog continued to have his way with the tax-supported furnishings.

Examples such as these may seem farfetched, but they do occur, and they underscore the need for controllers of behavior to understand the connection between specified responses and presumed outcomes. Consider your own experiences. When you were a child, were you ever punished for something for a reason you never really understood? Still, when an enraged parent three times your size shouted, "You know why you are being punished, don't you?" it was probably in your best interest at the moment to nod yes. Yet in such situations, the behavior and its consequences are not likely to be associated because of poorly defined operant relationships. For operant control to be effective, both the behaviors and the outcomes must be clearly outlined and the appropriate connections must be made.

Shaping

In the earlier example in which the rat learned to press the lever to receive food, you may have wondered what made the rat press the lever initially. Pressing levers that protrude into experimental chambers is not a natural behavior for a rat, and so it commonly does not occur with high probability. Furthermore, if you just leave the rat to its own devices, don't expect to get out of the lab early, because you will be around a long time before it will ever press that lever. Fortunately, there is an operant conditioning technique that permits the learning of a novel behavior to occur at an accelerated pace.

Through the process of **shaping**, experimenters or anyone else involved with training animals to perform can decrease the time required to learn the task. Shaping is achieved by reinforcing approximations to a goal behavior in a step-by-step fashion. Regarding the lever press, you begin by reinforcing

shaping reinforcing successive approximations to a goal of behavior any activity in the vicinity of the lever. Rats are dynamic creatures and will spontaneously make contact with the lever just from energetically moving about. After the animal learns to stay close to the lever, you elevate the criteria so that the rat must stay close and touch the lever with its paw. Eventually, you reinforce only partial depressions of the lever, and then later a full lever press hard enough to trigger the food dispenser. By reinforcing gradual improvements in performance, you ensure that the animal quickly adds a new behavior to its repertoire.

Deliberate acts of shaping also are necessary for many things that we humans do; even writing your name reflects a shaping process. In the beginning, you scrawl out a few symbols that appear rather like letters, but they are not really. Yet with encouragement, you gradually improve until you are able to offer a polished version. Similarly, learning to play a piano, moving from simple scales to classics, involves a systematic shaping process over a period of years.

Basic Training Procedures

It is becoming increasingly common to classify the various training procedures used in operant conditioning according to two main features: (a) whether that response produces or removes a stimulus, and (b) whether the stimulus is appetitive (positive) or aversive (negative). Figure 6–13 summarizes four basic conditioning paradigms formed by the interaction of these factors.

Positive Reinforcement. In **positive reinforcement**, also known as reward training, the emission of an operant response is followed by stimuli called positive reinforcers that make the actions that produce them more probable. Positive reinforcement is used extensively inside and outside the laboratory as a behavior control technique designed to increase responding. Earlier, we discussed how food worked as a positive reinforcer for increasing lever pressing in a rat. Similarly, congratulating a young girl after her first piano recital, patting your dog on the head after it successfully completes a new trick, and telling an employee that he or she has done a good job all involve positive reinforcement. In each example, an operant behavior results in something positive. The importance of this sort of reward is recognized by parents, educators, animal trainers, business executives, and in fact almost everyone who

positive reinforcement when actions that follow an operant response make responding more probable

Response Outcome		Appetitive	Aversive
Response produces stimulus		**Positive Reinforcement** • Rat presses lever for food • Employee receives praise for a job well done	**Punishment** • Rat runs to the end of a maze and receives electric shock • Political figure who has made a mistake suffers public contempt
Response prevents or eliminates stimulus		**Omission Training** • Rat presses lever and causes a scheduled delivery of a food pellet to be skipped • Misbehavior results in being sent to your room	**Negative Reinforcement** • Rat turns an activity wheel to terminate electric shock • Student studies to avoid failing an exam
		Appetitive	Aversive
		Type of Stimulus	

FIGURE 6–13
The four basic training procedures used in operant conditioning.

is a controller of behavior. When you want to encourage responding, you reward appropriate behaviors by dispensing positive reinforcers.

Punishment. When a response results in the production of an aversive stimulus, the conditioning procedure is called **punishment**. The effect of punishment is to suppress responses that have led to it. Some common punishing stimuli used in the animal laboratory are electric foot shock, a blast of air to the face, or loud noises. Unfortunately, the use of punishers in the human community is all too obvious, but we have more to say about this later.

Omission Training. Rewards for what we do right and punishments for what we do wrong are familiar techniques. But other methods are available that accomplish the same goals in terms of increasing or suppressing behavior rates. **Omission training** is one alternative to the use of punishment. In this procedure a positive reinforcer is given as long as an unwanted behavior does not occur. When the unwanted behavior occurs, it results in the omission of the next scheduled reward; that is, the response removes a positive stimulus. The effect of omission training is to decrease the likelihood that undesirable responses will occur again, and in that regard the result is the same as with punishment. With humans, grounding, being sent to your room, and not being able to watch TV all involve the loss of positive reinforcers that would have been attainable had the unwanted responses not occurred.

Of critical importance to the successful implementation of an omission program is what actually happens following the response. It does no good to take away one reinforcer and then replace it with one that is equally valued. Should a parent place a child in the corner of a room for misbehaving, only to discover later that the child has struck up a warm relationship with a friendly Japanese beetle and a companion daddy longlegs, behavior change should not be expected. This is similar to expelling a child from school for bad behavior and then realizing that the student spent the unexpected free time at the local fishing hole. There is no loss here, but rather a gain. So if omission training is to be used effectively as a control agent, care must be taken to ensure that the consequences of responding are what you intend them to be.

Negative Reinforcement. **Negative reinforcement** is a training procedure wherein operant behaviors terminate or postpone the delivery of aversive stimuli. As is true for any type of reinforcement manipulation, response probability increases. It is a general rule that more aversive stimuli produce greater performances than less aversive stimuli.

Examples of negative reinforcement abound in everyday life. Sometimes, the responses involved in such cases terminate aversive events that are already present, as when a window is closed to shut out traffic noise, or when a person takes aspirin to decrease headache pain. In other instances, negative reinforcement involves the removal of threatened aversive stimuli. Indeed, anyone who has ever studied to avoid failing an academic course has been controlled in this way.

Stimulus Control

In our earlier discussion of Pavlovian conditioning we mentioned the importance of the procedures of generalization and discrimination. These two phenomena are also of concern in operant conditioning, but they are usually dealt with as special cases of **stimulus control**. This concept presumes that only certain environmental events become defining features in conditioning. Under natural conditions, where there is no explicitly programmed discriminative stimulus (S^D) that signals reward availability, there is still a restricted set of

---

punishment aversive events that follow an operant response and that make responding less probable

omission training occurs when an operant response removes a positive event and thus becomes less probable

negative reinforcement occurs when an operant response removes an aversive event and thus becomes more probable

stimulus control an operant response occurs only in the presence of selective stimuli

stimuli that specify the conditions under which the response is likely to be reinforced. The lion learns through experience to hunt the wildebeest after a heavy rain, for the wildebeest is slowed by the muddy terrain and therefore makes easy prey. At the human level, we learn that one form of conduct is appropriate in church, another at parties, and so forth. On close examination, many such behaviors can be reduced to sophisticated instances of stimulus control.

In view of the demonstrated precision that is attainable with stimulus control training, it is not surprising that some investigators have cleverly sought to show how animals can become organic computers. Verhave (1966), in an attempt to liberate quality-control inspectors at a pharmaceutical company from the mindless task of monitoring defective capsules, offered pigeons in their place. Each bird was taught to scan capsules as they were moved past on an endless belt (see Figure 6–14). Through a careful process of discrimination training, the pigeons, which have exceptionally acute vision, became extraordinarily adept at identifying "skags." A skag is a capsule that should be discarded because it is off-color, has a piece of gelatin sticking out, has a dent in it, or has another defect. Rewarded with food for pecking a disk when a capsule was judged to be imperfect, the pigeons responded with 99% accuracy. No human being could maintain such accuracy, and pigeons work cheaper. Nevertheless, after a period of initial excitement on the part of some top corporate executives, the project was scrapped because of possible adverse publicity. After all, who would accept medicine inspected by pigeons?

Secondary Reinforcement

No one is likely to dispute that there are certain kinds of outcomes or reinforcers that are meaningful to every person on earth. Food, water, and a place to lie down at the close of an exhausting day are things we all need just to survive, and people understandably seek to obtain them. Because these reinforcers are natural and have biological relevance, they are called **primary reinforcers**. Primary reinforcers tend to be few in number, and they generally operate uniformly across species.

When an event acquires reinforcing properties because of an association with a primary reinforcer, that event is labeled a **secondary reinforcer**. Secondary reinforcers, also known as *conditioned reinforcers*, constitute a distinctive category of stimuli that determine much of what we do. They include books, music, art, report cards, attention, and even other people. Essentially all the elements having membership in this class of events are fundamentally neutral, but due to their conditioning history they have taken on added meaning and power.

Secondary reinforcers can be used in many different ways. For example, when previously neutral stimuli are presented as tokens (secondary reinforcers) that can be exchanged for backup primary reinforcers, they can be used effectively to modify behavior in the classroom.

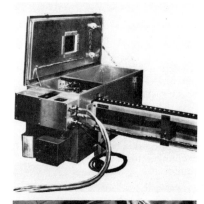

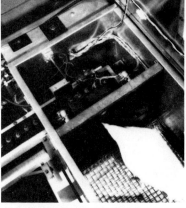

FIGURE 6–14
Top: Apparatus used by Verhave to monitor defective capsules. *Below:* A pigeon working inside the apparatus as a quality control inspector. (From Verhave, 1966.)

primary reinforcers natural events having biological relevance that are capable of increasing the probability of behaviors that produce them

secondary reinforcer a neutral event is paired with a primary reinforcer and takes on the properties of that primary reinforcer

> THINKING ABOUT
> # A Token Economy

Think back on your early years in school. What were your days like in the classroom then compared to now? Certainly college is more demanding, and the intensity level has jumped several notches since elementary school. Even the reward and feedback systems have changed. Often because of the large number of students in a class, a professor may seem indifferent to individual needs. This contrasts sharply with the attention and high-frequency reward schedule that likely was used when you first began your education. Recall all the decals, happy faces, and gold stars that were placed on your papers to punctuate your teachers' approval? As with all secondary reinforcers, these feedback stimuli were of no intrinsic value, but they did stand for something very important—success.

Another reward program that you may have been exposed to during the early grades is known as a *token economy system*. A **token economy** is said to exist when a variety of target behaviors are reinforced with poker chips, points marked on a sheet of paper, or some other secondary reinforcer (called a token) that can be traded in for different primary reward objects. Typically, the supply of exchange items, such as trinkets, marbles, and candy, are kept at a sort of "store," and the teacher dispenses these to worthy recipients who have earned the necessary tokens to complete the trade. For example, a student may get a check by his or her name each time a section is completed in a math workbook. When five checks are garnered, the student has a choice of a piece of candy, a magnet, a ribbon, balloons, or free time.

The educational psychology literature is full of examples of the successful implementation of token economy programs. In some instances, token economies are used with just one person. In other cases an entire class or even an entire school system may be placed on a token economy program. Most of the time real benefits are associated with token systems (Sullivan & O'Leary, 1990). Improvements in spelling, mathematics, and virtually every academic subject have been reported following the introduction of token economy programs, and in most cases the gains are lasting (Domjan, 1993). Outside the educational environment, token economy programs have proven effective in teaching skills to prison inmates, and they offer an effective alternative to treating schizophrenia and other psychiatric disorders (Glynn, 1990).

A case can be made that secondary reinforcement techniques involving token economies are more desirable than behavioral control programs using primary rewards. For one thing, presenting a person with a "menu" of primary reinforcers ensures that the individual will get something he or she really likes. Moreover, in most cases it is easier to dispense a secondary reinforcer (token) than a primary reinforcer. Think about attempting to teach a mentally retarded child to form words properly. Surely when the child forms the word appropriately, it is easier to give the child a poker chip to deposit in a container than it is to stop and give her or him some ice cream. Primary reinforcers often disrupt the continuity of the training session. Finally, secondary reinforcers are not as likely to cause satiation, as primary reinforcers can. A child may soon grow sick of candy. By giving the child candy only after several tokens have been collected, the training period can be extended.

Of course, token economy systems are not perfect. What happens when you take away the tokens? Can people become so dependent on the tokens that they will settle for nothing less? What other problems might there be with this system? Think about it; we will discuss some of these issues again in Chapter 9.

Generalized Reinforcers

Our discussion of token economies leads to another important point. Sometimes, a researcher, teacher, or therapist may be concerned that the reinforcer they have selected for controlling behavior either is of no value to the person or may lose its value. Under these conditions the ability to control behavior is lost. Tokens have an advantage in that they can be exchanged for so many different things that one of the options surely will look good. Therefore, with token systems the chances of losing control are not as great as they might be with some other procedure.

On a more general level, what we are talking about here are *generalized reinforcers*. Generalized reinforcers are secondary reinforcers that are associated with a wide variety of other reinforcers such as food, clothing, shelter, and luxury items. Money is a good example of a generalized reinforcer. A major advantage of generalized reinforcers is that motivation to respond is almost guaranteed. Think about it. Is there anything you would like to buy or a situation in which money would be useful to you? Perhaps a new book, or a replacement part for a computer, or a plant for your room would be nice. The point is that you can always find some use for a generalized reinforcer. Consequently, this type of reinforcer never loses its value, a quality that is extremely important for a behavior controller.

Chaining

With respect to the animal learning literature, one of the most famous studies of secondary (conditioned) reinforcement ever conducted is the now classic experiment by Wolfe (1936) that used primates in conventional parallel roles to humans. In a series of experiments, chimpanzees were taught to insert a chip into a vending machine (the "chimp-o-mat" pictured in Figure 6–15) to get a grape. After the secondary reinforcement properties of the chips were firmly established, the chips were used to reward the animals when they performed physical labors, such as moving heavy boxes or pulling a weighted lever. Interestingly, as the tokens became abundantly available, the chimps began to hoard them, just as some humans hoard money. An intriguing question arises: Are we going to the human version of the chimp-o-mat when we go to the local food market and exchange tokens (money) for vegetables, meat, and other commodities?

The use of secondary reinforcers in this example further illustrates a phenomenon known as **chaining**. Chaining occurs when a subject performs several different behaviors in sequence in order to obtain a reward. In the study by Wolfe, the chimps first had to work to obtain the token, then they had to place the token in the vending machine. Once the final behavior in the chain was accomplished, food (the primary reinforcer) became available.

Of course, most of the chained behaviors that occur in the span of our busy lives are far more complicated. You attend college for years, each semester building up credits (secondary reinforcers) that tell you to keep going until you eventually get to the one response (walking across the stage and receiving your diploma) that has been your objective from the beginning. Your degree, your sense of accomplishment, and the knowledge you have acquired during your college years have been made possible through chaining.

The fact that complex chains can also be formed by animals has been demonstrated by some quite resourceful rat trainers (see Figure 6–16). With astonishing ease, a rat named Barnabus, possessing no special pedigree, learned to master this complex chain: The animal was required to ascend a spiral staircase to a platform and then, after crossing a moat, climb a ladder to another platform. Next, upon pedaling over to yet another platform and ascending another staircase, Barnabus had to run through a tube to an elevator door, enter the elevator, and raise a flag. When the flag was at high mast, the elevator descended to the ground floor, whereupon a buzzer sounded, cueing Barnabus to scuttle over to a lever located on one of the walls and press it to receive food. After eating, Barnabus was ready for a second engagement.

FIGURE 6–15
The "chimp-o-mat." This chimp has learned to place a token (chip) in the vending machine in order to obtain a grape. Later, chips can be used as conditioned reinforcers when training the chimp to perform in other settings.

chaining several different behaviors must occur in sequence before a single reward is given to the last behavior in the sequence

continuous reinforcement training schedule in which every criterion response is rewarded

intermittent reinforcement training schedule in which some criterion responses produce rewards and some do not

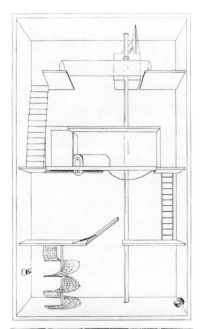

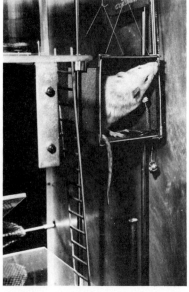

FIGURE 6–16
Top: The apparatus used to demonstrate chaining, with Barnabus the rat as subject. *Bottom:* Barnabus riding his elevator. (Pierrel & Sherran, 1958.)

Schedules of Reinforcement

The schedule of reinforcement is probably the most heavily researched topic in all of operant conditioning. By *schedule* we mean the program settled upon by the experimenter that specifies how and when rewards will be delivered. The significance of schedule variables derives from the fact that unique rates (number of responses per unit time) and patterns of responding are produced by selected schedule conditions.

Usually, we distinguish between two major types of reinforcement schedules, **continuous reinforcement** schedules and **intermittent reinforcement** schedules. The latter are also known as partial reinforcement schedules. Continuous schedules are defined as schedules that reinforce the occurrence of every operant behavior that satisfies an accepted criterion. Attending to a newborn infant's every whimper and giving food to a rat for every lever press are examples of continuous reinforcement schedules. However, rarely in the real world is a reward given following every response. Mom and Dad cannot always be around to satisfy their baby's every need, any more than a trout will always be available to the Alaskan brown bear that goes to the stream in quest of it. In the more typical case, reward items are found only occasionally. It is this occasional reinforcement of responding that defines intermittent reinforcement schedules, and it is this concept that deserves the greatest attention. The four most common intermittent schedules are as follows.

Fixed-Ratio (FR). In a *fixed-ratio* schedule, behavior is rewarded after a fixed number of responses have been made. Under an "FR-12," for example, every 12th response that satisfies a set criterion will be followed by a reinforcer, regardless of how much time has elapsed from the first to the last behavior. There are many circumstances where such schedules are used, both in the laboratory and ordinary work settings. A maid who receives payment for a specified number of hotel rooms cleaned, a migrant worker who is compensated for a certain number of bushels of fruit picked, or an industrial worker whose wages are adjusted according to unit output (piece work) are all responding according to FR schedules.

Fixed-Interval (FI). In a *fixed-interval* schedule, the subject is rewarded for the first response that occurs after a specified period of time has elapsed. Note that this does not mean that reinforcement is delivered for an FI-2 schedule every 2 min. Rather, it means that after 2 min has elapsed, the first criterion response to occur is reinforced regardless of how long it takes the subject to make it. Once the rewarded response occurs, the 2-min interval starts over. Not surprisingly, most animals eventually learn to discriminate the time relationship, so they stop responding for a period immediately after a reward is given and then start up again just before the 2-min mark.

What are some examples of FI schedules familiar to nonscientists? How about studying for an exam? Like the animal waiting for the appropriate interval to elapse, do you wait to respond (study) until just before the time the reward (exam grade) becomes available? Also, waiting for fruit to ripen on a tree is an example of an FI schedule. It is not very reinforcing to pluck an immature pear from a tree and bite into it. Only after a certain amount of time has passed will the fruit be ripe enough so that gathering and eating behaviors lead to reinforcing consequences. In another realm, the Namibian desert animals that hasten to position themselves properly for the early morning fog, and thereby collect the day's only water allotment, respond to fixed time constraints. Of course, under ordinary environmental conditions there are convenient cues such as calendars, clocks, and the position of the sun to function as signals (S^{D}s) that events are now favorable for responding.

This individual gathering berries may be responding according to a fixed-interval schedule of reinforcement. The response (gathering) leads to reinforcement (ripe berries) only after a certain amount of time has passed since the last season.

Variable-Ratio (VR).   Under *variable-ratio* schedule conditions, the number of responses required for reinforcement changes, depending on where the subject is in the schedule. Thus, although only a few responses may be required to obtain the first reward, a great many more may be necessary before the second is given, and so on to completion. Variable-ratio schedules are specified according to the average number of responses required for reward. For example, a VR-15 schedule may reward the 10th response, then the 20th, then the 15th, and so on, with the average continuing to be 15.

A familiar example of a VR schedule is provided by slot machines at gambling casinos. The number of lever pulls required to produce money from a machine varies. Sometimes only a few attempts produce a winner, yet on other occasions it seems getting another payoff takes forever. Also, think about the reward schedule for a person who sells door to door. Most of the time the person will encounter rejection, but occasionally the sales pitch produces a winner. In such an environment, the salesperson is working on a low-frequency VR schedule. Checking your mailbox is yet another example of a VR schedule. Some days you find mail the first time you check, yet on other days you make multiple trips before the mail is delivered. What other VR schedules can you think of that function in your life?

Variable-Interval (VI).   As one of the most widely used schedules in basic operant conditioning research, *variable-interval* schedules reward responses that occur after one given interval of time, then a different time interval, and still a different time interval until training stops. This schedule is described according to an average interval. For instance, a VI-4 schedule might reward the first response made after 2 min, then 6 min, then 3 min, and then 5 min, with the average being 4 min. Because prediction of the next interval in the sequence is not possible, discrimination of a set time interval does not occur. Consequently, the stop-and-start pattern of FI schedules is not evident in VI schedules. Rather, a stable rate of responding emerges and an even distribution of behaviors over time is apparent. Perhaps this is why farmers are so steady in their efforts to plant and harvest crops. Prices fluctuate on an irregular basis, so rewards sometimes occur close together and sometimes wide apart.

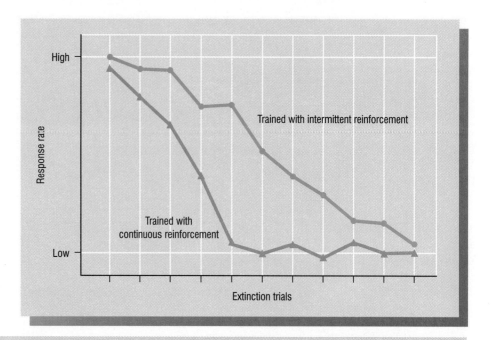

FIGURE 6–17
Typical pattern of response rates during operant extinction for subjects trained with either continuous or intermittent (partial) reinforcement.

operant extinction an operant response no longer produces a reinforcer

partial reinforcement effect the tendency for intermittent reinforcement schedules to produce greater resistance to extinction than continuous reinforcement schedules

With respect to the overall rates of responding produced by intermittent schedules during training, generally ratio schedules occasion higher rates of responding than interval schedules, and variable schedules occasion higher rates than fixed schedules. Moreover, this pattern still holds when the subject is placed on **operant extinction**; that is, when the response no longer produces reinforcement (for example, food does not follow a lever press), behaviors acquired under a VR schedule will continue to occur at a higher rate than, say, those behaviors acquired under an FI schedule. Psychologists often refer to such higher rates of responding during extinction as evidence of greater resistance to extinction.

This brings us to a final, but major, point regarding schedules of reinforcement. Although certain intermittent reinforcement schedules may result in greater resistance to extinction than others, all intermittent (partial) schedules will ultimately lead to greater resistance to extinction than a continuous reinforcement schedule (see Nation & Cooney, 1982; Pittenger et al., 1988). This phenomenon is often called the **partial reinforcement effect**. As shown in Figure 6–17, subjects trained under either intermittent or continuous reinforcement schedules will eventually stop responding if extinction continues for a very long time. But the point at which responding no longer occurs is dramatically different for the two general types of schedule conditions. Thus, if greater persistence is an issue when you attempt to teach a child to clean his or her room, and it usually is, it makes sense to reward the relevant activity intermittently rather than every time it occurs.

The Premack Principle

Until now we have discussed the concept of reinforcement from the traditional point of view that reinforcers are stimuli. University of Pennsylvania psychologist David Premack has stressed that reinforcers may be better conceptualized as responses. The argument is that food itself is not a reinforcer, but rather the activity of eating the food is what is reinforcing. Similarly, working math problems in the classroom may be reinforced by getting to play with friends out on the playground. The key is that recess as a stimulus event is not the reinforcer; it is only a condition that permits preferred behaviors to be performed.

Possibly even more important than questioning the identity of reinforcers was Premack's almost heretical claim that reinforcers are relative, being effective with some responses and not others. Premack set out to show that a reinforcer is any response that is independently more probable than the response that you are trying to condition. This expression is referred to as the **Premack principle**. Implicit in this statement is the notion that reinforcers can be moved up and down a hierarchy by environmental manipulation; that is, most any behavior can be made highly probable (a high-valued reinforcer) or improbable (a low-valued reinforcer) if the external conditions are structured properly.

Premack principle position that states that any high-probability behavior can be used as a reward for any lower-probability behavior

Experimental confirmation of this hypothesis was first provided in a basic animal learning study (Premack, 1962). When environmental restrictions made rats thirsty but not idle, the opportunity to drink water could be used to strengthen the activity of running in a wheel mounted on the side of the test cage. Alternatively, when the rats were restricted in terms of movement but had free access to water, then the opportunity to run in the wheel became a reinforcer for the behavior of drinking water. So, it seems that different events can be accorded different reinforcement status, depending on the conditions under which they are introduced.

The Premack principle circumvents many of the problems inherent in reinforcement applications by focusing on the need for individual training. When the Premack approach is used, what constitutes a reinforcer is individually determined, so you can feel relatively secure that what you are using as a reward is indeed valued. And if the truth be known, on many occasions it is almost impossible to know beforehand what people are going to like. A vivid illustration of the unpredictability of individual preferences is recalled by one of the authors of this textbook. The situation involved a child psychology research project in which three different incentives had to be scaled for value. Specifically, 5-year-olds and 9-year-olds were required to rate Hershey's kisses, marbles, and paper clips and rank them as high-valued, medium-valued, and low-valued incentives. What do you suspect the 5-year-olds picked as their favorite? Candy kisses? Marbles? Wrong, on both counts. Practically every child went for the paper clips as number one. Comments such as "I can use these to play with my magnet" and "Look, I can make a chain out of these," were common. By comparison, the 9-year-olds picked the candy kisses first and the paper clips last. In this context, Premack's argument that we must determine the value of a reinforcer on an individual basis seems like sound advice.

Despite its appeal, the Premack technique is not without shortcomings. For instance, what is considered a reinforcing activity one day may not be the next, even for the same person. Picture this scene: Brad has just offended the biggest guy in school, who also possesses a nasty disposition. Brad is informed that he will be dealt with at recess. Subsequently, Brad's social studies teacher instructs him that only when he completes his workbook may he go out to recess. Do you think this intended incentive is likely to motivate Brad to work on social studies?

AVERSIVE CONDITIONING

Thus far, the bulk of our coverage of learning phenomena has focused on what happens when positive reinforcers (rewards) are used to condition associations between or among stimulus and response events. But as we saw earlier in our discussion of basic training procedures, aversive conditioning also contributes to behavioral development, and the importance of unpleasantness as a control agent should not be ignored.

Escape/Avoidance Learning

Recall that negative reinforcers are aversive stimuli which, when terminated by a response, operate to increase the probability of the occurrence of that response. When animals or people are placed in stressful situations, they will engage in behaviors that have some promise of getting them out of such circumstances. Initially, reactions to aversive events are reflexive and thus often ill-suited to meet environmental demands. With continued effort, however, an appropriate response eventually occurs and terminates the noxious stimulation. This is an example of **escape learning**. Through negative reinforcement, we learn to get away from conditions that are painful or unpleasant. Examples of escape learning include moving indoors to an air-conditioned building on a hot day, taking medication to reduce cold symptoms, and turning off the TV when an absolutely dreadful situation comedy comes on.

Peril is everywhere in life, and we must learn to live in a world that is sometimes unsympathetic. But happily we do not have to actually encounter every negative event to profit and gain in the craft of staying alive. Through **avoidance learning**, the necessary coping responses can be acquired without undue physical suffering. Avoidance training involves using a signal or cue to alert the animal or person to impending danger (see Levis, 1989). This is conveniently illustrated by placing an experimentally naive rat in a chamber that has two compartments separated by a barrier (see Figure 6–18). One side has lights, which can be illuminated by control equipment. The floor consists of grid rods that can carry electric current to the rat. Training begins with the animal placed in the compartment that contains the lights. A light is then turned on and after 5 sec, a moderately intense electric shock begins and forces the rat to cross the barrier to the other safe side of the apparatus. After several sessions (trials) the animal learns that the shock can be avoided alto-

escape learning aversive conditioning procedure in which a response terminates a primary aversive event

avoidance learning aversive conditioning procedure in which a response terminates a conditioned aversive event

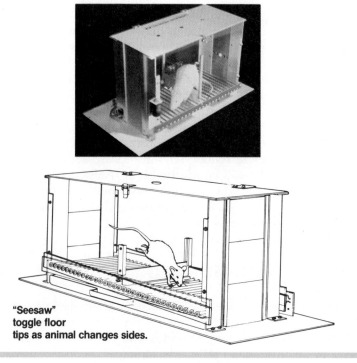

FIGURE 6–18
A shuttle cage is frequently used for avoidance conditioning. A tone or light cue may be used to warn the subject of an impending shock through the grid bars of the floor on his side of the cage. Shock is avoided and the intertrial timer is reset when the subject avoids the shock by moving to the other side.

"Seesaw"
toggle floor
tips as animal changes sides.

gether by fleeing to the safe side within 5 sec of the onset of the light in the shock compartment of the apparatus. Avoidance training is now complete.

Punishment

Punishment is another aversive control technique. As stated previously, the effect of punishment is to decrease the probability of the response that produces it. Unlike the case of escape/avoidance conditioning, where aversive stimuli are used to encourage responding, punishment uses aversive means to make a response unlikely. It follows from this distinction that the same aversive event may be appropriately labeled as a negative reinforcer (a stimulus that, when terminated, increases response strength) or punisher, depending on its use, and in fact may simultaneously function as both. A porcupine is a punisher for a dog that unwisely chooses to battle with it, and at the same time it becomes the negative reinforcer for the ensuing escape response when the dog is dispatched to safer quarters. In real-life settings, events are often structured like this. The wrong response results in aversive stimulation that persists until the correct response occurs.

For punishment to be effective, it must be *intense* and it must be *immediate* (Schwartz & Reisberg, 1991). Many parents make the mistake of issuing a mild reprimand following their child's misbehavior, only to see the misconduct reappear. When the behavior is repeated, a more severe punishment is given, and this cycle continues until both parent and child are out of control. Had the more severe form of punishment been used from the outset, it likely would have been more effective. The importance of the immediacy of punishment stems from the need to make the response–outcome connection. Sending a child to her or his room after misbehaving with the pronouncement that "You will be dealt with later," will probably be ineffective because by the time the punishment is meted out, the child may have forgotten the misdeed.

Even though psychologists uniformly recognize that a strong, quickly delivered punishment will suppress behavior, they are at odds about recommending its use. Proponents cite the many clinical cases in which punishment has worked effectively. Take autism as an example.

THINKING ABOUT
Autism

Autism is a psychological disorder in which a person has an intense or unusual need for preventing change, seeks social isolation, and seems unable to relate to others (Davison & Neale, 1990). Autistic people appear to have retreated to an internal world, and they will not permit anyone or anything to intervene. In children this condition is often called *infantile autism*; it is characterized by repetitive, self-injurious behavior.

Several years ago, Ivar Lovaas of the University of California at Los Angeles was working with an autistic girl named Beth. The recommended treatment for Beth was support and nurturing, aimed at restructuring her inner feelings. Beth's self-mutilation was a chief concern of the staff. She often beat her head on the sharp corners of furniture, tore her skin with her teeth or nails, or burned herself. One day, while attending to another task, Lovaas responded to Beth's biting and clawing reflexively. Out of frustration, when Beth began to harm herself, Lovaas turned around and slapped

autism disorder characterized by self-centered thought and self-mutilation

her on her rear, and yelled "Stop it!" Not accustomed to this treatment, Beth looked surprised and did not harm herself for nearly a minute. When she began to do it again, her behavior again met with a quick slap and a reprimand. Each time this exchange was reenacted, the time during which Beth refrained from hurting herself increased (Carr & Lovaas, 1983).

Reasoning that Beth was responding to these painful, but harmless, slaps as punishment, Lovaas moved to control the self-injurious behavior with an electrical prod. When Beth began to bite herself, a brief shock was administered. Although the shock was not strong enough to hurt Beth, it did have the intended effect of decreasing the undesirable behavior. In fact, Lovaas was able to accomplish more in a few days than had previously been achieved over the course of many months!

In Beth's case, the implementation of an aversive control technique actually brought forth a substantial improvement in her quality of life. Soon Beth was able to sit alone while eating, sleep without restraints, and enjoy the presence of other people. Nevertheless, there have been concerns about this form of behavioral control.

Think about it in a broader context. What might be your objections to this form of behavioral control? Do your objections justify recommending against the use of such programs?

Because punishment can produce negative side effects, Lovaas and others more recently have recommended that reward (positive reinforcement) techniques be used instead of punishment in the control of autistic behavior (Kay, 1990). Harsh environments that contain a heavy dose of aversive stimulation are known to foster hostility, aggression, and fear in animals and humans alike. Accordingly, any system that makes use of punishment as a control agent must be willing to accept an increase in these potentially destructive forces. It is not an issue of whether or not punishment works; it does. But along with the gains in control come the disturbing risks inherent in dealing with a volatile organism.

Controllability of Aversive Events

As we have indicated, when you deal with aversive control measures, you necessarily deal with stress. Certain types of aversive stimulation now appear to be more stressful than others. On the surface, bad situations that are controllable would seem easier to handle than bad situations that are uncontrollable, because events outside our influence sometimes add to our anxiety and make things generally worse.

This intuitive position was challenged years ago in a classic study by Brady (1958). In this investigation, aversive stimulation was delivered to pairs of monkeys. One of the monkeys controlled the pattern of stimulation to both animals, while the other had no control. Curiously, it was the "executive monkey" that developed the greater number of fear-related problems. At the time, the interpretation was that the added pressure of control created more stress, and so controllable aversive events were proclaimed to induce more anxiety than uncontrollable aversive events.

The next 25 years of research failed to confirm Brady's findings. Numerous demonstrations showed that when a CS was paired with controllable, escapable footshock in rats, that CS elicited *less* conditioned fear and passivity than the case in which the same CS was paired with uncontrollable, inescapable shock (Cook, Mineka, & Trumble, 1987). Why the apparent inconsistencies between the "executive monkey" findings and more recent reports? It seems that the key is the amount of time the organism is exposed to the aversive events (Abbott, Schoen, & Badia, 1984; Domjan, 1993). With brief exposure to the stressor, uncontrollable aversive events do cause more fear. But exposure to a bad situation for an extended period may cause controllable events (such as those in the Brady study) to result in greater fear than uncontrollable events. It may be the initial high anxiety created by an uncontrollable environment promotes tolerance (habituation) with extended exposure that is not realized in the controllable case (Mazur, 1990). Or, over the long term, it may be easier to accept the situation than to continue to struggle against adversity in an unresponsive environment. Whatever the reasons, many factors affect aversive conditioning, in terms of both the strength of the behavior and the emotions inherent to this form of learning.

Learned Helplessness

Another aspect of aversive conditioning that deserves attention is what happens when aversive events are programmed to occur independently of performance. The preliminary investigations in this area were carried out by psychologist Martin Seligman, now at the University of Pennsylvania. In one of the defining experiments (Seligman & Maier, 1967), dogs were used as subjects and assigned to one of three groups. Subjects in the escape group were immobilized by being placed in a hammocklike device, and then they were administered several strong electric shocks. The animals could terminate the shock by using their nose to press a panel located on either side of their head. The nose press, then, represented a normal escape reaction. A second group, the inescapable group, was put in the apparatus and given precisely the same shock pattern as the escape group, but these subjects were unable to turn off the shock. Rather, the shock ended independently of the dog's performance. A control group was placed in the hammock but given no shock. Subsequently, all dogs were given a routine escape/avoidance task similar to the one described previously. Here the animals received a warning signal followed by electric shock to a grid flooring. To avoid or escape the shock, the dogs merely had to cross over a hurdle to a safe compartment. This task was easily learned by escape and control subjects, but inescapable subjects failed to respond. The dogs that had previously been given inescapable shocks sat passively and repeatedly accepted an intense electric shock, when all they had to do was make a simple escape/avoidance hurdle jump.

Seligman and his co-workers have labeled this phenomenon **learned helplessness**. The reasoning is that exposure to the aversive noncontingency (stopping the shock was not controlled by responding) produces an expectancy that behavior cannot produce changes in the environment. Animals feel helpless because of their previous inability to control the shock, so later, even though conditions are now favorable for responding, that is, they could control the shock by escaping it, they transfer an expectancy of uncontrollability to the test situation. In other words, they don't think they can control the situation at all, even though they could if they would just try.

The concept of learned helplessness has generated an enormous amount of research, and its influence extends to many diverse areas of psychology. The basic principles of learned helplessness have been suggested as possible mechanisms in the development of such varied phenomena as human depression (Abramson, Seligman, & Teasdale, 1978).

Along these lines, the tendency toward developing learned helplessness has been shown to affect job-related performances. Seligman and Schulman (1986) found that people who have a personality style that renders them more vulnerable to helplessness do not make effective life insurance sales agents. In fact, the helplessness-prone agents sold only about half as many

learned helplessness decrease in responding after exposure to uncontrollable aversive events

policies as other agents, and they were less likely to remain on the job for more than one year. Apparently, when you believe you will fail, failure is indeed more likely. Such findings suggest that the learned helplessness model applies to many situations.

BIOLOGICAL CONSTRAINTS ON LEARNING

You may have noticed that much of what we know about the basic principles of classical conditioning and instrumental learning has come from experimental work with rats and pigeons. The reasons for using animals in psychological research are compelling, and we mentioned some of the more important ones in Chapter 1. But a broader issue along these lines has been a topic of debate in the psychology of learning. It relates to the principle of *equipotentiality*. The premise of equipotentiality states that the selection of the species, stimulus, response, reinforcer, and other aspects of the experimental preparation is arbitrary. It really does not matter what combination of variables you choose to include in your investigation, the basic processes underlying learning will be the same.

A considerable amount of evidence now challenges the principle of equipotentiality. As early as 1970 Seligman argued that the dimension of **preparedness** must be included in the analysis of conditioning. Preparedness refers to the idea that innate predispositions determine the conditionability of any two events (Klein & Mower, 1991). Some associations will be difficult to make, regardless of the duration of training. For example, you cannot teach a dog to cough. Try it! You may attempt to establish the cough as a conditioned reflex, or reinforce it some way, but you will not be able to strengthen this response in the animal. Similarly, you cannot teach a rat to back up to receive food, although rats rapidly learn to back up to avoid shock. At the other end of the conditioning spectrum is a natural propensity for some associations to form quickly and easily. This is evident from a classic study on conditioned taste aversion.

In a simple but elegantly controlled experiment conducted by Garcia and Koelling (1966), a group of rats were trained to drink from a spout that was built to produce flashing lights and a loud noise whenever a rat began to drink. A second group of animals drank saccharin water from the drinking tube, but without the external light and noise stimuli. At the same time they were drinking, one half of each group was made ill (either by radiation or by injection with a toxic substance), and one half of each group received electric foot shock. Subsequently, the rats were offered their respective solutions (bright light and noise with water, or saccharin water) as a test for conditioned aversion. The results are summarized in Figure 6-19. For the rats trained to consume water with lights and noise, only those rats that received shock showed an acquired dislike for the test solution. The opposite finding occurred with rats trained on saccharin water; that is, only those rats made ill developed an aversion to the test solution.

From the perspective of Pavlovian conditioning, the taste of saccharin and the audiovisual stimuli represent CSs. And shock and illness (nausea) constitute USs that naturally produce aversive reactions. According to a traditional view of classical conditioning, any combination of CSs and aversion USs should result in a conditioned aversion to the CS, given that the stimuli involved are of sufficient intensity and saliency. Obviously, this is not what happened. Rather it seems that associations were made between internal cues (taste, nausea) and external cues (audiovisual stimuli, shock), but crossover combinations produced no effect. That is, internal to external and external to internal connections were not made.

preparedness principle that states that events vary along a dimension of conditionability

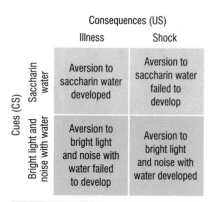

FIGURE 6-19
Summary of the results from a learning study by Garcia and Koelling (1966); see text for explanation.

Why were Garcia and Koelling's animals disposed to form certain connections and not others? Perhaps it has to do with what is biologically relevant in terms of survival. Clearly, it is adaptive to learn quickly that the poisoned food should be avoided. Thus, any process that facilitates a learned aversion to a specific food flavor and thus increases chances for survival should be retained among members of the species. This rationale accounts for the findings just reported, where it was shown that a taste CS, but not an audiovisual CS, produced conditioned aversion when paired with nausea. In the former case the two events are biologically relevant; in the latter case they are not.

The literature on taste aversion supports Seligman's position on preparedness and further calls into question the validity of the concept of equipotentiality. Biological predispositions apparently do determine what types of associations can be learned. Even in situations where preparedness is not a concern, biological determinants of behavior may intrude on the learning process. Consider the work of Keller and Marian Breland. To make their living the Brelands used operant techniques to train animals to perform circus acts, and generally they were very successful in their efforts. However, training did not always go smoothly (Breland & Breland, 1961). The Brelands describe one operation with a pig that ended in failure. The pig, apparently as charming and agreeable as possible for a pig, was presented with the task of putting a wooden disk into a piggy bank. Simple enough, and well within the range of the pig's ability, but the pig became unruly and obstinate. Instead of dropping the disk into the bank, the pig rooted the disk along the ground and was resistant to any attempts to get it to do otherwise (see Figure 6–20). So the Brelands abandoned the pig and substituted a raccoon. The raccoon did fine with one disk, but when required to deposit two disks for reward, performance deteriorated. The animal began to rub the disks together as if it were washing them. When the Brelands attempted to train a chicken to play baseball, things also went foul. All the chicken had to do was learn a simple sequence that consisted of pulling a chain that moved a bat so that a tiny ball was hit to the outfield. Then the chicken could run to first base. The chicken would hit the ball, but then, rather than run toward first, it would chase the ball, pecking it wildly.

Notice that in these illustrations preparedness is not the issue. The problems faced by the Brelands did not result from any difficulty in forming new associations. Rather, existing associations prevented new connections from being established. Because the existing behaviors are part of the animal's natural response profile, the intrusion of such innate responses in a learning situation is called **instinctive drift**. In such cases, the animal's performance drifts away from the reinforced behaviors toward instinctive behaviors. As a result, there are limits to classical conditioning and instrumental learning. In the next section we see that there is an alternative to these more traditional ways of interpreting learning phenomena.

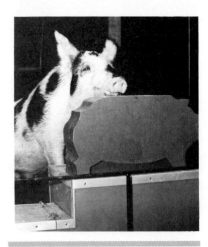

FIGURE 6–20
When Keller and Marian Breland attempted to reward this pig for depositing a wooden disk into the piggy bank, they discovered that the animal was often more concerned with rooting the disk along the ground than putting it into the bank. Apparently, in some cases inborn behaviors interfere with the acquisition of new, learned responses.

instinctive drift natural behavior intrudes on a training schedule, preventing the learned responses from occurring

COGNITIVE LEARNING

Over the past several years the discipline of psychology has experienced a resurgence of interest in higher mental processes. The behavioristic tradition that began with Thorndike and Watson served a needed housecleaning function, in that imprecise methods were replaced with observable, scientific methods. Yet the majority of psychologists today feel that radical behaviorism is excessively rigid in refusing to study mental structures and processes. To fill the void in our understanding of how people (and some animals) respond according to complex decisions, rules, strategies, and other uniquely mental events, the **cognitive learning** approach has reentered

cognitive learning learning that involves mental processes such as thinking and the development of decision rules

the scientific arena. In the sections that follow we discuss several different topics that underscore the importance of cognitive concepts.

Insight Learning

In a typical conditioning study we assume that experience works slowly to form habits, and that, consequently, learning is reflected by gradual improvements in performance over trials. As we have seen, there are many instances of changes in performance that occur in such a methodical fashion. But in some cases the solution to a problem occurs in an instant, with a sudden grasp of the concept. Surely you have had the experience of struggling with a math problem to the point of unspeakable frustration—then, bingo! It's as if you just walked out of a dull haze into the clear light of day. When the solution to a problem is arrived at suddenly like this, we speak of **insight learning**. Systematic research on insight and its effect on performance dates back to the 1920s and the investigations of Gestalt psychologist Wolfgang Köhler. In his classic volume entitled *The Mentality of Apes* (1925), Köhler describes two commonly referenced examples of insight learning.

> CASE 1. A piece of fruit was placed outside the cage of a chimpanzee, at a distance beyond the ape's reach. A stick that had been placed inside the cage was too short to use as a rake for getting the fruit, but it was of sufficient length to reach a second, longer stick that could reach the fruit. After several unsuccessful attempts to reach the fruit with the shorter stick, the chimp (named Sultan) withdrew and sat motionless. He gazed around for a moment and then there was a sudden flurry of activity, wherein the ape grasped the shorter stick, raked in the longer one, and then, without hesitation or miscue, secured the fruit with the longer stick.

> CASE 2. Six chimps (Sultan included) were placed in a cage where, in one corner, a banana was suspended, out of their reach. A small wooden box was positioned on the floor about 2 meters from the point where the food was hanging. After all six chimps made a number of fruitless efforts, one of them (Sultan again) suddenly pushed the box to a location directly under the banana "and springing upwards with all his force, tore down the banana" (Köhler, 1925).

Tool use among primates may further reflect a special case of insight. The now-famous report by Goodall (1971) documenting the use of probes by chimpanzees to gather termites certainly implies a sort of conscious awareness in an animal. When a chimpanzee carefully selects a branch, strips it of its leaves and side branches, breaks it at just the right length, and then carries it over to a termite mound on a fishing expedition, it seems reasonable to suspect that some type of mental activity has been taking place.

Tolman and Latent Learning

Edward C. Tolman (1886–1959) spent nearly all of his professional career at the University of California at Berkeley. For most of this time he stood alone in psychology as someone who advocated the scientific study of cognitive variables that influence performance. This meant rejecting S-R principles and installing S-S (stimulus–stimulus) principles in their place. Opposed to the idea that we associate environmental cues with specific behaviors, Tolman contended that we learn meanings, or the relation of one stimulus to another. In this model, responses are viewed only as convenient, purposeful acts that result in goal attainment.

Tolman's ideas received some preliminary support from experiments designed to show that learning occurs even when performance changes do not. This leads us to a discussion of the phenomenon of latent learning. **Latent learning** is defined as learning that occurs in the absence of apparent reward. Tolman believed that animals incorporate information about their

insight learning sudden awareness of the solution to a problem

latent learning learning in the absence of apparent reward

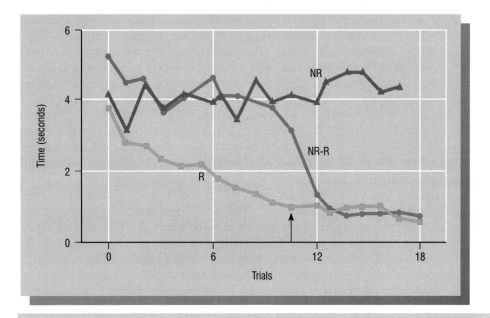

FIGURE 6-21
Results of the Tolman and Honzik (1930) latent learning experiment. The control group NR never received reward in the complex 14-unit maze. A second control group R always received reward in the maze. The experimental group NR-R did not receive reward for the initial 10 trials but then was shifted to reward for all remaining trials.

environment, almost incidentally, even when there is no explicit incentive to do so. In a maze, therefore, animals should form S-S associations just from exploring and moving about. They learn where one cue is relative to another and file facts away for later reference. Given an appropriate demand for an object, like food, they then retrieve the relevant maze information and respond accordingly. The prediction would be that dramatic one-trial increases in performance would occur, given the right training conditions.

The right training conditions were evidently present in a study by Tolman and Honzik (1930). One of three groups of rats was tested in a complex 14-unit maze, with food reward always available in the goal box. A second group received no reward in the maze. A third group received no reward in the maze until over half the training trials in the maze were completed. Then reward was made available on all remaining trials. As shown in Figure 6-21 the performances of subjects that were shifted from receiving no reward to receiving a reward improved immediately to the level of those subjects that had been given a reward throughout the training. It seems that the shifted subjects all along had learned as much as their control counterparts. It just took an appropriate incentive to motivate them to respond.

According to Tolman, the rats' experiences in the maze (with or without reward) were sufficient for the rats to form **cognitive maps**, or mental layouts, of the apparatus. The fact that the animals' performances were different initially was the result of differences in motivation, not learning. When reward was introduced for the shifted subjects, their motivational level suddenly was made comparable to that of the subjects that had already been getting rewards. With knowledge of the maze and incentive now equivalent for both of these groups, similar performances would be expected.

cognitive maps Tolman's idea that experiences create mental representations that act as guides for future responding

Abstract Learning

In addition to Tolman's work on latent learning, animal research in the area of **abstract learning** has shown that cognition is an important part of learning in a variety of species. Abstract learning is a form of learning in which the relations between and among stimuli are realized independently of the specific features of the stimuli (Spear et al., 1990). Consider, for example, the situation of an organism presented with the task of discriminating

abstract learning learning in which relations between and among stimuli are more important than the physical features of those stimuli

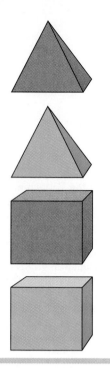

FIGURE 6–22
Stimuli used in studies of concept learning. Stimuli vary on two dimensions (shape and color), with two values on each dimension. All combinations may be presented during the experiment; the subject has to learn which relationships are correct and which ones are incorrect.

matching-to-sample procedure for studying abstract learning in which the subject must learn to respond to the stimulus just presented

oddity procedure for studying abstract learning in which the subject must learn to respond to a different stimulus from the one just presented

observational learning learning that takes place by watching another participant perform the learning task

"same" from "different." When any two identical stimuli selected from the array of items shown in Figure 6–22 are presented on a test trial, the animal must make a specific response. When green square and green square are presented at the same time, the animal, in this case a pigeon, must peck a disk in order to get a reward. Similarly, a reward can be obtained by pecking the disk when a red triangle is paired with a red triangle. By contrast, when dissimilar stimuli are presented together, a different response is required for a reward. For instance, when a green triangle and a green square occur together, the bird must operate a treadmill device to get the reward. Or, if a green triangle and a red triangle are presented at the same time, the "different" response (the treadmill response) is required.

The key in this form of learning is that the animal must learn to respond to the abstractions "The stimuli are alike" or "The stimuli are not alike." The actual stimulus events used in testing are arbitrary. Performance is determined not by a specific stimulus feature, but by a comparison along the dimension of *sameness*. In such comparisons, the organism is responding cognitively and independent of simple stimulus–response connections.

Two commonly used procedures for exploring abstract learning are **matching-to-sample** and **oddity** discriminations. Typically, in these procedures, as shown in Figure 6–23, a center key located on a wall panel in an operant chamber first lights up red or green. When the animal pecks this illuminated key (let's say it is a red key), the side keys—one red and one green—light up. If the problem is a matching problem, the animal is required to peck the red key for a reward. Conversely, in the oddity task the animal must peck the green key for a reward.

Using these techniques, psychologist Tony Wright and his colleagues at the University of Texas Health Science Center in Houston demonstrated that pigeons, as well as monkeys, can match-to-sample on the basis of learning abstract concepts (Wright et al., 1988). After animals had learned to match 152 different pictures of such things as a white martini, a red chicken, and a blue kettle, they tested to see if they would match something like a duck the first time they saw it. More than 80% of the time, the animals transferred responding on the basis of the decision rule. That is, the abstract concept "respond to the stimulus that looks like the sample" was learned and applied.

Animal cognition is an important research area. Learning specialists are beginning to realize that nonhuman species may use abstract assessments and comparisons to make decisions about the world they live in. Clearly, what we normally call intelligence is not the exclusive province of humankind. Even in simpler animals, we do not actually have to perform (behave) for learning to take place. In the next section, we see that the same is true of the most sophisticated human environments.

Observational Learning

Psychologist Albert Bandura of Stanford University was one of the first persons to document systematically the importance of **observational learning** (learning that takes place when one person watches another). Bandura demonstrated that if a child watches an adult behave aggressively, the child behaves aggressively as well. Considering these sorts of findings, it is not surprising that a chorus of complaints about violence on TV have come from parent and citizen groups. One has to be concerned that children who watch fights and killings in the sterile atmosphere of TV settings will model such aggressive displays. In addition to concerns over regular network programming, the controversy over the content of videos on Music Television (MTV) has created quite a flap among parents. MTV has come under the scrutiny of psychology researchers. For example, Sherman and Dominick (1986) have

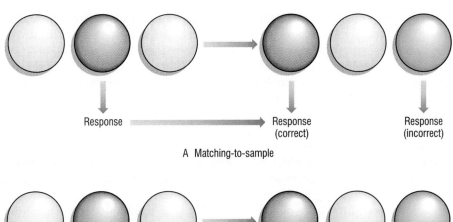

Response → Response (correct) → Response (incorrect)

A Matching-to-sample

Response → Response (incorrect) → Response (correct)

B Oddity

FIGURE 6–23
Matching-to-sample and oddity procedures. A central (red) key comes on and starts the trial. When a response is made to this key, the side keys (one red and one green) are illuminated. Responding correctly on the matching task requires that the subject respond to the red key, while the oddity task requires that a response be made to the green key.

conducted an analysis of MTV videos, and they report that over a 7-week period, violence was a dominant theme in 57% of the cases. Furthermore, 81% of the time the videos containing violence also included sexual imagery.

How all of this gets translated into reality is unclear. Some investigators, such as Freedman (1986), take the position that laboratory demonstrations of the effects of media violence on young viewers' attitudes are meaningless. The argument is that the results from actual field studies do not correspond to what happens in a contrived research environment. On the other hand, Friedrich-Cofer and Huston (1986) make a rather strong case for the validity of laboratory studies of TV violence and empirically question some of Freedman's conclusions. In the final analysis, perhaps the issue will have to be resolved on an individual basis. For some people, media violence may not be influential. For others, it could have a major impact. Which category are you in? Can you really answer this question?

As with instrumental learning, with observational learning it seems there are dispositions toward making some connections and not others. Cook and Mineka (1990) had observer rhesus monkeys watch a videotape of model monkeys responding fearfully to toy snakes. The observers were quick to acquire a fear of snakes just from watching the tapes. However, when the models reacted just as fearfully to artificial flowers, the observers gave no indication they were afraid of the flowers. Consistent with our earlier discussion of preparedness, these findings suggest that there may be biological constraints on cognitive learning, as well as on other forms of learning.

Perhaps one of the most noteworthy features of observational learning is the positive influence it has on human and animal behavior. Have you ever thought about how many of the things you know and how much of what you do result from watching someone else? Music appreciation and even musical performance certainly involve observational learning. Anyone who has ever taken a single piano lesson will recall that one of the first comments the teacher makes is, "Now, watch me, then I want you to try it." Through observation and repetition, and with continued effort, you learn to play. Similarly, when a young boy is faced with tying a knot in a tie for the first time (as many of us know, this constitutes one of the greatest challenges of youth), he is instructed by his father or someone else "to do it this way." You try, you try again, and after several spectacularly unsuccessful attempts, you finally tie the knot. Learning to throw a baseball, fix your hair, apply makeup, climb a tree, do needlepoint, and so many other things are accomplished as a result of watching someone else do it first. So, observational learning is certainly as influential in establishing positive associations as it is in determining the sort of fear reactions and negative connections just discussed.

Animals learn positive relations through observational learning as well. Students of animal behavior have watched for many years as offspring acquire the habits of the older members of the species through observation. For example, it is not uncommon to see a young bear that does not have a clue about how to catch fish stand on the bank of a river and watch with great interest as an older animal uses a particular technique to procure food. The naive observer learns where to stand in the river, when to make a move, and where to go with the food, simply by watching. Such examples are numerous throughout the animal kingdom, and surely observation is an important feature for animal survival.

Observational learning is a transmission of knowledge from member to member of a species, and from one generation to the next. Such instruction ensures that the same mistakes won't be made twice, and that we will not have to start from scratch and learn everything on a trial-and-error basis.

Artificial Intelligence and Parallel Distributed Processing

Cognitive scientists have recently begun to look more closely at computer models of learning, seeking similarities and differences between humans and machines (Bower, 1988). Because humans may process information in machinelike ways, we may be able to obtain clues about human thought by simulating thinking on computers. This line of reasoning has been the inspiration for one of the newest research fields in psychology, **artificial intelligence (AI)**. The term, of course, derives from the notion that intellectual thought can be mimicked with a machine.

artificial intelligence (AI) method of studying cognitive processes by simulating thought on computers

Without getting into the great complexities of AI research, we can say that because of it, many advances have been made in our understanding of how humans learn. But some see as a limitation of the AI perspective its traditional assumption that learning takes place in a serial fashion. That is, ideas occur, they are used, then they are discarded and replaced with new ones on a moment-to-moment basis. Surely this is a reasonable argument, but it fails to account for the fact that in many instances several items must be considered at once.

Take something as simple as catching a ball. You must gauge the trajectory of the object along with its weight and size, decide to catch it with one or two hands, and so on. All this seems to happen so fast that it is difficult to believe that the events are processed one after the other. But what if we assume that the events are interconnected in the cognitive apparatus, and that all of the corresponding mental units are activated at the same time? Then "catching the ball" becomes a stimulus situation that simultaneously switches on different parts of the brain that react to each other. Essentially, this is the view of the perspective known as **parallel distributed processing (PDP)**. PDP models represent a major departure from conventional schools of thought because they suggest that learning takes place in many different locations in the brain at the same time (Rumelhart et al., 1987). And physiological evidence supports this position (Goldman-Rakic, 1988). Cognitive learning, then, becomes an even more complicated phenomenon than previously believed. Uncovering the mechanisms of the mind has always been challenging, and now the task of learning about learning has gotten even tougher.

parallel distributed processing (PDP) position that states that learning takes place in many different regions of the brain at the same time

THINKING AHEAD . . .

In Paris I had brought three books by Henri Bergson: *L'Evolution creatrice, Matière et memoire,* and *Sur les Données immediates de la conscience,* and late one afternoon, sitting on deck, I was reading one of them. Suddenly I was startled by a very loud blast of a bugle. A member of a crew had come up behind me and had taken this customary way of announcing that dinner was served. After dinner I came back and began to read again. I went down the same page, and as I approached the point at which I had heard the blare of the bugle, I could feel perceptual and emotional responses slowly building up. The very thing Pavlov would have predicted (Skinner, 1976)!

This account of the impact of conditioning on human emotion comes from B. F. Skinner. It describes his experience at the age of 24 on a return cruise from Europe. With no formal training in psychology at the time, Skinner was nonetheless able to make the connection between environmental events and behavior. In many ways, each of us conducts a similar informal analysis. How many times have you found yourself thinking about previous experiences and the effect these experiences have had on the way you are today? So often, we see in ourselves a reflection of our past. The boy becomes the man, the girl becomes the woman, and each carries into adulthood the anxieties, uncertainties, strengths, talents, and bold emotions defined by earlier life events. We are who we are because we have learned to be.

As we have seen in this chapter, there have been a number of attempts to characterize the learning process. Almost a century ago Pavlov was formulating his ideas about what happens when two events are paired in time, and Thorndike was focusing on the consequences of responding. The next 50 years would witness a proliferation of animal and human laboratories designed to test the assertions of these and other general process models. The intent was to provide a science of behavior that was rooted solidly in an empirical literature. The last 50 years have been spent revising the early accounts; polishing rough spots; and, when necessary, charting entirely new theoretical courses. But one premise has remained: experience dictates future behavior.

The notion that our experiences in life determine what we think, do, and say presents an immensely provocative intellectual framework. If we accept that we are a product of our environment, what does it mean in terms of individual freedom? Do we really ever make a choice or are we simply acting out a script that was drafted over the course of our lives? Why did you undertake a study of psychology? Given your background and circumstance, could it have been otherwise? Have you ever done anything that was uniquely *yours*, or is it your stimulus history that is unique? Either way, does it make you less special?

In addition to such questions, there is the more profound issue of where we may be headed with our control technology. If we are programmable, what behavioral programs are appropriate for the future? It may be possible at some point to regulate thought with precise conditioning exercises and careful arrangement of environmental contingencies. Behavioral replicas would ensure compliance; there would be no civil disobedience, no discord, no antagonism, no diverting differences of opinion. Interested? Is this world to your liking? If it isn't, can the same forces that make it possible, be moved to prevent it? It's your *choice*.

Classical Conditioning

1. The Russian scientist Ivan Pavlov was the first person to discuss issues related to classical conditioning with others in the scientific community.

2. Classical conditioning is a form of learning in which two stimulus events are associated. Typically, a conditioned stimulus (CS) is paired with an unconditioned stimulus (US) that naturally produces an unconditioned response (UR). The result is that the conditioned stimulus acquires the capacity to elicit a new response (the conditioned response, or CR) similar in form to the unconditioned response.

3. The intensity of the CS and US plays a profound role in the acquisition and extinction of classically conditioned behaviors. As a rule, more intense stimuli produce greater conditioning. Another factor that affects conditioning is saliency. The more salient the stimuli, the more rapid the learning.

4. Classical conditioning may contribute to drug tolerance. Experimental psychologists and the medical community are working together to help prevent such effects when medication is given over a long period of time.

5. Generalization is the process whereby conditioned responses are transferred to novel stimuli on the basis of the similarity between stimuli. Generalization is restricted through discrimination training, which teaches the subject to respond to a select class of stimuli.

6. Blocking, along with other experiments testing the validity of Pavlovian principles, has caused psychologists to reconsider the idea that contiguity is the chief principle in classical conditioning. Recent advances have been made in understanding the biochemistry of classical conditioning.

Instrumental Learning

7. In instrumental learning the consequences of responding determine future response strength. This behavior and the conditions that affect it were investigated first by E. L. Thorndike and later by B. F. Skinner, who called it operant behavior.

8. Four basic operant conditioning paradigms are positive reinforcement, punishment, omission training, and negative reinforcement. Positive reinforcement involves following an operant response with a positive reinforcer, such as food or social praise. Punishment is said to occur when aversive consequences occur to responding. Omission training is the removal of a positive reinforcer following a response, whereas negative reinforcement involves the removal of an aversive stimulus (negative reinforcer) following a response. The effect of reward training and negative reinforcement is to increase response probability; the effect of punishment and omission training is to reduce response probability.

9. Neutral stimuli that are paired with primary reinforcers and thus acquire reinforcement properties are labeled secondary (conditioned) reinforcers. Token economy systems represent one way that secondary reinforcers can be used. Generalized reinforcers are secondary reinforcers that are associated with a variety of other reinforcers.

10. Intermittent (also known as partial) reinforcement results in greater resistance to extinction than continuous reinforcement. Intermittent reinforcement schedules include the fixed-ratio (FR), fixed-interval (FI), variable-ratio (VR), and variable-interval (VI) schedules.

11. The Premack principle, named for psychologist David Premack, states that a high-probability behavior can serve as a reinforcer for a low-probability behavior. This system permits the behavior controller to define reward on an individual basis.

Aversive Conditioning

12. Escape learning involves the acquisition of new responses that lead to the termination of primary aversive stimuli. By contrast, avoidance learning involves learning to respond to a cue or signal that predicts primary aversive stimulation. Punishment is another aversive conditioning technique, but it is used to discourage responding. For punishment to work, it must be intense and immediate. When aversive events are programmed independently of responding, learned helplessness often results and responding does not occur, even when it becomes advantageous to do so.

Biological Constraints on Learning

13. Biological constraints on learning are the limitations imposed on conditioning by the natural tendencies of animals to respond in certain ways. The discussion of preparedness and instinctive drift detailed two ways biology controls learning.

Cognitive Learning

14. Cognitive psychology, which examines mental processes as they relate to learning, has become popular once again. Insight learning, latent learning, abstract learning, and observational learning are four types of learning that are easily understood from within the framework of the cognitive perspective. Artificial intelligence (AI) and parallel distributed processing (PDP) models have recently emerged within the area of cognitive psychology.

Key Terms

learning (212)
classical conditioning (213)
unconditioned stimulus (US) (213)
unconditioned response (UR) (213)
conditioned stimulus (CS) (213)
conditioned response (CR) (213)
asymptote (214)
simultaneous conditioning (215)
delayed conditioning (215)
trace conditioning (215)
temporal conditioning (215)
backward conditioning (216)
extinction (216)

spontaneous recovery (216)
drug tolerance (217)
generalization (218)
discrimination (218)
second-order conditioning (219)
contiguity model (220)
contingency model (221)
blocking (221)
instrumental learning (223)
law of effect (224)
operant conditioning (224)
discriminative stimulus (S^D) (225)
shaping (226)
positive reinforcement (227)
punishment (228)

omission training (228)
negative reinforcement (228)
stimulus control (228)
primary reinforcers (229)
secondary reinforcer (229)
token economy (230)
chaining (231)
continuous reinforcement (232)
intermittent reinforcement (232)
operant extinction (234)
partial reinforcement effect (234)
Premack principle (235)
escape learning (236)

avoidance learning (236)
autism (237)
learned helplessness (239)
preparedness (240)
instinctive drift (241)
cognitive learning (241)
insight learning (242)
latent learning (242)
cognitive maps (243)
abstract learning (243)
matching-to-sample (244)
oddity (244)
observational learning (244)
artificial intelligence (AI) (246)
parallel distributed processing (PDP) (246)

Suggested Reading

Domjan, M. (1993). *The principles of animal learning and behavior*. Pacific Grove, CA: Brooks/Cole. A comprehensive textbook that covers the most recent research in the area of learning. The emphasis is on animal learning, but the basic principles discussed throughout the book are appropriate for human learning as well. This book is designed for the more experienced reader.

Hill, W. F. (1990). *Learning: A survey of psychological interpretations* (5th ed.). New York: Harper & Row. A very readable coverage of some of the major theories of learning. The focus is on traditional learning theories, but more recent developments are also discussed.

Martin, G., & Pear, J. (1988). *Behavior modification: What it is and how to do it* (3rd ed.). Englewood Cliffs, NJ: Prentice-Hall. Applied examples of how learning principles can be used to treat various disorders in humans. Numerous examples of learning applications in everyday life are also provided.

Skinner, B. F. (1974). *About behaviorism*. New York: Knopf. An overview of behaviorism and Skinner's version of it, written in a nonacademic style that is easily understood by a reader new to the area.

CHAPTER 7
Memory

Leslie H. was working late at an all-night convenience store when a man, bleeding from a cut on his face, pulled a gun on her and demanded money. Taking a little over $100 from the cash register, the gunman, holding the pistol to Leslie's head, ordered her into his car to prevent her from calling the police before his getaway. After driving several miles to an isolated spot outside of town, the gunman shoved her from the car and sped away, escaping. In all, Leslie was in the presence of the robber for over an hour, and she reported that during that time she did her best to memorize the man's face.

Leslie, an Asian woman, described the robber as a Caucasian man with dark freckles under his eyes, and gave other descriptive information as well. The police did a good job of finding lineup faces that fit the description, although it was 6 weeks before they finished constructing the photospread. The faces of the men in the lineup were all of Caucasian men with freckles, and although the freckles did not show up very well in the photospread, the two tattooed teardrops under the eyes on one face appeared as dark spots. Leslie identified that face, Karl S., as that of the gunman, beyond any doubt. Although Karl did not fit the victim's description in terms of height, weight, or voice, she later picked him out of a live lineup. Worse for Karl, an analysis of a blood stain taken from the convenience store found that the robber had a blood type consistent with Karl's, indicating that he could have been the gunman.

Convinced of his client's innocence in spite of the confidence that Leslie expressed when she identified Karl as the robber, the defense attorney engaged several independent laboratories to reanalyze the blood stain. Surprisingly, all of the laboratories found that the first blood test had been in error; biologically, Karl S. could not have been the robber. In spite of the victim's absolute certainty of her memory, the biological proof showed that she was clearly wrong, and the case was dismissed.

How could Leslie's memory have been so wrong when the circumstances might have suggested that her memory would be very clear? Does intense emotion really make memories vivid? Did the six-week delay before her seeing the lineup cause her to forget? Did Leslie's verbal description of the armed robber affect her later memory? Did the fact that Leslie was Asian and the robber was not affect her judgment?

These are examples of questions that memory researchers have posed to learn more about the functioning of human memory. This chapter will address these questions and many others related to theoretical approaches, empirical research, and applications of research in human memory.

THE INFORMATION PROCESSING PARADIGM

Scientists typically conduct their research within a *scientific paradigm*, which is a theoretical approach or world view of a domain of science. For example, when a chemist uses models made of multicolored Styrofoam balls connected with various pegs, exchanging some balls for others to represent chemical reactions, it reflects the way that scientists think of atoms and molecules and chemical bonds. No chemist really believes that molecules act exactly as Styrofoam balls, but the analogy is useful and convenient when speaking about chemistry.

Similarly, the scientific paradigm used by many who study human memory views the mind as a special type of computer, a human **information processing system**. No one really believes that the mind works exactly like a computer, but, as in the other sciences, an analogy can be very useful, both for thinking about the phenomena of interest and for describing them. The human information processing paradigm uses a set of descriptive terms for discussing memory, even though the correspondence between those terms and specific physiological systems is not yet known.

Information processing theories of memory often distinguish between three different stages: **encoding, storage,** and **retrieval**. Encoding refers to the mental processes that convert physical stimuli into a format that can be placed in memory, just as material must be typed before it can be saved in a computer's memory. To encode information successfully often requires **rehearsal** of the material, a process involving mental practice or review of the material being learned. Storage, which is also called "retention," is the process of holding or maintaining information in memory, just as a diskette stores information for a computer. Finally, when the stored information is needed, it can be retrieved from memory, which brings the information back momentarily into one's awareness. Similarly, a computer file can be retrieved from the disk on which it is permanently stored. These three basic stages can be used to describe other memory systems as well, such as the way that books can be printed (encoding), saved in a library (storage), and checked out by library users (retrieval).

In the information processing paradigm, memory is viewed as a system of **structures**, or information storage banks, and **processes**, the mental operations performed with the information in memory. There are many different information processing theories and models of memory, and not all of them

---

information processing system
human or computer memory system that encodes, stores, and retrieves bits of knowledge

encoding converting a stimulus to a form that can be stored in memory

storage retention or maintenance of information in memory

retrieval bringing stored knowledge into awareness

rehearsal conscious repetition or elaboration of information in short-term memory

structures memory storage systems

processes cognitive operations and procedures

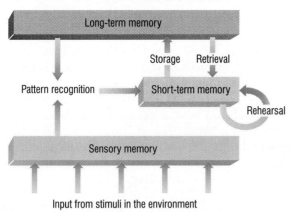

Human Information Processing System

Long-term memory

Storage Retrieval

Pattern recognition → Short-term memory

Rehearsal

Sensory memory

Input from stimuli in the environment

FIGURE 7–1
Diagrammatic representation of the information processing system.

propose the same memory structures and processes. The model shown in Figure 7–1 is a useful and popularly known one. It shows three memory structures, or stores, represented by boxes. Information is transferred among the memory stores by control processes, represented by the arrows.

This information processing theory of memory describes the processes of encoding, storage, and retrieval, in three distinct memory systems: **sensory memory, short-term memory**, and **long-term memory**. As shown in Figure 7–1, stimuli from the environment enter the system through sensory memory (also known as the *sensory register*). By the process of **pattern recognition** (see Chapter 4), the information is encoded and sent to short-term memory, where one becomes aware of the information. If it is rehearsed sufficiently, the information can enter long-term memory, where it is stored more permanently. If needed, the material can be retrieved, or brought back into awareness by being placed back into short-term memory.

We now turn to a more detailed discussion of this information processing model of memory.

sensory memory very brief memory for sensory information

short-term memory memory structure that holds a small amount of information in conscious awareness for a short time usually 1 min or less

long-term memory memory structure that stores information for long periods of time, allowing memory for material that has been out of consciousness for a long time

pattern recognition process of determining what an object is by finding a long-term memory that fits the object's sensory pattern

SENSORY MEMORY

When information becomes available to an organism, the initial step in processing begins with the *sensory register*. This component of the memory system is activated when environmental stimuli evoke the firing of receptor cells in specialized sensory organs, such as those contained in the eye or ear (refer to Chapter 3). Information held in the sensory register remains there only briefly, usually less than a second for visual stimuli and less than 4 sec for auditory stimuli.

Why is the sensory register needed? For the most part, it functions as a preliminary holding bin for further processing. If we assume that the memory mechanisms involved with coding and storage take time, it makes sense that information must remain long enough so that certain preliminary steps can be completed. Without sensory memory, we would not be aware of much of the information we receive—it would just come and go. Thus, sensory memory is important because it gives us time to review novel sources of information and to select key items to consider more extensively.

Although the majority of psychologists now believe that separate registers are associated with each of the primary senses, vision and hearing (audition) have received the most research attention. Accordingly, our discussion of sensory memory is restricted to studies of visual and auditory phenomena.

Visual Sensory Register

Much of what we now know about the visual sensory register we have learned from experiments conducted by George Sperling (Averbach & Sperling, 1961; Sperling, 1960). Sperling first designed an ingenious study to document some key features of the visual sensory register. Human subjects were shown a letter matrix such as the 3 (rows) × 4 (columns) example profiled in Figure 7–2 (below, left). But the visual array was flashed for only 50 milliseconds (msec), too brief a period for them to scan visually. When subjects were asked for a "whole report," that is, for all of the material, they could correctly recall only four or five items from the entire display. Then Sperling introduced a procedure known as the **partial report technique**. In this procedure, one of three distinctively different tones signals the subject to recall one of three rows of letters from the visual matrix. For instance, the participant may briefly view the display and then immediately hear tone 1 and be asked to recall the letters from row 1. On a subsequent trial, tone 2 is administered after the subject views the matrix, and the task is to recall the letters from row 2, and so on. Using the partial report technique, Sperling found that subjects accurately reported virtually all of the matrix. Sperling concluded that the whole of the visual array is stored in memory, but only briefly. When the report procedure is sufficiently concise, any section of the visual field can be retrieved. But when the recall procedure is lengthy, as in the whole report technique, much of the visual pattern decays or is automatically erased before a complete report can be filed.

As further evidence that information in the visual sensory register is held for only a brief duration, Sperling demonstrated that delaying the tone that signals recall in the partial report procedure produced substantial drops in performance. Figure 7–2 (below, right) shows what happened when the delay between the end of the visual matrix and the beginning of the signal to report (tone) was increased systematically up to 1 sec. The number of letters subjects could report declined markedly within .3 sec, and when the delay reached a full second, the number of letters subjects could recall was roughly equivalent to their performance under the whole report condition. Other investigators have reported slightly different results with stronger visual stimuli (Long & Beaton, 1982). But overall, it

partial report technique experimental method in which a cue indicates what part of a briefly presented visual display should be reported, used to measure the sensory register

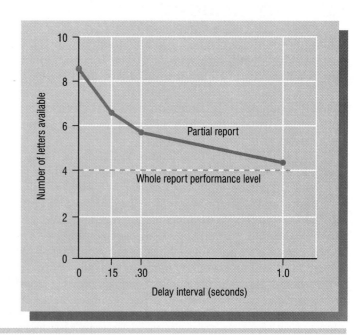

FIGURE 7–2
Left: Example of a letter matrix used in a partial report experiment. *Right*: The number of letters available (recalled) from such a matrix in the "partial report" situation under conditions of varying delay in the interval between the matrix presentation and the signal to report. The dashed line indicates the performance of subjects in the "whole report" condition. (Adapted from Sperling, 1960; see text for explanation.)

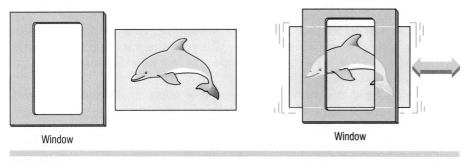

Window Window

FIGURE 7–3

Observing the visual sensory register. You can easily demonstrate the existence of your sensory register by constructing a simple device like the one shown here. On one piece of paper cut out a vertical window about 1 in. wide. On another strip of paper draw a figure that is wider than the window. Now move the figure rapidly back and forth from behind the window. If you wave it rapidly enough, you will see the entire figure, even though the figure is too wide for the window. Your visual sensory register holds one part of the figure while the rest of it moves into view, allowing you to see a complete image of the figure.

is safe to say that methods such as the partial report technique, which are designed to enhance recall of information from the visual sensory register, are no longer effective after a second or so has elapsed following the presentation of the stimulus.

Auditory Sensory Register

There is now substantial support that an auditory sensory register also exists, and that it functions in a similar way to the visual memory structure just discussed. Partial versus whole report techniques, modeled after those previously described for the visual sensory register, have established that information remains in the auditory sensory register for as long as 4 sec.

A real-life example can be used to illustrate how auditory sensory memory works. Think back to any lecture you have had in the past week. Regardless of the communicative talents of the professor or the inherent appeal of the subject matter about which he or she lectures, occasionally your mind is going to drift. Nonetheless, when a new term is mentioned, you usually are able to shift your focus back to the lecture. What is interesting is that you not only recall the new term but also recall what was said immediately before it. The reason for this is that even though the words delivered before the key term are no longer represented physically (in the form of sound waves), they remain in the auditory sensory register just long enough for you to recall them.

SHORT-TERM MEMORY

Although you may not be familiar with *short-term memory* as a psychological term, it is undoubtedly a concept that you know very well. It is the storage of only a few items in memory for a brief period. Short-term memory is what you use when you follow directions, look up a phone number, or mentally review a grocery list. Let's use the example of following directions to clarify what we mean. Assume that today is your very first full day of classes at college. Unless you have made a point of exploring the campus in detail prior to the beginning of school, you probably will have to ask someone where a particular classroom and building is located. Suppose you ask where the chemistry building is. A friend tells you to go to the bell tower, turn left toward the married students' apartments located just off campus, and there you should find the chemistry building, two buildings down on the right. Using rehearsal techniques, you keep this message in your head by replaying it often, as if it were a tape. The result is that you are able to make your way to class.

This example has two central points that relate to short-term memory. First, only a few events had to be remembered. Imagine what would happen if you asked directions to the Shwe Dagon Pagoda in Rangoon, Burma, and someone fed you a landmark-by-landmark description of every necessary move from your present location. You would suffer information overload and lose the early directional components before all the directions could be given! In our example, of course, the directions are simple and easily retained intact. A second issue is the length of time the information was available for recall. What might have happened had you run across an acquaintance on your way to the bell tower? If you stopped to talk, you might not have remembered the directions just given you. Information in short-term memory is usually lost unless it is continually repeated in memory.

The following analogy should help with respect to grasping the nature of the functional role played by short-term memory. Consider that you are sitting at your desk, prepared to draft a term paper on the successes and failures of the Ming Dynasty. You have thoroughly researched the topic, but most of your notes and articles are filed, according to specific reigns, in separate folders located in a cabinet adjacent to your desk. When you begin writing, you select only a couple of folders at a time, and you do this for several reasons. For one thing, you can keep your folders better organized; for another, you could not possibly get all the folders on the desktop at one time anyway. Half of them would fall off or get knocked off. Short-term memory is similarly constrained. You have a limited capacity (desktop), so only a few memory items (folders) can be accommodated at a given time. However, these items can be exchanged for new ones that are permanently located in long-term memory (the file cabinet). This organization provides an orderly method for processing a massive amount of information.

Now that we have learned some of the distinguishing characteristics of short-term memory, it would be worthwhile to examine some of the experimental evidence used to support or refute the validity of the assertions made in this area.

Duration of Short-Term Memory

Rarely in psychology does a single paradigm emerge as a dominant experimental force and dictate thought in an area for several decades. Yet this is precisely what happened with the Brown-Peterson paradigm introduced years ago in separate scientific reports (Brown, 1958; Peterson & Peterson, 1959). The technique, aimed at documenting the rapid deterioration and loss of information housed in short-term memory, is typified by some of the training trials administered by the Petersons. Trials began with a light cueing the subject that an item consisting of a nonsense syllable (consonant–vowel combinations, such as *BUK*) or a word was about to be presented. When the item was presented, the subject was asked to remember it and then to count backward from a particular number until a signal was given, at which time the subject was to report the original item. The mathematical task was considered a neutral exercise that simply took time and did not add to memory. The counting-backward task was carried out for successively greater 3-sec intervals, up to a maximum of 18 sec. Figure 7–4 shows the results from the trials that imposed varying retention intervals. Performance declined systematically with increasing delay before the recall task. The interpretation of this effect was that the math activity prevented the subject from repeating the item over and over during the retention interval. Without this rehearsal, the information that was obviously registered and stored, if only briefly, was lost. We may conclude from this study that some information is stored only momentarily, perhaps not more than 20 sec. Since this early work on the time limits associated with short-term memory, many other studies have confirmed these results.

Capacity of Short-Term Memory

The work of Nobel laureate Herbert Simon and his colleagues at Carnegie–Mellon University indicates that the capacity of short-term memory likely varies, depending on how the information is encoded (Zhang & Simon, 1985). When items are discriminated on the basis of how they sound (acoustical encoding), about seven items can be accommodated at once. However, when items are encoded based on how they look or what they mean (visual and semantic encoding), the capacity of short-term memory is reduced to around three items.

As a rule, when we have a name for something, even if it is a visual stimulus, we encode it acoustically. For example, when we see familiar numbers, letters, or some combination of the two, we process the information based on the sounds corresponding to each item. It follows that immediate memory in such cases can handle only about seven items. Once we reach seven a "no vacancy" sign goes up. This explains why your telephone number has only seven digits. Anything more in the way of information would create problems for short-term memory. Indeed, this was vividly demonstrated by Florida State University psychologist George Weaver in a study of a telephone company policy. Directory assistance operators were requested to say "Have a nice day" after giving out a telephone number. The operators may have been courteous, but they also made it more difficult for people to retain the phone numbers! Apparently, the added information exceeded the seven-item capacity of acoustical memory and everything was lost (Schilling & Weaver, 1983).

Actually, the notion of a seven-item acoustical and a three-item non-acoustical memory span refers to overlapping sensory inputs rather than isolated informational components. In this sense, an "item" is really a **chunk** of information (Miller, 1956). A chunk of information is a discrete, coherent unit compiled from smaller bits of data that share common properties and relationships. In most cases, chunking helps us assimilate information from the environment (Hirst, 1988). For example, an academic concept in chemistry, such as "the negative log of the hydrogen ion concentration," may be reduced to "pH," which is a single, unitary bit of information. On the other hand, chunking sometimes causes us to miss points of enrichment.

Consider two persons reacting to Grant Wood's famous painting *American Gothic*, reproduced in Figure 7–5. One person sees the painting as a simple expression of life in rural Iowa. The husband and his wife reflect the grimness and austerity of an elderly farm couple, and that is pretty much all there is to the painting. Here, the individual processes the painting as a chunk. By contrast, a second observer examines the painting in detail and notes that the painting is not about a couple at all. Rather, it is about a father and daughter. The daughter is portrayed as sexually repressed, yet the single strand of wayward hair snaking mischievously down her neck betrays a spark of defiance and suggests liberation. The pitchfork of the father is interpreted as a symbol of male sexuality and paternal dominance. In this latter case, chunking does not occur, and the artist's original intent is more fully appreciated (see Corn, 1983).

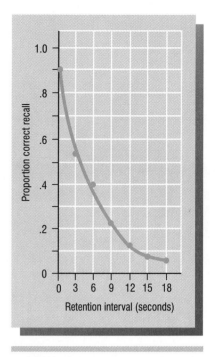

FIGURE 7–4
Proportion of items recalled correctly after various retention intervals. (Adapted from Peterson & Peterson, 1959.)

chunk meaningful or well-practiced unit of information

FIGURE 7–5
American Gothic by Grant Wood can be viewed more than one way. What do you see here?

Because of the limited storage capacity of short-term memory, complex material is often coded according to some scheme that will yield fewer, more meaningful units. An often cited example of the advantages afforded by this strategy comes from experiments conducted by Gordon Bower and his colleagues at Stanford University (Bower, 1972; Bower & Springston, 1970). All subjects in these studies were read aloud the following letters in a memory span task: *TVFBIJFKYMCA*. But one group received the letters clustered by pauses to form the pattern *TVF . . . BIJF . . . KY . . . MCA*. For a second group pauses occurred such that the sequences were heard as *TV . . . FBI . . . JFK . . . YMCA*. Despite the fact that the number of letters in each sequence was identical, the subject's memory in the second condition was dramatically superior. This result most likely occurred because in the first condition there were really 12 items to store (too many for acoustical short-term memory), whereas in the second there were essentially only 4 (well within the capacity of acoustical short-term memory); in the second sequence meaningful chunks were formed that facilitated processing.

In an especially powerful demonstration of chunking, Chase and Erickson (1982) reported the case history of S. F., who developed the astonishing ability to hold 82 digits in short-term memory at one time. This feat was accomplished by converting numerical digits to running times in various track events. For example, S. F., a former member of a championship college cross-country team, would remember 3492 as "3 minutes, 49.2 seconds, near world record mile time." In an elaborate system that developed across more than 200 hours of practice, S. F. was able to chunk sequences of numbers as a series of connected thoughts.

In everyday life, we use chunking when we package information in bundles and attach descriptive labels that we already know something about. We remember addresses, license plates, and a host of other items by coding

Read the following list of words in order, one word at a time. When you have seen each word once (don't look back!), take out a piece of paper. For 2 min, write down all the words from the list that you can, in any order you like.

1. SILICON
2. AARDVARK
3. AGNOSTIC
4. BORSCHT
5. ALLEGORY
6. BLARNEY
7. INERTIA
8. BOROUGH
9. CROQUET
10. ALMANAC
11. SHERIFF
12. TEQUILA
13. DEMOCRAT
14. CUPCAKE
15. NIRVANA

Read the following paragraph after you have recalled the list of words:

To score your free recall test, compare your list to the one in the book, checking each one you correctly recalled. Now, count the number you remembered out of the first five list items, the second five, and the last five. Compare the three totals; most people recall less from the middle of the list, as compared with recall of the beginning and the end. This is an example of a serial position effect.

FIGURE 7–6
Serial position effects in free recall.

---

the information into chunks to create less confusion. Even master chess players take advantage of chunking (see Ellis & Hunt, 1989). It seems that whereas a novice player must use all of the available short-term memory capacity to store the identity, color, and location of a few chess pieces, the master retrieves entire patterns (chunks). Thus, the master is able to consider more sophisticated strategies than the novice, even though the master expends no greater effort.

The Serial Position Phenomenon

Before reading this section, do the free recall exercise shown in Figure 7–6.

When a subject is given an ordered list of items to remember, the subject easily recalls items at the beginning of the list and items at the end of the list. The subject has the greatest difficulty remembering items in the middle of the list. As shown in Figure 7–7, the typical pattern of results accordingly takes on the form of a U-shaped function (the precise character of this curve may fluctuate depending on the methods used in research; see Nairne & Pusen, 1984). Because the location of items within the list seems to be the important variable, this effect has been labeled the **serial position phenomenon**.

How does an information processing model account for these surprising findings? One popular interpretation suggests that the serial position curve results from the interaction of both short-term and long-term memory. First, consider the great ability to recall items from the beginning of the list, a phenomenon known as the **primacy effect**. When an item is at the beginning of the list, the chances that you will rehearse it are good; and, as we discuss later, this rehearsal process causes information to be transferred to long-term memory. Items located later in the middle of the list enter short-term memory while this rehearsal process is going on; as a result, they are largely ignored. This rationale accounts for primacy and the subsequent

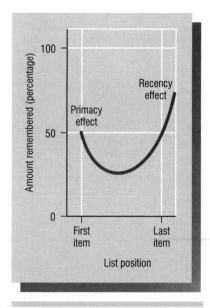

FIGURE 7–7
Idealized version of a serial position curve showing memory as a function of list position.

serial position phenomenon the finding that the position of an item in a sequence influences how well recalled it will be

primacy effect enhanced memory for items presented early in a sequential list

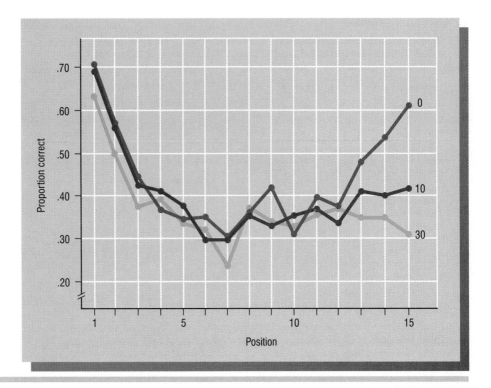

FIGURE 7–8
Serial position curves following delays of 0, 10, and 30 sec between the last item and the opportunity for recall. (From Glanzer & Cunitz, 1966.)

recency effect enhanced memory for items presented late in a sequential list

decline in recall, but what about the upswing in remembering items at the end of the list? This phenomenon, known as the **recency effect**, is thought to occur because items from the end of the list are still in short-term memory and readily available for retrieval.

Such a hypothesis is testable. Glanzer and Cunitz (1966) reasoned that the recency effect, if it is indeed a short-term memory phenomenon, should be affected if there was a time delay between the time the subject was shown the last item on the list and the beginning of the recall test. The idea here is that the information (items in the list) should decay after 30 sec or so because of the limited amount of time information was stored in short-term memory. Thus, Glanzer and Cunitz gave subjects a list of 15 words to remember, and then had the subjects perform a task that prevented them from rehearsing the lists for 0, 10, or 30 sec before they were asked to recall the complete list. As shown in Figure 7–8, the serial position curve did appear following 0 sec, but it was reduced or not present for the longer delays of 10 or 30 sec. Ostensibly, the delay left the primacy effect unaffected because this material was contained in long-term memory, but the recency effect was eliminated because of the excessive time demands imposed on short-term memory. Overall, then, the findings offer support for both short-term memory and a multistore information model such as that presented in Figure 7–1.

LONG-TERM MEMORY

Our focus until now has been on those aspects of memory that last for only short periods of time. Although our ability to extract key input features and to act on them immediately is necessary to our survival, more enduring long-term memories ultimately define reality for each of us. Do you recall advice that your parents gave you years ago about life's challenges? Many people do. Over the years each of us has benefited from the wisdom supplied by others, as well as from the wisdom that we have acquired on our own. But just consider for a moment how old some of these memories are. Also, think about the enormous capacity of long-term memory. Song titles, poetic expressions, and traces of home are among the vast number of items stored for later use. Thus, long-term memory has two important features: the lasting nature of the stored information and the great size of the repository.

In the sections that follow we examine the different types of information in long-term memory, as well as factors that affect the encoding or storage processes, and retrieval or the lack of it (forgetting).

Different Long-Term Memory Systems

In 1972, Endel Tulving made a distinction between two types of information stored in long-term memory. One type of memory, **episodic memory**, refers to long-term memory for events, or episodes that you have personally experienced. This type of memory includes, for example, your memory of your high school graduation, your dinner last Tuesday, and the last time you called home. As the repository of virtually all of your remembered experiences, episodic memory constitutes your living autobiography. Although memory of a few important events will remain with you for nearly your entire life, most episodic memories are highly susceptible to forgetting; you may remember last Tuesday's dinner right now, but you are likely to forget it a month from now.

episodic memory memory for personally experienced events, also called autobiographical memory

Tulving's second type of long-term memory is called **semantic memory**. This type of memory represents your general factual knowledge, such as the formula for computing the area of a circle, the role played by Harriet Tubman in the Underground Railroad, or the meaning of the word *skeptic*. Each of these memories is impersonal, with no definite reference to your own experiences. In contrast to episodic memory, semantic memory is not particularly susceptible to forgetting; if you know the formula for the area of a circle, you will probably still know it next month.

semantic memory memory for facts and other abstract knowledge

More recently, Tulving identified what he believes is a third long-term memory system called **procedural memory**. This refers to memory for skills and habits, such as tying your shoes or hitting a tennis ball. When performing such procedures, you are not consciously aware of each individual movement, nor are you actively thinking about how to combine the movements. In fact, asking your opponent about how she holds her arm when she serves is likely to make her aware of the movements, a good way to disrupt her well-learned skill.

procedural memory memory required for using skills and habits

To demonstrate this lack of awareness for procedural memories, try to describe how you tie your shoes. Do you cross the left lace over or under the right one? How do you pull the loop through without undoing the entire knot? Although most adults have no problem remembering how to tie their shoes, they find it very difficult to describe such memories without going through the motions, either physically or mentally, gaining awareness only by observing their own actions. The lack of awareness we have of such memories contrasts sharply with the direct awareness we have for memories of a conversation, an automobile accident, or a movie. The term for remembering that involves an awareness of one's memories has been termed **explicit memory**, and remembering without being aware of the memory is called **implicit memory** (e.g., Schacter, 1987).

explicit memory remembering that one is consciously aware of

implicit memory remembering or using knowledge without an awareness of remembering

Experimental studies of episodic memory have used primarily explicit tests, such as recall and recognition. These tests direct the subject's attention to the events that are to be recalled; therefore, they are called **direct measures** of memory (Richardson-Klavehn & Bjork, 1988). Psychologists have

direct measures memory tests that direct attention to the target memories being tested

Take a moment to complete some of the puzzles below. Fill in the three missing letters in each one to form a word. Spend about 10 sec. on each.

1. AN_T_ _Y	6. _C_OP_S	11. _NSO_NI_
2. BU_ _A_	7. EL_ _P_E	12. _A_DVA_K
3. _HI_MU_K	8. _E_UIL_	13. LE_TE_ _
4. _IRV_N_	9. T_IC_ _LE	14. _LA_ING_
5. E_PO_E_T	10. LE_ _OS_	15. _IG_E_T

Some of the words may seem easier than others, particularly numbers 4, 8, and 12. Those words were on the study list for the free recall test you took earlier in this chapter (p.259). The other words on this test would seem easier, too, if you had read them recently. Word fragment completion can be used as an implicit memory test, because it tests recent memory without referring to the events being tested. The influence of recent events (the words you studied on an earlier page) on a word fragment completion test is an implicit memory effect, because subjects in experiments do not need to be aware of the nature of the memory test; the effects of memory appear even if subjects do not realize that it is a memory test (answers are on p.289).

FIGURE 7–9
Word fragment completion.

indirect measures memory tests that reflect prior experience but that do not refer to the target memories being tested

now developed tests of implicit memory that are referred to as **indirect measures** of memory, which do not direct attention to the events in question. These indirect measures consist of tasks in which the subject's performance is biased or improved due to recent experience of which the subject is not aware. For an example of an indirect memory test, try the exercise shown in Figure 7–9.

Testing whether subjects are aware that they are remembering is usually accomplished by asking for subjective reports; that is, experimental participants are asked questions about the experiment, such as whether they noticed that some of the test words were from the previously studied list. Subjects are typically surprised to hear that some test words were indeed from a previously studied list. Other evidence that memory can occur without any awareness of remembering has been found with patients suffering from certain forms of amnesia. This topic will be discussed later in the chapter.

As a final note to the issue of separate memory systems, it should be pointed out that not all researchers agree that there are distinct systems. For example, some studies have shown that the same experimental manipulations have exactly the same effect on semantic and episodic memory (Craik, 1985; McKoon, Ratcliff, & Dell, 1986). It may be that these two types of memory have a common basis; some think of semantic memory as an accumulation of episodic events (Ratcliff & McKoon, 1986).

> THINKING ABOUT
> **Permanent Memory**

Have you ever sat back and thought about what your college training is intended to do? Perhaps your academic experiences will serve as a vehicle for personal growth and enrichment, or maybe obtaining a college degree will permit you to get a better-paying job. Whatever your thoughts on the matter, there is the implicit belief that the knowledge acquired during the period of your formal education will stay with you long after graduation; that is, most students enter the educational system with the idea that newly attained skills survive indefinitely. But do they? Just how much of what you are studying now will you remember 10 years from now? How much will you recall 50 years from today?

These were precisely the questions asked by psychologist Harry Bahrick in one of the few investigations available on long-term retention of semantic memory (Bahrick, 1984). In this study, which has already had a profound influence on the way we think about remembering and forgetting in naturalistic settings, 733 individuals were tested for their retention of Spanish learned in language courses at the high school or college level. One astonishing feature of this particular study was that the retention interval indeed did span 50 years. The findings from the various tests of reading comprehension, vocabulary, and grammar showed a very clear pattern; namely, memory of Spanish declined systematically for the first 3- to 6-year period, then there was virtually no memory loss over the next 30 years. Even after the subjects had first learned it, 50 years later, a large amount of the originally acquired information was retained. These results are even more remarkable when you consider that the majority of persons had not rehearsed their Spanish skills at any point after completing the course.

Bahrick interprets his results to mean that the storage of semantic memory (knowledge) involves separate processes. One process leads to the placement of materials in long-term memory for only a few years. The other process results in a **permastore state**, where the information is placed in a sort of mental concrete where it remains for life. The critical concept here is the either–or nature of the memory allocation. Material is tagged for permanent status and preserved, or it is passed over and permitted to weaken. For Bahrick, then, retention of academic facts reflects more than the degree of original learning. Somehow, selective pieces of information are assigned to what has been described as "a mental fallout shelter" (Neisser, 1984) and thereby preserved, or they are accorded reduced significance and thus given less protection.

permastore state condition in which long-term memories are permanently stored in a way that makes them highly resistant to forgetting

Obviously, it would be of great benefit to educators to know what sorts of conditions promote permastore learning and memory. That is, given that the objective of teaching is to impart a knowledge set that serves the student for a lifetime, it follows that instructors at all levels would seek to enhance the life span of acquired knowledge. Along these lines, Bahrick and Phelps (1987) have shown that permastore placement (retention over a period of decades) is more likely when learning sessions are 1 month apart, instead of 1 day apart. This would seem to question the wisdom of a college curriculum based on a system in which lectures are typically given every other day or so, over a period of 15 weeks. Bahrick's studies have now been well replicated and extended (e.g., Bahrick, 1992; Bahrick & Hall, 1991; Conway, Cohen, & Stanhope, 1991). Memory researchers will undoubtedly continue to influence educational approaches, as new discoveries are made.

Thinking back on your own education, what subject do you think has best stuck with you? In light of what you know about the permastore, why do you think that material has remained with you? Can you think of situations in which permastore memories could be a disadvantage? How would your oldest educational memories help you relearn material later in life?

ENCODING PROCESSES

Whatever the number of types of lasting memory, there remains the basic issue of how information is stored in long-term memory initially. What processes are involved in encoding information from short-term memory? What shortcuts help to facilitate storage? Actually, several somewhat interrelated activities must be considered. The encoding processes discussed in the following sections are especially important to understanding how information gets inside long-term memory.

Rehearsal Processes and Levels of Processing

During the Middle Ages, philosopher and theologian Thomas Aquinas stated that in order to remember events well it is necessary to "meditate frequently" on what we wish to recall (Yates, 1966). Unless we repeat items mentally in our heads, these items rapidly leave short-term memory and are lost altogether. In addition, rehearsal during short-term memory may serve the function of transferring information to long-term memory. When we repeat items over and over, we begin to see relationships with what we already know about the world. Consequently, we pull selected items out of short-term memory and weave them into a broader memory context.

According to one theory, the **levels of processing theory**, items are simply repeated in short-term memory or transferred to long-term memory on the basis of coding schemes that require different levels of processing (Craik & Lockhart, 1972). When information is processed at a surface level, as is happening now as you read this sentence, **shallow processing**, or *maintenance rehearsal*, is sufficient to keep the information in short-term memory long enough for you to evaluate its content. Should you need to place a part or all of this information in an existing long-term memory file (knowledge network), then **deep processing**, or *elaborative rehearsal*, is required. As we discuss later, the different levels of processing associated with maintenance rehearsal and elaborative rehearsal distinguish separate memory activities.

Maintenance Rehearsal

In addition to reading, another example of maintenance rehearsal is when you look up a phone number in the directory and repeat it to yourself until you have finished dialing. In this case, you are reciting numbers in your head until you no longer need them. At one time it was believed that this sort of simple repetition process would add significantly to long-term memory. In effect, just being exposed to the visual or hearing cue was seen as an aid to recall. Experimental evidence supporting this view was provided by Rundus (1971) in a study that showed subjects recalled a list of words better after they had the opportunity to rehearse the words out loud. But more recently it has become apparent that the contributions of shallow processing to long-term memory are nominal. In this regard, Glenberg, Smith, and Green (1977) found that the length of time subjects spent rehearsing verbal information was of little consequence when subjects were unaware that they would be tested on that information in a subsequent recall task. Apparently, merely experiencing something over and over keeps it active momentarily (short-term memory), but enduring impressions require more in-depth processing (long-term memory).

Practically speaking, the shallowness of maintenance rehearsal is illustrated by the following quick and simple memory task. It involves an ordinary push-button telephone. In addition to the numbers and letters presented on the dialing face, what other two symbols are present? Do the letters *ABC* correspond to the digit *1* or *2*? Which two letters of the alphabet have been omitted? Compare your answers to the correct answers provided in Figure 7–10.

Most people have difficulty with this telephone task. Yet, think of how often you have seen the dialing face of a telephone. You see it frequently, but you do not store all the visual details in memory because they do not seem that important. Again, we see that encoding information into long-term

levels of processing theory memory theory that states that more meaningful rehearsal makes material better remembered

shallow processing low level, rote, meaningless repetitive vocalization of a word; it maintains material in short-term memory, but results in poor long-term memory

deep processing meaningful elaboration of material in short-term memory, resulting in good long-term memory

memory requires a deeper level of processing that leads to more than automatic repetition.

Elaborative Rehearsal

Elaborative rehearsal is an encoding process that involves the formation of associations between new information and items already in the long-term store. As an example, the word *poverty* may mean different things to different people. For one person, poverty may be a distant concept that evokes images of starving children in Third World countries, government relief programs, and TV commercials requesting economic aid. Another person may think of poverty in a more personal way, having experienced it firsthand. Each of these individuals will therefore fit the same item into a different memory context. The process of elaboration serves to integrate the incoming information into a coherent network of thoughts and ideas. Subsequently, the entire record is quickly transferred to long-term memory.

One line of research on elaborative rehearsal indicates that elaboration networks are more useful when they are self-generated as opposed to externally generated. For example, Pressley et al. (1987) presented adult subjects with sentences such as "The fat man read the sign." Or, in the case where a precise external elaboration was produced, similar subjects were presented with the same base sentence, altered to read, "The fat man read the sign warning about thin ice." Relative to these two conditions, a third condition was employed where subjects first read the base sentence "The fat man read the sign," and then they were asked, "Why did that particular man do that?" With respect to learning and memory, the results clearly revealed that the *why* approach was superior. The reason, most likely, is that the elaborations we invent are richer and more thoroughly dimensioned than those imposed by someone or something else. This is one aspect of remembering that you may be able to use to improve your own memory. Rather than encoding information within an arbitrary knowledge base prescribed by a particular essay, mathematical formula, or scientific classification scheme, build your own linkages. Tie the material to informational sets you already have, and you may find that you are better able to recall details of the newly learned material.

Implicit in the preceding statements on elaboration is the notion that recall is progressively enhanced by the number of elaborations that new items generate. The more meaningful an item, the better it should be remembered. Consistent with this view, several investigations have shown that memory benefits from more elaborate encodings (Craik & Tulving, 1975; Richardson-Klavehn & Bjork, 1988). However, a number of reports indicate that memory performance may decrease as the number of prior associations with an item increases (Nelson, Bajo, & Casanova, 1985; Nelson & Friedrich, 1980). These findings paradoxically suggest that the more we know about something, the more difficult it is to remember some recently experienced part of that information set. This may be due to the fact that available memory resources are allocated to the related concepts as well as to the new concept to be remembered, thus weakening the encoding of the new item. In any event, this sort of paradoxical relation between set size (elaboration) and recall is observed only in isolated learning situations (Nelson et al., 1985). As a general rule, it is still safe to say that integrating new information into a larger information network helps to improve our memory.

Subjective Organization

Earlier we observed that chunking is an important process for short-term memory. In essence, chunking is an organizational phenomenon that involves

FIGURE 7–10
The push-button telephone dialing face presented above provides the answers to the telephone memory test.

The symbols * and # are present along with numbers and letters. The letters *ABC* correspond to digit *2*.
The letters *Q* and *Z* have been omitted.

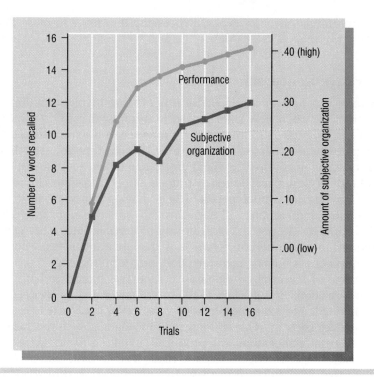

FIGURE 7–11
The number of words recalled from a 16-item list and the amount of subjective organization over trials in a free recall task. (Adapted from Tulving, 1962.)

subjective organization finding one's own way to categorize a set of seemingly unrelated items, resulting in improved recall

the creation of informational clusters, ultimately making storage easier. Organization is also important for long-term memory. When we order information in a way that is familiar to us, we increase the chances for encoding.

A great deal of research attention has focused on the aspect of organization that has to do with the spontaneous tendency for people to impose an organized framework on information that is presented randomly. This type of recoding process is called **subjective organization**. A free recall procedure is commonly employed as a testing technique in this area. With this technique, subjects are permitted to recall information in any order they wish. The suggestion is that the order present in the report reflects an underlying subjective attempt to organize the information for memory storage.

One of the classic experiments on this topic was conducted by Tulving (1962). Subjects in this study were repeatedly shown lists containing 16 unrelated words, such as *lagoon* and *cent*. Each of several separate lists had a different ordered arrangement of the same items. Following the presentation of a particular list, each subject was asked to recall as many items as possible in any order (free recall). Tulving discovered that subjects tended to recall certain words together, and that most of these fell into a common category. Moreover, the inclination toward this sort of subjective organization increased with the number of training trials (Figure 7–11). Interestingly, overall performance, defined in terms of the total number of items recalled, increased at the same rate as the amount of subjective organization. The combined results of this study strongly suggest that organization is a phenomenon that increases the chances that information will be transferred to long-term memory.

Imagery and Mnemonic Devices

Canadian psychologist Allan Paivio (1971) should receive credit for resuscitating the concept of imagery during the mid-1960s. As noted earlier, imagery is defined as a transformation process that converts different sources of information into a visual code. The scientific literature is full of examples of the helping effects of imagery on memory. For example, when word pairs are presented, they are better recalled when the subject is able to form a visual image that connects them. For example, *shoe* and *cook* are easier to remember together when you construct a mental picture of a chef looking over a boiling pot of water with a shoe in it. *Mad* and *book* can be connected by imagining a book cover with a frowning face.

In real life, mental imagery comes into play when we employ mnemonic devices as memory aids. **Mnemonic devices** are cues that improve memory by linking new organizational sets of information to memory elements that already exist.

mnemonic device method for enhancing memory

Mnemonic techniques are useful in any setting where large amounts of information must be processed and stored in long-term memory. In some cases, as with those involving children, mnemonics can be quite simple. As adults, we are capable of conjuring up incredibly elaborate schemes that improve our use of our memory capacity. Two well-known systems for mnemonic encoding are the method of loci and the peg-word method.

The **method of loci** is a technique that has been traced back to Simonides, an early Greek poet. As the story goes, through an act of good fortune, Simonides left a banquet hall moments before the walls collapsed, killing many people. Those killed were so crushed and disfigured that they were difficult to identify. But Simonides was able to identify the victims by mentally placing himself back in the hall. He remembered that one person was near a particular column, another was by a doorway, and so forth. Their names had been attached to certain locations in a visual array. By reinstating a mental image of the array, he was able to provide the names of the victims.

method of loci mnemonic device in which objects to be remembered are imagined in known locations

Thus, the method of loci involves the use of locations (loci) as memory cues. To make use of this method, you first have to think about a familiar set of places, or loci, that are ordered in such a way that you can move from one point to the next and still know where you are. Your house or apartment can often be used. Now, suppose you want to commit items from a shopping list to long-term memory. You simply place different items on the list in different locations throughout the house. Milk is on the front step, tomatoes are growing in the hallway, the den is overrun with green bean stalks, and a quilt made of eggs covers your bed (see Figure 7–12). Once these images are firmly in place, you can easily recall them with an imaginary walk through the house. Each location is a cue for a grocery item on the shopping list.

FIGURE 7–12
The method of loci. Mental pictures are formed with items placed in familiar locations. To retrieve the items, the person mentally moves in order from one location to the next.

peg-word approach mnemonic device in which objects to be remembered are associated with a numbered sequence of images

The **peg-word approach** is a mnemonic device similar to the method of loci, except that word cues are substituted for location cues. Typically, you learn a numerical rhyme such as the one presented in Figure 7–13. An object (peg word) is first associated with each number in a series. Then each item that is to be remembered is linked to a specific object or peg word in such a way that a unique visual image forms. To illustrate this technique, let's use the same list of grocery items that we just used in our discussion of the method of loci. Consistent with the rhyme, you imagine a bun with a milk center, a shoe that is made from tomatoes (red with green sprouting at the top), a tree with green bean vines suspended from each branch, and a door made from eggshells. When you recite "one is a bun, two is a shoe," and so on, the corresponding visual images are readily available from the long-term store. Admittedly, sometimes the peg-word mnemonic system can become ridiculous, but it is a very effective encoding technique and a great memory aid.

eidetic imagery rare and highly accurate memory ability in which a long-term memory can be remembered with as much detail as a sensory image

Although most psychologists agree that imagery is an important memory concept, this topic is not without controversy. One contentious issue relates to **eidetic imagery**, more familiarly known as photographic memory. Over 50 years ago, German scientists reported several cases involving young children who could apparently store a duplicate picture of a visual stimulus in memory in photographic detail (see Haber & Haber, 1964). These very talented children could examine a complex visual array and then, after it was removed, reproduce it exactly. The children attributed this amazing skill to the fact that the picture was "still in their minds." More recently, Richardson and Harris (1986) tracked "eidetic imagers" across four age categories and found that there is a systematic decline in eideticism from age 5 to age 13. Why this happens is not clear. No more certain is the notion that eidetic imagery occurs at all. Research in this area is difficult to replicate (Lieblich, 1979), and many psychologists question the methods of those who claim to measure it.

One is a bun.
Two is a shoe.
Three is a tree.
Four is a door.
Five is a hive.
Six is sticks.
Seven is heaven.
Eight is a gate.
Nine is a line.
Ten is a hen.

FIGURE 7–13
The peg-word approach. A rhyme such as this one associates an object (peg word) with each number in the rhyme. Then, each item to be remembered is linked to a peg word by forming a visual image that works as a retrieval aid when the rhyme is repeated.

RETRIEVAL

Thus far we have restricted our coverage of long-term memory to the acquisition and storage processes involved with encoding new sources of information. Assume for the moment, then, that the information is neatly locked away in some cranny of the long-term store. We now ask, How do we get it out? What factors determine how effectively it is retrieved?

Reconstruction

When we are required to retrieve information from long-term memory, many of the details will not be available for recall. Consequently, we embellish our report with fictitious events; that is, we fill in with material "that must have been." This process of combining actual details from the long-term store with items that seem to fit the occasion is the basis for what is known as **reconstructive memory**.

reconstructive memory piecing together memories by fitting them to a meaningful plan or organization

One of the classic studies of memory reconstruction was done by Sir Frederic Bartlett (1886–1969) over a half-century ago (Bartlett, 1932). British college students were required to read a folktale entitled "The War of the Ghosts." The story contained many details about the experiences and ultimate death of a warrior who found himself doing combat with ghosts. Bartlett had students recall the story immediately and then again after several hours or days had passed. The student versions of the story showed that they had stored a few key facts about the story and constructed a new story based on these few features. The main theme was still the same, yet no two stories were alike. Each person had apparently filled in with material from a personal knowledge base (the long-term store), thus creating a unique recollection.

More recent work on memory reconstruction has focused on where in the information-processing scheme the memory distortion takes place. Some evidence indicates that events are broken down and reconstituted when they are first stored. But other findings argue against an encoding interpretation of reconstructive changes and implicate retrieval mechanisms in the process. For example, Hasher and Griffin (1978) have shown that the recall of ambiguous stories is profoundly influenced by content clues given after a period of study and before testing. Specifically, if just before testing someone on a recall test you provide hints that the story was about a sailor, there is a high probability that the reader will remember the story as having involved a sailor, even when no such person was mentioned in the original script. Alternatively, if you provide a clue that indicates that the story was about a factory worker, then a factory worker will be woven into the memory fabric. Such data argue rather forcefully for changes during retrieval, inasmuch as the same information gets stored during the initial study sessions.

Context

You may have read an account of a trial where the victim or an observer returned to the scene of the crime under the direction of the court. The expressed hope in such cases is that by going back, recall of the events that took place in the specific context will be enhanced. In fact, there have been instances where the memory of an eyewitness has benefited from such an experience. Apparently, the context itself provides retrieval cues that aid recall.

Perhaps this line of reasoning explains a biographical incident reported by Dreistadt (1971), involving the famous composer Ludwig van Beethoven. Enroute to Vienna, Beethoven fell asleep in his coach and dreamed of going on a journey to Jerusalem, where he met a friend named Tobias van Haslinger. During his dream, Beethoven composed a short musical piece dedicated to Tobias. Upon awakening from the dream and departing the coach, he discovered that he was unable to recall the melody or words from the composition. Beethoven returned home the next day in the same coach. Then "in accordance with the laws of association of ideas the same canon [of music] flashed across" his mind again. This time he wrote it down.

Considerable scientific evidence also points to the importance of contextual retrieval cues (see Riccio & Richardson, 1984a, for a review). With 3-month-old infants, for example, learning to kick to produce movement in a crib (see Figure 7–14) was recalled better when the infants were tested in the same crib as compared to a distinctively different crib (Rovee-Collier, Griesler, & Earley, 1985). Apparently, from the very beginning our memories are linked to the surroundings where they are formed (Rovee-Collier, 1988).

In a study of environmental reinstatement (i.e., returning to an environment where learning took place) with older subjects, Texas A&M University psychologist Steven Smith and his colleagues had students learn a list of words in one room and then recall as many words as possible in the same room or another room that was conspicuously different (Smith, Glenberg, & Bjork, 1978). The results showed that memory was much better when the recall test was conducted in the same environment where the original learning took place (see Figure 7–15). In a follow-up investigation, Smith (1979) found that it was unnecessary to physically reinstate the same environmental cues to produce superior recall. Simply instructing subjects to remember the original learning environment improved their retention.

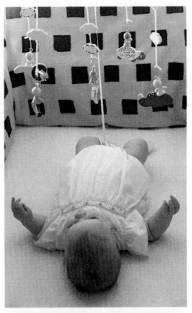

FIGURE 7–14
Two distinctively different cribs were used to test for contextual retrieval in 3-month-old infants. What the infants learned in one crib was recalled better if they were tested in the same crib rather than a different crib. (From Rovee-Collier, Griesler, & Earley, 1985.)

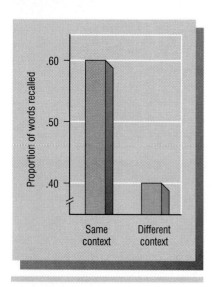

FIGURE 7–15
Proportion of words recalled from lists when testing occurred either in the same room where learning took place or in a different room. (Adapted from Smith, Glenberg, & Bjork, 1978.)

recognition tests memory tests, such as a multiple choice exam, in which a mixed set of correct memory targets and nontargets is given, and the task is to choose which are correct

outshining strong memory cue overpowers weaker cues, rendering them ineffective

state-dependent memory better memory for material tested in the same mental, emotional, or drug-induced state that was present when the material was learned

The practical significance of these findings may be important to you in a direct way. It would be ideal, for example, if you could take an examination in the precise physical location where you studied the material on which you were being tested. Your bookshelf, lamp, desk, and so forth would serve as added retrieval cues that would improve recall from long-term memory. But unless college professors experience a major shift in their thinking, the chances of your being granted permission to take an exam at your living quarters are pretty slim. But there is at least one thing you can do to help your memory. *Think* about the context where you studied; that is, mentally place yourself in that environment again and you may find that you do better on exams.

Although most experimental tests have shown that environmental reinstatement improves memory, some studies have not shown this effect, particularly when **recognition tests** have been used. In contrast to free recall, a recognition test shows you test items while you decide whether or not the item was on the list you studied. Although these negative findings have caused some to doubt the generality of context effects, it has since been shown that people use the associations among words in the studied lists to help them recognize words on a test. These associations are stronger memory cues than the background environmental cues; therefore, they overpower the weaker context cues, a phenomenon Smith (1988; 1993) refers to as **outshining**. When associations among list words are not stored (for example, when maintenance rehearsal is used), context effects show up even on a recognition test because the context cues are not outshone.

Actual field studies with eyewitnesses have shown that recognition of faces improves when the witness mentally reinstates environmental background cues (Krafka & Penrod, 1985) or when he or she returns physically to the original scene (Smith & Vela, 1992). When an eyewitness is asked to identify a criminal viewed at the scene of a crime, there is only a single test item, the suspect's face. There are no associative cues that can outshine the context cues, as can happen with a list of words. Contextual reinstatement, then, can be used to help eyewitnesses identify criminals. This topic will be considered further in the section on eyewitness memory.

State-Dependent Memory

Another line of research relating to retrieval from long-term memory has to do with contextual changes that occur internally. Specifically, it has been demonstrated that bodily conditions or states evoke contextual stimuli that influence how effectively memories are retrieved. The fascinating nature of the retrieval process in **state-dependent memory** is evident from drug studies that show the following surprising result: If you initially process information while you are under the influence of alcohol or marijuana, you will remember more during a memory test if you are drunk or stoned than you will if you are not intoxicated. Memory is best, it seems, when you recall information in the same physiological condition that you were in when you originally learned it. Drugs produce states that are defined by their own particular network of stimuli. These stimuli become associated with items during the encoding stage of information processing and later function as retrieval cues during a subsequent retention test.

Pharmacologically produced state-dependent memory seems to be a robust phenomenon not dramatically influenced by different types of drugs, dosage, or the specific type of material to be remembered (Horton & Mills, 1984). Moreover, when two or more drugs are included in the experiment, both must be present during the memory test in order to have maximum recall. For example, Lowe (1987) gave undergraduate volunteers both alcohol and caffeine and tested them for recall a day later under conditions where they were exposed to one or both drugs. The results indicated that the combined drug condition (identical to the original learning setting) produced the best performance.

Elsewhere, emotional mood states have been shown to influence memory processes in a fashion similar to the drug-dependent effects just cited (see Eich, 1989; Eich & Metcalfe, 1989). Bower (1981), for example, reports findings from a free recall task in which subjects learned a list of words under either a happy or sad mood state that had been induced through hypnosis. As shown in Figure 7–16 when subjects were *mood congruent* (in the same mood for both the learning and the testing phases of the experiment), they recalled more information than they did when they were *mood incongruent* (learning and testing were conducted in opposite mood circumstances). The sad–sad comparison is especially interesting in that it reveals the superiority of same-mood retrieval even when the mood is a negative affective state.

The obvious interpretation of these results, at least within a state dependency framework, is that emotion-produced cues become essential components of the information network during encoding. When these same cues are present during retrieval testing, recall is helped by added contextual cues. When the cues are absent, as they would be in the changed mood condition, much of the memory matrix would be missing and retrieval presumably would be more difficult. Perhaps this is why we can recall so many more negative words when we are depressed (Teasdale & Russell, 1983). And now there is evidence that clinically depressed patients become even more depressed when they hear words that are related to their negative mental state (Bower, 1987). When depressed persons are in the throes of a negative mood state, the negative affective stimuli quite literally remind them of other unpleasant events. The unfortunate product of all this, of course, is a blue funk that builds on itself. Such word-dependent research findings are causing many therapists to think more carefully about their dialogue with clients.

Retrieval Pathways

When a particular memory is immediately available, fetching it back to mind is an automatic process. But when a memory is obscure, locating it and bringing it into the short-term store can be very frustrating.

We have all had such exasperating experiences. We rack our brains trying to think of someone's name, the words to a song, or a historical fact. For example, we might think, what was the name of that river that Julius Caesar crossed in 49 B.C. that started the war with Gaul? Let's see, "crossing the (blank)" is used as a phrase that indicates commitment. Is it "crossing the Rubaiyat?" No, no, the *Rubaiyat* is a poem, not a river. It's something like that though. Rhine? Ruby? Rubicon? That's it! "Crossing the Rubicon" means "you are in it for keeps," because when Caesar crossed the Rubicon river and entered Gaul, he knew there was no turning back.

Groping around for a memory and then suddenly finding it after a series of "almost got it" sensations is known as the **tip-of-the-tongue (TOT) phenomenon**. As frustrating as it is to go through TOT experiences, they are extremely useful in improving our understanding of human memory. Investigations of TOT states have revealed that the pathway to memory retrieval is anything but haphazard (Brown & McNeill, 1966; Reason & Mycielska, 1982). People use word sounds and word meanings to home in on the target word. In the preceding paragraph, note the similarity in sound between *Rubaiyat* and *Rubicon*. And the Rhine is a river in Germany. These

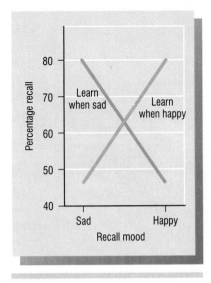

FIGURE 7–16
Percentage recall of material learned in either a happy or a sad mood, as a function of mood at time of recall. (Adapted from Bower, 1981.)

tip-of-the-tongue phenomenon memory retrieval failure in which recall seems imminent

items were not retrieved from memory coincidentally. They were part of a matrix that provided clues and gave direction to the memory search. TOT research is important because it tells us that information is stored in long-term memory in such a way that it is accessible by different routes. Events are catalogued by their distinguishing features; and when similarities occur, they are duly recorded. The resulting network is a vast array of word linkages that make TOT experiences possible. So the next time you have one, don't start jumping up and down as if you are on the brink of a sneeze. Relax, and enjoy the search. Each step along the retrieval pathway will tell you something about how elaborate your memory really is.

Apart from TOT research, recent investigations of retrieval processes have shown that episodic memory searches are aided by clues about a particular point in time. That is, if you are given specific information about a date, your ability to recall details of personal events of that day is quite impressive, even when the episode took place more than a year ago. One of the more interesting illustrations of this phenomenon relates to a challenge presented by former president Ronald Reagan in February 1987. In the midst of a press conference where President Reagan admitted to not remembering details of his involvement in meetings leading to the Iran–Contra scandal, the president said, "Everybody who can remember what they were doing on August 8, 1985, raise your hand." This statement, intended to imply that we cannot recall specific events that took place on specific dates in years past, raised an empirical question. Can we really remember that far back? To answer this question, Robert Reynolds and Harold Takooshian of Fordham University asked 35 undergraduate students to recall personal episodes from August 8, 1985. Although it had been 19 months, every person was able to give general information about his or her whereabouts on that day, and more than half of them could describe in detail what they had been doing (Reynolds & Takooshian, 1988). It took a few minutes to step back through time and reestablish some old connections, but in the final analysis, the retrieval pathways were intact and the personal events of that day were available for recall. So it seems that we are capable of retrieving specific information from a long time ago. Why don't you try it? Close your eyes and try to think back about where you were, and what you were doing, exactly 2 years ago today.

Of course, some dates in our lives don't require concentration—what was taking place comes to us in a flash.

MEMORY IN EVERYDAY SETTINGS: FLASHBULBS AND EYEWITNESSES

Flashbulb Memories

Do you remember what you were doing on Wednesday, January 16, 1991? That was the day that the bombing of Iraq began, Operation Desert Storm. For many Americans, the news and the television pictures of bombers and anti-aircraft fire produced vivid memories that are not easily forgotten. You may have no difficulty remembering immediately how you first heard the news that fateful January day. Indeed, you are probably able to recall in detail that moment in time, even though it was years ago.

The vivid recollection of shocking events such as the Gulf War, the San Francisco earthquake in 1989, and the *Challenger* mishap in 1986 is called a **flashbulb memory**. Brown and Kulik (1977) suggested the label for this phenomenon when they discovered that people had amazingly detailed memories associated with the announcement of the assassination of President

flashbulb memory vivid long-lasting memory, usually associated with an arousing event

John F. Kennedy. Even though years had passed since the assassination, people were able to describe, with great clarity, who they were talking to, where they were standing, and what happened immediately after hearing the news. It was as if a photograph had been snapped at the instant they learned of the shooting.

In addition to being fascinating, flashbulb memories pose some interesting theoretical questions. For instance, Brown and Kulik's claim that flashbulb memories are complete, accurate recollections immune to forgetting suggests that special mechanisms create these memories. In other words, ordinary memory functioning does not operate here. But evidence questions the validity of such an assertion. McCloskey, Wible, and Cohen (1988) gave a questionnaire to 50 faculty and students at Johns Hopkins University immediately after the *Challenger* explosion and again 9 months later. The results indicated that the so-called flashbulb memory is neither uniformly accurate nor immune to forgetting. These findings have raised the possibility that the superior recall of important, tragic events may stem from the perceived significance and distinctiveness of the experience. Therefore, such recall may follow an ordinary memory course.

Further evidence that flashbulb memories are like normal ones was provided by Weaver (1991), who tested memories of the beginning of the Persian Gulf War in 1991. For a class assignment, Weaver's students had recorded a normal event in their daily routine that coincidentally happened on the day war broke out. Collecting students' descriptions of their ordinary events, and descriptions of how they heard of the Gulf War, he found that

Shocking events produce flashbulb memories. These schoolchildren are watching on television the liftoff of the *Challenger* flight that moments later would claim the life of schoolteacher Christa McAuliffe and six other crew members. For years, the details of this tragic moment will be remembered.

the war-related events were more emotionally laden than the ordinary events. Testing both types of memories 3 months later, Weaver found that the ordinary events were recalled just as accurately as the Gulf War memories and that both types were equally susceptible to forgetting. In fact, the memories differed in only one respect: Students were much more confident in the accuracy of the Gulf War memories, even though those recollections were actually no more accurate than the ordinary ones.

Are highly emotional memories usually more accurate than less emotional ones, whether or not they seem like flashbulb memories? In many circumstances, they are. Apparently, one dimension of emotion, arousal, is associated with improved memory, but the other major dimension, pleasantness/unpleasantness, is not (Bradley, Greenwald, Petry, & Lang, 1992). High arousal may improve memory by improving consolidation (Baddeley, 1990), a topic to be discussed in a later section on amnesia.

A final consideration for flashbulb memories is the personal importance of the event. If you were *in* an earthquake, you might remember it better than if you *heard* about it on the news. That is exactly the result found in studies by Neisser, Winograd, and Weldon (1991) and Palmer, Schreiber, and Fox (1991). On October 18, 1989, a major earthquake struck northern California, causing a section of the Bay Bridge in San Francisco to collapse. People who were caught in the quake had, a year and a half later, more accurate memories of their experiences than those who had heard about the quake on the news. Still, there are no special mental mechanisms needed to explain the findings. Neisser et al. and Palmer et al. point out that the uniqueness of the real event differed from hearing a news story, there were constant reminders of the quake from damage in the subjects' environment, and there were frequent retellings of personal quake stories. These explanations are all perfectly normal reasons for the memories of the real event to remain so vivid.

Eyewitness Memory

One of the more interesting and controversial applications of the concept of memory retrieval concerns the interpretation of **eyewitness testimony**. A prominent researcher in this area has been Elizabeth Loftus of the University of Washington. Many years ago Loftus and Palmer (1974) demonstrated that the mere wording of a question could affect what an observer reported. In one experiment college students were asked to view a series of films, each depicting a traffic accident. Following this initial viewing, the students were asked to respond to a number of written questions, including one about the speed of the vehicles involved in the accident. This question took the general form: "How fast were the cars going when they _____ each other?" Different groups of subjects had one of the following words inserted in the blank: *bumped, collided, contacted, hit,* or *smashed.* A crucial comparison involved those students reading *smashed* as the verb as opposed to *contacted.* The results indicated that estimates of vehicle speed were elevated significantly when *smashed* was used in the question.

The importance of this finding is that it shows that the memory of an eyewitness can be altered by information received after the eyewitness sees an event take place. The danger, of course, is that a person's account of what really happened will depend to some degree on unrelated events that occur after the fact. For example, in a police interview, misinformation unwittingly given by an interviewer could be integrated into a person's memory and thereby modify his or her report (Loftus, 1983). Apparently, the risks here are especially great when there is already an element of uncertainty in the recollection of the events that actually took place (McEwan & Yuille, 1981).

eyewitness testimony report of the events witnessed at the scene of a crime

Needless to say, attorneys are excited by the idea that they may be able to control the reconstructive processes involved in memory retrieval by simply changing the way they phrase their questions. Perhaps even more relevant to the judicial process are the following disclosures made by Loftus (1984). Two variables that have received special attention from memory researchers of eyewitness testimony are the degree of violence in the criminal offense and the confidence the witnesses have in their testimony. Although the findings here are intriguing, they probably are not what you would expect; namely, violence interferes with memory retrieval, and there is absolutely no relationship between confidence and accuracy. The disconcerting thing, of course, is that jurors are not likely to be aware of these features of memory. Consequently, on the basis of eyewitness testimony, they act on criminal cases falsely secure in their judgments.

One other aspect of memory that has proven to be especially problematical for eyewitness testimony is the tendency for people to respond unidimensionally on the basis of racial characteristics. In other words, because people have difficulty distinguishing among people of other races (Loftus, 1984), they may mistake one person for another simply because the two persons possess a common trait. This can lead to misidentification in criminal cases. Such was the fate of William Bernard Jackson (see Figure 7–17). Jackson spent 5 years in prison for a rape he did not commit. Despite the confident testimony of the victim that Jackson was the assailant, another man who hardly looked like Jackson except that he was black and bearded was later discovered to be the true offender. Memory reconstruction, and justice in this instance, was grossly distorted by the excessive reliance on only a few cues (Tversky & Tuchlin, 1989).

So it seems clear that the testimony of adult witnesses must be viewed cautiously. What should we expect when the witness is a child? Are children any more or less reliable than their adult counterparts? The issue of the child witness has emerged as an exceedingly important topic in recent years, partly because of the much-publicized cases of sexual abuse among children in day-care centers. Often, with the aid of anatomically complete dolls and other techniques, investigators attempt to help children recount instances of abuse at the centers. However, serious questions remain about

FIGURE 7-17
A case of misidentification. William Jackson (*left*) was imprisoned for 5 years for two rapes committed by Dr. Edward Jackson, Jr. (*right*; no relation). Due to faulty memory retrieval, an eyewitness (one of the victims) wrongly identified William Jackson.

the children's competency as witnesses in such criminal cases (Quinn, 1986). The trauma of sexual abuse may distort recall, and the examiner may inadvertently cue the child, either by gestures or tone of voice. Future attempts to resolve legal issues in such cases will undoubtedly have to consider the impact of childhood stress reactions on the functioning of memory. As yet, however, this phenomenon is poorly understood.

THINKING ABOUT
Eyewitness Identification

eyewitness identification test in which a person who saw a crime tries to recognize a criminal from a lineup or a photospread

Eyewitness reporting of crimes is one of the foundations of evidence used in criminal investigations. **Eyewitness identification** refers to the situation in which a witness is asked to identify a perpetrator of a crime, usually from a live lineup or a photospread. A jury is likely to trust an eyewitness's memory, especially when the witness is certain about the identification. How reliable are eyewitness identifications?

Although there is no single standard operating procedure for constructing lineups and photospreads, an attempt is usually made to include not only the face of the suspect, but also other similar faces. These similar faces are referred to as **foils**. The foils usually consist of people who could not have committed the crime in question (for example, because they were in prison at the time). The eyewitness might then identify the suspect, a foil, or no one. The only choice that is clearly an error is a foil identification; it cannot be known whether the witness is correct or not if the suspect is identified. Therefore, experimental investigations of eyewitness identification in which the correct perpetrator is known beyond any doubt must use two different lineup conditions: a target-present lineup, in which the perpetrator's photo is in the lineup, and a target-absent condition, in which a photo of a similar face is substituted for the perpetrator's.

foil incorrect target inserted in an eyewitness lineup or photospread

Eyewitness identifications are highly susceptible to error. This is easy to show in a classroom demonstration in which a confederate runs into the class and stages an event such as a fake shooting incident with a cap gun. Student witnesses are typically poor at recalling the details of the incident, and their ability to identify the confederate is quite faulty. In one staged-event study, for example, Smith and Vela (1992) found that witnesses correctly identified the confederate from a photospread only 54% of the time. The errors were not at all innocuous; 30% of the errors were false identifications, evidence that might have convicted an innocent person in a genuine homicide case.

As faulty as eyewitness identification can be under normal circumstances, it can be made even worse by a number of factors. If the perpetrator wears a disguise, or if the witness gets only a brief look, accuracy suffers. A biased lineup or photospread can also cause error if, for example, only one suspect fits the original description or only one mug shot has a border around it. In the case of Leslie H., the armed robbery victim described at the beginning of the chapter, only one mug shot in the photospread showed "dark spots" on a suspect's face, as Leslie had described to the police. Particularly disturbing are findings that show that **cross-racial identifications** are especially poor; witnesses are worse at identifying faces of people who are racially different from themselves than they are at identifying faces of members of their own race (Malpass & Kravitz, 1969). Most of the poorer cross-racial errors are due to false identifications, rather than misses. This cross-racial bias is quite pervasive, occurring just as much for witnesses with little racial

cross-racial identification identification of a criminal suspect by a witness who is racially different from the suspect

prejudice as for highly prejudiced witnesses (Brigham & Barkowitz, 1978). Regardless of Leslie H.'s racial opinions, her attempt to identify a robber who was racially different from her may have contributed to her misidentification.

Identification is also less accurate if the witness was highly aroused or anxious during the crime. Although arousal improves memory in other contexts, as described for flashbulb memories, it interferes with an eyewitness's recognition memory (Brigham, Maass, Martinez, & Whittenberger, 1983). This poor memory is probably caused by a combination of factors, including confusion, focusing on the weapon, or focusing attention on a single object other than the criminal's face.

Information received by the witness after the event can also make recall worse, and it can interfere with remembering a face. Face recognition is poorer if a witness describes the face before attempting to identify the person in a photospread, a result called the *verbal overshadowing effect* (Schooler & Engstler-Schooler, 1990). Unfortunately, most criminal investigations involve getting descriptions of suspects from the first time the crime is reported; therefore, verbal overshadowing seems unavoidable. Interestingly, one way to overcome the problem is for a witness to make a snap judgment when viewing a mug shot, rather than a slower, more considered decision. Apparently, viewing mug shots is a case in which first impressions count.

One interesting source of error in eyewitness identification is called poor **calibration** of witnesses' memories. *Calibration* in this context means a relationship between how certain a witness professes to be and how accurate he or she really is. A well-calibrated witness who said, "That's him! I'm absolutely sure he's the one!" could be trusted by a jury. Unfortunately, witnesses are *not* well calibrated, a consistent finding in eyewitness identification studies (Wells & Murray, 1984). This means that you should not trust people's recollections just because they express certainty that their identifications are accurate; in the armed robbery case described earlier, Leslie H. was completely convinced of her identification, even though it was clearly incorrect. Such findings further shake our confidence in eyewitness memory. Calibration in other contexts will be discussed in Chapter 8.

calibration relationship or correlation between a rememberer's confidence that a memory is correct and the actual accuracy of the memory

Because eyewitness memory is so untrustworthy, should the judicial system throw it out altogether? Obviously not; many cases rely on eyewitness evidence. When a conviction rests solely on a single eyewitness's testimony, the evidence must be doubted. As *corroborating* evidence, however, eyewitness memory may be more reliable. Another answer is that investigators can use newly developed techniques for helping memory, such as improving photospreads and lineups, avoiding misleading questions, and using memory improvement techniques that have been reliably shown to enhance memories, even in genuine criminal investigations (Fisher, Geiselman, & Amador, 1989).

Have you ever witnessed a crime or an accident, or do you know someone who has? How much do you trust your own judgment, based on your memory as an eyewitness? Should juries in criminal trials be told about scientific evidence that casts doubt on the credibility of an eyewitness?

FORGETTING

In previous sections we talked about encoding, or how memory is stored in the first place, and we discussed memory retrieval. Now we turn to what happens when memory fails altogether, an event known more commonly as **forgetting**. Although forgetting occurs for all of us, recent evidence indicates

forgetting loss of information

that not all memories are lost at quite the same rate. For instance, in a study of everyday forgetting, Terry (1988) had 50 college students keep a diary of things they had forgotten over a period of several weeks. Interestingly, it was discovered that "forgetting to do something" was a much more common experience than forgetting a fact, name, or some other specific information. Perhaps because this kind of memory involves remembering the intent to do something rather than the recollection of something already done, fewer retrieval cues may be available when we try to remember to take a pencil to an examination or reset the alarm clock.

There is one case where forgetting a past action is almost as common as forgetting to perform a future one. This is true when we decide to store an important object in a special place. What would you do if your best friend gave you a wedding ring to hold until the ceremony a month from now? Would you put it in a jewelry box where someone else might find it? Or, would you hide it in a vase or in a light fixture? In all probability, you would do one of the latter, because you would see that as a safe and memorable storage location. In actuality, you are more likely to forget that the ring is in the light fixture, where it doesn't belong, than that the ring is in the jewelry box, where it does belong (Winograd & Soloway, 1986). The problem is that as time passes and ordinary memory loss occurs, the improbability of the hiding place makes it virtually impossible for us to tap into the appropriate retrieval network. We simply outsmart ourselves. In our enthusiasm to trick others, we ensure our own forgetfulness. So next time, be safe and store your cash and valuables in a safe-deposit box, not in the freezer.

Regardless of which memories are lost, the question remains of why forgetting occurs at all. What actually happens when memory fails? Generally we forget for one of two reasons: the information no longer resides in long-term memory, or, conversely, the information still exists but is not accessible. These two explanations for forgetting form the basis for the theoretical distinctions made in this area. In the next sections we review two basic models: the **decay theory** and the **interference theory** (see Figure 7–18). We also discuss the special cases of forgetting in the elderly and in those suffering from amnesia.

Decay Theory

Many philosophers have suggested that time heals all wounds, and there is surely some truth in this. But in addition to making us forget bad events,

decay theory theory that forgetting is caused by the passage of time

interference theory theory that forgetting is caused by learning similar material

Decay Theory	Interference Theory
Forgetting occurs because as time passes, the memory trace gradually fades away. A name you once knew, for instance, is no longer available for recall because the physiological basis for the memory has eroded.	Proactive interference: Material learned initially prevents you from recalling material learned later (for example, Spanish words interfere with your memory of French words that were learned later).
	Retroactive interference: Material learned after previously learned material prevents you from recalling the previously learned material (for example, you cannot remember someone's phone number given to you at the beginning of a party because activities that occurred later block your memory).

FIGURE 7–18
Theories of forgetting.

time also is responsible for the loss of other, more positive memories. How is it that time causes us to forget?

Perhaps the oldest account of the effects of the passage of time on forgetting comes from Hermann Ebbinghaus (1885/1964). Ebbinghaus was the first to study long-term memory in a systematic manner. Often using himself as a subject, Ebbinghaus found that his ability to remember a list of nonsense syllables diminished over the course of several hours. He discovered that "savings," defined as the amount of time saved in relearning the list, was reduced progressively for intervals up to 2 days (Figure 7–19). To explain such results, he suggested that disuse is accompanied by decay. That is, if memories are not practiced, they fade with time. Such a stance was based on the idea that a lasting physical change in the nervous system, called a memory trace, eventually eroded over time.

The decay model had advocates, but only for a period of about 20 years or so. Skeptics have since questioned the quantitative validity of the approach, meaning that our ability to measure decay is in doubt. Because the relevant physiological responses have not been specified, the decay position has been essentially an untestable one.

Interference Theory

A competing alternative to the decay theory focuses on retrieval failure. In this interference theory of forgetting, the information in question is believed to remain in long-term memory. Time-imposed retrieval difficulties (forgetting) are assumed to occur, however, because something prevents memory access. The interference theory of forgetting proposes that the "something" blocking the usual process of retrieval is present in the form of established associations that conflict with what we are trying to recall.

Typically, we talk of two different types of interference that contribute to such forgetting (refer to Figure 7–20). The first type, called **proactive interference**, is said to occur when material that you have learned under a previous condition decreases your ability to recall more recently learned material. An example that undoubtedly is painfully familiar to some of you is what happens when you enroll in a French course after taking a Spanish course. Your memory of Spanish interferes with your recall of the more recently acquired French, and this problem is accented when words or phrases sound alike. Similarly, an athlete may have difficulty acquiring new and better techniques because of previously learned bad habits. Procedural memories established early in training intrude on memories established later, and so execution is adversely affected.

Retroactive interference, by comparison, involves a quite different situation. In retroactive interference, your ability to recall information decreases because of activities that occur between the time you originally

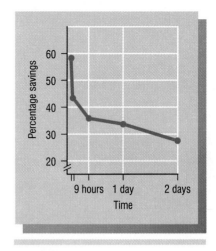

FIGURE 7–19
Retention of nonsense-syllable lists learned by Ebbinghaus. The "savings" measure reflects the amount of time saved in relearning the lists. (From Ebbinghaus, 1885.)

proactive interference forgetting due to previous learning

retroactive interference forgetting caused by learning material after the to-be-remembered episode

	Order in which events occur		
	1	2	3
Retroactive interference	Encounter to-be-remembered material	Encounter interfering material	Memory test for to-be-remembered material
Proactive interference	Encounter interfering material	Encounter to-be-remembered material	Memory test for to-be-remembered material

FIGURE 7–20
Sequence of events in retroactive and proactive interference. (Adapted from Ellis & Hunt, 1989.)

learned the information and the time you're tested on it. When you take a comprehensive final examination, for example, the material you learned early in the semester may be obscured by the material you covered more recently. For example, consider the address of your current residence. Do you think that 5 years from now you will be able to remember your post office box number or street address? Chances are that if you are living at a temporary address while attending college, you will have great difficulty remembering this information in the future. According to a retroactive interference account of forgetting, events that occur after you leave college will obscure the earlier memories of where you once lived.

Laboratory evidence offers strong support for the basic beliefs of interference theory. One of the more compelling scientific documents providing such support is a review of several experimental reports. In this review, Underwood (1957) analyzed the results from the studies named in Figure 7–21. Each report had been concerned with verbal learning and recall, but the experimental procedures were different with respect to the number of word lists that subjects learned before the one on which they were tested for retention. When Underwood plotted the percentage of items recalled from the most recent list as a function of the number of previous lists, a clear pattern emerged. Specifically, the more previous lists subjects had to learn, the less they remembered the last list they learned. The early material was apparently interfering with retrieval of information stored later. Thus, the Underwood summary offers a dramatic illustration of proactive interference.

The notion of retroactive interference also receives substantial support from scientific studies. As far back as 1924, Jenkins and Dallenbach examined the influence of immediate activity on recall. The inspiration for their research actually came from a reexamination of Ebbinghaus's forgetting curve (Figure 7–19). Close inspection revealed that the rate of forgetting decreased during the brief period following the 9-hr retention test. Realizing that Ebbinghaus was his own subject and assuming that, like everyone else, he had to sleep, Jenkins and Dallenbach deduced that this interruption in the rate of forgetting must have been due to the fact that he forgot less when he was asleep than when he was awake. When this hypothesis was tested on two Cornell graduate students, Jenkins and Dallenbach's suspicions were confirmed. When the students slept immediately after learning lists of 10 non-

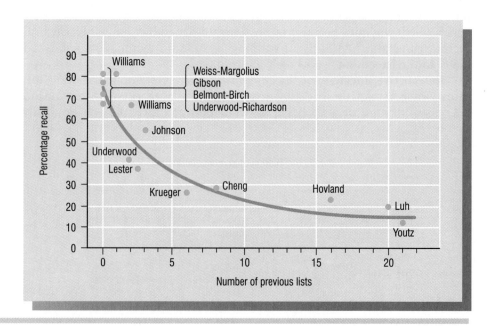

FIGURE 7–21
The percentage recall of items from the most recent list as a function of the number of previous lists encountered. Dots reflect the findings from different published reports. (From Underwood, 1957.)

sense syllables, as opposed to engaging in a routine activity, they had greater recall on tests given 4 and 8 hr later. In the terminology of interference theory, sleep, or the absence of activity, had decreased the amount of retroactive interference and increased the amount of information they remembered.

What does this say about your study habits? Perhaps you would retain more if you went directly to sleep following a late-night study session in the library or your room. "Winding down" by watching TV or reading a magazine article after studying may retroactively interfere with the recall of what you have just learned.

Forgetting Among the Elderly

Forgetfulness in old age is something that society takes for granted. We see our grandparents or elderly friends struggle to find their misplaced eyeglasses. Or they may forget where they put the flashlight or lock themselves out of their house or apartment. We assume that memory functioning just slips a notch once you turn 60, but how much research evidence supports this widely held belief? Actually, quite a bit, but the issue is not as clear as you may think. In a comprehensive study of the age and memory question, Light and Singh (1987) show that older adults are impaired on tasks that require a conscious effort to remember. However, when memory depends on automatic operations, elderly persons perform as well as people in their 20s. This means that an older person may have difficulty remembering the content of a newspaper article he or she is instructed to read, but the same person would have no problem remembering how to repair a sewing machine, having recently acquired the skill. Based on such findings, our perceptions of forgetfulness among the elderly probably are exaggerated. Older persons can learn and retain a vast amount of information, and even when memory loss occurs, it may not be a substantial loss (Craik, 1985).

Amnesia

In the following sections, a special type of forgetting, called amnesia, is discussed. There are some famous case histories that will help illustrate this type of forgetting.

Retrograde Amnesia.   The first clinical case history illustrates a form of memory disturbance called **retrograde amnesia**. In retrograde amnesia, the memory loss is for information acquired before the trauma that caused the amnesia. In the case of G. K., age 22, the trauma was the result of an unfortunate fall from a motorcycle (reported in Russell & Nathan, 1946). Although the X rays showed no fracture, within a week of the accident G. K. began to have memory problems. G. K. could not remember many of the events of his life over the previous 2 years, and when he returned to the village where he had been working, everything was unfamiliar. In effect, part of G. K.'s memory had been erased.

Case histories such as this and the following one reflect horrible human tragedy, of course, but they do help us understand better how basic memory functions. In truth, much of the experimental work on forgetting that is caused by trauma was inspired by such instances of personal misfortune. The most clear-cut example may rest with the topic of retrograde amnesia and electroconvulsive therapy (ECT). When an electric shock strong enough to elicit convulsions is administered to a person, the result is a loss of memory for events learned before the administration of the shock. As we discuss in Chapter 17, ECT is a form of treatment for certain types of psychopathology, and one of the unfortunate side effects is a memory loss. Why does it

retrograde amnesia inability to remember events explicitly that occurred before a trauma

consolidation processes occurring after an experience that stabilize memory for the event

occur? At one time it was suspected that ECT prevented **consolidation**; that is, memory events formed just before the shock treatment may not have had time to stabilize and become part of the permanent core. This consolidation-disruption hypothesis is not as popular as it once was, however, because cued-recall studies have recently indicated that the lost information can be brought forth under appropriate testing conditions. It now seems that retrograde amnesia may be due to retrieval failure caused by stress (Riccio & Richardson, 1984b).

Anterograde Amnesia. Second, consider the case of H. M. (refer also to Scoville & Milner, 1957). At the age of 7, H. M., a male, was knocked down by a bicycle, and he sustained damage (apparently minor) to his head. Three years later he began to have moderately intense seizures, and on his 16th birthday H. M. had his first major seizure. The frequency and severity of attacks increased over the next several years despite attempts to control the problem with anticonvulsant medications. Ultimately, in 1953, a medical decision was made to surgically remove most, but not all, of the hippocampus and the nearby amygdala. H. M. was 27 years old at the time.

Since his operation over 40 years ago, H. M. has been the focus of attention for several memory researchers, originally William Scoville and Brenda Milner and most recently Suzanne Corkin of the Massachusetts Institute of Technology (Corkin, 1984). Not long after the operation it became apparent that H. M. had trouble with new memories. This is a phenomenon known as **anterograde amnesia**, and for H. M. it means that he can explicitly remember only what he knew before 1953. His vocabulary remains the same; his concious knowledge of world events has not increased; he fails to remember that he just mowed the lawn; 30 min after a meal, he does not recall eating; and so on.

anterograde amnesia inability to remember new learning explicitly

Although it was once thought that patients with anterograde amnesia were unable to store new information in memory, new evidence shows that they forget only when direct memory tests are used. On indirect tests of

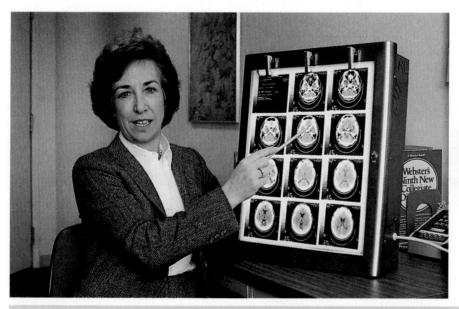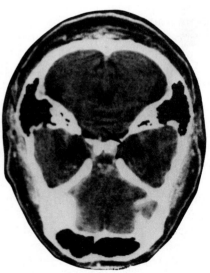

Above: Suzanne Corkin of MIT points to 1 of 11 CAT scans of the patient H. M. Because of recurrent, very intense seizures, part of H. M.'s temporal lobes were removed surgically, resulting in great memory impairment. *Right*: In this CAT scan of H. M.'s brain, the site of the lesion is shown by the arrow pointing to the red area.

memory, such as the word fragment completion task described earlier in this chapter, amnesic subjects often show the same level of memory performance as nonamnesic control subjects. Apparently, it is not a problem of storing new information, per se; the real problem is with explicit memory (Jacoby & Witherspoon, 1982; Squire, 1992; Tulving & Schachter, 1990). People with anterograde amnesia can learn skills, and they can learn through classical and operant conditioning. These amnesic subjects show that remembering is not always accompanied by an awareness of the memory.

Elsewhere, parallels have been drawn between people with anterograde amnesia and people with **Korsakoff's syndrome**, a disorder associated with chronic alcoholism (Mayes, 1988). It appears that the common denominator is a malfunctioning hippocampus. This brings us to the following very important point: Increasingly, neuroscience is unveiling the secrets of how memory works by establishing neurobiological relations among such varied processes as storage, retrieval, and forgetting. In the next section on biological memory structures, we provide brief coverage of what promises to be an exciting approach to understanding memory from a purely anatomical and chemical perspective.

Korsakoff's syndrome disorder associated with long-term alcoholism in which anterograde amnesia is found

MEMORY STRUCTURES: BIOLOGICAL PERSPECTIVES

Actually, the assumption that learning and memory phenomena are reducible to molecular analyses is not new. Lashley (1950) and Hebb (1949) advocated the biological bases of behavior years ago. What *is* new are convincing findings made possible by improved technology that localize neurophysiological substrates of selected memory events. During the remaining years of this century, you can expect to see further increases in research activity relating to biologically based models of memory. As our ability to detect bodily changes increases, so too will our ability to isolate discrete memory events. Let's see what has been happening regarding neuroanatomy and neurochemistry.

Neuroanatomy and Memory

Earlier in our discussion of different memory systems, we distinguished between *procedural* memories, which correspond roughly to habit formation, and memories based on stored representations (Tulving's *episodic* and *semantic* memories). Some very important findings have indicated that these different systems are physically distinct. Specifically, procedural memories seem to reside more in the cerebellum, whereas more cognitively based memories are associated with hippocampal and thalamic functions.

Cerebellum and Memory.   Stanford's Richard F. Thompson has come astonishingly close to isolating an individual memory pathway for procedural memory. Thompson (1986) and McCormick and Thompson (1984) report findings from experiments with rabbits that show that specific memories travel along highly localized neural circuits in the cerebellum. In one study, a classical conditioning procedure was used (see Chapter 6 for a discussion of classical conditioning). A tone (CS) and air puff to a rabbit's eye (US) were paired, and after a few trials the tone reliably evoked a conditioned eyeblink response. Thompson and his co-workers discovered that lesioning (surgically destroying) 1 cubic millimeter (mm^3) of brain tissue in the area of the cerebellum was sufficient to stop the learned eyeblink response. The loss proved to be specific to the association; that is, the ani-

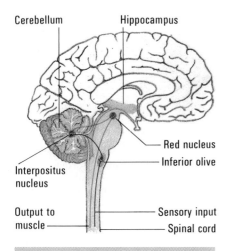

Cerebellum   Hippocampus

— Red nucleus
— Inferior olive

Interpositus
nucleus

Output to
muscle

— Sensory input
— Spinal cord

FIGURE 7–22
Mapping an individual memory
trace associated with a conditioned
eyeblink response. The memory of
the conditioned eyeblink apparently
originates as sensory information
arising at lower brain centers (inferior olive). With training, the information then takes a side route to a
tiny area in the cerebellum called
the interpositus nucleus. Here the
memory is converted to action. A
signal to respond is sent to the midbrain area called the red nucleus,
which, in turn, relays the activation
command to selected muscles.
(From Thompson, 1986.)

mal could still hear the tone, voluntary eyeblinks were still made, and so
forth. When Thompson recorded the activity of different cells and nerve
pathways in other brain areas, the details of the entire circuitry involved in
the conditioned eyeblink response came into focus (see Figure 7–22).

Interestingly, Thompson and his colleagues also observed that separate
lesions in the cerebellum resulted in disturbances peculiar to specific
response systems. For example, a lesion in one area disrupted a conditioned
eyeblink response, yet a conditioned leg movement was unaffected. A second lesion a millimeter closer to the midline (center) of the brain produced
the opposite result, namely, the conditioned leg movement was disrupted
but the eyeblink association remained intact. On the basis of such findings,
Thompson and his colleagues concluded that isolated procedural memories
have unique pathways in the cerebellum. It is important to note that other
investigators have surgically removed the hippocampus with no corresponding disturbance of such procedural memories (Farley & Alkon, 1985). This
offers further confirmation of the unique role played by the cerebellum in
the formation of procedural memories.

Hippocampus and Memory.   Now let us consider the relationships between
material structures and representational (episodic and semantic) memory.
The hippocampus is one of the chief structures involved here. Think back to
the case of H. M. Recall that H. M.'s surgery involved removing a large section of the hippocampus. It is now clear that the hippocampus plays a role in
the fixing of memories during the hours and days following learning (Squire
& Zola-Morgan, 1991). It is understandable, therefore, that H. M. would suffer memory losses of the sort just described. If you sat down and read a magazine and never encoded or stored the information, it would be like flour
passing through a sifter: the material would not be retained. Perhaps this
lack of processing that results from a dysfunctional hippocampus is the reason for H. M.'s inability to profit from articles he has just finished reading.

The idea that hippocampal damage is associated with these types of
encoding and storage failures has substantial experimental support. Patients
who have had bilateral hippocampal operations have been shown to exhibit
dramatic decreases in performance on tasks that require them to store numbers in long-term memory (Drachman & Arbit, 1966). Elsewhere, Squire
(1982) has reported that neurological patients with suspected hippocampal
disturbances manifest symptoms much like those reported for H. M. Of
course, not all of our evidence on hippocampal/memory interactions comes
from patients. Sometimes it comes from victims.

THINKING ABOUT

Effects of the Environment
on Memory

As a 49-year-old inspector for the Occupational Safety and Health Administration
(OSHA), E. B. was responsible for ensuring that proper safety precautions were
being taken by an industrial manufacturer of toluene, a chemical solvent. On a
routine inspection, a large vat of toluene spilled over and drenched E. B. from
head to toe. Within a matter of hours, E. B. began to suffer seizures and develop
severe tremors. He spent the next 6 months in a hospital, and he totally lost his
memory. Today, E. B. is disabled, and incapable of recounting the tragic events
that destroyed his life.

Fortunately, industrial accidents such as E. B.'s do not occur often. But when such catastrophes do happen, irreversible damage occurs. In the case of E. B., for instance, MRI tests (see Chapter 2) revealed that the hippocampus was permanently injured. Laboratory research tells us that chemicals such as toluene, trimethyltin, kainic acid, and a host of other compounds attack selected neural cells in the hippocampus (Tilson, 1987). When these cells are destroyed, the memory functions they control are lost permanently, unless some other brain region compensates for them.

Instances of extreme memory loss resulting from chemical poisoning raise questions about the risk of at least some memory dysfunction for all employees who work in polluted environments. Even though a worker may not be involved in an accident, recurrent exposure to low levels of contaminants may cause an insidious erosion of memory functioning. Indeed, memory losses among workers at lead-smelting plants do occur (Baker et al., 1983), and such effects seem to correlate positively with the concentration of metal residues in the blood.

At present, it is unclear whether low-level exposure to toxic agents produces the same degree of physical injury that is produced by acute, high concentrations, as was the case with E. B. Memory problems may derive from changes in neurotransmitter systems, structural abnormalities, or even changes in endocrine operations. In any event, the potential hazards of the workplace must be recognized and the necessary steps taken to protect against such things as chemically related memory loss.

Do you think we are living in a dangerous chemical environment? Do we have sufficient safeguards to protect us against pollution? Can we afford such safeguards?

Thalamus and Memory. Only in the last few years have memory theorists given the kind of attention to the thalamus that they have given to the hippocampus for 3 decades or more. The thalamus seems to be the structure that gives the order to "print" the memory initially (Mishkin, Malamut, & Bechevalier, 1984). When damage to the thalamus occurs, memory traces are never created, let alone stored in long-term memory. A key distinction needs to be made here: With hippocampal damage, the memory is formed, but due to insufficient elaboration the information is not appropriately encoded; with thalamic damage the memories never get formed at all.

Obviously, much work remains before new relationships are uncovered and old arguments are resolved. Nonetheless, neuroanatomical profiles of memory offer new ways of thinking about memory, and in most cases the ideas are rooted in the solid tradition of scientific observation.

Neurochemistry and Memory

In addition to recent advances concerned with the anatomy of memory, progress also has been made in understanding neurochemical systems involved in memory formation. One line of research links the neurotransmitter norepinephrine (refer to Chapter 2) to memory. Results from numerous animal studies show that memory impairment occurs when brain regions rich in norepinephrine are destroyed. Further evidence shows that a depletion of norepinephrine occurs in patients suffering from Korsakoff's syndrome, the alcohol disorder mentioned earlier. However, as noted elsewhere (Squire, 1988), so many other neural changes are evident among Korsakoff patients that it is hard to determine the precise cause of memory loss. Is it norepinephrine depletion, hippocampal cell death, cortical lesions, or what?

Also, we should mention what promises to be one of the most exciting findings in neuroscience in recent years. The story begins with a retired California postal worker who, having just had a coronary bypass operation, suffered a sudden loss of blood to his brain. R. B., as the patient is now known, completely lost his ability to form memories. Several years after the trauma, R. B. died, and an autopsy of his brain revealed that, contrary to expectation, only a tiny section of the hippocampus had been damaged. Closer inspection revealed that this brain region contained a high concentration of an unusual molecule called the *NMDA receptor*, named after the chemical, N-methyl D-aspartate, that is used to detect it (McGaugh, 1989). As it turns out, the NMDA receptor controls whether or not one brain cell communicates with the next. So when these receptors are inoperative, the neural network that constitutes a memory fails accordingly. Curiously, when the brain is overstimulated by wildfire electrical activity, NMDA receptors self-destruct. Perhaps this is why ECT treatments disrupt memory, as discussed earlier. In any event, scientists already are discovering that they can prevent learning and memory in animals by chemically blocking NMDA receptor activity. What will happen when we find a way to artificially stimulate this receptor in humans? Are we getting closer to having a memory pill? If so, do you see any potential ethical problems here?

THINKING AHEAD . . .

In this chapter we have seen that memory is involved in virtually every facet of our lives; we must remember what the answers are on an exam, when to take out the trash, how to ride a bicycle, who the star of a movie is, and where we left our keys last night. Psychologists are unable to observe memory directly, so they observe the various behaviors that accompany learning and remembering, much as the atomic physicist must observe the by-products of subatomic collisions to make inferences about the structure and dynamics of particles that are too small to see. Like physicists, psychologists construct models to represent the way they believe memory operates. Whether the correct model of memory involves particular subsystems or mental processes remains to be tested.

We now know a good deal about memory, in terms of both performance measures and biological relations of memory phenomena. In the past, the biological and behavioral approaches to memory have proceeded more or less independently, without much common ground. In recent years, however, that has begun to change; cognitive psychologists have turned to neuroscience in an effort to verify ideas about memory systems and phenomena, and biologically oriented researchers, in turn, are now interpreting patterns of neural communication in terms of the more macroscopic systems described by cognitive models. Although much remains to be learned, we can expect to see great advances in cognitive neuroscience in the coming years.

Along with an understanding of abstract systems of memory, we have seen an increased interest in ways that such theories can be applied, such as in education and the legal system. Studies of eyewitness memory, for example, are having an impact on the use of procedures for improving the witness's memory; for creating lineups that are freer from bias; and perhaps most important, for showing us when our memories, no matter how vivid they may seem, are simply wrong.

Finally, we consider the adaptive significance of memory. We may learn from our successes and failures, but that learning can be effective only if we remember to use it. The most fascinating paradox of human memory is that we can remember a plethora of details of events that appear to remain intact for a lifetime, whereas we seem to forget important things like course material, birthdays of relatives, and names of people we have just met, as if our minds held memories like a sieve holds water. What is the adaptive significance of forgetting? Although this question cannot be fully answered here, we can make a few guesses. For example, it may be useful to forget where you parked yesterday when you look for your car today, to forget the way to drive to last year's apartment when you are driving home tonight, and to forget the name of an old flame when whispering in your fiancé's ear. Memories of bad feelings and traumatic tragedies may be better put aside in many circumstances. Finally, forgetting may require us to concentrate on a limited set of thoughts, which may be critically important in helping us stick to a task, rather than idly wandering the endless rooms in the vast storehouse of memory.

Summary

The Information Processing Paradigm

1. According to the information-processing model of memory, three sequentially dependent stages are involved in memory processing. In the initial stage of encoding, sensory events are coded and changed to a format that permits further processing. In the second stage, storage, memory events are assigned individual memory locations. Finally, memory material is reclaimed during the retrieval stage.

Sensory Memory

2. The sensory registers hold information in store for only a sec or so. The purpose of the sensory registers is to keep the information represented long enough to complete the necessary encoding and storage steps.

Short-Term Memory

3. Short-term memory refers to a memory structure that holds a limited amount of information in memory for about 20 sec. Items must be continually rehearsed to be maintained in short-term memory.

Long-Term Memory

4. Events placed in long-term memory are available for recall even years later. One type of long-term memory, known as procedural memory, basically corresponds to habit formation. When long-term memory involves items that relate to specific events in one's life, we speak of episodic memory. By contrast, semantic memory concerns general knowledge that is stored on a long-term basis. Procedural memories are implicit, meaning they are remembered without awareness.

5. Recent research indicates that a form of long-term memory known as permastore may hold semantic items for as long as 50 years.

Encoding Processes

6. Maintenance rehearsal involves shallow processing and does not contribute much to long-term memory. Elaborative rehearsal involves deep processing and facilitates the transfer of information from short-term to long-term memory. This form of rehearsal involves forming associations between new items and items already in long-term memory.

7. Subjective organization and imagery are encoding processes that relate to the storage of material in the long-term store. The former makes storage easier by ordering information into meaningful clusters; the latter includes mnemonic systems that enhance memory quality by converting different sources of information into visual form.

Retrieval

8. One phenomenon that affects memory retrieval is reconstruction. Reconstructive memory refers to the tendency to fill in the actual details from long-term memory with items that seem to fit the occasion. This process often alters one's recollection of specific events in quite dramatic ways. Of particular interest is the way reconstructive processes influence eyewitness testimony.

9. Contextual retrieval is concerned with what happens when we learn in one environment and then recall the information in the same or a different environment. Generally, people remember better when training and testing occur in the same context. According to a state-dependent model, this context phenomenon extends to include drug states and different moods.

10. The tip-of-the-tongue (TOT) phenomenon occurs when we struggle to pull from memory an item that we can almost, but not quite, recall. This phenomenon can tell us something about how our memory system is organized.

Memory in Everyday Settings: Flashbulbs and Eyewitnesses

11. Episodic memory is facilitated by tragic events, often leading to flashbulb memories. Flashbulb memories are not especially different from ordinary memories, but they seem more vivid than memories lacking emotions and are generally remembered well. Eyewitness memories are often flawed. Cross-racial identifications are especially prone to error.

Forgetting

12. Memory failing altogether is known as forgetting. The decay theory of forgetting states that without practice, memory traces fade away. The alternative account, the interference theory of forgetting, suggests that memory loss occurs due to retrieval failure. Specifically, this model assumes that competing associations prevent the recall of information that still resides in long-term memory.

Memory Structures: Biological Perspectives

13. Technological advances have provided increased opportunities for memory investigations into the neuroanatomical and neurochemical bases of memory. Even industrial accidents that destroy certain brain regions have produced results that help us better understand the relation between brain structures and memory. Still in its infancy, this biological perspective on memory promises to play a significant research role in the future.

Key Terms

information processing
   system (252)
encoding (252)
storage (252)
retrieval (252)
rehearsal (252)
structures (252)
processes (252)
sensory memory
   (253)
short-term memory
   (253)
long-term memory
   (253)
pattern recognition
   (253)
partial report technique
   (254)
chunk (257)

serial position
   phenomenon (259)
primacy effect (259)
recency effect (260)
episodic memory (261)
semantic memory (261)
procedural memory
   (261)
explicit memory (261)
implicit memory (261)
direct measures (261)
indirect measures (262)
permastore state (263)
levels of processing
   theory (264)
shallow processing (264)
deep processing (264)
subjective organization
   (266)

mnemonic device (267)
method of loci (267)
peg-word approach
   (268)
eidetic imagery (268)
reconstructive memory
   (268)
recognition tests (270)
outshining (270)
state-dependent
   memory (270)
tip-of-the-tongue
   phenomenon (271)
flashbulb memory
   (272)
eyewitness testimony
   (274)
eyewitness
   identification (276)

foil (276)
cross-racial
   identification (276)
calibration (277)
forgetting (277)
decay theory (278)
interference theory
   (278)
proactive interference
   (279)
retroactive
   interference (279)
retrograde amnesia
   (281)
consolidation (282)
anterograde amnesia
   (282)
Korsakoff's syndrome
   (283)

Suggested Reading

Baddeley, A. (1990). *Human memory: Theory and practice.* Needham Heights, MA: Allyn and Bacon. A broad coverage of topics researched in human memory, including memory models, emotion and memory, amnesia, and treatment of memory problems.

Davies, G. M., & Thomson, D. M. (1988). *Memory in context: Context in memory.* New York: Wiley. An edited volume that provides coverage of recent research on the importance of contextual cues in memory. Along with chapters on the impact of environmental stimuli on recall, chapters on mood and memory and eyewitness identification are included.

Klatzky, R. L. (1984). *Memory and awareness: An information processing approach.* New York: Freeman. A basic discussion of memory processes and functions. Covers what memory can and cannot do, along with memory applications.

Loftus, E. F. (1979). *Eyewitness testimony.* Cambridge, MA: Harvard University Press. A review of a number of case histories of eyewitness reports of crime. The influence of suggestion, delay, and a host of other factors on retrieval is discussed, along with the implications of these events for legal issues.

Luria, A. A. (1960). *The mind of a mnemonist.* New York: Basic Books. An astonishing portrayal of one man's ability to use visual imagery to encode information. Examples of his exceptional memory are given, and the personal problems resulting from his anomaly are discussed.

Answers for Word Fragment Completion Test

1. anatomy	6. octopus	11. insomnia
2. bureau	7. ellipse	12. aardvark
3. chipmunk	8. tequila	13. lectern
4. nirvana	9. tricycle	14. flamingo
5. exponent	10. leprosy	15. pigment

CHAPTER 8
Thought and Language

The Caroline Islands, consisting of about 25 atolls and low islands, are located in an area of the central Pacific called Micronesia. The islands stretch across about 150 miles of an area that is over 99% water. There are almost no landmarks in the area, and if you travel from island to island by the customary canoe, what you see, essentially, is a vast featureless expanse of water in all directions. You might think it would be ill advised to set out from one of the islands in a canoe to get to another unseen island many miles away, on an excursion spanning several days, and with no navigational instruments! The chances seem too great of ending up lost on the immense ocean. Yet, that is exactly what Micronesian navigators do routinely, as they have done for centuries, and they rarely get lost. How do they do it?

One technique that navigators from Puluwat Island in the Carolines use is the idea of the "moving island." The navigator sees the canoe as a small stationary microcosm, the one stable point under the sky. As the water glides endlessly past the canoe on a voyage, islands and atolls are imagined to slip past at certain predictable rates, and in particular known patterns. Puluwat navigators use this mental model of moving islands to guide them on their journeys, day or night, where Westerners would never stray without scales, charts, sextants, compasses, and chronometers.

As technologies infiltrate the island cultures of the Pacific, navigators have come to rely less on the moving islands mental model and more on navigational instruments. Already, the model has been lost to many island groups near the Carolines, such as Polynesia and Melanesia. Fortunately, studies of Micronesian navigators have revealed and recorded this otherwise unknown and undocumented system of navigation. An understanding of this mental model has provided the knowledge for a renaissance of seafaring in the Pacific islands.

What are mental models? How do they help us understand and function in the world around us? These are examples of questions asked by cognitive psychologists, whose primary interest is thinking and the mind. This

◀ Thinking, and communication through language, increase our awareness.

chapter is divided into two major sections: thought and language. The section on thought will describe mental imagery, conceptualization, problem solving, and creativity. Language, one of our most important and uniquely human abilities, allows us to express our thoughts and understand the ideas of others.

THOUGHT

The literature on thought, sometimes colorful and controversial, dates back long before scientific psychology emerged. "I think, therefore I am," was the basic, self-evident truth from which the philosopher René Descartes began his proof of God and reality. The importance that Descartes and other philosophers attributed to thought reflects the fascination philosophers and psychologists have had with this topic throughout history. Progress on the psychological study of thought, however, has been difficult. As Bourne, Ekstrand, and Dominowski (1971) have written, "Thinking is one of those mysterious concepts that everyone understands and no one can explain." As a concept within psychology, thought has had a checkered existence. With the advent of behaviorism its study was deemphasized because of its obvious mentalistic qualities (see Figure 8–1). Yet with the growth of the cognitive psychology movement in the 1960s, thinking has once again become a respectable subject of study. Consequently, the number of studies on this topic has increased substantially in recent years. It is a complex topic that includes activities ranging from the fantasies associated with daydreaming to complex problem-solving activity. Our discussion of thinking in this chapter focuses primarily on the topics of methods for studying thinking, mental images, concepts and categories, problem solving, and creative thinking.

Methods for Studying Thinking

We tend to view thinking as an invisible process that goes on within the brain. When the EEG was invented in 1929, many psychologists believed that the key to thinking was at hand. The brain waves recorded on the EEG were assumed by some to be thoughts. To understand these EEG messages, one had only to break the code. It did not take long for scientists to abandon that idea, but the search for the neural basis of thinking continues, even though the task, at times, seems to be an impossible one. Consider the fact that there are billions of neurons in the human brain. Even if 10,000 electrodes could be placed in the human brain at the right locations, the information they would provide would not be sufficient to describe thinking. The complexity of the brain is dictated not only by the sheer number of cells, but also by factors such as the potential groupings of those cells. The combinations may be infinite, and some researchers have suggested that the patterning of neural connections differs from person to person (Hebb, 1980b).

Thinking can also be studied as a process intervening between some specified set of stimulus variables and the subsequent behavior. A profitable approach to studying thinking this way is the information processing approach (described in Chapter 7), which developed with the advent of computers. Computers have been assumed to have capabilities analogous to human thinking in that they code information, store it, act on it through various manipulations and transformations, retrieve information from their memory stores, and eventually reach some decision or initiate some action. Like any analogy, the computer analogy has many shortcomings in its ability to account for human thinking. Nevertheless, it has been a useful model in guiding research in this area (Gilhooly, 1982).

FIGURE 8–1
The Gestalt school of psychology did not abandon the study of thinking during behaviorism's heyday. Part of their approach to the study of thinking involved studying famous thinkers such as Albert Einstein (*top*), who happened to be a close friend of Max Wertheimer (*bottom*), the founder of Gestalt psychology (see Wertheimer, 1945).

More recently, a different type of computerized analogy known alternately as connectionist, neural network, or parallel distributed processing models of thought (also discussed in Chapter 6) has captured the attention of cognitive psychologists and computer scientists interested in artificial intelligence. Rather than characterizing thought as a rapid sequence of information processes that follow precisely defined logical rules, these **neural network models** emphasize the parallel, or simultaneous, nature of thought that occurs automatically, inexactly, and without our awareness. These models can learn, they can adapt to new situations, and they can deal with imprecise or incomplete information—abilities that "intelligent" computers usually do not have. Further, the neural network models are based on neuronlike systems, which are biological, whereas traditional information processing models are based upon artificially contrived computer codes. Although still fairly early in their development, and despite criticism by some cognitive psychologists (e.g., Fodor & Pylyshyn, 1988; Massaro, 1988), these neural network models show great promise for adding to our understanding of human thought (Rumelhart & McClelland, 1987).

> **neural network models** theories or models that use patterns of neural connectivity, activation, and inhibition as a system for describing cognitive processing

Metacognition.   Another way to study what people are thinking is to ask them about their thoughts. For example, would you be able to recognize the capitol of Australia if you saw the name in a list of Australian cities? Could you multiply two 2-digit numbers in your head? Are you better at learning lists of numbers or lists of words? Questions that ask about the workings of your own mind require you to use **metacognition**, which is defined as thinking about or awareness of one's own thoughts. A medical doctor can learn more (but not everything) about a human patient's ills by asking what the problem is, when it hurts, and in what situations the problem is most bothersome; a veterinarian cannot, because animals do not speak. Similarly, we may be able to learn more about the human mind (but not everything) by asking people about their metacognitions. Of course, in cognitive psychology, as in medicine, it is important to learn when metacognitions are accurate and when they are not.

> **metacognition** thinking or awareness of one's own thoughts

Methods of Studying Metacognition.   Cognitive psychologists study metacognition with **subjective reports**, a method in which subjects are asked to give some indication about their metacognition. At first glance, the subjective report may sound like introspection (see Chapter 1), another method requiring the subject to report mental events. Subjective reports differ considerably, however, particularly because of the way the data are used. Whereas introspection is used to describe the structures and processes of the mind, subjective reports are treated as performance measures. That is, just as we can measure the effect of practice on the number of problems that are solved, or the time needed to solve a problem, we can also look at the effects of practice on the subject's confidence, a subjective report.

> **subjective reports** metacognitions described by a subject

One technique that relies heavily on the subjective report is called the **think-aloud method**. In this method the subject is asked to say aloud what he or she is thinking as much as possible while working on some experimental task, such as problem solving. The record of what the subject says is called the subject's **protocol**, and the analysis of these protocols is referred to as **protocol analysis**. By systematically analyzing the protocols of many subjects, or even of the same subject many times, the researcher can examine patterns of cognition, such as how people solve various types of problems. A particularly important use of protocol analysis is to create an **expert system**, a computer program that makes decisions in some area of knowledge. For example, an expert system created from the subjective reports of medical diagnosticians might be used by other doctors. A different system

> **think-aloud method** technique in which subjects try to say out loud everything they are thinking

> **protocol** in an experiment, a subject's experimental record; refers to the spoken report in the think-aloud technique

> **protocol analysis** systematic analysis of subject protocols in order to find consistent patterns of cognition

> **expert system** computer program intended to process and interpret information in a specific area as an expert in that area would

metamemory awareness of one's memory

illusion of knowing an inaccurate overconfidence about one's knowledge and understanding

dual coding theory the theory that words can be stored in memory with a verbal code, an imagery code, or both

mental comparisons the use of mental imagery, rather than real objects, to compare two figures

might help a manufacturer decide on the most cost-effective body to put on an automobile.

An important consideration in determining the accuracy of metacognition is referred to as *calibration*. Your metacognition is calibrated if you can accurately predict your performance on a cognitive task, such as recognizing a name, solving a problem, or understanding a piece of text. In Chapter 7, for example, it was noted that eyewitnesses are not very good at predicting the accuracy of their identifications; thus, **metamemory** (i.e., metacognition about one's memories) is not well calibrated for eyewitness identification.

Another area in which people are often not well calibrated is text comprehension. Overconfidence about understanding a course textbook all too commonly leads students to perform poorly on exams. This common mistaken belief that you understand a text when you really do not is called the **illusion of knowing** (Glenberg et al., 1982).

These examples of poor calibration of metacognition show that we cannot rely solely on subjective reports as a method for studying thinking. We must also consider physiological measures and performance on tasks to study cognition adequately.

Mental Images in Thinking

Thinking is assumed to be made up of a number of mental processes in which events, objects, and ideas are manipulated in some symbolic way. In the earliest days of experimental psychology, Wundt proposed that thought is always accompanied by pictorial images. That view was not shared by Oswald Külpe (1862–1915), a former student of Wundt, who proposed that thinking could occur without mental pictures being present. This controversy of "imageless thought" occupied psychologists for several decades as they debated whether thinking involved pictures or words.

Today the validity of both visual and auditory processing is recognized in a contemporary view of thinking known as the **dual coding theory**. This theory proposes one system that is perceptual (primarily visual), uses images, and deals with objects and events that are largely nonverbal, and a second system that makes use of verbal symbols, or language. Dual coding theory proposes that these two systems interact regularly when we are thinking (Richardson, 1983).

Early researchers, such as Wundt and Külpe, studied thinking by asking subjects to report on their own mental processes when they were presented with problems to think about. But these investigators also used reaction time as a way to study thinking. They designed experiments of differing complexity and interpreted the differences in response times as reflecting the differences in the time required for mental processes to occur (recall the discussion of Wilhelm Wundt in Chapter 1). This latter technique, which is called *mental chronometry*, remains an important experimental procedure.

Perceptual Properties of Mental Images.   The most striking aspect of mental images is their similarity to perception, especially visual perception. Evidence of this similarity comes from an imaginative variety of laboratory procedures, such as **mental comparisons**, which describe a decision process in which we compare two or more things. "Weighing things in our mind" is a phrase we often use to describe this kind of mental process. Such comparisons might be complex, like thinking about several job offers, or simple, like deciding which of two dinners on a restaurant menu is cheaper. Cognitive psychologists have studied such comparisons and have made some interesting discoveries about this kind of mental activity. Which is bigger, a mouse or an elephant? A mouse or a rat? How do we answer such questions? Research shows that people actually imagine an elephant and a mouse and then compare those mental images. Given the two comparisons just suggested, would you expect them to be of comparable difficulty? It seems that it takes less time for a person to compare the mouse–elephant pair than the mouse–rat pair, because of the greater disparity of size in the first pair. This finding has given rise to the *symbolic distance effect* (Moyer & Bayer, 1976), which states that mental comparisons are made along some relevant dimension (e.g., size, color, pleasantness), and that the speed of the decision is inversely proportional to the distance between the items on that dimension. Thus, with respect to the dimension of cost, it would be easier to decide between a pair of items such as an original painting by Rembrandt and a toaster than between a sofa and a television (Paivio, 1980). Such studies not only provide information about the time required for mental comparisons and the dimensions that are used, but they also reveal the way imagery is used in thinking.

Other techniques have added to our knowledge about the way mental images are used in thinking. For example, does a rabbit have ears? In answering this question, we might form a mental image of a rabbit which we then examine. Interestingly, Stephen Kosslyn (1975, 1980, 1981) found that this question was answered faster if subjects had been picturing a rabbit next to a fly, rather than next to an elephant, just before the question was asked. Why? Because the rabbit next to a fly filled the "image space" (a sort of mental picture frame as shown in Figure 8–2); features are easier to "see" in a larger mental image because the details are relatively larger and clearer. The image of the rabbit next to an elephant was small and thus the details are more obscure. The type of imaging described for this situation is similar to looking at objects in your own environment.

In addition to these studies, **mental rotation** experiments have shown that rotating mental images follow the same patterns of results as those obtained when objects are actually rotated (Shepard & Cooper, 1982). Subjects were shown the letter *R* in a variety of orientations. Sometimes the letter was presented in its normal orientation, and sometimes backward. Other presentations involved turning the letter to the side or inverting it (see Figure 8–3). The subject's task was to say whether the letter was normal or backward. As shown in Figure 8–3, Shepard and Cooper found that the decision time increased steadily as the rotation approached 180°. These data suggest that subjects mentally rotate the letter to its upright position and then make the judgment of whether the letter is normal or backward. They make that judgment by comparing the stimulus against one they have stored

mental rotation laboratory task used to study mental imagery in which a figure must be turned in space to compare its similarity to a second figure

FIGURE 8–2
The kinds of mental images we might construct in thinking about a rabbit and fly together or a rabbit and elephant together. The time required for thinking (that is, answering the question about the rabbit's ears, as described in the text) is longer in the rabbit–elephant pair because the rabbit image is relatively smaller thus making the details in the image more obscure.

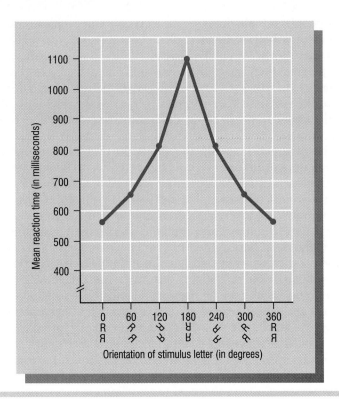

FIGURE 8–3
The graph shows that response times were longest for letters that were rotated 180°. Shepard and Cooper found that response times for normal letters were consistently 100 msec shorter than those for the letter's mirror image. (Adapted from Shepard & Cooper, 1982.)

in memory in the kind of template matching procedure similar to what we described in the chapter on perception. The initial step in mental rotation involves deciding left from right. That decision determines the direction in which the stimulus will be rotated (Corballis & McLaren, 1984). It has also been found that the capacity to rotate images is limited; three-dimensional shapes and complex objects take more time to be mentally manipulated (Bethell-Fox & Shepard, 1988; Shepard & Metzger, 1988).

The many correspondences between mental and perceptual images have been noted by psychologist Ronald Finke (1986), whose research has added significantly to the scientific literature on imagery. His research has shown that subjects experienced and responded to visual illusions similarly when the subjects imagined them and when they actually saw the physical stimuli. His results, and those of others such as Lynn Cooper and Roger Shepard, support the hypothesis that imaging is very much like visual perception. Finke suggests that imagery may be a normal preparatory process that occurs when one is expecting to see a particular object.

Concepts and Categories

If the tomato is a fruit, why do grocers always put tomatoes with the vegetables in the store? If you want to see the penguins at an unfamiliar zoo, do you look for the birds or the aquatic animals? When you look up the phone number of the place up the street that specializes in pizza and submarine sandwiches, do you check under "restaurant," "sandwich shops," or "pizza" in the Yellow Pages? Answering these questions requires us to classify and categorize information into conceptual categories. A **conceptual category** consists of a set of members (also called cases or instances), all of which are given the same label (such as "restaurant" or "monster").

The method used for classifying things into conceptual categories refers to the definition of a category. The simplest way to define categories is by *enumeration*. Using this method, one simply lists the members of the cate-

conceptual category set whose members are defined by rules

gory and checks the list to determine whether or not something fits into a category. For example, to find out if a baseball player is a Cardinal or a Yankee, we have only to check the team rosters. Enumeration will likewise work well for classifying New Jersey as a state, the Golden Gate Bridge as one of the wonders of the modern world, and "Thou shall not kill" as one of the Ten Commandments. Many categories, however, are too large to be easily enumerated. Examples include animals, dangerous things, people, chairs, and even (or odd) numbers.

Look at the following number:

73,864,026,876,104,479,014,065,264,119,745,765,220,578

You probably have never seen this particular number before. Other than merely repeating the digits, you probably cannot even say the number, because you may not know the number place names after trillions or quadrillions or quintillions. Still, even though you may not be able to say the number and even though you have never seen it before, you can probably classify it correctly as either an even number or an odd number. Why is this so easy? It is done by using **classification rules** for defining categories, rather than enumerating every possible even and odd number. Classification rules define the characteristics of category membership. In the case of numbers, the rule "if it ends in an odd digit, then it is an odd number, and if it ends in an even digit, it is even" can be used quickly and efficiently to classify any whole number.

classification rules guidelines for determining category membership, such as possessing certain features, fitting a cognitive structure, or resembling a prototype

Many different kinds of classification rules can be used to define categories. One type of classification rule is of the general form "if X has all of the defining attributes of a category, then it is an instance of that category." A **defining attribute** is a quality or a property that occurs in all members of a category. For example, all birds have the defining attributes of feathers, wings, and beaks.

defining attribute a feature unique to category members; that is, a feature possessed by all members of a category

Learning of Concepts.   Psychologists are interested not only in how concepts are used but also in how they are learned (see Figure 8–4). To find these answers, they have studied special concepts created for laboratory use. This procedure ensures that the subjects will not have had any prior famil-

FIGURE 8–4
Psychologists have used many tests to study how concepts are learned. In this one, either shape or color can be used as the defining attribute determining inclusion in the concept category.

iarity with the concept. A simplified version of this procedure is presented next. Look at the following nonsense syllables. Some of them are labeled "true" and others are labeled "false." Study these examples and try to discover what makes for a "true" syllable.

AEM	OLZ	EIX	FCT	AXC	HLZ	KYW	ORU
True	False	True	False	False	True	False	True

In an experimental situation the subject would probably be shown each of the nonsense syllables one at a time. When seeing each syllable, the subject would respond either "true" or "false." Then the experimenter would tell the subject the correct answer. Once the subject learns the concept, performance is essentially perfect.

Have you learned the concept yet? You have an advantage in that you can study the eight different syllables at once. The syllables have several different attributes. Because they are all composed of three letters, obviously that cannot be a defining attribute. No single letter or pairs of letters appear in all the true syllables, so that is not the answer. What about the shape of the letters? Some letters are composed totally of straight lines, for example, the letters *K* or *L* or *Z*, whereas other letters have a curved portion, such as the letters *C* or *D* or *S*. The first nonsense syllable on the left has all straight lines and it is true. The second nonsense syllable has a curved letter and it is false. Checking the 3rd, 4th, 5th, and 6th syllables shows this attribute to be accurate in distinguishing between the true and false syllables. But suddenly with syllables 7 and 8 it does not work. Thus, curvature or linearity of letters cannot be the defining attribute.

What about the relationship of consonants and vowels? The true nonsense syllable *AEM* has two vowels, which is the case for *EIX* and *ORU* as well. But *HLZ* is true and it has no vowels.

In learning concepts, people usually proceed in this manner. They typically focus on one attribute, generating some hypothesis about how this attribute determines the concept, although sometimes they may test several attributes at once. When their hypothesis is proved wrong, they form another hypothesis. This new hypothesis may involve the same attribute in a different way or it may involve a totally new attribute. The procedure is repeated again and again until the concept is learned. This method of learning concepts is called **hypothesis testing** (Bruner, Goodnow, & Austin, 1956) and is the most popular contemporary explanation of how concepts are learned (Medin & Smith, 1984).

What is the answer to our concept learning problem? The true syllables are those whose letters are arranged in alphabetical order reading from left to right. That is the defining attribute for nonsense syllables included in the true category. Thus, *OLZ* is false because *L* comes before *O* in the alphabet. Once you know the concept, we can show you syllables that are totally novel (new), and you can draw on your concept to deduce the right answer. For example, what about the nonsense syllable *EGV*? You know it is true, even though this may be the first time you have encountered that particular syllable. You are able to answer correctly in the same way that you knew the lengthy number presented earlier was an even number.

Learning what makes nonsense syllables true or false may seem trivial, but concepts have great value for us in learning about our world and in thinking. Concepts not only help us think more rapidly and efficiently and deal with novel situations, they also help us to learn faster and more economically. To use our lengthy number example again, there are at least two ways to learn which numbers are odd and which ones are even. One way is to learn the classification rule of the concept, that is, that even numbers end with a 0, 2, 4, 6, or 8. Another way to learn would be to memorize the even

hypothesis testing sequence of logical steps in which one evaluates the validity of a rule by examining relevant evidence

or odd label for each number by going through all the numbers: "12,301 is odd, 12,302 is even . . . 8,344,766 is even, 8,344,767 is odd," and so on. The value of learning concepts should be obvious!

Natural Categories.   The concept formation studies that flourished throughout the first half of this century were careful to use artificial materials and contrived tasks, such as the exercise you just did with the nonsense syllables. The reason for using these materials and tasks was to help ensure that laboratory measures would not be biased by subjects' experiences outside of the laboratory. The use of such sterile methods, however, runs the risk of eliminating the most important and interesting phenomena from our observations, that is, naturalistic everyday phenomena. Cognitive psychologist Ulric Neisser (1987) has been one of the strongest proponents of the *ecological approach* to the study of cognition, which stresses the importance of studying naturalistic phenomena.

This ecological approach appears to have grown out of the research of Eleanor Rosch, who suggested a basic change in the way concept categories have been studied. Rosch's 1970s research centers on **natural categories**, or concept categories used in everyday life, such as "bird" or "cup" rather than artificial categories such as "an alphabetized nonsense syllable." Natural categories are less precisely defined; often there is no strict set of classification rules. For example, a dolphin is like a fish in many ways; it is shaped like a fish, it lives in the sea, and it swims rapidly. A dolphin is a "sort of" fish, just as a magazine is a "sort of" book, and a toilet is a "sort of" piece of furniture.

natural categories conceptual groups seen in everyday life

When asked to use natural categories and name a vegetable, a piece of clothing, and a weapon, many more people answer "peas," "pants," and "gun," rather than "pumpkin," "apron," and "scissors." Those responses demonstrate typical examples that are most likely to occur as rapid associations. **Typicality** is an important factor for classification, referring both to **typical attributes** of categories (those categories found in most, but not all, members of a concept category, e.g., "flying" for the category "birds") and to typical examples of categories. For example, "sparrow" is a typical example of a bird, whereas "ostrich" is not. Typicality has been used to define *prototypes*, category members that are most representative of their categories. Prototypical examples (which contain more of the typical attributes than do other class members) are identified most quickly. So when you are asked if a sparrow is a bird, you say "yes" faster than you would if asked if an ostrich is a bird (Medin & Smith, 1984).

typicality degree to which an instance seems representative of a category

typical attributes features commonly possessed by members of a category

Conceptual Combination.   Although typicality is clearly important for classifying objects into single conceptual categories, it is not always useful when we consider combinations of categories. For example, consider the category "pets." Many people would rate "warm," "four-legged," "cuddly," and "furry" as typical attributes of this category, and "hard," "cold," "intelligent," and "talkative" as atypical of pets (although any of those are possible). On the other hand, "cold" would be very typical for the category "pet fish," "talkative" might be judged as typical for "pet birds," "intelligent" might be typical for "teacher's pet," and "hard" would be typical for "pet rocks." When words are combined, their combined meanings often produce concepts that are different from either concept alone (Hampton, 1987).

Many cases of combined concepts produce new concepts that consist of the union of the two component concepts. For example, although "cold" is not typical of pets, it is typical for "fish"; therefore, the combination "pet fish" is said to inherit the attribute "cold" from the category "fish." Similarly, "not eaten" is not typical for the category "fish," but it is typical for "pets."

Therefore, "not eaten" is typical for "pet fish," because the combination inherits "not eaten" from "pets."

On the other hand, conceptual combinations sometimes produce **emergent properties**, qualities that do not typically fit either component category alone, but that emerge when the concepts combine (Finke, Ward, & Smith, 1992). Using the previous example, the attribute "talks" is not typical for "birds" or "pets," but it is typical for "pet birds." Another example is "Communist," which in the 1980s was not typical of the categories "iron" or "curtain," but was typical of the combination "iron curtain." Combinations of concepts may be a useful method for generating creative ideas.

Basic Level Categories.   Rosch and her associates (Rosch et al., 1976) identified a special type of natural category called a basic level category. **Basic level categories** are special because they seem to be the first categories acquired in life, they are important in language comprehension, and they provide a perceptual means of differentiating categories. To help understand basic level categories, look at the listing of grocery items in Figure 8–5. It is arranged hierarchically, with the most general categories at the left and the most specific ones at the right.

Basic level categories are members of the superordinate categories, and subordinate categories are members of basic level categories. What is perceptually interesting is that members of basic level categories tend to look alike (e.g., apple pie, chocolate cream pie, and pecan pie), and each basic level category tends to look very different from other basic level categories (e.g., pies, apples, bread). This means that categories at the basic level are easy to differentiate from other categories, and the members of a basic level category are easy to classify, even with only visual perceptual information. A category that is easy to discriminate from other categories and whose members are easy to classify is also easy to learn. Researchers have noted that children usually learn basic level categories first, with superordinate and subordinate categories learned later (Neisser, 1987). Furthermore, because

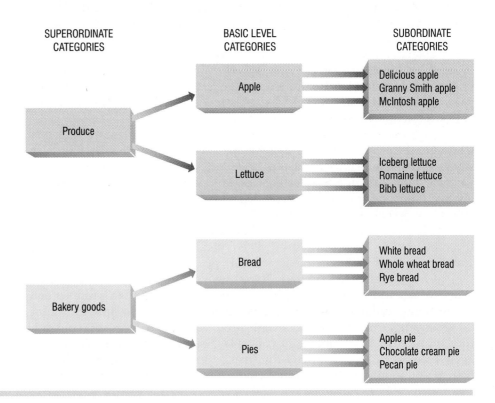

FIGURE 8–5
Levels of concept categories.

basic level categories are usually the first concepts learned, they obviously affect language comprehension. Which did you understand at the earliest age: "produce," "apple," or "McIntosh apple"? "Bakery goods," "pie," or "pecan pie"? Typically, we comprehend basic level category names before the names of categories at other levels.

Mental Models. The different approaches to concepts and categories we have already discussed describe category members but do not consider how a system works. A **mental model**, which is best described as a personal theory, is a concept about how a system functions. For example, you probably have mental models for the structures and workings of your car, vacuum cleaner, television, and calculator; for how trees grow; for why it rains; for how balls bounce; and for how to drive from where you are to the store and back. Each of your mental models explains a system, and you might be able to make predictions about those systems based on your model. For example, although you might never have seen a ball roll out of a coiled tube such as the one in Figure 8–6, you could probably figure it out based on your mental model of bodies in motion. Such mental models are sometimes referred to as "naive theories of motion" (McCloskey, 1983) or "intuitive physics."

Many people give incorrect answers to the question posed in Figure 8–6 (the correct trajectory is arrow 5), based on their mental models of how bodies in motion behave. Responses to questions such as the coiled tube and others suggest that most people believe in "impetus theory," which is simply the idea that a force applied to an object tends to set that object in motion. Many mistakenly believe that the curved path somehow gives the ball a "curvilinear impetus" that makes the ball continue to move in a curve after it leaves the tube.

Mental models do not need to be technically accurate, but they need to be functionally accurate if they are to be useful to us. For example, the Micronesian navigators described at the beginning of the chapter use a mental model that sees the canoe as stationary and the islands as moving. Obviously, this model lacks technical accuracy; the islands are not moving. However, if a navigator adopts the model during a voyage between islands, it is possible to navigate accurately in extremely difficult waters without instruments. Therefore, the moving island model represents a functionally accurate concept, even though it lacks technical accuracy.

Mental models tend to be incomplete. For example, you probably have a concept of how your car works, and you might be able to diagnose a number of problems that it might develop. However, unless you are a very knowledgeable mechanic, there are probably important gaps in your understanding. Mental models are not the same as scientific models, unless you are a scientist. Even then, the model may not be accurate. Because mental models are incomplete and unscientific, they are also naturally evolving. Whenever a model's inaccuracies and gaps fail to function properly, there is a need to develop the mental model further.

Problem Solving

The word *problem* can describe events as diverse as learning to tie your shoes, figuring out how to get a date with a particular individual, thinking of an eight-letter word that means the banishment of an evil spirit, trying to rearrange the furniture in your room, and reducing the threat of nuclear war in the world. **Problem solving** can be defined as a goal-directed process begun in the presence of some obstacles and the absence of an evident solution.

Problem solving is a popular activity for many people. Mystery readers want to be a step ahead of the novel's skilled detective and solve the murder

mental model personal theory or view of a domain of knowledge

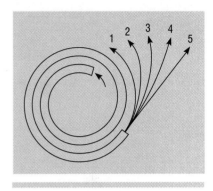

FIGURE 8–6
The curved metal tube in the diagram is lying flat and is shown as viewed from above. A metal ball is placed in the opening of the tube in the inner part of the spiral and is shot out of the tube at high speed. Which arrow (1–5) shows the correct trajectory of the ball when it emerges? (Answer is in text.)

problem solving set of mental procedures used for reaching a goal, state, or solution

before the solution is revealed by the author. Many popular games test the problem-solving skills of the players. Players of the game *Clue* work to narrow the list of locations, weapons, and suspects until they are ready to venture their guess—"Colonel Mustard did it in the library with the lead pipe." Newspaper readers use the daily feature *Jumble* to solve the various anagrams, which are jumbled arrays of letters that can be arranged to form words (see Table 8–1). Jigsaw puzzles are another popular form of problem solving. For some people, hobbies such as sewing or woodworking are interesting, in part because of the problem-solving aspects of those activities.

Psychologists have studied problem-solving activities to learn about the thinking processes that are going on when solutions are being sought. Among the earliest contributors to this field were the Gestalt psychologists (recall their contributions to the field of perception), who distinguished between two kinds of thinking in problem solving: *productive* and *reproductive* thinking. If the parts of a problem are viewed in a new way to reach a solution, then the thinking is described as productive. But when solving the problem involves the use of previously used solutions, then the thinking is reproductive. In the following discussion of problem solving we give examples of both kinds of thinking. Our focus is on the steps that are commonly used in problem solving and the obstacles to thinking that hinder problem solving.

Stages in Problem Solving.   Psychologists have viewed problem solving as a process of stages since Wallas, in 1926, first described his stage model. Techniques for studying problem solving have progressed enormously since that time. We have gone from having subjects verbally describe what they are thinking as they are engaged in solving the problem to using computers and artificial intelligence to simulate human problem solving. But problem solving is still viewed as involving a number of discrete stages, although there is disagreement over the number of stages required. Using what seems to be a consensus view, we identify the stages of problem solving as *preparation*, *production*, and *evaluation*. A fourth stage, *incubation*, is present in some problem-solving situations but not in others.

Preparation.   The initial, preparation stage of problem solving involves a great deal of information gathering, including an assessment that requires a clear definition of the problem. What is the problem? What are its starting and end points? What seem to be the obstacles? What kinds of information are needed to work toward a solution? If a problem seems familiar, reproductive thinking might lead to the conclusion that a previously successful solution may be successful again. Research has shown that one of the strengths of expert problem solvers is that they can draw on their considerable experience to generate reproductive solutions (Larkin et al., 1980). For such experienced problem solvers, the preparation stage may be a very brief one.

One key factor in the preparation stage is the assessment of how the problem is structured. Most problems can be represented in several ways, and one of these ways may lead to a faster solution. Consider the following example from psychologist Michael Posner (1973).

> Two train stations are fifty miles apart. At 2 P.M. one Saturday afternoon two trains start toward each other, one from each station. Just as the trains pull out of the station, a bird springs into the air in front of the first train and flies ahead to the front of the second train. When the bird reaches the second train it turns back and flies toward the first train. The bird continues to do this until the trains meet.
>
> If both trains travel at the rate of twenty-five miles per hour and the bird flies at a hundred miles per hour, how many miles will the bird have flown before the trains meet?

In the preparation stage, there are at least two ways to structure this problem. The final part of the problem asks how far the bird flies, a question that structures this problem in terms of distance. It can be solved that way. But a faster solution can be reached if the problem is structured in terms of time rather than distance. In this case you ask, "How much time will pass before the trains meet?" Because the stations are 50 miles apart and the trains are traveling at a speed of 25 mph, the trains will meet after 1 hr's time. You have been told that the bird flies at a speed of 100 mph; clearly, then, the answer to the problem is 100 miles. Again, the important step here is to structure the problem in a way that makes it easy to solve. The Posner problem is structured in terms of distance; the problem solver must overcome that structure and restructure the problem in other terms. The Gestalt psychologists considered this ability to restructure problems a key to successful problem solving.

Production.   In the second stage of problem solving, potential solutions are generated. The most primitive procedure used to find a solution is labeled *random search*. This search is carried out without any knowledge of what strategies might be most promising. In essence, it is a form of trial and error totally without guidance. The would-be solver tries one approach and then another and perhaps arrives, by chance, at a solution. This strategy can be likened to trying to open a combination lock without knowing the combination. A standard combination lock used on gym and school lockers has 40 numbered positions and requires a three-number sequence to open it. Without considering whether one starts rotating the dial left or right, and not even taking into account the number of rotations between each number in the sequence, how long would it take to open the lock using a random strategy? Well, there are 64,000 three-number possible combinations. Assuming it takes you 10 sec to try one combination of numbers, you could try all combinations in a little less than 178 hr. Of course, you might get lucky and hit the right combination after only 90 hr or so! A bank vault with 10 dials, each with 10 numbered positions, can also be opened in this way, assuming you have about 16,000 years to work at it (Hayes, 1978). Although time-consuming, these exhaustive searches guarantee solution of the problem. Researchers call any method that guarantees a solution to a problem an **algorithm**. Algorithms do not always involve exhaustive searches. For example, the rule for finding the area of a circle when you know the circumference is an algorithm. Using that algorithm allows the solution to be easily determined, and the problem solver does not even have to understand the algorithm. However, for most problems the only existing algorithm is exhaustive search.

algorithm a step-by-step procedure for solving a problem

A more fruitful approach is to select certain paths that offer the promise of a solution. These searches are called **heuristics** and are possible when the person has some knowledge and experience to draw on for the solution. Heuristic searches, the more commonly used strategies in problem solving, are the strategies psychologists have most often studied. These search techniques do not guarantee solution, as in the case of algorithms, but they substantially reduce the search time (see Table 8–2).

heuristics general rules, or rules of thumb, usually providing shortcuts in thinking

One often-used heuristic technique is referred to as **means–end analysis**. In this strategy, the difference between the present state and the desired state (the goal) is analyzed. The approach attempts to reduce that difference by dividing the problem into a number of subproblems that may have more manageable solutions. Suppose a first-year college student wants to be a physician. How can the student reduce the difference between these two states? In thinking about the problem, some of the following subproblems should be considered: getting to know professors well enough so that they can write knowledgeable letters of recommendation; getting some medically related experience as an undergraduate student to aid in the career decision;

means–end analysis view of problem solving that identifies subgoals that are necessary to achieve before reaching a solution

taking the best preparatory courses as an undergraduate; earning an undergraduate degree with good grades; choosing the right medical school; making a high score on the Medical College Admissions Test; having the money to go to medical school; getting admitted to medical school; doing well in medical school; and obtaining a prestigious residency after graduation. Each of these can be viewed as subgoals, and the student can begin to plan to accomplish each one. By using subgoals, the eventual goal of becoming a physician seems more manageable, and the planning that is involved in dealing with the subgoals makes the larger goal more attainable. The use of subproblems is an especially effective strategy when the problem itself is ill defined.

Another heuristic strategy involves *working backward* from the goal to the present condition. This strategy would not prove very effective for dealing with the problem in the preceding paragraph. Working backward is an effective strategy for certain types of problems, for example, proving theorems in plane geometry. If you work from the axioms, hundreds of theorems might be proven. Yet in working backward from the theorem itself, the number of possible paths to the axioms is relatively small. Solving mazes like the one shown in Figure 8–7 is a kind of problem for which working backward is an especially good strategy. On the other hand, working forward in the maze will lead you into a number of blind alleys, a problem that is reduced when the procedure is reversed. Heuristics other than the two we have discussed are also used in problem solving. Research has shown that effective problem solving often makes use of a combination of heuristic strategies.

Evaluation.   In this stage, the solution is evaluated in terms of its ability to satisfy the demands of the problem. If it meets all the criteria, then the problem is solved. If not, then the person goes back to the production stage to generate additional solutions. In some cases, several solutions may be generated,

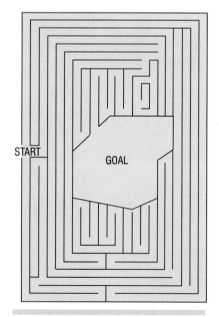

FIGURE 8-7
Most people would begin solving this maze by starting at the point labeled "start." A more effective strategy is to work backward from the "goal" area.

all of which solve the problem. Yet some solutions may be better than others; that is, they are more cost efficient, involve less time, are more humane, and so forth. These alternate solutions are compared at the evaluation stage.

Incubation. Some versions of the stages of problem solving include incubation as a stage, but others do not. The consensus view seems to be that the incubation stage is present only sometimes. Incubation occurs when the problem has been put aside; that is, when the individual stops thinking about the problem and engages in some other activity. During this incubation period the solution may suddenly appear, or a new approach may become apparent that leads the individual back to the production stage, where the solution is then achieved. Many people have experienced this phenomenon, and the literature is filled with anecdotal evidence of its existence. Unfortunately, incubation has eluded experimental psychologists who have tried to study the phenomenon (Olton, 1979). Only recently have methods been discovered for reliably observing incubation in the laboratory (Smith & Blankenship, 1989; 1991).

Researchers are unsure about what is happening during the incubation period that improves the chances of finding solutions, but there are several reasonable possibilities. The original idea was that when the problem solver takes a break from consciously working on a problem, the person continues unconsciously to work on the problem until the solution is reached. This hypothesis is difficult to test, because it is not clear how we might observe unconscious work. Another hypothesis is that the incubation period allows the person to recover from the mental fatigue that has built up from working on the problem. Although this fatigue hypothesis is plausible in many situations, laboratory experiments have found the incubation phenomenon to occur even after a brief initial problem-solving period (Smith & Blankenship, 1991). A third possibility is that when an unsolved problem is put aside, the part of the mind that is related to the problem remains activated, making it more sensitive to clues in the environment that could have a bearing on solving the problem (Yaniv & Meyer, 1987). Thus, during the incubation period, these chance encounters with clues may trigger a solution to the unsolved problem. A fourth hypothesis is that a person's thinking may become blocked, or "stuck in a rut," and the person continues trying to solve a problem in some way that cannot produce a solution. Incubation, then, allows the person to forget about the previous unproductive approach to the problem, and gets the person out of the rut long enough to discover a better approach. These hindrances to problem solving will be discussed more fully in the next section.

Hindrances in Problem Solving. Earlier we noted that prior experience can be an aid in problem solving; indeed, it is the very basis for reproductive thinking. Yet at times such experience can be a hindrance to problem solving, as in the cases of mental set and functional fixedness.

Mental Set. The tendency to react to new problems in the same way one dealt with old problems is called **mental set**. Such a habitual strategy is an effective one as long as the problems are of a similar nature. But some problems may only look similar. The result is that the individual uses a solution to the problem that does not work, or uses a complex strategy when a much simpler solution would have worked. This latter point is illustrated in the classic water jar experiment of Luchins (1942), outlined in Figure 8–8. Subjects found the complicated solution needed to solve the first problem and applied it to the second, and so forth. The seventh problem could have been solved by a much easier method, but the mental set kept the individual from seeing that.

mental set tendency to react to new problems with a habitual strategy

Problem	Jar A	Jar B	Jar C	Goal (oz)
1	21	127	3	100
2	14	163	25	99
3	18	43	10	5
4	9	42	6	21
5	20	59	4	31
6	12	75	3	57
7	23	49	3	20
8	15	39	3	18

FIGURE 8–8

Water jar problem. In the eight problems shown, the task is to use Jars *A, B,* and/or *C* to produce the exact amount of water shown under "Goal" for that problem row. In each problem row, the capacity of the three empty jars is given. One solution to Problem 1 is as follows: fill Jar *B* and pour from Jar *B* to fill Jar *A.* Jar *B* will now contain 106 oz. Now, pour *B* into *C,* empty *C,* and use *B* to fill *C* again. You are left with 100 oz in Jar *B* and have solved the problem. Now try Problem 2. You may note that a similar strategy will work here as well. In fact, the formula Goal = *B - A - 2C* will work for all eight problems shown, and most people, once they have found this successful strategy, will continue to use it. For Problems 7 and 8, however, a much simpler strategy will work: in Problem 7 you need only to fill *A* and then pour some of *A* into *C*; in Problem 8 you can fill *A* and *C* and pour both into *B.* Mental set is a hindrance to problem solving, and it prevents many people from seeing the simpler solutions to the last two problems. (Adapted from Luchins, 1942.)

Consider the following riddle. It was a dark and stormy night. A father was driving with his son around Dead Man's Curve when the car spun off the wet pavement into a tree. The man was killed instantly, but the son was still alive. He was rushed to the hospital and into the emergency room. The surgeon, on seeing the boy's face, ran out of the room shouting, "I cannot operate on this boy; he is my son!" How is this possible?

Typical answers suggest that the man was the boy's stepfather and that the surgeon was the biological father, or that the supposed father was in fact a grandfather or even a priest, or that the mother had lied about who the father was. These incorrect solutions have in common the assumption that the surgeon was male and was therefore the boy's father. Thus, a gender-role stereotype—that surgeons must be male—provides a mental set that prevents one from seeing the obvious solution: the surgeon is the boy's mother.

Some have dismissed the importance of mental set in applied settings, saying that demonstrations of the phenomenon rely on artificially tricky problems, whereas real-life creative problem solving does not (Weisberg, 1986). Studies of mechanical engineers as they design new inventions, however, have found pervasive effects of mental set, a phenomenon referred to as "design fixation" (Jansson & Smith, 1991). In these experiments, mechanical engineering students and professional engineers were given design problems such as, "Design a measuring cup that blind people can use" or "Design an inexpensive spillproof coffee cup that does not use a straw or a mouthpiece." It was hypothesized that if designers were shown example designs beforehand, as often happens in applied settings, then their creative designs would reflect a mental set or fixation caused by seeing the examples. Jansson and Smith's results showed clearly that features of the examples were much more likely to appear in the designs for those who saw the examples, even when the features were specifically forbidden and detrimental to the designs. For example, more than half of the subjects who saw the

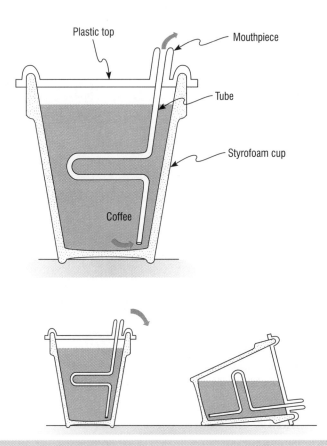

FIGURE 8–9
Diagram of a disposable spillproof coffee cup shown to some subjects to study design fixation. (From Jansson & Smith, 1991.)

example in Figure 8–9 created designs of cups with straws or mouthpieces, even though such devices were expressly ruled out in the instructions (mouthpieces would cause more scalding because they prevent air from being taken in with each sip). Only 11% of the control subjects who had not been shown example designs beforehand committed the same error. This same pattern of design fixation was found for a variety of design problems, whether students or professional engineers served as subjects. When questioned afterward, the professionals recognized design fixation as a detrimental factor they had seen affecting their work. Jansson and Smith's results demonstrate the importance of mental set in real-life problem-solving tasks.

Functional Fixedness.   Returning home after a stop at the service station, a professor saw steam coming out from under her hood. Raising the hood, she immediately saw the problem: the attendant had forgotten to replace the radiator cap. Replacing the water that had boiled out, and muttering a few choice words for the attendant, she realized that she needed a temporary spare radiator cap in order to get back to the station without the water boiling out again. After checking every odd object in her junk drawer and finding none that would cap the radiator, she suddenly hit upon the solution. Grabbing a potato from the pantry, she wedged the vegetable firmly into the opening—one size fits all!

Thinking of the potato demonstrated an ability to overcome a hindrance to problem solving called "functional fixedness," a term coined by Gestalt psychologist Karl Duncker. **Functional fixedness** refers to the difficulties people have in a problem-solving task when the problem calls for a novel use of a familiar object. Duncker's label was derived from the fact that the functional usefulness of objects seems fixed by our experience with them. One demonstration of this difficulty involves the problem of tying two strings

functional fixedness failure to think of unusual uses of an object different from the typical uses of that object

FIGURE 8-10
The problem is to tie the ends of the two strings together. To solve the problem the person is given a ball of cotton, a book of matches, and a pair of scissors. Successful solution requires that the subject view the scissors in a new way, namely as a pendulum bob. When the scissors are tied to the bottom of one string, the person can set the string pendulum in motion toward the other string. Then, by holding onto the other string, the person can catch the scissors when they swing by and attach the two strings.

together that hang from the ceiling and are too far apart for a person to grab one and then reach the other. See Figure 8-10 for a solution to the problem.

By understanding the factors that hinder problem solving (poor preparation, inability to restructure the problem, mental set, functional fixedness), psychologists hope to find ways of making people better problem solvers. One approach to better problem solving is to teach people to think more creatively.

Creative Thinking

Often creative thinking is viewed as a special case of problem solving. The special quality, however, is not the thinking process itself but the outcome of that thinking (Matlin, 1983). Most researchers have used the terms *creative thinking* and *creativity* interchangeably, and we will do so as well in our discussion. Defining creativity is difficult. Most definitions describe **creativity** in terms of the outcome, the final product. The consensus is that creative products should be (*a*) novel and (*b*) useful or valuable in some way—both aspects are important. These expectations hold whether the creative products are poems, paintings, scientific discoveries, or solutions to problems. For example, Charles Lamb, a nineteenth-century essayist, proposed a very novel solution to the problem of how to roast a pig. He suggested putting the pig in a house and then burning the house down (Matlin, 1983). By our definition, this response is not creative because it does not meet the criterion of utility. Newell, Shaw, and Simon (1962) agree with the criteria of novelty and usefulness and add three other conditions that they believe often characterize the products of creative thinking: (*a*) the solution requires the rejection of previously accepted ideas, (*b*) the solution is the result of intense motivation and persistence, and (*c*) the solution involves clarification of a problem that was ill defined. For them, creative thinking occurs when any one of these conditions exists in addition to novelty and usefulness.

Creative Cognition. A recently devised view of creativity is the creative cognition approach (Finke, Ward, & Smith, 1992). According to this point of view, there are patterns of cognition that set the stage for creative discoveries, patterns that can be found in people in all domains of creative endeavor. The reason that famous creative people have made their contributions in a single area, according to the creative cognition approach, is that in addition to thinking creatively, these individuals tend to acquire extensive expert knowledge in a single domain. This approach focuses not on creative products or people, but on creative thinking itself.

creativity process or product of novel, imaginative work on a problem, idea, artistic work, or invention

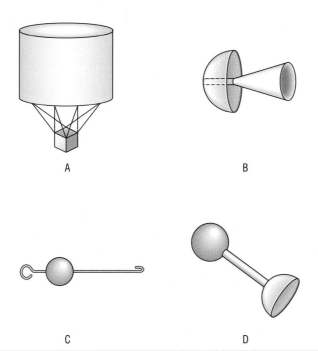

A

B

C

D

FIGURE 8–11
Four quick inventions constructed from simple shapes: (*A*) tension wind vane for measuring wind speed and direction (from a cube, wire, and cylinder); (*B*) contact lens remover (half-sphere, cone, and tube); (*C*) universal reacher (from hook, sphere, and wire); and (*D*) hamburger shaper (from a sphere, half-sphere, and cylinder). (From Finke, Ward, & Smith, 1992.)

Creative Visualization.   Imagery and visualization have often been cited as being instrumental in important creative discoveries. For example, Einstein is said to have discovered the concept of special relativity by picturing himself soaring at the speed of light. Likewise, Faraday's concept of electromagnetic fields, and Tesla's advances with alternating electrical current were all inspired by mental images.

Can mental images inspire creative ideas and inventions in people who are not necessarily as gifted as Einstein or Tesla? To examine the implications of creative imagery, Finke (1990) asked college students to try to combine simple shapes into pleasing mental images, then look for inventive ideas in the generated images. The elementary shapes consisted of simple geometric forms, such as a half-sphere, a hook, or a flexible tube. The figures imagined by students are referred to as preinventive forms, because interpretations of the forms can lead to inventive ideas. Examples of the images that students created in just a few minutes are shown in Figure 8–11. Although we are unlikely to see, in the patent office, creations based on a couple of minutes' work, Finke's creative visualization techniques may well produce ideas and refinements that are feasible for product development.

Insight.   The creative cognition approach has also turned its attention to the topic of **insight**. Gestalt psychologists described and demonstrated insight in learning and problem solving, as discussed in Chapter 6. More recently Robert Weisberg (Weisberg, 1986; 1992; Weisberg & Alba, 1981) has revived the idea of insight; he challenged the idea that insight is any special process. Weisberg asserted that individuals arrive at solutions to traditional insight problems in much the same way as they do for more mundane noninsight problems. He revived the subject in order to debunk what he refers to as the myth of insight. According to this position, remembering one's past experiences, not an abrupt reconceptualization of the problem, is the central factor in solving insight problems. Weisberg proposed that people solve problems by steadily accumulating knowledge that is relevant to the solution and that people remember what comes from memory bit by bit as they work on the problem.

insight sudden realization of an idea

Janet Metcalfe, however, has examined metacognitions as a way of assessing insight and noninsight processes (Metcalfe, 1986; Metcalfe & Weibe, 1987). In one study she found that subjects were unable to predict their eventual success on insight problems, whereas they could predict success on memory tasks. She concluded that subjects' lack of partial knowledge of solutions showed that solutions to insight problems involve a radical transformation in the subject's conceptualization of the problem, not a gradual accumulation of knowledge relevant to the problem. Metcalfe also tested metacognitions of impending solutions, asking subjects to rate how "warm" (close to solving the problem) they were every 10 sec during problem-solving tasks. This "on-line" metacognitive monitoring technique found that increases in warmth show the gradual incremental pattern described by Weisberg only for noninsight problems, such as algebra or logic problems that have multiple steps. With insight problems, however, problem solvers did not feel as if they were getting closer to the solutions as they worked on them. Rather, subjects felt completely stumped until only a few seconds before they were able to state the correct solutions to the insight problems. These results show that insight in problem solving is an abrupt process, not a gradual one.

THINKING ABOUT
Creativity

One aspect of creative cognition concerns conceptualization. For example, a method for generating new creative ideas is to explore combinations of concepts in search of novel ideas that might emerge from such combinations, as described earlier in this chapter. Try constructing and exploring combinations of the simple concepts shown in Table 8–3. Can you discover any interesting emergent properties?

Another consideration of creative conceptualization is that ideas and inventions, as imaginative and odd as they may sometimes seem, reflect an underlying conceptual structure. This is an idea that Ward (1991) has referred to as *structured imagination*. You might think that imagination is so personal and unique that the imaginative creations of different people would rarely look the same. To test this intuitive hypothesis, Ward asked college students to imagine a distant planet similar to Earth in size, terrain, and climate, and to

---

TABLE 8-3
Emergent Properties in Creative Cognition

Select any two of the following categories and make a phrase, such as "computer dog." Now, examine your phrases for new meanings that could not be predicted from either category alone. For example, a "computer dog" might be an animated dog, a computerized burglar alarm system, a four-legged robot that barks and rolls over, a person who hunts for bargains on computer sales, or a frankfurter sold at lunch counters at IBM. Explore the possibilities you discover.

computer	dog	date	song
school	car	garbage	clock
shoe	paper	medicine	tape
light	writing	travel	lunch
ball	store	stream	family

invent new creatures that might inhabit such a planet. Given the endless possibilities of creatures that could have been generated, the results were somewhat surprising; most of the ideas reflected an underlying concept of typical earth creatures. Although there was great variation and creativity shown in the creatures, it is interesting to note that almost all of them were bilaterally symmetric, had at least one major sense organ (usually eyes), a mouth, and at least one set of appendages (usually legs). In case you might think that truly creative ideas would not show these same conceptual constraints, try renting a good science fiction movie with extraterrestrial monsters, such as those in *Star Wars*. Ward's analyses of those movie creatures showed essentially the very same features seen in his experimental subjects. An example of a creature generated by Ward's subjects is shown in Figure 8–12.

The results of Ward's experiments also showed support of the theory of basic level categories. Generated creatures of supposedly different species varied a great deal in shape, as would be expected for members of different basic level categories. But, also consistent with the idea of basic level categories, students who were asked to draw a second member of the same invented species almost always used the same shape for both members. Even for their imaginative creations, subjects used basic level categories for familiar concepts.

If you were inventing creatures for a new science fiction movie, would you make them similar to creatures that are familiar to you? Could you identify with creatures in a movie if they had no legs, mouth, or sense organs? How would it change the shape of your creatures if you wanted to convey the idea that they are intelligent? How does the audience affect creative thinking?

FIGURE 8–12
An imaginary creature created for an imaginary planet similar to earth. (From Ward, 1991.)

Measuring Creativity.   One of the most interesting questions concerning creativity, and one of the reasons the term is so difficult to define, is how to measure it. The research on this question has focused largely on ways to identify creative individuals. One promising approach was developed by Mednick and Mednick (1967), using a test they devised called the Remote Associates Test, or RAT. Possibly you have seen examples of this test in game or puzzle books. In this test, words are presented in groups of three, such as *bowl*, *nail*, and *painting*. The task is to think of one word that is related to all three of these words. In this case the word is *finger*: finger bowl, fingernail, finger painting. Initial research on this test suggested that it correlated with creativity. For instance, one study (see Hayes, 1978) found that architecture students rated high in creativity by their professors achieved high RAT scores. However, although a few other studies have reported similarly positive results, the bulk of the evidence over the years suggests that there is little relationship, if any, between ability on the RAT and creativity.

Another reseacher in this area, J. P. Guilford (1967), has argued that a measure of creativity is a person's ability for divergent production. Guilford points out that most tests measure **convergent thinking**, in which the person uses the presented information and is asked to arrive at a single answer. In **divergent thinking**, the task is to generate as many answers as possible. (See the divergent-thinking task shown in Table 8–4.) This generation of various possible right answers is what Guilford calls "divergent production." Questions to measure divergent thinking might take the following form: If all television broadcasting were to cease, what could you do with a television set? Answers might include doorstop, planter, object to press flowers, aquarium, bookcase, new Olympic event called the TV-put, footstool, picture frame, toy chest, ship ballast, and baby crib. In a test like this, one measure of creativity might be the number of ideas generated in a specific time period

convergent thinking reasoning or problem solving that arrives at a single correct solution

divergent thinking finding multiple hypothetical problem solutions that are typically unusual ones (e.g., "In 5 minutes, write down all the things you can do with a brick"). But creativity implies originality, thus all answers would not be counted equally. A response like "You can use bricks for a bookshelf" would add to the count of total responses, but it would not be considered a creative response. But "A brick mobile to hang from the ceiling" would be considered creative. One of our colleagues suggested painting the brick to look like a thermostat and then gluing it to the wall to trick people. That, too, is a creative response, albeit a bit bizarre.

By now you have no doubt decided that creativity is some mysterious quality that cannot be identified or measured. Contributing to the problem is the very definition of what is creative behavior. History is filled with examples in which what appeared to be madness in one generation became the creativity of a later generation. Further, creativity as measured in the laboratory may not accurately reflect creativity in the real world, a criticism often leveled at laboratory studies of creative thinking.

Is creativity an all-or-none quality, or does it exist on a continuum? Studies support the position that most, if not all, of us have some potential for creative behavior. The research clearly indicates that people can enhance their creative behavior through various kinds of training programs. Organizations recognize this fact and have initiated programs to enhance creative thinking in their employees.

THINKING ABOUT
Brainstorming

Recognizing the importance of innovation and creativity in business, many corporations today are hiring consultants to help them enhance the creative-thinking skills of their employees (Rice, 1984). These programs have been found to vary widely in proven effectiveness, but some strategies have been shown to produce considerable improvement in creativity on the job (Basadur, Graen, & Green, 1982; G. A. Davis, 1982; Grossman, 1982).

Organizations are made up of people who form various groups within the organizational setting. The various groups are related to one another by an organizational structure. Greater numbers of people can be an advantage in problem solving, as more minds are present, but if the organizational structure is limiting—and most are—creative solutions to problems may be less likely to emerge. Researchers in this area talk a lot about "organizational climate" and its relation to creativity (Taylor, 1972). Use of the term *climate* in this way is meant to describe the atmosphere of the work setting: rigidity of the organizational structure, communication of company goals to employees, openness of management to employee suggestions, incentives for innovations, and so forth. Studies agree that some organizational climates are more conducive to creative thinking (Kirton & Pender, 1982; Mars, 1981).

Too many people seem comfortable with the assumption that change is to be avoided. "We've always done it that way" is the catchphrase indicative of this attitude. Creative solutions may also be discouraged when creative people are viewed as odd or weird. To enhance creativity, it is important to change these attitudes and to make visible efforts to reward employees for their creative suggestions. Bell Telephone Labs, Eastman Kodak, Goodyear, and Texas Instruments are companies that have major programs to encourage employee creativity. Bell Labs, a research unit that works primarily on problems of communication, has a speakers program that brings in experts in fields with no direct relevance to Bell projects. This program is designed to stimulate Bell researchers with new ideas (Rice, 1984).

One of the most popularly known techniques for creative problem solving in a group setting is **brainstorming** (Osborn, 1963). Brainstorming is regularly used in corporate and business settings, and has a specific set of rules. The four principles of a brainstorming group are:

brainstorming group technique for divergent thinking and idea generation

1. Judgment is deferred (put off for a later time); ideas should be freely generated without fear of criticism.
2. The more ideas, the better.
3. Ideas should be as wild, imaginative, and freewheeling as possible.
4. Ideas should be combined; creative ideas often result from novel combinations of familiar ideas.

Does brainstorming work? That depends on what you want out of it. If we compare the number of ideas generated by a group brainstorming a problem with the number of ideas generated by an equal number of people working individually on the problem, it is commonly found that the individuals get more ideas, overall (e.g., Diehl & Stroebe, 1987). This productivity loss in brainstorming groups was recognized even by Alex Osborn, the originator of the technique (Davis, 1986). Why, then, should people use brainstorming for creative problem solving if individuals can get more ideas by working independently?

There are at least three answers to this question. First, group creative problem solving can enhance the creative climate of an organization. Second, the brainstorming technique has a good track record. It has been used to save thousands of hours of labor at Denver's main post office; to increase sales for Heinz Foods, Reynolds Metals, and Aunt Jemima's cornmeal mix; and to invent the flashcube (Davis, 1986). Finally, and perhaps most important, brainstorming is undeniably fun.

Innovation is important in business, as it is a key element of competitiveness. Companies have long recognized the value of creative thinking, but they have not always been very good about eliciting it from their employees. ***Can you think of situations in which brainstorming would be useful? What could you do to encourage the most creative ideas from people in a brainstorming group?***

Having explored the theories and uses of thinking, we now turn to another fundamental part of human cognition—language.

LANGUAGE

Lytton Strachey, the English biographer, called language the most astonishing of all human abilities. Many psychologists consider it to be the accomplishment that sets humans apart from the rest of the animal kingdom. One cannot overstate the importance to human evolution of the development of spoken language and of the later emergence of written language (see Figure 8–13). Language provides another form of biological adaptation. It is not transmitted genetically, but it acts together with the adaptations of organic evolution, thus dramatically increasing adaptive potential (G. Miller, 1981). Language is an integral part of much of human functioning including communication, memory, and thought. Many psychologists agree that communication is the principal function of language, and that the need to communicate is probably the reason that spoken languages developed. It is estimated that there are approximately 5,000 different languages in the world today.

Before we proceed any further, we should clarify some of the terms we will be using. **Speech** is the act of speaking, a mechanical process for producing sounds. Usually these sounds are meaningful, in which case we can understand a person's speech, but meaningfulness is not a necessary requirement for speech. Gibberish is speech without meaning. Meaning is derived from **language**, which is a system of words and the rules for combining those words.

Language as Communication

Language is one of the forms of communication; it may be expressed in oral speech or through the printed word that you are reading at this moment. There are also ways of communication other than language, such as ges-

speech speaking, producing sounds for the purpose of communicating with language

language system of words, including meanings and rules for combining words

FIGURE 8–13
The Rosetta stone, now in the British Museum in London, is a black basalt slab bearing an inscription that was the key to the deciphering of Egyptian hieroglyphics and thus to the foundation of modern Egyptology. The tablet was inscribed in 196 B.C. and is a decree praising Egyptian king Ptolemy V. The decree appears in three scripts: hieroglyphic, demotic, and Greek. By using the Greek version, the translators were able to decipher the other two.

tures, sounds, and changes in animal coloration. Communication implies the transmission of information from one organism to another, and many animals have that capability. Some animals use pheromones, chemicals that have communication value within a particular species. Thus, an animal may signal to another the boundaries of its territory or the fact that it is sexually receptive. Animals use a variety of sounds in communication to signify approaching danger, to ward off intruders, to locate their young, and to court a potential mate. Animals, especially birds, also use a variety of body postures as a means of communication. Some of these communication systems are quite ingenious. For example, the Nobel Prize–winning biologist Karl von Frisch discovered how honeybee scouts were able to "tell" the other bees about the location of new sources of nectar. The scout bee does an elaborate dance in the shape of the figure eight. The number of revolutions the bee makes in the figure eight communicates the distance of the nectar source, and the orientation of the figure eight in relation to the sun tells the other bees the direction they should fly (see Figure 8–14).

Because animals other than humans have the ability to communicate, can we call this communication language? The answer depends largely on the definition of language that is used. Although there is some dispute, most psychologists agree that language is an ability restricted to humans. The communication systems of other animals consist of a relatively small number of signals related principally to the animal's survival. Some might argue that these animal communication systems are rudimentary languages, but even that assertion seems to misuse the label of language. In recent years, some psychologists have proposed that other primates, such as chimpanzees, are capable of learning and using human language (we discuss this controversial research in a later section of this chapter). But according to George Miller, language is uniquely human:

> The capacity for language made human culture possible, and culture, with all its social, artistic, technological and scientific innovations, set *Homo sapiens* apart from all other animals. It enabled this big-brained, loudmouthed, featherless biped to overrun the earth—to understand, and, through understanding, to control the adaptive process itself. (Miller, 1981)

In its communicative function, language allows us to teach, to learn, to read, to talk with friends, to tell stories, to enjoy motion pictures, to describe our feelings, and to know about our past in terms of our own life and the lives of those who preceded us. It is because of the gift of language that we are able to share much of the richness of human experience.

Irony. A good example of the richness of language as a uniquely human experience is the communication of **irony**. An ironic statement is one that states the opposite of what it actually intends to communicate. For example, when your professor tells you, "Oh, don't bother studying for the next exam; they aren't ever difficult," you should know by now that it means to hit the books harder than ever if you want to survive the course. How can you know that the professor's intended meaning is ironic? One way you could tell would be if the first two exams were deadly, it should be obvious that the professor's remark was **counterfactual**, or at odds with the true facts. Another clue could be the professor's tone of voice, which is usually a clue that a statement is intended ironically. The same statement made in different tones of voice can have entirely different meanings. Finally, irony can be detected more easily if the speaker and listener have some common ground; that is, if the speaker and listener have experiences or attitudes in common, irony is more easily detected. In this case, if poor exam scores had been a topic of class discussion, it would provide a common ground in which the

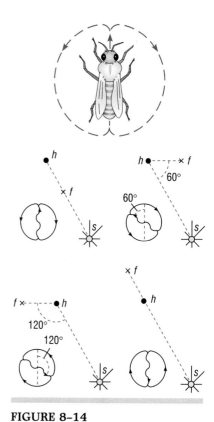

FIGURE 8–14
The dance of the honeybee is a most ingenious form of communication. The scout bee uses it to "tell" the other bees of the distance and direction of a new source of nectar. *h* = hive, *f* = feeding place, *s* = sun's position. At left of each diagram is shown how the bees dance on the perpendicular comb to indicate the direction of the feeding place with respect to the sun's position. (From von Frisch, 1950.)

irony statements in which the intended meaning is opposite of the stated meaning

counterfactual at odds with the facts

obvious counterfactual remark, that the previous exams were easy, would be easily noticed by the listeners. All of these clues show that the intended meaning is not always contained in the simple words that are spoken; sometimes the context of a statement is critical for proper understanding.

Irony in speech usually has three characteristic features: (*a*) a particular tone of voice, (*b*) victims, and (*c*) asymmetry of affect. Because an ironic tone of voice cannot easily be described in text, it must suffice to say that such a tone should differ from the speaker's normal or serious tone of voice; otherwise, it will not clearly alert the listener that an ironic meaning is intended. The victim of an ironic expression is the person, real or imagined, who is being ridiculed. Someone who speaks ironically typically pretends to be ignorant of the truth, as seen by the speaker. The victim is the real or hypothetical person who is implied to be ignorant of the truth. For example, if Thelma, who is helping her friend Hazel with the nine suitcases she is taking for a single overnight trip, asks ironically, "Are you sure you have everything you need?" Thelma pretends not to know that Hazel has packed more than she needs, and she implies that Hazel has been ignorant of this fact as well. Therefore, Hazel is the victim of this irony. Finally, irony is asymmetric, meaning that a positive statement is more likely to be interpreted as negative (e.g., saying on a cold rainy day, "What a nice day for our picnic!"), as compared to interpreting negative statements positively (saying on a sunny warm day, "What a lousy day for our picnic!").

Another language device used for conveying irony is echoic reminding (Kreuz & Glucksberg, 1989). With echoic reminding, the speaker echos or repeats something that the irony's victim might be imagined to say to remind the listener of the inferred attitudes or ignorance of the victim. For example, a teenage boy buys his bicycle unassembled, rather than spending an extra $3 to have it assembled. Bringing it home he tells his father, "It's no problem to assemble, Dad; the instructions say that it goes together as easy as 1–2–3." Six hours and a considerable amount of cursing later, the exhausted father hands the bicycle back to his son, grumbling, "It was no problem; as easy as 1–2–3." Clearly, the echoic adaptation of the son's earlier remark is intended as irony.

An interesting development in the use of ironic statements is the use of the word *Not*! after a statement. This device is used to assure the listener that a meaning is intended ironically. For example, the date who tells you, "I had a wonderful time this evening . . . Not!" wants to be perfectly clear about the ironic intent, rather than risk the mistake of being taken seriously. Perhaps the use of *Not*! indicates a breakdown in the subtlety of our communication, or perhaps it means that we have so little common ground that there is a great danger of misinterpreting ironic statements. Whatever it means, the appearance of new expressions like *Not*! shows that the public use of irony remains an important feature of communication in our society.

Spoken and Written Language

Psychologists, anthropologists, and linguists who have studied the evolution of language agree that spoken language grew in complexity over many generations. Initial languages probably consisted of words for certain commands and a number of nouns to signify various objects or events in the environment. Later developments involved the addition of other parts of speech as spoken language evolved from simple words, to two-word combinations, to complete sentences. Languages grew from several hundred words to many thousands of words. Words grew to mean more than just things; they denoted action and still later, relationships. This evolutionary development is not unlike the child's acquisition of language, which we will discuss shortly.

FIGURE 8–15
A storyteller in the Yaou village, Ivory Coast, keeps alive the tribe's history through his storytelling activities that serve as entertainment and instruction.

Spoken language was a great accomplishment, but it had some severe limitations. Specifically, it was restricted in terms of time and space. Spoken words were useful for those people in the presence of the speaker, but once spoken they were gone forever. They could only be approximated in the speech of others, and thus could be preserved only to some extent by repetition (see Figure 8–15). Written language changed all of this, creating a way for the broadest form of language use within a particular time period, as well as across many generations to follow.

Writing was invented about 5,000 years ago by the Sumerians, who lived in ancient Mesopotamia. Because of that invention, we are able to know about the rule of the Roman Caesars, enjoy the poetry of Elizabeth Barrett Browning, relive the struggle of the Northern Cheyenne Indians to return to their homeland, visit France or Kenya without leaving our living room, and learn a great deal about psychology.

With the development of written language, information was no longer simply a word-of-mouth affair. New generations could share in the knowledge and experiences of generations past, and by writing could pass on their information to future generations as well. The storehouse of written information today is enormous. For example, the libraries at Harvard University contain more than 10 million books, not to mention their extensive holdings in journals, newspapers, and materials on microfilm. In effect, libraries represent the permanent memories of those who have inhabited this planet; as such, they offer us a way to enhance our own limited memory stores.

Language Structure

In order to understand language as behavior we need to know something about the structure of language; mastery of language structure is important to our understanding of how language develops in the child. A linguist is someone who studies **semantics**, or the structure of language, including its meaning, and **grammar**, or a language's rules for combining and using words. The psychological study of language, called **psycholinguistics**, involves the study

semantics structure of language, the science of meanings

grammar a language's rules for using and combining words

psycholinguistics psychological approach to the study of language

Thought and Language 317

phonemes basic units of speech; pronunciation differences that affect meaning

morpheme smallest unit of meaning in a language

of both language structure and the psychological processes involved in language (Carroll, 1986).

Phonemes. All spoken languages contain a number of basic sounds, called phonemes. **Phonemes** refer to pronunciation differences that affect meaning (Tartter, 1986). Not all differences in pronunciation affect meaning; this is demonstrated by the fact that you can understand the same word spoken in different accents. Phonemes can be identified with minimal pairs, two words that are identical except for one sound which changes the meaning. For example, the sound "op" is shared by the words *mop* and *cop*; they are different words because the sounds "m" and "c" are different phonemes in the English language. It is estimated that there are as many as 100 different phonemes, although no language is thought to use more than about 80. The English language, for example, uses approximately 40 phonemes. Babies born into English-speaking families will utter phonemes other than those used in English, but those sounds will eventually disappear from their vocal repertoire. Table 8–5 offers some examples of English-language phonemes. You will see that the language has one *P* phoneme that is spoken by producing a slight puff of air. The language of northern China contains two *P* phonemes, one spoken with a puff of air and the other without. One of the difficulties adults face in learning another language is to pronounce those words that contain phonemes that do not exist in their native language. By definition, phonemes are not meaningful. It is the combination of these units of language that produces meaning.

Morphemes. The smallest unit of meaning in a language is called a **morpheme**. Typically morphemes are composed of two or more phonemes, but there are exceptions to that rule. The words *a* and *I* are morphemes, yet they are composed of a single phoneme. Morphemes include such words as *fly, paper, listen, book, nation,* and *keep*. Not all words are single morphemes though. *Flypaper* and *bookkeeping* are two words that are each composed of more than one morpheme. Remember that morphemes make up the smallest meaningful unit of language, thus *flypaper* has two morphemes, *fly* and *paper*. You might think that *bookkeeping* has two morphemes, but in fact it has three: *book, keep,* and *ing*. The first two morphemes are words, whereas the third one is an inflection.

An inflection is a special type of morpheme that is usually applied to the beginning or end of a word; inflections are chiefly suffixes and prefixes. The suffix *ing* creates a progressive of the verb and thus changes the meaning of the word. Other inflections are *ed, s, ness,* and *un*. Some languages make great use of inflections, a fact known to students of the German language. Even so, it is estimated that the English language has approximately 50,000 morphemes. Morphemes are the units from which we construct words, which are, in turn, grouped into phrases, which are further combined to form sentences. These are the building blocks of language.

Language Rules. Every language has its set of rules. It is amazing to note that speakers of a language learn to use the same set of rules in spite of the fact that no two people hear the same set of spoken utterances from which they could abstract those rules. This set of rules is frequently complex and ranges from the appropriateness of combining certain phonemes (*phonological rules*) to the grammatical rules that govern the combination of phrases, and the word changes appropriate to changes in verb tense. For example, phonological rules in English do not allow us to begin words with the letters *tk,* or *tv*. These combinations are permissible in the Russian language, however, which includes words such as *tkan* (meaning *cloth*) and *Tvar* (which is

TABLE 8-5
Examples of Some English-Language Phonemes

Symbol	Examples
p	*p*at, a*pp*le
b	*b*at, am*b*le
d	*d*ip, love*d*
g	*g*uard, o*g*re
f	*f*at, *ph*iloso*ph*y
s	*s*ap, pa*ss*, pea*c*e
z	*z*ip, pad*s*, *x*ylophone
y	*y*ou, ba*y*, f*eu*d
w	*w*itch, *qu*een
l	*l*eaf, pa*l*ace
ē	b*ee*t, b*ea*t, bel*ie*ve
i	b*i*t, *i*njury
ā	*a*te, b*ai*t, *eigh*t
u	b*oo*t, tw*o*, thr*ough*
U	p*u*t, f*oo*t, c*ou*ld
oy	b*oy*, d*oi*ly
ay	b*i*te, s*igh*t, *i*sland
š	*sh*oe, mu*sh*, dedu*c*tion

Source: Adapted from Moates & Schumacher, 1980.

a city in central Russia). If you were told to pick out the English word from among *tberopod*, *tceropod*, and *theropod*, you should have little difficulty in choosing the last word, because many English words begin with the phonological combination *th*. (Incidentally, a theropod was a flesh-eating dinosaur.) These phonological rules are the same heuristics used to solve anagrams.

Rules that deal with the formation and structure of words are called *morphological rules*; **syntax** is the set of rules that specifies how words are arranged in phrases and sentences. All of the rules of language structure are referred to collectively as grammar, and every language has its unique grammar.

In truth there are two systems of grammar. **Prescriptive grammar** is the formalized system of social prescriptions about the proper use of language. The journalist Edwin Newman is one of the more vocal advocates of following the prescriptive rules of our language (see his book *Strictly Speaking*, 1980). Prescriptive grammar forbids the use of contractions like *ain't* or double negatives such as "he didn't drink no coffee." These rules also say that we cannot use a preposition to end a sentence *with*.

Descriptive grammar comprises the rules of what some might call our natural speech. It is the system of rules that governs the use of everyday language. It is this kind of grammar that interests psycholinguists, for an understanding of these rules may reveal other processes, such as thought. In addition, these descriptive grammars tend to be unique to various dialects, some of which are the result of geographic, ethnic, and social class differences. The diversity of people is expressed in the various dialects of the same language, and that language diversity may be the clue to some interesting psychological differences.

We have said that syntax is the set of rules that regulates the combination of words into phrases and sentences. Certainly the order of words is important. Consider the following two phrases.

> three blind mice
> blind three mice

Even though the words are the same in both phrases, the meanings expressed by the two phrases are quite different (Moates & Schumacher, 1980). This example illustrates the relationship between syntax and semantics; meaning is dictated in this case by the order of the words in the two phrases.

Sentence Structure. The *phrase structure approach* to the study of sentences analyzes a sentence by dividing it, first, into its noun phrase and verb phrase and then further subdividing these two phrases. For unambiguous sentences this procedure works quite well. But consider the following sentence.

> Visiting relatives can be a nuisance.

After having read that sentence, are you clear about its meaning? Actually, it has two meanings. If *relatives* is the subject of the sentence, the sentence means that relatives who are visiting a person may be considered to be a nuisance. However, if *relatives* is the object of the sentence, and the subject is the act of visiting one's relatives, the sentence means that it can be a nuisance to visit one's relatives. The ambiguity of the sentence could be eliminated by wording it in one of two forms.

> Visiting relatives are a nuisance.
> Visiting relatives is a nuisance.

Use of the plural verb *are* makes it clear that the subject of the sentence is *relatives*. Use of the singular verb *is* indicates that *relatives* must be the object (Slobin, 1979).

syntax rules that specify how words are to be correctly arranged in phrases and sentences

prescriptive grammar formalized abstract system of grammatical rules

descriptive grammar rules that apply to natural language

Professor Noam Chomsky of the Massachusetts Institute of Technology.

surface structure actual words used in a phrase or sentence

deep structure meanings of the words in phrases or sentences

transformational grammar rules for determining which transformations in the wording of a sentence are possible without changing the meaning

babbling spontaneous and meaningless vocalization in infants

Ambiguous sentences such as these have led researchers to recognize that there are different structural levels in sentences. Noam Chomsky (1965), one of the leading linguists of the twentieth century, describes sentences in terms of their surface structure or their deep structure. The sentence as actually worded forms the **surface structure**, and every sentence has only one such structure. However, the meaning of a sentence constitutes its **deep structure**. Thus, a sentence that has three different meanings has three deep structures.

Chomsky has also demonstrated that one deep structure can be represented in many different surface structures. Suppose the meaning you wish to convey is that a psychologist reduced someone's test anxiety. That deep structure could be communicated in any of the following surface structures.

The psychologist reduced the client's test anxiety.
The client's test anxiety was reduced by the psychologist.
Reduction of the client's test anxiety was accomplished by the psychologist.

Each of these sentences is different in terms of actual wording (surface structure), but the meaning of each (deep structure) is the same.

Because of the potential ambiguity in the wording of sentences, Chomsky has rejected the phrase structure approach to sentence structure that analyzes sentences only at the surface structure level. His approach is called the *syntactic approach*, and it recognizes that different surface structures are produced by a set of rules that specify what transformations in the wording of the sentence are acceptable. He has labeled these rules **transformational grammar**. Studying these transformational rules not only leads to a better understanding of the structure of language but also provides us with knowledge about how meaning is communicated in sentences. Chomsky's views play an important role in the next section of this chapter.

Language Development

The college student who enrolls in the first semester of French may find learning a language quite a difficult process. How is it that this student learned the first language so easily and through so informal a procedure? The 4-year-old has taken no classes in the native tongue yet has a large vocabulary and a good understanding of the grammar of the language. Just how do we learn language? And is language learning just a matter of learning, or do innate factors play some role? We address some of these questions in this section.

Babbling. Newborn infants are quite capable of vocalization. Parents often comment that the baby "has a great set of lungs." These earliest vocalizations are principally in the form of crying, and they serve as important cues in communicating various needs to the parents. Most parents claim that they can distinguish their baby's various cries, such as a "hunger cry," or a "soaked diaper cry." The infant makes other kinds of sounds during happier times, and these noises are usually labeled cooing.

At about 6 months of age, babies begin to engage in **babbling**, a kind of vocal activity in which the infant spontaneously utters a number of sounds. These sounds represent the basic phonemes of language and include the utterance of some phonemes that will not be a part of the child's language. All infants babble (assuming nothing is wrong with their vocal apparatus), including infants who are born deaf. This fact suggests that babbling is not part of some communicative process, because deaf infants cannot hear the sounds from others (nor from themselves). Apparently, infants just naturally produce these sounds whether they can hear them or not. The nature of babbling

This father carries on a "conversation" with his 3-month-old son.

changes over time as certain sounds are made more frequently and others drop out of the infant's vocal repertoire. These changes are likely maintained by imitation; the infant repeats sounds it hears from other people. Babbling also begins to come under social control, meaning that an adult talking to or babbling to an infant can elicit babbling from the infant (Glenn & Cunningham, 1983). However, this progression does not occur for deaf children. Because they do not hear, their own vocal behavior eventually stops.

Babbling is vocalization, not verbalization, and as such it is really prelinguistic behavior. Nevertheless, babbling is an important precursor to language development. It gives infants the opportunity to exercise vocal capabilities and indicates, through the social attention most infants receive when they babble, the use of vocalization in communication.

Single-Word Stage. Most infants utter their first word around one year of age. Mother hopes it will be "Mama," father hopes it will be "Dada," and the baby's older brother spends hours trying to get the baby to say "Fred." First words mean that the infant is moving from vocalization to verbalization and that true language has begun. Some psychologists call this stage the beginning of *expressive language*, distinguishing it from *receptive language* in which children understand much of what is said to them but are not yet capable of talking. Two infants in the newspaper comics, Trixie (in the strip "Hi and Lois") and Marvin, have excellent receptive language abilities but are not yet able to speak.

Studies of babies' one-word utterances have shown that a pattern of word usage emerges that is quite consistent among infants (Greenfield & Smith, 1976). Earliest words are associated with actions, for example, "bye-bye" as the infant waves, "down" when the infant wants to get down from the high chair, or "bottle" when the infant wants a bottle. The last two examples are what psychologists call **holophrastic speech**, meaning that a single word is used to express some broader idea or sentence. Thus, the utterance "play" might mean, "I want you to play with me." Or "go" might mean, "Let's go ride in the car."

The next most common words used by infants tend to refer to objects, such as daddy or doggie. Toward the end of the one-word stage, infants use single words to indicate modification of events such as "again" to request

holophrastic speech use of single words to convey larger meanings that are usually expressed by fuller sentences

that something be done again. By the end of infancy, at 2 years of age, a typical child has a vocabulary of 50 words. Amazingly, that vocabulary may swell to as many as 1,000 words by the time the child is 3.

Two-Word Stage.   Most infants begin two-word utterances around the age of 2. The two-word stage is important because it signals the beginning use of sentences and marks the formal beginnings of grammar. On this latter point, infants arrange the two-word combinations in such a way as to indicate that they are beginning to learn some of the rules of language. These early two-word utterances include such statements as "milk gone," "mommy bye-bye," and "car dirty."

Syntax emerges in this stage, evidenced by the appropriate word order in a number of these two-word sentences. Most sentences are structured with the subject first, then the verb, then the object. When the child wants to get down from the high chair, the child is more likely to say "me down" than "down me." In asking for a ball to be thrown, the child says "throw ball," not "ball throw."

Not only does the child's vocabulary increase during this stage, but the types of sentences the child can use grow in number as well. Some two-word sentences are commands such as "want toy," whereas others describe a situation ("mommy go"). Eventually, the child learns about possession ("my toy," "daddy's shoe") and how to ask questions ("where puppy?").

Later Language Development.   It is difficult to specify exact ages for changes in language development; in fact, Roger Brown's (1973) research has shown that age is not a very good predictor of language skill in the child. Instead, Brown (see Figure 8–16) proposes a measure that he calls the *mean length of utterance* (MLU) to determine a child's stage of language development. This measure is calculated by averaging the number of morphemes per utterance. Using the MLU values, Brown divides language development into five stages; each stage represents increasing MLU values. Language development is, of course, more than just adding to the length of utterances. Advanced stages reflect the ability of children to produce more complex combinations of words, their growing use of various parts of speech, and increased sophistication with the grammar of the language. Sentences get longer so that it is possible for children to communicate more complex ideas. In addition, the inclusion of extra words means that the ambiguity of the sentences is diminished. Some prepositions—for example, *on*—will appear in early sentences, but articles such as *a* or *the* will not be used until later language development. The exact ages for when these items emerge in language development cannot be specified. What is important is that the *pattern* for each child seems to be essentially the same; that is, developmental stages occur in the same order in most children (Brown, 1973; Nelson, 1981). Further, cross-cultural research has shown that despite obvious differences in grammar and words among languages, the sequencing of language development is roughly the same in all.

In English, children learn grammatical rules first for regular verbs, and they then usually generalize the same rules to irregular verbs. Thus, a child may say, "I goed to the store." This inappropriate use of the rule is called *overgeneralization*, or overregularization, as when a child states, "I eated a cookie here last week." The child has learned to add the ending *ed* to a verb to make it past tense and so makes many errors such as "I runned all the way home." Commonly, to make plurals, an *s* is added, so the child talks about "putting shoes on my foots." Or, the child may hear a noun being used as a verb; for example, "John bats the ball." Assuming that all nouns can be used as verbs, the child, intending to communicate the fact that John swept

FIGURE 8–16
Roger Brown and one of his subjects in a small park adjoining William James Hall at Harvard University.

the floor with a broom, says "John broomed the floor" (Clark, 1982). Speech errors such as these indicate that grammar is being learned. Eventually, as language skills are refined, the child learns the endings for irregular verbs and the appropriate plural endings. At some point, language development is complete; grammar is essentially mastered.

Interestingly, although we learn to use the rules of language quite accurately, few, if any, of us can actually articulate all those rules. When we hear bad grammar, we can recognize it as bad and restate the sentence using correct grammar. But when asked to state the rule that was violated, many of us have trouble doing so. Thus, using the rules of grammar does not require that we be capable of stating those rules.

Theories of Language Acquisition

The basic conflict among researchers studying language involves the role of innate processes in language acquisition. No one denies that learning plays an important role. We have indicated already how children's language develops through modeling words and sentences they hear—that is, through imitation. It is also possible that some language development proceeds as a result of reinforcement and punishment, so that grammatically correct statements are praised whereas incorrect ones are verbally punished. For example, the utterance, "Daddy says the car doesn't have no gas" may be corrected by a statement such as, "No, that's not right; the car doesn't have *any* gas." Yet studies show that such communicative exchanges between parent and child rarely occur. Parents correct language errors of fact, but not of grammar. Thus, a more probable exchange would be the child saying, "Daddy is a soldier," and the father replying, "No, daddy is a sailor" (De Villiers, 1980).

The question remains, however, whether imitation and reward and punishment are sufficient means to account for all or even much of language development. Psychologist B. F. Skinner (1957) thought they were. Skinner believed that learning language requires innate mechanisms. He assumed some innate capacity to associate stimuli and responses, but beyond that he believed that language is learned through a shaping process. Thus, language moves from babbling to words to sentences through a process of reinforcing successive approximations (see Chapter 6).

Leading the opposition to Skinner's view has been Noam Chomsky. Chomsky (1959, 1968) argues that learning and imitation alone cannot account for language development, for children utter sentences that they could not have heard before. Further, Chomsky claims, verbal rewards and punishments rarely tell the child exactly what is right or wrong with an utterance. Parents often note the incorrectness of a child's utterance without actually correcting it. Or, even if the statement is corrected, the underlying rule that was violated may not be articulated to the child. As we noted earlier, language consists of a complex rule system, and these rules are rarely stated. Further, rules dictate the proper arrangements of words, and as we have seen, the same arrangement can produce different meanings or the same meaning can be produced from different arrangements. An understanding of these complexities, according to Chomsky, cannot be acquired through learning.

Chomsky's view, a nativist theory of language acquisition, proposes the inherent existence of a set of cognitive structures that prepare the child to learn language, a kind of inborn *language acquisition device*. Chomsky's theory holds that the brain is prewired for language learning, a view that is consistent with the finding that certain brain areas specialize in language development and production (e.g., Broca's area and Wernicke's area; see

Chapter 2). Neuroscientists have discovered an anatomical asymmetry in the temporal lobe of the human brain; the region known as Wernicke's area is noticeably larger on the left side of the brain, a difference that can be observed in human fetuses (Damasio & Geschwind, 1984). Recall that language ability resides primarily in the left cerebral hemisphere.

Chomsky is not arguing that humans are born with innate language; rather, he suggests, they have an innate ability to extract the grammatical rules of the language. In the nativist view, language learning occurs too rapidly to be explained by such processes as imitation or reinforcement. Despite the complexity of language, normal children learn their native language with relative ease, and this pattern of language development is similar for children in different cultures. Nativists interpret this similarity as evidence of biological programming.

Other evidence for Chomsky's theory comes from studies that demonstrate a critical period for optimal language learning, perhaps from birth to about age 6 (G. Miller, 1981). In addition, the fact that all languages have remarkably similar characteristics provides further support for Chomsky's views when one recognizes the vast cultural differences of the learning environments under which those languages were acquired. Even deaf children, deprived of the opportunity for imitation and verbal reinforcement, develop a form of gestural language (Feldman et al., 1978).

In summary, learning is probably only part of the story of language acquisition. Innate cognitive structures may provide the infant a basis for the hypothesis testing and rule learning that bring about language. These cognitive structures may be specific to language, or they may be part of an inherent cognitive complex that functions in other processes as well, such as thinking, remembering, and perceiving. Although scientists cannot as yet identify these innate structures, their proposed existence explains some aspects of language acquisition that other processes do not easily explain.

> THINKING ABOUT
> # Bilingual Education

A major controversy within American society today involves the issue of bilingual education. For many years, Canada has had to deal with this issue in respect to its English- and French-speaking citizens (see Gardner & Desrochers, 1981). The growth of the U.S. population of citizens of Hispanic origin, now numbering more than 12 million, has brought this question to the forefront of local and national politics. Advocates of bilingual education see this technique as a means of preventing Spanish-speaking children from being disadvantaged in the early school years, when they have not yet learned English. They can take their classes in their native tongue and learn English, in time, as a second language. Further, it is suggested, these students should take courses in the history of the culture of their origin, a step that many feel is important to bolster self-esteem as well as to preserve a part of that culture.

Opponents of bilingual education argue that the United States cannot afford to be a bilingual society, that the additional language implies additional costs. Further, they argue that delaying learning of English will only cause problems for citizens who seek employment and upward mobility in a society that rewards communication in standard English (Rotberg, 1982). Supporters of this view indicate studies that have shown the negative effects of bilingualism, principally slower overall language development and lower scores on intelligence tests (see Carringer, 1974). Bilingualism has been assumed to be a problem because (*a*) two languages present too heavy a cognitive burden, and (*b*) there will be negative transfer between the competing languages. Studies done before 1960 support these conclusions, but more recent research has offered a very different conclusion (Lambert, 1981).

These more recent studies, like earlier ones, have compared the abilities of monolingual and bilingual children. However, they have also done a better job of matching the two groups on some important variables, such as socio-economic status and educational opportunities. Cummins (1978) found that bilingual children were superior in their understanding of language structure, a finding replicated by Aronsson (1981), who also reported evidence for better overall cognitive development in bilinguals. Cathcart (1982) found that bilingual children performed better on tests of numbers and concepts of measurement and on tests of conservation (see Chapter 12). Other studies have shown that bilingualism produces a flexibility of thinking that leads to greater creativity (Carringer, 1974). Yet some studies (Titone, 1980) can find no cognitive differences at all. These recent studies should not be taken as conclusive evidence of the superiority of bilingualism or as support for the advantages of bilingual education. Nevertheless, they do call into question the findings of earlier research, and they argue for continued scrutiny of the issue.

How about you? Can you speak more than one language? Are there any advantages to being bilingual? Do you think that schools should offer courses in more than one language?

Whorf's Linguistic Relativity Hypothesis

Every language is different because each has its own phonemes, vocabulary, and rules. Although many words can be easily translated among many languages, there are some concepts that cannot be expressed in some languages. For example, neither the Shona language (spoken in Zimbabwe) nor Bassa (spoken in Liberia) have words that distinguish red from orange. Similarly, as we observed in Chapter 4, Eskimos have words for many types of snow that have no English equivalents, and the Hanuos in the Philippines have numerous words for different types and states of rice that have no direct English translations.

The **linguistic relativity hypothesis**, also named the Whorf–Sapir hypothesis after its founders, Benjamin Whorf and his professor, Edward Sapir, claims that the failure of words to translate into some languages shows that peoples' perceptions and conceptualizations of reality are influenced by their language. Thus, the hypothesis states that people fail to perceive the different types of colors, snow, or rice because of limitations in their language. The linguistic relativity hypothesis states that there are basic differences among languages, contrasting greatly with Chomsky's view of language acquisition, which emphasizes linguistic universals.

linguistic relativity hypothesis theory that a person's language determines and limits that person's experiences

Although many psychologists and anthropologists have been fascinated by Whorf's linguistic relativity hypothesis, empirical research on the subject indicates that it is probably false. For example, Rosch (1973) studied New Guinea natives whose language is Dani, a language that has only two different color words. Rosch found that the New Guineans could recognize colors that have common names in other languages, even though the colors have no names in Dani. Furthermore, skiers can learn to distinguish many different types of snow even if their native language has no distinct terms for the different types. The fact that you can perceive something even though your language has no words for it indicates that Whorf's hypothesis is not correct.

If the linguistic relativity hypothesis is incorrect, then why does the Eskimo language have so many words for different types of snow and English so few? Rather than language determining what we can perceive, a more likely explanation is that the most common objects and events in a culture's environment, whether they are snow, rice, or colors, determine the words that become incorporated into that culture's language (Solso, 1991).

The Ape Language Controversy

Earlier in this chapter we noted some of the forms of communication common to animals. Although animals can communicate danger, call for a mate, and signal the boundaries of their territory, these accomplishments do not display anything so complex as human language. Is any animal capable of learning a language system comparable to that used by humans? For years the answer to that question was a clear no, but in recent years the certainty of that answer has been challenged.

Not surprisingly, psychologists interested in this question have looked to other primates as subjects. Moreover, they have most often used chimpanzees, because many researchers regard the chimpanzee as the primate most similar to humans. Attempts to teach chimps to talk date back to the nineteenth century, but one of the most serious attempts was made in the 1930s by Winthrop and Luella Kellogg, who raised an infant chimp named Gua along with their infant son Donald (Kellogg & Kellogg, 1933). Gua had her own bedroom, high chair, and clothes identical to Donald's. In many ways Gua was treated like a human infant, and she achieved some skills that would not be typical of a chimp. However, she did not learn to talk. In fact, she could not utter a single humanlike word (Benjamin & Bruce, 1982). In the 7 years that followed, a number of other researchers tried teaching chimps to talk, with similarly disappointing results (see C. Hayes, 1951).

Failure in these early experiments was attributed to a number of suspected causes, including a lack of voluntary control over vocal behavior (Jolly, 1985). Then, in the 1960s, Allen and Beatrice Gardner initiated a new approach (see Figure 8–17). They decided to try to teach a chimp to communicate through the use of the sign language system used by humans who are deaf. The Gardners' first subject was a female chimp named Washoe. Washoe eventually learned to use more than 150 signs, an impressive vocabulary for a chimp, but far smaller than that possessed by a 3-year-old human child. She even combined her signs into a number of simple phrases such as "gimme toothbrush." Some of these phrases, such as "open eat drink" for the refrigerator, "dirty good" for her potty chair, and "water bird" for swans were original with Washoe, and different from the standard adult "cold box," "bowl chair," and "duck" that Washoe's human companions used as names for these objects (Fouts & Rigby, 1977; Gardner & Gardner, 1971). Other researchers using different techniques have reported similar results. For instance, David Premack worked with a chimp named Sarah who, instead of gesturing, used a set of more than 100 plastic shapes on a magnetic board. Sarah learned her plastic symbol vocabulary and was able to arrange the symbols on the magnet board to form simple sentences (Premack & Premack, 1972).

Do these accomplishments represent language learning? As far as the Gardners, Premacks, and some others are concerned, they do. But other researchers in this field disagree, criticizing the research on a number of methodological and interpretive points. Even the critics do not dispute the

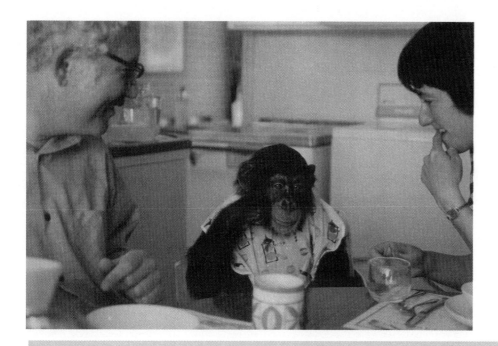

FIGURE 8–17
Moja, one of the chimps trained by Allen and Beatrice Gardner, makes the sign for apple.

fact that chimpanzees, gorillas, and orangutans can learn to use signs, but they do not agree that such usage is evidence of real language. Much of the "speech" of apes using these signs is in the form of demands: "give milk," "more banana," "hurry play." Some researchers have argued that such double signs are really only conditioned responses, gestures that the ape has learned to make to secure certain rewards. Thus, one gestural pattern is used if the ape wants a banana and another is used for milk. Critics argue that use of such signs does not demonstrate that the ape has the conceptual understanding that is at the heart of language, that is, that those signs actually stand for objects or actions. At this stage of the research, neither side can answer that question.

Another criticism of this research is that the trainers of these animals often give cues, perhaps unintentionally, that elicit the appropriate gestural responses from the animal in the testing situation. This phenomenon has a long history in psychology, dating to the beginning of this century when Clever Hans, a horse in Berlin, was amazing the public with his ability to solve mathematical problems by stamping out the correct answer with his foot (Fernald, 1984). A commission was appointed to study the horse, and eventually a psychologist, Oskar Pfungst, discovered the very subtle cues the trainer was inadvertently giving to his horse that caused the horse to stop stamping and thus arrive at the right answer. Although the cueing criticism is probably valid for some of the ape language studies, the results of more recent studies, using blind and double-blind control conditions, are not open to such criticism (Gardner & Gardner, 1980; Premack & Premack, 1983).

One major criticism of ape language surrounds the issue of grammar: Do apes learn to use the rules of language? The principal grammatical component of the English language is word order, and three-word statements are usually required to tell if the subject is using accurate grammar. Because most ape "utterances" are two words in length, the language sample is rather small. Further, the longer utterances do not show consistent arrangements of signs that would be indicative of rule learning in language. Indeed, the longer utterances do not even resemble those of children.

One of the critics of the ape language research is Herbert Terrace, who worked with a chimp that he named Nim Chimpsky (see Figure 8–18) after

FIGURE 8–18
Nim Chimpsky is shown signing "hug" to his teacher, Jean Baruck.

the linguist Noam Chomsky. Nim's longest utterance consisted of 16 signs: "Give orange me give eat orange me eat orange give me eat orange give me you." Such extensive language behavior was prompted by the reward of the orange being held out of Nim's reach (Jolly, 1985). Terrace found that 40% of Nim's signs were direct imitations, and only 12% of the signs occurred spontaneously. For Terrace (1979, 1985), ape signing shows little evidence, if any, of the ability to construct sentences, which would show some comprehension of grammar, an accomplishment that Terrace claims is a minimal requirement of language.

Roitblat's (1987) listing of the minimal characteristics of human language includes reference, grammar, productivity, situational freedom, and communication of new information. *Reference* means that signals stand for events, objects, and concepts, and it seems to be present at least in chimpanzees such as Washoe and Sarah. *Grammar*, as just discussed, probably does not occur in primate language, at least not beyond a crude two-word type of phrasing. *Productivity* refers to expressing novel ideas. Although a few instances of productivity have been seen in the communication of apes, they are far fewer than what would be seen in most young children. *Situational freedom* refers to the ability to use expressions which are not determined by the surrounding stimuli in a rigid way. Evidence that chimps have tried to lie to others (e.g., Roitblat, 1987) suggests at least a crude form of situational freedom; ideas expressed by the chimps referred to imaginary situations. *Communication of new information* means not simply repeating what someone else has been saying.

Regardless of the criteria we use to decide about the linguistic abilities of apes, two facts seem inescapable: (*a*) apes are capable of communicating, sometimes with the use of meaningful symbols, and (*b*) apes are *not* capable of the flexibility, sophistication, or creativity in the use of language which can be seen in most adult humans. Roitblat (1987) suggests that it is a mistake to ask whether or not animals are capable of human language because we can always construct criteria that animals will fail to meet. He suggests that it would be more fruitful simply to study the linguistic capabilities of animals in order to understand better the evolutionary determinants of our own language.

THINKING AHEAD . . .

Since the decades in which the study of mental processes was assumed to be scientifically impossible, cognitive psychologists have discovered a clever variety of tasks to learn much about the mind in terms of how it structures and represents knowledge, and how that knowledge is processed in various ways. Cognitive theories have been adopted by psychologists in many areas to explain such phenomena as intelligence, aging, group decision making, stereotypes and prejudice, and certain psychological disorders. The usefulness of cognitive models and theories can also be seen in applications in important areas outside of psychology, such as computer-assisted instruction, jury decision making, artificial intelligence (AI), and medical diagnosis.

One of the most promising new directions is cognitive neuroscience, a combination of ideas in cognitive psychology, computer science, and neuroscience. Now that cognitive psychologists have ideas about how thinking operates, and how thought is reflected in task performance, cognitive neuroscientists know what to look for in terms of brain functioning. Perhaps it will be discovered where in the brain, and by what physiological processes, certain types of cognition occur, such as mental imagery or insight.

Once we have considered human cognition, we can also examine the future of our understanding of thought in nonhuman entities, such as animals and computers. How intelligent are animals? Can we make computers with true intelligence? What rights and responsibilities should be given to intelligent animals or computers?

Summary

Thought

1. Thinking is studied as a cognitive process that intervenes between some stimulus inputs and subsequent behavior. Methods of studying thought include physiological measures, task performance, computer models, and subjective metacognitive reports.

2. Mental images bear striking similarities to perception, especially visual perception.

3. Thinking involves the classification and categorization of information into conceptual categories. Category membership is determined by classification rules. One such rule is a defining attribute, a quality that exists in all members of a category.

4. Natural categories are part of an ecological approach to the study of cognition and include basic level, superordinate, and subordinate categories. Conceptual combinations and mental models can be used to understand concepts. Combinations often give rise to emergent properties. Mental models are functional representations of categories.

5. Problem solving involves either productive thinking or, more commonly, reproductive thinking. Stages in problem solving include preparation, production, evaluation and, sometimes, incubation. Problem-solving strategies involve the use of algorithms and heuristics.

6. Mental set and functional fixedness are two hindrances to problem solving. Mental set occurs when habitual solutions keep the person from seeing simpler ones, and functional fixedness results from an inability to see novel uses for objects.

7. Creative thinking should produce results that are novel and useful or valuable. Creativity is usually associated with divergent thinking, which produces many possible solutions to a problem. Businesses recognize innovation as a key element of competitiveness and have adopted programs for their workers, such as brainstorming, that encourage creative thinking.

Language

8. Speech is the mechanical act of speaking, whereas language is a system of words and rules for combining words. Animals can communicate in a variety of ways, including the use of pheromones, but they do not possess a real language.

9. Semantics refers to the meanings of words, grammar to the rules for combination and proper usage of words. All languages contain a number of basic sounds called phonemes, which are combined to form meaningful language units called morphemes, which combine, in turn, to form words.

10. Phonological rules, morphological rules, and syntax are the three component rule systems of grammar.

11. The surface structure of a sentence lies in the words as they appear, but the deep structure of a sentence is the meaning of the words. Rules that specify the acceptable meaningful changes in sentence structure are called transformational grammar.

12. Acquisition of language begins with babbling, progresses to the use of single words, and then to two-word sentences.

13. Learning plays an important role in language in terms of imitation and reinforcement, but there is evidence to support the existence of some innate language structures.

14. Language can affect our recall of events, how we feel about ourselves and others, and how we think.

15. The advantages and disadvantages of bilingual education are still a subject of much debate. One finding seems clear, and that is that children under 5 years of age have better learning skills for a second language than do adults.

16. Chimpanzees can learn to use signs; whether this skill is an indication of actual language is open to controversy.

Key Terms

neural network models (293)

metacognition (293)

subjective reports (293)

think-aloud method (293)

protocol (293)

protocol analysis (293)

expert system (293)

metamemory (294)

illusion of knowing (294)

dual coding theory (294)

mental comparisons (294)

mental rotation (295)

conceptual category (296)

classification rules (297)

defining attribute (297)

hypothesis testing (298)

natural categories (299)

typicality (299)

typical attributes (299)

emergent properties (300)

basic level categories (300)

mental model (301)

problem solving (301)

algorithm (303)

heuristics (303)

means–end analysis (303)

mental set (305)

functional fixedness (307)

creativity (308)

insight (309)

convergent thinking (311)

divergent thinking (311)

brainstorming (313)

speech (314)

language (314)

irony (315)

counterfactual (315)

semantics (317)

grammar (317)

psycholinguistics (317)

phonemes (318)

morpheme (318)

syntax (319)

prescriptive grammar (319)

descriptive grammar (319)

surface structure (320)

deep structure (320)

transformational grammar (320)

babbling (320)

holophrastic speech (321)

linguistic relativity hypothesis (325)

Suggested Reading

Adams, J. L. (1979). *Conceptual blockbusting: A guide to better ideas* (2nd ed.). New York: Norton. A self-help manual to improve thinking by learning to overcome the various blocks that impede thinking and, especially, problem solving.

Bruner, J. (1983). *Child's talk: Learning to use language.* An easy-to-read yet scholarly account of language acquisition and development in children.

Mayer, R. E. (1992). *Thinking, problem solving, and cognition* (2nd ed.). San Francisco: Freeman. Like the Adams book, a discussion on learning how to solve problems better, but with a broad, research-based coverage of thinking.

Miller, G. A. (1981). *Language and speech.* San Francisco: Freeman. A very well written account of language acquisition and use, including some material on the evolution of language.

Roitblat, H. L. (1987). *Introduction to comparative cognition.* New York: Freeman. An evolutionary approach to animal cognition that covers not only apes but a broad range of other animals such as dolphins, parrots, and seals.

Solso, R. L. (1991). *Cognitive psychology* (3rd ed.). Needham Heights, MA: Allyn and Bacon. General coverage of broad field of cognitive psychology.

ANAGRAM ANSWERS FOR TABLE 8–1: afire, tulip, crack, kidnap, cattle, phobia, grain, curio, fetch, vestry, callow, corpse

ANAGRAM ANSWER FOR TABLE 8–2: operator

CHAPTER 9
Motivation and Emotion

As a member of the Pima Indian tribe in Arizona, B. K. Nashobi was committed to maintaining the customs and traditions of an honorable, historic way of life. B. K. shared in the reenactment of ancient rituals, the timeless expression of thanks for a good harvest, and the glorification of the art of Native American painters and craftsmen. Unfortunately, B. K. also shared another distinctive cultural feature with his Pima tribal members—he was extremely overweight.

The excessive weight carried by B. K. was surely a contributing factor to B. K.'s overall poor health. He had difficulty moving about and suffered from incessant lower back pain, high blood pressure, and continuing fatigue and even depression. Ultimately, B. K. had to lose weight to improve his quality of life. Voluntarily, B. K. went on an intense weight-loss program in which he consumed about half his usual daily amount of calories.

Initially, he experienced a sharp drop in weight and body fat. However, even though B. K. remained on a strict diet of reduced caloric intake, he began to regain the weight he had lost. How could this be happening? The simple rule is that if you maintain normal activity and decrease the amount of food you eat, you will lose weight. But in this case it wasn't working. Why?

The answer rests with basic metabolic characteristics that are peculiar to Pima adults. Hunger and weight specialists, and researchers, have long been aware of the tendency for Pima adults to be obese, and this unique cultural group has been the subject of many scientific investigations on weight control. As it turns out, the metabolism levels of heavy Pima adults are normal, unless their weight drops, at which point their metabolism rates diminish.

◀ People seek different goals, and respond differently, as they succeed
   and fail in attempting to reach their goals.

The result of this decreased metabolic activity is that less means more. That is, as weight comes off, metabolic processes shift and convert more of the available calories into fat (lipids). This pattern will continue until an appropriate amount of fat deposits are restored. Tribal members such as B. K. are thus fighting a losing battle. They eat less but remain overweight.

The problems experienced by B. K., a true case history, are linked to two aspects of behavior that are the focus of this chapter—*motivation* and *emotion*. Obviously, B. K. had a desire or motive to lose weight, or at least to attempt to lose weight. Why behavior occurs, or the motivational impetus for responding, has long been a concern among psychologists. As we shall see, although no single motivational approach has been completely successful, contemporary motivational models do help us better understand the reasons for our behavior, whether it be biologically or socially determined. Also, emotional reactions often tied to motivational behavior (such as B. K.'s depression) play an important role in everyday life.

Each of us continually grapples with motivations and emotions. As we succeed and fail in our attempts to accomplish certain things, we experience happiness and unhappiness, triumph and despair, tranquility and anger, and an array of other moods that affect our lives. In the following pages we examine the psychology of *wanting* and *feeling*—that is, motivation and emotion.

MOTIVATION: DEFINITION AND THEORY

motivation the why, or purpose behind responding

In a broad sense, **motivation** pertains to the reason for acting or responding. The term comes from the Latin *movere*, meaning "move," and it is what causes movement (behavior) that concerns us here. Although motivation has many facets, psychologists have been especially concerned with those influences that energize and direct responses. Simply stated, motivation determines how strong a behavior will be and the form it will take.

In the following sections we discuss a few of the different theoretical perspectives on motivation. Although none of the models answers all questions adequately, each helps us understand why we do the things we do.

Biological Determinism

ethologists scientists who view behavior as largely governed by instincts and other biologically determined events

Ethology. The idea that behavior is driven by forces that are uniquely biological, mechanistic, and innate is one of the oldest in all of psychology. In contemporary circles, scientists called **ethologists** talk about biologically determined behaviors within the framework of instincts. An **instinct** is a genetically programmed, adaptive behavior that is important for survival (Gould, 1986). Although instincts are triggered by environmental stimuli, they are believed to have their own energy source. And once an instinctive behavior begins, it typically is carried out to completion.

instinct a relatively stereotyped, genetically programmed behavior in a given species that is important to survival

The naturalistic observations of many different scientists, most prominently Konrad Lorenz and Niko Tinbergen (Figure 9–1), benefitted the ethological movement. Lorenz, Tinbergen, and their students carefully examined different species, particularly birds, fishes, and insects, over a period of several decades. Their findings have since become classics, and, along with the research of Karl von Frisch, resulted in their joint reception of a Nobel Prize in 1973.

fixed action patterns (FAPs) behavioral patterns that are identical across members of a species and are biologically determined

Among other important discoveries, they found that selective behavioral patterns are remarkably the same, or stereotyped, across members of the same species. This led Lorenz to formulate the concept of **fixed action pat-**

FIGURE 9–1
Konrad Lorenz (*left*) and Niko
Tinbergen (*right*).

terns (FAPs) (Grier & Burk, 1992). It seems that once a behavior starts, such as when geese attempt to retrieve an egg that has rolled out of the nest, it follows a very set and predictable course. More recent studies have indicated, however, that there is actually some minor variation in animal behavior. For that reason, researchers use the more contemporary term **modal action patterns (MAPs)**, which means that most animals, but not all, respond to certain environmental cues in a constant way.

Regarding the role of environmental cues, another important concept in ethology is that behaviors tend to be released by only one aspect of a stimulus. Appropriately, that one aspect that triggers the behavior is called a releaser, or a **sign stimulus** (Lorenz, 1981). Two classic illustrations of sign stimuli operating in the natural environment are profiled in Figures 9–2 and 9–3. Figure 9–2 depicts a test of the territorial threat response (in which the animal defends its territory) in male European robins. When a real robin lacking a red breast was presented as a test probe, no threatening displays were elicited from the subject. But when a bunch of red feathers clustered around a wire frame not resembling a bird was introduced, the fight was under way. Similarly, Figure 9–3 shows that only certain shapes of models elicited an escape response in young waterfowl. When the model had a short neck, much like that of a hawk, the waterfowl tried to escape. But when the model possessed a long neck, like that of a goose, the waterfowl did not try to escape. In these examples, the red feathers on the belly surface of the object, and the short neck feature of the model, represent sign stimuli.

Occasionally, one may observe the occurrence of MAPs in animals, even when appropriate environmental stimuli (sign stimuli) are not present. Often this results from inadequate opportunities to express the behavior. An example is when a bird, such as a canary, has been kept in a cage for an extended period with no chance to seek food naturally. When released into the open air, it may go through all the motions of catching, killing, and eating imaginary insects! This is an example of **vacuum behavior**, because it occurs independently of a true releaser. Biologist James Grier of North Dakota State University notes an even more remarkable illustration of vacuum behavior. Once, after giving his dog a new bone, Grier noticed that the animal began to go through the motions of digging a hole in the kitchen floor, in order to bury the bone. Of course, the dog was not really able to

modal action patterns (MAPs) behavioral patterns that occur among most members of a species and are biologically determined

sign stimulus an environmental releaser that serves as the triggering mechanism for instincts and other biologically driven behaviors

vacuum behavior when an instinct occurs independently of the appropriate environmental releaser, usually because of lack of opportunity to respond

FIGURE 9-2
Models used to test the effectiveness of a red breast as a sign stimulus for territorial threat displays in male European robins. (*A*) The mounted real robin without a red breast proved to be a less effective stimulus than (*B*) a tuft of red feathers. (Adapted from Lack, 1943.)

behavioral ecology study of the coexistence of several different species in one habitat

sociobiology evolutionary study of animal social behavior; advances the idea that animals respond to ensure their genetic survival

deposit the bone in the phantom hole, but this didn't stop him from carefully shoveling imaginary dirt over the bone and tamping it in place with his nose! The dog walked away, secure that the bone was hidden from view, then came back much later to retrieve his treasure—after digging once again through the imaginary pile of dirt (Grier & Burk, 1992).

These and other research examples point to the possibility of a biological account of behavior based on unlearned, predetermined causes. But ethology and the concept of instincts have been sharply criticized in recent years. Because of the complexity of human behavior, the number of suggested instincts has proliferated to an unreasonable number. The current tally includes instincts for fighting, loving, sleeping, jealousy, security, competition, and sex, and it continues to grow. In effect, behaviors are being relabeled, rather than explained.

Sociobiology and Other Evolutionary Models. The classic views of Lorenz, Tinbergen, and others have more recently given way to biological accounts of behavior that place greater emphasis on evolutionary phenomena. One modern theory is **behavioral ecology**, which examines the interaction among different species that coexist in a common environment. Also, the *theory of neuroethology* has gained favor among psychologists because it incorporates elements of neurophysiology, learning, memory, artificial intelligence (AI) (see Chapter 6), and related events. Overall, current biological models of motivation are tethered more to genetics and physiology than those of the past, and there is less emphasis on anecdotal, naturalistic reports.

Of all the relatively new evolutionary models of behavioral determinism, sociobiology probably has stimulated the most debate. **Sociobiology** is defined as the evolutionary study of animal social behavior (Grier & Burk, 1992). Sociobiologists argue that we respond to a genetic imperative to keep our genes alive, and this means we will do anything to ensure that our genetic material is passed on to the next generation (Wilson, 1975). In the extreme, this would even mean sacrificing one's own life so that the offspring carrying the genetic profile could survive. Such a rationale may explain why elderly members of nomadic Eskimo populations volunteer to remain behind when the rest of the group must travel. Too old to continue, these individuals refuse to jeopardize the welfare of the entire tribe by slowing its movement; so they stay back in a camp that for them is a way station to death. What may appear to be *altruism* is really behavior motivated by a desire to increase the chances

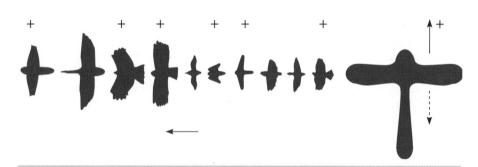

FIGURE 9-3
These models were used to test the escape response in young waterfowl. Models that elicited the escape response are shown with a plus (+) sign. The larger model at the extreme right elicited the escape response when flown in one direction but not the other. In cases where a response was obtained, the model possessed a short neck characteristic, much like that of a hawk. (From Tinbergen, 1948.)

for gene survival. Because they can quite literally live through their children, the aged forfeit the remainder of their lives.

One of the major motivational phenomena that sociobiology hopes to explain is *grouping*. Why do members of a common species band together? The sociobiology position shares a belief widely held by other models that groups form because there is strength in numbers. That is, more numbers mean increased resources for protection and for defending the young. But sociobiology takes a further step by suggesting that gregarious behavior is motivated by self-interests that place other members of the group at risk. For instance, an individual may join a group because this increases the chances that a predator will take a neighbor first (Grier & Burk, 1992). Such a "you-first" strategy is antithetical to the notion that grouping has evolved because it benefits the entire population, but it fits nicely with the rationale that behavior is motivated by the desire of the individual to stay alive at all costs.

Hull's Drive-Reduction Model

A somewhat more versatile account of motivation than the purely biological models is Clark Hull's (1884–1952) **drive-reduction model**. This perspective focuses on the concept of *homeostasis*, which is the tendency toward the maintenance of a relatively stable internal environment. According to Hull's system of motivation, responding occurs in an effort to restore homeostatic equilibrium that has been disturbed by internal or external events (Figure 9–4). The interaction between drives and needs is basic to this restoration. Specifically, Hull's primary motivational principle asserts that behavior is activated by an internal psychological drive state arising out of a psychological need. In this sense, tissue deficits (*needs*) provoke a desire in the organism (*drive*) that ultimately leads to purposeful responding. For example, when a bear is deprived of food, the need for nourishment creates the relevant hunger drive. Hunger, as a primary motive, is sufficient to cause the animal to search for food. When the bear finds food and eats, that response

drive-reduction model Hull's model, which states that motivation arises out of a need state

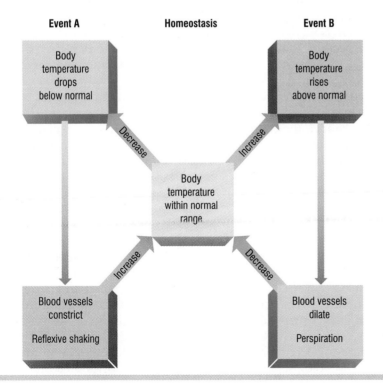

FIGURE 9–4
An example of homeostatic regulation. When event *A* occurs (for example, decrease in internal body temperature), internal changes are triggered that bring about a return to stable conditions. Separate internal regulatory processes are engaged by a sudden shift in the opposite direction (event *B*).

resupplies the tissue deficits, biological need is reduced (i.e., equilibrium is restored), and the hunger drive drops off accordingly. In the absence of the appropriate drive, the animal is not motivated to continue to forage, so responding ceases.

Numerous findings have tarnished the once sterling image of the drive-reduction model. For instance, many investigators have shown that animals will learn a new response when that response leads to an increase in the opportunity to explore (Butler, 1953). And how would Hull explain someone's wanting to learn to skydive? In these cases the motivational impetus for responding is associated with increasing, not decreasing, arousal.

Cognitive Consistency Theory

cognitive consistency theory the model that states that cognitive inconsistencies create tension and thus motivate the organism to respond

cognitive dissonance theory cognitive consistency model formulated by Festinger

Another homeostatic model that offers an alternative to Hull's motivational theory is cognitive consistency theory. **Cognitive consistency theory** maintains that the internal balance of beliefs, thoughts, and behavior determines the level of motivation. When cognitive inconsistencies occur, tension arises, and the result is behavior that is aimed at reducing tension.

Of the several cognitive consistency theories that have been advanced over the past several years, **cognitive dissonance theory** has generated the most research and gained the most widespread recognition (Festinger, 1957). This model asserts that when a person experiences two cognitions (thoughts) that are dissonant (inconsistent), a state of psychological discomfort results. This negative motivational state triggers specific mechanisms that are designed to reconcile thought discrepancies and thereby alleviate stress. For instance, consider what many parents experience when they are faced with decisions about moving to school districts with dramatically different features. A large school system with a high enrollment may afford greater scholastic opportunities, because the large student numbers justify more laboratories, equipment, and specialized courses. But a small school setting offers a better teacher–student ratio, and thus greater attention to the individual. How is this conflict resolved? Either choice is surely going to create some uncertainty and tension. Dissonance theory states that the resolution of such a conflict comes about by changing cognitions. Regardless of what decision is made, says the theory, there is a tendency to accentuate the positive aspects of that choice and to exaggerate the negative value of the alternative. The result is that dissonance, and the attendant psychological tension, is reduced.

The cognitive consistency rationale may be an improvement over Hull's approach in that it emphasizes thought and motivation more. However, as with Hull's model, the cognitive consistency view fails to explain why some behaviors occur that are designed to increase tension. So how do we account for motives aimed at increasing stimulation? Another motivational model, arousal theory, provides some clues.

Arousal Theory

We all recognize that different people prefer different levels of excitement. People who like a low level of activity find sufficient stimulation in reading, going for walks, and engaging in casual conversation. In sharp contrast, other people seem wired for thrills and intensive stimulation. We all know people who are sensation seekers—people who want to climb mountains, drive race cars, or run marathons. And, as contradictory as it may seem, such high levels of activity actually relax these individuals.

arousal theories models of motivation that argues that we all have optimal levels of stimulation that we try to maintain

In order to account for such pronounced differences in motivation and behavior, psychologists have proposed **arousal theories**. According to these models, each of us tries to maintain an optimal level of arousal. Although the optimal level varies from person to person, we seek to achieve a level of stimulation that is best for us. Departures in stimulation in either direction from the optimal point cause us to do what is necessary to bring activation levels back within the optimum range. A woman who has a low optimal level of arousal, for instance, may escape for a quiet weekend retreat when she is overloaded at work. In contrast, a man who needs a high level of stimulation may spend leisure time riding a motorcycle or listening to loud music (Zuckerman, 1984). The point is that in all cases, behavior is motivated by a desire to maintain a preferred level of arousal.

In addition to explaining sensation seeking, which the drive-reduction model fails to do, arousal theory provides a framework for understanding one of the oldest principles in psychology: the **Yerkes–Dodson law**. This law (refer to Figure 9–5) states that on tasks of moderate difficulty, increasing levels of arousal will increase performance up to a point, and then further arousal will have a detrimental effect on responding. By comparison, simple tasks can accommodate much higher levels of arousal before performance begins to fall off, and more difficult tasks require much lower levels of arousal for optimal performances. A good example of the harmful effects that excessive arousal has on difficult tasks is what happens to many college students when they take exams. Some students become so anxious about tests that they cannot perform. In one case familiar to one of the authors, a student was handed a "trace a drop of blood" problem in a comparative vertebrate anatomy class and had to follow the detailed vascular route of the flow of the blood in a cat. The student was trembling so much that he could not hold a pencil and write his answer, even though he knew it in great detail! In this instance, he eventually relaxed, completed the test, and made the highest grade in the class. However, in some cases test anxiety does not go away, and it can be extremely destructive. Although some arousal is probably needed for optimal performance, in certain circumstances it can be too much and lead to less efficient performance.

Incentive Theory

The biological, drive-reduction, and arousal theories of motivation have a common feature: they see the impetus for responding as internal. That is, behavior is believed to be *pushed* by events inside the organism. A contrasting viewpoint is maintained by **incentive theory**, which presumes that external stimuli motivate responding by *pulling* the behavior from the individual. Thus, positive incentives cause approach reactions, and negative incentives cause avoidance reactions.

Incentive theory argues that we are sufficiently motivated by goal attainment. It is unnecessary to propose that behavior is geared toward anything other than obtaining a specific reward (Mook, 1987). We read for enlightenment, we enjoy participating in social functions because it is pleasant to do so, and we eat ice cream because it tastes good. Along with the theoretical challenges that incentive theory presents, this deceptively simple doctrine raises some intriguing practical questions. For instance, under what conditions are tangible incentives (rewards) likely to produce better performance than intangible incentives such as approval or recognition? What happens when you shift from one incentive type to the other?

Intrinsic Versus Extrinsic Rewards.   Understanding the differences between tangible and intangible incentives involves the realization that activities are often rewarding, apart from any external stimulation they generate. For example, consider the hypothetical case of Calvin Blalock.

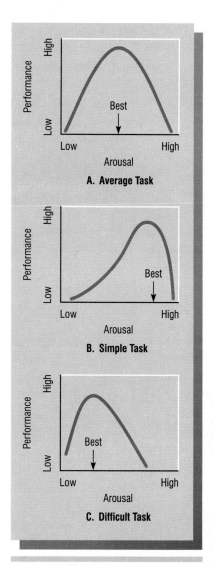

FIGURE 9–5
The Yerkes–Dodson law describes an inverted-U relationship between arousal and performance. (*A*) The optimal arousal changes according to the difficulty of the task required. For simple tasks (*B*) a higher arousal level is better for improved performance, but for difficult tasks (*C*) a lower arousal level is better. (From Houston, 1985.)

Yerkes–Dodson law principle that states that arousal will increase performance up to a point, then further increases will impair performance

incentive theory viewpoint on motivation that suggests that behavior is pulled rather than pushed

Calvin Blalock was professor of ancient Chinese history at a private midwestern college. Professor Blalock worked with such enthusiasm that his work became his life. He never seemed to relax, never took time off, and never went on vacation. Finally, his son convinced him to spend a summer in Europe, just traveling, sightseeing, and generally taking it easy. But fate intervened and Professor Blalock died of a heart attack one week prior to his scheduled departure on what was to be the first real vacation of his life. In a later conversation with the son, a family friend remarked about the tragedy, noting that Professor Blalock never really had a chance just to enjoy life. The son interrupted, "But he did enjoy life. He did exactly what he wanted to do all of his years. He worked continually, and it was his work that gave him the greatest pleasure."

How is it that hard work, or any other activity for that matter, can be rewarding in and of itself? It seems that certain behaviors offer *intrinsic rewards*, which means that they are interesting and fun to do even when they produce no external benefits. By contrast, *extrinsic rewards*, such as money, food, and public recognition, produce satisfaction independently of the behaviors that produce them. Whereas extrinsically motivated behavior appears to be controlled by external, tangible rewards, intrinsically motivated behavior comes from within, and the rewards are internal (Deci & Ryan, 1985).

As a rule, it is reasonable to expect that tangible rewards or social praise will serve as positive incentives for performance. If you want a child to acquire proper eating habits, you applaud when she or he behaves in a manner consistent with accepted dining standards. But sometimes introducing external rewards can backfire. When a behavior is maintained intrinsically, offering an extrinsic reward can have a detrimental effect because the external reward might replace the internal one and become the sole purpose for the behavior. When the external reward is later removed, the behavior may fall below levels that were consistently maintained before the external reward was given (Lepper, Greene, & Nisbett, 1973). An example of this extrinsic encroachment on intrinsic motivation is evident when a writer begins to pander to the wishes of his or her audience. As the brilliant Russian novelist Leo Tolstoy acknowledged (Solzhenitsyn, 1980), when a writer performs for profit, the essence of genius is lost. What must come from within is then being dictated by external demands. Accordingly, when

Some activities such as painting are intrinsically rewarding and fun to do even when they produce no external benefits.

those demands shift, so does the writer's behavior, sometimes to the point of abandoning writing altogether.

It is easy to see why there is so much concern about the negative impact that extrinsic rewards may have on intrinsic motivation. In educational settings, for instance, there have been concerns over the excessive reliance on external rewards in the classroom.

> ## THINKING ABOUT
> # Rewards in School

In today's educational market, it is common to reward academic achievement at all levels. For younger children, superior performances in the classroom are followed by an array of decals and happy faces. Or perhaps the "student of the month" has his or her picture appropriately placed on display. Clearly, such techniques are useful motivational devices that inspire children to do well (Gross & Shapiro, 1981). At the high school and college levels, similar reward systems are employed. Grades, honor rolls, dean's lists, and award assemblies are all designed to encourage academic excellence.

But are these reward systems really in the best interest of the student? Many educational psychologists doubt that they are. Numerous scientific reports indicate that academic performance is better when intrinsic rewards are used as opposed to extrinsic rewards (Lepper & Malone, 1986). In one instance where the educational goals involved teaching children about the addition and subtraction of fractions using an instructional computer, conventional "drill and practice" programs were less effective than educational games such as "Fraction Basketball" and "Torpedo" that were designed to appeal to the children's intrinsic interests (Lepper, 1985).

There is also the issue of what happens when we shift from external to internal rewards, as just discussed. There are many reports in the educational literature that show that extrinsic rewards can undermine what would ordinarily be accomplished with intrinsic reward programs (Domjan, 1993). Perhaps as Lepper and Greene (1978) have suggested, external rewards can produce an **overjustification effect**. Overjustification is said to occur when external compensation for a behavior becomes the sole basis for that behavior. The behavior is judged to be justified only so long as it pays off in money, candy, or some other tangible outcome. When the external reward is no longer available, intrinsic rewards that normally would sustain the behavior are deemed inadequate. Consequently, the behavior drops off or stops altogether. An example is what happens to a child who is paid for good grades. If this system breaks down, and it is likely to as the child grows older, the reason for learning will no longer be there. The child has so firmly associated academic performance with monetary gain that in its absence it makes no sense to even try to do well in school. The point is that had the external reward program never been implemented, intrinsic reinforcers such as pride and perceptions of self-worth probably would have maintained academic excellence indefinitely. When someone overjustifies an external reward, he or she is letting tangible incentives obscure less visible rewards that may be even more important.

Despite such concerns over intrinsic-extrinsic issues, not all the evidence recommends against the use of external rewards. For example, Dickinson (1974) followed the academic development of 50 fifth- and sixth-grade students who had participated in a token (extrinsic) reinforcement

overjustification effect when shifting from an external reward to an intrinsic reward, the desired behavior falls off substantially because responding is no longer deemed to be worthwhile

program where they were given extrinsic rewards of toys and a variety of privileges for completing their school assignments. When the program ended, the reading scores of the group that had received tokens were higher than the scores in a control group. In addition, the students who had received tokens continued to make greater gains than the control group during the 2-year period after the token program ended.

Regardless of the dynamics underlying intrinsic-extrinsic interactions, some people question the seriousness of the issue. First, even when performance decreases are noted following the removal of a reward, they appear to be brief and transitory. Second, evidence exists that external rewards can actually be used to increase intrinsic motivation, as with the case when gifted children are rewarded for creativity (D. J. Smith, 1986). And when a beginning reader receives a tangible reward for making the "ten-books-a-month club," he or she may be more likely to discover gradually the intrinsic satisfaction of reading. In such cases, external rewards are internalized and may enhance self-esteem.

So what do you think? As a parent, will you use external rewards when your child does well in school? How long would you be willing to continue them?

Maslow's Theory of Self-Actualization

What if, at this moment, you were asked to accompany someone on an extended excursion across a barren region of the Sudan in northeast Africa? The only stipulation is that you take along your own provisions. Assuming that this invitation is attractive to you, with what would you initially concern yourself? What needs would you be sure to satisfy? Well, considering the arid desert climate and the remoteness of the region, one of the first things you would probably choose to take along would be water. And, of course, you would need food, as well as medical supplies and perhaps some weapon with which you might defend yourself against marauding tribes common in the desert adventures that we see on TV. Oh yes, don't forget the reading material. *The Arabian Nights* would seem appropriate.

Notice the progression here. Your immediate concerns are for bodily needs and safety assurances. Only when these fundamental needs are satisfactorily addressed is one free to consider other needs, such as reading and entertainment. The same motivational profile holds true for an entire culture: When a country is threatened with famine or military takeover by a hostile neighbor, issues like transportation and literacy are incidental and not likely to receive much political attention.

Most theories of motivation make some minor provisions for ordering motives, but the central core of Abraham Maslow's theory of self-actualization is the notion of a hierarchy of needs (see Figure 9–6). Maslow (1970) proposed a need schema comprised of five interrelated levels. In order for needs higher on the scale to become relevant motivational concerns, needs contained in the lower levels must be satisfied. The most primitive and the most basic needs are physiological. Before we look to anything else, we must attend to breathing, eating, drinking, and procreation (sex). Given that these demands are satisfied, we then enter the level of safety needs and go about securing a safe, orderly, and supportive environment. There is little consolation in being safe, however, should a physiological need resurface. Our behavior adjusts to the prevailing deprivation conditions and satisfies the most pressing needs.

With physiological and safety needs met, belongingness and love become the most urgent concern: we seek out mates, friendships, and social

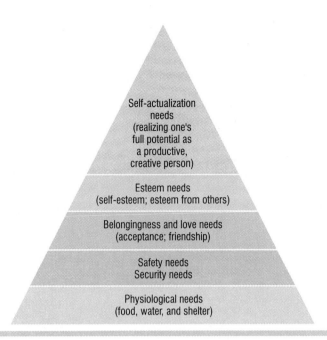

FIGURE 9–6
Maslow's need hierarchy proposes that more basic needs must be satisfied before it is possible to meet higher needs.

affiliations. Maslow was an optimist and saw people as basically good. He believed that people have a vast capacity for expressing kindness and love. But in order for individuals or groups to be in a position to display their genuine regard for others, their physiological needs must be met and they must be free of the corrupting influence of fear and uncertainty. After love and belongingness are esteem needs. Here, people's conduct is directed by approval. The goal is to achieve a combination of both self-esteem, wherein you think well of yourself, and the esteem of others, wherein others think well of you. Ultimately there is the need for **self-actualization**. With all other, lower needs satisfied, the individual aspires to be all that he or she can be. However, few of us realize our fullest potential because the more basic motives that go unfulfilled prevent us from totally ascending the hierarchy.

As with many of Maslow's contributions, the charm inherent in his model of motivation is the upward spirit that it embraces. He envisioned a world of people striving to attain an ideal state. But, as is also characteristic of much of Maslow's doctrine, his position on motivational hierarchies is without substantial empirical support. Exceptions to his rules, in both everyday life and the laboratory, continue to refute the theory. For instance, how is it that love can take precedence over safety? Yet, the romantic lore is rife with episodes where life is sacrificed for the sake of a higher plane. One is reminded of Sydney Carton in Charles Dickens's *A Tale of Two Cities* (1859/1962), who unselfishly volunteered for the guillotine to ensure the happiness of the woman he loved. Thus, if a motivational hierarchy such as Maslow's does exist, the different levels that define it certainly vary dramatically from person to person.

Now that we have gained some understanding of the basic motivational theories summarized in Table 9–1, let us move to a discussion of specific motives. We begin with hunger.

self-actualization Maslow's position that we all strive to be everything possible for us to be

HUNGER

The simplest position on hunger contends that we eat when our stomachs are empty and we stop eating when they are full. Cannon and Washburn (1912) were the first to investigate systematically such a straightforward account of

TABLE 9-1
Theories of Motivation

Theory	Description	Evaluation
Biological Determinism	Biological and genetic forces trigger predetermined actions. Instincts and unlearned behaviors occur mechanistically.	Although some behaviors are likely to be biologically determined, the complexity of human behavior demands a more flexible account of motivation.
Hull's Drive-Reduction Model	Needs arising out of tissue deficits generate drive states that motivate responding. Relevant behaviors continue to occur until the tissue deficits are restored and the drive state is reduced accordingly.	This approach fails to account for the fact that in some instances the motivation for responding is associated with increasing, not decreasing, stimulation.
Cognitive Consistency Theory	Imbalances in beliefs, thoughts, and behaviors create tension. The impetus for responding is tension reduction, and behavior persists until balance (cognitive equilibrium) is restored.	Linking motivation to cognitive processes seems reasonable, but the model (along with all other homeostatic models) fails to account for the fact that in some instances the motivation for responding is associated with increasing, not decreasing, tension.
Arousal Theory	Departures in stimulation from an optimal point motivate responding aimed at increasing or decreasing arousal until the optimal level of stimulation is reached.	The optimal point of arousal varies from person to person, and from one task to another.
Incentive Theory	External stimuli (incentives) pull the behavior rather than push it. Goal attainment is the primary motive.	In some instances tangible incentives work better; in others intangible incentives produce better performance. Shifting from one type of incentive system to another can cause problems.
Self-Actualization Theory	A hierarchy of needs, beginning with basic bodily and safety demands and progressing to needs for fulfillment, determines which behaviors occur.	On occasion, a person may choose to satisfy needs higher in the hierarchy (e.g., love) while disregarding needs lower in the hierarchy (e.g., safety).

hunger. Cannon convinced his co-worker Washburn to swallow a balloon that provided a fairly accurate index of stomach contractions. Cannon observed that his colleague's reports of feeling increased hunger coincided with increased stomach contractions. The evidence seemed conclusive. However, later work showed that both animals and people stopped eating even when the nerves from the stomach to the brain had been severed. With the signaling system inoperative, and with no other method of gauging fullness, eating should have continued but did not. Obviously, something other than stomach contraction must influence food ingestion.

Brain Mechanisms

One promising theory of hunger implicated the brain's hypothalamus as the neural basis for eating (see Stricker & Verbalis, 1987). Separate hypothalamic centers were thought to regulate food ingestion (hunger) and the discontinuation of eating (satiety). Specifically, the brain region known as the **lateral hypothalamic area** was identified as the "hunger center," and the **ventromedial nucleus of the hypothalamus (VMH)** was the "satiety center" (Grossman, 1975). Tumors in humans and laboratory-induced lesions in animals showed that destruction in very precise areas in these parts of the brain was associated with dramatic changes in eating habits and overall body weight (Carlson, 1991). Although we know now that neural mechanisms do not directly control hunger, they are important in the regulatory chain.

The extent to which the lateral hypothalamus is involved in the beginning and the continuation of eating is apparent from these animal studies, which show that surgical lesions of the area produce starvation, even though a food source is readily available (Teitelbuam & Epstein, 1962). Such a condition is known as *aphagia*. By way of contrast, electrical stimulation of the lateral hypothalamic area will cause an animal to begin eating even though it is already full (Hoebel, 1971).

Perhaps even more astounding is what happens following the destruction of the ventromedial hypothalamus (VMH). VMH-lesioned rats tend to eat excessively; they exhibit *hyperphagia*. On some occasions (see Figure 9–7), animals increase to three times their normal weight. One might think that such an animal would fill to a maximum and then pop, like an overinflated bicycle tire. However, attempts toward equilibrium persist. The animal's weight eventually levels off, and the animal may actually show an indifference to food unless it is a preferred source. What seems to be happening is that hypothalamic lesions adjust a homeostatic center up or down (Keesey & Powley, 1986).

Because of its simplicity, the notion of single controlling neural mechanisms for hunger and satiety is appealing. However, motivational phenomena rarely prove to be simply determined, and there is no reason to expect this case to be different. The current position in motivational psychology is that hypothalamic control per se does not exist, for it now appears that neurons from the hypothalamic areas discussed carry impulses to other parts of the body that do function as hunger control centers. Thus, the hypothalamus functions more as a dispatcher than as a regulator.

Hormonal Mechanisms

Important hunger and satiety signals may come from the hypothalamic area, but control of feeding is accomplished somewhere else, apparently in the endocrine system, specifically the pancreas and liver. Both these organs are crucial to maintaining proper glucose (blood sugar) balance. The pancreas secretes a hormone called **insulin** that facilitates the transfer of glucose from the blood into cells throughout the body. The liver, on the other hand, stores glucose in reserve in the form of *glycogen*. A hormone called **glucagon**, produced by the pancreas, serves to convert glycogen back to glucose, when it is needed. Normally, insulin and glucagon work in harmony to keep blood sugar levels within an optimal range. However, hypothalamic lesions disrupt the usual endocrine operations. With VMH lesions, for example, insulin secretions increase and glucagon secretions decrease (Kimble, 1988).

lateral hypothalamic area brain region once identified as the "hunger center"

ventromedial nucleus of the hypothalamus (VMH) brain region once identified as the "satiety center"

FIGURE 9–7
A hyperphagic rat following a VMH lesion. This animal weighs over 1,000 g (1 kilogram), which is about three times the normal amount.

insulin hormone produced by the pancreas that promotes the transfer of glucose to the tissues

glucagon hormone produced by the pancreas that serves to convert glycogen back to glucose

Consequently, everything in the way of blood sugar gets transferred to the cells (excess insulin) or remains in the liver (deficient glucagon). The result is a low level of glucose in the blood. Today there is widespread agreement that low blood glucose level is an important physiological stimulus for hunger.

There is now considerable evidence that specialized receptors, called **glucoreceptors**, are concentrated in the hypothalamus and the liver. These glucoreceptors are excited by extremely low or high blood sugar concentrations. When blood glucose levels drop, for instance, glucoreceptors in the liver fire at a high rate and these signals are sent to the brain, which interprets them as hunger. VMH lesions produce hyperphagia, therefore, not because the brain control center is destroyed, but rather because low blood sugar, caused by the neurally mediated disruption in endocrine operations (see preceding paragraph), triggers a feeding response. The animal gets stuck in an intake mode, and no matter how much glucose is taken in from the food source, blood glucose levels remain low. Everything will either infuse the tissues (due to excessive amounts of insulin) or be stored as glycogen (due to lack of glucagon). The animal continues to eat but remains hungry.

There is an excellent test of the hypothesis that hunger is controlled by such an endocrine network. Figure 9–8 graphically depicts what should happen to eating patterns after sectioning (cutting) the vagus nerve, the principal neural pathway that supplies the thoracic and abdominal regions of the body. Included in the vagus nerve are the neural circuits connecting the hypothalamic area with the liver and pancreas. With the vagus intact, therefore, destruction of VMH centers should evoke changes in pancreatic functioning that result in increased insulin production and decreased glucagon activity. Due to the resulting drop in blood glucose levels, hyperphagia should occur. But with the neural signal from the hypothalamic area surgically blocked (with the vagus cut), VMH lesions should leave the blood glucose levels unaffected; that is, insulin and glucagon hormones would exist in their usual amounts because the damage done at the hypothalamic level would never get reported to the pancreas. Therefore, no hyperphagia would be expected under such conditions. Such findings have been obtained (Powley, 1977).

Short-Term and Long-Term Cues

In addition to those investigations that implicate hormonal mechanisms in the control of eating, a significant amount of scientific research has been devoted to the role that short-term and long-term cues play in selecting and eating food (see Kandel, Schwartz, & Jessell, 1991). **Short-term cues** consist primarily of the properties of the food, and they include such stimuli as the taste and smell of the food, the texture and the temperature of food placed in the mouth, and the immediate chemical changes in the gastrointestinal tract and endocrine system we noted earlier. Short-term cues determine the size of the meals we eat, and as we discuss next, they may be instrumental in certain eating disorders such as obesity. When you stop eating because you feel full, or when you reject food because it tastes bad, your eating behavior is under the control of short-term cues.

Long-term cues, by comparison, regulate our overall body weight. Chief among the long-term cues that affect our intake of food is the level of fat that is stored in the body. The most popular present-day account of hunger and weight control relates to the notion of **set point**. Set point is the idea that each of us has an established body fat (lipid) level that remains fixed and that resists attempts to alter it. When fat deposits drop below set individual levels, hunger occurs and consequently we eat more. Should we try to shift the set point, metabolic changes will occur that prevent it. This phenomenon is exactly what happened in the case of B. K. that was mentioned at the beginning of this chapter.

glucoreceptors specialized receptors in the body that are sensitive to the amount of glucose present

short-term cues stimuli such as the color or taste of food that may determine meal size and frequency

long-term cues cues such as body fat that regulate overall body weight

set point the point established for each person that determines how much fat will be stored

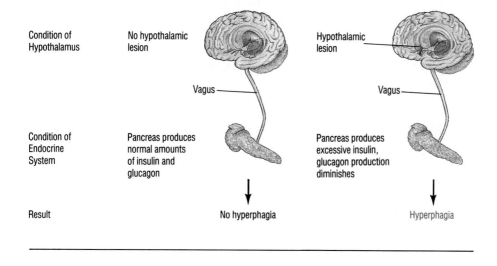

VAGUS NERVE INTACT

Condition of Hypothalamus	No hypothalamic lesion		Hypothalamic lesion	
Vagus			Vagus	
Condition of Endocrine System	Pancreas produces normal amounts of insulin and glucagon		Pancreas produces excessive insulin, glucagon production diminishes	
Result	No hyperphagia		Hyperphagia	

VAGUS NERVE CUT

Condition of Hypothalamus	No hypothalamic lesion		Hypothalamic lesion	
Vagus			Vagus	
Condition of Endocrine System	Pancreas produces normal amounts of insulin and glucagon		Pancreas produces normal amounts of insulin and glucagon	
Result	No hyperphagia		No hyperphagia	

FIGURE 9–8
The effects of hypothalamic lesions on hyperphagia with the vagus nerve intact (*top*) or cut (*bottom*).

Many people try to establish a new, lower set point by exercising, smoking, or taking one of the many diet medications that are available over the counter. On the whole, these efforts will be spectacularly unsuccessful, and they may even backfire. For example, when people self-impose a reduced-calorie diet over a long period, they run the risk of producing a long-term decline in metabolic rate (Kandel et al., 1991). These dieters can actually make themselves worse than they were at the start: If they continue on the low-calorie diet, they will regain the fat stores (weight) they lost briefly because of the aforementioned drop in metabolic conversion. If they resume normal eating habits, they will actually *gain* weight beyond their previously normal levels because the enduring decline in metabolism translates into the storage of more fat than was stored before the diet was begun. For someone looking for an excuse not to diet, such a realization is not likely to promote a reduction in meal size or frequency.

The importance of long-term cues and predetermined set levels of body fat in weight regulation is also evident from an adoption study reported by Stunkard et al. (1986). Based on their adult body size, people who were adopted as children were divided into four weight classes: thin, median weight, overweight, and obese. Comparisons with the biological parents revealed a strong positive relation between the weights of the adoptees and the weights of their mothers and fathers, yet no such relation was found for adoptees and their adoptive parents. These findings suggest that everyone conforms to a genetic mold shaped by the physiques of his or her parents. But this is not the whole story.

Eating Disorders

Obesity.   Clearly, biological influences do determine eating habits to some degree, but extreme cases of overeating that lead to obesity probably do not result exclusively from biological factors. Ample evidence exists that environmental factors play a major role for the 25 to 45% of adults in the United States who are clinically overweight or obese (Grinker, 1982). Moreover, the situation is no different for children.

Perhaps what we eat is one determinant of *obesity*. According to a report released a few years ago by a private consumer health advocacy group, children in the United States are getting cram courses every Saturday on unhealthy eating (Jacobson, 1992). In just 4 hr of network television cartoon programming, 222 junk-food commercials were shown. Sugar-coated cereals, candy, cookies, and high-fat fast foods were being advertized instead of fruits, vegetables, and grains. In this context, it is easy to believe reports of a 54% increase in obesity among elementary school children, just in the last 10 years. Even when children are not watching junk-food ads, TV habits themselves may promote weight gain. Gortmaker et al. (1987) report that the incidence of obesity increases by 2% with each additional hour spent sitting in front of the TV. Combine this pattern of inactivity at home with the minimum exercise requirements established by many schools, and the escalating numbers of obese children are easily understood. What can be done? How can we get children away from the TV set? One technique used by one of our colleagues was to place an electronic timing mechanism on the TV set at home. When the "hour allotment" had been used for the week, further access to the set was electronically denied. Along with declines in body weight, the academic performances of the children in this household increased.

Other environmental determinants of overeating and excessive weight gain relate to the potentially appealing properties of food stimuli. The extent to which external food cues are important in controlling eating in obese and normal people has been extensively studied by psychologist Stanley Schachter (see Schachter, 1968, 1971). The essence of Schachter's hypothesis is that the eating behavior of obese people is under the control of external factors, like the sight, smell, and taste of food. Conversely, people of normal weight are more likely to respond to the internal physiological cues associated with hunger or satiety.

Several studies have failed to support Schachter's earlier ideas (see Grinker, 1982; Rodin, 1986, for reviews). Current models focus more on why obese people have failed to learn, or choose to ignore, appropriate internal cues for eating. It now seems that in many cases overeating is related to deeper psychological problems that interfere with normal biological factors (Kolotkin et al., 1987).

Whatever the ultimate causes of obesity, the social consequences of being fat can be devastating. For instance, in interviews of college students, Verner and Krupka (1985) found that students are more reluctant to marry the obese than to marry cocaine users, ex-mental patients, shoplifters, the sexually promiscuous, communists, the blind, atheists, marijuana users, and the divorced. In fact, the status of obese persons was rated as similar to that of embezzlers and prostitutes. Given the evidence, cited earlier, that many weight problems have biological causes, such discrimination seems especially unfair and insensitive.

To confuse the issue even more, there is now some question about the health consequences of weight loss. Thinness not only may be an elusive and futile goal for most men and women, it actually may be dangerous to their health.

THINKING ABOUT
Dieting

As seems to be the case for many families, weight control had been an enduring problem for Sebrina and Geoffrey Dechman, as well as their two children. Finally, the family members agreed to a pact wherein they would eat only low-calorie, low-fat foods. The result: Sebrina lost over 15 lb over the next several months, and each of the children lost nearly 10; Geoffrey lost 106 lb, down from 300!

This story is true, and it is reenacted routinely throughout American society, where thinness and self-perfection have been the unofficial state religion for some time. People virtually starve themselves because not being thin may be interpreted as a public statement of weak will power. But recently, being skinny has come under criticism, and many health professionals think this criticism is long overdue.

Many of us can painfully testify about dieting experiences that failed, or even worse, made the situation worse. A statement released by the National Center for Health Statistics in 1992 indicates that only 10% of American dieters who lose 25 lb or more will keep the weight off for as long as 2 years. The cycle of dieting, regaining, more dieting, regaining once again, and so on can lead to unspeakable frustration, for the person is stressed by one circumstance or the other all the time. Now there are medical studies to indicate that this cycle also may be unhealthy. A *New England Journal of Medicine* report, published in 1991, shows that swinging through successive bouts of weight loss and gain may actually be associated with a shorter life expectancy (Brownell, 1991). In a study of 3,130 men and women, ages 30 to 62, researchers on the Framingham Heart Study found that so-called yo-yo dieters ran a 70% higher risk of dying from heart disease, relative to nondieters, even when the nondieters were overweight.

A number of physiological explanations have been offered for such findings, including the negative results associated with rapidly mobilizing fat stores. The real issue, however, lies not with the biological cause, but with the fact that Americans, especially women, may have become captive to a social prescription that is not only unworkable, but life threatening.

The realization that not everyone can, or even should, look like a willow has caused a sharp decline in the number of dieters (Figure 9–9). One of the more visible "never-again dieters" is television personality Oprah Winfrey, who lost and subsequently regained a great deal of weight. As many others are declaring, Oprah states that she is learning not to judge herself on the basis of her weight.

More tolerance for how much people weigh is also evident from the latest tables for "healthy weights" issued by the federal government in 1990 (Figure 9–10). These charts, which are often used by insurance companies

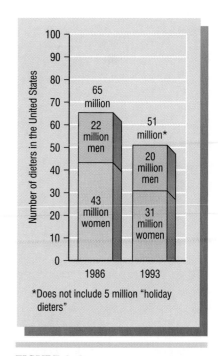

FIGURE 9–9
There has been a sharp decline in the number of dieters in the United States in recent years.

	Weight (pounds)	
Height	19 to 34 years	35 years and over
5'0"	97–128	108–138
5'1"	101–132	111–143
5'2"	104–137	115–148
5'3"	107–141	119–152
5'4"	111–146	122–157
5'5"	114–150	126–162
5'6"	118–155	130–167
5'7"	121–160	134–172
5'8"	125–164	138–178
5'9"	129–169	142–183
5'10"	132–174	146–188
5'11"	136–179	151–194
6'0"	140–184	155–199
6'1"	144–189	159–205
6'2"	148–195	164–210

FIGURE 9–10
Revised U.S. government figures for healthy weight, for men and women.

anorexia nervosa eating disorder characterized by self-imposed starvation

bulimia nervosa eating disorder in which a person eats large amounts of food, only to vomit or otherwise purge the system; results in extreme weight loss

and other agencies, allow for a range of 30 lb or more at each height, and up to a 16-lb gain after age 35. These changes reflect a more realistic appraisal of appropriate weight goals for most people. Still, there is resistance to relaxing weight standards. Young people continue to copy the slender female and muscular male models they see in magazines and on TV. In addition, the fashion industry, which is steeped in the thin tradition, could be financially at risk should preferences shift too rapidly.

Finally, it should be recognized that the pendulum should not swing too far and endorse excessive weight gain, which is as unhealthy as excessive weight loss. As with so many other facets of life, moderation seems to be the key. What would you recommend? Do you think dieting would be good for you? What about 20 years from now? Do you think it would be worthwhile to keep up with the rapidly changing literature in this area?

Anorexia Nervosa. Although excessive weight is a problem for many people, another segment of the population suffers from an eating disorder called **anorexia nervosa** that places them at the opposite end of the spectrum. In this disorder, people don't eat and so they lose too much weight. In a competitive environment such as a ballet company, it is easy to see how someone could fall victim to this condition because weight loss is associated with benefits. But more commonly, anorexia develops when there is no obvious incentive to lose weight. People who are already too thin see themselves as overweight and needing to diet, jog, take numerous exercise classes, or do whatever is necessary to "get their weight down." Often, the physical condition of these people spirals downward, and they lose weight to the point where it threatens their lives.

The physical symptoms of anorexia nervosa, in addition to the obvious emaciation, include tooth loss, hormonal imbalances, and weakness (Takai et al., 1989). These people are often self-destructive and sometimes suicidal. Because anorexics' attitudes toward eating are so rigid, some psychologists have suggested that their behaviors are actually a variant of another disturbance, *obsessive-compulsive disorder* (Holden, 1990). Regardless, intervention for anorexia is an absolute must.

The causes of anorexia nervosa have not been clearly determined. Many clinical psychologists believe that the disorder arises from an unstable self-concept. This position has support from reports that show a high degree of personality disturbance among people with anorexia (Kennedy, McVey, & Katz, 1990). Whatever the causes, the disorder is most common in young women (about 85% of the cases are adolescent females from white, middle- and upper-middle-class backgrounds), and it seems to be associated with a rejection of traditional feminine roles. Fortunately, in most instances treatment produces positive results and the person fully recovers, both physically and psychologically. Occasionally, however, the extent of the stress to the body is so great that it cannot be reversed. This happened to singer Karen Carpenter (Figure 9–11), who regained much of her weight before her death. The tissue damage caused by her severe dieting over a long period could not be mended, and she eventually succumbed to this psychological illness.

Bulimia Nervosa. Along with anorexia, a food-related disorder known as **bulimia nervosa** has been identified (see Spliegler & Guevrement, 1993). Unlike people with anorexia nervosa, people with bulimia nervosa do eat; in fact, they gorge. One is reminded of John Belushi's portrayal of Bluto at the cafeteria line in the movie *Animal House*. But after stuffing themselves, people with bulimia nervosa purge themselves by self-induced vomiting or with the use of laxatives (Halmi, 1987).

Perhaps nowhere is bulimia nervosa a greater problem than on college campuses. As with anorexia, women are more likely to have this disorder. A case familiar to the authors is typical of an all too common situation.

> Susan K. was a first-year college student majoring in sociology at a private school in the southwestern region of the United States. As happens with many new college students who acquire poor eating habits, Susan gained weight her first semester at school. She saw herself as someone who was not just overweight, but obese. She began to eat large amounts of food but then would induce vomiting or take laxatives to purge her system of food. Eventually, Susan weighed only 76 lb. Her family was forced to place her in a hospital, where she received adequate nutrition and began psychotherapy for her eating disorder. For the last 4 years, Susan's weight has been stable at about 100 lb, and she has relapsed into bulimia only once.

Of course, bulimia nervosa does occur outside of college campuses, but considering that as much as 10% of the female student population may suffer from the disorder, it is understandable that the bulk of the research on this important phenomenon has come from this special group. When it does occur it is accompanied by discoloration of the teeth, esophageal hernias, and laceration of the gastrointestinal track. Again, as is true for all of the eating disorders discussed here, improvement is possible with professional help.

FIGURE 9–11
Singer Karen Carpenter died as a result of complications associated with anorexia nervosa.

SEX

Compared to hunger, sexual motivation is less affected by deprivation. And there are other differences that distinguish these basic motives. For instance, an individual can survive without sex, but survival is impossible without food and water. Sexual activity is necessary not for the individual's survival but for the survival of the species. Another difference between sex and the other basic motives is that arousal of the sexual motive is itself a pleasurable experience. Arousal of hunger and thirst are generally considered to be unpleasant states. Also, the controlling forces in sex are more varied than for hunger and thirst. In our coverage of sex, we see that the brain, hormones, and the environment all influence sexual behavior.

Brain Mechanisms

The brain clearly plays a key role in regulating sexual behavior. The brain's control operates in two principal ways. First, the brain controls the activity of the *gonads* (sex glands)—testes in the male, ovaries in the female—by acting on the pituitary gland. Second, the brain responds to both gonadal hormones and external stimuli and thereby mediates the sex drive and sexual arousal.

Brain Control of Gonads. In a sexually mature animal, the gonads produce and release hormones that have a major influence on sexual behavior. The action of the gonads themselves is under the control of complex brain mechanisms that operate in a homeostatic feedback system. The hypothalamus secretes releasing factors into the bloodstream supplying the pituitary gland. These factors in turn stimulate or inhibit the pituitary's action for releasing other hormones into the circulatory system. Among the hormones produced by the pituitary are two **gonadotropic hormones**, hormones whose target organs are the gonads. One of the gonadotropic hormones, **follicle stimulating hormone (FSH)**, induces the maturation of ovarian follicles and induces

gonadotropic hormones hormones that have the gonads (sex organs) as their target

follicle stimulating hormone (FSH) gonadotropic hormone that induces the maturation of ovarian follicles and stimulates estrogen release and sperm production

the ovaries in the female to secrete the gonadal hormone *estrogen*, and stimulates sperm production in the male. Another gonadotropic hormone, **luteinizing hormone (LH)**, induces ovulation in the female and stimulates secretion of the gonadal hormone *testosterone* by the testes in the male.

Release of hormones by the gonads not only affects target organs such as the uterus and the prostate, but also helps to regulate the neuroendocrine feedback system. In other words, the level of circulating gonadal hormones affects the amount of gonadotropic hormones secreted by the pituitary. When there is a low level of gonadal hormones, greater amounts of FSH and LH are secreted in order to stimulate the release of more hormones by the gonads. When the level is high, the pituitary reduces the amount of LH and FSH secreted in order to reduce the amount of gonadal hormones released.

Brain Mediation of Sexual Responses. There are three ways the brain affects and controls sexual responses. First, we have seen some structures in the brain control the secretion of hormones that act directly on the gonads and thereby alter the sexual response system. These brain structures include the hypothalamus and the pituitary. Second, certain structures in the brain respond to gonadal hormones and control behavior through their action. For example, when the female hormone estradiol is administered to female rats, the hormone tends to accumulate in the hypothalamus and limbic structures such as the septum and amygdala (Carlson, 1991). Finally, there are brain structures that may not be sensitive to hormones but that nevertheless are involved in controlling sexual behavior. Older studies of specific brain areas have revealed that microelectrode stimulation of these areas elicits specific components of the sexual response. When electrodes are implanted in the anterior hypothalamus, male rats mount female rats with much greater frequency than normal, with markedly higher rates of intromission and ejaculation (Vaughan & Fisher, 1962).

Hormonal Mechanisms

The effects of hormones on sexual behavior, as we have already seen, are inextricably linked to a neuroendocrine feedback system that is quite complex. Some of these effects are fixed before birth. Differentiation of the sexes in terms of external genitalia occurs before birth and subsequently determines whether the child is reared as a male or a female. Genital differentiation is under hormonal control, and the presence of testosterone is required to differentiate male genitals (Beach, 1977).

Other hormonal effects are transitory, and they are linked to sexual behavior in the sexually mature individual. In species in which the female is sexually receptive only during specific periods, known as **estrus**, secretion of gonadal hormones makes the female more attractive to males, makes her more attracted to males, and induces her to assume postures of copulatory readiness. Also, experiments with diverse species show that treating females with estrogen makes them more attractive to males; when estrogen is withdrawn, attractiveness correspondingly declines (Beach, 1977). However, species differences in the role of hormonal control of sexual behavior are profound. In less complex mammals such as guinea pigs, rats, and hamsters, females mate only during estrus. In more complex species, such as dogs, estrus is a necessary but not sufficient condition for sex. Females in still more complex species, such as chimpanzees, often allow copulation at any stage of the menstrual cycle.

Early reports on the relationship between hormone levels and human sexual behavior show that some women report higher frequency of intercourse and orgasm when ovarian hormone levels are at their peak. But more recent evidence indicates that such women are in the minority, because sexual responsiveness for most women apparently is not linked to hormonal activity (Hoon, Bruce, & Kinchloe, 1982). The situation may be slightly different for males in that some recent evidence does show that testosterone is directly related to desire. For example, in a study of men who suffered from extremely low levels of testosterone, it was discovered that high doses of testosterone increased the men's sexual fantasies and restored their sexual desire (Davidson & Myers, 1988). However, the mechanics of sex such as genital arousal were unaffected by testosterone administration, so something other than hormones is obviously involved in the male sexual response.

Environmental Factors

For humans, the influence of social and physical stimuli on sexuality is profound. For now, we note that the role of smell in human sexual behavior may be more important than previously suspected. Of course, the perfume and cologne industry has operated under the belief for some time that particular odors are sexually alluring (see Figure 9–12). Extending the suspected connection between smell and sexuality, in 1988, Winnifred Cutler and George Preti of the University of Pennsylvania School of Medicine reported that male underarm odors affect women's menstrual cycles and, more generally, sexual health among females. A "soup" of aromatic essences taken from underarm pads worn by male volunteers resulted in more regular menstrual cycles and fewer infertility problems when applied to the skin under women's noses. Although such findings are new, and the precise mechanisms for the effects are unclear, continuing research on the issue of odor influences on human sexuality will be interesting to follow.

Now we turn to a group of human motives that, like sex, have highly social aspects. Let us begin with aggression.

FIGURE 9–12
Pictures from advertising agencies, such as this one showing an attractive woman holding a bottle of perfume, are commonly used to suggest a link between certain odors and sexual arousal.

AGGRESSION

One need only pick up a newspaper to see examples of hostility and aggression. The Rodney King incident in Los Angeles that sparked racial violence and riots, trouble in the Persian Gulf, subway violence in New York, a state senator in the Midwest punching out a colleague in a scuffle during a legislative session—these are but few of the many instances of human aggression.

Over the years, questions have arisen as to why so much aggressive behavior occurs. What are the origins of a motive that is so potentially destructive? Are we expressing a biological imperative, as Robert Ardrey suggests in his book *African Genesis* (1961), or do social forces dictate a level of aggression that is neither predetermined nor abiding? This issue is an exceedingly important one, of course, because in the biological case human aggression is natural and unalterable. Conversely, if aggression is socially determined, it is learned and therefore changeable. Either way, before we can discuss the motivational mechanisms underlying aggression, we first must agree on what it is. Accordingly, our discussion begins by defining aggression. Also, two different types of aggression are distinguished to help us understand the roots of this ubiquitous human motive.

Definition and Types of Aggression

We define *aggression* as the act of delivering an aversive stimulus to an unwilling victim. Note that this definition contains two distinguishing features. First, the action that is undertaken must be aversive and potentially

This sort of hostile aggression is often the result of frustration.

harmful. Some aversive events present in aggressive behavior are obvious, as when physical beatings or verbal abuse occurs. Other events may be less conspicuous but equally destructive. Second, the victim of aggression must be an unwilling participant. It clearly is not aggression when a victim provokes an attack that is designed to meet some perverse personal need.

Hostile Aggression. **Hostile aggression** is the type of aggression that is most commonly associated with acts of human violence. Here, there is a flagrant attempt to strike out against something or someone as a result of feeling pain, discomfort, or frustration (Eron, 1987). In addition to the examples used to open this section, consider highway aggression. When people in a hurry are faced with traffic delays, they can become angry and tempers may flare. The most trivial violation can lead to an argument, even fighting. Under such conditions, the object of aggression is often a convenient substitute for the real source of a person's irritation.

> **hostile aggression** form of aggression that results from frustration or discomfort, and that is not necessarily intended to produce benefits for the aggressor

In some cases, hostile reactions to discomfort are considerably more violent than what you see in highway aggression. In a study by Anderson and Anderson (1984) that looked at the relationship between ambient (outside) temperature and violent crime in the cities of Chicago and Houston, murder and rape offenses increased significantly when temperatures reached the mid-90s (see Figure 9–13). There was no corresponding increase in aggressive crimes of an instrumental nature such as robbery (see the following section). Also, it was observed that this increase in hostile aggressive crimes was most dramatic for Saturday, Sunday, and Monday. This latter result, of course, simply may reflect the greater availability of potential victims on weekends. In any event, it appears that the physical environment contributes significantly to aggressive behavior that is affected by discomfort and irritability.

We further note that a contagious pattern is common in hostile aggression. An initial act of violence often sets in motion a chain of events that culminates in an aggressive act directed toward a totally unsuspecting and innocent target. Consider what may happen between a brother and sister when the brother is reprimanded for misbehaving. Because he poured sand in his father's toolbox, the brother is not permitted to play with his friends.

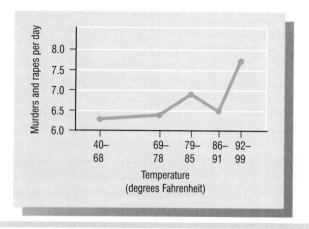

FIGURE 9-13
The effects of ambient temperature on violent crime in two major cities in the United States. As temperatures climb into the 90s, the number of murders and rapes committed each day increases sharply. (Adapted from Anderson & Anderson, 1984.)

Frustrated and filled with anger, the brother torments his younger sister by making fun of her and calling her names. Too small to retaliate, the younger sister takes it out on the family cat by picking him up by the head and tossing him across the room. In this case, the infectious nature of aggression has left an innocent cat wondering about the capriciousness of the world it lives in.

Instrumental Aggression. Sometimes people respond aggressively because their aggressive behavior has produced benefits in the past. This type of aggression is called **instrumental aggression** because it is instrumental in producing a desired result. Children may respond aggressively on the playground because by doing so, they get their way. Or, a thief may assault someone in a park because it is a way of getting money. In this type of aggression the violence is secondary to obtaining some other goal. So, unlike hostile aggression, instrumental aggression includes no explicit intent to inflict injury. Of course, in some circumstances aggression may be both hostile and instrumental. For example, a fight on the school playground may result as much from a need to gain respect from peers as it does from anger.

instrumental aggression aggression with the intent of gaining some personal benefit

Causes of Aggression

Psychologists have determined that a variety of factors contribute to aggression, including neural activation of certain brain regions such as the hypothalamus and amygdala (Beck, 1983), crowding (Freedman, Sears, & Carlsmith, 1981), media violence, and violent role models. But the fundamental question of what makes one person behave aggressively when others do not has not been answered satisfactorily. One promising line of research points out that aggression is more likely when a person is unable or unwilling to feel the hurt that his or her victim feels after an attack (Miller & Eisenberg, 1988). For example, the probability of child abuse goes up as the capacity for sympathy declines (Feshbach, 1987). It follows that as psychologists discover new methods for enhancing the capacity for sympathy, acts of aggression should decrease accordingly.

ACHIEVEMENT

Even among young children, it is easy to detect differences in desire to become and remain successful. In a Little League baseball game, some children are so intently determined to win that one worries about their mental state should they lose. At the same time, other children are indifferent to winning and losing, and may exhibit greater interest in an earthworm wriggling its way out of a hole behind second base. At the adult level these motivational disparities may take on a new form, but the degree of difference holds firm. Why do some people want to achieve more than others? How important is it to you to be number one?

These and similar questions are concerned with the area of achievement motivation. One of the first psychologists to study the need to achieve was Henry Murray (Murray, 1938). Murray developed a self-report assessment test to measure the desire to succeed. A person taking the test would be required to indicate agreement or disagreement with an item such as, "I set difficult goals for myself, which I attempt to reach." This early test provided a relatively objective index of the strength of an individual's motivation to excel. Later, psychologists David McClelland (McClelland, 1961) and John Atkinson (Atkinson & Birch, 1978), built on Murray's original ideas, and theorized that **need achievement** is but one of several motives linked to a *success–failure dichotomy*.

need achievement motive based on our desire to achieve at a certain level

Many psychologists feel that the major theoretical advances regarding achievement motivation have been due to the efforts of Atkinson (Weiner, 1980). Atkinson amended the conceptual thought in the area, suggesting that the need to avoid failure must be considered along with the hope for success. This means that many people are motivated to perform, not so much because they want to be successful, but rather because the prospect of failing is so loathsome. An example is the student who diligently applies himself or herself in an academic setting and maintains a high grade point average. Is the person attracted by the *A* or threatened by the *F*? It could be either reason or a combination of both that impels the person to study.

Thus, for Atkinson's theory of achievement motivation, goal-directed performance is jointly determined by the tendencies to achieve success and avoid failure (see McClelland, 1985b). This fundamental concept leads to some novel and quite curious predictions for human behavior: namely, if the achievement motive is greater in strength than the motive to avoid failure, then goal-directed responding is probable. However, should the fear of failure outweigh the need to be successful, then the person may abandon the goal altogether. Accordingly, task selection may vary depending on individual needs, and a number of hypotheses are possible. For example, people high in need achievement and low in fear of failure may select a task of moderate difficulty because extremely difficult tasks minimize the chances for success, and very easy tasks present few challenges, and therefore minimal satisfaction. On the other hand, people high in fear of failure and low in need achievement may select an easy task that virtually guarantees that failure can be avoided. Or, they may choose a very difficult task that would cause them minimal shame and embarrassment should they fail.

Over the years, the findings have consistently supported Atkinson's theoretical predictions about task selection by people high in need achievement. As shown in Figure 9–14, those persons expressing a strong need to be successful but with low fear of failure prefer tasks involving moderate risks (Hamilton, 1974). But the idea that persons high in fear of failure and low in need achievement will opt for very easy or very difficult tasks seems to be only half true. Students who were low in need achievement and high in fear of failure preferentially selected a high-risk difficult task but virtually never chose a low-risk easy task. Perhaps they perceived the easy task as too simple and felt its selection would invite derision or self-deprecation. The extremely difficult task, on the other hand, would be a safe choice because the high degree of failure inherent in the task would absolve them of any personal responsibility. In other words, it wouldn't be their fault if they failed.

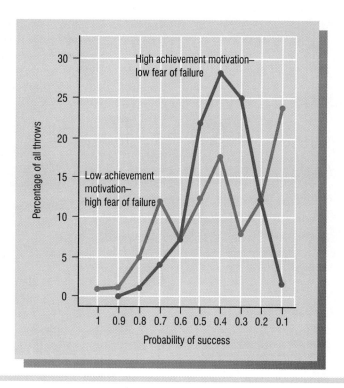

FIGURE 9-14
Preference for easy or difficult tasks in a ring-toss game for students varying in achievement motivation and fear of failure. Task difficulty, defined in terms of the probability of getting a ring on the peg, was varied by having the subject stand at different distances from the peg. (Adapted from Hamilton, 1974.)

Along with our needs to achieve and show competency, we apparently have a need to be with other people. Affiliation, discussed next, is the last of the specific motives we cover in this chapter.

AFFILIATION

Henry David Thoreau was a renowned naturalist. Yet he may have been a naturalist who responded to the world in an unnatural way. Thoreau was an inveterate loner who once stated, "The man I meet with is not often so instructive as the silence he breaks" (journal entry, January 7, 1857). But Thoreau's contempt for society and his passion for privacy are rarely expressed by other humans. Most people dislike being alone and, in fact, will go to great lengths to affiliate with others.

Reflect, if you will, on the affiliation patterns of your day thus far. Did you have breakfast with someone? At school, did you seek out someone from class to talk to before or after the lecture? Do you have plans this evening that include friends or a close companion? In all probability, the answer to all three questions is yes. College students are known to spend most of their time in groups. In one study, students at Ohio State University and the University of North Carolina were observed to be with one or more other persons over 66% of the time (Latané & Bidwell, 1977). Similar results were obtained by Deaux (1978), who found that students spend only about 25% of their waking moments alone.

The fact that college students are so strongly motivated to affiliate actually increases the potential for loneliness on campuses. Watching others have fun may just remind someone of how desperate his or her own isolated circumstances happen to be (Newcomb & Bentler, 1986). People who are alone on campus often attribute their predicament to "lack of opportunities," or they will say that "others have their own groups" (Peplau, Russell, & Heim, 1982). Such attributions may be more desirable than attributions

Most people enjoy being with others and sharing in the fun of group situations.

like "I'm too physically unattractive to make friends" or "I don't have sufficient self-confidence to be successful in a group setting." In the latter case, the person perceives loneliness as a personal rather than an institutional problem, and therefore the prospects for change are appreciably reduced.

Of course, college populations reflect the same basic motives as the broader social community. Business life, the home environment, church gatherings, and so forth all involve a need for affiliation, a need to be among kindred spirits. What causes this apparent need for company? Perhaps positive environmental experiences inculcate a desire to be with others. Clearly, many of the good things that happen to a person take place in the presence of another person. Even as an infant, one encounters warmth, food, love, and many other satisfying events in the company of a parent. Later, group situations take on added luster as the family, school, church, and other institutions become associated with people having fun with other people. Ultimately, other persons become conditioned cues for having a good time and enjoying life. In this sense, we are motivated to be around people because they remind us of how pleasant life can be.

MOTIVES IN CONFLICT

Our final comments on motivation are concerned with what happens when motives conflict. When you desire one object or outcome very much and there are no competing interests, your course is clear. You proceed without conflict and go about your business unencumbered. But it is actually rare that the direction of our activities is so simply determined. In most instances, we must deal at once with several different pressing needs. When these motives conflict with one another, the result can be stress and indecision.

German psychologist Kurt Lewin (1890–1947) was one of the first persons to classify conflicts by type. Figure 9–15 provides a diagrammatic representation of four of the most common kinds of conflicts at the human level. The first type of conflict is called the **approach–approach conflict**.

approach–approach conflict motivational conflict in which a person is caught between two equally attractive goals

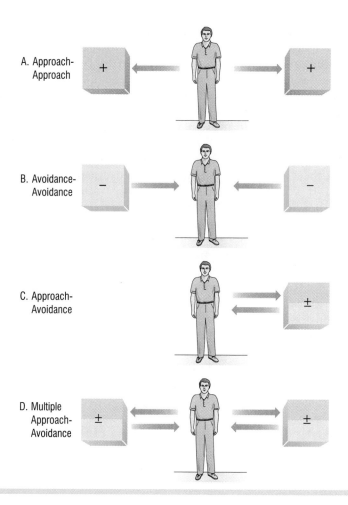

A. Approach-Approach

B. Avoidance-Avoidance

C. Approach-Avoidance

D. Multiple Approach-Avoidance

FIGURE 9–15
Four types of conflict: (*A*) the approach–approach conflict, with two equally desirable goals; (*B*) the avoidance–avoidance conflict, in which the person is caught between two negative goals; (*C*) the approach–avoidance conflict, in which a single goal possesses both positive and negative features; (*D*) the multiple approach–avoidance conflict, in which two or more goals have both positive and negative features.

When one goal is valued more than another, there is no conflict. But in approach–approach situations, the individual is pulled toward equally attractive goals. Conflict is produced, because you cannot have everything you want. For example, when the daughter of one of the authors of this textbook enrolled in her third semester in college, she listed all the courses she wanted for the term. She had reeled off 34 hours of coursework! Obviously, she had overloaded herself and had to omit some courses, much to her immediate displeasure. In approach–approach conflicts you can satisfy some needs but not others.

A second type of conflict involves unpleasant alternatives, each one as offensive and unattractive as the next. This sort of circumstance leads to an **avoidance–avoidance conflict**, in which a person can escape one misery or the other, but not both. Making decisions between studying and failing illustrates the point. Neither event may seem very inviting, but one of them must be accepted. Because the tendency to avoid negative events increases as you draw closer to them, a person caught in an avoidance–avoidance conflict often vacillates and behaves first one way and then the other.

A third type of conflict is the **approach–avoidance conflict**. In this situation a person is simultaneously attracted to and repelled by the same event or object. It is perhaps best exemplified by the young man or woman who develops cold feet at the altar. The individual may really love the prospective spouse and find sanctity in the institution of marriage. Yet, at the same time, getting married means giving up a certain amount of freedom. The real stress comes as you approach very near to the event. This is the time when the attraction and the aversion levels are at their respective peaks. Resolution of

avoidance–avoidance conflict motivational conflict in which the person is caught between two equally unattractive alternatives

approach–avoidance conflict motivational conflict in which a person is simultaneously attracted and repelled by a single event

multiple approach–avoidance conflict
motivational conflict that results
when a person must choose between
two or more events that have both
attractive and unattractive features

the conflict can only occur when one motive gains dominance over the other. Most likely a pattern will form where the individual repeatedly moves toward a goal then retreats to temporary comfort at the last moment.

Perhaps the most common of all motivational conflicts is the **multiple approach–avoidance conflict**. This occurs when a person must choose between two or more events, each with positive and negative features. Dating relationships often present such conflicts. For example, a woman who has dated a man steadily for a long period may still care for him very much, but the relationship may be growing a bit stale and boring. On the other hand, there are both positive and negative aspects to starting a new relationship. It would be romantically unfamiliar and exciting, but it would also mean a loss of security. Normally, these sorts of psychological tugs-of-war are resolved without incident. But in extreme cases, the emotional discomfort can be devastating.

As we mentioned at the beginning of this chapter, emotion is tied closely to motivation. As a scientific topic, emotion was studied in the earliest days of psychology. Research on emotions has persisted throughout the twentieth century, but during much of this time the topic has remained an issue outside the mainstream of experimental psychology. With the emergence of the cognitive psychology movement and its emphasis on studying mental events, this situation has changed. Today emotion is widely studied as a topic in its own right as well as one allied to learning, memory, motivation, personality, human development, communication, and psychopathology.

EMOTION: DEFINITION AND THEORY

The term *emotion* has caused problems for those who try to define it. Typically, emotion is defined as a feeling of pleasantness or unpleasantness, with the emphasis being on the person's awareness (conscious experience) of the emotional state. But this is only one aspect of an emotion. Two other factors describe an emotional occurrence: the changes in the nervous system reflected in physiological events, such as sweating, and the behavioral changes that are expressive of the emotion, particularly changes in facial expression. In other words, emotion involves (*a*) a *conscious experience*, (*b*) *physiological changes*, and (*c*) *behavioral acts*. But emotions are more than just pleasant and unpleasant; they also differ in intensity. For example, an emotion like fear can range from mild to extreme, from apprehension to terror. These different intensities are reflected in the conscious experience of the emotion as well as in the associated physiological and behavioral changes. Thus, a complete picture of emotion must include all three components.

Emotion-Related Physiological and Behavioral Changes

fight or flight syndrome emotional
changes that prepare an organism for
emergency responding

Unlike the conscious experience dimension of emotion, which is difficult to study scientifically, physiological and behavioral changes in emotion have been the focus of intensive empirical investigation. With respect to emotion and bodily changes, a pattern of changes referred to as the **fight or flight syndrome** is of special interest. In emergency situations, the autonomic nervous system (see Chapter 2) is activated, and the resulting increased blood flow to the skeletal muscles, the increased availability of epinephrine (also called adrenalin), and other physiological changes all prepare the body for action. When you are in an intense emotional state—whether fear, anger, or something else—you are capable of performing physically in a way that you could not ordinarily. Recall, for instance, the story from Chapter 2 in which the frightened farmer lifted the tractor off his son. You probably have had

Photograph Judged						
Judgment	Happiness	Disgust	Surprise	Sadness	Anger	Fear

Culture			Percent Who Agreed with Judgment			
99 Americans	97	92	95	84	67	85
40 Brazilians	95	97	87	59	90	67
119 Chileans	95	92	93	88	94	68
168 Argentinians	98	92	95	78	90	54
29 Japanese	100	90	100	62	90	66

FIGURE 9–16
The meaning of facial expressions is universal. This chart shows that people from five different cultures agree about the emotional meaning of certain facial expressions. (From Ekman, Friesen, & Ellsworth, 1972.)

the experience of jumping over a fence to flee a barking dog, or dodging a falling object, only to look back in disbelief that you moved so quickly. Emotions aid survival by providing us with brief periods of supernormal energy and strength.

One thing that has become clear is that facial expressions betray hidden feelings and communicate open displays of emotionality. As Figure 9–16 shows, faces around the world tell pretty much the same tale of happiness, disgust, surprise, sadness, anger, and fear. Charles Darwin was so impressed with the link between facial expressions and emotion that he suggested that it was part of our evolutionary endowment. Today the belief that facial expressions are innately determined is maintained by psychologists who call themselves **universalists**. Among the most active researchers who favor this notion is Paul Ekman of the University of California, San Francisco. Ekman hypothesizes that these facial expressions are programmed as a natural part of the emotion. That is, the particular facial musculature, known as the **facial affect program**, is tied to the other components of physiological arousal, which means that the expression is triggered physiologically (see Zajonc, 1985). Because all humans, regardless of culture, are members of the same species and thus share a common genetic heritage, the universalists assume that each emotion has a characteristic facial expression that is the same all over the world. Other universalist views extend to the nonverbal aspects of speech (pitch, loudness, rate) in the communication of emotion. These components of speech are called **prosodic features**, and an extensive review of the research on this topic supports similar usage across cultures (Frick, 1985).

Even though facial expressions are thought to be automatic reactions to emotions, Ekman acknowledges that it is possible for a person voluntarily to modify a facial expression that is physiologically wired to a particular emotion. In this regard, every culture has its unwritten rules for the proper display of emotion. A child losing in the final round of a spelling bee may feel incredibly sad but may alter a facial expression so as to appear less sad. Similarly, the winner may show a less intense expression of happiness than is felt. These unwritten rules about the proper display of emotion are learned as

universalists scientists who believe that emotional expression is innately prescribed

facial affect program the inborn facial muscle changes that go with the expression of particular emotions

prosodic features nonverbal components of speech that are universally present among all cultures

we grow up in our particular culture. Appropriately, Ekman calls these **display rules**. His research has shown that there may be two facial expressions to any emotion: The first one is the programmed expression and is the same in all cultures; the second one represents the alteration of the programmed expression by the display rules of that particular culture.

Extending the idea that emotional expressions can be inborn or learned, recent work by Ekman, Wallace Friesen, and their colleagues has focused on detecting differences between real and contrived emotions. Careful attention to physical features can tell you whether someone is sincere; consider smiling, for instance.

SPOTLIGHT ON RESEARCH
Counterfeit Smiles

We have all had the experience of listening to someone who seems to be saying one thing, but means another. On occasion, you can get the feeling that the person you are with is giving you false feedback about his or her real feelings. Is the laugh actually a laugh or is it forced? What is this person thinking?

There is current evidence that counterfeit smiles may be detectable. The astute observer can identify a fraud in a second, because people's true feelings are written all over their faces. Ekman, Friesen, and O'Sullivan (1988) studied videotapes of 31 student nurses who participated in an "honest" interview or a "deceptive" interview. When they were being honest, the nurses who had just watched a pleasant nature film were asked to describe their true feelings. When they were being dishonest, they were asked to fake positive emotions even though they had just watched a gruesome film showing amputations and burns.

As Figure 9–17 shows, the true smiles were very different from the deceitful smiles. Smiles reflecting actual pleasure were characterized by muscular changes that pulled the lip corners upward, raising the cheek and gathering the skin around the eye. Fake smiles, by comparison, were evident by a downward turn of the lip corners and an elevated upper lip. So, it may be possible to unmask false friends by keeping your eye on their lips and eyes.

Ekman has recently labeled the spontaneous smile that reflects true enjoyment the **Duchenne smile**, in honor of the anatomist Duchenne de Boulogue, who in 1862 was the first to show that different muscle groups are involved in genuine smiles and other types of smiles. Using prisoners as subjects, Duchenne electrically stimulated various facial muscles in an attempt to reproduce joyful smiles. He found that a combination of muscle contractions distinguishes true smiles from all other smiles. Based on the distinctiveness of the Duchenne smile, Ekman and his colleagues have been able to uncover a great deal about the expression of human emotions. For instance, there is now evidence that when people force smiles, they actually feel bad about it. When they experience pleasant emotions, brain activity in the left hemisphere is increased. Negative emotions are more likely to produce right-side activation. As it turns out, true smiles are correlated with left hemisphere activity, and deceitful smiles are correlated with right hemisphere activity (Ekman, Davidson, & Friesen, 1990). So, when you sense you are being misled, you are not the only one who finds it distasteful—the deceiver apparently feels as bad about it as you do!

Continuing examination of selective emotional expressions such as the Duchenne smile will help us better understand how and why humans com-

FIGURE 9–17
Sincere smiles and fake smiles are not the same. (*Left*) The facial expression associated with a genuinely felt happy smile, the Duchenne smile. (*Right*) The facial expression associated with an attempted smile when the person actually is experiencing negative feelings. Notice the differences in facial appearances around the eyes and the corners of the mouth. (From Ekman, Friesen, & O'Sullivan, 1988.)

municate through emotional behavior. Scientists and nonscientists alike have long been aware of the complexity of human emotions, a newly discovered part of which is the issue of truth in reporting.

We should mention that the universalist view is not without opposition. The so-called **relativists** believe that emotional expressions are learned. They point, for example, to research showing that the same facial expression is seen as sad when it is presented alongside a happy face, but it is seen as happy alongside a sadder face (Russell & Fehr, 1987). Such evidence calls into question the notion of a predetermined facial pattern corresponding to a given emotion. Both relativists and universalists probably are correct in some aspects of their doctrine, and more research is needed.

relativists scientists who, unlike the universalists, believe that most human emotions are learned

Nonverbal Communication.   Related to the physiology of emotional expression is the topic of nonverbal communication. As with the case of people's eyes or other facial features telling us whether they are sincere, other bodily gestures communicate certain emotions and dispositions.

Each of us has a unique style for communicating our feelings with a particular stance, voice inflection, or other overt behavioral event that involves the body. Close friends can often "read" each other's moods by watching hand movement or posture (Poyatos, 1983). People may clasp their hands tensely when they are anxious, or slump in a chair when they are feeling a bit depressed over some setback that has occurred during the day. It pays to be attentive in such cases, because such bodily clues may tell you more about how people are really feeling than they would be willing to disclose verbally.

It is clear that cultural differences play a major role in communicating emotions through nonverbal behavior. Different cultures and ethnic groups have their own unique mannerisms and styles for expressing a particular emotional status. For example, in imperial China a man registered surprise by stroking his moustache. Obviously, this behavior is very different from what you would see in a Western culture.

A great deal of attention has been given recently to the expressive styles of blacks, particularly black males. Author Richard Majors's book *Cool Pose* (1992) addresses the idea that certain black males have adopted behavioral styles that are intended to communicate very specific attitudes or feelings. A particular walk may be designed to intimidate, or the distance maintained between two people may be a physical indicator of acceptance. A large amount of the research reported by Majors suggests that many posturing and movement styles among black males are motivated by perceptions of oppression. When you feel you are a victim of social indifference or discrimination, you use your body to tell a story—a story of emotional discontent. In any event, it is becoming increasingly evident that nonverbal styles vary across distinctive cultural, ethnic, and racial groups, and we can expect research activity in this area to increase over the next several years.

Emotions do seem to be tied to behavioral and physiological changes. As we shall see in the following sections on theories of emotion, not everyone is in agreement about exactly how this link is made.

Evolutionary Theory

In his classic book, *The Expression of the Emotions in Man and Animals* (1872/1965), Charles Darwin set forth his ideas on emotion. Darwin was little concerned with physiology or with the subjective experience of emotion. Instead, he focused on the expression of emotion, as the title of his book suggests. Consistent with his views on evolution, he saw emotions as having adaptive significance for humans and animals. Emotional expressions, such as facial expressions and various body postures, serve as important forms of communication (see Figure 9–18) not only about what is happening but about what can be expected to happen. As such, these expressions aid the prediction of behavior, a fact that enhances survival. Darwin did not deny that certain expressions in emotion are learned, but he did assert that most emotional expressions are innate. Further, he argued that the recognition of these expressions is conspecific, meaning that wolves could recognize emotional expressions in other wolves, but not in humans. Likewise, people could interpret emotional expressions in other people but not in other animal species. Still, Darwin also noticed similarities between humans and other animals in certain emotional expressions and used this observation to bolster his view of humans as being descendants of more primitive animal species.

More recent developments in evolutionary theory have proposed that emotions are innate responses to specific stimuli (Izard, 1977). Supported by Paul Ekman's research on facial expression, modern evolutionary theory argues that emotions trigger a fixed physiological pattern that defines such varied phenomena as enjoyment, distress, contempt, fear, shame, and a host of other moods.

FIGURE 9–18
Facial expressions of emotion in humans and other animals show many similarities.

James–Lange Theory

William James, in 1884, and Danish physiologist Carl Lange, in 1885, independently proposed a similar theory of emotion that has come to bear both their names. At the time these two men wrote, the common view of emotion was that the perception of a situation gave rise to a subjective feeling that was, in turn, followed by a series of bodily changes. James and Lange turned this view around in an interpretation that still seems illogical. They argued that the bodily changes result from the perception of the situation, and that recognition of the bodily changes subsequently produces the subjective feeling. In the traditional view a person would see a bear, become frightened, and run. The bodily changes would occur as a result of the fright caused by seeing the bear. In the **James–Lange theory**, however, a person sees the bear, runs, and experiences fright upon recognizing the bodily changes that have been occurring. Thus, for James and Lange, emotion was the sensing of bodily changes, and it occurred only when those changes were perceived (Figure 9–19). James felt the theory was well supported by those cases in which emotions were experienced but no situation could be specified as the precipitating event. In other words, emotion (for example, anxiety) was experienced because the person sensed bodily changes, even though those changes were not necessarily the result of some external cause.

James–Lange theory historical account of emotion that suggests that bodily changes cause subjective feelings to occur

Cannon's Thalamic Theory

Walter B. Cannon (whose work on hunger was discussed earlier in this chapter) was an American physiologist whose research tested some of the tenets of the James–Lange theory. His work led him to reject the views of James and to propose his **thalamic theory**. Cannon conducted a series of studies in which he surgically blocked inputs to the brain from the visceral organs (for example, stomach, spleen, liver) and from the sympathetic divi-

thalamic theory Cannon's idea that the thalamic region in the brain controls emotional expression by simultaneously changing bodily events, thoughts, and feelings

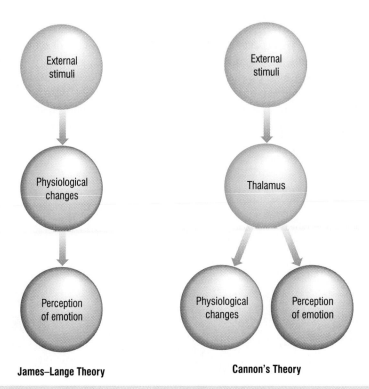

FIGURE 9–19
The determinants of emotion according to the contrasting theories of James–Lange and Cannon. The James–Lange theory proposes that emotions are produced by bodily (physiological) changes. Cannon's theory states that emotions and bodily changes are produced simultaneously by signals from the thalamus.

sion of the autonomic nervous system. He found that animals could produce emotional expressions such as fear, or pleasure in being stroked, in the absence of the physiological feedback to the brain. The James–Lange theory predicted the total elimination of emotion under the surgical conditions created by Cannon. Cannon's (1929) second criticism of James's theory was based on his finding that bodily changes in various emotions were very similar; James had argued for a separate pattern of bodily change for each different emotion. Further, Cannon showed that visceral events were often slow, and that subjects reported emotional experiences before the visceral changes could have been relayed to the brain.

These findings, plus other work, led Cannon to propose a theory of emotion that gave the thalamus a central role. In his view, the thalamus sent out impulses simultaneously to the cerebral cortex and to the visceral organs and skeletal muscles. Thus, the subjective awareness of the emotion and the bodily changes were said to occur together (see Figure 9–19). Part of the importance of Cannon's theory is that it began a long period of study in psychology that focused on the physiology of emotion. In the 1930s, J. W. Papez (1937) presented evidence that the hypothalamus is the brain region governing physiological arousal, and that the hippocampus regulates the subjective experience of emotion. Later work by Paul Maclean and others extended control centers to other limbic areas (amygdala, septum, and cingulate gyrus) and the cerebral cortex (Carlson, 1991).

Cognitive Theories

Although cognitive theories of emotion have existed for some time (see Ruckmick, 1936), there has been little interest in them until recently. One of the contemporary leaders in this camp is psychologist Stanley Schachter, who has proposed a **cognitive-physiological theory**. In Schachter's view three sources of information contribute to the experience of emotion. The first source is *bodily changes*; the brain receives input from the skeletal muscles and the visceral organs about various states of arousal. This input would be difficult to interpret without the second and third sources: *stimulus inputs* coming from the environment at any given moment, and information coming from *past experiences* in the form of memories of earlier, similar situations. According to Schachter, the person processes all three sources of information (physiological changes, current stimulus events, and memories) to arrive at the subjective emotional experience. In other words, the assignment of a label, such as *fear* or *sadness*, to the experience is a cognitive appraisal that makes sense of the physiological changes (see Figure 9–20).

cognitive-physiological theory idea proposed by Schachter that three events (bodily changes, current stimulus events, and memories) combine to determine emotional behavior

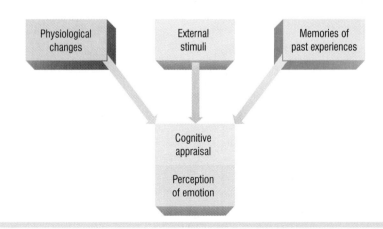

FIGURE 9–20
Schachter's cognitive-physiological theory of emotion holds that bodily changes, external stimulus input, and past experiences all impact on the process of labeling emotions.

Support for Schachter's theory comes from studies that used essentially the same experimental paradigm (Schachter & Singer, 1962). In these studies, subjects were injected with epinephrine (adrenalin), which produces physiological arousal that is manifested in a number of ways, including increases in heart rate and respiration. Some subjects were informed of what to expect from the injection, others were misinformed about its effects, some received no information, and some subjects were given a placebo injection of saline. Following the injection, a subject was placed with another subject who was, in actuality, a confederate of the experimenter. Sometimes the confederate acted angry, and at other times happy. Results showed that subjects in the uninformed and misinformed groups were more likely to interpret the arousal they experienced in light of the behavior of the confederate. In other words, when a confederate acted angry, the subject was likely to interpret physiological arousal as anger. These results are interesting because they show the importance of cognitive appraisal in situations where the felt bodily changes are ambiguous.

Although a number of psychologists are willing to grant cognitive factors a role in emotion, they are not willing to assign it the primary role that Schachter suggests. This reluctance is partly due to the fact that Schachter's placebo groups also reported emotional experiences consistent with the confederate's behavior in the absence of any physiological arousal. Some researchers have argued that the emotion felt by Schachter's subjects was because the subjects modeled the expressive behavior of the confederates, which, in turn, initiated neural feedback that triggered the emotional experience (Izard, 1971). To further confuse the issue, some studies have been unable to replicate the findings of the original Schachter studies (Marshall, 1976; Rogers & Deckner, 1975). A later review of 20 years of research on Schachter's theory suggests that it should be altered to minimize the role of peripheral arousal in the determination of emotion (Reisenzein, 1983). Despite these problems, however, most psychologists accept the notion that cognitive appraisal plays some role in emotional experiences.

SOME SPECIFIC EMOTIONS

Regardless of the theoretical scheme (see the summary in Table 9–2 on page 368) that is used in determining the origins of emotions, the distinctiveness of different emotions cannot be dismissed. Certain emotions such as fear and love have a character all their own. In the following sections, we present a brief review of what we know about these familiar affective states.

Fear and Anxiety

Carroll Izard (1979) has called *fear* the most dangerous of all emotional conditions, noting that a number of people in various cultures have literally been frightened to death. Fear ranges in intensity from mild to very intense. Intense fears that are also viewed as irrational—such as an intense fear of the dark—are labeled phobias; these are discussed in Chapters 16 and 17. *Anxiety* is an emotion very similar to fear. Many psychologists differentiate fear and anxiety in terms of the source of the unpleasantness. If the source can be specified, they call it fear. When a person feels frightened, uneasy, and apprehensive, yet is unable to say why, these psychologists usually label the person's emotion anxiety. We will not make much of that distinction here and will treat the two terms as the same.

Are humans born with fears? Psychologists think most fears are learned, with two possible exceptions: the fear of loud noises and the fear of falling.

TABLE 9-2
Theories of Emotion

Theory	Description	Evaluation
Evolutionary Theory	Emotions have adaptive significance and are treated as innate responses to specific stimuli.	Although some research points to the unlearned nature of emotion, at the human level learned (cultural) variables also play a role.
James–Lange Theory	Emotions arise out of bodily changes; e.g., when people see a bear, they run, and as they perceive that they are running from danger, they experience fright.	Because animals experience emotions such as fear and pleasure in the absence of physiological (bodily) feedback, emotions would appear to involve something more than just a set pattern of bodily changes.
Cannon's Thalamic Theory	The thalamus simultaneously signals the cerebral cortex, visceral organs, and skeletal muscles when emotional events are presented.	Although the thalamus is one brain region important to the expression of emotions, other brain areas such as the hippocampus, amygdala, and cortex also are involved.
Cognitive Theories	Physiological changes, current stimulus events, and memories are sources of information that are all processed before a subjective determination is used in labeling the emotion.	Cognitive appraisal is important and plays some role in emotional experiences, but it may not be a primary determinant of emotional behavior.

stranger anxiety fear of unfamiliar people in infants; usually develops after about 6 months of age

Newborn babies cry and show facial expressions and body postures characteristic of fear when exposed to those conditions. Research has shown that other fears begin to develop within the first year of life, toward the latter half of that year. For example, infants react to strangers by crying, but usually not until after the age of 6 months. This fear is often labeled **stranger anxiety** and develops in most, but not all, infants. As people grow older they fear different things. Fear of the dark and fear of animals typically are not seen in infants but do occur after about age 3. Fear of death is not common until around the age of 8, presumably when a child's conceptual abilities have reached a level that allows the child to understand the finality of death. Interestingly, children do not usually fear their own death; rather, they begin to worry about the death of their parents. Fear of imaginary creatures and imagined situations begins at about age 4 and continues to increase with age in conjunction with an increase in cognitive skills. A child may be less fearful than an adult in some situations because the adult is able to imagine more of the dangers inherent in the situation (Bowlby, 1973).

Although fear is an unpleasant emotion, it does play a positive role in behavior. Fear of failing in your psychology course might motivate you to study and thus enhance your performance. Fear of losing your job might prevent you from making disparaging remarks about your boss's ancestry. Fear can keep certain behaviors under control and can initiate the performance of desirable behaviors, including those that might enhance the probability of one's survival.

Love

> "By what do men live?" It was even awkward to answer out loud. Indecent somehow. "By love."

Thus did Yefrem Padduyev, a character in Aleksandr Solzhenitsyn's novel *The Cancer Ward* state simply and concisely the guiding force in his life. Love, although difficult to define, is perhaps the most powerful of all human emotions.

Part of the difficulty in defining love stems from the disagreement over how many types there are. Kemper (1978) says there are many distinct kinds of love, including romantic love, parent-infant love, brotherly love, and adulation by fans. Thus, it is possible for you to love your boyfriend or girlfriend, your father, your sister, and a famous actor, presumably loving each person in a different way.

Ellen Berscheid and Elaine Walster (1974) have distinguished two types of love: **romantic love** and **mature love**. The more exciting version is romantic love, which tends to have high physical arousal levels, high fantasy levels, and often a touch of jealousy. Romantic love tends not to last; as it fades, either the relationship ends or the love changes to mature love. Mature love is much less arousing; however, it is characterized by a strong communicative relationship of openness, is high in caring and intimacy, and typically endures.

We have discussed how important physiological arousal appears to be in most emotions, and we have noted the importance of arousal in love as well, particularly in romantic love. Schachter and Singer mentioned this relationship in a 1962 article in which they first proposed the cognitive theory discussed earlier. These investigators speculated that if a man experienced arousal (brought about, for example, by an injection of epinephrine) in the presence of a woman, he might interpret the arousal as love. Richard Dienstbier (1979), a psychologist at the University of Nebraska, tested this notion. Some of his male and female college student subjects were seated in a dental chair (which has unpleasant associations) and blindfolded. After the chair was rotated a number of times, it was suddenly tilted backward. Simultaneously, there was a loud crashing noise in the room. Following this procedure of arousal induction, subjects were asked (among other things) to rate the experimenter's attractiveness. When the experimenters were of the opposite sex, aroused subjects rated them significantly more attractive than did control subjects who had not been aroused. The subjects may have attributed their arousal to sexual arousal or maybe even love, either of which would have contributed to their higher attractiveness ratings for the opposite-sex experimenters.

Another theory of love has been proposed by Yale University's Robert Sternberg (1986), labeled the **triangular theory of love**. According to Sternberg, love consists of three components:

1. *Intimacy*, the feeling of closeness and bondedness
2. *Passion*, the drives that produce romance, physical attraction, and sexual intercourse
3. *Decision/commitment*, the decision that one loves another and the commitment to continue that relationship.

The amount of love that a person experiences is due to the strength of each of those three components. But the nature of the love is more complicated and depends on the interactive qualities of the components. Passion plays an

Romantic love.

romantic love love characterized by high physical arousal, fantasy, and occasional jealousy

mature love less arousing than romantic love, but more enduring

triangular theory of love Sternberg's theory, which states that love consists of intimacy, passion, and decision/commitment

important role in the beginning stages of some love relationships but may play less of a role as the relationship endures. That notion is similar to the distinction of romantic and mature love. But passion is not a component in some love relationships, such as love of one's children. Intimacy, on the other hand, seems important in almost all love relationships.

Sternberg has also distinguished between *liking* and *loving*. Although each is considered part of a larger interrelated complex, factors controlling each emotion often vary. For instance, in liking relationships people seek a steady diet of reinforcement (approval), but in a passionate love relationship reinforcement is intermittent (Sternberg, 1987). In the latter case, a long-term advantage is gained because of the increased resistance to extinction that goes with intermittent reinforcement experiences (see Chapter 6). Perhaps this contributes to the enduring nature of love. Anyway, insofar as such research brings us closer to understanding the complexities of love relationships, it is of profound significance.

THINKING AHEAD . . .

To be sure, the study of motivation and emotion is one of the oldest forms of psychological inquiry that has ever been initiated. Throughout time, women and men have been sensitive to events that determine why they behave and how they feel. From Eros to computer-dating services, we have attempted to decipher, reorder, and improve our understanding of the human condition. In addition to seeking, we find that experiencing defines a quality of existence that elevates life. Through motivation and emotion, we express the manifold tones of human behavior.

The complexity of motivational (wanting) and emotional (feeling) phenomena is apparent from our coverage here. Biological and environmental variables converge and dictate eating patterns, interactive styles, affiliations, and decision making. Virtually everything we do and feel is determined by unique patterns of desire that characterize our individuality. It makes one wonder about how we came to our particular berth, and it raises the even more mystical issue of where we are going from here. What changes are in store for us regarding our ability to alter human behavior by altering selective incentives? Is it possible that we may come to regulate emotional behavior so precisely that it becomes predictable, and therein limits spontaneity? Would you care to live in such a world?

One thing is certain. As with all aspects of behavior, motivational and emotional components will continue to evolve and change commensurate with the demands imposed on us as a species. Nothing remains the same forever, and no doubt the purpose and degree of pleasure in our lives will undergo review and continual redefinition.

Summary

Motivation: Definition and Theory

1. Motivation pertains to why behavior occurs. Two important features of motivation are that it energizes and directs behavior.
2. Ethology, sociobiology, and behavioral ecology are three biologically based accounts of motivation that argue that behavior is caused by innate forces.
3. Hull's drive-reduction model, cognitive consistency theory, and arousal theories all presume that behavior is pushed, whereas incentive theory states that behavior is pulled. Incentives may be either intrinsic or extrinsic, and shifting from one to the other may have a detrimental effect on performance.
4. Maslow has presented a theory of self-actualization, which arranges motives in a hierarchy, beginning with the most basic physiological needs and extending to the supreme need to be all that one can be (self-actualization). Problems for this model are associated with higher-level needs prevailing over those considered basic.

Hunger

5. At one time, hunger was believed to be regulated exclusively by brain mechanisms. The lateral hypothalamic area was identified as the hunger center, and the ventromedial nucleus of the hypothalamus was considered to be the satiety center. In addition to the research on short-term and long-term cues, recent research has indicated that hunger is controlled by a variety of mechanisms that include the endocrine system and a certain set point of fat.
6. Obesity is a hunger-related disorder that involves continued food ingestion beyond the point where a nutritional deficit exists. Obesity has been found to be influenced by a variety of bodily and environmental factors. Although dieting may make some sense in certain cases, it can also create major health problems. Anorexia nervosa and bulimia nervosa are two eating disorders that have serious negative side effects.

Sex

7. Sexuality is a complex motivational system including brain, hormonal, and environmental controls.

Aggression

8. Aggression is defined as the act of delivering an aversive stimulus to an unwilling victim. Hostile aggression is aggression that is triggered by discomfort and frustration. Instrumental aggression is intended to produce some benefit.

Achievement

9. Children as well as adults vary in terms of their need to be successful. The most recent evidence indicates that both need achievement and fear of failure affect goal-directed activity. Perhaps the most consistent finding is that persons high in need achievement will choose tasks of moderate difficulty when given the opportunity to select from a task-difficulty menu.

Affiliation

10. As a rule, people like to be around other people. That is, there is a need for affiliation in most of us. The tendency to affiliate among humans is likely due to conditioning.

Motives in Conflict

11. When motives conflict, stress and indecision can result. Four types of conflict have been postulated: approach–approach, avoidance–avoidance, approach–avoidance, and multiple approach–avoidance.

Emotion: Definition and Theory

12. Emotion is a special state, often an intense experience, that consists of a subjective awareness of an emotion, physiological changes, and behavioral changes.
13. Facial expressions are the principal means by which we observe emotions in others. Some facial expressions appear to be the result of biological programming and are thus universal. Every culture has a set of implicit guidelines about the expression of emotion. These display rules serve to modify facial expressions.
14. Nonverbal communication is also linked to emotional expression. Different cultures communicate emotions differently with particular poses and movement styles.
15. Theories of emotion include evolutionary theory, which states that emotional expression has adaptive significance; the James–Lange theory, which says that emotions occur in response to bodily changes; and Cannon's physiological model of emotion. Also, cognitive theories of emotion, which emphasize perceptual processes in emotional behavior, were discussed.

Some Specific Emotions

16. Fear is an unpleasant emotion that can nonetheless serve an important positive role in human behavior. Love is one of the most important of the pleasant emotions. Researchers agree that there are different kinds of love, such as romantic love and mature love.

Key Terms

motivation (334)
ethologists (334)
instinct (334)
fixed action patterns (FAPs) (334)
modal action patterns (MAPs) (335)
sign stimulus (335)
vacuum behavior (335)
behavioral ecology (336)
sociobiology (336)
drive-reduction model (337)
cognitive consistency theory (338)
cognitive dissonance theory (338)
arousal theories (338)
Yerkes–Dodson law (339)

incentive theory (339)
overjustification effect (341)
self-actualization (343)
lateral hypothalamic area (345)
ventromedial nucleus of the hypothalamus (VMH) (345)
insulin (345)
glucagon (345)
glucoreceptors (346)
short-term cues (346)
long-term cues (346)
set point (346)
anorexia nervosa (350)
bulimia nervosa (350)
gonadotropic hormone (351)

follicle stimulating hormone (FSH) (351)
luteinizing hormone (LH) (352)
estrus (352)
hostile aggression (354)
instrumental aggression (355)
need achievement (356)
approach–approach conflict (358)
avoidance–avoidance conflict (359)
approach–avoidance conflict (359)
multiple approach–avoidance conflict (360)

fight or flight syndrome (360)
universalists (361)
facial affect program (361)
prosodic features (361)
display rules (362)
Duchenne smile (362)
relativists (363)
James–Lange theory (365)
thalamic theory (365)
cognitive-physiological theory (366)
stranger anxiety (368)
romantic love (369)
mature love (369)
triangular theory of love (369)

Suggested Reading

Ekman, P., & Friesen, W. V. (1975). *Unmasking the face.* Englewood Cliffs, NJ: Prentice-Hall. A paperback manual on how to recognize emotion in facial expressions. The research on which this facial recognition program is based is described in a more research-oriented book by Paul Ekman, *Emotion in the human face* (2nd ed.). New York: Cambridge University Press, 1982.

Golding, W. (1954). *Lord of the flies.* New York: Putnam. An extremely successful novel that deals with innate tendencies toward human aggression. Due to an accident, children are isolated, with no adult supervision, and the result is a reversion to a primitive state of unbridled hostility.

Majors, R. (1992). *Cool pose.* New York: Maxwell Macmillan. This insightful account of the social and behavioral dilemmas that black males face in America offers an excellent entry into multicultural study of motivational and emotional phenomena.

Morris, D. (1967). *The naked ape.* New York: McGraw-Hill. In this ethologist's perspective on the nature of human behavior, numerous parallels are drawn between selected human acts and corresponding animal analogs.

CHAPTER 10
Personality

Stereotypes abound about the volatile or otherwise unusual personalities of artists. One artist who seems to have lived up to the reputation of the artistic personality was Vincent Van Gogh, the enigmatic nineteenth-century Dutch painter. The son of a minister, Vincent studied theology and worked as a lay missionary in a coal-mining district in Belgium before committing himself to art.

In February of 1888, Vincent moved to Arles, a small city in the south of France, where he produced some of his most famous paintings. Eight months later, the painter Paul Gauguin joined him in the little yellow house where he lived in Arles. The two artists apparently had a stormy relationship over the next few months, quarreling and bickering as they drank and painted together. In December, one of their quarrels escalated, and Van Gogh threatened Gauguin with a razor. Nothing much came of the incident. But the next day, Van Gogh carried out the act that is probably the single most salient piece of information about him: He cut off a part of his left ear and delivered it, wrapped in canvas and paper, to a prostitute in town.

Perhaps the bizarreness of this act explains why so many people are fascinated with Van Gogh and his work. We wonder why anybody would do such a thing. Luckily for psychobiographers, Van Gogh left a treasure trove of letters that give some insight into the artist's personality. They were written mostly to his brother Theo, on whom Van Gogh was dependent for both emo-

◀ Why do people act as they do? Personality includes an individual's characteristic ways of thinking and behaving in a variety of situations.

tional and financial support throughout his life. These letters have been edited and collected in a book entitled *Dear Theo*. In his first letter to Theo after the incident, Van Gogh seemed to believe that he had just "freaked out":

> I hope I have had simply an artist's freak, and then a lot of fever after very considerable loss of blood, as an artery was severed; my appetite came back at once, my digestion is all right, and my blood revives from day to day, so that from day to day serenity returns to my brain. I think I shall yet see calmer days here than in the year that is gone.

The serenity that he wished for eluded him, however. He spent time in St. Paul's Asylum in Saint-Rémy, where he continued to paint. One of his most vivid canvases, "Starry Night," the inspiration for Don McLean's popular song of the 1970s, dates from the St. Rémy period. Two years and seven months after the ear incident, Vincent shot himself in the stomach and died.

personologists psychologists who study personality

Within the field of psychology, the study of personality is perhaps the closest topic to the study of human nature. Why do people act as they do? **Personologists**, the label given to people who study personality, attempt to understand a person in totality. However, they must also grapple with isolated pieces of behavior, particularly those that are highly salient. Thus, personologists have had some interesting things to say about Van Gogh's personality and how it relates to his self-mutilation. But we are getting ahead of the story. First we must deal with the scientific meanings attached to the term *personality*.

THE MEANING OF PERSONALITY

personality organization of an individual's characteristics, attitudes, and habits

Personality is a fascinating area of study, but a difficult concept to define. In this chapter we define **personality** as the organization of an individual's distinguishing characteristics, attitudes, or habits; it includes the individual's unique ways of thinking, behaving, or otherwise experiencing the environment. The qualities that make up one's personality are relatively stable and organized into a totality.

With this definition of personality in mind, we can identify four separate tasks that personality psychologists have addressed (Runyan, 1988):

1. *To analyze individual and group differences.* Why are people different from each other? Are members of some groups more similar to each other than other groups? For example, are there personality dimensions that influence the way we experience life events such as the midlife transition?
2. *To understand particular individuals.* This is the task we are faced with when we consider Vincent Van Gogh. In fact, students tell us that this is a major reason that they take introductory psychology. They want to find out what makes people—themselves and others— do the things they do.
3. *To study selected personality processes.* There are many personality processes, including such things as altruism and sex-role differences. For example, are masculinity and femininity dimensions of personality that influence behavior in predictable ways?
4. *To develop general theories of personality.* Theories of personality are unified explanations for the totality of individual behavior. A large part of this chapter is devoted to general theories of personality.

Research Methods in Personality

Psychologists have approached the study of personality using a wide variety of research methods (see Table 10–1). Knowledge about people's personalities can be obtained from their everyday conduct, as is the case in *field studies*. People also reveal themselves through the products of their imaginations, and this technique is used when people take personality tests known as *projective tests* (described in Chapter 11). A straightforward approach to gathering personality data is to ask people to fill out *self-report inventories* about their characteristics. With this method, two risks are apparent: People may not be fully aware of what they are like; and if they are, they may wish to cover up some of the flaws they perceive. We gain information of a different sort about personality when we ask others for their impressions of specific people. This technique is known as the use of *observer reports* in research. *Psychobiography* relies primarily on verbal material, through interviews or other primary source material (Henwood & Pidgeon, 1992). Examples include life histories such as those in biographies and autobiographies, and archival material, such as Van Gogh's letters. Clinical case histories, on which many of the major theories are based, also fall into this category. The most carefully controlled information comes from behavior in *laboratory studies* of personality. Although control is maximized in laboratory studies, it is sometimes at the expense of naturalistic experiences.

No single source of information about personality is the ideal, correct source. All these methods are important for obtaining information about personality. Published research on personality, however, relies heavily on self-report inventories and laboratory studies with limited samples of people. Between 1980 and 1983, 85% of the research published in major journals used these two methods, and approximately two thirds of the research used undergraduate samples (Craik, 1986). However, there has been a trend in recent years toward greater use of biographical material in the study of personality (Alexander, 1988; McAdams, 1988).

Traits Versus Situations.   A long-standing debate in the psychology of personality centers on the issue of *consistency*. Was Van Gogh, for instance, always argumentative and histrionic, or did the particular situation he was in—living closely with another painter, being dependent on his brother— lead to a buildup of tension, and ultimately his outburst? In short, the debate

---

TABLE 10-1
Research Approaches in the Study of Personality

Type of Approach	Description
Field Studies	Observation of everyday conduct in natural settings.
Projective Tests	Products of the imagination elicited by having a person tell stories about ambiguous pictures or inkblots.
Self-Report Inventories	Person fills out questionnaires or inventories about him- or herself.
Observer Reports	Other people fill out questionnaires or inventories about a person.
Psychobiography	Life history material from biography, autobiography, archival material, and clinical case histories.
Laboratory Studies	Study of behavior in carefully controlled standard situations (experiments).

is about the consistency of traits across situations. Most people expect behavior to be relatively consistent from one situation to the next, and that assumption is at the heart of many theories of personality that are discussed in this chapter. This assumption reappears when we discuss personality disorders in Chapter 16. However, many researchers claim that there is very little trait consistency (Loevinger & Knoll, 1983; Mischel & Peake, 1982).

Much of the current research in personality is aimed at resolving the general controversies within personality psychology, such as the issue of traits versus situations (Pervin, 1985). Personality researchers have devoted a considerable amount of energy to the issue of consistency in human behavior. Personality theorists and researchers are particularly interested in what produces and maintains consistency in human behavior and what techniques can be used to alter the personality if there is a need to do so (Duke, 1986).

When traits are measured by personality tests of the type to be discussed in Chapter 11 and behavior is also observed, there is not always a strong correspondence between the behavior and the traits. For example, research indicates that friendliness varies a great deal from one situation to another (Mischel & Peake, 1982). Studies of this sort have led some psychologists to conclude that situations are more important in determining behavior than are personality traits. But it is also clear that powerful individual differences emerge among people who are in the same situation (Rorer & Widiger, 1983). Some students who live on the same hall in a dormitory are loud and aggressive; others are quiet and meek. Some are demanding; others are tolerant.

People so commonly assume that there are consistent traits from one situation to another that research suggesting otherwise comes as a surprise. Psychologists have looked for reasons for the inconsistent data, perhaps because psychologists, like most humans, tend to seek order in the universe. As we discuss in Chapter 14, people have a strong tendency to explain other people's behavior in terms of stable traits (Jones, 1979). The English language seems to reflect this bias; there are about 18,000 words in the English language for traits (Bem & Allen, 1974).

Do our language and our tendency to look for traits reflect or distort reality? There is no definite answer to this question, but there is some suggestive evidence. One study investigated the traits of friendliness and conscientiousness among college students. For example, students were asked, "In general, how friendly and outgoing are you?" and "How much do you vary from one situation to another in how friendly and outgoing you are?" Some of the students thought they were more consistent than others, as one might expect. For students who said they were very consistent in friendliness from one situation to another, there was a high degree of agreement among their own reports, their parents' and friends' reports, and their actual behavior (Bem & Allen, 1974). This finding was essentially replicated in the 1980s (Woodruffe, 1985).

Most psychologists now recognize that both traits and situations are important in determining behavior. Neither traits alone nor situational factors alone can account for the richness and complexity of human personality. Is Sean Penn by nature a bullying and aggressive person, or was this behavior elicited by tabloid photographers who followed him around when he was married to Madonna? Is Madonna a promiscuous, publicity-craving individual, or is that a persona that she carefully cultivates as a public image, one that bears little resemblance to her as a real person? The safe bet would be that traits and situations interact to produce the behavior we call personality. We will return to this issue later in the chapter.

Factor Analysis. The Greek physician Galen (A.D. 130–200) may be credited with initiating research and theory on personality types (Stelmack & Stalikas, 1991). Galen speculated that the relative mixture of four bodily

How much of the behavior of pop culture icons Sean Penn and Madonna is a reflection of enduring personality traits, and how much is it situationally determined? Could some of their public behavior be designed to create a persona that would ensure further publicity?

humors—blood, black bile, yellow bile, and phlegm—contributed to a person's temperament. Thus, a person with an overabundance of phlegm would be *phlegmatic*, that is, cool and calm or even tending toward the sluggish. A person with an overabundance of black bile would be *melancholic*, that is, gloomy, irritable, or depressed. Within contemporary psychology, the search continues for the smallest number of personality types that can accurately describe the full range of personalities.

The search for personality types, or factors, often relies on a statistical technique known as **factor analysis**. The logic of factor analysis is to take a large number of terms or items that appear to describe personality and reduce them to a much smaller number of overlapping traits. In practice, personality questionnaires in which people answer a long series of questions about themselves or others are intercorrelated. Thus, each question is correlated with all other questions in the set. Ultimately, a complicated statistical routine identifies clusters of questions that seem to go together. These clusters become the personality factors, or types.

Unfortunately, there is not a great deal of consensus among contemporary psychologists about how many personality factors there are, or indeed if there are any "true" personality types that transcend situations. The factors generated by the statistical routines depend on the original set of items on the personality questionnaires, among other things. However, many studies have produced five personality factors (Digman, 1990; Eysenck, 1991; Goldberg, 1990; Costa & McCrae, 1991). These five personality factors are extraversion, agreeableness, conscientiousness, emotional stability, and intellect (Goldberg, 1990). They are defined in Table 10–2.

Nomothetic Versus Idiographic Approaches.   In addition to the issue of traits and situations, personality research has also focused on the universality of traits. Most of this research has looked at personality traits that are assumed to apply universally, so that each person could theoretically be assessed in terms of the degree to which he or she possesses each trait. By this reasoning, everyone could be described in terms of the extent to which he or she exhibited extraversion, agreeableness, conscientiousness, and so on. This approach is called the **nomothetic approach**, referring to universal norms for a group.

nomothetic approach research method that uses group norms that are assumed to apply universally to study personality

On the other hand, some traits might be irrelevant to particular people, so that a nomothetic approach would be meaningless. Perhaps, for example, there are some personality variables, such as the tendency to monitor one's own behavior, that are not distributed throughout the population, but apply only to some people (Gangestad & Snyder, 1985). What is needed in this view is a more individualistic understanding of the personalities of particu-

---

TABLE 10-2
Five Personality Factors

Extraversion—interest is directed to other persons rather than to oneself.
Agreeableness—willingness to consent; helpfulness.
Conscientiousness—showing care and precision, and doing what one thinks is right.
Emotional stability—being relatively free of anxieties and other mood variations.
Intellect—ability to reason, understand, and perceive relationships among variables.

Sources: From Norman, 1963; Goldberg, 1990.

idiographic approach research method that uses idiosyncratic descriptions of individuals, without group norms, to study personality

Personality theorists now look for ways to combine nomothetic and idiographic approaches to personality. In some ways Luciano Pavarotti and Bruce Springsteen are alike, in other ways very different. Both have active musical careers, and both have Italian working-class origins.

theory organized set of principles that describe or explain a phenomenon

lar people—here we need an **idiographic approach**. This person-centered approach assumes that individuals are unique case histories (Allport, 1961).

Although we frequently acknowledge the idea that each person is unique, we also assume that psychological affinities exist between people. A social science that addressed only uniqueness and had nothing to say about general human tendencies would be of little use. Recent attempts to bridge the nomothetic and idiographic approaches to personality have emphasized the contributions of both (Silverstein, 1988). For example, we may speak of general human growth tendencies, developmental tasks, and personality factors that all humans exhibit to one degree or another. But we must also acknowledge the uniqueness of human experience. In what ways, for example are Luciano Pavarotti and Bruce Springsteen psychologically similar and in what ways unique? They are both singers, of course, one operatic and the other rock and roll. On his mother's side, Springsteen is of Italian descent, and Pavarotti was born in Italy. Both men come from working-class backgrounds. Yet each is also unique. Good biographies would reveal psychological portraits for each man that differed from those of all other human beings in some important respects.

Cross-Cultural Personality Research. The issue of nomothetic versus idiographic approaches to personality leads naturally to a discussion of cross-cultural research. If personality is truly nomothetic, one would expect that similar personality factors or types would appear in all cultures. After all, the particular experiences of a given culture—although they might influence individual differences in personality—should still be captured by a finite set of personality types.

In a recent study of personality structure across different cultures, using two different assessment techniques, the five personality factors listed in Table 10–2 were found for each of the cultures (Paunonen, Jackson, Trzebinski, & Forsterling, 1992). The four countries studied were Canada, Finland, Poland, and Germany. Although all of these cultures have a European tradition, they differ in customs, in their degree of development, in their economic system, as well as in their language. The fact that the five-factor model works for all of them supports the nomothetic point of view.

In another cross-cultural study, people in four countries were asked to recall an emotional experience that they had had, and to remember it as vividly as possible. Then they were asked to rate the experience on different dimensions. People in these four countries—the United States, Japan, Hong Kong, and the People's Republic of China—were very similar in their subjective experiences of emotion (Mauro, Sato, & Tucker, 1992). Again, this cross-cultural similarity supports the notion of universality in personality and emotional states.

Personality Theories in Psychology

A **theory** is an organized and systematic set of principles that describe or explain a phenomenon. Why are there so many theories? Would it not be preferable to have just one comprehensive theory of personality? Although there may be considerable evidence in support of a theory, in personality the principles involved have not been shown to occur with unvarying uniformity under the same conditions. If that were the case, the theory would be upgraded to the status of a law. There are no laws in personality psychology, and it is therefore useful to have a number of competing theories that can be compared and contrasted.

In general terms, we may distinguish three broad uses of personality theories. One use is embodied in the definition of the term *theory*. A theory should be useful in describing or explaining aspects of human personality. The second use is also very important; a theory should guide research in the area. A theory provides a set of principles from which hypotheses about human personality can be generated. The hypotheses, in turn, can be subjected to empirical test. The third use involves practical application. For example, a theory of personality provides a set of principles that may be used in clinical practice with individuals who may have psychological problems that can be traced to elements of their personalities.

As we explain in Chapter 17, personality theories have been particularly useful in clinical treatment settings. Indeed, many of the theories we examine in this chapter were derived from clinical practice, including the theories of Freud, Jung, and Rogers. There is a considerable amount of research on the various theories of personality covered in this chapter, but much of it is murky and flawed by methodological problems. Many of the theoretical principles are difficult to test empirically. It is exceedingly difficult, for example, to design a test for Freudian defense mechanisms or Rogerian unconditional positive regard.

Although many models of personality have generated empirical research, that has not been their greatest strength. Many followers of these theories have preferred clinical applications rather than empirical research. They believe that if a theory works to explain a particular quirk of personality and thereby helps to alleviate a symptom, its usefulness has been demonstrated even in the absence of empirical support. In this view, the description and explanation functions of theory are of greater importance.

In this chapter we review four broad categories of personality theories. In essence, each theory approaches the same information—the seemingly stable behavior patterns of individuals—and attempts to make sense out of it. To do so requires descriptions of relevant behavior, explanations for how such behavior came about, and predictions for future behavior.

Because different theorists have looked for very different aspects of personality, they have arrived at conclusions about personality that are very different. Viewpoints differ in part because of divergent views about human nature. As you will see, some psychologists believe that people are motivated primarily by sexual instincts, whereas others believe that people have higher motives, including motives to become self-actualized or to realize their full human potential, as discussed in Chapter 9. Having a number of different theories in personality psychology poses certain problems for evaluating competing alternative explanations for complex human behavior. How can one evaluate alternative explanations to find the one that is correct, or most nearly correct? Let us explore the issue of alternative explanations by examining a case study.

Van Gogh as a Case Study.   Consider the case that opened this chapter, that of Vincent Van Gogh (1853–1890), the troubled Dutch painter who created his most famous works in the south of France. The ear incident in Van Gogh's life has attracted a great deal of attention from personality theorists, resulting in a number of alternative explanations from a psychological point of view.

One explanation, for example, focuses on frustrating events in Van Gogh's life at the time, especially his inability to establish a living and working relationship with Gauguin and the recent engagement of Van Gogh's brother, Theo. (Van Gogh usually spent Christmas with Theo, but that year Theo planned to spend the holidays with his fiancée and her family.) These frustrating circumstances may have aroused aggressive impulses, first directed toward Gauguin, and then turned inward (Lubin, 1972). A competing explanation is that Van Gogh and Gauguin had both visited the prosti-

A self-portrait of Vincent Van Gogh entitled *Self-Portrait with Bandaged Ear*. There are many competing explanations of why Van Gogh cut off his ear and gave it to a prostitute. Such complex behavior poses a challenge for personality theories.

tute Rachel, and that she had teased Van Gogh about having oversized ears. In retaliation for this teasing, he sent her his ear as a ghoulish Christmas present (Lubin, 1972). Yet another explanation has a biological flavor. Van Gogh was a heavy drinker, and was particularly partial to absinthe, a bitter liqueur made from wormwood oil and anise that is now illegal in most countries. Anise contains the toxic chemical thujone, in the terpene class of chemicals. Having developed a taste for thujone, Van Gogh may even have begun eating some of his paints (Arnold, 1988). This point of view was suggested by the 1990 film about Van Gogh, "Vincent and Theo." Table 10–3 lists four additional interpretations of the event.

It is difficult to know how to make sense of so many interpretations of a single event. In the field of personality psychology, where each of several competing theories presents a particular view of human nature, the problem is compounded further by the variety and complexity of the behavior being considered. However, theories and explanations of complex behavior such as Van Gogh's can be evaluated according to certain criteria. These criteria include the theory's *explanatory power* in accounting for a number of different behaviors, and its *consistency* with all the relevant evidence and with

TABLE 10-3
Van Gogh's Self-Mutilation: Some Possible Explanations

1. One interpretation of the incident holds that Van Gogh, in a deranged state, was mimicking the bullfights he had seen in Arles, where the matador cut off the bull's ear and presented it, as an award, to a lady of his choice. According to this interpretation, Van Gogh simultaneously played the roles of defeated bull and victorious matador, and presented his own ear to the lady.

2. Just before Van Gogh's self-mutilation, the local newspaper had carried a number of articles about Jack the Ripper, a sexual sadist who mutilated prostitutes' bodies, sometimes cutting off their ears. Highly publicized crimes are sometimes emulated, and Van Gogh, in his own bizarre way, may have been such a copycat. But instead of mutilating another person, he turned on himself in a reversal of the role played by Jack the Ripper; Van Gogh presented the evidence of mutilation to a prostitute.

3. Another explanation centers around Oedipal themes, as dealt with in Freud's theory. Van Gogh, according to this view, may have wanted to attack Gauguin because in his mind Gauguin represented Van Gogh's hated father. But because Van Gogh also identified with his father, his self-mutilation simultaneously did violence to his father and punished himself for the act. Giving the remnant to the prostitute may have been a symbolic gift to his mother.

4. Finally, Van Gogh may have had auditory hallucinations during a psychotic episode and may have cut off the ear in an attempt to stop the frightening sounds. Later, when he was in the sanatorium, he mentioned hearing strange sounds and voices.

Source: Adapted from Lubin, 1972; Runyan, 1981.

what is known about human nature and behavior. We should also add *parsimony*, an insistence that the explanation or theory be stated as simply and economically as possible. When evaluated against these criteria, the competing hypotheses about Van Gogh's self-mutilation take on a new significance. One cannot simply select the information that fits a particular viewpoint; one must also examine the explanations critically, comparing one with another.

The explanation that Van Gogh cut off his ear in response to Rachel's teasing, for example, appears on critical analysis to be highly unlikely. No such report of teasing is presented in Van Gogh's letters or his extensive biographies or in Gauguin's own memoirs (Runyan, 1981). This explanation is not supported by known facts about Van Gogh's life. However, it is known that Van Gogh's mental breakdowns coincided with events in his relationship to his brother, Theo. The ear mutilation coincided with Theo's engagement, and two later breakdowns coincided with Theo's marriage and with the birth of his first child. Furthermore, it is clear from the record that Van Gogh was dependent on Theo for emotional and financial support, and the perceived loss of this support may have been a threat to his sanity (Runyan, 1981). There is also evidence that Van Gogh responded bizarrely to threats of loss of love. He once visited the parents of a woman he loved, and, putting his hand in the flame of a lamp, said, "Let me see her for as long as I can keep my hand in the flame."

In fact, it is likely that most complex human behaviors have more than one cause and more than one meaning, a concept referred to in Freudian theory as *overdetermination*. Furthermore, the people most intimately involved in any behavior—Van Gogh, in this case—may not be aware of all the causes. Personality theory thus has a very challenging task in trying to provide a comprehensive account of human emotion and its attendant behavior.

PSYCHOANALYTIC MODELS
OF PERSONALITY

psychoanalytic models theories of personality that locate the cause of behavior in unconscious motives

According to **psychoanalytic models** of personality, people are born with psychic energy that is transformed and redirected during their normal course of development into complex human behavior. In the psychoanalytic view, the human mind is an active agent, with divisions that keep some material from entering conscious experiencc. We consider in detail the psychosexual theory of Sigmund Freud and, to a lesser extent, Jung's analytical theory and feminist revisions of psychoanalysis.

Freud's Psychosexual Theory

Freud developed most of his theory through his studies of his patients, people who sought his help or were referred to him for help for psychological problems. These problems, he believed, were related to the ways that instinctual energy was channeled. For example, patients suffering from hysteria, a disorder in which physical symptoms are present without apparent organic basis, were suspected of allowing their sexual energy to build up without appropriately discharging it (Freud, 1905/1977).

life instinct (eros), including sexual impulses

According to Freud, there are two sources of instinctual energy that "are the ultimate cause of all activity" (1940/1949). One instinct accounts for feelings and behavior related to self-preservation and preservation of the species, including sexual behavior; Freud called this the **life instinct (eros)**. The other instinct, called the **death instinct (thanatos)**, impels the person toward aggression and destruction (Freud, 1920/1955). Most of Freud's work on personality was concerned with the life instinct, which also forms the core of this discussion. However, Freud's views on aggression and its place in civilization merit some attention as well.

death instinct (thanatos), including aggressive impulses

Thanatos.   Primitive people, according to Freud, had no restrictions on the expressions of their instincts. Social norms of decorum did not restrict them from expressing their sexual urges. Contemporary civilized societies, however, place fairly rigid restrictions on sexual expression. We can have intercourse only in appropriate places and with certain people, or we face severe social sanctions. Similarly, civilization limits the expression of our aggressive instincts.

Freud felt that aggression was a derivative of the death instinct, and that it could be channeled in two different directions. If directed toward the self, then the individual risks self-destruction. If directed away from the self, aggression is the result. Because the instinct demands some kind of expression, a decrease in aggression increases the risk of self-destruction (Freud, 1930/1961). Freud's views on aggression are controversial in a number of respects. For one thing, he tells us that civilization itself is part of our problem: "What we call our civilization is largely responsible for our misery, and we should be much happier if we gave it up and returned to primitive conditions."

id in Freud's theory, the part of the mental apparatus that demands immediate gratification

The Mental Apparatus.   Freud's model of the mind included three parts: the id, ego, and superego. The **id** is that part of the mental apparatus that demands immediate gratification of the individual's instinctual needs. The id's demands are unconscious and without specific direction. According to Freud, the id is the original part of the psychic apparatus. Infants are directed only by the id, which demands gratification according to the **pleasure principle**. The pleasure principle involves the wish for gratification without any regard for external reality.

pleasure principle wish for gratification for its own sake, without any regard for external reality

Under the influence of external reality, the mental apparatus undergoes a differentiation that results in the appearance of the **ego**, the rational buffer between reality and instinct. The ego directs thought that we usually regard as higher mental functioning. It stores information about past experiences and recalls it in dealing with the external world. The ego operates under the **reality principle** and uses anxiety to protect the individual from danger (Freud, 1940/1949). If the id demands pleasurable sensation, the ego may prompt a delay of gratification because the realities of the situation will not allow it. For example, a child in church might want to obtain the pleasurable sensation associated with urination. This id impulse will be delayed by the ego until the child is safely out of the church and into the bathroom. Finally, the **superego** is a moral system, or conscience, that develops at around the age of 5, incorporating parental values and rules. To id demands, the superego reply might be, "No, it's wrong to do that."

ego the part of the mental apparatus that acts as a rational buffer between instinct and reality, and also includes higher cognitive powers

reality principle use of past experience and anxiety to protect the individual from psychological conflicts

superego last part of the mental apparatus to develop, the part that operates as a conscience

Defense Mechanisms.   Because these three elements of the mental apparatus often make conflicting demands, it is necessary to bring about some compromises among them. The dynamic character of Freud's theory is particularly well illustrated by conflict among the elements of the mental apparatus. One of the ego's chief functions is to make these compromises through the use of **defense mechanisms**. The ego uses these techniques to resolve conflicts with the id and the superego and to guard against anxiety created by instinctual wishes (A. Freud, 1966).

defense mechanisms compromises initiated by the ego between demands of the id and the superego

Several of Freud's defense mechanisms are described in Table 10–4 on page 386. One of the most common defense mechanisms is *repression*. In this defense mechanism, the ego forces material out of the conscious mind. As a consequence, the individual is unaware of the material on any conscious level. If, for example, a child who was sexually abused by a family member had no memory of the incident in adulthood, Freud might ascribe the lack of memory to the defense mechanism of repression. The memory might simply be too painful to admit into conscious awareness.

> ### THINKING ABOUT
> # Repression

Freud's concept of repression has gained renewed respect in the last few years, based on recent research in social and cognitive psychology. Social psychologists argue that we have a strong tendency to maintain favorable views about ourselves. Freud's concept of repression concerns motivated forgetting as a self-protective mechanism. If we manage information in such a way as to fool others and even ourselves, then we are engaging in a kind of self-deception that is very close to repression.

For example, suppose that you have an argument with one of your close friends. On cooler reflection, after the argument has passed, you may look back and see some things in your behavior that you don't like. Maybe the argument had to do with your desire to do one thing, while your friend wanted to do another. Instead of rationally discussing the situation and arriving at a compromise, you insisted on getting your way. Later, you think you appeared selfish, and you don't like to think of yourself that way. Thus, you are in the position of simultaneously believing that you are selfish, and of wanting very much to believe that you are not selfish. Repression may be

Sigmund Freud on a stroll in the mountains with his daughter Anna. Freud's early life is of particular interest because so much of his theory emphasizes the importance of childhood events. Freud's mother, his father's second wife, was considerably younger than her husband. In fact, she was 2 years younger than her husband's oldest son by his first marriage. Sigmund was the first of eight children produced by this second marriage. Freud and his wife Martha Bernays had six children. Their daughter Anna (1895–1982) became one of Freud's most loyal followers in her own career as a psychoanalyst. When Freud was asked what he thought normal people should be able to do well, he replied, "to love and to work."

TABLE 10-4
Freudian Defense Mechanisms

Denial. A defense similar to repression, in which a person denies the reality of something that has happened. *Example:* Parents who have lost a child may continue to behave for a time as if the child were still alive, by keeping the child's room exactly as it was and speaking as if the child were still with them.

Displacement. Use of a substitute object as the target for an impulse. The substitute is often linked to the real target by some association. *Example:* A man who has been treated unfairly at work by a superior may take his anger and frustration out on his children. The associative link involves his dual role as inferior in the first instance, superior in the second.

Intellectualization. Dealing with psychological conflicts in an intellectual rather than overt behavioral or emotional manner. The aim is to gain mastery over instinctual impulses. *Example:* A teenager who has conflicts over sexual expression intensely studies medical textbooks on human sexuality.

Identification. Taking the attributes of another person and making them part of oneself as a protective defense. *Example:* Prisoners of war who are beaten by their captors may take on some of their captors' characteristics in an attempt to reduce their own punishment.

Projection. Attributing to someone else an impulse that in reality one is experiencing oneself. *Example:* People who are hostile or aggressive toward others may view the world as a hostile and aggressive place. (Note the similarity with paranoia, a symptom of certain psychological disorders discussed fully in Chapter 16.)

Rationalization. A defense for dealing with something that has already happened by constructing a false but plausible explanation for the behavior. Rationalization must result in actual self-deception to be effective. *Example:* A student who plagiarizes a paper may excuse the behavior by saying that the teacher's assignment was unreasonable, and anyway, everybody does it.

Reaction formation. An impulse is repressed and expressed as its opposite. *Example:* A child who hates an abusive parent may act with excessive tenderness and closeness toward the parent.

Regression. A return to an earlier, more childlike, form of behavior when a current pattern of behavior appears inadequate or unsatisfactory. *Example:* A child begins bedwetting again soon after the parents' attentions are diverted by the birth of another child.

Repression. Forcing unpleasant or emotional material out of conscious awareness. *Example:* A child who was sexually abused by a family member has no memory of the incident in adulthood.

Sublimation. Transforming frustrated urges, especially sexual urges, into more socially accepted forms of behavior. *Example:* An adolescent takes up horseback riding as a substitute for exaggerated sexual desires.

Source: Adapted from Fancher, 1973; A. Freud, 1966.

---

the answer to this dilemma; you deal with it by repressing the fact that the argument ever took place.

Psychologists who study this kind of impression management do not always refer to it as repression. For example, some social psychologists have written about maintaining "positive illusions" about the self (Taylor & Brown, 1988). They believe that it is actually healthier to maintain these self-deceptions than it would be to acknowledge all our faults. In this sense, paradoxically, mental health may not be best achieved through clear contact with reality. This is basically Freud's point. Defense mechanisms such as repression serve the useful function of protecting the ego.

Freud's concept of repression has begun to acquire some of the newer jargon of cognitive psychology. For example, it has been described as "motivated inaccessibility of disturbing cognitions" (Baumeister & Cairns, 1992,

p. 851). In Taylor and Brown's language, "both the social world and cognitive-processing mechanisms impose filters on incoming information that distort it in a positive direction; negative information may be isolated and represented in as unthreatening a manner as possible" (1988, p. 193).

How do these filters—this motivated inaccessibility—work in practice? Baumeister and Cairns (1992) researched this question by administering personality tests to a group of people, and then giving them false feedback that included negative characteristics. They hypothesized that people would respond to the threatening material by paying slight attention to it. If the negative information were presented publicly, however, they hypothesized that their subjects would attend to it very closely, in order to neutralize the information later. These researchers had previously classified their participants as "repressors"—those who had strong tendencies to avoid unpleasant information about the self—and "nonrepressors"—those who admitted negative information about the self. Their hypotheses were confirmed for the repressors. Later, when the repressors were asked to recall information in their personality profiles, they recalled more of the positive information and less of the negative than the nonrepressors. These results suggest that repression itself may be a personality trait, and that, as Freud suggested, it serves to protect the ego.

How objective are you able to be about your own character? Do you think it is a good thing to be totally honest with yourself? Why might humans have a tendency to repress some types of information?

Psychosexual Stages of Development.   In 1905, Freud published one of his most controversial and influential works, *Three Essays on the Theory of Sexuality*. In these essays, Freud argued that children are driven by a sexual instinct from birth (1905/1962). Freud's essays caused a sensation in the medical and psychological worlds. The behavior of children could no longer be viewed as completely innocent. Human psychological development, in the Freudian view, followed a biologically predetermined course, with different zones of the body being the major source of the sexual instinct at different stages of development. This notion is the key to Freud's psychosexual stages of development, which are outlined in Table 10–5 on page 388.

Oral Stage.   In the first year of life, the region around the infant's mouth is the primary source of erotic impulses. This first stage of psychosexual development is the **oral stage**. To get gratification—that is, to release the tension built up there—the infant nurses at the mother's breast, sucks its own thumb, or any other object. The controversy over Freud's work concerned his assertion that such mundane childhood events as thumb sucking and breast-feeding had sexual overtones.

oral stage Freud's first psychosexual stage, in which sexual gratification is centered on the mouth region

Freud believed that events in childhood determine, to a large extent, the personality of the adult. Events in the oral stage, for example, may be linked with particular patterns of behavior in adulthood. Adult oral behavior patterns included, according to Freud, drinking and smoking. We might add to this list pencil chewing, fingernail biting, gum chewing, and excessive eating.

Anal Stage.   Between the ages of 1 and 3, the primary source of erotic impulses is the anal region. This stage of development is called the **anal stage**. The child derives sexual pleasure from this region of the body, especially during elimination. The feces, products of this pleasurable act, become "gifts" to be given to or withheld from parents. Parents, in turn, demand that the child put aside the pleasure of elimination in favor of their own socialized wishes

anal stage psychosexual stage in Freud's theory in which sexual gratification is centered on the anal region

TABLE 10-5
Freud's Psychosexual Stages

Stage	Age	Major Characteristics
Oral	Birth–1	Mouth region primary erogenous zone; sucking for gratification; relative primacy of id.
Anal	1–3	Anus primary erogenous zone; elimination as form of gratification; feces as gifts; ego as aid in adaptation to external reality.
Phallic	3–5	*Boys:* Penis as source of sexual excitation; incestuous fantasies toward mother and rivalry with father, culminating in intense castration anxiety and sexual repression, as well as superego development.
		Girls: Clitoris as source of sexual excitation; anatomical enlightenment leads to castration complex (feeling that she has been castrated and is inferior to boys), culminating in repression of sexual instincts.
(Latency)	5–puberty	Latency is not a stage of psychosexuality per se, but rather a period of sexual repression during which the ego becomes significantly strengthened.
Adult Genital	Adolescence and adulthood	Development of sex-role identity and nonincestuous object choice.

(Freud, 1916/1924b). This state of affairs naturally causes a certain amount of conflict between parent and child.

Phallic Stage. Freud labeled the third stage of psychosexual development the **phallic stage** for both sexes, arguing that only the male genitals exert an influence on psychosexual development at this stage (Freud, 1940/1949). At around age 3, boys begin to experience sexual excitation primarily in the genital region. They also become attracted to their mothers as objects of sex-

phallic stage psychosexual stage in Freud's theory in which sexual gratification is centered on the genital region, and which emphasizes the penis or its "lack"

In Freudian theory, such adult behaviors as drinking, smoking, nail biting, and gum chewing characterize the oral personality type. These personalities can be traced to conflicts involving gratification in the oral stage of early infancy.

ual gratification. With the advent of sexual feelings toward their mothers, boys feel increasing rivalry with their fathers. Because of the parallels with the Greek legend of Oedipus depicted in Sophocles's tragedy *Oedipus Rex*, Freud called this the **Oedipal crisis**. (In the legend, Oedipus unwittingly kills his father and marries his mother.)

At the same time that boys feel attraction toward their mothers, they experience the inhibiting fear of castration, which intensifies throughout the phallic stage. Why, you may ask, would normal boys from normal households fear castration? Castration fears, according to Freud, arise from several sources. With the genital zone as the primary erogenous zone, boys engage in autoerotic behavior such as rubbing or stroking their penises. Such activity often brings strong disapproval from their parents, who may threaten boys with dire consequences unless they stop. Furthermore, boys assume that all children have penises until confronted with facts to the contrary. When they discover that girls do not have penises, they believe girls have suffered castration (Freud, 1916/1924a). Freud labeled the fear of castration that little boys experience the **castration complex**.

One of our friends, a psychiatrist, told us the following story about her son when he was 4 years old. She had observed him playing with himself in an autoerotic way, and had noticed that the behavior not only was increasing but also was occurring in circumstances that were embarrassing to her, such as when guests were present. Not wanting to engage the boy's castration fears, she proceeded gingerly to discuss the issue with him. She told him that it was perfectly all right to do what he was doing, but that he needed to understand that there were appropriate circumstances and inappropriate circumstances. She just wanted him to try to confine this behavior to private moments. Her son, feeling that he was being told to cut down on this pleasurable activity, blurted out, "But, mom! It's my best game!"

Castration anxiety intensifies throughout the phallic stage, building up to such an extent that it requires strong defensive measures. Boys nullify this anxiety primarily through identification with their fathers. This identification results in the emergence of the superego, that part of the mental apparatus that provides the rule system known as conscience. A second defensive maneuver is to repress all sexual impulses.

The sequence of events in the phallic stage for girls is somewhat different. In pregenital sexuality, mothers serve as love objects for both boys and girls. With the arrival of genital sexuality, boys can retain the same love object, but girls must switch to a male figure as a potential lover (Freud, 1933/1964).

The key to a sexual object choice for girls is the discovery of genital differences. One of Freud's most controversial assertions centers around the consequences that he believed followed this discovery. When girls discover the existence of the penis, they view themselves as anatomically inferior and believe that they must have been castrated. Furthermore, according to Freud, they blame their castration on their mothers. Girls blame their mothers partly because it was their mothers who "made" them, and partly because they may believe that their mothers castrated them in retaliation for being castrated themselves. **Penis envy** is Freud's label for the girl's reaction to the discovery of genital differences.

Freud argued that many aspects of later behavior and personality are traceable to the discovery of genital differences. Following this discovery, girls are prepared to choose love objects of the proper gender. "In girls, the discovery of the penis gives rise to penis-envy, which later changes into the wish for a man as the possessor of a penis" (Freud, 1916/1924a). The girl's father, the closest possessor of a penis, is a logical choice for fantasies of genital gratification. The parallel to the boy's Oedipal crisis for girls is known as the **Electra**

Oedipal crisis crisis that occurs during the phallic stage, when boys desire their mothers and fear their fathers, obsessing about castration fears

castration complex a boy's intense fear of losing his penis because of Oedipal desires

penis envy in Freud's theory, the girl's counterpart to castration anxiety, in which she views her sexual anatomy as inferior to a boy's

Electra crisis girl's counterpart to the Oedipal crisis; she desires her father and feels hostility toward her mother

Boys neutralize their castration anxiety by using the defense mechanism of identification with their fathers, according to Freudian theory.

crisis, named for the daughter of Agamemnon in Greek legend. (Agamemnon's wife Clytemnestra had betrayed him, and his daughter avenged his death by persuading her brother Orestes to kill her mother and her mother's lover.) In Freud's version of the Electra crisis, the wish for a penis translates symbolically into the wish for a baby (Freud, 1916/1924a). Thus, the compensation for her castration is the wishful fantasy of having a child by and for her father.

Several researchers have attempted to verify Freud's views on castration anxiety and penis envy. One such attempt involved interpreting the dreams of college students (Hall & Van de Castle, 1965/1973). The researchers analyzed over 1,900 dreams for imagery of castration anxiety and penis envy. As Figure 10–1 shows, college men had castration anxiety dreams far more often than did college women. College women had penis envy dreams somewhat more frequently.

However, critics of this study point out that some of the scoring criteria for castration anxiety could only apply to men (e.g., "inability or difficulty of the dreamer in using his penis"), and some of the criteria for scoring penis envy could only apply to women (e.g., "a female dreams that she is a man or has acquired male secondary sex characteristics"). The critics argued that there is a bias in the very language of Freud's concepts. They point out that one could just as well view men's dreams of castration as castration wishes, or women's dreams about phallic-shaped objects as penis anxiety (Eysenck & Wilson, 1973). Freud's assertions about the sequence of events in the phallic stage for girls, with their negative views about female development, have attracted scores of critics (for example, Gilligan, 1982; Janeway, 1974; Mead, 1974).

Later Course of Psychosexual Development.　Because it is devoid of strictly sexual content, the period of sexual repression that children experience in

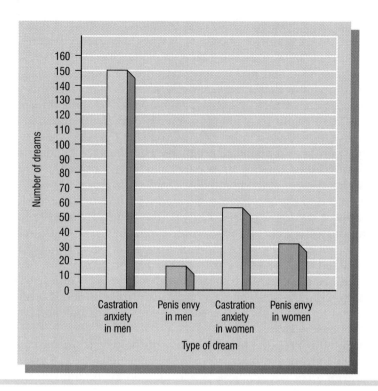

FIGURE 10–1
Some research claims to show greater castration anxiety themes in the dreams of male college students than female college students, and somewhat more penis envy themes in the dreams of the females. However, these results may have been obtained because of peculiarities in the coding schemes. (Adapted from Hall & Van de Castle, 1965/1973.)

late childhood, called *latency*, is not a psychosexual stage. With the physiological changes that occur at puberty comes a renewed interest in sexuality. The genital region is once again the primary source of excitation as people move into the fourth and final stage of psychosexual development, the stage of *adult genital sexuality*. In this stage, most people select heterosexual objects for gratification. Nevertheless, according to this model, some of the peculiarities of adult personality may be traced to the development of erotic impulses in childhood. For example, the anal-erotic character type in adulthood, which includes orderliness, obstinacy, and stubbornness, is traceable to the anal stage of psychosexual development (Freud, 1916/1924b).

Levels of Consciousness. One of the most enduring contributions of Freud's personality theory to modern psychology is the concept of unconscious mental life—aspects of the psyche of which people are themselves unaware. For Freud, all behavior, however trivial, was usually motivated by unconscious processes.

One example of unconscious processes at work comes from a casual conversation Freud had with a well-educated young man who was expressing pessimism about the state of the world. In the conversation, the young man quoted a line from Virgil's *The Aeneid*: "*Exoriare aliquis nostris ex ossibus ultor.*" (Literal translation, "Let someone arise from my bones as an avenger.") But the young man could not remember the word *aliquis* ("someone") in the line and had to ask Freud to supply it. He then challenged Freud to show how this trivial lapse of memory could have been motivated, even by unconscious processes. Freud took up the challenge, asking the young man to cooperate fully by concentrating on the word *aliquis* and reporting all associations he had to the word, with no censoring whatsoever (Fancher, 1973).

The young man's associations to the word included liquidity, liquids, and relics, and by an idiosyncratic train of thought his mind turned to St. Januarius, whose blood was kept in a vial in a church in Naples. It was reported that on a particular holy day, the blood liquified. If this event were delayed for any reason the people of Naples reportedly became agitated, hoping the miracle would take place soon. At this point, the young man blushed and said he had had an association too intimate to pass on. When Freud reminded him that a fair test of the theory of unconscious motivation required complete candor, the young man alluded to some information that a young woman might pass along to him. Freud then astounded the young man by correctly telling him he must be worried that the young woman had missed her period and might be pregnant. His clues, embedded in the associations, were blood flowing on a particular day, a calendar saint, and the hope that the miracle of the blood flow would take place.

Freud tried to explain the complicated workings of the mind by dividing it into levels of consciousness. *Conscious thought* in its most specific sense, concerns only material about which a person is momentarily aware. Workings of the mind that are available to awareness but that the person is not immediately aware of are part of the *preconscious*. You are probably familiar with Shakespeare's tragedy *Romeo and Juliet*. Until it was referred to at this moment, however, it was part of your preconscious level of awareness—available within that structure of your mind, but not part of your immediate consciousness.

According to Freud, a large majority of thought is *unconscious*. People are normally unaware of material in the unconscious level of awareness, but their behavior may nevertheless be strongly under its influence. According to this view, the young man's seemingly trivial forgetting of the word *aliquis* was influenced by unconscious mental processes. Unconscious thought has been repressed, barred from consciousness, because it is too emotion-provoking and anxiety-producing for people to handle. Unconscious thought often involves sexual matters, such as incestuous wishes or perversions. Freud believed that much of the pathological behavior he treated with psychoanalytic methods was determined by unconscious thought.

A Summary of Freud's Theory.   The major elements of Freud's theory have now been presented and are summarized in Table 10–6. These elements include a view of human nature as determined by instinctual forces, with behavior determined by motives of which people are largely ignorant. Personality is formed in early childhood through interaction in the family and through modification of the sexual instinct. The id is joined in childhood by the ego, and later by the superego, or conscience. The forces of the mind, borne of particular experiences in childhood, shape adult personality. Although Freud concentrated on abnormal behavior in a clinical practice, he believed that the same mechanisms governed normal and abnormal behavior.

Evaluation of Psychoanalytic Theory: Freud's Legacy.   The majority of psychologists today are not adherents to Freud's theory, and view its place in psychology primarily in historical terms. Nevertheless, Freud's legacy to the field of psychology is enormous. Several major contributions of this theoretical model continue to influence the field. Among these contributions is the view that childhood is an important stage in psychological development, and that much of what occurs in childhood will influence later functioning in adulthood. Before Freud, there was virtually no scientific attention devoted to human affectional systems. There is now a great deal of study of such phenomena as attachment and dependency, including the work of Harlow, Ainsworth, and Bowlby that we discuss in Chapter 13. This research tradition developed largely in response to Freud's theory (Lewis, 1984). Freud's insistence on the importance of childhood in determining later psychological development is now virtually accepted as a given.

TABLE 10-6
Summary of Sigmund Freud's Psychosexual Theory of Personality

View of Human Nature: People are driven by instincts; people are by nature uncivilized and must become civilized by redirecting sexual instincts into socially approved behavior.

Core of Personality: Personality is a dynamic entity determined by distributions of psychic energy. All behavior is motivated, much of it by unconscious elements of personality.

Developmental Aspects: People go through regular stages of psychosexual development (oral, anal, phallic, adult genital); events in childhood are of crucial importance in determining adult personality.

Major Concepts: The *id* is the part of the psychic apparatus that demands immediate gratification; the *ego* is the part of the psyche that modifies demands for gratification with practicalities of external reality; the *superego* is the part of the psyche that acts as a conscience, developing at the resolution of the Oedipal or Electra crisis. Sexual energy is known as *libido*; two major instinctual systems: life instincts and the death instinct.

Basis of the Theory: Work with patients who sought analysis of psychological problems.

Major Influences: Nineteenth-century determinism and positivism.

Major Sources for Summaries of the Theory: *A General Introduction to Psychoanalysis* (1917/1952); *New Introductory Lectures on Psychoanalysis* (1933/1964); *An Outline of Psychoanalysis* (1940/1949).

Carl Jung (1875–1961) was a Swiss psychoanalyst and contemporary of Sigmund Freud. Like Freud, Jung was trained in medicine and became interested in processes involved in the development of psychological disturbance. Jung was the first president of the International Psychoanalytic Association. However, he later resigned from the society after major disagreements with Freud about the nature of the dynamic processes in personality formation. Although Jung's contributions to psychodynamic theory have been overshadowed by Freud's, he is one of the giants in the field of personality psychology.

Freud was also a pioneer in establishing the role of sexuality as an important factor in psychological development. Before Freud, the notion that there might be important aspects of sexual development in childhood was barely acknowledged. We now recognize that sexuality is a major force in human psychological functioning, and that its influence begins long before puberty.

A third element in Freud's legacy to psychology is the importance of unconscious thinking. Although many psychologists might disagree about the exact nature of unconscious processes (e.g., Hilgard, 1977), most now accept their existence. Freud's insistence that much of mental life is not available to the individual's awareness may stand as his most enduring contribution to the field of psychology.

Jung's Analytical Theory

Carl Jung (1875–1961) was a contemporary of Freud who significantly revised the psychosexual account of personality in his own analytical psychology. Jung and Freud carried on a lively correspondence in the early 1900s in which they debated some of their differences about personality (McGuire, 1974). As Jung said, "When I was working on my book about the libido and approaching the end of the chapter 'The Sacrifice,' I knew in advance that its publication would cost me my friendship with Freud" (Jung, 1961, p. 162). Jung's most direct departure from Freud's theory concerned the issue of sexuality and the nature of the **libido**, the power behind the sexual instinct. Jung felt that Freud had applied the libido too broadly, giving it a position that was too central in the development of personality. Jung also constructed a view of the unconscious that was more elaborate than Freud's.

Levels of Awareness. In Jung's theory, the conscious mind is the ego. It includes all of the elements of the mind of which an individual is aware, including thoughts, perceptions, memories, and feelings. There are, how-

libido power behind the sexual instinct (eros)

ever, two separate unconscious regions of the mind, the personal unconscious and the collective unconscious.

The Personal Unconscious.   In Jung's system, there is a region of the mind, called the **personal unconscious**, that includes material outside an individual's current awareness. Some of this material has been repressed, or pushed out of awareness, because of its emotional content. Other material in the personal unconscious is accessible to awareness on demand, when the individual wishes to retrieve it. Material in the personal unconscious is highly individualized, based on personal experience.

The personal unconscious consists primarily of **complexes**, organized groups of feelings, thoughts, and memories that influence a person's experiences. A complex attracts some of the psychic energy and "behaves like a partial personality" (Jung, 1968). A complex may exert considerable influence over one's experience, depending on its strength. For example, people who are dominated by their mothers, like Franklin D. Roosevelt or like the fictional Cliff Claven on the TV program "Cheers," might be described as having a mother complex. Jung himself may have had a father complex, influential in his intense relationship with Freud (Alexander, 1982).

The Collective Unconscious.   One of Jung's most interesting departures from Freud's psychosexual theory is his concept of the **collective unconscious**. Whereas the personal unconscious is individualized and based on experience, the collective unconscious is a part of human genetic heritage, common to all people. The collective unconscious is composed of a number of universal thought forms, called **archetypes**. Because of the archetypes, individuals share similar psychological experiences and represent those experiences in similar ways in the imagination.

The archetypes of the collective unconscious are analogous to complexes in the personal unconscious. Some of the common fears people experience may be lodged in archetypes in the collective unconscious. For example, people are often afraid of the dark or of snakes. Such fears may be rooted in human prehistory, when darkness and reptiles posed a more realistic danger than they do today. Jung identified many archetypes, such as birth and rebirth, death, magic, God, the earth mother, the self, and anima and animus.

Anima and animus describe the feminine and masculine principles, respectively. In each male there exists an archetype of the female called the **anima**; and in each female, an archetype of the male called the **animus**. The male's anima influences his behavior, especially in emotional situations; the female's animus influences her behavior in more practical situations. In this respect, Jung subscribed to a stereotyped view of men as rational and women as emotional (Jung, 1936/1959). The **self archetype** connotes wholeness or unity of personality. The **mandala** is a frequent symbol of the unity of the self. *Mandala* is a Sanskrit word meaning circle; in psychology, according to Jung, the mandala can take the form of circular images in a variety of ways—painted, drawn, danced, or otherwise represented, as in Figure 10–2.

One of Jung's archetypes that has generated contemporary interest is the **shadow archetype**. By *shadow*, Jung meant the "negative" side of the personality, the collection of unpleasant qualities that people like to hide about themselves (Storr, 1983). Among other things, the shadow archetype may include guilt, shame, and embarrassment.

Dreams and other products of the imagination are primary sources of information about both complexes and archetypes. Jung believed that

---

personal unconscious in Jung's theory, the highly individualized material that has been repressed or pushed out of conscious awareness

complexes in Jung's theory, organized groups of feelings, thought, and memories in the personal unconscious

collective unconscious in Jung's theory, material outside of conscious awareness that is common to all people

archetypes in Jung's theory, organized groups of thoughts in the collective unconscious

anima in Jung's theory, the archetype of the female in each male

animus in Jung's theory, the archetype of the male in each female

self archetype sense of wholeness or unity of personality, according to Jung

mandala a type of circle symbolizing the self archetype, according to Jung

shadow archetype collection of unpleasant qualities that people like to hide about themselves; one of Jung's archetypes

---

FIGURE 10-2
Jung thought that the mandala, or magic circle, represented an archetype of the self. The mandala can take the form of circular images in a variety of ways. The mandala represented on the left is from a patient's drawing. The patient interpreted the four circles as representing separate functions of consciousness: thinking, feeling, sensation, and intuition. The snake has many symbolic interpretations; temptation, sexuality, and threat are among the most common. In the illustration on the right, we see the beginning of a tradition started in 1910 at the graduation ceremony of the Westover School in Middlebury, Connecticut. The graduates form a circle and clasp hands, at a time in their lives when identity and the self are important psychological issues.

dreams contain universal symbols because of their relationship to the collective unconscious. Therefore, dreams and other products of the imagination contain elements that have a universal interpretation. Compare, for example, the *Bird-Head* of German surrealist Max Ernst and an African mask of the Tusyan people, both shown in Figure 10–3 on page 396. Both portray flat rectangular heads, a straight horizontal mouth, small round eyes, and— their most extraordinary characteristic—a bird's head projecting from the forehead. Although Ernst was interested in ethnology, the resemblance between his *Bird-Head* and the Tusyan mask cannot be accounted for by any direct influence, because his *Bird-Head* was sculpted before any Tusyan masks appeared or were reproduced in Europe (Rubin, 1984). From a Jungian perspective, the appearance of both may have been influenced by psychological archetypes. Archetypes can be gleaned from studies of myths, folktales, art, religions, delusions, and trances. Jung's interest in archetypes led him to conduct detailed studies of mythology, religion, astrology, and even alchemy (Jung, 1939/1958; 1942–1957/1967).

Evaluation of Jung's Theory.   Like Freud's theory, Jung's analytical approach lacks empirical support. However, his theory has heavily influenced literature and the arts, especially the visual arts. His influence is perhaps most evident in surrealist painting, such as the works of Salvador Dali.

A summary of Jung's analytical theory is presented in Table 10–7 on page 397. Jung was a psychoanalytic theorist who emphasized unconscious

Jung's influence has been especially great in the visual arts. Surrealist painter Salvador Dali's painting "The Hallucinogenic Toreador" contains many startling images that may represent archetypes. The painting also has hidden images, such as the face that can be seen in partial shadow incorporating the form of the second Venus de Milo.

FIGURE 10–3
The similarity between (*top*) a primitive Tusyan mask and (*below*) surrealist Max Ernst's *Bird-Head* suggests an archetype at work. Both pieces are flat and rectangular, and both have a straight horizontal mouth and small round eyes. Their most extraordinary common characteristic is a bird's head projecting from the center of the forehead. Despite these striking similarities, Ernst had not seen the Tusyan mask when he completed the *Bird-Head*.

processes and the distribution of psychic energy. He placed less emphasis on sexual instincts than Freud and wrote persuasively of the collective unconscious and universal symbolism.

Adler's Individual Psychology

Like Jung, Alfred Adler (1870–1937) broke with Freud over the role of psychosexual forces in determining personality. Adler felt that sexual issues were just one of the ways in which personality expressed itself, and did not form the basis of personality as Freud had argued. Adler is known as an *ego*

TABLE 10-7
Summary of Carl Jung's Analytical Theory of Personality

View of Human Nature: People are heavily influenced by their genetic history. Goal of human life is the realization of full selfhood.

Core of Personality: Personality includes conscious experience as well as the personal and collective unconscious. The self, symbolized by the mandala, is a major archetype.

Developmental Aspects: There are no stages of development per se, but personal and collective experiences can dominate personality through complexes such as the mother complex. Therefore, childhood is a very important period in personality formation. However, full selfhood is not possible until a unity of all components of the personality is achieved in adulthood.

Major Concepts: The *ego* is conscious experience; the *personal unconscious* represents unconscious aspects of mental life based on personal experience; the *collective unconscious* contains universal thought patterns based on human genetic heritage. *Individuation* is the psychological process by which a person becomes an individual, a unified whole, including conscious and unconscious processes.

Basis of the Theory: Clinical practice; analysis of mythology and religion.

Major Influences: Sigmund Freud; Friedrich Nietzsche.

Major Sources of Summaries of the Theory: *Modern Man in Search of a Soul* (1933); *Two Essays on Analytical Psychology* (1953).

psychologist, meaning that he focused much more on the individual's conscious experience. People are aware of the motivations for their behavior much more than Freud thought, according to Adler (Ansbacher & Ansbacher, 1956). He replaced the highly sexualized motivation system of Freud's theory with a set of goals that he called **fictional finalisms**. They embody a future orientation, rather than being rooted in a person's psychosexual history.

These Adlerian goals are "fictional" in the sense that they may not be based entirely on reality, and yet they serve as guides for one's behavior nevertheless. For example, in our Western democratic society, we subscribe to the principle that "all people are created equal," and yet on some level we know that such a principle is not literally true. Still, the principle can serve as a useful guide to our behavior, moving us as individuals and as a society closer toward the ideal of equality (Hall, Lindzey, Loehlin, & Manosevitz, 1985).

From Adler's point of view, the key to understanding behavior resides in the concepts of *superiority* and *inferiority*. People feel inferior in a great many instances throughout their lives, especially when they encounter new tasks that they have not yet mastered. In college, for example, everyone feels inferior from time to time in some area of behavior, be it in the classroom, in the sports arena, or in the social sphere. We strive to overcome these feelings of inferiority and replace them with feelings of superiority. For Adler, superiority does not have the negative connotations of doing better than others and lording it over them, but rather striving to come as close as possible to one's own ideals. This part of Adler's theory was a strong influence on the humanistic perspective on motivation, such as Maslow's concept of self-actualization, discussed in the previous chapter.

Adler believed that several forces combined to produce the individual personality, including heredity, environmental circumstances, and the individual's own perception of the world. Our individual personalities come about because we each have a unique genetic makeup and a particular

fictional finalisms in Adler's theory, a set of idealized goals that motivate a person to strive for perfection

View of Human Nature: People are motivated by their tendency to want to achieve perfection. Genetics, environment, and individual interpretation of situations all contribute to personality.

Core of Personality: The *ego*, based primarily on conscious experience.

Developmental Aspects: No developmental stages, but people tend to strive for ideals, and their basic personality makeup is fixed in childhood.

Major Concepts: Fictional finalisms (precursors to the self-actualization of the humanists); superiority and inferiority, pulls and pushes for personality, respectively.

Basis of the Theory: Clinical practice.

Major Source of Summary of the Theory: Ansbacher & Ansbacher (Eds.), *The Individual Psychology of Alfred Adler* (1956).

social situation that differs from all others. With these major contributing factors in mind, Adler emphasized the concept of *birth order* as a determinant of personality. Adler argued that there are similarities among people who share a particular birth-order position. However, a person's personality is also greatly influenced by the overall climate within the family, in either a positive or a negative way. For example, firstborns tend to take responsibility for others when there is a favorable family situation, or to feel insecure and pessimistic when there is an unfavorable situation.

Evaluation of Adler's Theory. Adler's individual psychology of personality forms a bridge between the strictly psychoanalytic views of Freud and later developments in the study of personality, including feminist perspectives, humanistic perspectives, and even some of the biological approaches to personality, covered later in this chapter. Adler's theory is summarized in Table 10–8.

Adler's emphasis on striving for individual perfection—the "finalism" of his fictional finalism—led him to emphasize the equality of the sexes. In a letter of advice to his daughter and son-in-law, Adler wrote: "Don't allow either of you to become subordinate to the other. No one can stand this attitude" (Adler, 1978, p. 340). Adler's theory is far more democratic than Freud's, and anticipates some of the criticisms that are included in the feminist revisions of psychoanalytic theory, to which we turn next.

Feminist Revisions of Psychoanalysis

Much criticism has been directed against Freud's views about personality development in women. These views appear to be based on an antifemale bias, perhaps best understood in the context of the culture of Victorian Vienna. His ideas about penis envy and weaker superegos among women, for example, are interpretations that are not adequately supported by data.

Karen Horney. Karen Horney recognized in her criticisms of Freud's theory the cultural context in which he operated. "Not even a genius can entirely step out of his time" (Horney, 1939, p. 37). Horney broke with Freud over the male bias in his theorizing, especially his insistence that penis envy plays such a major role in the personality development of women. As she points out, there is almost no personality trait of women that Freud does not attribute to penis envy—from supposed feelings of inferiority to vanity. She finds this view of feminine psychology to be logically and empirically implausible: "It would require tremendous evidence to make it plausible that woman, physically built for specifically female functions, should be psychically determined by a wish for the attributes of the other sex" (Horney, 1939, p. 104).

Horney suggested that penis envy in women had its counterpart, womb envy, in men. **Womb envy** refers to the positive aspects of the procreative role that women experience and that men would like to experience. It includes an envy of pregnancy, motherhood, and the breasts and breastfeeding. Men may pour themselves into their creative work as an overcompensation for their small role in the creation of other human beings (Horney, 1926/1967).

Horney also emphasized culture to a far greater extent than Freud in speculating about gender differences in personality. Freud's account of personality is heavily biological; Horney's revision places emphasis on situational determinants of personality. Women have for centuries been assigned roles in economic and political systems that are more centered on home and family than the roles assigned to men. As a result, Horney argued, women have a more interpersonal and emotional personality makeup, in contrast to men, who have a more impersonal and matter-of-fact orientation to relationships.

Horney believed that because of these cultural circumstances, love plays a more significant role in the happiness and security of women than of men. As she put it, "There were, and to some extent still are, realistic reasons in our culture why woman is bound to overrate love and to expect more from it than it can possibly give, and why she is more afraid of losing love than man is" (Horney, 1939, p. 115).

Nancy Chodorow. Nancy Chodorow, a contemporary psychoanalytic theorist who takes a feminist perspective, also parts company with Freud over the issue of biological determinism. She points out several areas of Freud's theory that show an antifemale bias: "Freud denied women their own orgasms; he thought that women were without as great a sense of justice as men, that they were vain, jealous, full of shame, and have made no contributions to civilization except for weaving. He thought it was obvious that any three-year-old would think the masculine genitalia better than the feminine" (Chodorow, 1989, p. 166).

Despite the limitations of Freud's theory from a feminist perspective, Chodorow believes that the theory can be modified in ways that would make it more acceptable and useful as an account of personality development. Its strengths—which Freud himself often overlooked because of his own cultural blinders—include the notion that sexuality, including questions of gender and sexual orientation, is a continuous rather than a discrete variable. Nothing in the theory makes sexual object choice or particular form of sexual expression inevitable. It all depends on the particular experiences of the individual.

A feminist psychoanalytic theory, therefore, acknowledges that cultural socialization plays a large part in psychosexual stages in infancy. The fact that in most cultures, including ours, women play a larger role in socializing children than men affects the psychosexual development of both boys and girls. Both develop a primary dependency on their mothers. Boys later have to break those dependency ties more forcefully than girls in order to establish a masculine orientation. As Chodorow put it, "One indication of the continuing threat of an internalized femininity to males in our culture is the strength of both external and internal pressure on little boys to conform to masculine ideals and to reject identification with or participation in anything that seems feminine" (Chodorow, 1989, p. 36).

Although this perspective implies that socialization would be smoother for girls, because they identify with the female role from the start, societal pressures intervene. Girls are socialized partially into a traditional female role of compliance and dependency, and partially into a cultural ideal of

womb envy Horney's counterpart to penis envy; males envy females' procreative powers

Karen Horney (1895–1952) accepted many aspects of Freudian psychoanalysis, but believed that the theory incorporated too many male biases. In her feminist revision of the theory, she suggested that men envy the female role in reproduction and child care in a way that affects their psychological development—a counterpart to Freud's views about penis envy.

TABLE 10-9
Summary of Feminist Revisions of Psychoanalytic Theory

View of Human Nature: People are heavily influenced by instinctual pressures as well as by cultural socialization.

Core of Personality: Gender and sexual orientation are not fixed in any sense, except through particular experiences.

Developmental Aspects: Psychosexual stages, but outcomes determined more by culture than by biology. The fact that both boys and girls are mothered by women influences personality.

Major Concepts: Womb envy, the male counterpart to Freud's penis envy, in which males envy the female's procreative powers.

Basis of the Theory: Clinical experience as well as philosophical reactions to Freud.

Major Sources of Summaries of the Theory: Horney, *New Ways in Psychoanalysis* (1939); Chodorow, *Feminism and Psychoanalytic Theory* (1989).

achievement and success. They have, as a result, competing psychological pressures that can lead to role conflict. Matina Horner (1970) called this kind of role conflict "fear of success."

Chodorow's feminist revision of psychoanalysis contains suggestions for changes in our society's socialization practices that might lessen psychological conflict in men and women (see Table 10–9). To relieve the cycle of psychological oppression, Chodorow argues, both boys and girls should grow up in an environment that allows them to identify with more than one adult. Boys should see male role models take an active part in child care and other nurturing activities, and girls should see female role models who are involved in traditional areas of power and social control, in addition to child-care activities. "These arrangements could help to ensure that children of both sexes develop a sufficiently individuated and strong sense of self, as well as a positively valued and secure gender identity, that does not bog down either in ego-boundary confusion, low self-esteem, and overwhelming relatedness to others, or in compulsive denial of any connection to others or dependence upon them" (Chodorow, 1989, p. 65).

Evaluation of the Psychoanalytic Approach

A criticism that can be made of all the psychoanalytic personality theorists is their tendency to generalize about normal personality development from their work with neurotic patients. Freud's theory, for example, relies heavily on childhood events, yet Freud never studied children. He based much of his description of the Oedipus complex on an analysis of a child that he completed through correspondence with the child's father (Freud, 1909/1977a). Indeed, many of the assertions of psychoanalytic theory, such as Freud's concept of penis envy and Jung's archetypes, do not easily lend themselves to formulating testable hypotheses.

Most psychoanalytic theorists have been content to rely on the results of their therapeutic work as a test of their theories. If their techniques help to relieve symptoms, they claim, then the theory must be correct. This notion, of course, falls far short of the research support that most psychologists favor.

While the post-Freudian theorists rejected some of Freud's claims about sexual energy and about the role of childhood events in personality development, other schools of thought in psychology were looking at completely different accounts of personality. A second major theoretical orientation, to which we now turn, is behaviorism.

BEHAVIORISTIC MODELS OF PERSONALITY

The **behavioristic models** of personality grew out of instrumental learning theory, which was explored in detail in Chapter 6. Instrumental learning theory generally assumes that the behavior of all organisms—humans as well as lower animals—is lawful and predictable, based on an organism's history of reinforcement. The same is true of the behavioristic account of personality. Personality is assumed to be predictable from the individual's own particular history of reinforcement. The best-known behaviorist is B. F. Skinner. Other personality theorists of the behaviorist school include John Dollard and Neal Miller, who translated some of Freud's concepts into behavioristic terms, and Albert Bandura, whose social learning theory offers an influential model of personality.

behavioristic models personality theories that emphasize overt behavior, arguing that personality *is* behavior

Skinner's Operant Behaviorism

B. F. Skinner (1904–1990) was a pioneer in the systematic study of behavioral control in the form of contingencies of reinforcement (Skinner, 1969). His operant theory of learning was discussed in detail in Chapter 6. Skinner believed that personality must be viewed in terms of observable behavior. Mystical notions such as the superego or the collective unconscious are not observable. Therefore, they are not a part of the legitimate study of psychology. Instead, what people generally view as consistent traits of personality are in reality merely patterns of behavior under the control of particular contingencies of reinforcement.

In his book *About Behaviorism*, Skinner (1974) offered his definition of personality from the behavioristic perspective. "A self or personality is at best a repertoire of behavior imparted by an organized set of contingencies." In the debate over traits versus situations, Skinner came down heavily on the side of situations. For example, he argued that a young man might acquire a particular set of behaviors—some would call this set of behaviors his self or personality—in one situation, such as when he was with his family, because of the particular contingencies there. He might acquire a rather different set of behaviors—a different self or personality—in a different situation, for example, as a member of the armed forces, because that setting has a different set of contingencies. People learn to distinguish behaviors that will receive reinforcement in one type of situation but not in another, and they behave accordingly. Thus, according to Skinner, one's personality might be very different in different situations.

Consider the following example. Elliot is a 4-year-old who likes attention from his parents. When Elliot and his little sister play together quietly, looking at picture books or building with blocks, his parents ignore him. However, when Elliot paints his sister's face with grape jelly, his parents intervene with a great deal of attention. Elliot's behavior when he plays quietly is not reinforced with positive consequences, and hence it is less likely to be repeated. His behavior when he engages in outrageous activities is followed by the attention he craves, and thus has a higher probability of recurring. Over time, Elliot's behavior settles into patterns including aggressiveness and mischief. Behaviorists argue that the contingencies of reinforcement control the behavior.

Skinner's theory regards human behavior in as deterministic a fashion as Freudian theory, albeit in a different way. For Skinner, behavior is essentially determined by the history of reinforcement and punishment. Skinner gave credit to Freud for acknowledging that behavior can be understood in terms of what has preceded it. But Skinner argued that Freud introduced

After B. F. Skinner (1904–1990) completed his studies at Hamilton College, he entertained the idea of becoming a writer and moved to Greenwich Village in New York City to try writing fiction. He has judged this career exploration a failure: "I discovered the unhappy fact that I had nothing to say, and went on to graduate study in psychology, hoping to remedy that shortcoming" (*Current Biography*, 1964). And remedy it he did. Skinner became one of the major forces in psychology and the leading behaviorist of our time.

TABLE 10-10
Summary of B. F. Skinner's Operant Behavioristic Theory of Personality

View of Human Nature: All behavior is determined by a person's history of reinforcement. Nevertheless, people may be unaware of the factors that cause their behavior. Free will is a fiction; all behavior is determined.

Core of Personality: An individual's past history of reinforcement determines behavior; behavior *is* the personality. Skinner rejects all internal mechanisms such as ids and archetypes. Behavior can, in principle, be controlled by manipulating the environment.

Developmental Aspects: There are no stages of development. Behavior patterns are established through reinforcement and can be reversed or altered by changing the contingencies of reinforcement systematically. Intermittent reinforcement results in persistent behavior.

Major Concepts: An *operant* is a response that operates on the environment; *reinforcement* refers to presenting a reward or removing an aversive stimulus in order to strengthen a behavior; *extinction* occurs when the probability of a response is decreased through nonreinforcement.

Basis of Theory: Research with lower animals, especially pigeons and rats.

Major Influences: John Watson; E. L. Thorndike.

Major Source for Summary of the Theory: *Science and Human Behavior* (1953).

mentalistic language—including concepts such as the id, ego, and super-ego—for what amounts to different contingencies of reinforcement.

In many respects, Skinner's theory of personality, which is summarized in Table 10–10, is elegantly simple. By rejecting mentalistic concepts and relying entirely on behavior as the data of personality, the terminology is kept to a minimum.

Skinner's approach has important implications for therapy. Whereas the psychoanalytic theorists search for the traumas that disrupt normal patterns of development, leading to symptoms, the behaviorists attempt to modify behavior. According to the behaviorists, the behavior is the problem; it is not a symptom of some larger psychic catastrophe. This therapeutic approach, appropriately called behavior therapy, is covered in detail in Chapter 17.

Behavior therapy is a technique in which contingencies of reinforcement are systematically altered to bring about desired patterns of behavior and to remove undesired patterns. In a broad sense, education can also be defined in behavioral terms, as arranging contingencies so that the individual will acquire behaviors that will be useful in future situations. Skinner addressed the issue of education and its relation to personality when he described training procedures for self-control in an ideal community.

APPLYING PSYCHOLOGY
Personality Socialization in *Walden Two*

In his fictional account of a utopian community called Walden Two, B. F. Skinner elaborated on educational programs designed to influence character and emotions. *Walden Two* is an argument, through the medium of fiction, for using experimental methods to shape human behavior, including what we generally think of as personality. In the book, one of the chief planners of the community is a man named Frazier. As he takes a group of visitors on a tour, Frazier offers a critique of established practices for educating children:

> The behavior of the individual has been shaped according to revelations of "good conduct," never as the result of experimental study. But why not experiment? The questions are simple enough. What's the best behavior for the individual so far as the group is concerned? And how can the individual be induced to behave in that way? Why not explore these questions in a scientific spirit? (Skinner, 1948)

Frazier then explains that the great works on ethics and morals serve as guides to desirable behavior—works such as the New Testament and the writings of Plato, Confucius, Machiavelli, and Freud.

In Walden Two, the planners went a step beyond reading the great works. They instituted a program of scientific moral education, for example, by experimenting with techniques of self-control. Frazier describes one element of the children's training. They are given lollipops but are told that they can eat them later in the day only if they haven't licked the lollipop in the meantime.

> The children are urged to examine their own behavior while looking at the lollipops. This helps them to recognize the need for self-control. Then the lollipops are concealed, and the children are asked to notice any gain in happiness or any reduction in tension. Then a strong distraction is arranged—say, an interesting game. Later the children are reminded of the candy and encouraged to examine their reaction. The value of the distraction is generally obvious. (Skinner, 1948).

In a similar fashion, all desired behavioral goals are reached through deliberate engineering of the environment. Children will grow up to exhibit the full range of desired behaviors; that is, they will have personality characteristics to fit the society they live in. Although this approach to personality has its adherents, many people find the idea of deliberate shaping of personality or emotion offensive. Shaping of personality evokes images of "Big Brother," to use George Orwell's phrase. Bureaucratic government control over personality would create behavior that advances the aims of the state rather than the individual. Control offends our sense of individual liberty. Skinner's answer, in his controversial book *Beyond Freedom and Dignity* (1971), is that free will is an illusion. The problem is not to free people from control, but from certain kinds of control, which can be done only if we understand the contingencies that operate to control our behavior.

Bandura's Social Cognitive Theory

Albert Bandura and his colleagues also take the position that personality is acquired, or learned, behavior. Bandura extended the approach by placing learning in a social context. In particular, Bandura's insistence that behavior can be learned from mere observation is a significant departure from Skinner's behaviorist position.

An empirical demonstration of **observational learning** was presented in a study by Bandura, Ross, and Ross (1963). Nursery school children were allowed to watch an adult's unusual aggressive actions against an inflated Bobo doll—the kind that pops back up after it has been punched or knocked down. The adult models hit the doll with a hammer and kicked it, tossed it

observational learning modification of behavior through merely watching others perform the behavior, rather than from direct experience with reinforcement

FIGURE 10–4

(*Below*) Children who had observed an adult model hit a Bobo doll later behaved more aggressively against the doll than children who had not observed the model. The children who had observed the model also tended to hit the doll the same way the model had done. (*Right*) Children who had seen a live or filmed model were more aggressive than children in the control group, who had not seen a model. (Adapted from Bandura, Ross, & Ross, 1963.)

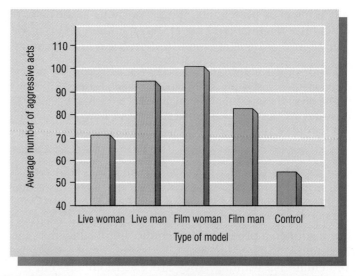

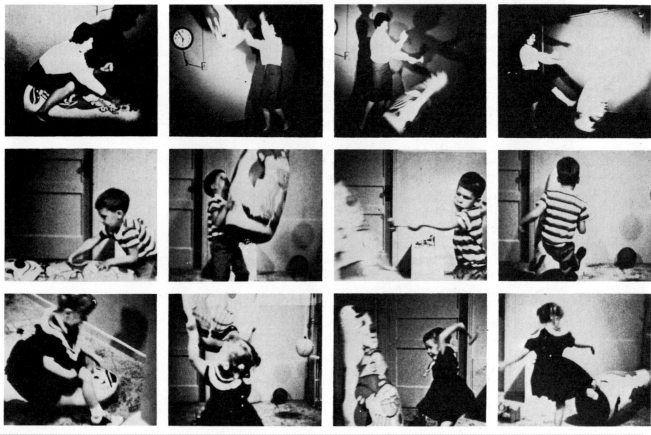

in the air, and even sat on it and punched it. After merely observing this behavior, the children were later allowed to play with toys that included the Bobo doll and hammer. The children who had observed the adult model, either live or on videotape, hit the doll more frequently than a control group who had not seen a model, as illustrated in Figure 10–4. They also tended to hit the doll the way they had observed the adult model do it. Bandura interpreted this study as demonstrating that the probability of behavior can be strengthened through observation. Indeed, in Bandura's approach to personality, much of one's behavior is learned and strengthened through imitation, which is a kind of observational learning.

Observational Learning and Television Violence

Bandura's studies of observational learning, particularly his demonstration that videotaped models are as powerful as live models in eliciting behavior, have disturbing implications for the effects of television on children, and adults, too, for that matter. Television is a powerful medium, both for entertainment and for education. Based on Bandura's studies, we should pay close attention to the content of televised models to which our children, and we, are exposed. The amount of violence on television could contribute to the violence played out daily on our streets.

Perhaps no aspect of everyday life is more common than watching television. In the average American household the television set is on more than 6 hours per day, and the average child between the ages of 2 and 11 watches it for about 3 hours daily. Estimates are that by high school graduation, the average American child will have spent 11,000 hours in the classroom and 15,000 hours watching television. Programs aimed specifically at children, such as Saturday morning cartoons, contain a great deal of violence. The National Institute of Mental Health's report on television and behavior estimates that children's weekend programs contain more violence than do prime-time shows (NIMH, 1982).

Hundreds of studies have examined the relationship between television violence and actual aggression among viewers. In one of these studies, more than 500 children in grades 1 through 5 participated in a short-term longitudinal study. Television viewing peaked in grades 3 and 4 among these children, with boys watching more than girls. The younger children, up to age 9, believed what they saw on television to be real; given what we know about cognitive development, this makes sense. Children who watched more television were more likely to be identified by peers as being aggressive, and the relationship between this measure and television viewing increased with age (Eron et al., 1983). Although these associations do not prove that viewing violence on television causes aggressiveness, they demonstrate a strong relationship between the two factors.

The Surgeon General of the United States, who reported on the effects of television on children, concluded that there was a cause-and-effect relationship between television violence and aggression. He testified before a Senate committee in 1972: "Certainly my interpretation is that there is a causative relationship between televised violence and subsequent antisocial behavior, and that the evidence is strong enough that it requires some action on the part of responsible authorities" (Liebert, Sprafkin, & Davidson, 1982).

Do you think the content of television should be more carefully regulated? Should the excessive violence depicted in children's cartoons be treated as a hazard to our nation's social health? Do you think your behavior has been influenced by the types of programs you watched as a child?

In recent years, Bandura (1986, 1989) has so significantly modified his social learning position that it now is called a **social cognitive theory**. In this approach, he has provided new insights into the trait–situation debate by proposing that three factors—personal factors (or traits), environmental

social cognitive theory Bandura's social learning theory, relating behavior to traits and situations

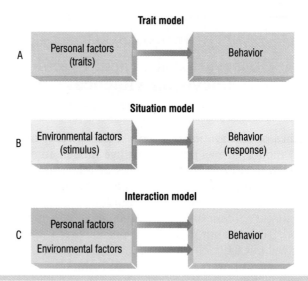

FIGURE 10–5
Theoretical relationships among traits, situations, and behavior.

triadic reciprocality Bandura's view that reciprocal influences among three factors—person, situation, and behavior—are necessary to account for personality

(or situational) factors, and behavior—exert reciprocal influence on each other. Trait approaches alone propose that internal dispositions cause behavior, as illustrated in Figure 10–5A. Bandura found such a simplistic view untenable: "People would have to be grossly inattentive to the world around them, obtuse, or indifferent to the personal and social effects of their conduct to act the same irrespective of the circumstances" (Bandura, 1986, p. 11).

Situational approaches alone, best illustrated by Skinner's views, propose that environmental circumstances elicit and control behavior, as shown in Figure 10–5B. This view, too, is untenable, because its takes away the power of human thought: "One can originate fanciful but coherent thoughts, as, for example, visualizing hippopotami gracefully navigating hang gliders over lunar craters" (Bandura, 1986, p. 18).

A simple interactionist model argues that both personal and environmental factors combine to produce behavior, as in Figure 10–5C. Although conceptually more sophisticated, the interactionist model also fails to account for how people can change the environment, and how such a change itself affects behavior. In 1992, the attention given to the world summit on the environment in Rio de Janeiro underscored just how much humans have altered the global environment, and how human behavior will have to adjust to those changes.

Bandura's model calls for **triadic reciprocality**, a view that all three factors influence each other, and that any simple interactionist view is inadequate to account for the variety of thought and behavior subsumed by the term *personality*. Bandura (1986) illustrated triadic reciprocality using TV viewing as an example. Personal preferences, based on internal dispositions, influence what one chooses to watch on TV ($P \rightarrow B$). Preferences, as communicated to TV networks and to advertisers, also influence what is broadcast, i.e., the environmental factor ($P \rightarrow E$). What is broadcast may also shape personal preferences ($E \rightarrow P$); and of course one must choose from among the broadcast alternatives, so that the environment influences behavior ($E \rightarrow B$). After the choice is made and a program is watched, it may alter the person to some extent, by influencing cognition or attitudes ($B \rightarrow P$). Networks also pay close attention to what people actually watch, through the monitoring of Nielsen ratings. Thus, behavior influences the environment in the future ($B \rightarrow E$). These aspects of Bandura's model are shown schematically in Figure 10–6.

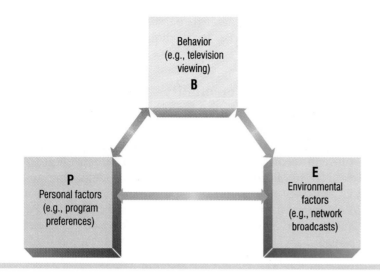

FIGURE 10-6
Diagram of the relations between the three classes of determinants in triadic reciprocal causation. (From Bandura, 1986.)

Evaluation of the Behavioristic Approach

One of the major criticisms of the behavioristic approach to personality is its very simplicity. Some psychologists argue that these few principles are too simplistic to account for the complexity of human personality. Furthermore, rejecting all internal psychological states as unworthy of study makes the behavior of human beings too mechanical. Critics point out that Skinner's position is based largely on work with pigeons and other lower animals; it appears highly risky to base much speculation about human personality on the behavior of pigeons in a laboratory cage. Bandura's new social cognitive theory goes so far beyond the ordinary behavioristic account of personality that in many ways it should be classified with the cognitive models discussed later. Bandura attempts to provide a grand synthesis of several aspects of psychology in this theory, especially cognitive, personality, and social psychology.

The behavioristic approach to personality of Skinner shares a strong determinism with psychoanalytic theories. Instead of basing the theory on work with disturbed patients, behaviorists base it on laboratory studies, primarily with lower animals. The next major category of personality theories, humanism, criticizes both of these views as too narrowly conceived and too negativistic.

HUMANISTIC MODELS OF PERSONALITY

Followers of psychoanalytic and behavioristic models of personality have sometimes treated personality as a battlefield, with loyalties that can obscure the aim of theorizing in the first place, which is a full understanding of the complexity of personality. **Humanistic models** propose that these two traditions have been negative in their outlook about human personality, and they believe that the battles interfere with learning the truth. Abraham Maslow, one of the humanistic theorists, put it this way:

> It is very difficult, I have found, to communicate to others my simultaneous respect for and impatience with these two comprehensive psychologies. So many people insist on being *either* pro-Freudian *or* anti-Freudian, pro-scientific-psychology *or* anti-scientific-psychology. In my opinion all such loyalty-positions are silly. Our job is to integrate these various truths into the *whole* truth, which should be our only loyalty. (Maslow, 1962)

humanistic models personality theories that focus on striving to attain the most positive aspects of living; called the Third Force, in opposition to psychoanalytic and behavioristic models

Because the humanistic approach to personality was put forward as an alternative to the two major forces in psychology, it is sometimes referred to as the Third Force.

Rogers's Self Theory of Personality

In Carl Rogers's view, *self-actualization* is a central theme. Self-actualization refers to the human being's tendency to fulfill his or her human potential, particularly with regard to the higher, positive motives such as belongingness and love. You will recall from Chapter 9 that self-actualization was also an important concept in Maslow's theory of motivation. According to Rogers, a basic growth tendency that is embedded in the human organism is entirely different in character from the inner nature of lower animals. People have very important learned needs, including the need for *positive regard*. The need for positive regard includes the need for being liked, the need for warmth, and the need for respect and sympathy from others. Parents play a particularly important role in providing positive regard to their offspring.

However, most positive regard is conditional upon behavior that is acceptable according to certain standards. For example, parents may withhold positive regard from a child who uses felt-tipped marking pens to draw animal pictures on the white cotton fabric of the living room sofa. For Rogers, the self-concept gets distorted by evaluations from others. According to his theory, if parents gave their children unconditional positive regard, they would grow up to be quite well adjusted. But no one grows up with consistently unconditional positive regard.

Rogers's personality theory, like many others, has provided a framework for the treatment of psychological disorders. In particular, Rogers's theory suggests a therapy based on unconditional positive regard. This concept is discussed in greater detail in Chapter 17. According to Rogers, the primary obstacle to actualization occurs because people strive so hard for positive regard. If one is overly concerned about the regard of others, then it is difficult to achieve actualization. Perhaps this is one reason why only 1% or so of the population shows evidence of being self-actualized (Maslow, 1970). A brief summary of Rogers's theory is included in Table 10–11.

Evaluation of the Humanistic Approach

The main criticism of the humanistic position is that it presents an overly optimistic view of human nature. The humanistic insistence on positive, or

---

TABLE 10-11
Summary of Carl Rogers's Self Theory of Personality

View of Human Nature: People are basically good, and if they received unconditional positive regard, they would be well adjusted. (Most positive regard is conditional upon certain standards of acceptability in behavior.)

Core of Personality: People strive to reach self-actualization.

Developmental Aspects: There are no stages of development. Sometimes the self-concept gets distorted through reactions from others, particularly significant others such as parents.

Major Concepts: The *phenomenal field* is the locus of all subjective experience; *positive regard (conditional* and *unconditional)* represents the affection and respect one person may hold for another.

Basis of Theory: Primarily clients in therapy.

Major Influences: Otto Rank, Sören Kierkegaard.

Major Source for Summary of the Theory: *On Becoming a Person* (1961).

at worst neutral, human motives is difficult to reconcile with the observation that so many people engage in destructive and antisocial behavior. In addition, the research presented by Maslow and some of the other humanists is less rigorous than the more scientifically oriented psychologists would like. For example, Rogers's and Maslow's concept of self-actualization is very difficult to study empirically. The next class of theories that we discuss, the cognitive models, are closely aligned with scientific studies of human information processing.

COGNITIVE MODELS OF PERSONALITY

Cognitive models view individual personality in terms of people's tendencies to process, interpret, and predict the world that they encounter. Cognitive theories currently are stimulating a great deal of research. Earlier we considered Bandura's social cognitive theory as a derivative of learning theory. Because Bandura's thinking was initially linked to instrumental learning theory, we classified his theory with behaviorism. However, his later thinking has moved much closer to cognitive models, and could as easily be classified here. In addition to Bandura's *social cognitive model*, there are two additional cognitive theories of personality: the *personal construct theory* of George Kelly and *attribution theory*. We discuss attribution theory in Chapter 14 on social psychology; here we describe only Kelly's approach.

cognitive models personality theories based on people's tendencies to process, interpret, and predict the world that they encounter

Kelly's Personal-Construct Theory of Personality

In the cognitive approach to personality, human nature is based neither on sexual instincts nor on histories of reinforcement. Rather, human nature is based on people's attempts to understand the world. In Kelly's (1955) approach, personality is best understood as the habitual way people make sense out of their experience of the world. In this approach, people act very much like rational scientists, encountering events and trying to understand and control them. Personality, then, becomes the person's habitual mode of understanding.

Personal Constructs. People attempt to predict and control the experiences of their lives by using their own individual system of **personal constructs**. Constructs are bipolar categories such as *black–white, smart–dumb, kind–unkind*, by which people can understand the world. People behave according to their system of construing, where *construe* means to interpret an event.

personal constructs bipolar categories (such as kind–unkind) through which people understand the world

In any given situation, some of these constructs take on a higher degree of importance, whereas others are subordinate. For example, consider the situation of a young man who has been invited to go sailing with friends. He has never before been on a sailboat, and furthermore, he is a little afraid of the water. When he is judging the captain's behavior, the construct of *competent–incompetent* will likely be of paramount importance; *generous–stingy* is likely to be relatively unimportant. In another situation, for instance when he is having an argument with his girlfriend, neither of these constructs is likely to be very important. Others, such as *forgiving–unforgiving*, might be crucial. Notice that the constructs are considered only from the subjective point of view of the individual. The person's judgment may or may not be accurate, but nevertheless, it is based on the individual's personal-construct system. This aspect of Kelly's theory has a parallel in psychoanalytic theory. Both approaches are highly subjective, taking the point of view of the individual and his or her interpretation of events (Warren, 1990).

People tend to apply constructs like attractive–unattractive in similar ways.

Fundamental Postulate. Kelly developed his theory with one fundamental postulate and 11 corollaries. Although all aspects of the theory cannot be covered here, the fundamental postulate is important enough to describe in more detail. The fundamental postulate states that people behave according to the way that they construe events, and that the way they will behave in similar situations in the future is predictable from the constructs that they currently use. To use a simple example, if Ellen thinks her boyfriend is being unfaithful to her (she construes him as unfaithful), she may keep close tabs on him in the future (she behaves in a distrustful manner because of her construction of the situation). Sometimes people get themselves into trouble because they misconstrue situations. For example, Ellen's boyfriend might be late meeting her for a date not because he is cheating on her, but because he stopped on his way to buy her a present. Think how Ellen would feel if she accused him of infidelity in that situation.

Kelly's personal constructs operate essentially as cognitive "schemas," or organized memory structures that can become determinants of social interaction. In some ways the core concepts that a person uses are similar to values, whereas less central constructs are more like beliefs (Horley, 1991). Schemas are currently receiving a great deal of research attention in personality (Singer & Kolligian, 1987). Sexual experience is one such schema. In one study more sexually experienced college students recalled arguments they had heard about sexual dilemmas differently than did sexually inexperienced students (Lewis, Gibbons, & Gerrard, 1986). In another study schemas of masculinity determined the way male students interpreted a film with masculine-stereotyped behaviors, such as lifting weights, but not a film of neutral behaviors, such as eating an apple (Markus, Smith, & Moreland, 1985). Kelly described how personal constructs, or schemas, develop and how they provide a basis for individual differences in his corollaries to the fundamental postulate.

Evaluation of the Cognitive Approach

Kelly's theory is summarized in Table 10–12. The theory has interesting implications for helping people to deal with personality problems. In this system, problems arise when people have unrealistic constructs or when

---

TABLE 10-12
Summary of George Kelly's Personal-Construct Theory of Personality

View of Human Nature: People are rational in their attempts to predict and control their experiences.

Core of Personality: People have an individualized system of personal constructs that they use to help them predict and control their experiences. People anticipate future events on the basis of their construct systems.

Developmental Aspects: There are no stages of development, but children do not have as elaborate systems of constructs as adults do. With experience and age, people acquire more elaborate and complex systems of personal constructs.

Major Concepts: *Personal constructs* are bipolar categories such as *black–white* or *smart–dumb* by which people can understand the world; people differ from each other in the ways that they construe events; constructs are useful for some situations and not for others, that is, they have a limited range; people continually revise and update their constructs.

Basis of Theory: Clinical practice.

Major Influences: Cognitive and experimental psychology.

Major Source for Summary of the Theory: *A Theory of Personality: The Psychology of Personal Constructs* (1955).

they misapply them. Therapy, then, is a matter of education—to get people to view the world differently and thereby open up new ways for dealing with others.

Kelly's construct model offers some valuable ways of thinking about the therapeutic situation. Family therapists, for example, often find it useful to inquire about the subjective interpretations each family member places on the events that are disturbing the whole family. Looking at the situation through the client's eyes—or rather through the client's construct system—is the essence of the constructive approach to therapy (Solas, 1991).

Cognitive approaches to personality, such as Kelly's, have been criticized as being too narrow in scope to account for the richness and vitality of human personality. According to critics, people are seen as lifeless, cognitive creatures. As one might expect, the behaviorists criticize this approach for its mentalistic concepts such as constructs, and the psychoanalytic theorists see cognitive theories of personality as far too neglectful of childhood as the major period for personality development.

BIOLOGICAL PERSPECTIVES ON PERSONALITY

Many of the theories of personality that we have reviewed have relied on biological aspects of development to explain personality differences. Freud, for example, set out to explain all of human personality, both normal and abnormal, in terms of the functioning of the nervous system. He called this early work his "Project for a Scientific Psychology" (Fancher, 1973). In addition, many of the elements of personality in the humanistic tradition, such as Maslow's hierarchy of needs, are based on biological drives. For this reason, we discussed Maslow's theory of personality in the previous chapter on motivation.

Sheldon's Somatotypes

William Sheldon (1899–1977), building on Kretschmer's (1921) work on body types, constructed one of the earliest biological models of personality. Sheldon's work is controversial in a number of respects, not the least of which was his methodology. Sheldon identified three body types by photographing thousands of college students in the nude—front, side, and rear shots (Sheldon, 1940). The three body types—endomorphs, mesomorphs, and ectomorphs—are each measured on a seven-point scale. An *endomorph* has a softly rounded, or fat, body type; *mesomorphs* have a greater preponderance of muscle and connective tissue; and *ectomorphs* are thin and frail in body composition.

From his nude photographs, Sheldon rated individuals on each of these body-type dimensions, using a seven-point scale. A person rated as a 7-1-1 would be extremely high on endomorphy and extremely low on the other two dimensions; such an individual would thus be classified as an extreme endomorph. A person with a rating of 1-7-1 would be an extreme mesomorph, and a person rated 1-1-7 would be an extreme ectomorph. Between these extremes are a great many less extreme body types with various mixtures of the three dimensions (such as 4-3-3 or 2-5-4). Sheldon called these numerical ratings **somatotypes**.

Using lists of personality traits, Sheldon looked for clusters of traits that were associated with different somatotypes. He argued that endomorphs tended to be sociable, amiable, and greedy for affection and approval. Mesomorphs were more inclined to be assertive, adventurous, and dominat-

somatotypes Sheldon's numerical ratings of body types, thought to influence personality

ing, and ectomorphs emotionally restrained, apprehensive, and secretive (Sheldon, 1942).

Evaluation of Sheldon's Biological Perspective

Sheldon's biological theory of somatotypes has some serious flaws. First of all, even if there is a relationship between somatotype and personality, the underlying mechanism may not be biological. An elementary lesson about correlations is that they do not address the issue of causation. Thus, we may assume ectomorphs are timid simply because of our tendency to stereotype. If we see someone with a thin body build, we may expect them to be timid, and look for evidence to support our stereotype while simultaneously ignoring information that disputes the stereotype. Sheldon did the somatotyping as well as the ratings of personality, thereby seriously compromising the scientific validity of his findings.

Although Sheldon's somatotype approach to personality has not held up well empirically, other biological approaches to personality are currently receiving a great deal of attention. In particular, attempts to link features of personality to genetic control constitute one of the most intense areas of current research.

Genetics and Personality

The controversy within the study of personality that we discussed earlier—the trait versus situation debate—also has biological implications. If traits are indeed aspects of personality that have stability over time and across circumstances, then one would hypothesize that they are highly heritable. *Heritability* refers to the degree to which a characteristic is inherited. It is most often studied by examining the difference in expression of a trait between monozygotic twins (who are identical in genetic makeup) and dizygotic twins (who are no more similar in genetic makeup than ordinary siblings, with about 50% shared genetic material).

Several studies in personality have taken this approach. One study, for example, looked at two personality characteristics—psychosocial instability and extraversion—in more than 12,000 twin pairs. Heritability estimates for both characteristics, and for both men and women, were over .50, indicating that about half of the variation in expression of these traits can be attributed to genetic factors (Floderus-Myrhed, Pedersen, & Rasmuson, 1980). Other studies have found similarly high heritability estimates for a number of personality traits (Pedersen, Plomin, McClearn, & Friberg, 1988; Tellegen et al., 1988).

THINKING ABOUT
The Heritability of Personality

Over the past decade, psychologists at the University of Minnesota have conducted what has become one of the most famous studies of twins of all time. The researchers have extensively tested hundreds of twin pairs, including identical twins reared either together or apart, on a battery of tests from physiological measurements to personality characteristics. In videotaped interviews with the twins, these researchers have discovered a number of extraordinary "coincidences," which may in fact have a biological (genetic) basis.

A few of their more striking examples of the similarity of twins reared apart will help to make this point. In one pair of twins reared apart, both members had consistently refused to vote, on the grounds that they were not sufficiently informed about political issues. Another pair of twins reared apart discovered, when they were reunited, that they both used the same brands of toothpaste, hair tonic, and cigarettes. Finally, the account the researchers gave of another pair is particularly striking: "Only two of the more than 200 individual twins reared apart were afraid to enter the acoustically shielded chamber used in our psychophysiology laboratory, but both separately agreed to continue if the door was wired open" (Lykken, McGue, Tellegen, & Bouchard, 1992, p. 1565). These two individuals constituted a pair of identical twins reared apart, who also showed a similar aspect of their personality at the beach, by always insisting on entering the water backwards, and always only up to their knees.

Surely some of these similarities are merely coincidences, such as the male pair of twins who had both divorced women named Linda, and then both married women named Betty (Lykken et al., 1992). But a biologically based explanation most likely accounts for a great deal of this similarity. The researchers proposed a rather complicated genetic model for how these similarities may come to exist, and why it is necessary to study identical twins to reveal the similarities. Their model suggests that individual differences in personality, idiosyncrasies of the type described in the previous examples, are determined by a particular *configuration* of genes, rather than the simple presence or absence of the gene somewhere in the person's genetic makeup.

Think of the genetic message as one huge "bar code" of the type used to scan products at the checkout counter. Half of the genetic bar code is contributed by the father and half by the mother, but the elements of the bar code are scrambled into a totally novel pattern when the egg and sperm unite at conception. Ordinary siblings share a great many of the elements of the genetic bar code, but the specific configuration of the information differs from one to another. Only among identical twins is the entire bar code sequence identical. Thus, although siblings may share specific genetic elements, these elements do not appear in the configuration required for the expression of an idiosyncratic trait in behavior. Identical twins do have that configuration, and thus they share behavioral idiosyncrasies that are controlled by genetic mechanisms. If this explanation is correct, then the task for researchers is to isolate the specific aspects of personality that are controlled by genetic mechanisms, and the degree to which the control is exerted.

Imagine biological research on personality projected many years into the future, when the human genome has been mapped in such a way that the chromosomal location for particular personality characteristics is known, and the specific configuration of genetic elements can be manipulated through genetic engineering. Do you think it would be desirable to be able to specify the personality makeup of your children? Would you want to "shop around" for the most desirable personality type? Might important chance elements of genetic diversity be lost if such a thing were possible?

Evaluation of Genetic Approaches to Personality

The more sophisticated biological approaches to personality are represented by the genetic theories. However, despite the high estimates of heritability for some personality traits, the trait versus situation debate is not completely resolved by the biological approach to personality. After all, even if 50% of the variation observed in some personality traits is due to genetic factors, that still leaves 50% due to other, presumably situational factors. As we have seen, theories of personality take different positions on the issue of traits and situations in the control of personality. No single model or explanation has proved completely adequate in explaining the incredible diversity of personality.

VAN GOGH'S EAR REVISITED

Early in this chapter we described several alternative explanations for a bizarre event in the life of Vincent Van Gogh, when he cut off a portion of his left ear and presented it to a prostitute. Now that we have reviewed the major theoretical orientations in personality psychology, we can return to Van Gogh as a case study and discuss the incident in terms of the kinds of information that each of the theories might seek in order to explain it. The comparison of the major personality models covered in this chapter presented in Table 10-13 may be helpful in examining how the theories differ, not only in their approach to a case like Van Gogh's, but in more general terms as well.

Psychoanalytic Theory

A Freudian interpretation of the ear mutilation would probably focus on Van Gogh's childhood as a source of relevant information. One explanation, noted in Table 10-3, holds that Van Gogh threatened Gauguin because Gauguin represented his father—a kind of Oedipal scenario played out in Van Gogh's troubled adulthood. The Freudian theorist who favored such an explanation would need to find information about Van Gogh's relationship with his father during his early childhood. We know from his letters that his relationship with his father was strained in adulthood. For example, he wrote to his brother, "My masculine intellect tells me that I must consider it an irrevocable, fatal fact that in the depth of our souls Father and I are irreconcilable" (New York Graphic Society, 1959, Vol. 2).

TABLE 10-13
Comparison of Different Models of Personality

Model	Description and View of Human Nature	Proponents
Psychoanalytic	People are driven by instincts, largely sexual; behavior is determined; people are passive. Development proceeds through four psychosexual stages (plus latency).	Freud, Jung, Horney, Chodorow
Behavioristic	Behavior *is* personality; all behavior is determined by history of reinforcement. Behavior is modified through changing contingencies.	Skinner (Bandura)
Humanistic	People are inherently good; society ruins them. Growth proceeds as people satisfy a hierarchy of motives and move toward self-actualization.	Maslow, Rogers
Cognitive	People are rational and want to predict and control their world; personal constructs help with prediction and control. Constructs develop and change through experience.	Kelly (Bandura)
Biological	Personality is determined by biological factors, such as body type, or genetics.	Sheldon, Lykken

This Freudian explanation also requires some compelling reason why Van Gogh might have seen Gauguin as representing a father figure, such as a link or similarity between the French painter and the elder Van Gogh. Because castration anxiety is a powerful force during the Oedipal years in Freudian theory, the cutting off of the ear as a symbolic castration takes on new significance, especially in light of the similarity between the Dutch word for ear and the slang term for penis, *lel* and *lul*, respectively.

Behavioristic Theory

The central concept in a behavioristic account of personality is reinforcement. On the surface, there seems to be little reinforcement value in cutting off one's ear, so obviously the behaviorist will have to look beyond the act itself to associated behaviors. We have seen, for example, that Van Gogh's brother was an important and supportive figure in his life. A behavioristic analysis of their relationship might turn up evidence that Van Gogh's dependent behaviors were rewarded with attention and solicitous behavior on the part of his brother. The self-mutilation might then have been in the service of recapturing Theo's attention, diverting it from his fiancée. Van Gogh's protestations to his brother that the mutilation should not have troubled him sound unconvincing. His first letter to Theo after returning home from the hospital contained these lines of apology for being the cause of Theo's having to rush to Arles: "I do so regret that you had all that trouble for such a trifle. Forgive me, who am after all probably the primary cause of it all. I did not foresee that it would be important enough for you to be told of it" (New York Graphic Society, 1959, Vol. 3).

Humanistic Theory

Self-mutilation is an irrational behavior that poses serious problems for any theory of personality, but perhaps especially so for humanistic theory. Humanism developed as a theoretical orientation out of frustration with prevailing negative views of human nature and with reliance on the study of abnormal behavior to explain all of human personality. But humanism acknowledges that there is a hierarchy of motives, and that not everyone has attained the highest level of self-actualization. Van Gogh's feelings of low self-worth show that he had not reached self-actualization, but his creativity may have been a reflection of his needs for self-esteem and self-actualization.

Carl Rogers, in fact, argued that creativity is a means people use to strive for self-actualization, and that it is a self-satisfying process by which people try to distill the essence of their perceptions of reality (Rogers, 1959). Van Gogh, for example, was motivated to paint not by a greed for money but by a need to express himself. Indeed, his paintings were not selling well enough for him to support himself fully.

The humanists recognize, however, that people do not always achieve self-actualization. Rogers, for example, might focus on Van Gogh's need for positive regard. The mutilation occurred at a time when Van Gogh thought he was losing the positive regard of two very important people in his life: his brother and Gauguin. The mutilation might then have been a cry for unconditional positive regard from these two people or a response to its loss.

Cognitive Theory

The cognitive theorist, who views personality in terms of the way people try to make sense out of the world, would likely try to find information about Van Gogh's state of mind at the time leading up to the incident. Van Gogh wrote to Theo on the very day of the self-mutilation, but it is only in hindsight that the letter reveals any portent of the day's dark events: "I think myself that Gauguin was a little out of sorts with the good town of Arles, the little yellow house where we work, and especially with me. As a matter of fact, there are bound to be grave difficulties to overcome here too, for him as well as for me. But these difficulties are more within ourselves than outside" (New York Graphic Society, 1959, Vol. 3).

Biological Approach

A biological approach to understanding Van Gogh's personality could take a number of turns, but two seem more plausible than the others. One involves a response to toxins. Van Gogh was heavily exposed to thujone, present in both the liqueur he drank and the paints he used. Behavioral toxicology, a growing subfield in psychology, is investigating the influence of several toxins on aspects of human behavior. Although we do not have enough infor-

Van Gogh's *The Church at Auvers*, painted the year he died. After Van Gogh cut off his ear, he continued to suffer bouts of psychological turmoil over the remaining 2 years of his life. Ultimately he was sent to a sanatorium at Saint Rémy. He continued to paint until he committed suicide by shooting himself in the stomach at the age of 37. Van Gogh's brother, Theo, collapsed at his grave and suffered a stroke shortly thereafter. Theo died the following January and was buried beside Vincent in the churchyard at Auvers, France.

mation at present to state with conviction that Van Gogh's personality was affected by exposure to toxins, it is a plausible hypothesis.

A second biological explanation emphasizes genetic factors that might have contributed to Van Gogh's volatile personality. Although behavior as specific as cutting off one's ear is not genetically preprogrammed, more global traits that are consistent with such behavior very likely are under genetic control, at least to some extent. The search for these genetic mechanisms, as we have said, is proceeding rapidly. If and when the specific genes are isolated, it might be possible to validate the presence of certain genes empirically by exhuming Van Gogh's body and taking a cell sample for genetic analysis. Such postmortem biological analyses are not unprecedented. In 1991, 141 years after President Zachary Taylor's death, his body was exhumed in order to test the hypothesis that he had been a victim of arsenic poisoning.

THINKING AHEAD . . .

We have discussed the incident in which Van Gogh cut off his ear in relation to various theories of personality, but we have said little about the possible relationship between creativity and personality. Many psychologists believe that highly creative individuals have distinct personality traits (Eysenck, 1983); some even believe that creativity may be correlated with madness (MacLagan, 1983). Such a view would be consistent with Van Gogh's life history. A number of studies suggest that highly creative people, such as poets, novelists, composers, and painters, are afflicted with psychological problems more frequently than people in the general population who are comparably intelligent (Andreason, 1987; Jamison, 1988; Richards, 1981). Some highly creative individuals who are known to have had psychological problems, especially disorders involving mania and depression, are poets Sylvia Plath and Edgar Allan Poe, painters Jackson Pollock and Mark Rothko, and composers Robert Schumann and Wolfgang Amadeus Mozart.

Although it seems clear that a link exists between creativity and some forms of psychological problems, which we discuss in Chapter 16, there are almost certainly multiple roads to creativity. Not all roads to creativity involve madness.

In fact, many empirical studies of the relationship between creativity and personality suggest a very positive personality profile for creative individuals. For example, children in India who were given tests of creative thinking as well as personality questionnaires were divided into highly creative and low creative groups. The children classified as highly creative were more outgoing, cooperative, attentive, adaptable, quick to learn, emotionally mature, and spontaneous than the children classified as low creative (Agarwal & Bohra, 1982).

Another study examined the relationship between creativity and personality among conservatory and university dance majors. In comparison to average college students, the dancers showed distinct personality profiles: they were more flexible, achieving, positive, intelligent, and dominating (Alter, 1984).

These studies suggest that creativity, far from indicating psychopathology, actually indicates a higher degree of psychological integration than is typically found among normal individuals. Indeed, some researchers contend that psychopathology is characterized by personality disorganization, whereas creativity is characterized by personality integration. According to one researcher (Storr, 1983), the creative process is similar to the process of personality development described by Carl Jung. Both processes seek new unities of elements that do not obviously go together, and both are always unfinished in some sense.

We do not have the exhaustive information that our various theorists would require in their search for an explanation of Van Gogh's self-mutilation or his creativity. Instead, we use the case as an illustration of how some of the theorists we have discussed might proceed. It would be satisfying to report that one of these theoretical approaches was obviously correct and the others false. But as we have said, there are no laws in personality psychology, so we must be content to encourage you to examine the theoretical accounts on their own merits, using as guides our criteria of explanatory power, consistency, and parsimony.

Summary

The Meaning of Personality

1. Personality is defined as the organization of an individual's distinguishing characteristics, attitudes, or habits. Personality may also include tendencies to think, behave, or otherwise experience the environment.

2. Psychologists have used a wide variety of research strategies to gather information about human personality. The most popular methods used in published research are self-report inventories and laboratory studies, but psychobiography has become increasingly popular.

3. Some psychologists favor a trait approach to personality, looking for consistent patterns of behavior from one situation to another. Other psychologists believe that personality is primarily a function of a particular situation. When traits are seen as universally applicable to everyone in some measure, the approach is nomothetic. In contrast, an idiographic approach describes personality in terms of unique individual traits.

4. From Galen's time nearly 2,000 years ago, people have looked for personality types that could be used to classify people. Contemporary psychologists continue in that tradition. Five factors are frequently mentioned: extraversion, agreeableness, conscientiousness, emotional stability, and intellect.

5. Cross-cultural research generally finds consistency in personality across different cultures.

6. Theories of personality are used to describe and explain human behavior, to generate research, and to provide principles for use in clinical practice. Theories can be evaluated on the basis of criteria such as explanatory power, consistency with relevant evidence, and parsimony. Currently, there are several alternative theories about human personality.

Psychoanalytic Models of Personality

7. The psychoanalytic model argues that psychic energy underlies the peculiarities of personality. The human mind is an active agent with some divisions that keep sensitive material from entering consciousness.

8. Freud's psychosexual theory is the best-known psychoanalytic theory. Freud concentrated on sexual energy as a determinant of personality. Instincts include the life instinct and the death instinct.

9. In Freud's theory, instincts require some kind of release. However, civilization frowns on blatant expression of sexual and aggressive behavior, part of the life and death instincts, respectively.

10. In Freud's psychosexual stages of development, even infants and young children are motivated by sexual impulses and move through regular stages of development: oral, anal, phallic, and adult genital. In the phallic stage, boys feel attraction toward their mothers and rivalry with their fathers, accompanied by intense castration anxiety. This is known as the Oedipal crisis. The counterpart for girls, the Electra crisis, is accompanied by penis envy. Divisions of the mind—id, ego, and superego—also develop at different points in childhood.

11. Jung's analytical psychology is also a psychoanalytic theory, but one with less emphasis on sexual energy. Jung was less insistent on childhood as the central stage of personality development. He felt that people need to fulfill their destiny or purpose; when they have done so, they are individuated. Jung divided the unconscious into the personal and the collective unconscious. The personal unconscious, based on individual experience, includes complexes—organized groups of feelings, thoughts, and memories that influence behavior. The collective unconscious is a part of human genetic heritage and includes archetypes, analogous to the complexes, but common to all people.

12. Adler's individual theory moves even further from Freud's sexual motivation to form a bridge with later humanistic theories. Adler's concept of fictional finalism proposes that people have idealized goals that push them to strive for perfection.

13. Freud's view of development has been criticized for a strong antifemale bias. Feminist revisions of psychoanalysis include those of Karen Horney and Nancy Chodorow. Both of these theorists emphasize culture to a far greater extent than Freud. The way boys and girls are socialized and the role of women in child-care arrangements have implications for psychosexual development. A feminist perspective on psychoanalysis sees gender and sexuality in more flexible terms than Freud did, and also offers hope for cultural change.

Behavioristic Models of Personality

14. Behaviorists reject any mentalistic concepts in personality and focus entirely on behavior. They are often concerned with reinforcement, punishment, and extinction of behavior.

15. Behaviorist B. F. Skinner formulated his personality views from studies with laboratory animals.

He believed that history of reinforcement is the central factor in developing behavior patterns that people have come to call personality.

16. In *Walden Two*, B. F. Skinner's fictional account of a utopian community, behavioral goals are reached through deliberate engineering of the environment. The community decides what personality characteristics are desirable and designs situations to shape these characteristics through appropriate reinforcement schedules.

17. Other behavioristic accounts include the social cognitive theory of Bandura, which includes the concept of observational learning. It also emphasizes reciprocal influences among personal, environmental, and behavioral factors.

Humanistic Models of Personality

18. Humanistic theorists reject both psychoanalytic and behavioristic views as too pessimistic about human nature. This approach is sometimes called the Third Force.

19. Humanistic approaches include Rogers's self theory of personality. Rogers emphasizes the individual's need for positive regard, arguing that if positive regard were given unconditionally, people would emerge psychologically healthy.

Cognitive Models of Personality

20. Cognitive theories view individual personality in terms of people's tendencies to process, interpret, and make sense out of the world that they encounter. Kelly's constructs are similar to schemas, organized memory structures that can determine aspects of social interaction. Schemas are currently receiving a great deal of research attention.

21. Kelly's personal-construct theory describes human nature as being rational, like a scientific approach that includes the goal of understanding people and events in the world. People's personalities are best described in terms of habitual modes of understanding the world through the use of constructs, bipolar categories such as *smart–dumb*, *kind–unkind*, or *forgiving–unforgiving*.

Biological Perspectives on Personality

22. The biological approach holds that personality derives primarily from biological factors such as body type or genetics. Sheldon's theory linked personality to body type, while modern biological theories emphasize genetics. Genetic control of personality is thought to be quite complex, involving specific configurations of genes.

Van Gogh's Ear Revisited

23. Each major theory would look for different things in attempting to explain a complex event such as Van Gogh's self-mutilation. At present, no single theory can be taken as true. Instead, each must be individually evaluated for explanatory power, consistency, and parsimony.

24. Studies of creativity suggest that, far from indicating psychopathology, creativity is associated with a desirable cluster of personality traits.

Key Terms

personologists (376)
personality (376)
factor analysis (379)
nomothetic approach (379)
idiographic approach (380)
theory (380)
psychoanalytic models (384)
life instinct (eros) (384)
death instinct (thanatos) (384)
id (384)
pleasure principle (384)

ego (385)
reality principle (385)
superego (385)
defense mechanisms (385)
oral stage (387)
anal stage (387)
phallic stage (388)
Oedipal crisis (389)
castration complex (389)
penis envy (389)
Electra crisis (389)
libido (393)

personal unconscious (394)
complexes (394)
collective unconscious (394)
archetypes (394)
anima (394)
animus (394)
self archetype (394)
mandala (394)
shadow archetype (394)
fictional finalisms (397)
womb envy (399)

behavioristic models (401)
observational learning (403)
social cognitive theory (405)
triadic reciprocality (406)
humanistic models (407)
cognitive models (409)
personal constructs (409)
somatotypes (411)

Suggested Reading

Bandura, A. (1986). *Social foundations of thought and action: A social cognitive theory*. Englewood Cliffs, NJ: Prentice-Hall. Bandura's attempt to integrate the study of personality with cognitive and social psychology.

Chodorow, N. (1989). *Feminism and psychoanalytic theory*. New Haven, CT: Yale University Press. One of the feminist revisions of Freud's psychoanalytic theory. Instead of rejecting all of the theory, Chodorow modifies it to retain its basic elements while eliminating some of its sexism.

Freud, S. (1949). *An outline of psycho-analysis*. New York: Norton. A brief outline of psychoanalytic theory written by Freud not long before his death. (Original work published 1940)

Gay, P. (1988). *Freud: A life for our time*. New York: Norton. A compelling biography of Sigmund Freud that places him in social and political context, as well as traces the development of his theory.

Kelly, G. A. (1955). *The psychology of personal constructs*. New York: Norton. A good summary of the major cognitive approach to personality, although the terminology and mode of exposition of this work may be difficult for the beginning student.

Lubin, A. J. (1972). *Stranger on the earth: A psychological biography of Vincent Van Gogh*. New York: Holt, Rinehart & Winston. An exercise in psychobiography, this work explores the alternative explanations of Van Gogh's self-mutilation in the context of his personality.

Rogers, C. (1961). *On becoming a person*. Boston: Houghton Mifflin. A detailed account of Rogers's humanistic theory of personality.

Skinner, B. F. (1953). *Science and human behavior*. New York: Free Press. Although not specifically a work on personality theory, this book provides a solid overview of Skinner's behavioristic approach to the wide spectrum of human behavior.

CHAPTER 11
Intelligence and Personality Assessment

Oliver Sacks, the real-life neuropsychologist portrayed by Robin Williams in the film *Awakenings*, has written a series of essays about his patients. The cases are often moving and eloquent, and reveal some of the advances made in understanding the human mind as well as some of the mysteries still to be solved.

One of Sacks's patients was named Rebecca. Rebecca was 19 at the time she was referred to his clinic. She was clumsy and uncoordinated, and, according to reports from her grandmother, was quite limited in the kinds of skills she could learn. For example, she could not reliably open a door with a key or put on her clothes the right way—often getting them on backwards. Her speech often came out in small bursts, and it was difficult for her to sustain a narrative. Although she loved stories, and had tried hard to learn to read, she had never been able to acquire this skill. She relied on her grandmother, with whom she lived, to read stories to her.

When a person such as Rebecca is referred to a psychological clinic, she undergoes a "psychological evaluation," including a battery of tests, to assess her level of functioning. On standardized intelligence tests, Rebecca scored an average IQ of less than 60, an estimate of intelligence that—as we shall see later in this chapter—places her in the classification of mental retardation.

In his evaluation of Rebecca, Dr. Sacks saw primarily her limitations: her inability to perform calculations, her clumsy behavior, her low IQ. But later, he observed her in other contexts and saw a different person. One April morning, outside of the clinic, he saw her as a calm and composed young woman enjoying a beautiful spring day, unencumbered by labels like "retardation," a person not defined by deficits revealed on psychological tests. He learned that she enjoyed going to the synagogue with her grandmother, and that she appreciated the religious rituals involved. He learned that she liked dancing, and that when she danced, her clumsiness disap-

◀ Testing—especially the testing of intelligence and personality—is one of the most pervasive contributions of psychology to modern life.

peared. He learned that when her beloved grandmother died, Rebecca experienced a deep sense of grief, and understood her loss.

After her grandmother's death, Rebecca underwent a change. She knew that she did not want to remain in the classes and workshops designed to help people who are mentally retarded to learn basic skills. These classes had always been frustrating for her, and they now became more so. She approached Dr. Sacks and—using language filled with an elegant metaphor—told him she wanted to leave those classes. "I'm like a sort of living carpet," she said. "I need a pattern, a design, like you have on that carpet. I come apart, I unravel, unless there's a design. I must have meaning. The classes, the odd jobs have no meaning. What I really love is the theatre" (Sacks, 1985, pp. 175–176). So Sacks helped her leave the workshops and enroll in a special theatre group, where she has thrived.

Rebecca's case was something of a revelation for Sacks, showing him the limitations of psychological testing. As he put it, "Our approach, our 'evaluations,' are ridiculously inadequate. They only show us deficits, they do not show us powers; they only show us puzzles and schemata, when we need to see music, narrative, play, a being conducting itself spontaneously in its own natural way" (Sacks, 1985, p. 172).

It may seem strange to you that we open our chapter on psychological assessment by pointing out its weaknesses. But Rebecca's story carries a lesson we would do well to remember: By classifying people using our assessment procedures, we lose something; we lose some of the richness of behavior that makes us human. Tests have their uses, as we hope to convince you in this chapter. They can, however, be overused and misused, and this, too, is important for you to understand.

New tests are being marketed all the time. If they are to be effective, these tests must be constructed carefully. One of the aims of this chapter is to make you a better consumer of tests of psychological concepts such as personality and intelligence. In order for you to evaluate claims about psychological assessment devices, you need to know how the tests were standardized, how realiability and validity were assessed, and who the test is targeted for, among other things. These concepts are treated in this chapter.

FUNCTIONS AND CHARACTERISTICS OF PSYCHOLOGICAL TESTS

psychometrics scientific approach to measurement of psychological characteristics

standardized test set of tasks administered under controlled conditions

The word *test* comes from the Latin *testum*, meaning "earthen vessel." The meaning derives from the ancient practice of using earthen vessels in the examination of precious metals. The standardized psychological testing movement has a much more recent history. Within contemporary psychology, the field of psychological assessment is known as **psychometrics**. A **standardized test** is a task or group of tasks, administered under controlled conditions, used to assess a person's knowledge, skill, or other psychological characteristic. Standardized psychological testing grew out of the concern in the nineteenth century for providing more humane treatment to persons judged to be mentally ill or mentally retarded. Instruments were needed to identify people who fit into these categories, and to differentiate between them.

These early beginnings have burgeoned into a formidable movement; psychological testing has now become the most pervasive aspect of applied psychology, and perhaps the most controversial as well. The objective of psychological assessment is to obtain as pure an estimate as possible of a specified characteristic, be it intelligence, creativity, leadership potential, or

Psychological testing has become one of the most pervasive and controversial aspects of applied psychology. Psychological tests are now given for virtually every kind of selection and screening situation.

whatever. Psychological tests now exist for virtually every kind of selection and screening situation imaginable—from alcoholism screening to work-environment preferences, from achievement motivation to values assessment. New tests continue to be developed all the time, some of them for highly specific purposes. Recent tests, for example, have been designed to measure fear of AIDS and homophobia (Bouton et al., 1987), police cynicism (Regoli, Crank, & Rivera, 1990), and even the attitudes of rural people toward poultry farming as a career (Reddy & Reddy, 1986).

Individual Differences

In the most general sense, psychological tests are used to measure differences among individuals. The English scientist and mathematician Sir Francis Galton (1822–1911) developed much of the underlying logic of measuring individual differences. Galton, a cousin of Charles Darwin, strongly believed that differences between people were inherited, including differences in intelligence. In addition, he thought these differences might be represented by the Gaussian, or normal, distribution. (The German mathematician Karl Friedrich Gauss [1777–1855] had discovered that measurement errors for physical quantities, such as planetary positions, formed a distribution that was bell shaped and that had a line dividing the bell into two equal halves.) Galton, instead of using the **normal distribution** to differentiate true values from false ones due to measurement error, used it to represent the distribution of true scores for the members of a population. Galton and others assumed that many human characteristics were normally distributed, including height, weight, and intelligence.

In Galton's application of the logic of the normal distribution to height, for example, he argued that if a million men stood against a wall, and each had a dot marked to represent height, the dots would concentrate at the point of average height, as shown in Figure 11–1 on page 426. As Galton (1869–1978) put it, "The dots will be found to be ranged so symmetrically on either side of the line of average, that the lower half of the diagram will be almost a precise reflection of the upper." When the notion of units of deviation from the average (see Appendix A) is added to this symmetry, one has the basic idea of the normal distribution.

normal distribution bell-shaped distribution of scores, divided at the mean into two equal halves

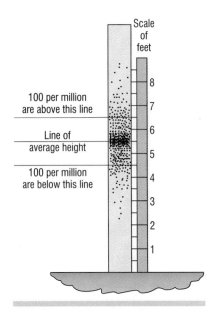

FIGURE 11-1

In Galton's hypothetical data on the distribution of height, if a million men stood against a wall to have their height marked, most of the observations would fall around a mean of approximately 66 in. (an average man's height when Galton made his observations in 1869). Galton's hypothetical marks on the wall illustrate the normal distribution of human characteristics such as height. (From Galton, 1869/1978).

People are drawn to touch the sharp edge of the East Building of the National Gallery of Art in Washington, DC. Their hands have left marks on the building in a pattern similar to Galton's distribution of height.

Indeed, the normal distribution rests on the assumption of population differences that vary around a mean (arithmetic average) for a given characteristic. Tests, then, are used to locate an individual's standing on a distribution relative to other members of that population. Not all psychological tests assume that the characteristics they are measuring are normally distributed, but they are all aimed at measuring differences among people or differences within the same person at different times.

In a more specific sense, the rich variety of tests indicates their numerous uses. As we have already emphasized, one of the uses of psychological tests is to identify intellectual differences among people. The early history of test development reveals that identifying intellectual deficits was a major goal of testing, and educational institutions remain among the heaviest users of tests. In addition to testing for achievement in the various subject areas, schools use tests to identify children who need special educational treatment, such as the learning disabled or the academically gifted. Educational institutions also use tests to screen applicants for admission to educational programs, as any aspiring college student who has taken the Scholastic Aptitude Test (SAT) or American College Testing Program test (ACT) knows.

Psychological tests are also heavily used to select and classify personnel in industrial and military settings. Allocation of human resources in the economy has become a multifaceted enterprise with social and political overtones; it also has implications for economic productivity. Personnel selection has become a discipline in its own right, focusing on selection, assessment, and evaluation of people for specific jobs and on predicting the performance of these selected people in their jobs (Zedeck & Cascio, 1984).

A very broad use of testing involves the identification of individual differences in personality. The goals of such testing are many and varied: to aid in counseling and therapy for psychological problems, to identify temperaments that are suited for different careers, to classify people into groups for research purposes, even to select candidates for certain forms of surgery. Recipients of artificial hearts, for example, are selected in part because of their personality profiles.

In the course of this chapter, we examine in some detail the assessment of two major dimensions of human mental functioning: intelligence and personality. However, the assessment of these human psychological characteristics is of little value without some means of interpreting the test results. We discuss some issues involved in test interpretation next.

Issues of Test Interpretation

A score on a test such as the SAT means little without background information that helps to evaluate the test score. We need to know how and for what purpose the test was designed, whose scores are being used for comparative purposes, whether the score is easily affected by extraneous factors (such as the characteristics of the person giving the test), and how the score is related to behavior in the real world. These issues influence how the test results are interpreted.

Test Construction and Standardization. The initial stages of test construction are laborious and time-consuming. The first step is to write a detailed definition of the construct to be measured by the test (Anastasi, 1986). Then, the authors must write a large number of items, bearing in mind what the test is intended to measure. For example, an early battery of tests for predicting success in college, developed by Cattell (1890/1966) before the SAT and ACT, included tests of sensory capability and judgment of elapsed time. The items on Cattell's simple mental tests bore little theoretical relationship to what he wanted to measure, and research later showed that the tests as a group were useless as indicators of intellectual capacity.

After many items are written, they must be tried out on a pilot group of examinees who are comparable to those people who will ultimately be taking the tests. Items that do not successfully discriminate between people can be eliminated after the pilot testing. For example, if everyone in the pilot group answers a given item in a particular way, the item must be discarded; it adds no information to the test because it does not discriminate between people. Psychological assessment is, above all, about individual differences.

After pilot testing is completed, the test authors draw up a final version of the test that includes only those items that show good discrimination. **Norms**, or standards for achievement on the test, are established by giving the test, initially, to a large number of people who are as similar as possible to the group who will eventually take the test. The group of people who take the test to establish norms, referred to as the **standardization sample**, must be carefully selected to be representative of people for whom the test is intended.

Consider, as an example, one of the tests of personality that focuses on emotional adjustment, the Minnesota Multiphasic Personality Inventory (MMPI). The MMPI was designed to be a screening device for people with specific psychological problems, such as depression. For purposes of standardization, the test was originally given, in hospitals at the University of Minnesota, to patients whose pathologies fell into distinct categories, and the scores were compared to the scores of a normal group. In this instance, the normal group consisted of about 700 relatives and friends of the patients who visited them in their hospitals (Groth-Marnat, 1984). The original group on which the MMPI was standardized was not representative of the normal population as a whole and therefore does not provide adequate comparative norms. The revised version of this test, the MMPI-2, was standardized using a far more representative sample (Butcher et al., 1989). We discuss the MMPI-2 in more detail later.

In constructing some tests, enough items are generated for alternate, equivalent versions of the test. Equivalent forms, theoretically, yield approximately the same score when taken by the same individuals. Equivalent forms are useful for a number of research purposes, including retesting the same individuals at different times.

Characteristics of Test Scores.   Test scores cannot be usefully interpreted unless they are reliable and valid. **Reliability** refers to the repeatability and consistency of the test scores; **validity** refers to the test score's relationship to actual behavior or psychological characteristics in the area the test is supposedly measuring. Although reliability is essential for a test to be valid, validity is the ultimate measure of the usefulness of a test. Reliability and validity are usually expressed in terms of the correlation coefficient, a statistic described in detail in Appendix A.

Reliability.   Some measurement error can be expected with any test. Even measurements of highly objective physical characteristics have some error associated with them. If you weighed yourself on the bathroom scale every hour during the day, you would find minor variations in your weight, some due to the measuring instrument (the scale), some due to actual fluctuations in the construct of interest (your weight), and some perhaps due to errors of the examiner (you). Overall, however, the actual scores on this test would be very consistent from one time to the next—that is, the reliability would be high. Measurement error is usually much greater when assessing psychological characteristics. Nevertheless, reliability is an essential ingredient for a useful test. Without consistency of measurement, you cannot be sure a test is

norms standards for achievement on tests

standardization sample group of individuals used to establish a test's norms

reliability consistency, or repeatability, of test scores

validity correspondence between a test score and the characteristic the test is supposed to measure

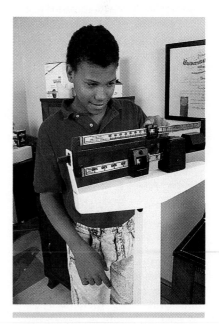

Even measures of highly objective physical characteristics such as weight are not perfectly reliable. If one were to weigh oneself several times during the day, some measurement error would derive from the measuring instrument (the scales), and some fluctuations would occur because of subtle changes in the characteristic itself (one's weight). Fluctuations in weight might also result from errors of the examiner (the individual who records the weight).

| TABLE 11-1 | | |
| Types of Reliability | | |

Testing Sessions Required	Test Forms Required	
	One	Two
One	Split-half	Equivalent-form (immediate)
Two	Test–retest	Equivalent-form (delayed)

Source: Adapted from Anastasi, 1988

measuring anything meaningful. An unreliable test may simply result in a highly individualized response based on whim or fleeting circumstance.

A number of ways exist to measure the reliability of a test. Three of the more popular methods are test–retest procedures, split-half procedures, and equivalent-form procedures. In **test–retest reliability**, the same test is administered to the same individuals at two different times. High correlations between the two sets of scores indicate that the test scores are consistent and hence reliable. If the retest is given after only a short interval, however, the people who took the test may remember their earlier answers and simply repeat them without actually rethinking the test. In that case, the test–retest reliability is artificially inflated.

In **split-half reliability**, the two halves of a test are separately scored and then correlated with each other. For example, even-numbered and odd-numbered items might be scored separately and then examined for their consistency. Similar patterns of scoring on the two parts of the test show good split-half reliability, a strong indication that the overall test is reliable. **Equivalent-form reliability** can be calculated when there are two parallel forms of a test. Both forms are administered to the same people, and correlation coefficients are calculated. High correlations indicate that the measurement of the construct under study is consistent. Equivalent-form reliabilities are available only for the relatively few tests that have alternate forms, such as the SAT. The types of reliability are summarized in Table 11–1.

Validity. As noted earlier, *validity* refers to whether a test measures what it is supposed to measure. In other words, validity assesses the relationship between the test and the behavior or construct of interest. Psychologists over the years have used a number of different measures of validity, which generally fall into three major categories: criterion-related validity, content-related validity, and construct validity.

Criterion-related validity checks the score on the test against the individual's performance in a given area of functioning—that is, against a criterion. Suppose, for example, that we wanted to design a test to measure the construct of *honesty*. If we were about to hire an employee who would be unsupervised in handling large amounts of cash, such a measure would be valuable to us. Our task, then, would be to design a valid test of honesty. The test would measure a psychological characteristic (an honest disposition), and in order for it to be valid, it would have to be evaluated against some criterion, such as performing honestly in a given situation. These relationships are illustrated in Figure 11–2. Criterion-related validity may be assessed against future performance, as in *predictive validity*, or against current performance, as in *concurrent validity*.

In **predictive validity**, future performance in a particular area is referred to as the criterion. Predictive validity is of major importance when a test is

test–retest reliability correspondence between two administrations of the same test to the same people

split-half reliability correspondence between two halves of the same test

equivalent-form reliability correspondence between two alternate versions of a test

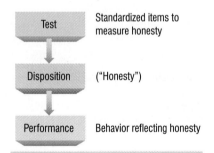

FIGURE 11–2
Criterion-related validity. For a test of honesty to be valid, standardized items on the tests would need to show a relationship to the disposition of honesty, and be reflected in the individual's actual behavior.

criterion-related validity correspondence between a test score and some independent measure of the characteristic it is designed to test

predictive validity validity measure in which a test score is associated with future performance in the area of interest used to select people who are likely to succeed in a training program or other educational experience. The SAT, for example, is used for selecting people who are likely to succeed in college. To assess its predictive validity, one would have to choose a measure indicative of college success and correlate that measure with scores on the SAT. Grade point average (GPA) is usually selected as a criterion measure of college success, and GPA and SAT scores generally do show modest to high correlations, indicating the SAT's moderate predictive validity. Nevertheless, high school grades are more valid predictors of college success than SAT scores (DuBois, 1972).

When tests are used to decide if someone already meets a criterion, rather than to predict future performance, we refer to **concurrent validity**. In the case of the MMPI, for example, the criterion is whether people can be separated meaningfully into categories of psychological diagnosis. To assess such concurrent validity, groups of individuals who fall into the categories are given the test and compared to people who do not fall into the categories. People who have been diagnosed as having specific psychological disorders tend to show characteristic profiles on the MMPI, indicating some concurrent validity.

> **concurrent validity** validity measure in which a test score is associated with current performance in the area of interest

In addition to criterion-related validity, a second major type of validity is **content-related validity**, which concerns whether a test covers the full range of conceptual material it is designed to test. Content validity is particularly important in academic testing. For example, if you have an upcoming biology test covering a group of five chapters, you would expect a more or less even distribution of questions from all the chapters. If the questions you were tested on came only from the first two chapters in the group, the content validity of the test would be low. Your comprehension of the full range of the material would not be adequately assessed through such a test.

> **content-related validity** correspondence between a test and the full range of material it is designed to test

Another aspect of the content of a test is **face validity**, an indicator of whether the test items superficially measure a given characteristic, rather than whether they actually are measuring the characteristic. Face validity, then, is more involved with appearances than with validity in the technical sense. As an example, a bricklaying test has good face validity as a selection test for construction workers, but not for members of a sailing team.

> **face validity** superficial relationship between test items and the tested characteristic

Essentially, *criterion-related validity* refers to the diagnostic utility of a test, and *content-related validity* refers to its relevance or its coverage of the characteristic in question. The "true" validity of the test is the domain of **construct validity**, the extent to which the test measures a given characteristic, trait, or construct (Anastasi, 1986). Consider, by way of example, a hypothetical test of the construct of quantitative reasoning. Let's call it the Quantitative Reasoning Test, or QuaRT. Many sources of information are useful in determining such a test's construct validity, including correlations between the test and other, related tests, such as the quantitative portion of the SAT. In addition, factor analysis of all the items on the test should identify factors that make theoretical sense and that are related to each other, such as computational skill and proportional reasoning. If the QuaRT is a valid measure of quantitative reasoning, it should also show low correlations with unrelated or independent constructs, such as vocabulary or comprehension of metaphors. Experimental interventions designed to raise or lower the test score, such as intensive classes in quantitative reasoning, can also show whether or not a test has construct validity. The different types of validity are summarized in Table 11–2 on page 430.

> **construct validity** the major element of a test's usefulness; the correspondence between a test and the tested characteristic or trait

By now it should be clear to you that the validity of a test depends heavily on its reliability. Test scores that vary greatly from one testing to another are of little use in assessing behavior or predicting performance, because there is little assurance that the test is really measuring a stable characteristic. In other words, the variability in test scores might have more to do with a flaw in the test itself than with a changing psychological characteristic.

TABLE 11-2
Different Measures of a Test's Validity

Type of Measure	Meaning of Measure
Criterion-Related Validity	Assessment of the diagnostic utility of a test
Predictive Validity	Correlation between test score and future performance
Concurrent Validity	Correlation between test score and current performance
Content-Related Validity	Assessment of relevance of coverage for the specified construct
Content Validity	Assessment of whether the coverage of the test is balanced and fair
Face Validity	Assessment of whether the test seems superficially to be measuring the construct
Construct Validity	"True" validity of a test: extent to which it measures a given characteristic, trait, or construct

Increasing a Test's Reliability and Validity. Because test scores are often used in ways that influence people's future lives, it is very important that a test's reliability and validity be sufficiently high. The most obvious method to increase reliability and validity is to add items to the test. An example may help to clarify this point. Suppose the final examination for your psychology class consisted of only four multiple-choice items. Because of chance factors in item selection, you might do poorly on such a test, even if you knew the material very well, because each item would account for 25% of the total score.

Reliability coefficients between this 4-item exam and an alternate form that also contained four items would likely be low. In addition, the content validity of the test would be low, because it would not contain enough items to provide a test of the full spectrum of the material in psychology. You would not have a great deal of confidence that the test could predict your future success in psychology courses. However, if the test contained 200 items instead of 4, its reliability as well as content and predictive validity would be significantly increased, provided, of course, that the items were good ones.

Reliability and validity can also be increased through **item analyses**, where each item on a test is examined for its correlation with the total score. If the correlation between an item and the total score is low, the item may not be measuring the conceptual material the test was designed to measure. Another possibility is that a particular item may be so easy or so difficult that it contributes nothing to the test. Item analyses are useful in revising tests to ensure greater reliability and validity and to ensure their fairness as assessment instruments.

item analysis procedure for evaluating tests by correlating each test item with the total test score

THE NATURE OF INTELLIGENCE

Most people have implicit views about what constitutes intelligence. They describe one friend as being "really smart" and another as "a hard worker but not very bright." Most people endorse the notion that there are individual differences in intelligence, and that there is a continuum of intellectual abilities along which people can be roughly ordered. Defining intelligence

A bricklaying test would not have good face validity for picking members of the America's Cup yacht-racing team. *Face validity* refers to whether a test seems to measure a given construct superficially.

precisely is exceedingly difficult. Nevertheless, we must explore the nature of intelligence before we can meaningfully discuss its assessment.

Experts have historically disagreed about the nature of intelligence. In the 1920s, for example, several experts were asked to define intelligence, and they provided a wide range of definitions; 65 years later, another group of experts was asked the same question, with a similar variety of responses (Sternberg & Detterman, 1986; Sternberg & Powell, 1982).

In 1923, psychologist E. G. Boring defined intelligence as "what the tests test," thus providing an operational definition that circumvented some of the frustration over definitions. Boring's definition has been influential for a number of years, although it illustrates the lack of consensus among experts whose work has touched so many aspects of people's lives. For our purposes, we define **intelligence** as the capacity to acquire and use knowledge, a capacity that is supported by a host of cognitive activities such as perception, memory storage and retrieval, reasoning, problem solving, and creativity. By our definition, intelligence is not the individual's storehouse of knowledge itself, but rather the capacity to acquire and use it.

intelligence capacity to acquire and use knowledge

As a *capacity*, or a potential, intelligence cannot be measured directly, because in a sense it is an abstraction, a capacity that results from information processing: acquiring, storing in memory, retrieving, combining, comparing, and using information in new contexts (Humphreys, 1979). Intelligence can be measured indirectly, because the best indicator of the capacity to acquire

We cannot directly assess intelligence, which is an abstraction or a capacity. Similarly we cannot directly assess running ability but must rely on current running speeds and records of past performance.

and use knowledge is the knowledge that an individual has already acquired, measured on a comparative basis. Keep in mind, however, that the knowledge that an individual has already acquired is affected by many factors, including opportunities provided in home and school environments, motivation, and even physical health. The measurement of pure intellectual capacity is virtually impossible.

An analogy may help to clarify this point. All healthy people possess the organ systems that allow them to run—the musculature, the cardio-pulmonary system, the nervous system for coordination, and so on. However, people generally accept the notion of individual differences in running ability, recognizing that not everyone is a good candidate to run competitively. Some people are not motivated to run; some have not grown up in environments that stressed competitive sports; and some would rather spend their leisure time doing other activities. Suppose we wanted to assess running ability, defined in terms of the likelihood of winning an Olympic marathon. Presumably, any healthy individual could be trained to run a marathon, but the Olympic committee must select for its team only those who have the best running ability and the greatest potential for winning. They cannot directly assess an individual's ultimate running ability, but they can indirectly assess it by looking at current running speeds and past records of performance in marathons.

So it is with intelligence. All healthy people possess the cognitive apparatus for acquiring and using information, but we can only estimate that capacity based on knowledge already acquired. Our definition leaves open the question of whether people come into the world with identical intellectual capacities that develop differently depending on background, experience, and motivation, or whether people are born with different intellectual capacities. This question is certainly not a trivial one, and we discuss the controversy that surrounds it later in the chapter. Regardless of how this controversy may be ultimately resolved, we do know that individual differences in the capacity to acquire and use information can be assessed indirectly.

Theories of Intelligence

Theories of intelligence can be distinguished on the basis of a number of characteristics, such as the nature of the specific abilities that make up intelligence and the number of abilities included; the role of cognitive capacities, such as the speed at which an individual processes information; and the role of factors that go beyond specific abilities and cognitive capacities, such as the environmental context. We will examine theories of intelligence in three broad categories: ability theories, cognitive theories, and contextual theories.

Ability Theories. Most of the traditional theories of intelligence are *ability theories*. That is, they view intelligence in terms of a collection of abilities that can be measured and that serve as the basis for individual differences. This view of intelligence is sometimes referred to as the *psychometric* view, because it is so heavily influenced by measurement issues (*metric* refers to measurement, and *psycho* refers to psychological constructs such as intelligence).

Ability theories of intelligence have traditionally divided on the issue of whether intelligence is one general capacity or whether it is made up of a number of separate capacities. If intelligence is one composite capacity, then it is sensible to summarize its assessment with one number, such as an IQ (intelligence quotient). If, however, it is made up of a number of separate abilities, then one summary measure is misleading. There is little consensus, however, about the number of abilities involved. On the low end of the scale, for example, is Spearman's general intelligence theory.

FIGURE 11-3
In Spearman's model of intelligence, g is the general intellectual ability required for various specific abilities. In this diagram, quite a lot of general intelligence is necessary for the specific ability marked s_1, less for s_2, and not very much at all for s_3.

Spearman's General Intelligence Theory. British psychologist Charles Spearman argued that all activities share one common factor, called **general intelligence**, or simply *g*. However, there are additional **specific abilities**, or *s*, that may require more or less of the *g* factor. General intelligence is essentially the cognitive fuel required for various specific abilities; the more fuel that is required, the greater the correlations between *g* and *s*.

Figure 11–3 illustrates Spearman's model of intelligence. The *g* factor, required for all cognitive activities, is shaded. The amount of *g* required for *s* factors is indicated by the extent of overlap in the diagram. Thus, a factor such as s_1 is very similar to general intelligence, whereas s_3 hardly requires general intelligence at all.

Most people's ordinary understanding of the term *intelligence* follows Spearman's ideas rather closely. The word is, after all, a singular noun, which implies that it is one thing (Brody, 1985). Furthermore, we generally assume that intelligence and achievement are quite different. Many intelligent people do not achieve up to their capacity because of lack of motivation, interest, and so on.

From the perspective of Spearman's theory of general intelligence, assessment requires the construction of a test that gauges general intelligence without becoming clouded by the various specific abilities. Ideally, such a test should be highly abstract and free of cultural biases. The most successful such test of intelligence is Raven's Progressive Matrices, a series of abstract patterns with one piece missing. The examinee must identify the missing piece in a multiple-choice array. A sample item is shown in Figure 11–4. Correlations with other intelligence tests suggest that the Raven matrices do share a common factor with them.

Thurstone's Primary Mental Abilities. Other psychologists reject the notion that one general factor fuels specific abilities. Instead, they reason that there are a number of intellectual abilities, each of which is important. These abilities are not, however, dependent on one overarching general ability. Each individual has a different pattern of intellectual strengths and weaknesses. One person might be exceptionally competent at one intellectual task and quite weak on another. L. L. Thurstone argued for a small set of perhaps six or seven **primary mental abilities**, factors that together make up the elusive concept of intelligence. Thurstone and other investigators provided evidence for several factors; the most frequently mentioned are listed in Table 11–3.

---

general intelligence (g) common intellectual factor shared by all cognitive processes, which theoretically can be summarized with one number

specific abilities (s) individual intellectual functions that are thought to depend on *g*

primary mental abilities Thurstone's small set of intellectual capabilities identified through factor analysis; similar to Gardner's multiple intelligences and Fodor's modules

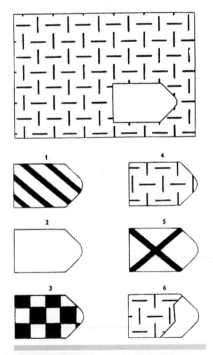

FIGURE 11–4
There have been several attempts to design culture-fair tests of general intelligence (*g*). One such attempt, Raven's Progressive Matrices, requires the examinee to look at a series of abstract items in which one piece is missing, and determine from the pattern which piece in a multiple-choice array it is. A sample item is shown here. (*Answer*: 4)

TABLE 11-3
Examples of Thurstone's Primary Mental Abilities

Verbal comprehension. A factor in tests of such things as verbal reasoning, reasoning by analogy, and reading comprehension

Word fluency. Facility with words in special contexts, such as anagrams, rhyming, or naming as many words as possible beginning with the letter *v*

Number ability. Arithmetic computation

Spatial ability. The ability to mentally manipulate and visualize geometric relations, and similar abilities

Associative memory. The ability to make random paired associations that require rote memory

Perceptual speed. The ability to grasp visual details quickly

General reasoning ability. Found, for example, in tests requiring the subject to find a rule, as in a number series

Gardner's Multiple Intelligences.   Howard Gardner has argued for several relatively autonomous human intellectual capacities in his theory of *multiple intelligences* (Gardner, 1983). Although the precise number of "intelligences" has not been settled, there are probably between a half dozen and a dozen that can be combined in many ways by individuals and by cultures. Gardner proposed a set of intelligences that included linguistic intelligence, musical intelligence, logical-mathematical intelligence, spatial intelligence, and bodily kinesthetic intelligence. Perhaps Rebecca, Oliver Sacks's patient, had a kind of intelligence—awareness of nature, sensitivity to emotion—not tapped by the usual tests of intelligence. Another cognitive scientist, Jerry Fodor, proposed that intelligence, in addition to a central processor akin to Spearman's *g*, consists of several distinct and independent *modules* within the mind, each operating with its own rules and processes (Fodor, 1983).

Guilford's Three-Factor Structure of the Intellect.   On the high end of the scale of number of abilities is J. P. Guilford's cubic model of the structure of intelligence (Figure 11–5). His model assumes that three separate factors make up any individual intellectual activity. These factors are *operations*, which refer to what the individual does, such as remembering and evaluating; *contents*, which refer to the material on which the individual performs these operations, such as symbols or words (semantics); and *products*, the basic forms in which one can fit information, such as classes and implications (Guilford, 1985).

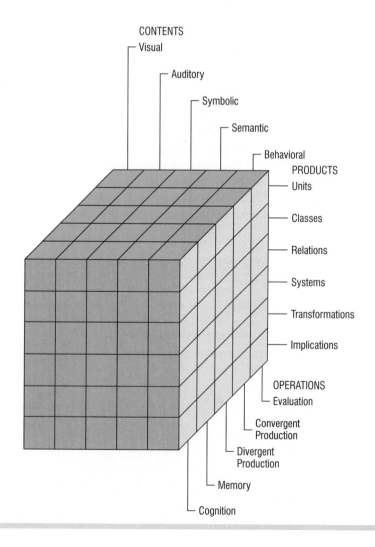

FIGURE 11–5
Guilford's model of intelligence assumes three separate factors that make up any individual intellectual activity: *operations* are what the individual does, such as remember; *contents* are what the individual works with, such as symbols; and *products* are the basic forms in which the information is fit, such as classes. The model calls for 150 separate cognitive abilities. (From Guilford, 1985.)

Guilford's cube contains five operations, six products, and five contents, for a total of 150 categories, and each category has at least one intellectual ability associated with it. Such a model calls for a dazzling array of abilities that can potentially be assessed. Consider the intersection of Guilford's factors that lead to just one of the 150 pieces of the cube: divergent thinking (or creativity) with symbolic content and systems as products. Guilford called this intersection "expressional fluency" and offered the following as a way of measuring it (Guilford, 1959). The task is to produce a sentence, given a particular set of initial letters of the words.

W ——————   C ——————   E ——————   N —————— .

Answers might be "We can eat nuts," or "Where could Earl navigate?" or "Will Carol enjoy notoriety?" Here the individual creates (operation) meaningful, but novel, sentences (products) using words (contents). This, however, leaves 149 additional aspects of intelligence to describe, a task that even Guilford himself never completed and that is well beyond the scope of this chapter.

The ability theories of intelligence just described are summarized in Table 11–4. This table also includes notes on measurement of intelligence implied by each of the theories.

Cognitive Theories.   Many of the models just reviewed rely on **factor analysis**, in which many different tasks are given and intercorrelated. Patterns of items that tend to go together can then be isolated as factors. The concept of cognitive competencies has recently attracted a great deal of attention. As cognitive psychology has gained influence, theorists of intelligence have

factor analysis statistical technique for isolating clusters of items (factors) on a test

TABLE 11-4
Summary of Ability Theories of Intelligence

Number of Abilities	Theorist	Notes on Measurement
One	Spearman	General intelligence (or g) can be summarized with one score such as an IQ score.
	Raven	General intelligence should be measured with a highly abstract, culture-fair test.
Several (6–12)	Thurstone	Several interrelated mental abilities form the basis of intelligence. Tests can be developed for each major ability.
	Gardner	There is no single intelligence. Separate "intelligences" can be found in a variety of combinations in individuals and in cultures. Theoretically, each intelligence (such as musical intelligence) could be measured.
	Fodor	There is a central mental processor in the mind, plus several modules, each of which could theoretically be measured, yielding an overall measure of intelligence, plus several primary abilities.
Many	Guilford	Five operations, six products, and five contents form a three-factor model with 150 categories of intelligence, each of which, theoretically, can be measured.

looked to elementary cognitive processes as the key to intelligence. These processes might include, for example, short-term memory scanning or long-term memory retrieval, or even speed with which information is scanned and encoded (Kranzler & Jensen, 1991).

Many researchers are currently interested in reaction time as a factor that might account for individual differences in intelligence. Reaction time is a measure of how fast a person can react to a specific stimulus; for example, we can measure how fast someone can press a button when a light comes on. Reaction time appears to be associated with several aspects of intelligence (Lindley, Smith, & Thomas, 1988; Smith & Stanley, 1983).

Although our language indicates that we recognize an element of speed in intelligence, as when people who are mentally retarded are referred to as "slow" or the mentally cunning are called "quick-witted," it is somehow unsatisfying to view reaction time as a measure of intelligence. For one thing, it seems to have little face validity; for another, it penalizes older people whose reactions have slowed, but whose intellects are still sharp. Still, one rationale for a reaction-time factor in intelligence is that it indicates the efficiency with which one can perform very basic cognitive operations that are, in turn, necessary for other kinds of cognitive and intellectual activity (Vernon, 1983). In fact, the reaction times of adults whose tested intelligence is in the superior range are faster than those of average adults (Meeker, 1985). It should be noted that many intelligence tests have a time limit and therefore assume that the speed with which one can carry out the operations involved is an aspect of intelligence.

Philip Vernon, a proponent of the information-processing notion of intelligence, has argued that biological indexes of central nervous system activity can provide the most direct measures of intelligence (Vernon, 1991). Such measures, taken while the individual solves cognitive problems, include the time it takes the brain to respond to stimuli measured by EEGs, glucose metabolism measured by PET scans, and speed of nerve electrical activity using reaction-time tasks. These measures require validation, of course. Vernon reported high correlations between these measures and a standardized intelligence test (Vernon & Mori, 1992). PET scans, for example, show that people who are more intelligent, as measured by traditional tests, solve more problems during a given period of time and use less energy, as indicated by glucose metabolism, than less intelligent people (Vernon, 1991); see Chapter 2.

Contextual Theories.   The two previous types of theories of intelligence—ability theories and cognitive theories—are presumed to apply universally. Abilities and cognitive processes are thought to be present to some degree in all people, and the task for measurement is to assess individual differences in the abilities and processes. The third category of intelligence theories that we examine takes a somewhat different view. While acknowledging that there may be universal aspects to intelligence, these theories also assume that much of intelligence is influenced by the cultural context. What is relevant for one type of cultural setting may be useless, or even maladaptive, in another. The most sophisticated and influential of the contextual theories is Sternberg's (1985) theory.

Sternberg's Triarchic Theory of Intelligence.   Sternberg's triarchic ("three-part") theory includes three major dimensions of intelligence. The most global of these dimensions is the *contextual dimension*, which relates intelligence to the external world in which the individual lives. The kinds of behavior that are intelligent depend on the cultural context. Thus, intelligence has a relativistic aspect to it. As an example, consider map-reading skills, which are highly relevant for people who must travel long distances and who are frequently required to find their way around unfamiliar places. Such skills

TABLE 11-5
Examples of Sternberg's Insight Problems

1. If you have black socks and brown socks in your drawer, mixed in the ratio of 4 to 5, how many socks will you have to take out to make sure of having a pair of socks the same color?

2. Suppose you and I have the same amount of money. How much must I give you so that you have 10 dollars more than I?

3. Water lilies double in area every 24 hours. At the beginning of the summer there is 1 water lily on a lake. It takes 60 days for the lake to become covered with water lilies. On what day is the lake half-covered?

4. A farmer has 17 sheep. All but 9 broke through a hole in the fence and wandered away. How many were left?

Note: Answers appear on page 461.
Source: Sternberg, 1985, p. 81.

would be critical in judging the intelligence of people who need them for their survival, but irrelevant to people whose lives are spent in familiar locations. There is also an element of historical relativity to the contextual dimension. Computer skills formed no special part of intelligence a few decades ago, but now they have assumed a prominent place in intelligent behavior for most people in a highly technological cultural context (Sternberg, 1985).

The second element of Sternberg's triarchic theory is the *experiential dimension*. This dimension of intelligence explores the link between behavior in a specific situation, and experience with that situation. It includes the ability to deal with new situations and to show insight, which is essentially the application of information acquired in the past to new problems. For example, a physician shows intelligence along the experiential dimension when she applies her knowledge from past cases to a current set of symptoms one of her patients has. A microbiologist shows experiential intelligence when he uses past knowledge about viruses (such as the tissues they infect or their general shape and structure) to identify a newly discovered virus like the human immunodeficiency virus (HIV). Insight also can be assessed for less specialized experiential knowledge. How well can you solve the insight problems in Table 11–5?

The third and final aspect of Sternberg's triarchic theory is the *componential dimension*, which refers to the activities, or components, of intelligence—the set of mental mechanisms from which intelligent behavior is derived. Sternberg's (1985) description of components is similar to the cognitive theories of intelligence, described earlier. Although fairly complicated, these components are elementary information processes that come into play when a person tries to solve a task or problem. Taken together, the three dimensions of intelligence converge to indicate individual differences in intelligence.

ASSESSMENT OF INTELLIGENCE AND ABILITY

There are a number of ways of classifying intelligence and ability tests, with some overlap among the types. Some tests are administered individually, whereas others are administered in groups. Other classifications include aptitude versus achievement tests and speed versus power tests. In this section we look briefly at these classifications of tests and at some examples of each.

Types of Tests for Intelligence and Ability

Individual Versus Group Tests. The original tests of intelligence were **individual tests**; that is, they were administered individually in a one-to-one situation. **Group tests** did not appear until a mass testing program was developed during World War I. Individual tests are used today for somewhat different purposes than are group tests. In general, they are used more for diagnostic purposes and for evaluating individuals who may be suspected of having special characteristics, such as being gifted or retarded. Group tests, on the other hand, are used in mass testing programs, particularly in the educational system and in the military services.

Individual tests have a number of different types of items, some of which require detailed scoring procedures and careful judgment on the part of the examiner. Because individual tests are given in one-to-one settings, examiners have a greater opportunity to observe the person taking the test; they can more easily detect someone who is ill or otherwise having a bad day. Both the restricted format and the lack of examiner contact may keep a person from working up to full potential on a group intelligence test. The major individual intelligence tests are the Stanford–Binet and the Wechsler scales.

The Stanford–Binet Intelligence Scale. In 1904, Alfred Binet (1857–1911) was appointed by the Minister of Public Instruction in Paris, France, to study procedures for the education of mentally retarded children. Binet and his colleagues began developing a set of items to test intelligence. These items were directed at what Binet considered important mental functions, such as judgment, reasoning, and comprehension—items that emphasized verbal skills.

The result was a series of items arranged in order of increasing difficulty; the items were selected by testing them on a sample of normal children and on some children and adults who were mentally retarded (Anastasi, 1988). Binet grouped the items by level, so that, for example, the items on the 4-year level were passed by 80 to 90% of the 4-year-olds. An individual's score could then be expressed in terms of **mental age**, a score corresponding to the average age of the normal children whose performance on the test was equal to his or her own. The cornerstone of Binet's method of assessing intelligence was the assumption that people are normal if they can perform tasks that people their age can usually perform, retarded

individual tests tests that are administered by a trained examiner to only one person at a time

group tests tests that are administered to several people at the same time

mental age score corresponding to the average number of items passed by a given age group, corresponding to chronological age of that group

Individual tests of intelligence are administered by trained examiners in a face-to-face situation. They involve many different types of tasks, from vocabulary to block design and pattern arrangement.

if they can only perform tasks that match the performance of persons younger than themselves, and accelerated if their performance level is better than that of persons their own age (Terman & Merrill, 1973).

Lewis Terman (1877–1956), who was at Stanford University, translated and revised the Binet scales in 1916 for use in the United States. The resulting test came to be known as the **Stanford–Binet Intelligence Scale**. It was this individually administered test that first used a formula developed by William Stern for calculating an **intelligence quotient**, or **IQ**, a ratio between mental age (MA) and chronological age (CA).

$$IQ = \frac{MA}{CA} \times 100$$

Using this formula, a 12-year-old child scoring a mental age of 15 has an IQ of 125, whereas a 12-year-old scoring a mental age of 10 has an IQ of 83. Most people of a given age are expected to achieve an IQ score very near to 100, plus or minus a few points. Subsequent developments in IQ measurement made use of Galton's ideas about the normal distribution of human characteristics, as we discuss later in the chapter. The Stanford–Binet now computes a composite score known as the *standard age score*.

The Stanford–Binet has been revised periodically since it was brought to the United States in 1916. The most recent—and most radical—revision was in 1986. It is an individually administered test and requires an examiner who has been trained in the administration and scoring of the 15 subtests that make up the scale. A manual provides detailed instructions for administering the Stanford–Binet to people from age 2 to adult (Thorndike, Hagen, & Sattler, 1986). Individuals at most of the age levels are given all 15 subtests. When younger children are tested, however, subtests that are beyond their skills, such as verbal relations and equation building, are omitted. The 15 subtests of the Stanford–Binet are listed in Table 11–6 (page 440).

There are reasons why a psychologist might opt to use the Stanford–Binet over other individual intelligence tests. Because the test has been around for so long, comparative norms on the test are available for a considerable time span. Such norms are useful for charting trends within the population as a whole on a single instrument. In addition, the Stanford–Binet is the test of choice when individuals are to be tested over a considerable time span. No other individual test can be administered at so many different ages (Laurent, Swerdlik, & Ryburn, 1992). The test is also useful for assessing other factors about individuals than their intellectual level. The close interaction between the test taker and the test administrator allows the administrator to observe carefully the test taker's approach to problems, work methods, self-confidence, persistence, and so forth. In a way, the Stanford–Binet allows the examiner to make inferences about a person's personality characteristics (Zimmerman & Woo-Sam, 1985).

On the negative side, the Stanford–Binet attempts to do too much. It covers such a wide age range—age 2 to adult—that it may not be able adequately to measure intelligence at all ages. Some of the standardization procedures were less than ideal as well. For example, many of the samples of normal individuals were from higher social class groups than the general population, obscuring possible social class biases in the test. Among exceptional individuals, the test's validity measures were consistently poor, as shown by correlations with other measures of intelligence. In other words, the Stanford–Binet may not be a good test for identifying exceptional individuals, especially those who are gifted (Laurent et al., 1992).

The Wechsler Scales. The other major individual tests, the **Wechsler intelligence scales**, differ from the Stanford–Binet in an important respect.

Stanford–Binet Intelligence Scale an individual test of intelligence, based on Binet's original test, that measures performance in 15 areas

intelligence quotient (IQ) ratio between mental age and chronological age, times 100

Wechsler intelligence scales three separate individual intelligence tests, each geared to a different age group

TABLE 11-6
The Subtests of the Stanford–Binet Intelligence Scale

1. Vocabulary (*Example:* Examinee must define words such as *mundane*.)
2. Bead Memory (*Example:* Examinee must reproduce a pattern of differently shaped beads on a stalk after seeing a prototype for a brief time.)
3. Quantitative (*Example:* Using large dice, individual must answer questions that require counting and more advanced quantitative manipulations.)
4. Memory for Sentences (*Example:* Examinee listens to a sentence such as "Bob did not want to leave the ballgame," and then repeats it to the examiner.)
5. Pattern Analysis (*Example:* With a set of patterned cubes, examinee must reproduce a pattern under a time limit.)
6. Comprehension (*Example:* Examinee must provide a reasonable answer to questions of the type, "Why do people brush their teeth?")
7. Absurdities (*Example:* Examinee must identify "what is wrong" with a picture of some absurd action such as wearing a hat upside down.)
8. Memory for Digits (*Example:* Examiner reads a series of numbers to examinee, who must say them back exactly as they were read.)
9. Copying (*Example:* Examinee must reproduce a simple block pattern, such as a tower of three blocks.)
10. Memory for Objects (*Example:* Examinee must point to drawings of a set of common objects in the exact order that the examiner showed them to the examinee.)
11. Matrices (*Example:* Examinee must complete a block pattern with one block that most logically fits with the pattern of three other blocks.)
12. Number Series (*Example:* Examinee must complete a number series, such as 1, 2, 3, 4, ___ , with the appropriate number.)
13. Paper Folding and Cutting (*Example:* Examinee must choose from a set of drawings what a folded piece of paper that had been cut would look like when unfolded.)
14. Verbal Relations (*Example:* Examinee must tell how three things, such as boots, sandals, and sneakers, are alike yet different from a fourth thing, such as gloves.)
15. Equation Building (*Example:* Examinee must rearrange number and arithmetical symbols so that they make sense, such as rearranging 1 2 3 = + to 1 + 2 = 3.)

Note: These examples are not identical to actual items, but are very similar.
Source: Thorndike, Hagen, & Sattler, 1986.

Instead of one test for the entire age range, the Wechsler scales include three separate tests, each designed for a particular age group. The revised Wechsler Preschool and Primary Scale of Intelligence (WPPSI-R) covers the age range from 4 to 6½ years. The third edition of the Wechsler Intelligence Scale for Children (WISC-III) is for children ages 6 to 16. The revised Wechsler Adult Intelligence Scale (WAIS-R) is designed for people in late adolescence or adulthood.

Scores on the Wechsler scales use the term **deviation IQ**. (*Deviation* refers to the statistic known as the "standard deviation," a measure of variability of scores around a mean that can be interpreted in terms of the normal distribution. The standard deviation is discussed fully in Appendix A.) For each

deviation IQ score achieved on an intelligence test, interpreted in terms of the normal distribution's standard deviation

age group on the Wechsler, the mean of the distribution is set at 100, and the standard deviation at 15. A score can then be interpreted in terms of the mathematical properties of the normal distribution, shown in Figure 11–6.

The Wechsler scales are the most widely used individual intelligence tests. The WAIS-R, for example, ranks second overall among all types of psychological tests for frequency of use in five different settings: psychiatric hospitals, community mental health centers, counseling centers, centers for developmentally disabled and mentally retarded persons, and veterans hospitals. The ranking for the Stanford–Binet, by contrast, is 18 (Lubin, Larsen, Matarazzo, & Seever, 1985). Two major strengths of the Wechsler contribute to its popularity. It can be used as a general diagnostic tool, beyond yielding an overall score for "intelligence," by examining the patterns of scores on subtests. Moreover, targeting specific age groups with different versions of the test is seen as a major advantage over the Stanford–Binet.

Group Tests. There are several noteworthy differences between individual and group tests of intelligence. The most obvious difference concerns the numbers of people who may be tested. Whereas individual tests are always limited to one examinee at a time, group tests can be administered to as many people as will comfortably fit into a testing room. Furthermore, individual tests require a highly trained examiner; group tests can be administered by anyone who can read the simple instructions that are provided by the test manufacturer. Scoring is generally more objective on the group tests, for they are almost always written in a multiple-choice format. In group testing of intelligence and ability, the examiner's role is greatly simplified to one of reading instructions and timing subtests. Examples of group tests include those used to screen recruits in the armed services, such as the Armed Services Vocational Aptitude Battery (ASVAB), and test batteries used to assess ability in school settings, such as the California Test of Mental Maturity (CTMM).

Aptitude Versus Achievement Tests. The classification of tests into aptitude or achievement tests is based primarily on the degree to which a test is intended to evaluate past learning. **Aptitude tests** are designed to predict

aptitude tests assessments of ability (or set of abilities) in different areas of functioning

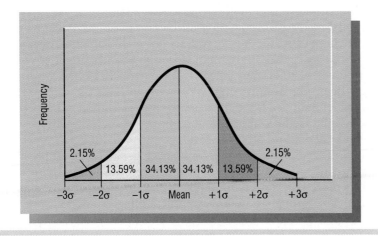

FIGURE 11–6
Scores on intelligence tests such as the Wechsler are now interpreted in terms of standard deviation (σ) units. The mean is set at 100 and the standard deviation at 15. A score of 115 on the Wechsler, for example, is one standard deviation above the mean. Because the mean and median are the same in a normal distribution, 50% of cases fall on each side of a score of 100; and between the mean and one standard deviation (either below or above the mean) fall 34% of cases. Therefore, a score of 115 is at the 84th percentile. In comparative terms, this means that a person scoring 115 performed equal to or better than 84% of the population of the same age.

whether one can profit from admission to an educational program or course of study. As such, they are intended to measure a global ability or set of abilities.

Achievement tests, on the other hand, are intended as evaluations of performance in specific programs of instruction that have already been completed, to see if given levels of mastery of material have been achieved. Periodic college course examinations are good examples of achievement tests. Standardized examples include the tests prepared by the College Board for assigning credit in certain academic subjects. Some colleges assign credit on the basis of scores on the CLEP (College-Level Examination Program) and AP (Advanced Placement) tests.

The Scholastic Aptitude Test. One of the best known group aptitude tests is the Scholastic Aptitude Test (SAT). Since the mid-1920s, when the SAT was first developed, literally millions of individuals have taken this test. Of all the group tests, the SAT ranks as the most technically polished test. The SAT was designed not specifically to measure intelligence, but to measure aptitude for college work. Recall, however, our earlier definition of intelligence as the capacity to acquire and use knowledge. The SAT is broken down into two major components, verbal and mathematical, and a separate score is reported for each. Each of the SAT subscores has a mean set at 500 and a standard deviation set at 100. Thus, a score of 600 is one standard deviation above the mean.

The standardization sample for the SAT was a group of more than 10,000 students who took the test in 1941 (DuBois, 1972). Although several newer forms of the test have been used since then, they are each statistically equated with the form standardized in 1941. Although the mean score of groups taking the test from year to year may vary, a score of 500 on any form of the test corresponds to the mean of the 1941 reference sample (Anastasi, 1988). Therefore, the interpretation of test scores maintains some continuity over time, even though the mean and standard deviation in any given year may differ considerably from the fixed reference group.

Throughout the 1980s, average SAT scores remained fairly steady, but by the early 1990s, they had reached new lows. The average verbal score in 1991 was 422; the average math score was 474 (De Witt, 1991). The decline has been attributed to a broadening of the population of students taking the test and to changes in the home and school environment (Anastasi, 1988). The low verbal scores are often blamed on the abandonment of recreational reading in favor of television viewing (De Witt, 1991). The decline in SAT scores has been alarming to many professionals in psychological assessment. As one of them said, the figures indicate "a decline in non-IQ personal traits, motivation, self-discipline, and so forth, of such magnitude as to constitute a national disaster" (Flynn, 1984).

Many professionals also criticize the SAT itself. The multiple-choice format, they argue, may not allow students to show their true aptitudes. Emphasis is placed on test-taking skills, rather than higher level skills such as critical analysis. In one study, for example, college students were randomly assigned to one of two groups. One group took a version of the SAT with items on reading comprehension of prose passages. These students read the passages and then answered multiple-choice questions based on them. The other group answered the same questions, without having read the passages. Even this group scored significantly above chance, indicating that those items may be sensitive to test-taking savvy rather than actually measuring comprehension (Katz, Lautenschlager, Blackburn, & Harris, 1990).

These and other criticisms have prompted the College Board, which administers the test, to make some fundamental changes. The College

achievement tests assessments of performance in specific programs of instruction; tests in college courses illustrate achievement tests

Board announced in 1990 that it would begin using a new version of the SAT in 1994. The new test, collectively known as the Scholastic Assessment Test (SAT) has two components, SAT I: Reasoning Tests and a series of achievement tests, known as SAT II: Subject Tests. The SAT I includes some items that require short answers rather than multiple choice. For example, some of the math items require computation and short answers, and students may use electronic calculators. The SAT II includes more achievement areas than the old test, such as Japanese, Chinese, and non-Western history. A writing test with an essay is also an option (Leslie & Rosenberg, 1990).

Speed Versus Power Tests. Sometimes it is important to measure how fast an individual can perform certain tasks; tests that are designed to measure this aspect of behavior are called **speed tests**. A speed test is one that provides a number of items, all relatively easy and within the capabilities of the people taking the test, but only a small amount of time, so that no one could finish all the items. For example, an arithmetic teacher might be interested in how well individuals can perform certain arithmetic operations. By providing a large number of items and a small amount of time, the teacher can elicit individual differences in the speed of calculation.

speed tests assessments of how fast an individual can perform certain tasks

Power tests, on the other hand, are used to assess level of ability or mastery of a body of material. In power tests, ample time is allowed so that every individual can attempt all items on the test, but the items range from very easy to very difficult. The most difficult items on the test are unlikely to be solved by anyone taking the test. A perfect score is impossible on either speed or power tests, and consequently, these tests provide a basis for examinees to indicate how much they are able to accomplish. For example, if examinees had been able to finish all the items or solve all the problems, the examiner would not know how much more they could have accomplished had the test been structured beyond their limits.

power tests assessments of an individual's level of ability or mastery of material

One rarely finds a pure speed or a pure power test. Most standardized tests incorporate elements of both speed and power in the assessment of ability or of achievement, because most tests have a time limit as well as a set of items varying in level of difficulty. Even when tests are timed, however, speed may not play much of a role in performance on the test. For example, if students are given 2 hours to complete an examination but everyone finishes within an hour and a half, speed was not a factor in determining the final score.

The choice of intelligence test depends very heavily on the purposes and uses to which the scores will be put. To find the best prospects for college admission, one would choose a standardized group aptitude test, probably one that had elements of both speed and power. The SAT is an example of such a test. To assess the mastery of material in an educational program, which some might describe as finding the most "intelligent" students, a group achievement test would likely be chosen; and if speed of performance were not a relevant factor, it would be a power test. To evaluate an individual for admission to a program for gifted students, one might select an individual aptitude test that had both speed and power elements. What we mean by intelligence, therefore, cannot be summarized by one quick and easy measure. This highly complex concept is measured in a wide variety of ways, depending upon specific circumstances.

As we mentioned earlier, a major rationale for the development of intelligence tests was to identify children who needed special educational assistance, such as those with mental retardation. In 1978 a new law, Public Law 94–142, went into effect in the United States that radically changed the way public schools treat children with mental retardation.

mental retardation deficits in intellectual development that are partly assessed by intelligence tests

This chapter opened with Oliver Sacks's account of Rebecca, a young woman whose intelligence test scores and adaptive behavior classified her as having mental retardation. Professional associations such as the American Association on Mental Retardation (AAMR) define **mental retardation** in terms of limitations in adaptive skills (such as communication, self-care, health and safety, and so on), as well as in terms of tested intelligence (AAMR, 1992).

One part of the definition is that mental retardation "is characterized by significantly subaverage intellectual functioning" (AAMR, 1992, p. 5). Intellectual functioning is measured by one or more of the individually administered tests for general intelligence, such as the Wechsler scales or the Stanford-Binet. Cut-off scores for a classification of mental retardation are set at 70 to 75 or below. Mental retardation becomes noticeable usually in childhood, certainly by the age of 18, according to the AAMR.

People with mental retardation frequently have other handicapping conditions as well, particularly those with greater degrees of retardation. Individuals with moderate to profound retardation also usually have speech and language handicaps. People with mental retardation therefore form a special population that poses particular challenges to the educational system. Before enactment of the Education for All Handicapped Children Act, known as **Public Law (PL) 94–142**, only a small proportion of school-age children with moderate, severe, or profound mental retardation received any public school education. PL 94–142 mandates education for all school-age children, regardless of the degree of severity of the handicapping condition.

Public Law (PL) 94–142 Education for All Handicapped Children Act, mandating education for all children regardless of their handicapping condition

Furthermore, the provisions of PL 94–142 provide safeguards in the evaluation procedures used to classify people as mentally retarded. Among the provisions is the statement that classification is not to be based on a single determinant, such as a score on an IQ test, and that assessments can be made only by licensed professionals (Grossman, 1983).

Changes in the educational system brought about by this legislation have dramatically improved the lives of people who are mentally retarded. Before 1978, basically only two options existed for individuals with pronounced degrees of retardation: they could be cared for at home, or they could be placed in institutions. Now all children are entitled to an education appropriate to their level of functioning. Tests designed to measure intelligence are used as one tool for matching children with appropriate educational strategies—the original purpose for which they were intended.

Do you think this is a good use of intelligence tests? In what ways is there a potential for their misuse?

Since Public Law 94–142 went into effect in 1978, public schools have greatly improved their programs for special children such as those with Down syndrome. Many of these children now participate in regular classroom activities.

ASSESSMENT OF PERSONALITY

Most people have implicit views of what personality is, just as they have implicit definitions of intelligence. But, as we discussed in Chapter 10, many different theories of personality exist. Different theories of personality have been based on different assumptions about human nature; on studies with diverse populations—clients seeking treatment, healthy and happy adults, rats and pigeons; and on different focuses of analysis, such as emotions, behaviors, and cognitions.

Assessment of personality characteristics therefore depends heavily upon which type of personality theory is selected as the focus of study. Psychoanalytic theorists, for example, who subscribe to notions of the power of unconscious motivation, are likely to assess personality indirectly. Because they believe that major elements of personality are hidden even from the individual under study, only indirect methods of assessment are appropriate. Behaviorists, on the other hand, are likely to approach personality directly by observing characteristic behaviors. Psychoanalytic theorists are more likely to look for traits; behaviorists are more likely to look for situational measures for personality. The assessment of personality is, therefore, a complicated business. Indeed, the enterprise of assessing personality is big business. There are now hundreds of tests designed to measure different aspects of human personality. In this section of the chapter we discuss three major approaches to assessing personality: self-report inventories, projective techniques, and behavioral assessment.

Self-Report Inventories

The most frequently used instruments for assessing personality are **self-report inventories**, which require individuals to answer a series of questions about themselves. One assumption underlying self-report inventories is that people know themselves better than anyone else knows them, and that they are therefore in the best position to provide personality information. Self-report inventories often contain a very large number of items that can be grouped into various categories of personal functioning.

The Minnesota Multiphasic Personality Inventory. The most widely used psychological test is a self-report inventory called the **Minnesota Multiphasic Personality Inventory, or MMPI-2**, which we briefly described earlier. The MMPI-2 consists of more than 500 statements that individuals must respond to as being either "true" or "false" with respect to themselves, or indicate that they "cannot say." The items cover a very large territory, ranging from family and marital issues to psychosomatic symptoms and political attitudes. Three sample items are:

I like dramatics.
I certainly feel useless at times.
I am sure I am being talked about.

The MMPI-2 yields scores on the 10 subscales and 3 response-tendency subscales listed in Table 11–7.

The MMPI-2 is an **empirical scale**, which means that the items actually differentiate among groups of people. The MMPI-2 differentiates between those who have been diagnosed with psychological disorders and those who have not (Butcher et al., 1989). The procedure for establishing an empirical scale is fairly straightforward. A group of diagnosed patients is selected to take the test. Their pattern of answers to the questions is compared to that of a nonclinical group who also take the test. Items that differentiate between the two groups then form the basis for a subscale. For example, items that differentiate between patients diagnosed with paranoia and normal individuals form the *paranoia* subscale. There is often some logic to the grouping of items, as when individuals diagnosed with paranoia answer true to the item "I am sure I am being talked about." However, as long as the groups answer the items differently, items can be included on the subscale whether or not they demonstrate any theoretical relevance.

self-report inventories personality measures in which individuals answer a series of questions about themselves

Minnesota Multiphasic Personality Inventory (MMPI-2) the most widely used self-report inventory of personality

empirical scale test in which groups with known differences answer items differentially

TABLE 11-7
Scales of the Minnesota Multiphasic Personality Inventory

Ten subscales of psychological functioning
   Hypochondriasis
   Depression
   Hysteria
   Psychopathic deviate
   Masculinity–Femininity
   Paranoia
   Psychasthenia
   Schizophrenia
   Hypomania
   Social introversion

Three response–tendency subscales
   Lie Score
   Validity Score
   Correction Score

The MMPI has proved to be an enormously popular test, but it has gone beyond its original purpose of differentiating between individuals diagnosed as having psychological disorders and normal individuals. Today it is frequently used as a test of personality functioning for normal populations. Standardization for the second edition included samples of people that were much more representative of the population as a whole than the original standardization done in the 1940s (Butcher et al., 1989). The second edition also updated and reworded items to eliminate sexist language. The MMPI-2 can be administered using written booklets, audio cassettes, or computers.

Other Self-Report Inventories.   A host of other self-report inventories assess characteristics that are related to personality. These include personality inventories for use with normal individuals, such as the California Psychological Inventory; sex-role inventories, such as the Bem Sex-Role Inventory; values scales, such as the Allport–Vernon–Lindzey Study of Values; and even scales designed to assess the need for thrill seeking, such as Zuckerman's Sensation Seeking Scale.

In the previous chapter, we discussed personality factors that were based on the statistical technique of factor analysis, and concluded that consensus is emerging for five basic factors. One of the self-report inventories of personality purports to measure these five personality factors. This test was originally based on the theory that there were only three personality factors—neuroticism, extraversion, and openness—and was called the NEO Inventory. Later studies indicated two additional factors—agreeableness and conscientiousness—and the name became the NEO Personality Inventory, or NEO-PI. The authors of this test take a strong stand about the universal nature of personality: "Truly basic dimensions of personality ought to be universal—found in both sexes, in all races, in various age groups, in different cultures" (Costa & McCrae, 1992a, p. 657).

The NEO-PI is gaining ground as one of the standard tests of personality, especially geared for normal populations. Two forms of the test are available. One is the traditional self-report inventory; the second form, with items written in the third person, is for observer reports of someone else's personality makeup (Costa & McCrae, 1992b). Table 11–8 lists the five fac-

Self-report inventories are designed to allow individuals to report on their own feelings and personality characteristics. Zuckerman's Sensation Seeking Scale, for example, is aimed at identifying those people who have a high need for adventure. This sky surfer would likely score very high on the Sensation Seeking Scale.

TABLE 11-8
NEO-PI Personality Factors and Associated Traits

Neuroticism	Extraversion	Openness	Agreeableness	Conscientiousness
Anxiety	Warmth	Fantasy	Trust	Competence
Angry hostility	Gregariousness	Aesthetics	Straightforwardness	Order
Depression	Assertiveness	Feelings	Altruism	Dutifulness
Self-consciousness	Activity	Actions	Compliance	Achievement striving
Impulsiveness	Excitement seeking	Ideas	Modesty	Self-discipline
Vulnerability	Positive emotions	Values	Tender-mindedness	Deliberation

Source: Costa & McCrae, 1992a, p. 654.

tors of the NEO-PI, along with several traits that combine to constitute each factor.

Strengths and Weaknesses of Self-Report Inventories.   Self-report inventories are easily administered and provide a quick assessment of some aspects of personality. Their very ease of use has led to a problem of overuse. Some employers, for example, require personality tests such as the MMPI-2 before an employee can be hired. The test was not designed as a screening device for employment and should not be used for such purposes. The availability of computer-based scoring and interpretation of the MMPI-2 increases the risks for such abuse, because interpretation is complex and should be done only by trained clinicians (Anastasi, 1988).

THINKING ABOUT
Faking a Personality Profile

Using inventories that people fill out about themselves to measure personality characteristics raises an interesting question: Can people fake a personality profile? Some criminals, for example, have an incentive to appear to be legally insane. If judged sane, they might be sentenced to life in prison rather than to treatment in a psychiatric hospital. Thus, the question of faking a particular personality profile is a critical one in applied settings such as clinical assessment of defendants in murder cases.

On personality inventories, it is often obvious which answer appears, on the surface at least, to be the more socially desirable answer. In this sense, personality inventories may not be *self-reports* as much as they are *self-presentations* of what is thought to be socially desirable (Hogan & Nicholson, 1988). How would you expect someone interested in faking a poor personality profile to answer the MMPI-2 item "I have strange and peculiar thoughts"? To correct for this tendency, some self-report inventories, most notably the MMPI-2, contain a *lie scale*, several items that almost everyone who is telling the truth would answer as false. (A potential lie scale item might be "I never tell a lie.") A person who answers a large proportion of these items as true is assumed to be lying on other parts of the test as well. The MMPI-2 *correction score* is composed of a set of items that indicate attempts by the test taker to fake a good score.

But are these subscales for faking valid? That is, do they actually succeed in identifying correctly those individuals who are faking? Furnham (1990) gave four different career-interest self-report inventories (a category that does not include the MMPI-2) to several individuals who were asked to fill them out in four different ways. In addition to answering honestly, they were to fake the ideal personality profile for three different jobs (librarian, advertising executive, banker). Furnham found that a different personality profile emerged for each of these four instructions, which leads one to conclude that it is possible to fake scores on at least some of the self-report inventories.

The inventories that Furnham used were designed for career counseling, based on the assumption that different personality profiles are suited to specific types of occupations. These particular tests are rarely used in clinical settings to help determine something as weighty as legal insanity. Another recent study used a battery of psychological tests that are more extensively used for clinical assessment. The test battery consisted of the MMPI, the Bender Gestalt, and a new test of lying called the Malingering Scale.

This test battery was given to men jailed in a medium-security prison and to men hospitalized on the psychiatric unit of a VA hospital. The psychiatric patients and a control group of prisoners were given standard instructions for the psychological tests, so that they were answering the questions as honestly as any similar group would have been expected to do. The experimental group, however, received special instructions:

> In this experiment you will be taking some psychological tests. But we *do not* want you to take them in the usual way. Instead, we want you to pretend that you are insane, that is, crazy. In other words, you are to answer the test questions in the way you think an insane person would. (Schretlen, Wilkins, Van Gorp, & Bobholz, 1992)

They were also told that if they succeeded in faking without being caught, they would receive $15, but if they were identified as fakers, they would receive only $2.

This experimental design allows comparison of the pattern of personality deviance on the clinical subscales. The experimental fakers produced a pattern of deviance at least as great as the psychiatric patients and more deviant than the inmate control group on every measure. Thus, they did manage to fake a profile of insanity. However, when various indexes of faking from the three tests in the battery were combined, 80% of the fakers were correctly identified as faking by coders blind to their experimental condition, whereas none of the inmates not assigned to the faking group were misidentified as fakers. Thus it is possible to fake a poor personality profile, but at least under some conditions, the faking can be detected with a high degree of accuracy.

Under what circumstances do you think you would be tempted to fake responses on a self-report test? How far do you think researchers should go in designing ways to detect faking?

Projective Techniques

projective techniques ambiguous and unstructured tasks used to assess personality

Projective techniques involve relatively ambiguous and unstructured tasks to assess personality characteristics. If you were given a projective test, you might be asked to describe what you saw in an inkblot or to tell a story about an ambiguous picture. The assumption that underlies projective techniques is that your own personality characteristics are projected onto the

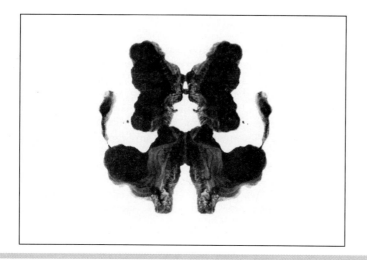

task. When the task is unstructured and ambiguous, what you see in the ambiguous form is presumed to be a function of your own personality.

Projective techniques were designed primarily for use by trained examiners who wished to assess problems in personality. Many psychologists, especially those in the psychoanalytic tradition, assume that much of personality is influenced by unconscious motivation; therefore, individuals will not be fully aware of what they are projecting onto the ambiguous task. A more direct approach, such as the self-report inventory, bypasses this unconscious motivation. Some clinicians argue that it is desirable to provide a task that the examinee cannot readily figure out, because it is less easy to fake a task that is not clear in the first place. Two of the most popular projective techniques are inkblots and the Thematic Apperception Test.

Inkblot Techniques. **Inkblot techniques**, such as the Rorschach and the Holtzman, provide an examinee with cards on which elaborate inkblots are reproduced. For example, look at Figure 11–7. A person taking the inkblot test is shown several inkblots of this type, and the examiner says, "Tell me what you see, what it might be." As the person responds, the examiner makes a verbatim record of what is said and notes certain characteristics of the responses. For example, the examiner notes how the examinee holds the card, how long he or she takes to respond, the nature of any overt emotional response, and other aspects of behavior. Some clinicians believe that these incidental features of test administration are more important than the actual content of an examinee's responses (Korchin & Schuldberg, 1981). Most inkblots are bilaterally symmetrical (that is, when folded in the middle, the two halves form a mirror image); some are in black, white, and shades of gray, and some contain colors. The most popular systems for scoring and interpreting inkblot responses address the major elements described in Table 11–9 on page 450.

inkblot techniques projective personality tests whose stimuli are smeared ink patterns

The Thematic Apperception Test. More emphasis is placed on the **Thematic Apperception Test**, or **TAT**, than on any other projective method for assessing personality characteristics (Piotrowski & Keller, 1984). The TAT, developed by personality theorist Henry A. Murray and his colleague Christiana Morgan (Morgan & Murray, 1935), consists of a series of 20 cards. Nineteen of them contain pictures that are ambiguous, similar to the example presented in Figure 11–8 on page 450. The remaining card is blank, and the examinee must make up a story with no stimulus at all. The examinee instructs the indi-

Thematic Apperception Test (TAT) projective personality test whose stimuli are ambiguous pictures

TABLE 11-9
Major Elements Used in Scoring and Interpreting Inkblot Responses

Location	The part of the inkblot used in the response: whole blot, common detail, unusual detail, white space, etc.
Determinants	Element of the inkblot that determines the nature of the response: form, color, shading, perception of movement, etc.
Content	Categories attributed to the ambiguous forms: human figures, parts of human figures, animal figures, anatomical diagrams, plants, clouds, X-rays, maps, blood, etc.
Popularity	Based on empirical experience with inkblots, responses are categorized on the basis of the frequency with which they have been used by people in general or by specific subgroups of the population.

vidual being tested, "Tell what has led up to the event shown in the picture, describe what is happening at the moment, what the characters are feeling and thinking; and then give the outcome" (Janis et al., 1969).

The TAT is based on several assumptions about personality and its measurement. Again, because the stimuli—here, pictures—are ambiguous, individuals are assumed to project their own feelings into the stories they tell. These feelings may be derived from motivation that is unconscious, and hence hidden from the individuals themselves. With a whole series of ambiguous pictures, it is assumed that themes can be extracted from the stories that have meaning for the individual examinee's personality. Scoring the TAT is therefore done primarily through content analysis of the stories produced, and it relies heavily on subjective clinical judgment.

Consider the following response to the ambiguous picture in Figure 11–8:

> Down in Yucatan, Mayans or Incas—where family life was different from what we know—more like in India today, where marriages are apart from the wishes of the participants or anything like that, this young couple of about 17–18 years old—the man's a very sensitive sort, an artist; therefore, he must have been . . . very much in love with this very charming girl. Since custom . . . Well, the idea is, somehow they got together, she had a baby—but since the marriage hadn't been sanctioned, the elders of the tribe were outraged. They couldn't have the baby, since they had violated all the taboos, etc. It would be taken by the boy's mother, who felt worst about it, to be reared by a priest in one of the temples. The couple were driven out of the place and were never heard of again. This is where the baby's being taken away. The girl's pretty much crushed; he'd like to do something about it, but there's nothing he can. (Janis et al., 1969)

The theme of this story is one that recurs in Western culture: the theme of sacred versus secular love. Like the story of Adam and Eve in the Garden of Eden, forbidden love leads to expulsion. The boy and girl were driven away never to be heard from again. The story suggests an inner conflict over the expression of sexual motivation, but such an interpretation requires analyzing the content of stories to several ambiguous pictures.

Strengths and Weaknesses of Projective Techniques. Projective techniques have generated a wide variety of research on various clinical syndromes, and this must be counted as one of their achievements. It is helpful to be able to estimate the degree to which a test such as an inkblot can differentiate between normal individuals and those suffering from various psychological disorders. Inkblots and the TAT remain very popular tests among clinicians for purposes of diagnosis. Because the purposes of projective

FIGURE 11–8
A picture similar to those presented in the TAT. The pictures are ambiguous in nature, so that an individual can project his or her own feelings onto the scene.

techniques are disguised, there are no correct answers to the items. Faking is therefore less of a problem than it is on self-report inventories.

Although apperception tests and inkblot techniques are popular instruments among clinicians, they lack rigor in terms of their psychometric properties such as norms and reliability. People respond to projective tests with complex verbal material that does not yield an objective score. It is therefore difficult to estimate reliability accurately. The multitude of ways of scoring inkblots and their relatively small standardization samples pose problems for the interpretation and the validity of results (Dana, 1978).

The projective tests were designed to help clinicians identify personality problems; as a result, they appear skewed toward identifying weaknesses rather than strengths in personality profiles (Greenwald, 1990). Because so much of the interpretation of the inkblot and the TAT responses is a matter of clinical judgment, the clinician is more the focus of these techniques than the instruments themselves (Korchin & Schuldberg, 1981).

Behavior Assessment

Critics of projective techniques argue that a more direct approach to personality eliminates some of the problems of subjective scoring. In addition, many psychologists prefer to examine observable behavior, rather than attempt to measure unconscious motivation. As we saw in Chapter 10, many personality theorists believe that the situation determines the behavior we refer to as personality, rather than stable traits of the individual. As a result, they favor the development of behavior techniques for assessing personality, such as naturalistic observation, situation tests, and observation in structured settings.

For example, many developmental psychologists believe that personality is shaped by the experiences that one has throughout childhood. Accordingly, naturalistic observation of families as they interact with each other in their homes may reveal clues about the relationship between specific environmental circumstances and personality characteristics. There are many studies in this tradition. In one study, for example, 3- to 5-year-old children were videotaped with their parents at home in a free-play situation. Investigators found a relationship between parents' behavior in the home and teachers' ratings of the children's popularity, with more popular children having engaging, directive, and stimulating parents (MacDonald & Parke, 1984).

Situational tests and other behavioral measures have good face validity for aspects of personality that may be observed in overt behavior. They are less popular in personality research that emphasizes unconscious aspects of motivation. Behavioral assessments are more frequently used in developmental and social psychology than in personality research or diagnosis. Their main weakness is that they cannot be generalized beyond the specific situation in which they are used. Because many personality theories focus on traits that are assumed to generalize across situations, behavioral assessment is less popular than global trait measures, such as self-report inventories and projective techniques.

After 2 decades of research on the trait versus situation debate in personality, it seems clear that both are important in determining individual characteristics. Assessment techniques such as self-report inventories and behavioral or observational methods seek different types of information about the person. When combined, these sources of information will yield a more complete picture of the individual (Moskowitz, 1986). Table 11–10 contains a summary of different types of personality tests.

Researchers who are interested in the relationship between environmental circumstances and personality often employ naturalistic observation techniques. Investigators have found that more popular children have engaging, directive, and stimulating parents. This mother, for example, asks her son questions about the pictures they see in catalogs.

TABLE 11-10
Tests to Assess Personality

Categories and Examples of Tests	Measurement Notes
Self-Report Inventories	
Minnesota Multiphasic Personality Inventory (MMPI–2)	Over 500 items to which examinee responds yes or no.
NEO Personality Inventory (NEO-PI)	Assesses five personality factors: neuroticism, extraversion, openness, agreeableness, and conscientiousness.
Bem Sex-Role Inventory	Identifies sex-role orientation (masculine, feminine, androgynous, and undifferentiated).
Projective Techniques	
Inkblots (Rorschach and Holtzman)	Unstructured inkblots (usually bilaterally symmetrical) on which the examinee projects elements of personality.
Thematic Apperception Test (TAT)	Ambiguous pictures about which the examinee tells a story. Themes theoretically reveal aspects of personality.
Behavioral Assessment	
Situational tests Interviews Naturalistic observations	Samples of behavior in situations that are as comparable as possible.

SOCIAL ISSUES IN PSYCHOLOGICAL ASSESSMENT

As we said earlier, the objective of psychological assessment is to obtain as pure an estimate as possible of a specified characteristic. Because testing takes place within a social context, however, extraneous factors—such as the anxiety level of the individual being tested or the degree of familiarity with the examiner—may affect the outcome of the test. A great deal of debate, some of it highly charged with emotion, has been devoted to social characteristics, such as race, and their contribution to assessment, especially to the testing of intelligence. In this section, we review some of the social issues involved in psychological assessment, including methods of test administration, characteristics of the examinee, and the background experience of the examinee.

A key issue in testing is to provide standard testing conditions. A fair comparison of individuals on a given test requires that they each have an equivalent opportunity to perform at their best on the test. Part of the interpretation of test scores must rest on the assumption that the testing conditions were similar from one situation to the next in terms of such characteristics as lighting, the demeanor of the examiner, comfort of surroundings, heating and ventilation, and so forth. When tests are given in groups, proctors must assure that everyone is working on the correct section of the test at the same time, and that distractions from others in the room are kept to a minimum. In practice, testing conditions vary a great deal from one testing to another, despite efforts to keep them uniform. The variability of testing conditions introduces sources of error into scores achieved on tests. Our discussion focuses on just a few of the many possible types of variability in testing conditions.

Examiner Familiarity

In individually administered tests, there is close one-to-one interaction between the examiner and the individual being tested. Sometimes people are intimidated or frightened by testing situations in which they must give answers to a stranger. When children are being tested, this problem may be especially acute. One study examined how the familiarity of the examiners contributed to children's test scores on an individually administered test developed especially for the study. The children in this study performed significantly better on the test when they were tested by an examiner who was familiar to them (Fuchs et al., 1984).

Situational factors, such as the race and sex of the examiner, may inadvertently complicate the assessment of intelligence and personality. For example, when white examiners test black children individually, the black children may view these examiners as less familiar than would white children. This difference in the method of test administration may give white children an unintended advantage in overall average scoring because most examiners are white.

A similar point can be made about the sex of the examiner. For example, research suggests that examinees give more responses on personality tests like inkblots when tested by examiners who are the same sex as the examinees. Researchers gave inkblot tests to boys and girls between 6 and 12 years of age and found that boys were more responsive when tested by men, and girls more responsive when tested by women (Greenberg & Gordon, 1983). Interpersonal factors such as familiarity can therefore play an important role in testing, complicating the unbiased estimate of the characteristics of interest.

When examiners are unfamiliar to children being tested, the children may not perform as well. White examiners may be less familiar to black children, and thus inadvertently give white children an edge in scoring.

Characteristics of the Examinee

In addition to the factors related to test administration, characteristics of the examinee may affect the test results. People may differ systematically on the amount of anxiety they experience in testing situations because of their own particular personality makeup. In addition, whether the different social characteristics of the examinees affect psychological assessment, particularly the assessment of intelligence, has been one of the most heated and controversial aspects of testing.

Test Anxiety. People become anxious in testing situations to different degrees. A moderate amount of test anxiety may actually facilitate test performance for simple tasks. However, when test anxiety surpasses a certain level, then it begins to have a debilitating effect on difficult tasks. Students who score high on measures of test anxiety have lower grade point averages, for example. In addition, it appears that women are more likely to suffer from debilitating test anxiety than men (Couch, Garber, & Turner, 1983).

Good test administration calls for well-trained examiners, and part of their training relates to the establishment of rapport with people taking the test. Test anxiety is generally not as high when there is good rapport between examiner and examinee, thereby reducing the contribution of this variable to the test results (Anastasi, 1988).

Age. A fair assessment of psychological characteristics among older people is becoming increasingly important as the median age of the population rises. According to some estimates, half of the population in the United States will

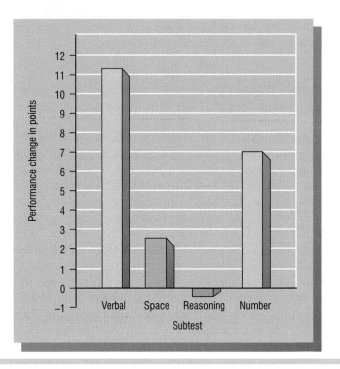

FIGURE 11-9
Adults over the age of 70 performed better on intelligence tests that had large print than they did on small-print versions of the same test. The gain was particularly noticeable on verbal and number subtests. (Adapted from Popkin, Schaie, & Krauss, 1983.)

be over 50 by the turn of the century (Rimmer & Myers, 1982). As we will see in Chapter 12, regular and expected changes in physical characteristics occur with age. Many of these age-related changes may have an impact on the responses given to tests. For example, visual acuity declines with age and reaction time slows. Both of these factors would have important effects on the results of timed written tests that are taken by older adults. In fact, adults over 70 do significantly better on a standardized test that has larger print and greater readability than they do on a small-print version of the same test (Popkin et al., 1983). Performance gains are particularly great on verbal and number subtests, as shown in Figure 11–9. Because the size of print and readability presumably have nothing to do with intelligence, the characteristic being measured, these factors introduce extraneous and irrelevant information into testing, reducing the reliability and validity of the test.

Sex. The best-known intelligence tests—the Stanford–Binet and the Wechsler scales—were standardized in a way that eliminated items that showed large sex differences (Willerman, 1979). It is therefore unreasonable to question whether there are sex differences in intelligence based on studies using these tests. Not surprisingly, large-scale studies show equivalent full-scale scores for males and females on the Stanford–Binet and the Wechsler (Reynolds et al., 1987; Tyler, 1965). Patterns of scoring on the subtests, however, do reveal some average sex differences, with women generally outperforming men on verbal subtests, and men generally doing better than women on mathematical and quantitative subtests (Maccoby & Jacklin, 1974).

The SAT also shows sex differences, with men doing better on both the verbal and the math portions than women. Because the criterion measure of the SAT's validity is grades in college, and since women get better grades than men, on the average, this sex difference poses a problem for validity as well as potential bias (Seligman, 1992).

Race. Racial differences in intelligence have been among the most controversial aspects of the entire psychological assessment movement. A general finding in the area of intelligence testing is that blacks score lower on the tests, on the average, than whites. Many authorities quote the difference at about 15 points, or about one standard deviation on the major intelligence tests (Mackenzie, 1984; Reynolds et al., 1987). How can we account for this average difference in performance? Much of the debate over this issue has centered on the contributions of heredity and environment to the development of intelligence.

A Nature–Nurture Issue.   The debate over nature versus nurture is one of the enduring controversies in developmental psychology. This issue has also been a central focus in discussions of race differences in intelligence. Arthur Jensen provoked a round of debate over the nature–nurture issue in intelligence when he published an article concluding that intelligence (or, more specifically, IQ) was largely heritable. "The preponderance of the evidence," he concluded, "is less consistent with a strictly environmental hypothesis than with a genetic hypothesis, which of course, does not exclude the influence of environment or its interaction with genetic factors" (Jensen, 1969).

One important source of information for Jensen's conclusion was studies of identical twins who were separated soon after birth and reared apart in different social environments. Research on separated identical twins is controversial because such cases are quite rare and probably not representative of the larger population (Mackenzie, 1984). In addition, some of the twin research that has been published is tainted with the scandal of falsified data. The work of Cyril Burt in England, on which Jensen based some of his conclusions about the heritability of IQ, was apparently deliberately faked (Gould, 1981; Kamin, 1974).

However, there are a number of scientifically respectable studies of the genetic contribution to intelligence, such as the Colorado Adoption Project, involving more than 200 adoptive and 200 nonadoptive families. Data from this project support the conclusion that there is a genetic contribution to intelligence, and that heritability of intelligence is more evident among adults than among children and adolescents (DeFries et al., 1987). If genes control neurological development, as these researchers speculate, then intellectual differences become more pronounced over time because they are based on information-processing structures within the nervous system.

A somewhat different pattern of results was found in the Minnesota Transracial Adoption Study (Weinberg, Scarr, & Waldman, 1992). This study examined the IQ scores of black and interracial children (i.e., those with one black parent) who were adopted into white upper-middle-class families, and compared their scores to adopted white children and to biological children from the same families. The birth children scored, on average, higher than the adopted children, whether they were black, interracial, or white. However, the adopted black children scored higher than the average for black children being reared in the black community, and higher than the average for white children in the same geographical area.

When the children were followed up 10 years later, the average IQs for all groups—biological children, adopted black and interracial children, and adopted white children—had all gone down, presumably due to revisions in the tests. However, there were no differences between the groups in the average decline in IQ scores. Although these researchers acknowledge that there is a genetic component to IQ variations among children, they argue that "the social environment maintains a dominant role in determining the average IQ level of black and interracial children" (Weinberg et al., 1992, p. 133). When children are raised in the culture of the test, which happens to be the white middle- to upper-middle-class culture, their scores are reflective of their upbringing. Based on the results of this study, racial differences in IQ variation can be attributed primarily to cultural rather than to genetic factors.

Considerable IQ variation exists even within biological families. Thus, many of the environmental factors that contribute to intelligence differences among people are not due to differences between families as much as to differences within families. Some potential within-family influences on intelligence are listed in Table 11–11.

One very important point must be kept in mind when reviewing research on the heritability of intelligence: even if intelligence has a significant genetic component, the interpretation of racial differences in tested intelligence is still a separate issue. Moreover, a strong interaction between genetic and environmental contributions to intelligence is likely. Intelligence testing has to be viewed within the context of its social and political aspects.

Because of the social and political implications, some researchers believe that psychometricians should not even study race differences in intelligence. In a recent editorial on this question, one psychologist answered the question about studying race differences this way: we should study race differences *"if the research is appropriately motivated, honestly done, and adequately communicated"* (Loehlin, 1992, p. 1). These are big *if*s that have rarely been achieved in the contributions to this topic thus far.

Although standardized IQ tests yield an average difference between black and white populations taking the test, there is considerable overlap in the two distributions. Furthermore, in recent years there has been a narrowing of the gap between black and white average scores on standardized aptitude and achievement tests in elementary and secondary schools. While the average SAT verbal and math scores have declined nationwide since 1976, the scores for black students have increased, by 19 points in the verbal component and by 31 points in math ("Blacks' average," 1991). IQ scores on the Wechsler and Stanford–Binet scales among adults remain at about a one-

TABLE 11-11
Potential Within-Family Sources of Environmental Influence on Intelligence

Accidental Factors
　　Teratogenic agents (discussed in Chapter 12)
　　Physical illness
　　Prenatal and postnatal trauma
　　Separation
Sibling Interaction
　　Differential interaction with siblings
　　Lack of identification with siblings
Family Structure
　　Birth order
　　Sibling spacing
　　Total number of children
　　Presence of extended family members
Parental Treatment
　　Differential treatment of children
　　Interactions of parent and child characteristics
Extrafamilial Networks
　　Peer group members not shared by siblings
　　Relatives
　　Teachers
　　Television

Source: Adapted from Bouchard & Segal, 1985, Table 25.

standard-deviation difference between the races, but among children the gap is narrowing (Vincent, 1991).

Even within the white population, intelligence tests yield a wide range of individual variation. As psychologist Leon Kamin, a critic of the testing movement in the United States, summarized the situation, "To attribute racial differences to genetic factors, granted the overwhelming cultural–environmental differences between races, is to compound folly with malice" (Kamin, 1974). Other reviewers encourage moving away from the limited and ideological question of race differences to questions concerned with identifying the determinants of intellectual level (Mackenzie, 1984).

Although genetic factors may be one determinant of performance on intelligence tests, it is clear that background experience is another determinant. Not even the staunchest advocate of heritability would deny that experience plays a role in psychological assessment. With respect to the narrowing gap between black and white students on standardized tests like the SAT, most explanations have focused on improved social conditions for blacks, such as relative improvement in income and reduction in dropout rates for black students (Jones, 1984). The narrowing gap is clearly not attributable to changes in genetic makeup. The debate over race differences in intelligence testing has not been limited to the issue of heritability. Many critics of testing believe that the tests themselves may be biased against minority groups.

THINKING ABOUT
Psychological Assessment in Different Cultures

Psychological tests are designed to measure differences among people, but they are also designed by psychologists who are themselves members of a cultural group. To what extent is it possible to use these measures with people who grew up in very different cultural contexts? Because so many views about intelligence and personality make predictions about what is universal among humans, the issue of measurement in different cultural groups is an important one.

But when psychologists try to tackle the problem of measurement in different cultures, they run into a host of problems. Perhaps the most obvious is language. Setting aside the differences in literacy rates from one society to another—a very real problem in itself—it is often impossible to find equivalents for concepts from one language to another.

The logic used by people in different cultures to "know" something may also differ. In Western society, we tend to use formal logic derived from Greek philosophy. But other peoples may substitute other forms of "knowing." Consider the attempt to assess the thinking of a member of the Kpelle culture in Liberia; the individual had gone through secondary school, and took part in the following assessment interview:

RESEARCHER: At one time, spider went to a feast. He was told to answer this question before he could eat any of the food. The question is: Spider and black deer always eat together. Spider is eating. Is black deer eating?

KPELLE SUBJECT: Were they in the bush?

RESEARCHER: Yes.

KPELLE SUBJECT: They were eating together?

RESEARCHER: Spider and black deer always eat together. Spider is eating. Is black deer eating?

KPELLE SUBJECT: But I was not there. How can I answer such a question? (quoted in Segall, 1979, pp. 127–128).

Assessing either intelligence or personality characteristics may also be derailed by different standards of what is supposed to happen in a social interaction. People in India, for example, are socialized to be polite to strangers and to answer questions the way they think a questioner wants them to answer. They might have less regard for the correct answer than for the answer they think is desired, out of politeness (Sternberg, 1988). Incidentally, retarded children in the United States show this same tendency toward giving answers they think the interviewer wants them to give. For the rest of us in America, apparently outscoring our peers is more important than being courteous!

Think about the amount of experience you have had in taking tests of various kinds. Test taking is so much a part of our culture that it seems reasonable and natural for some authority to require us to take a test, and we comply with a minimum of grumbling. But we may be the odd ones with respect to test taking. Requests to answer peculiar questions may appear quite bizarre to people in other cultural contexts. The people involved may humor us, or ignore us, or even try to trick us when we approach them with our test batteries.

Do you think it is reasonable to try to test people from very different cultures with assessment instruments developed in our own country? If the people from other cultures score lower than we do as a group, does that mean we have higher levels of intelligence or better personalities? If they score higher, would we be likely to continue to use the tests? To what extent do you think we should take these points into consideration when we test different minority groups within our own larger society?

Research on Test Bias. Unfortunately, research on subcultural bias in standardized intelligence tests is inconclusive. A researcher attempted to determine the issue of racial bias by studying a group of black and white children in Georgia longitudinally, over a period of 6 years. He found that the rank order of item difficulty was the same for the two races, and he concluded that the WISC is not culturally biased against blacks (Miele, 1979). In a review of bias in the WISC, researchers found that some studies revealed bias, whereas other studies did not (Murray & Mishra, 1983). For example, a study with Mexican-American and Anglo–American children found that about 13% of items on the information, similarities, and vocabulary subtests of the WISC were biased against the Mexican-American children (Mishra, 1983).

Perhaps the more important issue here is overreliance on IQ tests. Some critics charge that we do not understand intelligence well enough to test it (Miller-Jones, 1989). The score on an intelligence test is an abstraction that only indirectly reflects an aptitude for acquiring and using knowledge. In a way, heavy reliance on IQ scores causes us to neglect other human traits—such as altruism, courtesy, and sympathy—that are very important in their own right (Willerman, 1979).

Whatever the motives behind the development and widespread use of psychological tests, it is clear that there are social and political implications of testing. The social context in which the test occurs, as well as the cultural characteristics of the individuals being tested and factors in their backgrounds, can affect test results. Although a test may have excellent predictive validity, there is no guarantee that the results of the test will be used wisely, or in the best social and political interests of the population as a whole.

THINKING AHEAD . . .

As we have seen, psychological assessment devices are widely used in a variety of situations, from job placement to educational selection to identification of personality characteristics. By the turn of the century, psychological assessment will undoubtedly have made technological gains for even wider and more sophisticated uses.

It is likely that by the year 2000, intelligence tests will still be used to predict success in settings thought to require intellectual capabilities. However, this rather narrow purpose may be supplemented by other purposes, such as to predict an individual's competence in everyday reasoning and to predict school failure before it occurs (Brown & French, 1979). As research into cognitive functioning becomes more sophisticated, test questions will likely be designed to assess specific cognitive activities thought to be related to overall intelligence. Tests may be aimed at neural efficiency, measuring such things as brain wave patterns to specific stimulus configurations, in an attempt to find the neurological basis for general intelligence (Turnbull, 1979).

Computers are playing an increasingly important role in the area of psychological assessment. The Navy Personnel Research and Development Center, for example, has begun to develop computerized test systems that will greatly enhance the information from multiple-choice questions, by collecting data on how long it takes to answer each item, controlling duration of each item, permitting free responses from the examinee, presenting animated items, and assessing psychomotor coordination (Wolfe, 1986). Computer administration of self-report inventories can also measure how long it takes to answer items, which may provide additional clues about emotionally meaningful questions (Temple & Geisinger, 1990). It may become even more difficult to fake a score on a self-report inventory with computer latency data.

A typical testing station at the turn of the century is likely to include, at a minimum, a color display screen linked to a computer, a response keyboard for the examinee, and a response device similar to current computer-game joysticks. Supplementary material is likely to include physiological measuring devices such as caps for measuring brain waves and brain metabolism, and more complex response apparatuses, such as eye-movement tracking devices. The computer may tailor an individual's test battery to fit the purposes of the test, the type of assessment to be done, and the particular characteristics of the examinee (Hunt, 1982).

Computer analyses of performance can be immediately carried out, with reference to norms for a particular population stored in the computer for ready access. Already, computer scoring of personality tests such as the MMPI is widespread, although feedback is not now immediate and the personality assessments that result have not yet demonstrated validity (Lanyon, 1984; Moreland, 1990).

In the long run, however, computerized testing and interpretation may prove more efficient than testing by psychologists. Clients who have taken computer-interactive personality tests have responded favorably to them (Ben-Porath & Butcher, 1986). The kits used for intelligence testing in the 1990s may be all but obsolete by the beginning of the next century. If electronic psychological assessment is to surpass gimmickry, however, research must focus more specifically on the precise nature of constructs tested. It will not be enough to define intelligence as "what the tests test."

Summary

Functions and Characteristics of Psychological Tests

1. Testing for certain purposes has a long history, but standardized testing is relatively recent. Standardized tests are tasks or groups of tasks administered under standard conditions for assessing knowledge, skill, or other psychological characteristics.

2. An early pioneer in psychological assessment was Francis Galton, who viewed the normal distribution as a representation of the distribution of true scores for the members of a population.

3. Practically speaking, standardized tests are used to measure differences among individuals, or differences in one individual at different times. For tests to be useful, they must be carefully constructed and standardized. Interpretation of scores is based on norms from a standardization sample. Good tests are reliable; that is, they yield scores that are repeatable for an individual, rather than highly inconsistent from testing to testing. They are also valid, meaning that they are actually measuring the behavior or characteristic they are designed to measure.

The Nature of Intelligence

4. Although there are many tests designed to measure intelligence, there is no single agreed-upon definition of intelligence. We define intelligence in this chapter as the capacity to acquire and use knowledge.

5. A number of theories of intelligence have influenced its measurement. These theories fall into three general categories. Ability theories look for specific patterns of ability. Spearman proposed a general intellectual ability and several specific abilities that rely on general intelligence. Thurstone preferred the notion of several primary mental abilities, but no single general ability. Gardner proposed a set of less than a dozen "intelligences." Guilford proposed a model of intelligence that contained 150 specific abilities.

6. Cognitive theories of intelligence suppose that information processing forms the heart of the construct. Reaction time and speed of nerve transmission are examples of cognitive processing.

7. Contextual theories of intelligence, such as Sternberg's, require us to include context in our understanding of intelligence.

Assessment of Intelligence and Ability

8. Intelligence and ability tests can be classified in many different and overlapping ways. Individual tests are administered to one person at a time by a qualified examiner, whereas group tests are administered in groups. The two major individual tests of intelligence are the Stanford–Binet and the Wechsler scales. Group tests of intelligence include the Armed Services Vocational Aptitude Battery and the California Test of Mental Maturity.

9. Other classifications include aptitude versus achievement tests, and speed versus power tests. Aptitude tests are intended to measure potential for future performance; achievement tests are intended to measure the amount of information learned. Speed tests measure how fast one can solve items on a test, and power tests measure the extent of one's ability or achievement.

10. The Education for All Handicapped Children Act of 1975 (PL 94–142) dramatically changed the educational opportunities for children who are classified as having mental retardation. PL 94–142 mandated education for all school-age children, regardless of degree of handicap, and provided safeguards on the IQ testing of such children.

Assessment of Personality

11. Assessment of personality also suffers from a lack of agreed-upon definitions and theories. The most popular methods of assessing personality are self-report inventories, projective techniques, and behavioral assessment.

12. Self-report inventories require examinees to answer a series of questions about themselves. Popular instruments include the Minnesota Multiphasic Personality Inventory, the NEO Personality Inventory, and a host of other inventories of a more specialized nature, such as sex-role inventories.

13. Concern exists about the possibilities of faking good or bad scores on self-report inventories such as the MMPI-2. Research suggests that it is possible to fake scores, but that various checks such as "lie scales" can identify people who faked their scores.

14. Projective techniques are often preferred by psychologists who subscribe to the notion of unconscious motivation. A relatively ambiguous task is given to the examinee, who presumably projects elements of personality onto it. Examples include the various inkblot tests and the Thematic Apperception Test.

15. Behavioral assessment, where the individual's behavior is directly observed, is generally preferred by behaviorally oriented psychologists. Naturalistic observation, structured observation, and situation tests are examples of behavioral assessment techniques.

Social Issues in Psychological Assessment

16. The ideal psychological assessment procedure provides a pure estimate of the characteristic to be measured, be it intelligence or some aspect of personality. Many social issues complicate this pure estimate, however, and become potential sources of error in the interpretation of scores. For example, when examinees are familiar with the person administering the test, their scores tend to be higher.

17. Other problems with testing include test anxiety, and differences in age, race, and sex. Race differences in intelligence are among the most contro-versial topics in psychology. Research claiming that intelligence is largely heritable received much criticism when it was discovered that one of the major figures in this field, Cyril Burt, had falsified twin-study data that purported to show a large genetic component to intelligence.

18. There are many social policy implications from data on race differences in intelligence.

19. Technological advances are expected in the field of psychological assessment in the next few years. By the year 2000, a typical testing station is likely to include computer terminals and a special appa-ratus to measure brain activity.

Key Terms

psychometrics (424)
standardized test (424)
normal distribution (425)
norms (427)
standardization sample (427)
reliability (427)
validity (427)
test–retest reliability (428)
split-half reliability (428)
equivalent-form reliability (428)
criterion-related validity (428)

predictive validity (428)
concurrent validity (429)
content-related validity (429)
face validity (429)
construct validity (429)
item analysis (430)
intelligence (431)
general intelligence (g) (433)
specific abilities (s) (433)
primary mental abilities (433)
factor analysis (435)

individual tests (438)
group tests (438)
mental age (438)
Stanford–Binet Intelligence Scale (439)
intelligence quotient (IQ) (439)
Wechsler intelligence scales (439)
deviation IQ (440)
aptitude tests (441)
achievement tests (442)
speed tests (443)
power tests (443)

mental retardation (444)
Public Law (PL) 94–142 (444)
self-report inventories (445)
Minnesota Multiphasic Personality Inventory (MMPI-2) (445)
empirical scale (445)
projective techniques (448)
inkblot techniques (449)
Thematic Apperception Test (TAT) (449)

Suggested Reading

Anastasi A. (1988). *Psychological testing* (6th ed.). New York: Macmillan. A major textbook on psychological testing that covers general issues such as reliability and validity and offers detailed information on a num-ber of specific psychological tests.

Fancher, R. E. (1985). *The intelligence men: Makers of the IQ controversy.* New York: Norton. A discussion of many controversial issues in the nature–nurture debate over intelligence and the validity of tests used to measure intelligence. Several major figures in the measurement of intelligence are discussed, including Binet, Spearman, and Terman.

Gardner, H. (1983). *Frames of mind: The theory of multiple intelligences.* New York: Basic Books. A theory of intel-ligence that rejects the notion of one overall ability in favor of several independent intellectual domains. Also reviews a number of other contributions to intelligence and its measurement.

Kamin, L. (1974). *The science and politics of IQ.* Potomac, MD: Erlbaum. A major critique of the intelligence-test-ing movement that points out some of the political ramifications of testing.

Sternberg, R. J. (1985). *Beyond IQ: A triarchic theory of human intelligence.* New York: Cambridge University Press. A comprehensive account of Sternberg's contextual approach to intelligence.

ANSWERS TO QUESTIONS IN TABLE 11–5:
1. 3   2. $5   3. 59   4. 9

CHAPTER 12
Physical and Cognitive Development

Hat makes a cat a cat? Could a cat ever be anything other than a cat? These questions may sound overly philosophical for a course in psychology, but they are the sorts of questions that sometimes are asked of children to investigate the ways they think.

Rheta De Vries devised an ingenious, if somewhat devious, method to investigate the "cat identity" issue. She wanted to see if children understood that some aspects of identity are not changeable. A cat is a cat, and cannot suddenly be transformed into a dog or a rabbit. But in De Vries's study, something very much like that happened. She trained a black cat named Maynard to tolerate wearing a mask over its head, representing either a rabbit or a mean-looking dog. The cat underwent this "transformation" behind a screen that obscured its head and forelegs, but left its hindquarters and tail visible. After the transformation, children between the ages of 3 and 6 were asked a series of questions to probe their understanding of identity—of the constancy of "catness."

Mark, who was 3 years and 8 months old and very bright according to intelligence test scores, observed the cat-to-rabbit transformation and exclaimed, "He's a bunny rabbit! Hi! Hi! Hi!" Addressing the animal directly, he said, "Bunny rabbit, I like you." And then to the researcher, "Lock him up! Lock him up!" The researcher asked why, and Mark answered, "Cause he frighten everybody."

One might conclude several things from this interview. For one thing, in comparison to how an adult would likely react, Mark's response to the transformation is immature. It appears that Mark had no clue that the cat was still a cat. Later in the interview, he seemed to confirm this interpretation further by requesting that the researcher make the animal into something

◀ As people grow up physically and mature, their thinking also changes.

else, as if she had some magical power over animal identity. "Make him out a monkey this time! Make him out something else" (De Vries, 1969, p. 18).

In an interview with a 6-year-old, by contrast, the child searched immediately for some plausible way to explain how Maynard appeared to become a dog all of a sudden. "That's probably a fake head," he said, as he touched the dog mask. "Oooh! I felt that nose. It's wood! How come the nose is made out of wood? Maybe this head comes off" (De Vries, 1969, p. 20).

Younger and older children do perform differently on tasks like this one. How do we explain these differences? Is it simply that younger children are more suggestible and more easily tricked by a clever researcher like De Vries? Or is there a more fundamental difference, one involving totally different types of thinking at different points in the life cycle? This is the point of view of some developmental psychologists, as we shall see later in the chapter.

It seems obvious that people change as they grow older. Our goal in this chapter and the next is to examine some of the major elements of developmental change and try to account for them. Do we change on the basis of experience, or through genetic programming? Do we change in small ways on a continuous basis, or do we go through more radical reorganizations in our developmental trajectories? Are the principles governing developmental change universal, or is there an important contribution from culture?

In this chapter we examine the physical and cognitive dimensions of human growth and development. Our aim is to isolate the typical sequences of human development, so that we are in a better position to understand and appreciate the range of human behavior. In the following chapter, we turn to life-cycle changes in social development. Knowing more about human development and its underlying processes may help us to find solutions to problems in development, when the typical trajectory of human growth is disturbed in some way. Let us begin, then, with an overview of major themes in developmental psychology.

THEMES IN DEVELOPMENTAL PSYCHOLOGY

developmental psychology study of changes in domains of behavior from conception to death

As a first step toward understanding the life cycle, we look at some of the enduring themes in developmental psychology. **Developmental psychology** is the study of changes in physical, cognitive, and social behaviors from conception to death. Two controversies have been particularly persistent in developmental psychology: (a) the nature versus nurture debate and (b) the issue of continuity versus discontinuity in development.

Nature Versus Nurture

Have you ever wondered why some people appear to be more outgoing than others, or why some infants begin walking and talking earlier than their peers? Is it because of differences in their genetic endowment or because of the different circumstances in which they grew up? Psychologists have argued, from the very beginnings of the discipline, over the relative importance of heredity and environment in human development.

The heredity versus environment issue is popularly known as the "nature versus nurture" question. To frame the question this way suggests that characteristics of human development are controlled either by nature (heredity) or by nurture (environment). A **nature position** on human development, for example, argues that growth and development are genetically programmed. When the genetic blueprint is laid down at conception, the plan for psychological and behavioral characteristics is determined. Development consists of a biological unfolding. Individual differences among us are due to genetic differences.

The **nurture position** focuses on the diversity among human beings across time and culture, and argues that these differences are so enormous that rearing conditions, experiences, and historical events account for the differences among people. Thus, psychological characteristics such as personality and intelligence are a function of environmental experiences.

Nature versus nurture has been a major organizing theme in developmental psychology, but we now recognize that human development is not an "either–or" proposition. Both heredity and environment exert their influences, and in highly complex ways. To assume that development in any given sphere, such as personality or intelligence, is due to only one of these influences would be extremely misleading.

The nature–nurture controversy is nowhere more apparent than in the area of intellectual ability. Although the controversy has by no means been settled, it seems clear that both nature and nurture are important factors in determining intelligence. Estimates of genetic stability in measures of intelligence from early childhood to adulthood are high, as shown in data from the Colorado Adoption Project of over 200 adoptive and 200 biological families (DeFries, Plomin, & LaBuda, 1987). Social environment also exerts its influence on intelligence. For example, a substantial relationship exists between social class and school success among adopted children. The higher the social class of the adopting families, the better the school performance of adopted children (Duyme, 1988).

Twin Studies.   As discussed in previous chapters, twin studies have often been used to estimate the relative contributions of heredity and environment. Twins are created in one of two ways. They may result after one sperm cell fertilizes one egg cell. The zygote then splits into two separate cells, which in effect become two genetically identical individuals. These twins are called **monozygotic (MZ)**, or identical, twins. In the other case, two separate egg cells are fertilized at the same time, each by different sperm cells. These fertilizations result in two zygotes, and the twins are called **dizygotic (DZ)**, or fraternal, twins. These twins share about 50% of their genetic material, the same as ordinary siblings.

The logic of twin studies exploits this accident of reproductive biology. Twin studies typically compare MZ and DZ twins who have been reared apart or together on various measures of interest. The magnitude of the similarities between the different types of twin pairs yields valuable information about the effects of heredity and environment. To the extent that heredity is important, one would expect MZ twins to be more similar to each other than DZ twins. To the extent that environment is important, one would expect twins reared together to be more similar than twins reared apart.

In a major study of twins and adoption in Sweden, researchers examined correlations from pairs of twins on a test known as the Family Environment Scale (Plomin, McClearn, Pedersen, Nesselroade, & Bergeman, 1988). In Table 12–1, you see the correlations from several subscales of this test. (Remember that a correlation can vary from -1.00 to +1.00, and that the higher the absolute value of the correlation, the stronger the degree of association; see Appendix A for further elaboration of the correlation coefficient.) The magnitude of the correlations is higher for MZ twins than for DZ twins, indicating a

TABLE 12-1
Correlations for Identical and Fraternal Twins Reared Apart or Together

	MZ		DZ	
	Apart	**Together**	**Apart**	**Together**
Cohesion	.41	.60	.32	.43
Expressiveness	.22	.45	.07	.25
Conflict	.35	.58	.18	.46
Achievement orientation	.39	.45	.16	.31
Cultural orientation	.33	.61	.22	.43
Recreational orientation	.38	.60	.28	.47
Organization	.12	.53	.17	.32
Control	−.03	.52	.21	.29

Source: Plomin, McClearn, Pederson, Nesselroade, & Bergeman, 1988, p. 741.

genetic component for these characteristics. In addition, the magnitude of the correlations for twins reared together is greater than for those reared apart, indicating an environmental contribution as well (also see Chapter 2).

To complicate matters further, genetic and environmental effects are not static; that is, their influence changes as the individual matures. In a review of more than 100 published twin studies of intelligence and personality variables, the typical pattern of higher correlations for MZ than DZ twins was found (McCartney, Harris, & Bernieri, 1990). In addition, higher twin correlations were observed for intelligence than for personality variables. These correlations might be higher because there is a greater degree of genetic control over intelligence, or they could be due to more sophisticated, and hence more reliable, measures of intelligence than of personality. But the most important finding from this study was that as twins get older, they become less similar to each other. In other words, as twins get older, environmental influences that they have not shared become more important in determining their behavior.

Identical (or monozygotic) twins have the same genetic material, and have a very similar appearance. They may also be similar in a number of psychological characteristics. Twins are often used in studies of the contributions of heredity and environment to behavior.

Continuity Versus Discontinuity

The second major controversy in the study of human development can be stated in question form: Does development proceed smoothly in a different pattern and direction for each individual, depending on particular experiences in the family and the culture? Or does development occur in universal stages that are discontinuous—that is, discrete and separate from one another? Those who support the **continuity position** argue that development is very gradual and that there are few, if any, dramatic and noticeable shifts in development. Each person seems to grow at an individual rate without any obvious restructurings from one day to the next. Most learning theorists, such as B. F. Skinner and his followers (see Chapter 6), accept the continuity position.

The **discontinuity position** proposes stages in domains such as cognitive and moral development. Shakespeare poetically captured the discontinuity notion in his "seven ages" description of human development in the play *As You Like It*. Many everyday expressions in our language suggest a discontinuity or stage position: "It's just a phase she's going through" or "I'll be glad when he outgrows this stage!"

To some degree, the assumption of either a continuity or a discontinuity position may be influenced by the methods chosen to study human development. Unfortunately, no convenient and agreed-upon technique for studying this issue exists, similar to the twin studies for studying nature and nurture. A number of popular research approaches have evolved, however, and we turn to a discussion of the major techniques in the next section.

THE STUDY OF DEVELOPMENTAL PHENOMENA: LIFE-CYCLE CHANGES

Over the past decades, researchers have increasingly realized that human development is a complex phenomenon, incorporating both nature and nurture, both stages and individual differences. Furthermore, developmental issues should be viewed in the context of the human life span. What happens in one developmental period is influenced by earlier phases of life and will, in turn, have an effect on what is to come. For this reason, in recent years the study of human development has come to be called *life-span developmental psychology*.

Cross-Sectional Research

One way of approaching the field of developmental psychology is to look at changes in psychological phenomena across the entire life. Such an approach, however, requires research strategies that yield information about age-related changes. The most frequently used technique for studying age changes in functioning is **cross-sectional research**, which takes a slice, as it were, or a cross-section, of the population at a given time and assumes that a difference among different age groups can be attributed to age. By that reasoning, the characteristics exhibited by 50-year-olds today could be expected to show up in 20-year-olds 30 years hence. For example, cross-sectional studies of adult intelligence indicate that intelligence peaks in the mid-30s, levels off and remains constant until about 50, and then declines continuously (Schaie, 1983).

Cohort Effects. People born at different time periods differ in ways that cannot be attributed to their age. For example, people who are living today

continuity position position that development is gradual or continuous

discontinuity position position that development occurs in discrete, or discontinuous, stages

All the world's a stage,
And all the men and women
merely players.
They have their exits and their
entrances,
And one man in his time plays
many parts,
His acts being seven ages. At first
the infant,
Mewling and puking in the nurse's
arms.
Then the whining schoolboy,
with his satchel
And shining morning face,
creeping like snail
Unwillingly to school. And then
the lover,
Sighing like furnace, with a
woeful ballad
Made to his mistress' eyebrow.
Then a soldier,
Full of strange oaths, and bearded
like the pard,
Jealous in honour, sudden and
quick in quarrel,
Seeking the bubble reputation
Even in the cannon's mouth. And
then the justice,
In fair round belly with good
capon lin'd,
With eyes severe and beard of
formal cut,
Full of wise saws and modern
instances,
And so he plays his part. The
sixth age shifts
Into the lean and slipper'd
pantaloon,
With spectacles on nose and
pouch on side,
His youthful hose, well sav'd, a
world too wide
For his shrunk shank; and his big
manly voice,
Turning again toward childish
treble, pipes
And whistles in his sound. Last
scene of all,
That ends this strange eventful
history,
Is second childishness and mere
oblivion,
Sans teeth, sans eyes, sans taste,
sans everything.
(From Shakespeare's *As You Like It*,
Act II, Scene 7, lines 139–166)

cross-sectional research developmental research technique in which different age groups are all tested at the same time

and who are in their 60s and 70s typically grew up without television in their homes. Furthermore, on the average they have less formal education than individuals born in subsequent decades. These are differences in their experience that result from being members of different birth cohorts. (A *cohort* is a group of people born at about the same time. For example, the majority of first-year college students in 1993 were born in 1975; collectively, they are referred to as the 1975 birth cohort.) These cohort differences might explain the difference in their performance on intelligence tests.

It is possible, for example, that older cohorts score lower on intelligence tests than younger cohorts because they had fewer years of education, on the average. In fact, the ability of older persons to recall prose passages is about as good as that of young people who have not gone to college but whose verbal abilities are similar to those of college students. College students do significantly better on these recall tasks than either the old or the noncollege young (Ratner et al., 1987). Many tasks that appear on intelligence tests are similar to tasks encountered in school. Cross-sectional research might mislead us into thinking that intelligence declines in middle adulthood, when in fact age differences can reflect the experiences of different cohorts that have nothing to do with aging itself. Thus, we would attribute the results to **cohort effects**, research findings that are based on the time that people were born and their subsequent experiences rather than on their ages per se.

Cross-sectional studies may also indicate that adults process information in more sophisticated ways than young people. Adolescents, when asked to recall the elements of a prose passage and then to summarize it are very good at recalling the basic propositions of the passage. Their summaries show good memory for detail, but tend to ignore the implied psychological and metaphorical meanings of the passage. Mature adults, on the other hand, are about as good at remembering detail, but are much more likely to summarize the metaphorical and psychological content (Adams, 1991). Table 12–2 gives examples of these cohort differences from cross-sectional research.

Sometimes it is possible to control for effects that can be attributed to cohort differences. It seems quite reasonable, for example, to suppose that

cohort effects observed group differences that are based on the time people were born (their birth cohort)

TABLE 12-2
Story Content Summaries from Individuals in Three Age Groups

Summary from 13-year-old:
Once there was a stream. The stream made a journey and was stopped by a desert. When the stream tried to pass the desert it was absorbed by the sand. A voice said that the wind had to carry the stream over the desert. The stream doubted it but later agreed to let the wind carry him over. The wind carried the stream over and the stream never forgot what the voice said.

Summary from 39-year-old:
I believe what this story was trying to say was that there are times when everyone needs help and must sometimes make changes to reach their goals. Some people may resist change for a long time until they realize that certain things are beyond their control and they need assistance. When this is finally achieved and they can accept help and trust from someone, they can master things even as large as a desert.

Summary from 65-year-old:
The essence of the story is that in order to accomplish one's goals, one sometimes has to sacrifice one's individuality and join forces with others moving in similar directions.

Source: Adams, 1991, p. 333.

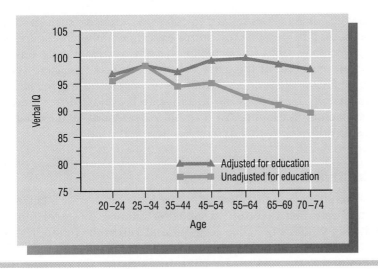

FIGURE 12–1A
One cohort difference that logically could have a bearing on IQ is educational level. When educational level was controlled, verbal IQ scores were about the same for people across the age range from their 20s to their 70s; when educational level was not controlled, a slight decline was shown. (Kaufman et al., 1989.)

differences in formal education might help to explain generational differences in intelligence test scores. In one study of adult intelligence, verbal and performance intelligence, sometimes referred to as different aspects of "IQ," or intelligence quotient, were measured in individuals in seven different age groups, from ages 20–24 to ages 70–74. Their pattern of performance was compared when all individuals, of all different educational levels, were included in the analysis, and then separately with educational level controlled.

As Figure 12–1A shows, verbal IQ declined slightly from ages 25–34 into the 70s when education was not controlled. But with a control for education, this decline disappeared entirely (Kaufman et al., 1989). In other words, people with similar educational backgrounds did not show a decline in intelligence across the life span. Performance IQ is measured somewhat differently than verbal IQ. The performance items are timed, so that a person achieves a higher score when solutions are arrived at quickly. Performance IQ, in contrast to verbal IQ, declines more dramatically with age, and appears to be less affected by differences in educational level, as shown in Figure 12–1B. This pattern, where nontimed performance remains steady over age, whereas timed performance declines, is called the classic aging pattern in intelligence (Botwinick, 1977).

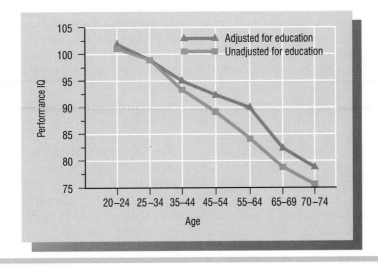

FIGURE 12–1B
Performance IQ scores appear less affected by educational level than verbal IQ scores. Performance IQ shows a similar decline from the 20s to the 70s, whether adjusted for education or not. (Kaufman et al., 1989.)

Although some factors related to cohort differences, such as educational differences, may be possible to control experimentally, others are true confounding variables (that is, variables that are systematically linked to the independent variable, in this case cohort). Because television was simply unavailable for the older cohorts, there is no way to control for its effects. In addition, it may be impossible to tell which cohort differences are the important factors to examine. As a result, researchers have looked for other ways to study developmental differences across the life span.

Longitudinal Research

longitudinal research developmental research technique in which participants are tested over a period of time using the same or similar tests

One obvious strategy is to follow the same individuals over a period of time, testing and retesting them on variables of interest. In developmental psychology, this strategy is called **longitudinal research**. In studies of intelligence, for example, participants are given a battery of tests at periodic intervals throughout their lives. Longitudinal studies, in contrast to cross-sectional studies, do not reveal as much decline in intelligence in adulthood, although some decline becomes evident after age 60 (Schaie & Hertzog, 1983).

Longitudinal studies have their own drawbacks. One major problem with them is that participants may drop out of the study for various reasons that could have an impact on the outcome of the study. If intelligence is related to education, and education is in turn related to access to the health care system, then more educated individuals (who would score higher on the tests) may have better health, and thus be more readily available to participate in the research. The *differential dropout rate* would complicate the interpretation of the longitudinal findings.

Another problem with longitudinal studies is that their actual tests and measures may change over time. One study, aimed at discovering clues about how individuals explain positive and negative events in their lives, chose people over the age of 55 (with an average age of 72) to participate. They were asked to recall a positive or negative event in their recent lives and to answer a series of questions about how they dealt with the event. Their explanations were coded by independent observers for explanatory style, such as attributing the event to some stable characteristic about themselves ("I'm just not good at handling stress, I guess").

Because it's not possible to have people time travel to their earlier lives, how can we obtain information about explanatory styles from their youth? The researchers selected only individuals who had kept diaries or old letters from earlier in their lives (an average of 52 years earlier) that dealt with positive or negative events, and coded that material using the same coding scheme. They found a fairly high degree of consistency in people's explanations for negative events, but not for positive events (Burns & Seligman, 1989). This stability across time, the authors suggested, might be an enduring risk factor for depression or for poor health.

Notice, however, that the materials used to arrive at this conclusion are somewhat different for the two time periods. Letters without probing questions were used for the youth measure, and scenarios with follow-up questions in the older age period. Note also the restrictions on the sample. Only people who met stringent criteria for having kept specific types of material from their youth were included. These criteria would likely overlook some social class groups. Is it really fair to infer stability or instability over time based on material that is really different for the two time periods, and from individuals who are highly selected in the first place?

Longitudinal studies are also very expensive and time-consuming to conduct. One solution to the problem of interpreting cross-sectional and longitudinal studies is to combine their methods in a technique known as **cohort-sequential research** (Schaie, 1983). In this type of research, several age groups (cohorts) are tested periodically. At any given time of testing, cross-sectional comparisons are possible, but in addition, each cohort is tested at intervals, permitting longitudinal comparisons.

In this chapter we survey life-cycle changes in two major areas that affect psychological functioning: physical and cognitive development. (The following chapter is devoted to a detailed discussion of social development.) *Physical development* encompasses the growth of the body, including changes in the brain that are likely to affect behavior. *Cognitive development* incorporates the vast array of changes in the ways that human beings think and perceive, as they move from infancy to adulthood and old age.

cohort-sequential research developmental research strategy that combines longitudinal and cross-sectional research

PHYSICAL DEVELOPMENT

It is a commonplace observation that people change in rather dramatic ways as they grow older. And yet, most people view themselves as being the "same" from one part of the life cycle to another. Although we maintain a sense of continuous identity about who we are, most of us do notice modest changes in our physical appearance with aging. Let us look at some of the most obvious physical changes that people go through and the ways that these changes affect other aspects of their being.

Conception

When does life begin? When does one become a person? These questions have provoked heated moral and philosophical debates, which have no obvious or easy answers. Whatever the answers to these difficult questions may be, we can, at least, describe the sequence of physical changes in the organism before birth. These changes start at the moment of conception, when one male *sperm* cell reaches and fertilizes a female egg, or *ovum*, usually a few hours after sexual intercourse.

Genetic material from both male and female, carried by the sperm and ovum, respectively, combine to produce a new, one-celled organism, called a *zygote*. After about a day, the zygote begins to undergo cell division, producing a multicellular organism called a *blastula*. The blastula travels down the female's fallopian tube into the uterus, where it floats for several days and then attaches itself to the wall of the uterus. This early phase of pregnancy lasts about 2 weeks.

Phases of Pregnancy

The average length of a pregnancy in humans is 280 days, or 40 weeks, measured from the first day of the last menstrual period before conception. After the first 2 weeks, a pregnancy is sometimes divided into two major phases: the period of the embryo and the period of the fetus.

The Period of the Embryo. During the phase of prenatal development from the 2nd through about the 8th week of pregnancy, the organism is referred to as an *embryo*. During this period of pregnancy, cells begin to specialize in a way that will ultimately result in the major organ systems, following the genetic plan laid down at conception. Embryonic growth and development are orderly, following a predictable timetable and sequence. Growth proceeds first from the head downward, in a sequence called **cephalo-caudal development** (the term means "head-to-tail"), and from the

cephalo-caudal development sequence of prenatal development from the head downward

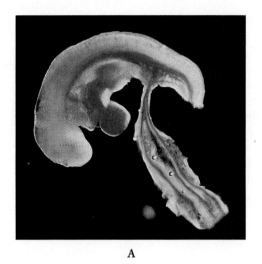

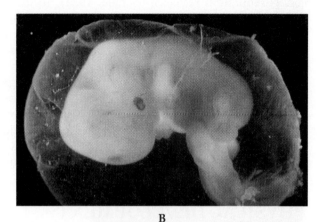

A

B

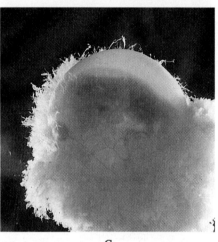

C

FIGURE 12–2
Human embryos at (*A*) 4, (*B*) 6, and (*C*) 8 weeks postconception. At 4 weeks, notice the rudimentary brain and backbone. At 6 weeks, the head is proportionally very large and quite distinct from the body. Note the dark eye disk in the head. Also note that limbs have begun to form, and indentations have begun to appear that will eventually develop into fingers. At 8 weeks, notice the progress in development of the arms and hands, in comparison to legs and feet. Limb buds are not discernible at all at 4 weeks. At 8 weeks the embryo is still less than 4 in. (10 cm) long.

proximo-distal development sequence of prenatal development from the inside outward

inside outward, in a sequence called **proximo-distal development** (this term means "near-to-far"). This sequencing results in the embryo having a head larger than its body. The embryonic head is about half the size of the entire organism. Embryonic development is shown in Figure 12–2.

Most of the major organ systems and structures of the body begin at least rudimentary development during the period of the embryo. The central nervous system and the heart are distinguishable during the 3rd week of pregnancy; eyes, ears, arms, and legs become distinguishable during the 5th week. Gonads appear during the 7th week, but at this early stage they are not clearly distinguishable as male or female.

The Period of the Fetus. After about 8 weeks of pregnancy, the organism is referred to as a *fetus*. The fetal period is characterized by accelerated development of organ systems such as the liver and heart, and further overall growth. Early in the fetal period the heart begins beating, and the pregnant woman can detect the fetus's first movements.

age of viability gestational age (about 6 months) when a fetus has a chance of survival outside the womb

At the end of 6 months of pregnancy, the fetus has achieved a length of approximately 12 in. (30.5 cm). Six months is also the **age of viability** of the fetus, which means that it has a chance to survive if born prematurely. This chance for survival, however, is only about 50%. A considerable amount of prenatal development must still take place.

During the final 3 months of pregnancy, the fetus grows in size, and organ systems mature and begin to function. The fetus more than doubles its

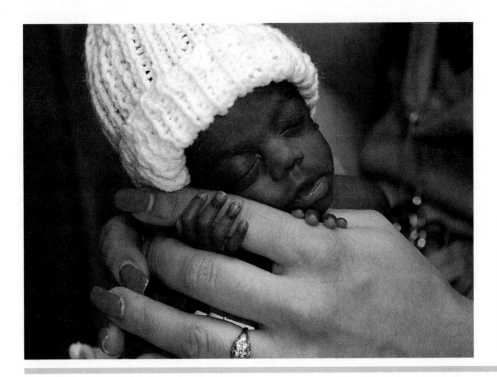

Infants who are born after only 6 months of gestational age (near the end of the second trimester of pregnancy) are at grave risk. They have poorly developed lungs and incomplete heart structures, and are often jaundiced from immature livers. They are also tiny.

weight during the last 3 months of the fetal period. In particular, much of the brain's growth occurs during this phase of pregnancy. At birth an average infant in the United States is about 20 in. (50.8 cm) long and weighs approximately 7.5 lb (3,400 gm) (U.S. Bureau of the Census, 1984).

The developmental processes that transform the microscopic fertilized ovum into a baby weighing several pounds at birth are truly remarkable. Our review has stressed typical development. Some atypical aspects of prenatal development can occur when toxins or disease agents cross the placenta and cause birth defects. But the risks of these types of birth defects can be reduced through an understanding of these causal agents, known as teratogens, and a modification of behavior to avoid them.

SPOTLIGHT ON RESEARCH
Teratogens

People who are contemplating having children, as the vast majority of us eventually do, should be aware of research that has burgeoned in the last 40 years on exposure to hazards that may harm the developing organism during the prenatal period. Substances that can cause birth defects if the embryo or fetus is exposed to them are called **teratogens**. Disease agents, such as viruses and bacteria; drugs, such as alcohol and nicotine; and environmental agents, such as radiation and pollution, all have potential harmful effects on the development of the embryo or fetus. Several teratogens have their most pronounced effects at critical periods during pregnancy. For example, it is during the 1st trimester that diseases are especially serious. German measles, or rubella, affects physical development most markedly during this phase of pregnancy. It may cause blindness or heart damage, because these organ systems are just beginning to develop at this time. If a

teratogens substances that cause birth defects

woman contracts rubella later in pregnancy, teratogenic effects such as mild retardation may still occur (Hardy, 1973).

A number of other diseases may cause birth defects if there is prenatal exposure, including mumps, chicken pox, acquired immune deficiency syndrome (AIDS), syphilis, and some types of influenza. In some cases, birth defects may be severe even though the woman was not very ill during pregnancy. The effects of *toxoplasmosis* (caused by a parasite found in insufficiently cooked meat and in cat feces), for example, are usually minor for an adult woman. If she is pregnant, however, the teratogenic effects may be severe, including serious brain damage and blindness.

Women who are alcoholics particularly risk having infants who are physically affected or mentally impaired. Alcohol is clearly a teratogen, and its most severe effects may vary from malformations, growth deficiency, and behavioral abnormalities to spontaneous abortion and stillbirth. Some infants born to women who are alcoholic suffer from **fetal alcohol syndrome**, characterized by unusual facial features such as widely spaced eyes, a thin upper lip, and a short nose. It is estimated that from about 33 to 43% of infants born to women who are alcoholic suffer from this syndrome (Streissguth et al., 1980). Even when alcohol is consumed in moderation, as in social drinking, it may still act as a teratogen—perhaps through compromising the nervous system of the developing fetus—and affect the infant's cognitive capacities (Streissguth, Barr, & Martin, 1983).

Many other drugs also act as teratogens. Teratogenic effects of cocaine use during pregnancy have now been well documented. Among the effects are smaller size, including smaller head circumference; an increased risk of seizures and localized brain destruction; impaired ability to perform simple perceptual tasks such as finding the source of a sound; and abnormal reflexes (Chasnoff & Griffith, 1989; Chasnoff, Griffith, MacGregor, Dirkes, & Burns, 1989). Direct teratogenic effects of cocaine are most likely due to a change in synaptic transmission in the fetal brain (Lester et al., 1991). PCP ("angel dust") is a teratogen that produces effects similar to those of cocaine (Tabor, Smith-Wallace, & Yonekura, 1990).

Mothers who smoke cigarettes are more likely to have low-birthweight or premature infants, which places the infants at greater risk in the early postnatal period. Longitudinal studies that have followed infants born to mothers who smoke suggest that these children are more likely to experience a number of problems, from temper tantrums to asthma, as they grow into childhood (Butler & Goldring, 1986).

Teratogenic effects of drugs are not limited to physical damage; behavioral disturbances are also common. This growing field of psychology is referred to as *behavioral teratology* (Gilden & Bodewitz, 1991). For example, cigarette smoking or marijuana use during pregnancy is associated with problems in language development and lower scores on cognitive tests (Fried & Watkinson, 1990).

Although additional research is needed on the effects of prenatal exposure to drugs, any drug might potentially have teratogenic effects. The labels on common cold remedies, for example, carry cautionary warnings to pregnant women. Even drugs that are prescribed to aid pregnancy may have teratogenic effects. For example, millions of women in the United States have been treated with progestins and estrogens to avoid spontaneous abortion. Yet prenatal exposure to progestin has been linked to the development of aggression, especially in boys (Reinisch, 1981). In the early 1960s, the drug thalidomide was given to thousands of pregnant women to help prevent nausea and insomnia. Tragically, many women who took this drug during the early part of pregnancy gave birth to babies with physical deformities such as missing ears, arms, and legs. Prenatal exposure to environmental

fetal alcohol syndrome disorder caused by prenatal exposure to alcohol

Children who are born to mothers who drank heavily during pregnancy often exhibit fetal alcohol syndrome. The physical signs of this disorder include widely spaced eyes, a thin upper lip, and a short flat nose. Psychological signs may include varying degrees of mental retardation.

toxins, for example, by eating fish from lakes polluted with polychlorinated biphenyls (PCBs), can also have teratogenic effects, including deficits in memory later in infancy (Jacobson et al., 1985).

We hope that readers of this book who contemplate having children will remember this information about avoiding hazards during pregnancy, so that preventable tragedies involving birth defects will not occur.

Growth During Infancy and Childhood

Growth is greater during infancy than in any other period of postnatal life. However, growth rate declines throughout the period of childhood until it spurts again in adolescence. The change in growth rate can be seen in the typical curve for growth in height presented in Figure 12–3. Although there is a steep decline in the rate of growth over the first 2 years of life, growth rate is still higher at this time than at any other period, reflecting the fact that this is indeed a period of rapid gains. The decline tapers off in early childhood.

The brain is not completely developed even in full-term newborn infants. A great deal of brain development takes place in the first few months of postnatal life; and, in fact, brain growth continues at least until adolescence, and perhaps into adulthood. You will recall from Chapter 2 that some nerve fibers in the brain develop myelin sheaths. Many of these

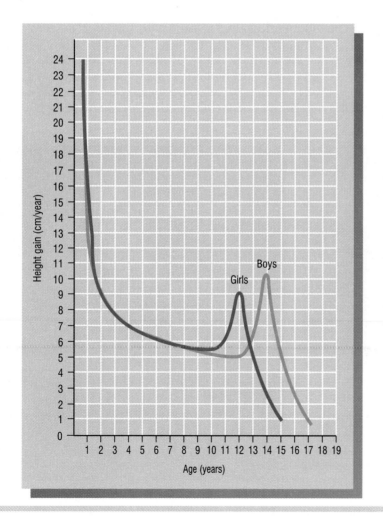

FIGURE 12–3
Growth curves for height in boys and girls reflect the very rapid growth of infancy, a tapering off in childhood, and a second growth spurt in adolescence, which occurs 2 years earlier for girls than for boys. (From Tanner, 1978.)

nerve fibers have not become myelinated by the time of birth. The process of myelination continues for years, especially in the reticular formation and parts of the forebrain (Tanner, 1978).

Motor development proceeds regularly and rapidly throughout the period of infancy. Between 3 and 5 months of age, most infants can lift their heads while lying on their stomachs, roll over, and sit with their heads steady when propped up. By the first year of life, most infants are able to walk while holding on to someone or something, and, by about 14 months of age, they are able to stand well on their own. By the second birthday, most infants can walk up steps and kick a ball forward (Frankenburg, Frandal, Sciarillo, & Burgess, 1981).

Physical growth continues at a regular rate during childhood, accompanied by continued development of the central nervous system. By age 5, children have attained roughly 90% of their adult brain weight. Brain weight, of course, is only a crude measure of information-processing capability.

During childhood, large muscle capability, sometimes called *gross motor coordination*, matures rapidly. Gross motor coordination includes running, jumping, and other active movements associated with childhood play. *Fine motor coordination*, the ability to use small muscles smoothly in such discrete behaviors as writing with a pencil or handling small objects, develops more slowly, throughout childhood.

Cultural Variation in Motor Development. More similarities than differences characterize infants from various ethnic and racial groups. For example, infants attain the milestones of motor development on approximately the same schedule worldwide. In fact, more variation is likely to be seen *within* ethnic groups than *between* the groups (Konner, 1991). That does not mean, however, that cultural variation does not exist. It does exist, and much of it is due to environmental differences. *Culture* in this sense refers to a collection of different things, including socioeconomic status, family structure, attitudes and beliefs about child rearing, and so on (Garcia Coll, 1990).

Large muscle capabilities mature rapidly during childhood. Gross motor coordination for active movements, such as running and kicking, matures earlier than fine motor coordination for making the finer movements associated with coloring or writing.

Comparisons across ethnic groups in the United States must be undertaken with caution, because of the heterogeneity of ethnic groups with respect to these and a number of other important factors. Ethnic groups differ in the degree to which they have adopted the dominant culture, in the period of time since large numbers of them immigrated into the United States, in their choice about immigration, in social class, and in other important respects (Harrison, Wilson, Pine, Chan, & Buriel, 1990). Still, it is important to examine cultural variation, so that diversity can be viewed as an asset, rather than a barrier, to understanding development.

Consider some ethnic differences in beliefs about child rearing. African-American and Mexican-American parents expect their infants to overcome dependency earlier than Anglo-American parents; Mexican-American parents are less authoritarian than either of the other two groups. Chinese-American parents exercise more parental control and encourage more independence in their infants than Anglo-American parents. Yet when socioeconomic status is controlled, parents from these different ethnic groups behave in very similar ways in their actual child-rearing techniques (Garcia Coll, 1990; Lin & Fu, 1990).

Some Native-American parents have traditionally used cradle boards in the care of their infants up until about 6 months of age. These boards restrict the movement of the infants dramatically, especially in comparison to how other ethnic groups provide opportunities for movement. This practice may reflect a different idea about infant responsiveness. Navajo mothers, for example, are more silent and passive in their interactions with infants than African-American or Anglo-American parents. At the same time, Navajo infants are less irritable and more self-soothing than African-American and Anglo-American infants (Garcia Coll, 1990).

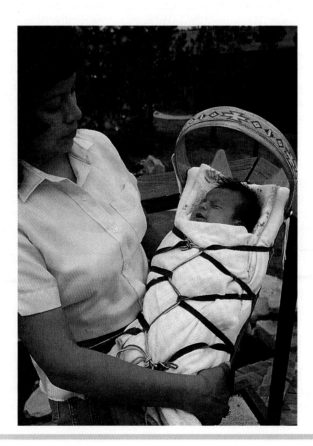

Child-rearing practices differ across cultural groups, and are probably related to different views about infant responsiveness. Navajo mothers have traditionally bound their infants into cradle boards, and they are more passive in their interactions with their infants than African-American and white mothers in the United States.

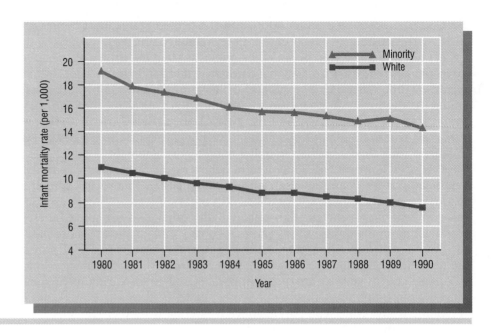

FIGURE 12-4
Ethnic groups have shown consistent differences in infant mortality rates. Although there has been an overall decline in infant mortality rates over the last decade, the average difference between white and minority infants has continued. Just under 8 white infants (per 1,000) die in infancy, compared to 14 minority infants. (From the National Center for Health Statistics, 1993.)

In some cultural groups, puberty is a time for a special ceremony marking the transition into a period of life when reproduction is a possibility. This Apache girl's puberty ceremony involves being painted with earth, symbolizing a unity with nature and natural processes.

menarche onset of a girl's first menstruation

One alarming ethnic group difference concerns infant mortality rates. Although infant mortality in the United States has declined among white and among ethnic minority groups over the past decade, the gap between the groups has remained relatively constant (see Figure 12–4). Just under 8 white infants per 1,000 die in infancy, compared to more than 14 per 1,000 among all minority groups combined (National Center for Health Statistics, 1993). These differences are likely due to differences in the economic status of the ethnic group. Because ethnic minority groups are more likely to suffer economically than the white majority, they are less able to afford adequate prenatal and postnatal care.

Poverty affects parenting in a number of important ways beyond health status. It increases the psychological distress of parents and makes it harder for them to maintain consistent and supportive behavior toward their children, which in turn disrupts the child's emotional functioning (McLoyd, 1990).

Puberty

One of the most intense physical transformations of the entire life cycle occurs in early adolescence, with the changes associated with *puberty*. Over a 2-year period there is rapid height and weight gain, development of secondary sex characteristics such as pubic hair, maturation of the reproductive system, and muscle development that renders the body more adultlike in appearance. The physical transformation of the body at adolescence marks the end of childhood and the transition into adulthood.

Do you remember 6th grade, when the girls had suddenly become taller and seemed to be developing a mature appearance more rapidly than the boys? One of the interesting oddities of developmental physiology is the fact that boys and girls seem to be on a different developmental timetable. In infancy, girls are precocious compared to boys in both physical and cognitive dimensions. In adolescence, girls are ahead of boys, in the physical changes of puberty, by an average of 2 years. The peak growth spurt, for example, occurs at an average age of 12 for girls, 14 for boys (Marshall & Tanner, 1970).

A girl's first menstruation, known as **menarche**, is the event that most dramatically signals the point of transition from childhood to sexual maturity. Three research findings about menarche seem clear. First, there is a great deal of individual variation in the age of menarche, with an average in the United States of about 12½ (Warren, 1983). Second, there is also a great deal of cultural variation. The average age of menarche in Nigeria, for example, is 13½, and in Zimbabwe 14¼ (Akinboye, 1984). Third, the average age of menarche has decreased over the last 100 years or so. For Anglo-American girls in the mid-1800s, average age of menarche was just over 16, compared to the current 12½ (Frisch, 1983; Warren, 1983).

There is no event during puberty that is a male equivalent of menarche, although first ejaculation is a close approximation. For most boys, however, this event occurs during sleep as a *nocturnal emission*, or in more popular terms, a "wet dream." In the United States the average age for first ejaculation is between 13 and 14.

THINKING ABOUT
Pubertal Development

Puberty has an impact on the adolescent's developing sense of self. Pubertal status also affects the adolescent's relationships within the family. Pubertal status is measured in a variety of ways in the research that has been published on the topic. Some researchers, for example, ask adolescents to rate their degree of physical development, often by indicating how similar their development is to photographs of the typical stages of puberty (Dorn, Susman, Nottelmann, Inoff-Germain, & Chrousos, 1990). Other researchers ask trained observers to make surreptitious ratings of pubertal development by looking for signs such as facial shape and hair, body proportion, and chest and hip development (Steinberg, 1987).

As pubertal development progresses, interaction shows signs of strain among families of adolescent boys and girls. Both sons' and daughters' relationships with the mother, in particular, become less cohesive. One way of measuring family cohesiveness is to videotape discussions within a family triad (mother, father, and adolescent child), and to code these interactions for such things as number of interruptions, explanations of points of view, deference, and so on. When such discussions are held at intervals as the adolescent progresses toward the peak of pubertal change and beyond, an interesting pattern emerges. As the adolescent shows more intense signs of puberty, conflict increases, particularly with the mother. Eventually, the mother begins to defer more to the adolescent as a way of reducing the level of conflict (Steinberg, 1989).

Adolescent girls sense more conflict with their families than boys. They report less parental acceptance and greater intensity of conflict with their mothers. Some positive effects occur as well, with both boys and girls reporting greater emotional autonomy as puberty progresses (Steinberg, 1987).

Studies of the effects of puberty on family interaction have focused largely on white, middle-class families, which limits the generalizability of the findings. Most likely, family interaction during adolescence is moderated by a number of factors other than puberty, including the gender of the adolescent and of the parent, the family structure and presence of siblings, and ethnicity. As noted, almost no research has been done to date on the influence of puberty on family interaction in nonwhite families. Without such studies, it is impossible to discuss meaningfully the boundaries of what constitutes "normative" development (Paikoff & Brooks-Gunn, 1991).

Why do you think conflict might increase between adolescents and parents during puberty? Could conflict be a way of ensuring the transition toward independence? What part do you think sexuality might play in generating conflict?

Physical Changes in Adulthood

Most physical and sensory capacities peak in early adulthood, and then begin a gradual decline that lasts throughout adulthood and old age. Heart and lung capacity, muscular strength, visual and auditory acuity, and even touch sensitivity are among the capacities showing this pattern of gradual decline, of about 1% a year, throughout adulthood (Bromley, 1974). Despite the gradual loss of physical and sensory capacities, most people barely notice these changes as they age. There is a strong sense of continuity in one's perception of oneself throughout the life cycle.

That is not to say, however, that signs of aging go unnoticed. Most people begin to develop some wrinkles, especially around the eyes, during their late 20s and 30s. Changes in the hair also typically begin to occur by the 30s, until they are noticeable in most people by the age of 40. These changes include thinning for men and graying for both sexes.

With advanced age, there is progressively greater weakness in muscles and changes in the chemical composition of bones, resulting in a slight loss in height and some stooping. Many of the most notable changes in old age involve the skin: increased paleness and wrinkling, dryness, and changes in texture, including the development of pigmented skin spots.

menopause cessation of menstruation in middle age

Reproductive Changes. At around the age of 50, women experience a change in their reproductive systems known as **menopause**, when ovulation ceases and the body produces lower levels of the female hormone estrogen. The period of about 2 or 3 years during which the body adjusts to this change is known as the *climacteric*. The old term for this period—"change of life"—generally connoted a change for the worse. Research on women's

Physical changes are apparent with aging, but there is still a vibrancy and vitality in the smile and twinkling eyes of artist Beatrice Wood at age 100. Many of the physical changes of aging involve the skin— wrinkling and dryness and changes in texture.

reactions toward menopause suggests, however, that this is not necessarily the case. In fact, many women describe positive changes in their lives after menopause (Datan, Rodeheaver, & Hughes, 1987; Neugarten et al., 1963).

Women who have stopped menstruating show no dramatic emotional differences in comparison to those who have not stopped menstruating (Berkun, 1986). A more important factor seems to be women's expectations about menopause. Those who expect unpleasant symptoms such as hot flashes or night sweats are more likely to develop those symptoms, as is consistent with the self-fulfilling prophecy (Adler, 1991).

Men do not undergo any sudden downward shift in reproductive capability, but they do show changes in reproductive physiology with aging. Although men may produce sperm cells throughout their lives, the number of cells they produce decreases. Sexual drive also decreases with age, and older men find it more difficult to become aroused. However, both men and women can and do continue to enjoy sexual relations into advanced age.

SPOTLIGHT ON RESEARCH
Neuroanatomy and Alzheimer's Disease

Some of the physical changes associated with aging involve the central nervous system, particularly the brain. All of these changes in neuroanatomy are more extensive in the roughly 3% of older people who suffer from senile dementia than in older people who remain healthy. **Senile dementia** involves confusion, memory loss, and other aspects of cognitive deterioration. Neural changes associated with one form of senile dementia, **Alzheimer's disease**, are of two major types (Price, Whitehouse, & Struble, 1985). First, changes in neurotransmitter systems have been detected. Over a decade ago, it was discovered that Alzheimer's sufferers had 60 to 90% reductions in an enzyme that is needed to make the neurotransmitter acetylcholine (Davies & Maloney, 1976). The source of this problem lies in a small region of the brain located near the hippocampus (Mesulam et al., 1983). Autopsies of Alzheimer's victims reveal that up to 75% of the neurons in this area are abnormal and dysfunctional.

Structural changes constitute the second kind of brain abnormality seen in Alzheimer's sufferers. Bundles of neural material called *neurofibrillary tangles* and neuronal debris referred to as *senile plaques* exist in profusion among these patients (Price, Whitehouse, & Struble, 1985). At one time it was thought that aluminum might play a major role in the development of Alzheimer's. But subsequent findings have failed to confirm the suspected link between aluminum and the disease (Markesbery et al., 1981). In fact, new research suggests that aluminum might even be a candidate in the treatment of Alzheimer's disease. This research, although preliminary, implicates a protein molecule called amyloid that makes cell membranes vulnerable to an influx of calcium. The protein helps to kill brain cells, which then become a part of the neurofibrillary tangles and plaques. To counteract this problem, scientists are searching for a chemical to block the action of the amyloid protein. Two chemicals so far appear promising, and one of them is aluminum (Arispe, Rojas, & Pollard, 1993).

Elderly individuals who have not been diagnosed with Alzheimer's disease, and who are otherwise healthy and not medicated with drugs that impair cognition, sometimes show a focal slowing of the EEG in the left tem-

senile dementia syndrome involving cognitive deterioration with aging

Alzheimer's disease form of senile dementia with severe memory loss and progressive deterioration

poral lobe (Rice, Buchsbaum, Hardy, & Burgwald, 1991). These EEG patterns are correlated with impaired memory performance but not with other cognitive impairment. These data hint at left temporal lobe changes as early signs of Alzheimer's disease that has not progressed far enough for a diagnosis. To test this hypothesis, researchers could do a *prospective study*, which involves following groups of individuals who are identified by the temporal EEG pattern as at risk to see if they develop the disorder. To date, no such prospective studies of the left temporal EEG pattern have been conducted.

The most striking symptom of Alzheimer's disease is loss of memory. Victims become confused and disoriented. They may repeat questions they just asked or get lost just going around the block. Additional symptoms of the early stages of the disorder include apathy and withdrawal. In later stages, the individual may lose social judgment, indicated by the use of obscene or indecorous language and by sexual references or overtures that are out of character. Memory problems intensify and may pose some danger, as for instance when one forgets to turn off a burner on the kitchen stove. Personal hygiene and appearance may deteriorate. In advanced stages of the disorder, the person shows profound losses of mental functions and physical control and may become agitated and even violent.

The current challenge for brain researchers is to clarify what is really happening in Alzheimer's disease. Now that researchers have identified the chemical and structural elements of the disease, they must explain how these factors relate to the abnormal behavior associated with Alzheimer's. Also, the question of why only a small percentage of older persons get the disease needs to be answered. Is it due to genetic factors, infection, or lifestyle factors? We do know that the rate of decline of cognitive skills differs greatly among individuals. Those who have a history of alcohol abuse decline more sharply than their counterparts who do not, for example (Teri, Hughes, & Larson, 1990). Answers to the riddle of Alzheimer's disease are desperately needed, so that we as a society will be better equipped to handle the problems of an aging population.

Life Expectancy

As we mentioned earlier, aging is characterized by progressive changes in a number of physical characteristics. With the progressive changes of aging, the body declines physically, and ultimately each of us can expect to die. The joy of life is in the living of it, but ultimately all good things come to an end. How long can we expect to live?

The good news is that life expectancy has increased regularly over the past decades, and has reached an all-time high of 75.4 years (for infants born in 1990). Life expectancy represents the average number of years that a group of infants would live if the age-specific death rates that prevailed in the year they were born continued throughout their lives.

The bad news is that life expectancy is not evenly distributed in the population. Life expectancy varies, of course, with birth cohort. The life expectancy of an infant born in 1994 is quite different from the life expectancy of infants born in 1944, or of people who have reached the age of 90 in 1994. Sex and ethnic group membership also have a considerable bearing on life expectancy. The 1990 birth cohort of white females has a life expectancy of 79.4, compared to 72.7 for white males, 73.6 for black females, and 64.5 for black males. Thus, there is a gap of almost 15 years in life expectancy between white females and black males (National Center for Health Statistics, 1993).

Life Expectancy and Ethnicity.   Information on the experience of aging for different ethnic groups in the United States is sorely lacking. The gap in research is particularly striking for Native-American groups. Collectively, Native-American groups—with Cherokee, Navajo, Sioux, and Chippewa constituting the largest subgroups—total between one and a half to two million people (Harrison et al., 1990). Although they are often grouped together in discussions about ethnic experience, they are quite heterogeneous. Before they were forced off their lands, they lived in hundreds of different and diverse tribal societies. Presently, Native Americans continue to constitute a diverse population.

All minority groups in the American "melting pot" have been pressured to some extent to adopt the values and practices of so-called mainstream society, but perhaps none more so than Native Americans. Their resistance has intensifed the prejudice and discrimination that they have had to endure. Contact with mainstream society may have had some negative consequences for the health status of Native Americans. Incidences of obesity and diabetes among Native Americans, for example, have reached high levels in the 20th century, and are thought to be related to the disruption in their traditional life-styles (Markides & Mindel, 1987).

Although it is clear that life expectancy at birth varies dramatically by ethnic group, life expectancy after one has reached an advanced age shows little variation by ethnic group. By around age 75, for example, the average number of years remaining is about the same (approximately 9 to 11) for African Americans and Anglo-Americans (National Center for Health Statistics, 1993).

COGNITIVE DEVELOPMENT

Cognition refers to thinking. In this next section, we examine patterns of thinking across the lifespan. It is probably obvious to you that you know more today than you did in grammar school or even in high school. Most people do increase their stores of facts and information as they grow into adulthood. But are you actually thinking in a different way than you used to? Most authorities on cognitive development believe that you are, even though this aspect of cognitive development is not as obvious as the increase in information. The different reactions of 3- and 6-year-olds to the "cat identity" problem that opened this chapter might result from differences in the *way* people think as they grow older. In this section, we survey some of the major milestones in human cognitive development, starting with cognitive beginnings in infancy.

Cognitive Beginnings

William James, the great American psychologist of the turn of the century (see Chapter 1), speculated that the world of the infant is a "blooming, buzzing confusion." Infants do lack the sophisticated cognitive systems of older children and adults, but their world is far from a total confusion. Even newborn babies can sense and process information about their world. For example, you probably have seen very young infants react with apparent discomfort to experiences such as being bathed in water that is too hot or tasting food that they do not like.

If the infant's world is not a "blooming, buzzing confusion," how can it best be characterized? This is the question that researchers have addressed in the last few decades of intense study into the developmental period of infancy. The results of that effort reveal an individual who is surprisingly capable of extracting information about the world, even in the first moments after birth. In fact, the senses are capable of functioning even before birth, with touch, taste, and smell developing earlier than hearing and vision (Hall & Oppenheim, 1987).

Neonates (literally meaning "newborns") respond to taste and smell stimuli quite clearly. For example, infants respond differently to cotton swabs saturated with either sweet- or sour-tasting substances. Similarly, they react more positively to whiffs of pleasant aromas than they do to acrid smells. The sense of touch is also well developed in newborns. Rhythmic stroking is one way to calm a fussing infant.

Development of Hearing. The development of hearing precedes the development of sight both structurally and functionally in humans. By about the 25th week after conception the hearing system is operating on a rudimentary level, and it is quite mature at birth. Sight, by contrast, is still immature at birth (Lewkowicz, 1988a). Newborn infants prefer their mother's voice to a strange woman's voice even at birth (DeCasper & Fifer, 1980). Many researchers believe this preference is due to the infant's ability to hear and become familiar with her voice prenatally. Newborn infants respond differently to sounds that are continuous, such as "Aaaahhhh," than to sounds that are pulsed, such as "Ah–ah–ah–ah" (Clarkson & Berg, 1983). Infants are especially responsive to higher frequencies, which may be one reason why adults modify the pitch of their voices when they interact with them (Grieser & Kuhl, 1988; Jacobson et al., 1983). The infant's sensitivity to sound is important in the subsequent development of language.

During at least the first 6 months of life, hearing is the dominant sense for human infants. When confronted with both auditory and visual stimuli such as flashing checkerboards and pulsing sounds, infants pay more attention to the sounds. By 7 months of age, infants are able to locate the objects that are making sounds even in the dark, as shown by their reaching movements in the correct direction. They also have good distance perception for sounds. In a darkened room, infants reached in the direction of a noise-making object (a plastic container filled with popcorn kernels) within their grasp, but did not reach when the object was beyond their grasp (Clifton, Perris, & Bullinger, 1991).

Development of Sight. By the age of 10 months, the developmental shift to visual prominence that characterizes adults has already begun (Lewkowicz, 1988b). Neonatal vision is not as good as adult vision. During just the 1st year of life, however, visual acuity becomes three to four times better than it was at birth (Aslin & Smith, 1988). Still, young infants can see, and they show keen interest in their visual world.

Researchers once believed that vision was relatively poor because infants had trouble focusing on objects unless they were in a narrow range of distances from the eyes, about 8 to 10 in. (20 to 25 cm). Now it appears that accommodation is not "fixed" at any particular distance, but that the visual system provides different information when it is immature (Aslin & Smith, 1988). Thus, the developmental prominence of vision that will appear later awaits the maturity of the visual system. Although vision may not be the most prominent sense for young infants, its prominence in adulthood has led researchers to study it more heavily than any of the other senses (Hay, 1986).

Between the ages of 3 and 6 months, infants perfect the ability to reach for an object and grasp it, a milestone that psychologists refer to as **visually directed reaching** (White, Castle, & Held, 1964). After visually directed reaching abilities develop, almost every object that is small enough makes

visually directed reaching ability guided by sight to reach for and grasp an object

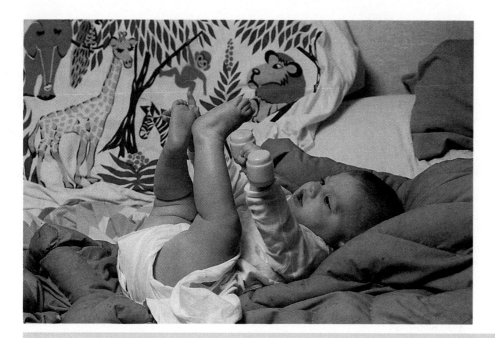

Between the ages of 3 and 6 months, infants perfect their visually directed reaching. They can visually guide their hands toward an object and grasp it, coordinating visual and tactile feedback in one smooth and purposeful movement.

its way to the infant's mouth. In general, infants become more alert and exploratory, using hearing, vision, touch, and taste to examine objects in their world.

Perception of Patterns in Infancy.   As described in Chapter 3, research with other species has revealed specialized cells that react selectively to certain specific stimulus patterns. Sophisticated equipment can monitor a single neuron in selected areas—say, the visual area—of the nervous systems of lower animals. Because nerve cells in the visual area seem to respond to specific features in the environment, these nerve cells have been called **feature detectors**.

Although the single-cell recording techniques used with lower animals are inappropriate with human infants, there is growing evidence that humans possess specialized visual areas that contain cells more sensitive to some perceptual properties than others. These properties include orientation, color, direction of movement, and curvature, among others (Treisman & Gormican, 1988). How do we know what features infants respond to? Methods for researching pattern perception in infants are obviously different from those used with lower animals. Two popular research techniques are habituation and preference.

Habituation and Preference.   In the **habituation technique**, infants are repeatedly shown a stimulus until their response to it declines in frequency or intensity. Then they are presented with a new stimulus in which one feature has been altered. If they detect the change in that feature, they may show a different pattern of response. For example, curvature is a perceptual feature to which infants respond. In a habituation study of curvature, infants were shown a straight stimulus line and over time, indicated habituation by looking less at the straight line (Figure 12–5A). Following habituation, they were shown a curved line, and they increased their looking time, or *dishabituated*, indicating that curved patterns capture their attention (Hopkins et al., 1976).

In order to learn what patterns interest infants, the **preference technique** exploits infants' tendencies to look more often and longer at one stimulus than another. In one preference study (Fantz & Nevis, 1967) researchers

feature detectors brain cells that respond to specific stimulus characteristics

habituation technique research technique in which a person is repeatedly exposed to one stimulus, followed by the introduction of a novel stimulus

preference technique research technique in which two stimuli are presented simultaneously and the person's responses to each are measured

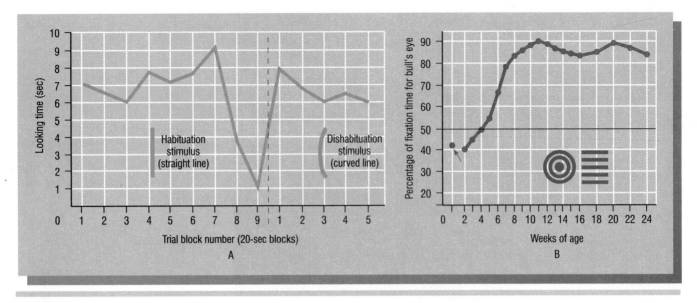

FIGURE 12–5

(*A*) In the habituation technique, infants are repeatedly shown a stimulus until their responses to it decrease. They are then shown a new stimulus with some feature altered. Here, habituation of looking time occurs for a straight-line stimulus, followed by dishabituation of looking time for a new, curved stimulus line. (*B*) In the preference technique, infants have the opportunity to look at two stimuli at once. Looking preferences are shown here for infants between the ages of 2 and 24 weeks for a bull's-eye pattern and an arrangement of straight lines. By about 8 weeks there is a strong preference for the more curvilinear pattern. (Adapted from Hopkins, 1974, and Fantz & Nevis, 1967.)

visual cliff apparatus used to test for depth perception in infants and animals

placed two patterns at a time in a mechanism above the infant's crib and measured the amount of time the infant looked at each. If an infant looks at each pattern about the same amount of time, no preference is demonstrated. Preference is shown, however, if the infant looks longer at one pattern than at the other. One pair of such stimuli is shown in Figure 12–5B. Very young infants showed no particular preference for either stimulus, but by 2 months infants registered a strong preference for the bull's-eye pattern. The curvilinear pattern of the bull's-eye is one factor accounting for this preference (Ruff & Birch, 1974).

You may have noticed a young infant staring intently at the facelike features of a stuffed animal. Several researchers have confirmed the infant's preference for facelike patterns (Fantz, 1961; Langsdorf et al., 1983). The fact that infants respond universally to facial patterns suggests that something about the stimulus characteristics of the face is important in eliciting their attention. A limited set of perceptual properties may be especially effective in engaging the attention of infants. Perception of these simple features, in turn, may lead to more sophisticated cognitive activities in later infancy and childhood.

Many researchers have attempted to isolate patterns that infants prefer or perceive. For example, in addition to curvature, infants like high contrast, complex stimuli with large elements, and stimuli that move. Infants also perceive differences in stimulus orientation (Bornstein, Krinsky, & Benasich, 1986; Humphrey & Humphrey, 1986), and, by about 3 months of age, they even have reasonably adultlike color vision (Banks & Salapatek, 1983).

Some perceptual patterns are difficult to assess in very young infants. It is difficult, for example, to establish firmly whether or not infants have a natural fear of heights before they are able to move around on their own. Most species that can move around soon after birth, such as goats and chickens, show a fear of venturing out over a deep side of the **visual cliff** (an apparatus that appears to have both a deep and a shallow side, as described in Chapter 4). However, human infants cannot practically be tested on the visual cliff until they are able to crawl. By that time most infants do avoid the deep side of the visual cliff. Their fear suggests that depth is an important perceptual feature for them (Gibson & Walk, 1960). You might think that such a perceptual ability would be very useful in helping infants avoid dangerous places; unfortunately, it is not an ability that can be relied on to keep exploring infants from falling off chairs or down stairs. Depth perception may be relatively poor in younger infants because they do not have *stereopsis* (the ability to perceive depth based on retinal disparity), perhaps because they lack the necessary neural mechanism (Aslin & Smith, 1988). Maturation of the nervous system continues well after birth.

Infants begin to obtain information about the environment by exploring it, using all their available senses to do so. With exploration comes the discovery that the environment contains regular perceptual information that we can use (Gibson, 1988). For example, it is useful to discover that a floor provides support but water does not, or that water can be used for drinking and cleaning, but wood cannot. With perceptual development, more and more of these regularities are learned, eventually resulting in a perceptual system of great subtlety and variety (Gibson & Spelke, 1983).

Cognitive Growth in Later Infancy and Childhood

Older infants have built up a set of expectancies about the world and objects in it, based on their own observations and experiences. These expectancies lead to surprise when the infants encounter new situations that are different from their expectations. Violations of expectations can sometimes lead to frustration. In one study (Alessandri, Sullivan, & Lewis, 1990), infants were placed in an infant seat in front of a projection screen, with a Velcro wrist band connected to a string. First their baseline level of hand waving was recorded, followed by a learning phase in which their hand-waving activated slides projected onto a screen.

During the learning phase, infants increased their hand waving as they learned the connection between moving their hands and activating the slides. This phase sets up an expectancy about the results of their behavior. After the expectancy is firmly established, infants enter an extinction phase, in which no slides are presented when they wave their hands. In this phase, their hand waving increased four times what it had been during baseline, indicating their reaction to the violation of their expectations. As shown in Figure 12–6, their hand waving returned to the level in the first learning phase after the connection between hand waving and slides was restored.

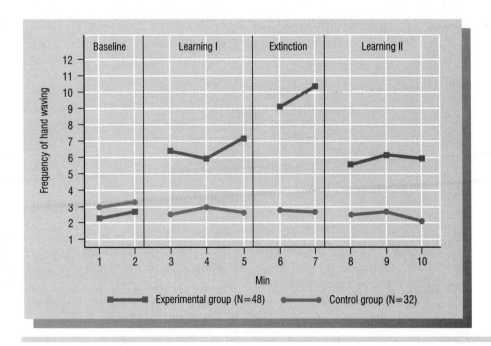

FIGURE 12–6
When infants in the experimental group had their hands attached to a Velcro wrist band that activated slides when they waved their hands, they quickly learned to alter their behavior to activate the slides. The extinction phase (when the hand waving no longer activated the slides) shows the infants reaction to frustration: Their hand waving increased dramatically. (From Alessandri, Sullivan, & Lewis, 1990.)

This study of infant reaction to violations of their expectations showed a significant age effect, with older infants waving their hands more than younger infants (Alessandri et al., 1990). The increase in hand waving may result from the infants' frustrated expectations, a finding that is even more evident among older infants.

Toward the end of the first year of life, or soon thereafter, infants begin to produce meaningful words. This marks their entrance into a new world of cognitive competence, one in which language plays an important role. The cognitive accomplishments associated with human language development are truly astonishing. At around age 2, for example, there is a spurt in vocabulary development such that children begin learning between 10 and 20 new words each day for several years (Miller & Gildea, 1987). (Language development was described more fully in Chapter 8.) Once language development is under way, adults can communicate with children on an entirely different level, beginning some of the direct teaching that will fill so much of their later lives.

APPLYING PSYCHOLOGY
Preschool Education

The practical importance of developmental psychology is nowhere more apparent than in the schools. An understanding of how children develop cognitively and socially is a prerequisite to structuring a curriculum that will maximize their potential for learning. Literally thousands of research projects have been conducted that bear directly on the practical application of developmental psychology to education.

Academic programs aimed specifically at young children grew out of the Head Start program that began in 1964 as a nationwide effort to make up for early deficits experienced by economically and socially disadvantaged children. In the 30 years since Head Start began, there have been numerous attempts to evaluate the effectiveness of the program, but there is little agreement about that effectiveness.

One study, for example, compared four different types of Head Start programs:

1. The Bereiter–Engelmann program, a highly structured program developed at the University of Illinois
2. The Demonstration and Research Center for Early Education (DARCEE), a structured program developed at George Peabody College in Nashville
3. A Montessori program that is child centered and oriented to discovery learning
4. A regular Head Start program, child centered and somewhat individualized.

All programs except the Montessori one assume that disadvantaged children have major motivational problems, including lack of persistence and distractibility, and attempt to overcome them.

Participants were evaluated during kindergarten and again in first and second grade and compared to a control group of children who were similarly disadvantaged but who had not participated in any Head Start program. On some measures, such as reading tests, children in all of the Head Start programs performed better than the control group. But on other measures, there was no apparent pattern to the results. Even the reading score improvement did not last into second grade, when the control group did about as well as any of the Head Start groups (Miller & Dyer, 1975). In other studies, in which adjustments were made for initial differences in social background and intellectual functioning, Head Start students showed significantly larger gains in achievement in areas necessary for later school performance (Lee, Brooks-Gunn, & Schnur, 1988). Effects of Head Start on general cognitive measures and on analytical ability were sustained into the first grade (Lee, Brooks-Gunn, Schnur, & Liaw, 1990).

Family involvement is very important in intervention programs to help disadvantaged children, but family involvement alone may not be enough to reverse the problems encountered in the educational setting by disadvantaged children. This point was demonstrated in a study that began in 1978 and followed children who had participated in an intervention program in North Carolina (Wasik, Ramey, Bryant, & Sparling, 1990). Sixty-five families with children at risk for educational failure participated, and were randomly assigned to one of three groups.

The first group attended a child development educational center with a specific developmental curriculum, and also had a family education program that involved regular home visitors who assisted with information about child development, encouraged and modeled positive parent–child interactions, and promoted coping strategies for problems. The second group received only the family education component of the program, without the educational center attendance. The third group served as a control group, and received neither the educational center intervention nor the family education program.

The children in the first group, who attended the educational day-care center and who also participated in the family education component of the program, performed significantly better on cognitive tasks in follow-up tests up to the age of 4½. The family education component alone was not sufficient to change the child's performance on cognitive measures or parents' attitudes about developmental issues; this group did not differ significantly from the no-intervention control group (Wasik et al., 1990).

Early education programs, initially aimed at disadvantaged students, have now entered the mainstream. In 1966, 60% of 5-year-olds attended kindergarten programs, compared to 82% in the mid-1980s. In addition, there has been a thousandfold increase in nursery schools in the United States since the mid-1960s (Elkind, 1987). Some authorities on childhood education, such as David Elkind of Tufts University, believe that the vast majority of children are being rushed into educational experiences at the expense of their enjoyment of childhood. In an age when both parents in many families must work, some type of day care is inevitable. But day care need not mean an academically oriented school atmosphere. Stringent academic programs for young children are an example of the "miseducation" of the young, in Elkind's view.

The argument about timing of education is related to the issue of stages in cognitive growth. Attempting to teach children before they have attained the appropriate level of developmental readiness is not just a mistake, according to this view. It results in frustration for the child that may ultimately lower motivation for school achievement. Boys, who are developmentally behind girls from the start, may be particularly vulnerable to this negative effect of early educational intervention.

Since large-scale Head Start preschool programs were introduced in the 1960s, preschool experiences have entered the mainstream. Some authorities on child development criticize the rush toward academic preparation of the young.

Piaget's Cognitive-Developmental Theory

The issue of developmental readiness for specific educational activities suggests a stagelike approach to cognitive development. In other words, a child would have to reach a certain stage of cognitive development to be ready to understand the logic of particular educational lessons. Jean Piaget (1896–1980), a Swiss developmental psychologist, has been one of the most influential developmental theorists. He divided human cognitive growth into four developmental stages. His theory provides a useful framework for understanding cognitive development. As one of the enduring controversies in developmental psychology suggests, many psychologists believe that human thinking proceeds through discrete stages, characterized by qualitatively different forms of thinking. Cognitive development, in this view, is not simply a matter of learning more facts and strategies as one grows older. Rather, transformations occur in the *way* a person thinks.

Piaget believed that human thinking was an adaptive process, in which the native cognitive powers that humans possess adapt to a particular environment. Piaget's four developmental stages are (*a*) the sensory–motor stage of infancy, (*b*) the preoperational stage of early childhood, (*c*) concrete operations in late childhood, and (*d*) formal operations beginning in early adolescence and lasting throughout the remainder of life.

The Sensory–Motor Stage.   Piaget called the cognitive world of the infant the *sensory–motor stage*, reflecting the infant's tendency to experience the world in terms of basic senses (sensory) and action (motor). One may think of very young infants as having basic action patterns as their cognitive equipment. This equipment represents a set of **cognitive structures**, the means by which humans acquire and apply knowledge about their world. Piaget described the acquisition of information as **assimilation**—the use of available cognitive structures to gain information about the world. Cognitive structures become progressively more elaborate as infants acquire more information. These structures are modified when the infant encounters greater complexity in the environment. This modification based on experience is called

cognitive structures means by which humans acquire and apply knowledge about the world

assimilation using one's cognitive structures to take in (or assimilate) information about the environment

490   *Chapter 12*

Jean Piaget rejected the highly controlled laboratory methods favored by American psychologists and chose instead the clinical method, essentially a probing interview in which the child's thought is followed wherever it may lead. He is shown here with some children in Harlem, on one of his rare visits to the United States.

accommodation. As infants mature, they must modify their reflexes and other cognitive structures to meet the demands of the environment.

From Reflexes to Circular Reactions.   In the beginning, infants use reflexes, such as sucking, to gain information about the world. In early infancy, of course, these actions are automatic; babies are not deliberately attempting to learn anything. Infants gradually acquire the ability to explore their environment nonreflexively. They engage in repetitive, almost stereotyped, movements that Piaget called **circular reactions**. They may touch their noses, then their eyes, in a repetitive, exploratory fashion. For example, Piaget described a repetitive sequence he observed his son Laurent performing at the age of 2 months: "Laurent constantly pulls at his face before, during, or after sucking his fingers. This behavior slowly gains interest for its own sake and thus gives rise to two distinct habits. (He holds his nose with four fingers while sucking his thumb)" (Piaget, 1952).

Object Permanence.   In the latter half of their 1st year of life, infants show evidence of **object permanence**. That is, they come to understand that objects continue to exist even when they are hidden under obstacles or otherwise out of range of the senses. When younger infants who are playing with a desirable toy have it gently removed from their hands and hidden under a cloth directly in front of them, they act as if the toy had ceased to exist. Older infants are likely to search for the toy, demonstrating their understanding of object permanence. Object permanence also extends to the perception of people. Young infants live in a world in which people literally come and go; alternately, people exist and then cease to exist for them. Older infants appreciate that people continue to exist when they are out of sight.

By the end of the sensory–motor period of development in the 2nd year of life, infants are capable of simple forms of intelligent deduction. With a minimum of outside influence, they begin to solve simple problems on their own. The appearance of intelligent, intentional activities and the development

accommodation modification of one's cognitive structures based on experience

circular reactions in Piaget's theory, repetitive action patterns in infancy

object permanence in Piaget's theory, the realization that objects continue to exist even when they are out of range of the senses

of symbolic activity such as language signal the transition into the second major period of development in Piaget's theory: the preoperational stage.

Preoperational Thinking.   Between the ages of about 1½ and 6 years, children exhibit a mode of thinking that is in many respects different from that of either infants or older children. Their thought is characterized by primitive, prelogical elements such as cognitive egocentrism, animism, and artificialism. The thinking of later childhood and beyond makes use of logical operations. Early childhood thought, which lacks these operations, is thus termed **preoperational thinking**.

Egocentrism.   One of Piaget's studies of preoperational thinking required the use of a three-dimensional model of three mountains, each clearly distinguishable from the other. As illustrated in Figure 12–7, the smallest mountain

Side view

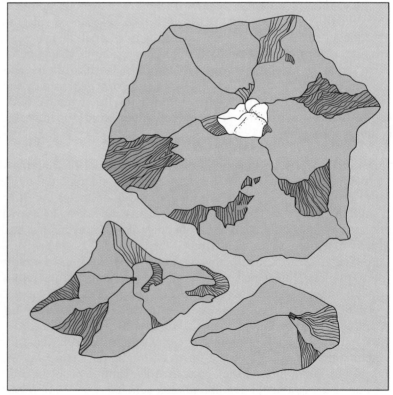

View from above

preoperational thinking in Piaget's theory, thinking that precedes logical reasoning, characterizing young children

FIGURE 12–7
The apparatus for Piaget's "mountains" task for studying egocentrism. The smallest mountain has a little house on it, and the middle mountain has a little red cross at the top. The highest mountain is snow-capped, and the child must describe the scene from a perspective other than his or her own. (From Piaget & Inhelder, 1948/1967.)

had a little house on its summit, the middle-sized mountain had a red cross at the top, and the highest mountain was a snow-capped peak. An interviewer placed a small doll at various places around this model and asked the child to pick from a set of pictures what the doll would see from those vantage points. Young children consistently picked the picture that reflected what they saw from where they were standing, not the one that showed what the doll would see from its position (Piaget & Inhelder, 1948/1967).

Some psychologists believe children have difficulty with this task not because of their cognitive egocentrism, but because the task doesn't make much sense to them. Children may simply be unable to comprehend a situation that seems divorced from any reality they have experienced (Ford, 1985). One critic put it, "The 'mountains' task is abstract in a psychologically very important sense: in the sense that it is abstracted from all basic human purposes and feelings and endeavors. It is totally cold-blooded. In the veins of three-year-olds, the blood still runs warm" (Donaldson, 1978). It seems clear that preoperational-stage children behave egocentrically in situations such as described by Piaget. This does not necessarily mean they are unable to learn to behave less egocentrically with greater experience.

Animism. Preoperational thought also reflects, to some degree, **animism**. Children have a tendency to attribute life to inanimate things—to those things that are useful to humans, such as furnaces, and to things that move around, such as automobiles (Piaget, 1964/1967). Animistic thinking disappears only gradually. In later stages, children attribute life only to things that move spontaneously, such as the wind.

animism attributing life to inanimate things

Artificialism. **Artificialism** is a third characteristic of preoperational thinking. Children have a tendency to believe that everything is the product of human creation (or of a divinity acting the same way that humans do). Causality apart from human activity is inconceivable. Six-year-old Roy, for example, told Piaget that the sun began "because it knew that life had begun," and that it was made of fire "because there was a fire up there." When asked how a fire happened to start in the sky, Roy replied, "It was lighted with a match" that God threw away (Piaget, 1929/1965).

artificialism belief that everything is a product of human creation

Concrete–Operational Thinking. The stage of **concrete–operational thinking** begins at about the age of 6, and continues until early adolescence. The characteristics of preoperational thought—egocentrism, animism, artificialism—break down and are superseded by a more logical form of thinking. However, the logic is still tied to concrete reality.

concrete-operational thinking in Piaget's theory, logical thinking that is tied to concrete reality

Earlier, we mentioned the concept of developmental readiness for education. Presumably children are not developmentally ready for the experiences of the educational system until they have reached the concrete operations stage. Attempts to train children to use reasoning beyond their current stage before they are developmentally prepared have had very limited success (Adey & Shayer, 1990; Snyder & Feldman, 1977). It is no accident that entry into first grade is age linked and that it tends to occur at about the transition into concrete operations.

In Piaget's theory, the development of operational thinking builds on the accomplishments of the previous stages. **Operations** are defined as internalized actions. They are actions similar to the sensory–motor acts of infancy, but now they take place in the child's mind. In addition, operations are very general kinds of activities, such as combining, classifying, and ordering. These operations are, in turn, integrated into a logical system that includes such characteristics as **reversibility**. As the name implies, reversibility refers to the negation of an action. For example, if we are given five apples and these are

operations in Piaget's theory, internalized actions

reversibility logical negation of an operation

combined with two more apples, the action of combining them can be reversed—two apples can be taken away, and once again we have five apples.

Conservation.   Concrete–operational thought is represented by the child's ability to solve the **conservation problems**. *Conservation* refers to the principle that matter does not increase or decrease because of a change in form. One of Piaget's most famous series of problems, illustrated in Figure 12–8, involves conservation of quantities of liquid. A child is presented with three beakers. Two are the same, short and wide; the third is tall and thin. Liquid is poured into the two equal-sized beakers, and the child agrees that there is the same amount of liquid in both of them. Then, the child is cautioned to watch carefully as the liquid is poured from one of the short, wide beakers into the tall, thin one, where it rises to a higher level. The child is now asked some version of the question, "Is there the same amount of liquid in these two beakers, or is there more in one than there is in the other?"

Preoperational children, usually younger than 6 years old, consistently reply there there is more liquid in one beaker than the other. They have failed to appreciate that the *amount* of liquid did not change despite a difference in *level* to which the liquid rises. Their perception typically centers on the height of the water level, and they reply that the tall beaker has more. Concrete–operational children, by contrast, reply that there is still the same amount of liquid despite its being poured into another glass. Furthermore, they appreciate the logical necessity that there is the same amount of liquid, for after all, "you only poured it." Questioning of children on this problem has proceeded along several different lines. In this case, it appears that the form of the question does not matter much for the outcome; preoperational children fail to conserve, whereas concrete–operational children answer correctly.

Questioning does seem to matter on some of the other problems used to assess conservation. Preoperational children are said to lack conservation of number. They are unable to appreciate number equivalence unless the objects in question are matched one for one. For example, a child might be shown five toy elephants and five peanuts, with the elephants spread out and the peanuts bunched together. The child is asked, in the standard Piagetian question: "Are there more elephants than peanuts, the same number of elephants and peanuts, or more peanuts than elephants?" In one study using this technique, only 2 of 14 children under 5 years old made the correct equivalence judgment. But when they were asked to connect the elephants and the peanuts with string before deciding, 12 of 15 children were correct (Fuson, Secada, & Hall, 1983).

Generally, however, children shift toward an appreciation of conservation during the concrete–operational stage, if questions are not deliberately misleading. Let's look at an example in the area of conservation of number. When children judge two arrays of dots and then watch as the position (but not the number) of dots changes in one column, young children (ages 3 to 4) are unable to tell if there are the same number of dots beyond the level of random guessing, whereas older children (ages 6 to 7) show conservation of number by recognizing that there are the same number of dots despite rearrangement (Halford & Boyle, 1985).

Most children of concrete–operational age treat Piaget's conservation problems as obvious and logically necessary truths (Miller, 1986). For example, the 6-year-old who knew that Maynard the cat could not be transformed into a dog understood the logical necessity of the constancy of "catness." Appreciation of conservation and other cognitive accomplishments that characterize the concrete–operational stage may be responsible for children's questioning the reality of our culture's mythical figures such as Santa Claus, the Easter bunny, and the tooth fairy. A child who appreciates conser-

conservation problems Piaget's testing procedures for the concept that amount remains the same despite surface changes in form

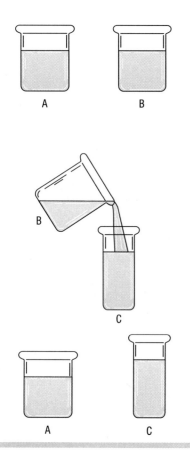

FIGURE 12–8
A typical sequence for studying conservation of liquid quantity involves getting the child's agreement that two equal-sized beakers contain the same amount of water. Water is then poured from one of the beakers into a differently shaped beaker while the child observes. The child is asked if there is the same amount of liquid in the two beakers, or if there is more in one than in the other.

vation will realize that Santa could not possibly deliver presents all over the world in a single night, and that his presence in every parade and department store is logically suspicious (Fehr, 1976). For many generations, children in America have discovered that Santa Claus is a myth at about the age at which concrete operations begin, between 6 and 7, according to research from one community in Nebraska (Benjamin, Langley, & Hall, 1979).

Class Inclusion. Likewise, concrete–operational children succeed on Piaget's class-inclusion problems, whereas preoperational children are baffled by them. The form of these problems is always the same. The child is presented with an array of items that clearly have some characteristic that distinguishes one from another but that are nevertheless included in the same class. For example, the child is given three roses and two tulips and is told, "Here are some flowers. There are some roses and some tulips, but they are all flowers. Now, are there more roses, or more flowers?" Preoperational children are clearly confused by this problem and consistently answer, "More roses." Young children may be baffled by this problem in part because of the way the question is asked. In fact, adults are sometimes initially confused by the question, until stress is given to the word *flowers*.

Before the advances in logical thinking associated with concrete operations, children readily accept the reality of Santa Claus. After about age 6, however, children's logical systems will no longer support the Santa Claus myth.

Formal–Operational Thinking. Concrete operations are tied to reality. In the next cognitive stage, the fourth and final one in Piaget's scheme, the logical system becomes even more elaborate, with the ability to think hypothetically and abstractly. Piaget called this final stage of development **formal–operational thinking**. The difference between child and adolescent logic is both a qualitative and quantitative difference and one that has a major significance for cognitive development in general (Piaget, 1972). Many other psychologists have also confirmed the greater use of logic among adolescents as compared to children (Miller, 1986; Moshman, 1977; Shantz, 1967).

In comparison to the way children think, adolescent thought involves several new characteristics. First, adolescents are better able to use formal principles of logic than younger children. The growth of logical thought is illustrated by one of Piaget's tests to measure formal reasoning called the "billiard game" (Inhelder & Piaget, 1958). A special apparatus is used when questioning children, but the basic physical relationships are the same as those in a standard billiard game. In Figure 12–9, aficionados of billiards will see immediately that hitting a billiard ball from point *x* to point 0 (against the

formal–operational thinking in Piaget's theory, hypothetical and abstract thinking that appears in adolescence and continues throughout adulthood

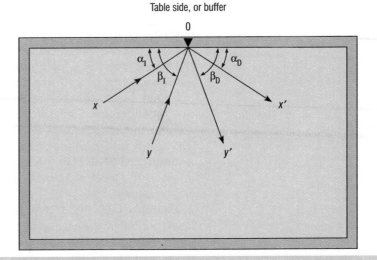

FIGURE 12–9
The billiard game. A billiard ball hit from point *x* to 0 against the buffer will deflect through point *x*', angle α_I = angle α_D. Similarly, a ball hit from point *y* to point 0 against the buffer will deflect through point *y*'; angle β_I = angle β_D. (Based on a discussion in Inhelder & Piaget, 1958.)

buffer) will deflect it through point *x'*. A hit from point *y*, on the other hand, will deflect it through point *y'*. Pool sharks can make use of this predictable relationship even if they cannot put it into words: the angle of incidence is equal to the angle of deflection, independent of the force of the hit.

Adolescents, in contrast to younger children, begin to formulate hypotheses as they try to figure out the billiard game. When they figure it out, they view the relationship as a logical necessity, confident in the generality of the relationship between angles of incidence and deflection. One of Piaget's adolescent subjects illustrates the use of logic:

> It depends on the buffer, too; it has to be good and straight—and also on the plane—it has to be completely horizontal. But if the buffer were oblique, you would have to trace a perpendicular to the buffer and you would still have to take the same distance [to the line and from it] up to the target. The law would be the same. . . . The law doesn't vary. (Inhelder & Piaget, 1958, p. 12)

A second advance in adolescent thinking is reasoning about hypothetical situations. Older adolescents have no trouble reasoning about propositions that are contrary to fact (such as "All purple snails have straw feet. I have a purple snail; what are its feet made of?"), whereas younger adolescents have trouble with such propositions (Markovits & Vachon, 1989).

Third, adolescent thinking is becoming introspective. Adolescents think about thinking itself far more than children do. This last characteristic of adolescent thinking may be related to self-consciousness, a form of egocentrism that increases during adolescence. Some adolescents are obsessed with their own mental processes, attributing their own thoughts to others. Teenagers, in fact, have more difficulty than 9-year-olds remembering whether they actually said something or only thought about it (Foley, Johnson, & Raye, 1983). Adolescent egocentrism also includes the feeling that other people are thinking and talking about them, sometimes referred to as the "imaginary audience" (Gray & Hudson, 1984).

Beginning in adolescence, people often exhibit a **personal fable**—an exaggerated belief in their own uniqueness and immortality (Elkind, 1967). Adolescents may write diaries for posterity, confide in their own personal god, and believe that bad things "can't happen to me"—all aspects of the personal fable. The fact that adolescents often engage in sexual activities without using birth control may be more understandable in this context. If they believe that unwanted consequences, such as pregnancy or sexually transmitted diseases, can't happen to them, then precaution won't seem necessary. In the age of AIDS, this aspect of the personal fable could have frightening implications. Research with adolescents in Australia suggests that there is a link between cognitive maturity and fears about exposure to the AIDS virus, with the more cognitively mature adolescents showing greater fear—and presumably more willingness to take safer sex precautions (Peterson & Murphy, 1990). Apparently people never completely set aside their personal fables. Adolescents and adults appear about equally likely to underestimate the risks associated with their behavior (Quadrel, Fischoff, & Davis, 1993).

Inhelder and Piaget implied that most adolescents achieve formal–operational thought. Subsequent researchers, however, have found that formal thought is far from universal, even among older adolescents and adults. For example, 37% of 11th-graders in one study failed several physical science tasks at the level of formal operations (Keating & Clark, 1980). In another study, almost 25% of college students failed a formal reasoning problem in probability (Murray & Armstrong, 1978). Although adolescents and adults may not solve the stringent natural science problems devised by Inhelder and Piaget, they can still think logically, hypothetically, and abstractly, all aspects of formal–operational thinking.

personal fable exaggerated belief in one's own uniqueness and immortality, especially evident among adolescents

Summary and Critique of Piaget's Stages of Cognitive Development.
Piaget's four stages of cognitive development are outlined in Table 12–3. The sensory–motor action patterns of infancy are overshadowed in early childhood by internalized representations of objects and events, and by the symbolic representation that language makes possible. In later childhood, true operations—internalized actions that are reversible—are applied to situations in concrete reality. Beginning in adolescence, true operations of abstract thought can be applied to hypothetical as well as actual events. Formal–operational thought is the highest stage of thinking described by Piaget.

The characteristics of cognition just presented suggest that thought is different from one stage of the life cycle to another in important and predictable ways. Piaget has proposed that human thinking proceeds through four stages, characterized by qualitatively different modes of thinking. Cognitive development, in this view, is not simply a matter of learning more facts and strategies as one grows older. Rather, there are transformations in the *way* a person thinks.

As we mentioned at the beginning of this chapter, the issue of continuity versus discontinuity is a persistent controversy in developmental psychology. Piaget maintained his belief in the discontinuity of development, characterized by discrete stages, throughout his remarkable career. Some psychologists believe that Piaget refused to consider alternative accounts of development that might have been more consistent with the data. Considerable evidence suggests that children have more cognitive competence than Piaget's theory would predict.

For example, the animistic nature of preoperational thinking has been questioned by some researchers. In one study 3- and 4-year-old children were shown photographs of unfamiliar objects such as strange mammals, nonmammalian animals, statues with animal-like parts, wheeled vehicles, and rigid objects (Massey & Gelman, 1988). They were asked in each instance if the pictured object could go up and down a hill by itself, a question designed to tap animistic thinking. Although the mammals and the statues are similar in appearance, and the nonmammals are very different from either, the children grouped the mammals and nonmammals together for their movement prediction. Both 3- and 4-year-olds were significantly above chance in the accuracy of their answers, with an overall accuracy rate of 68%. The older children were especially good at this task, despite the fact

TABLE 12-3
Summary of Piaget's Stages of Cognitive Development

Stage (and Age)	Salient Characteristics
• Stage I **Sensory–motor stage** (Birth to age 1½)	Sensory–motor action schemes, such as sucking, grasping. Reflexes. Circular reactions. Object permanence.
• Stage II **Preoperational stage** (Ages 1½ to 6)	Internalized representations of objects and events. Symbolic representation and language. Egocentrism, animism, and artificialism.
• Stage III **Concrete–operations stage** (Age 6 to puberty)	True operations applied to objects in concrete reality. Reversibility, conservation, and class inclusion.
• Stage IV **Formal–operations stage** (Adolescence and adulthood)	Hypothetical and deductive thinking. Propositional logic.

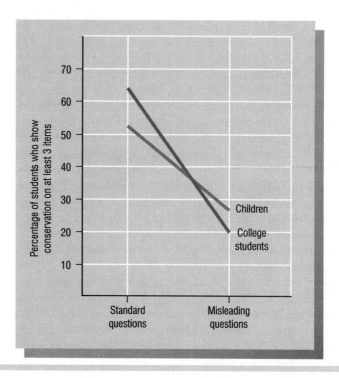

FIGURE 12–10
Both college students and children can be easily thrown off by misleading questions on conservation of weight. (From Winer, Hemphill, & Craig, 1988.)

that they should have been squarely in the preoperations stage according to Piaget's theory. If stages of cognitive development exist, it is likely that they exist as dominant tendencies rather than the absolutes that Piaget suggested (Gelman & Baillargeon, 1983).

Piaget's stages are far from absolute. Even college students fail some of Piaget's conservation questions, particularly when the questions are misleading. An example of a *standard* question for addressing conservation is: "When do you weigh the most, when you are walking or running—or do you weigh the same regardless of how you are moving?" A *misleading* question suggests that only one alternative can be correct, even though that is counter to logic: "When do you weigh the most—when you are walking or running?" When researchers score the answers, they take into account the reasoning. For example, some students say a person weighs less when running because of sweating, an answer that is scored as showing conservation. As shown in Figure 12–10, both children and college students are easily thrown off by the misleading questions (Winer, Hemphill, & Craig, 1988). If anything, the college students are more confused by the misleading questions.

Piaget has also been criticized for his views on the origin of cognitive structures, which he argued were constructed by the child, rather than inherited. What is present at birth, according to Piaget, are the cognitive functions of assimilation and accommodation. Critics doubt that development would proceed along the same course for all normal children if inherited structures did not somehow guide cognitive functioning (Gelman & Baillargeon, 1983). Thus, we see that Piaget's theory confronts, but does not resolve, the two major controversies that we discussed at the beginning of the chapter—continuity versus discontinuity and nature versus nurture.

Cognitive Changes in Adulthood

Although Piaget's cognitive stage theory has been an influential model of development, it leaves the impression that there are no further developments in thinking that are important after adolescence. It also implies that all normal adolescents and adults consistently use formal–operational reasoning. Both of these impressions are likely false.

It is clear that not all adults use formal–operational thinking consistently, even when they are able to use it some of the time. Average adults, ages 20 to 55, who were tested on problems in logical combinations and on proportionality failed, in some studies, to use formal–operational thinking a majority of the time (Dulit, 1975; Tomlinson-Keasey & Keasey, 1972). However, the criteria for formal operations outlined by Inhelder and Piaget (1958), with their heavy loading of natural science experiments, may be too stringent to account for the everyday thinking of most adults.

Many older adults show some declines in cognitive processes, particularly those involving some aspects of memory (Foos, 1989; Lehman & Mellinger, 1984). Others continue to perform well on cognitive tasks, despite declines in sensory capabilities and in reaction time. Changes in cognitive functioning are stable in some areas, such as the interpretation of proverbs, and discontinuous in others. For example, verbal recall abilities decline from the 30s to the 50s, but then remain stable until the 70s. It seems likely that selective brain changes account for some of these patterns (Albert, Duffy, & Naeser, 1987).

A study of everyday memory illustrates the changes that may occur with age (West & Crook, 1990). For this study, volunteers between the ages of 18 and 85 were recruited from newspaper advertisements in Washington, DC. Their task was to remember several series of numbers, with either 3, 7, or 10 digits in each number. Note that these number series correspond to the lengths of area codes, local telephone numbers, and long-distance numbers, respectively. Virtually all the people in all age groups could remember the area codes, but there was a substantial difference between the youngest and the oldest age groups in the average number of recalled digits of the local numbers. The long-distance number memory differences were even more dramatic. These age differences are illustrated in Figure 12–11. A special feature of this research project was the auditory presentation of the stimuli to be remembered. The findings indicated that when the numbers were presented in chunks, the performance of the older subjects was significantly better. The directory assistance procedures for giving out numbers via com-

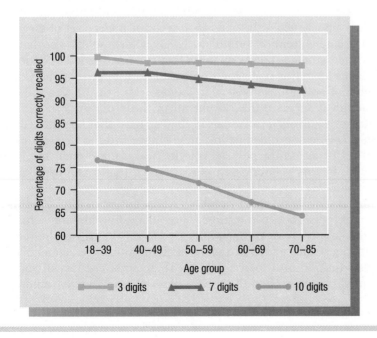

FIGURE 12–11
A study of everyday memory. Individuals in age groups from early to late adulthood attempted to remember number series of 3, 7, or 10 digits (the number of digits in area codes, local telephone numbers, and long-distance numbers, respectively). Recall in all age groups was close to perfect for area codes. For local numbers, performance was still high, with older individuals having slightly more difficulty. Older participants were noticeably poorer at remembering the longer strings of digits, however. (From West & Crook, 1990.)

puters in a nonchunked way thus presents a special memory disadvantage for older individuals.

Reaction time for cognitive processing is surely a factor in some of the tested declines in intelligence. This point was demonstrated in a unique study involving a group of men who had been given intelligence tests as army recruits in World War II and then were given the same tests 40 years later. For some men the retest was administered under the original time limits; others took the test with double the time allotment. There was a reliable but minor decline in intelligence under the regular time limits. But when extra time was allowed, scores actually showed improvement (Schwartzman et al., 1987). We discussed the issue of "speed tests" (those with time limits) in Chapter 11.

Part of the decline in cognitive abilities is also likely to be a function of practice, following the old adage "use it or lose it." In one study, aging rats raised in a complex, toy-filled environment were found to have thicker cerebral cortexes and more branching in their dendrites than rats reared in regular cages (Black et al., 1987). Among humans, declines in some intellectual abilities have been shown to be reversible with only a few hours of training. This result is particularly impressive given that the decline in abilities took place over many years (Schaie & Willis, 1986). Older adults, aged 55 to 91, also demonstrated that exercise is an important factor in cognitive performance. Those who were more physically active in exercise programs performed better on reaction time, working memory, and reasoning tasks than those who did not (Clarkson-Smith & Hartley, 1990).

Older adults differ in a number of respects from younger people, and many of these factors might influence performance on cognitive tasks. For example, in comparison to young adults, older individuals tend to have poorer health, less education, greater cautiousness, less experience with tests, and slower reaction times. Perhaps older adults find the sort of problem given to them silly or beneath their dignity. Perhaps they are merely further removed from the practice one gets with problems of this sort in school. Also, older adults may simply have less attentional capacity to devote to cognitive puzzles. In one study, young and old adults (average ages of 20 and 69, respectively) were asked to search through lists of letters for a set of target letters. The older participants did not do as well on this admittedly pointless and boring task as the young adults did. In addition, they performed particularly poorly when they had to search for a large set of targets, which required greater attention (Madden, 1983). Older adults also have greater difficulty than younger adults on tasks that require divided attention. Mental activity takes longer as one grows older, and this effect may be amplified by the number of operations involved in the task (McDowd & Craik, 1988).

Although it seems unlikely that all of these differences can be easily eliminated or controlled in research, they suggest that cognitive differences between younger and older people might have little to do with changes in intellectual functioning per se. Intellectual competence might remain unchanged, but its reflection in performance could change dramatically (Datan et al., 1987).

Some researchers, most notably Gisela Labouvie-Vief (1986), believe that the differences between younger and older adult thinking actually reveal developmental progress. Young adults tend to rely heavily on literal and even rigid thinking. Older adults are more likely to introduce elements of subjectivity and intuition into their thinking. Their apparent loss of some logical powers might actually be in the service of a richer cognitive framework.

THINKING AHEAD . . .

Developmental research has increased enormously in the last 2 decades. The growth has been especially impressive in studies of infants and of older adults. In fact, most college courses in human development 20 years ago were called "child development" courses; now they are more likely to be called "life-span development" courses.

Developmental issues have come to play a larger role in all areas of psychology. Studies of the impact of brain structures on behavior often look at the developmental implications. For example, what happens if a part of the brain is destroyed early in life, as opposed to later in life? Or in the study of language, how do systems of communication develop early in childhood? In the study of memory, how does the memory system change with age, and how malleable is it? In abnormal psychology, how is it that some individuals develop psychological disorders, and what role did early experience play in determining the pattern of symptoms that an individual exhibits?

Through research in developmental psychology, we are learning how people develop normally, including physical timetables of matura-tion for the brain. Basic research in physical and cognitive development helps us to understand what to expect at different points in the life cycle, and ultimately to understand the underlying mechanisms—genetics, biochemistry, learning, family rearing, and so forth. The practical application of this kind of knowledge is endless. It will help us to nurture creativity; to reduce the debilitating effects of racism; to facilitate the education of all our children, with and without handicaps; and to ease the plight of individuals afflicted with Alzheimer's disease.

Finally, we need to acknowledge the limitations of our understanding of human development. We are especially lacking in information about the developmental differences experienced by ethnic minority populations. The population of the United States, 250 million strong and growing, is made up of many different groups, varying in color and creed, in values and beliefs, and in prospects for growth and development. We need to understand more about our differences so that we can respect the things that divide us and strive for the things that unite us.

Summary

Themes in Developmental Psychology

1. Persistent controversies in developmental psychology include the nature versus nurture and continuity versus discontinuity arguments. There is a growing consensus that development is a product of both heredity and environment, as well as of maturation and experience, and that there are both continuities and discontinuities in behavioral development.

The Study of Developmental Phenomena: Life-Cycle Changes

2. Life-span developmental psychology is the study of changes in psychological phenomena, such as thinking, dreaming, and social behavior, over the course of the life cycle. The two main strategies for studying life-span development are cross-sectional studies, in which a cross section of age groups is studied at a given time, and longitudinal studies, in which the same people are periodically retested over a long period of time. The two strategies sometimes yield different results because of cohort effects, findings that are based on the time people were born and their subsequent experiences, rather than their ages per se.

Physical Development

3. Prenatal growth during pregnancy proceeds in an orderly fashion, from head to tail (cephalo-caudal development) and from inside to outside (proximo-distal development).

4. Teratogens are substances, such as viruses, drugs, or pollutants, that can cause birth defects. Alcohol is a powerful teratogen that sometimes causes physical and mental impairment.

5. Growth is rapid in infancy but tapers off throughout childhood until the second major growth spurt at adolescence. Reliable sex differences in maturation rates have been observed.

6. More similarities than differences characterize infant motor development. Poverty, however, has negative effects on developmental outcome in a number of ways. Minority infants, who are more likely to suffer ill effects of poverty, have higher mortality rates than majority infants.

7. Girls reach puberty ahead of boys by about 2 years. Studies of family interaction indicate that as puberty progresses, increases in conflict are observed in the family. The conflict is especially pronounced with mothers.

8. There is some decline in physical and sensory capacities throughout adulthood, but the change is gradual. More discontinuous changes occur in the reproductive system for women at around the age of 50, when ovulation ceases at menopause. Men continue to produce sperm cells, and both sexes may remain sexually active in old age.

9. Life expectancy has increased, but it is not evenly distributed in the population. Women have a longer life expectancy at birth than men, and Caucasians have a longer life expectancy than members of most minority groups.

Cognitive Development

10. Newborn infants have good sensory capabilities and seem particularly prone to pay attention to certain patterns or distinctive features in the environment, such as movement, curvature, orientation, and high-pitched sounds. Cognitive accomplishments associated with language, especially in the 2nd year of life, are truly astonishing.

11. The practical importance of developmental psychology is especially great in educational settings. In recent years, many programs have been designed to facilitate cognitive development in early childhood. A case in point is the nationwide Head Start program.

12. Piaget proposed a stage theory of cognitive development, characterized by the development of cognitive structures—the means of acquiring and applying knowledge about the world. In Piaget's four stages of cognition, the sensory–motor action patterns of infancy are overshadowed in early childhood by internalized representations of events, although intelligence remains preoperational. Logical operations such as reversibility appear in later childhood in the concrete–operational stage of intelligence. In adolescence and adulthood, true operations of hypothetical and abstract thought appear in the formal–operational stage.

13. In comparison to childhood thought, adolescent thinking is more logical, more hypothetical, and more reflective.

14. Some cognitive declines, especially in memory and in logical thinking, appear to characterize later adulthood. Adult thinking may be richer in subjectivity and intuition, however.

Key Terms

developmental psychology (464)

nature position (465)

nurture position (465)

monozygotic (MZ) (465)

dizygotic (DZ) (465)

continuity position (467)

discontinuity position (467)

cross-sectional research (467)

cohort effects (468)

longitudinal research (470)

cohort-sequential research (471)

cephalo-caudal development (471)

proximo-distal development (472)

age of viability (472)

teratogens (473)

fetal alcohol syndrome (474)

menarche (478)

menopause (480)

senile dementia (481)

Alzheimer's disease (481)

visually directed reaching (484)

feature detectors (485)

habituation technique (485)

preference technique (485)

visual cliff (486)

cognitive structures (490)

assimilation (490)

accommodation (491)

circular reactions (491)

object permanence (491)

preoperational thinking (492)

animism (493)

artificialism (493)

concrete–operational thinking (493)

operations (493)

reversibility (493)

conservation problems (494)

formal–operational thinking (495)

personal fable (496)

Suggested Reading

Elkind, D. (1987). *Miseducation: Preschoolers at risk*. New York: Knopf. A warning to parents and early childhood specialists that academic programs at too early an age might have negative consequences in the long run.

Konner, M. (1991). *Childhood*. Boston: Little Brown. A book that served as a companion to the Public Broadcasting System's series on childhood. Konner, an anthropologist, includes abundant material on childhood in other cultures.

Markides, K. S., & Mindel, C. H. (1987). *Aging and ethnicity*. Newbury Park, CA: Sage. An overview of the differences in the experience of aging, including physical and health-related issues, among ethnic minority populations in the United States.

Piaget, J. (1967). *Six psychological studies* (A. Tenzer, Trans.). New York: Vintage. (Original work published 1964). Six essays, varying in length, on such aspects of Piaget's theory as the cognitive stages, language and thought, and the concept of equilibrium.

Siegler, R. S. (1991). *Children's thinking* (2nd ed.). Englewood Cliffs, NJ: Prentice-Hall. An overview of a variety of aspects of cognitive development in childhood.

Tanner, J. M. (1978). *Fetus into man: Physical growth from conception to maturity*. Cambridge, MA: Harvard University Press. A summary of physical changes from conception through puberty. The book focuses primarily on normal development, but it includes information on growth disorders as well.

CHAPTER 13
Social Development

Psychologists and other professionals who are interested in the welfare of children have sometimes studied the effects of extreme rearing conditions on later development. These conditions can be dramatically unfavorable, and occasionally truly awful. In the latter category falls the case of "Genie," who appeared with her blind mother in the Los Angeles County welfare office in 1970 (Rymer, 1992). (Genie's mother had been seeking welfare assistance for herself.) Genie's father, who committed suicide shortly after authorities discovered her, had subjected her to the most horrendous conditions almost from birth until her rescue at age 13. By day she had been harnessed to a potty chair in a back bedroom of her family's home with virtually no visual or auditory stimulation and barely adequate nourishment. At night she was placed in a sleeping bag that restricted her movement, and the bag, in turn, was put into a crib covered with wire mesh.

These arrangements constituted her entire world—devoid of social interchange, playmates, toys or noisemakers, loving embraces from parents, outdoor walks, and the rhythms of the seasons. What would be the result of such an upbringing on social development? One of the psychologists who first evaluated Genie, Dr. James Kent, described his reaction this way: "As far as I'm concerned, Genie was the most profoundly damaged child I've ever seen. There has been nothing in other cases to approach it" (Rymer, 1992, p. 63).

Genie, unfortunately, is not the only child to have suffered the abuses of profound isolation, although she is one of the most famous cases in the twentieth century. The scientific community seized upon Genie's case to

◀ Social aspects of developmental change extend from earliest infancy to advanced age.

help answer some elusive questions about human nature and its relation to upbringing. Dr. David Rigler, a professor of pediatrics and psychology who ultimately became a foster parent to Genie, summed up the importance of her case for psychology shortly after she was found: "Theories of child development hold that there are essential experiences for achievement of normal psychological and physical growth. If this child can be assisted to develop in social, and other areas, this provides useful information regarding the critical role of early experience which is of potential benefit to other deprived children" (Rymer, 1992, p. 69).

Genie's case recaps some of the enduring controversies of developmental psychology that we studied in the previous chapter, such as nature versus nurture and continuity versus discontinuity. One might ask, for example, if Genie's early behavior reflected a developmental delay, perhaps genetically linked, to which her father responded with abuse. Although his behavior would be equally reprehensible in that situation, her subsequent retardation might not be an outcome of the extreme rearing she had endured as much as it was a condition she already had. One might also ask if Genie's condition could be reversed if she were placed in a nurturing and supportive environment. If not, perhaps she had missed some critical developmental milestones during those years in which she was kept isolated—developmental milestones that could not subsequently be made up.

One intense and emotional case study cannot answer these perplexing questions in a scientifically satisfying manner, but it can offer some suggestions. As we shall see, Genie was ultimately unable to overcome her early extreme rearing conditions. Whether her rearing conditions were alone responsible for her plight, we will never know. But combining what we know from other studies with the dramatic aspects of this case, it seems clear that her rearing conditions greatly influenced her later behavior.

In this chapter, we tackle the issues underlying social development across the life span, from the social beginnings in infancy to the psychological processes involved with death and dying. Along the way we also examine some changes in the American family structure and their impact on social development. Our discussions begin with the emergence of social awareness in infancy.

INFANCY: SOCIAL BEGINNINGS

The cognitive level of very young infants makes intentional social behavior unlikely. For example, infants may smile in a wide variety of situations, not all of them social. Newborns sometimes smile when they are asleep, and older infants smile when they recognize a familiar object (Kagan, 1971). Before 3 or 4 months, the smile may not be truly social—intentionally directed at another person. Indeed, some psychologists believe that social behavior is not intentional until near the first birthday (Frye et al., 1983).

Very young infants do take part in social interchanges, however, whether intentionally or not. **Social interchanges** are patterns of social interaction that have reciprocal influence—the behavior of each person affects and is in turn affected by the other. For example, as shown in Figure 13–1, infants appear to imitate very simple acts, such as opening the mouth and sticking out the tongue (Jacobson, 1979; Kaitz et al., 1988; Meltzoff & Moore, 1983). These simple social interchanges serve to regulate the behavior of both infants and the adults who may be interacting with them. As we saw in Chapter 12, infants come into the world equipped with preferences for specific features in the environment. Among other things, they have a

social interchange pattern of social behavior between individuals who have reciprocal influence on each other

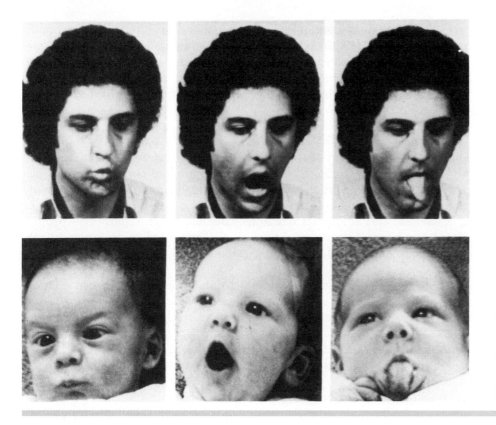

FIGURE 13-1
Infants are able to imitate very simple
acts, such as sticking out the tongue
or opening the mouth. Nevertheless,
the imitation requires perceptual and
motor coordination that until recently
many psychologists did not believe
infants possessed.

strong preference for looking at human faces, and this preference has a powerful effect on adults (Brazelton, 1982).

A growing body of research into social interchanges, particularly between mothers and young infants, shows that influence is reciprocal. That is, mother and infant are both influential in sustaining the interaction. Behaviors such as smiling, eye contact, touching, and changing facial expressions influence the nature of the interaction, sometimes in very subtle ways (Cohn & Tronick, 1988; Fogel, Toda, & Kawai, 1988; Symons & Moran, 1987).

Adults may be more likely to respond to and care for infants given their distinctive body shape and facial features (see Figure 13–2). A large head and

FIGURE 13–2
The distinctive head shapes of infants may bring about nurturing responses from their parents and other caregivers. Infants of many species have large heads, large eyes, and fat cheeks.

eyes, fat cheeks, and a small body seem to elicit more nurturant responses from adults (Hess, 1970). When pairs of drawings in a variety of sizes and shapes, depicting newborns and older children are presented to adults, the adults are more likely to pick the younger-looking drawing as the one they would choose to defend from attack or to hug or cuddle (Alley, 1983).

Attachment to Caregivers

Shortly after World War II, John Bowlby, a prominent British psychiatrist, began studying why infants develop strong emotional bonds with their primary caregivers and why they often display anxiety and distress when separated from them. Bowlby (1969, 1973) proposed that the specific sequence of behavioral and emotional reactions associated with separation—protest, despair, and detachment—might reflect the operation of an innate attachment system designed to keep young, vulnerable infants physically close to their caregivers.

Bowlby called the process by which infants establish a close relationship with those people who provide most of their care **attachment**. Some psychologists believe that the process begins shortly after birth, when close physical contact between mother and infant fosters **bonding**—the creation of an emotional relationship that will affect both parent and child in the months and years ahead (Klaus, 1978). However, this bonding takes place more on the part of caregivers than infants. Mothers who have spent only an hour with their newborns can recognize their infants at a better-than-chance level by touch alone—without any odor or other non-touch cues (Kaitz et al., 1992).

Bowlby's observations and theoretical ideas about attachment were converted into a systematic assessment procedure by Mary Ainsworth and her colleagues (Ainsworth & Bell, 1970). Attachment implies physical closeness, which is one of the ways it is manifested in infancy. When infants are frightened, they may seek contact with their caregivers, usually parents. When they are in a strange situation or some unfamiliar place, the mere presence of a parent may serve to keep them calm (Ainsworth & Wittig, 1969). Thus, to assess infant attachment to caregivers, Ainsworth designed a "strange situation" with several episodes in which the parent leaves a child alone or with a stranger and then returns. The infant's behavior at the separation and subsequent reunion is carefully recorded in order to classify the infant's style of attachment.

Using this procedure, Ainsworth identified three primary styles of attachment (Ainsworth et al., 1978). Infants who show **secure attachment** relationships with their primary caregivers use them as a base of security to reduce feelings of distress and anxiety when they are upset. Other infants make inconsistent, conflicted, and ambivalent attempts to receive emotional support from their caregivers when they are upset, actions that seem to reflect their uncertainty about the caregiver's availability and supportiveness. These infants are described as showing **resistant attachment**. Finally, infants who neither seek support from their primary caregivers nor use them to manage and dissipate anxiety when it arises show **avoidant attachment**.

Most infants can be classified into a style of attachment with the strange situation procedure. The majority of infants—roughly 70%—are securely attached. Another 20% or so are avoidant, and about 10% are resistant (Ainsworth et al., 1978). Table 13–1 summarizes the reactions of infants in these three categories to their caregivers after a brief episode of separation.

Experience and Infant Attachment. Bowlby's and Ainsworth's views about attachment are heavily influenced by evolutionary concepts. There is

attachment process by which infants establish a close relationship with caregivers

bonding process of caregivers establishing an emotional tie to infants shortly after birth

secure attachment style of attachment in which infants use their primary caregiver as a base of security to reduce distress

resistant attachment style of attachment in which infants make inconsistent and ambivalent use of caregivers in strange situations

avoidant attachment style of attachment in which infants neither seek support from nor show distress toward caregivers in strange situations

TABLE 13-1
Styles of Attachment Exhibited by Children in the "Strange Situation"

Secure Attachment: After separation, infant actively attempts to get close to caretaker, through seeking proximity, contact, or social interaction.
Avoidant Attachment: After separation, infant avoids or ignores caretaker.
Resistant Attachment: After separation, infant is angry or unable to be calmed by the caretaker.

Young children who are securely attached to their caregivers seek contact with them when they are frightened or when they are in a strange or novel situation.

obvious survival value to a strong attachment bond that keeps an infant close to its caregivers. But the particular style of attachment that develops between caregivers and infants may be influenced by a number of experiential factors. For example, attachment style may be similar from one generation to the next. One study of this phenomenon asked pregnant women to describe as fully as possible, in an interview, their own childhood attachment experiences. Subsequently, after their infants were born and had reached one year of age, Ainsworth's strange situation was used to classify their infants' attachment styles. The mothers' self-reported attachment experiences correctly predicted their infants' styles of attachment 75% of the time (Fonagy, Steele, & Steele, 1991).

The consistency of attachment style across generations does not mean that the style is unchangeable, however. The social support that caregivers receive in their child-rearing situation might logically affect their attachment relationship to the child. For example, when mothers receive help from other family members, such as the father, older children, or extended family members, they have infants who are more securely attached (Crockenberg, 1981). The impact of social support was tested experimentally by randomly assigning pregnant women to either an experimental or a control group. The experimental group of women were given social support and information by volunteer coaches before their children were born and throughout the first year of the child's life. Women in the control group, matched on demographic factors such as income and education, had no volunteer coaches. At 14 months, the infants of the mothers in the experimental group were more securely attached than the infants of the mothers in the control group (Jacobson & Frye, 1991). This study shows that attachment style can be modified by experience—in this case the experience of the mothers.

Day Care and Attachment. What is the impact of day care on attachment between infants and mothers? In the 1990s, it is expected that 75% of women with school-aged children will be in the work force (Silverstein, 1991). This figure is a dramatic increase over figures from earlier generations, and can be explained by a number of factors. More marriages are ending in divorce, and women who have custody of the children need to work to support the family; more families in the 1990s are single-parent families; and more women expect to combine family life with careers. Arrangements must be made for child care either outside the home or by someone other than the mother in the home. A great deal of debate has centered on the question of how day-care arrangements affect the attachment relationship between mothers and young children.

Unfortunately, the data on this issue are not completely consistent, but most studies indicate that young children whose mothers work outside the home show more insecure attachment (either resistant or avoidant) in the strange situation (e.g., Belsky & Rovine, 1988; Clarke-Stewart, 1989). However, the differences in percentages of infants who are insecurely attached based on their mothers' work status are quite modest; according to data from several studies, 36% of infants whose mothers worked full time were insecurely attached, compared to 29% whose mothers worked part time or not at all. Furthermore, children in day care were advanced in some areas, such as in measures of intellectual development (Clarke-Stewart, 1989).

The debate about the effect of mothers' employment on attachment style also perpetuates the notion, partly traceable to Freud, that mothers are critical to the psychological and emotional health of children. This view constitutes a bias with three faulty assumptions: (1) fathers are relatively unimportant; (2) mothers can be blamed when things go wrong; and (3) the mother is the only viable caregiver for young children. Looking at child-care arrangements cross-culturally shows that many societies have adopted patterns different from ours. In hunter-gatherer societies, for example, young children are cared for not by mothers but by groups of older children of both sexes (Silverstein, 1991). Much of our thinking about child care needs modification. Perhaps we should stop searching for what can go wrong if mothers work, and begin looking for ways to ensure day care of high quality for the children of all working parents.

Some studies suggest that infants adapt to repeated separations from their mothers by showing less distress. For example, the distress shown by infants and toddlers when their mothers left them to attend professional conferences over a period of several days decreased with repeated separations (Field, 1991). Although more time in day care may increase the likelihood of an insecure attachment to the mother, the child may still develop a secure attachment relationship to the professional caregiver (Goosens & van Ijzendoorn, 1990). At any rate, as one reviewer put it, "Maternal employment is a reality. The issue today, therefore, is not whether infants should be in day care but how to make their experiences there and at home supportive of their development and of their parents' peace of mind" (Clarke-Stewart, 1989, pp. 271–272).

Child-rearing beliefs and practices differ from culture to culture. But there are also many similarities in care-giving practices from one culture to another.

Culture and Attachment.   Different experiences that are linked to beliefs about child rearing may also influence attachment style. Child-rearing beliefs differ to some extent by social class, as well as cross-culturally. These cultural beliefs may underlie some of the cross-cultural variation observed in attachment. In western Europe, avoidant attachment is relatively more common, whereas resistant attachment is more common in Israel and Japan (van IJzendoorn & Kroonenberg, 1988). The Israeli kibbutz, characterized by a collectivist ideology in which infants experience close relationships with parents and professional caretakers, but have few opportunities to interact with strangers, produces the most distress; a very large percentage of these infants are classified as resistant (Sagi, van IJzendoorn, & Koren-Karie, 1991).

The closeness of contact experienced by infants when their caregivers carry and hold them may also influence the style of attachment. In an experimental test of this idea, a group of mothers were randomly assigned to carry their infants in soft baby carriers to promote more physical contact, whereas another group were instructed to carry their infants in hard infant seats that reduced physical contact. In the strange situation test given at 13 months, significantly more of the infants in the soft-carrier group were securely attached than those in the hard-carrier group (Anisfeld et al., 1990).

SPOTLIGHT ON RESEARCH
Monkeys and Contact Comfort

The soft and hard infant seats used in the carrying study just described are reminiscent of the treatments received by groups of infant Rhesus monkeys in a series of classic experiments by Harry Harlow. Harlow was interested in which variables might lead to an attachment bond between a mother and an infant. One popular hypothesis of the 1940s and 1950s was that attachment grew out of the feeding situation. Such a prediction might be made from the perspective of either learning theory or psychoanalytic theory. In learning theory, a caregiver becomes a secondary reinforcer in the feeding situation, leading to a greater probability of infants seeking to be close to the caregiver. In psychoanalytic theory, the oral stage is the first stage of psychosexual development, and leads to a strong identification with the mother that makes the child want to be close to her.

Harlow tested some of these theoretical principles by providing infant monkeys with two "surrogate mothers"—a concept that now means something quite different from what it did when Harlow used the term in the 1950s. His surrogates were either a construction of wire mesh with a square head or a similar construction covered in terrycloth with a round head (see Figure 13–3). Both surrogates were the same general size and tilted at a slight angle. Furthermore, both could be outfitted with a bottle stuck roughly in the center of the surrogate's "chest." Harlow could then systematically test the power of the feeding situation to elicit attachment. To which surrogate would the infant monkeys cling? Where would they go in times of stress?

Harlow found that even when the wire surrogate fed them, infant monkeys overwhelmingly preferred the cloth surrogate and were comforted by its presence in a strange situation (Harlow & Zimmerman, 1959). (Harlow's strange situation—strange for a monkey—was a noisy, battery-operated

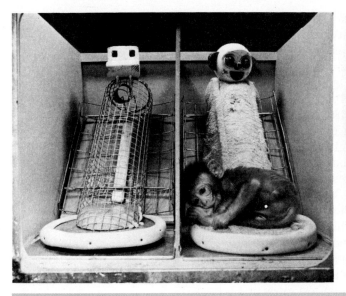

FIGURE 13–3
(*Left*) Infant monkeys prefer to stick close to a cloth surrogate mother, even if the wire mother fed the infant from a bottle stuck in her chest. (*Right*) They also ran to the cloth mother in frightening situations, much as human children do in strange laboratory situations.

contact comfort need for close contact with a "caregiver" experienced by infant monkeys (and perhaps humans)

bear, or a large cricket-like creature.) He speculated that infant monkeys experience a need for **contact comfort** that is independent of feeding. The same sort of need may well apply to human infants, and may help to shape the infant's attachment style.

The Father's Role in Attachment. Most of the research on attachment has been directed toward the mother–child relationship. What about the father's role in attachment? One approach to this question is to examine the amount of time fathers spend with their infants and the type of activities they engage in. Although there is a great deal of individual variation among fathers in the amount of time they spend with their infants, studies indicate that the time is short for most fathers, both in absolute terms and in comparison to mothers. Estimates of the amount of time fathers spend actually interacting with their infants on weekdays range between averages of 15 and 50 minutes. By contrast, for mothers who hold full-time jobs outside the home, the interaction time seldom falls below 1 hour (Ninio & Rinott, 1988). In one study of father–infant interaction, less than half of the fathers performed even a single caretaking chore (such as diapering or putting the child to bed) over a 2-day period (Ninio & Rinott, 1988).

A few studies have investigated the relationship between fathers' interactions with their young infants and the style of attachment they develop, measured with Ainsworth's strange situation. Fathers who interact more with their infants and who have a more positive attitude about their role are more likely to have infants who are securely attached in later infancy (Cox et al., 1992). Other researchers have found a relationship between the infant's style of attachment to one parent and its style of attachment to the other (Fox, Kimmerly, & Schafer, 1991). If infants were insecurely attached to their fathers, then they also were likely to be insecurely attached to their mothers.

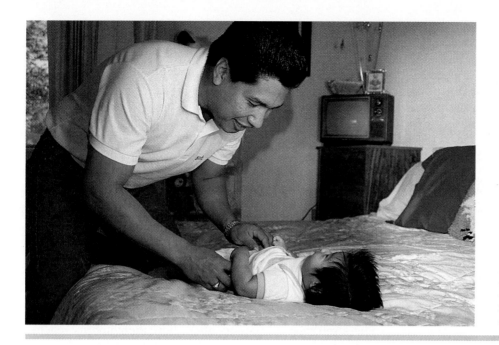

Most studies of father–infant interaction indicate that fathers spend considerably less time than mothers in routine caretaking duties such as diapering, bathing, and feeding.

Attachment Beyond Infancy. Attachment style also shows developmental continuity into childhood. Children whose attachment style had been measured during infancy with Ainsworth's strange situation returned to the laboratory with their parents at age 6. A version of the strange situation, adapted for older children, revealed an attachment style to mothers at age 6 that was predictable in 84% of the cases from the style exhibited in infancy. Attachment to fathers was predictable from infancy in only 61% of the cases (Main & Cassidy, 1988).

The surface characteristics of attachment behavior change in regular ways during the life span (Ainsworth, 1989). Some of these changes are undoubtedly related to patterns of cognitive development, including the child's ability to comprehend parental motives in their child-rearing techniques. The onset of adolescence, with the associated pubertal and hormonal changes, probably alters children's relationships with their parents even further, as we shall see later in this chapter. Nevertheless, a considerable body of research suggests that attachment style in infancy may be reflected in later social behavior. Attachment style in infancy may even influence the nature of romantic relationships in adulthood, a point that we explore in the next chapter, on social psychology.

Anxieties in Infancy

Two milestones of infant social development involve fears. Most North American infants, late in the first year of life, express **stranger anxiety**. This fear may be so strong that infants cry when an unfamiliar person approaches them, even if their parents are nearby. The second fear, called **separation anxiety**, peaks around the middle of the second year of life. Young children may become very upset at any separation from their parents. However, although a majority of children exhibit these childhood fears, they are not inevitable (Corter, 1976). These anxieties gradually decrease, although some social inhibition and shyness may remain.

Stranger anxiety and separation anxiety are obviously relevant to discussions of attachment style, especially as it is measured by Ainsworth's strange situation. Recall that her assessment involves several episodes, in an unfamil-

stranger anxiety typical fear of strangers that infants exhibit during the second half of the first year of life

separation anxiety typical fear of separation from caregivers that infants exhibit late in the second year of life

iar environment, in which the caregiver leaves the infant alone or with an adult stranger. The stronger the child's degree of stranger and separation anxiety, the more likely he or she will be to show distress in this situation.

Stranger and separation anxieties are also linked to cognitive development. Both depend to a certain extent on the child's appreciation of *person permanence*, the belief that people continue to exist even when they are out of sight. This concept derives from Piaget's cognitive developmental theory. Piaget placed its development late in the first year of life.

Infant Temperament

temperament an infant's personality disposition that affects patterns of interaction from early infancy

An infant's style of attachment, while changeable, appears to be a relatively stable characteristic having continuity from one period of life to another. **Temperament** is a similar concept used to describe an infant's relatively stable patterns of interaction from very early in life. Temperament is generally considered to be an innate style of behaving that can be observed in the ways infants interact with their parents. Some babies seem to be very easy to care for, while others are described as "difficult." The psychologists who are most noted for their work on infant temperament are Thomas, Chess, and Birch (1970).

These researchers interviewed parents about how their infants reacted in routine caregiving situations that required close interpersonal contact, such as bathing and feeding. Based on their interviews, Thomas, Chess, and Birch argued that infants differ, even from the earliest weeks of life, along nine dimensions of personality. These nine dimensions include activity level and rhythmicity of behavior, adaptability, quality of mood, distractibility, and so on. The nine dimensions are listed and described in Table 13–2.

One of Thomas, Chess, and Birch's dimensions of temperament is approach–withdrawal. Some babies are fascinated by anything new, delighting in novelty; others are timid about new experiences, and withdraw from such situations. This dimension of infant personality is currently under increased scrutiny as a biologically based characteristic, which Kagan (1992) calls *inhibi-*

TABLE 13-2
Nine Categories of Infant Temperament

Activity level. Physical activity level of the infant, including sleep–wake cycles and activity during routines such as bathing, eating, playing, and dressing.

Regularity. The predictability of the infant's behavior, e.g., in terms of bedtimes and feeding patterns.

Approach or withdrawal. Initial response to a new stimulus situation, such as a new food or toy. Approach is indicated by smiling and verbalizing, reaching, etc.; withdrawal is indicated by crying, fussing, or moving away.

Adaptability. Reaction to new stimulus situations over a period of time (as opposed to the initial reaction).

Threshold of responsiveness. The level of intensity of a stimulus situation that is required to provoke a response, whether the response is positive or negative.

Intensity of reaction. The energy level of the response, regardless of whether it is positive or negative.

Quality of mood. The amount of pleasant, joyful, and friendly behavior shown by the infant.

Distractibility. Effectiveness of extraneous stimulus in interfering with ongoing behavior.

Attention span and persistence. Length of time the infant pursues an activity, and continues to pursue an activity even in the face of obstacles.

Source: Thomas & Chess, 1977, pp. 21–22.

tion. In more ordinary conversation, we would call the dimension *shyness.* Kagan believes that behavioral indicators of inhibition show up very early in life, and that the characteristic shows stability over time. For example, toddlers who were extremely inhibited were also shy and inhibited with a peer later in childhood (Kagan, Reznick, & Snidman, 1988; Kochanska & Radke-Yarrow, 1992). It is possible that these inhibited children will grow up to be introverted adults. As we shall see, however, stage models of development support the notion of developmental discontinuities, major shifts that occur in social development despite superficial similarities from one part of the life cycle to another.

Inhibited children reveal their wariness to newness in a variety of ways; they show increased heart rate and muscle tension, and grow quiet. The mother of a child whom Kagan observed as an infant described him this way: "If something is new and different, his inclination is to be quiet and watch—he's aware of it, and he has coping strategies. His friends don't see him as shy. But it's unfamiliarity that is the cause of his behavior. Not just new people, but *newness*" (Galvin, 1992). After testing infants in a variety of situations, Kagan estimated that about 15% are extremely inhibited, and about 20% are extremely uninhibited, with the majority falling somewhere in between. Kagan has outlined the characteristic differences between inhibited and uninhibited children, and has speculated about their continuity into adolescence and adulthood. These descriptions are listed in Table 13–3.

TABLE 13-3
Characteristic Differences Between Inhibited and Uninhibited Children

Inhibited child	Uninhibited child
In infancy, shows high levels of agitation and irritability in response to the unfamiliar.	In infancy, low levels of agitation and minimal irritability in response to the unfamiliar. Smiles frequently.
In unfamiliar situations, remains quiet; stays close to mother. Heart rate and muscle tension increase with novel events or psychological stress. Large rise in diastolic blood pressure when posture changes from sitting to standing.	Small rise in heart rate or muscle tension in response to novelty or psychological stress. Highly variable heart rate at rest.
In response to mild psychological stress, larger dilation of eye pupils; right side of face becomes cooler.	Greater cooling on left side of face in response to mild stress.
Higher secretion of cortisol, a stress-related hormone. Prone to allergies, especially hay fever and eczema.	
Likely to have blue eyes and ectomorphic (tall, thin) build.	Likely to have brown eyes and mesomorphic body build.
Concerned with doing the "right thing" and not violating standards. Sensitive to reprimand.	Spontaneously verbal; speaks quickly and easily in unfamiliar situations with unfamiliar people.
In adolescence or adulthood . . .	
Not likely to be delinquent. Begin to date in late adolescence; likely to marry later than most in age group.	
Likely to take a job involving minimal uncertainty (e.g., bureaucratic).	Likely to take moderate- to high-risk jobs (e.g., entrepreneur).
At risk for panic disorder and agoraphobia in adulthood.	

Source: Galvin, 1992, p. 43.

CHILDHOOD: A WIDENING SOCIAL WORLD

The disparity between mothers' and fathers' infant caretaking activities that we noted previously extends into childhood. Mothers interact more with their children and are more involved in caregiving than are fathers. Fathers are somewhat more involved in playing with the children, especially outdoor play. Despite these differences in parental roles, an interview and observational study of families in which the oldest child was 6 or 7 indicated few differences in the child's response to mothers versus fathers (Russell & Russell, 1987).

Whereas parents are the focus of social interaction in infancy, in childhood—especially after school entry—this focus shifts more and more to peers. Other children serve as models for imitation, as play partners, and perhaps as vehicles for emotional development. Harlow and his colleagues demonstrated this latter point with Rhesus monkeys. Infant monkeys who were deprived of any mothering by an adult monkey nevertheless were able to develop more or less normal social skills if they were allowed to play with other monkeys the same age (Suomi & Harlow, 1972).

Regularities in the developmental shift toward a wider social world in childhood are illustrated in a study of students in fourth, seventh, and tenth grades, and college. For fourth graders, parents were viewed as the most frequent providers of social support. In seventh grade, same-sex peers were as likely as parents to be perceived as providing social support. By the tenth grade, same-sex peers had surpassed parents as the main social support system. Among college students, romantic partners, friends, and mothers all received high ratings for social support (Furman & Buhrmester, 1992).

Gender and Peer Relationships in Childhood

As the previous study indicates, peers of the same sex play a particularly important role in social development. Friendships in childhood are overwhelmingly with other children of the same sex. This sex bias in friendship increases during the childhood years, at least up to the sixth grade (Hayden-Thomson, Rubin, & Hymel, 1987). When boys and girls are paired with other same-sex children, different styles of interaction for the two sexes emerge in

Fathers interact somewhat differently with their children than mothers. They are more likely to play with them—especially outdoors—than to engage in routine care activities.

Friendships in early childhood tend overwhelmingly to be with other children of the same sex. This young girl has invited her special friends—all girls—to her birthday party.

laboratory settings. For example, pairs of girls engage in more information exchange and less disagreement than boys (Furman, 1987). Some of these sex differences also show up in natural settings like playgrounds. Boys play more competitive games and tolerate disputes better than girls (Lever, 1976).

Another typical situation that children encounter is joining a peer group that is already engaged in play. In one study, children were observed attempting to join other peers, either relatively familiar or unfamiliar, who were playing a board game. Boys were somewhat more active and assertive in the way they approached their peers than girls. Girls who were already part of the group were more attentive to the newcomers than boys, who were more likely to ignore the newcomers (Borja-Alvarez, Zarbatany, & Pepper, 1991). These observations support some of the stereotypes of gender-based behavior in childhood. Boys are seen as more individualistic and assertive; girls are seen as more socially sensitive and responsive (Gilligan, 1982).

Explanations about sex differences in behavior abound, but critical tests of hypotheses about these differences are hard to construct. Although there may be biological bases to the differences, it is also clear that socialization practices favor sex differences. Parents respond differently to boys and girls, differentially rewarding them for behaviors that follow sex stereotypes (Lytton & Romney, 1991). For example, boys are rewarded more for playing with blocks, manipulating objects, and playing with transportation toys. Girls are rewarded more for playing with dolls, dancing, and asking for help (Fagot, 1978). Parents react more positively to boys when they behave aggressively. However, the different reactions of parents are much less noticeable by the time their children reach age 5 (Fagot & Hagen, 1991).

Social Play in Childhood

The ways that young children play when they are in groups, such as in nursery schools or kindergartens, reveal a great deal about their level of social participation. Children become more socially involved in their play as they grow older, according to researchers who have systematically observed their behavior. In a classic observational study, Mildred Parten (1932) observed children in a nursery-school setting over the course of a year, and

TABLE 13-4
Parten's Categories of Social Play in Childhood

Unoccupied behavior. Child does not appear to be playing. Child may watch other children from a distance, without asking questions or attempting to get involved. Child engages in aimless activities. Examples: casual glancing; standing around; wandering; getting on and off a chair; tugging on clothing.

Solitary play. Child plays alone even if other children are close and playing with different toys. Child makes no effort to speak with or interact with others. Examples: drawing at a table alone, or where other children are engaging in activities other than drawing; playing with a gerbil when no other children are around.

Onlooker behavior. Child stays near others and watches them play, and may even ask questions or make comments, but does not take part in the play itself. Watchfulness here is not aimless as it is in unoccupied behavior, and the child is closer to others and actually interacting with them verbally from time to time. Examples: standing on fringes of dress-up corner; watching two children play house, and asking them "Why you do that?"

Parallel play. Child plays independently within a few feet of other children and with similar toys, but without trying to influence the other children or being influenced by them. There is no real interaction between the children. Examples: playing with a bucket and shovel in sandbox where other children also have buckets and shovels, but with no interaction between children; drawing at a table where other children are also independently drawing.

Associative play. Child plays with other children in similar or identical activity but with no division of labor or organization. There may be influence attempts or taking and giving of material. Examples: holding hands on playground; running after another child on playground; following another child on a tricycle, but in no organized game.

Cooperative play. Child plays in an organized group that is making something or playing a structured game. There is division of labor, with some children leading or taking different roles. All children appear to understand that they are playing the same game. Examples: enacting a part in a joint fantasy, such as being mommy in a household corner; assisting another with a project.

Source: Parten, 1932.

found that their play patterns could be summarized into six categories of increasing social complexity (see Table 13–4).

At the lowest levels, children are either *unoccupied* and wandering aimlessly or are engaged in *solitary play* without attempting to interact with other children. A higher level of complexity includes *onlooker behavior*, in which children stand near other children and observe what they are doing without interacting, and *parallel play*, in which children play near each other in similar ways with similar toys, but still without interacting. The two most complex categories of play are *associative play*, in which the children in a group all participate in the same activity yet without any clear set of directions or rules, and *cooperative play*, which includes the give-and-take interaction involved when there are clear roles that members of the group must play in a structured activity. Researchers are still using Parten's scheme for observing play behavior in childhood; her categories have held up well over time.

Social Rejection and Loneliness

Parten's categories of unoccupied and solitary play may reflect children's social immaturity at the preschool level. Another possibility is that these play categories are simply alternatives to more organized play (Harper & Huie, 1985). Some children, however, may be uninvolved because they are rejected by other children. Peer rejection is usually measured using a tech-

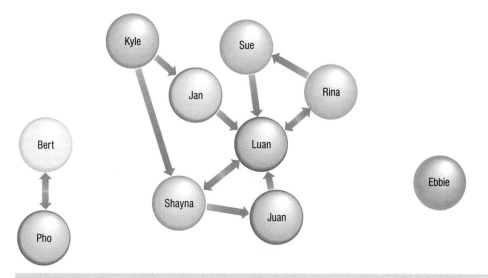

FIGURE 13-4
Sociometric choices in a playgroup can indicate popularity. This sociometric analysis indicates that Luan is the most popular child in the playgroup. Bert and Pho form their own subgroup. Kyle and Ebbie are the most isolated children, because they are chosen by no other members of the group.

nique known as **sociometric analysis**. All members of a group of children—a classroom or playgroup, for example—indicate which children in the group they would most like to spend time with; see Figure 13–4 for an example. This technique is used to identify the children about whom there is consensus as to social standing in the group, either popular, average, or unpopular.

In one recent study using sociometric analysis, kindergarten and first-grade children were assessed for social standing, and were also interviewed about their understanding of loneliness. Nearly all of the children understood the concept of loneliness. As one might expect, the children who were less well accepted by the group were the most lonely (Cassidy & Asher, 1992). Among somewhat older children, in sixth grade, those who were more isolated perceived their school friendships to be less supportive. Although having positive relationships with their brothers and sisters helped these children to compensate for social isolation at school, the isolated children were less well adjusted overall than more socially involved children (East & Rook, 1992).

sociometric analysis research technique for finding which children in a playgroup are popular or rejected

FAMILY ISSUES

At several points in this chapter, family issues have formed the basis of the discussion. Indeed, the opening vignette for this chapter, on "Genie," revolved around severe social deprivation within a dysfunctional family. In addition, we have discussed attachment to caregivers within the family, and the positive effects of close sibling relationships on isolated children. But families are changing within our culture, and psychologists are exploring the effects of these changes on social development.

The Changing American Family

If a "traditional" family is defined as a heterosexual couple who are married, with children under the age of 18, living together in a household, only about one fourth of families in the United States fit the definition, according to the 1990 census. The number of households headed by a single parent continued to grow throughout the 1980s, although at a slower pace than in the 1970s. At the 1990 census, there were 9.7 million single-parent households in the United States, the vast majority of them headed by women

("Census finds," 1991). Estimates are that in the 1990s, 60% of children will spend some part of their childhood in a single-parent family (Silverstein, 1991).

Marriage and birth rates have both declined, while divorce rates and out-of-wedlock births have increased (Melton & Wilcox, 1989). These trends have an impact on the character of the "typical" family, and also potentially influence the patterns of social development of all members of the family. One potential impact of social changes in the family concerns the role of women in the labor force.

THINKING ABOUT
Latchkey Children

The traditional family structure in which the father worked full-time to support the family and the mother remained in the home to care for the children, has all but disappeared. In the 1990s, 75% of mothers of school-aged children work outside the home (Silverstein, 1991). What is the impact of this social change on the socialization of children and on their relationship with their parents?

latchkey children children who return from school to unsupervised homes

There has been much attention in the media to **latchkey children**, those who must return from school to an unsupervised home. Estimates put the number of self-care, or latchkey, children between the ages of 6 and 13 at 2 to 5 million (Fosarelli, 1984). Some psychologists believe that this lack of supervision may lead to psychological and behavioral problems, perhaps even to juvenile delinquency. Others argue that self-care children show greater maturity, self-reliance, and responsibility. There are few formal studies comparing self-care children to adult-supervised children, but the available evidence suggests that there are no significant differences between the two groups on such measures as self-esteem, social adjustment, or interpersonal relations (Rodman, Pratto, & Nelson, 1985).

Self-care children can be further divided into groups, however. Some self-care children go to an unsupervised home after school, where they remain alone or with other siblings. These are the traditional latchkey children (Rodman, Pratto, & Nelson, 1988). Others go to a friend's house where they are also unsupervised but in the company of peers. Still others just "hang out" at malls, arcades, or libraries. In one study of these groups, latchkey children who were at home were not significantly different on susceptibility to peer pressure from children who were home with a parent. The other two groups were much more vulnerable to peer pressure for antisocial activities (Steinberg, 1986). Self-care per se is therefore probably not as important as the setting in which the self-care takes place. Parental knowledge of the child's whereabouts is also likely to be an important factor in determining the child's behavior.

The greater number of women in the labor force underscores a restructuring of the family in American society. It seems clear that we are unlikely to return to the traditional family pattern. But because the mother has traditionally taken the lead in socializing children, what may change is the pattern of socialization that children experience. In addition, women will have different experiences of the adult life cycle than their mothers and grandmothers. In any event, studies to date have not supported the dire predictions of those who felt that mothers working outside the home would have psychologically vulnerable children.

The need for day care and for after-school care is one by-product of the restructuring of the American family. How do you think we as a nation can best address the need for adequate child care? How should the costs of child care be measured against the benefits? What are some of the benefits likely to be? Who should bear the costs?

Parental Discipline

Regardless of their employment status, parents tend to adopt a disciplinary style with their children that derives from their views about child rearing and from their own experiences as children. Diana Baumrind (1971) has identified three major disciplinary styles that characterize most parents (see Table 13–5). The most strict disciplinary style is called **authoritarian**. Parents who use this style expect complete obedience from their children to absolute rules that they have set up. Authoritarian parents tend to rely on physical punishment, and do not allow any "back talk" or verbal give-and-take from their children.

Parents who use a second disciplinary style, known as **authoritative**, also have rules for their children to follow, but in a more flexible, issue-oriented way. These parents tend to explain the reasoning behind their rules, rather than simply stating the rules as absolutes. Parents who are authoritative exercise some control over their children and discipline them when they break rules, but the discipline is likely to be flexible and to "fit the crime."

The third disciplinary style identified by Baumrind is permissive. More recent research suggests a need to divide this category into two types, indulgent and neglectful. **Indulgent** parents make few demands on their children, with few rules or elements of control in the children's lives. When their children's impulses and actions go beyond the indulgent parents' wishes, the parents rarely punish them, although they may talk to them. The parents' focus is on getting children to regulate their own behavior. Thus they act more as resources than as controlling or socializing agents. **Neglectful** parents, on the other hand, simply pay little attention to their children (Lamborn et al., 1991).

As you might expect, different parenting styles are associated with different outcomes in children's behavior (Baumrind, 1971; Lamborn et al., 1991). Children of authoritarian parents tend to be less trusting and contented, and

authoritarian parenting style in which absolute rules for child behavior are set up, and physical punishment is common

authoritative parenting style in which rules are flexible and reasoning is commonly used

indulgent a permissive parenting style having few rules or demands for children

neglectful parenting style in which children are largely ignored

---

TABLE 13-5
Parenting Styles and Their Outcomes

Authoritarian. Autocratic rule by parents, with absolute rules for children. Rule violations often result in physical punishment.	Outcomes: social withdrawal; lack of trust; shy and quarrelsome; aggression, especially boys.
Authoritative. Flexible rules and flexible punishments. Reasoning frequently used to regulate child's behavior.	Outcomes: outgoing and friendly; socially active; independent; creative; self-reliance and self-control.
Indulgent. Few rules or demands placed on children. Little punishment of any kind.	Outcomes: dependent; nonaggressive; more sexually active in adolescence; compliant; noncreative.
Neglectful. Little attention of any kind is paid to the child.	Outcomes: aggressive; impulsive; disobedient; lack of direction.

Source: Adapted from Vander Zanden, 1989.

more withdrawn, than other children. Although the philosophy behind permissive parenting is to foster autonomous control, children of permissive parents tend to show the least self-control and are also less self-reliant and exploratory. The best behavioral outcomes are associated with authoritative parenting. These children are more often self-reliant, self-controlled, exploratory, and contented, when compared with children whose parents use the other styles of discipline. In a recent study with young children, for example, mothers who combined control with guidance, as authoritative parents do, got their children to do what they wanted without defiance more frequently than mothers using other strategies (Crockenberg & Litman, 1990).

Although most of the research on parental discipline style has focused on its impact on young children, some studies suggest that the effects carry over into adolescence and early adulthood. Self-esteem among college students, for example, is positively associated with authoritative parenting and negatively associated with authoritarian parenting (Buri, 1989). Even sexual activity may be related to parenting style. In a study of over 2,000 adolescents' perceptions of parental strictness and rules, those who thought their parents were permissive had the highest rates of sexual activity, while those whose parents were perceived to be authoritative had the lowest (Miller et al., 1986).

> ### THINKING ABOUT
> # Child Abuse and Neglect

Genie's case, with which this chapter began, raises questions about the role of parenting in social development, and especially about the effects of abuse. The kind of abuse that Genie endured, however, went so far beyond child abuse as we usually encounter it that the lessons we can draw from her case are limited. It does appear, however, that child abuse occurs more frequently in families that use authoritarian parenting styles than in families that use other styles.

Several important distinctions need to be made in discussing the generic term *child abuse*. **Child neglect** refers to a lack of adequate care for the physical, social, and emotional development of the child. **Child abuse**, on the other hand, refers to physical injury or harm done to a child, usually by caregivers. (These children are sometimes referred to as "battered children.") **Child sexual abuse** is a special category of abuse in which minor children are subjected to any one of several types of sexual exploitation, including inappropriate touching or fondling; taking nude photographs; having sexual acts performed in their presence; and being subjected to oral sex, sodomy, or intercourse. Also included within the federal Child Abuse Prevention and Treatment Act of 1974 is the category of **psychological maltreatment**, or "mental injury." This category includes mental cruelty, emotional abuse, and emotional maltreatment, and is the most difficult of the categories to define or to identify (Garrison, 1987).

The scope of the problem of abuse and neglect is enormous. Federal officials estimate that about 1 million children each year are victims of neglect or physical or sexual abuse, with most cases involving neglect. However, psychological maltreatment is probably even more prevalent, and may even be more destructive than other forms of abuse. One might argue that psychological maltreatment is always present when a child experiences physical abuse. Studies that have attempted to disentangle the separate effects of physical and psychological maltreatment suggest that psychologi-

child neglect lack of adequate care for physical, social, and emotional development

child abuse physical injury or harm to children

child sexual abuse sexual exploitation of minor children

psychological maltreatment mental cruelty, emotional abuse, and emotional mistreatment of children

cal maltreatment is more detrimental to the social and emotional development of children than the severity of injury in physical abuse (Claussen & Crittenden, 1991). Of all the categories, psychological maltreatment receives the least attention from professionals and from researchers, in part because it is so hard to identify (Hart & Brassard, 1987).

Physically abused children suffer a variety of consequences that have an impact on their social functioning, including low self-esteem, aggression, withdrawal, and general adjustment problems (Kaufman & Cicchetti, 1989; Wodarski et al., 1990). The long-term consequences of physical abuse are highly variable, with some victims remaining traumatized and barely able to function even in adulthood, and others leading normal lives, raising families, holding jobs, and functioning socially. As a group, victims scored high on measures of resentment and suspiciousness, even those who were functioning well socially (Martin & Elmer, 1992).

Infants who have suffered physical abuse or neglect, or both, show distorted reactions in Ainsworth's strange situation. These results have prompted some researchers to add an entirely new attachment category known as **disorganized attachment**. These infants blend contradictory features of other categories. For example, they may show exaggerated attempts to be near the caregiver, followed by strong avoidance; or they may be dazed and disoriented during a reunion episode with a parent (Carlson et al., 1989).

disorganized attachment distorted form of attachment shown by abused or neglected children characterized by exaggerated approach toward and avoidance of caregivers

Recently, the first national survey of adults with a history of child sexual abuse was completed. Surprisingly large numbers of adults say they were victims of sexual abuse as children. More women than men reported abuse: 27% of women and 16% of men. Perpetrators of abuse were also disproportionately male, in 83% of the cases involving male victims and in 98% of the cases involving female victims (Finkelhor et al., 1990) (see Figure 13–5).

Long-term consequences of childhood sexual abuse appear more consistently negative than consequences of physical abuse. Adult women who were sexually abused as children suffer more from sexual problems, depression, anxiety, fear, and suicidal tendencies than women from similar backgrounds who were not abused. Adult men who were sexually abused as children often have problems with sexual functioning (Beitchman et al., 1992; Lanktree, Briere, & Zaidi, 1991).

One of the most disturbing aspects of the information available on child abuse and neglect is that there tends to be a cycle of abuse from one generation to another (Simons et al., 1991). As we saw earlier, intergenerational

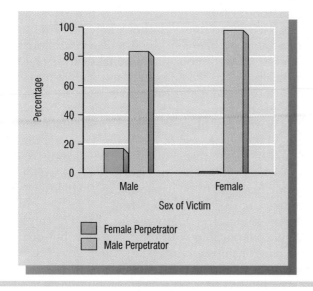

FIGURE 13–5
Both male and female victims of sexual abuse are likely to have been abused by male perpetrators. When the victim is female, the perpetrator is male in more than 98% of the cases. (*Source*: Finkelhor et al., 1990.)

communication of attachment style can be modified through effective social support. Social support also seems to modify the tendency of child abuse to occur across generations of the same family. One study of mothers who were abused as children (according to their retrospective reports) showed that three situations appeared to be effective in helping them to break the cycle of abuse. These three situations were (1) having an emotionally supportive relationship with a mate; (2) receiving emotional support from a nonabusive adult during their own childhoods; and (3) receiving therapy sometime during their lives (Egeland, Jacobvitz, & Sroufe, 1988). Clearly there is a critical need for programs of intervention for abusive families.

Based on these findings, what types of intervention do you think might work in helping to break the cycle of abuse? What types of social support could be offered to parents in highly stressful life situations, for example for those who are single parents, or poor?

Effects of Divorce on Social Development

Divorce is a fact of life for an increasing number of families, many of them with young children. The rate of divorce in the United States rose precipitously from the mid-1960s to 1980, and then leveled off or showed a modest decline. In human terms, the data indicate that approximately half of all children born around 1980 can expect to experience their parents' divorce and spend an average of 5 years in a single-parent household before they are 18 years old (Hetherington, Stanley-Hagan, & Anderson, 1989).

What are the effects of parental divorce on children's social development? Some developmental psychologists hypothesize that divorce will have a negative impact on children in the short or long term. Longitudinal studies offer the most promise for helping to understand the consequences of divorce on social development, and Mavis Hetherington has taken the lead in conducting these studies.

In the early 1980s, Hetherington and her colleagues began a longitudinal study of 144 middle-class white families, each with a 4-year-old child. Half of these families had gone through a divorce, and the mothers had custody of the children; the other half had not gone through a divorce. Half of the children in the study were boys and half were girls. Thus, Hetherington was able to examine the children's adjustment following divorce, for boys and girls separately, at 2 months, 1 year, 2 years, and 6 years following the divorce (Hetherington, 1989).

All involved parties—mothers, fathers, sons, and daughters—experienced some adjustment problems in the first 2 years following the divorce. Many of the children showed signs of emotional distress and had difficulties relating to their peers. But at the end of 2 years, they were considerably less distressed. Boys, more frequently than girls, continued to show signs of social problems even after 2 years, however. For example, boys from divorced families were more likely than boys from intact families to act out and be antisocial in the home, and to have poor peer relationships in school (Hetherington, 1989). Remember, however, that all of these divorced families were ones in which the mother had custody of the children. The lasting negative effects for boys might be explained by their losing the continuous contact and influence of their same-sex parent.

When mothers remarried following the divorce, stepfathers initially reported a difficult relationship with their stepsons, but one that improved over time. Their relationships with stepdaughters, however, remained rocky or even deteriorated over time. Many stepfathers who experienced difficulties with their stepchildren adopted a defeatist attitude after a while, making comments like, "I married her, not her kids," or "That's their mother's problem not mine" (Hetherington, 1989, p. 7).

The 6-year follow-up was particularly interesting, because it occurred at the time the children were entering adolescence, and it allowed Hetherington to look at longer-term effects of divorce. One lesson of this longitudinal study is that there is a great deal of variability in outcomes. Some individuals are more affected socially by the experience than others. But there were some interesting regularities in the data.

Hetherington was able to identify three major patterns of behavior in the adolescent children that were associated with the experience of divorce 6 years earlier. The most negative outcome occurred in a group of adolescents who exhibited an *aggressive and insecure* behavioral pattern. This pattern showed up in the home, in school, and with peers, and was characterized by impulsive behavior and irritability, alternating with sullen withdrawal. A large majority of these individuals (70%) did not have any close friends. One suggestion from Hetherington's data is that temperamental differences among these children were intensified by the divorce experience; they had been "temperamentally difficult" early in life (Hetherington, 1989, p. 11). The parenting style used with these children was rarely authoritative; rather, it was likely to have been neglectful or authoritarian. Three times as many boys as girls showed this aggressive and insecure pattern.

The second pattern of long-term response to divorce was more positive. Hetherington described this pattern as *competent but opportunistic*. These adolescents showed high self-esteem and good adjustment. They had few behavior problems and were popular in school and with friends. However, they had a manipulative streak, using disagreements between parents for their own gains. Many in this group had a close relationship with one parent and a neglectful relationship with the other, usually opposite-sex, parent. They developed friendships, but usually not long-lasting ones. Girls and boys were about equally represented in this group.

The third pattern was a *competent and caring* orientation. These adolescents were also well adjusted and high in self-esteem, and were popular with friends. These individuals showed more helping and sharing behavior than any of the other groups. They had more stable friendships than the opportunistic adolescents, and often made friends with children who had been rejected or neglected by others. Almost all of these adolescents were girls.

Hetherington (1989) describes these three outcomes with the labels "losers," "survivors," and "winners." Clearly the insecure and aggressive children are the losers. The competent but opportunistic adolescents are survivors, yet they have some serious interpersonal difficulties. The competent and caring adolescents seem to be the winners in the trauma of divorce. These differing outcomes seem to be associated with gender; with some basic characteristics of the child, such as temperament; and with the quality of their relationships with others, especially parents and siblings. The variability in reactions to parental divorce is an important lesson, and is often obscured by a media focus on the negative outcomes following a divorce. One single mother expressed her exasperation with the negative images presented in the media this way:

> I get really upset and resentful over all the media talk about the negative effects of divorce on children. I resent the tube telling me, and my kids, that "children of divorced parents don't make good peer relationships and do poorly in school, and they're likely to live a life of crime." That's *garbage*! The media ignores the fact that we have crazy people running around who grew up in the so-called normal family. (quoted in Barber & Eccles, 1992)

This mother would like us to remember that there are some winners—people who successfully adjust—in the aftermath of a divorce.

In fact, the conflict and stress within an intact family may have negative effects on children that are as great or greater than the effects of divorce. Studies that have examined personality characteristics of children indicate that some of the negative behaviors that are attributed to divorce—impulsiveness, aggressiveness, and so on—are evident *before* the divorce occurs. These effects are particularly striking in boys, and in some cases are apparent as much as 11 years before the divorce (Block, Block, & Gjerde, 1986). A fair generalization seems to be that family *structure*—intact, divorced, single-parent, and so on—is less important than family *functioning*—the quality of interaction and degree of stress present in day-to-day life.

ADOLESCENCE: SOCIAL TRANSITIONS

Although social development is a continuous process throughout the life cycle, there are developmental shifts in social interaction. The social world of the infant is a dependency relationship to parents. During childhood, a strong bond to parents remains, but during the school years there is increasing interaction within the peer group, especially same-sex peers. During adolescence, the balance of power between parents and peers in social influence appears to even out. This developmental shift is followed, later in adolescence, by an emphasis on romantic interaction.

Parent and Peer Interaction

Adolescents as a group do not show a uniform pattern of interaction with their parents, a point that is obvious from the discussion of divorce. Some adolescents seem to have harmonious relationships with their parents, without experiencing any major disagreements. Other adolescents bicker with their parents constantly, although most of the conflicts between parents and adolescents tend to be over small issues, such as schoolwork and general irritations, rather than larger issues such as drugs and politics (Montemayor, 1982).

G. Stanley Hall, author of the first textbook on adolescence and a central figure in the history of American psychology, viewed adolescence as a period of storm and stress. "Adolescence is a new birth," he wrote. "The qualities of body and soul that now emerge are far newer. Development is less gradual and more saltatory, suggestive of some ancient period of storm and stress when old moorings were broken and a higher level attained" (Hall, 1904, p. xiii). The new birth leads the adolescent to want to get away, to conquer new territory. "At the dawn of adolescence this impulse to migrate or wander shows a great and sudden increase. Home seems narrow, monotonous, intolerable, and the street and the motley passers-by interest and invite to be up and away" (Hall, 1904, p. 377). Hall's storm-and-stress view echoes through English literary works with adolescent characters, especially male characters. Portrayals of adolescence in works of Shakespeare, Milton, Wordsworth, Coleridge, and Dickens, to name a few, present the themes of turbulence, excess, and passion (Violato & Wiley, 1990).

In recent years, a major research focus on parent and peer interaction has been the variable of pubertal status and its relation to conflict. Although the notion of a major generation gap involving high levels of conflict is a myth (Petersen, 1988), increased conflict within families appears as the adolescent experiences the physical changes of puberty (Paikoff & Brooks-Gunn, 1991). It is not clear what variables are responsible for this increase in conflict. One suggestion from research is that concentrations of sex hormones influence the adolescent's personality, perhaps in ways that would increase the likelihood of conflict, such as through greater aggressiveness

Ceremonies that mark adolescence sometimes symbolize a "birth" into a new role. In the Irian Jaya Highlands of New Guinea, boys at adolescence were traditionally initiated into warrior roles by participating in real conflicts. This practice has now been supplanted by mock battles or archery competitions.

(Udry & Tolbert, 1988). In human evolution, separation from the family may have been needed to reduce the risks of inbreeding and to increase genetic diversity. Thus, conflict may be an evolved mechanism for increasing the distance between adolescents and their families (Caine, 1986). Conflict may also arise from parents' ambivalence about their children's increased interest in sexuality.

Laboratory and home-based observational research has elaborated on the course of conflict and its relations to adolescent development. Before puberty, adolescent boys are very low in the family dominance hierarchy, with mother and father maintaining about equal positions. But after puberty, the dominance hierarchy shifts, with the boys moving up in the hierarchy to a position below the level of their fathers and above the level of their mothers (Steinberg, 1981). In studies of conflict within the family, boys showed the most conflict when they were alone with their mothers. Presence of the father actually seemed to improve the quality of mother–son interaction, perhaps because when the father is present the mother's problems with disciplining the adolescent boy diminish (Gjerde, 1986).

Patterns of conflict vary when adolescents interact with their mothers versus fathers (Steinberg, 1988; Youniss & Smollar, 1985). In general, more conflict occurs between mothers and both sons and daughters. Paradoxically, however, the mother's relationship to the adolescent is also viewed as the more intimate one. Both adolescent girls and boys are likely to identify their mothers as the parent with whom they would discuss important personal issues. One indication of the greater degree of intimacy in relationships with mothers is seen in adolescents' perceptions of the ways in which their parents meet their material and emotional needs. Both sons and daughters feel their material needs are met by both parents. But adolescents, especially daughters, report dramatically more often that their mothers meet their emotional needs (Youniss & Smollar, 1985). Adolescent daughters have very few conflicts with their fathers. For both, problems typically arise, instead, because they ignore each other. Adolescent sons experience more conflict with their fathers, usually over issues such as the son's failure to meet paternal expectations or insubordination in pointing out the father's character flaws.

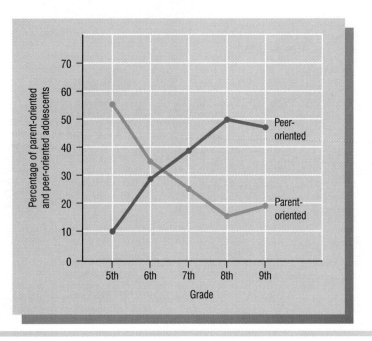

FIGURE 13–6
Parent and peer orientation undergo shifts in early adolescence, with peer orientation stronger in a majority of teenagers beginning in sixth grade. (Adapted from Steinberg & Silverberg, 1986.)

In adolescence, social influence shifts from a family orientation to an orientation in which peers exert considerably more influence than they had before (see Figure 13–6). This shift in orientation occurs at about age 12 or 13, when peer orientation becomes stronger than family orientation (Steinberg & Silverberg, 1986). Although adolescents show more and more autonomy from their parents, they are influenced by their parents or by peers at different times, depending on the situation. In general, the more important the situation is perceived to be, the more likely adolescents are to comply with their parents' wishes (Sebald & White, 1980). Parents have a particularly strong influence on adolescents' educational plans (Kandel & Lesser, 1969).

Although adolescents progress more and more toward psychological autonomy from their parents, they spend about as much time with their parents as they do with their peers. The activities they engage in, however, are very different. The time they spend with their parents is generally taken up in household routines in which little communication takes place: household chores, eating, watching television. They spend time with their peers, on the other hand, playing games and talking (Montemayor, 1982).

Sibling Relationships

It is clear that parents and peers play a central role in the social development of children, but what about siblings? As Sutton-Smith and Rosenberg remarked, "Common sense dictates that our brothers and sisters, our siblings, have some effect upon our personality and development" (1970, p. 1). One of the themes in Western literary tradition is a power struggle between siblings, at least male siblings. Thus, Cain and Abel, the first siblings in the biblical account of creation, were a highly disagreeable pair, and Cain finally killed his brother.

Studying children in four grade levels—3rd, 6th, 9th, and 12th—Buhrmester and Furman (1990) discovered some imbalances in sibling relationships, especially for the younger children. In the higher grades, adolescents said they experienced less companionship, intimacy, and affection with their siblings than did students in the lower grades. But there was a trend toward more balanced and equal sibling relationships with increasing

Although common sense tells us that siblings have an effect on personality development, the precise mechanisms are not clear. One's position in the family as well as the gender relationships are likely to affect personality formation.

age. The relationships also became less intense with increasing age, presumably as adolescents began the transition away from the family and toward the larger social world.

Even within the same family, siblings have very different experiences. When sibling pairs between the ages of 11 and 17 are compared on how well adjusted they are, the more adjusted are closer to their mothers and are friendlier with both friends and siblings than the siblings who are less well adjusted (Daniels et al., 1985).

Friendship and Dating in Adolescence

Social development in early adolescence seems to favor same-sex friendships (Berndt, 1982). A large part of adolescent social interaction occurs with members of the same sex and revolves around shared interests, as well as emotional support and empathy. Some sex differences in patterns of friendship continue into early adulthood. For example, female roommates in college express more emotion and less general information than do male roommates (Ginsburg & Gottman, 1986). In late adolescence, there is a shift toward more sexual interests and close friendships with members of both sexes.

Activities with peers may psychologically benefit adolescents in a variety of ways. For example, research indicates that peer activities provide a context for sociability and a sense of belonging to a group, promote a sense of the integrity of the self, and provide opportunities for instructing and learning (Zarbatany, Hartmann, & Rankin, 1990). The degree of intimacy within a friendship is consistently associated with adjustment and competence, and appears to become increasingly important over the preadolescent and adolescent years, as the individual makes the transition away from a family orientation and toward a peer orientation (Buhrmester, 1990; Morison & Masten, 1991).

Support for the psychological benefits of friendship is suggested in a study in which adolescents in sixth grade were videotaped in pairs with either friends or acquaintances. Physiological measures, such as heart rate and saliva cortisol (associated with stress) were also collected. Pairs of friends were more active, positive, involved, relaxed, and playful than pairs of acquaintances, and physiological measures indicated lower levels of stress (Field et al., 1992).

Dating has become a social institution in the United States and serves diverse functions, as you probably know from your own dating experiences. The traditional date—a prearranged event initiated and paid for by a male, with acceptance and veto power exercised by a female—may be a rare phenomenon. In more contemporary dates, couples still prearrange activities to do together, often as informal group dates involving several couples and some singles.

Adolescents mention a number of functions of dating, from recreation to mate selection, when they describe their most important reasons for dating. Male and female adolescents attribute very similar meanings to dates (Hansen, 1977; Roscoe, Diana, & Brooks, 1987). However, there are some developmental differences in adolescents' perceptions of the functions of dates. The most popular function of dating for early adolescents of both sexes is recreation. By late adolescence the most popular function has shifted to intimacy. The most striking sex difference concerns the role of sexual activity as a dating function. Males are much more likely than females to emphasize its importance, especially in middle and late adolescence (Roscoe et al., 1987).

Relationships often go beyond mere dating and develop into stronger attachments. Like the benefits associated with friendships, these more intense relationships are important opportunities for enhancing self-esteem and learning about one's self in a social context. And, just as a disruption of the attachment relationship in childhood causes distress, adolescents may suffer from social distress when their dating relationships end. Adults often minimize or even trivialize the experience of distress in the face of breakups in adolescent relationships, using such stock phrases as, "You're too young to understand what love is," or "You'll look back and wonder what you ever saw in this person" (Kaczmarek & Backlund, 1991, p. 253). Most professionals who work with adolescents suggest that adults develop a more understanding approach that acknowledges real feelings of loss when adolescents break up with someone.

Norms of dating have changed somewhat over the past few decades, but a number of rituals and norms are still associated with dating. Adolescents attending their senior prom at Valley High School in Louisville, Kentucky, dress in similar ways and engage in some of the other expected behaviors associated with dating.

Adolescent Sexuality

Sexual interest is present before the hormonal changes associated with puberty, but it does increase at that time. Adolescent sexual experience can take a variety of forms, from masturbation to sexual interaction with a partner. Evidence suggests that a predictable progression in sexual experience occurs from necking, to feeling breasts through clothing, to feeling breasts directly, to feeling sex organs directly, to intercourse (Miller & Moore, 1990).

Data from national surveys indicate that by age 15, between a quarter and a third of adolescents have had sex; by age 19, more than 80% of adolescents have had sex. At each age, somewhat more males than females report experiencing intercourse (Miller & Moore, 1990). Adolescents have likely been fantasizing about sex for some time before they have their first experience with a partner. However, about half of them report that their first sexual experience was unplanned; they say that it "just happened." After it happens, however, it is likely to happen again. About two thirds of adolescents report having sex again within 6 months of their first experiences (Miller & Moore, 1990).

Adolescent experience with intercourse takes on greater significance in the age of AIDS. Loss of virginity in adolescence is frequently an unplanned event, and sexual intercourse is often an unprotected event as well. Although increasing numbers of adolescents are using condoms the first time they have intercourse, fewer than half of teenage couples actually use condoms during their first sexual experiences (Ventura et al., 1992). Among all sexually active adolescents, fewer than one third use condoms, which provide the greatest protection—after abstinence—against exposure to HIV, the virus that causes AIDS (Moore & Barling, 1991). In the United States, adolescents are one of the fastest-growing risk groups for HIV infection (DiClemente, 1990).

In the United States, the teenage pregnancy rate is increasing and has reached very high levels. More than 100 women out of every 1,000 between the ages of 15 and 17 become pregnant (Ventura et al., 1992). In comparison to other industrialized countries studied in the 1980s, the United States has the highest rates of teenage pregnancy. The other countries in the comparison—England and Wales, France, Canada, Sweden, and The Netherlands—have better sex education programs, which is one factor used to explain the differences (Jones et al., 1986).

Several factors are related to the start of sexual activity in adolescence. We have already mentioned physical changes at puberty as influences on sexual motivation. In addition, some personality characteristics appear related to sexual behavior. Sexually active adolescents place a higher value on independence and a lower value on academic achievement than those who have not yet experienced intercourse (Donovan & Jessor, 1985). Some family variables also have an impact on adolescent sexual experience. For example, mothers who experience sexual intercourse earlier have daughters who experience intercourse earlier as well, perhaps because of modeling. Furthermore, more highly educated parents tend to have adolescents who are less sexually experienced. Single-parent families appear to have adolescent children—especially daughters—who begin sexual activity at an earlier age than adolescents from two-parent families (Miller & Moore, 1990).

The development of sexual identity is often difficult for adolescents, but perhaps especially for the 10% or so who are gay or lesbian. Although relatively few studies have explored the social meanings attached to sexual orientation for gay and lesbian adolescents, those studies that do exist suggest that adolescence may be a difficult time for them. Often gay and lesbian adolescents learn to hide their sexual orientations for fear of ridicule, ostracism, or worse. Some gay and lesbian adolescents attempt to adopt a heterosexual orientation, or hope that they will grow out of their attraction to people of the same sex. One gay male who tried dating girls in high school put it this way: "I thought it was a matter of time before I could make my straightness happen" (Gordon & Gilgun, 1987, p. 157). In his 20s, he finally came to terms with his sexual orientation, as is the case for many gay men and lesbians.

Moral Development

One of the major themes of social development, especially in adolescence, is moral development. The most influential research program on moral development was that of Lawrence Kohlberg (1927–1987). Kohlberg's research on moral judgment was heavily influenced by Piaget's cognitive–developmental approach. Like Piaget, Kohlberg used the clinical method to assess an individual's level of moral thought. His method relied on responses to verbal descriptions of standard moral dilemmas and to follow-up probe questions, which were used for classifying moral reasoning into stages. Kohlberg questioned people on the moral aspects of difficult issues, for example, the commitment involved in a promise, the acceptability of mercy killing, and the value of human life.

preconventional level Kohlberg's level of moral judgment in which moral issues are decided on the basis of individualistic factors rather than social standards

Preconventional Level. Responses to Kohlberg's moral dilemmas fall into three levels of moral judgment: preconventional, conventional, and postconventional. At the **preconventional level**, individuals recognize labels of "good" and "bad," "right" and "wrong," but do not interpret these labels in terms of social standards. In his longitudinal study of moral judgment, Kohlberg (1976) reinterviewed several participants at different points in time. At age 10, Joe, one of the participants, was asked, "Why shouldn't you steal from a store?" Joe's preconventional response was: "It's not good to steal from the store. It's against the law. Someone could see you and call the police" (Kohlberg, 1976). Preconventional morality, which is exemplified by most children, some adolescents, and many adolescent and adult criminals, begins to emerge during the preschool years (Fischer, 1983).

conventional level Kohlberg's level of moral judgment in which moral issues are judged on the basis of social expectations or social norms

Conventional Level. Individuals at the **conventional level** make moral judgments on the basis of expectations—those of the family, the social group, or the nation at large. Maintaining conventional expectations has a moral value in its own right. At age 17, Joe's conventional-level response to the question about stealing from a store was: "It's a matter of law. It's one of our rules that we're trying to help to protect everyone. It's something that's needed in our society. If we didn't have these laws, people would steal, they wouldn't have to work for a living and our whole society would get out of kilter" (Kohlberg, 1976). Conventional morality is the level shown by most adolescents and adults in American society (Colby et al., 1983).

postconventional level Kohlberg's level of moral judgment in which moral issues are decided through universal principles that go beyond norms or laws

Postconventional Level. Moral judgments at the **postconventional level** transcend the authority of persons or conformity to groups. Now, values and principles guide moral judgments. Individuals at this level may understand and accept society's rules and laws but tend to view them in terms of the underlying principles. Not many people reach this level of moral reasoning. When Joe was asked at age 24 about stealing from a store, the following dialogue took place (Kohlberg, 1976):

JOE: "It's violating another person's rights, in this case to property."
INTERVIEWER: "Does the law enter?"

JOE: "Well, the law in most cases is based on what is morally right so it's not a separate subject, it's a consideration."

INTERVIEWER: "What does morality or morally right mean to you?"

JOE: "Recognizing the rights of other individuals, first to life and then to do as he pleases as long as it doesn't interfere with somebody else's rights."

Each level of moral judgment has one or two stages of moral development (see Table 13-6). Kohlberg's theory takes a strong position on the continuity–discontinuity controversy in developmental psychology. According to Kohlberg, the model meets the requirements of a discontinuous stage theory: stages occur in a fixed sequence and are qualitatively different yet logically related, and within a given stage thinking shows some consistency. Although there is some controversy about whether Kohlberg's stages are as fixed as he suggested (Kurtines & Greif, 1974), there is evidence that, across many different types of cultures, moral judgment evolves through a sequence of changes that could be described as stages (Snarey, 1985).

Sex Differences in Moral Judgment. One of the problems with Kohlberg's conception of moral development centers around sex differences. In deriving his basic model, Kohlberg interviewed only males beginning in early adolescence. Later, when females were interviewed, their answers seemed at first to indicate that they attained the higher stages of moral judgment less frequently than males (Kohlberg, 1969). Carol Gilligan, one of Kohlberg's colleagues at Harvard, took issue with this finding, arguing that developmental theory may

TABLE 13-6
Kohlberg's Stages of Moral Judgment

Level I **Preconventional Level**	**What Is Right**
Stage 1 Heteronomous	Avoidance of breaking rules backed by punishment; obedience for its own sake; and avoidance of physical damage to persons and property.
Stage 2 Instrumental individualism, purpose, and exchange	Following rules only when it is to someone's immediate interest; acting to meet one's own interests and needs and letting others do the same. Right is what's fair, what's an equal exchange, a deal, an agreement.

Level II **Conventional Level**	**What Is Right**
Stage 3 Mutual interpersonal expectations, interpersonal conformity	Living up to what is expected by people close to you or what people generally expect of people in your role as son, brother, friend, etc. "Being good" is important and means having good motives, showing concern about others. It also means keeping mutual relationships, such as trust, loyalty, respect, and gratitude.
Stage 4 Social system and conscience	Fulfilling the actual duties to which you have agreed. Laws are to be upheld except in extreme cases where they conflict with other fixed social duties. Right is also contributing to society, the group, or institution.

Level III **Postconventional Level**	**What Is Right**
Stage 5 Social contract orientation or utility and individual rights	Being aware that people hold a variety of values and opinions, that most values and rules are relative to your group. These relative rules should usually be upheld, however, in the interest of impartiality and because they are the social contract. Some nonrelative values and rights like *life* and *liberty*, however, must be upheld in any society and regardless of majority opinion.

Source: Adapted from Kohlberg, 1985.

have persistently misrepresented females—from Freud through Erikson and Piaget to Kohlberg. Gilligan argued that women's greater interpersonal focus, which Kohlberg felt was indicative of lower-stage reasoning, may be on a par with men's tendency to emphasize rules. Citing the case of moral judgment, she stated that "the very traits that traditionally have defined the 'goodness' of women, their care for and sensitivity to the needs of others, are those that mark them as deficient in moral development" (Gilligan, 1982). The fact that women are more concerned about interpersonal issues than men has been demonstrated in many psychological studies (Douvan & Adelson, 1966; Hodgson & Fischer, 1981; Kurdek & Krile, 1982).

Women's Different Voices. Gilligan was one of the first scholars to raise the possibility that men and women have different "voices"—that is, different approaches to and perceptions of the moral and psychological world. *Sociolinguistics* is a field that has examined differences in patterns of language by different social and ethnic groups, including sex differences. Many of these studies indicate that women do have a different linguistic style than men, characterized by differences in both form and content. The form includes more qualifications and questioning; the content includes a greater concern for practical and everyday activities, and more emphasis on interpersonal topics (Belenky et al., 1986).

The emphasis in male theories of development on autonomy, independence, and achievement may not be mirrored in the experiences of women. When women are interviewed about their lives and their educational experiences, they often describe a more personal orientation than men. A woman who participated in one of these studies put it this way:

> I think women care about things that relate to their lives personally. I think the more involvement they have in something that affects them personally, the more they're going to explore it and the more they're going to be able to give and to get out of it. I think that men—because they're male they haven't been put down all the time for their sex, so they can go into any subject with confidence, saying "I can learn about this" or "I have the intellect to understand this." Whereas I think women don't deal with things that way. I think they break down an issue and pick out what it is about it that has happened to them or they can relate to in some way, and that's how they start to explore it. (Belenky et al., 1986, p. 202)

The crisis of identity in adolescence for men may be rooted in separation from others to find a self that is distinct. For women, in contrast, it may be a relational crisis in which they must give up their own voice, suppressing it "for the sake of becoming a good woman and having relationships" (Brown & Gilligan, 1992, p. 2). Using the male model of development as the norm—as is the case in such theories as Freud's, Erikson's, and Kohlberg's—places women in the position of having either to conform their voices to those of men or to see themselves as somehow different and flawed. Neither of these alternatives is very desirable, and may place young women psychologically at risk during the adolescent struggle for identity (Brown & Gilligan, 1992). What is needed is a developmental scheme that offers respect and support for different patterns of social development for males and females, so that one is not judged in terms of the other and women are not forced to conform to male patterns.

Moral judgment and moral behavior are important aspects of social and personality development. The exact nature of the stages and their sequences in moral and social development remain open to question, especially patterns that may differ in important respects for men and women. However these issues are resolved, it is clear that moral development is not fixed at adolescence, but rather continues throughout adulthood.

ADULTHOOD: THE MIDDLE YEARS

Research on adult development shows that in early adulthood most people make their preliminary choices for their adult lives—looking for a mate and settling on a first job or career. In one longitudinal study of adult male development (Levinson, 1978), the 20s were experienced as a time of entering into the adult world by making career and marriage commitments. For many participants in this study, the age of 30 was a psychological turning point—stressful for some—requiring review of one's preliminary life choices.

Levinson's views on adult male development are illustrated in Figure 13–7. According to Levinson, both men and women have a "social clock" that exerts pressure for structuring life events. The **social clock** incorporates a society's shared judgments of the appropriateness of different behaviors as a function of age. For example, most people are expected to get married sometime in their 20s. Part of the similarity in the age of life events and transitions that Levinson found for men is likely a function of the social clock.

For women, the social clock differs in some respects. The traditional feminine social clock, which characterized a majority of women (53%) in one longitudinal study, is marriage in the early 20s with one or more children within 6 years after graduation (Helson, Mitchell, & Moane, 1984). Another significant group of these women (21%) followed this pattern somewhat later, having children beyond 6 years after graduation. Another, nontraditional, group (22%) followed a "masculine occupational clock," with professional training and advancement in their careers by the age of 28.

social clock society's shared judgment of the appropriate timing for various behaviors, such as getting married or having children

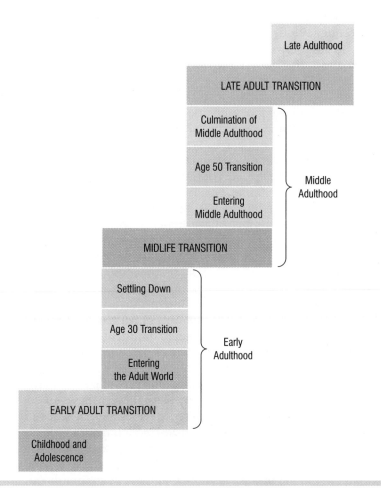

FIGURE 13–7
Levinson's scheme of development in men shows major transitions that often occur at specified times in development. The midlife transition, for example, often occurs at around the age of 40, until age 45, and the process may involve a very satisfying restructuring or a genuine social upheaval. (Adapted from Levinson, 1978, 1986.)

Data from the National Survey of Family Growth indicate that some aspects of the social clock have shifted over the past 2 decades. For example, the marriage rate for women has dropped by more than 25% since 1970; a parallel shift has been that the age of first marriage has risen steadily over the same period. Thus, the social clock is not obeyed as strictly as it was in the past.

Are these social clocks associated with different personality characteristics? Is one pattern psychologically healthier than the others? The answers to these questions are not as simple as we might hope. In the longitudinal study previously described, women on the two traditional feminine social clocks were very similar to each other in personality characteristics. The nontraditional women, however, differed from them in some respects. They tended to score higher in dominance, self-acceptance, independence, and empathy (Helson et al., 1984).

Midlife Crisis

midlife crisis heightened sensitivity to aging and mortality that occurs in middle age

A new term entered our vocabulary a decade or so ago, the "midlife crisis." This concept is very much related to the social clock, because it sets up the expectation that a person in our culture will experience some sort of crisis when he or she enters midlife. The **midlife crisis** occurs when people become sensitized to their own aging and are confronted, usually in some dramatic way, with their own mortality (Ciernia, 1985a; Schalin, 1985). Midlife generally includes the age span from about 35 to 55, and the midlife crisis is presumed to be most likely when a person turns 40 or shortly thereafter.

One would predict that a midlife crisis would be associated with a greater frequency of problems such as alcoholism, divorce, and suicide (Ciernia, 1985b). However, rates of alcoholism actually decrease with age. The divorce rate has gone up for everyone, but the relative percentage of divorces is greater among younger men than among middle-aged men. Suicide rates decline somewhat in the middle years, and increase with old age. These data indicate that a midlife crisis, to the extent that it exists at all, is not necessarily a traumatic experience.

Women at midlife appear in some ways to be a more heterogenous group than men at midlife because of the different social clocks for career involvement. Some have had continuously low levels of involvement in employment outside the home. Others have switched from low involvement, while establishing their families, to high involvement, after their children were a little older. Still others have managed to integrate several roles— worker, mother, wife, and volunteer—successfully for years. Integrating many roles is not easy. It requires planning combined with personal adaptation (Cole & Zuckerman, 1987). For many women, individual fulfillment may require achievement in roles both inside and outside the home, whereas for others, individual fulfillment may come primarily through achievement in one of these areas. Patterns of personal fulfillment are somewhat different for these groups of women, but there is no evidence that one pattern is healthier than others in terms of personality characteristics associated with it (Hornstein, 1986).

postparenthood phase of the family cycle after the youngest child has left home, leaving an "empty nest"

During the course of the life cycle, a majority of people marry and have children. Although most of us do not view these aspects of social life as "tasks," they frequently are considered developmental tasks of the adult years. Families as well as individuals have developmental histories, histories that can be divided into important phases. Examples of phases of the family cycle are the periods from marriage to the birth of the first child; from the birth of the first to the birth of last child; and the **postparenthood**, or "empty

The majority of people in our culture marry and have children. Indeed, a number of people remarry after divorces or deaths of spouses. This couple, in their 70s, is getting married in front of their families. Collectively they have 11 children from previous marriages, as well as 38 grandchildren and 30 great-grandchildren.

nest," phase after the last child has left home. Although many people believe that the postparenthood phase is a depressing period for parents, studies suggest the opposite. Parents evaluate it as a good time in their lives. In one study, a majority of parents (76%) rated postparenthood as "better" or "as good as" any other phase of the family cycle (Deutscher, 1964). National surveys conducted by the Gallup and Roper organizations in the 1970s indicate that more women in the postparenthood phase say they are "very happy" than those who are still actively involved in parenting, even when their ages are matched. These data are illustrated in Figure 13–8.

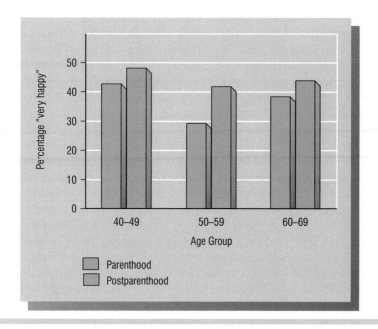

FIGURE 13–8
More parents report that they are "very happy" during the postparenthood (or "empty nest" phase) than they do when their children are still living at home. (Adapted from Glenn, 1975.)

Retirement calls for social readjustment. Individuals who maintain active social lives in retirement are more satisfied with their lives, and may even live longer.

ADULTHOOD: AGING

Retirement from a job or career is an important life-cycle event that occurs for many individuals as they age. This event requires considerable social readjustment. Following retirement, individuals frequently have fewer social contacts than they had previously, and some retirees may show signs of depression. Those retirees who maintain active social networks, by joining or retaining membership in organized social groups, are more satisfied with their lives. Many observers believe the relatively high rate of suicide among the elderly is a function of reduced social relationships. There are fewer suicide attempts among older people who maintain strong ties to family and community than among those who do not (Bock, 1972).

During the 1960s, the civil rights movement included as one of its important elements equal employment opportunity for women and minorities. In 1967, the Age Discrimination in Employment Act extended equal employment protection to older workers, prohibiting discrimination against those aged 40 to 65. However, companies could still require that their workers retire at the age of 65, in effect allowing discrimination based on age beyond 65. In the late 1970s, this upper limit was raised to age 70, and in 1986, the age ceiling was removed altogether, so that no mandatory retirement age was possible for most occupations (Quadagno & Hardy, 1991). More and more older workers may opt to remain on the job and retain their accustomed social networks, rather than to retire. The overall impact of these changes in employment laws is unclear at this time.

In many societies, old age is viewed as a time of wisdom and potential for spiritual growth, but also as a time of physical decline and weakness. These views of old age are common in European and American stage views of development, and are also apparent in ancient Indian and Chinese writings (Ikels et al., 1992). Recently, a team of anthropologists (Ikels et al.,

1992) investigated perceptions of aging by ordinary individuals in seven different locations: Swarthmore (PA) and Momence (IL) in the United States; Hong Kong; Blessington and Clifden in Ireland; and among the Herero and !Kung people in Botswana, Africa.

Interestingly—and perhaps distressingly—old age was viewed as the least desirable time of life by a majority of individuals interviewed in each location (Ikels et al., 1992). Apparently the attainment of wisdom in old age did not offset the physical decline associated with aging. Negative judgments of aging were particularly strong in Botswana, perhaps because the societies investigated there require physical strength for social participation to a greater extent than more industrialized societies. Among the Herero and !Kung, for example, physical exertion is required in everyday life as a part of subsistence. In the two communities in the United States and in Ireland, the negative evaluation of old age was less strong, but still evident.

Death and Dying

An inevitable part of the life cycle is death, a subject that psychologists have neglected until recent years. It is now recognized that death is an event of such enormous psychological impact, both for the dying person and for the bereaved, that it deserves closer study. Elisabeth Kübler-Ross, a psychiatrist who became interested in the psychological impact of terminal illness, identified several reactions to dying exhibited by her patients. Many people who learn they have a terminal illness deny its existence at first and try to live as they had before they knew they were sick. Initial denial is often followed by anger and feelings of "Why me?" A whole range of other emotional reactions are also possible: depression, hope, terror, envy, pretense—even a yearning for death. In most terminally ill individuals, dying evokes predominately negative emotions such as sadness, fear, anger, and depression, which occur in no particular order (Schulz & Schlarb, 1988). In the previous chapter, we discussed the increase in life expectancy in the United States. One consequence of this increase may be a greater degree of predictability to death and dying. The probability of

Customs regarding funerals and mourning vary from one cultural group to another. Mourners in Ireland follow the coffin quietly on its journey to the cemetery. In Yunnan Province, China, some mourners bow under the coffin as it passes, as others set off firecrackers in the hope of keeping evil spirits away.

death increases as we grow older. Nevertheless, as a culture we have developed an attitude of denial and avoidance of death.

In the United States, rituals surrounding death have become somewhat more impersonal, with the deceased typically remaining in funeral homes for "viewings," rather than being transported to their own homes. Funerals also have less ritual associated with them now than in previous generations (Markides & Mindel, 1987). Practices and beliefs surrounding death vary among ethnic groups within North America as well as cross-culturally.

Ethnic Differences.   African Americans and Anglo-Americans appear to depend less on family support following the death of a family member or friend than Mexican Americans or Japanese Americans. The role of the church among African Americans, however, seems to be stronger. Among Mexican Americans, in particular, "when death occurs, there appears to be more overt outpouring of emotions by a larger network of kin than is found with the other groups" (Markides & Mindel, 1987, p. 164). Other ethnic groups may also have distinct attitudes and beliefs about death and dying.

As with other aspects of social development, it is difficult to generalize about the death-related experiences of ethnic groups; this difficulty is perhaps greatest for Native Americans because of the great diversity from tribe to tribe. For example, little fear and anxiety about death are evident among the Chiricahua or Jicarilla Apache, whereas death is greatly feared among the Pueblo and the Navajo. Some Native American groups, such as the Navajo, bury their dead quickly and without great ceremony, and minimize contact between the deceased and members of their families (Markides & Mindel, 1987).

Hospice Care.   Dying is not simply a physical process. Psychological dimensions of dying include the need to minimize physical distress; the need to feel in control of one's life and to feel secure and autonomous; the need to sustain interpersonal attachments; and the need to sustain some degree of spiritual energy and hope (Corr, 1991–1992; Fry, 1990).

In recent years, in England, the United States, and Canada, there has been a growing concern to provide support for dying patients and their families. The **hospice care** movement attempts to provide for the terminally ill through a network of support services based in the community (Buckingham, 1983). Terminally ill patients for whom medicine offers little hope move into alternative facilities or are cared for at home with the support provided by the hospice movement. In the mid-1980s approximately 100,000 people were cared for in hospice programs each year in the United States (Schulz & Schlarb, 1988). The hospice movement benefits not only the dying patient, who is allowed to die with dignity, but the patient's family as well. The hospice movement, in short, facilitates the needs associated with the psychological elements of dying. Studies indicate that hospice patients, in comparison to patients in acute-care facilities, have less anxiety, feelings of helplessness, and guilt (Buckingham, 1983).

hospice care community-based support services for the terminally ill and their families

ERIKSON'S LIFE-CYCLE APPROACH TO PSYCHOSOCIAL DEVELOPMENT

We have considered some of the milestones of social development in several eras of life in this chapter, from infancy to old age. Erik Erikson's theory of human development is one of the few that has considered the entire life span, and developmental tasks associated with each of its stages.

Working within the psychoanalytic tradition, Erikson modified Freud's stages of development, focusing more attention on the social concerns of each stage of the life cycle than on the sexual evolution Freud proposed. (We considered Freud's psychosexual theory in detail in Chapter 10.) In Erikson's model, each of eight stages of the life cycle has a dominant theme or task, which can result in a positive or negative outcome. Tension builds up as a kind of psychological crisis, which must be resolved. One way to think of crisis resolution is to view it as a **developmental task** that must be solved before psychological growth can proceed. Although this crisis may be experienced as a very unpleasant psychological state, Erikson did not view it as debilitating. Rather, it is "a necessary turning point, a crucial moment, when development must move one way or another, marshalling resources of growth, recovery, and further differentiation" (Erikson, 1968).

developmental task issue that must be resolved before social development can proceed, illustrated by Erikson's crises at each stage of development

Tasks of Infancy

In infancy, the crisis—or developmental task to be solved—is one of **trust versus mistrust**. In this initial stage of development, which lasts for about the 1st year of life, the infant's primary social interaction is with the parents, especially the mother. The infant's helplessness and need to be fed provoke the crisis of trust. A relatively favorable outcome results in a sense of trust in life-sustaining care, as well as trust of others in a broader sense. Trust based on the continuity provided by others also facilitates trust in oneself. A relatively unfavorable outcome results in a cynical mistrust of others and perhaps in oneself as well.

trust versus mistrust Erikson's first normative crisis of infancy, a period of helplessness and dependency

The crisis of **autonomy versus shame and doubt** confronts the child during the 2nd year of life. The primary form of social interaction continues to be with parents, but now the issue of interaction centers around toilet training. Children in Erikson's second stage develop modes of "holding on" and "letting go," developing, in the process, the beginnings of an autonomous will. Autonomy is the positive outcome of this crisis, but shame and doubt—especially in the context of toilet training—form the negative aspect.

autonomy versus shame and doubt crisis of later infancy, centered on toilet training and the child's will

Tasks of Childhood

Between the ages of 3 and 5, according to Erikson, children experience the crisis of **initiative versus guilt**. In Erikson's formulation, this stage includes strong sexual interest but is important for other reasons as well. Children are by now able to walk around and explore things on their own. At this age they begin to make longer forays into the outside world, attending nursery school or beginning kindergarten. These advances in competence can result in a sense of initiative for doing things and a sense of guilt for having gone too far. The conflict between these two feelings is the essence of the crisis of early childhood.

initiative versus guilt early childhood crisis that requires the child to manage a strong attraction to the opposite-sex parent, roughly corresponding to Freud's phallic stage

Entering school marks an important transition in the social life of a child and leads to the next crisis, between the ages of 6 and puberty, called **industry versus inferiority**. Throughout the elementary school years children attempt to master the information and skills necessary for life in their culture. In the process they may either become increasingly satisfied with their competence, gaining a sense of industry, or be marred by failure, succumbing to a sense of inferiority. Erikson's stages of psychosocial development build one upon the other, just as Piaget's early cognitive stages are

industry versus inferiority crisis of later childhood, corresponding to school entry, when children must learn many new skills that can affect self-esteem

Throughout the elementary school years children attempt to master the information and skills necessary for life in their culture.

integrated into the later ones. For example, a child comes to school with a family history, including a history of encouragement or discouragement about performing the kinds of tasks required in school.

Task of Adolescence

identity versus role confusion crisis of adolescence, when self-definition is the crucial issue

Beginning with puberty, adolescents enter a new stage of psychosocial development that is focused around the crisis of **identity versus role confusion**. They face the task of figuring out what role they will prepare for in the adult world ahead. In short, they suffer a crisis of identity, one that is prolonged in a highly technological society with many years of educational preparation. The most positive outcome of the crisis is an optimal sense of identity achievement, a feeling of psychosocial well-being that results from an examination of the alternatives, followed by a commitment to one alternative within the range of possibilities. Negative outcomes include an inability to make commitments to any roles, or the development of a negative identity marked by commitment to a role the individual considers bad or inappropriate.

Tasks of Adulthood

intimacy versus isolation crisis of early adulthood, when commitment to another person in a relationship is central

Commitment to another person is stressed in early adulthood in Erikson's theory. The crisis for resolution at this stage is **intimacy versus isolation**, which builds upon the identity commitments made in adolescence. People begin the developmental task of finding a person with whom they can share their lives. Intimacy refers to more than sexual intimacy, although that is a part of it; it also encompasses emotional sharing. The counterpoint to intimacy at this stage is isolation; this result sometimes comes about when people avoid social contacts that could lead to intimacy.

The crisis of middle adulthood in Erikson's theory is that of **generativity versus stagnation**. As we saw earlier, Daniel Levinson (1986) has studied men and women at midlife. A common developmental pattern was people's fear in middle adulthood that they would not be able to express some aspects of their personalities. Erikson has also stressed the importance of midlife. People in midlife need to be productive, creative, and involved in helping younger generations with their future. These goals make up the central focus of generativity, which may include producing and providing for children and generally helping to guide the next generation (Snarey et al., 1987). The opposite pole of the crisis, stagnation, refers to the sense of productive failure that sometimes arises when adults see themselves on a meaningless treadmill, expending a lot of effort but going nowhere.

generativity versus stagnation middle-age crisis of involvement in guiding future generations and generally being productive

The life cycle culminates in Erikson's eighth stage, where the crisis is **ego integrity versus despair**. The human tendency for self-evaluation expresses itself in the years of late adulthood through a review of one's life. The most positive outcome of such a self-review is ego integrity: "The acceptance of one's one and only life cycle as something that had to be and that, by necessity, permitted of no substitutions" (Erikson, 1963). Despair is the negative outcome of this review, accompanied by feelings of leaving nothing of value behind and of dread for death.

ego integrity versus despair crisis of old age, when life review takes place

A cornerstone of Erikson's developmental theory is its emphasis on multiple possibilities for human social and personality development. Between the two extreme outcomes of the eight crises that Erikson charted, there are many possibilities for developmental change (Meacham & Santilli, 1982). The resolution is never completely clear-cut. One does not come out of infancy with an orientation of pure trust or pure mistrust. In this sense, what is normal about human development is the sequence of social issues around which these crises revolve, not the nature of the outcome itself.

Critical Appraisal of Erikson's Theory

Erikson based his theory primarily on his clinical intuition, rather than on empirical studies of people in various stages of the life cycle. Most of the research that Erikson's theory has spawned has concerned the identity crisis in adolescence. A great deal of that research has corroborated many aspects of this stage as outlined by Erikson, particularly the elements of crisis and commitment (Marcia, 1966).

Several problems remain with Erikson's theory, however. Two of these problems are particularly central to a critical appraisal of the theory. One concerns the lack of any agreed-upon set of instruments to measure the various aspects of Erikson's theory. A wide variety of measurement devices has been used, even to measure the crisis of the single stage of adolescence (Grotevant, 1985). A second problem concerns the issue of continuity and discontinuity in development. Erikson implies that the eight stages must occur in the particular order in which they appear in Table 13–7. Few age guidelines exist, however, particularly for the later stages. In addition, Erikson suggests that the sequence may differ in some respects for men and women. Women, he suggests, may define their identities through relationships, thus experiencing the crisis of intimacy before the crisis of identity. There are many critics of this view of "woman's place in a man's life cycle" (Gilligan, 1982).

This and the previous chapter have charted human development in physical, cognitive, and social domains. Although we have separated our

TABLE 13-7
Erikson's Eight Stages of the Life Cycle

Normative Crisis	Age	Major Characteristics
Trust vs. mistrust	0–1	Primary social interaction with mothering caretaker; oral concerns; trust in life-sustaining care, including feeding.
Autonomy vs. shame and doubt	1–2	Primary social interaction with parents; toilet training; "holding on" and "letting go" and the beginnings of autonomous will.
Initiative vs. guilt	3–5	Primary social interactions with nuclear family; beginnings of "Oedipal" feelings; development of language and locomotion; development of conscience as governor of initiative.
Industry vs. inferiority	6–puberty	Primary social interaction outside home among peers and teachers; school-age assessment of task ability.
Identity vs. role confusion	Adolescence	Primary social interaction with peers, culminating in heterosexual friendship; psychological moratorium from adult commitments; identity crisis; consolidation of resolutions of previous four stages into coherent sense of self.
Intimacy vs. isolation	Early adulthood	Primary social interaction in intimate relationship with member of opposite sex; adult role commitments accepted, including commitment to another person.
Generativity vs. stagnation	Middle adulthood	Primary social concern in establishing and guiding future generation; productivity and creativity.
Ego integrity vs. despair	Late adulthood	Primary social concern is a reflective one; coming to terms with one's place in the (now nearly complete) life cycle, and with one's relationships with others; "I am what survives of me."

Source: Adapted from Erikson, 1968, Chapter 3.

life-span coverage into these three areas, readers should be aware that it is, in a sense, a false division. In reality, human beings develop holistically, and changes in one area inevitably affect development in other areas. Human life is "a strange eventful history," to use Shakespeare's phrase, in which all areas of development are integrated.

THINKING AHEAD . . .

Developmental *change* has become a central concern in several areas of psychology over the past several years. The growth of developmental concerns is reflected in our decision to expand coverage of human development from one chapter, in previous editions of this book, to two chapters in this edition.

As you review what you have already studied in this book, and as you read what is yet to come, consider some of the developmental aspects of psychology. For example, how do brain structures and functioning change over time? In Chapter 12 we discussed several neurological changes with aging, such as the growth of tangles and plaques that are implicated in Alzheimer's disease—a disease with profound social as well as physical alterations in a person's life. We have also seen that sensory processes undergo age changes, with losses in most of the senses, including vision and hearing. These changes, too, alter a person's social world.

Even circadian rhythms differ from one part of the life cycle to another. The amount of time you can expect to spend in REM sleep—and therefore dreaming—is reduced as you grow older. What might be some of the social ramifications of this developmental change? To anticipate some of the material still to come in this book, what is the impact of aging on psychological problems? Are you more at risk for developing psychological disorders in different parts of the life cycle? What reasons would you give to justify your predictions about changes in vulnerability by age?

Genie, the young victim of profound social deprivation whom we met at the beginning of this chapter, posed a real challenge to developmental psychologists. What would the great theorists of developmental psychology have said about Genie? How does her sad case help us to understand the mysteries of growth and development? Unfortunately, Genie's case does not satisfactorily illuminate the issues. Perhaps it raises more questions than it answers. In any case, Genie, now in her early thirties, lives in a home for retarded adults. After a childhood of almost total social isolation, she made some progress toward entering a normal life, but ultimately was unable to maintain her existence outside a semi-institutional context.

Summary

Infancy: Social Beginnings

1. Social behavior begins soon after birth, even if it is not intentional until later in infancy. Social interchanges are patterns of social interaction that have reciprocal influence; infant behavior, for example, helps to solidify the emotional bonding between parent and child that will lead to the close emotional relationship known as attachment.

2. The social world of infants is focused on the dependency relationship they have with their parents. Infants show a style of attachment to their caregivers, based on their behavior in a laboratory assessment known as the "strange situation." They are classified as either securely attached, resistant, or avoidant.

3. Infant attachment style is based in part on experience. There are cultural variations in style of attachment, and infants adapt to separation from their caregivers after being repeatedly separated, as is the case for children in day care.

4. Harlow's research with infant monkeys suggests comparisons with human infants. Infant monkeys deprived of real mothers preferred a soft surrogate, as opposed to a wire mesh one, even if the latter provided nourishment. Harlow concluded that monkeys need contact comfort.

5. Fathers develop strong attachment relationships with their infants and are also important figures in the social development of their children.

6. An infant's attachment style with caregivers has some developmental continuity into later stages of development.

7. Stranger anxiety and separation anxiety, two typical fears of infancy, are related to cognitive development and to attachment style.

8. Infant temperamental differences appear to develop very early in life, and perhaps may be innate. The dimension of inhibition, or shyness, has been researched extensively in recent years.

Childhood: A Widening Social World

9. In childhood the focus of social interaction shifts more and more away from parents and toward the peer group.

10. Friendships in childhood are overwhelmingly with same-sex peers. Gender differences in social play may be a function of genetic differences, socialization differences, or a combination of the two.

11. In childhood, social play is an important facet of development. Regularities in type of social play are seen in childhood, from solitary play through cooperative play, following Parten's classification system.

12. Children as well as adults experience loneliness. Positive peer relationships are important in help-ing children to avoid loneliness. Social rejection by peers is a predictor of loneliness.

Family Issues

13. Traditional families (heterosexual couples with minor children in the household) are now a minority of all families in the United States.

14. Changes in the family and in sex roles have had an impact on some issues in human development. With greater numbers of women in the work force now than in previous decades, alternative child-care arrangements are necessary. Studies indicate that latchkey children, those who care for themselves after school, do not differ significantly from other children on measures of self-esteem, adjustment, and interpersonal relationships.

15. The style of parental discipline—authoritarian, authoritative, or permissive/indulgent and permissive/neglectful—affects the social development of children in a number of ways. The best developmental outcome for children is associated with authoritative parenting.

16. Child abuse and neglect have become vast social problems. Abuse and neglect occur in a variety of forms, from physical abuse, to sexual abuse, to psychological maltreatment, to neglect. Studies indicate that each type of abuse may have its own harmful outcomes on social development.

17. Approximately half of all children born in the 1980s will experience their parents' divorce and live in a single-parent household for some period. Most children are affected by divorce in the short term. Some children will suffer long-term effects as well. These effects are influenced by variables such as their gender, their age at the time of the divorce, whether their parents remarry, and the gender of the custodial parent.

Adolescence: Social Transitions

18. With puberty comes increasing conflict with parents. G. Stanley Hall, a pioneer in American psychology, saw adolescence as an inevitably stormy and stressful period.

19. Sibling relationships may help to alleviate some of the social problems that children have in school. Sibling relationships appear to become less intense with age, presumably as adolescents make the transition from a family orientation to a peer orientation.

20. Friendships and romantic relationships in adolescence help to convey self-esteem and a sense of belonging. Breakups of romantic relationships can have a negative effect on adolescents that is similar to a grief reaction.

21. Sexual interest increases at puberty, and by age 19, 80% of adolescents report that they have had intercourse. The teenage pregnancy rate has

increased; adolescents are also becoming a high-risk group for HIV infection.

22. A major theme of adolescence is moral questioning. Kohlberg has provided a model of moral development in which people progress from a preconventional level, where labels of "good" and "bad" operate in the absence of genuine social standards, to a conventional level of social norms and laws, to a postconventional level, where underlying principles guide moral judgments.

Adulthood: The Middle Years

23. Levinson's studies of adult social development indicate important restructurings at predictable ages in the adult life cycle. Many of these transitions are consistent with Erikson's psychosocial theory. Part of the social clock for many individuals is a midlife crisis, in which one confronts the inevitability of mortality. A midlife crisis does not, however, appear to be inevitable, and when it occurs, it need not be traumatizing.

Adulthood: Aging

24. Many people have fewer social contacts after retirement, but those retirees who maintain stronger ties lead more satisfying lives. The mandatory retirement age was lifted in 1986, creating the possibility that more people will continue to work in their advanced years.

25. Cross-cultural studies indicate that old age is seen as a time of wisdom, but also of physical decline. It is viewed as an undesirable time of life in many societies, especially those where physical exertion is an important part of everyday life.

26. An inevitable part of the life cycle is death. A hospice movement has grown in the United States, England, and Canada that allows terminally ill patients to die with dignity at home or in sheltered-care facilities.

Erikson's Life-Cycle Approach to Psychosocial Development

27. Erikson has outlined eight stages of social development, each of which has a dominant social theme and a crisis—a developmental task that must be solved for continued psychological growth. His theory is one of the most highly developed accounts with a life-span focus.

══ Key Terms ══

social interchange (506)
attachment (508)
bonding (508)
secure attachment (508)
resistant attachment (508)
avoidant attachment (508)
contact comfort (512)
stranger anxiety (513)
separation anxiety (513)
temperament (514)

sociometric analysis (519)
latchkey children (520)
authoritarian (521)
authoritative (521)
indulgent (521)
neglectful (521)
child neglect (522)
child abuse (522)
child sexual abuse (522)
psychological maltreatment (522)
disorganized attachment (523)

preconventional level (532)
conventional level (532)
postconventional level (532)
social clock (535)
midlife crisis (536)
postparenthood (536)
hospice care (540)
developmental task (541)
trust versus mistrust (541)

autonomy vs. shame and doubt (541)
initiative versus guilt (541)
industry versus inferiority (541)
identity versus role confusion (542)
intimacy versus isolation (542)
generativity versus stagnation (543)
ego integrity versus despair (543)

══ Suggested Reading ══

Brazelton, T. B., & Cramer, B. G. (1990). *The earliest relationship*. New York: Addison-Wesley. A book on the parent–child relationship, beginning prenatally and extending into infancy. Both social interaction studies and case studies are presented. The senior author is one of the country's foremost pediatricians.

Erikson, E. (Ed.). (1978). *Adulthood*. New York: Norton. A collection of 15 essays, edited by Erik Erikson, on adulthood. The collection is diverse, with several essays examining adulthood in other cultures, as well as approaching the study of adulthood from multidisciplinary perspectives.

Gulotta, T. P., Adams, G. R., & Montemayor, R. (Eds.). (1993). *Adolescent sexuality*. Newbury Park, CA: Sage. A collection of eight chapters focusing on different aspects of adolescent sexuality, from anatomy, physiology, and gender issues to the promotion of sexual responsibility.

Kagan, J. (1984). *The nature of the child*. New York: Basic Books. A view of childhood that suggests that humans have a lifelong capacity for change. The book also discusses moral development and the influence of the family on child development.

Whiting, B. B., & Whiting, J. W. M. (1975). *Children of six cultures: A psycho-cultural analysis*. Cambridge, MA: Harvard University Press. Studies of social development, gender, and culture in Kenya, Okinawa, India, the Philippines, Mexico, and the United States.

CHAPTER 14
Social Psychology

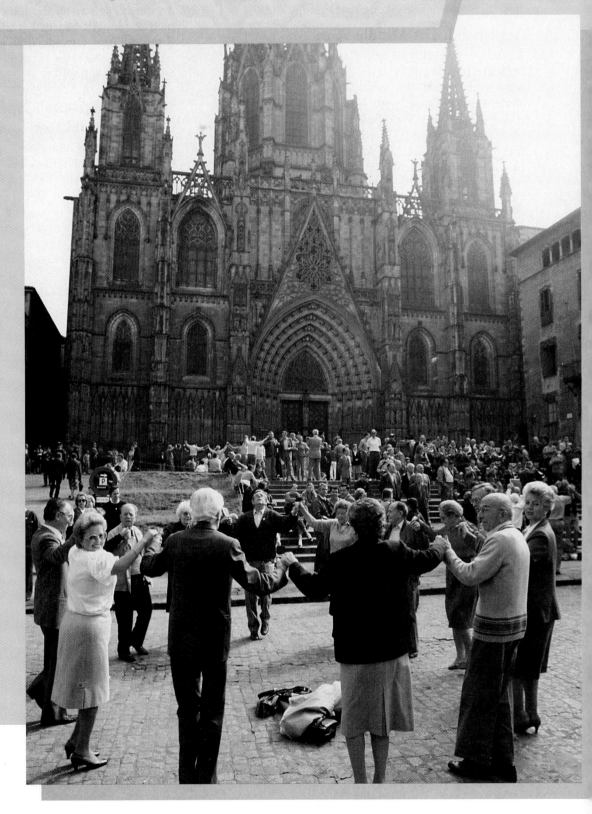

On a warm night in March of 1991, the Los Angeles police stopped an African-American man named Rodney King after a high-speed car chase. What had started as a fairly routine procedure quickly escalated, and additional squad cars were called to the scene. While several other officers looked on, four of the officers severely beat Rodney King. What made this incident unique was not that it happened, but that it was video-taped by an onlooker from a nearby apartment. The videotape showed that King had been repeatedly hit with a nightstick long after he appeared to pose no physical threat to officers around him.

When the major news networks showed the videotape on television, citizens throughout the country were bewildered, stunned, and angered. How could individuals sworn to uphold the law seem callously to break it? Why did so many officers beat King, apparently brutally? Were they evil people? Were they obeying orders from someone on the scene? Were they simply conforming to the social norms that they thought applied to this situation? Why did so many motorists pass by without stopping to investigate? Did they not want to "get involved"? What kind of person would stand by and watch another human being beaten senseless? Would a white motorist have received the same treatment? How often do these violent beatings occur? Could they be racially motivated?

Following the incident, four officers were indicted on criminal charges based largely on the videotape. When they came to trial, many people felt certain that the officers would be punished for using excessive force. However, all four officers were acquitted. (although two were later convicted of violating King's civil rights in a Federal trial). Thus, the use of excessive force that so many people had interpreted from viewing the tape was not shared by the all-white jury in the officers' criminal trial. After the acquittal, the worst rioting occurred in Los Angeles since the Watts riots of

◀ People are social animals, and they behave differently when they are in the company of others than when they are alone.

1965. Over several days, dozens of people were killed and damage estimates ran in the hundreds of millions of dollars.

When the rioting was broadcast on television, citizens from around the country were once again bewildered, stunned, and angered. How could normally law-abiding people break so many laws in such a violent and destructive fashion? Why did they do things during the riots that they never would have done normally? Why did so many people who live near the riot-torn areas fail to stop looters or assist the police in curtailing property damage? Could a situation like the Los Angeles riots spread to other parts of the country?

The Rodney King incident highlights several themes that are central to what social psychology is all about. Social psychology asks such questions as, when do people act on their attitudes about what is proper, law-abiding conduct, and why do they occasionally deviate from these attitudes? How does the presence of other people influence how one behaves in a social or group setting? Why is there conflict between members of different ethnic groups, and how can it be lessened? Why and under what conditions do people obey authority figures? Under what circumstances will people disobey authority figures? What social and environmental factors influence conformity to group pressure? These are weighty questions that have an impact on all of us; they are the sorts of questions that the discipline of social psychology attempts to answer through research.

social psychology scientific study of how people think about, influence, and relate to one another

Social psychology is the scientific study of how people think about, influence, and relate to one another. More specifically, it focuses on how the thoughts, feelings, and behavior of one individual affect other individuals in different social contexts. Whenever possible, social psychologists attempt to identify and explain the underlying psychological mechanisms that account for individual behavior within a given social setting. These mechanisms may include biological, perceptual, motivational, developmental, personality, cognitive, and a host of other factors.

Social behavior is full of variety. It includes the darker forces within human behavior such as aggression and prejudice, as well as the more positive sides of social life, such as romantic attraction, friendship, and altruism. Because so much of human and animal behavior is social behavior, our coverage in this chapter is necessarily selective. We discuss four major topics in this chapter: *social cognition*, which concerns the ways thinking and social behavior interact; *group processes*, where the focus is on the social context for individual behavior; *friendship and romantic attraction*, including sexuality and the development of sexual orientation; and *gender and sex roles*, where the discussion centers around the ways the social categories of gender influence behavior.

SOCIAL COGNITION

social cognition study of how individuals gather, process, retrieve, and interpret information about different aspects of their social environment

Social cognition refers to the ways that individuals gather, use, and interpret information about social aspects of their world (Taylor, 1976). It is concerned with the ways that cognitive elements, such as attitudes, beliefs, and values, shape our social behavior. In this section, we first examine information about attitudes and attitude change, including techniques of persuasion. Next, we examine interpersonal perception and attribution: the ways people perceive the causes of social behavior and the ways in which this perception influences their own behavior.

Attitudes and Attitude Change

An **attitude** is a relatively stable system of beliefs and feelings about something. Social psychologists are interested in any attitudes that affect social behavior, including attitudes about certain types or classes of people, religious groups, or racial groups. A great deal of research has been conducted on questions such as, How are attitudes formed? What is the relationship between attitudes and personality? How can attitudes be changed?

The Formation of Attitudes.   People obviously are not born with a set of attitudes. Attitudes must be learned through many of the principles of learning that we described in Chapter 6, including operant conditioning, modeling, and classical conditioning. Operant conditioning accounts for the development of attitudes when children are praised for expressing attitudes that their mentors—such as parents and teachers—want them to hold and punished for expressing attitudes that are viewed as inappropriate. Children also model the attitudes that are expressed by people with whom they identify. Parents, schools, the media, and other significant influences on children contribute to their socialization. Finally, children sometimes acquire attitudes when certain people or objects are repeatedly associated with positive or negative experiences (Staats & Staats, 1958). If such experiences are pleasant, positive attitudes develop; if they are unpleasant, negative attitudes emerge.

Attitudes and Behavior.   Most of us assume that if we know how someone thinks and feels about another person or group, we can predict her or his behavior toward that person or group. For example, if we know that a senator holds homophobic attitudes, we would predict that he or she will be opposed to lifting the ban on gays and lesbians in the military. Indeed, knowing someone's attitudes does help in the prediction of behavior (Cialdini, Petty, & Cacioppo, 1981). Attitudes, however, are far from perfect as predictors of behavior. In the early 1930s, a sociologist named LaPiere (1934) toured the country with a Chinese couple for several months. They went from town to town, looking for accommodations at motels, hotels, campgrounds, and restaurants. LaPiere was aware that, in the 1930s, many Americans held prejudicial attitudes toward Asians. Nonetheless, the couple was accommo-

attitude relatively stable and enduring system of feelings and beliefs about a given person, object, or event

A person's attitudes are highly influenced by the environment in which he or she grows up. These youngsters on Israel's West Bank are likely to have very different attitudes about street violence than children growing up in a typical American suburb.

dated and treated well at virtually every place they stopped. Six months after the trip, LaPiere sent questionnaires to the owners of each establishment asking them if they would serve a Chinese couple. To his amazement, nearly 90% of the respondents said no! Although some observers raised methodological questions about the study, a review of the research on the correspondence between attitudes and behavior revealed that attitudes tend to predict behavior rather weakly (Wicker, 1969). Indeed, knowing someone's attitudes does help slightly in the prediction of behavior (Cialdini, Petty, & Cacioppo, 1981).

One way to think of attitudes is in terms of structures in long-term memory (Tourangeau & Rasinski, 1988). Attitudes form a network of interconnected elements—beliefs, memories of experiences, general propositions, images, and feelings. Attitudes about one issue are therefore related to a cluster of issues with some connection to the primary attitude. For example, people who hold either a prolife or a prochoice attitude on abortion are likely to have related views on issues such as sex roles, sexuality, and parenthood, as indicated in Table 14–1.

Attitudes are sometimes poor predictors of future behavior for four reasons (Rajecki, 1982). First, it is often difficult to measure attitudes accurately. People may describe their attitudes in terms of what they think others want to hear or what is socially desirable, rather than how they truly feel. Second, general attitude measures are often used to predict how a given person will behave in a specific situation on a single day. Global measures are notoriously poor predictors of single future events. Third, people are not always aware of the relevance of certain attitudes for their behavior. Once they are made aware that certain attitudes imply certain actions, the correspondence between attitudes and behavior increases. Fourth, personality differences may influence the degree to which people's behavior can be predicted from their attitudes.

Cognitive Dissonance. Not only can attitudes affect how people behave; the way in which people behave can alter what they believe. According to Leon Festinger (1957), people are motivated to maintain consistency among their beliefs, attitudes, and behavior. When an inconsistency arises, it creates a sense of psychological tension known as **cognitive dissonance** that motivates people to restore consistency. Festinger's theory of cognitive dissonance (see Chapter 9) accounts for situations in which changes in a per-

cognitive dissonance theory proposes that when individuals behave contrary to their attitudes and beliefs, they feel anxious and are motivated to change their attitudes to conform to their actions

---

TABLE 14-1
Interconnectedness of Attitudes: The Case of Prolife and Prochoice Views on Abortion

Topic	Prolife View	Prochoice View
Sex roles	Men and women are different.	Men and women are equal and similar.
Meaning of sex	The purpose of sex is reproduction.	The purpose of sex is to foster intimacy.
Parenthood	Parenthood is a natural function, not a social role.	Parenthood means giving the child one's best resources.
Premarital sex	Sex outside of marriage is wrong.	Teenage parenthood is the problem, not teenage sex.
Abortion	Abortion breaks divine law.	Abortion is a matter of individual choice.

Source: Tourangeau & Rasinski, 1988.

son's behavior produce corresponding changes in their attitudes. In a classic study, Festinger and Carlsmith (1959) gave undergraduate students some exceedingly boring and monotonous tasks to perform. After completing them, students were told the study was over. However, the researcher asked them if they would do him a favor—tell the next student coming in for the study (actually a member of the research team) that it really was fun and exciting. In essence, students were asked to tell a small lie. Half of them were told they would receive $20 for "assisting" the researcher, and the other half were told they would get $1 for doing so.

After telling the lie, students were asked to rate the boring task that they had just endured. Students who were promised $20 for lying indicated that the task was dull and monotonous; those who were promised $1 gave it much higher ratings. The attitudes of these latter students had, in effect, been changed by the behavior they just performed—telling a lie for very little monetary incentive. According to Festinger and Carlsmith, the $1 payoff was insufficient justification for misleading the next participant, and it induced a state of *cognitive dissonance* or discomfort (e.g., "I just told someone a lie for no good reason, and the experiment really *was* boring"). To resolve this dilemma, students who were promised only $1 reevaluated their attitude toward the experiment and brought it in line with their behavior. Because $20 provided ample justification for misleading someone about a relatively trivial event, students who were promised $20 felt no cognitive dissonance and did not change their attitudes.

Researchers have identified five conditions that are necessary for the creation of cognitive dissonance (Cooper & Fazio, 1984). First, the behavior in question must violate the performers' attitudes or beliefs. Second, the behavior must have unwanted, negative consequences for either themselves or other individuals. Third, they must feel personally responsible for the unpleasant consequences of their actions. In order to feel personally responsible, they must believe that the negative consequences of their actions were somehow foreseeable. Fourth, they must experience physiological arousal, such as increased heart rate or nervousness. And fifth, they must attribute their arousal to their actions. If all of these conditions are met, individuals will experience a state of cognitive dissonance.

Attitude Change and Persuasion. Advertising campaigns try to exploit the information available about how attitudes are formed in order to persuade people that a product is superior. Market researchers, for example, assess the public's attitudes toward competing products. Suppose such researchers find that Brands W and X are rated highly, but Brands Y and Z are not. If they wish to sell Brand X, they may design campaigns to increase the public's rating of that product, and to decrease the rating of Brand W. If Brand W is rated very highly, advertisers are probably better off trying to reduce those ratings (Jaccard, 1981). The major beer and soft-drink manufacturers frequently devalue their competitors' products as a strategy for improving consumers' attitudes about their own product.

One approach to studying attitude change is to focus on cognitive responses in a persuasion campaign (Cooper & Croyle, 1984). Campaigns of persuasion try to present arguments that will convince listeners to alter their attitudes in the desired direction. The effectiveness of these campaigns varies, depending on the characteristics of the source of the communication, characteristics of the communication itself, and characteristics of the listener.

Source of Communication. Persuasion campaigns are more effective when communicators are viewed as experts on the topic they are talking about (Maddux & Rogers, 1980). Television advertisements for painkillers often have actors posing as physicians praising their products; one campaign placed a well-known race-car driver in an ad to describe the road-handling ability of a particular brand of tires.

The credibility of a communicator is also affected by perceptions of how trustworthy he or she is. If communicators are perceived to be biased in their views, they are less effective in changing others' attitudes (Eagly, Wood, & Chaiken, 1978). However, if the communicator takes a position contrary to what is expected from his or her past behavior, seemingly on the basis of overwhelming evidence, then the campaign is more effective.

The likability and attractiveness of communicators also enhance the effectiveness of persuasion, particularly when communicators are more conspicuous, as is the case when they are on videotape as opposed to in print (Chaiken & Eagly, 1983). Popular entertainers are often selected for advertising or persuasion campaigns because of these characteristics. Manufacturers of sports apparel and equipment, for example, pay athletes enormous sums of money to wear and promote their products.

Characteristics of the Communication. Several characteristics of the communication itself are important in helping to change attitudes. To change attitudes, a communication should not differ too much from the listener's own position. It is unlikely that any campaign would convince an ardent member of the National Rifle Association (NRA) that private ownership of guns should be banned. It might be possible, however, to modify such a person's position on ordering assault rifles by mail; perhaps NRA members could be persuaded that everyone would be safer if it were more difficult to purchase weapons that are so frequently used in violent crimes.

Should campaigns of persuasion present both sides of an argument, or should they concentrate only on their own position? The answer to this question appears to depend on the initial position of the listener. If the listener already agrees with the position being advocated, one-sided arguments appear to strengthen the attitude even further. If the listener initially disagrees, then two-sided arguments are generally more effective (Hovland, Lumsdaine, & Sheffield, 1949). If a person is asked to take a position after hearing only one side of an argument, the person has greater resistance to any new arguments that are presented (Hovland, 1958).

Frequent exposure to a persuasive campaign, up to a point, increases its effectiveness. In fact, there is empirical support for the **mere exposure effect**, the tendency to become more favorably disposed toward people or attitudes merely by coming into repeated contact with them (Zajonc, 1968). This finding may help you understand why you encounter the same advertisement over and over again on television. It also explains why, in the electronic age, money for media advertising is so important for successful political campaigns.

The effects of emotional appeals in persuasive messages can be very complicated. Messages about smoking that emphasize health risks are designed to arouse fear; messages that show starving children in Somalia are designed to arouse compassion. A classic study by Janis and Feshbach (1953) demonstrated that these kinds of campaigns work as long as the emotion is not overly intense. Students were presented with three different forms of a lecture on tooth decay and oral hygiene. In each lecture, the same essential information on the causes of tooth decay was presented, but the lectures differed in the amount of fear they aroused. The lecture that was designed to arouse only a little fear barely mentioned the consequences of tooth neglect. In the lecture that was designed to arouse greater fear, however, listeners were told that poor hygiene could cause infection and lead to diseases such as arthritic paralysis, kidney damage, and total blindness. When fear arousal was high, the effectiveness of the communication was

mere exposure effect tendency to like something or someone more following repeated exposure to it or them

---

TABLE 14-2
Effects of Communicator, Communication, and Listener on Attitude Change

Communicator

Campaigns are generally more effective when the communicator
a. is viewed as an expert.
b. is credible.
c. is likable and attractive.

Communication

Campaigns are generally more effective when the communication
a. is not very different from the listener's own position.
b. offers a one-sided argument for the listener who already is, to some extent, in agreement on the issue.
c. offers a two-sided argument for the listener who disagrees.
d. is presented frequently.
e. contains messages that are not excessively emotional and that provide information on how to reduce emotion.

Listener

Campaigns are generally more effective when the listener
a. actively processes information in the message.
b. hears a personally relevant message.

significantly lower than when fear arousal was low. Emotional appeals are also more effective if listeners are provided with concrete recommendations for action, such as effective ways to stop smoking or details on how to contribute to relief for the children in Somalia (Janis & Feshbach, 1953).

Characteristics of the Listener.   Even though attitudes sometimes change by virtue of mere exposure, attitude change is more enduring when listeners have been actively processing the content of the persuasive message (Cialdini et al., 1981). Active processing is likely to occur when the focus of the persuasive message has a high degree of personal relevance for the listener. For example, college students are likely to be highly involved in messages about the importance of passing comprehensive examinations as a requirement for graduation; family members of homicide victims are likely to actively process arguments against the effectiveness of the death penalty as a deterrent to crime. Table 14–2 summarizes the effects that the characteristics of the communicator, the communication, and the listener have on changing attitudes.

A Model of Persuasion.   One model of persuasion proposes that attitude change occurs via one of two different routes (Petty & Cacioppo, 1981). According to this **elaboration likelihood model**, the **central route** to persuasion takes place when an individual carefully thinks about the issues and arguments to which he or she has been exposed. The **peripheral route** occurs when persuasion results from concerns that are not relevant to the issue, such as the desire to make a good impression on others, the attractiveness of the message's source, or one's current social role. New attitudes formed via the central route tend to be more stable and last longer, particularly if individuals put some effort into thinking about the issues involved when they initially acquire the attitudes. Attitudes formed via the peripheral route tend to be stable only so long as the cues associated with their development remain important. For example, if you develop a positive attitude toward rap music only because the person you are going out with likes it, your attitude toward rap may change quickly when you break up with that person. Enduring attitude change, therefore, depends on the extent to which issues and arguments are elaborated or pondered during the initial stages of attitude formation.

elaboration likelihood model model of persuasion that specifies how attitudes become more stable and enduring following effortful thinking about persuasive arguments

central route route to persuasion in the elaboration likelihood model in which persuasion occurs due to deliberate, effortful thinking about the arguments to which one has been exposed

peripheral route route to persuasion in the elaboration likelihood model in which persuasion occurs due to factors not associated with the content of persuasive arguments

Attribution Processes

People often want to explain their own social behavior as well as the social behavior of others. A compelling body of research on what is called **attribution theory**, which evolved out of work by Fritz Heider (1958), has examined people's inferences about the causes of behavior. According to attribution theory, people behave much like intuitive scientists in their attempts to find the causes of behavior. Although the theory does not resolve the trait versus situation debate that we encountered in Chapter 10, it does deal with the ways in which people make judgments about inferring the causes of behavior from either traits or situations.

attribution theory theory that specifies how people make inferences about the causes of behavior

The Nature of Attribution.   Attributions can be made about any behavior, from bedwetting to winning a tennis match. In order to illustrate some of the issues in attribution theory, consider the tragedy that occurred in the Persian Gulf on July 3, 1988. U.S. warships, including the USS *Vincennes*, had been patrolling the waters, looking out especially for Iranian and Iraqi air and sea attacks on neutral merchant vessels. There had been much tension in the area, and the *Vincennes* itself had been involved that day with Iranian gunboats. On the fateful day, sailors monitoring sophisticated instruments aboard the *Vincennes* reported an Iranian jet approaching in an attack mode. Only a brief time was available to Admiral Will Rogers III, the ship's captain, for making a critical decision—either to leave the plane alone and risk a direct attack or to shoot it down. He gave the order to shoot it down. It turned out to be a civilian aircraft, and all 290 passengers were killed.

How are the actions of the *Vincennes* crew, especially its captain, to be understood? In explaining the behavior, we tend to make one of two general types of attribution. A **person attribution** places the cause of behavior in a person's character, basing it on some internal trait or characteristic. Person attributions can be stable or unstable. A lingering trait that is difficult to change would be considered a stable, internal cause. Perhaps Admiral Rogers is a sadistic, war-mongering person, as the Iranian government asserted in its early reactions to the tragedy. A temporary internal state, such as mood, or acute illness, would constitute an unstable, internal cause. If Admiral Rogers had been drunk or drugged at the time of the incident, we might make an internal attribution that would be due to temporary, or unstable, characteristics.

A **situation attribution**, on the other hand, locates the cause of behavior in the particular situation, rather than in the person. Situation attributions may also be due to either stable or unstable causes. In the case of the *Vincennes*, we might infer that the cause of the decision to shoot down the approaching plane was related to the combatlike situation, taking into account recent engagements of the *Vincennes*—an unstable, situation attribution. Or we might question the adequacy of the electronic equipment on board the *Vincennes* for dealing with any emergency situation—a stable, situational attribution. In the days and weeks following July 3, 1988, the U.S. government and the media suggested virtually all of these hypotheses for explaining the tragedy.

Factors Determining Type of Attribution.   One of the major figures in the study of attribution has been Harold Kelley, who proposed that three factors help to determine whether one will make person or situation attributions. These factors are distinctiveness, consensus, and consistency (Kelley, 1967).

To help explain these factors, let us suppose that a college student named Sharon takes a chemistry test. **Distinctiveness** means that a response is specific to a particular situation. Suppose Sharon fails a chemistry midterm but passes all her other midterm exams. Her performance in chemistry is high in distinctiveness; it is unlike her performance in any other subject. **Consensus** refers to the similarity of response from one person to another. Suppose almost everyone in the class failed the chemistry test in question. In that case, Sharon's response would be characterized by a high degree of consensus. **Consistency** is the tendency to respond the same way in similar circumstances. Suppose that when Sharon took her next chemistry test, she failed that also. Her performance would show consistency.

These three types of information—distinctiveness, consensus, and consistency—combine to influence the type of attribution that will be made. Table 14–3 contains a list of the four most common types of attribution and corresponding information on distinctiveness, consensus, and consistency. When all three factors are high, a stable, situation attribution is the likely result. Perhaps Sharon's chemistry professor has unreasonable expectations for students or is simply a very tough instructor.

When all three factors are low, we tend to make unstable, person attributions. What if Sharon failed chemistry and history midterms (low distinctiveness), she was one of the few students to fail the chemistry test (low consensus), and she passed the next chemistry test (low consistency)? Here we would likely place the cause of her behavior in internal, but unstable,

person attribution attribution that locates the cause of behavior in a person's character or dispositional nature

situation attribution attribution that locates the cause of behavior in a person's environmental surroundings

distinctiveness term from Kelley's attribution model that indicates the extent to which a response is unique to a given situation

consensus term from Kelley's attribution model that indicates the extent to which a response is similar across different people

consistency term from Kelley's attribution model that indicates the extent to which a person's response is the same in similar situations over time

TABLE 14-3
Types of Attribution and Their Relationship to Distinctiveness, Consensus, and Consistency Information

Types of Attribution	Distinctiveness	Consensus	Consistency
Person—stable	Low	Low	High
Situation—stable	High	High	High
Person—unstable	Low	Low	Low
Situation—unstable	High	High	Low

Source: Adapted from Brown, 1986.

causes. Perhaps she had a few bad days and was ill during history and chemistry midterm season. However, when the next set of tests came up, she was back to a high level of performance.

When distinctiveness and consensus are both low and consistency is high, we tend to make stable, person attributions. Sharon fails chemistry and biology midterms (low distinctiveness), she is one of the few students to fail the chemistry test (low consensus), and Sharon also fails the next chemistry test (high consistency). Most of us who had this information would probably advise Sharon to major in something other than chemistry because of a lack of talent in that direction—a stable, person attribution.

Unstable situation attributions are likely to be made when distinctiveness and consensus information are high but consistency is low. Sharon fails chemistry but passes her other midterms (high distinctiveness), most students fail the chemistry midterm (high consensus), and Sharon passes the next chemistry test (low consistency). This information suggests that the chemistry midterm was particularly difficult—an unstable, situation attribution. Table 14–4 lists some possible person and situation attributions one might use in trying to find the cause for exam failure (Lunt, 1988).

You probably noticed that all combinations of distinctiveness, consensus, and consistency are not included in Table 14–3 or in the preceding discussion. However, the four we have discussed are the most likely attributions that people make. Other types of attribution involve complicated interactions of person and situation, and of stable and unstable causes, and are beyond the scope of this chapter. Furthermore, we do not always have information on all three factors. For example, we may know only that Sharon failed her chemistry test and passed all her other midterms, without any information regarding other students' performance on that test or Sharon's performance on other chemistry work. But when information is available, consistency seems to be the strongest of the three factors in influ-

TABLE 14-4
Perceived Causal Structure of Exam Failure: Person and Situation Attributions

	Stable Causes	Unstable Causes
Person	Low aptitude	Poor time management
	Hates studying	Sick on test day
Situation	Biased teacher	Bad luck: studied wrong material
	Difficult course	Lost class notes

Source: Adapted from Lunt, 1988.

encing attributions, especially in situations that emphasize a person's behavior (Zuckerman & Feldman, 1984).

Biases in Attributional Processes.   Attributions are cognitive processes. In a sense, they serve the twin purposes of providing an understanding of social events and of defending the self against threatening interpretations of the social environment. To understand this latter function, we must review some common biases in attribution processes.

Self-Serving Bias.   According to the attributional concept of the **self-serving bias**, people accept greater personal responsibility for positive outcomes than for negative ones. This attributional bias occurs in many areas of life, including sports. Following an important win, for instance, individual members of sports teams frequently attribute the victory to the brilliance of their own personal play during decisive moments of the contest. After a loss, however, they often blame defeat on events that are either external to them (mediocre play by other members) or beyond their personal control (poor officiating). To the extent that team members take more personal credit for success than for failure, these attributions are self-serving in nature.

Person attributions following success presumably help to maintain the positive feelings associated with self-esteem. Situation attributions following failure, on the other hand, serve to reduce the negative feelings associated with personal failure. A related explanation involves self-presentation. The self-serving bias leads to attributions designed to win approval from others through presenting oneself in the most positive light. However, when people believe that they may have their attributions challenged or evaluated by experts, the tendency for self-serving bias declines (Harvey & Weary, 1984).

Other data suggest that mental health is maintained in part by an overly positive self-image (Taylor & Brown, 1988). The self-serving bias filters incoming information and distorts it in a positive direction. Negative information is thus isolated and rendered harmless and nonthreatening to one's self-esteem.

self-serving bias tendency for people to take greater personal responsibility for positive outcomes than for negative ones

People tend to take more personal credit for success than for failure, the so-called self-serving bias in attribution processes. If this soccer team wins its match, the coach is more likely to cite personal contributions than if the team loses.

The self-serving bias may be particularly adaptive in situations with a potential for a lot of negative feedback. In the parent–child relationship, for example, mothers are more likely to attribute their children's desirable behavior to stable, personal characteristics, and their undesirable behavior to transitory, situational factors (Gretarsson & Gelfand, 1988). Causal attributions for success in the job market are likely to be perceived as personal and stable, whereas attributions for unemployment are likely to be seen as situational and unstable (Schaufeli, 1988).

Fundamental Attribution Error. The **fundamental attribution error** reflects the fact that people are more inclined to make person attributions than situation attributions when evaluating the actions of other people (Ross, 1977). For instance, when someone makes a critical remark about us, we are more likely to attribute the statement to the person's cruel and brutal character rather than to his or her transient mood or situational norms that may have called for a frank evaluation. In retrospect, the term *error* may be an improper description of this phenomenon. We cannot legitimately call the attribution an error unless there are clear ways of deciding on its accuracy, and in most cases that is not possible (Harvey & Weary, 1984).

The tendency to attribute behavior to internal, dispositional causes declines when there is a perception of little choice for behavior (Ajzen & Fishbein, 1983). For example, if a commanding officer orders a soldier to kill a prisoner, there may be little perceived choice for the soldier's behavior; in that case a situation attribution becomes more likely (although we may question the soldier's moral development). If it is the soldier's decision to harm a prisoner, however, it is perceived that the soldier had a choice of action, and person attributions become more likely; the soldier is judged to be cruel and inhuman.

We have briefly covered many different aspects of the complex cognitive processing involved in attribution, and Table 14–5 summarizes these aspects. Let us turn now to a discussion of some of the consequences of attribution.

Consequences of Attribution. People may alter their behavior based on the attributions they make about themselves and others. In a classic study of the consequences of attribution, Kelley (1950) presented college students

fundamental attribution error tendency for people to make person attributions rather than situation attributions when evaluating others

---

TABLE 14-5
Summary of Several Aspects of Attribution Processes

Types of Attribution

Person attribution. Places cause of behavior in a person's character.
Situation attribution. Places cause of behavior in a particular situation.

Factors Determining Type of Attribution

Distinctiveness. Response is specific to a particular situation.
Consistency. Response is the same in similar circumstances.
Consensus. Response is the same from one person to another.

Biases in Attributional Processes

Self-serving bias. People accept personal responsibility (person attributions) for their successes and blame failures on circumstances (situation attributions).
Fundamental attribution error. People tend to make person attributions about other people's behavior and fail to take the situation sufficiently into account.

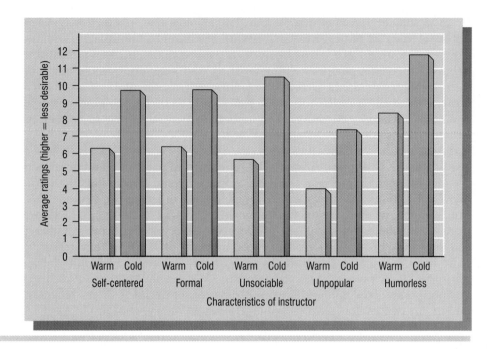

FIGURE 14-1
Students who were told that a visiting instructor was "rather cold" rated him more negatively after class than students who were told he was "rather warm." Their view of his behavior was biased by these labels, and they attributed much of his later behavior to this one characteristic. Those who were told the instructor was "rather cold" rated him as more self-centered, formal, unsociable, unpopular, and humorless. (Adapted from Kelley, 1950.)

with information about a visiting instructor. Embedded within the information presented to some of the students was the phrase that the instructor was "rather warm"; for other students, the phrase "rather cold" was inserted. There was no other difference in the information given to the students before the instructor appeared. The instructor actually behaved the same way for both groups of students. However, that single phrase altered the students' behavior in interacting with the instructor. The students who had been told the instructor was warm asked more questions during class and gave more positive impressions of him after class, as shown in Figure 14-1. Apparently, they attributed characteristics of his behavior to the warm or cold facet of his character and altered their judgments and behavior accordingly. Teachers may also alter their behavior on the basis of attributions they make about their students' abilities.

SPOTLIGHT ON RESEARCH
The Self-Fulfilling Prophecy

Many teachers assume that intelligence test scores (of the kind we discussed in Chapter 11) reveal information about stable, personal characteristics of their students. Such assumptions have an impact on the educational enterprise, because the characteristics implied by the scores are difficult to change. Teacher behavior, in turn, may affect the motivation of the students.

Should teachers have access to their students' IQ scores from standardized tests of intelligence? The arguments in favor include the following: Teachers can better provide for the educational needs of students in their classrooms if they know their academic potential; teachers could more effectively instruct children in ability groupings based on test scores; the more information teachers have about their students, the better they can instruct them.

But what of the social-psychological side of the issue? Perhaps this information biases the teacher's treatment of students, so that rather than living up to their potential, they do only what the teacher expects of them. This notion was tested in a field experiment in a public elementary school in California (Rosenthal & Jacobson, 1968).

In the spring semester, students in several grades were given a test that supposedly predicted whether they might "bloom" academically during the next school year. Teachers were told that the test, called the "Harvard Test of Inflected Acquisition," was a valid predictor of "blooming." At the start of the next academic year, researchers told the teachers that they "might find it of interest to know which of their children were about to bloom," and they were given lists of names of children in their classes who had supposedly been identified by the Harvard Test. In fact, the children were selected randomly.

At the end of the school year, children identified as potential bloomers showed greater gains on tested IQ and improved reading performance in comparison to other children. In addition, teachers rated them as more intellectually curious, happier, and less in need of social approval. These effects were especially strong for children in the lower grades.

Teachers' expectations for their students' performance may have a very strong effect on what children do in the classroom, as well as on the ways teachers evaluate student performance. This effect appears to be an example of a **self-fulfilling prophecy** at work. Teachers may have unwittingly spent more time with these special pupils, encouraged them more, and otherwise communicated their expectations for improved performance, which came to be reflected in the actual behavior of the children.

self-fulfilling prophecy tendency for people to elicit behavior from others that conforms to their own personal expectations

The reverse is also likely to be true. When teachers expect less, as they might if they encountered a relatively low intelligence test score, they probably get less. It is for that reason that many people prefer that teachers not have access to children's IQ scores.

Social cognition has a profound effect on human social behavior. We have presented information on just two aspects of social cognition—attitudes and attribution—in order to suggest some of the intricacies in the relationship between thinking and social behavior. The study of the effects of cognition on social behavior is crucial for the field of social psychology. Among other things, social cognition influences how people perceive and think about their behavior in groups, but group processes are generally studied as a separate phenomenon.

GROUP PROCESSES

Individuals are affected by the presence of other people, and sometimes they behave differently simply because other people are around. Much of our social life takes place in the presence of other people, either in groups of people we know or around collections of strangers.

A **group** consists of two or more people who interact with one another in such a way that each person influences and is influenced by the other(s). The individuals who make up the group must be aware of each other in a way that implies some continuity to the relationship, even if brief. Thus, not all collections of people are referred to as groups; for example, shoppers near the checkout lane in a grocery store are not a group because there is no continuity to the relationship and there is little dynamic interaction among them. However, the exact criteria for calling a collection of people a group are fuzzy: "Some, but not all, multiperson aggregates are groups; but some

group two or more individuals who interact in such a manner that each person influences the other(s) and is influenced in return

(Left) A Little League baseball team is an example of a group, a collection of people who dynamically interact with each other and have some continuity. *(Right)* Collections of people without these characteristics, such as people who are riding on a "Tilt-A-Whirl," are not groups.

norms rules that apply to every member of a group

roles norms that apply to specific members of a group who occupy special positions within it

reference groups groups to which people relate and/or want to belong

of them are 'groupier' than others; and all of them are 'groupier' at some times than at other times" (McGrath & Kravitz, 1982).

A few examples may be useful. Little League baseball teams, members of a church's youth fellowship, members of a rock band, and pairs of police officers who patrol together all represent groups—people involved in a dynamic, reciprocal interaction with each other over time. People riding together in an elevator or camping in the same national park campground or working in the library at the same time do not constitute groups. If some emergency were to arise, however, any of these collections of people might begin an interaction that would create a short-term group with a fixed purpose.

Behavior within specific groups is often enforced through sanctions for misbehavior and rewards for appropriate behavior. **Norms**, defined as rules that apply to all group members, often develop within such groups. For example, it is a norm within most households that children, up to a certain age, must obey the rules and expectations established by their parents. **Roles**, defined as norms that apply to specific persons who occupy different positions in the group, frequently emerge once global norms have been developed. For instance, different children within a given family often carry out specialized roles (e.g., taking out the trash, cleaning the bathroom) to ensure the smooth functioning of the family unit. Social psychologists have observed some of these aspects of social life and have attempted through research to chart some of the principles governing group behavior.

Effects of the Presence of Others on Individual Behavior

We clearly alter our behavior when we are aware that we are around other people. We try not to look foolish; we try to impress other people; we behave in socially acceptable ways. Sometimes when we are alone, we act as if we had dropped our guard. Indeed, there may even be a fading of social norms when we are around other people whom we know very well. On the other hand, we sometimes anticipate how we would behave if we were to become a member of some elite group, even though we may not know how people in the group behave. In this case we may speak of **reference groups**, those groups to which people relate themselves or to which they aspire to relate themselves psychologically (Sherif, 1953).

Social Facilitation. The effect of others' presence was the focus of one of the first deliberate experiments in social psychology. In this experiment,

The presence of observers increases performance of some well-learned behaviors such as running.

Triplett (1898) examined the effects of competition on behavior. Triplett had children wind a fishing reel several times, either alone or competing in pairs, and found that children's performance improved in competition. Triplett's experiment is interesting because it shows that a social context, such as competition with another person, may alter behavior.

Triplett's experiment involved only two individuals at a time, and they were competing with each other. This is a very simple social context, but there are other contexts in which people might influence each other's behavior. In one variation, Allport (1920) had individuals work on a series of tasks either alone in a little room or in a group around a large table. He found that working in the group improved performance on some tasks and hindered performance on others. He labeled the improvement in performance that took place while working in a group **social facilitation**.

Why would the presence of other people improve a person's performance on some tasks and hinder performance on others? One suggestion is that the presence of other people increases one's level of motivation. Increased motivation, in turn, improves performance if the response is well learned; if not, performance may be hindered by the increased motivation (Zajonc, 1965). This notion has been tested in several experiments. One measure of motivation is physiological arousal. When subjects were asked to perform a complex motor task, either alone or with an audience of 10 people, they showed more physiological arousal, as shown by sweaty palms, when there was an audience.

It seems likely that people do better in the presence of others because they want to look good in their eyes. However, if a response is not well learned, the presence of others may actually hinder performance. Zajonc (1965), reviewing studies with such disparate species as humans, albino rats, chickens, ants, and cockroaches, has found data to support two generalizations: (1) the presence of others improves the performance of well-learned behaviors, but (2) it inhibits the learning and performance of new responses.

Laboratory studies of social behavior, such as those just described, have been supplemented with **field studies** (studies done in real-life settings). In one field study, runners were observed on a footpath without their knowing it. They were unobtrusively filmed and randomly allocated to groups, so that

social facilitation tendency for individuals to perform better in the presence of other people

field studies studies conducted in everyday, real-world settings

they were either running with no one else in sight; running, for part of the course, with a young woman in sight whose back was turned to the runner; or running with the young woman facing the runner. The woman was placed in such a way that she was not visible to the runner for the first half of the course, allowing the measurement of running speed before and after her presence was known. Runners increased their speed when the woman was facing them more often than they did when she had her back to them or when they were running alone (Worringham & Messick, 1983). It was the specific awareness of being observed that facilitated performance.

Deindividuation.　The effect of the group on individual behavior may also have a sinister side. The presence of others can weaken normal restraints on behavior and lead to socially prohibited acts. In extreme cases, an individual in a group may become so caught up that he or she loses a sense of individual responsibility, and a kind of mob psychology takes over. This loss of self-restraint is referred to as **deindividuation**.

deindividuation loss of self-restraint that occurs under conditions of arousal, novelty, and anonymity

The presence of others allows for more anonymity and diffusion of responsibility. In turn, these conditions may reduce self-awareness, weaken restraints, and reduce concern over social evaluation (Zimbardo, 1969). The stage is then set for antisocial behavior, as shown in Figure 14–2.

Anonymity is often fostered by wearing uniforms, which make one individual member of a group look much like any other. Uniforms also lead to a spirit of group cohesion and belongingness. The violence of groups like the Ku Klux Klan may be facilitated by uniforms that hide individual identity and thus leave the individual unaccountable for his or her behavior.

Members of groups are obviously not always violent. Members of the Hare Krishna cult, the Peace Corps, and the medical staffs of metropolitan hospitals are just a few examples of peaceful groups. Even members of these groups, however, may experience deindividuation and subordinate their own personal values and feelings to identification with the group. Deindividuation is most likely to occur when individuals find themselves in a new unstructured situation; feel anonymous or "hidden" in a crowd; experience sensory overload; focus on the present as opposed to the past or future; or become physically involved in what they are doing (Zimbardo, 1970).

Conformity.　Groups exert a strong influence on their members to go along with the crowd. The tendency to match one's behavior to that of others is called **conformity**. People conform by adopting the social norms or customs of the larger group. Changing fashions in dress and hair style illustrate conformity. It would have been extremely unusual in the 1950s, for example, for a young man to wear an earring, but it is commonplace today. Most people feel pressure to go along with the fashion trend that is operative at the time for their group.

conformity tendency for people to match their behavior to that of other members of a group

Solomon Asch conducted a classic series of studies of conformity that have been replicated many times. Asch (1956) studied the effects of group pressure on perceptual judgments. His technique required the use of confederates, all of whom stated an obviously incorrect judgment before the turn of the individual whose behavior was being investigated. About three fourths of the college students who participated in Asch's study went along with the incorrect group judgment. The mean number of errors with groups of different sizes is illustrated in Figure 14–3 (p. 566), along with one of the stimulus sets.

Variations of the Asch experiment suggest that the social impact of the group varies as a function of its size, the degree of unanimity in the group, and the degree to which one's nonconforming behavior can be hidden from scrutiny. People evaluate their opinions and behavior against the standards

FIGURE 14–2
Steps leading to antisocial behavior following deindividuation. Deindividuation results from the sense of anonymity and diffusion of responsibility that may come about when a group takes precedence over the individual. It may lead to a reduction in self-awareness, weakened restraints, and a reduction in concern over self-evaluation. Antisocial behavior may follow.

Groups exert strong influences toward conformity, including matters of dress. Groups as diverse as the KKK or inner-city high school cliques show conformity in dress.

of a reference group. If they find major differences, they feel pressure to conform—or to change reference groups.

Since Asch's work, attention has shifted to the flip side of conformity: Under what circumstances are people who hold minority opinions in a group able to resist conforming to, and occasionally even to change the beliefs of, people who hold majority opinions? Research on *minority influence* was launched by Serge Moscovici, who sought to understand how a small band of disenchanted French college students was able to bring about some major social and political reforms in France following demonstrations

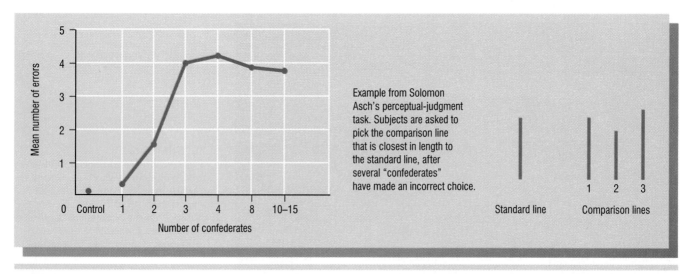

Example from Solomon Asch's perceptual-judgment task. Subjects are asked to pick the comparison line that is closest in length to the standard line, after several "confederates" have made an incorrect choice.

FIGURE 14–3
People often conform to a group's opinion even though it reflects obviously incorrect perceptual judgments such as those pictured in this figure. When the group reaches a size of about three other people, the number of errors peaks and remains at about the same level with increasing group sizes. (Adapted from Asch, 1956.)

in May of 1968. Four major insights have come from research on minority influence (Nemeth, 1992). First, minorities can successfully influence majorities, and their degree of influence depends on the particular way in which they argue their position. If they adopt a strong and consistent stance, they are much more likely to change the opinion of the majority (Moscovici, Lage, & Naffrechoux, 1969; Mungy, 1982). Second, majorities often experience doubts about the legitimacy of their opinions, particularly when they encounter confident and persistent opposition (Kiesler & Pallack, 1975). Third, minorities often exert influence on majorities privately and behind the scenes rather than publicly (Nemeth & Wachtler, 1974). Finally, minorities do not necessarily have to be liked in order to be persuasive (Nemeth, Wachtler, & Endicott, 1977).

Obedience.   Whereas conformity results from the pressure exerted by a reference group, **obedience** refers to the tendency for people to comply with orders, real or implied, given by someone who is supposedly in a position of authority. Some of the darkest moments in human history can be linked with the pressure to comply with orders. In Nazi Germany, the horror of the Holocaust can hardly be understood because of its scope. Yet the officers and soldiers who supervised the murder of millions of people said that they were following orders.

obedience tendency for people to comply with orders, either real or imagined, from an authority figure

The U.S. involvement in Vietnam provides another example. In March 1969, hundreds of civilians in the village of My Lai, South Vietnam, were killed by American soldiers. The first impulse most people have is to try to make some sense out of this kind of human behavior. One tendency is to attribute the behavior to something wrong with the individuals involved: "They must have been crazy or sick to massacre innocent civilians." But the soldiers themselves saw the situation differently; they were acting in an abnormal environment, and they maintained that most people would have behaved the same way. The soldiers perceived themselves as victims of an intolerable situation, under orders to search for and destroy an enemy who was so elusive that they could not know who or where that enemy might be. (Recall our earlier discussion of person and situation attributions.)

Stanley Milgram (1974), in a series of controversial studies, examined in a laboratory setting some conditions under which normal people can be induced to inflict harm on other people. Milgram placed advertisements in a newspaper and sent out letters to persons listed in the telephone directory requesting participants for "a scientific study of memory and learning." Upon arriving at the laboratory, a participant met a researcher, another supposed participant (who was actually a confederate of Milgram), and saw the supposed research setup. A rigged drawing was held to determine who would play the roles of "learner" and "teacher" in the experiment; in fact, the actual participant was always the "teacher." The "learner" was then strapped into a chair that would supposedly deliver an electric shock to the learner's arm, while the subject of the experiment watched. No shocks, however, were ever actually delivered.

Would normal people who had answered ads to benefit the scientific study of learning deliver what were seemingly lethal—or at the very least highly dangerous—shocks to an innocent victim even though the latter demanded to be let out of the experiment? When Milgram asked people, including psychiatrists, college students, and middle-class adults, to predict how many people could be induced to proceed all the way through the 30 positions on the shock generator, they predicted that only a pathological fringe—perhaps 1 or 2%—would do so.

In fact, more than 60% of the men who participated in the study were fully obedient, even when the learner–victim yelled out in pain and protest.

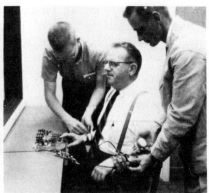

(*Left*) The shock generator used in Milgram's studies had 30 toggle switches, going from 15 volts (labeled "slight shock") to 450 volts (labeled "danger: severe shock XXX"). (*Right*) The learner being strapped into a chair in the presence of the subject.

Figure 14–4 presents the percentages of obedience for subjects in several variations of the study. Women as teachers were no more, or less, obedient than men. When the victim was placed closer to the subject so as to be visible, the percentage of obedience fell somewhat, to 40%. Almost one third of the subjects (30%) were fully obedient even when they physically had to force the victim's hand onto a shock plate.

Several important factors contribute to obedience in this, and similar, situations. In the first phase of the study, participants see themselves transformed into agents of the scientific authority figure. They acknowledge that the authority figure knows more about what is going on than they do, they accept prepayment for their participation, and they invest their own time and trouble to come to the laboratory. These factors contribute to a shift in perspective, in which the participants see themselves as instruments for carrying out the wishes of a higher-status person. They feel that the responsibility for what happens rests with the experimenter, not with themselves.

The comments of some of the participants in Milgram's study illustrate the shift in personal responsibility that takes place. After the learner–victim screamed, and then became quiet, not even answering the questions, one participant said to the experimenter, "Something's happened to that man in there. You better check in on him, sir. He won't answer or nothing." When the experimenter told the participant to continue, the participant asked, "You accept all responsibility?" The experimenter answered, "The responsibility is mine. Correct. Please go on." And the subject continued all the way

FIGURE 14–4
Obedience in Milgram's study was defined as willingness to administer the full 450 volts to the learner. Just over 60% of men and women subjects in the study were fully obedient. About 40% were obedient when the learner was visible, and almost one third were obedient even when the learner's hand had to be forced onto a shock plate. (From Milgram, 1974.)

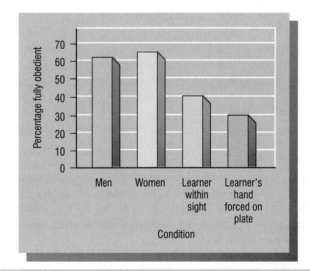

Strong leaders, both good and bad, are capable of commanding a great deal of obedience. The Ayatollah Khomeini was such a leader. The scene at his funeral was an emotional outpouring that sometimes degenerated into deindividuated violence.

through the shock generator, to 450 volts, without getting any other answer from the learner. Later the participant said, "What if he's dead in there? I mean, he told me he can't stand the shock, sir. I don't mean to be rude, but I think you should look in on him" (Milgram, 1974).

The binding factors in this situation are very strong. The experimenter, supposedly an authority on what is going on, keeps telling the subjects that "the experiment requires that you continue." To refuse to go on requires that a subject reject the experimenter's competence and authority. Furthermore, once involved in the situation, one has an investment in it. Terminating the session is not only interpersonally awkward, it is also an admission that the participant's behavior up to that point has been wrong.

The Milgram studies raise disturbing questions about the extent to which ordinary individuals may be induced by a malevolent authority, such as an Adolph Hitler, to behave in reprehensible ways. The psychological forces that allow social interaction to proceed smoothly in the vast majority of situations may be the same forces that maintain negative social behavior as well. Milgram's studies suggest that the heinous events of other places and other times cannot be dismissed so easily as something "that could never happen here."

Prosocial Behavior. The Milgram studies suggest some of the factors that can induce people to harm others, but what about factors that promote helping? **Prosocial behavior** is behavior that benefits other people. The form of help can be minimal and involve little risk to the helper, such as letting someone who is in a big hurry cut in front in a bank line, or it can be a major effort involving risk, such as trying to save someone from drowning in a swift river current. Although it would be comforting to think that some people have altruistic personalities—dispositions to be compassionate and helpful to others in distress—there is little evidence that that is the case (Batson et al., 1986). However, there may be particular circumstances that increase the likelihood of behaving altruistically.

Social psychologists are interested in the circumstances under which people come to the aid of others. One area of study—**bystander intervention**—focuses on the factors responsible for an individual's helping others in distress. Does the presence of others affect the likelihood of bystander intervention?

prosocial behavior behavior that benefits other people

bystander intervention research that focuses on when and under what conditions individuals help others in need of assistance

One evening in 1964, a woman named Kitty Genovese was stabbed to death on a darkened street in Queens, New York. When her attacker first stabbed her, Ms. Genovese began screaming loudly and awakened some people in nearby apartments. They turned on their lights and peered out their windows, witnessing part of the attack. Although the lights initially scared off the assailant, no one came out to help, and no one called the police. The killer returned and stabbed the woman again. A total of 38 people had looked out on the scene, but no one had intervened. Ms. Genovese died on the street.

The event touched off a flood of research on the conditions leading up to helping others in a crisis. Since that attack, approximately a thousand articles or books on bystander intervention have been written, and the general conclusion is that the 38 people who watched in Queens on that evening behaved as most people do in similar circumstances. People are reluctant to become involved in someone else's crisis.

The Kitty Genovese murder led a number of researchers to investigate in laboratory settings the factors involved in helping another person in distress. In one of the studies, male students thought they were participating in market research (Latané & Darley, 1970). They filled out questionnaires in one of the following four conditions: alone, with another participant, with a friend, or with a male confederate of the experimenter who remained unresponsive throughout a concocted emergency. The emergency consisted of having the young woman who had given the instructions on market research go next door, climb on a chair, fall off, and scream. She cried out for help, saying that she could not move. A majority of the participants who were working alone came to the woman's rescue (although not all of them did). However, when more than one person was present, the amount of helping was reduced substantially, as Figure 14–5 shows. Only 7% of the participants who were with a passive confederate helped the woman.

One explanation for these striking results is diffusion of responsibility. It appears that one person witnessing an emergency feels a great deal of responsibility to help. When a group of people witness an emergency, it is as if the responsibility becomes diffused throughout the group, so that any individual member feels a decreased responsibility to help. According to the principle of **diffusion of responsibility**, the larger the number of witnesses

diffusion of responsibility situation in which individuals in a group assume less personal responsibility for helping a victim as the group becomes larger

FIGURE 14–5
In a laboratory study of bystander intervention, probability of helping was greatest when a lone individual or two friends together witnessed an emergency. Helping was less likely when two strangers witnessed the emergency, and least likely when the emergency occurred in the company of an unresponsive confederate of the experimenter.

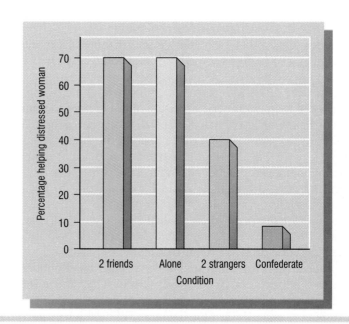

(or bystanders), the less likely it is that any one of them will intervene. The 38 witnesses to Kitty Genovese's murder knew there were other observers, and each one of them chose not to become involved, perhaps because they felt someone else should take the responsibility.

Bystanders often refuse to become involved because of a perception of danger to themselves or because they think others will hold them responsible for what happens to the person in distress. One experiment showed that people adopting the perspective of a helper following an accident expected to be held accountable by onlookers, an expectation that increased in proportion to the number of bystanders present. Individuals adopting the perspective of onlookers did indeed hold the helper responsible, a tendency that increased as the number of onlookers increased (Cacioppo, Petty, & Losch, 1986).

Another possible explanation for nonintervention may be found in the concept of **pluralistic ignorance**, a feeling that one should not intervene if other people are not doing so. People take their cues on how to behave from watching other people. The nonintervention of others may indicate to a person that the situation is not one that calls for action. The strikingly low level of helping observed among individuals who were placed with a nonresponsive confederate of the experimenter could be explained by pluralistic ignorance. These participants may have checked to see what their partner was doing and how he or she was reacting; discovering no response, they too remained unresponsive.

These accounts might lead one to conclude that the human predicament is a sorry one, indeed. However, there are some bright spots to human social behavior. In fact, there are some conditions in which the likelihood of prosocial behavior is high. There are also notable examples of individual heroism, in which people have helped others under conditions of great peril. During World War II a number of individuals, Jews and non-Jews alike, risked their own lives to help save others from the mass slaughter by the Nazis. Altruism is also illustrated by modern-day medical heroes and heroines who donate one of their healthy kidneys, thus facing major surgery and an increased lifetime risk to themselves for needing dialysis. Bone marrow donors also face painful medical procedures in order to help others.

Do people behave in a prosocial manner mainly because of selfless, *altruistic* motives, or for more self-centered, *egoistic* reasons? One model of egoism and altruism attempts to specify the situations in which people will behave on each of these motives (Batson, 1987). If people observe someone in distress and experience strong personal distress themselves, they are more likely to help the other person in order to reduce their own distress (egoistic motive). On the other hand, if people observe someone in need and immediately feel strong empathy for them, projecting how they would feel in similar circumstances, they will focus on reducing the other's distress purely to relieve the other's suffering (altruistic motive). Recent findings tend to support this egoism/altruism model, although some researchers still question whether people ever engage in truly altruistic acts (Schaller & Cialdini, 1988).

The previous sections have addressed the effects of other people on individual behavior. Social psychology is also concerned with the interactions among different groups of people. One focus of research on intergroup relations has been prejudice. Social psychologists are especially interested in ways to reduce prejudice. We consider some of these issues in the next section.

pluralistic ignorance tendency not to intervene in a situation based on the fact that others are not intervening

Intergroup Relations

Sometimes two or more groups come into contact with each other, creating the potential for either conflict or cooperation. A special form of group interaction that has captured the attention of sociologists, laypeople, and

prejudice unjustified negative attitudes that one person holds about another based exclusively on the person's membership in a social group

discrimination unjustified negative behavior directed toward others based solely on their membership in a social group

stereotypes mental images in which specific mental, physical, and behavioral traits are uncritically attributed to others based solely on their membership in a social group

psychologists alike is the conflict that can occur between racial and ethnic groups. The history of the United States resounds with ethnic hostility; it is a sad fact of our heritage. Ethnic hostility is, in fact, a worldwide problem, with numerous examples: Croats versus Serbs in Bosnia, Palestinians versus Jews in Israel, Muslims versus Hindus in India. What have social psychologists contributed to the understanding of prejudice and intergroup hostility?

Prejudice. **Prejudice** is defined as unjustified negative attitudes that one person has about another based solely on the person's membership in a social group, such as a religious or ethnic minority. Prejudice is witnessed in behavior in the form of **discrimination**, and it tends to be perpetuated in part by **stereotypes**—mental images in which specific psychological, physical, and behavioral traits are attributed uncritically to members of a social group.

At different periods in our history, there has been considerable agreement about the assignment of stereotypic traits to various ethnic, national, religious, and gender groups. In a study undertaken over 60 years ago, college students assigned fairly consistent stereotypical traits to 10 national groups (Katz & Braly, 1933). More than half of the students agreed, for example, that Germans were scientifically minded and industrious, Italians were artistic, and the English were good sports. Similar agreement on stereotypical characteristics of the two sexes has been demonstrated (Rosenkrantz et al., 1968). However, consistent trait assignment does not mean that stereotypes are accurate. Rather, people somehow develop the same mental pictures based on oversimplified opinions and, strangely enough, seem to have little awareness that these stereotypes influence their behavior (Hepburn & Locksley, 1983).

Stereotypes are a part of the cognitive apparatus. When people encounter someone for the first time, they tend to attribute characteristics and personality traits to that individual on the basis of very limited information. One piece of information is membership in a social category—Methodist, for example, or black, or woman—and that information is used to make predictions about the person's behavior. Recall the discussion that opened this chapter, the incident involving the beating of motorist Rodney King by Los Angeles police officers. One speculation about the beating was that the officers responded to King's race more than to his actual behavior. Considerable disagreement surfaced at the subsequent trials of the officers about whether this explanation was accurate, but it is clear that race leads people to assume things about other people that may not be accurate and that may be quite unfair.

The Development of Racial Prejudice. Children appear to be sensitive to racial differences at an early age, perhaps as young as 4 or 5. The values, beliefs, and stereotypes that help to nourish prejudice are learned in the home and through other major agents of socialization. In some cultural contexts, traits assigned to minority groups by members of the majority group may be adopted by the minorities themselves, creating a heightened problem of prejudice. Black children in the 1940s, for example, said that they looked more like a black doll than a white doll, but they preferred to play with the white doll and thought it was "better" (Clark & Clark, 1947). This research was cited in the Supreme Court's historic 1954 decision, *Brown v. Board of Education of Topeka*, which declared segregated schools unconstitutional. In the 1980s, following 3 decades in which struggles for civil rights by minority groups achieved a measure of success, these patterns of preference were not seen. Black children were more likely to prefer the black doll (Tajfel, 1982).

School integration can successfully reduce prejudice when integration is endorsed by those in authority, competition across racial lines is minimized, status is equivalent, and contact permits learning about others as individuals.

Reducing Prejudice and Discrimination.   Following the landmark Supreme Court decision of 1954 eliminating segregated public schools, many people hoped that increased contact between races would reduce prejudice and discrimination. In social psychology the term **contact theory** is used to express this view (Pettigrew, 1969). As is evident from the history of racial tension in the United States, contact alone has not always been sufficient to eliminate tension, and indeed it sometimes increases it. Several social scientists prepared a statement for the Supreme Court outlining some necessary conditions for achieving real integration. These conditions include (1) firm endorsement of integration by those in authority, (2) absence of competition among members of the different racial groups, (3) equivalence of status of the different groups, and (4) interracial contacts that would permit learning about each other as individuals (Gerard, 1983). Both laboratory and field studies have provided evidence for the contact hypothesis when these conditions are met (Cook, 1985). Although it is possible to achieve these conditions, merely putting racial groups with a history of antagonism together will not assure a reduction in prejudice.

contact theory theory that proposes that equal-status contact between antagonistic groups should lower tension and breed greater harmony

If only a few minority group members enter a previously all-white school system, they may be seen as unrepresentative of their group as a whole and hence may be ineffective in reducing stereotypes despite evidence that they do not match the stereotypes (Weber & Crocker, 1983). Contact alone will not erase intergroup conflict as long as the social system maintains status and power differences among the racial groups (Tajfel, 1982).

In the 1950s, a series of field studies demonstrated the power of common goals in reducing prejudice. These studies of intergroup conflict were conducted by social psychologist Muzafer Sherif and his colleagues (Sherif, 1958/1965). The participants in the studies were boys in a camp setting, mostly 11 or 12 years old. Sherif first created distinct groups from previously unacquainted boys by giving each group a task that could be solved only at the expense of another group. Sherif (1958/1965) described what happened:

> Members of each group developed hostile attitudes and highly unfavorable stereotypes toward the other group and its members. In fact, attitudes of social distance between the groups became so definite that they wanted to have nothing further to do with each other. . . . Conflict was manifested in

derogatory name-calling and invectives, flare-ups of physical conflict, and raids on each other's cabins and territory.

In order to reduce intergroup conflict, Sherif next introduced **superordinate goals**, tasks that were important to both groups but that could only be solved if they cooperated. Among these superordinate tasks were solving a water shortage problem that affected the whole camp, and getting the food delivery truck in running shape. After the superordinate goals were introduced, intergroup conflict and prejudice declined dramatically. In a sense, superordinate goals serve to erase the distinctions between the groups, creating one large, cooperating group (Tajfel, 1982).

Since Sherif's famous study, contact theory has been successfully applied to several social problems. One study, for example, identified highly prejudiced white women and hired half of them to work closely with an African American for 2 hours a day over a 3-week period on an important project. Several months later, these women's attitudes toward African Americans were reassessed in a different context. Forty percent of the women who took part in the project showed a significant reduction in prejudice, whereas only 12% of the women who did not participate were less prejudiced. The conclusion: Fairly intimate, equal-status contact geared toward achieving a common, superordinate goal noticeably reduces prejudice.

These principles also have been used in elementary schools. Elliott Aronson and his colleagues (1978) have developed a cooperative learning method known as the **jigsaw classroom**. School children are placed in small groups that are mixed racially and academically. Each group divides the material to be learned among its members, much like a jigsaw puzzle. Each student is responsible for learning one piece of the puzzle, after which he or she must teach it to other group members. Regardless of race, aptitude, or skill, everyone must master his or her piece of the learning puzzle in order to complete the overall task of the group. Children in jigsaw classrooms, compared to those in regular classrooms, tend to be less prejudiced, like each other more, like school more, and have higher self-esteem.

Ethnocentrism.   The tendency to evaluate one's own groups, especially racial, ethnic, or national groups, as superior is referred to as **ethnocentrism**. (Special cases of ethnocentrism are racism and sexism.) Experimental studies of intergroup competition illustrate the tendency to rate one's own group higher. In one study, college students listened to taped discussions on the issue of whether to retain standardized college admissions tests. Some were told they were listening to a group they would later join, others that they were hearing a competing group. Students who thought they heard their own group changed their attitude toward the position advocated on the tape (Mackie & Cooper, 1984).

Cognitive processes related to ethnocentrism accentuate the differences between different groups and minimize differences within groups (Tajfel, 1982). Group members are assumed to hold more similar attitudes than they actually do, a phenomenon referred to as **out-group homogeneity**. For example, when men are asked what most women are like, they often assume erroneously that women—as a group—have more similar attitudes and behave in a more uniform fashion than men. The reverse also is true: When evaluating men, women fall prey to the perception that men tend to be more alike in attitudes and behaviors than women (Rothbart, 1993). Out-group homogeneity is particularly strong when there is a likelihood of competition between groups (Judd & Park, 1988). Ethnocentrism persists, however, even when cooperation is anticipated.

Most attempts to reduce ethnocentrism have focused on the groups themselves. Face-to-face contact between the groups, introduction of cooperative tasks and superordinate goals, and persuasive campaigns to change attitudes are all techniques that have been used. There is also a kind of psychological algebra of group interaction. For example, out-groups differ on how far away they are from the in-group in terms of attitudes, behaviors, and characteristics. If a new out-group can be introduced that is more extreme, it may bring two competing groups closer together (Wilder & Thompson, 1988). In the world of politics, this polarization effect is illustrated by Saddam Hussein's Iraq. There were many rival factions within Iraq that threatened to undermine Saddam Hussein's authority. But the Persian Gulf War united several internal Iraqi factions against the United States as an external enemy and solidified Saddam Hussein's rule.

Group Task Performance

Groups can serve a variety of functions. They can help individuals establish and perpetuate their social identity; they can fulfill people's social and emotional needs; and they can allow individuals to complete tasks and accomplish goals that would be difficult to achieve without assistance from others. Given the paramount importance of this latter function in modern society, most research on groups has focused on how decisions are made in groups and how group members approach different kinds of tasks.

Jury Studies.   Much of the work on task performance has concentrated on decision making by juries. Most jury studies are actually of mock juries, composed either of people drawn from the jury rolls or of college students. In early studies they listened to tapes of real trials and then deliberated (Strodtbeck, James, & Hawkins, 1958). Those studies indicated that people who have high status, such as an impressive occupation, tend to have a great effect on the group's deliberations. Many of these studies indicate that juries actually operate on a rule of "very strong majority" rather than "unanimity." Thus, if eight or so jurors achieve consensus, the rest are likely to go along (McGrath & Kravitz, 1982).

The actual size of juries is a factor that might influence the process of decision making. Smaller juries appear to have less adequate deliberations and are therefore more likely to convict an innocent person (Monahan & Loftus, 1982). This information is important, given that many states have recently proposed to reduce the size of juries to save tax dollars. According to this research, such action could have unfortunate effects on the judicial system.

Jurors have difficult decisions to make on the basis of testimony that is often conflicting. One argument maintains that jurors are too willing to believe the testimony of eyewitnesses. Witnesses are often recruited by one side or the other in an adversarial process. Their role—either for the defense or for the prosecution—may actually alter their testimony. For example, college students were shown a 5-min slide and audio presentation of an argument and subsequent fight in a bar. Then they were assigned as witnesses, either for one of the two participants or for neither (Vidmar & Laird, 1983). Student judges rated the testimony of witnesses for each participant as more favorable to their party compared to the testimony provided by neutral witnesses.

Mock jury deliberations also indicate a leniency bias, where proacquittal factions have a stronger influence than proconviction factions of equal size. In one study, 60 mock juries were manipulated with respect to predeliberation opinions. Each jury had two members for conviction and two for acquittal, with the remaining eight members undecided. The decisions following deliberation were uneven, with proacquittal forces stronger than proconviction, as shown in Figure 14–6 (MacCoun & Kerr, 1988).

FIGURE 14-6

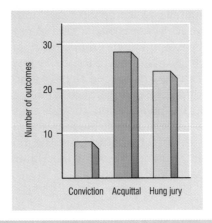

FIGURE 14-6
Outcomes of deliberation of 60 mock juries show proacquittal forces stronger than proconviction forces. There was also a large number of "hung" juries, which were unable to agree on a verdict after deliberation. Studies of mock juries indicate that people who have high status, such as those with prestigious occupations, tend to have a disproportionate effect on the group's deliberations.

group polarization tendency for decisions made by groups to be more extreme than those made by individuals

Polarization.   When groups make a decision following a discussion, the group decision is often more extreme than the average of the positions of all of the members of the group before the discussion. This effect is referred to as **group polarization**, because the decision is more extreme, or polarized. Group polarization is true almost by definition for juries that are required to reach consensus on the guilt or innocence of a defendant. Unless all the jurors agree at the outset, they are bound to reach a more extreme decision than the average of the opinions they held before they deliberated.

However, group polarization occurs in a wide variety of tasks, from gambling to allocating rewards, and over a wide range of issues and group sizes (Gray & Stafford, 1988; McGrath & Kravitz, 1982). In most of these situations, too, it appears that group discussion leads individual members to shift toward a more extreme version of the position they favored in the beginning.

Why does group polarization occur? Three possible reasons have been suggested (Myers, 1978). First, individual members of groups may feel less personal responsibility for group decisions, and this diffusion of responsibility may produce more extreme group positions. Second, individuals often prefer to adopt somewhat extreme positions in groups in order to appear unique and progressive. During discussions, group members may compare one another's extreme positions, and then they may slowly alter their own personal opinions in a more extreme direction. As a result, the group opinion becomes more extreme. Third, individuals typically shift their personal opinions toward the side of an issue that has the strongest arguments. More extreme and avant-garde positions often may generate stronger and more convincing arguments.

Because people spend a large part of their lives in groups, it is important to recognize the effects of group processes, both on individual members of the group and in terms of intergroup action. Much of the material in this chapter thus far has painted a rather negative picture of human beings as social animals. But there are more positive sides to human social interaction, such as friendship and romantic attraction.

FRIENDSHIP AND ROMANTIC ATTRACTION

Everyone operates within a social network in which some people become closer friends than others. A particularly interesting social problem is posed for beginning college students or business executives who must relocate, for they generally do not have a set of friends in their new environmental context. They must build relationships from among people in their social network. In addition, new romantic relationships may also need to be begun in an unfamiliar environment with unfamiliar norms. How do people go about building friendships? How do they become involved in romantic relationships? How do people handle the lack of friendships and the resulting loneliness? These are some of the issues we focus on in this section.

The Acquaintance Process

People are generally likely to become friends with others who have similar characteristics, who reside in close proximity, and who return their liking (Berscheid, 1985). These three factors serve as the major reasons most relationships initially develop.

Similarity, Proximity, and Reciprocal Liking. Several studies have demonstrated that *similarity* is important in the formation of friendships. In laboratory studies, people fill out questionnaires that assess their attitudes on a variety of topics. Some time later, they are given information about other people's attitudes on the same topics, and they indicate how well they think they would like these people (Byrne & Nelson, 1965). In one such study (Gonzales et al., 1983), college students were randomly assigned to one of three conditions of attitude similarity: 0%, 50%, or 100%. They were given the responses of strangers on an attitude survey that matched their own responses by these amounts. Then they were asked about their personal feelings about the stranger. The results are shown in Figure 14–7. They indicate that there is a strong relationship between being attracted to others and a similarity of attitudes. Furthermore, the students' estimates of how much the stranger would like them parallel their own levels of attraction.

A second feature of major importance in forming friendships is *proximity*, or physical closeness of people in the social network. Studies of friendship formation in housing facilities, for example, suggest that people who interact more frequently are more likely to develop friendships. College roommates are particularly likely to become close friends (Newcomb, 1966).

A third factor of considerable importance in the development of friendships is *reciprocal liking*, or the degree to which two people sense strong mutual attraction to one another. During the very early stages of the development of a relationship, one person's liking for another strongly depends on the perception that the person is liked equally in return (Kenny & Nasby, 1980).

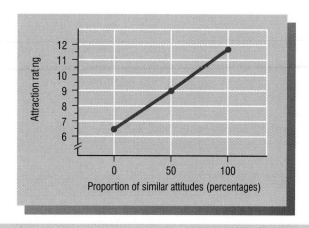

FIGURE 14–7
Attitude similarity plays an important role in attraction. When students were led to believe that they had very similar attitudes to those of a stranger, they were more attracted to the stranger than when attitudes were dissimilar. (From Gonzales et al., 1983.)

Self-Disclosure and Liking.   As people come to like each other more, they tell each other more intimate details about themselves. As friendships and relationships progress, there is more reciprocal self-disclosure (McGrath & Kravitz, 1982). In addition, there is evidence that people like others who seem to have disclosed more about themselves (Burger, 1981). Even children tend to reveal more about themselves when others have done the same with them (Cohn & Strassberg, 1983). Women appear to be somewhat more likely to reveal intimate details about themselves than men (Grigsby & Weatherley, 1983), especially early in the development of a relationship.

A high level of intimacy in self-disclosure in a relationship generally takes some time. If a stranger approaches you in a shoe store and declares, "My father died of syphilis, and now I have it too!" you are unlikely to make a revealing disclosure in return. Excessive intimacy in inappropriate situations arouses anxiety, which may result in a desire to terminate all social interaction (Hansen & Schuldt, 1982).

Romantic Attraction

Elizabeth Barrett Browning began one of her best-known poems with the line, "How do I love thee? Let me count the ways." Browning might be surprised to learn that social psychologists have asked similar questions about love and that they too have tried to count the ways. One of the most influential attempts to enumerate the kinds of love is that of Sheila Lee (1977), who proposed that there are six types of love (listed and described in Table 14–6).

Several researchers have attempted to establish the psychological reality of Lee's six types of love. One approach is to design questionnaires that address the dimensions of love, using the technique of factor analysis to see if the responses fall into six distinct clusters. Indeed, questionnaire data do fit this pattern and do show some differences between men and women in their styles of loving (Hendrick & Hendrick, 1986; Richardson, Medvin, & Hammock, 1988). Men are more likely than women to engage in a playfully manipulative and deceptive kind of love (*ludus*). Women more frequently endorse love as friendship (*storge*), love as a rational calculation (*pragma*), and love as an emotionally intense experience (*mania*).

The style of love endorsed by couples is related to the likelihood of their continuing in a relationship. If couples have similar styles of loving, they are more likely to stay together. They also are more likely to report satisfaction with the relationship if it includes a strong component of passion and commitment (*eros*). When members of a couple disagree on the eros and ludus components of love, they are more likely to break up (Hendrick, Hendrick, & Adler, 1988). Another attempt to list the types of love is that of Robert Sternberg, whose triangular theory of love was discussed in Chapter 9.

Other researchers have concentrated on the processes involved in initiating a romantic relationship. The processes involved in romantic attraction are similar to those in friendship formation. Similarity in attitudes and interests, physical proximity, and reciprocal liking are perhaps more important in a romantic relationship than they are in a friendship. When married couples, for example, were asked about the characteristics they would prefer their spouses to have, partners shared strong preferences for several characteristics such as religiosity and liking for children (Buss & Barnes, 1986). In the initial stages of romantic involvement, physical attractiveness assumes an important role (Rubin, 1973).

However, some sex differences in preferences for certain mate attributes do exist. Surveying men and women from 37 different cultures worldwide, David Buss (1989) has found that women in most cultures place somewhat greater importance on financial capacity, ambition, and industriousness when

TABLE 14-6
Lee's Six Types of Love: Definitions and Questionnaire Items

Eros	*Passion and commitment.* Strong physical component, early attraction, intense emotion, strong commitment to lover.
	    My lover and I were attracted to each other immediately after we first met.
	    Our lovemaking is very intense and satisfying.

Ludus	*Game playing.* Love is an interaction game to be played with diverse partners; manipulation and deception are acceptable.
	    I try to keep my lover a little uncertain about my commitment.
	    I have sometimes had to keep two of my lovers from finding out about each other.

Storge	*Love as friendship.* Inclination to merge love and friendship; solid and enduring.
	    It is hard to say exactly where friendship ends and love begins.
	    Love is really a deep friendship, not a mysterious, mystical emotion.

Pragma	*Calculated mate selection.* Rational calculation about the desired attributes of a lover; love planning; computer matching.
	    I consider what a person is going to become in life before I commit myself.
	    It is best to love someone with a similar background.

Mania	*Emotional intensity.* "Symptom love" based on uncertainty of self and others; puppy love.
	    When things aren't right between my lover and me, my stomach gets upset.
	    When I am in love, I have trouble concentrating on anything else.

Agape	*Selfless caring.* All-giving, nondemanding, self-abnegation.
	    I try to use my own strength to help my lover through difficult times.
	    I would rather suffer myself than let my lover suffer.

Sources: Adapted from Hendrick & Hendrick, 1986; Lee, 1977; Richardson, Medvin, & Hammock, 1988.

evaluating men as marriage partners. Men, on the other hand, put slightly more weight on physical attractiveness and youth when rating women.

SPOTLIGHT ON RESEARCH
Attachment Style and Commitment in Relationships

In Chapter 13, we discussed three major styles of attachment that children exhibit toward their caregivers (Ainsworth et al., 1978). *Securely attached* children use their caretakers as a base of security to reduce feelings of distress and anxiety when they are upset. *Resistantly attached* children make inconsistent, conflicted, and ambivalent attempts to receive emotional support from their caregivers when they are upset, actions that seem to reflect their uncertainty about the caregiver's availability and supportiveness. *Avoidantly attached* children neither seek support from the caregivers nor use them to manage and get rid of anxiety when it arises.

Hazan and Shaver (1987) recently have identified these same three basic styles in adults. When it comes to romantic relationships, securely attached adults view themselves as valued and worthy of others' concern, support, and affection. They also view romantic partners as accessible, reliable, trustworthy, and well intentioned. As a result, securely attached people develop closeness with others easily, they feel comfortable depending on others and having others depend on them, and they rarely are concerned about being abandoned or about others becoming too close (Hazan & Shaver, 1987). Not surprisingly, their romantic relationships tend to be characterized by more frequent positive emotions (Simpson, 1990); by higher levels of trust, commitment, satisfaction, and closeness (Collins & Read, 1990); and by happy, positive, and trusting styles of love (Hendrick & Hendrick, 1989; Levy & Davis, 1988).

Resistantly attached adults consider themselves to be misunderstood and unappreciated, and significant others to be undependable and either unwilling or unable to pledge themselves to committed, long-term relationships. They believe that others are reluctant to become as close as they would like, they frequently worry that their romantic partners do not truly love them or will leave them, and they often desire to be extremely close to others (Hazan & Shaver, 1987). Hence, their relationships tend to be characterized by more frequent negative emotions (Simpson, 1990); lower levels of trust, commitment, satisfaction, and closeness (Collins & Read, 1990); and obsessive, preoccupied, and jealous forms of love (Hendrick & Hendrick, 1989; Levy & Davis, 1988).

Avoidantly attached adults perceive themselves as being aloof, emotionally distant from others, and skeptical in nature. Moreover, they see significant others as unreliable and overly eager to make long-term commitments to relationships. Accordingly, avoidant persons are uncomfortable being close to others, they find it difficult to completely trust and depend on them, and they become apprehensive whenever anyone gets too close (Hazan & Shaver, 1987). As a result, their relationships tend to be defined by more frequent negative emotions, and lower levels of trust, commitment, satisfaction, and closeness (Collins & Read, 1990; Simpson, 1990). The negative nature of their relationships, however, appears to stem from acute fear of intimacy rather than from obsessive preoccupation with their romantic partners (Hazan & Shaver, 1987).

Behavioral evidence in support of these three styles is beginning to mount. After measuring the attachment style of each member of 83 dating couples, Simpson, Rholes, and Nelligan (1992) told the female member of each couple that she was going to participate in a study known to provoke "stress and anxiety" in most people. Females then waited alone with their male partners in a "waiting room" for the study to begin, at which time they were unobtrusively videotaped. Independent observers then rated each woman according to how upset she appeared to be about the impending study and how much support she sought from her partner. Men were rated according to how much support they actually offered. Results revealed that securely attached women who appeared more distressed actively sought more comfort and support from their romantic partners. Avoidantly attached women who were more distressed, on the other hand, sought less reassurance and support. Furthermore, securely attached men provided more reassurance and support as their partners appeared more distressed, whereas avoidantly attached men offered less support.

Sexual Behavior

Sexual behavior is a component of complex interpersonal interaction. As such, it includes elements of physiological responding and elements of psychosocial significance for the individuals involved. A full understanding of sexual inter-action must include the psychosocial factors as well as the physiological.

Psychosocial Tactics of Sex.   Human courtship rituals include tactics that people use, consciously or unconsciously, to attract mates. David Buss asked college undergraduates to describe some of the tactics that people use to attract mates. From their answers Buss isolated 23 distinct types of tactics, from displaying resources, wearing stylish clothes, and touching, to showing off and displaying strength. Buss (1988) argued that these tactics are consistent with an evolutionary explanation of human psychosexual behavior. Each individual is seen as being in competition with other same-sex individuals for mating opportunities with the opposite sex. Among humans, such competition might include skill at locating mates, behaving in ways that effectively attract the attention of the opposite sex, acquiring resources that are highly desired by the opposite sex, and altering appearance to attract the opposite sex.

Men and women should differ in their reproductive strategies according to this evolutionary interpretation of psychosexuality. The male reproductive strategy is to maximize copulatory opportunities. From an evolutionary point of view that emphasizes "reproductive success," the male has little to lose and much to gain by copulating with many females. The female reproductive strategy is to maximize choice and wait for the best mate with the greatest investment in helping to care for offspring. Her reproductive success hinges on the ability to ensure survival of her offspring through their reproductive years, and help from a mate is therefore critical. Buss found a high degree of similarity in the use of tactics men and women use to attract mates, but there were some differences consistent with the evolutionary interpretation. Males were more likely to use tactics involving display of resources, in effect impressing the

Tactics of sexual attraction include display of resources, as in driving flashy cars or wearing revealing clothing. Some observers believe that display of resources is a socio-biological signal that one can invest in future offspring.

female with an ability to invest in future offspring. Females, on the other hand, were more likely to use tactics involving displays of health and attractiveness, in effect showing their suitability for producing offspring (Buss, 1988).

Many of the tactics of sexual attraction are also consistent with a learning approach to sexual behavior. Perhaps men and women adopt different strategies simply because they have been socialized differently. Because the consequences of pregnancy are far greater for women than for men, women may have been socialized through the ages to ignore sexual cues to a greater extent than men. Their sexual behavior is more closely scrutinized by agents of socialization such as parents because of these consequences. Norms about the kind of behavior that is acceptable reinforce the biological consequences.

In either position—the evolutionary sociobiological position or the sexual socialization position—one would expect men and women to differ in their responses to sexual situations. When men and women view videotaped interactions between couples, they differ in their sexual interpretations. Both men and women are good at differentiating between interactions that are just friendly and those that involve sexual intent, but men perceive more sexual interest in both male and female participants in social interactions than do women (Shotland & Craig, 1988). Whether men have a greater sexual appetite, or whether they have been reared to expect a greater sexual appetite, is open to question.

Men and women also rate photographs of couples in a way that suggests different sexual connotations. In a study in which 10 photographs of couples in a cafeteria were rated, men thought the couples were more seductive, sexy, and promiscuous than women did. Men also expressed more sexual attraction to the opposite-sex member of the couple in the photographs (Abbey & Melby, 1986). Gender differences in response to sexual situations suggest differences in the ways women and men play their sexual roles.

Decisions surrounding sexual behavior, whether they are arrived at rationally or haphazardly, are influenced by several important factors in a person's life. These factors include the perceived behavior in reference groups or the nature of the relationship within which sex occurs. The act of first intercourse, for example, has meaning far beyond its pleasurable physical aspect. For many people, sex may be a form of escapism from pressures at home or at the office, from economic troubles, or from loneliness.

People tend to adopt standards and behavior that they think characterize their reference groups. Among college students, other students of the same sex are a powerful reference group. Indeed, peer group influence on sexual behavior and standards increases during the college years (Mirande, 1968). The perceived sexual behavior of friends was examined in a study of college students at the University of Wisconsin. One of the strongest factors associated with sexual behavior of the participants was friends' sexual experience. The incidence of premarital intercourse increased for each additional friend who was perceived as sexually experienced among both men and women (Schulz et al., 1977).

Sexual Orientation. In twentieth-century Western society, many people still regard homosexuality as perverse and disapprove of its expression in behavior. The Kinsey reports, the first large-scale surveys of sexual behavior in the United States, indicated that despite widespread condemnation, same-sex sexual experience was relatively common. One of the most surprising findings in the two Kinsey volumes was that about 37% of males and about 20% of females had at least one sexual experience with a person of the same sex at some time in their lives (Kinsey, Pomeroy, & Martin, 1948; Kinsey et al., 1953). Based on his surveys, Kinsey argued that the labels "homosexual" and "heterosexual" are misleading and obscure the variety in human sexual behavior. He proposed instead a rating scale based on a continuum of sexual experience.

Studies of sexual orientation often ignore this continuum, treating anyone with same-sex sexual experience, however slight, as "homosexual." In reality, individuals who are exclusively attracted to members of the same or opposite sex are likely to differ systematically from individuals who fall in the middle of the continuum. Those in the middle of the continuum are referred to as bisexual—that is, equally attracted to people of either sex.

Social Issues in Sexual Orientation.   Many opinions about sexual behavior between members of the same sex are apparent, and a great many of them are negative. Most churches consider homosexuality a sin, many states consider it a crime, and until recently, many mental health professionals have considered it a sickness. The phrase "until recently" is an important one, for it shows that considerations about sexual practices, including homosexuality, change with time and culture. The psychiatric community no longer considers homosexuality a psychological disorder. In classical Greece, homosexual relationships were openly accepted, at least among the upper classes (Flacelière, 1960). In ancient Rome, homosexuality apparently was openly accepted, as it is in some contemporary Melanesian cultures (Money, 1987).

Despite the greater visibility of gay men and lesbians since the beginning of the gay liberation movement, most sexologists agree that the prevalence of homosexuality has not increased since the publication of the Kinsey reports (Chilman, 1983; Hunt, 1974). Estimates of the percentages of individuals who are predominately or exclusively attracted to members of their own sex vary widely, from lows of 1 or 2% to highs of 20% or more. A reasonable estimate seems to be that around 10% of males and fewer females—perhaps half as many—are primarily attracted to people of the same sex. Many more people, however, have some sexual experience with people of the same gender in their lifetimes, as Kinsey's data indicated about 40 years ago.

The wide range of speculations about the origins of homosexuality generally fit within two major perspectives. One perspective holds that sexual orientation is a product of learning, either through the type of family situation an individual grew up in or through early experiences with sexual behavior. The other perspective holds that sexual orientation is biologically determined.

Sexual Orientation and Learning.   Early attempts to understand the development of an individual's sexual orientation often focused on the family and suggested that childhood experiences predisposed individuals to be either homosexual or heterosexual. A frequent stereotype was that gay men, and perhaps lesbians, grew up in families with a weak or absent father and a strong, domineering mother. Scientific evidence does not support this family predisposition view of sexual orientation (Bell, Weinberg, & Hammersmith, 1981).

A few studies have been done to see if homosexual and heterosexual individuals differ in their early experiences; these studies are aimed at isolating factors that contribute to the adoption of one sexual orientation or another. In one study, 28 gay men and 22 heterosexual men were asked about sexual activity in four age periods: childhood, preadolescence, adolescence, and early adulthood. Gay men reported more sexual experiences with other males in childhood and preadolescence, but they often shifted to both male and female partners in adolescence and early adulthood. Data from this research show that at each age level, a minority of gay men had sexual experience exclusively with members of their own gender (Manosevitz, 1972). During adolescence, close same-sex friendships are common and often very important to the psychological development of young people. Some of these friendships include sexual interaction. However, there is no clear evidence that such experimentation is linked to adult sexual orientation.

The 1993 March on Washington for lesbian, gay, and bisexual rights and liberation makes its way past the White House. The march attracted several hundred thousand demonstrators. Since the beginning of the gay liberation movement in the late 1960s, homosexuality in the United States has been more visible.

Sexual Orientation and Biology.   One biological explanation that attracted some followers several years ago was the notion that sexual orientation is genetically based. This explanation became popular after a geneticist published reports that studies of sexual orientation in sets of identical twins revealed a perfect concordance rate. That is, if one twin was identified as homosexual, then the other was homosexual also. However, it is clear from observation alone that sexual orientation is not under complete genetic control. In addition, environmental factors such as fetal hormone levels might also account for similarities between twins (Brown, 1986).

Studies of hormone levels in homosexuals and heterosexuals provide the basis for another type of biological explanation. Some studies have found, for example, that gay men have lower levels of the male hormone testosterone than do heterosexual men, whereas lesbians have higher levels of testosterone than heterosexual women (Bell et al., 1981). The issues raised by this type of research are complex and controversial. The findings are not always consistent, and even if they were, an association between two factors, such as hormone levels and sexual orientation, does not demonstrate causality. Perhaps same-sex sexual behavior accounts for the difference in hormone levels, rather than vice versa. A great deal of current speculation about the origins of sexual orientation centers on the role of prenatal sex hormones. Human sexual orientation undoubtedly is influenced by socialization, but prenatal hormone influences may alter individual susceptibility to sexual stimuli in the environment (Money, 1987).

Taken together, the studies to date provide some interesting clues about sexual orientation, but they do not completely clarify the issues. It would appear that the family situation is only weakly associated with sexual orientation, if at all. Early sexual experience is more common among gay men, but no one knows why this is the case (Elias & Gebhard, 1969). There is probably not any single cause or route to either homosexuality or heterosexuality.

Loneliness

Social psychologists have studied factors associated with interpersonal attraction and friendship extensively because of their unquestioned importance in

Loneliness is a subjective experience. People sometimes feel lonely even when there are many people around.

everyday social life. Ironically, the importance of social relationships becomes most strongly evident when they are either absent or deficient.

Loneliness is perhaps the most widely studied social deficiency. It typically occurs during important life transitions (such as moving away to college) and major life disruptions (such as the loss of a long-term romantic partner). Loneliness is defined as a feeling of deprivation stemming from unsatisfactory social relations with others (Perlman & Peplau, 1981). Two distinct types of loneliness exist (Weiss, 1973): *social isolation* (which is felt when social contacts are too infrequent) and *emotional isolation* (which is experienced when in-depth, close relationships are lacking).

There are three major elements in the experience of loneliness. First, and most obvious, loneliness is a result of *perceived deficits in social relationships*. Second, the experience is *subjective*. People sometimes feel lonely even when many people are around, and sometimes people who are alone do not feel lonely. Third, loneliness is an *unpleasant and distressing* experience (Peplau & Perlman, 1982).

Questionnaires about loneliness have yielded some information about the nature of this subjective experience. People who are lonely feel several negative reactions. They feel desperate and depressed, experience impatient boredom, and have low self-esteem (Rubenstein & Shaver, 1982). When they are asked about their reasons for feeling lonely, their answers seem to fall into five clusters (see Table 14–7). Having nothing to do, feeling bored, and having no lover or spouse appear to be major reasons for the experience of loneliness. Because self-disclosure is associated with forming friendships and building relationships, a relative lack of disclosure appears to be a factor in loneliness (Berg & Peplau, 1982; Solano, Batten, & Parish, 1982).

For many people the first year in college is a time when they must make adjustments to a completely new and different social environment, and many first-year students report feelings of loneliness. Among the contributing causes are *personality factors*, such as low self-esteem and shyness; *social factors*, such as the lack of established social networks; and *environmental factors*, such as large, impersonal classes and overcrowded high-rise dormitories (Cutrona, 1982).

loneliness feeling of deprivation resulting from unsatisfactory social relations with others

TABLE 14-7
Some Factors Associated with the Experience of Loneliness

Being Unattached	Alienation	Dislocation	Forced Isolation	Being Alone
Having no spouse	Feeling different	Being far from home	Being housebound	Coming home to an empty house
Having no sexual partner	Being misunderstood	Being in new job or school	Being hospitalized	Being alone
Breaking up with partner	Not being needed	Moving too often	Having no transportation	
	Having no close friends	Traveling often		

Source: Rubenstein & Shaver, 1982.

People who are lonely attempt to make sense out of this unpleasant psychological state. Recall from our discussion of attribution processes that people tend to look for causes of their social experience. In the study of loneliness, three dimensions help to clarify attributions and their effects. One dimension concerns the *locus* of the cause, either within the person or within the situation. A second dimension concerns the *stability* of the cause, whether it is enduring and stable, or momentary. And finally, a third dimension concerns whether the person can exert any *control* over the experience (Peplau, Miceli, & Morasch, 1982). The particular matrix of attributions that people have will influence their psychological reaction to loneliness. For example, someone who views loneliness as resulting from personal, stable causes (such as being unattractive) is more likely to feel helpless and depressed than someone who views loneliness as a result of a lack of effort—a personal and unstable cause and something over which the individual has control.

GENDER AND SEX ROLES

Throughout this chapter, we have noted several differences between the social behaviors of men and women. For instance, we have observed that conversations between female roommates tend to be more emotional and expressive than those between male roommates; that men and women show some striking differences in the tactics they use to attract potential mates; and that men tend to view interpersonal situations in sexual terms more than women. Gender is a ubiquitous social category that has different and sometimes profound effects on the way men and women behave. Moreover, it is a social category that people *expect* to affect behavior. College students, for example, frequently infer that men are more aggressive, dominant, and competitive than women, whereas women are more talkative, tactful, and emotional than men (Rosenkrantz et al., 1968).

Sex Differences in Social Behavior

The fact that people expect men and women to differ in their social behavior does not necessarily mean that they actually do differ. We have already seen the power of expectancy effects associated with the self-fulfilling prophecy. To what extent do studies show a difference in social behavior between men and women? To answer this question, we look at studies on sex differences in two social domains: aggression and prosocial behavior.

Aggression. Eleanor Maccoby and Carol Nagy Jacklin published a comprehensive review of sex differences in 1974. They concluded that sex differences

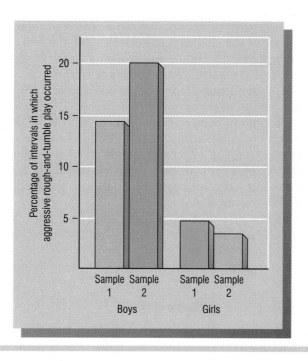

FIGURE 14-8
Boys in two different samples of nursery school children engaged in more aggressive rough-and-tumble play than girls. (Maccoby, 1988.)

in aggressive behavior, with males showing more aggression than females, were well established in all cultures where aggression had been studied. A study of play among 4½-year-old children illustrates the difference (Maccoby, 1988). In two different samples of children, boys engaged in much more aggressive rough-and-tumble play, such as wrestling or jumping on another child who was bouncing on a trampoline, than did girls. These data are shown in Figure 14-8.

Other reviewers agree that men are more aggressive than women, although the overall sex difference is not especially great in the typical short-term social psychology study (Eagly, 1987). In a form of aggression that occurs within the family context, men and women engage in child abuse with about equal frequency (Eagly, 1987). However, men are far more often involved in violent crime against strangers. Evidence also suggests that men and women think differently about aggression. Women report more guilt and anxiety over aggressive impulses and experience more concern about danger to themselves.

In sum, research has revealed that males are more aggressive than females. Nevertheless, the overall effect is not as large as common stereotypes suggest. We now turn to a more positive form of social behavior, prosocial actions.

Prosocial Behavior.   Earlier in this chapter we discussed prosocial behavior and some of the methods for studying it. After Kitty Genovese was murdered in New York, studies addressed bystander intervention in emergencies. One of the independent variables in the bystander intervention studies is gender. Consider the following situation. A hitchhiker is standing in the rain waiting for a ride, holding a sign that says "Going to a wedding." Would you give this person a ride? Would it make any difference to you if the hitchhiker was male or female? Would you predict that men or women drivers would be more likely to help by offering a ride?

In fact, more men than women indicated they would offer the hitchhiker a ride (Hope & Jackson, 1988). Also, both men and women indicated that they would be more likely to give a ride to a male, rather than a female, hitchhiker. At first it might seem counterintuitive that men would be more likely to help the hitchhiker than women, who are viewed stereotypically as more nurturant. However, the need for intervention in this situation is not as great as in some of the studies that have simulated medical emergencies. Furthermore, the driver who might intervene faces a risk. We have all read news stories about drivers being attacked, raped, or murdered by hitchhikers to whom they offered rides. Because of these factors, this situation poses some problems as a test of sex differences in prosocial behavior.

Most of the studies of helping are similar to this one in that they involve short-term encounters with strangers. The finding that men are more likely to help than women is a consistent one (Eagly, 1987; Senneker & Hendrick, 1983). However, none of the studies involves long-term caring in a close relationship. Perhaps the latter type of situation would elicit greater amounts of helping from women than from men.

Our brief review of sex differences in social behavior has shown that there are some average group differences between males and females, both in negative social behavior such as aggression and positive social behavior such as assistance to strangers. How can these sex differences best be explained?

Explanations for Sex Differences

The social category of gender is obvious and pervasive. All known languages have terms for men and women, boys and girls. All known cultures differentiate between roles men and women will play in society, even though there is a great deal of variety in the way the roles are assigned. Gender is one of the most extensively studied independent variables in the field of social psychology. And yet psychologists still do not fully agree on how reliable and important sex differences are or on what their explanations might be. A number of possible explanations have appeared over the years, from Freud's assertion that "biology is destiny" to Margaret Mead's hypothesis that sex differences are a matter of cultural assignment and socialization.

Explanations of sex differences, more than most other social behavior, are heavily influenced by the scientific and political pressures of the times. In the 1970s, after some of the successes of the women's movement, social psychology seemed ready to dismiss sex differences as largely overrated and unproven. In *The Psychology of Sex Differences* (1974), Maccoby and Jacklin advanced this position and influenced a whole generation of researchers.

A shift that reemphasized sex differences in social behavior emerged in the 1980s. A pivotal publication in this shift was Carol Gilligan's critique of traditional theories of human development. Gilligan (1982) argued that men and women approach the social world differently. Women emphasize caring and nurturance in their approach to the world, whereas men are more competitive and individualistic.

Within social psychology, explanations of sex differences that favor distant causes, such as heredity and early childhood socialization, are now deemphasized in favor of explanations that stress more immediate influences on behavior such as social interaction, roles, and cognitive factors (Eagly, 1987; Hargreaves, 1986). Social psychologists stress that sex differences are highly variable and dependent on the social context in which they occur (Deaux & Major, 1987). Women can be aggressive and aloof in some circumstances, and men can be tender and compassionate. Our analysis of prosocial behavior is a good example. Men may be more likely to help strangers in distress than women, whereas women may be more likely to nurture and care for others in close relationships. Perhaps the task of social psychology for the 1990s is to isolate the variables that are most likely to lead to sex differences in particular types of social interaction, with a goal of facilitating positive social interaction and understanding for all of us.

THINKING AHEAD . . .

As we noted at the outset of this chapter, social psychology encompasses an incredibly diverse array of social behavior. It ranges from aggression to altruism, from cooperation and conflict occurring within dyads (two people, such as married partners), to similar interactions occurring between large groups; and from how individuals *think* about people, objects, and events to how they genuinely *feel* about them. Given this diversity, where is the field of social psychology headed in the next decade?

Chances are that the field will move in several new directions. Research on persuasion and attitude change will continue to test and refine the elaboration likelihood model, linking the model to psychophysiological responses that may directly affect short- and long-term attitude changes. More attention also is likely to be devoted to understanding the kinds of factors that sustain and consolidate long-term attitude change. Such research is badly needed if we are to make significant progress in reducing prejudice and discrimination.

Research on groups currently is addressing how and under what circumstances members who hold deviant opinions or viewpoints can change the opinions held by a majority of the members during group decision making.

The study of close relationships is likely to follow several paths. Investigators will continue to examine how adult attachment styles systematically influence the nature, harmony, and ultimate stability of romantic relationships, especially marriages. Future research will continue to test and refine models of mate selection. Research will also continue into the determinants of sexual orientation.

Research on sex and gender will further clarify the precise variables that are most and least likely to yield sex differences in behavior in specific types of social settings. Undoubtedly, this work will pit social-learning and evolutionary models against one another in an attempt to determine when and under what conditions these models best account for observed sex differences in behavior.

Social Cognition

1. *Social cognition* refers to the ways that individuals gather, use, and interpret information about the social aspects of their world. Social cognition includes attitude formation and change, and attribution processes.

2. Attitudes are relatively stable systems of beliefs and feelings about something. Attitude instability occurs because of personality differences, the way attitudes are measured, how relevant they are in the immediate situation, and whether individuals have recently behaved in a way that is contrary to them.

3. Persuasion campaigns attempt to exploit what is known about attitudes to convince people to alter attitudes in a desired direction. The effectiveness of persuasion campaigns varies as a function of characteristics of the source of communication, characteristics of the communication itself, and characteristics of the listener.

4. According to the elaboration likelihood model, two routes to persuasion exist: a central route that involves careful, deliberate thought about an issue, and a peripheral route in which perceivers focus on circumstances that are not relevant to the issues.

5. Attribution processes are involved in causal explanations. Person attributions place the causes of behavior within the person; situation attributions place causes of behavior in the situation. Distinctiveness, consistency, and consensus are factors that determine the type of attribution.

6. *Self-serving bias* refers to people's tendency to accept greater personal responsibility for their successes than for their failures, making person attributions for the former and situation attributions for the latter. *Fundamental attribution error* refers to the tendency to make person attributions about other people's behavior.

7. Teachers may unwittingly alter their behavior toward students on the basis of attributions about student ability. When the result is lower or higher performance of students, a self-fulfilling prophecy is at work.

Group Processes

8. A group consists of two or more people in dynamic interaction with each other. People's behavior is altered by group membership, or even by the desire to be a member of a reference group. Norms are rules that apply to all group members. Roles are rules that apply to specific group members.

9. Enhancement of performance in the presence of others is known as social facilitation. Social facilitation occurs when a response is already well learned; learning and performing new responses are more difficult when other people are watching.

10. Deindividuation, which occurs in some group contexts, encompasses a loss of self-restraint and individual responsibility that may lead to antisocial behavior.

11. People feel strong pressure to go along with the consensus of a collection of people, a tendency referred to as conformity. The flip side of conformity is minority influence, which examines when and under what circumstances minority members in groups exert persuasive influence over majority members. Obedience, on the other hand, is the tendency for people to comply with orders of an authority.

12. People often fail to come to the aid of others in distress because of a sense of diffusion of responsibility and pluralistic ignorance. The result of these tendencies is that people are less likely to help when others are around than when they are lone witnesses to an emergency. Current research seeks to determine whether prosocial behavior has altruistic or egoistic origins.

13. Prejudice is a set of negative attitudes toward members of particular social groups. The behavioral expression of prejudice is discrimination. It is maintained in part by stereotypes—standardized mental pictures of members of a group that are based on oversimplified and uncritical judgments.

14. Contact between members of social groups will probably not reduce prejudice by itself. Groups need to be convinced that they have common goals, authority figures must endorse equality, and status and power need to be equivalent to effectively reduce prejudice and discrimination. These principles have been used in the jigsaw classroom.

15. The tendency to evaluate one's own group as superior is called ethnocentrism. Racism and sexism are specific forms of ethnocentrism.

16. Some groups, such as juries, come into existence to perform a specific task. High-status members have a strong impact on such groups.

17. When groups make a decision following a discussion, the group's decision is often more extreme than the average of the individual group members' decisions before the discussion. This tendency is called group polarization, and it occurs in a wide variety of situations.

Friendship and Romantic Attraction

18. People are particularly likely to become friends with others who are similar to themselves in attitudes, interests, age, and other characteristics. They are also more likely to become friends with others who live nearby and who like them in turn.

19. Social psychologists have attempted to enumerate, through research, different kinds of love. Couples who have similar orientations to love have stronger relationships. Lee proposed six types of love.
20. Men and women behave similarly in the tactics of courtship they use. However, there are some differences that are consistent with both evolutionary and socialization interpretations. Men interpret more situations as sexual than women.
21. Norms for sexual behavior are somewhat different for men and women, so that gender affects sexual role playing.
22. Loneliness, which results from a perceived lack of social relationships, is an unpleasant and distressing experience. Two types of loneliness exist: social isolation and emotional isolation.

Gender and Sex Roles

23. Gender is an important variable in research in social psychology. People hold expectations that social behavior will vary as a function of gender.
24. Men and women show average differences in behavior in several social domains, including aggression (males are more aggressive) and prosocial behavior (men are more likely to help strangers in short-term laboratory studies).
25. A wide variety of explanations for sex differences in social behavior have been offered. Contemporary social psychology emphasizes immediate influences on social behavior, such as social interaction, roles, and cognitive orientation.

Key Terms

social psychology (550)
social cognition (550)
attitude (551)
cognitive dissonance (552)
mere exposure effect (554)
elaboration likelihood model (555)
central route (555)
peripheral route (555)
attribution theory (555)

person attribution (556)
situation attribution (556)
distinctiveness (556)
consensus (556)
consistency (556)
self-serving bias (558)
fundamental attribution error (559)
self-fulfilling prophecy (561)
group (561)
norms (562)
roles (562)

reference groups (562)
social facilitation (563)
field studies (563)
deindividuation (564)
conformity (564)
obedience (567)
prosocial behavior (569)
bystander intervention (569)
diffusion of responsibility (570)
pluralistic ignorance (571)

prejudice (572)
discrimination (572)
stereotypes (572)
contact theory (573)
superordinate goals (574)
jigsaw classroom (574)
ethnocentrism (574)
out-group homogeneity (574)
group polarization (576)
loneliness (585)

Suggested Reading

Aronson, E. (1992). *The social animal* (6th ed.). San Francisco: Freeman. An exploration and review of topics in social psychology including conformity, persuasion and propaganda, prejudice, and attraction.

Brehm, S. S., & Kassin, S. M. (1993). *Social psychology* (2nd ed.). Boston: Houghton Mifflin. An excellent social psychology introductory text.

Chilman, C. S. (1983). *Adolescent sexuality in contemporary society*. New York: Wiley. A review of issues in adolescent sexuality including psychosocial factors, sex education, and contraceptive use.

Milgram, S. (1974). *Obedience to authority*. New York: Harper & Row. The major statement of Milgram's research on obedience, exploring variations of his research paradigm and setting the work on obedience in a larger context.

Rosenthal, R., & Jacobson, L. (1968). *Pygmalion in the classroom: Teacher expectations and pupils' intellectual development*. New York: Holt, Rinehart & Winston. A report of a comprehensive study on the social effects of releasing aptitude scores to teachers.

Rubin, Z. (1973). *Liking and loving: An invitation to social psychology*. New York: Holt, Rinehart & Winston. An introduction to social psychology that concentrates on the attraction process in friendship and romance.

CHAPTER 15
Health, Stress, and Coping

We are becoming ever more aware of how intimately our own physical and psychological health depend on the "health and well-being" of the world around us. Physicist James Lovelock and microbiologist Lynn Margulis have proposed the *Gaia hypothesis*, which argues that the earth is a living creature and should not be studied using traditional geological procedures but rather through geophysiology, " . . . the science of bodily processes applied to the planet Earth" (Joseph, 1990, p. 2). Interdependence is one of Margulis's major themes. She writes:

> The consortial quality of the individual pre-empts the notion of independence. For example, what appears to be a single wood-eating termite is comprised of billions of microbes, a few kinds of which do the actual digesting of the cellulose of the wood. Gaia is the same sort of consortial entity, but it is far more complex. Consortia, associations, partnerships, symbioses, and competitions in the interaction between organisms extend to the global scale. Living and nonliving matter, self, and environment are nicely interconnected.

It is interesting that many cultures, foremost among them the Native Americans, have long maintained this perspective and consequently could not understand the exploitive behavior of the Europeans.

> The white people never cared for land or deer or bear. When we Indians kill meat, we eat it all up. When we dig roots we make little holes. When we build houses, we make little holes. When we burn grass for grasshoppers, we don't ruin things. We shake down acorns and pine nuts. We don't chop down trees. We only use dead wood. But the White people plow up the ground, pull down the trees, kill everything. The tree says, "Don't. I am sore. Don't hurt me." But they chop it down and cut it up. The spirit of the land hates them. They blast out trees and stir it up to its depths. They saw up the trees. That hurts them. The Indians never hurt anything, but the White people destroy all. They blast

◀ Psychological factors can affect people's health, and help to determine how they cope with stress.

rocks and scatter them on the ground. The rock says, "Don't. You are hurting me." But the White people pay no attention. When the Indians use rocks, they take little round ones for their cooking. . . . How can the spirit of the earth like the White man? . . . Everywhere the White man has touched it, it is sore. (quoted in T. C. McLuhan, *Touch the Earth*, p. 15)

To Native Americans the Europeans' adversarial relationship with the world around them seemed unhealthy.

And in Japan today a new disease is emerging, called *karoshi*.

. . . the nation that has taken the sting out of the word "workaholic," producing 10 percent of the world's exports with just 2 percent of its population is suddenly obsessed with a deadly phenomenon known as *karoshi*. That's the Japanese word for "death from overwork." Tetsunojo Uethata, the medical authority who coined the word defines *karoshi* as a "condition in which psychologically unsound work processes are allowed to continue in a way that disrupts the worker's normal work and life rhythms, leading to a buildup of fatigue in the body and a chronic condition of overwork accompanied by a worsening of pre-existent high blood pressure and a hardening of the arteries and finally resulting in a fatal breakdown." Translation: all work and no play can really wreck one's health, even in Japan. (*U.S. News and World Report*, March 18, 1991)

Perhaps the Japanese could benefit from the Hopi, who have a word for "life that calls for another way of living"; it is *koyannisquatsi* (ko-yaa-nis-katsi) and means "life out of balance." If our lives are unhealthy, whether physically or psychologically, they are by definition lives out of balance. *Koyannisquatsi* is one of the themes we will explore in this chapter on psychological health.

THE ROLE OF PSYCHOLOGY IN HEALTH AND ILLNESS

The relationship between the mind and body is a topic that philosophers have debated since at least as early as the time of Plato. Some philosophers consider the mind and body to be separate and distinct, a philosophical position known as **dualism**. Others, however, believe it is impossible to separate the interacting influences of mind and body.

> **dualism** philosophical position that assumes that mind and body are separate and distinct

Traditionally, health has been considered a state related to the body, and hence the domain of physicians who deal with the physical causes and cures of diseases. Psychology has traditionally had a limited role in dealing with sickness, chiefly concerning itself with the minds of healthy individuals or with "mental illness." As we discuss in Chapters 16 and 17, many psychologists have even adopted a medical model when dealing with the mind. Now these traditional views are beginning to change.

More and more researchers are gathering evidence that the mind and body interact in complex ways that affect our feelings, thoughts, and behavior. There is also growing evidence that the interaction of the mind and body can have an impact on our health and play an important role in the development and course of illness.

> **behavioral medicine** new approach to health, incorporating knowledge from the medical, behavioral, and social sciences

Within the past 2 decades a new discipline has emerged that unites the mind and body in understanding health and treating illness. The new discipline, **behavioral medicine**, is broadly defined as an interdisciplinary field that incorporates knowledge from the medical, behavioral, and social sciences to promote health and prevent illness. As interest in behavioral medicine has increased, so has interest in the role that psychological factors play in the processes of health and illness. In the late 1970s the field of **health psychology** was established as a distinct area of study in psychology. Whereas

> **health psychology** distinct from behavioral medicine in that it is specifically involved with the role of psychology in health and illness

behavioral medicine is an interdisciplinary field in the study of health and illness, health psychology specifically involves the role of psychology in health and illness.

Health and Life-Style

In 1900 the leading causes of death in the United States were pneumonia and influenza, and tuberculosis. Since 1900 advances in medical technology have allowed us to virtually eliminate the ravages of these infectious diseases (although tuberculosis is again on the rise in metropolitan areas). As shown in Table 15–1, the leading causes of death in the United States in the 1980s were heart disease and cancer (Matarazzo, 1984). Assessment of changes in the leading causes of death from 1900 to 1980 reveals a trend toward illnesses related to life-style and behavior. Common behavioral and life-style patterns that are considered risk factors for the development of heart disease and cancer include cigarette smoking, diet, obesity, and stress. Most of us have a relative or friend who has been advised to quit smoking or drinking or has been told to stop eating fried foods and cut down on cholesterol. Although we realize that certain habits are harmful to our health, we also know how difficult it is to give up those habits, but we must change them if we are to change our lives. Nowhere is this more evident than in our eating and exercise habits.

As indicated in the book *The Paleolithic Prescription* (see the application section of the same title later in this chapter), our nutritional and exercise needs have changed very little in the last 30,000 years, but our ability to meet those needs has changed dramatically. In the natural environment that shaped human physiology, sugar and fat were particularly rare resources and therefore highly prized. Sugar is a simple carbohydrate that provides an

Dr. Ellen Langer of Harvard University is a pioneer in the new field of health psychology, the study of the role of psychological factors in health and illness.

The Paleolithic Prescription approach to health that argues that understanding our health needs begins with understanding our evolutionary history

TABLE 15-1
The Ten Leading Causes of Death in the United States in 1900, 1940, and 1980

Cause of Death	1900	1940	1980
Pneumonia and influenza	1	5	6
Tuberculosis (all forms)	2	7	
Diarrhea, enteritis, and ulceration of the intestines	3		
Diseases of the heart	4	1	1
Intracranial lesions of vascular origin	5	3	
Nephritis (all forms)	6	4	
All accidents	7	6	4
Cancer	8	2	2
Senility	9		
Diphtheria	10		
Diabetes mellitus		8	7
Motor vehicle accidents		9	
Premature birth		10	
Cardiovascular diseases			3
Chronic, obstructive pulmonary diseases			5
Cirrhosis of the liver			8
Atherosclerosis			9
Suicide			10

Source: Matarazzo, 1984.

genetic predisposition hereditary tendency

immediate source of energy. Fat is efficient because it is stored directly as fat, while carbohydrates and protein must be converted to fat before they can be stored. Our ancestral body wisdom says, "eat as much sugar and fat as you can because there isn't much of it and it enhances survival." The problem is that although we have a naturally useful **genetic predisposition** to consume sugar and fat, we have created a culture in which there is an unnatural abundance of sugar and fat. Compare, for example, the percentage of fat and calories in domestic and wild animals shown in Table 15–2. The meat in that hamburger you had for lunch was at least 50% fat. As the old saying goes, you are what you eat, and what modern humans are in the habit of eating is "fat."

While our sugar and fat intake has increased drastically, our consumption of complex carbohydrates (vegetables, breads, pasta, and so forth) has decreased significantly. Overweight people trying to diet often complain that they simply lack the energy to exercise, and this is true. The less they eat, the less fuel they have. Consequently, they consume fewer and fewer calories and still fail to lose weight because the energy requirements of their bodies are also decreasing.

Life in balance means eating high-energy foods (complex carbohydrates) *and* expending large amounts of energy. The American College of Sports Medicine recently proclaimed inactivity as this nation's number one health hazard. This is certainly true for physical health, but, as we emphasize in this chapter, physical and psychological health are intimately intertwined; you can't discuss one without considering the other. Developing good nutritional and exercise habits affects not only the longevity of life but also its quality. With advances in medicine, life expectancy has dramatically increased, as we saw in Chapter 12. However, living a longer life is of diminished value if we must live it infirmed. What we all want is a better quality of life, now and in the future. Understanding the "paleolithic prescription"—the need for naturalness in activities and diet—is a necessary first step if we want to change bad living habits and acquire good ones.

The effect of life-style on health and illness was demonstrated forcefully in the Alameda County (California) Study (Belloc & Breslaw, 1972). A research team studied over 6,000 adults in Alameda County over a period of

---

TABLE 15-2
A Comparison of the Fat Content in Domestic and Wild Meats

	Fat (%)	Calories (per 6 oz serving)
Beef		
Beef, eye of round, roasted	26	286
Beef, bottom round (pot roast), roasted	28	291
Ground beef, extra lean, broiled, medium	58	435
Prime rib, roasted	58	481
Beef, tenderloin, broiled	62	495
Wild Game (all roasted)		
Bison (buffalo)	15	243
Antelope	16	255
Venison	18	269
Wild boar	24	272
Rabbit	34	262

Source: USDA Handbooks 8-17 and 8-13

5½ years. Participants were asked to list how many of the following seven health practices they observed:

- Sleeping 7 to 8 hours daily
- Eating breakfast almost every day
- Rarely or never eating between meals
- Maintaining normal weight (adjusted for height, age, and sex)
- Never smoking cigarettes
- Moderately or never using alcohol
- Engaging in regular physical activity

Using correlational measures, the relationship between these health habits and mortality was examined, and the results were dramatic (Belloc, 1973). Individuals between the ages of 40 and 80 who practiced all or nearly all of the health behaviors were much less likely to die during the study period than those who practiced none or few of the health behaviors. However, behaviors that impaired health, such as smoking, drinking, poor diet, and lack of exercise, are complicated for a number of reasons. They are influenced by social factors, such as peer pressure, belief systems, and other social-psychological processes that can affect both the practice of healthy behaviors and health itself (Krantz, Grungerg, & Baum, 1985). Many of these health-threatening behaviors are also highly reinforcing in the short run; their long-term negative effects may not appear until the distant future.

THINKING ABOUT
The Paleolithic Prescription

In pondering what it means to be "human," Emerson said, "First, be a good animal." This is a good prescription for life, but it needs modification for the psychologist studying behavior, who might say something like this: "If you desire to understand the human animal, first understand the animal human."

Since the time of John Stuart Mill (1806–1873), the battle cry of ethology (see Chapter 9) has been "Know your organism." This dictum seems relevant in the context of Emerson's concern for humanness as well. If we are to know Emerson's "good animal," we need to understand humans in the context of their evolutionary history. This is the concern of Eaton, Shostak, and Konner (1988) in their book, *The Paleolithic Prescription*. They maintain that to understand our genes we must understand the relationship genes had with the environment that influenced their selection. What were humans like 40,000 years ago? Most of our health-related problems result because of a conflict between our biology and our culture.

Our relationship to the environment—the foods we eat and the types of physical exercise we engage in—are further examples of our changed world. The problem is that our genes don't know it. They are programming us today in much the same way they have been programming humans for at least 40,000 years. Genetically, our bodies now are virtually the same as they were then. Except that "then" was a world we had spent hundreds of thousands of years adapting to, a world we had gradually responded to with subtle alterations in our genetic constitution, a world to which we had slowly molded a reasonably close fit. "Now" is so radically different—its demands so new—that our very old human design has not had time to adapt.

If we want to improve the quality of our lives, we should strive for "naturalness" in our activities and diet. The Paleolithic Prescription calls for a natural diet of (*a*) high protein (approximately 20% of consumed calories); (*b*) low-fat (20%) (domestic meat contains seven times as much fat as natural game); (*c*) high carbohydrates (60%), a majority from complex carbohydrates; and (*d*) high fiber intake with the majority from soluble fibers, fruits, vegetables, and oats. An article by Eaton and Konner, 1985, titled "Paleolithic Nutrition: A Consideration of its Nature and Current Implications" published in the *New England Journal of Medicine*, is largely responsible for the current oat bran fad.

In addition to a change in diet, the authors of *The Paleolithic Prescription* recommend that we significantly increase the amount of time we spend exercising. They suggest 30–90 minutes of an aerobic exercise, like running, at least three times a week, accompanied by resistance training, like weight lifting, an additional three times weekly. As they note, the Paleolithic life was physically demanding for both males and females, and our bodies are still programmed for action.

The Paleolithic Prescription is highly recommended to those wanting to understand Emerson's "good animal," and as a consequence, how to significantly improve both the longevity and the quality of life.

How well do your diet and activities match those called for in* The Paleolithic Prescription? *Given the benefits—both psychological and physical—associated with vigorous exercise, why do you think more people don't engage in regular exercise programs?

Psychological Control and Health

Common to both behavioral medicine and health psychology is a desire to understand how behavior, cognition, and emotion affect health and how they can be used to prevent illness. Health psychologists attempt to find ways of altering behavior, thought, or emotion so that becoming ill will be less likely. Thus, coping strategies that will allow the individual to exert greater control over these facets of psychological life are a major part of health psychology. What are the psychological processes involved in changing behavior such as stopping smoking, altering diet, getting more exercise, or changing the way one thinks and feels about health-related matters?

At this point we need to look more precisely at different types of psychological control and their effect on health. One way of thinking about control is in terms of what actually comes under the control of the individual. For our purposes, three types of psychological control are important: behavioral control, cognitive control, and information control (Thompson, 1981).

Behavioral Control. John Young was the first space shuttle pilot. Landing a glider the size of a building was considered a very scary business. When asked if he was nervous, he said no, he was simply doing his job. You get scared, he said, only when you don't know what to do next. When people exercise **behavioral control**, they believe that they have available to them a response that can affect their health status or their experience of stress.

Beliefs about how much control people actually have over their health-related behavior differ from individual to individual. Are people with alcoholism responsible for beginning drinking, or does that activity lie outside their control? Are smokers responsible for initiating their habit? Are obese people considered to be in control of their behavior problems? Similarly, beliefs differ about responsibility for changing behaviors once they have

behavioral control belief that one has available responses that can affect health status or the experience of stress

		Yes	No
Is the person responsible for changing the behavior?	Yes	Character model	Compensatory model
	No	Enlightenment model	Medical model

FIGURE 15–1
Models of health-related behavior.
(From Brickman et al., 1982.)

begun. Can a person change on his or her own initiative? Why don't smokers just stop smoking, or drinkers stop drinking? Overall models of health-related behavior can be considered in terms of these beliefs about control and therefore about responsibility, as shown in Figure 15–1 (Brickman et al., 1982). Knowing the model of behavioral control that people subscribe to helps in predicting how they will respond to health-threatening behaviors.

When people are viewed as having personal control over the initiation of a behavior and over its change, then health-threatening behaviors are seen as a function of character. If smokers, alcoholics, and the obese are thought to be responsible for initiating and changing their behavior, then their condition must be a result of a weak character. If they don't stop what they are doing, it's their own fault. This view of health-related behaviors is a common one; people often blame alcoholics or smokers for their own misfortunes. The tobacco industry has promoted this view of smoking, for example, and they seldom lose lawsuits brought by smokers or their survivors because juries generally agree with this *character model*.

The *enlightenment model* corresponds to beliefs that the individual controls the start of a behavior, but not its change. Alcoholics Anonymous and many other social-support groups accept this model, arguing that change can come about only through the intervention of a higher power, even though the person is responsible for having begun to drink or overeat or smoke.

The dominant treatment approach for addictive behaviors is the *medical model*, which holds that these behaviors signify a disease over which the individual has little control, either for initiating or changing the behavior. Diseases are generally thought of as progressive and are often seen as having a genetic component. Medical intervention is necessary, because the individual cannot change through personal initiative.

The model that is most in keeping with health psychology is the *compensatory model*. Here people are viewed as having relatively little control over the initiation of addictive behavior. They may be genetically predisposed or may have other biological or learning factors outside their own control in the beginning. But they can take an active role in changing these behaviors once they are aware of their destructive power and of their own effectiveness in dealing with them. Although rates of successful intervention for smoking and obesity are low when there is therapeutic intervention (through a medical model), self-cure rates, which are more likely based on a compensatory model, appear to be much higher (Schachter, 1982).

Cognitive Control. Psychological control is concerned not only with overt behavior. Another type of control, **cognitive control**, involves the belief that one has cognitive strategies that can affect outcomes related to health and stress. Ignoring pain, controlling physiological responses, and reappraising health threats are all cognitive control strategies. Research indicates that cognitive control can reduce anxiety and physiological arousal, reduce per-

cognitive control belief that one has cognitive strategies that can affect outcomes related to health and stress

ceived pain, and increase tolerance to pain (Thompson, 1981). If you were to close your eyes and think about a long walk along a warm beach during your next visit to the dentist's office, you would be using a cognitive strategy.

A considerable body of literature now shows a relationship between cognitive factors and the experience of depression, as we discuss further in Chapter 17. For example, events that are perceived as controllable cause fewer feelings of upset and less depression than events perceived to be uncontrollable (Brown & Siegel, 1988). In general, negative cognitive style seems more a cause than a symptom of depression (Parry & Brewin, 1988).

Cognitive mechanisms in depression and other health issues are related to *attribution theory*, a theory that examines the causal structure used to interpret events (see Chapter 14). Are negative events attributable to internal characteristics of the person, or to the situation? Are they stable over time, or unstable? Are they controllable, or not controllable? Take the example of obesity. If the obese individual views the cause as due to internal factors ("that's just the way I am") that are stable over time ("I've been overweight all my life") and uncontrollable ("no matter how hard I try, I can't lose weight"), then success in future dieting programs is unlikely. People who are faced with life-threatening illnesses such as coronary heart disease adjust better when their attributions about their situation include greater cognitive control (Turnquist, Harvey, & Andersen, 1988).

Recent evidence reviewed by Tennen and Affleck (1990) suggests that "blaming others for one's misfortune is associated with impairments in emotional well-being and physical health" (p. 209). People who have experienced life-threatening events adapt better if they perceive themselves as somehow the cause of their misfortune. This type of attribution is called **behavioral self-blame** and seems to offer the victim "both a sense of control over future threats and the image of a reliable world" (p. 226). On the other hand, Tennen and Affleck speculate that blaming others "shatters either the illusion of self-sufficiency or one's belief in a benign world and the reliability of others. Blaming others appears to offer no adaptational benefits while wresting a great emotional cost" (p. 226). Keep this research in mind while reading about Seligman's theory of learned optimism later in this chapter.

Cognitive control can be a powerful coping strategy for dealing with pain, stress, or other health-related situations. Bandura and his colleagues investigated a cognitive control strategy that involved diverting attention away from a painful stimulus, specifically, plunging one's hand into ice water. As shown in Figure 15–2, pain tolerance increased almost 60% in the cognitive control group, compared to an increase of less than 10% in groups that received either a placebo or no treatment (Bandura et al., 1988).

Information Control.   **Information control** is conceptually different from behavioral and cognitive control because the individual does not actually exert real control over the situation. Instead, information control refers to communications about the nature of health-related situations given to the potential recipient of a stressful event. For example, the individual might be warned that something was about to cause pain or be told exactly what to expect before, during, and after a surgical procedure. Research indicates that many individuals experience some benefits when they are given warning information, but the benefits are not as dramatic as in behavioral or cognitive control. Indeed, many individuals say they feel more anxious because they are always waiting for the warning signal (Thompson, 1981).

Loss of Psychological Control with Aging.   As people grow older, they change in a number of ways, several of which we discussed in Chapters 12

behavioral self-blame perceiving one's self as the cause of misfortune

information control communications about the nature of health-related situations given to the potential recipient of stressful events

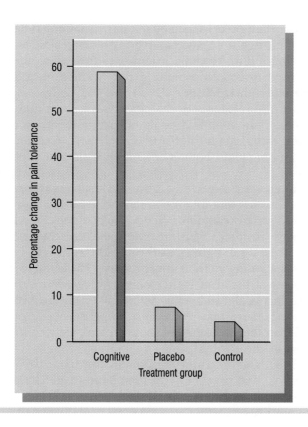

and 13. Many of the changes experienced by an aging population have an impact on health. Among these factors is psychological control.

Old age may affect perceived psychological control for a number of reasons (Rodin, 1986). Often the loss of friends may mean the loss of feedback about one's social self. Retirement, in addition, may result in the loss of feedback about one's competence. Increasing needs for assistance further undermine one's sense of psychological control. In general, medical care restricts a person's self-control, and older people have more contact with the health-care delivery system than younger people. Many people consider the move to a nursing home as the ultimate loss of psychological control, and about 5% of people over 65 in this country live in some type of residential-care facility. Living in a nursing home intensifies dependency and lack of control over one's own life. Institutionalized adults frequently lose any say over their diet, dress, room decoration, and daily activities.

Few places establish as much control over a person's existence as the typical nursing home for the elderly. Even residents who are not infirm are cared for in a routine established by the institution, with little or no choice or input from the residents themselves. Several psychologists with an interest in the relationship between psychology and health have speculated that loss of control may have a negative impact on health, quite independent from the biological aging process. Among these psychologists are Ellen Langer and Judith Rodin, who decided to test directly the effects of control on health and well-being in a nursing home environment (Langer & Rodin, 1976).

For their field experiment on psychological control, Langer and Rodin selected a respected nursing care facility in Connecticut with a cooperative staff. They targeted two nonadjacent floors of the facility, the second and the fourth. The residents of one floor were given opportunities for increased control over their daily lives, although to most of us these opportunities appear minimal. They could have the furniture arranged in their rooms as

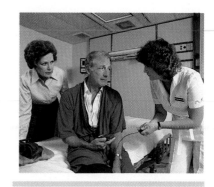

Feelings of loss of psychological control often accompany aging, partly because the individual has increased needs for assistance. For example, older people have more frequent contact with the health-care delivery system.

they liked, rather than prearranged by the staff. They could decide when and how to spend their free time, such as visiting other residents, watching television, scheduling a film, reading, listening to the radio, and so forth. And they were allowed to choose a plant, if they wanted it, and told that they should take care of it themselves.

By contrast, the residents of the comparison floor had their furniture arranged for them. Although they could engage in the same activities as the residents of the experimental floor, they had more regimented schedules. They were also given plants, but not of their choosing; the staff cared for their plants.

The two floors were selected because the residents were similar to each other in characteristics that might be relevant to health, such as age, severity of illness, and sex distribution. After 3 weeks of these modest experimental manipulations, residents were interviewed about their activities, happiness, and life in general. Nurses also rated the residents on a number of characteristics, including general improvement. These nurses were unaware of the hypotheses of the study. After only 3 weeks, more than 70% of the comparison residents showed some deterioration in their health status. In dramatic contrast, more than 90% of the experimental group, whose perceived control over their lives had become greater, showed improvement. As the population of the United States ages over the next two decades, we would do well to bear in mind the conclusion from this study that the decline in physical and psychological functioning typically associated with aging can be slowed down or reversed when aged individuals assume more control over their lives.

Health and Personality

If it is true that those things perceived as real are real in their consequences, then what a person believes *can* cause illness or even death, as it did for the Biami tribesman from New Guinea pictured in Figure 15–3. What we believe to be true about ourselves and the world we live in is influenced by our personalities. A number of health psychologists and physicians are investigating the relation between personality traits and health outcomes

FIGURE 15–3
The belief that things are real may be so powerful that they actually become real. This tribesman in Papua New Guinea believed that sorcery had been used on him, and he lay down and died, despite apparent physical health.

using correlational methods. Of special interest to health psychologists is the personality–behavioral style known as Type A.

Type A Personality. Two physicians, Meyer Friedman and Ray Rosenman (1974), have described a personality pattern that they believe characterizes people who are at high risk for heart problems. This coronary-prone personality, known as **Type A**, characterizes a person who eats, walks, and does almost everything fast. Type A individuals also have rapid speech patterns and often finish other people's sentences. In addition, they are hostile, competitive, and strongly achievement oriented. People with Type A personalities get jumpy and irritated at small delays in their lives, such as waiting in supermarket checkout lines. They often do several activities simultaneously, such as eating while reading their work assignments or studying language tapes while driving to work. They frequently work long hours and have trouble just doing nothing. Despite this striving, they are frequently dissatisfied with life.

Type A personality highly motivated to achieve, competitive, impatient, fast paced, and more prone to heart problems

Type B Personality. **Type B** personalities, by contrast, are characterized by a calm and relaxed style, very much the opposite of Type A (Krantz et al., 1985; Matthews, 1982). It should be noted that people with so-called Type A and Type B personalities do not always behave differently. When doing jobs under a deadline or when engaged in a nonfrustrating task, Type As and Type Bs often perform similarly (Glass, 1977).

Type B personality calm, relaxed, patient, and at a lower risk for heart problems than a Type A personality

Recent results from the Family Heart Study in Portland, Oregon, have suggested a link between Type A behavior patterns in fathers and sons (Weidner et al., 1988). No such links were found for daughters and either parent, or for mothers and sons. Perhaps the significant correlations between fathers and sons are a result of modeling and imitation, or perhaps they are suggestive of a genetic link. In either case, these results should be followed up by other investigators to see if the suggested link is reliable and is a cause for concern and intervention.

Studies correlating the incidence of heart attack with personality type have shown that people with Type A personalities are more than twice as likely to have coronary problems as those with Type B personalities (Cooper, Detre, & Weiss, 1981). Even so, only about 14% of the people categorized as Type A will actually suffer a heart attack. One of the authors of this text, a noted Type A, offers a purely untested assertion about the stress suffered by the Type A personality. He claims that coronary problems in Type A people are caused by the fact that there are too many Type B people in the world!

Recently, the links between Type A and coronary heart disease have been challenged (Fischman, 1987). Doubts about the link between Type A and heart disease have led researchers to take a less global view of the Type A personality and to focus more specifically on its component parts. The elements of hostility and cynicism are personality traits that researchers have identified as significant risk factors in the Type A personality that can contribute to heart disease.

Results of a controversial study suggest that some of the traits of the Type A personality may actually protect against some of the devastation of a heart attack after it has occurred (Ragland & Brand, 1988). Following a group of 257 men with both Type A and Type B personalities for a period of 13 years, these researchers found that although Type As had significantly more heart attacks than Type Bs, the Type As were only 58% as likely as Type Bs to die from those attacks. One explanation for this may be that Type A individuals are able to use their hard-driving, aggressive style to manage their health and medical problems.

Generality Theory. The discussion of the Type A personality assumes that psychological traits such as competitiveness, hostility, and anger predispose

specificity theory in health psychology, the view that certain personality traits may predispose individuals to specific health problems

generality theory in health psychology, the view that psychological characteristics can leave individuals vulnerable to a variety of illnesses

individuals to specific health problems. Such an assumption is an example of **specificity theory** in health psychology, which states that certain traits are related to specific illnesses. In contrast, **generality theory** assumes that psychological characteristics can leave individuals vulnerable to a variety of illnesses. According to generality theory, for example, feelings of loss and a tendency to give up can lead to any number of health problems. The occurrence of loss along with a tendency to give up can create feelings of helplessness and hopelessness (Engel, 1968). Health risks following loss may be linked to an increase in parasympathetic nervous system activity and a decrease in sympathetic nervous system activity (Engel & Schmale, 1972).

Vulnerability to a variety of illnesses may also result from the effect of emotional trauma and other psychological variables on the immune system. A new specialty within health psychology, known by the label *psychoimmunology*, as discussed in Chapter 2, explores links between psychological factors and the immune system's response. Stress and psychological trauma have a suppressing effect on the human immune system through a number of mechanisms (Krantz et al., 1985). Stress reduces the number of *lymphocytes*, which play an important role in the body's production of antibodies to fight disease. Stress also lowers the level of *interferon*, a cellular protein produced in response to infection that inhibits viral growth; many medical researchers believe that interferon can reduce cancer risk. In addition, stress increases the level of some hormones that may alter the immune system, such as the *corticosteroids*.

Physical and psychological adaptation to psychological stress is a complex phenomenon. Researchers have shown that a number of situations with psychological overtones lead to decreases in the response of the immune system. Among these are surgery, sleep deprivation, learned helplessness, and bereavement (Krantz et al., 1985). However, as we discuss in the next section, some stresses have both adaptive and nonadaptive characteristics.

THINKING ABOUT
The Functions of Grief

grief intense emotional suffering, usually caused by loss

Before 1960 there was little research on grief, perhaps because many people want to avoid the subject of death. However, as psychologists have become more interested in the processes of aging and the psychological issues related to growing old, interest in this emotion has increased. **Grief** refers to intense emotional suffering, usually caused by loss. The loss may be temporary, as in separation, or permanent, as in death. We tend to think of the loss that brings about grief as the loss of a person or perhaps of a beloved animal, but other kinds of losses may cause grief: loss of some personal quality such as memory, intellectual skills, self-esteem, or physical attractiveness; loss of some object such as money or one's homeland; and loss due to developmental processes, such as weaning and loss of the only-child status when a sibling arrives (Peretz, 1970).

Despite its unpleasantness as an emotion, grief serves some very important functions. Because grief is unpleasant, it is something we all want to avoid if possible. Yet grief reinforces group cohesiveness by encouraging individuals not to separate from the group—whether family, friends, or the community. Historically, such a function has had obvious survival value. Grief has adaptive functions for the individual as well. By grieving, an individual deals with a loss and, eventually, adjusts to it. Grief also provides the individual with a way to acknowledge the loss publicly and to pay homage to the person who was lost. Such a public display of emotion can elicit feelings of empathy and concern from the community and thus afford the grieving person much-needed support during difficult times. Further, grief shows others that the bereaved person is a caring person, adding to the communicative value of grief. Grief may motivate the person to recover the lost object, if in fact it can be recovered, as in the case of separation. Finally, grief is important because it promotes personal growth. When social relationships are broken due to death or separation, the person may turn the loss to eventual advantage with increased maturity and even enhanced self-esteem.

But adjustment to major losses can also pose risks to health. For example, people who have encountered major tragedies in their lives may have an increased risk of sudden death, a phenomenon documented by Engel (1971). Less dramatically, traumatic emotional events can also aggravate respiratory, gastrointestinal, and cardiovascular disorders (Taylor, 1986).

Studies of people who have experienced losses have shown that grief usually, but not always, occurs in three stages. The first stage, labeled *protest and yearning*, involves a "protest over the fact of bereavement and an intense yearning after or urge to recover the lost object" (Averill, 1979b). This stage is followed by a stage labeled *disorganization and despair*, a slow process in which the loss is accepted, as the person abandons efforts to recover the lost object. The final stage, *detachment and reorganization*, is marked by a final emotional detachment from the lost object and the formation of new life goals and perspectives.

If public grieving is a useful psychological process, how might our cultural practices for funerals impede the grieving process? Do other cultures have funeral practices that might lead to more psychologically beneficial grieving? When is grief an adaptive and useful process, and when is it detrimental to health and well-being?

Addictive Behaviors and Health

Early in this chapter we listed seven health practices that are related to maintaining good health, among them, not smoking and moderate or no use of alcohol. Nicotine and alcohol are widely used—and abused—substances in our society. Alcohol and tobacco are so common in our society that we tend to forget that they are drugs that can be addictive and harmful to our health. Within health psychology, a great deal of attention has been paid to the dangers of alcohol and tobacco use, because the use of these substances involves behavior that can potentially be changed.

Addictive behaviors are repetitive behavior patterns that increase the risk of disease and associated personal and social problems (Marlatt & Baer, 1988). Addictive behaviors include drinking, smoking, abusing other substances, overeating, and perhaps gambling. Addictive behaviors can lead to loss of control, when the individual cannot stop or decrease using substances despite trying. All of the addictive behaviors provide both short-term rewards and long-term costs, including health problems.

Substance use disorders are classified in the American Psychiatric Association's manual of mental disorders (DSM-IV), which we discuss in Chapter 16. However, these disorders differ in some interesting ways from disorders in other categories. First, the behavior problems in this category result from an individual ingesting chemical substances to the point where normal life is seriously disrupted. Second, a majority of Americans use drugs such as alcohol and caffeine, but do so at a level below that diagnosed

substance use disorder involves abuse of or dependence on drugs or alcohol

as abuse. Our first task, then, is to explore the diagnostic criteria for substance abuse. Following that discussion, we concentrate on the abuse of two particular substances, alcohol and tobacco. Use of these drugs was also discussed in Chapter 5.

Diagnostic Criteria for Substance Abuse and Dependence.   DSM-IV describes two levels of substance use disorders. The more serious is called substance dependence, whereas the other is a category known as substance abuse. **Substance abuse** is more likely among people who have recently begun using the substance and is more characteristic of substances that do not have physical withdrawal signs associated with them, such as marijuana, cocaine, and hallucinogens.

The diagnosis of **substance dependence** is made when an individual shows several symptoms that have been present in one 12-month period. The symptoms include taking the substance in larger amounts than intended or for a longer period of time; desire to cut down or control the substance; reduction of social, occupational, or recreational activities because of substance use; continued use despite social, psychological, or physical problems associated with it; and characteristic withdrawal symptoms.

Alcohol Abuse and Dependence.   Alcohol is the most used and most abused drug in American society. More than 90% of Americans try alcohol at some point in their lives. Estimates of problem drinking vary, but it is probable that about 10% of the population have relatively serious social or medical problems associated with alcohol use, and about 5% are actually addicted to alcohol. About half of all automobile fatalities are alcohol related.

As noted in Chapter 5, alcohol is basically a central nervous system depressant. However, the initial effect of alcohol intoxication is usually more like that of a stimulant: The individual experiences a sense of well-being, hyperactivity, is more sociable, and has lowered inhibitions. People who are shy and uncomfortable in social situations may become uncharacteristically sociable. As intoxication progresses, however, behavior becomes more and more depressed and withdrawn. With sufficient dosages, unconsciousness results.

substance abuse use of a chemical substance on a regular and continuous basis to the point that it interferes with work and family life

substance dependence serious substance use disorder diagnosed when an individual desires to reduce intake of the substance but is unable to do so, and suffers impairment of social, occupational, or recreational activities as a result of the substance

About half of all automobile fatalities are alcohol related. Because the alcohol-related accident rate is particularly high among teenagers, most states have raised the legal drinking age to 21.

There may be genetic predispositions toward alcoholism, although the data are not conclusive (Merikangas et al., 1985). The sons of fathers with alcohol dependence have characteristic brain waves that are associated with alcoholism before the boys have ever used alcohol (Begleiter et al., 1984). Evidence also suggests that individuals who are at high risk for alcoholism may have a biological predisposition to experience more pronounced stress-reducing effects from drinking (Sher & Levenson, 1982). In addition, more males than females are diagnosed as alcohol abusers. Critics of this biologically oriented research on alcohol dependence point out that environmental influences have been underemphasized, however. Children in families where there is a parent with alcohol dependence also experience family conflict, social isolation, and even parental neglect (Searles, 1988).

Alcohol dependence affects every member of the family, and children may be especially vulnerable. Children from families where alcoholism was present have been compared on a number of measures to children from families without any history of alcoholism. The children of families with alcoholism did not score as well on 9 of 17 tests of such characteristics as intelligence, cognitive achievement, psychological and physical health, hyperactivity, and self-esteem (Bennett, Wolin, & Reiss, 1988).

Risk for developing alcoholism is greater for people who begin drinking heavily in adolescence. Other risk factors contributing to drug abuse among young people include poor academic performance, psychological distress, low interest in religion, low self-esteem, and the perception of a lack of parental love (Bry et al., 1982; Chassin, Mann, & Sher, 1988). As Figure 15–4 shows, the more risk factors involved, the greater the extent of substance abuse.

Excessive use of alcohol has been linked to a number of health problems. Among these are cirrhosis of the liver; cancers of some types, especially of the alimentary–digestive systems; and fetal alcohol syndrome in children born to mothers with alcohol dependence (described in Chapter 12) (Taylor, 1986). Chronic alcohol abuse can also lead to brain changes and associated psychological disorders. Korsakoff's syndrome, characterized by severe memory loss, strikes some chronic alcoholics. Alcoholics also have significantly enlarged brain sulci (the shallow grooves separating convolutions in the cortex) in comparison to people who are not alcoholic (Pfefferbaum et al., 1988).

Cigarette Smoking. Research findings continue to document the health hazards associated with cigarette smoking. Smoking is the single most pre-

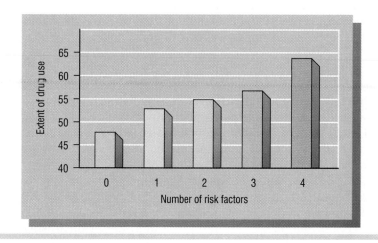

FIGURE 15–4
Extent of drug (including alcohol) use in adolescence is greater with a higher number of risk factors. Risk factors include heavy drinking beginning in adolescence, poor academic performance, low religiosity, psychological distress, low self-esteem, and perception of lack of parental love. (Adapted from Bry, McKeon, & Pandina, 1982.)

ventable cause of mortality and illness in the United States, affecting one in three people (Krantz et al., 1985). Smoking is associated with increased risks of lung, nose, mouth, throat, and bladder cancer. It is also associated with heart disease, emphysema, bronchitis, strokes, and vascular disease. In addition, pregnant women who smoke have more stillbirths and underweight babies than those who do not smoke (U.S. Public Health Service, 1979). Even people who do not smoke are not safe from the smoking behavior of others. Recent evidence has shown an increased risk of health problems from **passive smoking**, the inhalation of others' cigarette smoke.

As discussed in Chapter 5, nicotine is a stimulant. When it is inhaled in tobacco smoke, it is quickly absorbed into the lining of the lungs and carried by the blood into the brain. Within 7 seconds after it is inhaled, nicotine reaches the brain and alters the neurochemical action of selected neurons, producing increased alertness. There are corresponding increases in heart rate and blood pressure. As blood vessels constrict, circulation is reduced to the body's extremities and there is a decrease in skin temperature. At high levels, nicotine can trigger the release of endorphins, which bring about a sense of pleasure and relaxation (Pomerleau, 1980).

Given all the documented health hazards associated with cigarette smoking, why do people smoke? The answer is not a simple one. People smoke for a variety of reasons, including the pleasurable sensations just described. Several models can be used to understand smoking behavior. The *social learning model*, discussed in Chapter 10 (Bandura, 1977b), suggests that smoking is reinforced through peer approval and media depictions of the glamour associated with smoking. Eysenck's (1982) *arousal model* asserts that smoking causes arousal and that socially extroverted people who seek arousal are more likely to become smokers. Schachter (1980) has proposed an *addiction model* that states that people become addicted to nicotine and continue to smoke in order to maintain sufficient nicotine levels and avoid withdrawal. *Personality models* relate smoking to the personality characteristics of the smokers, much as the Type A personality is related to individuals prone to coronary heart disease. Some data suggest, for example, that people who return to smoking after they have been diagnosed with coronary heart disease score high on antisocial tendencies, aggression, and self-destructiveness, and that they may even thrive on social disapproval (Bass, 1988).

Although some research support exists for parts of each of these models, none of them can adequately explain smoking behavior. What we can say is that cigarette smoking involves a complex interaction of biological, psychological, and social factors and that quitting is difficult. A large majority of people who try to stop smoking eventually return to their habit. When people do stop, it is likely to be a result of their own efforts. Table 15–3 lists some of the pertinent findings on efforts to quit smoking.

Some people may begin smoking because of the glamorous advertising campaigns for smoking. This ad, for example, suggests that smoking is refreshing and is associated with attractive people.

Sexual Behavior and Health: The AIDS Crisis

Although many infectious diseases, such as poliomyelitis, have been all but eliminated as health risks in developed countries, sexually transmitted diseases are still rampant. Most of these diseases can be effectively treated. But in the early 1980s, a killer disease entered the world's consciousness—a behaviorally transmitted disease (Morin, 1988).

On June 5, 1981, the Centers for Disease Control in Atlanta, Georgia, reported the initial cases of the disease that would become known as **acquired immune deficiency syndrome**, or **AIDS**. In the months that followed, pieces of the puzzle fell into place until the medical world realized the horror of the situation. This new disease had a lengthy period of incuba-

TABLE 15-3
Data on Trying to Quit Smoking

- Over 70% of smokers who attend intensive cessation programs resume regular smoking within 12 months.
- Most of these smokers resume within the first 3 months following cessation.
- Most smokers who succeed in refraining from smoking in the long term will have made a number of unsuccessful previous attempts at cessation.
- Over 90% of smokers who stop do so by their own efforts, rather than with any specific aid or formal assistance.
- It is argued that self-initiated attempts at smoking cessation are more likely to be successful in the long term than are attempts with formal assistance.
- Smokers who relapse following cessation often report that negative emotional states (e.g., frustration, anxiety, anger, depression) or social pressures are what precipitate the relapse.
- Smokers who have a small number of cigarettes after stopping may experience a guilt reaction, believing that they have violated an absolute standard, and are therefore smokers again. This is known as the abstinence violation effect.

Source: Adapted from Owen, Halford, & Gilbert, 1986.

tion, perhaps as long as 10 years. Infected individuals could therefore spread the disease for years before becoming aware of any AIDS symptoms. The disease was spread by contact with infected semen and blood, initially affecting gay and bisexual men, intravenous drug users, and other people receiving infected blood in transfusions. (In Africa the disease is most prevalent among heterosexuals.) And the ultimate of horrors: apparently, all who contracted the disease would die.

AIDS cases were diagnosed worldwide, causing the international medical community to mobilize in search of the cause. The long-awaited announcement came in April 1984 when it was discovered that AIDS was caused by a virus labeled *human immunodeficiency virus,* or *HIV.* This discovery led some authorities to predict that an AIDS vaccine would be developed within 2 years. But that optimism quickly vanished as the complexity of HIV was discovered.

HIV does not actually destroy the immune system. In fact, the B-cells of the immune system, which actually attack invading bacteria and viruses, are

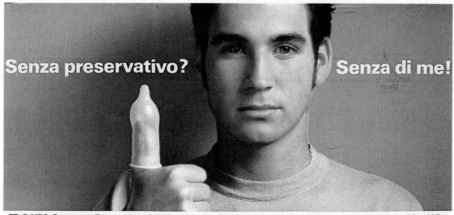

STOP AIDS. Campagna di prevenzione dell'Aiuto Aids Svizzero, in collaborazione con l'Ufficio federale della sanità pubblica.

Because the spread of AIDS is linked to risky sexual behavior, the role of psychology in this health crisis is to help change people's behavior. Raising awareness about alternatives, for example, through condom ads, is one approach. This ad campaign was sponsored by the government of Switzerland.

not harmed by HIV. Instead, HIV attacks the T-4 cells, also called *helper cells*, which signal the B-cells to attack. Thus, with the T-4 cells inoperative, invading germs wreak havoc on the body, because the immune system is incapable of fighting the infections (Batchelor, 1988). Research on HIV and the nature of the immune system continues at a furious pace, and much has been learned in recent years. Still, most experts believe that an AIDS vaccine is a distant goal, not likely to be reached in the near future.

So why is this disease discussed in a textbook on psychology? The answer to that question should be obvious: AIDS is caused by a virus, but the disease is spread to others through behavior. Change behavior, and you can significantly reduce the spread of the disease. Thus, psychology's role in fighting AIDS is a crucial one while research continues on effective pharmacological treatments.

One approach to behavior change is to educate people about the spread of AIDS, particularly those groups most at risk. Various local and national organizations have attempted to do this through the distribution of posters and booklets. In an attempt to raise national awareness, the U.S. Surgeon General's Office prepared an eight-page brochure on AIDS that was mailed to 107 million households in 1988. It was a public information campaign unprecedented in the history of the United States, indicative of the government's desire to slow the rising death toll. (By the end of 1992, there were 242,000 AIDS cases in the United States, and 600,000 worldwide, with estimates of 13 million infected with HIV worldwide.)

But does merely informing people about how AIDS is spread cause them to alter their behavior? Many psychologists doubted the effectiveness of the mass mailing, arguing that the $17 million it cost could have been better used in programs targeted at those people most likely to contract the disease. But proponents argued that everyone who practiced unsafe behaviors was potentially at risk. The public needed to understand that AIDS was not a disease restricted to gay men and IV drug users (Hostetler, 1988).

Psychologists began their work on AIDS by investigating the behaviors that placed people at risk, principally sexual intercourse and sharing of infected needles by drug users. Although the majority of cases in the United States were initially among homosexual and bisexual men (77%), that per-

Magic Johnson, the celebrity basketball player who contracted AIDS, became a spokesperson for AIDS awareness after his illness was disclosed.

centage has been dropping as more heterosexuals—men and women—have contracted the disease. Indeed, worldwide the principal way in which AIDS is spread is through heterosexual sex (Batchelor, 1988). Psychological research has focused on ways to convince people to practice "safe" sexual behavior.

Some of the work under way is targeted at (*a*) developing assertiveness in people so that they can resist coercion to engage in high-risk sexual behaviors; (*b*) understanding why women infected with AIDS choose to become pregnant, knowing there is a 50% chance the baby will be born with the disease; (*c*) counseling adolescents about safe sex, because they tend to believe, falsely, that they are not at risk; (*d*) changing community norms about acceptable sexual practices; and (*e*) discovering why some people refuse to change their dangerous sexual practices (Landers, 1988; Morin, 1988).

The outcome of these research efforts remains to be determined. But already there is evidence that high-risk behaviors are changing. For example, gay men report more monogamy, more frequent condom use, and less frequent anal sex (Ginzburg, Fleming, & Miller, 1988; Stall, Coates, & Hoff, 1988). Among heterosexuals the changes have not been as dramatic, probably because they do not view themselves as being at risk. Condom use among heterosexuals has increased, however (DeBuono et al., 1990).

Earlier in this chapter we discussed the growing relationship between health problems and life-style. In many respects, AIDS clearly fits with the other killers of the late twentieth century (such as heart disease and cancer) in that a change in life-style can reduce a person's risk of contracting the disease. The stress associated with the disease exacerbates the problem, perhaps even producing further damage to the immune system (recall the discussion of immunosuppression earlier and in Chapter 2). Related psychological issues include the need to change public and governmental attitudes to marshal support for AIDS prevention and treatment, as well as the facilitation of counseling and social support as part of a broad program of patient care (Baum & Nesselhof, 1988). Thus, both psychological researchers and practitioners are involved in attempts to prevent the disease where possible and deal with its reality where necessary.

STRESS

We have seen that certain behavioral and personality characteristics are psychological factors that contribute to health problems. Perhaps the best-known source of illness is **stress**, which is defined as the individual's reaction to environmental events that are aversive and threaten the person's well-being. In truth, stress is not an easy concept to define because it refers both to stimulus events and to responses, that is, how a person reacts to those events. Many events are stressful, from a hurricane to the death of a child to an exam. However, the actual stress experienced from such events depends on a number of personal factors that will define how the individual interprets the event (recall our earlier discussion of control) and what coping mechanisms are available (we discuss coping mechanisms in the next section). Thus, stress is an interactive process of environmental stimuli and a person's responses to them (see Kessler, Price, & Wortman, 1985).

stress physiological and psychological responses to excessive stimulation, usually of an unpleasant nature

Sources of Stress

Sources of stress, or the stimuli that produce stress, are known as *stressors*. The list of potential stressors is virtually limitless and includes drugs, exercise, marriage, examinations, job searches, childbearing, competition, aging, procrastination, disease, vacations, dieting, excessive eating, insufficient sleep, lottery winnings, house purchases, dating, and earthquakes (see Figure 15–5). Note that many of these stressors represent changes that can occur in a person's life.

Major Versus Minor Stressors.   The *Social Readjustment Rating Scale* (Holmes & Rahe, 1967) represents an important attempt to quantify stress in relation to what has been called **life change events**, and has been used in many studies of physical and psychological health.[*] The typical procedure used in these investigations is to select a large and varied sample of subjects and ask them to rank a list of life change events. In one study (Rahe, 1975), the subjects were told that they were to rank 42 life change events on a scale of 0 to 100, from the least stressful to the most stressful. To provide some common reference for the scale, the subjects were told to assign a value of 50 for marriage, and to scale the other 41 events in reference to that value. Ratings were averaged across the subjects and were categorized into four groups of events: family, personal, work, and financial. It is certainly not surprising that the death of a spouse and divorce rank as the most stressful events. An expanded version of the Holmes and Rahe Scale is presented on pages 613–614 so that you can assess your own level of stress.

Although most of the life change events on the Social Readjustment Rating Scale would be perceived negatively, some are clearly positive, such as taking a vacation or getting married. Still, these events serve as stressors, even though they have less psychological and physical impact than the more negative events (Sarason & Spielberger, 1979). Some events may entail both positive and negative features. A change in residence may reflect a higher standard of living but a loss of neighborhood friends. Changing to a different line of work may bring new opportunities for advancement, work that is diverse rather than routine, and increased salary, but it may also create fears about failure in the new job, a loss of job security, and worry about acceptance in the new field. Recall our discussion of motives in conflict in Chapter 9. Conflict is a stressor.

Procedurally, the scaling of life change events has been used to study the relationship between stress and health where the *sum* of the life changes during a specified period of time is used to predict subsequent changes in health. While a simple sum of the life change events is used in the Holmes and Rahe scale, Brinbaum and Sotoodeh (1991) have recently suggested that such combinations of stressful events are not equal to the sum of each of the separate events. The impact of a particular event seems to vary as a function of other events that have changed the individual's life. This certainly complicates the picture, but Brinbaum and Sotoodeh have devised alternative scaling procedures that offer more refined predictions.

Major changes in life are not the only stressors people experience. Stress comes in smaller packages, in the form of the frustrations and conflicts that are part of everyday life. Research by Richard Lazarus (1981) assigns a major role to these minor stresses. Because they are so common, Lazarus believes these stressors may play a larger role in our physical and psychological well-being than the major life changes discussed earlier.

What are the stressors most common to college students? Not surprisingly, they center around concern about making good grades, having friends, and getting a good job after college. According to Lazarus (1981), college students asked about their principal concerns listed anxiety about wasting time, concern over meeting high academic standards, and loneliness. In addition, the amount of stress students experience outside the class-

life change events positive and negative changes in the individual's living routine

FIGURE 15–5
For many people, their jobs are a major source of stress. Chief stressors are work overload, work pressure, responsibility for other people, role conflict and ambiguity, inability to develop satisfying social relationships at work, perceived inadequate career development, and lack of control over work (see Taylor, 1986).

[*]   Brinbaum and Sotoodeh (1991) point out that this scale has achieved the distinction of being represented in virtually every recent introductory psychology textbook.

What follows is the Social Readjustment Rating Scale reprinted from Blake, Fry, and Pesjack (1984). It is an expanded version of the Holmes and Rahe scale. To complete the questionnaire, indicate the number of times during the last 12 months you have experienced each of the events described (maximum frequency is 5), then multiply this number by the value associated with the event and total your score.

Event	Value	Frequency	Total
1. Death of a spouse, lover, or child	94	_____	_____
2. Death of a parent or sibling	88	_____	_____
3. Beginning formal higher education	84	_____	_____
4. Death of a close friend	83	_____	_____
5. Miscarriage or stillbirth of pregnancy of self, spouse, or lover	83	_____	_____
6. Jail sentence	82	_____	_____
7. Divorce or marital separation	82	_____	_____
8. Unwanted pregnancy of self, spouse, or lover	80	_____	_____
9. Abortion of unwanted pregnancy of self, spouse, or lover	80	_____	_____
10. Detention in jail or other institution	79	_____	_____
11. Change in dating activity	79	_____	_____
12. Death of a close relative	79	_____	_____
13. Change in marital situation other than divorce or separation	78	_____	_____
14. Separation from significant other whom you like very much	77	_____	_____
15. Change in health status or behavior of spouse or lover	77	_____	_____
16. Academic failure	77	_____	_____
17. Major violation of the law and subsequent arrest	76	_____	_____
18. Marrying or living with lover against parents' wishes	75	_____	_____
19. Change in love relationship or important friendship	74	_____	_____
20. Change in health status or behavior of a parent or sibling	73	_____	_____
21. Change in feelings of loneliness, insecurity, anxiety, boredom	73	_____	_____
22. Change in marital status of parents	73	_____	_____
23. Acquiring a visible deformity	72	_____	_____
24. Change in ability to communicate with a significant other whom you like very much	71	_____	_____
25. Hospitalization of a parent or sibling	70	_____	_____
26. Reconciliation of marital or love relationship	68	_____	_____
27. Release from jail or other institution	68	_____	_____
28. Graduation from college	68	_____	_____
29. Major personal injury or illness	68	_____	_____

Event	Value	Frequency	Total
30. Wanted pregnancy of self, spouse or lover	67	_____	_____
31. Change in number or type of arguments with spouse or lover	67	_____	_____
32. Marrying or living with lover with parents' approval	66	_____	_____
33. Gaining a new family member through birth or adoption	65	_____	_____
34. Preparing for an important exam or writing a major paper	65	_____	_____
35. Major financial difficulties	65	_____	_____
36. Change in the health status or behavior of a close relative or close friend	65	_____	_____
37. Change in academic status	64	_____	_____
38. Change in amount and nature of interpersonal conflicts	63	_____	_____
39. Change in relationship with members of your immediate family	62	_____	_____
40. Change in own personality	62	_____	_____
41. Hospitalization of yourself or a close relative	61	_____	_____
42. Change in course of study, major field, vocational goals, or work status	60	_____	_____
43. Change in own financial status	59	_____	_____
44. Change in status of divorced or widowed parent	59	_____	_____
45. Change in number or type of arguments between parents	59	_____	_____
46. Change in acceptance by peers, identification with peers, or social pressure by peers	58	_____	_____
47. Change in general outlook on life	57	_____	_____
48. Beginning or ceasing service in the armed forces	57	_____	_____
49. Change in attitudes toward friends	56	_____	_____
50. Change in living arrangements, conditions, or environment	55	_____	_____
51. Change in frequency or nature of sexual experiences	55	_____	_____
52. Change in parents' financial status	55	_____	_____
53. Change in amount or nature of pressure from parents	55	_____	_____

Social Readjustment Scale (continued)

Event	Value	Frequency	Total
54. Change in degree of interest in college or attitudes toward education	55	___	___
55. Change in the number of personal or social relationships you've formed or dissolved	55	___	___
56. Change in relationship with siblings	54	___	___
57. Change in mobility or reliability of transportation	54	___	___
58. Academic success	54	___	___
59. Change to a new college or university	54	___	___
60. Change in feelings of self-reliance, independence, or amount of self-discipline	53	___	___
61. Change in number or type of arguments with roommate	52	___	___
62. Spouse or lover beginning or ceasing work outside the home	52	___	___
63. Change in frequency of use or amounts of drugs other than alcohol, tobacco, or marijuana	51	___	___
64. Change in sexual morality, beliefs, or attitudes	50	___	___
65. Change in responsibility at work	50	___	___
66. Change in amount or nature of social activities	50	___	___
67. Change in dependencies on parents	50	___	___
68. Change from academic work to practical fieldwork experience or internship	50	___	___
69. Change in amount of material possessions and concomitant responsibilities	50	___	___
70. Change in routine at college or work	49	___	___
71. Change in amount of leisure time	49	___	___
72. Change in amount of in-law trouble	49	___	___
73. Outstanding personal achievement	49	___	___
74. Change in family structure other than parental divorce or separation	48	___	___
75. Change in attitude toward drugs	48	___	___

Event	Value	Frequency	Total
76. Change in amount and nature of competition with same sex	48	___	___
77. Improvement of own health	47	___	___
78. Change in responsibilities at home	47	___	___
79. Change in study habits	46	___	___
80. Change in number or type of arguments or conflicts with close relatives	46	___	___
81. Change in sleeping habits	46	___	___
82. Change in frequency of use or amounts of alcohol	45	___	___
83. Change in social status	45	___	___
84. Change in frequency of use or amounts of tobacco	45	___	___
85. Change in awareness of activities in external world	45	___	___
86. Change in religious affiliation	44	___	___
87. Change in type of gratifying activities	43	___	___
88. Change in amount or nature of physical activities	43	___	___
89. Change in address or residence	43	___	___
90. Change in amount or nature of recreational activities	43	___	___
91. Change in frequency of use or amounts of marijuana	43	___	___
92. Change in social demands or responsibilities due to your age	43	___	___
93. Court appearance for legal violation	40	___	___
94. Change in weight or eating habits	39	___	___
95. Change in religious activities	37	___	___
96. Change in political views or affiliations	34	___	___
97. Change in driving pattern or conditions	33	___	___
98. Minor violation of the law	31	___	___
99. Vacation or travel	30	___	___
100. Change in number of family get-togethers	30	___	___

Interpretive Scale

Major Stress	above 5,500
Moderate Stress	3,501–5,500
Mild Stress	1,501–3,500
Minor Stress	below 1,500

Source: Blake, Fry, & Pesjack, 1984.

room has a definite effect on their classroom performance (DeMeuse, 1985). Often professors forget that fact, assuming that students exist in an academic vacuum.

Emergency Situations. Another category of stressors includes natural disasters and other emergency situations that make extreme physiological and psychological demands on the individual. Stressors in this category include fires, tornados, floods, and wars. Exposure to some of these stressors may be brief (fire), whereas the period of exposure for others may be long (war). Although these stressors are not commonly experienced by most people, psychologists are interested in them for a variety of reasons, including discovering ways to help people readjust to normal life after these experiences. Using methods of naturalistic observation, psychologists have studied war veterans, particularly those who fought in Vietnam, and survivors of a number of disasters such as Hurricane Andrew in 1992, the 1985 earthquake in Mexico City, or a flood in West Virginia.

In the West Virginia disaster, researchers studied the survivors of a flood in 1972 that killed 125 people in a community and left another 4,000 homeless. The results of the study, conducted 3 years after the flood, showed that 80% of the survivors had some severe psychological problems, a condition known as *post-traumatic stress disorder* (see Chapter 16). Some of these people may have had some problems before the flood, but it is likely that most of their difficulties were the result of the disaster experience. The psychological legacy of the disaster included a heightened fear of death; nightmares, with death by drowning a common theme; reduced social relationships; reduced emotionality, a change that has been called **psychological numbing**; and guilt over the fact that they had lived while others had died (Lifton & Olson, 1976; Titchener & Kapp, 1976). (See Figure 15–6.)

> **psychological numbing** reduction in the capacity to experience emotions

Recently the APA established a special task force to deal with the survivors of disasters. The goals of the task force focus on ensuring that communities have the psychological resources to deal with disasters after the fact and helping communities in potential disaster areas plan for possible emergencies.

In summary, there are many sources of stress in the world, some major and some minor. Many are associated with life changes, others are the

FIGURE 15–6
Hurricane Andrew, the killer storm of the 1992 hurricane season, left a path of destruction in southern Florida. Such disasters leave behind much physical damage, but the psychological consequences of such stressful events are longer lasting.

result of common frustrations and conflicts, and some are the result of disasters. Everyone experiences stress; it cannot be avoided. But its effects can be lessened, as we see in the next section that discusses stress management in the workplace.

THINKING ABOUT
Stress in the Workplace

As we saw at the beginning of this chapter, a major source of stress is one's job. Job stress is partly due to characteristics of the person in the job, as well as to other workers in the job setting, but jobs carry their own inherent levels of stress. Some jobs are classified as high-stress occupations, such as secretary, farm owner, social worker, sales manager, and firefighter. Low-stress jobs include farm laborer, heavy equipment operator, child-care worker, and college professor (M. Smith, 1978). These classifications are based on self-reports of job-related stress by workers in these various occupations.

Because certain jobs are especially stressful, they exact a heavy physical and psychological toll from people who serve in those occupations. Consequently, psychologists have focused considerable attention on dealing with this particular kind of occupational stress. The complex of treatment methods that has developed to deal with job stress is often labeled **stress management**, and it includes meditation, relaxation techniques, biofeedback, exercise programs, group therapy, behavior modification, social networking, and others. As research in this field has progressed, there has been a growing emphasis on the notion of stress prevention. Ideally the approach is to eliminate the stressors inherent in a job situation. In many cases, however, that simply is not possible. An alternative strategy is to acknowledge the inevitability of the job stress and to prepare the worker to anticipate the stressors and to deal more effectively with them. This kind of preventative program has been called **stress inoculation** (Meichenbaum & Novaco, 1978).

Ray Novaco (1977) has used stress inoculation with police officers to teach them how to deal with their anger. Simply controlling anger may not be healthy, and the police officer may experience even greater stress at feeling unable to vent that emotion. It is therefore important to train these workers to react in ways that will make the anger less likely to occur. Situations are used that the officer is likely to encounter, such as a drunk vomiting in the police car, a citizen refusing to help, or someone shouting obscenities or even physically assaulting an officer.

The procedure used by Novaco with the police officers involved three stages. The first, *cognitive preparation*, helped the officers understand the inevitable situations they would face and their own reactions to these stressors. Second, the officers met together and with the psychologist to discuss various situations and how they should be handled, a stage labeled *skill acquisition and rehearsal*. Finally, the officers were able to practice the coping techniques learned in stage 2 in a series of *simulated job-related incidents* that gradually increased in terms of their crisis quality (see Figure 15–7).

This kind of program holds great promise for stress management, especially in those job situations where the stress cannot be eliminated or even reduced substantially. It succeeds by causing workers to restructure their jobs cognitively; that is, workers learn to think about their jobs in new ways.

stress management complex of treatment methods developed to deal with job stress

stress inoculation program that prepares the individual to anticipate stressors, acknowledge their inevitability, and thus deal more rationally with the stress

Furthermore, the group training procedures help the workers realize that they share common problems, and the acquisition of new job skills builds the kind of competence that can effectively reduce stress. It is very likely that these kinds of programs will find even greater use as they are applied to a wider range of occupations.

How can some of the techniques for reducing stress in the workplace be aplied to college stress? Can you list the major stressors inherent in college life? What types of cognitive preparation and skill acquisition and rehearsal might be useful for reducing college stress? Should orientation programs at college include simulated college-related stress incidents?

FIGURE 15–7
Police psychologist Harvey Goldstein (*left*) works with the Prince Georges County Police Department in Maryland. He is one of many psychologists who work with people having high-stress jobs, helping those individuals cope with the stressors that are inherent in their jobs. Psychologists may not be able to reduce the stressors, but they can reduce stress by changing the way the person reacts to the stressors.

Models of Stress

Consider the following series of events. It is the day of your final exam in psychology. You stayed up late last night finishing your reading but fell asleep before reviewing your class notes. It is time to head for campus. You jump in your car and put your open notebook on the seat next to you. While you are driving, you glance repeatedly at your notes. Suddenly you look up and see the brake lights of the car ahead of you looming ever closer. Startled, you slam on your brakes, stopping inches short of the car ahead. Almost immediately you are aware that your heart is racing and your breathing has increased. Realizing that getting into an accident would be an expensive excuse for missing an exam, you close your notebook and pay attention to the road.

Recall from earlier chapters that the physiological changes that accompany a perceived danger or threat prepare the individual to respond to that danger. In the preceding example, the perception of the stopped car and the potential for an accident caused an increase in autonomic nervous system and endocrine activity that resulted in increased arousal. The response was to step on the brakes quickly. Our scenario is an example of the *fight or flight response*, which you encountered in Chapter 9. This response was first described by Walter Cannon, who saw it as adaptive because it prepares the organism to respond quickly to danger. However, it can also be detrimental because sustained physiological and psychological arousal can eventually impair health and cause illness. Cannon's work on stress incorporated both the physiological and psychological aspects of the stress response. His description of the fight or flight response was one of the earliest models of stress and the one from which most modern models have been developed. Since the time of Cannon, two models of stress have dominated the literature. One is a biological model proposed by Hans Selye, and the other is a psychological model developed by Richard Lazarus.

Selye's Model. According to Selye (1956), stress is a physiological response to noxious stimuli, that is, stressors. His work on stress began with experiments on rats. Selye observed that prolonged exposure to stressors produced predictable responses: enlarged adrenal glands, a shrunken thymus, and ulceration of the stomach's lining. These changes suggested extended activity from the autonomic nervous system and its regulation of endocrine function, particularly the release of epinephrine (adrenalin) from the adrenal glands. Selye argued that the response to the stressor was *nonspecific*, meaning that the organism responded to all stressors with the same initial physiological reactions, as explained in the following analogy:

Suppose that all possible accesses to a bank building are connected with a police station by an elaborate burglar-alarm system. When a burglar enters the bank, no matter what his personal characteristics are—whether he is small or tall, lean or stout—and no matter which door or window he opens to enter, he will set off the same alarm. The primary change is therefore nonspecifically induced from anywhere by anyone. The pattern of resulting secondary change, on the other hand, is highly specific. It is always in a certain police station that the burglar alarm will ring and policemen will then rush to the bank along a specified route according to a predetermined plan to prevent robbery. (Selye, 1956)

Using the concept of the nonspecific response, Selye developed a model of stress which he called the **general adaptation syndrome (GAS)**. The GAS consists of three stages, as shown in Figure 15–8. First to occur is the *alarm stage* in which the body prepares itself for immediate response by activating the sympathetic division of the autonomic nervous system. This initial reaction is quite general in that it produces physiological and biochemical changes throughout much of the body.

The second part of the GAS is more focused and is called the *resistance stage*. In this stage the organism attempts to cope with the specific stressor by focusing the body's resources on the particular stressor. Although this stage may deal effectively with the source of stress, it also weakens the body's ability to deal with other stressors. Studies have shown that even mild stressors introduced in the resistance stage, when the body is battling another stressor, may cause serious problems for the individual. Under continued and persistent stress, the body experiences the wear and tear of ongoing physiological arousal. This situation taxes the body's resources and can be a precursor to stress-related disorders such as ulcers and hypertension. Selye hypothesized that prolonged resistance to stress can increase the risk of infection due to a weakening of the immune system, an issue we discussed earlier.

The body's ability to resist stress has obvious limits. The final phase of the GAS is known as the *exhaustion stage*. In this stage, the organism can no longer resist the stressors and begins to break down. During the exhaustion stage the parasympathetic branch of the autonomic nervous system is activated in response to the increased levels of sympathetic activity experienced in the earlier stages. The low level of functioning experienced during the exhaustion stage can result in reactions ranging from depression to shock to death. Fortunately, most stress situations do not reach this final stage. In summary, Selye's GAS model describes a physiological system that provides an immediate coping response for any form of stress and a more focused coping response to deal with the particular stressor (see Figure 15–9).

Lazarus's Model. Unlike Selye's GAS, Richard Lazarus's model of stress developed from his work with humans, and it emphasizes psychological variables, namely, the cognitive processes of perception and thought. Lazarus (1966, 1982, 1984) argued that it is neither the stressor nor the response that best defines stress. Rather, it is the individual's perception and

general adaptation syndrome (GAS)
Selye's proposed model of the body's emergency reaction to stressful situations: alarm reaction, resistance, and exhaustion

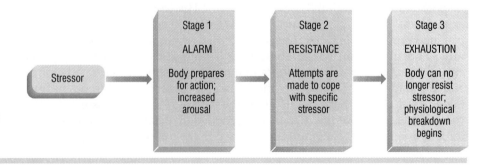

FIGURE 15–8
Selye's general adaptation syndrome (GAS) includes three stages in responding to stress.

FIGURE 15-9
Fires are stressors that can invoke the general adaptation syndrome. This fire victim is in the resistance phase of coping with a specific stressor, and is being attended by paramedics.

appraisal of the situation that is a significant determinant of whether or not stress will be experienced. For example, Tom may enjoy public speaking, whereas Nancy finds it terrifying. According to Lazarus, events in and of themselves do not produce stress; it is the individual's appraisal of the event that creates the stress.

Lazarus's model of stress is presented in Figure 15–10. When an individual is confronted with challenge, **primary appraisal** occurs. During primary appraisal the individual attempts to determine how the event will affect her or his well-being. Some events are perceived as positive and beneficial and thus are not likely to create stress. However, other events are viewed negatively and thus are perceived as harmful or threatening. This appraisal of the event also generates emotions such as fear, anger, or excitement.

The next stage, **secondary appraisal**, involves determining whether one's coping capacities are sufficient to meet the demands of a potentially harmful event. An important part of this stage is the individual's review and analysis of the response alternatives available to him or her. This second stage of the model is more important than the first, because even if the individual identifies the event as harmful in the primary appraisal, secondary appraisal may convince the individual that adequate coping responses are available, thus minimizing the effect of the stressor.

Secondary appraisal can also lead to the acquisition of new coping responses. For example, recall Tom and Nancy's different opinions with regard to public speaking. They both enroll in a psychology class and learn from the course syllabus that an oral presentation is required for the class.

primary appraisal first stage in Lazarus's model of stress in which the individual attempts to determine how the stressor will affect well-being

secondary appraisal second stage in Lazarus's model of stress in which the individual attempts to determine whether coping capacities are sufficient and to select the best coping strategy

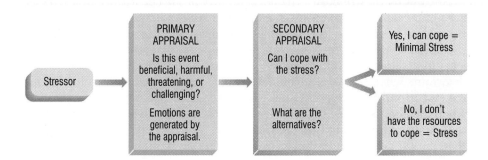

FIGURE 15–10
The cognitive–psychological model of stress developed by Richard Lazarus emphasizes the processes of appraisal as the primary determinant of stress.

When Nancy reads this, she feels some fear and imagines making a fool of herself in front of the class. Thus, Nancy's primary appraisal of public speaking is that it is a threat to her psychological well-being. After class she shares her fears with Tom and is surprised when he says he welcomes the opportunity to speak in front of the class because he is considering a career in broadcasting. Tom's primary appraisal is that public speaking is beneficial to him and is in his best interests.

As part of secondary appraisal, Nancy begins to consider her options. She can drop the course and thus avoid having to give her speech. Recalling her previous public speaking efforts, she remembers the times she presented reports to several high school committees and the part she once had in a school play. On those occasions she had felt quite anxious, but her friends and teachers had praised the job she did. Nancy decides to respond to an announcement in the school newspaper and join a group to help students reduce their anxiety about public speaking. As a result of the secondary appraisal, Nancy feels less anxious. It helped her to recall that she had handled such stress in the past and gave her confidence that she could do it again. Her appraisal also led her to take some steps to further reduce her anxiety by adding to her coping abilities. This two-stage appraisal process helps us identify potential stressors, evaluate coping strategies, and make decisions about dealing with the stress.

Although the two models of stress we have described here are quite different, they are not necessarily antagonistic. It is easy to see how a biological system to cope with stress would have obvious evolutionary advantages in enhancing survival. Yet the nature of the human cerebral cortex allows for decisional processes in dealing with stress, rather than automatic biological reactions that are characteristic of lower organisms. A synthesis of the two models provides for an immediate, probably nonspecific, preparation for dealing with stressors; it is followed by an intelligent appraisal of the situation that may redirect the physiological reactions and institute appropriate behaviors. As humans, we have behavioral options, even though we may not always make intelligent decisions in dealing with stressors.

Determinants of the Stress Reaction

The two models just described can account for how people respond in stressful situations. However, they do not tell the whole story. Other factors can play a role in determining the intensity of the response to stressors.

Intensity and Duration of Stressor.   Obviously, the *intensity* and *duration* of the stressor affect the intensity of the stress reaction. Stressors that exist for long periods usually do so because the individual is not permitted to escape the stressful situation (such as combat), or because the person is coping so poorly that the stressor remains.

Predictability of Stressor.   The *predictability* of the occurrence of a stressor is as important as its intensity. A number of studies have found that subjects report less stress when they are able to predict the occurrence of the stressor (Folkman, 1984). For example, one study exposed two groups of human subjects to a series of electric shocks. The experimental group was allowed to determine when the shocks would occur and how intense they would be; the control group received the identical pattern of shocks but knew neither when the shocks would occur nor what their intensity would be. Subjects in the experimental group judged the shocks to be significantly less intense than did the control group subjects (Staub, Tursky, & Schwartz, 1971).

Rats behave in a similar way. In a study by Badia, Culbertson, and Harsh (1973), rats could press a lever that produced a warning tone before each shock was delivered. If the rats did not depress the lever, the shocks occurred without warning. Rats clearly preferred the predictable shocks, and surprisingly, they maintained this preference even when those shocks were stronger in intensity and longer in duration than the unpredictable shocks. Other findings indicate that the physiological reactions that accompany stress are less pronounced for predictable shocks than for unpredictable ones (Abbott, Schoen, & Badia, 1984).

Motivation of Person.   *Motivation* is another important variable that affects the intensity of stress responses. Stressors experienced by a soldier trying to stay alive during combat (see Schultz, 1985) and those experienced in the midst of heated athletic competition may be minimized, if not ignored altogether, when personal motivation is high. For instance, a football player may sustain a painful injury during the game, yet not notice the injury until after the game has concluded. At that point, the stress experienced may still be low if it is offset by the elation of an important victory. Another way to view this situation is to realize that stress is but one state, and the effects of stress can only be assessed when the other existing cognitive and emotional states are considered.

Competency of Person.   The intensity of stress is also determined by the *competency* of the person experiencing the stress. In truth, actual competence may not be as important as the person's belief in her or his ability to handle a stressful situation. For people who must face stressful situations, such as firefighters and other emergency personnel, training serves to help them not only do a more professional job but also manage the stress that is inherent in that job, as we have discussed earlier. Students who are prepared for an exam, and thus feel competent, do not experience as much stress as students who are not prepared (see Figure 15–11).

Social Support.   Another important factor in moderating stress intensity is *social support*, that is, the social network from which people can draw emotional support in times of stress. The death of a child or of a spouse is an extremely stressful event, yet the intensity can be lessened with strong social-support groups, such as friends and relatives who can help the person through those tough times. In some cases people who have experienced similar stressful events have formed groups, for example, parents whose children have been killed by a drunk driver. The fact that others have gone through a similar stressful event can provide the understanding and credibility of support needed to reduce the intensity of the stress and perhaps to speed the readjustment process. The importance of social support is underscored by studies demonstrating that people with strong social ties (family, relatives, friends, group memberships) have longer life expectancies and suffer fewer stress-produced disorders than people who lack that social support (Antonovsky, 1979). (Figure 15–12 on the next page is a diagram of the factors affecting the intensity of the stress response.) We say more about social support as a coping mechanism later in this chapter.

Stress: An Inevitability

Thus far we have described a number of psychological factors related to illness; the concept of stress subsumes many of those. Selye was one of the first to observe that stress-related diseases, such as high blood pressure,

FIGURE 15–11
Many colleges and universities, recognizing that college life can be extremely stressful, have established stress management programs for students. Some follow the model in which students are educated about the nature of stress, then given training in methods to cope with the stress, and then made to practice those skills in real-life, stressful situations. In general, these programs have been very successful (Taylor, 1986).

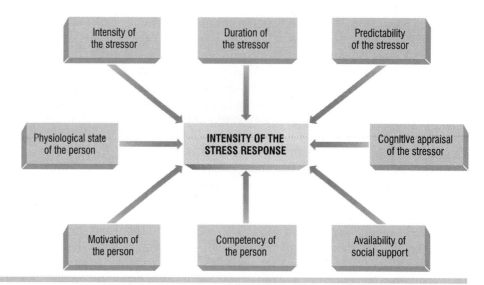

FIGURE 15–12
Factors that contribute to the intensity of the stress response.

often began during the stage of resistance when the body was especially susceptible. Ulcers, some forms of kidney disease, headaches (both tension and migraine forms), and respiratory disorders, such as asthma, are all associated with stress.

In some cases stress may actually be the cause of the disease, but more likely it is a condition that contributes to the problem, perhaps by triggering an attack from a dormant disease process. This last point is reinforced by studies that link stress and the onset of cancer (Sklar & Anisman, 1981). Finally, as discussed earlier, there is good evidence that stress increases susceptibility to infectious diseases by weakening the body's immune system (Jemmott & Locke, 1984). Among the many pieces of supporting evidence for this contention is the fact that most stress-related diseases are those for which an immune system is known to exist.

In this section we have reviewed the various sources of stress that people experience and the physiological and psychological reactions to those stressors. We have described how stress can be an important determinant in a number of physiological disorders. Its psychological consequences are many (recall our discussion of the flood survivors) and include nightmares, guilt, impaired sociability, loss of self-esteem, depression, insomnia, and a number of variables related to performance ability (see Glass & Singer, 1972). In our analysis, we have treated stress as a largely negative force, something to be avoided if possible.

But is there a positive side to stress? Perhaps there is. After all, many people seem to derive pleasure from activities that are stress inducing, for example, skydiving or bullfighting. Perhaps in the evolutionary scheme of things, some amount of stress seeking has been selected for on a genetic basis. Early humans who took chances, challenging the unknown, may have enhanced their survival opportunities (Averill, 1973). Mastery of the environment appears to be an important part of human behavior, and that mastery necessarily involves some induction of stress. Yet tolerance levels for stress must not be exceeded, at least not for very long, without serious consequences. Because of these potential consequences, methods for coping with stress remain a crucial concern for psychologists as a means of promoting human welfare. In the remainder of this chapter we describe the principal mechanisms for coping effectively with stress. Given that we cannot completely avoid stress, how can we seek to minimize its effects?

COPING

Coping may be defined as those behaviors and thoughts that an individual uses to handle anticipated stress or stress that already has occurred. Coping is usually thought of as a response to stress, yet as this definition indicates, it is more than that. It is also a means to avoid the experience of stress or to prepare for it in such a way as to minimize its effects. People use many coping strategies, far too many to cover in this chapter. We begin this section by providing a classification scheme, a taxonomy of coping strategies, and then we discuss selected examples of some of those strategies. Our discussion does not include unconscious strategies such as defense mechanisms, which were covered in Chapter 10.

coping behaviors and thoughts that enable an individual to handle stress or anticipated stress

Types of Coping Responses

Our taxonomy comes from the work of Arthur Stone and John Neale (1984), who have delineated eight categories of coping methods. Their research has demonstrated that in responding to stressful situations, people employ one strategy in about half of the problems they face, but for the other problems they use two or more strategies. In fact, in about 11% of the stress situations they studied, people used from four to seven different **coping strategies**. Table 15–4 shows the frequency of use of all eight coping categories.

coping strategies Stone and Neale identified eight different categories that define the various methods individuals use to handle stress

The most frequently used strategy is *direct action* in which the person thinks about the problem and then tries to do something to solve it. In the second strategy, *acceptance*, the person accepts the fact that the stress has occurred and that nothing can be done about it. Some people use strategies that involve *distraction*, in which they get involved in other activities or force themselves to think about other topics. Some use the cognitive strategy of *situation redefinition*, in which the person attempts to think about the problem in a different way so as to make the stress more acceptable. Another strategy is *catharsis*, in which pent-up emotions are released as a means of reducing the stress. Some people use *relaxation* techniques as a way of reducing the stress they are experiencing or expect to experience. A seventh category is the use of *social support*. With this strategy the stress is reduced by the support received from friends and loved ones or professionals such as psychologists and physicians. The eighth category includes *religious strategies*, in which the person seeks spiritual comfort, which may be from friends or from a minister.

What determines which coping strategy a person will use? Personality plays a role; people use strategies that fit them. Past experience is also important, for some coping strategies may have been more successful than others. Availability of resources for coping is important. Further, the situation itself determines what coping strategies are adopted (McCrae, 1984).

Coping by Direct Action. As shown in Table 15–4, Stone and Neale (1984) found direct action to be the most commonly used coping strategy. Within this category there are many approaches. As we discussed earlier, conflict is one of the sources of stress. Not surprisingly, behaviors that are designed to resolve the conflict are stress reducing. Suppose that you and your roommate both like to study in your room. The problem is that your roommate likes to study while listening to music, whereas you prefer absolute quiet. Under these circumstances, stress is created. A number of responses on your part are possible. You could hide your roommate's cassette tapes. You could study in the library. You could study in your room after your roommate has

TABLE 15-4
Frequency of Use of Various Coping Strategies by 2,370 Adults

Coping Category	Frequency of Use (%)
Direct action	46
Acceptance	30
Distraction	27
Situation redefinition	25
Catharsis	25
Relaxation	17
Social Support	15
Religious strategies	6

Source: Stone & Neale, 1984.

gone to sleep or before she or he wakes up. Although all of these responses might allow you to study, they would not eliminate the stress. One way to reduce the stress would be to work out a compromise in which half of the hours each evening were quiet hours, but music could be played during the other half of the evening. Or you could ask your roommate to wear earphones. There is nothing terribly creative about these solutions. But the solutions to most of the problems we face do not require much imagination—just a little dispassionate analysis and some willingness to bend. We usually label this type of solution *conflict resolution*, and it is the substance of which long-term relationships are made.

Another coping strategy in the direct action category is *assertiveness*. Some people will buy anything that someone tries to sell. They just cannot say no to the sales pitch, even though later they are very distressed that they made a foolish purchase. If lack of assertiveness is a continuing source of stress for someone, an obvious strategy is to become assertive. Psychologists and others have developed training procedures to help people develop their assertive behavior.

Some direct action strategies may involve engaging in the very behavior that is stress producing. After an automobile accident, just being in a car may be stressful, to say nothing of having to drive again. A successful strategy might first involve just sitting in the car while it is parked, then taking short rides as a passenger in low-traffic areas, then rides in more traffic, gradually working up to driving again. Similarly, people who experience stress from public speaking may reduce that stress through gaining more experience, or, which is even better, by taking a course in public-speaking skills. Recall that *feeling* competent can reduce the intensity of emotion.

An important part of any coping strategy is the kind of cognitive appraisal described by Lazarus. Yet it is especially important in direct action approaches, which require an accurate identification of the source of stress and an appraisal of behavioral options.

Social Support.   Earlier we mentioned that social support can moderate the intensity of a stress reaction. *Social support* refers to the feeling that we are important to and valued by others. By nature we are social beings; we seek the company of others and form complex social and interpersonal networks. Family and friends help us mark important events, sharing with us our joys and sorrows. Births, graduations, marriages, illnesses, and deaths are but some of life's occurrences that cause us to seek out others and share our lives with them. Hause (1984) has described four types of social support:

1. *Emotional concern* involving the expression of empathy, caring, and concern
2. *Instrumental aid*, such as giving money and other forms of material assistance
3. *Information*, which includes giving advice and directions
4. *Appraisal*, which refers to giving feedback to others that is relevant to their own self-evaluation.

All four types of support are important; however, they may come from different sources in a person's support network.

All cultures have evolved social-support systems to facilitate coping with stress. The death of people close to us is the most significant life-change event any of us will ever have to contend with. It is not surprising, then, that elaborate rituals accompany this experience (see Figure 15–13).

FIGURE 15-13
Elaborate rituals often accompany significant life changes, such as funerals. The rituals, such as this Balinese creation ceremony, may serve as social-support mechanisms for coping with the stress of change.

Can it be that relationships with others can protect a person from stress and illness? Earlier we noted that people with strong social support are less likely to die prematurely than those who lack such support systems. Social support can reduce the negative effects of stressful events such as unemployment, surgery, or grief (Krantz et al., 1985). Further, for people under high stress, social support has been shown to reduce such health problems as high blood pressure, ulcers, headaches, and indigestion (Gentry & Kobasa, 1984).

Social-support networks can include family, friends, co-workers, social organizations, and religious groups. Traditionally, the nuclear family, the church, and the community have been the primary sources of social support. However, as our society has become more mobile and diversified, these supports have not always been readily available. For people suffering from medical and serious psychological problems, social supports may be significantly reduced. Needed support can be acquired through counseling and psychotherapy, but such services can be expensive, and thus unaffordable for many. Government and privately supported social service agencies exist to provide low-cost assistance, but because of limited budgets, they cannot always meet the needs of those in distress.

In response to the increased need for social support and the costs of professional help, self-help or support groups are becoming increasingly popular. A **support group** is a collection of people with a similar concern who band together to share their problems and help one another. These groups generally provide regular, free meetings where people discuss their difficulties and successes in an empathic, supportive atmosphere. Alcoholics

support group people with a similar concern who band together to share their problems and help one another

Anonymous (AA), as noted earlier, is a well-known self-help group that supports recovering alcoholics in their attempts to remain sober.

Relaxation Training. A frequent indicator of stress is the feeling of muscular tension. One popular way to reduce that tension is **relaxation training**, a set of techniques that teach individuals how to relax their muscles voluntarily. One such technique is *progressive relaxation*, a training program developed by Edmund Jacobsen in the 1930s. It involves step-by-step relaxation of various muscles of the body. The subject begins by relaxing the hands, then the arms, shoulders, neck, face, and scalp, and then moving gradually down the body to the toes. The procedure requires the person to flex the muscles before relaxing them so that the individual can attend better to the differences between relaxed versus tensed muscles. The method is easily learned and can help individuals feel more relaxed in situations that elicit stress (Holland & Tarlow, 1980). Progressive relaxation has been shown to be helpful in the control of headache, pain, asthma, insomnia, and hypertension. Thus, it can reduce both the effects of those problems and the stimulus conditions that might lead to them (Lavey & Taylor, 1985).

Relaxation can be used with a variety of techniques to eliminate psychological problems and reduce stress. *Systematic desensitization* is a therapeutic technique that combines relaxation training with behavior therapy to help people overcome anxiety and phobias. We discuss this technique in detail in Chapter 17. Relaxation is also used in conjunction with imagery techniques, such as *guided imagery*, that are used to reduce pain, thus lowering stress. In using guided imagery, individuals are asked to visualize a scene that is peaceful and relaxing and to focus their attention on that image as fully as they can (Lyles et al., 1982). Many users of this technique report that it reduces their pain. Its effects probably are produced because the pleasantness of the imagery improves a person's mood and provides a distraction from pain. Use of this imagery may also give the person a sense of control that aids in the reduction of stress. However, its actual effectiveness is impossible to ascertain because it is almost always used in conjunction with other treatments such as pain medication (Taylor, 1986).

Meditation. Typically, meditation is viewed as a relaxation technique that people use as a way of coping with existing stress or preventing stress from occurring. But it can function in other ways. The popularity of meditation is a relatively recent phenomenon in America, although forms of meditation have been practiced in many Eastern countries for centuries. **Meditation** is an altered state of consciousness in which the individual may try to increase awareness and to achieve bodily relaxation, as well as relaxation of the mind (see Figure 15–14). Most types of meditation can be placed in one of two classes. *Opening-up meditation* requires the subject to achieve a clear mind by eliminating all thoughts and thus becoming especially receptive to new experiences. In *concentrative meditation*, the person focuses attention intensively on a single sound, idea, object, or action of the body, such as breathing (Naranjo & Ornstein, 1977).

A number of claims have been made for the benefits of meditation, including the elimination of depression and anxiety, greater resistance to fatigue, improved sexual potency, greater creativity, reduction of sympathetic nervous system activity (or enhancement of parasympathetic activity), greater social skills, better mental efficiency, a shift in brain dominance, and feelings akin to religious experiences. Not surprisingly, many of these claims have not held up under scientific scrutiny.

The claims of meditation can be summarized in three categories: (*a*) increased cognitive awareness, (*b*) increased cognitive relaxation, and (*c*)

relaxation training set of techniques that teach individuals how to relax their muscles voluntarily as a way of reducing stress

meditation altered state of consciousness used to achieve bodily awareness and relaxation

increased somatic (body) relaxation. The first two of these are difficult to test because of a lack of appropriate dependent variables. Studies that have reported positive results have relied essentially on verbal report measures, mostly from subjects committed to meditation. The third claim, that of somatic relaxation, has been better researched by recording changes in such measures as rate of respiration, blood pressure, muscle activity (EMG), heart rate, and electrical activity in the skin. A number of studies have reported reductions in these measures during and following meditation exercises. But is it the meditation that produces these changes? David Holmes (1984) of the University of Kansas has analyzed the research literature. He notes that if one looks at only those studies with appropriate controls (such as a control group whose subjects rested or slept), meditating subjects do no better than control subjects. In other words, resting in bed for 20 minutes produces the same reduction in somatic arousal as engaging in 20 minutes of meditation. Furthermore, Holmes noted that the reductions for both groups are very small for the majority of subjects.

What then can be said about meditation as a means for reducing stress? With respect to the physiological changes that appear to accompany enhanced relaxation, the changes are small and may be no better than those derived from just resting. With regard to changes in mood, the situation is more difficult to interpret. Many meditators claim they derive great personal benefits in terms of improved mood as a result of their meditative sessions. Thus, whether or not scientific studies confirm their belief is quite irrelevant for them.

FIGURE 15–14
One can engage in meditation in many ways, including this classic yoga position—for those limber enough to achieve it.

Biofeedback Training. It is a well-established fact that internal, autonomic nervous system responses are controllable through classical conditioning (see Chapter 6). Intestinal contractions, heart rate, and blood pressure (vasoconstriction–vasodilation) are reflexively linked to many strong primary stimuli, and neutral events paired with these stimuli also can cause changes in the internal environment. More controversial is the idea that such autonomic behaviors can be brought under *instrumental* control; that is, those behaviors that are believed to be involuntary apparently may be conditioned using traditional instrumental techniques like reward and punishment (see Domjan, 1993).

The question of instrumental autonomic conditioning first received experimental attention from a group of investigators directed by Neal E. Miller at Rockefeller University. In one of the early experiments (Miller & Carmona, 1967), nonlaboratory dogs were successfully trained to increase or decrease salivation in order to receive water as a reinforcer. Note that for these conditions the salivation response acts on the environment to produce a change, and as such it should not be considered as a classically conditioned response. Elsewhere, DiCara and Miller (1968) provided evidence of instrumental conditioning of autonomic responses. Rats made selective vasodilation responses in their ears in order to receive positive reinforcement in the form of direct electrical stimulation to a part of the brain. In essence, the rat was able to learn how to control its blood pressure by relaxing certain vessels in order to receive reinforcement. When rewards or other sources of information are used as outcomes to instrumentally condition autonomic reactions that promote health, the intervention procedure is referred to as **biofeedback training**.

Amazingly popular, despite unreliable scientific evidence, biofeedback training helps people monitor and control an assortment of autonomically based disorders such as chronic tension, lower backache, and epilepsy (Qualls & Sheehan, 1981). Extensive investigations also have been conducted regarding the use of instrumental techniques in alleviating the suffering asso-

biofeedback training intervention procedure in which a person is taught to monitor and control an internal and normally automatic function such as heart rate

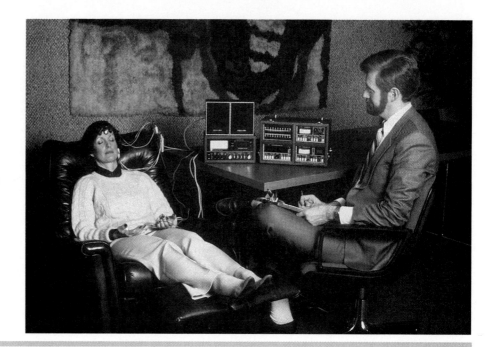

FIGURE 15-15
The technique of "hand warming" is commonly used in the treatment of migraine headaches. The patient is connected to a monitor with thermosensors (here the sensors are attached to the little finger of each hand) that are sensitive to blood flow at the extremities. The patient learns to divert blood volume from the head; consequently, blood pressure in the head diminishes and pain decreases.

ciated with migraine headaches. Unlike tension headaches that are muscle related, migraines seem to be produced by pressure-induced capillary breakage (Adams, Feuerstein, & Fowler, 1980). Treatment usually takes the form of conditioning "hand warming," using a biofeedback temperature trainer (see Figure 15–15). Thermosensors are placed on the fingers and connected to a monitor that provides visual or auditory feedback about temperature levels. The aim of the therapy is to increase finger temperature by increasing the blood flow at the extremities, thereby diverting blood volume from the head. As blood pressure in the head decreases, vascular damage (pain) diminishes and the migraine patient enjoys relief. In one report, 60% of the migraine cases that were treated by this method were judged as improved at the end of treatment (see L. Miller, 1978). Unfortunately, some researchers have been unable to find such positive results using biofeedback (Roberts, 1985). Moreover, even the validity of the early animal findings on instrumental conditioning of autonomic behaviors is now in doubt (for a review of this issue see Dworkin & Miller, 1986).

Although further research is needed to clarify the mechanisms involved in the treatment of stress and illness using biofeedback training, another important issue must be considered—the cost of such treatment. Biofeedback, like relaxation and meditation, can be practiced at home without extensive professional help. The obvious implication is that biofeedback and other self-management techniques can be applied to problems such as headaches, hypertension, and pain control without incurring large medical expenses. For example, in a study of migraine headache sufferers, Kenneth Holroyd and his associates (1988) compared patients who were treated solely by pharmacological means (drug therapy) with patients who practiced only behavioral treatments (relaxation training and biofeedback training) in their homes. The less expensive home-based behavioral treatments proved as effective or more so (52% improvement) than the medical treatments (41% improvement).

Researchers and practitioners will continue to debate the effectiveness of such techniques and the mechanisms that underlie their operation. Yet, as health care costs continue to rise, the use of home-based interventions such as biofeedback and relaxation training probably will remain popular. These techniques can be useful in many situations, including test anxiety.

Coping with Test Anxiety

A source of stress for many people, including a number of college students, is test anxiety, an unpleasant state that has physiological, cognitive, and behavioral components. *Test anxiety* refers to the distress one experiences when being evaluated or when thinking about prospective evaluation situations, which typically leads to reduced performance. People usually experience test anxiety during formalized testing or in other situations where they are being evaluated. Research has shown that test anxiety has its roots in childhood, during the preschool and early school years. Parents often play a role in its development by creating unreasonably high expectations for the child. Because the child's performance rarely meets the expectations, the child learns to fear the testing situation because of the anticipated failure (Dusek, 1980).

Most people, if not all, are anxious about testing, and indeed some measure of anxiety can enhance performance. But some people are so anxious about tests that they may become ill before or during a test or freeze during a test and perform quite poorly; the anxiety is so overwhelming that it blocks their ability to think. Irwin Sarason (1980) has developed a 37-item scale called the Test Anxiety Scale (TAS) that is designed to identify persons who have varying degrees of test anxiety. Sample questions are, "While taking an important exam, I find myself thinking of how much brighter the other students are than I am" and "I sometimes feel my heart beating very fast during important exams."

The first item reflects the negative thinking that is characteristic of people with high test anxiety; highly test-anxious subjects include many negative statements in describing themselves (Lang, Mueller, & Nelson, 1983). The second item is indicative of the physiological responses that accompany test anxiety. Highly anxious persons may perspire heavily, have stomach pains, and experience difficulty in breathing; some may even become so ill that they vomit (Holroyd & Appel, 1980).

Traditionally, most treatments of persons with severe test anxiety have focused on physiological arousal. Relaxation techniques including biofeedback have been used. But some studies of treatment approaches point to the importance of a comprehensive treatment effort that deals not only with the physiological arousal, but with the negative thinking (Lang et al., 1983; Sarason, 1984). Highly anxious subjects worry a lot before tests. During the test they wonder how other people are doing, and they think of things unrelated to the content of the test. They think negative thoughts about their ability. Past successes still may not give them any confidence on a new test. Thus, a crucial element of effective treatment for these people is restructuring the way they think about themselves. In other words, self-perception must be changed. **Cognitive behavior modification** techniques (discussed more fully in Chapter 17) are forms of treatment that are designed to do just that. These techniques try to show people that their thoughts are irrational and to shape their thinking from negative patterns to more positive ones. Coupled with some of the relaxation therapies, these techniques are proving very successful for people troubled with excessive test anxiety.

Text anxiety exists to some degree in everyone. But for some individuals, the anxiety level can be so high that performance is seriously affected. Most colleges and universities offer programs to help students cope with this kind of anxiety. Such programs are typically administered through the counseling center.

cognitive behavior modification therapy technique designed to change people's self-perceptions, that is, the way people think about themselves

The Hardy Personality

The announcer in the 1991 World Series commented on how calm and effective Atlanta's phenomenal young pitcher, Steve Avery, was under pressure.

The closer the game, the more crucial the pitch, the more calm and mechanical he seemed to get, as if he were being fueled by the stress of the situation. Is it possible that stress can in fact make a person more **psychologically hardy**?

Kobasa (1979) studied business executives who, in spite of increasing stress, were particularly resistent to illness. Kobasa found that psychologically hardy individuals were high in the three Cs of hardiness: *commitment*, *challenge*, and *control*.

In terms of commitment, the hardy personality is involved in the task at hand instead of experiencing alienation and a lack of control. Whenever Steve Avery was not pitching and forced to watch from the dugout, he was a nervous wreck, prompting the announcer to remark, "I guess there's good pressure and bad pressure." Avery would rather have been involved. Regarding change, hardy individuals are challenged by it. They believe in and seek change rather than stability. Change is not avoided as a threat to security, but rather sought as an opportunity for growth. Perceived control is the third factor contributing to psychological hardiness. According to Kobasa, hardy individuals believe that their actions matter. They attempt to influence their lives rather than remaining passive and helpless.

Evidence is beginning to emerge regarding the hardy personality in relation to learned helplessness and **learned optimism**. Seligman (1990) argues that each of us developed a unique optimistic or pessimistic **explanatory style** early in life and that we use this style in explaining the misfortunes of everyday living. Seligman presents evidence that suggests that an optimistic explanatory style is related to higher achievement and improved health. In his book *Learned Optimism*, Seligman (1990) argues that optimism is essential for a healthy and successful life and is in large measure the consequence of our explanatory style. More specifically, Seligman identifies three dimensions of explanatory style that can be used to describe how people think about themselves: *permanence*, *pervasiveness*, and *personalization*.

Permanence refers to our perception of ourselves in relation to the passage of time. People who are pessimistic tend to give up and explain their misfortune as a permanent state of affairs, using words like *always* and *never* to explain their situation to themselves. Optimists, on the other hand, explain bad events as temporary, focusing on some specific situational cause for their misfortune. Interestingly, Seligman suggests that exactly the reverse is true for the way we explain good events. Pessimists will focus on the temporary, "I was lucky this time," while optimists will see good things as permanent, "I am talented."

A similar reversal is observed with regard to the dimension of *pervasiveness*, which refers to space rather than time. The pessimist explains bad events as universal, "Teachers are out to get me" and good events as specific, "I did this job well." The explanatory style of the optimist is just the opposite. Bad events are explained in terms of specifics, "This teacher is out to get me" and good events as universals, "I do my job well."

Personalization refers to an internal (blaming yourself) versus external (blaming others or circumstances) explanatory style. According to Seligman, people with low self-esteem tend to blame themselves for bad events and fail to take credit for good events, while people with high self-esteem explain away bad events by focusing on external causes and internalize good events. Notice, however, that this contradicts the research on "blaming others for one's misfortune," reviewed by Tennen and Affleck (1990), in which blaming others was associated with impaired psychological health.

Seligman states emphatically that the Hope Score is the single most important score on his test. "People who make permanent *and* universal explanations for their troubles tend to collapse under pressure, both for a long time and across situations" (p. 49).

THINKING AHEAD . . .

If you have visited any bookstores lately, you might have noticed that more and more space is being devoted to the psychology section. Self-help books on psychological health are a very big business, but often the advice given is contradictory. One of the things we have repeatedly emphasized in these "Thinking Ahead" sections is that to be effective in today's society you must learn to be a critical consumer of information. You need to know how to separate the wheat from the chaff. Although there is a danger in "appealing to authority," within professions there are select groups of individuals who have earned the respect and admiration of their peers, and we can use their collective authority to guide our own decision making.

One of the most prestigious of these select groups of authorities is the National Research Council. This council of scientists recently formed a committee to evaluate the expanding body of information from cognitive, social, and brain sciences that is available about the techniques that are used to enhance human performance. The council looked at the evidence on altering mental states to enhance performance and how best to prepare to perform under pressure, of particular interest for health psychology. What they found is very significant for the consumer of information (*APS Observer*, 1991). Among other things, members of the council examined three techniques used to alter mental states and to improve performance: subliminal self-help tapes, meditation, and pain management.

Subliminal self-help tapes (audiotapes that supposedly have embedded messages to help a person alter behavior) have been highly successful in the marketplace, with sales in one recent year (1988) exceeding $50 million. Their market success has not been matched, however, in tests of their effectiveness. Claims that these tapes can change attitudes and behavior in desirable directions have not held up well under scrutiny (*APS Observer*, 1991). Some short-term laboratory studies do indicate that these tapes can alter performance on simple tasks without the individual's awareness. However, these results do not extend to long-term changes in complex behaviors such as smoking, depression, or self-confidence. Any positive effects of the subliminal tapes are likely a result of placebo or expectancy effects. In fact, careful analyses of the acoustical characteristics of some of the tapes indicate that there are no subliminal messages on them at all!

The council also could not find empirical support for special effects of *meditation* for reducing stress, controlling arousal, or enhancing self-efficacy. In some cases meditation did help with those things, but so did other forms of rest and relaxation, as we discussed earlier in this chapter.

Claims about psychological *techniques to manage pain* have more empirical support than the other two techniques assessed by the National Research Council. People can be taught ways to cope with physical pain other than the use of drugs. Cognitive factors, for example, can influence the perceived intensity of the pain, and how manageable it seems. The subjective experience of pain can also be reduced through relaxation techniques, information about what to expect, and enhancement of the person's sense of control over the situation.

When psychology is sold in bookstores and other outlets, it is a "buyer-beware" market. Very often you hear the advocates of subliminal self-help and meditation argue that there is no evidence that it *doesn't* work. As critical consumers of information, we should demand more than such an argument because it is an *argument from a null set*, that is, arguing without evidence. Science includes methods and procedures designed to evaluate evidence. Without evidence, claims about self-help products are nothing more than marketing strategies. It is invalid to say that because scientists have been unable to prove that subliminal messages do not affect behavior, such approaches must work, just as it would be invalid to say that because scientists have been unable to prove that whales are not telepathic, whales must have this ability. The "you can't prove it's wrong" list is infinitely long. If scientists want to argue for the telepathic ability of whales, then it is their responsibility to present evidence for such an ability. We need to be equally demanding as critical consumers of psychological self-help infomation.

The Role of Psychology in Health and Illness

1. Behavioral medicine is an interdisciplinary field that incorporates knowledge from the medical, behavioral, and social sciences to promote health and prevent illness. Health psychology specifically deals with the role of psychology in health and illness.

2. Over the last several decades, data on causes of death show trends toward illnesses related to lifestyle and behavior. As we learn more about ourselves and our environment, we have discovered the importance of balance and harmony for health and well-being. Our relationship to the environment, the foods we eat, the type of work we do, and how we spend our leisure time often conflict with the way our bodies were designed to function, which can lead to undesirable consequences.

3. When people can exert greater control over health-related aspects of their lives, their health status is improved. Types of control include behavioral control, where individuals have available responses that can affect their health status; cognitive control, where beliefs can affect outcomes related to health and stress; and informational control, where the individual is given information about what to expect in health-related situations. The power of psychological control to affect health status is illustrated in studies of control in nursing homes.

4. Health status has been correlated with certain personality characteristics, and interest has increased in the hypothesis that specific diseases are correlated with particular personality and behavioral types. Cardiovascular disease seems related to the Type A behavior pattern that includes feeling time pressured, hostile, competitive, and achievement oriented.

5. Grief is intense emotional suffering that has both adaptive and nonadaptive aspects. On the nonadaptive side are relationships between grief and sudden death, or less drastically, respiratory, digestive, and cardiovascular disorders.

6. Addictive behaviors are repetitive behavior patterns that increase the risk of disease and associated personal and social problems. Smoking and drinking are two addictive behaviors with major implications for health status. Alcohol abuse is one of the most serious health problems for contemporary American culture.

7. Sexual behavior can also affect health status. The 1980s and 1990s have emphasized the importance of behavior change in the area of sexuality because the HIV virus has been linked to AIDS. Relatively simple forms of behavior change, such as the use of condoms, can reduce the risk of exposure to HIV.

Stress

8. Stress is manifested in terms of psychological and physiological problems. Events that cause stress are called stressors and include a number of events related to changes in life. Although major life changes such as divorce are stressful, the minor stressors of everyday life have also been shown to produce intense stress. Other sources of stress include frustration, conflict, and emergency situations, such as disasters.

9. Stress management includes techniques, such as stress inoculation, that help people better cope with stress in those occupations where the stress cannot be substantially reduced.

10. Two contemporary models of stress emphasize biological factors (Selye) and cognitive factors (Lazarus). Selye proposes a general adaptation syndrome as a biological response to stressful situations. Lazarus emphasizes the role played by cognitive appraisal in identifying the nature of the stress and deciding among coping alternatives.

11. Factors related to the intensity of the stress reaction include intensity and duration of the stressor, predictability of its occurrence, motivation and competence of the person, and the social support available to the person.

Coping

12. Coping with stress involves a great number of strategies. Most common is some form of direct action taken to deal with the stressor. Direct action solutions include techniques such as conflict resolution and assertiveness.

13. Social support is important for coping with stress. Groups of people with similar stressors who band together to help one another are called support groups.

14. Relaxation training involves learning muscular relaxation, and it can be an effective coping strategy alone or in conjunction with other techniques. Meditation, a related technique, can be used to reduce stress or prevent its occurrence by relaxing the body and/or mind. Biofeedback training seeks to reduce stress by inducing muscle relaxation or vasodilation as a result of instrumental learning.

15. Test anxiety is accompanied by negative thoughts and physiological symptoms such as sweating and

stomach pains. Cognitive behavior modification and relaxation techniques are used to treat excessive test anxiety.

16. New evidence suggests that the psychologically hardy person is high in commitment, challenge, and control and reacts positively to most stressful situations. This type of hardiness is also related to an optimistic or pessimistic explanatory style that is learned early in life.

17. Self-help psychology is very big business, but it is a buyer-beware marketplace. Particular concern is warranted in the areas of subliminal self-help and meditation.

Key Terms

dualism (594)
behavioral medicine (594)
health psychology (594)
The Paleolithic Prescription (595)
genetic predisposition (596)
behavioral control (598)
cognitive control (599)
behavioral self-blame (600)
information control (600)

Type A personality (603)
Type B personality (603)
specificity theory (604)
generality theory (604)
grief (604)
substance use disorder (605)
substance abuse (606)
substance dependence (606)
passive smoking (608)
acquired immune deficiency syndrome (AIDS) (608)

stress (611)
life change events (612)
psychological numbing (615)
stress management (616)
stress inoculation (616)
general adaptation syndrome (GAS) (618)
primary appraisal (619)
secondary appraisal (619)

coping (623)
coping strategies (623)
support group (625)
relaxation training (626)
meditation (626)
biofeedback training (627)
cognitive behavior modification (629)
psychologically hardy (630)
learned optimism (630)
explanatory style (630)

Suggested Reading

Lazarus, R. S., & Folkman, S. (1984). *Stress, appraisal, and coping*. New York: Springer. A thorough account of Lazarus's model of stress, emphasizing the role of appraisal processes in coping with stress.

Selye, H. (1974). *Stress Without distress*. Philadelphia: Lippincott. A paperback book written for laypeople by a leading authority on stress. It focuses on how to minimize the stress in your life and how to deal effectively with the stress that you cannot eliminate.

Shilts, R. (1987). *And the band played on*. New York: St. Martin's. A gripping and powerful book that describes the events leading up to the discovery of the deadly AIDS virus. It is loaded with psychological lessons concerning the health field.

Watson, D. L., & Tharp, R. G. (1993). *Self-directed behavior*. Pacific Grove, CA: Brooks/Cole. This book is designed to help the readers help themselves. By understanding themselves and regulating their own behavior, they learn to manage stress and improve the quality of life.

CHAPTER 16
Psychological Disorders

One has to look no further than the newspaper to find instances of bizarre behavior. Consider, for example, the case of David Koresh, the leader of the Branch Davidian cult in Waco, Texas. Koresh convinced his fellow cult members that he was a messiah and that God had instructed him to begin a "House of David" with many wives. Accordingly, he was the only man in the Branch Davidian compound allowed to have sex with women; his "wives" ranged in age from 12 to 67. Koresh's predecessor as leader of the cult may have been even odder. He once challenged Koresh to a contest to see which one of them could raise the corpse of an 85-year-old woman from the dead. Koresh refused the challenge.

Or consider Jeffrey Dahmer. On July 22, 1991, Milwaukee police arrested Jeffrey Dahmer for murder. In apartment 213 in the Oxford Apartments, Dahmer's residence, police detectives found the remains of 11 of his 17 victims. The tale that unfolded after Dahmer's arrest was scarcely believable, including, as it did, accounts of dismemberment, cannibalism, and amateur lobotomies performed in a crude attempt to create "sex zombies."

How are we to evaluate these types of behavior from a psychological point of view? Do they indicate a serious disturbance, a psychological disorder? Would psychologists view these examples of odd behavior differently from other professionals, such as psychiatrists or attorneys? One of the professionals who testified at Dahmer's sanity trial, Dr. Frederick Berlin, Director of the Sexual Disorders Clinic at Johns Hopkins University, concluded "If this isn't mental illness, from my point of view, I don't know what is" (Walsh, 1992).

◀ Psychologists recognize a wide spectrum of psychological disorders, from major depression to antisocial personality disorder.

Psychologists, psychiatrists, and legal experts, however, often speak in different technical languages. Dahmer obviously displayed behavior that was massively disturbed; Dr. Berlin concluded, from his point of view in the medical specialty of psychiatry, that this behavior constituted mental illness. Psychologists, from their training outside of medicine, are likely to view Dahmer's behavior as constituting a psychological disorder, which is not necessarily the same thing as a medical illness. Legal experts, on the other hand, ask whether a person such as Dahmer can appreciate the wrongfulness of his conduct, and they typically speak of "insanity" rather than mental illness or psychological disorders.

These various professional groups often have a difficult time appreciating each others' points of view, and the result is a good deal of murkiness surrounding the concept of psychological disorders within the legal system. Dahmer's jury, for example, concluded that he was legally sane at the time of the murders. Although we are not able to untangle all of the issues involved in classifying behavior into categories like "mental illness," "psychological disorder," and "insanity," in this chapter we provide you with a basic understanding of the concept of psychological disorders, and the wide territory that these disorders cover.

DEFINING AND DIAGNOSING PSYCHOLOGICAL DISORDERS

One way that people have traditionally viewed the oddities of behavior that get called psychological disorders is to refer to them as *abnormal*. But defining abnormality is not easy. *Abnormal* literally means "away from the rule" or "out of the ordinary." These senses of the term imply that any atypical behavior is abnormal behavior. Hence, some people label any unusual behavior as abnormal, although few of us would wish to inhabit a world in which everyone behaved in the same way. Within psychology, we need to go beyond calling behavior abnormal; that term is derogatory, and implies that we should all conform to some imaginary standard that would eliminate much of the desirable diversity of behavior that humans exhibit.

Social context, for example, is one factor that people take into account when they evaluate someone's behavior as abnormal. Behavior occurs within a social context, and abnormal behavior is generally deemed socially unacceptable within the framework in which it occurs. Walking nude through a supermarket is socially unacceptable and might get one arrested, but walking nude in a college dormitory is somewhat more acceptable, and walking nude in a nudist colony is socially expected. The issue of socially unacceptable behavior is a delicate one. Psychological disorders must represent more than a disagreement between an individual and society. For example, before the end of the Cold War, the Soviet Union confined political dissidents in psychiatric facilities. Were these dissidents suffering from psychological disorders just because they objected to the policies of their government? Views about what constitutes abnormal behavior change with time and circumstance. Prehistoric people viewed abnormal behavior as a manifestation of supernatural forces acting on the body. Evil spirits, demons, witches, and magicians were thought to cause abnormal behavior. Within our own society, we see examples of eccentric behavior all the time. People handle poisonous snakes as a test of faith, undergo plastic surgery to make themselves look like Elvis, or leave their estates to their cats. Should we label all instances of eccentric behavior as abnormal, or pin a label such as "mental disorder" on it?

Labels such as "mental disorder" or "abnormal behavior" should be used with extreme caution. Among other things, *mental disorder* is a very misleading term that perpetuates a distinction between mind and body that has outgrown its usefulness. Acceptable alternatives to the term are not obvious, however, leading one group of psychologists and psychiatrists to declare, almost plaintively, "Can anyone suggest better terms for us? We have been largely unsuccessful in fashioning more desirable substitutes" (Frances et al., 1991, p. 409).

Labels of mental illness have been used to justify repression, subjugation, and even slaughter of those who were different. For example, when European explorers encountered Native-American tribes, they often viewed their behavior as abnormal. One instance is the tradition of the *berdache*, a role that was particularly puzzling to the Europeans, who viewed it as aberrant on many levels. The *berdache* role refers to a biological male who does not fill the typical male role, but rather expresses androgyny, which mixes typical male and female behaviors (Williams, 1992). Some of the *berdache*'s work was woman's work, but, in addition, the *berdache* performed ceremonial roles and was treated with respect for his wisdom and spirituality. Jesuit missionary Joseph François Lafitau wrote of the *berdaches* in 1724, condemning them for their behavior. He wrote incredulously that the Indians themselves did not share his view: "They believe they are honored. They participate in all religious ceremonies, and this profession of an extraordinary life causes them to be regarded as people of a higher order, and above the common man" (quoted in Williams, 1992, p. 17). Vasco de Balboa, on an expedition across Panama, had several *berdaches* killed and eaten by his dogs (Williams, 1992). Why did the European explorers view the *berdache* tradition as abnormal? If the term had been in their vocabulary, would they have labeled it a psychological disorder? Any working definition of *psychological disorder* should be presented with a strong warning to guard against using it in a culturally insensitive way.

Having said that, we must attempt to provide a working definition. Instead of *mental disorder* or *abnormal behavior*, we prefer the term **psychological disorder**, and define it as an involuntary impairment in psychological

psychological disorder involuntary impairment in psychological functioning, including cognitive, affective, and behavioral functioning

An engraving of the incident in which Spanish explorer Balboa ordered his dogs to eat Indian *berdaches* alive. The engraving, done in 1594, was based on an account of the incident written in the 1540s.

functioning, which is meant to include thinking, feeling, and behaving. Examples of persons having psychological disorders would include those who "are hindered in their ability to adapt flexibly to stress, to make optimal life decisions, to fulfill desired potentials, or to sustain meaningful or satisfying relationships as a result of impairment in cognitive, affective, or behavioral functioning over which they have insufficient control" (Widiger & Trull, 1991, p. 112). In addition, the impairment in behavior is not a response that could reasonably be expected because of external events (Wakefield, 1992). As an example, impairment in mood (i.e., "affective functioning") could reasonably be expected in response to the death of a close relative, and thus grief is not a psychological disorder.

Impairment in psychological functioning includes the concept of **maladaptive behavior**. Maladaptive behavior is behavior that is counterproductive or interferes with functioning in some important way. For example, maladaptive behavior patterns make it difficult for a person to find or keep employment or to maintain ties with other people. Symptoms of maladaptive behavior include distorted belief systems ("telephone poles are evil aliens from another planet") or short attention spans (a child's inability to focus attention long enough to benefit from a classroom lesson). In addition, any behavior that poses a threat to others or to oneself is considered maladaptive.

The behavior associated with a psychological disorder is frequently disturbing to the individual who exhibits the behavior. For example, people who are depressed are very unhappy about their psychological state, and yet they are simply unable to be happy. Similarly, people with agoraphobia, who are afraid of leaving their homes, may desperately wish they could behave more like other people. However, people with some psychological disorders are not unhappy because they are unaware that a problem exists. People with severe mental retardation or with some forms of schizophrenia may not realize they have a psychological disorder.

This discussion should lead you to conclude that it is a very complex task to define and describe psychological disorders. Two cautions that apply throughout this chapter illustrate this complexity. One involves the risks inherent in labeling. "Diagnosing" and categorizing psychological disorders, although meant to be helpful in guiding treatment, distort and tend to make an abstract diagnosis a real "thing" (Widiger & Trull, 1991). To label someone is to change the way others view that person. The second caution is that no clear dividing line exists between "normal" and "abnormal." By "diagnosing" a set of behaviors as a particular psychological disorder, we are implying that some clear line of demarcation separates the normal from the abnormal. In reality, behavior lies on a continuum and is not easily divided into diagnostic categories. With these cautions in mind, we proceed to a discussion of approaches to studying psychological disorders.

Contemporary Views of Psychological Disorders

A wide range of approaches to psychological disorders exists in the contemporary research literature. Although we can discuss the approaches separately and view them as distinct, they are not so easily separable when we confront behavior problems in the real world. In this section we look briefly at five contemporary models of psychological disorders.

Biomedical Model. Chief among the contemporary views of psychological disorders is the **biomedical model**, which is especially prominent in the medical specialty of psychiatry. The biomedical perspective is used to explain problems in brain biochemistry, genetic abnormalities, and problems within the physical structure of the brain. Proponents of this position believe that

maladaptive behavior behavior that is counterproductive or interferes with functioning in some important way, such as in employment or maintaining social ties

biomedical model view that psychological disorders are traceable to physical abnormalities, such as brain biochemistry, genetic abnormalities, or brain structure defects

most, if not all, psychological disorders are ultimately traceable to biomedical problems and should be treated like any other disease. Critics of this position object to a *medical model* for psychological disorders; they believe that a disease orientation leads to overusing drugs to treat behavioral problems.

Research into biological aspects of psychological disorders has proceeded feverishly over the past few decades. For example, since the discovery in the mid-1970s of brain neuropeptides (naturally occurring compounds that influence neural functioning, discussed in Chapter 2), many researchers have examined the possible role of neuropeptides in psychological disorders. Despite claims of elevated levels of neuropeptides in the cerebrospinal fluid of some psychiatric patients, no conclusive evidence yet exists that these brain peptides *cause* psychological disorders (Nemeroff & Bissette, 1986). The search for molecular bases of psychological disorders continues unabated, in what one observer called the "remedicalization of psychiatry" (Horvath, 1986).

Cognitive Model. Although biomedical research into psychological disorders is one of the most intense contemporary areas of study, it is not the only one. Cognitive approaches to psychological disorders, particularly to depression, are also receiving widespread attention. The **cognitive model** looks at psychological problems as unusual ways of thinking about the world, including faulty perceptions of oneself and others and inappropriate belief systems. For example, some researchers report that a negative cognitive style, in which individuals view the world with fatalistic pessimism, is a contributing cause to depression (Parry & Brewin, 1988).

cognitive model view that psychological disorders result from unusual ways of thinking, such as inappropriate belief systems

Psychoanalytic Model. The **psychoanalytic model** holds that psychological disorders emerge from internal psychological conflicts that are often hidden from the individual who experiences them. These conflicts are traceable to events in early childhood; they lead to a predisposition to develop psychological disorders in adulthood when stress exceeds some threshold. According to this model, psychological disorders may be caused by traumatic events that have been pushed out of conscious thought but resurface in the form of psychological symptoms. To relieve the disorder fully, these traumatic events must be brought into conscious thinking and dealt with.

psychoanalytic model view that psychological disorders emerge from internal psychological conflicts that are unconscious, and often arise from childhood trauma

Behavioral Model. The view that an individual's early experiences contribute to the development of psychological disorders has a long tradition in psychology, both from the psychoanalytic perspective and in the behavioral model. The **behavioral model** attempts to trace psychological problems to faulty contingencies of reinforcement, where improper behavior is rewarded or proper behavior is ignored or punished. For example, peculiar rearing conditions and family treatment may reward behavior that later is identified as a symptom of a psychological disorder. Another explanation from the behavioral perspective involves parental modeling of problem behavior, such as abusing drugs and alcohol. Even when the behavior of parents does not directly resemble the child's problem behavior, it still might be a factor in the cause of a psychological disorder. For example, overprotective parents who show little warmth toward their children may contribute to the development of schizophrenia (Kendler, 1988).

behavioral model view that psychological disorders are a result of faulty contingencies of reinforcement

Sociological Model. Another contemporary approach to psychological disorders is the **sociological model**, in which variables such as social class, gender and sex roles, and rural–urban environments contribute to the development of psychological disorders. Depression, for example, is more common among people in lower socioeconomic groups and among women, perhaps because they have fewer options for dealing with the stress of daily living.

sociological model view that variables such as social class, gender, and rural–urban contexts contribute to the development of psychological disorders

Researchers who approach psychological disorders from a sociological model examine the contribution of such variables as social class and rural–urban contexts to the development of disorders. These unemployed people are waiting in line for meals provided by volunteers at Lafayette Park, across from the White House, in Washington, DC.

Although psychologists sometimes have a tendency to subscribe to one of these positions to the exclusion of the others, it is likely that a number of different approaches contribute to the explanation of the cause and course of psychological disorders. In understanding depression, for example, there may well be genetic and hormonal factors that contribute to the cause. But other factors are almost surely at work as well, including people's gender roles, social class, history of reinforcement, and the way they think about their problems (Alloy et al., 1988).

Historically, folk explanations have been proposed for abnormal behavior. There has long been speculation about the role of such things as astrology and planetary movements in causing psychological disorders. One of these folk views centers on the role of the moon in causing madness.

SPOTLIGHT ON RESEARCH
A Folk Model—The Moon and Madness

One folk view holds that psychological disorders can be traced to phases of the moon. Indeed, the words *lunacy* and *lunatic* are derived from *luna*, the Latin word for "moon." A number of problem behaviors have been attributed to moon phases, including alcoholism, epilepsy, somnambulism (sleepwalking), suicide, homicide, and lycanthropy—a psychological disorder in which a person thinks he or she is a wolf (Rotton & Kelly, 1985).

Several mechanisms have been proposed to explain a lunar effect on behavior. Some people speculate that the moon acts on bodily fluids in essentially the same way that it influences the tides. Others believe that the effect is totally accidental, arising from the time before electricity when the light of the full moon allowed people to go out and behave in bizarre ways that they could not do on moonless nights. Still others think that many areas of human behavior are affected by the light, and that specific structures of the brain respond to exposure to light. The counterargument is, of course, that the moon does not provide much light, even less light than a 100-watt bulb (Rotton & Kelly, 1985).

The folklore about the effect of the moon on problem behavior is so strong that some crisis hotlines and police stations post warnings about the approach of a full moon. Hypotheses about the moon and problem behavior have not been limited to folklore, however. There are some adherents to the lunar hypothesis among members of the scientific community, and they have published a number of reports about the lunar effect (e.g., Garzino, 1982).

Campbell and Beets (1978) published a review of this research and concluded that there is no relationship between the lunar phases and human behavior. Their review touched off a debate about statistical issues in the moon studies and in their own analyses of them. Another review of the lunar studies (Rotton & Kelly, 1985) focused on statistical reanalyses of 118 sets of data from 37 separate empirical reports. Relationships among the phases of the moon, the type of lunar cycle, geographical features such as population density, and several criteria of problem behavior (including mental hospital admissions, psychiatric disturbances, calls to crisis hotlines, homicides, and other criminal offenses) were examined.

Although the researchers did find a few significant effects suggesting an association between the moon and some problem behaviors, the effects were extremely small, accounting for no more than 1% of the variation in behavior termed "lunacy." Apparently we will have to search in places closer to home for explanations of psychological disorders.

Several mechanisms have been proposed to explain a lunar effect on behavior. Some people speculate that the moon acts on bodily fluids in essentially the same way that it influences the tides.

Categorizing Psychological Disorders

Human beings seemingly have a natural tendency to classify objects in their world. (In Chapter 8 we discussed concept formation as one of the central aspects of human thought.) In virtually all of the sciences, classification schemes are used to help bring order to the subject matter. Thus, in chemistry the periodic tables arrange the elements according to their atomic numbers; in biology the Linnaean binomial classification system gives two names (hence "binomial") to each species (e.g., humans are *Homo sapiens*).

Within psychology, there have been several attempts to categorize and systematize psychological disorders, to help with diagnosis and treatment. Emil Kraepelin (1856–1926) in the late 1800s created an early comprehensive system of diagnosis for psychological disorders. Kraepelin's system relied heavily on the description of symptoms in much the same way that a medical diagnosis does. The tradition of listing symptoms that form a **syndrome**, or collection of symptoms, has continued to the present day.

syndrome collection of symptoms associated with a disorder

The Diagnostic and Statistical Manual (DSM). In 1952, the APA published the first of its categorization systems, the *Diagnostic and Statistical Manual of Mental Disorders* (DSM). The latest revision of this document, published in 1994, is the fourth edition, and is popularly known as **DSM-IV**. Although the most widely accepted standard for classifying psychological disorders in use in the United States, the DSM is not the only system. In other countries, the classification system of choice is the *International Classification of Diseases* (ICD-10), published by the World Health Organization. In fact, the United States has a treaty obligation with the World Health Organization to maintain consistent terminology and coding between its diagnostic system and the international one (American Psychiatric Association, 1991).

DSM-IV fourth edition of the *Diagnostic and Statistical Manual of Mental Disorders* published by the APA in 1994

As we have seen, categorizing psychological disorders under various diagnostic labels, is a controversial undertaking. Categorization offers the advantage of enabling psychologists to look for common characteristics of individuals whose behavior closely resembles the description of a particular syndrome. Common characteristics might include biological markers (biological factors associated with a disorder that may or may not be linked to its cause), family history, childhood trauma, similar social circumstances, or a host of other characteristics that could provide clues about the cause and treatment of the disorder. An analogous situation arose in the identification of AIDS in 1981. After the diagnostic category was identified, health professionals suspected a number of possible causes before they finally isolated the human immunodeficiency virus and its transmission through body fluids (Shilts, 1987). Diagnosing people who might then be studied for clues about cause and cure seems a rational and socially useful way to proceed.

On the other hand, there are pitfalls to this procedure in psychology. Diagnostic categories come and go with the various editions of the *Diagnostic and Statistical Manual*. Even the popular diagnostic label "neurosis" disappeared in 1980 with the publication of DSM-III.

The authors of the *Diagnostic and Statistical Manual* have been careful to warn against some of these dangers. They caution that there may be no sharp boundary between one diagnostic category and another, or even between a diagnostic category and normal behavior. The authors of the manual also warn against thinking that the diagnostic labels apply to people instead of disorders. People may have schizophrenia or an alcohol dependence, but they are not somehow transformed into their disorder, as implied in the labels "schizophrenic" and "alcoholic" (American Psychiatric Association, 1987).

The *Diagnostic and Statistical Manual* is a formidable document that includes descriptions for well over 200 different psychological disorders. Clinicians and researchers who use the manual must narrow down a diagnosis to the appropriate disorder or disorders. In the following sections of this chapter, we review many of the major diagnostic categories of the manual. Our necessarily selective coverage describes major diagnostic categories, illustrates many categories with case material, and provides information on etiology (causes). Research on etiology from all five of the contemporary perspectives on psychological disorders is proceeding rapidly, and we review some of it as we describe the categories. The presumed causes for psychological disorders may also suggest ways to treat them. We discuss approaches to treating psychological disorders in the next chapter.

Warning: Intern's Syndrome.   Before we plunge into these descriptions, a note of warning: Do not look too closely for a diagnosis of your own behavior or the behavior of your friends in the descriptions of these syndromes. Despite the tendency to view behavior as either normal or abnormal that is inherent in a classification scheme for "disorders," there is almost certainly a continuum that characterizes the behavior we are diagnosing. Some people abstain from drinking alcohol; others are chronic alcohol abusers. Between these two extremes lies a continuum of alcohol use. Some people are rarely or never depressed; others experience frequent bouts of severe depression. Between these two extremes lies a continuum of mood. Where should the line be drawn in categorizing the drinking behavior as alcoholism or the emotional state as clinical depression? Psychologists have no easy answer to this question.

Furthermore, it is the rare individual who has never worried about some aspect of his or her behavior. Throughout the years that the authors of this book have been teaching psychology, students have expressed fears that they had an appalling variety of psychological disorders, from the bipolar disorder of mania and depression to an obsessive-compulsive personality disorder. In most cases, the students were merely afflicted with "**intern's syndrome**," the tendency to attribute to themselves the symptoms they were learning about in their training on the clinical syndromes. (For those individuals who are worried that they are suffering from a psychological disorder, help is available on most college campuses in a personal counseling center.)

intern's syndrome tendency to believe that one has a disorder that one has been studying

ANXIETY AND DISSOCIATION DISORDERS

This first major category of psychological disorder that we consider includes problems that interfere with everyday life, such as irrational fears and anxieties, and ailments that result when people react to severe traumas in their lives by developing psychological disorders. These disorders may be severe, but they are not necessarily debilitating. Research on and understanding of these disorders have become more refined over the years. When Freud was a private therapist in Vienna, these disorders were known as "neuroses," and they were all considered to be products of anxiety. The third edition of the *Diagnostic and Statistical Manual* eliminated the label of "neurosis" because it was too vague to describe the wide variety of disorders it was meant to include.

Anxiety Disorders

People with **anxiety disorders** commonly experience heightened levels of anxiety, sometimes to highly specific circumstances (as in phobias), and sometimes in a more general way. In many cases, these disorders are further complicated by a history of alcohol or drug use to reduce the anxiety.

anxiety disorders class of disorders whose major symptom is heightened levels of uneasiness or apprehension

Phobic Disorders.   **Phobias** are specific irrational fears of objects or situations. The person with a phobia usually recognizes that the fear is dispropor-

phobias irrational fears of objects or situations

tionate to the actual degree of danger involved, but the fear is so intense that the person may go to great lengths to avoid that object or situation. For example, a 28-year-old woman was so afraid of thunderstorms that she sought psychiatric treatment for the problem. Of course, many people become anxious during violent thunderstorms, but this woman's reaction far exceeded the usual fear. She would become anxious for days if she heard a forecast of thunderstorms for later in the week. She especially feared lightning, even though she knew that it was highly improbable that she would be struck (Spitzer et al., 1981).

specific phobia any one of several specific irrational fears, such as fear of spiders

Specific Phobia. The case just described is an example of a **specific phobia**, the diagnostic label for any one of several specific phobias. Most phobias involve objects or situations that pose some degree of danger, and thus they have some evolutionary significance (McNally, 1987). Among the most common specific phobias are fear of animals, such as snakes and dogs (called *zoophobia*); fear of enclosed places like elevators (*claustrophobia*); and fear of high places (*acrophobia*). The manual assigns a separate diagnostic category to two other phobias: agoraphobia and social phobia.

agoraphobia fear of public places from which there is no easy escape

Agoraphobia. **Agoraphobia** primarily involves a fear of public places from which there is no easy means of escape, or where help might be difficult to obtain in an emergency. (*Agora* is the Greek term for "marketplace.") Agoraphobia can be triggered by common situations such as being in a store, on a crowded street, in a tunnel or on a bridge, or even on a vehicle of public transportation. As is characteristic of the phobic disorders, agoraphobia dominates many aspects of the sufferer's existence. In later stages of the disorder, the person who has agoraphobia may even refuse to leave home. Depression is also a frequent complicating factor in this disorder.

social phobia irrational fear of situations that might lead to embarrassment, such as public speaking

Social Phobia. A person with a **social phobia** avoids situations that may lead to embarrassment in front of other people. The mere prospect of such a situation makes the individual feel highly anxious; the individual avoids the situation if at all possible. Among the more common situations that elicit social phobias are speaking or eating in public and using public toilets. People usually have only one social phobia, although it may accompany agoraphobia or specific phobia. It should be emphasized that many people are somewhat anxious in social situations such as public speaking, and that this reaction is quite normal. A person suffering from a social phobia, however, knows the fear is disproportionate and irrational. In addition, the disorder may limit or impair the person's career or social life.

Factors Associated with Phobic Disorders. The causes of phobic disorders are not clear at this time. One of Freud's celebrated cases was that of a little boy who would not leave the house because of his fear of horses. (In horse-and-buggy days, this was a more serious problem than it would be today.) Freud analyzed the boy's fear in terms of symbolic sexual content, and he felt that the boy was really afraid of his father's retaliation for his Oedipal wishes. (We discussed Freud's theory in detail in Chapter 10.) However, the boy had witnessed a frightening accident in the city streets that involved horses, and thus he might have been showing conditioned fear. A completely different line of reasoning holds that phobic disorders may have a genetic basis. For example, a greater risk of psychological problems exists among the relatives of people with agoraphobia than among nonanxious controls (Harris et al., 1983).

panic disorder disorder characterized by physiological anxiety responses that come on suddenly and unexpectedly

Panic Disorder. Closely associated with phobic disorders is **panic disorder**, characterized by recurrent panic attacks. Unlike phobias, which are triggered by specific situations, panic attacks come seemingly out of the blue. The unexpected nature of the attack is the essential feature of the disorder, with symptoms of apprehension, heart palpitations or chest pain, choking or smothering, dizziness, numbness and tingling in the hands or feet, sweating, and trembling. Although these symptoms come on quite suddenly and unpredictably, long-term sufferers may begin to feel anxious in anticipation of an attack.

Panic disorder is frequently associated with agoraphobia, perhaps because the individual begins to fear and avoid situations where a panic attack might occur. Panic disorder is much more common with agoraphobia than without it (American Psychiatric Association, 1987).

The case of Anne S. illustrates panic disorder with agoraphobia. Anne, a 45-year-old woman, went to a psychiatric clinic because she had been experiencing attacks of panic over a 2-year period. She had seen a family physician, who found nothing physically wrong and prescribed a mild tranquilizer. Initially, she found some relief from the tranquilizer. Gradually, however, it became less effective, and she turned to alcohol to relieve her anxiety. She got into the habit of having a cocktail or two at lunchtime and several drinks around dinner time. Eventually, she found herself drinking throughout the day to relieve her anxiety. Anne's anxiety attacks continued, and she began to dread leaving the house for fear she would have a panic attack in public. Thus, she avoided going to movies, stores, or social events with friends because of her fear of a panic attack and the embarrassment it would bring her (Spitzer, 1983).

The cause or causes of panic disorder are not clear at this time, but the disorder is made worse by caffeine. Individuals diagnosed as having panic disorder are more likely to feel anxious, nervous, nauseous, restless, and agitated after consuming caffeine (Lee et al., 1988). There is also evidence from PET scans (discussed in Chapter 2) that unequal blood flow to a part of the brain believed to control anxiety may be a physiological cause of panic disorder (Reiman et al., 1984) (see Figure 16–1 on page 646). Panic disorder may have a genetic basis. Monozygotic (identical) twins are twice as likely to share this disorder as dizygotic (fraternal) twins (Torgersen, 1983).

Although panic disorder may have genetic and other biological factors associated with its cause, psychological factors are also likely to contribute. One suggestion is that panic disorder is a conditioned "fear of fear." (One is reminded of the famous line from President Franklin Roosevelt's first inaugural address: "The only thing we have to fear is fear itself.") Conditioned fear of fear is based on principles of Pavlovian conditioning (as discussed in Chapter 6). After a person experiences the internal sensations associated with a panic attack, any similar sensations, even of a much lower intensity, that occur in the future may be interpreted as the onset of a panic attack, which in turn triggers a panic attack (McNally, 1990).

Post-Traumatic Stress Disorder. When people experience a traumatic event, they sometimes suffer later from **post-traumatic stress disorder**. They relive the terrible experience through recurrent memories or dreams, or through a feeling that they are suddenly back in the traumatic situation all over again. In addition, they avoid activities or situations that remind them of the trauma. Their emotions are usually somewhat numbed, and they lose interest in doing their usual activities. Other common effects are sleep disturbances and a decreased interest in sex. Many types of trauma may lead to post-traumatic stress disorder, including rape, natural disasters such as tornadoes or floods, or accidents such as fires or airplane crashes. It is now common practice for officials to set up counseling programs to help survivors deal with the shock of disasters such as airplane crashes or floods.

(*Top*) Agoraphobia, the most prevalent phobic disorder for which people seek treatment, involves fear of public places such as crowded subways or stores. Because of the disorder, many people with agoraphobia refuse to leave their houses. (*Bottom*) Other people suffer from acrophobia, a fear of high places. This man is obviously not troubled by acrophobia. Acrophobia is one of several specific fears classified under the label of "specific phobia."

post-traumatic stress disorder anxiety disorder in which a traumatic experience such as a plane crash or an earthquake is relived through flashbacks or dreams

FIGURE 16-1

Evidence from PET scans shows that people with panic disorder have unequal blood flow in the right and left sides of the brain. The left half of this figure shows a patient's cerebral blood flow, whereas the right half indicates the difference between left and right cerebral blood flow. Note the bright spot in the lower center of the right side, indicating greater blood flow in the right parahippocampal region, a part of the brain involved in mediating anxiety. People with no history of panic disorder do not show this pattern of unequal blood flow. (From Reiman et al., 1984.)

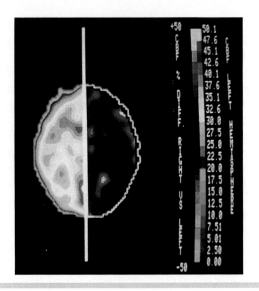

In 1988 Armenia suffered a devastating earthquake that destroyed whole villages and killed approximately 25,000 people. Survivors of such disasters are at risk for developing post-traumatic stress disorder.

obsessive-compulsive disorder disorder characterized by recurring thoughts that invade consciousness or behaviors the person feels compelled to perform

In a recent review of the research on psychological impairment following disasters of various types, Rubonis and Bickman (1991) identified a number of methodological problems. One problem concerns how data on post-trauma responses are obtained. Many of the studies simply ask those who experienced the trauma about their psychological adjustment before and after the trauma. In these retrospective studies, people estimate a greater magnitude of psychological impairment than people in studies that include independent estimates of impairment or a nondisaster control group. In other words, people are likely to inflate the effects of the disaster. Most studies also lump together males and females and people of diverse age groups who might reasonably be expected to respond differently to disasters. Nevertheless, experiencing a disaster does seem to be related to subsequent psychopathology. Compared to the adjustment of victims before the disaster and to control groups, there is an increase of psychological symptoms of about 17% following disasters (Rubonis & Bickman, 1991).

In recent years, post-traumatic stress disorder has frequently been associated with combat service in the Vietnam War, especially among those who saw significant amounts of combat (Foy et al., 1984). Vietnam veterans in general have poorer psychological health compared to military veterans of the same era (1964–1973) who did not serve in Vietnam, and especially compared to nonveterans (Kaylor, King, & King, 1987). These differences in psychological adjustment hold up despite controlling for premilitary experiences.

Obsessive-Compulsive Disorder. **Obsessive-compulsive disorder** is characterized by recurring thoughts or activities that the person cannot control. An *obsession* is an unwelcome and involuntary thought, one that the individual knows is not imposed from some outside source but rather is a product of his or her own mind. Most commonly, obsessions involve thoughts of violence, such as harming or killing a loved one; thoughts of contaminations from various diseases; and thoughts involving doubts, for example, wondering if one has hit a pedestrian on the street. A *compulsion* is an apparent need to repeat a particular behavior, even though it is a behavior that the person expressly wishes to avoid. Common compulsions are repetitive hand washing and counting. Not all compulsive behaviors are diagnosed as obsessive-compulsive disorder. For example, compulsive eating, drinking, gambling, and sexuality are placed into other diagnostic categories (Karno & Golding, 1991). Typically, obsessive-compulsive disorders begin in adolescence or early adulthood. Both obsessions and compulsions may occur in the disorder, although they may also occur separately.

The case of 13-year-old Ted illustrates an obsessive-compulsive disorder in which both obsessions and compulsions are present. Ted insisted on the perfect placement of objects in his room. For example: "He can spend 3 hours 'centering' the toilet paper roll on its holder or rearranging his bed and other objects in his room. When placing objects down, such as books or shoelaces after tying them, he picks them up and replaces them several times until they are straight" (Spitzer, 1983, p. 15). Ted's case also involved obsessions about contamination and disease: "He needed to know who had prepared his food before eating. He picked up his food with paper if his hands were not washed and placed the last piece of food back, fearing it was 'drugged.' At 11 he began to wear two layers of clothing, even in sweltering heat, so he would avoid 'catching pneumonia' " (Spitzer, 1983, p. 16).

Obsessive-compulsive disorder appears to have some associated psychophysical complaints, although these may be effects of the disorder rather than predisposing factors. You will recall from Chapter 5 that people go through regular stages of sleep. Compared to people who have no psychological disorder, people with obsessive-compulsive disorder get less sleep, spend a smaller percentage of time in sleep stage 4, and go into REM sleep more quickly (Insel et al., 1982). People with obsessive-compulsive disorder are also subject to high levels of physical arousal. Some researchers speculate that overarousal may be responsible for their excessive worrying and overresponse to situations perceived as threatening (Turner, Beidel, & Nathan, 1985). Recent studies of obsessive-compulsive disorder have revealed that it is more common than formerly suspected, afflicting perhaps as many as 1 in 40 people (Karno & Golding, 1991).

Somatoform Disorders

The term *somatic* refers to the body; **somatoform disorders** are those in which there are physical, or bodily, symptoms but no known organic or physiological pathology. The disorders are therefore presumed to have a psychological origin.

Many physical complaints have a psychological component to them. When their organic pathology can be identified using standard laboratory procedures, as in "psychophysiological" disorders such as neurodermatitis, asthma, gastric ulcer, and ulcerative colitis, they are not classified as somatoform disorders.

somatoform disorders a class of disorders with physical symptoms but no known organic or physiological pathology

Conversion Disorder. An apparently rather common psychological ailment at the turn of the century was *hysteria*, a disorder in which a physical symptom such as blindness or partial paralysis appeared, without any physical basis. *Hysteria* comes from the Greek word for "uterus" or "womb"; it was felt that the disorder was caused by the uterus wandering from its natural location to some other part of the body, where it caused physical ailments. Because of this peculiar view about causes, it was assumed that men were not afflicted with hysteria. Hysteria is now known as a conversion disorder, partly because the term *hysteria*, with its association with the uterus, is so inaccurate.

In **conversion disorder**, psychological problems somehow get converted into physical symptoms. Converting a psychological problem into a physical symptom is thought to benefit the person by keeping a conflict out of awareness, or by allowing the person to avoid some emotionally painful situation. Physical symptoms in conversion disorder are usually neurological and may include paralysis, blindness, or a lack of feeling in the limbs.

conversion disorder somatoform disorder in which emotional problems are converted into physical symptoms

Hypochondriasis.   People suffering from **hypochondriasis** have an unrealistic belief that they have a disease, despite medical consultations to the contrary. Individuals with hypochondriasis are preoccupied with their bodily processes, such as their heartbeat, and with minor physical symptoms, such as coughs, taking them to be signs of serious illness. They often go from one physician to another without finding a diagnosis that meets with their approval.

All of the somatoform disorders are presumed to have a psychological, rather than a physical, basis. However, sufferers may find this a meaningless distinction. To the sufferer, the physical pain associated with conversion disorder, or the symptoms leading to frequent medical consultations, are real.

Dissociative Disorders

Dissociative disorders involve a break, or dissociation, in conscious experience, identity, or memory. Earlier we discussed the continuum between psychological disorders and normal everyday experience. Dissociative experiences illustrate that continuum well. In everyday life, people are able to perform several actions simultaneously, without being aware in retrospect of the specific features of one or more of the actions. It is possible, for example, to drive competently and carry on a meaningful conversation at the same time. After a few minutes of intense conversation, the driver may be unable to recall anything about the features of the road just traveled. Such an experience is a mild form of dissociation. In more extreme circumstances, a person may be unable to remember any of the events of several days following some kind of disaster. Although the distinction between these two extreme situations is presumably linked to the capability to become aware of events if one wanted to, there is clearly a similarity between these two examples that suggests a continuum of experience (Spiegel & Cardeña, 1991).

Dissociative disorders share many features with somatoform disorders, particularly conversion disorder, and with post-traumatic stress disorder. All appear to be psychological adaptations to emotional or traumatic events. Whereas conversion disorder involves converting a psychological problem into physical symptoms, dissociative disorders manage to block conscious awareness of a traumatic experience. Most experts attribute dissociative disorders to great stress or trauma of some kind, such as childhood sexual

In everyday life, people sometimes exhibit dissociative behavior when they perform routine tasks without specific awareness. Driving for many people is a highly automatic behavior; people can drive and carry on a conversation at the same time.

abuse. Thus, there is a close relationship between post-traumatic stress disorder and dissociative disorders (Spiegel & Cardeña, 1991). It is likely that in the next few years, all of these disorders will be grouped together as "disorders of psychological trauma" (Davidson & Foa, 1991). In the next few paragraphs, we discuss two of the dissociative disorders, dissociative amnesia and multiple personality.

Dissociative Amnesia. The term *psychogenic* essentially means caused by psychological factors, and *amnesia* means a loss of memory. **Dissociative amnesia** is psychogenic and usually comes on suddenly following a major stress such as the loss of a job or a threat of physical injury. Dissociative amnesia is common in wartime and in natural disasters but apparently is rare in more usual circumstances (American Psychiatric Association, 1987). During episodes of dissociative amnesia, the individual may be disoriented, wandering from room to room or place to place in a purposeless fashion.

> **dissociative amnesia** sudden loss of memory following a major stress or trauma

A young man, 18 years old, illustrates dissociative amnesia (Spitzer et al., 1981). Police brought him into a hospital, where he was observed to be exhausted, sunburned, and disoriented. He thought the date was 3 days earlier than it actually was, and he had no memory for what had taken place during the lost days. Doctors, however, could find no physical basis for the loss of memory. Under the "truth serum" drug, sodium amytal, the young man was able to give an account of what had happened—an account that suggested a psychological basis for his loss of memory. He had been sailing with some close friends when they were surprised by a sudden severe storm. None among the group was experienced enough at sailing to handle the boat during the violent weather, and he alone had used a life jacket and tie line. All his friends were washed away, and he drifted alone for 3 days until the Coast Guard picked him up. The whole ordeal was blocked out of his conscious experience.

Multiple Personality. To most observers **multiple personality** appears to be a very strange and perplexing disorder. It is characterized by two or more distinct personalities within a single individual, each of them having periods of dominance. Transitions from one personality to another are often triggered by traumatic or stressful events. The pattern of interaction among the personalities varies. In some cases, they are not aware of each other's existence; in others, they eavesdrop when their rivals are dominant. The subpersonalities are usually very different from each other. The subpersonalities appear to serve the purpose of dissociating the self from highly emotional and traumatic events from which there is no other apparent escape. Diagnosed cases of multiple personality are three to nine times more frequent among women than men (American Psychiatric Association, 1987). (Multiple personality is distinct from schizophrenia, a disorder that is discussed later. Many people mistakenly think schizophrenia means split personality. The term *split personality* more nearly conforms to the syndrome of multiple personality.)

> **multiple personality** dissociative identity disorder characterized by two or more distinct personalities within one person

Several studies have indicated a strong association between childhood abuse or other traumatic experiences and multiple personality disorder. Some studies have found that more than 90% of cases of multiple personality disorder involved significant childhood trauma, with incest being the most common form (Spiegel & Cardeña, 1991). Recall, however, the problems of retrospective accounts cited earlier in connection with post-traumatic stress disorder; virtually all of the data on childhood events come from retrospective self-reports.

Paula S., a 38-year-old divorced woman with two adolescent children, is an example of a person with multiple personality disorder (Oltmanns, Neale, & Davison, 1986). She sought the professional advice of a psychologist after a series of disturbing events, such as frequent memory lapses, and difficulty in her coursework at college. She also occasionally found beer cans and whisky bottles in the back seat of her car and woke up with hangoverlike headaches, even though she didn't drink. Under hypnosis, Paula revealed four subpersonalities, none of which she was aware of in her conscious life. "Sherry" was a brassy woman in her 30s who knew all about Paula and sometimes substituted for her in classes. "Janet" was an adolescent who occasionally watched over the third subpersonality, 5-year-old "Caroline." Finally, "Heather" was a 23-year-old subpersonality who was very much in love with an older neighbor and who made sexual advances to him, without any other personality's knowledge. Like many cases of multiple personality, Paula's involved sexual abuse as a child. Her father had forced a sexual relationship on her from the time she was 5 years old until after her marriage and the birth of her first child.

It is difficult to imagine just how complicated, not to say bizarre, the life of a person with multiple personality can get. In Paula's case, "Sherry" even made promises to Paula's two children, to get them out of her hair, even though she had no intention of keeping the promises and Paula herself was unaware of them. Naturally, her children thought she was making the promises herself and were annoyed when she denied any knowledge of them. Other people viewed Paula as erratic and unpredictable, as indeed she was under the influence of so many subpersonalities.

Over the last several pages, we have reviewed anxiety states, obsessive-compulsive disorder, somatoform disorders, and dissociative disorders. The basic symptoms of these disorders make up different syndromes. However, they do have elements in common, such as the experience of anxiety and the fact that they are reactions to traumatic events. Next, we turn to disorders that involve moods, the so-called mood disorders.

MOOD DISORDERS

Mood disorders are the most common psychological disorders. Approximately 20% of the population have a bout of serious mood disturbance at some point in their lives (Hirschfeld & Cross, 1982). The most common mood disturbance is depression, which is sometimes called the common cold of psychological disorders. Like the cold, it occurs frequently in the general population but is still a poorly understood disorder. Also like the cold, depression varies in severity; some people are much more seriously affected than others.

Two major types of mood disorder are depression and bipolar disorder. In the latter disorder, mood fluctuates between unusual elation and depression. Because mood shifts from one extreme, or pole, to another, this syndrome is called **bipolar disorder**. Major depression, on the other hand, is referred to as **unipolar depression**, because mood remains at one bleak extreme.

Major Depression

Everyone gets depressed occasionally, because life does not always go according to one's plans or because of the inevitable losses and hardships

bipolar disorder mood disorder in which mood fluctuates between extremes of elation and depression

unipolar depression major depression, in which mood is at one bleak extreme of sadness

that are interspersed with the joys and triumphs of life. But a normal depressed mood is different from the despair of clinical depression. Major depression includes more symptoms, is more devastating to one's routine, and lasts longer than normal depression. Causes of major depression may also be different from the causes of normal variations in mood; we discuss causes of major depression later in this section.

The primary symptom of major depression is an overwhelming feeling of sadness. Other symptoms include loss of interest in almost all of one's usual activities; feelings of self-blame, worthlessness, and guilt; fatigue, so that even the smallest task may seem to require too much effort; loss of appetite; disturbances in one's usual pattern of sleep; difficulty in concentrating and greater distractibility; and suicidal thoughts or attempts. To be classified as an episode of major depression, several of these symptoms must be present nearly every day for a period of at least 2 weeks.

Major depression is also commonly accompanied by excessive crying, excessive concern about one's physical health, and even by delusions and hallucinations. Depression also intensifies feelings of wanting to be held, particularly among women (Stein & Sanfilipo, 1985). About twice as many women as men suffer from unipolar depression. This sex ratio is apparently not a result of a greater tendency on the part of women to seek help for their problems, because the same ratio characterizes groups of people who do not receive treatment and groups of those who are receiving treatment (Hirschfeld & Cross, 1982; Nolen-Hoeksema, 1987).

Consider the case of Janet M., a 30-year-old woman who had been divorced from her husband, David, for a year (Oltmanns et al., 1986). Janet and her three children lived in a comfortable house that was part of the divorce settlement, and Janet had been attending university classes but had stopped because she felt unable to concentrate on her work. In discussions with a psychologist, Janet said she felt completely unable to control her youngest son and that the situation was getting worse. She had felt "down in the dumps" after her divorce, and the depressed mood had gotten worse as time went on.

She now spent a great deal of time brooding about the breakup of her marriage: Maybe she shouldn't have gone back to school and strained the relationship. Maybe she shouldn't have criticized her husband. Maybe she should have tried to show more interest in sports. Maybe she shouldn't have spent so much money on clothes. In short, she felt it all must have been her fault, and if that marriage had failed, she might never be able to have another relationship. These bleak feelings, with loss of self-esteem, self-blame, loss of interest in regular activities, and loss of ability to concentrate, are all characteristic of major depression.

Cognitive Changes in Major Depression.   Patterns of thinking may be altered in several ways during an episode of major depression (Beck, 1987). As we discussed in Chapter 7, people who are depressed retrieve negative thoughts from memory more rapidly than nondepressed people. Depressed people often have negative automatic thoughts, unwelcome thoughts that they cannot seem to put out of their minds. However, when bouts of depression are over, the negative automatic thoughts disappear (Eaves & Rush, 1984). The cognitive style associated with depression appears to come and go with the disorder (Hamilton & Abramson, 1983; Segal, 1988).

Many of the symptoms of major depression have cognitive aspects. Included among these symptoms is an increase in negative thoughts about the self, increased feelings of helplessness, and a reduced ability to recall

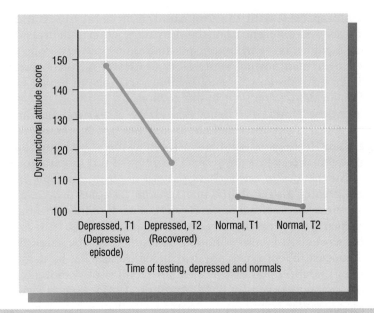

FIGURE 16-2
People who are experiencing episodes of major depression undergo cognitive changes such as an increase in maladaptive attitudes. However, when they have recovered from the depressive episode, their thinking is not significantly different from that of normal individuals. (T1 = first testing; T2 = second testing.) (From Hamilton & Abramson, 1983.)

events with happier overtones (Haaga, Dyck, & Ernst, 1991). People who are depressed show a larger number of negative attitudes than they do when they have recovered from the depression. In addition, research has shown that their postdepression negative attitudes do not differ significantly from those of normal people in control groups whose attitudes were measured at two different times, as shown in Figure 16–2.

A theory in social psychology—*attribution theory*—concerns the explanations that people assign to their own and others' behavior. (We discussed attribution theory in detail in Chapter 14.) According to this theory, when bad events occur that a person cannot control, depression may result because the person expects future events to be beyond control as well (Brewin, 1985). There is some evidence that people who are prone to depression are more likely to attribute blame to themselves and to view themselves as helpless in a greater variety of situations than do people who are not depression prone (Abramson et al., 1978; Raps et al., 1982). They also rate themselves lower in social skills than healthy individuals (Haley, 1985). People who are depressed also respond differently to feedback about success and failure than do those who are not depressed. Depressed people tend to magnify the importance of feedback about failure, in contrast to nondepressed individuals, who magnify feedback about success (Wenzlaff & Grozier, 1988). The relationship between explanatory style and depression may work both ways. People who tend to attribute blame to themselves are more likely to become depressed, and people who are depressed are more likely to attribute blame to themselves (Peterson & Seligman, 1984).

Seasonal Depression. Some people suffer from seasonal depression, also known as **seasonal affective disorder (SAD)**. Seasonal affective disorder is characterized by recurrent depression during a particular season of the year. People who have winter depression, for example, slow down, generally oversleep and overeat, and crave carbohydrates during the winter months (Garvey, Wesner, & Godes, 1988; Wurtman & Wurtman, 1989).

There is speculation that reduced levels of light contribute to winter depression (Rosenthal et al., 1985). A clue to the role of light in winter depression is the improvement in mood among patients who undergo light

seasonal affective disorder (SAD)
recurrent mood shifts, usually depression, during particular seasons of the year

therapy that approximates the illumination from sunlight on a clear spring day. Artificially extending the length of the day for individuals with winter depression leads within a few days to an improvement in mood that lasts throughout treatment. When treatment is discontinued, a relapse occurs (James et al., 1985; Rosenthal et al., 1985).

Searching for the Causes of Depression.   Depression may be triggered by a stressful event in a person's life, such as the loss of a job or breakup of a marriage. Depression may be especially likely when the stressful event disrupts a role that had been an important basis for a person's sense of self (Barnett & Gotlib, 1988; Oatley & Bolton, 1985). For example, if marriage conveys a sense of self-worth to one of the partners, and the marriage breaks up, then depression may be a likely result. Depressed individuals have experienced more recent stressful events such as family illnesses than nondepressed individuals (Billings, Cronkite, & Moos, 1983). Death of a loved one usually brings on a period of grief and bereavement that is very similar to the depressive syndrome. Such a change in mood is normal and expected when a major loss occurs. However, if grief becomes prolonged and severe, it may indicate major depression (American Psychiatric Association, 1987).

But stressful life events alone do not explain major depression. In recent years, researchers have devoted considerable attention to possible biological factors associated with depression. One of the most encouraging lines of investigation is the search for neurochemical bases of depression. The search began in part because of several observations that seemed to indicate a biochemical role. For example, a side effect of some medications is depression. Also, menopause in women, which is accompanied by hormonal changes, is sometimes associated with shifts in mood. Mood shifts may also accompany the cyclic hormonal changes in menstruation. Tension, mood shifts, and other symptoms preceding menstruation are popularly known as *premenstrual syndrome*, or *PMS*. The *Diagnostic and Statistical Manual (DSM-IV)* even includes a diagnosis related to the mood shifts of menstruation, although this category, *premenstrual dysphoric disorder*, has not been without its critics. Premenstrual dysphoric disorder is only diagnosed when it interferes dramatically with work or with typical social activities, and when mood undergoes dramatic shifts (American Psychiatric Association, 1993).

Exposure to high-intensity light for an hour or so in the morning can relieve some of the symptoms of winter depression.

Depression may be triggered by a highly stressful event, such as the death of a loved one. A period of grief and bereavement is normal and expected following the death of a close friend or relative. However, if grief is prolonged and severe, it may indicate major depression.

Critics argue that including such a category as a psychological disorder has the potential for stigmatizing women for a hormonal or gynecological, as opposed to a psychological, condition.

Shortages of some specific neurotransmitters, notably serotonin, have been linked to clinical depression (Wurtman & Wurtman, 1989). The action of neurotransmitters, which was described in Chapter 2, helps to regulate not only mood, but all physical and psychological processes. Although an association between shortages of specific transmitters and depression has been demonstrated, the issue of cause and effect is not yet settled. It is possible that environmental stress and its attendant alteration in mood influence the amount of neurotransmitter in the brain, rather than the other way around. What is clear, however, is that drugs that increase the level of these neurotransmitters in the brain alleviate the symptoms of major depression for many people.

Genetic factors have also been hypothesized to be related to major depression. Family history studies suggest that major depression, especially in its more severe forms, tends to cluster in families (Klein, 1990). The disparity in rates of major depression by sex have suggested that the disorder may have a sex-linked form of genetic transmission, but firm evidence to support such a view is lacking at this time (Faraone, Kremen, & Tsuang, 1990).

Other biological hypotheses about depression include the notion that brain asymmetry may be involved and that normal circadian rhythms have been disrupted. Some researchers have noted an increase in right hemisphere activity and a decrease in left hemisphere activity in depression (Gerner & Bunney, 1986). Evidence for disruption of circadian cycles comes from observations that depression often has a seasonal onset, recurs periodically, and often disrupts sleep–wake cycles (Healy & Williams, 1988).

Bipolar Disorder

The vast majority of cases of depression—more than 90%—are unipolar. The remaining cases involve moods that alternate between episodes of depression and mania, and are referred to as bipolar disorder. (Diagnostic manuals prior to DSM-III referred to this syndrome as manic–depressive psychosis.) During the depressive phase, the symptoms that we have already described apply. Bipolar disorder is diagnosed when a manic episode occurs in an individual with a history of one or more depressive episodes. Mania by itself, without any depression, is a rare occurrence.

Manic Episodes in Bipolar Disorder. A manic episode is in many ways the opposite extreme of a depressive episode. Mood is elevated and may be described as unusually cheerful or euphoric. In addition, the individual is likely to be hyperactive. In marked contrast to depression, mania is characterized by increased sociability, but social interaction is likely to be domineering and demanding. Individuals with manic hyperactivity are likely to engage in odd or bizarre behavior, such as reckless driving, buying sprees, and sexual escapades uncharacteristic of the person. Thought and speech in manic episodes are also unusual. Speech is loud and rapid, usually including jokes and plays on words that may be difficult to interpret. Thought, reflected in the speech, may jump rapidly from one topic to another, with few apparent connections. All of these symptoms occur in the context of changes in the individual's self-evaluation, which is typically grandiose and unrealistic.

For example, George W. was a 35-year-old man admitted to a hospital with a diagnosis of bipolar disorder. Although he had not slept for three nights, his behavior was described as follows:

[George] was talking a mile a minute. He harangued the other patients and ward staff, declaring that he was the coach of the U.S. Olympic track team and offering to hold tryouts for the other patients in the hospital. His movements were rapid and somewhat erratic as he paced the halls of the ward and explored every room. At the slightest provocation, he flew into a rage. When an attendant blocked his entrance to the nursing station, he threatened to report her to the president of the Olympic committee. (Oltmanns et al., 1986)

Manic episodes do not last as long as depressive episodes, and they end more abruptly. A manic episode typically lasts from a few days to a few weeks. There is no single pattern of mood change common to those who have bipolar disorder. Some begin with a depressive episode, others with a manic episode. Some return to normal moods before cycling into the opposite extreme, others do not. About 15% of the cases of bipolar disorder involve *rapid cycling*—regular, frequent, and almost continuous cycling between mania and depression. Such cases are particularly difficult to treat (Wehr et al., 1988). Unlike unipolar depression, bipolar disorder is equally common among men and women.

In many ways bipolar disorder is more serious than unipolar depression. Figure 16–3 shows the results from one study of outcomes for the two disorders. Far more of the people who had manic–depressive episodes were continuously incapacitated than were those who had unipolar depression, and only about half as many people with bipolar disorder had recovered (McGlashan, 1984).

Biological Vulnerability to Bipolar Disorder.   Scientists have been searching for several years for the possible biological markers of unipolar depression and bipolar disorder. One promising lead concerns evidence that there is a genetically transmitted sensitivity to the neurotransmitter acetylcholine among patients with bipolar disorder and their relatives who have other psychological disorders (Nadi, Nurnberger, & Gershon, 1984). Researchers took skin samples from individuals suffering from bipolar disorder and their relatives and from normal volunteers, and grew several generations of skin cells in the laboratory to eliminate any drug effects. There were significantly more acetylcholine receptors in the skin of the patients with bipolar disorder than in that of the volunteers. If there are also more acetylcholine receptors in the brains of these individuals, as the researchers speculate, then individuals with bipolar disorder

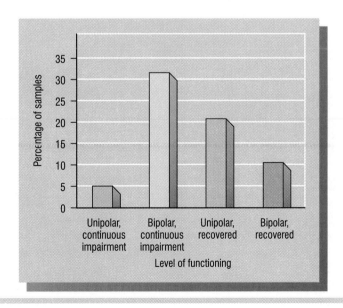

FIGURE 16–3
Bipolar disorder is more serious than major depression in outcome and prognosis. About six times more individuals with bipolar disorder show continuous impairment, compared to those with major depression. Half as many individuals with bipolar disorder show full recovery. (From McGlashan, 1984.)

A crowd of onlookers has gathered to watch as a young man is rescued by emergency workers during a suicide attempt. The suicide rate has increased over the last several years, especially among young people.

may be supersensitive to any of this group of neurotransmitters (Snyder, 1984). There is also some enlargement of one of the ventricles in the brain, where cerebrospinal fluid circulates, in bipolar disorder (Dewan et al., 1988).

> ## THINKING ABOUT
> # Suicide

One of the major risks in depression is suicide. Many people who are suffering from major depression have suicidal thoughts. Although not everyone who commits suicide is depressed, a majority are. No other psychological disorder has as great a risk of death associated with it as depression (Pokorny, 1964). We should not, however, link suicide too strongly with depression. Just as not everyone who commits suicide is depressed, so most people who are depressed do not attempt suicide (Baumeister, 1990).

The number of people who are officially listed as suicides has increased over the last few years, especially among adolescents and young adults. Figure 16–4 documents the increase for people from 15 to 24 years old. But the statistics graphed in Figure 16–4 are only the documented cases of suicide. About 30,000 people a year are counted as suicides, but estimates of the actual number of suicides are much higher, 100,000 or more. The discrepancy is accounted for by a number of factors: single-car accidents may have been suicides; family physicians may be unwilling to list suicide as a cause of death; and some coroners do not count a death as suicide unless the person left a note, which occurs only in about 15% of cases.

The data in Figure 16–4 graphically document a sex difference in suicidal behavior. Many people believe that men who attempt suicide are actually more intent on killing themselves than women who attempt suicide. One basis for this conclusion is that men are twice as likely as women to choose the more violent and immediately lethal method of shooting, whereas women are four times more likely than men to use drugs or poison. Men who attempt suicide are also more likely to have economic problems as stressors and are three times more likely to be substance abusers (Rich et al., 1988).

FIGURE 16–4
Suicide rates have increased dramatically over the last 3 decades in the age group from 15 to 24, especially among males. And while the suicide rate for young women has doubled, it has more than tripled among young men. This graph shows the rates for white males (M) and females (F). (Adapted from Klagsbrun, 1976; U.S. Bureau of the Census, 1992.)

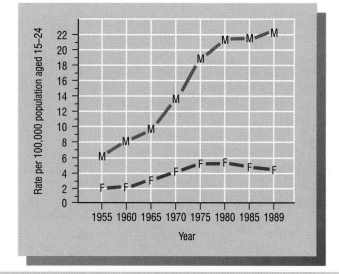

What if you know someone whom you suspect is thinking about suicide? What should you do? It is important to know what is true and what is myth in the area of suicidal behavior. Available research and the experience of professionals in crisis centers and in psychological clinics suggest that there are several common misconceptions about suicidal behavior. One misconception is that people who talk about suicide will not actually try to kill themselves. In fact, repeated threats of suicide provide a signal that an individual is having serious suicidal thoughts. Threats may even be an attempt to communicate that something is wrong. Dismissing a threat under the misconception that it means the person is not really serious would therefore tell the person that the attempt at communication was a failure. The next step in the communication process might be an actual suicide attempt.

A related misconception is that you should not talk about suicide in front of a potentially suicidal person, because you might give the person ideas. In fact, the potentially suicidal person already has the idea. Talking about suicide and showing that you care might actually help the person by focusing realistically on the problems at hand.

Another misconception is that when a person becomes cheerful after a period of depression, the danger of suicide has passed. In fact, the cheerful mood may simply reflect the relief experienced by a person who has come to a decision to attempt suicide. Frequently, a person's mood improves before a serious suicide attempt. A further misconception, however, is that once a person makes a decision to commit suicide, there is nothing you can do to reverse it. Many suicide attempts are desperate bids for communication. They are often preceded by signals. It may be possible to prevent many suicides by recognizing that the troubled person has problems and by helping the person to deal with them.

Some of the danger signs of suicide include the following. The potentially suicidal person may give away some of his or her prized possessions. The person may withdraw from ordinary activities and become apathetic. The person may also talk about specific plans for committing suicide, and may seem not to care about the effect suicide would have on friends and family. Another danger sign of suicide is a previous suicide attempt; most professionals believe the first attempt is the hardest.

If you believe you know someone who is at risk for attempting suicide, do something to help. You can try talking to the person. You should be a good listener and acknowledge the feelings the person is expressing, rather than trying to debate with him or her about suicide. "Suicide is wrong" is probably not going to be a compelling argument for someone who has reached this state of personal crisis. Don't be afraid to let the person know that his or her words or behavior scare you. Communicate how you feel, too. But by talking about it, you may be able to get the person through the immediate crisis. However, don't take more onto your own shoulders than you can handle. If you think the risk of suicide is real and immediate, get help. Let a counselor know about your fears, or get the suicidal person to an emergency room or to a professional, or call a crisis hotline. Most of all, don't worry that you will do the wrong thing. Showing your concern and acting honestly on the basis of it can never be the wrong thing.

What would you want your friends to do to help you if you were feeling suicidal? What resources are there at your college for helping someone through a crisis? What are the numbers for the crisis hotlines in your area? What three people can you think of who might be available to help you through a crisis?

Sadness and malaise are of course real to virtually anyone who has experienced normal depression at one time or another. But these moods are much more severe in the affective disorders during a depressive episode. The dark undercurrents of depression persist continuously for weeks. The individual comes to think of himself or herself as worthless and as living in a hopeless situation. But a greater understanding of affective disorders may be on the horizon. Recent research into biochemical markers and cognitive changes in depression seems more promising for this disorder than for any other at the present time.

PSYCHOSEXUAL DISORDERS

Much of human sexuality is grounded in society's attitudes and values about what is acceptable and appropriate. Indeed, some sexual activities that are considered normal by a large number of people, such as oral or anal sexual contact, are nevertheless illegal in many states. Masturbation, which is now considered normal and, in the age of AIDS, even a desirable sexual outlet, was once believed to be a precursor of madness. Sexual views change with time and place. Previous editions of the DSM included homosexuality as a psychosexual disorder. It is no longer considered a psychological problem.

The clinical term for sexual arousal to objects or activities not normally considered erotic is **paraphilia**. (*Para* means "beside" or "beyond," and *philia* means "love"; hence, *paraphilia* refers to sexuality that is beyond love.) More than 30 distinct paraphilias have been described in the literature on sexuality (Money, 1984). They can generally be divided into three groups: (1) arousal to nonhuman objects, (2) arousal based on suffering or humiliation experienced by oneself or one's partner, or (3) arousal to children or other nonconsenting persons.

Sexual Arousal to Nonhuman Objects

When people are sexually aroused by inanimate objects, they are said to exhibit **fetishism**. A fetish is an object believed to possess magical powers; sexual fetishes are objects whose power resides in their ability to arouse sexual feeling. Very few women appear to have fetishes (Katchadourian, 1989). Men's common fetishes include bras, women's underpants, stockings, and high-heeled shoes. These objects are frequently used in masturbation rituals in which they are held, fondled, or smelled (American Psychiatric Association, 1987). Articles of clothing, especially undergarments, are preferred if they have been worn.

Again, fetishism illustrates the continuity between normal and abnormal behavior. Many men get some erotic charge out of lacy undergarments or bikini underpants. However, these objects are erotically charged because of their association with sexual situations, and it is the sexual interaction that is the ultimate goal. But it may be impossible for a person with a fetish to be aroused without the object present (Katchadourian, 1989).

Sexual interaction with animals may be classified as a paraphilia if it occurs repeatedly or if it is the exclusive technique for sexual expression (Katchadourian, 1989). **Zoophilia** is the term applied to this paraphilia; it is also sometimes known as *bestiality*. Sexual interaction with animals may be more common than many people would think, but is most likely a sexual outlet when other, more conventional options are not available.

Arousal Based on Suffering or Humiliation

Among the most frequently mentioned paraphilias are sadism and masochism. **Sadism**, named for the practices of the Marquis de Sade (1740–1814), refers to

paraphilia sexual arousal to objects or activities not usually considered erotic

fetishism psychosexual disorder involving sexual arousal to inanimate objects such as, for men, bras and high-heeled shoes

zoophilia sexual interaction with animals, also known as bestiality

sadism sexual gratification through inflicting pain, injury, or humiliation on another

obtaining sexual gratification through inflicting pain, injury, or humiliation on others. **Masochism**, named for the Austrian novelist Leopold von Sacher-Masoch (1835–1895) who first described it, refers to deriving sexual gratification from being hurt or humiliated. Sadism appears to be more common among men; masochism is somewhat more common among women. These sexual activities, however, rarely come to the attention of psychological clinics (Christie Brown, 1983).

Most of the paraphilias are more common among men than among women. **Exhibitionism**, for example—the phenomenon of obtaining gratification through showing one's genitals to unwilling observers—is much more common among men and represents more than one third of the arrests for sex crimes. Exhibitionism may be a particularly blatant form of attention seeking, derived from feelings of insecurity or insignificance.

> Pete W.'s case is a good illustration of exhibitionism. Pete, at age 34, was arrested for sexual assault after he had stopped to help a woman who was looking at the engine of her car on the side of a highway. After adjusting her fan belt, Pete exposed himself to her and began masturbating. His history of exhibitionism dated back to his adolescence, when he first exposed himself in public, after an unsuccessful attempt at intercourse. His favorite targets were teenaged girls. His sexual urges increased at times of stress, such as during exams or work pressures. Although Pete married when he was 24, his marriage had become increasingly unsatisfying. His wife knew nothing of his exhibitionism until his arrest (Oltmanns et al., 1986).

Arousal to Nonconsenting Persons

Most people seek sexual partners who are within relatively the same age group. Some paraphilias involve seeking unwilling partners who are inappropriate in terms of age. **Pedophilia** involves an adult or adolescent who seeks a child as a sexual partner. The incidence of pedophilia is unknown, but surveys conducted in the last few years indicate that it may be a more serious social problem than had previously been thought. More than a fourth of women and about a sixth of men report having been sexually victimized to one degree or another as children (Finkelhor et al., 1990). Evidence is accumulating that child sexual abuse results in very disturbing psychological problems, such as depression, anxiety, feelings of isolation, and impaired sexual behavior in a substantial proportion of victims (Browne & Finkelhor, 1986).

As we have said, sexual norms change over time. When clinicians wrote about sexual pathologies at the turn of the century, they viewed any form of sexual interaction that was not aimed at reproduction as a deviation. Neither experts in the field nor the general public are likely to be so harsh in their judgments in the 1990s. Many authorities believe that unusual sexual practices are on a continuum with more common sexual behavior. The individual who is aroused by watching a willing partner undress, for example, under more extreme circumstances might be labeled a *voyeur* (more commonly known as a "peeping Tom"). Some sexual variations are completely unacceptable in our society. Rape and pedophilia, for example, are intolerable because they do not involve consent and are physically and emotionally harmful to others.

SCHIZOPHRENIC DISORDERS

In schizophrenic disorders, there is a major problem in reality testing, which means that the individual's perceptions of reality are greatly dis-

masochism sexual gratification from being hurt or humiliated

exhibitionism sexual gratification from exposing one's genitals to unwilling others

pedophilia seeking a child as a sexual partner (by an adolescent or adult)

torted. As a result, the individual may reach grossly inappropriate conclusions. For example, a woman whose friend had died in an automobile accident subsequently showed a failure in reality testing that reflected underlying schizophrenia. She believed that her friend had not died after all, and that the funeral had been staged in an elaborate plot to deceive her. Eventually, her conception of this plot was so elaborate that she thought ultrasound beams were being aimed at her and that her own life was in peril (Spitzer et al., 1981). False beliefs not based on external reality, such as those experienced by this woman, are called **delusions**. Another sign of a failure in reality testing may be **hallucinations**, perceptions that occur in the absence of sensory stimulation, such as hearing nonexistent voices.

The **schizophrenias** include several closely related disorders of thinking that result in severe behavior disturbances. Psychotic failures in reality testing are apparent during active phases of schizophrenia. Usually there are delusions or hallucinations, or both, and incoherent and illogical thinking. In work and other social relations, people with schizophrenia show marked deterioration in several areas of psychological functioning. Thinking and perception are impaired, emotional expression is dulled or flattened, and sense of self may be altered to the extent that the person loses a sense of identity. Some of these characteristics may be represented in the art of people who have schizophrenia, which differs in some ways from the art of normal individuals (Arnheim, 1986; see also Figure 16–5). Other symptoms may include unusual motor behavior, with the individual assuming odd postures or developing unusual mannerisms or facial expressions.

Schizophrenia can be a particularly debilitating psychological disorder. Schizophrenia accounts for about one half of all patients in psychiatric hospitals in the United States. Estimates of the prevalence of schizophrenia are fairly uniform from one culture to another and cluster at about 1% of the population. For the United States, that equals a total of about 2.5 million people with schizophrenia alone.

Historical Views of Schizophrenia

When German psychiatrist Emil Kraepelin produced a systematic set of diagnostic categories for psychological disorders in the late 1800s, he identified a disorder that included delusions, hallucinations, and bizarre behavior, in which the individual's condition worsened as time went on. Because Kraepelin thought the disorder invariably began in adolescence, he called it *dementia praecox*, or "premature impairment of mental powers." Kraepelin was incorrect in his thinking that the disorder always began in adolescence; we now know that the disorder may first appear well into adulthood, although it usually appears before the age of 45. Kraepelin's view that the disorder worsens with time is also not necessarily the case.

To avoid Kraepelin's misleading label regarding the age of onset, Swiss psychiatrist Eugen Bleuler (1857–1939) applied the term *schizophrenia* to the disorder. This label has also caused a certain amount of confusion as a description of the disorder. *Schizo* literally means "split," and *phrenia* refers to the mind. Bleuler meant to imply that the mind is split from reality or from its own perception, but many people mistakenly think schizophrenia means split personality. Nevertheless, Bleuler's term has remained the diagnostic label for the disorder. Both Bleuler and Kraepelin believed that schizophrenia was caused by a biomedical problem.

The American Psychiatric Association has also contributed to the conceptual murkiness of the diagnosis of schizophrenia, by changing the diagnostic criteria for schizophrenia from one edition of the diagnostic manual to another. Thus, a person diagnosed with schizophrenia before the DSM-III

delusions false beliefs not based on external reality

hallucinations perceptions in the absence of sensory stimulation

schizophrenias class of closely related disorders of thinking with severe behavioral disturbances

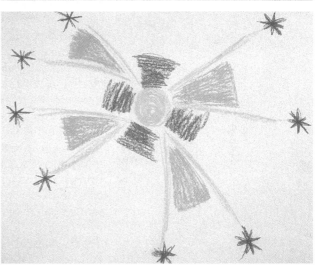

appeared in 1980 is not necessarily comparable to a person so diagnosed between 1980 and 1994. Additional changes in DSM-IV make the post-1994 population different again. Criteria from the various editions of the diagnostic manual have been fairly poor at predicting an individual's psychological outcome within 2 years of the diagnosis. The lack of such short-term stability calls into question the reality of the diagnosis. As one critic put it, "We must now surely consider the possibility that we have somehow managed in this case to carve out a category that has no counterpart in nature's table of organization" (Carson, 1991, p. 305).

FIGURE 16–5
Art therapist Barry Cohen uses patients' drawings to help him assess their problems. His preliminary studies suggest that the drawings of patients with schizophrenia (*left*), in comparison to those of normal controls (*right*), use less space and less blended color. In addition, patients with schizophrenia are far more likely to write on their drawings. (From Cohen, 1985.)

APPLYING PSYCHOLOGY
Implications of Diagnostic Labeling

In a classic study, David Rosenhan (1973) investigated some of the complexities associated with categorizing people as sane or insane. He and seven of his colleagues presented themselves to the admitting offices of 12 different psychiatric hospitals in five different states. None of the eight "pseudopatients" had had psychological problems beyond those that any normal individual experiences. Their purpose was to see if their sanity would be immediately detected by the professional staffs of these hospitals. During their appointments with the admissions offices, all the pseudopatients described the same symptoms, namely, that they had been hearing voices. The voices were unclear, but seemed to be saying, "empty," "hollow," and "thud." Otherwise, they told the truth about their backgrounds, feelings, and experiences, with two minor concealments. They used pseudonyms so that if a psychiatric diagnosis were made, it would not follow them later; and the four pseudopatients who had advanced training in psychology concealed that fact by stating that they had an alternate occupation.

In their 12 encounters with psychiatric admissions offices, none of the pseudopatients was detected to be sane. All were admitted, and in 11 of the 12 cases, the diagnosis was schizophrenia. A part of the procedure of this study was that the pseudopatients had to get out of the psychiatric hospital on their own, through behaving sanely. Length of hospitalizations ranged from 7 to 52 days, with a mean of 19 days.

There are a number of important points made by this study, among them the power of a diagnostic label. Diagnosed with schizophrenia, the pseudopatients were assumed to be "schizophrenic," a category that implies a set of traits that reside in the person rather than in the situation. At discharge, all of the pseudopatients were said to be "in remission." In psychiatric jargon, *remission* means that the "illness" remains, but that no symptoms are currently in evidence. Thus, even when they were discharged, these patients were not presumed to be sane by the professionals who dealt with them. Furthermore, their behavior inside the mental hospital was interpreted as a symptom of their disorder, rather than in terms of the context of an abnormal environment. Pseudopatients who kept notes of their experiences, for example, were described on their charts as "engaging in writing behavior."

The pseudopatients in Rosenhan's study experienced a strong sense of depersonalization in the abnormal context of the mental hospital. Staff members frequently treated them and the other, "real," patients as if they were not present, or as if they were somehow without awareness or feelings. Staff members avoided any casual conversation with the patients. On one occasion that Rosenhan himself witnessed as a pseudopatient, a "real" patient was beaten for approaching an attendant and saying to him, "I like you."

Rosenhan's sobering study should give everyone in the psychological community some important issues to think about. Rosenhan posed the central point, "The question of whether the sane can be distinguished from the insane (and whether degrees of insanity can be distinguished from each other) is a simple matter: Do the salient characteristics that lead to diagnoses reside in the patients themselves or in the environments and contexts in which observers find them?" (Rosenhan, 1973, p. 251). Twenty years later, the answer to Rosenhan's question is still not obvious.

Nevertheless, diagnoses of schizophrenia continue to be made, and research on this puzzling disorder continues. Because of the attention it receives, schizophrenia has been described as the disorder "that is at the absolute center, by almost any measure, of the entire mental health research and practice enterprise" (Carson, 1991, p. 305). We therefore need to know as much as we can about the signs, symptoms, and causes of this psychological disorder.

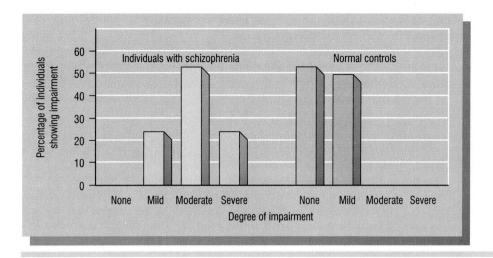

FIGURE 16–6
In comparison with normal controls, individuals who have schizophrenia suffer a great deal of cognitive impairment. In one study, none of the individuals with schizophrenia was completely free of cognitive impairment; more than half of the normal controls were free of impairment. (From Taylor & Abrams, 1984.)

Disordered Thought in Schizophrenia

People with schizophrenia characteristically have disordered thought, both in its form and content. The form of thinking may become loose, so that speech becomes incoherent. Examples of statements of one person with schizophrenia illustrate this incoherence: "My mother does not accreditize me"; "The hospital will have my records if they are consortive; they must have a litigation department" (Spitzer et al., 1981). There may also be a deterioration in formal thought processes such as memory (Calev, 1984). Figure 16–6 compares the degree of cognitive impairment on several tasks for individuals with schizophrenia and for normal control individuals. As you can see, patients with schizophrenia were much more severely impaired in their performance on cognitive tasks.

Typically, the content of thinking is also affected, especially in terms of delusions. People with schizophrenia often experience **delusions of persecution**, believing that others wish to harm them in some way, such as spreading false rumors about them. **Delusions of reference** are also common; these delusions involve attributing unusual personal significance to people or events. For example, a person with schizophrenia might believe that everyone in a room is thinking mocking thoughts about him or her. Individuals with schizophrenia may also believe that their every thought is broadcast to other people, or that their thoughts are not really their own but are inserted into their heads by some external force.

delusions of persecution false beliefs that people wish to harm one in some way

delusions of reference false beliefs that others are controlling one's behavior

Types of Schizophrenia

Much of the preceding discussion has implied that schizophrenia is one psychological disorder. Along with the diagnostic criteria, different subtypes of schizophrenia shift from one edition of the diagnostic manual to another. Many experts believe that schizophrenia is really a family of disorders that vary in severity. At this point it is unclear whether schizophrenia is one disorder or many disorders (Heinrichs, 1993). Although there are a number of classification schemes for schizophrenia, four subvarieties are usually mentioned, and each of them could conceivably have a different cause.

Disorganized Schizophrenia. Like all the schizophrenias, **disorganized schizophrenia** includes symptoms of severely disordered thinking. Language may be particularly incoherent, and there is unusual emotional expression. Individuals may appear extremely silly, bursting into giggles and laughter,

disorganized schizophrenia disorder involving severely disordered thinking, incoherent language, and unusual emotional expression

or they may appear depressed. Other common symptoms include grimaces, hypochondria, and peculiar mannerisms.

> Robert B., a 23-year-old man whose parents persuaded him to enter a psychiatric hospital, is a case in point. Robert was described as follows at the time of his hospital admission:
>
> His voice tone was expressionless, without feeling, and he grimaced as he spoke. He answered questions in a peculiar and illogical way. He said that concentrating on the questions was like "looking into a bright sun." When asked, "How have you been feeling?" he answered, "I'm as sure as you can help me as I have ice cubes in my ears." When asked to telephone his family, he refused because "insects come out of the little holes." . . . He described himself as a "urine reservoir," and received "messages" directing his diet and his personal hygiene from the ward television set. He believed that soap commercials, for example, were warning him against using excessive amounts of colored soap. (Spitzer, 1983)

The disordered thinking, incoherent speech, fragmented delusions, grimaces, and concern with bodily processes are all common characteristics of disorganized schizophrenia.

Catatonic Schizophrenia. A type of schizophrenia that is not as common now as it was a few decades ago is **catatonic schizophrenia**. It may be less common now because of the widespread use of psychoactive drugs, which mask the symptoms of this disorder particularly well. In this type of schizophrenia, the individual may show rigid postures or wild excitement, or may alternate between these two states. Sometimes these individuals' postures are characterized by *waxy flexibility*, in which they hold a particular posture for long periods of time and can be passively molded into a new posture, which they will then continue to hold. In addition, they often exhibit inappropriate negativism. When asked to open their mouths, they may clench their jaws, for example.

Paranoid Schizophrenia. **Paranoid schizophrenia** is dominated by delusions of persecution. The symptoms may also include argumentativeness, violence, and confusion about gender identity or extreme fear of being thought a homosexual. The age of onset of the paranoid type of schizophrenia tends to be somewhat later than onset of the other types, and features are more stable over time. Some individuals with the paranoid type of schizophrenia manage to function reasonably well if they do not act on their delusions.

Undifferentiated Schizophrenia. This final category is essentially a leftover category of schizophrenia. In **undifferentiated schizophrenia** there are clear indications of disordered thinking that are characteristic of schizophrenia, but additional criteria for the other types are not present.

The Search for Causes of Schizophrenia

Schizophrenia is one of the most heavily researched psychological disorders. Several factors have been proposed as causes of schizophrenia, from biochemical imbalances in the brain to faulty family relationships and the socioeconomic environment. Although a great deal of interesting research has been carried out, to date no single factor has been isolated as the cause of schizophrenia. In this section we examine some of the current research into schizophrenia.

catatonic schizophrenia disorder involving unusual motor behavior, such as rigidity, occasionally alternating with wild excitement

paranoid schizophrenia disorder dominated by delusions of persecution

undifferentiated schizophrenia disorder characterized by disordered thinking, but without other criteria for a specific subtype of schizophrenia

Genetic Relationships.   A popular line of research in recent years has been the search for a genetic link in schizophrenia. Several approaches to the study of genetic relationships have been used. Overall, results of this research seem to support the existence of a genetic basis for the disorder. For example, identical twins are more likely to share diagnoses of schizophrenia than fraternal twins, whether the twins are reared apart or together. The greater the severity of schizophrenia, the more pronounced this relationship is. Furthermore, children whose parents both have schizophrenia are three times more likely to develop the disorder than are children with only one parent with schizophrenia, whether the children are reared with their parents or not. Children who are reared by an adoptive parent with schizophrenia but whose biological parents are normal do not have a higher rate of schizophrenia (Kestenbaum, 1981). The most convincing evidence for a genetic relationship comes from research showing a characteristic defect on chromosome 5 among family members who have some types of schizophrenia (Sherrington et al., 1988).

The Dopamine Hypothesis.   When Kraepelin investigated the disorder he called dementia praecox, he felt that it was caused by biochemical imbalances that originated in the sex glands in adolescence and adversely affected the brain. Another biochemical focus of interest and research in schizophrenia is dopamine, a specific neurotransmitter in the brain. The **dopamine hypothesis** holds that schizophrenia is associated with elevated levels of dopamine in the brain.

dopamine hypothesis view that schizophrenia is associated with elevated levels of the neurotransmitter dopamine

Evidence for the dopamine hypothesis comes from studies of the effects of increasing or decreasing levels of brain dopamine, as shown in Figure 16–7. First, drugs that decrease the amount of dopamine in the brain alleviate

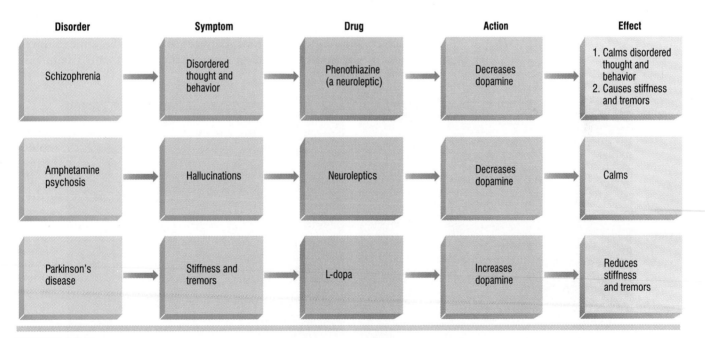

FIGURE 16–7
Evidence for the dopamine hypothesis comes from studying the effects of increasing or decreasing the levels of dopamine in the brain. Phenothiazine (or neuroleptic) drug therapy for schizophrenia decreases the amount of dopamine and relieves symptoms of the disorder. Amphetamine psychosis, which has symptoms similar to schizophrenia, is also relieved by neuroleptic drugs. People with Parkinson's disease often suffer from stiffness and tremors that are relieved by drugs that increase brain dopamine. Schizophrenic patients who have taken neuroleptics for a long period of time (and thus have lower levels of dopamine) also frequently develop stiffness and tremors. (From Seligman & Rosenhan, 1983.)

some of the symptoms of schizophrenia (Heinrichs, 1993). Second, amphetamine psychosis, a disorder resulting from taking large doses of amphetamines (speed), has symptoms very similar to schizophrenia, including hallucinations; amphetamine psychosis is also relieved by drugs that reduce the amount of brain dopamine. And finally, people with schizophrenia who have taken phenothiazines for a long period of time sometimes develop stiffness and tremors similar to those found in Parkinson's disease. Sufferers of Parkinson's disease are often treated with a drug, L-dopa, that increases the amount of brain dopamine, thereby reducing stiffness and tremors. The action of drugs on schizophrenia and Parkinson's disease, therefore, is opposite and parallel. Elevated levels of dopamine seem to result in symptoms of schizophrenia, and the disorder is alleviated when dopamine is reduced through drug therapy.

Brain Structure and Function.   Recent advances in the measurement of brain structure and function have set the stage for comparing normal individuals with those suffering from schizophrenia. One brain-imaging technique, the CAT scan, uses many low-energy X rays of the living brain taken at a number of different points and integrated into pictures by a computer. Studies using this technique show that many individuals with schizophrenia have enlarged brain ventricles, compared to normal persons (Raz & Raz, 1990; Rossi et al., 1988; Shelton et al., 1988). Some researchers believe a link exists between the enlarged ventricles and the lower frequency of alpha waves observed among individuals with schizophrenia (Karson, Coppola, & Daniel, 1988). Studies using PET scans (described in Chapter 2) indicate that people with schizophrenia have a decreased level of frontal lobe metabolic activity, as shown in Figure 16–8 (Farkas et al., 1984; Wolkin et al., 1988). You will recall from Chapter 2 that the frontal lobes are involved in human abilities to make judgments and to map out plans for solving problems.

Research supports an association between frontal lobe abnormalities and changes in personality, including unrestrained and tactless behavior,

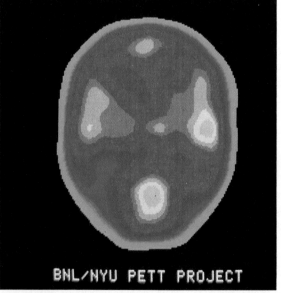

FIGURE 16–8
The dark colors in the PET scan of the individual with schizophrenia (*left*) indicate less use of sugar, and thus lower levels of brain activity, than the bright colors in the normal control individual's PET scan (*right*).

mood changes, blunted emotions, and a deterioration of memory and intellectual abilities (Stuss & Benson, 1984). Individuals with schizophrenia also show impairment in sensory integration, coordination, and the ability to perform sequential motor acts (Heinrichs & Buchanan, 1988).

Other comparisons of normal individuals and those with schizophrenia reveal potential differences in brain functioning as well. For example, people with schizophrenia who were not taking medication had more blood flow in the left hemisphere when they were not solving problems than normal individuals (Gur et al., 1985). This finding suggests that brain asymmetries might somehow be implicated, either as a cause or a result, in schizophrenia. An additional clue that supports this hypothesis is an incidence of left-handedness that is three times higher among people with schizophrenia than among the general population (Manoach, Maher, & Manschreck, 1988).

Environmental Stress.   Approaches to schizophrenia have not been exclusively biomedical. Even studies of identical twins show that more than half these pairs do not share diagnoses of schizophrenia. Because they do share all genetic material, there must be environmental factors that also contribute to the disorder, either by protecting constitutionally vulnerable individuals or by precipitating symptoms of the disorder (Kestenbaum, 1981). One way of conceptualizing the relationship between the environment and schizophrenia is through the concept of stress. A *stress hypothesis* holds that individuals are genetically vulnerable to the disorder. When environmental stressors are severe enough, the individual may experience physiological and biochemical changes and show symptoms of the disorder. The stress hypothesis therefore links several pieces of research on schizophrenia.

Faulty patterns of family interaction are likely candidates for stress that could contribute to the development of schizophrenia. In some families, for example, parents present their children with mutually contradictory messages, known as **double binds**. In these families, children cannot fulfill their parents' wishes and cannot escape the situation. A child may be told, for example, to study alone in his or her room and then be punished for not being sociable. (*Catch-22*, the term coined by Joseph Heller in his novel of the same name, is synonymous with the double bind.)

Onset of schizophrenia appears to be related to other family variables as well. Family members of people with schizophrenia frequently hold attitudes that are highly critical and may become emotionally overinvolved or overprotective. Individuals who have had schizophrenia and whose relatives fit these patterns are three or four times more likely to have relapses than other patients (Miklowitz et al., 1986). In addition to problems within the family, the stress of living in impoverished circumstances may contribute to the cause of schizophrenia. In one study of this relationship (Hollingshead & Redlich, 1958), a detailed psychiatric census of all patients in treatment was taken in one community—New Haven, Connecticut—over a 6-month period. Each patient was carefully classified as belonging to one of five social class positions on the basis of area of residence, education, and occupation. Among the patients with schizophrenia, there was a striking association between the disorder and social class position. The rate of schizophrenia in the lowest social class was almost triple the rate for the social class just above it.

Researchers in the New Haven study wanted to make sure that individuals with schizophrenia were not overrepresented in the lower social class because they had drifted downward after they had developed the disorder. To check this possibility, they researched the social class background of each individual before the development of the disorder. They found no evidence of a significant drift into the lower social classes with the onset of

double bind message or expectation with mutually contradictory elements

schizophrenia. Data from the New Haven study strongly suggest a social class factor in the development of schizophrenia.

Symptoms of most of the psychological disorders we have discussed up to this point can occur at any time in the life cycle, although typically the symptoms do not become apparent until sometime in adulthood. For the next class of disorders, however, the symptoms are linked to particular ages (as in the developmental disorders), or begin in childhood or adolescence and continue throughout life (as in the personality disorders).

DEVELOPMENTAL AND PERSONALITY DISORDERS

Developmental and personality disorders differ from the syndromes that we have described so far in two major respects. First, these disorders, especially the personality disorders, tend not to be as obvious or disruptive as disorders such as major depression or schizophrenia. Second, developmental and personality disorders involve enduring traits. Recall that in Chapter 10 we defined *traits* as relatively enduring patterns of behavior that occur in a wide variety of situations, or distinctive qualities or characteristics of particular people. We noted that trait theories differ from situational theories in viewing behavior as a function of internal characteristics of the person rather than as a result of particular situational circumstances. The classification of developmental and personality disorders relies on the notion of traits as both enduring and maladaptive, resulting in social and occupational impairment to varying degrees. Because most of the developmental and personality disorders involve enduring traits, they generally manifest themselves by childhood or adolescence and continue throughout adult life.

Developmental Disorders

developmental disorders class of disorders containing a wide variety of problems that first become evident in infancy, childhood, or adolescence

Developmental disorders encompass a wide variety of psychological problems that first become evident in infancy, childhood, or adolescence. The essential feature of this group of disorders as a whole involves disturbance in the acquisition of cognitive, language, motor, or social skills. An understanding of normal developmental patterns (discussed in chapters 12 and 13) is essential for evaluating the developmental disorders. For example, in order to classify someone as having mental retardation, defined as general intellectual functioning significantly below average, we must have an appreciation for average intellectual development. In Chapter 11 we discussed the definition and assessment of mental retardation.

Many symptoms or behavioral oddities in childhood may be isolated problems requiring little special attention, or they may be part of a larger syndrome. To some degree, childhood behavioral oddities may even be part of all normal development and may disappear without any treatment (Kazdin, 1989). Some of these symptoms are listed and defined in Table 16–1.

autistic disorder serious developmental disorder characterized by gross impairment in social interaction and communication

Autistic Disorder. Developmental disorders may, however, be more serious. For example, **autistic disorder** is a serious developmental disorder that begins in infancy or childhood. Autistic disorder includes marked impairment in social interaction, for example showing no imitation or no need for comforting in times of distress; impairment in verbal and nonverbal communication, for example repetitive and stereotyped speech or stiffening when being held; and abnormally restricted activities and interests, such as unreasonable insistence on following detailed routines (American Psychiatric Association, 1987).

TABLE 16-1
Special Symptoms Associated with Childhood (Normal at Some Ages;
Symptoms of Psychological Problems at Other Ages)

Enuresis	Wetting clothing during the day past age 3, or nocturnal wetting past age 5. Prevalence in the United States past the age of 11 about 6%. In most cases the symptoms will eventually go away without treatment.
Encopresis	Fecal soiling past age 3. Prevalence about 1–1.5%, with a 5:1 male:female ratio. In a supportive environment, no or minimal treatment is necessary in most cases.
Tics	Recurrent involuntary spasms of particular skeletal muscle groups. Prevalence about 5% in childhood, 1% at age 12. Most tics disappear without treatment. *Tourette's syndrome* is a more severe form of tic disorder, which may involve involuntary uttering of obscenities.
Stuttering	Disturbance in the flow of speech, with repetition of speech sounds and avoidance rituals to keep from using certain speech patterns. Prevalence in preschool about 4%, in school about 2%.
Thumb sucking	Prevalence in preschool about 60–85%, reduced to 20% by age 6. Usually disappears on its own; there are very few teenage thumbsuckers.
Nail biting	Usually begins by age 5, but rarely defined as a symptom unless it interferes with activities or is combined with other symptoms. Peak prevalence occurs between ages 12 and 14, but even about 24% of adults bite their fingernails. This behavior seems primarily associated with anxiety.

Source: Adapted from M. MacKay, 1981.

Academic Skills Disorders.   Another category of developmental disorders is **academic skills disorders**; these involve impairment in specific skills that are appropriate for a child of a given age. The impairment is not due to mental retardation, inadequate education, or sensory deficits such as visual or auditory impairment. This grouping includes *developmental arithmetic disorder, developmental writing disorder,* and *developmental reading disorder* (sometimes referred to as *dyslexia*). The most common of the skills disorders is dyslexia, which affects between 2 and 8% of all schoolchildren (American Psychiatric Association, 1987). Dyslexia is described more fully in Chapter 3.

academic skills disorders disorders characterized by impairment in specific academic skills, such as reading (dyslexia)

Attention Deficit/Hyperactivity Disorder.   Another developmental disorder that results in academic difficulties is **attention deficit/hyperactivity disorder (ADHD)** characterized by inattention, impulsivity, and hyperactivity. These symptoms generally appear in most situations, such as at school, home, and with friends, but in some instances they may appear in only one of the situations. The symptoms are usually worse when sustained attention is required, for example, during lessons at school. About 3% of children have attention deficit/hyperactivity disorder, and it is six to nine times more common among boys than among girls (American Psychiatric Association, 1987). The disorder generally persists throughout childhood, and in many cases, some signs of it continue in adulthood (Henker & Whalen, 1989).

attention deficit/hyperactivity disorder (ADHD) disorder characterized by inattention, impulsivity, and exaggerated motor behavior

Disorders of Aging.   The developmental disorders we have just described manifest themselves in childhood. Other psychological disorders associated with developmental processes, such as *senile dementia*, do not manifest themselves until late adulthood. Psychological disorders of aging are still poorly understood. Many of these disorders are undoubtedly a part of the physiological changes associated with aging; others are caused or worsened by social changes that accompany aging, such as retirement, loss of a spouse, and other losses in social support systems. As the median age of our population creeps upward, we must come to grips with the psychological problems of an older citizenry.

Personality Disorders

personality disorders disorders characterized by inflexible personal traits that cause noticeable impairment or subjective distress

Personality disorders are diagnosed when personality traits are inflexible and maladaptive, and cause noticeable impairment or subjective distress. People with personality disorders may be able to function reasonably well socially, although they may seem peculiar to people who interact with them. People with personality disorders generally deny that they have any problem, and they rarely come to the attention of a psychologist or psychiatrist unless close friends or relatives urge them to seek help out of concern or irritation. People with personality disorders may show a variety of symptoms: odd or eccentric behavior; emotional, dramatic, or erratic behavior; or anxious and fearful behavior. The personality disorders are listed in Table 16–2, along with the basic beliefs and behaviors that characterize them. Several of the personality disorders are described in greater detail below.

Avoidant Personality Disorder. People with *avoidant personality disorder* view themselves as inadequate or incompetent socially and academically. They are afraid that other people will discover their inadequacies and expose them to ridicule or criticize them for their failures. As a consequence, they tend to shy away from social situations and avoid contact with others as much as possible. People with this disorder might like very much to be close to others, but their fears about the reactions to their perceived failure keep them from seeking closeness. Their belief systems may include the following elements: "I am no good . . . worthless . . . unlovable. If people got close to me, they would discover the 'real me' and would reject me—that would be intolerable" (Beck, Freeman, & associates, 1990, p. 43).

Dependent Personality Disorder. In some ways, the characteristics of the *dependent personality disorder* are similar to those of the avoidant personality disorder. Both view themselves in negative terms; people with dependent personality disorder think of themselves as helpless, weak, and incompetent.

TABLE 16-2
Basic Beliefs and Behaviors Associated with Personality Disorders

Personality Disorder	Basic Beliefs/Attitudes	Behavior
Dependent	I am helpless.	Attachment
Avoidant	I may get hurt.	Avoidance
Passive-aggressive	I could be stepped on.	Resistance
Paranoid	People are potential adversaries.	Wariness
Narcissistic	I am special.	Self-aggrandizement
Histrionic	I need to impress.	Dramatics
Obsessive-compulsive	Errors are bad. I must not err.	Perfectionism
Antisocial	People are there to be taken.	Attack
Schizoid	I need plenty of space.	Isolation

Source: Beck, Freeman, & Associates, 1990, p. 26.

However, whereas the strategy of people with avoidant personality disorder is to avoid others, the strategy of people with dependent personality disorder is to cling to others, seeking a relationship in which the other person is perceived as stronger, and as a figure of support. People with dependent personality disorder often experience anxiety, in the form of fears that others will abandon them or that they will be unable to survive on their own. Their belief systems may include the following elements: "If I am abandoned, I will die. If I am not loved, I will always be unhappy" (Beck, Freeman, & associates, 1990, p. 45).

Obsessive-Compulsive Personality Disorder. People with this disorder share some of the characteristics of people with obsessive-compulsive disorder, which we discussed earlier; however, their symptoms are not as serious, overall, as those seen in obsessive-compulsive disorder. People with *obsessive-compulsive personality disorder* have a strong need to be perfectionists; however, this need is coupled with a view of themselves as inadequate to perform as they think they should. They also view others as falling short of their standards of perfection. Others are often perceived as irresponsible or incompetent. It is hard to live up to the standards set by people with obsessive-compulsive personality disorder. Their belief systems may include: "I need order, systems, and rules in order to survive. If I fail in this, I am a failure as a person" (Beck, Freeman, & associates, 1990, p. 47). Unwelcome thoughts often enter the consciousness of people with obsessive-compulsive personality disorder. These unwelcome thoughts typically involve self-criticism, such as "I am really stupid," or "Why can't I do anything right?" Because it is so hard to achieve the standards set by people with obsessive-compulsive personality disorder, they often experience regret and disappointment about their own or others' behavior.

Schizoid Personality Disorder. One of the main characteristics of people with *schizoid personality disorder* is that they are loners. They view themselves as self-sufficient, and view others with suspicion. Other people may make too many demands on them, or attempt to entangle them in relationships they do not want. Among their beliefs may be the following: "Close relationships with other people are unrewarding and messy. If I get too close to people, they will get their hooks into me" (Beck, Freeman, & associates, 1990, pp. 51–52).

Personality disorders are collectively characterized by difficulty with social adjustment and social functioning of varying degrees of severity. One area that is often affected is occupational functioning. People with schizoid personality disorder, for example, often have difficulty in the workplace, especially when the work includes interpersonal interaction.

Narcissistic Personality Disorder. Feelings of special status are the chief characteristics of *narcissistic personality disorder*. People with this disorder view themselves as special, almost as royalty. They seek recognition of their special status from other people, and become frustrated or manipulative when this acknowledgment is not forthcoming. People with narcissistic personality disorder believe that they are exempt from the rules that other people must live by. Their beliefs may include the following: "I'm superior to others and they should acknowledge this. I'm above the rules" (Beck, Freeman, & associates, 1990, p. 49).

One candidate for narcissistic personality disorder might be David Koresh, the "messiah" of the Branch Davidian cult in Waco, Texas, whom we discussed at the beginning of this chapter. Koresh presented himself to his followers as the new messiah, and required that they live in the cult by his rules. He was the only one allowed television and air conditioning in his room, for example. Another of his rules was that he was the only man allowed sexual access to the women in the cult. Some of Koresh's visions, however, seem to

Gary Gilmore, convicted of the murder of two young men in Utah in 1976, had a background consistent with antisocial personality disorder. He showed early trouble in school, began drinking at an early age, abused a variety of illegal drugs, and experimented early with sex. By age 16, he had been arrested for a serious criminal offense.

go beyond something as mundane as narcissistic personality disorder. For example, he viewed himself as the final angel of the apocalypse, the agent of God who would bring about the end of the world (Kantrowitz et al., 1993). This pattern of thinking appears more characteristic of the schizophrenias.

Antisocial Personality Disorder.   People with *antisocial personality disorder* also break the rules, but their motives are somewhat different from those with narcissistic personality disorder. Whereas people with narcissistic personality disorder view themselves as better than everyone else and above the rules, people with antisocial personality disorder think that "It's a dog-eat-dog world," and they are justified in breaking rules to get what they want. They frequently think that society has mistreated them, and that it is acceptable for them to fight back to get what they want. Among their beliefs are: "I need to be the aggressor or I will be the victim. Get the other guy before he gets you" (Beck, Freeman, & associates, 1990, pp. 48–49).

Antisocial personality disorder is much more common among males than it is among females (American Psychiatric Association, 1987). People with this disorder often spend a large part of their lives in institutions, such as detention centers or prisons, because they run afoul of the law in acting out their beliefs. However, people with this diagnosis are not the only ones whose behavior may get them into trouble with the law. In the beginning of this chapter, we discussed the competing views about odd behavior among psychologists, psychiatrists, and legal experts. How does the legal system view psychological disorders?

THINKING ABOUT
The Law and Psychological Disorders

For individuals who have committed crimes, like Jeffrey Dahmer, professionals in the legal system may wish to determine whether the person was legally insane at the time the crimes were committed ("Judge Orders," 1991). (Note that "insanity" is a legal concept, and may mean something entirely different from "psychological disorder.") Psychologists and psychiatrists often testify in court proceedings, attempting to reconstruct the state of mind of the individual up to and during the time the crime was committed. Although court cases involving insanity pleas often receive much media coverage—as did Dahmer's case—they are actually rare; only about 1 out of 400 homicide cases involves an insanity defense (Rosenhan & Seligman, 1989). When insanity pleas are invoked, an additional complication is that the procedures to judge insanity differ from state to state.

Historically, three tests have been used by the courts to determine if an individual is to be judged legally insane. The first test originated in England in an 1843 court case, and is named for the defendant, accused murderer Daniel M'Naghten. M'Naghten had claimed to hear a voice from God telling him to kill the prime minister. (M'Naghten actually killed another man he mistakenly thought was the prime minister.) After psychiatric testimony was offered, the judges in the case formulated a test for insanity now known as the *M'Naghten Rule*: "It must be clearly proved that, at the time of the committing of the act, the party accused was laboring under such a defect of reason, from disease of the mind, as not to know the nature and quality of the act he was doing; or, if he did know it, that he did not know he was doing what was wrong" (Rosenhan & Seligman, 1989, p. 621). Many states in the United States still use the M'Naghten rule.

The M'Naghten Rule cites "disease of the mind" as a part of the test for insanity, but it goes on to specify that the defendant must be able to judge right from wrong. The second test for insanity, the *Durham Test*, eliminated this right–wrong judgment and focused directly on "mental disease": The Durham Test stated that "an accused is not criminally responsible if his unlawful act was the product of mental disease or mental defect" (Rosenhan & Seligman, 1989, p. 622). Although it remained in effect in several states for 18 years, the Durham Test was ultimately withdrawn for a number of reasons. For one thing, it was not clear from its wording which of the disorders listed in the *Diagnostic and Statistical Manual of Mental Disorders* would qualify as a mental disease or defect. Would something like agoraphobia or dependent personality disorder justify a ruling of insanity? The Durham Test also forced the courts to rely very heavily on the expert testimony of psychologists and psychiatrists in determining sanity, and agreement among them was hard to come by—as indeed it still is.

The last of the tests for insanity, the *American Law Institute (ALI) Rule*, is considered to be more specific than the Durham Test. The ALI Rule has two parts. Part 1 sets the limits for responsibility for one's action—one must be unable to appreciate wrongfulness or unable to conform to the law to be judged legally insane. Part 2, which has been modified in subsequent court cases, attempts to define "mental disease or defect":

1. A person is not responsible for criminal conduct if, at the time of such conduct, as a result of mental disease or defect, he lacks substantial capacity either to appreciate the criminality (wrongfulness) of his conduct or to conform his conduct to the requirements of law.

2. The terms "mental disease or defect" do not include an abnormality manifested only by repeated criminal or otherwise antisocial conduct. A mental disease or defect includes any abnormal condition of the mind which substantially affects mental or emotional processes and substantially impairs behavior controls (Rosenhan & Seligman, 1989, p. 623).

The ALI Rule is the test for insanity used in all federal appeals courts, and in 30 state courts as well.

How would Jeffrey Dahmer's case be decided, using these tests of insanity? His defense attorneys presented a strategy in which they acknowledged guilt at the outset of the trial. Thus, his trial was not concerned with his guilt or innocence—he admitted guilt. Rather, it was a trial to judge whether he was sane or insane. A person judged "guilty but mentally ill" is sentenced to commitment in a mental institution rather than in a prison. As we said earlier, Dahmer's jury concluded that he was legally sane.

Thus, despite modification of the rules for determining sanity in the courts, a good deal of disagreement still exists about the meaning of that concept. "Insanity" is clearly not the same thing that psychologists mean when they talk about psychological disorders. Many psychological problems that people experience are commonplace, and almost no one would argue that having some of these psychological disorders should lead to a label of "insanity." Many psychologists also continue to object to the medical model that is promoted by labels such as "mental disease or defect."

What do you think about these issues? Under what circumstances do you think it would be appropriate for the legal system to treat a person differently because of having a psychological disorder? Does the concept of "guilty but mentally ill" make sense to you? If a person has diminished responsibility because of a psychological disorder, is it possible for him or her to be guilty in the same sense as a person who has no disorder? How does diminished responsibility differ for people who have a psychological disorder, and for those who are mentally retarded?

THINKING AHEAD . . .

It would be comforting to believe that psychological disorders have clear boundaries that distinguish the behavior associated with them from normal behavior. But no such boundary exists. Rather, there is a continuum between the normal and the abnormal. Furthermore, the interpretation of what constitutes a psychological disorder occurs within a cultural context, such that definitions of abnormality vary with time and place.

All of these points are cautions against hasty judgments about psychological disorders. We must be careful to distinguish between behavior that is eccentric or unusual or that brings disapproval, and behavior that genuinely needs professional treatment. Some people—psychologists and nonpsychologists alike—are quick to apply diagnostic labels to unusual behavior. Perhaps, to paraphrase one researcher, if people are able to function well in work, love, and play, they ought not to be diagnosed as having a psychological disorder, no matter how eccentric their life-style (Kirmayer, 1983).

Even though we have still not firmly settled the definitional issues inherent in examining problem behavior, we must attempt to understand as much as we can of the causes of psychological problems. The anguish is very real for people who are very depressed, who cannot control their sexual impulses, or who exhibit the signs of a variety of other psychological disorders. The pace of research into psychological disorders has increased over the last few years, particularly in the search for biological markers for the disorders. Many promising leads have been found in the search for causes, but precise causes have been isolated for only a small number of psychological disorders. It is important to understand that even if biological markers are found for a given disorder, a strict cause-and-effect relationship still has not been demonstrated. Some disorders may hinge on a combination of biological predispositions and environmental triggers; in other cases biological markers may be a result, rather than a cause, of the disorder. Research on biological aspects of psychological problems should not blind us to the tremendous importance of nonbiological factors. Psychologists and psychiatrists have to guard against "losing the mind" in their search for principles of abnormal behavior (Reiser, 1988).

Although many of the traditional definitions of psychological health have relied on the concept of contact with reality, a touch of illusion may not be such a bad thing. When the illusion is in the form of an overly positive, rather than negative, self-image, individuals show an increased ability to care for others, are more happy and contented, and are more creative and productive (Taylor & Brown, 1988). And most people are somewhat "out of touch with reality" in this positive sense. Most of us view ourselves as better than others, view our close friends as better than average, and even rate ourselves as more competent than independent observers rate us.

Our tendency to overrate ourselves is unfortunately all too often coupled with a tendency to discriminate against those whose psychological lives are more troubled than our own. Even when people who have received treatment for psychological problems no longer show any signs of abnormal behavior, they are frequently discriminated against in such important areas of their lives as employment and housing (Melton & Garrison, 1987). Thus, social and legal changes are needed to make the world a richer place for all of us.

Summary

Defining and Diagnosing Psychological Disorders

1. Abnormal behavior is difficult to define adequately, partly because there is no clear dividing line between normal and abnormal behavior. Psychological disorders are diagnosed on the basis of behavior and thoughts, and are defined as involuntary impairment in psychological functioning, including thinking, feeling, and behaving.

2. Contemporary views of psychological disorders include the biomedical models and cognitive and behavioral approaches. Each may help explain the development of a pattern of symptoms.

3. Folk explanations for psychological disorders also have a long history. Chief among the folk explanations is the notion that phases of the moon cause madness (lunacy). Careful analyses of research on madness and the moon provide little evidence to support such a relationship.

4. The APA's *Diagnostic and Statistical Manual of Mental Disorders* (DSM) has undergone periodic revision since first published in 1952; the most recent revision is the fourth edition, known as DSM-IV, published in 1994.

Anxiety and Dissociation Disorders

5. Disorders of anxiety and dissociation often involve irrational fears and anxieties and ailments in which people react to severe traumas by developing one of a number of dissociative reactions. Included are anxiety disorders such as phobias (irrational fears), obsessive-compulsive disorder, somatoform disorders, and dissociative disorders such as multiple personality.

Mood Disorders

6. Mood disorders, the most common psychological disorders, involve major disturbances in mood. There are two major types of affective disorder. Major depression, sometimes called unipolar depression, is a long-lasting mood disturbance in which an individual loses interest in almost all activities. Bipolar disorder involves mood changes from deep depression to elation and hyperactivity.

7. Current research on mood disorders indicates that there is a biochemical component, possibly a sensitivity to neurotransmitters such as acetylcholine.

8. Suicide is a risk associated with depression and some of the other psychological disorders. Research on suicide has exposed some of the myths about this behavior. Despite some people's notions that those who threaten suicide will not actually attempt it, threats may be an attempt to communicate. If the communication fails, they may carry out the attempt. Cheerful moods are also no guarantee that a person will not attempt suicide; when mood improves following a depression, it may signal a decision to attempt suicide. Danger signs of suicide include giving away possessions, talking about specific suicide plans, appearing not to care about the effect of suicide on friends and family, and having previously attempted suicide.

Psychosexual Disorders

9. Psychosexual behavior is interpreted in terms of society's attitudes and values. Some forms of sexual behavior are considered psychological disorders. These include the paraphilias, sexual arousal to objects or activities not normally considered erotic.

Schizophrenic Disorders

10. In schizophrenic disorders, individuals experience major difficulties in reality testing, where perceptions of reality are distorted. Common symptoms include delusions, or false beliefs not based on external reality, and hallucinations, perceptions in the absence of sensory stimulation.

11. The schizophrenias include several closely related disorders of thinking that result in severe behavior disturbances. Subvarieties are disorganized, paranoid, catatonic, and undifferentiated schizophrenia.

12. Research on the causes of schizophrenia suggests that genetic factors as well as brain mechanisms are involved. One promising lead indicates that there is an excess of the neurotransmitter dopamine in the brains of people with schizophrenia. Social factors also appear to play a role in the cause of the disorder.

13. It is surprisingly difficult for professionals to distinguish normal behavior from behavior that they would label as a psychological disorder. Rosenhan's research with pseudopatients—people who went to admissions offices of psychiatric hospitals with one symptom (hearing voices say "empty, hollow, thud")—were all admitted, usually with a diagnosis of schizophrenia. Such a psychiatric label is difficult to shake; Rosenhan's pseudopatients were released with the label "schizophrenia in remission"—i.e., present but without symptoms.

Developmental and Personality Disorders

14. Developmental and personality disorders tend to be less obtrusive than the other clinical syndromes and involve enduring traits that first appear in childhood or adolescence.

15. Developmental disorders are essentially exaggerations of normal development. Some are quite pervasive and serious, such as autistic disorder, whereas others may have minimal impact on one's life, such as developmental reading disorder (dyslexia).

16. People with inflexible and maladaptive personalities may be diagnosed as having one of the personality disorders. These people are usually able to function occupationally, but they often appear peculiar to others.

17. Personality disorders include avoidant personality disorder, in which individuals view themselves as inadequate or incompetent and avoid others for fear of rejection; dependent personality disorder, in which people view themselves as incompetent to live independently, and cling emotionally to others; and narcissistic personality disorder, in which people view themselves as special and above the rules that others must live by.

18. Sometimes the legal system must try to determine whether a person is legally insane. Several insanity tests have been used. The M'Naghten Rule requires that when a person committed a crime, he or she must have had a "disease of the mind" that prevented knowing that the crime was wrong, or being unable to distinguish between right and wrong. A newer test, the American Law Institute Rule, requires that a person have a "mental disease or defect" that prevents him or her from appreciating the wrongfulness of the act or from conforming to the law. In practice, all of these tests for legal insanity have been difficult to apply.

Key Terms

psychological disorder (637)
maladaptive behavior (638)
biomedical model (638)
cognitive model (639)
psychoanalytic model (639)
behavioral model (639)
sociological model (639)
syndrome (642)
DSM-IV (642)
intern's syndrome (643)
anxiety disorders (643)
phobias (643)
specific phobia (644)
agoraphobia (644)
social phobia (644)

panic disorder (644)
post-traumatic stress disorder (645)
obsessive-compulsive disorder (646)
somatoform disorders (647)
conversion disorder (647)
hypochondriasis (648)
dissociative disorders (648)
dissociative amnesia (649)
multiple personality (649)
bipolar disorder (650)
unipolar depression (650)

seasonal affective disorder (SAD) (652)
paraphilia (658)
fetishism (658)
zoophilia (658)
sadism (658)
masochism (659)
exhibitionism (659)
pedophilia (659)
delusions (660)
hallucinations (660)
schizophrenias (660)
delusions of persecution (663)
delusions of reference (663)
disorganized schizophrenia (663)

catatonic schizophrenia (664)
paranoid schizophrenia (664)
undifferentiated schizophrenia (664)
dopamine hypothesis (665)
double bind (667)
developmental disorders (668)
autistic disorder (668)
academic skills disorders (669)
attention deficit/hyperactivity disorder (669)
personality disorders (670)

Suggested Reading

American Psychiatric Association. (1994). *Diagnostic and statistical manual of mental disorders* (4th ed. rev.). Washington, DC: Author. A volume, also known as DSM-IV, providing a comprehensive set of criteria for use in diagnosing psychological disorders.

Kety, S. S. (1974). From rationalization to reason. *American Journal of Psychiatry, 131,* 957–963. A short paper in which Kety argues for the medical model for viewing abnormal behavior. The focus of the paper is schizophrenia.

Oltmanns, T. F., Neale, J. M., & Davison, G. C. (1986). *Case studies in abnormal psychology* (2nd ed.). New York: Wiley. A series of 20 detailed case studies of psychological disorders, including biographical information, social history, and a discussion of the treatment of the disorder.

Rosenhan, D. L. (1973). On being sane in insane places. *Science, 179,* 250–258. The fascinating description of Rosenhan's research project in which pseudopatients went to admissions departments of psychiatric hospitals reporting a single symptom. All were admitted, most with a diagnosis of schizophrenia.

Szasz, T. (1961). *The myth of mental illness.* New York: Harper & Row. A book in which Szasz takes a point of view directly opposed to that of Kety. He argues that mental illness is a myth, and that behavior we label abnormal is really explainable by circumstances. Abnormal behavior is not, therefore, a medical construct.

CHAPTER 17
Treatment of Psychological Disorders

The culture of the Wakuria tribe of the western and northeastern border lands of the Serengeti Plain in Africa has remained largely unchanged over the last 2 centuries. Isolated by geographical remoteness, and committed to preserving their heritage, the Wakuria people fall outside the influence of the industrialized world. Garment making, agriculture, and every other aspect of daily existence, including medical treatment, continue along a traditional course. Even disturbances in behavior are treated according to routine procedures set forth by ancestors.

The case of Kilunda Sala illustrates the approach that the Wakuria people take in treating psychological disorders. Kilunda is a 23-year-old male who had the misfortune to be born with a deformed left foot. Although the affliction is not disabling, it does limit Kilunda's mobility. The impact of this physical impairment might be insignificant in other societies, but in the Wakuria community it has profound consequences. Unlike his peers, Kilunda is unable to participate in hunts, dances, and other activities essential to defining the male role in the tribe. The continuing struggle to resolve his socially prescribed reduced role among fellow tribesmen has left Kilunda depressed and stripped of the will to live. Most of Kilunda's day is spent alone, lying on the grass floor of his shelter. He refuses food, and his general health has deteriorated to a point where he might die.

An elder tribesman responsible for the health of tribal members is consulted; he makes a gruel from a variety of herbs, roots, and berries and forces Kilunda to eat it. For several weeks, Kilunda's condition fails to change, but then he noticeably begins to improve. His appetite is better, his speech is stronger, and he is more hopeful. Eventually, with the support of the tribal community, Kilunda's depression is lifted and he assumes a constructive role as a tool and implement maker. The primitive medication consisting of a concoction of ingredients known only to the tribal "therapist" has, perhaps, saved Kilunda's life.

◀ A variety of different treatment approaches are available to help those who suffer from one or more psychological disorders.

This case history involving human suffering and depression is instructive in several ways. For one thing, it shows that emotional disturbances and negative moods are not exclusive to so-called modern societies. Grappling with the stresses that are inherent to the human condition is a worldwide phenomenon, and the devastation that comes with failure, disappointment, the end of close relationships, and other life crises is uniform across all peoples. When we think of disordered behavior, we tend to think of it in the context of contemporary Western civilization. But what about other, less visible populations? Do you believe that psychotic reactions such as schizophrenia and bipolar mood disorders, discussed in the previous chapter, occur among the nomadic herdsmen in the highlands of Tibet? Do Tanzanians exhibit panic disorder? Behavioral and emotional disturbances do occur among these people, of course, but their treatment, or the lack of it, may not receive the attention that is ordinarily given by some cultures.

Another aspect of Kilunda Sala's treatment that should be mentioned is the use of plants and other materials in treating what is actually a mental illness. Although this may seem unscientific and voodoo-like, we must consider that the benefits may derive from legitimate, but at present undefined, biochemical or physiological properties of the ingredients contained in the herbs, roots, and berries. That scientists have not identified the relevant chemical agents that produce change does not mean that such chemicals do not exist in these treatments. Consider the now famous case of the *rauwolfia plant*, historically used by physicians in India to treat severe psychological disorders. Extractions from the root of the plant were used to control the mental excitement of certain types of psychotic disturbances long before modern chemotherapy began. Later, Swiss researchers isolated and synthesized the plant's active ingredient, *reserpine*. Although it is not used much today because of its negative side effects, reserpine was used medicinally for many years by psychiatrists throughout the world before better drugs became available.

Unhappily, Kilunda's depression is common around the world, and nowhere is it more conspicuous than on a college campus. The transition to college life is a stormy period for many young people. At the age of 18, you are required to make major social adjustments while being thrust into a very competitive academic atmosphere. Often for the first time, you must wash your own clothes, prepare your own meals, and keep track of a monthly budget. All this creates stress that occasionally becomes intense. In addition, you might have an identity problem. At home everyone knew you, and you had the security of established, close-knit friendships. But at college, particularly at a large school, events may seem regimented and depersonalized. You may feel like an unattached form who moves from place to place to meet arbitrary demands.

Combine these aggravations with the emotional high tides produced by a wilted romance, throw in a dash of grade-related anxiety, and it comes as no surprise that college students often suffer severe psychological unrest. But where do most students go for help? Unfortunately, many do not go anywhere. Almost half the population of troubled students choose not to seek treatment; even when they do seek treatment, they often terminate it prematurely (Martin, McNair, & Hight, 1988). These findings are especially alarming, because over two thirds of all students are estimated to experience depression at some point during their college tenure (Beck & Young, 1978).

In an effort to reach students in need of psychological treatment, most colleges and universities today provide personal counseling centers on campus. Over the years these centers have moved away from focusing on career

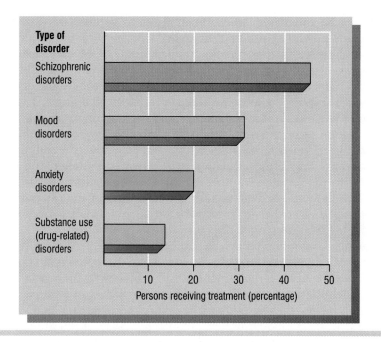

Type of disorder

- Schizophrenic disorders
- Mood disorders
- Anxiety disorders
- Substance use (drug-related) disorders

Persons receiving treatment (percentage)

FIGURE 17–1
Regardless of the severity of the disorder, fewer than half those in need of treatment ever obtain it. (From Shapiro et al., 1984.)

counseling and have assumed an actual therapy role (Clary & Fristad, 1987). Many of the services offered on campus are equal in sophistication to the best treatment techniques used in public or private hospital settings. In fact, it is becoming increasingly common to find clinical and counseling psychologists employed in college personal counseling centers. These counseling centers may also have a variety of crisis-intervention tapes that structure sessions over a period of weeks, or even months. Depression, test anxiety, and even some types of sexual disturbances can sometimes be treated effectively by these audiovisual packages.

So, treatment is attainable, and in most instances is free to students. Why, then, do so few students avail themselves of campus mental health services? One likely explanation is that many students are simply unaware that their college offers such a service. Several years ago, Benjamin and Romano (1980) completed a comprehensive study of counseling centers across the United States, and discovered that more than 85% of students nationwide were not even aware that their colleges offered counseling services. You should make a point of familiarizing yourself with the counseling center at your school. If you do not need the service, a friend might.

Of course, college students are not the only people who need psychological treatment and do not get it. As Figure 17–1 shows, even when the level of personality disturbance is extreme, more than half of all people who need treatment fail to receive it. With milder disorders, the statistics are much worse. Accordingly, we have decided to begin our coverage of the treatment of psychological disorders with a section on how the general population may successfully enter therapy.

SEEKING THERAPY

When people move from one city to another, one of the first items on their agenda is an inquiry about medical services. Few of us have any problem asking questions such as "Who is your doctor?" and "Is she competent?" Health care is critical, and it is important for us to identify these resources so that in times of emergency we can make the correct decisions.

Unhappily, this desire to establish a health support network does not often include mental health professionals. This fact is especially disquieting in light of data released by the National Institute of Mental Health. In the most comprehensive study of mental health problems in the United States ever completed, the NIMH investigators concluded that about one third of all Americans suffer from some form of acute psychological disorder at some point in their lives (Regier et al., 1988). Although alcohol and drug abuse continue to be the most common problem, 15% of the adult population have experienced anxiety disorders, and 8% have suffered major bouts of depression. And these statistics are even higher when the sample is restricted to persons below the age of 45. These alarming—and unexpected—numbers are of even greater concern when one realizes that so few people in need of treatment ever seek professional help. Why? What prevents people from entering therapy?

A major reason people are reluctant to seek treatment probably is the social stigma still associated with psychological disorders. Many people suspect that friends and even family members will view them as weak and permanently debilitated if they admit they are having emotional problems. So rather than betray their situation by seeking therapy, they choose to try to solve their problems by themselves. Ironically, riding it out alone may leave one with a false sense of frailty that ultimately contributes to the stigma that prevented the person from seeking help in the first place.

Another factor that may discourage people from seeking therapy is bewilderment. Because most people are unfamiliar with the entire psychotherapy process, they have no idea about what to do, whom to contact, how much it will cost, and so forth. Consequently, many individuals with psychological problems seek help from clergy and other paraprofessionals. Actually, the available research on the comparative effectiveness of such helpers, relative to professionals, indicates that paraprofessionals function remarkably well as therapists (Hattie, Sharpley, & Rogers, 1984). But this is true primarily in a counseling environment, and not a clinical environment. The former is concerned with relatively mild disturbances (personal adjustment problems, family crises, situational stress); the latter often deals with severe cases of pathology (total thought disorganization, psychotic episodes).

Those persons who receive treatment for psychological disturbance in a conventional therapeutic environment may find some surprises. For one thing, rather than dealing with just a single individual, treatment involves a team of mental health professionals, each with a specialized skill. A psychiatric social worker may explore features within the family unit that may have contributed to the disorder. A clinical psychologist and a psychiatrist may be brought in to provide needed therapy and medication. So modern treatment approaches use a variety of sophisticated techniques to help clients. In order to understand just how far we have come in this regard, it is necessary to gain some historical perspective on the treatment of psychological problems.

HISTORICAL ATTEMPTS AT TREATMENT

In the sections that follow we discuss the development of mental health treatment since early times. As we note, the history of treatment has been checkered; at times compassion and sympathy prevailed, but at other points mentally disturbed persons were brutalized. Ultimately, decency and good sense triumphed, and clients were offered real hope for improvement.

Our Primitive Ancestors

Even before written records, crude attempts at dealing with mental abnormalities were made. Evidence to this effect exists in the form of numerous Stone Age skulls that have been retrieved from anthropological digging sites. As shown in Figure 17–2, human skulls with sizable sections of bone chipped away have been discovered among the skeletal remains of people who lived over 500,000 years ago. Inasmuch as such holes appear to have been carefully formed and are of uniform shape, it would seem that they were cut with the intention of helping, rather than hurting, the person. Perhaps, as some argue, these deftly executed skull surgeries were conducted with the simple objective of removing bone particles resulting from a head injury (Leahey, 1986). But many other scientists now suggest that the holes are the result of a delicate operation known as *trephining*, where evil spirits that inhabited the brain were permitted to flee. Interestingly, such an approach must have presumed the brain to be the major control center for behavior—not bad, for psychologists and physicians who practiced over half a million years ago.

Hippocrates and Galen

Hippocrates, born in ancient Greece in the fifth century B.C., about 30 years before Plato, was probably the first physician to make an attempt to separate medicine as a science from magic and religion (Ehrenwald, 1976). In an effort to focus attention on bodily processes and away from supernatural interpretations of physical and psychological maladies, followers of the teachings of Hippocrates claimed that psychological illnesses arose when basic body humors (black bile, yellow bile, blood, and phlegm) were in conflict or out of balance. The recommended treatments were designed to restore the proper balances and thereby alleviate the source of the affliction. For example, because persons who were excessively cheerful and jubilant were thought to have too much blood, the treatment of choice for them was bloodletting. Not surprisingly, such techniques did in fact produce the intended result; that is, draining blood from someone did render the person less cheerful. Of course, over the long haul such procedures proved to be largely ineffective, and they were dropped from the physician's list of possible treatments. But other techniques, such as warm baths and music therapy, have continued. Ultimately, Hippocrates and his students provided an immense service to psychological treatment by suggesting that psychological disorders could be controlled without magical intervention.

Hippocrates was followed 700 years later by Galen (A.D. 130–200), a Greek physician who practiced in Rome. (See Chapter 1.) It was Galen who gave us the following medical jewel:

> All who drink this remedy recover in a short time, except those whom it does not help, who all die and have no relief from any other medicine. Therefore it is obvious that it fails only in incurable cases. (Quoted by Eysenck, 1960)

Although Galen's medical education might have benefited from a course in elementary logic, we should not underestimate his impact on psychological therapies. Galen, cited as an authority for centuries, believed that patients do not just get better on their own but must take medicine for noticeable improvement to be realized. Taken together, the views of Hippocrates and Galen lead to the following conclusion: There must be therapeutic intervention whereby a person, an event, or a drug is introduced to produce the needed behavioral changes. Historically speaking, then, it is safe to say that much of contemporary psychological therapy is rooted in the Greek healing tradition.

FIGURE 17–2
(*Top*) In the primitive procedure of trephining, a section of the skull was carefully cut away. It is believed that the opening was made to permit evil spirits to escape. (*Bottom*) Front view of trephined skull from Peru showing partial healing, which indicates that the patient survived the procedure.

The Middle Ages

After the decline of Greek civilization, Roman medical authorities continued to treat individuals with kindness and understanding. But once the Roman Empire fell, much of what had been achieved through medical science was reversed by European theologians. For many centuries following Roman times, people who were suffering from various sorts of psychological disturbances were persecuted as witches. Why women were singled out as victims has never really been determined, but the state of hostility was so bizarre that even when a man was afflicted with psychological disturbance, some woman in his household was blamed for his condition. The widespread belief that women were more sensitive and impressionable than men and thus more vulnerable to possession by fallen angels, devils, and demonic spirits may have prejudiced the church against them to some degree. More important was the publication of the *Malleus Maleficarum* (known as the "Witches' Hammer") in 1484. This book by two Dominican monks, Heinrich Kramer and James Sprenger, served as an inquisition manual. The result was that the governments of Europe, submissive to the authority of the Catholic church, officially sanctioned the burning of women at the stake. This gruesome tragedy occurred thousands of times over the next few hundred years.

A plea for help finally came from Johann Weyer in 1563. Convinced that these women were innocent, Weyer eagerly attempted to establish that their minds had become deranged due to faulty metabolism and disease. Eventually, the idea that emotionally disturbed people were sick and not possessed by demonic forces did gain advocates. However, it took more than 200 years for mental hospitals to replace prisons as suitable quarters for people with severe psychological disorders.

1792—A Turning Point

When people began to view mental illness as a medical issue, there remained the problem of where to place the sick. Where were these people to be kept, and how were they to be prevented from hurting themselves or others? Tragically, the first solution adopted was to place them in dungeons where they were often restrained by shackles, chains, wooden cribs, or other devices that were equally oppressive and punitive (see Figure 17–3).

This reproduction from *The Witches' Hammer* illustrates one of the recommended methods for dealing with mentally disturbed persons believed to be possessed by demons—burning.

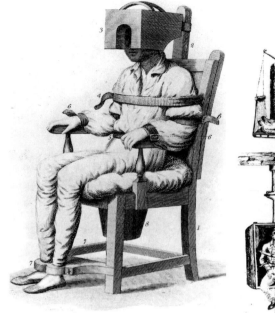

FIGURE 17–3
Early methods for treating psychological disturbance: (*A*) a crib for violent patients; (*B*) a "tranquilizing chair" used to restrain individuals showing symptoms of mania; (*C*) a circulating swing used to restore "balance" in those proclaimed to be "off balance."

A

B

C

The objective was to isolate these troubled people from society. So although the mentally disturbed were no longer being whipped or burned at the stake, neither were they receiving any treatments that might make them better. It was a French physician, Philippe Pinel, who finally launched a genuine mental health program.

In 1792 Pinel, caught up in the energetic spirit of the French Revolution, asked for and received permission to try an experiment at an asylum in Paris. Profoundly influenced by a former patient named Jean-Baptiste Pussin, Pinel directed a program of humanism based on tenderness, compassion, and patient respect. Although evidence indicates that it was Pussin, and not Pinel, who was actually responsible for removing the chains from patients (Sarason & Sarason, 1989), it was Pinel's leadership that truly fueled the reform. Patients were given better diets and were moved from darkness to rooms with open windows. The results were astonishing. The dramatic improvements that were witnessed led to calls for radical changes. A policy of humane treatment for "lunatics" was soon enforced throughout western Europe.

In the United States, the reforms that began with Pinel were continued by Benjamin Rush, known as the father of American psychiatry, and a Massachusetts schoolteacher, Dorothea Dix. In the 1800s, Dix traveled throughout America urging lawmakers to set aside funds to improve conditions for the psychologically disturbed. She argued against mere medical treatment and in favor of good exercise, good diet, and meaningful employment. Largely due to her tireless efforts, many new hospitals were established where patients were treated with dignity and respect.

Dorothea Dix (1802–1887), shown here, was an early reformer in the mental health movement begun in the 1800s in the United States.

PRESENT-DAY TREATMENT

Psychological services have come a long way since early humans first attempted to heal the mind by opening the skull to allow evil spirits to escape. Increased hygiene, good nutrition, and competent training programs for clinical psychology are but a few of the advances made over the course of more than a century of the modernization of therapy. Today this process of change and reevaluation continues. Among the most prominent issues in the world of contemporary psychological treatment are those relating to *prevention* and *deinstitutionalization*.

Prevention

Until the mid-1960s, many mental health professionals subscribed to the adage "If it ain't broke, don't fix it." They believed they should administer psychological services only when the level of functioning was so reduced as to produce serious debilitation (Carson, Butcher, & Coleman, 1992). According to this attitude, premature intervention might interrupt the normal course of events that would lead the person to seek the most suitable form of therapy. However, such a perspective on mental health obscured the potential risks of waiting too long before attempting treatment. Without treatment, the amount of distress may increase to dangerously high levels and accelerate the breakdown of psychological defense systems. Consequently, the illness can worsen to a point where the effectiveness of the treatment is compromised or a secondary behavioral abnormality emerges. Such concerns have evoked a chorus of professional requests for more training programs on prevention, both in the United States and Canada.

Such efforts, however noble, do have some liabilities. The most conspicuous difficulty rests with covering the enormous costs inherent in preventive care. It takes substantial time and money to manage the emotional surveillance being recommended. And with recent trends toward reducing federal spending, it is going to be even more difficult to secure needed funds from government agencies. Further, even if monetary resources were available, it is doubtful whether the specific causal factors of psychological disorders are understood well enough to permit the use of specific preventive techniques. In the 1990s it has become clear that psychological disorders are multiply determined, which means that it is rare to be able to point to just one cause, and that in many cases we may not be able to identify all the factors involved in the expression of the problem. Genetic predispositions, life events, and numerous other variables may contribute to disturbed behavior patterns. Because of the complexity of the issue, prevention is necessarily made more difficult. Still, we must continue our struggle to do what we can, and preempt psychological problems when possible.

Deinstitutionalization

An even more controversial topic than prevention is the decreasing number of patients in public hospitals. As shown in Figure 17–4, by 1985, the number of patients in state and locally supported hospitals had decreased by over 300,000 since the mid-1950s. Fewer public hospital beds are now occupied by mental patients than at any point since the turn of the century. But such statistics may be deceptive, as others have noted (Bassuk & Gerson, 1978). For one thing, the possibility of a shift to private hospital placement has not been fully investigated (Kiesler, 1982b).

Whereas some mental health professionals assert that the deinstitutionalization process is the result of more effective treatment, others point to the droves of homeless people in our larger cities who live on the streets and in flophouses. Consider what it would be like to have no home and be on the street, in any circumstances. You would never know whether or not you would eat on a given day; you would have no place to go during a snowstorm, and no health care. The plight of the homeless is even worse for people suffering from psychological disorders; they are confused, have limited

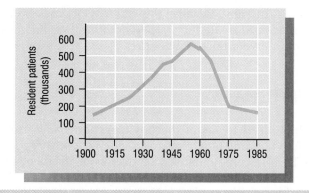

FIGURE 17-4
The inpatient population of state and locally supported mental hospitals from 1900 to 1985. Since the 1950s, the number of resident patients has decreased by two thirds. (From Bassuk & Gerson, 1978; Kiesler, 1982a, 1982b.)

resources, and are afraid. For most of us, coming in out of the cold is a physical reality, but for the homeless it may be only a dream, and for those with psychological disorders it may be literally unimaginable. So, deinstitutionalization, in many instances, creates additional stress, and the services that were once provided are no longer available.

Studies show that as many as 25% of homeless patients are no longer being cared for properly (Krauthammer, 1985). Even when support services are provided outside the institution, treatment is often inadequate and shamefully ineffective. In one long-term study of the lives of people with schizophrenia in the era of deinstitutionalization, for example, treatment outside the hospital was found to be inconsistent, with no continuity across sessions (Richardson, Craig, & Haugland, 1985).

More recent approaches have advocated that houses rather than community centers be provided for people with psychological disorders (Engler & Goldman, 1992). The belief is that if people live in a "real home" with the appropriate support, instead of a segregated community shelter, their chances for recovery improve. But even in these cases people are likely to be functionally isolated from mainstream society, and their chances for full social integration remain slim. There are unmistakable shortcomings in current mental health practices. That fewer people are in public mental hospitals today compared to 30 years ago may be a false indicator of better care if the integrity of the mental health network is adversely affected.

Treatment specialists continually grapple with these sorts of problems: When and where do we provide psychological intervention? How should treatment be carried out? What are the best methods of therapeutic intervention? Indeed, are there best methods or only different ones? Does therapy even work? Let us examine the various forms of treatment advocated by present-day therapists.

The organization of material in this chapter reflects the differences of opinion among therapists about the nature of psychological disorders. Some persons, as described in the section on the biomedical model in the preceding chapter, prefer to consider mental illness a disease. Consistent with this position, *biomedical therapy* seeks to improve a patient's mental state by changing events at an anatomical or neurochemical level. In this sense, the patient is viewed mechanistically, much like an automobile in need of repair. The objective in these cases is literally to restore the body and thus restore mental health. By contrast, the practice of *psychotherapy* assumes that psychological disturbance derives from invalid perceptions of the self and the world, inappropriate belief systems, internal conflicts, and an acquired repertory of maladaptive behaviors. Accordingly, psychotherapy places less emphasis on the biological aspects of treatment than does biomedical (somatic) therapy. Because the majority of cases involving psychological disturbance are treated using psychotherapy techniques, we discuss these treatment intervention strategies first.

PSYCHOTHERAPY

Unlike the biomedical forms of therapy, psychotherapy uses noninvasive (outside the body) treatment techniques to change the way people think and behave. When we become confused or disillusioned about one thing, our outlook on the rest of the world often changes as well. In moderate form, adjustment problems may produce only mild emotional discomfort or minor thought disturbances. In extreme cases, however, events are not seen realistically, and imagined experiences are substituted for what really happens. Under these conditions, biological change is not the solution. What is needed is a change of point of view. Perceptions of self-worth, meaningfulness, and enrichment must be dealt with systematically, along with the problem behaviors.

Psychotherapy techniques differ substantially in format and their underlying principles, but all share the same basic premise: that maladaptive behavior can be changed by environmental experience. In the discussion that follows we review the many different ways that experience can be used to modify disordered thinking and responding.

Psychoanalytic Therapy

psychoanalysis treatment originating with Sigmund Freud, designed to alleviate unconscious conflicts

In its classical form, psychoanalytic therapy consists of **psychoanalysis**, which is a treatment technique originated by Sigmund Freud. In some ways, psychoanalysis is compatible with the somatic (biomedical) view of psychological disorders, because it assumes that behavioral disturbances reflect symptoms of an underlying pathology. With psychoanalysis, however, the underlying causes are mental in nature.

In psychoanalysis, the therapist, or analyst as she or he is more often called, works intensively with the patient on a one-on-one basis. Conversations with the analyst represent the typical mode of therapeutic exchange. Sometimes traditional psychoanalytic techniques may be incorporated into other treatment methodologies. When this happens the intervention strategy is known as **psychodynamic psychotherapy** (Wolberg, 1982).

psychodynamic psychotherapy treatment technique that combines elements of classical psychoanalysis and other traditional forms of treatment

At the core of classical psychoanalysis is the notion that emotional problems arise from conflicting needs, impulses, and drives. As we saw in the earlier chapter on personality (Chapter 10), such forces are believed to reside in the unconscious. Submerged there, and relegated to eternal competition, unresolved conflicts are ultimately expressed as the symptoms we see in behavior disorders. The task of the analyst is to help the patient gain insight into the nature of the hidden motivational conflicts. Awareness does not come easily, however, for numerous personality defenses create **resistance**. Resistance is the reluctance on the part of the patient to permit the analyst to probe certain regions of the mind. The successful analyst overcomes the forces of resistance and frees inner desires from their repressive chains.

resistance in psychoanalytic therapy, client reluctance to accept the therapist's interpretations

free association in psychoanalytic therapy, the procedure whereby clients are encouraged to report freely anything that enters their minds

Free Association. Practicing psychoanalysts are likely to employ **free association** as a common analytical tool. Free association is a talking technique in which the patient is asked to say anything and everything that comes to mind. In general, the patient is also asked to lie comfortably on a couch or sofa (see Figure 17–5). The analyst sits in a chair situated close to the patient but out of the patient's visual field. This tactic serves two useful purposes. It

FIGURE 17–5
Freud's consulting room in Vienna, Austria. His patients reclined on this couch during their psychoanalytic sessions, while Freud sat in the chair to the left of the couch, where the patients could not see him.

facilitates the patient–analyst dialogue, and it spares the therapist the embarrassment of staring. As the session progresses, the patient is urged to keep saying whatever comes to mind. Nothing is considered too trivial, nor should anything be held back. Contained in this free flow of associations are disjointed thoughts and seemingly unrelated, sometimes ridiculous, remarks. But the skilled analyst often can create a coherent picture and decipher the unconscious code. What appears to be meaningless talk is understood to be unconscious material cloaked by resistance. Using the free associations as explanatory tools, the analyst leads the patient to an understanding of inner conflicts. With a more secure grasp of the genuine feelings involved, the patient can better address those problems that are the real source of the emotional disturbance.

Dreams.   According to Freud, dreams are another source of unconscious material that may contain clues to deep-seated psychological disturbance. When treating a patient, an analyst is alert to two different types of dream content: the manifest content and the latent content. Recall from Chapter 5 that the manifest content is that part of the dream that we can report. But psychoanalytic theory says that these reports are distorted images of underlying unconscious episodes that comprise the dream's latent content. Once again, the analyst must render an interpretation. Care must be taken to analyze the manifest content for symbols of repressed fears, anxieties, or potentially destructive motives.

Transference.   One of the most important processes in psychoanalysis is the concept of transference. **Transference** reflects a strong feeling a patient develops toward the analyst, which likely occurs as a result of an increased sense of intimacy following the client's self-disclosure, and the analyst's listening and caring (Young, 1990). Feelings involved in transference can be either positive (e.g., sexual attraction) or negative (e.g., contempt).

transference psychological phenomenon that occurs when clients develop strong feelings toward their analysts; reflects unresolved past conflicts

The psychoanalytic view of transference is that it reflects unresolved conflicts from the past. Love for a cold, rejecting father may be transferred as genuine affection for the analyst. Conversely, the client may see in the analyst evidence of a mean-spirited sister who was a rival for attention; as a result the client may be rude to the analyst. The analyst actually encourages this transfer, especially when it allows the client to relive an extremely emotional moment within the safe context of the therapy environment. Four types of transference are recognized: *superego transference*, in which the client projects the authority of a parent or some other controlling agent onto the analyst; *ego transference*, in which the client overidentifies with the analyst; *ego ideal transference*, in which the analyst is viewed as the perfect person; and *id transference*, in which the client projects basic childhood wants and needs, such as nurturance and attention.

Of course, strong negative feelings toward an analyst can cause a client to leave therapy prematurely. But such feelings can also help the analyst find out about unresolved conflicts from the client's past, and for this reason transference is viewed as crucial to the success of psychoanalytic psychotherapy.

Modern Psychoanalytic Perspective. It should be mentioned that although psychoanalysis began with Freud, it did not stop with him. Psychoanalysis should not be considered as a therapy technique in its final form. Rather, it is a continually expanding and changing model. A good example of how psychoanalysis changes to accommodate contemporary beliefs is the recent inclusion of more cognitive variables in the model. For example, many modern psychoanalytic analysts consider the phenomenon of transference just discussed to reflect distorted cognitions (Corey, Corey, & Callanan, 1988). Later in this chapter, we will see that this view is in line with more traditional interpretations of disordered and irrational thinking.

Along with the incorporation of cognitive elements, such as perceptual judgments and attitude formation, into the therapeutic process, *modern psychoanalysis* differs from classical psychoanalysis in several other respects. For one thing, the two approaches have somewhat different therapeutic objectives. In classical psychoanalysis the analyst interprets problems for the patient and leads the patient to an awareness of fundamental conflicts. In contrast to this focus on interpretation, modern psychoanalysis emphasizes the patient's need for personal growth. The belief here is that the patient must identify unmet maturational needs, and it is up to the analyst to show the patient how those needs can be satisfied.

Symptom Substitution. As mentioned, the traditional psychoanalytic model holds that the symptoms of a disorder are mere outward expressions of more basic psychological problems. Accordingly, psychoanalysts are disinclined to treat symptoms. When a patient has a stuttering problem, for instance, the therapist is not likely to focus on correcting the stammer. The reasoning from a psychoanalytic point of view is that stuttering, as one symptom of psychological conflict, can be replaced easily by another symptom (*symptom substitution*). Therefore, the analyst usually prefers to use a technique that treats the underlying causes of the disorder.

Those who see the symptoms of an illness as the illness per se criticize this point of view. Pointing to the lack of evidence for the notion of symptom substitution, some psychologists, most notably the behaviorists (discussed next), claim that psychoanalytic procedures delay treatment unnecessarily. With stuttering, for example, why not address the problem directly without regard to cause? This would mean more immediate treatment benefits for the patient. Implicit in the stance taken by the behaviorists is that perceptible, surface characteristics define learned psychological adjustment problems. Accordingly, the objective of treatment here is behavior change through relearning. The next section shows just how varied such relearning exercises can be.

Behavior Therapy

Behavior therapy involves the application of learning principles to the treatment of psychological disorders. In Chapter 6 we discussed how environmental experiences strengthen associations between stimulus and response events. Now we consider how the techniques employed in classical conditioning and instrumental learning can be used to treat psychological disturbances.

In our earlier chapter on learning we saw how Albert acquired a fear of a white rat when the rat was associated with an aversive loud noise. Only 4 years after the report of that study, Mary Cover Jones (1924) published the first behavioral prescription for eliminating childhood fears (phobias) like those exhibited by Albert. Following clues from John Watson about the development of such fears, Jones recommended "reconditioning" by having children eat in the presence of the object that elicited fear. The suggestion was that the more recent positive experience with food would foster a new associative connection between the object and the feeling of satisfaction. Instead of the object being associated with something stressful, the object predicts something pleasant.

Jones and others were quick to show that this technique was effective in reducing the symptoms of several different types of childhood phobias. And with experimental psychology emerging as a scientific force, the number of possible applications of these learning concepts expanded. As a result, modern behavior therapy offers a mixture of treatment strategies that are as versatile as the learning principles that underlie them. We discuss a few of them in the following sections.

Systematic Desensitization. In a series of experiments completed in 1948, Joseph Wolpe found that adult anxiety disorders could be successfully treated by using the same response competition strategy set forth for children by Mary Cover Jones. By substituting muscle relaxation for feeding activities, Wolpe used the method of **systematic desensitization** to break down old habits and replace them with new ones. Systematic desensitization replaces an old response to a stimulus with a new response to that stimulus, using classical conditioning techniques.

At the very core of the systematic desensitization technique is a classical conditioning procedure known as **counterconditioning**. Typically, counterconditioning is accomplished by pairing stimuli of different strengths that are known to evoke competing behaviors. As a rule, the stronger response elicited by the stronger cue will dominate and eventually condition (connect) to both stimuli (see Figure 17–6). Thus, the old response to the weaker stimulus is replaced (counterconditioned) with a new, stronger response.

systematic desensitization counterconditioning procedure developed by Wolpe that eliminates the reaction of fear to a stimulus by replacing it with a relaxation response to the stimulus that elicited the fear

counterconditioning method that replaces an old response to a stimulus with a new response, using the techniques of classical conditioning

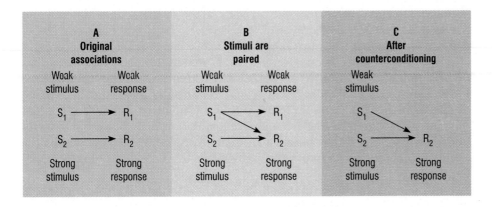

FIGURE 17–6
The basic model of counterconditioning used in behavior therapy. (*A*) The original associations involve a weaker stimulus–response connection (e.g., anxiety reaction) and a stronger stimulus–response connection (e.g., relaxation). (*B*) When the stimuli that cause each response are paired, the stronger of the two responses begins to connect to the weaker stimulus as well as the stronger stimulus. (*C*) Eventually, the originally weaker response is replaced with the new, stronger response (e.g., the previously anxiety-eliciting stimulus now evokes relaxation).

With systematic desensitization, counterconditioning takes place when the patient is taught to relax in the presence of weak anxiety-arousing stimuli. The presentation of weak stimuli assures that counterconditioning proceeds in the proper direction. Eventually, the relaxation response, because it is stronger than the anxiety reaction, connects to the cues that previously evoked anxiety. Thus, when those stimuli recur either in actual or imagined form, a feeling of relaxation is experienced. By gradually introducing stronger anxiety-eliciting stimuli, they too can be counterconditioned.

In clinical practice, the levels of anxiety are often quite high. As a result, the therapist must be especially careful to control the strength of the anxiety-eliciting cues presented during therapy. This necessitates the construction of an **anxiety hierarchy**. Anxiety hierarchies are lists of frightening events ranked according to the degree of severity. Typically, each successive item in the list is described by the client as increasingly fear-evoking.

In systematic desensitization the client learns to relax in the presence of item number 1, then item 2, and so on, working through the list. Although it is much more convenient to conduct desensitization using imagined stimuli, patients commonly report problems maintaining the images. Therefore, desensitization training often employs the actual use of the feared objects (a technique known as **in vivo desensitization**), or the patient observes someone else making contact with the object in a nonthreatening context (refer to the modeling approach discussed later in this chapter). Most therapists agree that the best results are obtained in cases where the client actually participates in the treatment activities (Bandura, 1977a). Seeing a person remain calm when a snake slithers across his or her foot is quite different from experiencing that calmness yourself.

Flooding and Implosive Therapy. We have just reviewed a technique whereby an undesirable anxiety reaction is replaced with a more desirable alternative through counterconditioning. Anxiety reactions can also be reduced by invoking the principle of extinction. If anxiety disorders like phobias reflect acquired connections between neutral events and threatening environmental stimuli, then phobic cues should regain their neutral status if they are presented over and over again in the absence of threatening stimuli. In classical conditioning terminology, the CS loses the ability to evoke the CR of fear when it is no longer paired with the US.

Flooding is one technique that uses extinction to treat anxiety disorders. **Flooding** is a sometimes harsh procedure that exposes the patient to real-life encounters with anxiety-eliciting stimuli and simply prevents escape. The oldest recorded account of this treatment involves a young woman who was intensely frightened by traveling in a car (see Crafts et al., 1938). Her physician ordered that she be driven to his office for treatment, a distance of more than 50 miles. He cured her before she arrived. Although she suffered intensely in the early part of the ride, her fear of traveling weakened as the trip continued. She had learned that there was nothing especially dangerous about traveling.

Because flooding produces such high anxiety levels, many therapists favor another extinction approach called **implosive therapy** (Stampfl & Levis, 1967). Unlike flooding, which may require the patient to experience events in real-life settings, implosive therapy involves having the patient imagine high-anxiety scenes from an exaggerated unrealistic verbal description that is given by the therapist. Although implosive therapy causes the client considerable discomfort, it usually is less than the discomfort of flooding.

In contrast to desensitization, in which attempts are made to avoid undue levels of felt anxiety, flooding and implosion create massive amounts of anxiety and allow it to decrease. Through presenting the fear-eliciting cue

anxiety hierarchy list of fear-evoking events and images, ranked according to severity

in vivo desensitization counterconditioning procedure that uses the actual fear-eliciting stimulus during treatment rather than an imagined form of the event

flooding extinction procedure designed to treat phobias in which the actual fear-eliciting stimuli (CS) are presented in a nonthreatening context (no US is present)

implosive therapy extinction procedure designed to treat phobias in which the fear-eliciting events are presented in an imagined form in an unrealistic setting (the CS) and blocking any attempts to escape, the therapist forces the patient to experience the CS in the absence of a pairing with an aversive US. Ultimately, CS extinction occurs and the anxiety is lost. Because flooding and implosive techniques seem to be more effective with younger patients, the usefulness of such procedures with older age groups has been questioned (Foa et al., 1983). But on the whole these strategies seem to produce beneficial results with minimal negative side effects (Boyd & Levis, 1983).

Aversion Therapy.   Our previous discussion of behavior therapy has centered on the elimination of an undesirable emotion or response. For instance, desensitization training aims to reduce anxiety reactions through counterconditioning. Flooding and implosion are designed to decrease fear and escape through extinction training. Yet it is sometimes helpful for the patient to learn a new fear rather than lose an old one. To this end, **aversion therapy** associates an aversive stimulus with an unwanted behavior.

aversion therapy the use of aversive events to alter the strength of a behavior

Two areas in which aversion therapy is commonly used are disorders relating to inappropriate sexual behavior and alcoholism. Cases that fall into these large categories are especially difficult to treat because the reinforcers that control the behavior are so strong. An example of the use of aversion therapy with a sexual disorder is found in a typical treatment routine used for child molesters. The client is presented with pictures or slides of children in various poses, and at the same time an electric shock is delivered through electrodes attached to a forearm or leg. When the picture or slide is turned off, so is the shock. Thus, a painful event is associated with children, and relief is associated with their absence. Of course, you do not want the client to go through life experiencing conditioned anxiety every time a child happens along. To avoid this, the therapist delivers a shock only when sexual arousal is exhibited in the presence of events such as pictures of attractive children. Eventually, the combination of sexual excitement and the image of a child come to evoke the conditioned response of anxiety. Thus, interest in the child as a sexual object declines.

Aversion therapy can also be used to treat alcohol disorders (Nathan & Skinstad, 1987). Typically, a drug like emetine is administered to the patient. *Emetine* produces no harmful effects. But when emetine and alcohol are present in the blood at the same time, the person becomes increasingly nauseated. Therefore, a patient on emetine who chooses to drink should expect to have an uncomfortable hour or two. As Figure 17–7 shows, alcohol itself eventually comes to elicit a conditioned nausea reaction due to its recurrent pairings with sickness. In some instances even the smell of alcohol, or a casual reference to a favorite bar, may produce similar discomfort. Not surprisingly, some patients are inspired to avoid all contact with alcohol—at least this is what happens in some cases. For others, aversion therapy using emetine or an alternative chemical agent such as *Antabuse* (generic name, disulfiram) produces no decreases in voluntary alcohol intake. Perhaps the greatest problem is that patients stop using the drug therapy. Thus, the aversive conditioning operation is no longer in effect.

Although electric shock and drug applications are the most common unpleasant stimuli employed in aversion therapy, numerous other aversive stimuli have been used. Vile-smelling potions, bright lights, tickling, and even shame and embarrassment have been used for purposes of aversive conditioning (Martin & Pear, 1988).

Instrumental Techniques.   We have thus far discussed desensitization, flooding, and aversion therapy. Each of these techniques uses some variant of classical conditioning procedures. But instrumental conditioning is also widely used in behavior therapy. Behavior studies point out that outcomes

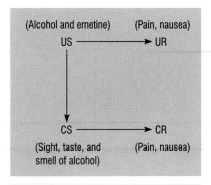

FIGURE 17–7
Aversion therapy for alcohol abuse. When the drug emetine is present in the blood, alcohol triggers extremely unpleasant reactions. Consequently, a CS related to drinking becomes associated with an US associated with intense discomfort.

of responding are important both for the formation of desirable behavior and the elimination of undesirable behavior.

The use of positive reinforcement to encourage appropriate behavior is evident from a case history summarized by Martin and Pear (1988).

> The case involved a six-year-old boy named Darren who was extremely uncooperative with his parents. Darren, rather than his parents, was the force in the home that determined what was to be done, and who was going to do it. Darren would push his mother away when he did not want her near him, or issue excessive verbal commands such as "No, that's wrong. Do it this way." At a treatment clinic at the University of Washington, Darren's mother was carefully instructed to be very positive and supportive when Darren behaved in a cooperative manner, and to ignore his demands. After only a couple of sessions, Darren began to cooperate with his mother and he quit ordering her to do things his way. In this demonstration of the application of instrumental conditioning in behavior therapy, it is apparent that Darren's improvement " . . . was due to the positive consequences provided by the mother following instances of Darren's cooperative behavior."

Although positive reinforcement techniques have been used successfully to produce impressive therapeutic results in the training of desired behaviors, removing positive reinforcement can be used as an effective technique for eliminating undesirable behaviors. An excellent example of the potential uses of extinction training is available from a classic study on bedtime crying reported by Williams (1959).

> A 21-month-old boy had tantrums every night when his parents put him to bed. The child totally controlled the parents and made them stay in the room with him until he fell asleep. The tantrum behavior, it seems, was being maintained by the reinforcing consequences of parental attention. Therefore, treatment for the tantrums involved the removal of the reinforcer; that is, the parents were instructed to put the child to bed and not go back into the room. They were further told to keep a record of the length of each crying or screaming episode and to graph the results. The first night was a horrible ordeal for both the child and the parents. However, dramatic drops in the duration of crying were noted on subsequent nights [see Figure 17–8]. The behavior that was once reinforced by the parents had been extinguished.

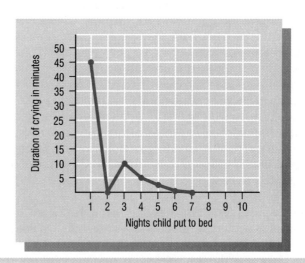

FIGURE 17–8
Extinction of crying episodes in a 21-month-old child who had tantrums when he was put to bed each night. (Adapted from Williams, 1959.)

Extinction as a treatment technique has also been used in instances where the behavior was acquired through negative reinforcement. Consider the following case history of a young girl who vomited recurrently:

Laura was a nine-year-old girl diagnosed as suffering from mental retardation, cerebral palsy, aphasia, hyperirritability, and brain damage. She was admitted to Rainer School, an institution for the retarded, about ten months before our observation began. According to Laura's dormitory nurse, Laura vomited at a moderate rate upon admission, but within a few weeks the rate declined to its present level of "a couple times a month."

Approximately six months after she was admitted, Laura was enrolled in the school program in a developmental level class that met three hours a day. After about a month, Laura began to vomit occasionally in class, and within three months, vomiting became practically an everyday occurrence. Among other consequences, the teacher returned Laura to her dormitory whenever Laura vomited on her own dress, which happened fairly frequently. Drug therapy was initiated but had no effect. At the end of the third month Laura was temporarily dropped from school because of her vomiting.

Reasoning that Laura's vomiting was an instrumental response that permitted her to get out of a stressful situation (the classroom), the psychologist called in on the case placed Laura on an extinction schedule. That is, when Laura vomited, she was forced to remain in the classroom. As a result, Laura's rate of vomiting declined from a daily high of 21 vomits early in treatment to zero by the end of treatment. By removing the source of reinforcement (escape from the classroom), the undesirable instrumental response was eliminated. (Wolf et al., 1965)

Cognitive–Behavior Therapy

Modeling.   In Chapters 6 and 10, we discussed the influence that Albert Bandura has had on learning theory. What has been termed *social learning theory* has had a profound impact on the way psychologists view the learning process, and on treatment approaches as well. Traditionally, practicing behavior therapists had denied that uniquely mental events existed, so of course there had been no attempt to include cognitions, beliefs, and other mental operations as part of the treatment package. Today, many therapists have departed from such a restrictive stance and argue that *information* about some event is often as useful as experience of that event. The implication is that progress in therapy can be made by presenting purely mental representations of phobic objects, depressing situations, and so on. This procedure has come to be known as **modeling**.

Originally, modeling was suggested only for use with snake phobias (Bandura, Blanchard, & Ritter, 1969). The idea behind it was that simply by watching someone else react calmly to snakes, a phobic client could learn that most snakes are harmless. The success of this procedure was immediately apparent, and it has been used more recently to teach the mentally retarded to care for themselves, and to teach drug abusers how to resist social pressures from peers (Wixted, Belleck, & Hersen, 1990). In many instances, modeling techniques involve **role playing**, in which clients are asked to act out a particular scene. For example, clients who are being treated for chronic cocaine abuse may be encouraged to play out a role in which they not only resist an offer of cocaine, but also attempt to educate the person offering the drug about the dangers of repeated drug use.

modeling therapy technique based on the use of observational learning

role playing modeling technique in which the client is asked to act out a particular activity or behavioral sequence

rational–emotive therapy (RET) treatment technique advanced by Albert Ellis that forces the patient to be more realistic in evaluating circumstances

Albert Ellis.

Rational–Emotive Therapy. Psychotherapist Albert Ellis (Ellis, 1962; Ellis & Grieger, 1986) has designed a cognitive–behavioral model that is known as **rational–emotive therapy (RET)**. The basic premise of RET is that emotional disturbances derive from unrealistic assumptions about the way the world is ordered. Some people impose exacting self-commands such as "I must never express my anger" or "I must excel on every examination I take." Such unattainable standards of perfection inevitably lead to disappointment and a profusion of negative self-statements. A consistent erosion of rational thinking occurs, and eventually the person "catastrophizes"; that is, the patient exaggerates a negative circumstance and responds as if conditions were worse than they really are.

The strategy on the part of RET practitioners is to break down negative thinking and substitute positive thinking in its place. This may consist of confronting the client rather openly with the ridiculous nature of his or her thoughts. For instance, someone who reports that he or she has failed miserably as a person for doing so little to help the world's starving population may elicit responses from the therapist such as, "Why is it that you alone should shoulder the burden of all humanity? It's silly to cast yourself as such a paragon of virtue." This approach may seem a bit unkind, but it has met with appreciable success. Recent scientific studies of the effectiveness of RET confirm that the procedure works with a wide variety of disorders such as depression and phobic reactions. In all instances, the goal is to get clients to think about their problems realistically. Everyone has difficulties and life stress is inevitable, but any situation can be managed.

Consistent with the trend in other treatment models, RET has broadened its recommendation on what types of treatment procedures can be used. Basic instrumental and classical conditioning techniques are used in combination with thought-restructuring procedures to produce a more fully integrated person (Carson, Butcher, & Coleman, 1992). The objective is still to change the way people feel about themselves, but a greater variety of treatment tools are used to achieve this result.

Stress-Inoculation Therapy. *Stress-inoculation therapy* is another model that employs cognitive–behavioral methods that are designed to restructure inappropriate thinking (Meichenbaum, 1977). In some ways the stress-inoculation approach is similar to RET, because it attempts to shift the client's internal focus from negative to positive self-statements. In contrast to RET, however, stress-inoculation therapy makes no attempt to completely eliminate negative self-commentary. Rather, self-instructional training teaches the client to use negative feelings and thoughts as cues to make positive self-statements. When you step before a group to deliver a speech and you start feeling your knees bumping against one another, tell yourself, "I can do this. I am an effective speaker and I will perform well. Besides, most everyone is a little nervous being on stage in front of a large group of unfamiliar people."

Recent investigations have shown that stress-inoculation therapy is especially effective when several clients are treated together (we will discuss group therapy in more detail later in this chapter). For example, Heimberg (1990) reports the case of J, a 23-year-old male who had a fear of meeting and talking to women he would like to date. Using some of the techniques just outlined, negative comments such as "I'll be incredibly anxious" or "She won't talk to me" were shifted to more confident statements about J's social skill. The support from others who understood and were sympathetic seemed to facilitate J's progress, and he in turn was able to offer them encouragement through his own advancement. Such findings are promising, but it should be kept in mind that one client in five will fail to benefit from cognitive–behavioral treatment. In addition, even though J was successfully treated, he continued to report social anxiety attacks for many months after his treatment was stopped. This is not an indictment of cognitive–behavior therapies, of course, for research shows that these procedures compare favorably with other approaches (Tyrer et al., 1988). Rather, we simply wish to acknowledge that specific therapeutic models have limits. Often, the therapist must try several different interventions before "the right one" is identified.

Cognitive Therapy.   One rather unique type of therapy that is often included in the list of popular cognitive–behavioral models is **cognitive therapy**. Although many writers and practitioners have contributed to the intellectual framework of cognitive therapy over the years, in the 1990s the term is often used to refer to the treatment focus advanced by psychiatrist Aaron Beck of the University of Pennsylvania. Beck's original formulation was designed to provide an understanding of depression, and his therapeutic technique has been most consistently applied to this disorder.

The premise of cognitive therapy is that depression results from distorted thinking, and the distortions tend to occur along three dimensions (Beck et al., 1979). Negative views of the self, of the world or experience, and of the future form what is known as the *cognitive triad*. As Figure 17–9 shows, the triad can be viewed as a triangle. Within the triangle, a person occupies a space that reflects the importance of a particular factor. A patient described at point "B" would hold distorted negative perceptions of the world and the future (e.g., "It's a mean, narrow, and trivial world, and it's never going to get better"). By contrast, a patient concerned with self and her or his world, but not the future, would occupy position "A" in the triad. ("I'm no good and I live in a world that is no good"). Now, consider point "C." What type of person would fall here? What negative statements would you anticipate hearing from this patient?

By paying attention to the special features of the triad, the therapist can determine the appropriate focus for treatment. Visually presenting the problems that the therapy will address helps the patient understand why certain things are being done; it also helps the therapist stay on track. The ultimate goal is to break down distortions and replace them with more realistic, positive attitudes. The attempt is to make people believe they are winners in a fair-minded world that is always improving. Although the cognitive therapy model has not stimulated much research, many practicing psychologists and psychiatrists have testified that the techniques are useful in a therapeutic environment.

Before leaving these sections on therapy that focus on behavior change, we should acknowledge that behavior is not always the end point of treatment. Sometimes behavior *is* the treatment.

cognitive therapy Aaron Beck's position that treatment of depression requires the restructuring of the patient's invalid perceptions of the self, the future, and the world or experience

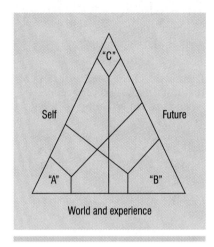

FIGURE 17–9
Graphic representation of the cognitive triad proposed by Aaron Beck. (See text for details.)

◄ THINKING ABOUT
Exercise as Therapy ►

There is something that each of us can do as part of our daily routine that may confer some degree of protection against mental disturbance. It is not an expensive venture, it is not fattening, and it could even increase your longevity. It is, in a word, exercise.

There is little question that we are in the throes of a fitness craze. Indeed, we are awash with jogging tracks, tennis clubs, softball teams, and a

Exercise has been used as a form of therapy. People seem to feel better when they are active.

proliferation of sports clothing that even includes athletic underwear. It remains to be seen if this predilection for exercise will survive, or if, in the words of Calvin Trillin, a journalist for *The New Yorker*, "this too will pass and our natural inclination toward sloth will reassert itself."

Actually, there is growing evidence that strengthens the argument that activity is healthful. Even under normal circumstances people report that they feel good after vigorous physical activity. In addition, exercise may elevate moods in clinically depressed clients (Simons et al., 1985). In several well-controlled studies of the effects of exercise on mood, it has been shown that exercise programs that last 6–20 weeks are associated with decreased depression and greater feelings of self-esteem (Morgan, 1985). Intense physical exertion may result in changes in brain chemistry that are likely to make people feel better (Morgan & Raglin, 1985). It is also possible that improvements are not produced by the exercise per se, but rather by the feelings of accomplishment that go with sticking to a tough workout schedule.

Whatever the mechanism, therapists and organizational officials are increasingly aware that more than mood is improved by exercise. Vigorous exercise classes have been shown to enhance cognitive functioning and the ability to solve difficult mental tasks (Lightman & Poser, 1988). A team of Canadian scientists found that aerobic exercise increased work efficiency in a job setting (Long & Haney, 1988). Exercising at work breaks up the day, causing a positive shift in attitude toward getting things done.

Outside purely clinical and occupational gains, the therapeutic benefits of exercise have also been demonstrated in studies of older populations. Retired people who swim, walk, bike, or just generally keep on the move are happier and have fewer health-related problems than their inactive counterparts. The importance of remaining active beyond the age of 60 cannot be overstated.

So, what does this mean to you? Do you think it is a good idea to exercise on a regular basis? Are you currently involved in an exercise routine, and do you have a sense that it serves your mental as well as your physical health? What kind of programs do you think are most likely to produce lasting benefits? Along these lines, what are some of the problems of overdoing exercise?

Humanistic Therapy

All the psychotherapy approaches discussed up to now view behavior essentially as outside the control of the individual. For psychoanalysis, symptoms are outward expressions of the unconscious; and for behavioral therapies, the person is at the whim of controlling external events. This idea, that mental disorders are due to forces outside the individual's control, is not without opposition, however. Likewise, some therapists object to the idea that treatment must be regimented and depersonalized. **Humanistic therapy**, in contrast to other treatment models, places much more of the responsibility of treatment on the person. In this regard, each person is seen as a unique, dignified individual capable of choice and free will. The goals of therapy are those that patients select for themselves and that help in understanding the real meaning of human existence. There are many variants of humanistic therapy, but client-centered therapy, existential analysis, and Gestalt therapy have achieved the widest acclaim.

Client-Centered Therapy. **Client-centered therapy**, also known as *person-centered therapy*, allows the client, rather than the therapist, to direct treat-

humanistic therapy general term for a class of therapy approaches that focus on getting patients to accept the responsibility for their improvement

client-centered therapy humanistic approach to treatment developed by Carl Rogers; emphasizes acceptance and unconditional positive regard

ment. It was the innovation of Carl Rogers in the 1950s. In what was then an unreceptive climate, Rogers argued that people in general are capable of considerable awareness as to the nature of their own problems. Therapy, therefore, should focus on structuring the client's world so that the natural healing process can unfold. By permitting the course of treatment to follow the feelings and ideas of the clients, people are encouraged to be themselves, and more important, to accept themselves as they are.

In order to accomplish the objective of helping one to become more self-accepting, the Rogerian method encourages a feeling of total support, or *unconditional positive regard*, as we noted in Chapter 10. When clients become immersed in this nonjudgmental atmosphere of warmth and compassion, they feel free to communicate their honest values or attitudes. The therapist does not interrupt but occasionally reflects the comments of the client for the dual purposes of recognition and clarification. Recognition is achieved in the sense that the client gains an intimate understanding of personal attributes. Clarification occurs when the meaning of certain feelings becomes clear and, eventually, more acceptable. For the first time the client sees the whole self, the good and bad, the popular and the distasteful.

In its original format, client-centered training employed a technique in which the therapist simply mirrored the comments of the client. The following excerpt from an actual treatment session illustrates this therapeutic approach:

CLIENT: I just want to run away and die.
THERAPIST: M-hm, m-hm, m-hm. It isn't even that you want to get away from here to something. You just want to leave here and go away and die in a corner, hm?
[Silence of 30 sec]
THERAPIST: I guess as I let that soak in I really do sense how, how deep that feeling sounds, that you—I guess the image that comes to my mind is sort of a, a wounded animal that wants to crawl away and die. It sounds as though that's kind of the way you feel that you just want to get away from here and, and vanish. Perish. Not exist.
[Silence of 1 min]
CLIENT: [Almost inaudibly] All day yesterday and all morning I wished I were dead. I even prayed last night that I could die.
THERAPIST: I think I caught all of that, that—for a couple of days now you've just wished you could be dead and you've even prayed for that—I guess that—one way this strikes me is that to live is such an awful thing to you, you just wish you could die, and not live.
[Silence of 1 min, 12 sec]
THERAPIST: So that you've been just wishing and wishing that you were not living. You wish that life would pass away from you.
[Silence of 30 sec]
CLIENT: I wish it more'n anything else I've ever wished around here.
THERAPIST: M-hm, m-hm, m-hm. I guess you've wished for lots of things, but boy! It seems as though this wish to not live is deeper and stronger than anything you ever wished before.
[Silence of 1 min, 36 sec]
THERAPIST: Can't help but wonder whether it's still true that some things this friend said to you—are those still part of the thing that makes you feel so awful?
CLIENT: In general, yes.
THERAPIST: M-hm.
[Silence of 47 sec]
THERAPIST: The way I'm understanding that is that in a general way the fact that he felt you were no good has just set off a whole flood of feeling in you that makes you really wish, wish you weren't alive. Is that—somewhere near it?
CLIENT: I ain't no good to nobody, or I ain't no good for nothin', so what's the use of living?
THERAPIST: M-hm. You feel, "I'm not any good to another living person, so—why should I go on living?"

[Silence of 21 sec]

THERAPIST: And I guess a part of that is that—here I'm kind of guessing and you can set me straight. I guess a part of that is that you felt, "I tried to be good for something as far as he was concerned. I really tried. And now—if I'm no good to him, if he feels I'm no good, then that proves I'm just no good to anybody." Is that, uh—anywhere near it? (Reprinted from *A Silent Young Man*, Carl R. Rogers, 1967)

Perhaps one of the most conspicuous oversights on the part of Rogerian followers has been the absence of a systematic research program. Rogers clearly sensed this. In one of his last papers published before his death in 1987, Rogers (1986) called for more solid research to be conducted on the essential elements of client-centered therapy. His fear, surely justified, was that without scientific challenges the approach is destined to become too narrow, dogmatic, and restrictive.

Existential Analysis. Rollo May and Viktor Frankl are two key people who have embraced an existential component in treatment. In many respects **existential analysis** overlaps with client-centered therapy, in that both emphasize personal responsibility and acceptance. But there is a major difference in the two treatment approaches. Whereas a client-centered therapist may seek to bring forth a previously obscure event, the existential therapist attempts to gain for clients something they have never had: an awareness of the meaning and importance of their lives.

In a fast-paced, depersonalized society it is easy to become lost. We may feel that we are submerged in a pool of humanity. Questions such as "Why am I here?" or "Does my life in itself mean anything?" emerge amidst suspicions of meaninglessness. The resulting feelings of alienation can lead to despair and confusion. To correct this, the existential therapist uses whatever technique works to force the client to actively pursue a course that yields meaning (Norcross, 1987). But the responsibility of choosing such a path to an authentic and meaningful life falls squarely on the shoulders of the client. It is the client alone who must cast off the feelings of aimlessness. The therapist continually insists that the client has free choice. The therapist tells the client the following: You can do anything you wish, however desperate the circumstances, you are free to adopt a more satisfactory way of living. Meaning comes through choice, and choice through acceptance of responsibility.

Gestalt Therapy. Still another form of humanistic therapy is **Gestalt therapy**, founded by Frederick (Fritz) Perls (1893–1970). The word *Gestalt* (meaning "whole") is used because treatment emphasizes the total integration of physical and mental processes. Clients are taught to recognize obscure mind and body elements that they have not examined before.

Gestalt therapy acknowledges the importance of early life experiences, but treatment focuses on the here and now (Perls, 1969). What has happened in the past, however harsh and undeserved, cannot be changed. Internal conflicts can be resolved only by selecting an effective strategy that brings past traumas into an urgent personal context. The complete self must be confronted and dealt with as a whole. In order to make the patient aware of some of the minor fragments that comprise parts of the whole person, the therapist may ask the patient to exaggerate subtle movements or amplify speech patterns that the patient rarely uses. This may take the form of acting out a familiar personal role while sitting in one chair and a less conspicuous role in another. Or patients may be encouraged to hold a conversation with parts of their bodies, if those parts are sources of tension. All of this is designed to enhance the patient's awareness; that is, the person must come

existential analysis humanistic approach to treatment that attempts to help the client gain a sense of purpose and meaning

Gestalt therapy humanistic approach to treatment in which the client is encouraged to come into contact with the whole self

In Gestalt therapy, feelings of intimacy may be enhanced through self-awareness and acceptance.

in touch with what he or she is doing and feeling. Harmon (1974) provides an example of how the therapists may work toward accomplishing this goal:

> The therapist may say to a patient, "What are you aware of now?" "What is your present awareness?" "What is your now?" Or the therapist may direct the patient's awareness to some specific segment of his behavior, for example, "What is your hand doing?" "Were you aware of smiling when you told me about the rough time you had?" . . . Awareness is an attempt to get the patient in touch with all of himself so that he can utilize all of his potential.

Ultimately, Gestalt therapy permits all aspects of one's being to be identified, and an image of completeness is restored. The key is that clients learn to accept themselves. In contrast to the client-centered and existential approaches, Gestalt therapy is more intensive and directed. An array of techniques is used by the therapist, including the reenactment of dreams and role-playing formats like those just described. But as with the other humanistic therapies, the Gestalt model places the responsibility for change on the individual.

Gestalt therapy continues to evolve as a treatment strategy, incorporating many of the features that have become popular in other forms of psychotherapy. The changing nature of Gestalt therapy is illustrated by the fact that many treatment sessions now include a group format. Couples and other small groups of six to eight people explore interpersonal difficulties, and define common solutions by increasing their awareness and acceptance of who they are as individuals (O'Leary & Page, 1990). As we see in the next section, the group concept used in Gestalt therapy is also used in other treatment groups.

Group Psychotherapy

Some years ago, group psychotherapy was used only when there were not enough staff people to conduct one-on-one therapy. We now know that the group procedure is useful in itself simply because some people respond more openly in a group format (Kirkley et al., 1985). In addition, the group represents a social reality that is a closer approximation of what the patient must deal with outside the confines of the treatment setting. The client must come to grips with interacting in a complex environment where people express different biases and social predilections, and this is a treatment dimension that is

Family therapy helps both parents and children to better understand the nature of their problems.

difficult to address in individual psychotherapy. Family–marital therapy and self-help therapy are examples of group psychotherapy.

Family and Marital Therapy. Many group therapies involve relationship treatments that include marital partners or parents and children. **Family therapy** is based on the recognition that a person's family is perhaps the most important, and potentially influential, force in one's life. The biological and emotional ties between and among family members increase the chances for devastation and despair. When an acquaintance fails to meet your expectations, you may be disappointed, but you are not likely to experience the agony that comes with parental neglect or the loss of a child to drug addiction. No pain hurts worse than one that accompanies family torment.

Because the therapeutic environment associated with treating family members is often an intense one, the therapist must exercise caution in controlling the dialogue between and among family members. Naturally, what is expressed during a session goes home with the clients. Moreover, individual family members may interpret a therapist's remarks as favoritism, or they may see themselves as being cast in an unpopular role. Because of the unique nature of family therapy, training programs in this area recommend that therapists gain additional experience regarding such issues as the importance of confidentiality, objectivity, and the impact their own values may have on different family members (Miller, Scott, & Searight, 1990).

Although the intensity of family relationships presents some special problems, it also renders the family as one of the most important tools in psychotherapy. Because support from other family members is such a powerful reinforcer, family approval can be used effectively to promote change. The approach has been successful in treating problems ranging from drug abuse to compulsive eating. Underlying all successful family therapy cases is the increased understanding that comes with increased communication.

A special type of family therapy is *marital therapy*. Marital therapy focuses directly on the interaction between married couples and attempts to resolve conflicts that can lead to separation and divorce. Because marital discord can have negative effects on children within the immediate family, and even on extended family members, effective intervention and treatment for

family therapy group therapy that focuses on the family unit and makes use of these bonds to treat individual members of the family

struggling married couples is essential. Yet, despite the recognized importance of marital therapy, not much is known about the theoretical mechanisms that contribute to successful change and improvement in a marriage.

What is known about approaches to marital therapy is based largely on the work of Snyder and Wills (1989) and Snyder, Wills, and Grady-Fletcher (1991). These researchers followed the marital status and marital satisfaction of 59 couples over a 4-year period after their treatment was stopped. In this well-controlled study, some couples who were having marital problems received *behavioral marital therapy*, while others received *insight-oriented marital therapy*. Behavioral marital therapy uses reinforcement and conditioning strategies to teach marital partners how to communicate with each other, and to say more positive things to each other. Through the rewarding feedback that is received, a spouse learns to make more constructive remarks, and fewer negative exchanges occur. In contrast, insight-oriented marital therapy seeks to teach the couple how to interact in a mature, autonomous manner by resolving hidden or unconscious sources of conflict. Techniques that are used in this form of therapy may include instructions in listening and caring, but the real thrust of the treatment is to have people understand the reasons for their behavior and the consequences it has for a successful marriage.

Both behavioral marital therapy and insight-oriented marital therapy show improvement at a 2-month follow-up after therapy is terminated. Obviously, though, the goal is a lasting relationship in which the effects of treatment last longer than a few months. With this in mind, Snyder and his colleagues published the only long-term (4-year follow-up) data to date in the area of marital and family therapy (Snyder et al., 1991). The results are shown in Figure 17–10. It is clear that both behavioral marital therapy and insight-oriented therapy produced substantial benefits at the point that treatment was terminated. But by the end of 4 years, it seemed that the couples

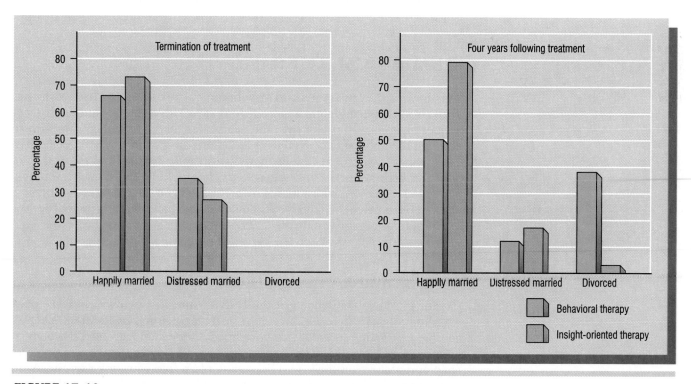

FIGURE 17–10
Percentages of happily married, distressed married, or divorced couples in behavioral and insight-oriented marital therapy conditions at termination and at 4-year follow-up.

who had received insight-oriented therapy were better off (38% of the couples in the behavior therapy group had divorced, compared with only 3% in the insight-oriented group).

Such studies on marital and family therapy are difficult to complete because of problems associated with staying in touch with the participants, expenses, and so forth. But they are essential to understanding the most critical aspects of effective treatment in an area of immense importance—keeping a family together.

Self-Help Therapy.   Perhaps the most rapidly expanding type of group therapy is the **self-help group**, as we noted in Chapter 15. Self-help groups are support groups without professionally trained leaders. In stark contrast to more traditional therapies, the self-help strategy is not designed to unravel mysteries or broach basic conflicts. Rather, the self-help setting hopes to increase understanding and facilitate acceptance by bringing together a group of people who may have common problems. Alcoholics Anonymous (AA) and other substance-abuse groups are familiar examples. Elsewhere, self-help groups have formed to discuss such diverse problems as loneliness, caring for physically handicapped children, and the stresses of being a single parent. Perhaps even more familiar in your community are the crisis-intervention centers and telephone hotlines that are staffed by volunteers who hope to help rape victims. Such groups provide confidential advice to persons who may have nowhere else to turn for help.

Bereavement is yet another area where self-help groups have provided needed support. A parent who suffers the terrible tragedy of losing a son or daughter may elicit a special type of compassion from someone who has experienced a similar loss. The problem, of course, is that in extremely stressful cases, as in the death of a loved one, the level of emotional disturbance may require professional intervention. Because of this, it has been suggested that professionals and self-help groups work within the framework of a team concept (Marmar et al., 1988).

self-help group sessions involving persons who share a common problem; no professional leader is present

BIOMEDICAL THERAPY

Our coverage of treatment of psychological disorders to this point has focused on psychological interventions (see Table 17-1), and such techniques have proved useful over the years. But there is another approach to treating mental disturbance that is tied more directly to physiology and biochemistry. In the next few sections we discuss biomedical therapies, in terms of both strengths and weaknesses. It should be noted that the procedures described in this section are performed only by physicians. Indeed, the use of some of the techniques covered here has been a principal source of division among many medical and psychological professionals who hold sharply conflicting views on the nature of psychological disorders.

Electroconvulsive Therapy (ECT)

Treatments involving shock to the body of one sort or another were used hundreds of years ago. We have discussed bloodletting. In addition to bloodletting, physicians surgically removed body organs and stressed the body in numerous other imaginative ways. Disease was even forced on people to help cure them. But these practices were often free-wheeling exercises with minimal control, thus involving considerable danger. A decisive giant step toward safe use of shock treatments was taken in 1933 at the University of Vienna when Sakel observed that insulin-induced hypoglycemic comas

TABLE 17-1
Summary of Psychotherapy

Therapy	Description	Advantages/Disadvantages
Psychoanalytic Therapy	Classical technique involves the analyst and client working intensively to gain insight into the nature of hidden conflicts. Modern psychoanalysis focuses more on meeting the patient's needs for personal growth.	Deep fundamental conflicts may be resolved, but treatment can be lengthy and expensive.
Behavior Therapy	Classical conditioning and instrumental learning techniques are employed to change disordered behavior.	Effective with less severe forms of disturbance, but in certain psychotic reactions medication is likely to be the preferred treatment.
Cognitive–Behavior Therapy	Cognitions, beliefs, and other mental operations are used in treatment to restructure thought processes.	Flexible and works well in some cases. Yet some clients seem unresponsive to this form of intervention.
Humanistic Therapy	The responsibility for behavior change is placed on the client; each person has the freedom of choice to define his or her own meaning and awareness.	Self-awareness and acceptance may be increased, although the goals of therapy are often vague, so it is difficult to monitor improvement.
Group Psychotherapy	Six to eight people are treated in a group; typically the therapist is responsible for controlling the direction of the session and maintaining focus.	People may speak out in a group, and a group situation is a closer approximation to reality. However, group situations can be emotionally charged and turn into vicious personal assaults.

improved the dispositions of psychotic patients (Carson, Butcher, & Coleman, 1992). The sudden drop in blood sugar and the coincident convulsions elicited by excessive insulin mysteriously decreased the episodes of thought disturbance among schizophrenics. The advantage of the insulin shock technique was that the degree of convulsive and seizure activity could be medically regulated.

Shortly after insulin shock treatments were introduced, Italian physicians Ugo Cerletti and Lucio Bini began experimenting with animals by using electrical currents instead of insulin to produce convulsions. In preliminary investigations, these researchers positioned electrodes in the mouth and anus of an animal and then administered an electric shock. This method produced the hoped-for brain seizure, but half the subjects died during the experiment. Reasoning that the current must be passing through the heart, and therefore causing cardiac arrest, Cerletti and Bini decided to apply the electrodes to the head. No animals died with this method, and yet the seizures were as pronounced as before (Kalinowsky, 1980). In April 1938, Cerletti and Bini applied their electrodes to a human, a schizophrenic patient. With repeated applications the patient showed marked improvement. Shortly thereafter the use of electrically induced brain seizures in

electroconvulsive therapy (ECT) use of electrically induced brain seizures to improve the disposition of severely disturbed patients

bilateral ECT simultaneous stimulation of both cerebral hemispheres during electroconvulsive therapy

mental health treatment was hailed as a breakthrough. Today, this technique is known as **electroconvulsive therapy (ECT)**.

Bilateral ECT.   The method of ECT treatment that is most commonly taught in psychiatric quarters is to attach electrodes to each side of the head (see Figure 17–11). This approach, which is known as **bilateral ECT**, involves the simultaneous stimulation of both cerebral hemispheres. Typically, an alternating electric current ranging from 70 to 120 volts is applied for about a half second to the temporal lobes (Kolb & Whishaw, 1990). During the course of treatment, which usually is 3 or 4 weeks, the patient receives ECT applications twice a week. Although muscle relaxants and tranquilizers are now used to control body convulsions and seizures, limited physical changes are unavoidable. Visually, you would expect to see the following pattern within a given ECT session: immediately upon stimulation, the patient's back arches; if the arms remain free of restraints, they may elevate sharply, and the slow rhythmic convulsions that begin in the upper extremities spread to the whole body. Because the muscles tighten, the patient might have difficulty breathing and may have to receive artificial respiration. The treatment session is over in just a few minutes, and the patient is moved to a comfortable area where she or he is monitored and allowed to recover.

Benefits of ECT.   Many students who are introduced to ECT have an initial repulsion to what on the surface appears to be a treatment only slightly in advance of barbarism. A great many professionals share this concern. Why, then, do we use ECT? Originally, a major factor favoring the use of ECT was economics. Physicians in public health care institutions were faced with more patients than they could treat (Beveridge & Renvoise, 1990). ECT offered a cheap, effective method for controlling patients' symptoms, in addition to putting them in a position to benefit from other forms of therapeutic intervention. Also, one must consider the fact that the treatment works, and in many instances it works when nothing else does (Rollin, 1990). In present-day treatment hospitals, ECT is often used when patients have not responded to other forms of therapy. There is no denying the results in terms of improving disposition and behavior. With such favorable therapeutic outcomes, it is not surprising that the number of ECT treatments has increased dramatically over the last decade.

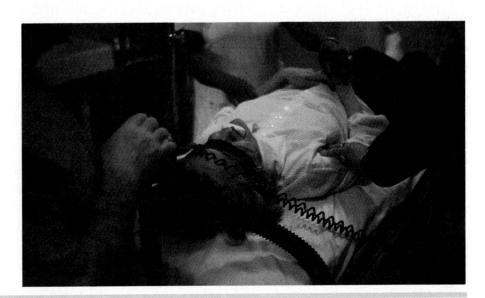

FIGURE 17–11
A patient undergoing bilateral electroconvulsive therapy may suffer side effects.

The development of new instruments and procedures that have permitted practitioners to transform unresponsive, withdrawn patients into receptive, interactive individuals who are more amenable to other forms of therapy has made ECT even more attractive as a treatment option. Precisely why such patient benefits occur is not fully understood. It has been suggested that ECT may produce changes in blood flow to the brain and therein alter cognitive functioning (Silfverskiold, Rosen, & Risberg, 1987), or that ECT sessions may cause a sudden release of endorphins (Misiasek et al., 1984). (Recall from Chapter 2 that endorphins are thought to decrease perceived pain and discomfort.)

Drawbacks of ECT.   With the acknowledged benefits of ECT come problems. Specifically, ECT can produce any of a long list of undesirable side effects (Breggin, 1979). Memory impairment seems to occur even with the standard number of treatments, and this effect seems to be cumulative, getting worse with each application (Kolb & Whishaw, 1990). Studies of ECT treatment performed on animals show that cell deaths occur in both the hippocampus and the amygdala following the electricity-induced seizures. These brain structures are involved in memory formation. Although this has not been reliably confirmed in humans that have had ECT, there is growing concern that the disorientation and memory impairment observed in older people may be caused by their repeated ECT applications. This alarm becomes even greater when considering that some patients have had as many as 100 ECT treatment sessions. Within the context of this discussion about memory disturbances that might be related to ECT, it is appropriate, if somewhat unsettling, to note that writer Ernest Hemingway suffered substantial memory loss during those long, fallow months before his suicide; he had received many ECT treatments for depression (refer to *How It Was* by Mary Welsh Hemingway, 1976).

Apart from possible memory side effects, treatment specialists have questioned the safety of ECT from a purely medical perspective. It is an established fact that very few psychiatry residency programs that teach medical doctors how to administer ECT actually provide formal training in anesthesia administration. Yet, in a recent survey of 100 psychiatrists using the technique, in almost 99% of the cases the psychiatrist, and not an anesthesiologist, gave the ECT patient the necessary anesthetic before electrical stimulation (Perlman, Loper, & Tillery, 1990). Although there have been few incidents to date, considerable disagreement exists in the medical community concerning the acceptability of psychiatrists functioning in a role for which they are poorly trained.

Finally, there is the lingering controversy over how best to apply the ECT electrical current. We have noted that the more common case involves bilateral electrode placement. By contrast, an increasingly popular alternative is **unilateral ECT**, in which electrodes are placed on just one side of the head, commonly the side of the nondominant hemisphere. The rationale underlying the unilateral method is that if the area of electrical impact is restricted, confusion and memory disturbance can be held to a minimum. A number of scientific studies have supported this view (Rosenberg & Pettenati, 1984; Squire & Slater, 1983). But experts have also observed that the treatment effectiveness of unilateral ECT is less than that associated with bilateral applications (Abrams et al., 1983). Thus, the therapist is presented with a procedural tightrope, where a balance between benefits and costs must be maintained.

unilateral ECT stimulation of only one cerebral hemisphere during electroconvulsive therapy

Psychosurgery

Psychosurgery is defined as "a destruction of some region of the brain in order to alleviate severe, and otherwise intractable, psychiatric disorders"

psychosurgery brain surgery that is designed to change the behavior of profoundly disturbed patients

(Valenstein, 1980). As we mentioned in our earlier discussion of trephining, the idea that brain surgery can alleviate behavior problems is a concept that dates back several thousand years. But it was only in the latter part of the nineteenth century that psychosurgery began to be performed in a systematic, scientific manner (Berrios, 1990). At that time, a number of British physicians surgically removed sections of the skull and extracted parts of the brain. The ultimate goal in those early surgeries was to relieve "pressure" on the CNS. Later, psychosurgery procedures were more directly aimed at lesioning (destroying) tissue that was associated with known behavioral patterns. In any event, this form of biomedical therapy has always been controversial. Although psychosurgery operations are no longer performed routinely, they are still recommended by some medical professionals.

Because it is often difficult to obtain precise records about specific surgeries, it is difficult to estimate exactly how many psychosurgeries are performed each year. Valenstein (1980) estimates that in the United States approximately 400 operations were performed in a 3-year period in the 1970s. A present-day figure would likely be substantially lower. The rate tends to be a bit higher in England, and somewhat lower in Canada (Kolb & Whishaw, 1990).

Part of the concern over the use of psychosurgery techniques stems from events that took place more than 50 years ago. Unhappily, many thousands of innocent patients were left disabled. This tragedy was given a strong assist, if unwittingly, by Walter Freeman and James Watts. On September 14, 1936, Freeman and Watts performed the first **prefrontal lobotomy** in the United States. The prefrontal lobotomy involves cutting major nerve pathways in the frontal lobes of the brain. One variation of this procedure is shown in Figure 17–12.

Despite the lack of information about the long-term side effects of the prefrontal lobotomy, tens of thousands of operations were performed on mental patients between the mid-1930s and 1955. Peak episodes involved as many as 50 surgeries a day at a single hospital. Although numerous reports testified

prefrontal lobotomy surgical procedure in which major pathways to the frontal brain region are cut

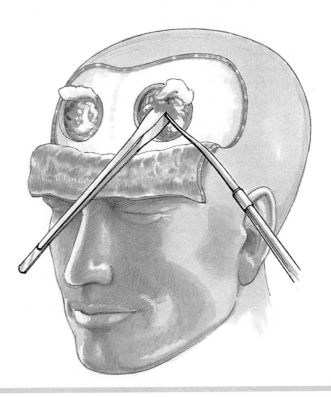

FIGURE 17–12
The "undercutting" version of the prefrontal lobotomy, introduced by William Scoville. The frontal lobes are forced upward by a spatula inserted through openings in the skull. Nerve pathways are then destroyed with a surgical instrument. (Adapted from Asenjo, 1963.)

to the early successes of lobotomy operations, most of these were based on sloppy, nonobjective casual observations that could not withstand scientific scrutiny. As the months and years passed, it gradually became clear that the lobotomy was not working—patients simply were not improving. In fact, there was growing evidence that lobotomies might even make patients' conditions worse. Eventually, the trickle of reports citing the negative behavioral effects produced by lobotomies became a flood. Postoperative patients were described as vegetative, indifferent, and without a desire to do anything or to try something new. The frequency of psychotic displays had been reduced, but many times at the expense of the whole person.

The bitter memories of the prefrontal lobotomy tragedy have caused many professionals to argue vigorously against the use of psychosurgery. In his 1986 book *Great and Desperate Cures: The Rise and Decline of Psychosurgery and Other Radical Treatments for Mental Illness*, Elliot Valenstein acknowledges the frailty of the scientific foundation on which the case for psychosurgery is built. Inappropriate control procedures and outright misrepresentation of facts have called into question the validity of psychosurgery techniques (Carlson, 1991). In addition, recent evidence indicates that even when psychosurgical operations are effective in terms of reducing one set of symptoms, a raft of new disordered behaviors often emerge. For instance, when the temporal lobe of the brain is removed in an attempt to control epilepsy, the result is often the development of a schizophrenia-like psychosis (Roberts, Done, & Crow, 1990).

However, there are benefits to psychosurgery, such as for cases in which there appears to be no alternative. Take the case of a 19-year-old male who was suffering from *Tourette syndrome*, as reported by Robertson, Doran, Trimble, and Lees (1990). In the early stages of the disorder, a person has multiple tics and twitches, then begins to yell word sounds that make little or no sense. In the progressive stages of the disorder, the person yells obscenities. Robertson and colleagues report in their case history that their patient's Tourette reactions were so strong that they could not be controlled by medication. The decision was made to cut nerve tracks in the limbic region of the brain, with favorable results. The patient's abusive behavior decreased, as did the frequency of his tics.

The status of psychosurgery has also benefited from advances in surgical equipment and the careful refinement of surgical techniques. For example, with the aid of MRI techniques (see Chapter 2), Mindus and associates (1987) used radiation to produce very precise brain lesions that resulted in positive outcomes. Still, ethical problems remain because psychosurgery techniques destroy brain cells that cannot regenerate, so the effects are irreversible. Accordingly, many physicians and most psychologists continue to criticize such operations.

Chemotherapy

Using drugs to treat psychological disorders is a less controversial form of biomedical therapy than either ECT or psychosurgery. In the last several years there have been major changes in the ways that drugs are used to help the mentally ill. When medicines were first prescribed for patients, the goal was to give immediate relief from symptoms. Tranquilizers were given to anxious patients to alleviate nervous discomfort, and stimulants were administered to depressed individuals to get them going again. The ultimate purpose was to use drugs to improve the emotional status of the individual so that he or she would be more amenable to conversations with a psychiatrist or clinical psychologist. Now, the objective of drug treatment, or **chemotherapy** as it is more commonly called, is to treat the symptoms of the disorder directly.

chemotherapy use of chemicals in the form of medicinal drugs to alleviate symptoms of behavioral disorders

chlorpromazine one of the first antipsychotic drugs used to treat severely disturbed patients

One of the first successful uses of medication to combat mental illness, rather than just to control it, was reported in 1952. Two French psychiatrists, Jean Delay and Pierre Deniker, showed that a drug called **chlorpromazine** was effective in treating the symptoms of a psychotic patient. Successive treatments of 10 more patients were equally dramatic, and the special psychological action of the drug was soon realized. The French psychiatrists proposed the term *neuroleptics* for the newly discovered class of drugs that included chlorpromazine and similar compounds.

psychotropic drugs chemicals that are known to produce pronounced changes in emotion, behavior, and other psychological phenomena

Shortly after the advances made with neuroleptics, other therapeutic chemicals began to emerge, especially those designed for use with anxiety disorders. Eventually, drug researchers discovered dozens of chemicals that could be used safely and efficiently in the treatment of mental illness. Collectively, these chemicals are called **psychotropic drugs** because their impact focuses on the psychological makeup of the individual (see Table 17–2 for a list of some of the more commonly prescribed psychotropic drugs). We will discuss four types of chemicals that are currently used in chemotherapy: (*a*) the antipsychotic compounds, (*b*) the antianxiety compounds, (*c*) the antidepressants, and (*d*) the metallic agent lithium, considered by some to be a miracle drug for the treatment of mood disturbances involving manic symptoms.

antipsychotics class of drugs that are used in the treatment of different forms of psychosis

Antipsychotic Compounds. As previously indicated, the term *neuroleptic* has been used to refer to the class of drugs used in treating psychotic reactions. But this term, which means "clasping the neuron," is a term used more often in Europe than North America. In North America, these drugs are known as **antipsychotics**.

TABLE 17-2
Common Psychotropic Drugs

Generic Name	Some Trade Names	Type of Disorder Treated
Antipsychotic Compounds		
Chlorpromazine	Thorazine	Used to treat psychotic disorders involving such symptoms as extreme delusions and hallucinations
Haloperidol	Haldol	
Molindone	Moban	
Thioridazine	Mellaril	
Thiothixene	Navane	
Antianxiety Compounds		
Alprazolam	Xanax	Used with nonpsychotic cases in which symptoms include moderate tenseness and anxiety
Chlordiazepoxide	Librium	
Diazepam	Valium	
Meprobamate	Miltown	
Antidepressant Compounds		
Amitriptyline	Elavil	Used primarily with severe cases of unipolar depression
Imipramine	Presamine	
	Tofranil	
Phenelzine	Nardil	
Antimania (Bipolar) Compounds		
Lithium carbonate	Lithane	Used commonly with bipolar affective cases; especially useful for extreme manic symptoms
	Lithotabs	

The antipsychotics are usually divided into **phenothiazines** and **nonphenothiazines** (McKim, 1991). Chlorpromazine, marketed under the trade name Thorazine or Largactil, is the most commonly prescribed phenothiazine drug. Another common phenothiazine is thioridazine (Mellaril), and like chlorpromazine, it has been used successfully to treat schizophrenia. Haloperidol (Haldol) is the most commonly administered nonphenothiazine drug. In most cases these drugs are taken orally, but they occasionally will be given in the form of a *depot* (slow-dissolving) injection. The latter method is used only when agitated schizophrenic patients cannot be relied upon to take their medication.

Regardless of classification, all antipsychotic compounds have the same neurochemical effect: they block dopamine receptors (Carlson, 1991). In Chapter 16, we discussed the dopamine hypothesis of schizophrenia, noting that levels of this transmitter are exceptionally high in schizophrenic patients. It now appears that the antipsychotics help such patients by blocking a particular type of dopamine receptor called a D_2 receptor (Horger, et al., 1991). In effect, the drug brings dopamine activity back into a normal range. As Figure 17–13 shows, there is a strong relationship between the potency of various antipsychotics and how strongly they interfere with dopamine transmission.

Many new antipsychotic compounds are now available in addition to the phenothiazines, but there is no clear indication that they are improvements over the old drugs. New and old antipsychotic medications share certain benefits and risks. The benefits are obvious—reduction and control of psychotic symptoms. The risks are more insidious and usually are evident only after prolonged use of the drugs (Kimble, 1988). But the risks are real, and in some cases the consequences can be severe motor impairment or, depending on the age of the patient, even worse.

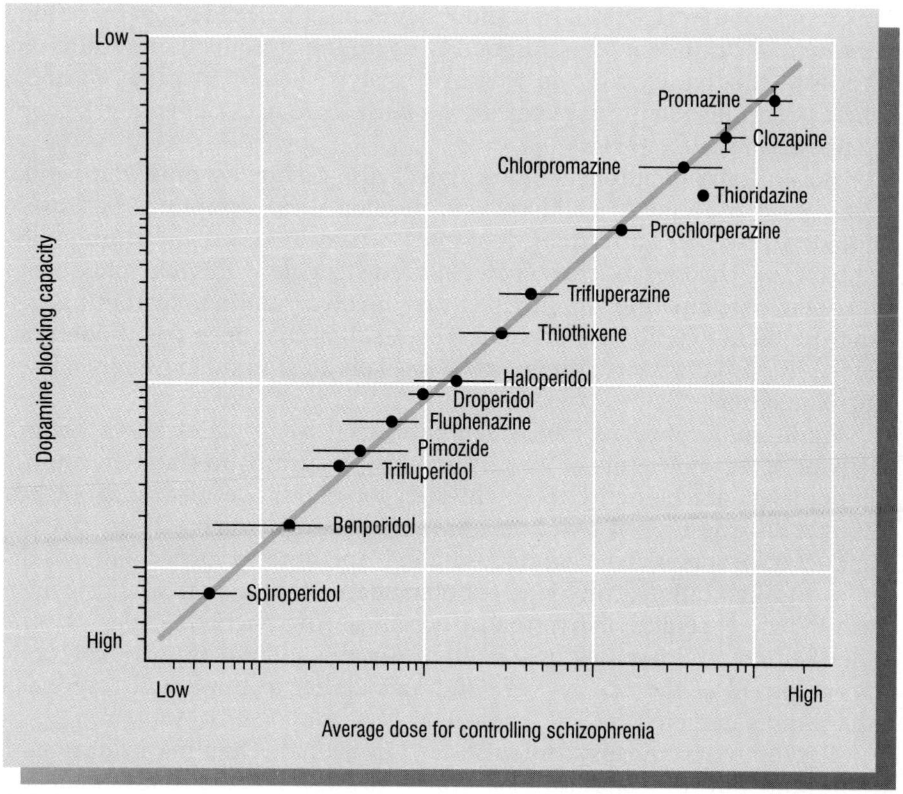

phenothiazines one of the major divisions of antipsychotic compounds that includes such chemicals as chlorpromazine and thioridazine

nonphenothiazines one of the major divisions of antipsychotic compounds that includes haloperidol

FIGURE 17–13
Relation between dopamine blocking and the therapeutic effectiveness of various antipsychotic drugs: the greater the blocking capacity of the drug, the more effective (the lower the required dose of) the drug. (Adapted from McKim, 1991.)

tardive dyskinesia side effect of chronic application of antipsychotic medication; characterized by uncontrollable jerking

For many years, treatment specialists have been aware of the disturbing side effects associated with the recurrent use of antipsychotic medications. The most thoroughly documented effect associated with the long-term use of antipsychotic agents such as phenothiazines and butyrophenones is a disorder known as **tardive dyskinesia**. The term comes from the French and Greek, and means "late-appearing, abnormal movements." A conservative estimate is that about 25% of all adults who take antipsychotic drugs over a period of months and years will eventually develop tardive dyskinesia. The disorder causes excessive movements, especially of the face and tongue. The result can be gross disfigurement, and the individual even has trouble eating. As the condition develops, the individual's entire body is affected, and he or she will eventually begin to jerk and writhe uncontrollably, even when asleep.

Tardive dyskinesia is more likely to occur in females than males, and is very difficult to treat. Decreasing or stopping drug treatment may not be the solution, for two reasons. First, the condition for which the drug was prescribed remains, and, second, stopping drug use does not always reduce the symptoms of tardive dyskinesia. Recently the picture has become even more complicated.

A team of psychologists headed by Mary Ann Richardson in New York has determined that as many as one third of all the children and adolescents treated with antipsychotic medication develop symptoms of Parkinsonism (see our discussion of this disorder in Chapter 2). This figure contrasts sharply with the development of tardive dyskinesia in this age range, for which only one in eight children show symptoms. It would appear that long-term use of antipsychotic compounds has different effects on adults and children; tardive dyskinesia is more likely to occur in older patients, whereas Parkinsonian symptoms are more likely to occur in younger people (Richardson et al., 1991).

Because the symptoms of Parkinson's disease involve muscular rigidity and slowed movement, children who develop these symptoms because of repeated antipsychotic drug treatments may take on a "zombie"-like appearance. Understandably, such children struggle with their schoolwork, and their participation in activities that involve running, swimming, and other physical exertion is curtailed. The result is that once the children are placed in outpatient programs, they are likely to stop taking their medication altogether.

Additional concerns have been expressed by psychiatrist C. Thomas Gaultier of the University of North Carolina. According to Gaultier, antipsychotic drugs are being given to children for childhood disorders, such as conduct disorders, even when they have no legitimate medical use. Because conduct disorders involve fighting, stealing, and other behavior patterns disruptive to institutional life, it is understandable that a staff would want to curb the violence and aggression by administering phenothiazines or some other form of antipsychotic medication. But this intervention is likely to be accomplished at the expense of children's ability to think and respond to other events in their lives.

Psychiatrists and psychologists are in a bind. Quelling symptoms is important, but how should it be done? Whatever the ultimate decision, recent findings, such as those cited here, underscore the need to look carefully at treatments across different age ranges. Apparently, chemotherapy affects neural pathways differently at different developmental stages.

Consider the importance of such findings for other select populations. Is it possible that men and women may respond differently to the same medication? What about the issue of ethnic and cultural diversity? We know that separate cultures respond in dramatically different ways to psychotherapy. Is it possible that reactions to chemotherapy may be similarly diverse?

Antianxiety Compounds.   The **antianxiety compounds**, also known as the minor tranquilizers, have two distinguishing features in addition to their anxiolytic effect (their ability to reduce anxiety). First, all of the antianxiety agents are also muscle relaxants; second, they are all anticonvulsant to some degree. Although reduced anxiety and fewer convulsions are desirable, sometimes the effect on muscle groups is so strong that it causes weakness, or even temporary paralysis.

Barbiturates and meprobamate compounds (such as Miltown and Equanil) were used for years to keep anxiety levels low, but the most popular antianxiety drugs today are the **benzodiazepines**. In 1963 diazepam (Valium) was first marketed as medication for anxiety. This marked the most significant shift toward the use of benzodiazepine treatment. Today, alprazolam (Xanax) is the most commonly prescribed benzodiazepine.

All the benzodiazepines appear to affect the same neural mechanism. In the human nervous system, chemicals that stimulate the movement of chloride ions inside the neural cell make it more difficult to excite the cell. This is how the inhibitory neurotransmitter GABA, discussed in Chapter 2, works to slow the rate of neural transmission. When GABA molecules bind to receptors on a postsynaptic nerve cell, chloride particles rush inside the cell, and consequently the neuron does not send an impulse that otherwise might be sent. The benzodiazepines function to increase the capacity of GABA to promote chloride influx. For instance, when Xanax is in the system, GABA activity increases and nervous excitement decreases. This produces the experience of relief and a sort of mellowness, and frees the person from the throes of anxiety.

No one contests the anxiety-reducing properties of chemicals such as Valium and Xanax. They are effective in alleviating everything from test anxiety to severe emotional stress that accompanies the loss of a loved one. The problem with the benzodiazepines is not their use, but their abuse. As a society we are conditioned to reach for a pill at the first sign of discomfort: you have a mild headache, take aspirin; you have a sinus condition, take an antihistamine; you are feeling a bit unhinged, pop a Valium. The point is that we may be too reliant on chemical control of our emotions, and such an approach to coping can backfire for a couple of reasons. First, a psychological dependence on antianxiety drugs can occur when they are used too often and in too great amounts (Carson, Butcher, & Coleman, 1992). A second, perhaps more debilitating factor is that treatment for the true source of the anxiety is delayed. Valium and other antianxiety agents may help a person through difficult times, but their chronic use is probably not in the best interest of the anxious individual.

Antidepressant Compounds.   Everyone from time to time feels a little down, and it is not even unusual to suffer periodic bouts of depression. But, as we discussed in Chapter 16, enduring negative mood states can be debilitating and can ravage the will to live. When acute depressions become life

antianxiety compounds general class of chemicals that are designed to decrease the level of stress an individual feels

barbiturates antianxiety agents that include the drug Miltown

benzodiazepines antianxiety drugs that relieve anxiety by enhancing GABA transmission

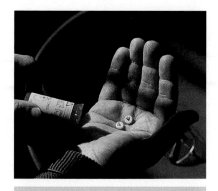

This person is about to take Valium before going to bed. Although it may be helpful in many cases, such tranquilizers are often used excessively.

threatening, the therapist must intervene at once and act quickly to elevate the patient's mood. A variety of treatments may be effective in reversing depressive symptoms in the long run, but suicidal feelings need immediate attention. Antidepressants cannot lift spirits overnight, but they can elevate mood within a matter of 1 or 2 weeks, and sometimes this can mean the difference between life and death.

Antidepressants have traditionally fallen into one of two classes. There are the **tricyclic antidepressants**, such as amitriptyline (Elavil) and imipramine (Tofranil), as well as the **monoamine oxidase (MAO) inhibitors**, such as phenelzine (Nardil). These chemicals are often used today instead of ECT. Although they do produce changes in heart rate, blood pressure, and body weight, on the whole they are safe and effective (Fernström, Krowinski, & Kupfer, 1987). Historically, the tricyclics appeared first on the pharmaceutical market, with the initial therapeutic application occurring in Switzerland in 1957 (Kalinowsky, Hippius, & Klein, 1982).

The tricyclic antidepressants and MAO inhibitors accomplish the same thing in the body, but via different mechanisms. Both types of chemicals cause certain types of neurotransmitters to remain in the synaptic cleft longer, thus enhancing neural transmission. The tricyclics accomplish this the same way cocaine does: they block transmitter reuptake (see Chapter 5). The MAO inhibitors do not disturb reuptake patterns, but they do reduce MAO, the enzyme that breaks down several different neurotransmitters (McKim, 1991). In both cases, depression is countered by chemically induced activation of the CNS.

As noted earlier, the *traditional* classification of antidepressants has been restricted to tricyclics or MAO inhibitors. More recently, however, a third kind of antidepressant has appeared that does not technically conform to either class. As we shall see, this new type of medication has created quite a debate.

tricyclic antidepressants general class of drugs that are designed to elevate mood; work by blocking the reuptake of different neurotransmitters

monoamine oxidase (MAO) inhibitors general class of drugs that are designed to elevate mood; work by inhibiting an enzyme that breaks down different neurotransmitters

---

SPOTLIGHT ON RESEARCH
To Use or Not to Use Prozac?

Prozac antidepressant that blocks the reuptake of the neurotransmitter serotonin; controversial because it may cause violence and promote suicide

Prozac (florextine hydrochloride) is an antidepressant that is chemically different from the other antidepressant medications. Unlike the tricyclics and MAO inhibitors, which work on several different transmitter systems, Prozac selectively acts on the serotonin system to block the reuptake of this neurotransmitter from the synaptic cleft.

Prozac was introduced in December 1987 (Cowley et al., 1990). The popularity of the drug is evident from the fact that its U.S. sales topped $350 million in 1989, which is more than the amount spent on *all* antidepressants only 2 years earlier. By some estimates, sales of Prozac should exceed $1 billion by the middle of this decade.

Why the enormous popularity? Clearly, the press accounts of the effectiveness of Prozac helped promote the use of the drug. *New York Magazine* hailed Prozac as a "wonder drug," and a *Newsweek* article called it a "breakthrough." Most of the reasons for recommending the use of Prozac have been based on a legitimate decrease in the side effects that occur with other antidepressant medicines. And, as a rule, Prozac is safer to administer than other forms of medication that can be toxic when the dose is too high (Cowley et al., 1990).

Given this positive profile, one might expect that there would be minimal controversy regarding the use of Prozac. But the opposite is true. Prozac is one of the most publicly debated drugs placed on the market.

Much of the clamor over the use of the drug has come from unscientific claims that the drug triggers obsessive and suicidal behavior (Burton, 1991). Some quasi-religious groups such as the Scientologists have even called it a "killer drug." Although there is some empirical evidence that suicide attempts are linked to disturbances in serotonin transmission (Ricci & Wellman, 1990), there appears to be minimal, statistically reliable evidence that Prozac increases the risk of violent misconduct or suicide.

Despite the meager scientific evidence linking suicidal thoughts and Prozac, some clinicians do report that they have seen evidence that their depressed clients seem more preoccupied with suicidal thoughts. For example, Teicher and his psychiatric colleagues have presented six case histories in which Prozac treatment did make the suicidal thoughts of their depressed patients more intense (Teicher, Glod, & Cole, 1990). But as Chouinard (1991) notes, such reports have been flawed by the fact that the patients were already suicidal, and on other medicines that may have chemically interfered with the medicinal advantages of Prozac.

This important debate will certainly continue. Considering the incidence of depression, it is a debate that must yield solid, useful evidence, one way or the other.

What is your opinion on the matter? Is Prozac a dangerous drug? Should a patient be given a choice between Prozac and some other drug, or is this the responsibility of the clinician? Most important, would you take Prozac if it were prescribed?

Apart from the Prozac issue, basing the effectiveness of antidepressant drugs on a neurochemical rationale provides a logical framework for understanding how antidepressant drugs elevate mood and increase psychomotor performance, but there remains the sticky issue of *therapeutic lag*. That is, the changes in enzyme activity and transmitter availability occur within minutes after taking medication. But as we mentioned previously, the benefits of antidepressants are not realized for a week or more. Why? What is causing the delay? Scientists have been unable to answer this important question, and until a satisfactory account of therapeutic lag is available, alternative models for the impact of antidepressant drugs must be explored (Cooper, Bloom, & Roth, 1986).

Lithium. **Lithium** is an alkali metal that is administered therapeutically in the form of lithium carbonate. The usefulness of the drug in treating mood disturbances was discovered by accident. The Australian researcher John Cade administered the chemical to rats in the 1940s as a buffer against another chemical he was testing. He noticed that lithium made the animals calm down, so he tried it with some manic patients and the result was astounding. Patients who had been resistant to treatment improved markedly. It took several decades for the treatment to be adopted worldwide, but today lithium carbonate treatment is proclaimed to be a very desirable form of therapy for reducing the symptoms of bipolar affective disorders (see Chapter 16).

lithium metal that is used for medical purposes to treat mood disorders, most notably mania

Lithium does alleviate depression in some bipolar patients, but it is generally more effective in preventing manic episodes than depressive episodes. For this reason lithium is sometimes referred to as "the mania drug." At the same time, significant therapeutic benefits are obtained with manic patients in only about 75% of cases (Prien, 1980). People exhibiting manic symptoms who do not respond to lithium are typically treated by methods other than chemotherapy, because alternative drugs are not likely to work either.

Although lithium treatments for disorders other than mania have not produced consistently positive results, on occasion the drug has been useful in treating both schizophrenia and alcoholism. At least for younger patients, lithium has also been shown to reduce aggression and combative behavior (Barklage & Jefferson, 1987).

In recent years, a growing number of therapists have questioned the wisdom of administering lithium, despite its demonstrated ability to control manic phases of most patients' disorders. For one thing, how lithium works, biochemically speaking, is not fully understood. And as the history of biomedical therapy shows, when bodily interventions are conducted in the dark, tragedies can occur. Too, there is the issue of lithium poisoning with long-term use (Decina, Schlegel, & Fieve, 1987). Hands and feet may swell, tremors may occur, and sexual performance may decline. Because of such disturbances, lithium treatments must be monitored carefully.

EVALUATION OF TREATMENT STRATEGIES

We have devoted a substantial amount of space in this chapter to therapy techniques. By now it should be clear that both psychotherapy and biomedical (see Table 17–3) treatment packages for helping people with psychological disorders are many in number and varied in format. We now return to the question: Does therapy produce real benefits?

Effectiveness of Treatment

The argument about the real value of psychological therapies was initially fueled by a report filed by Hans Eysenck (1952). At the time, it was considered impudent even to challenge the efficacy of treatment, and practitioners quickly rose to defend their successful records, citing numerous case histories in which "cures" were achieved. But Eysenck's astonishing review of over 7,000 cases called into question the true reasons for these improvements. The quarrel was not so much with the notion that people improved under treatment; rather, it was argued that the treatment process was unrelated to recovery. The client would have progressed anyway, without therapy. Offering evidence to support his claims, Eysenck showed that the number of improved persons found among those waiting to receive treatment matched the figures reported for persons actually treated.

Even though Eysenck probably overstated his case and underestimated the value of therapy, his position has had a positive effect nonetheless. The alarm Eysenck set off has stimulated more research on the effectiveness of therapy. One of the more often referenced studies reporting findings favorable to adult treatment intervention is a report by Smith and Glass (1977). In an ambitious project that transformed the data from 375 studies of the effectiveness of psychotherapy to a common metric, substantial improvements were noted for all methods of treatment other than Gestalt training (see Figure 17–14). The fact that Gestalt therapy produced somewhat less positive results than other therapies may derive more from the difficulty associated with identifying genuine change than from the fact that such change failed to occur. In other words, the goals of Gestalt therapy are so poorly delineated that routine scientific analysis sometimes cannot detect successful intervention (Rowe, 1980). At any rate, other programs of therapy reviewed by Smith and Glass produced results that showed that the average treated person was better off than 75% of the untreated people.

TABLE 17-3
Summary of Biomedical Therapy

Therapy	Description	Advantages/Disadvantages
Electroconvulsive Therapy	Brain seizures are produced by electrical stimulation.	Severe depression lifts, thereby rendering the patient more responsive to other forms of therapy. However, memory loss and neurological damage may occur.
Psychosurgery	Brain tissue is surgically destroyed.	Behavioral improvements may occur, but the brain cells that are destroyed do not regenerate, so the effects are irreversible.
Chemotherapy	Chemicals (drugs) are administered.	Antipsychotic compounds, antianxiety compounds, antidepressant compounds, and lithium have all been shown to be effective in treating disordered behavior. However, negative side effects (e.g., muscle spasms, swelling, disturbance in sexual behavior) may occur. Also, the mechanisms underlying drug treatments are not fully understood.

Another report on the effectiveness of psychotherapy with adult patients shows that the success of treatment occurs much faster than previously expected (Howard et al., 1986). As shown in Figure 17–15 on page 718, approximately 50% of the clients were measurably improved by the end of 8 sessions. And, about 75% of the clients improved by the end of a 6-month period (26 sessions at 1 session per week). These figures, based on comparisons with nontreated controls, reflect a shift in emphasis in modern psychotherapy. The expensive, long-term treatments that were common years ago are being replaced with brief, more efficient techniques. Indeed, there is evidence that some forms of extended therapy may even harm clients

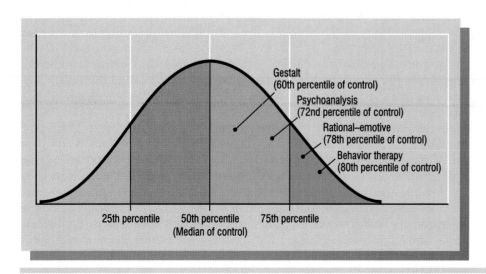

Gestalt
(60th percentile of control)
Psychoanalysis
(72nd percentile of control)
Rational–emotive
(78th percentile of control)
Behavior therapy
(80th percentile of control)

25th percentile   50th percentile   75th percentile
(Median of control)

FIGURE 17-14
A summary of 375 studies (primarily involving adult patients) of the effects of psychotherapy relative to nontreated controls. The median status (midpoint) of populations of treated patients is plotted against the population of controls. When a treatment median falls at a percentile above the control median (50th percentile), a positive treatment effect is indicated. (Adapted from Smith & Glass, 1977.)

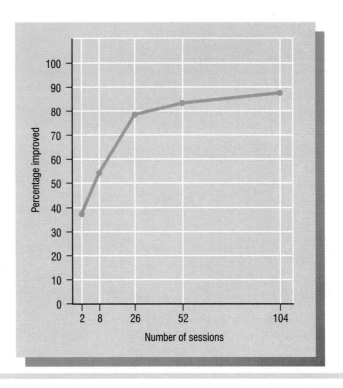

FIGURE 17–15
Relationship between number of sessions of psychotherapy and percentage of patients improved. (Adapted from Howard et al., 1986.)

(Lambert, Shapiro, & Bergin, 1986). Consequently, greater attention is focused on quick results in today's treatment of adult psychological disorders.

Psychotherapy also seems to benefit children who have psychological problems. Casey and Berman (1985) examined 75 studies in which disturbed children treated with different forms of psychotherapy were compared with similar children who were not treated. Once again, the positive effects of treatment were observed with virtually all forms of psychotherapy. Because some psychologists have argued that developmental factors (cognitive and intellectual limitations) may hinder the effectiveness of treatment with children, the report by Casey and Berman is especially significant.

Therapist Variables in Treatment

One factor that is often overlooked in the research on treatment evaluation is the characteristics of the therapist. Does interactive style affect the success of treatment? What about the age and gender of the therapist? Is the socioeconomic background of the therapist likely to influence the effectiveness of the treatment?

A comprehensive review of therapist variables in treatment indicates that although the effects are usually weak, attributes of the therapist actually do affect the therapeutic process (Beutler, Crago, & Arizmendi, 1986). For example, evidence exists that clients feel more satisfied at the end of treatment when they are of the same gender as their therapist. Moreover, improvement is likely to occur more rapidly when the therapist and client are of the same sex. Even the posture and dress of the therapist can make a difference. In some cases formal therapist attire and demeanor work better; however, in other cases informal dress and a relaxed atmosphere are likely to be more effective. Because client preferences probably determine the direction of difference along these lines, it is impossible to say beforehand which approach is better. But it is clear that therapist characteristics must be considered when one attempts to match the client and treatment suitably.

Client Variables in Treatment

Additional evaluation questions relate to the appropriateness of given therapies for specific types of disorders and for selected individuals. Which treatments are most useful with which cases? Are there certain people who are more likely to benefit from one form of therapy than others?

As shown in Figure 17–14, on an overall basis there are only slight differences among therapies regarding treatment effectiveness. Yet, when you examine the results in greater detail, a different picture emerges. It now seems clear that psychotherapies are most effective when the disorder involves less severe psychopathology. For example, certain types of anxiety reactions and some forms of nonpsychotic depression are perhaps best treated by behavioral techniques (Garfield, 1986; Tyrer et al., 1988). And, as we observed previously, insight-oriented therapy is especially effective in treating moderate marital problems (Snyder et al., 1991). But in cases of more extreme disturbance, such as schizophrenia or bipolar affective disorders (Fink, 1988), the patients may be more responsive to biomedical therapies (chemotherapy, ECT). This is not to say, of course, that psychotherapy is inappropriate for all psychotic cases, nor should chemical intervention be overlooked as a viable technique for controlling anxiety. However, recognizable trends can and should be used in planning treatment.

Cultural Background of the Client.   In addition to being sensitive to matching therapies to particular disorders, mental health service providers must be sensitive to the role of culture and cultural techniques in therapy. Several years ago Stanley Sue of the University of California, Los Angeles, studied more than 14,000 clients in 17 community health centers and discovered some alarming statistics. About half the ethnic-minority clients had dropped out of treatment prematurely, compared to only 30% for whites. On closer inspection, it became apparent that part of the reason for this difference was the stereotypes the predominantly white therapists had about the different racial groups. Because the therapists were ignorant of the traditions and values of diverse cultural groups, they were unable to use this information as an effective therapeutic tool.

More recently, it has been shown that matching racial and ethnic backgrounds of the client and therapist can improve therapeutic success rates (Sue & Zane, 1987). People tend to respond more openly and discuss their problems when they feel that the therapist has a genuine understanding of the world they live in and the unique pressures they face. Consequently, recommendations for contemporary training programs include (a) the inclusion of more ethnic therapists who are bilingual, (b) more training for all therapists about the specific traits and values of diverse cultures, and (c) the modification of traditional forms of therapy because they are validated on whites. With a greater awareness of the needs and desires of diverse cultural populations, more effective therapies can be developed and serve *all* people.

Other Client Variables.   Regardless of the particular strategy selected for treatment, as a general rule the client's response to the intervention will probably depend on how long she or he has had the disorder. Specifically, when a disorder develops slowly, the chances the client will improve rapidly are not likely to be as great as they would be had the disorder developed quickly. Also, how old the client was when he or she first developed the disorder can be an important factor in determining treatment success. For example, it has been shown that when mania develops in an adult, the chances for a fast recovery are better than they are when the disorder begins during adolescence (McGlashan, 1988).

Other findings show that treatment is sometimes more effective at home or when it is conducted by several different therapists. All of this accents the complex nature of treating behavioral disorders. In light of this fact, it is not surprising that 30–40% of all therapists in the United States identify themselves as *eclectic* (Goldfried, Greenberg, & Marmar, 1990). The eclectic approach to treatment uses whichever strategy works. There is no philosophical commitment to any one technique.

Whatever the treatment style or format, the important point to be made here is that therapy is worthwhile. Psychological problems can be dealt with effectively, and suffering can be reduced. Earlier in this chapter, we discussed the disinclination to seek treatment on the part of people in need of help. Our hope is that we have communicated the importance and value of intervention, and encouraged a more active role in assisting those who want to get better.

THINKING AHEAD . . .

Even before written records of history were made available on the social and behavioral evolution of humankind, evidence of the need for treating psychological disorders was left for posterity. As we have seen in this chapter, early methods of treatment were necessarily crude, and reflected the ignorance of a primitive ancestry. Chipping holes in people's heads or tormenting them with confinement or physical insults can hardly be viewed as helpful. How far removed are some of today's intervention strategies from such barbarous applications? As suggested previously, is it really in the best interest of patients to send electrical currents through their brains, thereby inducing seizures that have unknown consequences? Or, is it helpful to remove selective brain regions with sophisticated technical surgical tools? Even though improved behavior may result, can this legitimately be marketed as *therapy*? Also worth consideration is the immense uncertainty associated with introducing chemicals in the form of drug therapy, which, on an individual basis, may cause side effects more disturbing than the affliction. What are we doing? Where are we headed?

These questions are very much on the minds of treatment specialists throughout the world. No one enjoys causing discomfort to a patient, even if the long-term gains justify the use of an invasive procedure. No one feels good about recommending a drug when its full range of bio-chemical changes are not understood. But there simply may be no alternatives. You either employ the existing technology, or let the patient suffer and ride out a disorder until an acceptable treatment comes along.

Implicit in this chapter is the belief that treatment of psychological disorders will advance over time, in the same fashion that treatment of purely biological disorders improves through research and discovery. What can we expect? Certainly we can anticipate the availability of more sophisticated chemotherapy applications. But, ultimately, is this an answer? Are we just buying time, or are we really producing enduring behavior changes? What of the psychotherapeutic interventions? Will elements of the models of today be recognizable in the treatment packages of tomorrow? More important, as our ability to change the biology of the organism increases, will nonmedical forms of therapy even exist? If we adopt a purely medical or biochemical approach to treating behavior disorders, what must we forfeit in terms of human compassion, sensitivity, and warmth?

Psychological disturbances are not going away. We can work to control them, but we cannot eliminate them. The task for all of us will be to define a treatment agenda that is suitable for the patient and yet does not compromise a most precious human quality—caring.

Summary

Seeking Therapy

1. Because of certain myths surrounding psychological illness, and because many prospective clients are unaware of how to go about seeking treatment, less than half of those persons in the United States who need treatment ever receive it.

Historical Attempts at Treatment

2. Historically, psychological disorders were viewed as being due to demonic possession. During the Middle Ages, many innocent women were burned at the stake as witches, under the authority of the church. It was Philippe Pinel, in a 1792 experiment in France, who was one of the first to introduce humane treatment for those suffering from mental disorders.

Present-Day Treatment

3. Today, the emphasis in the mental health field is on prevention and deinstitutionalization. Efforts are being made to detect early warning signs and to treat more people in the community. The growing number of homeless people is a major concern in present-day treatment, inasmuch as many of these people are suffering from psychological disorders.

Psychotherapy

4. Psychotherapy uses noninvasive techniques to alter an individual's thinking and behavior. Along with changes in behavior, changes in one's perceptions of self-worth and meaningfulness are the goals of therapy.

5. Psychoanalytic therapy is a form of psychotherapy that was originated by Sigmund Freud. Treatment is based on helping the client gain insight by overcoming forces of resistance. Common psychoanalytic tools include free association, dream interpretation, and transference. Modern psychoanalytic techniques focus less on fundamental conflicts and more on meeting individual needs for personal growth.

6. Behavior therapy involves the systematic use of learning principles to bring about improvement in functioning. Some important behavioral techniques are systematic desensitization, implosion, flooding, and aversion therapy; all of these are linked in some way to classical conditioning. Instrumental techniques that focus on response outcomes are also used to treat mental disorders.

7. Cognitive–behavior therapy incorporates cognitions, beliefs, and other mental operations into the treatment regimen. Included in the list of cognitive models discussed were rational–emotive therapy (RET), stress–inoculation therapy, and cognitive therapy.

8. Client-centered therapy is a form of humanistic treatment that lets the individual, rather than the therapist, direct the treatment process. Fundamental to this intervention strategy is the notion of unconditional positive regard, which represents an attitude of total acceptance on the part of the therapist. Other humanistic techniques are existential analysis and Gestalt therapy.

9. The self-help group therapeutic environment has the advantage of being economical, and some people are more open in group situations. Family therapy is another example of a group treatment approach that has produced benefits. Marital therapy is a special case of family therapy that focuses on treating couples. Recent evidence indicates that insight-oriented therapy is especially successful in producing long-term benefits for couples experiencing marital problems. Self-help groups that lack professionally trained leaders also have produced positive results in narrowly defined areas where a specific type of support is needed. Occasionally, as in peer group therapy, a team concept is used where the self-help group operates with a professional as a consultant.

Biomedical Therapy

10. Biomedical therapies produce physical changes in the body. Electroconvulsive therapy (ECT) is a biomedical treatment that uses electric shock to treat depression. Another perhaps more controversial approach involves psychosurgery, in which certain brain regions are destroyed in order to improve the patient's disposition. A third form of biomedical therapy, chemotherapy, uses drugs to treat mental disorders. The four types of chemicals mentioned were the antipsychotic compounds, the antianxiety compounds, the antidepressants, and lithium. Prolonged use of some drugs may result in severe side effects, such as tardive dyskinesia.

Evaluation of Treatment Strategies

11. Overall, we conclude that treatment interventions can help people recover from psychological disorders. With regard to identifying a treatment most likely to be effective, it is important to consider the nature of the disorder as well as therapist and client characteristics. Also, the time of onset of the disorder and the age of the client may contribute to an individual's response to treatment.

Key Terms

psychoanalysis (688)
psychodynamic
    psychotherapy (688)
resistance (688)
free association (688)
transference (689)
systematic
    desensitization (691)
counterconditioning
    (691)
anxiety hierarchy (692)
in vivo desensitization
    (692)
flooding (692)
implosive therapy (692)

aversion therapy (693)
modeling (695)
role playing (695)
rational–emotive
    therapy (RET) (696)
cognitive therapy (697)
humanistic therapy
    (698)
client-centered therapy
    (698)
existential analysis
    (700)
Gestalt therapy (700)
family therapy (702)
self-help group (704)

electroconvulsive
    therapy (ECT) (706)
bilateral ECT (706)
unilateral ECT (707)
psychosurgery (707)
prefrontal lobotomy
    (708)
chemotherapy (709)
chlorpromazine (710)
psychotropic drugs
    (710)
antipsychotics (710)
phenothiazines (711)
nonphenothiazines
    (711)

tardive dyskinesia
    (712)
antianxiety compounds
    (713)
barbiturates (713)
benzodiazepines
    (713)
tricyclic
    antidepressants
    (714)
monoamine oxidase
    (MAO) inhibitors
    (714)
Prozac (714)
lithium (715)

Suggested Reading

Freud, S. (1953). *The interpretation of dreams*. In *Standard edition*, vols. 4, 5. London: Hogarth. A fascinating series of case histories involving mysterious psychological conflicts that present themselves in dreams. The psychoanalytic interpretation of dream content is especially instructive regarding the intricacies of the unconscious.

Lindner, R. (1954). *The fifty-minute hour*. New York: Holt, Rinehart & Winston. An engaging collection of psychoanalytic tales that take the reader through therapy and reveal the exhilaration and devastation of treatment.

McKim, W. A. (1991). *Drugs and behavior*. Englewood Cliffs, NJ: Prentice-Hall. For someone interested in psychopharmacology, this is an ideal primer. The author assumes no sophistication in biochemistry or neurochemistry on the part of the reader. The text focuses on substrates of drug treatment and the mechanisms of action of alcohol, benzodiazepines, caffeine, tobacco, and hallucinogenic drugs.

Zilbergeld, B. (1983). *The shrinking of America: Myths of psychological change*. Boston: Little, Brown. A personal view of what it is like to be a clinical psychologist. This book presents a number of challenges to many of the popular misconceptions associated with mental health treatment.

APPENDIX A

Statistics

In his region, Cedric Inman was an outstanding salesperson for a successful electronics firm that specializes in computer hardware. His performance for the year had been so strong, in fact, that Cedric was awarded an all-expenses-paid trip for two to Las Vegas. While neither Cedric nor his wife had ever been to a casino, they were looking forward to this getaway.

After arriving in Las Vegas, the Inmans decided to try their hand at a blackjack table. As inexperienced gamblers, they found this game the easiest to follow, and if things didn't go their way, they could get out quickly.

Predictably, the blackjack game did not turn in favor of these newcomers, and soon Cedric realized that he had lost over $1,000. His wife pleaded with him to leave the game and cut their losses, but rather than quit and accept the loss, Cedric insisted on remaining. "It's O.K. It's a game of chance, and eventually the law of averages will take over. My turn to win is due, and if I get out now, I will have walked away when the odds were in my favor."

The reluctance of Cedric Inman to leave the blackjack game demonstrates a phenomenon known as "the gambler's fallacy." People assume that the occurrence of event A influences the probability of event B, even though events A and B are independent. But this is not

true. The fact that Cedric Inman had lost several hands in succession in no way altered the likelihood of his winning the next hand. The probability of getting a particular card, or series of cards, on a given hand is independent of everything that went on before it. People like Cedric and the gamblers fallacy cause the casino business to flourish.

Reporting and interpreting numbers are important to all of us in our daily lives, but these activities are of even greater significance to the psychology researcher who must collect, summarize, and interpret large amounts of experimental data. In this section of the book we attempt to show how the use of statistical methods can improve psychologists' understanding of behavior.

SCALES OF MEASUREMENT

If we were interested in studying the effects of age and sex on attitudes toward helping others, we might choose to film males and females of different ages assisting a confederate who has just dropped a bag of groceries. But in order to understand what is really happening, we would have to reduce the events on film to numbers. By

725

TABLE A-1
Characteristics and Examples of Measurement Scales

Scale	Distinguishing Features	Applicable Situations
Nominal	Names and places objects in mutually exclusive categories; no reference to how objects differ	Numerals on sports uniforms, diagnostic labels, taxonomy in biology
Ordinal	Names and specifies differences along some dimension; unequal distances between scale values	Hardness of minerals, level of human aggression, house numbers, ranking of top tennis professionals
Interval	Names and specifies differences along some dimension; constant difference between scale values; lacks absolute zero point	Temperature, scores on many psychological tests
Ratio	Names and specifies differences along some dimension; constant difference between scale values; assumes absolute zero point	Height, weight, time, distance (most physical measurements)

doing so, we could analyze the data in more sophisticated ways that permit arithmetic manipulations, and thus more precise comparisons. But to get the numbers, we have to use a scale. A scale assigns numbers to observed events.

Beginning with the most elementary scale of measurement and proceeding to the most elaborate, we discuss nominal, ordinal, interval, and ratio scales in the next few sections (see Table A–1 for a summary chart).

Nominal Scales

Nominal scales of measurement use numbers or other symbols to name objects or events. About all that can be accomplished with a nominal scale is to classify data according to categories. In classifying mental patients, for example, we may label one patient as "paranoid schizophrenic" and another as "depressive" and so on. Notice that this descriptive process says nothing about the degree of psychological impairment. With this scale of measurement you have no information that suggests that one disorder is more severe than the other. Rather, you merely state that they are different. Even if you use numbers to replace the diagnostic labels, you still have a data set that can be distinguished only by membership in designated categories. Therefore, regardless of how many observations are made, nothing other than naming is possible with a nominal scale of measurement.

Ordinal Scales

When a scale names objects or events and also permits distinctions to be made along some dimension, the scale is termed an **ordinal scale**. Because ordinal scales spec-

ify differences according to direction, it has become fairly common to attribute "greater than" and "less than" features to ordinal scales.

Because the distances between values in the ordinal scale are unequal, ordinal data are most useful when a dramatic separation between scale values occurs. Take the ranking of criminal offenses, for example. It makes sense to say that armed robbery is a more severe crime than shoplifting, and there are advantages to being able to make such a distinction. Insofar as the judicial system aims to match the penalty to the crime, it seems appropriate to react more harshly to robbery than to shoplifting. The judgement, however, as to *how much* stiffer the penalty should be in the case of robbery must be made subjectively. No one can pretend to measure objectively the degrees of difference in the seriousness between and among crimes. So with ordinal data, we can say that there are differences along some dimension, but we have no precise information about how much difference there is.

Interval Scales

Interval scales have all the properties of the two scales we have just discussed, and they have the additional property of permitting evaluations of how much difference there is in a comparison. Interval scales are so constructed that there are equal (constant) differences between scores. For example, the difference between a 4 and an 8 is equivalent to the difference between an 8 and a 12.

Another feature of interval scales is that they have an arbitrary zero point. This means that a score of zero corresponds to a convenient starting point for the scale and does not necessarily indicate a true absence of the event being measured. A good example of an interval scale is the Celsius thermometer. A value of zero is not intended to indicate the complete absence of heat. Rather, 0°C merely refers to the point at which water freezes.

Sometimes, it is unclear exactly which type of scale is being used by a psychologist. The data may fall between two scales, as in the case of test scores on the SAT, administered to many prospective college students. A score of 600 on the verbal component of the SAT is 50 points greater than a score of 550; in this sense we gain some measure of how much separation there is between the two scores. Similarly, a score of 550 is 50 points greater than 500, and so on. It seems, then, that the scores of the SAT conform to certain features of interval scaling. But on closer inspection, we see that the 50-point separation between 600 and 550 does not mean the same as the 50-point separation between 550 and 500. Because more examinees score between 500 and 550 than between 550 and 600, unit increases (higher scores) at the upper end of the range carry greater distinction than scores lower in the range. This implies that the score *values* on the SAT are unequal. Therefore, are SAT data ordinal or interval? In such ambiguous cases the more sophisticated scale often is presumed to apply, because it permits more extensive statistical analyses to be performed.

Ratio Scales

A scale that does have an absolute zero point is more likely to involve physical than psychological measurements. It is called a **ratio scale**. In addition to an absolute zero point, ratio scales have all the properties of the aforementioned scales. Although ratio scale operations usually take place in a physical realm, psychologists use these too. For instance, when a psychologist records weight loss following the introduction of an intervention technique designed to treat obesity, he or she is using a ratio scale.

Because ratio statements are possible with this most sophisticated form of measurement, it is acceptable to make reference to one value as being twice or three times that of another. Although many people describe their lower-level data in such terms, technically it is inaccurate to do so. Thus, when an advertisement claims that a product can decrease lower back pain by one half, recognize that there may be a misunderstanding of scaling operations.

SAMPLING

Scaling makes the researcher's task easier by packaging the data in a more usable form, but large collections of data still present formidable problems. Typically, the issue is one of time and resources. The group membership is often so enormous that it would take forever to collect the data, regardless of what type of scale is used.

For example, you want to record the attitude toward capital punishment of all persons ranging in age between 25 and 35 now living in Michigan. Because there are a great number of people in this age group in Michigan, it is unlikely that you can interview each of them. Indeed, were you to attempt this, before you finished your interviews, the attitudes of those persons questioned early in the study might have changed. Thus, the validity of your results would be compromised.

There is an alternative method that may make it possible to assess these attitudes. Specifically, we could use a technique called **sampling**. Sampling involves the selection of some, but not all, of the members of the larger **population**. A population includes all relevant cases; in this instance, all people in Michigan between 25 and 35. If we could select and test a **sample**, that is, a subset of the population, it might tell us something about the larger population.

There is no question that sample data are easier to manage than population data. The amount of labor required in collecting and recording data is reduced in proportion to the fraction of the population studied. But are the data from the sample likely to be representative of the population? It depends on how the sample is drawn.

One way to draw a sample that reflects the character of the general population is to use a **random sampling procedure**. The sample created by randomly selecting population values is generally representative of the larger population because every member of the population has an equal chance of being selected for the sample distribution. To maintain the integrity of the random sample, however, two criteria must be met: (1) every population member must be identified, and (2) the selection process must be truly without bias. Meeting these criteria is not always easy, because some populations have a vast membership, and it is often difficult to ensure that each element of the population has an equal probability of being selected for the sample. Even when these conditions are met, a large number of sample observations usually is required before the sample reflects the true values of the population. Still, the random sample is one of the more useful research techniques in psychology.

In some cases, **stratified samples** may be more representative of the general population than random samples. Stratified samples are formed by randomly sampling within restricted categories of the population. This provides some assurance that subgroup characteristics are represented in proportion to their frequency in the population.

Stratifying is especially valuable when subgroups display markedly different patterns of scores. In the aforementioned Michigan study, for example, male and female attitudes toward capital punishment might differ substantially, and the overrepresentation of one subgroup would distort the entire sample. This problem is particularly acute when the sample size is relatively small. To control for this, we could stratify by sex and sample numbers within the male and female categories that correspond to the parallel percentages in the population. This stratified selection technique increases the confidence that our sample will represent the population from which it is drawn.

Thus, the stratified sample has an advantage over the random sample in that biases due to chance factors are less likely to occur. But to justify the use of stratified samples, the investigator must know precisely how the population is configured with respect to key variables that may affect the project findings. Unfortunately, this information often is unavailable in psychological research.

DESCRIPTIVE STATISTICS

Up to this point we have considered issues that relate primarily to the measurement and collection of data. Now we must address how best to describe a data set once we complete the task of gathering information.

Descriptive statistics are concerned with organizing and summarizing large amounts of data, in order to communicate the main features of the data set more effectively. The techniques discussed here are standard ways of expressing complex data sets in simple terms.

Frequency Distributions

Suppose we are interested in describing the final grade distribution for a political science class consisting of 84 students. One method for summarizing the data is to count the number of *A*s, *B*s, and so forth. This produces a **frequency distribution**. Table A–2 presents such a distribution where the possible scores (grades) are listed in one column and the numbers of students receiving each score are listed in a second parallel column. It is immediately apparent from the frequency distribution that most of the people in the class received a *B* or a *C*. Thus, simply by counting the frequency of each score, we learn something about the character of the class.

Frequency distributions are easily converted to bar graphs, or **histograms**. The data from Table A–2 are presented in the form of a histogram in Figure A–1. As a rule, the frequency variable is plotted on the vertical axis (the **ordinate**), and the actual scores (grades) are

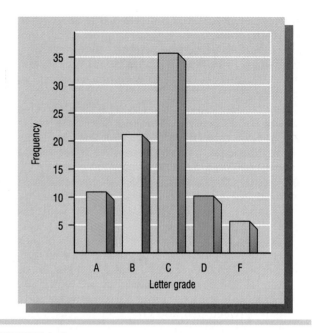

FIGURE A–1
Histogram for the distribution of scores (letter grades) of 84 political science students.

plotted on the horizontal axis (the **abscissa**). The top of the bar corresponds to the frequency of a particular score value. One of the advantages of the histogram is that it provides the viewer with a geometric, rather than a numerical, display. For many people, these graphic representations are quite familiar and thus easily understood.

Although histograms may be more familiar in non-scientific circles, **frequency polygons** are more commonly used by research psychologists to present frequency distributions in graphic form. A frequency polygon is essentially a line graph that is created by connecting individual locations that define the highest point represented by each bar in the histogram. Enter a dot at the top center of each bar, drop out the bars, connect the dots, and you have a frequency polygon.

In many ways, frequency distributions are like people. They come in an assortment of shapes and sizes; some are bold and provocative, others seem rather bland and evoke minimal interest. Along these lines, symmetry, or the lack of it, is especially conspicuous in frequency distributions, and consequently in the frequency polygons derived from them. Figure A–2A shows a polygon where scores are symmetrical; that is, cut in half, the two sides of the distribution are identical in shape. But many distributions are **skewed distributions**, which means they tail off in one direction or the other. As a rule, skewness is defined in the direction of the tail. Figure A–2B shows what a **positively skewed** frequency polygon looks like. This type of distribution may result following the administration of a very difficult examination. High scores would be unlikely, and most scores would fall at the lower end of the distribution. Conversely, the **negatively skewed** polygon shown in Figure A–2C indicates that low scores occurred infrequently. This pattern might be

TABLE A-2
Frequency Distribution for Grades of 84 Students Enrolled in a Political Science Class

Grade	Frequency
A	12
B	21
C	35
D	10
F	6

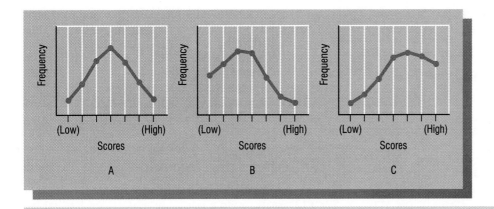

FIGURE A–2
Three frequency polygons: (*A*) symmetrical, (*B*) positively skewed, and (*C*) negatively skewed.

observed when the results from an unusually easy examination are graphed.

Percentiles

As we noted earlier, the SAT is a college entrance examination. When a prospective student receives her or his scores, the report most likely shows a raw score (such as a 600 on the verbal component) and a **percentile score**. A percentile is the score at or below which a given percent of the cases lie. For example, an SAT verbal score of 600 may have corresponded to the 80th percentile. This would mean that 80% of all persons taking the SAT scored 600 or below on the verbal component of the test.

Percentiles are distinguished from group frequency distributions in that they provide information about the relative position of individual scores in the distribution. When frequency distributions are reported alone, specific measurements often lose their meaning. On the other hand, percentiles communicate a notion of rank and therein give meaning to a particular score. For example, assume that you have recently taken an English quiz, and a frequency polygon for the class scores is posted along with individual numerical grades. You see that you scored 86 on the quiz, and from the polygon it is clear that only a few other students made such a high grade. Your 86 may not seem like a great score until you discover that it corresponds to the 94th percentile and earns you a letter grade of *A*.

Measures of Central Tendency

As noted, frequency polygons are useful for describing general features of a group of scores, and percentiles tell us more about the meaning of selected individual scores within the group distribution. Now we ask, is there one value that best characterizes the group? Is there a single number that we can use to distinguish one group from another?

To answer these questions we must understand the concept of central tendency. **Central tendency** refers to the high probability that most scores will concentrate in the center of a distribution, and that relatively few scores will fall at the extremes. The distribution of height and weight among males in the United States illustrates the point. Think about the last time you were at an airport or bus terminal. Some people may have been very tall, or conspicuously short, and therefore you noticed them. Similarly, an extremely overweight person or an unusually thin person may have caught your eye. But for the most part, people were between the extremes; they were the same general height or weight, and it was difficult to distinguish them on this basis.

Three measures of central tendency have been devised to yield a single representative score that provides the most useful information about a group. They are the mean, the median, and the mode. Each measure characterizes unique features of a distribution.

Mean. The **mean** is a statistical concept with which you may be familiar. It is simply the arithmetic average; that is, each score from the distribution is added, and then the sum is divided by the total number of observations in the distribution. When dealing with an entire population, the Greek letter μ is used as a symbol for the mean. Conversely, when only a sample from the population is being considered, the symbol $\overline{X}$ is used to refer to the sample mean. Statisticians express the computational formula for the sample mean as:

$$\overline{X} = \frac{\Sigma X}{N}$$

where

$\overline{X}$ = mean
Σ = Greek capital letter sigma, representing "the sum of"
X = raw (actual) score in the distribution
N = number of observations in the distribution

Alas, the mean has proven to be the nemesis of many a college student. For instance, suppose an average of 70% is the minimum needed for a *C* letter grade. Further suppose that you have three good exam scores of 78, 86, and 72 in English literature. Unfortunately, your fourth and last exam is a 46. To calculate the course mean you sum each raw score X:

$$78 + 86 + 72 + 46 = \Sigma X$$

Then you divide by the number of observations: $N = 4$

$$\overline{X} = \frac{282}{4} = 70.5$$

On this occasion you just made it; your mean course grade qualifies as a C.

The mean is the most commonly reported central tendency statistic. The principal value of knowing $\overline{X}$ is that so many other statistical operations have it as a formula requirement. You often need the mean before you can take additional analytical steps. Also, the mean is easily understood by the general public. Despite these attractions, however, reporting the mean sometimes can be misleading and distort the true picture. When extreme scores occur, for example, the value of the mean is altered drastically. This is evident from Table A–3 which contains data on the distribution of family income for households on a single block in Comanche, Oklahoma (a hypothetical case). For whatever reason, the Turner household is noticeably different from the rest of the distribution. First, notice the mean income for the block. The average annual income is $83,016. But without the Turners in the distribution, the block mean drops to $32,852 per year. Clearly, extreme scores can distort the mean, and this is especially true when the size of the distribution is small.

Median. When the distribution is highly skewed, that is, when there are extreme scores in one direction, it is preferable to report the **median** instead of the mean. The median is the middle value in a ranked set of scores; that is, half the scores are lower than or equal to the median ("median" is another label for the 50th percentile).

If we reexamine the data reported in Table A–3, we can see very quickly why the median is a better indicator than the mean of group characteristics under skewed conditions. First, we rank the 7 household income scores. The middle score, in this case the fourth one, turns out to be $33,006. Clearly, this value provides a more realistic estimate of how much money families on the block earn each year. The Turners remain in the distribution, but their extreme score does not bias the median in the same way that it does the mean.

The median is easy to figure when the number of observations in the distribution is odd. In our example that included 7 scores, 3 scores fall below the median and 3 fall above it. But what happens when you have an even number of scores? For example, what would the median be for those households living on the block in Comanche, Oklahoma, should the Martins, who earn $28,612 yearly, build a house on that vacant lot that has been unoccupied for years? Now that we have 8 households to consider, there is no actual middle score. To arrive at a median, we must calculate the midpoint between the 4th and 5th scores. Accordingly, we add $29,917 and $33,006 and divide by 2. The median in this case turns out to be $31,462.

The arithmetic expression $(N + 1)/2$, where N is the number of scores, can be used in locating the median. When N is an odd number, this quantity tells you the exact position of the middle score. With 21 scores, for example, the median is the 11th score in the rank-ordered list of values, that is, $(21 + 1)/2$. When N is even, the $(N + 1)/2$ rule tells you that the median is halfway between two ranked scores. With 22 scores, for example, the median falls at 11.5, that is, $(22 + 1)/2$. Add the 11th and 12th scores and divide by 2 and you will have the median.

Mode. When the most typical score is of interest, the mode is the most appropriate measure of central tendency to report. The **mode** is the most frequently occurring score. Because the mode is concerned only with the buildup of scores at one point along the distribution, scores added to the distribution do not necessarily change its value.

Most distributions are **unimodal**, that is, one score occurs more frequently than the others. Occasionally,

---

TABLE A-3
Hypothetical Distribution of Annual Family Income for Households on a Single City Block in Comanche, Oklahoma

Household	Annual Family Income
The Turners	$384,000
The Smiths	43,641
The Waltons	38,722
The Thompsons	33,006
The Robertsons	29,917
The Hunters	27,511
The Duvalls	24,312

$\overline{X}$ inclusive of all households = $\Sigma X/N$ = (581,109)/7 = $83,016
$\overline{X}$ with Turner household deleted = $\Sigma X/N$ = (197,109)/6 = $32,852

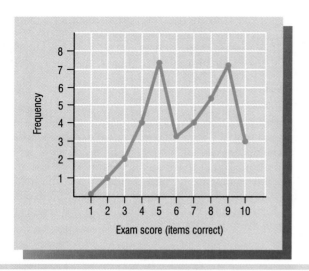

FIGURE A–3
Hypothetical bimodal frequency distribution for a classroom of 31 gifted students taking a 10-item social studies examination.

however, a **bimodal** distribution occurs where two scores occur more often than other scores. Bimodal patterns sometimes appear in gifted and talented classes in school, especially in the lower grades. In many of these classes ability is not an issue inasmuch as everyone is capable of performing at a high level. The variable that distinguishes students is interest. Quite simply, it is a matter of which students are motivated to excel. Unlike ability, which tends to be varied and widely distributed in the general population, interest is more apt to approach a dichotomy. It is either there at a given point in time, or it is not. Consequently, scores in a gifted class may cluster at the upper and lower ends of the scale, reflecting the respective performances of interested and noninterested students. Figure A–3 shows a hypothetical bimodal frequency distribution that could result should a gifted class of 31 students be given a 10-item social studies examination. Notice that one mode is at 5 and the other is at 9.

Before leaving this section on measures of central tendency, a comment is in order concerning the relation between central tendency measures and measurement scales. Depending on the scaling technique used, certain measures of central tendency may lose their meaning and present inappropriate information. For example, if a nominal scale involving diagnostic categories assigns values of 1 to paranoid schizophrenic patients, 2 to depressed patients, and so on, what does a mean of 1.5 connote? Is the average patient a paranoid depressive? Of course not. Nominal conversions do not even imply a common dimension, so it is inaccurate to speak of averages. But the mode would provide a reasonable statistic here. It would tell us the most frequently occurring disorder. Thus, it is important to have some grasp of scaling operations prior to making decisions about how best to report your data. As a general rule, more sophisticated scales permit more elaborate statistical techniques to be employed.

Measures of Variability

Karen and Amy, sisters whose ages differ by 4 years, attended the same college. Each graduated with a degree in computer science, finishing with an identical 3.2 overall grade point average. Moreover, Karen and Amy have both completed their respective courses of study in eight regular semesters, with no summer school required.

On the basis of their records, it would seem that Karen and Amy had similar academic records. But closer inspection of their transcripts reveals a quite different picture. Table A–4 profiles the semester grade point average for each young woman across the 4 years of college. We see that Karen, the older of the two, had an up-and-down college life, at least with respect to grades. Some semesters she was on the dean's honor list (fall of 1st year, spring of 3rd year), yet on one occasion she performed so poorly that she dropped below a *C* average for the semester (fall of 2nd year). On the other hand, Amy performed consistently throughout her college tenure. She never made the dean's list, but neither did she have a semester where she performed poorly.

The cases of Karen and Amy illustrate how two separate distributions can have identical measures of central tendency and yet be quite different in character. In order to better appreciate a distribution, then, we need information about the spread of scores within the distribution in addition to the central tendency value. The spread, or dispersion, of scores within a distribution is commonly referred to as **variability**. *Homogeneous* distributions are those that have only slight variability (Amy's scores); *heterogeneous* distributions have high

TABLE A-4
Semester and Overall Grade Point Averages for Karen and Amy in College

Year (Semester)	Karen	Amy
First Year		
Fall	4.0	3.1
Spring	2.3	3.3
Second Year		
Fall	1.8	3.2
Spring	3.8	2.9
Third Year		
Fall	3.4	3.3
Spring	4.0	3.4
Fourth Year		
Fall	2.9	3.1
Spring	3.4	3.3
Overall Grade Point Average	3.2	3.2

degrees of variability (Karen's scores). The three statistics frequently used to express variability are the range, the variance, and the standard deviation.

Range. The **range** is defined simply as the highest score in the distribution minus the lowest score in the distribution. The range is the easiest of the variability measures to calculate, and in some cases the range statistic can be very useful. For the distribution of scores shown in Table A–4, for example, we can quickly see that the range for Karen's grade point average is 2.2 (4.0 - 1.8), whereas the range for Amy's scores is 0.5 (3.4 - 2.9). Immediately we have some indication of the greater variability of Karen's grades relative to Amy's. But the range value can also be misleading. The problem is that it is determined solely by two values. Thus, an extreme value projects a misleading image concerning variability features of the distribution.

Variance. A much more useful statistic for measuring variability involves an assessment of the average difference between individual scores in the distribution and the mean. This measure yields a statistic known as the variance. Technically speaking, the **variance** is defined as the average of the squared deviations about the mean. In order to better understand the concept of variance, we shall take it step by step in terms of both logic and calculations. First, we need to address the notion of deviation scores. A deviation score is derived for each raw score (X) by calculating the difference between the raw score and the mean of the distribution ($\bar{X}$). Of course, if all scores in the distribution are the same, then $X - \bar{X}$, also written as x, will always equal zero; that is, each score is the same as the average score and there is no deviation. But with a set of heterogeneous data

where scores occur that are great distances from the mean, deviation scores necessarily take on larger values.

It is always true that if we add all the deviation scores, they will sum to zero; that is, the positive values of x will be canceled out by the negative values of x. To avoid this, we can square each deviation score and then add the resulting squared scores. We now have an indication of deviation of raw scores about the mean. But we want to know the mean deviation, or, in other words, the average distance of each score from the mean of the total distribution. To get this statistic we must take the sum of the squared deviations and divide by N, which in this case corresponds to the number of deviation scores. In final form, the formula for calculating the mean of the squared deviations about the mean is:

$$\frac{\Sigma x^2}{N}$$

This gives the variance.

To illustrate the calculation of the variance, we show in Table A–5 two height distributions. The first distribution is for six 9-year-olds enrolled in the third grade, and the other distribution is for the same children 4 years later when they were in the seventh grade. In Chapter 12 we discussed growth spurts that commonly occur among children during early adolescence. It is apparent from the second distribution that some spurts are more dramatic than others. Even though the six children were of the same approximate height at age 9, substantial differences in height were evident at age 13. This greater variance of height among teenagers that is mathematically demonstrated in Table A–5 is undoubtedly a source of great anxiety for many young people, for whom self-consciousness is often a problem.

TABLE A-5
Computation of the Variance and Standard Deviation for Two Sets of Height Scores

Heights of Six 9-Year-Olds (Third Grade)			Heights of Same Children 4 Years Later (Seventh Grade)		
X (Inches)	$x = X - \bar{X}$	x^2	X (Inches)	$x = X - \bar{X}$	x^2
54	0	0	70	+ 7	49
52	- 2	4	57	- 6	36
54	0	0	59	- 4	16
53	- 1	1	58	- 5	25
55	+ 1	1	66	+ 3	9
56	+ 2	4	68	+ 5	25
$\bar{X} = \Sigma X/N$	$\Sigma x = 0$	$\Sigma x^2 = 10$	$\bar{X} = \Sigma X/N$	$\Sigma x = 0$	$\Sigma x^2 = 160$
$\bar{X} = 324/6$			$\bar{X} = 378/6$		
$\bar{X} = 54$			$\bar{X} = 63$		

Variance = $\Sigma x^2/N = 10/6 = 1.67$	Variance = $\Sigma x^2/N = 160/6 = 26.67$
Standard deviation = $\sqrt{\text{variance}}$	Standard deviation = $\sqrt{\text{variance}}$
$SD = \sqrt{1.67} = 1.29$	$SD = \sqrt{26.67} = 5.16$

Standard Deviation. The **standard deviation**, obtained by taking the square root of the variance, is the measure of variability about the mean that is used most often in psychological research. Typically, the lower case Greek letter sigma (σ) is used to designate the standard deviation of a population. When dealing with a sample, *SD* is used as the symbol for the sample standard deviation, which is an estimate of σ.

The chief advantage of using the *SD* as opposed to the variance is that the *SD* is on the same scale of measurement as the raw scores in the original distribution. For example, the *SD* values reported for the distributions in Table A–5 are expressed in inches, as are the original height measurements. As we discuss later, a second advantage of reporting variability in terms of *SD* is that for many distributions we know approximately what percentage of the scores lie within one, two, or three *SD*s about the mean. Thus, *SD* values often communicate more than just information about variability.

Transforming Data

It is frequently desirable to compare scores across distributions. The following case history is one that is familiar to the authors, and it serves to illustrate the problems that arise when you must consider scores from different distributions.

> Randall was a senior psychology major who was faced with making a decision about graduate school. He wanted to continue in psychology, but he was equally attracted to graduate study in biology. Randall's roommate, having watched him agonize over the issue for several weeks, offered a way out. The roommate suggested that Randall go in the direction of his greater aptitude. "You have two major exams coming up, one in history of psychology, the other in genetics. Let your performance make your decision for you. Go with the discipline that is associated with the higher score."
>
> Although performance in a single course is rarely a good predictor of future academic success, Randall was desperate. And this idea seemed as reasonable as anything else that he had considered. So Randall decided to go with it, and he made a score of 84% on the biology exam and 44% on the psychology test. His route was clear, *he would go for a Ph.D. in psychology.*

If Randall scored higher in the biology course, why didn't he keep his agreement to go with his greater aptitude? Actually, he did. But to follow the reasoning here, we must understand **z scores**. By definition, z scores are values that indicate how far a raw score (*X*) deviates from the mean of the distribution in *SD* units. The equation for calculating a z score is:

$$z = \frac{X - \overline{X}}{SD}$$

It follows that if we know the mean and *SD* of a distribution, we can solve for the z score corresponding to a given *X*.

One of the principal uses of z scores is to convert scores from different distributions to a common metric. This means that different raw score values taken from distributions with very different characteristics can be transformed and compared on the same scale. Randall's case represents one instance where comparisons were derived from scores taken from dramatically different distributions. Let's look more closely at the biology exam. The mean ($\overline{X}$) on this exam was 80% with a *SD* of 4%. This means that Randall's score on the genetics test was +1 *SD* unit above the class average.

$$z = \frac{84 - 80}{4} = +1$$

However, the $\overline{X}$ on the history of psychology exam was 38% with a *SD* of 2%. This placed Randall's score +3 *SD* units above the class mean.

$$z = \frac{44 - 38}{2} = +3$$

When we transform the raw scores and compare them on a common scale, Randall's performance in history of psychology is clearly better. In retrospect, his decision makes sense.

Thus, if we want to know more about the relative position of a specific score within the overall distribution, z scores can help. Also, notice from the formula that it is possible to obtain a raw score when we know the z score. You just solve for the unknown. This feature is discussed further in the next section on the normal curve.

The Normal Curve

One of the most useful tools in all of statistics is the **normal distribution**, or normal curve. From Figure A–4 we see that the normal distribution is shaped rather like a bell—rounded on top, then tapering off at each end in symmetrical fashion. This bell-shaped curve reflects a distribution wherein scores close to the population mean (written as μ) accumulate in substantially greater numbers than scores that are distant from the mean. It is important to recognize that the normal curve is really characterizing a theoretical distribution. It is generated by a mathematical equation, and it assumes an infinite number of observations, or scores.

If the normal curve is theoretical, then why is it so important for psychology researchers? The answer is that many of the phenomena studied by psychologists approximate the normal curve. For example, IQ (see discussion in Chapter 11), athletic ability, and college entrance scores all conform to this pattern of the normal distribution. Thus, those statistical operations that hold for the normal curve can be considered valid for many empirical (actually recorded) distributions.

Look again at Figure A–4. Notice that the units of measurement along the baseline of the normal curve are standard deviations. Because the normal distribution has μ (the population mean) equal to 0 and σ (the population standard deviation) equal to 1, the *SD* values of the normal distribution correspond to z scores of the same value. This leads us to one of the most important characteristics of the normal curve: the area under the curve lying between any two z scores is a fixed amount. This means that the percentage of the total frequency can be determined on the basis of z-score manipulations. For example, we see from Figure A–4 that 34.13% of all cases

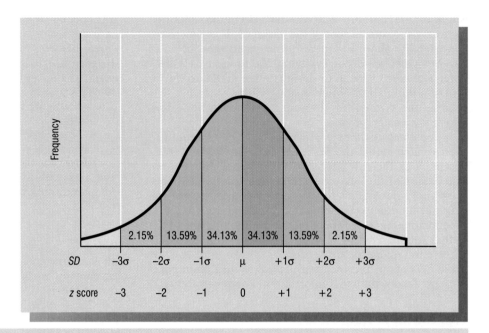

FIGURE A–4
The normal curve characterizes a theoretical distribution (the normal distribution) with μ = 0 and σ = 1. Accordingly, scores within the distribution defined in terms of standard deviation units are expressed as z scores with the same value.

fall between 0 (the mean) and z = +1.00. Because the normal curve is symmetrical, it follows that 68.26% of all cases lie between z = -1.00 and z = +1.00. In a like manner, we are able to determine that approximately 95% of the total distribution falls within plus or minus two z scores from the mean, and about 99%, or virtually all of the scores, lie within the range of z = -3.00 and z = +3.00.

It sometimes helps to have concrete examples when dealing with statistical principles. For convenience, let's use IQ to illustrate a point. Although IQ is a normally distributed variable, we cannot use IQ scores directly to answer questions that pertain to the normal curve. The reason is that scores must be in the form of z to enter

the normal distribution. Fortunately, if we know the $\bar{X}$ and the SD of the IQ distribution, we can calculate z for each IQ score. Such a transformation is displayed in Figure A–5 using the formula for z. We see that with a $\bar{X}$ of 100 and a SD of 15, an IQ of 115 falls at z = +1.00, 130 corresponds to z = +2.00, and so forth. Now we can make use of the normal curve. For example, we are now in a position to assert that approximately 68% of the population have IQs between 85 and 115 (that is, plus or minus one z score).

Another potential use of the normal curve deserves mention. What if you have the percentage figure but need to know the corresponding raw score value? For example, what if you knew that you wanted to exclude

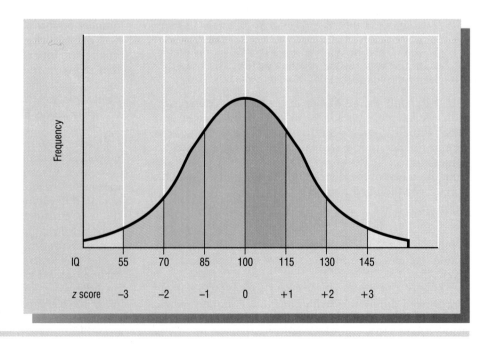

FIGURE A–5
A normal distribution of IQs ($\bar{X}$ = 100; SD = 15) and their corresponding z-score equivalents. Refer to Figure A–4 for the percentages of the distribution falling between specific z-score values.

the lower 84% of the distribution but you needed to identify the appropriate cutoff value? Again, the z score formula may be used. But this time we already have the z value; that is, from the normal curve we know that 84% of the distribution falls below $z = +1.00$ (the 50% below the mean plus the 34% between the mean and $z = +1.00$). Therefore, if our question relates to the IQ distribution just cited, then:

$$+1 = \frac{X - 100}{15}$$

When we solve for the raw score (X) algebraically, we find that an IQ of 115 is the cutoff score for excluding 84% of the population. Thus, in this instance we are able to make a decision about an empirical distribution because of certain features known to exist for a theoretical distribution.

CORRELATION

Psychologists are often interested in investigating phenomena over which they have minimal control. For instance, in Chapter 9 we mentioned research findings that examined the effects of heat on human aggression among city dwellers. In such cases the researcher has no control over the independent variable being investigated. That is, ambient temperature conditions will change in nonsystematic ways. In the absence of tight experimental control, correlation techniques are often used to describe and predict behavioral events.

Correlation, as we noted in Chapter 1, refers to the interrelation between two or more events, or variables. Specifically, when two or more events vary together, they are said to be correlated. When one event changes in value as another event changes, and when those changes are in the same direction, a **positive correlation** exists. An example would be the relation between cigarette smoking and lung diseases. Among habitual smokers, it has been established that as the number of cigarettes smoked increases, so does the incidence of lung cancer and emphysema. Thus, a positive correlation exists here. A **negative correlation**, conversely, is evident when high scores on one measure are associated with low scores on the other. Take age and sleep as an example. As discussed in Chapter 5, as we get older we require less sleep. The variables are therefore negatively correlated: As age increases, the number of hours spent in sleep diminishes.

When you have only a few scores associated with each variable, you can gain some sense of the correlation by just glancing at the data. But more often than not there are too many scores to get a feel for the relation between variables. Under such conditions a **scatter plot**, or scatter diagram, can be helpful. A scatter plot is formed by representing each individual's score on both variables with a single point on a graph. The variable designated X is traditionally plotted along the horizontal axis, whereas the variable Y is usually plotted along the vertical axis. A better visual profile of the correlation

between X and Y is provided by extending a **line of best fit** through the data plots. This line goes through the middle of the points on the scatter plot. With a high (strong) correlation most of the points on the graph fall close to the line of best fit. In contrast, with a low (weak) correlation, points on the graph fall great distances from the line. Figure A–6 contains scatter plots for hypothetical correlations that would be described as (a) high positive, (b) low positive, (c) high negative, (d) low negative, and (e) a zero correlation (variables are unrelated).

The Correlation Coefficient

Thus far in this section we have used illustrations and graphs to describe correlation in fairly general terms. In some cases, an imprecise feel for the relation between variables is all that is required. On numerous occasions, however, much more exactness is demanded. A researcher concerned with linking IQ to creativity may want to know the precise nature of the correlation between intelligence test scores and scores on a measure of artistic ability. Or, an industrial–organizational psychologist may want something more than a trend to confirm the validity of a newly developed test for assessing job-related skills. When an exact measure of correlation is needed, a **correlation coefficient** must be calculated.

The *Pearson product–moment correlation coefficient*, denoted by the symbol r, is the statistic used most often to express the degree of correlation in numerical terms. Named for statistician Karl Pearson, the value of r ranges between 0 (zero) and ± 1.00. Positive numbers reflect positive correlations, and negative numbers reflect negative correlations. With either type, the closer to the anchor values (-1.00 or +1.00), the stronger (higher) the correlation. Indeed, correlations of -1.00 and +1.00, should they ever be obtained, show perfect correlations.

Recognize that it is the *value* of the correlation coefficient, not the sign, that expresses the strength of the relationship between two variables. This means that a high negative correlation can be just as useful for making judgments as a high positive correlation. For instance, assume you have a choice between two stockbrokers. Broker A makes accurate predictions more often than not, and in fact you have determined that the correlation between Broker A's predictions and subsequent changes in the market is +.68. Broker B, on the other hand, never seems to make correct predictions. When selected stocks are predicted to go up in value, they fall; and when others are predicted to drop in price, their value escalates. Indeed, the negative correlation here stands at a rather remarkable -.92. Whom do you choose to advise you? Do not hesitate; go with the loser (Broker B) and do exactly the opposite of what is recommended. The reason for this decision derives from the amount of information provided by each broker's prediction. Because Broker B is virtually never right, a forecast that the market will take an upward swing almost guarantees a market plunge, and vice versa. Broker A is less reliable. Events are predicted more accurately, but with less consistency than the wrong

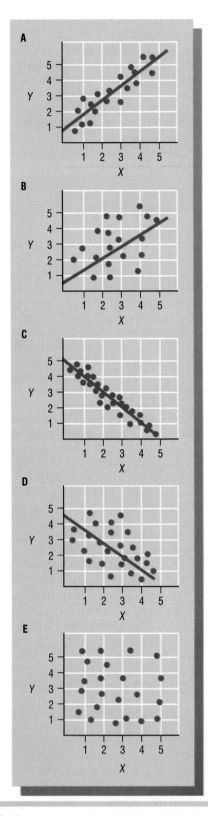

predictions made by Broker B. In this case the high value of the negative correlation provides more useful information than the moderate value of the positive correlation. The sign is of secondary importance.

There are several different formulas for calculating the correlation coefficient. Because of its mathematical simplicity, and because it includes concepts already discussed, we present the formula that uses z scores. The formula is:

$$r_{xy} = \frac{\Sigma z_x z_y}{N}$$

The correlation coefficient (r_{xy}) is equal to the sum of the products of individual z scores for each raw score value x and y divided by the number of times x and y are paired (N). This means that for each paired observation (remember, with correlation each subject or event must register a value for each variable), every raw score x and y must be converted to a z value by subtracting the raw score from the respective X or Y distribution mean and dividing by the appropriate SD. Once the transformation is complete, the product of z_x and z_y is found for each pair of scores. All the products are then added, and the total is divided by the number of $z_x z_y$ observations to yield an average known as r_{xy}.

From the formula we see that a positive value for r_{xy} occurs when x increases as y increases (z_x and z_y are both positive) or when x decreases as y decreases (z_x and z_y are both negative). A negative value for r_{xy} occurs when the balance of z_x and z_y pairs is at odds (positives and negatives are multiplied).

An example of the computation of r_{xy} is presented in Table A–6. The question of interest concerns the correlation between cumulative grade point average and starting annual salary. Six petroleum engineering students (three male and three female) were selected for analysis. From our calculations, we see that the correlation between grade point and salary is high and positive (r_{xy} = +.79). This would imply that students who do well in their college coursework also get higher starting salaries.

Interpreting Correlation

Perhaps the most common mistake that is made with correlational statistics is to assume causality. That is, when two events are highly correlated, a person may think that one event causes a change in the other. *But correlation does not imply causation.* As we have stated previously, correlation tells us about only the extent to which two events vary together. Some correlations, of course, are not likely to be misinterpreted because common sense argues against a cause and effect relationship. This is the case for the positive relation that exists between body weight and the ability to perform on the violin. No one is likely to assert too strongly that weight gain promotes musical talent. Yet there is a high positive correlation between body weight and musical expression, simply because as we grow older and bigger (gain weight), we become more sophisticated in the use of musical instruments.

The potential for erroneous conclusions is also evident from scientific investigations. For example, it has

FIGURE A–6
Scatter plots and lines of best fit for five hypothetical cases involving correlations between variables X and Y. The graphs reflect (*A*) a high (strong) positive correlation, (*B*) a low (weak) positive correlation, (*C*) a high negative correlation, (*D*) a low negative correlation, and (*E*) a zero correlation.

TABLE A-6
Computation of Correlation Coefficient Based on Grade Point Averages and
Salaries for Six Petroleum Engineering Graduates

Graduate	(Variable X) Cumulative Grade Point Average	(Variable Y) Starting Annual Salary (in dollars)	z_x	z_y	$z_x z_y$
Laura	2.85	$25,000	− .62	− .56	+ .347
Hillel	3.40	28,600	+ .75	+ .63	+ .472
Jennifer	3.71	31,750	+ 1.52	+ 1.67	+ 2.538
Jason	2.94	26,450	− .40	− .08	+ .032
Juanita	3.11	24,900	+ .02	− .60	− .012
Eric	2.59	23,500	− 1.27	− 1.06	+ 1.346
Sum	18.60	160,200	0	0	4.723
$\overline{X}$	3.10	26,700	0	0	.79
SD	.40	3,018			

$$\Sigma z_x z_y = 4.723 \qquad r_{xy} = \frac{\Sigma z_x z_y}{N} = \frac{4.723}{6} = + .79$$

$$N = 6$$

been observed that the average alcohol intake for humans is highly correlated ($r = +.53$) with blood lead concentrations (Grandjean, Olsen, & Hollnagel, 1981). It is tempting to say that alcohol causes increased lead absorption, perhaps by way of inducing tissue damage along the intestinal wall. But even if such tissue damage were observed, factors other than alcohol could be causing the increased accumulation of lead in the blood. Maybe people who live in urban areas, where the chances of lead contamination are high due to automobile emissions, also drink more because of their sociocultural values and beliefs. In any event, you cannot specify a causal relationship on the basis of the high correlation.

A second word of caution is in order. Although it is true that correlation does not imply causation, neither does it preclude it. Earlier we used the example of cigarette smoking and lung diseases to illustrate a positive correlation. Because the evidence here is correlational in nature, it is inappropriate to say that smoking causes lung cancer. But it is equally inappropriate to argue that no causal relation exists because smoking and cancer are only correlated. The point is that correlation is neutral with respect to the issue of whether or not one variable causes another.

Prediction

Finally, we note that one advantage of knowing that two variables are correlated is that sometimes a score on one variable may be predicted from a score on the other variable. For instance, if we know that the correlation coefficient between the verbal and quantitative components of a college entrance exam is $+.63$, then given a verbal score we should be able to predict a quantitative score, at least

within reasonable bounds. As a rule, the higher the correlation coefficient, the more accurate our prediction is.

INFERENTIAL STATISTICS

Thus far we have focused on statistical concepts that permit conclusions to be drawn about the data set that has actually been collected. In this regard, we note that the operations we have identified involve the use of values within the distribution; therefore, unless a calculation error is made, the validity of the statistics should not be questioned. However, most psychologists are faced with much broader problems than those associated with expressing the character of a given set of data. A clinical psychologist examining the comparative effectiveness of two different therapeutic strategies by using two different groups of 10 persons diagnosed as schizophrenic is not interested in only those 20 isolated cases. Rather, the investigator is interested in the relative value of the respective therapies for all persons with schizophrenia. Similarly, the experimental psychologist observing enhanced learning among 12 rats treated with a test drug hopes to discover a relationship that is relevant to more than just these 12 animals. The goal in such cases is to make more general statements about an entire population based on conclusions drawn from a sample. This process of reasoning from the particular to the general involves what has come to be called *statistical inference*.

Sampling Error

The use of inferential statistics presents a new set of problems. Unlike descriptive statistics, statistical inference presumes that mistakes can be made even when calculations are performed flawlessly. This perspective has evolved out of practical concerns associated with collecting every possible observation from a very large group or population. As mentioned earlier in this appendix, in many instances it is just not feasible to obtain a measurement for every member of the population. We must resort to sampling, where we draw a small number of cases from the population. Still, as just discussed, our ultimate objective is to make statements about the population. The issue is one of representativeness. Do the descriptive values of the sample (the mean, standard deviation) really reflect the values of the broader distribution of scores? Due to **sampling error**, we cannot be absolutely sure. Sampling error refers to the discrepancy between the true values of the population and those estimates of population values based on sample characteristics.

We can illustrate sampling error using a hypothetical population of age scores for Nobel Prize winners living in the United States. For the sake of simplicity, assume that there are only 24 such persons of the ages shown in Table A–7. The mean of this population of 24 scores is 62.5 years. On one occasion suppose we draw (on a random basis) a sample comprised of the following five ages: 37, 49, 48, 53, and 41. The sample mean in this case is 45.6, and it is a very poor estimate of the population mean. On a separate occasion, assume we randomly sample five other ages from the distribution: 48, 80, 62, 56, and 64. The mean of this sample is 62 years, very close to the actual mean of the population, which is 62.5. Thus, we see that because of sampling error, sample estimates may or may not provide valid clues about the true character of the population.

We accept that in many, if not most, cases in psychological research we are not ever likely to know the actual value of the population mean. How, then, can we be confident that our estimates based on sample statistics represent anything more than wild guesses? First, accuracy in estimating population values improves as sample size increases. Had we drawn samples of 10 observations from the distribution of scores shown in Table A–7 instead of 5, for instance, the chances of getting a distorted picture of the population would have diminished. This is why survey researchers such as those who take public opinion polls place more faith in larger samples. Also, with the use of some sophisticated statistical techniques that need not be explored here, it is possible to express a range around the sample mean within which the true population mean will almost certainly fall. Because this range expands as the sample standard deviation increases, samples that contain widely varied scores are often not of much help with respect to estimating population values.

Differences Between Means

Given that a sample mean of sufficient size provides us with a reasonable idea about the range of scores that encompass the true population mean, how is it that we are better able to deal with research issues like those mentioned earlier? For example, how does the process of estimation relate to determining whether or not Therapy A is a more effective intervention strategy for treating persons with schizophrenia than Therapy B? First, we must recognize that in such cases we are quite possibly faced with estimating two population values, not one. In other words, we must determine the population mean for each sample based on the estimates provided by the respective sample means. On the basis of these predicted population values, we then must determine if the difference between the sample means of the two therapy conditions reflects the fact that the samples were drawn from populations with noticeably different characteristics. In this regard, we must be aware of the possibility that the samples come from the same population and that the difference in means is due to sampling error. In the former case (different populations), we can conclude that our therapy approaches really do produce different treatment benefits, whereas in the latter case (same population) we must accept that neither approach is preferred over the other.

Critical to this process of deciding whether two sample means come from the same or different populations is the aforementioned range that ostensibly contains the population mean. After the respective ranges have been identified for each sample mean, we can feel fairly secure that sample mean values that fall within one range but not the other come from different populations. We are less certain when sample mean values exist within overlapping ranges. In such instances the mean differences simply may be due to chance (sampling error). Complex statistical tests permit psychologists and other scientists to determine the probability that differences in sample mean values occurred because of chance. Convention is that when the probability of a chance explanation of the results falls below .05 (5 times out of 100), the differences are **statistically significant**. That is, on the basis of our statistical analysis, we can feel confident that the sample means have been drawn from different populations. And depending on how confident we want to be, we can make the criterion for statistical significance even more stringent. In any event, keep in mind that statistical operations are merely tools that psychologists use to help them gain answers to meaningful questions. If the proper questions are not asked, no statistical manipulation—regardless of how elegant it may be—will produce a worthwhile result.

TABLE A-7
Ages of 24 Nobel Prize Winners Living in the United States (a Hypothetical Distribution)

37	48	61	53
58	56	41	59
62	74	69	49
64	82	84	78
46	71	74	68
70	80	56	60

THINKING AHEAD . . .

The true advantage of psychological statistics is that they can be used as tools to help us better understand the nature of the world around us. In this appendix, we have seen that descriptive and inferential statistics help us organize our data sets and make meaningful decisions about the significance of our findings. Statistics facilitate the flow of information and thereby make it possible for scientists and nonscientists alike to build a more substantial knowledge base.

Because the development of new statistical techniques necessarily moves at a slower pace than other areas within the discipline of psychology, there may be an inclination to think of the field as static and unchanging. That is, some may think that we are locked into using the basic statistical strategies that have been around for many years. Clearly this is not the case. Although the sophisticated statistical instruments of tomorrow may build on those available today, new analytical methods are definitely forthcoming. Such methods likely will be tethered to entirely new theoretical statistics models, and the various assumptions that underlie the use of the statistic may differ vastly from current assumptions.

Also, a world that is increasingly more complex will require everyone to gain an understanding of statistical concepts. Consumers, ranchers, salespersons, political analysts, and psychologists will need to be even better informed than they are now about the application of statistical methodology. How do you think this will affect you? Will the information explosion and the demand for understanding statistics affect your job? In regard to your personal life, how could even routine events such as shopping and driving a car be influenced by statistical developments? You are not just a number, but you might want to understand what being just a number can mean.

Summary

Scales of Measurement

1. In order to better analyze behavioral results, we often must assign numbers to observed behavioral events. To do this, we employ one of four scales: nominal, ordinal, interval, and ratio.

Sampling

2. Sampling is a process whereby some, but not all, members of a population are selected for analysis. Random samples and stratified samples are two of the more common sampling procedures.

Descriptive Statistics

3. Descriptive statistics permit us to describe distributions of scores in simple terms. Frequency distributions and percentiles are two such statistical methods that provide summaries of large data sets.

4. Additional descriptive measures are measures of central tendency: the mean (arithmetic average), the median (the middle score), and the mode (the most typical score).

5. In order to determine the amount of spread in a distribution, we report measures of variability. These include the range, defined as the highest minus the lowest score; the variance, which is the average of the squared deviations about the mean; and the standard deviation, calculated as the square root of the variance.

6. Psychologists have found the normal curve useful for interpreting the meaning of statistical results. The normal curve reflects a theoretical distribution that is symmetrical and bell shaped. We enter the distribution by way of z scores, which are transformed scores that relate individual raw scores within a distribution to the remaining scores in that distribution.

Correlation

7. Correlation tells us the extent to which two or more events vary together. Positive correlations indicate that as one variable changes in a given direction, a second variable also changes in that same direction. Negative correlations reflect an inverse relationship. Precise numerical estimates of the degree of correlation are expressed by a correlation coefficient, such as the Pearson r.

Inferential Statistics

8. Inferential statistics permit us to draw conclusions about population values on the basis of observed sample characteristics. With samples of sufficient size we can use sample mean values to estimate a range of scores that likely includes the true population mean. Tests of statistical significance allow us to make decisions about whether two samples come from the same or different populations.

Key Terms

nominal scales (726)
ordinal scales (726)
interval scales (726)
ratio scales (727)
sampling (727)
population (727)
sample (727)
random sampling
  procedure (727)
stratified samples (727)
descriptive statistics
  (728)

frequency distribution
  (728)
histograms (728)
ordinate (728)
abscissa (728)
frequency polygons (728)
skewed distribution
  (728)
positively skewed (728)
negatively skewed (728)
percentile score (729)
central tendency (729)

mean (729)
median (730)
mode (730)
unimodal (730)
bimodal (731)
variability (731)
range (732)
variance (732)
standard deviation (733)
z scores (733)
normal distribution
  (733)

correlation (735)
positive correlation
  (735)
negative correlation
  (735)
scatter plot (735)
line of best fit (735)
correlation coefficient
  (735)
sampling error (738)
statistically significant
  (738)

Suggested Reading

Bruning, J. L., & Kintz, B. L. (1987). *Computational handbook of statistics* (rev. ed.). Glenview, IL: Scott, Foresman. A simple cookbook approach on how to perform various statistical tests. Examples of how and when each test is used are described for descriptive and inferential statistics.

Huff, D. (1954). *How to lie with statistics*. New York: Norton. An excellent book for the beginning reader of statistical concepts. The use and misuse of statistics are covered.

Lehman, E. H. (1978). *Statistics: A guide to the unknown* (2nd ed.). San Francisco: Holden-Day. A series of essays on the application of statistical principles in diverse settings.

Spatz, C. (1993). *Basic statistics: Tales of distributions*. Pacific Grove, CA: Brooks/Cole. This elementary statistics text is an ideal book for undergraduates in the social sciences who want to gain more sophistication regarding the calculation and appropriate use of inferential statistics. The book assumes minimal background in mathematics and provides many good applied illustrations of the use of statistics in the real world.

APPENDIX B

Industrial–Organizational Psychology

Maxine A. Warnath
PROFESSOR OF PSYCHOLOGY,
WESTERN OREGON STATE COLLEGE

At a meeting sponsored by the Moscow Chamber of Commerce, Jean is talking with Vladimir Borisovich, who is the president of a consulting business in Moscow, Russia. Vladimir conducts workshops with Russian women and men who want to begin their own businesses. Private business ownership is relatively new in Russia, a by-product of *perestroika* and *glasnost*. Vladimir was one of the first to begin a business; he has 4 years' experience in business ownership. Jean is a member of a delegation of human resource and personnel management specialists from the United States who have traveled to meet with their Russian counterparts to exchange information and share ideas. She is an industrial–organizational psychologist and the owner of a private organizational consulting firm.

Jean wants to know what topics Vladimir includes in his training sessions. Vladimir says that he includes everything necessary to know in order to have a successful business. The topics include "who you need to contact to get permission to open the business," "who you should speak to about finding some space in which to conduct the business," "where you can get some money to help with the financing (preferably hard currency from Europe or the United States)," and so on. Jean noticed that Vladimir did not talk at all about areas of importance to industrial–organizational psychologists in the United States, such as how the business should be organized and structured or what incentive programs are used. She then recalled that in other discussions with chief executive officers in Moscow, the main motivational orientation comprised the concepts of reward and punishment, benefits for those who do adequate work, and suspension or firing when the work was less than adequate. These differences and others in the nature of employer–employee relationships and practices between Russia and the United States are just a few of the many Jean observed in her work in Russia. She decided to propose a program to the Association of Chief Executives of Moscow, in which industrial–organizational psychologists from the United States would work cooperatively with Russian business owners to improve the human resource practices and structural design of the newly privatized Russian companies. This cooperative endeavor would increase the likelihood of profitability and, consequently, the success of the new Russian business ventures, as well as improve the daily work life of Russian employees.

INTRODUCTION TO INDUSTRIAL–ORGANIZATIONAL PSYCHOLOGY

The specialty area in psychology known as **industrial–organizational (I/O) psychology** studies both the individual and the organizations in which individuals work. It is one of the most rapidly growing areas in psychological research and application. There is good reason for this growth. The workplace is an integral part of our lives; most of us spend at least one fourth of our daily time in a workplace that is a complex social psychological environment. The application of psychological concepts and theories to work settings can make that experience more positive for both the employer and the employee. As employers, managers, supervisors, or executive officers, we use I/O psychology to understand the employees with whom we work and the processes involved in developing the organization into a cohesive unit. As employees, we use I/O psychology to better understand our work setting and co-workers and thus make the workplace more comfortable, enjoyable, and profitable.

The most varying and complex aspect of business relates to people. Businesses often invest huge sums of money to install state-of-the-art equipment and technology, but neglect to invest enough in training to enable those who operate the equipment to do so efficiently. In other cases, a large investment in the training enterprise shows no measurable improvement in employee productivity because the wrong people are selected for the training. Men and women not only operate the machines on the production line, but also make the decisions concerning what products to develop, which markets to target, future trends, needed services, and other decisions that make the difference between business success and failure. In addition to the human resource policies, the structure of the organization also has an enormous impact on the quality and level of the output of the workforce.*

The most complex aspects of business relate to people. Businesses are increasingly realizing the need to deal with the "whole person" in the work environment. One way to do this is to provide exercise facilities within the company for employees to use during breaks.

I/O PSYCHOLOGISTS

I/O psychologists do many things. They help companies recruit and select the people who are best qualified to fill job openings, help structure organizations so that they can function most effectively (e.g., suggest communication patterns, structure reporting relationships), plan incentive programs, and develop procedures to resolve conflict. They also plan training and development programs, provide clinical and counseling psychological services through employee assistance programs, and implement decision-making processes and team-building programs. In a survey conducted by the Society for Industrial and Organizational Psychology (SIOP), the following five specialty areas of I/O psychologists were identified:

1. *Individual evaluation.* Includes employee selection, job analysis, testing, and performance appraisal
2. *Training.* Training and program evaluation combined with military and engineering psychology
3. *Organizational behavior.* Includes motivation, productivity, and job satisfaction
4. *Organizational development.* Group and organizational issues and areas related to managerial roles, such as power and decision making
5. *Employee development.* Career and family issues, including stress and counseling (Howard, 1990).

PSYCHOLOGICAL THEORIES IN I/O PSYCHOLOGY

Many basic psychological theories are used in the work of I/O psychologists. Theories regarding motivation (see Chapter 9) are the basis for the development of incentive programs and also relate to employee productivity. Social cognition theories and research on attitudes and values (see Chapter 14) help us understand diversity in

---

* Due to space limitations, it is not possible to cover all aspects of I/O psychology in this appendix. This brief overview attempts to introduce you to as many topics as possible. A list of suggested readings is provided at the end of the appendix as a resource for those who want additional information.

the workplace, and lead to processes for incorporating employees from many different cultural backgrounds and preparing executives for work in global settings (Black & Mendenhall, 1990; Shao & Hill, 1992; Von Glinow & Milliman, 1990). Attribution processes (see Chapter 14) help to explain some of the misunderstandings that happen in everyday work settings. The contribution of the research on group processes is very important in developing programs on conflict resolution (including learning negotiation and arbitration skills) and decision-making processes: It is the foundation for team-building programs. Developmental psychology and learning theories (see Chapters 6, 12, and 13) provide information useful in career management and adult learning. Concepts of individual differences (see Chapter 10) and assessment instruments that measure these differences (see Chapter 11) assist I/O psychologists in the hiring and placement process, determining training needs, and making decisions regarding promotions. Knowledge about the relationship of organizational structure to effective communication and decision making is used to assist companies in restructuring to meet the needs of an ever-changing society. Understanding theories about change as an ongoing positive process for organizational growth enables a company to meet the needs of changing economic environments. **Action research** is an important tool for I/O psychologists. It involves diagnosing the weaknesses of an organization, determining the nature of the changes that are necessary in that particular setting, and analyzing the best way to implement those changes.

INDIVIDUAL EVALUATION

Personnel Selection

Most of us have come into contact with a human resource professional through the hiring process as an applicant for a job. Let's look at the other side of the process. One of the critical responsibilities of the human resource department in a business is to select from many applicants the one person who is most likely to be productive and successful in a specific position. To help in the prediction of this success, human resource directors can use a variety of strategies and assessment instruments. The hiring process is only one of the personnel selection tasks. **Personnel selection** also includes placing the newly hired employee in a specific job or position and, later, making recommendations about promotions, lateral transfers, and global assignments. During these processes, questions are raised about whether the employee is ready to be promoted; about whether the employee has the requisite skills, talents, and characteristics; and about other similar concerns. There are some assessment tools used to assist the human resource director in answering these questions. Among the traditional predictive tools are interviews, biodata forms (biographical forms that request background information about the applicant), ability and aptitude tests, and personality tests (Anastasi, 1989; McEvoy & Beatty, 1989;

Rothstein et al., 1990; Russell et al., 1990). More recently, companies have begun to use additional predictors such as preemployment drug testing and integrity/honesty tests (Arnold, 1991; Bergmann et al., 1990; Jacobs & Zimmer, 1991; Jones & Terris, 1991; Konovsky & Cropanzano, 1991; Miller et al., 1990; Murphy et al., 1991; Normand et al., 1990; Ryan & Sackett, 1991; Scrivner, 1991). Most companies do not use all of these assessment tools, but will select those that best fit the jobs they are attempting to fill. The assessment instruments must meet scientific validity and reliability criteria so as to guarantee that the decisions are fair and not biased toward or against any applicants (Gottfredson & Sharf, 1988). In general, the more closely an assessment instrument is related to the job, the less potentially biased it will be.

Job Analysis. A carefully developed **job analysis** should be completed before new employees are recruited. The job analysis describes the tasks and duties of the job and worker qualifications such as the knowledge, skills, and personality characteristics. It can be used to provide information for a job description that appears in an employment ad and to help determine which assessment instruments should be used in screening applicants. For example, a major U.S. company placed an ad in the Moscow, Russia, paper for an entry level position; 20,000 applications were received. When the company added the qualification "fluency in English language required," the application pool was reduced to 4,000. It would have saved much time and energy on the part of both applicants and personnel officers had the original ad included that vital piece of information (Warnath, 1992).

Job analysis information is also important in selecting the tests that are used to screen applicants. The more closely the selection instruments are related to the

A careful job analysis helps to match workers with particular jobs. Here, a quality control worker monitors the production line at a beer brewing plant in Pennsylvania.

743

requirements of the job, the less likely the company will be faced with legal challenges to their selection procedures.

Downsizing.   One of the business "facts of life" in recent years has been downsizing, or reduction in force (RIF). Downsizing is now also being called "rightsizing" as companies are required to reduce their workforce to meet the economic and technological realities of the day. Even companies that in the past had virtually guaranteed lifetime employment have had to revise their company policies. Downsizing has an impact not only on the employees who are laid off, but also on those who remain with the company. Research has shown that an important factor in the whole process is fairness. If the survivors who continue to work at the company and those who are laid off perceive that the procedures for making the decisions have been fair, then the negative impact of the layoffs is diminished (Brockner, 1992). This perception of fairness would be enhanced if these changes were carefully planned and the appropriate predictors and assessment instruments were used.

TRAINING AND EMPLOYEE DEVELOPMENT

One of the motivating influences a manager can provide for workers is that of training and development. Training in its many aspects has become increasingly important in the workplace. In the first half of the 20th century it was not unusual for a person to be hired for a job, learn the skills and responsibilities of that job, and then do the same basic tasks for the bulk of his or her working life. Change was minimal and occurred slowly, a condition that is no longer true. In present-day businesses, change is constant and rapid. Technological advances in machinery, electronics, and office equipment require learning new skills, techniques, and thinking processes throughout life. In contrast to the past, when a person who changed jobs more than two or three times was considered unstable, it is now a sign of growth not only to change jobs, but even to change careers.

Most companies train employees on specific equipment, with techniques necessary to fulfill the job. Other learning programs are developmental or educational and do not concentrate on specific job-related skills and knowledge. Rather they concentrate on the development of the individual as a whole, and are related to the individual's personal career goals as well as to the needs of the organization (Carnevale et al., 1990). The important concept behind the trend of these developmental activities is the recognition in recent years that learning is lifelong and that adults of any age can benefit from educational programs (Cross, 1981; Feller, 1991; Wexley & Latham, 1991).

In the same way that job analysis provides information to hire employees with the right skills for a particular job, a training needs analysis is useful in matching the changing requirements of the organization with the talents, skills, and characteristics of employees. A training needs analysis will show where there is a difference between the performance expectations of the organization and the actual performance of the worker and, therefore, a need to train the worker. This analysis is done at the organizational, operational, and individual levels before instructional content is developed. Information from a thorough job analysis can be used as the basis for the training needs analysis (Carnevale et al., 1990; Goldstein, 1986).

Career Development.   Career development is another motivating influence the organization can provide. Career planning for employees recognizes that the individual worker has aspirations and life goals. If these aspirations and goals of the employee overlap with the mission and needs of the organization, a long and mutually profitable association can result. If they don't, the employee is likely to move on to another organization that is more congruent. In either scenario, the individual and the organization benefit from the career planning program. Mutual planning of careers (the employee's work future) is typical of the modern organization's emphasis on acknowledging employees as resources with skills, abilities, and knowledge who can contribute to the organization's success. This mutuality of planning and decision making requires a broader view of the nature of power relationships in organizations than the typical attitude in former years (Arthur et al., 1989; Hall, 1986, 1990; Liebowitz et al., 1986; Sekaran & Hall, 1989).

ORGANIZATIONAL BEHAVIOR

Motivation

A question frequently asked of I/O consultants by managers and supervisors is, "How can I motivate my workers to work more efficiently?" In the first place, it is not possible for someone actually to motivate someone else. Using the definition of motivation given earlier in this book (see Chapter 9), what can be done is to provide the "influences that energize and direct responses." Then the question becomes "What influences should I provide so that my workers become energized and direct their energies into productive channels?" This second question recognizes that control of behavior is within the individual.

Some of the basic theories on motivation are discussed in Chapter 9. In addition, I/O psychologists also apply the principles of equity and expectancy theories. *Equity theory* refers to the basic relationship of inputs and outputs as perceived by individuals. If workers perceive that what they receive from the company in terms of compensation, praise, or other internal satisfactions (job outputs) equals what they perceive they have given the company in enthusiasm, energy, and productivity (job inputs), they will feel satisfied. This is a highly individual phenomenon and is based on the person's perceptions of the situation (Walster et al., 1978). *Expectancy theory* is based on economic principles: A worker will make conscious choices about his or her behavior in the workplace and, after thinking through the alternatives and their associated payoffs, will choose the alternative with the highest payoff (Landy & Becker, 1987).

Power and Politics in the Workplace

Sources of Power. Power is a factor in all of our relationships, yet it is perhaps the most misunderstood variable in interpersonal relations. It is a major factor in many of the problems in organizational settings that I/O psychologists are brought in to solve. Some of the commonly used definitions of **power** include references to influence, resources, or the ability to get things done. Power is variously seen as the holding of key resources and the ability to influence others to behave in a particular way. It is also the way in which one is perceived by others. The classic description of the sources of social power came from French and Raven (1959). They described power as stemming from reward, coercive, legitimate, referent, and expert sources. Reward, coercive, and legitimate power sources are those we think of most frequently in relation to the workplace. Reward power means that the powerholder can provide something valued by the other person. Coercive power is the opposite of reward power; it is the ability to punish the other person. Legitimate power refers to the concept that the powerholder has a legitimate title or role (French & Bell, 1990; Raven, 1990).

Reward Power. When a manager tells a worker that he or she will receive a bonus if the work is done by the deadline and with no errors, the manager is exercising reward power. Rewards can be bonuses, gifts, extra time off, job enrichment, or career path advancement. They can also be greetings and smiles of approval. There are several keys to the effective use of reward power: (1) the reward must be something the powerholder can actually provide, (2) the reward must be something valued by the receiver, and (3) the relationship between the reward and the behavior should be clear.

Coercive Power. Coercion is in many ways the opposite of the use of rewards in a power situation. It is the use of insults, threats, punishments, and the removal of privileges in the attempt to control the employee. "Management by fear" is often used in business to "motivate" employees. Typical statements made by managers who use this approach include "You should have known this wouldn't work, you dummy," "You'd better get this done on time, or you'll really be in trouble," and "Anyone with even half a brain would have understood this without asking so many questions."

Legitimate Power. Legitimate power is sometimes known as role, designated, legal, or position power. An example of the use of legitimate power can be seen in the following exchange. A manager tells an employee to perform a task in a specific way. The employee asks whether it can be done somewhat differently or perhaps questions the need to do it at all. Using legitimate power, the manager's response is "I'm the manager, don't ask questions, just do it." This form of power relies heavily on a hierarchical organizational structure.

Expert Power. Expert power is an intrinsic power resource. It is the exclusive, or almost exclusive, knowledge of something that is needed. When the delivery van won't start, the copier jams, or the computer is down, the most powerful person in the company is the person who has the appropriate skills and knowledge to solve the problem. The young associate in an accounting firm can gain recognition and perhaps a promotion by knowing some aspect of tax law or accounting procedure that no one else in the company understands. It is an intrinsic power resource because it resides within the person.

Referent Power. Referent power is also an intrinsic power resource. Others want to identify with this powerholder. The referent powerholder has credibility, has integrity, is perceived as fair, and often serves as a role model or mentor for others. Referent power develops over time as a result of the way in which the person works with other people. In the workplace, managers can become referent powerholders by providing opportunities for employees to use their resources in the common effort of working together to achieve an organizational goal (Warnath, 1987).

Outcomes of Use of Power. What are the outcomes of each of these power resources? There are short- and long-term outcomes for each. For reward power, the short-term outcome is positive. If rewards are used to foster cooperative work, the participants will feel good about themselves, each other, and the work they are doing. If reward power is overused as a long-term strategy, employees may begin to feel manipulated. If rewards are used to foster ultra-competitiveness between employees, long-term outcomes can be extremely negative for the company, because teamwork will be discouraged.

Coercive power will get the work done; performance will improve in the short term as workers scramble to "find out what the boss wants." Although productivity may initially increase, it will level off. Creativity is stifled because employees are afraid to take risks, morale is low, resentment increases, and absenteeism and turnover are high. In extreme cases employees might sabotage work, sell valuable information to competitors (industrial espionage), and steal equipment and materials from the company.

The use of legitimate or role power needs to be accompanied by expertise and competence. The work will be done in the short term, but resentment and negativism will develop if the legitimate power is accompanied only by reward and coercive sources. This combination of legitimate (role), reward, and coercive power is commonly found in traditional organizations that have a narrow hierarchical structure. It is often accompanied by the belief that workers have to be prodded into doing their jobs. Most Russian factories use this combination of

Russian workers are accustomed to a combination of reward, coercion, and legitimate power in the workplace. As the new possibilities of a free-market economy become realized in Russia, organizations will have to adapt and change some elements of the power structure. These budding capitalists in Russia are beginning to integrate new technologies into their business.

reward, coercion, and legitimate power. Jean, the I/O psychologist, asked Ludmilla how absenteeism is handled in her factory. Ludmilla, the personnel director of the factory in Moscow, said: "We have no absenteeism problem. If a worker is absent, he is fired." Ludmilla then continued to say: "On the other hand, if a worker does adequate work, the factory provides child care. With a good record, the worker can expect to get an apartment, four weeks of vacation at a factory-owned resort on the Black Sea, and possibly a car." This is an example of the combined use of coercive power (firing the employee) with reward power (child care, apartment, vacation, car) exercised by a legitimate role-power person (personnel director of the factory).

Expert and referent power are positive for both the long- and short-term outcomes. Newer, more participative and less hierarchical organizations make good use of referent and expert power, along with the belief in the integrity and worth of each employee (Likert, 1967, 1979; McGregor, 1960). This shift in the forms of power used in organizations has an impact on the attitudes of employees toward their work and their managers. It can also have an impact on the constructs workers hold about the nature of power itself (Warnath, 1987).

The Nature of Power.   Many people believe that power is corrupting. They point to all the people who have used power to hurt and exploit others or to help themselves at the expense of others. Daily newspapers and television programs provide plenty of evidence to support that belief. In actuality, power has no value of its own. It is neither positive nor negative. Whether power corrupts is dependent on the value system of the person who exercises the power and the organization within which the power is exercised. For example, a sentence completion test was administered to 500 employees from different types of organizations. They were asked to complete the sentence: "A powerful person is _____." The responses were then separated into two groups: group 1, whose respondents worked in traditional, hierarchical organizations, and group 2, who worked in organizations that were implementing participative management techniques. Group 1 responses used words such as *insensitive, vindictive, unprincipled, untrustworthy, obnoxious, stubborn, aloof, hateful*, and *greedy*. Group 2 responses used words such as *mentor, knowledgeable, idea generator, ethical, innovative, tolerant, supportive, future oriented, flexible, charismatic*, and *growth oriented* (Warnath, 1987). Further discussion with the respondents revealed that the responses in group 1 reflected negative attitudes toward work, while those in group 2 reflected positive work attitudes. Thus the two sets of responses suggest differences in attitudes of employees in the two types of organizations. Negative attitudes toward work can result in decreased productivity, absenteeism, and increased turnover.

In traditional organizations, the amount of power you have is calculated by your span of control (the number of people who are dependent on you). The more people depend on you, the more powerful you are. This interpretation of power assumes that power is hierarchically arranged. The man or woman at the top of the organization is the all-powerful person in the organization with a legitimate power source. He or she controls the rewards and coercions available in the organization and decides how they are to be used. In contrast, expert and referent power are emphasized in participative organizations, and power is shared throughout the organization. Employees are encouraged to be less dependent and to exercise initiative and expertise. As managers share power with employees, the managers gain stature and power by being perceived by employees as referent power sources. The responses of group 2 in the sentence completion test are typical descriptions of referent power. Reward power is also used, but the source of the rewards is distributed among different levels of the organization and not located in just one or two key people. Coercion is used sparingly for severe problems and only after all other approaches have been tried without success. Intelligent use of power in an organization can have beneficial outcomes for both the organization and the individual employees.

ORGANIZATIONAL THEORY AND DEVELOPMENT

What is an organization? The word *organization* has been used throughout this appendix, and it is time that we explain it. It is not a simple task, because the study of organizations is multidisciplinary, and there are as many ways of explaining organizations as there are academic disciplines that study them: anthropology, sociology, economics, political science, and psychology, among others. For the purposes of this book, we will focus on the psychological approach to theories of organizations. One of the widely accepted definitions is that of Katz and Kahn (1966): "an organization is a social device for efficiently accomplishing through group means some stated purpose." I/O psychologists study and work with organizations of all types that consist of groups of people who are attempting to accomplish the purposes of the organization. This definition encompasses both the public and the private sectors—social service agencies, retail stores, manufacturing enterprises, and professional firms (physicians, lawyers, accountants, etc.). The key to understanding the work of I/O psychologists is the word *efficiently* used in the Katz and Kahn definition. I/O psychologists are concerned with how organizations can accomplish their goals most efficiently and effectively. The interpretations of *efficient* and *effective* have changed over the years as psychology has gained more knowledge about human beings.

Traditional Organizations

Early in the 20th century Frederick Taylor (1911), a pioneer in industrial psychology, and others promoted what has been called a classical approach to modern bureaucratic organizations. The classical approach made certain assumptions about human beings in relation to work. The underlying assumptions were that most workers do not like to work and that they lack intelligence and motivation. Following from those assumptions was the need for very close supervision, breaking down work into basic simple standardized tasks, and discouraging the worker from doing anything not specifically within his or her job description. There

was clear hierarchical command and central decision making. Supervisors and managers were not to be concerned with personal characteristics of workers; individual differences were of little or no importance. Incentives were in the form of rewards for technical proficiency (Weber, 1946). This mechanistic view of the relationship between worker and boss prevailed for many years and was labeled **Theory X** by McGregor in 1960. In contrast, McGregor described a **Theory Y**, which is viewed as an early approach to participative management and is part of the human relations or human resources approach. The Theory Y manager is more supportive and trusts employees. This attitude stems from a different set of assumptions about human nature and motivation than those believed by the Theory X manager. Theory Y assumptions are that human beings are not lazy; they will work hard and accept responsibility; they want to be useful and productive; and that, for many people, work is a primary source of satisfaction. The role of managers in Theory Y is to identify conditions that evoke this intrinsic motivation of employees. It implies providing a climate in organizations that allows employees to function as adults rather than as dependent children (McGregor, 1960).

Participative Organizations

Building on these concepts of employees as adults who are intrinsically motivated, Likert developed his System-4 theory (Likert, 1979). **System-4 theory** describes four major orientations to organization design: System 1, exploitive authoritative; System 2, benevolent authoritative; System 3, consultative; and System 4, participative group. This theory represents a continuum from task-centered, autocratic leadership in System 1 to employee-centered, democratic, participative leadership in System 4. Most work settings in Russia fit into System 1, the exploitive authoritative category. The motivational orientation is fear and need for money and status. It ignores other motives. There is tight control of information, attitudes are hostile, and mistrust is prevalent. Decisions are made at the top, orders are given by the boss, and there is overt compliance with covert resistance. In the United States, some companies still operate at the System-1 level, but increasingly businesses are recognizing the benefits of involving employees at all levels in the process of work, leading to the System-4 level, the participative group category. The motivational orientation at this level includes both intrinsic and extrinsic motives, but does not include fear. Trust is more prevalent, and attitudes toward the workplace are favorable. There is much cooperative teamwork, with substantial upward, downward, and lateral influence. Because the employees participate in goal setting and decision making, there is full acceptance of goals and decisions. Information moves in all directions, with no attempt to control it or engage in the distribution of disinformation (Bowers, 1977). Systems theory as developed by Likert (1967) is useful as a tool for understanding organizations and diagnosing organizational problems. Contingency theories add the element of the organization's environment to internal variables in the determination of an organization's effectiveness and provide an additional dimension on which to measure organizations (see Fiedler, 1964, 1978; Lawrence & Lorsch, 1967; Robbins, 1990).

Organizational Interventions

The systems and contingency theories of organizations assume a complex, dynamic organization in which change is a fact of life. Individuals and organizations sometimes consider change to be disruptive. However, if change is planned for and managed, it has great potential for growth both for individuals and for organizations. **Organization development (OD)** is a behavioral science approach to planning and managing change in organizations. OD practitioners accept certain basic values, which include the belief that individuals seek personal growth and development, given an environment that is supportive and challenging. Employees are capable of far more contribution to their organizations than the more traditional hierarchical forms of organizational relationships have believed. OD interventions can be targeted at different parts of the organization. French and Bell (1990) describe five levels of intervention designed to improve effectiveness: (1) individual, (2) dyads/triads (conflict resolution, negotiation), (3) teams and work groups, (4) intergroup relations, and (5) total organization. Many strategies and techniques are used, including process consulting, team building, role analysis, techno-structural changes, and force field analysis. These strategies and levels of intervention are geared to developing processes and understanding in the employees and employers that will enable them to use change as a positive influence for growth and development. The best use of OD is as a continuing process that uses behavioral science technology and follows an action research model (Bolman & Deal, 1992; Burke, 1993; Fagenson & Burke, 1990a; 1990b; Manz et al., 1990).

Implementing OD procedures incorporates democratic values in the workplace and provides employees with choices and the opportunity for participating in decision making at different levels of the organization. This approach places more control over work life in the hands of the worker. The end result of successful OD intervention in an organization is to give workers more control in their work lives, which results in a healthier, less stressful environment and, in turn, results in a healthier, more productive organization.

Action Research

The ongoing work and life of an organization cannot be stopped to do traditional experimental research. Action research was initially proposed by Kurt Lewin (1945) as a tool for those engaged in social change and is used by OD practitioners to plan and manage change in organizations. As defined by French and Bell (1990),

[A]ction research is the process of systematically collecting research data about an ongoing system relative to some objective, goal, or need of that system; feeding these data back into the system; taking actions by altering selected variables within the system based both on the data and on hypotheses; and evaluating the results of actions by collecting more data. (99)

The "action" part of the term *action research* refers to actions taken to solve real problems faced by a specific organization. "Research" refers to the research done on that action to determine its effectiveness and to add to the body of knowledge and theory in the field (French & Bell, 1990). Organizations are interested in the solution of their immediate problems. The I/O psychologists who do action research are equally interested in solving the organization's problems and adding to the knowledge and theory base of the field. There is also an educational mission involved. The goal of the OD specialist is to encourage the organization to incorporate the action research process as part of the ongoing activity of the organization. By doing so, the organization will be better equipped to deal with or head off future problems.

TRANSNATIONAL I/O PSYCHOLOGY

Often when we think about companies that do business outside the borders of the United States we assume that they are multinational companies. However, global competition and marketing are found at many levels of business and government, and national borders are becoming quite fluid in terms of goods and services. I/O psychologists are involved in transnational consulting and research and are not constrained by national borders. I/O psychologists from the United States can be found in many countries as consultants to organizations and governments in the development of organizational structure and design, training and incentive programs, and all the areas discussed earlier in this appendix. In addition, I/O psychologists prepare executives who will be moving to other countries to work.

It must be understood that the research, principles, and practices discussed in this appendix are based on values and assumptions of the United States. The I/O psychologist who consults globally must be aware that each culture has its own values and belief systems. Kiggundu (1986) reviewed 25 case studies and found that the application of sociotechnical systems theory has run into difficulty because of basic differences in values and belief systems. According to Kiggundu: "Organizations in developing countries exhibit dysfunctional modes of conflict management, closer social and emotional interactions, intergroup rivalry, little capacity for openness, trust, and the rational expression of feelings, and well established hierarchical and status barriers"

(Kiggundu, 1986). Government plays a more important role in organizations in developing countries, and the measures of performance and organizational goals are not clearly defined. Therefore, to be successful in transnational settings, I/O psychologists must understand and respect cultural differences (Kiggundu, 1986; Shao & Hill, 1992; Trice & Beyer, 1993).

I/O PSYCHOLOGY AS A CAREER

For those who are thinking about a career in psychology, the area of I/O psychology provides a growing, developing specialty in which you can work with people in their everyday lives, building a work environment that is healthier for the individual and productive for the organization. There are doctoral-level programs in many universities in the United States. Some are located in psychology departments, some in business departments. The Society for Industrial and Organizational Psychology (1989) has several booklets that provide information regarding graduate training competency areas and institutions providing graduate programs. SIOP is a division within the APA (Division 14) and is affiliated with the American Psychological Society (APS). "Its goal is to promote human welfare through the various applications of psychology to all types of organizations providing goods and services, such as manufacturing concerns, commercial enterprises, labor unions or trade associations and public agencies" (SIOP, 1991).

I/O psychologists from the United States are working with businesses and organizations in many countries. Here an I/O psychologist works as a consultant with Toyota in Japan.

As global economies develop, there is increasing need for cooperation across national borders. This business executive in Japan discusses strategies for involving U.S. businesses in her company's enterprise.

THINKING AHEAD . . .

Many organizations will look quite different in the year 2000, and flexibility will be the key to success. We are accustomed to thinking of working in a central location with others in close proximity, and with face-to-face communication. Typical images in cartoons about the workplace show several employees clustered around the water fountain or coffee machine exchanging both casual conversation and business information. The traditional manager sits at a slight distance from this casual group in his or her office, communicating with employees in a more formal setting. In more recent years, managers followed the principle of "MBWA" (**m**anaging **b**y **w**alking or **w**andering **a**round), and participated in the informal exchanges. Manufacturing enterprises have been characterized by the image of the ever-moving assembly line with workers doing repetitive actions as the line moved forward. However, much of this is changing. Assembly lines are more automated, with machines doing much of the work formerly done by human beings. Many manufacturing plants use robots to move equipment and supplies around the plant, and only one or two employees are needed to oversee the mechanical operations.

Offices have also been automated: computers, printers, OCRs (optical character recognition scanners), e-mail (electronic mail), voice-mail, fax machines, copiers, and so forth. Computers have been around since the mid-1940s, but the "electronic revolution" is a 1980s phenomenon. The electronic revolution accompanied the emergence of the "information age" in the United States, where knowledge and information transmission are important. With the advent of portable electronic devices (laptop computers, printers, modems, cellular phones, etc.), it is no longer necessary for employees to be located in a central setting.

Telecommuting is one way in which organizations are utilizing the new technology. It is the process whereby employees in locations separate from the central office transmit their work to the central office through computers, modems, e-mail, and fax machines. Therefore, traditional management processes no longer apply when managing employees who are not physically in the office. It is difficult to "manage by walking around" when your employees are located anywhere from 35 miles to thousands of miles away. New approaches need to be developed that have a more fluid concept of time and space. Offices have begun to move into more flexible scheduling to meet employees' needs, a first step in the recognition of this new fluidity. Inherent in this approach to management is the acceptance of the employee as intrinsically motivated and self-initiating.

In terms of organization theory, however, telecommuting with employees in many different locations raises some interesting questions. If we consider the organization as a social-psychological entity in which people interact on a regular basis, have shared goals, make decisions to achieve those goals, and receive certain social benefits from being a member of that organization, how will the increase in telecommuting affect that experience? The members of the organization can still communicate, have shared goals, make decisions together through the available electronic means, and achieve the organizational goals. But in what way will the social benefits be altered? Many of the current human resource functions, such as performance appraisals leading to training and development recommendations, promotions, and transfers, or career planning and management, are based on knowledge of the way employees function on a daily basis and not on production factors. When does computer monitoring of individual production invade employee privacy? Will the trend toward telecommuting reduce the social and personal benefits now being derived from the interpersonal interaction that occurs daily in the workplace? When does an organization cease to be an organization and become simply a collection of people doing discrete pieces of work, with only a handful of staff in the central office to coordinate the work? These are questions that I/O psychologists will need to address in the near future.

Summary

Introduction to Industrial–Organizational Psychology

1. I/O psychologists research and apply psychological concepts and theories as they are related to the world of work. The most complex aspect of the work setting is human beings: employees, managers, customers. All of the areas of psychology covered in this textbook can be included in the work of I/O psychologists: motivation, development, learning, thought and memory, and so on.

Individual Evaluation

2. Individual evaluation is used when selecting and placing personnel; in career planning; and in making decisions about training, downsizing, and other personnel functions.

Organizational Behavior

3. Theories about motivation are very important; employees who are motivated tend to produce more and work together more effectively.
4. Understanding power relationships in the work setting can be an invaluable tool not only for the manager, but also for every employee. Researchers have determined that power is often misunderstood and used ineffectively.

Organizational Theory and Development

5. There are many differences between the traditional organizational structure and function of the early 20th century and those of today. The change is toward more participation and empowerment of workers.
6. Organizational interventions are used by I/O psychologists to assist organizations in planning for change. The I/O psychologists diagnose problems organizations may have and work with them to develop adaptive processes.
7. Action research was a process developed to enable researchers to study and consult with organizations while the organization continued to do its work. Although the multiple variables cannot be controlled as well as they can in the laboratory, action research has the advantage of being done in a real-life setting.

Transnational I/O Psychology

8. We live in a world that is growing increasingly smaller through electronic communication and easier travel opportunities. I/O psychology is of value throughout the world, adapting basic principles to specific cultural differences.

Key Terms

industrial-organizational (I/O) psychology (742)
action research (743)
personnel selection (743)

job analysis (743)
organization development (OD) (748)

power (745)
System-4 theory (747)
Theory X and Theory Y (747)

Suggested Reading

Bergmann, T. J., Mundt, D. H., & Illgen, E. F. (1990). The evaluation of honesty tests and means for their evaluation. *Employee Responsibilities and Rights Journal, 3*(3), pp. 215–223.

Burke, W. W. (1993). *Organization development: A normative view.* Reading, MA: Addison-Wesley. An easy to read, but thorough introduction to the way in which some I/O psychologists work with organizations to solve organizational problems and plan for change.

French, W. L., & Bell, C. H., Jr. (1990). *Organization Development* (4th ed.). New Jersey: Prentice-Hall, Inc.

Miner, J. B. (1992). *Industrial–organizational psychology.* New York: McGraw-Hill. An excellent comprehensive and basic textbook covering the many aspects of I/O psychology.

Trice, H. M., & Beyer, J. M. (1993). *The culture of work organizations.* Englewood Cliffs, NJ: Prentice-Hall. A multidisciplinary approach to understanding the cultural side of the work world.

APPENDIX C

Psychology Resources in the Library

Choosing a Topic
Beginning the Search
Location of Psychology Books and Journals
Using Psychology Journals
Some Representative Psychology Journals
More Detailed Sources on Library Work in Psychology
Some Helpful Guides to Better Writing

If you have been given an assignment to write a paper in your psychology course, this appendix will not tell you how to write that paper, but it should help you find the materials you need. Further, the information provided here will be helpful if you are looking for reading materials beyond the coverage of this book.

Our goals are to describe the psychology resources available in most college and university libraries, and to inform you of the indexes, abstracts, and other sources that will make your search for information faster, more systematic, and more fruitful. We will also describe some other books written specifically to aid students seeking psychology materials in the library.

CHOOSING A TOPIC

Perhaps your instructor has given you a topic for your paper. In that case you are ready to begin your library research. If not, you are faced with the immediate problem of selecting a topic. That decision is not an easy one, but it is one you should begin immediately. You want to spend the bulk of your time researching and writing the paper, not trying to think of a topic. You might browse through this book looking for an idea, but it would be better to ask yourself what it is about psychology that interests you. Most everyone is intrigued about some aspects of psychology, and that curiosity is a good starting place for a paper. You can begin with a broad topic and generate a series of questions. For example, consider the topic of child abuse. Are particular personality traits associated with parents who abuse their children? Are fathers more likely than mothers to be abusive? What about stepfathers or stepmothers? Are certain kinds of children more likely to be abused? Why do these children put up with abuse? Is child abuse only physical, or can it involve exclusively verbal abuse? What are the conse-quences of child abuse for the personality development of the child? What treatments are used for abusive adults?

We hope these questions do not produce a rash of papers on child abuse. Our point is to illustrate the kinds of questions that can be generated by any topic. If you are allowed to choose your own topic, then certainly you should select one that interests you. It is also important to choose a subject that you can cover in the time allotted or within the page constraints that may be provided by your instructor. We cannot speak for all instructors, but our preference is for a paper on a narrow topic well researched and written, rather than one on a broad topic, which might not be adequately covered. But follow the wishes of your instructor. It is better to get such questions answered before you begin. Again, the rules are *choose early* (before someone else checks out all the books you need) and *choose wisely* (select a topic that is doable, given time constraints and page limitations).

BEGINNING THE SEARCH

Your library search should begin with the key term (or terms) of your topic. Such terms will be your entry into the subject index of the card catalog in your library (whether the catalog is on cards or a computer terminal screen). For example, if your topic were the toxic effects of lead on memory, you could begin by searching terms such as *lead* (or *lead toxicity*), *toxicology*, and *memory*. If you have access to a computer search system, you may be able to search all those terms at once. We will say more about that later.

Sometimes the terms you are using are not the same ones being used in the subject index of the card catalog. Thus, you may have to try some related terms.

One helpful source for terms used in publications on psychology is the *Thesaurus of Psychological Index Terms* (the sixth edition was published in 1991). Usually this book is located among the reference materials in the library; often it is housed with a monthly publication called *Psychological Abstracts*. The *Thesaurus* is a collection of terms with information about other terms that are narrower, broader, or related. It is a book designed for use with topical searches in *Psychological Abstracts*, but it can be used for other search purposes. For example, if you were looking for a specific form of psychotherapy, looking up the term would provide the following: *analytical psychotherapy, client-centered therapy, existential therapy, Gestalt therapy, play therapy,* and 40 others. By using the *Thesaurus* you should be able to narrow your search to a few of the most profitable terms.

LOCATION OF PSYCHOLOGY BOOKS AND JOURNALS

Most libraries shelve psychology books and journals together in the appropriate areas, but some house the two separately. Journals that are more than a few years old are usually bound and can be found in the library stacks. More recent journal issues (typically those from the current year) may be found in a separate area, often called the Current Periodicals Room. And some older issues of journals may be found on microfilm or microfiche in that department of your library.

Most libraries today use the Library of Congress (LC) classification system for shelving books and journals. Before the LC system became popular in the 1960s, libraries used the Dewey Decimal System. Some libraries never converted their collection; they simply began cataloging new books using the LC system. If your library is like that, it means you will find some sources cataloged in Dewey numbers and some cataloged in the letter/number combinations of the LC system. Most psychology books are found in the 150s in the Dewey system and in the BF section in the LC system. But psychology is a diverse field, a fact recognized by both systems. Thus you find psychology materials scattered throughout the library. Table C–1 provides a partial listing of these areas, showing both Dewey and LC designations.

USING PSYCHOLOGY JOURNALS

It is impossible to give an accurate count of the number of psychology journals currently being published, but the number would be in the hundreds. Because psychology is related to so many other fields, articles on psychology appear in journals in diverse fields such as nursing, engineering, marketing, history, religion, education, and biochemistry. Researching a particular topic through all of these journals would be an impossible task for any individual. Fortunately, there is an easier way to make that search—you can use *Psychological Abstracts* (also called *PA*). This journal is published monthly by the APA. It can be found in most college libraries, usually in the reference section.

The editors of *PA* employ a small army of readers who scan approximately 1,000 journals a year looking for psychology articles. These articles, more than 30,000 annually, are briefly described in *PA* (an abstract is a summary). Further, the description includes a complete reference to allow the reader to locate the article in the journal in which it appeared. Articles are grouped according to subject categories within each monthly issue. Subject and author indexes are included to assist you in your search. These indexes are also published annually, and in a still larger cumulative index on a three-year basis. The three-year indexes provide a particularly quick way to find the articles on your subject (or author). The subject index lists a number of articles under each subject heading. Each article is described in four to five key words or phrases, with two numbers, one indicating the volume number of the *PA* containing the abstract, and the other indicating the number of the abstract itself. By reading the abstracts you can decide if the article is or is not important for your purposes. From your work with *PA* you can generate a list of journal references that you can take to the journal stacks to find the articles themselves.

There is a still easier way to do this kind of literature search. Several computer data bases include the titles and authors published in *PA*. In general, these computer-based abstracts contain articles published after 1967 (*PA* began publication in 1927), but for most student needs, the recent literature should suffice. The most useful of the computer-based search systems is called *PsycLIT*, which uses CD-ROM technology and is available today in many college and university libraries. *PsycLIT* covers the psychological literature from 1974 to the present, and the disks typically are updated each year. This system allows you to search authors and key words in the abstracts of the articles as well as their titles. The system is very user friendly, so that if you know even a little about computers, you should be able to use this important search tool.

The advantage of the computer systems is that the user can search for a number of key terms simultaneously. For example, you might be researching a paper on *emotional development* in *adolescents* who are raised by *single parents*. By using these three key terms in a single search, you can ask the computer to give you a listing of all articles that have dealt with these subjects. A search like that is an obvious timesaver. If you are interested, ask a faculty member in your psychology department or a reference librarian about the availability of such a system on your campus.

TABLE C-1
Distribution of Psychology-Related Materials Throughout the Library
(Library of Congress and Dewey Decimal Classification Systems)

Library of Congress Class.	Subject Area	Dewey Decimal Class.
RC512–571	Abnormal psychology and psychiatric disorders	616.852–616.89
BF636–637	Applied psychology	158
Q334–336	Artificial intelligence	006.3
BF721–723	Child psychology	155.4
BF311	Cognition	153.4
BF660–678	Comparative psychology	156
LB1051–1091	Educational psychology	370.15
HQ503–1064	Family (social groups)	306.8
IA167	Human factors	620.82
HF5548.8	Industrial psychology	158.7
BF501–504	Motivation	153.8
BF1001–1999	Parapsychology and the occult	133
BF231–299	Perception	153.7
BF698	Personality	155.2
HF5549	Personnel management	658.3
QP351–495	Physiological psychology	152
HV689	Psychiatric social work	362.2
BF455–463	Psycholinguistics (psychology of language)	401.9
RC475–510	Psychotherapy	616.89
RC435–510	Psychotherapy and psychiatry	616.89
BF231–299	Sensory perception	152.1
HM251–291	Social psychology	302
LC4601–4803	Special education (mentally handicapped and learning disabled children)	371.92
QA278	Statistics (correlation)	519.5
BF39–39.2	psychometrics	150.151
BF237	psychophysics	152.8
HQ1206–1216	Women, psychology of	155.633

Source: Adapted from Reed & Baxter, 1992

Whether you search in *PA* yourself or use a computer system to do it for you, a good starting point is the *Thesaurus* we mentioned earlier, because it lists the subject terms used by *PA*. For example, if you looked for *bruxism* (a disorder involving grinding of the teeth, especially during sleep) in *PA*, you would not find any listing. However, looking up *bruxism* in the *Thesaurus* tells you that *PA* uses the phrase *nocturnal teeth grinding* for bruxism. The *Thesaurus* also gives you other terms to aid in your search. If you look up the term *learning disorder*, you will find the suggestion that you also search the related topics of developmental disabilities, educational diagnosis, and mental disorders. This reference work also notes narrower, but related, categories such as dyslexia, learning disabilities, and reading disabilities.

SOME REPRESENTATIVE PSYCHOLOGY JOURNALS

Sometimes psychology professors want their students to read one or more journal articles on the science and theory of psychology. They may even allow students to select articles related to their own interests. You may be asked to write a brief paper on the article you read, perhaps giving your reaction to what you read, evaluating the methods or conclusions of the article, or relating it to some part of your textbook. To assist you in locating journals suitable for such tasks, we have provided, in Table C–2, a partial listing of journals by topic area. These journals represent some of the best in their respective fields, and are likely to be found in most college libraries.

TABLE C-2
Selected Psychology Journals, by Topic Area

General/Theory
American Psychologist
Psychological Bulletin
Psychological Review
Science

Physiological Psychology
Behavioral Neuroscience
Physiological Psychology
Physiology and Behavior
Psychophysiology

Sensory Processes/Perception
Journal of Experimental Psychology: Human Perception and Performance
Perception and Psychophysics
Vision Research

Learning
Animal Learning and Behavior
Journal of Experimental Psychology: General
Journal of the Experimental Analysis of Behavior

Memory, Language, and Thought
Cognitive Psychology
Journal of Experimental Psychology: Learning, Memory and Cognition
Journal of Verbal Learning and Verbal Behavior
Memory and Cognition

Motivation and Emotion
Learning and Motivation
Motivation and Emotion

Development
Child Development
Developmental Psychology
Psychology and Aging

Abnormal Psychology
Archives of General Psychiatry
Journal of Abnormal Child Psychology
Journal of Abnormal Psychology
Journal of Nervous and Mental Disease

Psychological Treatment
Behavior Research and Therapy
Behavior Therapy
Journal of Consulting and Clinical Psychology
Journal of Counseling Psychology

Personality/Social Psychology
Journal of Experimental Social Psychology
Journal of Personality
Journal of Personality and Social Psychology
Journal of Social Issues
Personality and Social Psychology Bulletin

Industrial/Organizational Psychology
Journal of Applied Psychology
Organizational Behavior and Human Decision Processes
Personnel Psychology

Other Fields
Behavior Genetics
Journal of Educational Psychology
Journal of Humanistic Psychology
Journal of Mathematical Psychology
Journal of the History of the Behavioral Sciences
Psychology of Women Quarterly
Psychopharmacology
Sex Roles
Sleep

MORE DETAILED SOURCES ON LIBRARY WORK IN PSYCHOLOGY

Our account of library research in psychology has been intentionally brief, but most of what you should need to begin work on a paper is contained in this appendix. If you need more help, consult one of the following, more extensive accounts:

Bell, J. E. (1971). *A guide to library research in psychology*. Dubuque, IA: William C. Brown. This book describes the many specialized resources in psychology available in the library. It lists books and journals in all psychology fields. It provides a list of the Library of Congress classification codes for psychological fields, and it includes a chapter on writing a library research paper.

Reed, J. G., & Baxter, P. M. (1992). *Library use: A handbook for psychology* (2nd ed.). Washington, DC: American Psychological Association. This book offers information on selecting and defining a topic, using *PA* and other related abstracts, and using government documents. It also offers advice on citation searching, interlibrary loans, and computer searches. It is a thorough and up-to-date guide for the student doing library research in psychology.

SOME HELPFUL GUIDES TO BETTER WRITING

There are many books available to assist you in developing better writing habits. We mention three here that we think are especially helpful. Any one of these would be a good permanent addition for your desk. The first one is intended specifically for writing psychology papers; the other two are more general manuals of writing style.

Jolley, J. M., Murray, J. D., & Keller, P. A. (1984). *How to write psychology papers*. Sarasota, FL: The Professional Resource Exchange. Contains chapters on writing term papers, preparing research reports, writing clearly, and using the library.

Maimon, E. P., Belcher, G. L., Heran, G. W., Nodine, B. F., & O'Connor, F. W. (1982). *Writing in the arts and sciences*. Boston: Little Brown. An excellent guide to writing for college undergraduates, this book includes a section on doing library research.

Strunk, W., & White, E. B. (1979). *The elements of style* (3rd ed.). New York: Macmillan. This classic, 92-page book is one of the most popular style manuals ever written. Its concise form and complete index offer ready help on most of the common problems in writing.

Glossary

abnormal behavior. Behavior that is unusual in the context in which it occurs and that interferes with an individual's functioning in society.

abscissa. A graph's horizontal axis.

absolute threshold. The point at which a stimulus can be detected 50% of the time.

abstract learning. Learning in which relations between and among stimuli are more important than the physical features of those stimuli.

academic skills disorders. Disorders that involve impairment of specific skills appropriate for a child of a given age, but not due to mental retardation, inadequate education, or sensory deficits.

acceptance. A coping strategy in which a person accepts the fact that stress has occurred and that nothing can be done about it.

accommodation. A monocular depth cue in which the ciliary muscles change the shape of the lens according to the depth of visual focus. In Piaget's theory, modification of cognitive structures to meet the demands of the environment.

achievement tests. Tests that evaluate an individual's mastery of specific programs of instruction.

acrophobia. Fear of high places.

action potential. The sequence of transient shifts in the electrical potential of a neuron caused by a stimulus.

activation-synthesis hypothesis. The notion that dream content reflects a synthesis of the neural activation that occurs during REM sleep.

adaptive nonresponding theory. The proposition that sleep, as a form of non-responding, originally had adaptive significance insofar as it prevented early humans from risking their lives by wandering about in the dark.

adaptive specialization. The process by which a specialized learning mechanism evolves in a given species.

addiction. Psychological or physiological dependence on a drug.

additive color. A color mixture that is based on the addition of light wavelengths. Additive primary colors are red, green, and blue.

adrenal glands. A pair of endocrine glands, each located above a kidney, that are essential to both physiological and psychological functioning.

adult genital sexuality. Freud's last stage of psychosexual development.

aerial perspective. A monocular depth cue in which atmospheric haze causes changes in the coloration of distant objects.

afferent. Neurons that send a signal toward the brain or spinal cord.

age of viability. The end of the second trimester of pregnancy; the point at which there is a chance for a fetus to survive if born prematurely.

aggression. The act of delivering an aversive stimulus to an unwilling victim.

agoraphobia. Fear of public or other places that lack easy means of escape in which help might be difficult to obtain in an emergency.

AIDS. Acquired immune deficiency syndrome (AIDS) is a viral disease transmitted by infected semen and blood. Incubation of the disease averages around 10 years before symptoms appear; death appears certain in all cases.

aim. In Freudian theory, the goal of an instinct to achieve gratification.

albedo. The portion of light reaching a surface that is reflected back to the eye.

algorithm. Any method that guarantees a solution to a problem.

all-or-none law. A rule governing neural transmission that states that with a given level of stimulation an impulse occurs at full strength or not at all.

alpha waves. Brain waves of 8–12 cycles per second that are common in relaxed states, including drowsiness.

altered state of consciousness. Any state of consciousness other than normal waking consciousness.

altruism. The performance of behavior that is designed to benefit another person, sometimes at personal sacrifice to the actor.

Alzheimer's disease. A disease associated with the aging process; one symptom is memory loss.

amnesia. Forgetting under conditions of severe psychological or physical trauma.

anaclitic depression. Depression in infants and children associated with the loss of a parent or primary caretaker.

anal stage. Freud's second stage of psychosexual development in which the child derives pleasure from the anal region of the body, especially during elimination.

anima. According to Jung, the archetype of the female that exists within the male unconscious.

animism. A characteristic of Piaget's preoperational stage, in which children attribute life to inanimate things.

animus. According to Jung, the archetype of the male that exists within the female unconscious.

anorexia nervosa. An eating disorder in which people restrict their food intake even though they are underweight.

anosmia. The total absence of the sense of smell, usually caused by brain tumors or head injuries.

Antabuse. A drug that produces intense nausea when it is present in the bloodstream along with alcohol; used in the treatment of alcoholism.

anterograde amnesia. A condition in which a person has trouble forming new memories but retains old memories.

antianxiety compounds. Minor tranquilizers used to reduce anxiety; they also act as muscle relaxants and anticonvulsants.

antipsychotics. Class of drugs that are used in the treatment of different forms of psychosis.

antisocial personality disorder. A psychological disorder characterized by behavior that is harmful to other people or to society and that persists from adolescence throughout adulthood.

anxiety disorders. Disorders involving heightened levels of uneasiness, apprehension, or fear.

anxiety hierarchy. A list of frightening events ranked according to severity, used in systematic desensitization. See also *systematic desensitization*.

aphagia. Starvation that occurs, despite the availability of food, because of surgical lesions of the hypothalamus.

apparent movement. Illusory movement of a stationary object or the misperception of the direction of movement in a moving object.

approach–approach conflict. A conflict in which an organism is pulled toward equally attractive goals.

approach–avoidance conflict. A conflict in which an organism is simultaneously attracted to and repelled by the same event or object.

aptitude tests. Global measures of experience that are used to predict whether an individual can profit from an educational program or course of study.

archetypes. According to Jung, a number of universal thought forms that are part of the collective unconscious.

arousal theory. The notion, according to Berlyne, that people seek to maintain a preferred level of arousal or activation.

artificial intelligence (AI). The use of machines to mimic intellectual thought in humans.

artificialism. A characteristic of Piaget's preoperational stage, in which children tend to believe that everything is the product of human creation.

assimilation. The use of available cognitive structures to gain information about the world.

asymmetry of function. The difference in purpose and organization of the right and left cerebral hemispheres of the brain.

asymptote. A leveling-off or plateau that signifies that for a given set of experimental conditions, maximum learning has taken place.

attachment. The process by which an infant establishes a close emotional relationship with the person or persons who provide most of the infant's care.

attention. The focus of consciousness on a particular stimulus or event.

attention deficit/hyperactivity disorder (AD/HD). A disorder where the person is unable to focus attention for normal lengths of time, and often shows a pattern of elevated activity.

attitude. A relatively stable collection of beliefs and feelings about a person or a thing.

attribution theory. A theory in social psychology that people make inferences about the causes of behavior, and tend to locate the causes of behavior either within the person or the situation.

auditory cortex. A portion of the temporal lobe that receives inputs from the auditory nerve and processes auditory information.

auditory localization. The ability to locate the direction and distance of a sound source, usually by interaural differences in intensity of the sound and its time of arrival.

auditory nerve. One of the two branches of the eighth cranial nerve (the other is the vestibular nerve), which carries neural information from the hair cells in the cochlea to the auditory cortex.

authoritarian. Parenting style in which absolute rules for child behaviors are set up, and physical punishment is common.

authoritarian personality. A personality style characterized by rigid opinions and, often, prejudiced attitudes; this sort of person may either wield absolute authority or submit totally to others' authority.

authoritative. Parenting style in which rules are flexible and reasoning is commonly used.

autism. A severe childhood disorder associated with self-injurious behavior, language impairment, and lack of social responsiveness. See *autistic disorder*.

autistic disorder. A serious developmental disorder with marked impairment in social interaction and communication, and with abnormally restricted activities and interests.

autokinetic effect. The perceived movement of a stationary point of light in an otherwise darkened room.

automatic processing. The completion of routine and consistent tasks without conscious attention to them.

autonomic nervous system. One of two involuntary subdivisions of the peripheral nervous system; concerned primarily with the body's functioning.

autonomy versus shame and doubt. In Erikson's theory, the crisis of the second year of life, provoked by the conflict over toilet training.

aversion therapy. A type of behavior therapy in which an aversive stimulus is associated with an unwanted behavior.

avoidance–avoidance conflict. A conflict in which an organism is confronted with two unpleasant alternatives.

avoidance learning. Learning to respond to a cue or signal that predicts aversive stimuli (impending danger).

avoidant attachment. Style of attachment in which infants neither seek support from nor show distress toward caregivers in strange situations.

axon. A cylinder-like fiber that is often the largest component of the neuron and that transmits signals to other neurons.

babbling. Spontaneous vocal activity of infants that begins around six months of age.

backward conditioning. In classical conditioning, presenting the unconditioned stimulus before the conditioned stimulus.

balance theory. The theory that people strive for consistency in their interpersonal relationships; they want to be around people who like and dislike the same things that they do.

barbiturates. Also referred to as sedatives, these drugs are strong central nervous system depressants used to reduce anxiety or irritability.

basal ganglia. A set of structures located in the forebrain between the thalamus and the brain's outer shell that are involved with motor behavior.

basic level categories. Existing conceptually between subordinate and superordinate categories, these categories are important in language comprehension and for providing a perceptual means of differentiating categories. They are likely the first conceptual categories acquired in life.

basic research. Research that is undertaken to add to a science's store of knowledge and that has no immediate application.

basilar membrane. The membrane in the inner ear that contains the auditory receptors.

behavior ecology. Study of the coexistence of several different species in one habitat.

behavior therapy. A form of psychotherapy that makes systematic use of learning principles in order to bring about improvement in psychological functioning.

behavioral control. The belief that one has available responses that can affect health status or the experience of stress.

behavioral genetics. The field of psychology that clarifies the role inheritance plays in behavioral development.

behavioral medicine. An interdisciplinary field that incorporates knowledge from the medical, behavioral, and social sciences to promote health and prevent illness.

behavioral model. In abnormal psychology, the view that abnormal behavior is a function of faulty contingencies of reinforcement.

behavioral self-blame. Perceiving one's self as the cause of misfortune.

behavioral toxicology. The study of the effects of poisons on behavior.

behaviorism. A school of psychological thought, established by John B. Watson, that advocates the study of observable behavior rather than unobservable mental processes.

behaviorist approach. An approach to psychological study that emphasizes observable behaviors and excludes the study of unobservable events such as mental processes.

behavioristic models. In personality, models based on instrumental learning theory that assume that personality characteristics are a function of the individual's history of reinforcement.

benzodiazepines. Drugs, such as Valium and Librium, that produce relief of anxiety through increased inhibition of brain activity.

Békésy's theory. An auditory place theory that accounts for pitch perception in terms of the action of a traveling wave in the basilar membrane.

beta-endorphins. Opiate-like substances that occur naturally in the human nervous system.

bilateral ECT. ECT that is administered simultaneously to both cerebral hemispheres. See also *electroconvulsive therapy*.

bimodal. A distribution of scores in which two modes (most frequent scores) appear.

binocular cues. Depth perception cues that require the functioning of both eyes.

binocular disparity. A binocular depth cue that takes account of the disparate images on each retina; effective to a maximum of about 1,000 feet.

biofeedback training. An intervention procedure in which a person is taught to monitor and control an internal and normally automatic function such as heart rate.

biological approach. An approach to psychological study that seeks to understand behavior by describing it in terms of its underlying neurological, biochemical, and neuromuscular causes.

biomedical model. In abnormal psychology, the view that abnormal behavior is a function of physiological problems such as genetic abnormalities or problems in brain biochemistry.

biomedical therapy. Therapy that seeks to improve a patient's mental state by changing events at an anatomical or neurochemical level.

bipolar cells. Secondary cells in the retina that connect rods and cones to the ganglion cells.

bipolar disorder. A mood disorder characterized by fluctuations of mood between unusual excitement and serious depression.

bisexual. Sexual orientation in which an individual is attracted to members of the same and opposite sexes.

blind spot. An area of the retina containing no receptors, where the optic nerve exits the back of the eye.

blocking. The inability to condition a second stimulus because of prior conditioning to another stimulus that is also present during training.

bonding. The creation of an emotional relationship between parent and child shortly after birth.

bottom-up processing. In perception, information processing that begins at the receptor level and continues to the higher brain centers.

brain stem. The portion of the central nervous system in which the spinal cord meets the brain.

brainstorming. A popular technique for creative problem solving that encourages the generation of many ideas in an environment free of judgment and criticism.

brightness. The psychological dimension of color related to light intensity.

Broca's area. The section of the brain's left frontal lobe that relates to expressive language.

bulimia nervosa. An eating disorder in which people overeat and then purge themselves by self-induced vomiting or the use of laxatives.

bystander intervention. Research that focuses on when and under what conditions individuals help others in need of assistance.

calibration. Relationship or correlation between a rememberer's confidence that a memory is correct and the actual accuracy of the memory.

Cannon's thalamic theory. The theory that the thalamus sends impulses simultaneously to the cerebral cortex and the visceral organs, with the result that subjective awareness and bodily changes occur simultaneously in the experience of emotion.

castration complex. A Freudian concept that holds that boys between the ages of about two and six fear castration because of desire for their mothers and competition with their fathers. See also *Oedipal crisis*.

catatonic schizophrenia. Schizophrenia characterized sometimes by rigid postures, sometimes by wild excitement, or by alternations between the two.

catharsis. A strategy for coping in which pent-up emotions are released as a means of reducing stress.

central fissure. A canyon in the brain that demarcates the frontal and parietal lobes.

central nervous system (CNS). A subdivision of the nervous system, consisting of the brain and the spinal cord.

central route. Route to persuasion in the elaboration likelihood model in which persuasion occurs due to deliberate, effortful thinking about the arguments to which one has been exposed.

central tendency. The high probability that most scores will concentrate in the center of a distribution and that relatively few will fall at the extremes.

cephalo-caudal development. Direction of prenatal development that proceeds from the head downward. See also *proximo-distal development*.

cerebellum. A section of the hindbrain that is essential to coordinated movements in standing, walking, and other muscular activities.

cerebral cortex. The immensely complex part of the forebrain that constitutes two-thirds the weight of the nervous system and envelops the underlying sections of the brain.

chaining. The performance of several different behaviors in sequence in an effort to obtain reward.

chemotherapy. The use of drugs to treat illness.

child abuse. Physical injury or harm to children.

child neglect. Lack of adequate care for physical, social, and emotional development.

child sexual abuse. Sexual exploitation of minor children.

chlorpromazine. A drug found effective in treating psychotic disorders that involve symptoms such as extreme delusions and hallucinations.

chromosomes. Strands of material, aligned in pairs and located in the cell nucleus, that carry the organism's genes.

chunk. A discrete, coherent memory unit compiled of smaller bits of data that share common properties and relationships.

circadian rhythms. Physiological or behavioral patterns that fluctuate on an approximately 24-hour cycle.

circular reactions. According to Piaget, repetitive actions that infants acquire while engaging in a nonreflexive exploration of the environment.

classical conditioning. Learning that takes place when two or more stimuli are associated together.

classification rules. A rule or set of rules that define the characteristics of membership in a particular conceptual category.

claustrophobia. Fear of enclosed places, such as elevators.

client-centered (nondirective) therapy. A humanistic method of psychotherapy that lets the client rather than the therapist direct the treatment process.

clinical neuropsychology. A branch of psychology associated with interpreting various brain disorders.

clinical psychology. A branch of psychology that focuses on the diagnosis and treatment of psychological disorders, as well as on research into the causes and treatment of such disorders.

closure. The tendency to fill in information that is missing from a perceptual array by closing the gaps; a principle of Gestalt psychology.

cochlea. The coiled set of chambers in the inner ear containing the auditory hair cells.

cognitive appraisal of stress. A two-stage process in which a person first decides if the stress demands a response, and then chooses an available coping strategy.

cognitive approach. An approach to psychological theory and research that emphasizes the scientific study of mental processes such as thinking, memory, problem solving, and learning.

cognitive behavior modification. A therapy technique designed to change people's self-perceptions, that is, the way people think about themselves.

cognitive consistency theory. A motivational theory that states that tension arising out of conflicting thoughts motivates behavior in an attempt to reduce that tension.

cognitive control. The belief that one has cognitive strategies that can affect outcomes related to health and stress.

cognitive dissonance theory. A model that asserts that when a person experiences two motivational cognitions (thoughts) that are inconsistent, a state of psychological discomfort results; thus he or she is motivated to restore equilibrium.

cognitive learning. Learning in animals and humans that involves uniquely mental events such as rule formation and strategies for goal attainment.

cognitive maps. The mental layout of an apparatus or of an environment.

cognitive model. In abnormal psychology, the view that abnormal behavior is a function of unusual ways of thinking about the world. In personality psychology, models that view individual personality in terms of people's tendencies to process, interpret, and make sense out of the world.

cognitive-physiological theory. The theory, proposed by Schachter, that emotion as experienced is the result of interpreting physiological events within the body in the light of both ongoing environmental events and memories of past events.

cognitive psychology (cognitive learning). The study of higher mental structures and processes, including complex decisions, strategies, and other uniquely mental events.

cognitive structures. In Piaget's theory, the means by which human beings acquire and apply knowledge about their worlds.

cohort effects. Behavioral and psychological effects that are based on the time that people were born and their subsequent experiences, rather than on their age.

cohort-sequential research. Developmental research strategy that combines longitudinal and cross-sectional methods.

collective unconscious. Composed of a number of universal thought forms, the collective unconscious is a part of human genetic heritage that is common to all people. This is Jung's explanation for why each individual has similar psychological experiences.

complex cells. Cells in the visual cortex that react to a moving line of light in a particular orientation.

complexes. According to Jung, an organized group of feelings, thoughts, and memories that influences a person's experiences and is part of the personal unconscious.

compulsion. A ritualistic and stereotyped behavior that an individual feels compelled to perform repetitively.

computerized axial tomography (CAT). An X-ray scanning technique that converts X-ray pictures to a visual code that a computer can read.

computer assisted instruction (CAI). A training technique that requires a student to interact with a computer containing special systems programs and instructional materials. The computer records and analyzes student responses and determines subsequent presentations of information based on learning needs.

conceptual category. A set of members (things, cases, instances) possessing some common attributes that are given the same label.

concordant. A term used to describe twins who share a trait that may be heritable, such as schizophrenia.

concrete–operational thinking. According to Piaget, the stage between the age of about six and early adolescence in which more logical thinking appears.

concurrent validity. A measure of a test's meaningfulness based on whether people can be accurately assessed for the presence of traits.

conditioned reinforcer. A neutral stimulus that acquires reinforcing properties because of its association with a primary reinforcer.

conditioned response (CR). A reaction that resembles the original response, but which is a response to a neutral cue (conditioned stimulus, or CS) associated with the unconditioned stimulus (US).

conditioned stimulus (CS). A neutral cue that, when paired with the unconditioned stimulus, elicits a conditioned response.

conductive deafness. Deafness produced by a loss of conductive properties in the ear, usually the result of damage to the ossicles in the middle ear.

cones. Visual receptors that respond to differences in the wavelength of light, or what we call "color."

conformity. The act of adopting the social norms or customs of a larger social group.

confounding variables. Any variable that could possibly influence an experimental outcome. Such variables must be controlled or eliminated in an experiment.

conscious thought. In Freudian theory, thought of which the individual is aware.

consciousness. The state of awareness of the world and of the self.

consensus. A factor that helps determine type of attribution; the similarity of a response from one person to another. See also *attribution theory*.

conservation problems. In Piaget's theory, problems that assess the child's ability to understand that the amount of certain substances remains the same even though they have undergone physical transformations.

consistency. A factor that helps determine type of attribution; the tendency to respond in the same way in similar circumstances. See also *attribution theory*.

consolidation. The stabilizing of memory events prior to placement into long-term memory.

construct validity. The "true" validity of a test, that is, the extent to which the test measures a given characteristic, trait, or construct.

contact comfort. The infant's need for contact, independent of feeding.

contact theory. A theory that increased contact between races will reduce prejudice and discrimination.

content-related validity. A measure of a test's meaningfulness that is concerned with whether the test covers a full range of conceptual material that is being tested.

contiguity model. A model of classical conditioning that says that learned associations are formed when two events occur together in time and space.

contingency model. A model of classical conditioning that says that learning occurs when one event reliably predicts the occurrence of the other.

contingency theory. A type of theory which holds that characteristics of one or more events or entities will vary depending on characteristics of other events or entities.

continuity position. The position in developmental psychology that growth and development are very gradual and that there are no dramatic shifts in development. See also *discontinuity position*.

continuous reinforcement. Schedules that reinforce the occurrence of every operant behavior that satisfies an accepted criterion.

contrast theory. The theory that brightness constancy occurs when adjacent objects are available for comparison.

control group. In an experiment, the group that serves as a basis for the comparison of results with the experimental group, and also serves to eliminate alternate explanations of the results.

controlled processing. Refers to the fact that conscious attention is required on the part of the subject in those situations where stimuli and responses vary.

conventional level. According to Kohlberg's theory, the level of moral judgment at which individuals make moral judgments on the basis of expectations—from the family, the social group, or the nation at large.

convergence. An important binocular cue for depth in which coordination of the extrinsic eye muscles produces visual images in comparable portions of the retinas of each eye.

convergent thinking. A type of thinking required to solve problems that have a single correct solution.

conversion disorder. A psychological disorder characterized by physical symptoms such as blindness or paralysis that have no known organic basis.

coping. Behaviors and thoughts that enable an individual to handle stress or anticipated stress.

coping strategies. Stone and Neale identified eight different categories that define the various methods individuals use to handle stress.

cornea. A transparent bulge in the sclera of the eye that, in conjunction with the lens, focuses the image on the retina.

corpus callosum. A bundle of neurons positioned immediately below the large longitudinal fissure that separates the two brain hemispheres; connects the hemispheres so that neural messages can flow freely between them.

correlation. A statistical technique that measures the strength of a relationship between two variables.

correlation coefficient. A number ranging from -1.0 to +1.0 that expresses the degree of association—either positive or negative—between two variables.

counseling psychology. A branch of applied psychology involved in treatment and research on psychological problems associated with adjustment in areas such as marriage, career, and school.

counterbalancing. An experimental technique designed to control for the effect of order; two or more conditions or treatments are administered to separate groups in different orders.

counterconditioning. The process of pairing stimuli of different strengths that are known to evoke competing behaviors so that an old response to the original stimulus is replaced by a new, stronger response.

counterfactual. At odds with the facts.

creativity. Artistic or intellectual inventiveness that results in some novel and valuable product.

criterion. A performance measure or standard by which behavior is judged.

criterion-related validity. A form of validity that checks scores on a test against performance in a given area of functioning. Criterion-related validity includes both predictive validity and concurrent validity.

cross-racial identification. Identification of a criminal suspect by a witness who is racially different from the suspect.

cross-sectional research. A type of developmental research that tests people of different ages at the same time.

dark adaptation. A retinal chemical change due principally to changes in rods, but also involving cones; occurs when the eyes are adjusting to very low levels of illumination. The eyes are maximally sensitive to light when completely dark adapted.

death instinct. See *thanatos*.

debriefing. Informing subjects, at the end of an experiment, about the purposes of the research, including the hypotheses tested, the anticipated results, and their significance.

decay theory. The theory that memories that are not rehearsed fade with time.

deep processing. A level of processing, as with elaborative rehearsal, that promotes transfer to long-term memory.

deep structure. The meaning, or meanings, of a sentence. See also *surface structure*.

defense mechanisms. According to Freud, mental processes that the ego uses to avoid conflicts with the id and superego and to guard against anxiety created by instinctual wishes.

defining attributes. Qualities that exist in all members of a class.

deindividuation. The phenomenon in which the presence of others weakens restraints people ordinarily feel and may lead to socially prohibited behavior.

deinstitutionalization. The shift toward decreasing the population of psychiatric patients in psychiatric hospitals.

delayed conditioning. A technique in which a conditioned stimulus is introduced prior to the onset of the unconditioned stimulus, yet remains at least until the onset of the unconditioned stimulus.

delirium tremens (the DTs). Symptoms such as visual hallucinations, irritability, headaches, and fever that accompany withdrawal from alcohol.

delta wave. Brain waves of 1/2–2 cycles per second that are characteristic of stages 3 and 4 of NREM sleep. See also *NREM sleep*.

delusional disorder. Disorder in which an individual exhibits false beliefs that have no factual basis, but with no additional impairment of cognitive processes.

delusions. False beliefs that are not based on external reality.

delusions of persecution. The false beliefs that others wish to harm one, as, for example, to spread false rumors about one.

delusions of reference. Delusions in which the person attributes unusual personal significance to people or events.

dementia. See *senile dementia*.

dementia praecox. A term coined by Kraepelin to describe what we now call schizophrenia; the term denoted premature impairment of mental processes. See also *schizophrenia*.

dendrites. Branchlike structures of a neuron that interact with other neurons or receptors in order to gather information.

dependent variable. The variable that the researcher chooses to measure. Usually a response measure, it is expected to be influenced by the independent variable.

depersonalization. A state, often brought about by the drug PCP, that involves feelings of estrangement from others and from the environment.

depolarization. A change in membrane potential that defines a neural impulse.

depressants. Drugs that have a sedative effect on the central nervous system; for example, alcohol, barbiturates, and hypnotics.

dermis. Middle layer of the three layers of skin, composed of living cells.

descriptive grammar. The system of rules that governs the use of everyday language.

descriptive statistics. The use of selected techniques for organizing and summarizing large amounts of data in order to communicate the main features of a data set more effectively.

developmental disorders. Disorders that involve disturbances in the acquisition of cognitive, language, motor, or social skills, and that first become evident in infancy, childhood, or adolescence.

developmental psychology. A field of psychology emphasizing the changes in behavior that occur as a result of developmental processes such as maturation and experience.

developmental task. Something that must be resolved before continued psychological growth can proceed.

deviation IQ. Intelligence test scores presented in standard-deviation units, interpreted in terms of the normal distribution. See also *standard age score*.

dichotic listening. A technique used in studying selective attention, whereby a subject wearing headphones receives two different auditory messages, one in each ear. Typically, the subject is asked to attend to only one message.

dichromacy. A form of color blindness in which the person has trouble distinguishing reds from greens, or blues from yellows.

difference threshold. The minimal change in stimulation that can be reliably detected 50% of the time.

differentiation. A process by which one event or object/entity is separated or discriminated from other events or objects.

diffusion of responsibility. The social phenomenon in which individual group members feel a decreased responsibility to help in an emergency because the responsibility becomes spread throughout the group.

direct action. A coping strategy in which a person directly tries to solve the problem.

direct measures. Memory tests that direct attention to the target memories being tested.

discontinuity position. The position in developmental psychology that growth and development involve discrete shifts in functioning, often described as stages of development. See also *continuity position*.

discrimination. In perception, the ability to detect and respond to a select class of stimuli. In social psychology, the behavioral expression of prejudice.

discriminative stimulus (S^D). A cue or signal indicating that responding will be reinforced.

dishabituation. The phenomenon of increased responding to a new stimulus following decreased attention to an earlier stimulus.

disorganized attachment. Distorted form of attachment shown by abused or neglected children characterized by exaggerated approach toward and avoidance of caregivers.

disorganized schizophrenia. Schizophrenia characterized by symptoms of severely disordered thinking, such as incoherent language and unusual emotional expression.

display rules. According to Ekman, the culturally learned rules that operate unconsciously in defining appropriate displays of emotion and the necessary modifications of those displays.

dissociative amnesia. A loss of memory caused by psychological factors.

dissociative disorders. Disorders involving a break in conscious experience, identity, or memory.

distal stimulus. The stimulus as it actually exists in the perceptual world.

distinctiveness. A factor that helps determine type of attribution; when a response is specific to a particular situation. See also *attribution theory*.

distraction. A coping strategy in which a person gets involved in other activities or thinks about other topics.

divergent thinking. Creative thinking, in which a subject is asked to generate as many novel solutions to a problem as possible.

divided attention. The ability to monitor simultaneously more than one message or to respond to more than one stimulus.

dizygotic twins. Twins who share no more genetic material than ordinary siblings because they developed from separate zygotes. Also called *fraternal twins*.

dominant gene. A gene that rules over the recessive gene to determine the outward appearance, or phenotype, of the organism.

dopamine hypothesis. The line of reasoning that schizophrenia is associated with elevated levels of dopamine in the brain.

dorsal root. The back side of a spinal nerve where incoming sensory information is registered and enters the spinal cord.

double bind. A situation in which two mutually contradictory messages are given.

double blind. A control technique in experimentation where neither the experimenter nor the subjects are aware of the subjects' group assignment. See also *single blind*.

double standard. The term used when different regulatory norms are applied to two different groups.

Down syndrome. A mental deficiency that results from an extra chromosome on the 21st pair.

drive-reduction model. The theory that responding occurs systematically in order to reduce and to maintain a homeostatic balance.

drug tolerance. The decrease in the pharmacological effects of a drug that accompanies long-term use of the drug.

DSM-IV. The fourth edition of the *Diagnostic and Statistical Manual of Mental Disorders*, published by the American Psychological Association in 1994.

dual coding theory. The theory that thinking is a result of two interacting systems of information processing, one perceptual (primarily visual) and the other verbal.

dualism. A philosophical position that considers the mind and body to be distinct entities.

Duchenne smile. Facial changes that accompany a genuine smile; involves upward turn of the corners of the lips and cheek elevation.

dynorphins. Naturally occurring (endogenous) pain killers.

dyslexia. An impairment in the ability to read.

ecological theory of perception. James Gibson's theory emphasizing that perceptual responses can be explained fully by the information in distal stimulation.

effectors. Glands and muscles that respond to efferent neurons to produce changes in either the internal or external environment.

efferent. Neurons that send signals away from the brain and spinal cord to effectors. Also called *motor neurons*.

ego. According to Freud, the part of the mental apparatus that controls id demands for pleasurable sensation through pragmatic considerations.

ego integrity versus despair. In Erikson's theory, the crisis of late adulthood, based on the human tendency for self-evaluation.

eidetic imagery. An ability, now questioned, to look at a visual stimulus, such as a page of text, and then reproduce it exactly.

elaboration likelihood model. Model of persuasion that specifies how attitudes become more stable and enduring following effortful thinking about persuasive arguments.

Electra crisis. In Freudian theory, a psychosexual crisis that girls experience in the phallic stage, characterized by attraction to their fathers as objects of sexual gratification and rivalry with their mothers.

electroconvulsive therapy (ECT). The biomedical treatment for some psychological disorders, primarily depression, by a series of administered electrical shocks.

electroencephalograph (EEG) computerized classification scheme. An imaging technique that plots abnormal brain activity as a function of differences in brain wave patterns relative to controls.

electromyogram (EMG). The record of muscle activity that is used to assess the occurrence of REM sleep. See also *REM sleep*.

elevation. A monocular depth cue in which objects below the horizon are seen as farther away the higher their elevation is in the visual field.

embryo. The human organism in the earliest phase of prenatal development, lasting about 8 weeks after conception.

emergent properties. Attributes possessed by a combination of components, but not possessed by any of the individual components.

emotion. A feeling of pleasantness or unpleasantness that is manifested in conscious experience, as well as accompanying behavioral and psychological changes.

empirical scale. A test whose items were selected so that they differentiate between selected groups in the population; the MMPI is one example.

empiricism. A philosophy which holds that knowledge should be acquired by careful observation.

employee assistance programs (EAP). Formal measures sponsored by an employer to help employees with their personal and work-related problems. Typical problems include physical and mental health, financial, legal, drug, and marital difficulties.

encoding. The initial stage of memory in which sensory events are coded and changed to a format that makes additional processing possible.

encounter group. A group psychotherapy technique that requires members—usually strangers to each other—to make comments on the styles and personalities of others in the group.

endocrine system. A system of glands that secrete their chemical products in the bloodstream.

enkephalins. Naturally occurring (endogenous) pain killers.

environmental psychology. A branch of psychology that deals with the effects of different environments on human behavior.

epidermis. Outermost of the three layers of skin, composed of dead cells.

epinephrine. A hormone released from the adrenal glands when stimulated by the autonomic nervous system; also called *adrenalin*. When a person is frightened or aroused, the release of epinephrine aids the body's effort to respond to environmental demands by such means as increasing blood flow, heart rate, and blood sugar levels.

episodic memory. Memory based on personal events that have taken place during a person's life.

equivalent-form reliability. A measure of test scores' consistency, determined from administering two parallel forms of a test to the same people.

eros. According to Freud, the instinct that accounts for feelings and behavior related to survival, such as sexuality. Sometimes called the *life instinct*.

escape learning. Learning how to terminate aversive stimuli through negative reinforcement.

estrogen. The hormone produced primarily by the female ovaries.

estrus. In infrahuman animals, a specific period when the female is sexually receptive.

ethnocentrism. The tendency to evaluate one's own group—especially a racial, ethnic, or national group—as superior.

ethologists. Scientists who study animal behavior in the natural environment.

evaluation apprehension. The concern people experience when they are about to be evaluated by others.

excitation. A reaction to the synaptic buildup of neurotransmitters in which the neural signal continues in the post-synaptic neuron.

executive coaching. Training for executives that teaches them how to deal effectively and appropriately with employees.

executive outplacement. Counseling business executives who have been terminated or relocated.

exhibitionism. Obtaining sexual gratification through showing one's genitals to unwilling observers.

existential analysis. A type of humanistic psychotherapy in which therapists help clients gain an awareness of the meaning and importance of their lives.

exocrine glands. Glands that secrete their products into local body cavities.

expectancy theories. A type of theory which holds that behavior is a function of cognitive anticipations that arise in response to specific features of stimulus situations.

experience corollary. In Kelly's theory, the notion that people continually revise and update their personality constructs on the basis of their experience.

experiment. A scientific procedure in which one manipulates certain variables (independent variables), while observing the effects of that manipulation on other variables (dependent variables).

experimental extinction. A procedure that demonstrates the neutrality of the conditioned stimulus by presenting the conditioned stimulus repeatedly without pairing it with the unconditioned stimulus.

experimental group. In an experiment, the group that receives the actual treatment condition.

experimental psychology. A broad field of psychology in which research is typically conducted in a laboratory setting.

expert system. Computer program intended to process and interpret information in a specific area as an expert in that area would.

explanatory style. The "self talk" we use to explain life change events.

explicit memory. Remembering that one is consciously aware of.

ex post facto method. A research method that selects subjects on the basis of a pre-existing set of conditions. In this kind of study, the independent variable has already been manipulated and is thus not under control of the experimenter.

expressive aphasia. A condition, caused by damage to brain cells in Broca's area, in which the patient continues to understand speech but has difficulty speaking.

extinction. Classical conditioning procedure in which, following initial acquisition training, the CS is repeatedly presented without US pairings.

extrinsic rewards. Response outcomes that are satisfying independent of the events that produce them.

eyewitness identification. Test in which a person who saw a crime tries to recognize a criminal from a lineup or a photospread.

eyewitness testimony. Evidence given by someone who witnesses a crime; events that occur after an incident takes place may influence the way an eyewitness reconstructs a report of what occurred originally.

face validity. A measure of the meaningfulness of a test based on test items that appear, on the surface, to be measuring a given construct.

facial affect program. The particular patterning of the facial musculature associated with specific emotions.

facial blends. Facial expressions of combinations of emotions, exhibited in different parts of the face; for example, sadness-anger or happiness-surprise.

factor analysis. A statistical technique in which many different tests and measures are administered and intercorrelated in order to discover what measures tend to go together and can thus be isolated as factors.

family therapy. Therapy where family members play a significant role in treatment of psychological disorders.

father complex. According to Jung, the psychological orientation of a person who is dominated by past experiences with his or her father.

fear. A feeling of apprehension, uneasiness, or dread.

feature-analysis theory. A theory of pattern perception that proposes that patterns are identified by a stepwise perceptual and decisional analysis of their distinctive features.

feature detectors. Specialized nerve cells in the visual cortex that respond selectively to specific stimulus patterns in the visual environment.

fetal alcohol syndrome. A condition of some infants born to women who are alcoholics, characterized by unusual facial features such as widely spaced eyes, thin upper lip, a short nose, and mental retardation.

fetishism. Psychological disorder involving sexual arousal to inanimate objects such as, for men, bras and high-heeled shoes.

fetus. The human organism in the later phases of prenatal development, from about the 9th week after conception to birth.

fictional finalisms. In Adler's theory, a set of idealized goals that motivate a person to strive for perfection.

field studies. Studies carried out in real-life settings.

fight or flight syndrome. Pattern of autonomic nervous system arousal that prepares the body for action.

figure-ground perception. The tendency to differentiate the perceptual world into a focus (the figure) embedded in a background (the ground).

fissures. Canyons in the brain that mark the outer surface of the cortex.

fixed action patterns (FAPs). Behavioral patterns that are identical across members of a species and are biologically determined.

fixed interval schedule (FI). Schedule in which reward is given for the first response to occur after a specified period of time has elapsed.

fixed ratio schedule (FR). Schedule in which behavior is rewarded after a fixed number of responses have been executed.

flashbacks. Hallucinations that take place long after the stimulating event, such as use of a drug; a problem among LSD users.

flashbulb memory. When memory retrieval is aided by a personal event (often a tragedy) so extraordinary that recall occurs in great detail.

flooding. A behavioral technique that uses extinction to treat anxiety disorders by inducing real-life encounters with anxiety-eliciting stimuli without providing the opportunity to escape.

foil. Incorrect target inserted in an eyewitness lineup or photospread.

follicle stimulating hormone (FSH). One of the gonadotropic hormones that induces the maturation of the ovarian follicle and the secretion of the gonadal hormone estrogen by the ovaries in the female, and stimulates the production of sperm in the male.

forebrain. A subdivision of the brain consisting of the thalamus, hypothalamus, basal ganglia, limbic system, and cerebral cortex.

forgetting. When memory fails and previously learned material is no longer available for recall.

formal–operational thinking. According to Piaget, the cognitive stage of adolescence and adulthood in which the logical system is more elaborate, and hypothetical thinking is possible.

Fourier analysis. Analysis of a stimulus into its component sine waves.

fovea. A small region in the retina consisting entirely of cones, where visual acuity is best due to lack of visual summation.

free association. A talking technique in psychoanalysis in which the therapist encourages the patient to say the first thing that comes to mind in order to reveal inner conflicts.

free recall. A technique in which subjects are asked to recall information in any order they wish.

free running rhythms. The natural rhythms that, in the absence of any time cues, determine cycles for sleep and waking.

frequency. In sound waves, the rate at which the air is expanded and contracted; closely corresponds to the psychological dimension of pitch.

frequency distribution. A summary of a data set that shows how often each score occurred.

frequency polygons. A line graph that is used by research psychologists to present frequency distributions.

frequency theory. The theory, according to Rutherford, that differences in pitch are due to differences in the firing rate of the auditory nerve.

frontal lobes. Areas in the left and right cerebral hemispheres that are located above the lateral fissure and in front of the central fissure.

functional fixedness. A hindrance in problem solving in which a person thinks of objects as having very specific functions, and is unable to see the potential uses of various objects in novel situations.

functionalism. A system of American psychology, associated with William James and others, that emphasized the study of the functions of consciousness.

fundamental attribution error. An attributional bias that people are more likely to make person attributions than situation attributions about other people's behavior.

ganglion cells. The secondary cells in the retina whose axonal processes form the optic nerve.

gate control theory. Proposes pain is modulated by a spinal gate that determines whether a pain signal is allowed to go on to the brain.

gender identity disorders. Disorders in which an individual feels trapped in a body of the wrong gender.

general adaptation syndrome (GAS). Selye's proposed model of the body's emergency reaction to stressful situations: alarm reaction, resistance, and exhaustion.

general intelligence (g). Spearman's notion of a global cognitive factor from which all cognitive activities spring.

generality theory. In health psychology, the view that psychological characteristics can leave individuals vulnerable to a variety of illnesses. See also *specificity theory*.

generalization. When a CR occurs to stimuli that are rather like the original training CS, even though these events have never been paired with the US.

generalized anxiety disorder. A psychological disorder characterized by anxiety lingering as a generalized feeling of tension or apprehension.

generativity versus stagnation. In Erikson's theory, the crisis of middle adulthood, provoked by the need to be productive and creative.

genes. The basic units that are responsible for our hereditary traits and that are located within the chromosomes.

genetic predisposition. Hereditary tendency.

genotype. The internal genetic composition.

Gestalt psychology. A German system of psychology, originated by Wertheimer, that argued for the study of consciousness as an integrated whole as opposed to an analysis of its elements.

Gestalt therapy. A humanistic therapy that teaches the client to recognize obscure mind and body elements that have gone unexamined.

glial cells. Supportive cells in the nervous system that help protect neurons from harmful chemical and physical stimulation.

glucagon. A hormone produced by the pancreas that serves to convert glycogen back to glucose when it is needed.

glucocorticoids. Hormones released by the adrenal glands that produce dramatic changes in glucose metabolism.

glucoreceptors. Specialized receptors, concentrated in the hypothalamus and the liver, that are excited by low or high glucose concentrations in the blood.

goal setting. Refers to several techniques which rest on the premise that effective performance can be produced if the goals of the task are clearly detailed to and accepted by an individual.

gonadal hormones. Hormones secreted from the ovaries and testes.

gonadotropic hormones. Hormones, produced by the pituitary gland, whose target organs are the gonads.

good continuation. A principle of perception that states that lines are perceived as continuing in direction or form.

grammar. Language rules for combination and use of words.

grief. Intense emotional suffering, usually caused by loss.

group. Two or more people in dynamic interaction with each other.

group matching. A control technique that seeks to eliminate the potential imbalance of relevant variables by assigning subjects to specific groups based on a matching of those variables.

group polarization. The social phenomenon that occurs when, following a discussion, a group makes a decision that is more extreme than the average of the positions of all the members of the group prior to the discussion.

group tests. Tests that can be given to many people at once, used particularly in the educational system and in the military.

growth hormone. One of the hormones released from the anterior pituitary. Also called *somatotropin*.

habituation. A decrease in sensory sensitivity that occurs at the neural level. Responsiveness will suddenly reappear if the stimulation level is increased or decreased.

habituation technique. A technique in which infants are repeatedly shown a stimulus until their response to it declines.

hair cells. Located on the basilar membrane in the cochlea, these cells are the actual receptors for hearing.

hallucinations. Perceptions in the absence of sensory stimulation, such as the hearing of nonexistent voices.

hallucinogens. A class of drugs, also called psychedelic drugs, that distorts the perception of reality, usually producing vivid hallucinations.

hardiness. A personality type combining three traits—control, commitment, and challenge—which seems to promote good health and resist stress.

harmonics. Sounds that are produced due to sympathetic vibration in conjunction with the fundamental sound; also called *overtones*.

health psychology. A subdiscipline that involves the role of psychology in promoting health-related behaviors.

hemispheres. The two halves of the human brain.

heritability of traits. The phenomenon of passing from one generation to the next certain aptitudes or behavioral tendencies.

heterosexual. Sexual orientation in which an individual is attracted primarily to members of the opposite sex.

heuristic. Problem solving strategy that draws on the person's past experiences, helping to select paths that are more likely to lead to solutions.

hidden observer. A phenomenon in hypnosis that demonstrates the existence of two levels of consciousness, one of which is typically concealed.

higher-order conditioning. See *second-order conditioning*.

hindbrain. The most primitive subdivision of the brain, made up of the medulla oblongata, pons, and cerebellum.

hippocampus. Part of the limbic system that is involved in the recognition of new objects, memory, inhibitory learning, and decision making.

histogram. A bar graph that shows a frequency distribution.

histrionic personality disorder. A personality disorder characterized by overly dramatic reactions to minor situations; seen by others as vain and shallow individuals.

holophrastic speech. In young children, the use of a single word to express some broader idea.

homeostasis. The body's tendency to maintain a relatively stable environment.

homosexual. Sexual orientation in which an individual is attracted primarily to members of the same sex.

hormones. Secreted products from the endocrine system that circulate in the bloodstream to influence parts of the body.

hospice care. Support for dying patients and their families through a network of support services based in the community.

hostile aggression. Aggression that results when a person feels pain or frustration.

hue. The psychological dimension of color related to the physical wavelength of light.

human factors psychology (Also known as human engineering). The design and modification of equipment and equipment systems to make them safer, easier to use, and better adapted to the needs of human users and operators.

humanistic approach. An approach to psychological theory and treatment that views human behavior as the result of free will and an innate striving to achieve one's full potential.

humanistic models. In personality, models that emphasize the individual's humanity and higher motives such as self-actualization.

humanistic psychotherapy (humanistic therapy). Therapy that places the responsibility of treatment on the patient, emphasizing the patient's ability to select his or her own goals and exercise free will in attaining them.

Huntington's chorea. A deadly disease that results from the deterioration of basal ganglia cells in the brain.

hypercomplex cells. Visual cortex cells that react to moving lines of light of a specific length, and to moving corners and angles in particular orientations.

hyperphagia. Overeating that occurs because of lesions in the ventromedial hypothalamus.

hypnosis. An altered state of consciousness usually induced by a hypnotist. The subject is relaxed and extremely suggestible.

hypnotic age regression. A controversial hypnotic technique in which suggestion is used to take subjects back to earlier times in their lives.

hypnotics. A category of depressant drugs used to help people sleep.

hypochondriasis. A disorder characterized by an unrealistic belief that one has a disease, despite medical opinion to the contrary.

hypothalamus. The tiny neural mass in the forebrain, between the thalamus and pituitary gland, that is involved in the regulation of emotions, sexual activity, and food and water intake.

hypothesis. An idea about how things work or why things happen the way they do. Scientific hypotheses must be stated in such a way as to be testable.

hypothesis testing. In concept formation, the trial and error approach to discovering the determining attributes of a concept.

hysteria. A disorder in which an actual physical symptom, such as blindness or partial paralysis, is without physical basis.

id. According to Freud, the part of the mental apparatus that demands immediate gratification of the instincts.

identity versus role confusion. In Erikson's theory, the crisis of adolescence, provoked by the need to figure out what one will do with one's life.

idiographic approach. Personality research that analyzes individuals intensively as case histories.

illusion of knowing. An inaccurate overconfidence about one's knowledge and understanding.

imagery. A transformation process that converts different sources of information into visual form.

immunosuppression. A decrease in the responsiveness of the immune system due to psychological stress, believed to be mediated by opiates.

impetus. In Freudian theory, the strength of an instinct.

implicit memory. Remembering or using knowledge without an awareness of remembering.

implosive therapy. A behavioral technique that requires the patient to imagine a fear-eliciting event in an approximate form.

impulse. The signal caused by the depolarization of a neuron.

incentive theory. A motivational theory that says that behavior is pulled, rather than pushed, and that goal attainment is the purpose of responding.

independent variable. In an experiment, the variable an experimenter chooses to manipulate. Usually a stimulus variable, it is expected to influence the dependent variable.

indirect measures. Memory tests that reflect prior experience but that do not refer to the target memories being tested.

individuality corollary. In Kelly's theory, the notion that people differ from each other in their construction of events.

individual tests. Tests administered individually in a one-to-one situation.

individuation. According to Jung, a state in which every system of the human being has developed to its fullest potential.

indulgent. A permissive parenting style having few rules or demands for children.

industrial–organizational psychology. A field of applied psychology that studies behavior in the work setting.

industry versus inferiority. In Erikson's theory, the crisis of later childhood provoked by the child's entry into school.

inferior colliculi. Sections of the midbrain that consist of large relay nuclei involved in hearing.

inferential statistics. Tests that assess the likelihood that the differences obtained in an experiment could have occurred by chance. These statistics also allow generalizations from a sample to the population of which it is a part.

information control. Communications about the nature of health-related situations given to the potential recipient of stressful events.

information processing system. Human or computer memory system that encodes, stores, and retrieves bits of knowledge.

initiative versus guilt. In Erikson's theory, the crisis between the ages of 3 and 5 provoked by the child's sexual interests.

inkblot technique. A projective technique in which the examinee is asked to tell the examiner what he or she sees in an inkblot. The examiner observes not only the response but the way in which the examinee responds, to gain information about the examinee's personality. See also *projective technique*.

innate. Features or traits that exist from birth.

insight. Sudden realization of an idea.

insight learning. Learning that is marked by a sudden grasp of a concept and, usually, an immediate performance change.

insomnia. Difficulty in falling asleep and/or problems with maintaining sleep.

instinct. A genetically programmed behavior that is adaptive and important to the survival of both the individual and the species at large. It has its own energy source and typically is carried out to completion once it is released by a sign stimulus.

instinctive drift. Natural behavior intrudes on a training schedule, preventing the learned responses from occurring.

instrumental aggression. Aggression that occurs because it produces a desired result, or goal attainment.

instrumental learning. Learning in which a response produces a change in the environment that ultimately affects the probability that a response will recur.

insulin. A hormone secreted by the pancreas that facilitates the transfer of glucose from the blood into cells throughout the body.

insulin shock. A physically traumatic treatment with excessive insulin that induces seizure activity in order to improve the disposition of psychotic patients.

integration. A process by which one event or object/entity is organized into or coordinated with other events or objects.

intelligence. The capacity to acquire and use knowledge, based on cognitive activities such as perception, memory storage and retrieval, reasoning, problem solving, and creativity.

intelligence quotient (IQ). A ratio between mental age and chronological age. Stern's formula for IQ was MA/CA x 100.

interaction. The combined effects of two or more independent variables on a dependent variable.

interaction effect. Observed differences in the dependent variable that occur as a result of the combined influence of two or more independent variables.

interference hypothesis. In dream recall, the proposal that dream content is forgotten because of interfering events that occur upon awakening and throughout the day.

interference theory. The theory that forgetting occurs because something blocks the usual process of retrieval.

intermittent reinforcement. A schedule involving only the occasional reinforcement of an accepted criterion of behavior. Also called *partial reinforcement*.

intern's syndrome. Tendency to believe that one has a disorder that one has been studying.

interneurons. Neurons in the central nervous system that transmit stimulus signals from afferent neurons to other interneurons or to efferent neurons.

interposition. A monocular depth cue in which a nearer object is seen to overlap, and thus obscure, part of an object farther away.

interval scales. A scale of measurement that names and specifies differences along a dimension. Equal distances between scale values are assumed.

intimacy versus isolation. In Erikson's theory, the crisis of early adulthood, provoked by the need for commitment to another person.

intrinsic rewards. Activities that are interesting and fun to do even though they produce no external benefits.

introspection. A technique of self-observation in which a person undergoes an experience and then describes the personal nature of that experience.

in vivo desensitization. Employment of actual feared objects in the process of desensitization training.

iris. The pigmented portion of the eye that controls the amount of light entering the eye.

irony. Statements in which the intended meaning is opposite of the stated meaning.

item analysis. Procedure for evaluating tests by correlating each test item with the total test score.

James–Lange theory. Proposal that the perception of bodily changes gives rise to the experience of emotion.

jigsaw classroom. Learning method used in elementary and secondary schools in which different members of a group learn separate components, after which each person teaches his or her segment to the group; group success depends on the contributions of all members.

job analysis. A systematic appraisal of the requirements of a specific job.

job satisfaction. Workers' feelings about their jobs that can be assessed by I/O psychologists; usually workers are satisfied with some aspects of their jobs and unhappy about others.

job specification. A listing of the relevant skills and personal characteristics of a person well suited for a particular job.

key word approach. A mnemonic encoding system involving the use of words as memory cues.

kinesthetic system. Composed of receptors in the joints and ligaments, this system communicates information about the movement and location of body parts.

Klinefelter's syndrome. A condition that occurs when there is an extra X chromosome present in the sex chromosomes (23rd pair).

Korsakoff's syndrome. Amnesia due to a malfunctioning limbic system in the brain; associated with chronic alcoholism.

language. A system of words, word meanings, and the rules for combining those words.

latchkey children. Children who return from school to an unsupervised home.

latency. According to Freud, the period of sexual repression that children experience in late childhood.

latent content. According to Freud, the hidden meaning of dreams that is represented symbolically in the version recalled by the dreamer.

latent inhibition. When a conditioned stimulus is presented alone prior to being paired with an unconditioned stimulus, it makes it more difficult to get conditioning, relative to the case where no conditioned stimulus preexposure occurs.

latent learning. Learning that occurs in the absence of apparent reward.

lateral fissure. A canyon in the side of the brain that demarcates the temporal and frontal lobes of the brain.

lateral geniculate body. Located in the thalamus, this center sharpens the contrast of the visual image and organizes its features (before they are reassembled in the cortex).

lateral hypothalamic area. A section of the hypothalamus that is identified as the hunger center because it is thought to regulate food ingestion.

law of effect. Thorndike's principle that the environmental consequence of the response determines whether or not a stimulus-response connection will form.

laws of grouping. Perceptual organizing tendencies that group objects according to principles of similarity (like objects are grouped together) and proximity (near objects are grouped together).

Law of Prägnanz. The tendency to perceive things in the simplest form possible. Also known as the *law of simplicity*.

learned helplessness. Ceasing to respond because of prior inability to effect change.

learned optimism. Seligman's description of a particularly effective explanatory style.

learning. A relatively permanent change in behavior or knowledge that occurs as a result of experience.

lens. The translucent body located behind the pupil that changes its shape in order to focus images on the retina.

lesion. Damage to the nervous system.

levels of processing theory. A theory that says that the depth of processing (shallow or deep processing) determines the likelihood that material will be placed in long-term memory.

libido. According to Freud, the power behind the sexual instinct.

life change events. Events that can be especially stressful, such as death of a spouse, marriage, job troubles, or a vacation.

life instinct. See *eros*.

life span developmental psychology. The study of human development that takes into account all phases of the life cycle and their effects on each other.

light adaptation. A decrease in the sensitivity of the eye in conditions of increased illumination, produced to a large extent by chemical changes in the retina.

lightness constancy. The fact that object lightness tends to be perceived as unchanging, despite changes in the amount of light striking the surface of an object.

Likert's organizational system. See *organizational system*.

limbic system. An aggregate of brain structures that is involved in the control of the emotions, including behavioral inhibition and behavioral response to stimuli.

limbic system theory of emotion. A physiological theory of emotion emphasizing the role of limbic system structures such as the hypothalamus, amygdala, septum, and cingulate gyrus.

line of best fit. A line that is extended through the middle of the points on a scatter plot to give a visual profile of the correlation between two variables.

linear perspective. A monocular depth cue produced by the fact that parallel lines appear to converge in the distance.

linguistic relativity hypothesis. Theory that a person's language determines and limits that person's experiences.

lip reading. Also called speech reading, a procedure in which deaf individuals can understand speech by observing movements of the lips, jaw, Adam's apple, and other facial features. Accuracy ranges from 30% to 85%.

lithium. A drug used to treat mood disturbances (mania).

loneliness. Feeling of deprivation resulting from unsatisfactory social relations with others.

longitudinal fissure. The central fissure that runs from the front to the back of the brain, dividing it into two symmetrical hemispheres. See also *fissures*.

longitudinal research. A method of developmental research that tests and retests the same people over an extended period of time.

long-term cues. Cues such as body fat that regulate overall body weight.

long-term memory. A component of the memory system of great capacity that holds lasting information.

loudness. A psychological dimension of sound, principally determined by the amplitude of the sound wave.

lucid dreaming. Dreaming in which one is aware of one's dream and, possibly, able to control dream content.

luteinizing hormone (LH). One of the gonadotropic hormones that induces ovulation in the female and stimulates secretion of the gonadal hormone testosterone by the testes in the male.

magnetic resonance imaging (MRI). An imaging technique that sends a radio signal and disperses hydrogen atoms and records their realignment.

major depression. A long-lasting mood disturbance in which an individual feels overwhelming sadness, listlessness, self-blame, and guilt.

maladaptive behavior. Behavior that is counterproductive, interferes with functioning in society, and may be in need of intervention.

management by objectives (MBO). The establishment of clear objectives for improved work performance; working with employees to see that those objectives are reached.

management training. Procedures for training managers, including on-the-job training in which a trainee is assigned as assistant to an experienced manager, and then is transferred to a different mentor.

mandala. According to Jung, a magic circle that represents the archetype of the self.

manic episode. A phase during which the individual is unusually excited, hyperactive, and increasingly social.

manifest content. The dream content as actually recalled by the dreamer.

MAO inhibitors. A class of antidepressants, such as Nardil, that is often used instead of ECT to treat depression.

masochism. Deriving sexual gratification from being hurt or humiliated.

matching-to-sample. Procedure for studying abstract learning in which the subject must learn to respond to the stimulus just presented.

mature love. Love that characterizes enduring relationships. It is high in caring and intimacy and characterized by openness of communication.

mean. The arithmetic average of scores in a distribution.

means–end analysis. A heuristic technique that seeks to divide problems into a number of subproblems that may have more manageable solutions.

mechanism. A philosophy which holds that all phenomena in the universe are machine-like and thus explainable by physical events.

median. The middle value in a ranked set of scores.

meditation. Altered state of consciousness used to achieve bodily awareness and relaxation.

medulla oblongata. The relatively small section of the hindbrain that regulates vital activities such as breathing, swallowing, blood circulation, skeletal muscle contraction, and coordination.

menarche. A girl's first menstruation.

menopause. The cessation of ovulation and menstruation that women experience in middle age.

mental age. In testing, an individual's mental development expressed in terms of the average chronological age of individuals of corresponding mental ability.

mental comparisons. A decisional process in which we compare two or more objects in our mind.

mental model. Personal theory or view of a domain of knowledge.

mental practice. Used by many competitive athletes, this technique involves the rehearsal of the athletic performance in mental images depicting perfect performance.

mental retardation. Deficits in mental functioning that become apparent during development and that are manifested in tested intelligence.

mental rotation. A component of visual thinking in which subjects mentally alter the orientation of objects.

mental set. The tendency to approach new problems with strategies used for solving similar problems in the past. Mental set can hinder problem solving.

mere exposure effect. The tendency to become more favorably disposed toward a person or an attitude merely by coming into repeated contact with it.

metacognition. Thinking or awareness of one's own thoughts.

metamemory. Awareness of one's memory.

method of loci. A mnemonic encoding system involving the use of locations as memory cues.

microsleeps. Brief (2–5 sec.) bursts of sleep that intrude into wakefulness.

midbrain. A subdivision of the brain that includes the reticular formation.

midlife crises. Heightened sensitivity to aging and mortality that occurs in middle age.

Minnesota Multiphasic Personality Inventory (MMPI-2). A self-report inventory for assessing personality.

mnemonic devices. Cues that enhance memory by linking new organizational sets of information to memory elements that already exist.

modal action patterns (MAPs). Behavioral patterns that occur among most members of a species and are biologically determined.

mode. The score that occurs most often in a distribution.

modeling. Therapy technique based on the use of observational learning.

monoamine oxidase (MAO) inhibitors. Antidepressant drugs, such as Nardil, that elevate mood by altering neurotransmitter activity.

monochromacy. Total color blindness.

monozygotic twins. Twins who have the same genetic makeup because they come from a single zygote. Also called *identical twins.*

morale. In industrial/organizational psychology, the feeling that workers have of belonging to a group (the company) and striving to make it a success.

morpheme. The smallest unit of language that has meaning.

mother complex. According to Jung, a psychological orientation in a person who is dominated by past experiences with his or her mother.

motion parallax. A monocular depth cue in which near objects are seen as moving more rapidly than far objects when the viewer's own head is moving.

motivation. The purpose for responding. Motivation determines how strong a behavior will be, and it determines what form it will take.

motor cortex. A section of the frontal lobe, located close to the central fissure, that is responsible for controlling movements in different parts of the body.

multi-cultural approach. The study of psychological phenomena across diverse cultures, populations, and groups.

multimodal therapy. A form of treatment where a variety of therapy approaches are used to bring about improvement in a single case.

multiple approach–avoidance conflict. A motivational conflict in which a person must choose between two or more events, each of which has positive and negative features.

multiple personality. A disorder in which a single individual gives expression to two or more distinct personalities, each of which has periods of dominance.

myelin sheath. A tube around the axon, composed of cells that aid in the rate of transmission of information along the distance of the axon.

naloxone. A drug that counters the effects of beta-endorphins.

narcissistic personality disorder. A personality disorder characterized by an exaggerated sense of self-importance and demands for attention.

narcotic. A class of drugs derived from the opium poppy. Includes opium, heroin, morphine, and codeine.

natural categories. Conceptual categories that are used in everyday life; an emphasis of the ecological approach to cognition.

naturalistic observation. A research method in which the researcher attempts to observe behavior in its natural setting without altering or interfering with the behavior of the subjects being studied.

nature position. A position in developmental psychology that holds that growth and development are genetically programmed. See also *nurture position.*

need achievement. The motivation to achieve.

needs assessment. An analysis of education or training requirements that is based ideally on a complete evaluation of the tasks, competencies, and environment of a specific job.

negative automatic thoughts. Unwelcome thoughts that a person cannot put out of mind; frequently occur in major depression.

negative correlation. A correlation that occurs when high scores on one measure are associated with low scores on another.

negatively skewed. Describes a distribution in which low scores occur infrequently.

negative reinforcement. Removal of an aversive stimulus following a certain desirable response.

neglectful. Parenting style in which children are largely ignored.

neural network models. Models of thinking that emphasize the parallel, or simultaneous, nature of thought that occurs automatically, inexactly, and without awareness.

neuroglia (glial cells). Supporting cells that insulate neurons from harmful physical and chemical stimuli.

neurofibrillary tangles. Bundles of neural material found in victims of Alzheimer's disease.

neuromodulators. Chemicals that set the level of excitability of neuronal activity in the brain and elsewhere.

neurons. Individual nerve cells that communicate either directly or indirectly to produce integrated response patterns.

neuroscience. Scientific study of the nervous system.

neurotransmitters. Chemical substances, located inside the terminal buttons of the presynaptic neuron, that diffuse across the synaptic cleft to transmit a neural signal.

night terror. A type of nightmare most common in preschoolers in which the child awakens screaming and shows disorientation with respect to the surroundings. There is no recall of dream content.

NMDA receptor. A memory molecule that determines whether or not one brain cell communicates with another.

nodes of Ranvier. The gaps in the myelin sheath that permit the neural signal to skip quickly down the nerve cell fiber.

noise. Has two meanings in psychology: (a) the background stimulation in perception against which the signal is judged, (b) noxious auditory stimulation chiefly produced by excessive amplitude.

nominal scales. A scale of measurement that uses numbers or other symbols to classify objects or events according to categories.

nomothetic approach. An approach in personality research that analyzes personality characteristics according to the universal norms of the group.

nonphenothiazines. One of the major divisions of antipsychotic compounds that includes haloperidol.

non-rapid eye movement (NREM) sleep. See *NREM sleep.*

norepinephrine. A hormone released by the adrenal glands when stimulated by the autonomic nervous system; also called *noradrenalin.*

normal distribution. A bilaterally symmetrical distribution in which the mean, the mode, and the median are the same. The graph of this distribution is characterized by the normal curve, which is bell-shaped.

norms. The test result standards that are established by giving the test to a large number of people who are as similar as possible to the group for whom the test is intended. See also *standardization sample.*

NREM sleep. The part of sleep, divided into stages 1, 2, 3, and 4, that occupies approximately 75 percent of the sleep period. Non-rapid eye movement sleep.

nucleus basalis. A small region of the brain located near the hippocampus that may be associated with Alzheimer's disease.

nurture position. A position in developmental psychology that holds that growth and development are a function of environmental factors. See also *nature position.*

obedience. The tendency for people to comply with orders, real or implied, given by someone who is supposedly in authority.

object. In Freudian theory, the means through which an instinct is gratified.

object permanence. According to Piaget, the concept, mastered by infants in the latter half of the first year, that objects continue to exist even when they are hidden under obstacles or otherwise out of range of the senses.

observational learning. According to social learning theory, behavior that is learned from watching and imitating the actions of other people. Also called *modeling.*

obsession. A thought or idea that an individual cannot put out of mind, no matter how hard he or she tries.

obsessive-compulsive disorder. A disorder characterized by recurrent thoughts that invade consciousness involuntarily, or activities that seemingly must be performed.

occipital lobes. A section of the cerebral cortex, located at the back of the brain, which deals with the reception and analysis of visual stimuli.

oddity. Procedure for studying abstract learning in which the subject must learn to respond to a different stimulus from the one just presented.

Oedipal crisis. According to Freud, a psychosexual crisis that boys experience during the phallic stage, characterized by attraction to their mothers as objects of sexual gratification and intense rivalry with their fathers.

olfaction. The sense of smell.

olfactory bulb. Part of the limbic system that contains the cells that oversee the sense of smell.

olfactory cells. The receptor cells for smell, located in the olfactory epithelium of each nostril.

omission training. The scheduled delivery of a positive reinforcer as long as a certain behavior does not appear.

operant conditioning. A form of conditioning described in B. F. Skinner's experimental analysis of behavior that emphasizes the importance of the consequences of responding.

operant extinction. Discontinuing reinforcement for a certain response.

operations. According to Piaget, internalized actions that are similar to the sensory-motor acts of infancy but that take place in the child's mind.

opioid peptides. A general class of naturally occurring painkillers that are formed from short chains of amino acids.

opponent-process color theory. Hering's theory that color is due to two types of cones, one sensitive to red–green experiences and the other to blue–yellow experiences.

opponent process theory. Solomon's view that there are two opposing brain processes that maintain emotional homeostasis.

optic chiasm. The point in the visual system where the optic nerves from the two eyes join. At that point nerves from the nasal sides of the retinas cross to the other side of the brain.

optic nerve. The cranial nerve that carries visual information from the receptors in the eyes to the thalamus, and eventually to the visual cortex.

optimal level of arousal. The level of arousal at which performance is best. See also *Yerkes-Dodson law.*

oral stage. Freud's first stage of psychosexual development in which the mouth region is a major source of gratification, primarily through sucking.

ordinal scale. A scale of measurement that names and specifies differences along some dimension. Unequal distances between scale values are assumed.

ordinate. A graph's vertical axis.

organismic variables. The collection of the organism's personal characteristics that affect the selection of information from the environment.

organizational behavior. Behavior in the work environment that involves such varied activities as shaping corporate strategies, determining personnel moves, and decision making.

organizational behavioral management (OBM). The use of operant (instrumental) conditioning procedures in the business community, in an effort to promote behavior change.

organizational climate. The nature of the work environment as defined by the clarity of rules, the organizational structure, and the personalities of the workers involved.

organizational development. Refers to a field of endeavor which, in sum, seeks to change organizations to make them more effective over long periods of time.

organizational diagnosis. A thorough study of the policies, practices, and people of a company to determine the causes of a company's problems and to devise a plan to reduce or eliminate those problems.

organizational system. Likert's four-fold scheme for classifying organizational climate and procedures, used to help in organizational diagnosis and development.

ossicles. The three small bones of the middle ear that conduct sound from the eardrum to the cochlea.

out-group homogeneity. The tendency for people to see members of groups different from their own as more similar than they actually are.

outshining. Strong memory cue overpowers weaker cues, rendering them ineffective.

ovaries. Female reproductive organs that produce eggs and certain hormones, such as estrogen.

overdetermination. A Freudian concept that states that most complex human behaviors have more than one cause and more than one meaning.

overjustification effect. When the introduction of external rewards decreases the incentive value of intrinsic rewards and causes performance declines.

overtones. See *harmonics*.

oxytocin. A hormone released from the pituitary gland that affects the production of breast milk.

The Paleolithic Prescription. Approach to health that argues that understanding our health needs begins with understanding our evolutionary history.

panic disorder. An anxiety state characterized by recurrent panic attacks that seem to occur suddenly and unpredictably.

parallel distributed processing (PDP). A model of cognitive learning that assumes that several parallel associations are formed at once, as opposed to single associations forming in serial fashion.

paranoid disorder. A disorder whose symptoms include delusions of persecution that are generally organized around one central theme.

paranoid schizophrenia. Schizophrenia dominated by delusions of persecution.

paraphilia. Sexual arousal to objects or activities not normally considered erotic.

parasympathetic nervous system. A subdivision of the autonomic nervous system that counteracts the effects of the sympathetic subdivision, restoring the body to a balanced state by decreasing heart rate and blood flow to the extremities and increasing digestive processes.

parietal lobes. Areas in the left and right cerebral hemispheres located in the brain region immediately behind the central fissure.

Parkinson's disease. A disorder associated with degeneration of substantia nigra that progressively leads to movement problems, including difficulties with walking and fine motor skills.

partial reinforcement effect. The greater persistence during extinction following partial reinforcement training compared to continuous reinforcement training.

partial report technique. A procedure designed to show that a complete report is available from the sensory register when appropriate cues are used to signal recall of specific sections of material.

passive smoking. Inhalation of others' cigarette smoke.

pattern. A collection of stimuli arranged in a reasonably specific way.

pattern perception. See *pattern recognition*.

pattern recognition. A memory process that compares new information with long-term information.

pattern theory. Sensations are coded by the pattern of activity in a group of receptors.

pedophilia. A psychosexual disorder in which an adult or adolescent desires a child as a sexual partner.

peer group therapy. A form of therapy where someone of the same age or circumstance is involved in the treatment process along with a professional counselor.

peg-word approach. A mnemonic encoding system involving the use of words as memory cues.

penis envy. According to Freud, the feeling of anatomical inferiority that girls experience when they discover the existence of the penis.

percentile score. The score at or below which a given percent of cases lie.

perception. The selective extraction and interpretation of information from the environment.

perceptive deafness. Deafness due to damage to the auditory hair cells, the auditory nerve, or the auditory cortex.

perceptual learning. An increase in the ability to extract information from the environment.

perceptual organization. A set of processes that group the smaller units of the perceptual world into larger ones.

performance appraisal. Regular (usually annual) sessions that supervisors have with employees to tell them what is good and bad about their performance.

peripheral nervous system (PNS). A subdivision of the nervous system that consists of neural fibers outside the brain and spinal cord.

peripheral route. Route to persuasion in the elaboration likelihood model in which persuasion occurs due to factors not associated with the content of persuasive arguments.

permanence. Explanatory style in relation to the passage of time.

permastore state. Memories that are available after as long as 50 years. These lasting memories seem to be given special protection against forgetting.

person attribution. A type of attribution that places the cause of behavior in a person's character, basing it on some internal trait. See also *situation attribution*.

personal constructs. In Kelly's theory, bipolar descriptions (such as black-white, smart-dumb) that people use as labels to help them categorize and interpret the world.

personal fable. Exaggerated beliefs about one's own uniqueness and immortality.

personal unconscious. According to Jung, a region of each individual's personality that includes material that has been repressed because of its emotional context.

personality. The organization of an individual's distinguishing characteristics, attitudes, and habits.

personality disorders. Syndromes that encompass traits that are both enduring and maladaptive, resulting in social or occupational impairment.

personologists. Psychologists who study personality.

pervasiveness. Explanatory style in relation to space, either universal or specific.

phallic stage. In Freudian theory, the third stage of psychosexual development when children desire the parent of the opposite sex.

phenomenal experience. An individual's subjective experience of reality.

phenothiazines. A class of chemicals used in the treatment of psychosis.

phenotype. The outward appearance of the organism.

pheromones. Conspecific odors given off by animals and used to communicate with other animals regarding such matters as food trails, territory, and sexual receptivity.

phi phenomenon. A kind of stroboscopic movement, first reported by Wertheimer, that is produced when successive flashes of two lights are seen as a single light moving between the two points.

phobia. A specific irrational fear that interferes with everyday functioning by causing the individual to avoid the situation in which the object of the fear is found.

phonemes. The basic sounds of language.

physiological addiction. Drug addiction in which bodily changes require the continued use of the drug.

pitch. The psychological dimension associated primarily with the frequency of sound, but also influenced somewhat by sound intensity.

pituitary. The master endocrine gland, located beneath the hypothalamus, that serves to link the nervous system with the endocrine system.

placebo. A substance that has no physiological effect on a person, and that is commonly used as a control technique in drug experimentation.

place theory. A theory of pitch, originally proposed by Helmholtz, that differences in pitch are the result of stimulation of different areas of the basilar membrane.

plaques. See *senile plaques*.

pleasure principle. According to Freud, the governing principle of the id that demands immediate gratification.

pluralistic ignorance. A cause of nonintervention; occurs when a group of people, witnessing an emergency, feel that they should not intervene if other people are not doing so.

polarized. The state of a neural membrane when the neuron is not being stimulated.

polygraph. An instrument that measures changes in autonomic nervous system responses. Often used in lie detection.

pons. The section of the hindbrain that bridges higher and lower brain regions and consists of brain nuclei (nerve cell bodies) that are important in several activities, such as the formation of facial expressions.

population. A distribution of scores in which all relevant cases are represented.

positive correlation. A correlation that occurs when two variables change in value in the same direction.

positively skewed. Describes a distribution in which high scores occur infrequently.

positive regard. According to Rogers, the need to be liked; the need for warmth, respect, and sympathy from others.

positive reinforcement. Operant reward training where a response is increased in strength when it produces a positive outcome.

positron emission tomography (PET). An imaging technique that uses radioactive sugar to plot brain activity.

postconventional level. According to Kohlberg, the level of moral judgment that is guided by values and principles and therefore transcends the authority of persons or conformity to groups.

post-Freudian theorists. Followers of Freud who view behavior as being motivated by unconscious forces.

posthypnotic amnesia. A phenomenon in which the person forgets what was said or done during hypnosis in response to the hypnotist's suggestion.

posthypnotic suggestions. Suggestions given to a hypnotized subject that are to be carried out on cue when the person is no longer hypnotized.

postparenthood. Phase of the family circle after the youngest child has left home, leaving an "empty nest".

post-traumatic stress disorder. A psychological disorder in which an individual relives a traumatic event through recurrent memories, dreams, or through a feeling that he or she is suddenly back in the terrifying situation.

power tests. Tests that are used to assess the ability or mastery of a body of material by allowing ample time so that every individual can attempt all items on the test; items range from very easy to very difficult.

preconscious. Cognitive material that is available to awareness but that the person is not immediately aware of.

preconventional level. According to Kohlberg, the level of moral judgment in which individuals recognize labels of good and bad, right and wrong, but do not interpret these labels in terms of social standards.

predictive validity. A measure of the meaningfulness of a test through predicting future performance in a particular area.

preference technique. A technique that exploits infants' preference for looking at one stimulus over another to find the patterns that interest them.

prefrontal cortex. A section of the cerebral cortex, located in the front of the brain, that is responsible for our ability to make judgments and solve problems.

prefrontal lobotomy. Somatic treatment that involves the surgical destruction of major pathways in the frontal region of the brain.

prejudice. A negative, preconceived attitude toward members of particular social groups, such as ethnic or religious minorities.

Premack principle. The principle that a high probability response can serve as reward for an independently lower probability behavior.

premotor cortex. A section of the frontal region, located close to the forehead, that controls manual dexterity.

preoperational thinking. According to Piaget, early childhood thought characterized by animism, artificialism, and lack of logical operations.

preparedness. Principle that states that events vary along a dimension of conditionability.

prescriptive grammar. The formalized system of social prescriptions about the proper use of language.

prevention. The rendering of psychological services in order to preempt unnecessary suffering before stress reaches dangerously high levels.

primacy effect. The finding that items at the beginning of a list are recalled with greater frequency than items in the middle of the list. See also *recency effect*.

primary appraisal. The first stage in Lazarus's model of stress in which the individual attempts to determine how the stressor will affect well being.

primary mental abilities. A small set of cognitive factors, identified by Thurstone, that together make up the concept of intelligence.

primary reinforcers. Natural events having biological relevance that are capable of increasing the probability of behaviors that produce them.

primary visual cortex. A section of the cerebral cortex, located in the occipital area, that is responsible for vision.

proactive interference. Forgetting that occurs when material learned under a previous condition produces a decrement in the recall of more recently learned material.

problem solving. The act of achieving a goal in the presence of some obstacles and in the absence of an evident solution.

procedural memory. Stimulus–response memory that involves the formation and retention of habits.

processes. Cognitive operations and procedures.

projective technique. A technique used to assess personality characteristics in which the individual is given a relatively ambiguous and unstructured task to perform, on the theory that inner thoughts, feelings, and conflicts will be *projected* onto the stimulus.

prosocial behavior. Behavior that benefits other people.

prosodic features (of speech). Nonverbal components of speech, such as pitch, loudness, and rate, which are used in the communication of emotion.

protocol. In an experiment, a subject's experimental record; refers to the spoken report in the think-aloud technique.

protocol analysis. Systematic analysis of subject protocols in order to find consistent patterns of cognition.

prototypes. Members (things, events, etc.) that are most representative of their category.

prototype-matching theory. The theory that proposes that patterns are identified by being compared against a set of prototypical patterns stored in memory.

proximal stimulus. The retinal image of an object, as opposed to the object as it actually exists in the world.

proximity. The tendency to group stimuli on the basis of how physically near they are to one another.

proximo-distal development. The direction of prenatal development that proceeds from the inside outward. See also *cephalo-caudal development*.

Prozac. Antidepressant that blocks the reuptake of the neurotransmitter serotonin; controversial because it may cause violence and promote suicide.

psychoactive drugs. Drugs that produce changes in consciousness, perception, and mood.

psychoanalysis. Treatment technique originating with Sigmund Freud that involves intensive therapeutic exchange between the analyst and patient on a one-to-one basis.

psychoanalytic approach. Approach to psychology that views unconscious processes as the primary determinants of behavior.

psychoanalytic model(s). In abnormal psychology, the view that abnormal behavior is a function of internal psychological conflicts that are traceable to events in early childhood. In personality, models derived from Freud that emphasize psychic energy that is transformed and redirected during development into complex human behavior.

psychodynamic psychotherapy. The use of traditional psychological techniques to supplement classical psychoanalysis.

psychogenic fugue state. An extreme form of psychogenic amnesia in which the person loses all memory of the past and takes up a new identity.

psychogenic pain disorder. A psychological disorder in which the predominant symptom is pain, although the pain has no physical basis.

psychoimmunology. The study of the interrelation of the brain, behavior, and the immune system.

psycholinguistics. The psychological study of language structure; also, the psychological processes involved in language.

psychological addiction. Drug addiction that is assumed to have no physiological basis; continued use of the drug is required because of the addict's desire to experience pleasure or to avoid pain.

psychological climate. An individual's personal, subjective representation of the characteristics of an organization. It is how a person perceives the conditions of an organization.

psychological disorder. A disorder, usually expressed in a collection of symptoms, that results in an individual's psychological distress and/or the serious impairment of one or more important areas of functioning.

psychological maltreatment. Mental cruelty, emotional abuse, and emotional mistreatment of children.

psychological numbing. A reduction in the capacity to experience emotions.

psychological tests. Devices (often paper and pencil tests) that measure individuals on some psychological dimension, such as intelligence.

psychologically hardy. Individuals who are especially resistant to illness in spite of increased stress.

psychology. The systematic study of behavior and mental processes.

psychometric psychology. The field of psychology that involves the measurement of various behaviors, usually with psychological tests.

psychometrics. Branch of psychology involved with psychological assessment.

psychoimmunology. A specialty within health psychology that explores links between psychological factors and the immune system's response.

psychosexual dysfunction. A problem in normal sexual responding; examples include impotence and frigidity.

psychosocial dwarfism. Dwarfism that occurs when the growth hormone somatotropin is repressed due to emotional deprivation and severe forms of psychological stress.

psychosurgery. A destruction of brain tissue for the purpose of improving behavior.

psychotherapy. A noninvasive form of therapy that presumes that psychological disturbance derives from inappropriate thoughts and behavior.

psychotropic drugs. Chemicals used in the treatment of psychological disorders.

puberty. The period of physical transformation at early adolescence that results in maturation of the reproductive system, growth in height and weight, and development of secondary sex characteristics.

Public Law (PL) 94–142. The Education for All Handicapped Children Act that mandates education for all school-age children regardless of degree of handicapping condition.

punishment. Following a response with an aversive stimulus in order to suppress the response.

pupil. The opening of the iris of the eye that is one of the factors regulating the amount of light entering the eye. It dilates in low illumination and constricts in high illumination.

quality of work life (QWL). A cooperative movement between some managers and union leaders to improve job satisfaction and morale by making psychological changes in the work environment.

randomization. A control technique in experimentation that selects and assigns subjects to various groups in a way that minimizes any bias.

random sampling procedure. A procedure used to create a sample that ensures that every member of the population has an equal chance of being selected for the sample distribution.

range. The difference between the highest and lowest scores in the distribution.

range corollary. Kelly's statement that constructs are useful for only a finite range of events because they are situational (i.e., a construct applied to one situation may not apply to another).

rapid-eye-movement sleep. See *REM sleep*.

rational–emotive therapy (RET). Originated by Ellis, a process of restructuring irrational thought processes and replacing negative thinking with positive thinking.

rationalism. A philosophy that asserts knowledge can be acquired through reason and common sense.

ratio scale. A scale of measurement that names and specifies differences along a dimension and has an absolute zero point. Equal differences between scale values are assumed.

reaction time. A measure of how fast one can react to a specific stimulus.

reality principle. According to Freud, the ego may impose a delay of gratification if the id demands pleasurable sensation in an unsuitable situation.

reality testing. Testing one's perceptions of the world against those of others; psychotic individuals generally fail at reality testing and have greatly distorted perceptions of the world.

receiver operating characteristics. Decisional factors associated with an individual that affect thresholds.

recency effect. The finding that items at the end of a list are recalled with greater frequency than items in the middle of the list. See also *primacy effect*.

receptive aphasia. A language problem resulting from damage to the nervous system in the temporal-parietal cortex (Wernicke's area).

receptive field. Specific area of the retina tied to a particular optic nerve fiber and represented at higher levels in the visual system.

receptors. Specialized cells that are sensitive to different forms of energy. These cells act as transducers, converting one form of energy into the electrochemical signals used in the nervous system. Receptors include rods and cones, taste cells, and hair cells.

recessive gene. A weaker, as opposed to a stronger (dominant) gene. In any gene pair, the recessive gene controls individual characteristics only when the other gene is also recessive.

recognition by components. A feature-analysis model of pattern perception that explains object perception in terms of a system of basic shapes called geons.

recognition memory. Memory that is based on making discriminations among items physically represented in the environment.

recognition tests. Memory tests, such as a multiple choice exam, in which a mixed set of correct memory targets and nontargets is given, and the task is to choose which are correct.

reconstructive memory. The process of combining actual details from long-term memory with items that seem to fit the occasion.

reference groups. Groups that people relate themselves to psychologically or to which they aspire to relate themselves.

reflexes. Automatic responses that occur under highly specific stimulus situations.

refractory period. The short time period following the onset of the action potential, during which a second action potential cannot begin.

rehearsal. The repeating of information in memory.

reinforcer. An event that will increase the rate of responses that produce it (positive reinforcer) or remove it (negative reinforcer).

relative brightness. A monocular depth cue based on the fact that brighter objects are typically closer than dimmer objects.

relativists. Scientists who believe that facial expressions are learned.

relaxation. A coping strategy for dealing with stress, usually involving the reduction of muscle tension.

relaxation training. A set of techniques that teach individuals how to relax their muscles voluntarily as a way of reducing stress.

reliability. A characteristic of a psychological test that is a measure of the consistency and repeatability of test scores.

religious strategies. Coping strategies in which a person seeks spiritual comfort to reduce stress.

REM nightmares. Disturbing dreams that occur as part of REM sleep; subjects usually have good recall for these dreams.

REM sleep. REM sleep, also called rapid eye movement sleep, occurs approximately 4 to 5 times in an 8-hour sleep period and is associated with dreaming.

repression hypothesis. Freud's proposal that dreams are forgotten as a defensive act to keep the dreamer from experiencing troublesome dream content.

reserpine. The active ingredient of the root of the rauwolfia plant, used in the treatment of some severe psychological disorders.

resistance. Personality defenses created to cover motivational conflicts.

resistant attachment. Style of attachment in which infants make inconsistent and ambivalent use of caregivers in strange situations.

response rate. The percentage of subjects who complete and return a survey instrument; low response rates make surveys difficult to interpret accurately.

resting potential. Electrical charge on the neural membrane when the neuron is not being fired.

restorative theory. The theory that the function of sleep is to replenish the processes of mind and body that become depleted during the waking activities of the day.

reticular formation. The complex system of branching neurons in the midbrain involved in controlling levels of arousal.

retina. The specialized tissue at the back of the eye containing the photoreceptors (rods and cones) and secondary cells (bipolar and ganglion cells).

retrieval. Memory process in which previously stored material is reclaimed due to a present demand.

retroactive interference. A deficit in recall due to interpolated activities between original learning and testing.

retrograde amnesia. Memory loss of information acquired prior to a traumatic incident.

reversibility. In Piaget's theory, the negation of an action.

rods. Specialized receptor cells in the retina that respond to differences in the intensity of light.

role playing. The rehearsing or acting-out of certain behavior sequences by the client and the therapist.

roles. Norms that apply to specific members of a group who occupy special positions within it.

romantic love. A passionate form of love found in beginning love relationships. It is high in physical arousal and fantasy, and often includes jealousy.

sadism. Deriving sexual gratification through inflicting pain, injury, or humiliation on others.

salience hypothesis. The hypothesis that emotionally arousing dreams are more easily recalled.

sample. A group of items (e.g., subjects) selected from the total set known as the population. Typically, samples are selected in order to allow experimental results to be generalized to a population.

sampling. The selection of a few individuals from a population for the ultimate purpose of assessing the characteristics of the population.

sampling error. The discrepancy between the true values of a population and the estimates of those population values based on sample characteristics.

saturation. The complexity of light as determined by the number of wavelengths of which it is composed.

scatter plot. A graph that is used to indicate a general pattern of correlation between two variables. Also called *scatter diagram*.

schizoid personality disorder. A personality disorder in which the individual has difficulty maintaining social relationships and is generally indifferent to other people's feelings.

schizophrenia. A psychological disorder characterized by seriously disturbed patterns of thinking and failures at reality testing.

schizophrenogenic family. A family whose patterns of interactions may be so bizarre that they contribute to the development of schizophrenia by a member of the family.

school psychology. A branch of applied psychology concerned with the intellectual, social, and emotional development of elementary- and secondary-school-age children.

scientific method. The precise and rigorous testing of hypotheses that are experimentally testable. This method also requires that experiments be repeatable and that results can be independently verified by others.

scientific paradigm. Theoretical approach or world view of a domain of science.

seasonal affective disorder (SAD). A psychological disorder characterized by recurrent depression in particular seasons of the year.

secondary appraisal. The second stage in Lazarus's model of stress in which the individual attempts to determine whether coping capacities are sufficient and to select the best coping strategy.

secondary reinforcer. See *conditioned reinforcer*.

second-order conditioning. A procedure in which a conditioned stimulus is paired with an unconditioned stimulus and repeatedly followed by a second, neutral stimulus in order to evoke an indirect association with the unconditioned stimulus. Also called *higher-order conditioning*.

secure attachment. Style of attachment in which infants use their primary caregiver as a base of security to reduce distress.

selective attention. The ability to focus on one stimulus while excluding other stimuli that are present.

selective sleep deprivation. A method that seeks to deprive the individual of only certain kinds of sleep, typically REM sleep.

self-actualization. According to Maslow and Rogers, the human tendency to fulfill one's potential, particularly with regard to the higher positive motives. Can only occur when all of the more basic needs are satisfied.

self archetype. According to Jung, unity of opposites that connotes wholeness of personality.

self-fulfilling prophecy. The phenomenon that a person's performance matches the expectations that people communicate about that performance.

self-help groups. Groups that lack professionally trained leaders and that try to facilitate group acceptance by bringing together people who may share common problems.

self-report inventories. Techniques used for assessing personality in which individuals answer a series of questions about themselves.

self-serving bias. An attributional bias by which people accept greater personal responsibility for positive outcomes than for negative ones.

semantics. The branch of linguistics concerned with the meanings of words.

semantic memory. Memory for impersonal items with no definite reference to the self, such as mathematical formulas.

semi-permeable. The status of a cell membrane that allows the passage of certain particles in one direction only.

senile dementia. Cognitive deterioration, including memory loss and confusion, that occurs in a small percentage of the elderly population as a result of brain changes.

senile plaques. Neuronal debris found in the central nervous system of Alzheimer's disease sufferers.

sensitivity training. Group therapy sessions that are designed to promote the feelings of group cohesion through touching, holding hands, sustaining eye contact, and other means of breaking down defenses.

sensory adaptation. The decline in receptor activity when stimuli are unchanging.

sensory memory. Very brief memory for sensory information.

sensory-motor period. According to Piaget, the infancy period in which the cognitive world is experienced in terms of basic senses (sensory) and in terms of action (motor).

sensory register. The initial component of the memory system; a brief holding bin for information until it is reviewed for coding and storage.

sensory system. A network of receptors, neural pathways, and brain areas that process information in a single sensory modality.

separation anxiety. An infant's fear of being separated from its caregivers that usually peaks late in the second year of life.

serial position phenomenon. The finding that people can easily remember the beginning and end of a list of items but have difficulty recalling the middle of the list. See also *primacy effect* and *recency effect*.

set. An organismic variable that is a kind of perceptual readiness, in which the subject has an expectancy about what is to happen.

set point. A regulatory mechanism that determines the amount of fat we carry in our bodies. When fat deposits fall below the set point, hunger results; when fat deposits are over the set point, we stop eating.

sex chromosomes. The 23rd pair of chromosomes, which determines the sex of the offspring.

sexist language. Language that excludes a sex (usually female) by using pronouns and terms related only to the other.

sexual role playing. Patterns of behavior involved in sexual interaction that males and females engage in differentially.

shadow archetype. Collection of unpleasant qualities that people like to hide about themselves; one of Jung's archetypes.

shallow processing. A low level of processing, as with maintenance rehearsal, that does not promote transfer to long-term memory.

shape constancy. An example of perceptual constancy in which the perceived shape of an object remains constant despite changes in the shape of the retinal image of that object.

shaping. The systematic reinforcement of successive approximations to a goal-oriented behavior.

short-term cues. Stimuli such as the color or taste of food that may determine meal size and frequency.

short-term memory. A component of the memory system that holds only a few items in memory for a brief period.

signal detection theory. An approach to threshold measurement that measures detection of a signal in a background of noise.

sign stimulus. A stimulus that is a triggering event for a certain behavior.

silent extinction. The repeated presentation of the conditioned stimulus during extinction beyond the time required to eliminate the conditioned response.

simple cells. Cells in the visual cortex that respond to a small spot of light or to a line of light in a particular orientation.

simple phobia. A diagnostic label for any one of several specific phobias, such as claustrophobia.

simultaneous conditioning. The procedure in which the onset of the conditioned stimulus and the unconditioned stimulus occur at the same time.

single blind. A control technique in which subjects in various groups are unaware of their group assignment, but the experimenter is aware. See also *double blind*.

situation attribution. A type of attribution that locates the cause of behavior in the particular situation. See also *person attribution*.

situation redefinition. A coping strategy in which a person attempts to think about the problem in a different way that can make the stress more acceptable.

size constancy. A kind of perceptual constancy in which the perceived size of an object remains constant despite changes in the size of the retinal image of that object.

size-distance invariance hypothesis. Based on the known invariant relationship between size and distance (i.e., the retinal image size of objects decreases as object distance increases), this hypothesis explains the existence of size constancy.

skewed distribution. A nonsymmetrical distribution that tails off in one direction or another. See also *positively skewed* and *negatively skewed*.

sleep deprivation. The elimination or reduction of sleep for an extended period of time.

sleep latency. The amount of time it takes to fall asleep, which tends to increase with age. Long sleep latency is the chief complaint in insomnia sufferers.

slow wave sleep (sws). A label for stages 3 and 4 of NREM sleep, dominated by slow frequency, or delta, brain waves. (Also called *delta sleep*.)

social clock. Society's shared judgment of the appropriateness of certain behaviors, such as marriage, as a function of age.

social cognition. The ways that individuals gather, use, and interpret information about the social aspects of their world.

social cognitive theory. Bandura's social learning theory relating behavior to traits and situations.

social desirability. The phenomenon in self-report data, especially survey research, when respondents do not answer truthfully but instead answer questions in order to make themselves appear in a more favorable light.

social facilitation. The social phenomenon of improved performance that occurs due to the presence of others.

social interchanges. Patterns of social interaction characterized by reciprocal influence.

social phobia. Fear of situations that may lead to embarrassment because of observation by others.

social psychology. A field of psychology that studies how social conditions affect the behavior of individuals.

social support. A coping strategy in which stress is reduced by the support received from friends and loved ones as well as professionals, such as psychologists and physicians.

sociobiology. An account of behavior that assumes that human and animal activity is based on a biological imperative to ensure survival of genetic material.

sociogenic hypothesis. The notion that sociological factors, such as living in impoverished circumstances, contribute to the cause of schizophrenia.

sociological model. In abnormal psychology, the view that abnormal behavior is a function of variables such as social class or rural-urban contexts.

sociometric analysis. Research technique for finding which children in a playgroup are popular or rejected.

soma. The neural cell body, which contains the nucleus and is primarily concerned with the regulatory functions of the cell.

somatic nervous system. A subdivision of the peripheral nervous system that is comprised of both sensory and motor neurons that are involved in the control of voluntary muscle groups.

somatosensory area. A section of the brain, located in the front part of the parietal lobe, that deals with sensations of touch, pressure, pain, temperature, itch, and muscle tension.

somatoform disorder. A psychological disorder in which physical symptoms have no known organic or physiological pathology.

somatotropin. See *growth hormone*.

somatotypes. Sheldon's numerical ratings of body types, thought to influence personality.

somesthetic perception. The perception of skin sensations such as pain or cold, as well as the perception of body position.

sound waves. The pattern of compression and expansion of air molecules that produces a sound.

source. In Freudian theory, the region of the body where an instinct originates.

specific abilities (s). In Spearman's theory of intelligence, cognitive activities that require varying amounts of general intelligence.

specificity theory. In health psychology, the view that certain personality traits may predispose individuals to specific health problems. See also *generality theory*.

speech. The act of speaking, a mechanical process for producing sounds.

speed test. A test that measures how fast an individual can perform certain tasks by providing a number of items, all relatively easy and within the capabilities of the people taking the test, but only a small amount of time, so that no one can finish all the items.

spinal nerve. A component of the spinal cord, consisting of converging dorsal and ventral roots.

split-half reliability. A measure of the consistency of a test, in which two halves of the test are separately scored and then correlated with each other.

spontaneous recovery. The phenomenon in which, following a period of no training, a previously extinguished conditioned response suddenly reappears.

standard age score (SAS). The standardized score on the Stanford-Binet Intelligence Scale, comparable to the deviation IQ. See also *deviation IQ*.

standard deviation. The measure of variability that is used most often in psychology research; defined as the square root of the variance.

standardization sample. A group of people who take a test to establish norms and who must be carefully selected to be representative of the people for whom the test is intended. See also *norms*.

standardized test. A task or group of tasks administered under standard conditions for assessing a person's knowledge, skill, or other psychological characteristic.

Stanford–Binet Intelligence Scale. An individually administered intelligence test developed by Terman from Binet's original French version.

state-dependent memory. The notion that we are more likely to recall certain stimuli or events when we are in the same physiological or psychological state as when we first learned the material.

statistical inference. Making general statements about populations based on conclusions drawn from samples.

statistically significant. Following an inferential statistics test, differences are reported that cannot only be due to chance.

stereopsis. A process in which the brain combines the two disparate images from the eyes; an important process for depth perception.

stereotypes. Standardized mental pictures of members of a group that are based on oversimplified and uncritical judgments.

Stevens's power law. A law relating perceptual judgments with changes in physical stimuli that is accurate across a wide range of sensory stimuli.

stimulants. A class of drugs that increases arousal by aiding the release of CNS neurotransmitters; includes amphetamines and cocaine.

stimulus control. A situation in which operant responding occurs only in the presence of a restricted set of stimulus conditions that lead to reinforcement.

stimulus generalization. The principle that states that when a stimulus is conditioned to elicit a response, other similar stimuli will also evoke the same response.

stimulus variables. Those qualities that are a part of stimulus objects themselves, such as texture, shape, and temperature.

storage. Memory process in which the incoming material is assigned a location and usually remains there until it is needed or is lost altogether.

stranger anxiety. The fear of strangers that develops in infants after the age of about six months.

stratified samples. Samples that are formed by collecting items within restricted categories of a population.

stress. The physiological and psychological responses to excessive stimulation, usually of an unpleasant nature.

stress inoculation. A program that prepares the individual to anticipate stressors, acknowledge their inevitability, and thus deal more rationally with the stress. In therapy, a method that attempts to shift the patient's internal focus from negative to positive self-statements, without attempting to eliminate negative self-commentary.

stress management. The complex of treatment methods developed to deal with job stress.

stress reaction. A pattern of bodily responses to the activation of the autonomic nervous system.

stroboscopic movement. A form of apparent movement produced by the rapid presentation of a succession of still images, such as in motion pictures.

structuralism. The earliest of scientific approaches to psychology, associated with Wundt and Titchener, that advocated studying consciousness by analyzing it into its basic structural elements.

structures. Memory storage systems.

subcutaneous tissue. Inner layer of the three layers of skin.

subjective organization. The spontaneous tendency for people to impose an organized framework on information that is presented randomly.

subjective reports. Metacognitions described by a subject.

subliminal perception. Perception that is below threshold.

substance abuse. Use of chemical substances on a regular and continuous basis to the point that they interfere with work and family life.

substance dependence. A serious substance use disorder diagnosed when an individual desires to reduce intake of the substance but is unable to do so, and suffers impairment of social, occupational, or recreational activities as a result of the substance.

substance P. A pain neurotransmitter that is abundant in sensory pain tracts.

substance use disorders. Disorders involving abuse of or dependence on drugs or alcohol.

subtractive color. Color mixture based on the subtraction of light wavelengths, such as in paint mixtures. Primary subtractive colors are red, blue, and yellow.

summation. A neuronal process in which information is lost through a reduction process. In the case of vision, many rods and cones connect with fewer bipolar cells and still fewer ganglion cells. The result is more efficient visual

processing but a loss of some information.

superego. According to Freud, the conscience that develops around the age of five and that involves the incorporation of parental values and rules.

superior colliculi. Sections of the midbrain that help coordinate whole body movements to visual stimuli.

superordinate goals. Tasks that are important to two groups and that can be solved only if the groups cooperate. Such goals can reduce group conflict.

support group. A collection of people with a similar concern who band together to share their problems and help one another.

surface structure. Sentences as actually worded. See also *deep structure*.

survey method. Use of questionnaires, interviews, and opinion polls to secure information about behavior, attitudes, and beliefs.

sympathetic nervous system. A subdivision of the autonomic nervous system that functions as an alarm system, providing increased blood flow to skeletal muscles and, at the same time, releasing epinephrine from the adrenal glands.

symptom substitution. The (rare) replacement of one symptom that has been eliminated by therapy with another.

synapse. The point where two or more neurons interconnect.

synaptic cleft. The area between the terminal buttons of one neuron and the dendritic ends of another.

syndrome. A collection of symptoms of a psychological disorder.

syntax. The set of rules that specifies how words are arranged in phrases and sentences.

systematic desensitization. The behavioral method of learning to relax in the presence of anxiety-arousing stimuli so that the anxiety reaction is replaced by relaxation in the presence of the previously anxiety-evoking cues.

tardive dyskinesia. A disorder that results from the longterm use of antipsychotic medication. Symptoms include uncontrollable jerking and writhing.

taste buds. Sensory sites for taste located mostly on the tongue but also on portions of the throat and soft palate; each taste bud contains approximately 20 taste cells that are the actual taste receptors.

taste cells. Taste receptors that are located on the taste buds of the tongue.

tectorial membrane. A membrane in the cochlea, acting in concert with the basilar membrane, whose shearing action serves to stimulate the hair cells in audition.

temperament. An infant's personality disposition that affects patterns of interaction from early infancy.

temporal conditioning. The presentation of the unconditioned stimulus alone at discrete time intervals, causing time to become the conditioned stimulus.

temporal lobe. A section of the cerebral cortex, located below the lateral fissure, that deals with the recording and interpreting of auditory sensations, memory processing, and the formation of personality traits.

teratogen. A substance that can cause birth defects in the embryo or fetus.

terminal buttons. Microscopic knobs located on the tiny fingerlike projections at the end of the axon that release the neurotransmitter.

test anxiety. Stress that causes difficulty in preparing for an exam, as well as actually taking the exam.

testes. The male reproductive glands that produce sperm and sex hormones such as testosterone.

testosterone. The hormone produced primarily by the male testes.

test–retest reliability. A measure of a test's consistency, in which the same test is administered to the same individuals at two different times and the scores correlated with each other.

texture gradient. A monocular cue for depth in which the texture of a surface receding in the distance changes in clarity, getting more blurred at farther distances.

thalamic theory. Cannon's idea that the thalamic region in the brain controls emotional expression by simultaneously changing bodily events, thoughts, and feelings.

thalamus. The large section of the forebrain that relays all auditory, visual, and touch sensory signals to different areas of the cortex.

thanatos. According to Freud, the instinct toward destructiveness. Also called the *death instinct*.

Thematic Apperception Test (TAT). A projective technique in which individuals are asked to make up a story from an ambiguous picture; the technique assumes that individuals project their own feelings into the stories they tell. See also *projective technique*.

theory. In science, an organized explanatory account based on a collection of facts. Scientific theory is a major source for testable hypotheses.

Theory X. The view of worker motivation held by most business people, according to McGregor, that workers are inferior beings who must be directed from above and who like this better than taking responsibility.

Theory Y. McGregor's alternative to Theory X, which assumes that workers have much the same motivation as employers, including needs for self-esteem, control over working conditions, and opportunities to express ideas, as well as pay.

theta waves. Brain waves of 3–7 cycles per second that are common in stage 1 of NREM sleep.

think-aloud method. Technique in which subjects try to say out loud everything they are thinking.

third force. The humanistic approach to personality, which offers an alternative to Freudian and behavioral psychology.

threshold. The point at which a membrane will depolarize when a sufficient volume of an excitatory neurotransmitter collects on the dendrites of the postsynaptic cell.

thyroid gland. An endocrine gland that secretes thyroxin, which is essential to energy utilization.

thyroid-stimulating hormone. One of the hormones released from the anterior pituitary.

timbre. The complexity of sound determined by its composition of different frequencies.

tip-of-the-tongue phenomenon. The experience of almost remembering something but not quite being able to retrieve it. The information may become available suddenly.

token economy. The use of conditioned reinforcers to alter behavior in a classroom setting.

tolerance. A resistance to drug effects that develops with the continued use of many drugs. Thus, drug dosages must be increased to produce the desired effects.

top-down processing. The information processing in perception that begins in the higher brain centers and proceeds to the receptors, usually because the perceiver has some kind of perceptual readiness or set.

trace conditioning. The technique in which the onset of the conditioned stimulus occurs prior to the onset of the unconditioned stimulus, and the conditioned stimulus stops before the unconditioned stimulus is actually presented.

training. A learning experience that is intended to alter or enhance performance of a task or set of tasks.

transference. A process in psychoanalysis whereby the patient attributes personality traits and behavioral characteristics to the analyst that are actually more descriptive of some other person in the patient's life.

transformational grammar. A set of rules that specify what transformations or changes are acceptable in the wording of a sentence.

transsexualism. A disorder in which an individual insists that he or she be treated as a member of the opposite sex.

transvestites. Individuals who obtain sexual gratification from dressing in the clothing of the opposite sex.

trephining. The primitive practice of boring holes in the skull to release "evil spirits" from the brain.

triadic reciprocality. Bandura's view that reciprocal influences among three factors—person, situation, and behavior—are necessary to account for behavior.

triangular theory of love. A view of love being composed of three elements: intimacy, passion, and decision/commitment. These elements combine in different ways to produce different kinds of love.

tricyclic antidepressants. A class of antidepressant drugs, such as Elavil or Tofranil, that are often used in treating depression.

trigeminal sense. A chemoreceptor system in the nose that plays a secondary role in taste and smell perception.

trust versus mistrust. In Erikson's theory, the crisis of early infancy provoked by a sense of helplessness and the need to be fed.

Turner's syndrome. A condition that occurs when only a single X chromosome is present in the sex chromosomes (23rd pair).

twin studies. A method for studying the effect of genetics on behavior in which two different people having the same genotype are placed in different environments to see if they exhibit similarities in behavior.

tympanic membrane. Also known as the eardrum, this membrane vibrates to sounds entering the ear and passes the sound waves to the ossicles connected to the eardrum.

Type A personality. The Type A person is highly motivated to achieve, competitive, impatient, fast paced, and more prone to heart problems.

Type B personality. These individuals are calm, relaxed, patient, and at a lower risk for heart problems than a Type A personality.

typical attributes. Attributes that are associated with most members of a class, but not all.

typicality. An important factor for category classification that refers to both typical attributes and typical examples.

unconditional positive regard. A nonjudgmental attitude of total acceptance on the part of the therapist that is fundamental to client-centered therapy.

unconditioned response (UR). A reaction to an unconditioned stimulus that takes place even when there has been no previous training.

unconditioned stimulus (US). An event that reflexively produces an unconditioned response, even when there has been no previous training.

unconscious. In Freudian theory, a vast region of an individual's mental life that has been pushed out of awareness.

undifferentiated schizophrenia. Schizophrenia in which there are clear indications of disordered thinking as well as signs of other types of schizophrenia.

unilateral ECT. ECT that is administered to only one side of the head in order to minimize memory disturbance.

unimodal. Describes a distribution in which one score occurs more than others.

unipolar depression. A major depression in which mood remains at the bleak extreme of extended and overwhelming hopelessness. See also *major depression.*

universalists. Scientists who believe that facial expressions are innately determined.

unobtrusive measures. Data that can be collected without the cooperation and knowledge of the subject, and without interfering with the behavior being studied.

vacuum behavior. When an instinct occurs independently of the appropriate environmental releaser, usually because of lack of opportunity to respond.

validity. A characteristic of a psychological test that describes how well a test measures what it is supposed to measure.

variability. The dispersion of scores within a distribution.

variable interval schedule (VI). Schedule in which responses are rewarded when they occur after a variable time interval has elapsed.

variable ratio schedule (VR). Schedule in which the number of responses required for reinforcement varies.

variance. A statistic for measuring variability; the average of the squared deviations about the mean.

vasopressin. A hormone released from the pituitary gland that affects internal water balance.

ventral root. The front side of a spinal nerve where motor output originates.

ventromedial nucleus of the hypothalamus (VMH). A section of the hypothalamus often identified as the satiety center because it is involved in the discontinuation of eating.

vestibular system. Located in the inner ear, this system is concerned with the sense of balance and knowledge of body position.

visible spectrum. The band of electromagnetic energy, ranging from red to violet, that can be perceived by the human eye.

visual acuity. The ability to make fine visual discriminations among objects in the visual field. Acuity is best when objects are focused on the fovea.

visual agnosia. A condition that may occur when the occipital lobe is damaged, resulting in an inability to combine individual impressions into complex patterns.

visual cliff. An apparatus for testing depth perception.

visual cortex. That portion of the occipital lobe of the brain that receives inputs from the optic nerves.

visual substitution system (VSS). A matrix of vibrating pins attached to the skin of a blind person to simulate shapes and brightness in a tactile form.

visual thinking. Thinking composed of mental images that are visual in nature.

visually directed reaching. An infant's ability to reach for an object and grasp it that becomes perfected between the age of three and six months.

volley principle. An auditory theory proposing that auditory neurons alternate in firing patterns that could simulate sound frequencies. An adjunct to frequency theory.

voyeurism. Obtaining sexual gratification through the observation of other people who are nude, undressing, or engaging in sexual activities.

waxy flexibility. A characteristic of catatonic schizophrenia that entails holding a particular posture for long periods of time and allowing the body to be molded to a new posture.

Weber's Law. A nineteenth-century psychophysical law relating changes in perception to changes in sensory stimulation. The law, which was replaced by Stevens's power law, was accurate in the middle ranges of stimulation but not at the extremes.

Wechsler intelligence scales. A series of individually administered intelligence tests designed for specific age groups.

Wernicke's area. An area in the temporalparietal cortex that is the center for understanding language.

whole report. A sensory memory technique in which the individual is asked to recall all of the memorized material.

Whorfian hypothesis. The argument that language is the principal determinant of how a person thinks about the world.

withdrawal. The physical and psychological distress experienced by a drug addict when drug use ceases. Symptoms include chills, sweating, nausea, and cramps.

womb envy. According to Horney, the positive aspects of the female reproductive role that women experience and that men would like to experience.

working backward. A heuristic strategy that involves working from the goal to the present condition.

Yerkes–Dodson law. A description of the relationship between emotional level and task performance which suggests, among other things, that high arousal facilitates performance on difficult tasks.

Young–Helmholtz color theory. The theory, proposed by Young and modified later by Helmholtz, that color is produced by three different cones maximally sensitive to red, green, and blue.

z scores. Values that indicate how far a raw score in a distribution deviates from the mean of the distribution in standard deviation units.

zoophilia. Sexual interaction with animals, also known as beastiality.

References

Abbey, A., & Melby, C. (1986). The effects of nonverbal cues on gender differences in perceptions of sexual intent. *Sex Roles, 15,* 283–298.

Abbey, A., & Dickson, J. W. (1983). Research and development work climate and innovation in semiconductors. *Academy of Management Journal, 26,* 362–368.

Abbott, B. B., Schoen, L. S., & Badia, P. (1984). Predictable and unpredictable shock: Behavioral measures of aversion and physiological measures of stress. *Psychological Bulletin, 96,* 45–71.

Abel, E. L. (1980). *Marihuana: The first twelve thousand years.* New York: Plenum.

Abrams, R., Taylor, M. A., Faber, R., Ts'o, T. O. T., Williams, R. A., & Almy, G. (1983). Bilateral versus unilateral electroconvulsive therapy: Efficacy in melancholia. *American Journal of Psychiatry, 140,* 463–465.

Abramson, L. Y., Seligman, M. E. P., & Teasdale, J. D. (1978). Learned helplessness in humans: Critique and reformulation. *Journal of Abnormal Psychology, 87,* 49–74.

Adams, C. (1991). Qualitative age differences in memory for text: A life-span developmental perspective. *Psychology of Aging, 6,* 323–336.

Adams, H. E., Feuerstein, M., & Fowler, J. L. (1980). Migraine headache: Review of parameters, etiology, and intervention. *Psychological Bulletin, 87,* 217–237.

Adams, J. L. (1979). *Conceptual blockbusting: A guide to better ideas* (2nd ed.). New York: Norton.

Adams, K. L., & Ware, N. C. (1979). Sexism and the English language: The linguistic implications of being a woman. In J. Freeman (Ed.), *Women: A feminist perspective* (pp. 487–504). Palo Alto, CA: Mayfield.

Adey, P., & Shayer, M. (1990). Accelerating the development of formal thinking in middle and high school students. *Journal of Research in Science Teaching, 27,* 267–285.

Adler, A. (1978). Cooperation between the sexes. In H. L. Ansbacher & R. R. Ansbacher (Eds. and Trans.), *Writings on women, love and marriage, sexuality and its disorders.* Garden City, NY: Doubleday.

Adler, R., Felton, D., & Cohen, N. (1990). Interactions between the brain and the immune system. *Annual Review of Pharmacology and Toxicology, 30,* 71–94.

Adler, T. (1991, July). Women's expectations are menopause villains. *APA Monitor,* p. 14.

Agarwal, S., & Bohra, S. P. (1982). Study of the personality pattern of high and low creative children. *Child Psychiatry Quarterly, 15,* 136–139.

Ainsworth, M. D. S. (1989). Attachments beyond infancy. *American Psychologist, 44,* 709–716.

Ainsworth, M. D. S., & Bell, S. M. (1970). Attachment, exploration and separation illustrated by the behavior of one-year-olds in a strange situation. *Child Development, 41,* 49–67.

Ainsworth, M. D. S., Blehar, M. C., Waters, E., & Wall, S. (1978). *Patterns of attachment: A psychological study of the strange situation.* Hillsdale, NJ: Erlbaum.

Ainsworth, M. D. S., & Wittig, B. (1969). Attachment and exploratory behavior of one-year-olds in a strange situation. In B. M. Foss (Ed.), *Determinants of infant behavior* (Vol. 4, pp. 111–137). London: Methuen.

Ajzen, I., & Fishbein, M. (1980). *Understanding attitudes and predicting social behavior.* Englewood Cliffs, NJ: Prentice-Hall.

Ajzen, I., & Fishbein, M. (1983). Relevance and availability in the attribution process. In J. Jaspers, F. D. Finchan, & M. Hewstone (Eds.), *Attribution theory and research: Conceptual, developmental and social dimensions.* New York: Academic Press.

Akerstedt, T. (1988). Sleepiness as a consequence of shift work. *Sleep, 11,* 17–34.

Akinboye, J. O. (1984). Secondary sexual characteristics and normal puberty in Nigerian and Zimbabwian adolescents. *Adolescence, 19,* 483–492.

Albert, M., Duffy, F., & Naeser, M. (1987). Nonlinear changes in cognition with age and their neuropsychologic correlates. *Canadian Journal of Psychology, 41,* 141–157.

Alessandri, S. M., Sullivan, M. W., & Lewis, M. (1990). Violation of expectancy and frustration in early infancy. *Developmental Psychology, 26,* 738–744.

Alexander, I. (1982). The Freud-Jung relationship—The other side of Oedipus and countertransference. *American Psychologist, 37,* 1009–1018.

Alexander, I. (1988). Personality, psychological assessment, and psychobiography. *Journal of Personality, 56,* 265–294.

Algom, D., & Cohen-Raz, L. (1987). Sensory and cognitive factors in the processing of visual velocity. *Journal of Experimental Psychology: Human Perception and Performance, 13,* 3–13.

Alkon, D. L., Ikeno, H., Dworkin, J., MacPhie, D. L., Olds, J. L., Lederhedler, L., Matzel, L., Schreurs, B. G., Kuzirian, A., Collin, C., & Yamoah, E. (1990). Contraction of neuronal branching volume: An anatomic correlate of Pavlovian conditioning. *Proceedings of the National Academy of Sciences of the U.S.A., 87,* 1611–1614.

Alley, T. R. (1983). Growth-produced changes in body shape and size as determinants of perceived age and adult caregiving. *Child Development, 54,* 241–248.

Alloy, L. B., Abramson, L. Y., Metalsky, G. I., & Hartlage, S. (1988). The hopelessness theory of depression: Attributional aspects. *British Journal of Clinical Psychology, 27,* 5–21.

Allport, F. H. (1920). The influence of the group upon association and thought. *Journal of Experimental Psychology, 3,* 159–182.

Allport, G. W. (1961). *Pattern and growth in personality.* New York: Holt, Rinehart, & Winston.

Allport, G. W., Vernon, P. E., & Lindzey, G. (1960). *Study of values: A scale for measuring the dominant interests in personality* (3rd ed.). Boston: Houghton-Mifflin.

Alter, J. B. (1984). Creativity profile of university and conservatory dance students. *Journal of Personality Assessment, 48,* 153–158.

American Association on Mental Retardation. (1992). *Mental retardation: Definition, classification, and systems of supports* (9th ed.). Washington, DC: Author.

American Psychiatric Association. (1980). *Diagnostic and statistical manual of mental disorders* (3rd ed.). Washington, DC: Author.

American Psychiatric Association. (1987). *Diagnostic and statistical manual of mental disorders* (3rd rev. ed.). Washington, DC: Author.

American Psychiatric Association. (1994). DSM-IV draft criteria. Washington, DC: Author.

American Psychiatric Association (1991). *Diagnostic and statistical manual: IV. Options book: Work in progress.* Washington, DC: Author.

American Psychological Association. (1982). *Ethical principles in the conduct of research with human participants.* Washington, DC: Author.

American Psychological Association. (1984). *Behavioral research with animals.* Washington, DC: Author.

American Psychological Association. (1993). *American Psychological Association Ethics Code.* Washington, DC: Author.

Amoore, J. E. (1970). *Molecular basis of odor.* Springfield, IL: Charles C. Thomas.

Anastasi, A. (1986). Evolving concepts of test validation. *Annual Review of Psychology, 37,* 1–15.

Anastasi, A. (1988). Psychological testing (6th ed.). New York: Macmillan.

Anastasi, A. (1989). Ability testing in the 1980s and beyond: Some major trends. *Public Personnel Management Journal, 18,* 471–484.

Anch, A. M., Browman, C. P., Mitler, M., & Walsh, J. K. (1988). *Sleep: A scientific perspective.* Englewood Cliffs, NJ: Prentice-Hall.

Anderson, C. A., & Anderson, D. C. (1984). Ambient temperature and violent crime: Tests of the linear and curvilinear hypotheses. *Journal of Personality and Social Psychology, 46,* 91–97.

Andreason, N. (1987). Creativity and mental illness: Prevalence rates in writers and their first-degree relatives. *American Journal of Psychiatry, 144,* 1288–1294.

Andrews, L. B. (1984, February). Exhibit A: Language. *Psychology Today,* pp. 28–33.

Anisfeld, E., Casper, V., Nozyce, M., & Cunningham, N. (1990). Does infant carrying promote attachment? An experimental study of the effects of increased physical contact on the development of attachment. *Child Development, 61,* 1617–1627.

Anno, M. (1975). *Anno's alphabet.* New York: Thomas Y. Crowell.

Ansbacher, H. L., & Ansbacher, R. R. (Eds.). (1956). *The individual psychology of Alfred Adler.* New York: Basic Books.

Antonovsky, A. (1979). *Health, stress and coping.* San Francisco: Jossey-Bass.

Antrobus, J. (1983). REM and NREM sleep reports: Comparison of word frequencies by cognitive classes. *Psychophysiology, 20,* 562–568.

Ardrey, R. (1961). *African genesis.* New York: Atheneum.

Arispe, N., Rojas, E., & Pollard, H. B. (1993). Alzheimer disease amyloid ß protein forms calcium channels in bilayer membranes: Blockade by tromethamine and aluminium. *Proceedings of the National Academy of Sciences of the U.S.A., 90,* 567–571.

Arnheim, R. (1986). The artistry of psychotics. *American Scientist, 74,* 48–54.

Arnold, D. W. (1991). To test or not to test: Legal issues in integrity testing. Special Issue: Integrity testing. *Forensic Reports, 4*(2), 213–224.

Arnold, W. N. (1988). Vincent van Gogh and the thujone connection. *Journal of the American Medical Association, 260,* 3042–3044.

Aronin, N., Coslovsky, R., & Leeman, S. E. (1986). Substance P and neurotensin. *Annual Review of Physiology, 48,* 537–549.

Aronson, E., Blaney, N., Stephan, C., Sikes, J., & Snapp, M. (1978). *The jigsaw classroom.* Beverly Hills, CA: Sage.

Aronsson, K. (1981). The bilingual preschooler as grammarian: Children's paraphrases of ungrammatical sentences. *Psychological Research Bulletin, Land University,* No. 21.

Asch, S. E. (1956). Studies of independence and submission to group pressure: I. A minority of one against a unanimous majority. *Psychological Monographs, 70*(9, Whole No. 416).

Asch, S. E. (1965). Effects of group pressure upon the modification and distortion of judgments. In H. Proshansky & B. Seidenberg (Eds.), *Basic studies in social psychology.* New York: Holt, Rinehart, & Winston.

Asenjo, A. (1963). *Neurosurgical techniques.* Springfield, IL: Charles C. Thomas.

Aserinsky, E., & Kleitman, N. (1953). Regularly occurring periods of eye motility and concomitant phenomena during sleep. *Science, 118,* 273–274.

Asken, J. J., & Raham, D. C. (1983). Resident performance and sleep deprivation: A review. *Journal of Medical Education, 58,* 382–388.

Aslin, R. N. (1977). Development of binocular fixation in human infants. *Journal of Experimental Child Psychology, 23,* 133–150.

Aslin, R. N., & Smith, L. B. (1988). Perceptual development. *Annual Review of Psychology, 39,* 435–473.

Atkinson, J. W., & Birch, D. (1978). *An introduction to motivation* (2nd ed.). New York: Van Nostrand-Reinhold.

Atkinson, R. C., & Shiffrin, R. M. (1977). Human memory: A proposed system and its control processes. In G. W. Bower (Ed.), *Human memory: Basic processes.* New York: Academic Press.

Atwater, E. (1983). *Adolescence.* Englewood Cliffs, NJ: Prentice-Hall.

Averbach, E., & Sperling, G. (1961). Short-term storage of information in vision. In C. Cheng (Ed.), *Fourth London Symposium on Information Theory.* London: Butterworth.

Averill, J. R. (1973). Personal control over aversive stimuli and its relationship to stress. *Psychological Bulletin, 80,* 286–303.

Averill, J. R. (1979a). Anger. In H. Howe & R. A. Dienstbier (Eds.), *Nebraska Symposium on Motivation, 1978* (pp. 1–80). Lincoln: University of Nebraska Press.

Averill, J. R. (1979b). The functions of grief. In C. Izard (Ed.), *Emotions in personality and psychopathology* (pp. 339–368). New York: Plenum.

Bach-y-Rita, P. (1982). Sensory substitution in rehabilitation. In L. Illis, M. Sedwick, & H. Granville (Eds.), *Rehabilitation of the neurological patient.* Oxford: Blackwell.

Baddeley, A. (1990). *Human memory: Theory and practice.* Needham Heights, MA: Allyn & Bacon.

Badia, P., Culbertson, S., & Harsh, J. (1973). Choice of longer or stronger signalled shock over shorter or weaker unsignalled shock. *Journal of the Experimental Analysis of Behavior, 19,* 25–33.

Bahill, A. T., & LaRitz, T. (1984). Why can't batters keep their eyes on the ball? *American Scientist, 72,* 249–253.

Bahrick, H. P. (1984). Semantic memory content in permastore: Fifty years of memory for Spanish learned in school. *Journal of Experimental Psychology: General, 113,* 1–26.

Bahrick, H. P. (1992). Stabilized memory of unrehearsed knowledge. *Journal of Experimental Psychology: General, 121,* 112–113.

Bahrick, H. P., & Hall, L. K. (1991). Lifetime maintenance of high school mathematics content. *Journal of Experimental Psychology: General, 120,* 20–33.

Bahrick, H. P., & Phelps, E. (1987). Retention of Spanish vocabulary over 8 years. *Journal of Experimental Psychology: Learning, Memory, and Cognition, 13,* 344–349.

Baird, J. C., & Wagner, M. (1982). The moon illusion. 1. How high is the sky? *Journal of Experimental Psychology: General, 111,* 296–303.

Baker, E. L., Feldman, R. G., White, R. F., & Harley, J. P. (1983). The role of occupational lead exposure in the genesis of psychiatric and behavioral disturbances. *Acta Psychologica Scandinavica, 67*(Suppl. 303), 38–48.

Bandura, A. (1977a). Self-efficacy: Toward a unifying theory of behavioral change. *Psychological Review, 84,* 191–215.

Bandura, A. (1977b). *Social learning theory.* Englewood Cliffs, NJ: Prentice-Hall.

Bandura, A. (1986). *Social foundations of thought and action: A social cognitive theory.* Englewood Cliffs, NJ: Prentice-Hall.

Bandura, A. (1989). Human agency in social cognitive theory. *American Psychologist, 44,* 1175–1184.

Bandura, A., Blanchard, E., and Ritter, T. (1969). Influence of models' reinforcement contingencies in the acquisition of imitative responses. *Journal of Personality and Social Psychology, 1,* 589–595.

Bandura, A., O'Leary, A., Taylor, C. B., Gauthier, J., & Gossard, D. (1988). Perceived self-efficacy and pain control: Opioid and non-opioid mechanisms. *Journal of Personality and Social Psychology, 53,* 563–571.

Bandura, A., Ross, D. M., & Ross, S. A. (1963). Imitation of film-mediated aggressive models. *Journal of Abnormal and Social Psychology, 66,* 3–11.

Banks, M. S., & Salapatek, P. (1983). Infant visual perception. In M. M. Haith & J. J. Campos (Eds.), *Mussen's handbook of child psychology: Vol. 2. Infancy and developmental psychobiology* (4th ed., pp. 435–571). New York: Wiley.

Barber, B. L., & Eccles, J. S. (1992). Long-term influence of divorce and single parenting on adolescent family- and work-related values, behaviors, and aspirations. *Psychological Bulletin, 111,* 108–126.

Barklage, N. E., & Jefferson, J. W. (1987). Alternative uses of lithium in psychiatry. *Psychosomatics, 28,* 239–256.

Barlow, H. B. (1982). Physiology of the retina. In H. B. Barlow & J. D. Mollon (Eds.), *The senses.* London: Cambridge University Press.

Barnett, P. A., & Gotlib, I. H. (1988). Psychosocial functioning and depression: Distinguishing among antecedents, concomitants, and consequences. *Psychological Bulletin, 104,* 97–126.

Barone, J. J., & Roberts, H. (1984). Human consumption of caffeine. In P. B. Dews (Ed.), *Caffeine: Perspectives from recent research* (pp. 59–73). New York: Springer-Verlag.

Barron, F. (1955). The disposition toward originality. *Journal of Abnormal and Social Psychology, 51,* 478–485.

Barron, F., & Harrington, D. M. (1981). Creativity, intelligence and personality. *Annual Review of Psychology, 32,* 439–476.

Bartlett, F. C. (1932). *Remembering: A study in experimental and social psychology.* New York: Cambridge University Press.

Bartley, S. H. (1972). *Perception in everyday life.* New York: Harper & Row.

Bartoshuk, L. M. (1978). Gustatory system. In R. B. Masterson (Ed.), *Handbook of behavioral neurobiology* (Vol. 1). New York: Plenum.

Basadur, M., Graen, G. B., & Green, S. G. (1982). Training in creative problem solving: Effects of ideation and problem finding and solving in an industrial research organization. *Organizational Behavior and Human Performance, 30,* 41–70.

Bass, C. (1988). Personality correlates of smoking behavior in men with heart disease. *Personality and Individual Differences, 9,* 397–400.

Bassuk, E. L., & Gerson, S. (1978). Deinstitutionalization and mental health services. *Scientific American, 238,* 46–53.

Batchelor, W. F. (1988). AIDS 1988: The science and the limits of science. *American Psychologist, 43,* 853–858.

Batson, C. D. (1987). Prosocial motivation: Is it ever truly altruistic? In L. Berkowitz (Ed.), *Advances in experimental social psychology* (Vol. 20). Orlando, FL: Academic Press.

Batson, C. D., Bolen, M. H., Cross, J. A., & Neuringer-Benefiel, H. E. (1986). Where is the altruism in altruistic personality? *Journal of Personality and Social Psychology, 50,* 212–220.

Baum, A., & Nesselhof, S. E. A. (1988). Psychological research and the prevention, etiology, and treatment of AIDS. *American Psychologist, 43,* 900–906.

Baumeister, R. F. (1990). Suicide as escape from self. *Psychological Review, 97,* 90–113.

Baumeister, R. F., & Cairns, K. J. (1992). Repression and self-presentation when audience interferes with self-deceptive strategies. *Journal of Personality and Social Psychology, 62,* 851–862.

Baumhover, A. H. (1966). Eradication of the screwworm. *JAMA, Journal of the American Medical Association, 196,* 240–248.

Baumrind, D. (1971). Current patterns of parental authority. *Developmental Psychology Monographs, 4*(1, Part 2).

Baxter, D. W., & Olszewski, J. (1960). Congenital insensitivity to pain. *Brain, 83,* 381–393.

Beach, F. A. (1977). Hormonal control of sex-related behavior. In F. A. Beach (Ed.), *Human sexuality in four perspectives* (pp. 247–267). Baltimore: Johns Hopkins University Press.

Beck, A. T. (1987). Cognitive models of depression: New perspectives. *Journal of Cognitive Psychotherapy: An International Quarterly, 1,* 5–37.

Beck, A. T., Freeman, A., & Associates. (1990). *Cognitive therapy of personality disorders.* New York: Guilford Press.

Beck, A. T., Rush, B. T., Shaw, R. D., and Emery, A. F. (1979). Distorted thinking in the development of depression. *Archives of General Psychiatry, 36,* 103–132.

Beck, A. T., & Young, J. E. (1978, September). College blues. *Psychology Today,* pp. 80–92.

Beck, R. C. (1983). *Motivation: Theories and principles* (2nd ed.). Englewood Cliffs, NJ: Prentice-Hall.

Becklen, R., Wallach, H., & Nitzberg, D. (1984). A limitation of position constancy. *Journal of Experimental Psychology: Human Perception and Performance, 10,* 712–723.

Beckwith, J., Geller, L., & Sarkar, S. (1991, April 12). IQ and heredity. *Science,* p. 191.

Beecher, H. K. (1959). *Measurement of subjective responses.* New York: Oxford University Press.

Beehr, T., & Newman, J. (1978). Job stress, employee health, and organizational effectiveness. *Personnel Psychology, 31,* 665–699.

Begleiter, H., Porjesz, B., Bihari, B., & Kissin, B. (1984). Event-related brain potentials in boys at risk for alcoholism. *Science, 225,* 1493–1495.

Beitchman, J. H., Zucker, K. J., Hood, J. E., da Costa, G. A., Akman, D., & Cassavia, E. (1992). A review of the long-term effects of child sexual abuse. *Child Abuse and Neglect, 16,* 101–118.

Békésy, G. von (1960). *Experiments in hearing.* New York: McGraw-Hill.

Belenky, M. F., Clinchy, B. M., Goldberger, N. R., & Tarule, J. M. (1986). *Women's ways of knowing: The development of self, voice, and mind.* New York: Basic Books.

Belkin, G. S. (1988). *Introduction to counseling.* Dubuque, IA: W. C. Brown.

Bell, A. P., Weinberg, M. S., & Hammersmith, S. F. (1981). *Sexual preference.* Bloomington: Indiana University Press.

Belloc, N. B. (1973). Relationship of health practices and mortality. *Preventive Medicine, 2,* 67–81.

Belloc, N. B., & Breslaw, L. (1972). Relationship of physical health status and health practices. *Preventive Medicine, 1,* 409–421.

Belsky, J., & Rovine, M. J. (1988). Nonmaternal care in the first year of life and the security of infant-parent attachment. *Child Development, 59,* 157–167.

Bem, D., & Allen, A. (1974). On predicting some of the people some of the time: The search for cross-situational consistencies in behavior. *Psychological Review, 81,* 506–520.

Bem, S. (1974). The measurement of psychological androgyny. *Journal of Consulting and Clinical Psychology, 42,* 155–162.

Benbow, C. P., & Stanley, J. C. (1983). Sex differences in mathematical reasoning ability. *Science, 222,* 1029–1031.

Benjamin, E. R., & Romano, J. L. (1980). Counseling services in an open-door college: Faculty and student perceptions. *Journal of College Student Personnel, 21,* 14–22.

Benjamin, L. T. (1988). *History of psychology: Original sources and contemporary research.* New York: McGraw-Hill.

Benjamin, L. T., & Bruce, D. (1982). From bottle-fed chimp to bottlenose dolphin: A contemporary appraisal of Winthrop Kellogg. *Psychological Record, 32,* 461–482.

Benjamin, L. T., Langley, J., & Hall, R. (1979, December). Santa now and then. *Psychology Today,* pp. 36–44.

Bennett, L. A., Wolin, S. J., & Reiss, D. (1988). Cognitive behavioral, and emotional problems among school-age children of alcoholic parents. *American Journal of Psychiatry, 145,* 185–190.

Ben-Porath, Y., & Butcher, J. (1986). Computers in personality assessment. *Computers in Human Behavior, 2,* 167–182.

Benson, A. J. (1982). The vestibular sensory system. In H. B. Barlow & J. D. Mollon (Eds.), *The senses.* London: Cambridge University Press.

Berg, J. H, & Peplau, L. A. (1982). Loneliness: The relationship of self-disclosure and androgyny. *Personality and Social Psychology Bulletin, 8,* 624–630.

Bergmann, T. J., Mundt, D. H., & Illgen, E. F. (1990). The evaluation of honesty tests and means for their evaluation. *Employee Responsibilities and Rights Journal, 3*(3), pp. 215–223.

Berkun, C. S. (1986). In behalf of women over 40: Understanding the importance of the menopause. *Social Work, 31,* 378–384.

Berman, J. S., Miller, R. C., & Massman, P. J. (1985). Cognitive therapy versus systematic desensitization: Is one treatment superior? *Psychological Bulletin, 97,* 451–461.

Berndt, T. J. (1982). The features and effects of friendship in early adolescence. *Child Development, 53,* 1447–1460.

Berrios, G. E. (1990). A British contribution to the history of functional brain surgery. *Journal of Psychopharmacology, 4,* 140–143.

Berscheid, E. (1985). Interpersonal attraction. In G. Lindzey & E. Aronson (Eds.), *The handbook of social psychology.* New York: Random House.

Berscheid, E., & Walster, E. (1974). Physical attractiveness. In L. Berkowitz (Ed.), *Advances in experimental social psychology* (Vol. 7, pp. 157–215). New York: Academic Press.

Bersoff, D. N. (1981). Testing and the law. *American Psychologist, 36,* 1047–1056.

Bertelson, A. D., & Walsh, J. K. (1987). Insomnia. In J. Gackenbach (Ed.), *Sleep and dreams: A sourcebook.* New York: Garland.

Bethell-Fox, C. E., & Shepard, S. (1988). Mental rotation: Effects of stimulus complexity and familiarity. *Journal of Experimental Psychology: Human Perception and Performance, 14,* 12–23.

Beutler, L. E., Crago, M., & Arizmendi, T. G. (1986). Research on therapist variables in psychotherapy. In S. L. Garfield & A. E. Bergin (Eds.), *Handbook of psychotherapy and behavior change.* New York: Wiley.

Bevan, W. (1964). Subliminal stimulation: A pervasive problem for psychology. *Psychological Bulletin, 61,* 89–99.

Beveridge, A., & Renvoise, E. (1990). Electricity and British psychology in the nineteenth century. *Journal of Psychopharmacology, 4,* 145–151.

Bhanji, S. (1979). Anorexia nervosa: Physicians' and psychiatrists' opinion and practice. *Journal of Psychosomatic Research, 23,* 7–11.

Biederman, I. (1981). On the semantics of a glance at a scene. In M. Kubovy & J. Pomerantz (Eds.), *Perceptual organization.* Hillsdale, NJ: Erlbaum.

Biederman, I. (1987). Recognition-by-components: A theory of human image understanding. *Psychological Review, 94,* 115–147.

Billings, A. G., Cronkite, R. C., & Moos, R. H. (1983). Social-environmental factors in unipolar depression: Comparisons of depressed patients and non-depressed controls. *Journal of Abnormal Psychology, 92,* 119–133.

Black, J., Greenough, W., Anderson, B., & Isaacs, K. (1987). Environment and the aging brain. *Canadian Journal of Psychology, 41,* 111–130.

Black, J. S., & Mendenhall, M. (1990). Cross-cultural training effectiveness: A review and a theoretical framework for future research. *Academic Management Review, 15,* 113–136.

Blake, P, Fry, R., & Pesjack, M. (1984). *Self-assessment and behavior change manual.* New York: Random House.

Blake, R. (1987). Boarding home residents: New underclass in the mental health system. *Health and Social Work, 12,* 85–90.

Blane, H. T., & Leonard, K. E. (1987). *Psychological theories of drinking and alcoholism.* New York: Guilford Press.

Block, J. H., Block, J., & Gjerde, P. F. (1986). The personality of children prior to divorce: A prospective study. *Child Development, 57,* 827–840.

Bock, E. W. (1972). Aging and suicide: The significance of marital, kinship, and alternative relations. *Family Coordinator, 21,* 71–79.

Bolman, L. G., & Deal, T. E. (1992). What makes a team work? *Organizational Dynamics, 21,* 34–44.

Bon, L., Benassi, C., & Morigi, M. (1983). Rapid eye movements in the kitten. *Electroencephalography and Clinical Neurophysiology, 55,* 601–603.

Borbely, A. (1986). *Secrets of sleep.* New York: Basic Books.

Boring, E. G. (1923). Intelligence as the tests test it. *New Republic, 35,* 35–37.

Borja-Alvarez, T., Zarbatany, L., & Pepper, S. (1991). Contributions of male and female guests and hosts to peer group entry. *Child Development, 62,* 1079–1090.

Borkovec, T. D. (1982). Insomnia. *Journal of Consulting and Clinical Psychology, 50,* 880–895.

Bornstein, M. H., Krinsky, S. J., & Benasich, A. A. (1986). Fine orientation discrimination and shape constancy in young infants. *Journal of Experimental Child Psychology, 41,* 49–60.

Botwinick, J. (1977). Intellectual abilities. In J. E. Birren & K. W. Schaie (Eds.), *Handbook of the psychology of aging.* New York: Van Nostrand-Reinhold.

Botwinick, J. (1983). Intellectual abilities. In J. E. Birren & K. W. Schaie (Eds.), *Handbook of the psychology of aging* (pp. 580–605). New York: Van Nostrand-Reinhold.

Bouchard, T., Jr., Lykken, D. T., McGue, M., Segal, N. L., & Tellegen, A. (1990). Sources of human psychological differences; The Minnesota Study of Twins Reared Apart. *Science, 250,* 223–228.

Bouchard, T., Jr., & Segal, N. (1985). Environment and IQ. In B. B. Wolman (Ed.), *Handbook of intelligence: Theories, measurements, and applications* (pp. 391–464). New York: Wiley.

Boudreau, J. W., & Berger, C. J. (1985). Decision-theoretic utility analysis applied to employee separations and acquisitions. *Journal of Applied Psychology, 70,* 581–612.

Boudreau, J. W., & Rynes, S. L. (1985). Role of recruitment in staffing utility analysis. *Journal of Applied Psychology, 70,* 354–366.

Bourne, L. E., Ekstrand, B. R., & Dominowski, R. L. (1971). *The psychology of thinking.* Englewood Cliffs, NJ: Prentice-Hall.

Bousfield, W. A. (1955). Lope de Vega on early conditioning. *American Psychologist, 10,* 828.

Bouton, R., Gallagher, P., Garlinghouse, P., Leal, T., et al. (1987). Scales for measuring fear of AIDS and homophobia. *Journal of Personality Assessment, 51,* 606–614.

Bower, B. (1988). The brain in the machine. *Science News, 134,* 344–345.

Bower, B. (1990). Antipsychotics evoke youthful concerns. *Science News, 140,* 276.

Bower, B. (1992). Gene in the bottle. *Science News, 140,* 190–191.

Bower, G. H. (1972). Mental imagery and associative learning. In L. W. Gregg (Ed.), *Cognition and learning in memory*. New York: Wiley.

Bower, G. H. (1981). Mood and memory. *American Psychologist, 36*, 129–148.

Bower, G. H. (1987). Commentary on mood and memory. *Behavior Research and Therapy, 25*, 443–455.

Bower, G. H., & Springston, F. (1970). Pauses as recording points in letter series. *Journal of Experimental Psychology, 83*, 421–430.

Bowers, D. G. (1977). *Systems of organization: Management of the human resource*. Ann Arbor: University of Michigan Press.

Bowlby, J. (1969). *Attachment and loss: Vol. 1. Attachment*. New York: Basic Books.

Bowlby, J. (1973). *Attachment and loss: Vol. 2. Separation, anxiety and anger*. New York: Basic Books.

Boyd, T., & Levis, D. J. (1983). Exposure is a necessary condition for fear reduction: A reply to de Silva and Rachmann. *Behavior Research and Therapy, 21*, 143–149.

Boynton, R. M. (1971). Color vision. In J. W. Kling & L. A. Riggs (Eds.), *Woodworth and Schlosberg's experimental psychology* (3rd ed.). New York: Holt, Rinehart, & Winston.

Braddick, O. (1986). Mapping of motion perception. *Nature (London), 320*, 680–681.

Bradley, M. M., Greenwald, M. K., Petry, M. C., & Lang, P. J. (1992). Remembering pictures: Pleasure and arousal in memory. *Journal of Experimental Psychology: Learning, Memory, and Cognition, 18*, 379–390.

Brady, J. V. (1958). Ulcers in "executive" monkeys. *Scientific American, 199*, 95–100.

Braine, L. G. (1978). A new slant on orientation perception. *American Psychologist, 33*, 10–22.

Branham, F. L. (1983). How to evaluate executive outplacement services. *Personnel Journal, 62*, 323–326.

Braun, K. L., & Rose, C. L. (1987). Geriatric patient outcomes and costs in three settings: Nursing home, foster family, and own home. *Journal of the American Geriatrics Society, 35*, 387–397.

Brayshaw, N. D., & Brayshaw, D. D. (1986). Thyroid hypofunction in premenstrual syndrome. *New England Journal of Medicine, 315*, 1486–1487.

Brazelton, T. B. (1982). Joint regulation of neonate-parent behavior. In E. Z. Tronic (Ed.), *Social interchange in infancy: Affect, cognition, and communication* (pp. 7–22). Baltimore: University Park Press.

Breggin, P. R. (1979). *Electroshock: Its brain disabling effects*. New York: Springer-Verlag.

Breland, K., & Breland, M. (1961). Misbehavior of organisms. *American Psychologist, 16*, 681–684.

Brewin, C. R. (1985). Depression and causal attributions: What is their relation? *Psychological Bulletin, 98*, 297–309.

Brickman, P., Rabinowitz, V. C., Karuza, J., Coates, D., Cohn, E., & Kidder, L. (1982). Models of helping and coping. *American Psychologist, 37*, 368–384.

Brigham, J. C., & Barkowitz, P. (1970). Do "they all look alike"? The effect of race, sex, experience, and attitudes on the ability to recognize faces. *Journal of Applied Social Psychology, 8*, 306–318.

Brigham, J. C., Maass, A., Martinez, D., & Whittenberger, G. (1983). The effect of arousal on facial recognition. *Basic and Applied Social Psychology, 4*, 279–293.

Brinbaum, M. E., & Sotoodeh, J. R. (1991). Measurement of stress: Scaling the magnitudes of life changes. *Psychological Science, 2*(4), 236–243.

Broadbent, D. E. (1957). A mechanical model for human attention and immediate memory. *Psychological Review, 64*, 205–215.

Broadbent, D. E. (1987). Structure and strategies: Where are we now? *Psychological Research, 49*, 73–79.

Broca, P. (1865). Sur le seige de la faculte du langage articule. *Bulletin of the Society of Anthropology, 6*, 377–396.

Brockner, J. (1992). Managing the effects of layoffs on survivors. *California Management Review, 34*(2), 9–28.

Brody, N. (1985). The validity of tests of intelligence. In B. B. Wolman (Ed.), *Handbook of intelligence: Theories, measurements, and applications* (pp. 353–389). New York: Wiley.

Bromley, D. B. (1974). *The psychology of human aging* (2nd ed.). New York: Penguin.

Bronstein, P., & Quina, K. (1991). *Teaching a psychology of people: Resources for gender and sociocultural awareness*. Washington, DC: American Psychological Association.

Brou, P., Sciascia, T. R., Linden, L., & Lettvin, J. Y. (1986, September). The color of things. *Scientific American, 225*, 84–91.

Broughton, R. (1989). Sleep, napping, and narcolepsy. In *Narcolepsy: Third International Symposium*. Oak Park, IL: Matrix Communications.

Brown, A. L., & French, L. A. (1979). The zone of potential development: Implications for intelligence testing in the year 2000. *Intelligence, 3*, 255–273.

Brown, E. L., & Deffenbacher, K. (1979). *Perception and the senses*. New York: Oxford.

Brown, J. A. (1958). Some tests of the decay theory of immediate memory. *Quarterly Journal of Experimental Psychology, 10*, 12–21.

Brown, J. D., & Siegel, J. M. (1988). Attributions for negative life events and depression: The role of perceived control. *Journal of Personality and Social Psychology, 54*, 316–322.

Brown, J. W. (1988). *Classics in neuropsychology: Agnosia and apraxia*. Hillsdale, NJ: Erlbaum.

Brown, L. M., & Gilligan, C. (1992). *Meeting at the crossroads: Women's psychology and girls' development*. Cambridge, MA: Harvard University Press.

Brown, R. (1965). *Social psychology*. New York: Free Press.

Brown, R. (1973). *A first language: The early stages*. Cambridge, MA: Harvard University Press.

Brown, R. (1986). *Social psychology* (2nd ed.). New York: Free Press.

Brown, R., & Kulik, J. A. (1977). Flashbulb memories. *Cognition, 5*, 73–99.

Brown, R., & McNeill, D. (1966). The "tip of the tongue" phenomenon. *Journal of Verbal Learning and Verbal Behavior, 5*, 325–337.

Browne, A., & Finkelhor, D. (1986). Impact of child sexual abuse: A review of the research. *Psychological Bulletin, 99*, 66–77.

Brownell, K. (1991). Dieting. *New England Journal of Medicine, 46*, 469–481.

Bruce, V., & Green, P. (1985). *Visual perception: Physiology, psychology, and ecology*. Hillsdale, NJ: Erlbaum.

Bruner, J. S., Goodnow, J. J., & Austin, G. A. (1956). *A study of thinking*. New York: Wiley.

Bry, B. H., McKeon, P., & Pandina, R. J. (1982). Extent of drug use as a function of number of risk factors. *Journal of Abnormal Psychology, 91*, 273–279.

Buck, R. (1988). *Human motivation and emotion* (2nd ed.). New York: Wiley.

Buckingham, R. W. (1983). Hospice care in the United States: The process begins. *Omega: Journal of Death and Dying, 13*, 159–171.

Buhrmester, D. (1990). Intimacy of friendship, interpersonal competence, and adjustment during preadolescence and adolescence. *Child Development, 61*, 1101–1111.

Buhrmester, D., & Fuhrman, W. (1990). Age differences in perceptions of sibling relationships in childhood and adolescence. *Child Development, 61*, 1387–1398.

Bunnell, D. E., Bevier, W., & Horvath, S. M. (1983). Effects of exhaustive exercise on the sleep of men and women. *Psychophysiology, 20*, 50–58.

Burger, J. M. (1981). Self-disclosure and liking during initial encounters: An attributional approach. *Social Behavior and Personality, 9*, 179–183.

Buri, J. R. (1989). Self-esteem and appraisals of parental behavior. *Journal of Adolescent Research, 4,* 33–49.

Burke, W. W. (1993). *Organizational development: A normative view.* Reading, MA: Addison-Wesley.

Burns, M. O., & Seligman, M. E. (1989). Explanatory style across the life span: Evidence for stability over 52 years. *Journal of Personality and Social Psychology, 56,* 471–477.

Burr, D., & Ross, J. (1986). Visual processing of motion. *Trends in Neuroscience, 9,* 304–307.

Burton, T. M. (1991). *Anti-depressant of Eli Lilly loses sales after attack by sect.* (Reprinted from Wall Street Journal). Princeton, NJ: Dow Jones Reprint Service.

Buss, D. M. (1988). The evolution of human intrasexual competition: Tactics of mate attraction. *Journal of Personality and Social Psychology, 54,* 616–628.

Buss, D. M. (1989). Sex differences in human mate preferences: Evolutionary hypotheses tested in 37 cultures. *Behavioral and Brain Sciences, 12,* 1–49.

Buss, D. M., & Barnes, M. (1986). Preferences in human mate selection. *Journal of Personality and Social Psychology, 50,* 559–570.

Butcher, J. N., Dahlström, W. G., Graham, J. R., Tellegen, A., & Kalmmer, B. (1989). *MMPI-2: Manual for administration and scoring.* Minneapolis: University of Minnesota Press.

Butler, N., & Golding, J. (1986). *From birth to five: A study of the health and behavior of Britain's five-year-olds.* Oxford: Pergamon.

Butler, R. A. (1953). Discrimination learning by rhesus monkeys to visual-exploration motivation. *Journal of Comparative and Physiological Psychology, 46,* 95–98.

Byrne, D., & Nelson, D. (1965). Attraction as a linear function of proportion of positive reinforcements. *Journal of Personality and Social Psychology, 1,* 659–663.

Cacioppo, J. T., Petty, R. E., & Losch, M. E. (1986). Attributions of responsibility for helping and doing harm: Evidence for confusion of responsibility. *Journal of Personality and Social Psychology, 50,* 100–105.

Caine, N. (1986). Behavior during puberty and adolescence. In G. Mitchell & J. Erwin (Eds.), *Comparative primate biology: Vol. 2A. Behavior, conservation, and ecology* (pp. 327–361). New York: Alan R. Liss.

Calabrese, J. R., Kling, M. A., & Gold, P. W. (1987). Alterations in immunocompetence during stress, bereavement, and depression: Focus on neuroendocrine regulations. *American Journal of Psychiatry, 144,* 1123–1134.

Calev, A. (1984). Recall and recognition in chronic nondemented schizophrenics: Use of matched tasks. *Journal of Abnormal Psychology, 93,* 172–177.

Campbell, D. E., & Beets, J. L. (1978). Lunacy and the moon. *Psychological Bulletin, 85,* 1123–1129.

Campbell, J. P., & Pritchard, R. D. (1983). Motivation theory in industrial and organizational psychology. In M. D. Dunnette (Ed.), *Handbook of industrial and organizational psychology* (pp. 63–130). New York: Wiley.

Campbell, R. (1986). The lateralization of lip-read sounds: A first look. *Brain and Cognition, 5,* 1–21.

Campbell, R., & Dobb, B. (1980). Hearing by eye. *Quarterly Journal of Experimental Psychology, 32,* 85–99.

Campos, J. J., Langer, A., & Krowitz, A. (1970). Cardiac responses on the visual cliff in prelocomotor human infants. *Science, 170,* 196–197.

Cannon, W. B. (1929). *Bodily changes in pain, hunger, fear and rage.* New York: Appleton.

Cannon, W. B., & Washburn, A. L. (1912). An explanation of hunger. *American Journal of Physiology, 29,* 441–454.

Carlson, J. G., & Hill, K. D. (1987). The effect of gaming on attendance and attitude. *Personnel Psychology, 35,* 63–73.

Carlson, N. R. (1988). *Foundations of physiological psychology.* Boston: Allyn & Bacon.

Carlson, N. R. (1991). *Physiology and behavior.* Boston: Allyn & Bacon.

Carlson, V., Cicchetti, D., Barnett, D., & Braunwald, K. (1989). Disorganized/disoriented attachment relationships in maltreated infants. *Developmental Psychology, 25,* 525–531.

Carman, G. J., Mealey, L., Thompson, S. T., & Thompson, M. A. (1984). Patterns in the distribution of REM sleep in normal human sleep. *Sleep, 7,* 347–355.

Carnevale, A. P., Gainer, L. J., and Villet, J. (1990). *Training in America: The organization and strategic role of training.* San Francisco: Jossey-Bass.

Caro, T. M., & Borgerhoff-Hubler, M. (1987). The problem of adaptation in the study of human behavior. *Ethnology and Sociobiology, 8,* 61–72.

Carpenter, E. (1980). If Wittgenstein had been an Eskimo. *Natural History, 89,* 72–77.

Carr, E. G., & Lovaas, D. I. (1983). Contingent electric shock treatment for severe behavior problems. In S. Axelrod & J. Apsche (Eds.), *The effects of punishment on human behavior.* New York: Academic Press.

Carringer, D. C. (1974). Creative thinking abilities of Mexican youth: The relationship of bilingualism. *Journal of Cross-Cultural Psychology, 5,* 492–504.

Carroll, D. W. (1986). *Psychology of language.* Monterey, CA: Brooks/Cole.

Carson, R. C. (1991). Dilemmas in the pathway of the DSM-IV. *Journal of Abnormal Psychology, 100,* 302–307.

Carson, R. C., Butcher, J. N., & Coleman, J. C. (1992). *Abnormal psychology and modern life.* (9th ed.) New York: HarperCollins.

Carver, R. P. (1981). *Reading comprehension and reading theory.* Springfield, IL: Charles C. Thomas.

Casey, R. J., & Berman, J. S. (1985). The outcome of psychotherapy with children. *Psychological Bulletin, 98,* 388–400.

Cassidy, J., & Asher, S. R. (1992). Loneliness and peer relations in young children. *Child Development, 63,* 350–365.

Castro, J. (1986, March 17). Battling the enemy within. *Time,* pp. 52–55, 57–59, 61.

Cathcart, W. G. (1982). Effects of a bilingual instructional program on conceptual development in primary school children. *Alberta Journal of Educational Research, 28,* 31–43.

Cattell, J. M. (1966). James McKeen Cattell (1860–1944) on mental tests, 1890. In R. J. Hernstein & E. G. Boring (Eds.), *A sourcebook in this history of psychology* (pp. 423–427). Cambridge, MA: Harvard University Press. (Original work published 1890).

Chaiken, S., & Eagly, A. H. (1983). Communication modality as a determinant of persuasion: The role of communicator salience. *Journal of Personality and Social Psychology, 45,* 241–256.

Chapanis, A. (1965). *Man-machine engineering.* Belmont, CA: Wadsworth.

Chase, W. G., & Erickson, K. A. (1982). Skill and working memory. In G. H. Bower (Ed.), *Psychology of learning and motivation* (Vol. 16, pp. 1–58). New York: Academic Press.

Chasnoff, I. J., & Griffith, D. R. (1989). Cocaine: Clinical studies of pregnancy and the newborn. *Annals of the New York Academy of Sciences, 562,* 260–266.

Chasnoff, I. J., Griffith, D. R., MacGregor, S., Dirkes, K., & Burns, K. A. (1989). Temporal patterns of cocaine use in pregnancy. *Journal of the American Medical Association, 261,* 1741–1744.

Chassin, L., Mann, L. M., & Sher, K. J. (1988). Self-awareness theory, family history of alcoholism, and adolescent alcohol involvement. *Journal of Abnormal Psychology, 97,* 206–217.

Cherry, E. (1953). Some experiments on the recognition of speech with one and with two ears. *Journal of the Acoustical Society of America, 25,* 975–979.

Chilman, C. S. (1983). *Adolescent sexuality in contemporary society.* New York: Wiley.

Chodorow, N. J. (1989). *Feminism and psychoanalytic theory.* New Haven, CT: Yale University Press.

Chomsky, N. (1959). A review of B. F. Skinner's "Verbal behavior." *Language, 35*, 26–58.

Chomsky, N. (1965). *Aspects of the theory of syntax*. Cambridge, MA: MIT Press.

Chomsky, N. (1968). *Language and mind*. New York: Harcourt, Brace & World.

Chouinard, G. (1991). Flouxetine and the preoccupation with suicide. *American Journal of Psychiatry, 148*, 1258–1259.

Christie Brown, J. R. W. (1983). Paraphilias: Sadomasochism, fetishism, transvestism, and transsexuality. *British Journal of Psychiatry, 143*, 227–231.

Chusmir, L. H. (1985). Motivation of managers: Is gender a factor? *Psychology of Woman Quarterly, 9*, 153–159.

Chusmir, L. H., & Koberg, C. S. (1986). Creativity differences among managers. *Journal of Vocational Behavior, 29*, 240–253.

Cialdini, R. B., Petty, E., & Cacioppo, J. T. (1981). Attitude and attitude change. *Annual Review of Psychology, 32*, 357–404.

Ciernia, J. R. (1985a). Death concern and businessmen's mid-life crisis. *Psychological Reports, 56*, 83–87.

Ciernia, J. R. (1985b). Myths about male midlife crises. *Psychological Reports, 56*, 1003–1007.

Clark, E. V. (1982). The young world-maker: A case study of innovation in the child's lexicon. In E. Warner & L. R. Gleitman (Eds.), *Language acquisition: State of the art*. London: Cambridge University Press.

Clark, K. B., & Clark, M. P. (1947). Racial identification and preference in Negro children. In T. M. Newcomb & E. L. Hartley (Eds.), *Readings in social psychology*. New York: Holt, Rinehart, & Winston.

Clarke-Stewart, K. A. (1989). Infant day care: Maligned or malignant? *American Psychologist, 44*, 266–273.

Clarkson, M. G., & Berg, W. K. (1983). Cardiac orienting and vowel discrimination in newborns: Crucial stimulus parameters. *Child Development, 54*, 162–171.

Clarkson-Smith, L., & Hartley, A. A. (1990). Structural equation models of relationships between exercise and cognitive abilities. *Psychology and Aging, 5*, 437–446.

Clary, E. G., & Fristad, M. A. (1987). Predictors of psychological help seeking on a college campus. *Journal of College Student Personnel, 28*, 180–181.

Claussen, A. H., & Crittenden, P. M. (1991). Physical and psychological maltreatment: Relations among types of maltreatment. *Child Abuse and Neglect, 15*, 5–18.

Clifton, R., Perris, E., & Bullinger, A. (1991). Infants' perception of auditory space. *Developmental Psychology, 27*, 187–197.

Cogan, R. (1980a). Effects of childbirth preparation. *Clinical Obstetrics and Gynecology, 23*, 1–14.

Cogan, R. (1980b). Endorphins and analgesia. *ICEA Review, 4*, 1–7.

Cohen, B. (1985, April). In C. Turkington. Therapist seeks correlation between diagnosis, drawings. *APA Monitor*, pp. 34–36.

Cohen, D. B. (1970). Current research on the frequency of dream recall. *Psychological Bulletin, 73*, 433–440.

Cohen, D. B. (1974). Toward a theory of dream recall. *Psychological Bulletin, 81*, 138–154.

Cohen, D. B. (1979). *Sleep and dreaming: Origin, nature and functions*. New York: Pergamon.

Cohen, J. (1992, January 3). Why can't scientists agree? *USA Weekend*, pp. 20–22.

Cohen, L. B., DeLoache, J. S., & Strauss, M. S. (1979). Infant visual perception. In J. D. Osofsky (Ed.), *Handbook of infant development*. New York: Wiley.

Cohen, S. (1981a). Marijuana legalization: Solution or dissolution. *American Journal of Drug and Alcohol Abuse, 8*, 283–290.

Cohen, S. (1981b, October). Sound effects on behavior. *Psychology Today*, pp. 38–49.

Cohn, J. F., & Tronick, E. Z. (1988). Mother-infant face-to-face interaction: Influence is bidirectional and unrelated to periodic cycles in either partner's behavior. *Developmental Psychology, 24*, 386–392.

Cohn, N. B., & Strassberg, D. S. (1983). Self-disclosure reciprocity among preadolescents. *Personality and Social Psychology Bulletin, 9*, 97–102.

Cohn, T. E., & Lasley, D. J. (1986). Visual sensitivity. *Annual Review of Psychology, 37*, 495–521.

Colby, A., Kohlberg, L., Gibbs, J., & Lieberman, M. (1983). A longitudinal study of moral development. *Monographs of the Society for Research in Child Development, 48*(1–2, Serial No. 200).

Cole, J., & Zuckerman, H. (1987). Marriage, motherhood and research performance in science. *Scientific American, 256*, 119–125.

Coleman, M., & Webber, J. (1988). Behavior problems? Try groups. *Academic Therapy, 23*, 265–275.

Coleman, R. M. (1986). *Wide awake at 3:00 a.m.: By choice or by chance?* New York: Freeman.

Collings, V. B. (1974). Human taste response as a function of locus on the tongue and soft palate. *Perception and Psychophysics, 16*, 169–174.

Collins, N. L., & Read, S. J. (1990). Adult attachment, working models, and relationship quality in dating couples. *Journal of Personality and Social Psychology, 58*, 644–663.

Conway, M. A., Cohen, G., & Stanhope, N. (1991). On the very long-term retention of knowledge acquired through formal education: Twelve years of cognitive psychology. *Journal of Experimental Psychology: General, 120*, 358ff.

Cook, M., & Mineka, S. (1990). Selective associations in the observational conditioning of fear in the rhesus monkey. *Journal of Experimental Psychology: Animal Behavior Processes, 16*, 372–389.

Cook, M., Mineka, S., & Trumble, D. (1987). The role of response-produced and exteroceptive feedback in the attenuation of fear over the course of avoidance learning. *Journal of Experimental Psychology: Animal Behavior Processes, 13*, 239–249.

Cook, S. W. (1985). Experimenting on social issues: The case of school desegregation. *American Psychologist, 40*, 452–460.

Cooper, J., Bloom, F. E., & Roth, R. H. (1990). *The biochemical basis of neuropharmacology* (5th ed.). New York: Oxford University Press.

Cooper, J., & Croyle, R. T. (1984). Attitudes and attitude change. *Annual Review of Psychology, 35*, 395–426.

Cooper, J., & Fazio, R. H. (1984). A new look at dissonance theory. In L. Berkowitz (Ed.), *Advances in experimental social psychology* (Vol. 17). New York: Academic Press.

Cooper, L. M. (1979). Hypnotic amnesia. In E. Fromm & R. E. Shor (Eds.), *Hypnosis: Developments in research and new perspectives* (2nd ed.). New York: Aldine.

Cooper, M. L., Russell, M., & George, W. H. (1988). Coping, expectancies, and alcohol abuse: A test of social learning formulations. *Journal of Abnormal Psychology, 97*, 218–230.

Cooper, T., Detre, T., & Weiss, S. M. (1981). Coronary-prone behavior and coronary heart disease: A critical review. *Circulation, 63*, 1199–1215.

Corballis, M. C. (1983). *Human laterality*. New York: Academic Press.

Corballis, M. C., & McLaren, R. (1984). Minding one's P's and Q's: Mental rotation and mirror-image discrimination. *Journal of Experimental Psychology: Human Perception and Performance, 10*, 318–327.

Coren, S. (1969). Brightness contrast as a function of figure ground relations. *Journal of Experimental Psychology, 80*, 517–524.

Coren, S., & Ward, L. M. (1989). *Sensation & perception*, 3rd edition. New York: Harcourt Brace Jovanovich.

Corey, G., Corey, M. S., & Callanan, P. (1988). *Issues and ethics in the helping professions*. Monterey, CA: Brooks/Cole.

Corkin, S. (1984). Lasting consequences of bilateral medial temporal lobectomy: Clinical course and experimental findings in H. M. *Seminars in Neurology, 4,* 249–259.

Corliss, R. (1982). The new ideal beauty. *Time, 102,* 72–77.

Corn, W. M. (1983). *Grant Wood: The regionalist vision.* New Haven, CT: Yale University Press.

Corr, C. A. (1991–1992). A task-based approach to coping with dying. *Omega, 24*(2), 81–94.

Corter, C. M. (1976). The nature of mother's absence and the infant's response to brief separations. *Developmental Psychology, 12,* 428–434.

Cory, T. L., Ormiston, D. W., Simmel, E., & Dainoff, M. (1975). Predicting the frequency of dream recall. *Journal of Abnormal Psychology, 84,* 261–266.

Costa, P. T., Jr., & McCrae, R. R. (1992a). Four ways five factors are basic. *Personality and Individual Differences, 13,* 653–665.

Costa, P. T., Jr., & McCrae, R. R. (1992b). Normal personality assessment in clinical practice: The NEO Personality Inventory. *Psychological Assessment, 4,* 5–13.

Couch, J. V., Garber, T. B., & Turner, W. E. (1983). Facilitating and debilitating test anxiety and academic achievement. *Psychological Record, 33,* 237–244.

Coven, S., and Ward, L. M. (1989). *Sensation and perception* (3rd ed.). San Diego: Harcourt Brace Jovanovich.

Cowart, B. J. (1981). Development of taste perception in humans: Sensitivity and preference throughout the life span. *Psychological Bulletin, 90,* 43–73.

Cowley, G. (1988, May 23). The wisdom of animals. *Newsweek,* pp. 52–59.

Cowley, G., Springen, K., Leonard, E., Robins, K., & Gorden, J. (1990, March 26). The promise of Prozac. *Newsweek,* pp. 38–41.

Cox, M. J., Owen, M. T., Henderson, V. K., & Margande, N. A. (1992). Prediction of infant-father and infant-mother attachment. *Developmental Psychology, 28,* 474–483.

Crafts, L. W., Schneirla, T. C., Robinson, E. E., & Gilbert, R. W. (1938). *Recent experiments in psychology.* New York: McGraw-Hill.

Craik, F. I. M. (1985). Paradigms in human memory research. In L.-G. Nilsson & T. Archer (Eds.), *Perspectives in learning and memory.* Hillsdale, NJ: Erlbaum.

Craik, F. I. M., & Lockhart, R. S. (1972). Levels of processing: A framework for memory research. *Journal of Verbal Learning and Verbal Behavior, 11,* 671–684.

Craik, F. I. M., & Tulving, E. (1975). Depth of processing and retention of words in episodic memory. *Journal of Experimental Psychology, 104,* 268–294.

Craik, K. (1986). Personality research methods: An historical perspective. *Journal of Personality, 54,* 18–51.

Crick, F., & Mitchison, G. (1983). The function of dream sleep. *Nature (London), 304,* 111–114.

Crockenberg, S., & Litman, C. (1990). Autonomy as competence in 2-year-olds: Maternal correlates of child defiance, compliance, and self-assertion. *Developmental Psychology, 26,* 961–971.

Crockenberg, S. B. (1981). Infant irritability, mother responsiveness, and social support influences on the security of infant-mother attachment. *Child Development, 52,* 857–865.

Cromie, S., & Johns, S. (1983). Irish entrepreneurs: Some personality characteristics. *Journal of Occupational Behavior, 4,* 317–324.

Cronin-Golomb, A. (1986). Comprehension of abstract concepts in right and left hemispheres of complete commissurotomy subjects. *Neuropsychologia, 24,* 881–887.

Cross, K. P. (1981). *Adults as learners.* San Francisco: Jossey-Bass.

Cummins, J. (1978). Bilingualism and the development of metalinguistic awareness. *Journal of Cross-Cultural Psychology, 9,* 131–149.

Cunningham, S. (1984, May). Genovese: 20 years later, few heed a stranger's cries. *APA Monitor,* p. 30.

Cutrona, C. E. (1982). Transition to college: Loneliness and the process of social adjustment. In L. A. Peplau & D. Perlman (Eds.), *Loneliness: A sourcebook of current theory, research and therapy.* New York: Wiley.

Cutting, J. E. (1987a). Perception and information. *Annual Review of Psychology, 38,* 61–90.

Cutting, J. E. (1987b). Rigidity in cinema seen from the front row, side aisle. *Journal of Experimental Psychology: Human Perception and Performance, 13,* 323–324.

Czeisler, C. A., Kronauer, R., Allen, J. S., Duffy, J. F., Jewett, M. E., Brown, E. N., & Ronda, J. M. (1989). Bright light induction of strong (Type O) resetting of the human circadian pacemaker. *Science, 216,* 1328–1331.

Czeisler, C. A., Moore-Ede, M. C., & Coleman, R. M. (1982). Rotating shift work schedules that disrupt sleep are improved by applying circadian principles. *Science, 217,* 460–462.

Daiss, S. R., Bertelson, A. D., & Benjamin, L. T. (1986). Napping versus resting: Effects on performance and mood. *Psychophysiology, 23,* 82–86.

Damasio, A. R., & Geschwind, N. (1984). The neural basis of language. *Annual Review of Neuroscience, 7,* 127–146.

Dana, R. H. (1978). The rorschach. In O. K. Buros (Ed.), *The Eighth Mental Measurements Yearbook* (pp. 1040– 1042). Highland Park, NJ: Gryphon Press.

Dance, K. A., & Neufeld, R. W. J. (1988). Aptitude-treatment interaction research in the clinical setting: A review of attempts to dispel the "patient uniformity" myth. *Psychological Bulletin, 104,* 192–213.

Daniel, W. F., Crovitz, H. F., & Weiner, R. D. (1987). Neurological aspects of disorientation. *Cortex, 23,* 169–187.

Daniels, D., Dunn, J., Furstenberg, F. F., Jr., & Plomin, R. (1985). Environmental differences within the family and adjustment differences within pairs of adolescent siblings. *Child Development, 56,* 764–774.

Darwin, C. (1962). *The expression of the emotions in man and animals.* Chicago: University of Chicago Press. (Original work published 1872).

Datan, N., Rodeheaver, D., & Hughes, F. (1987). Adult development and aging. *Annual Review of Psychology, 38,* 153–180.

Davidson, G. C., & Neale, J. M. (1990). *Abnormal psychology.* New York: Wiley.

Davidson, J., & Myers, L. S. (1988). Endocrine factors in sexual psychophysiology. In R. C. Rosen & J. G. Beck (Eds.), *Patterns of sexual arousal: Psychophysiological processes and clinical applications.* New York: Guilford Press.

Davidson, J. R. T., & Foa, E. B. (1991). Diagnostic issues in posttraumatic stress disorder: Considerations for the DSM-IV. *Journal of Abnormal Psychology, 100,* 346–355.

Davies, P., & Maloney, A. J. F. (1976). Selective loss of central cholinergic neurons in Alzheimer's disease. *Lancet, 2,* 1403.

Davis, B. L. (1982). The PCP epidemic: A critical review. *International Journal of the Addictions, 17,* 1137–1156.

Davis, G. A. (1982). A model for teaching for creative development. *Roeper Review, 5,* 27–29.

Davis, G. A. (1986). *Creativity is forever* (2nd ed.). Dubuque, IA: Kendall/Hunt.

Davison, G. C., & Neale, J. M. (1990). *Abnormal psychology.* New York: Wiley.

Deaux, K. (1978, May). *Sex-related patterns of social interaction.* Paper presented at the meeting of the Midwestern Psychological Association, Chicago.

Deaux, K., & Major, B. (1987). Putting gender into context: An interactive model of gender-related behavior. *Psychological Review, 94,* 369–389.

DeBuono, B. A., Zinner, S. H., Daamen, M., & McCormack, W. M. (1990). Sexual behavior of college women in 1975, 1986, and 1989. *New England Journal of Medicine, 322,* 821–825.

DeCasper, A., & Fifer, W. (1980). Of human bonding: Newborns prefer their mothers' voices. *Science, 208,* 1174–1176.

Deci, E. L., & Ryan, R. M. (1985). *Intrinsic motivation and self-determination in human behavior.* New York: Plenum.

Decina, P., Schlegel, A. M., & Fieve, R. R. (1987). Lithium poisoning. *New York State Journal of Medicine, 87,* 230–231.

DeFries, J., Plomin, R., & LaBuda, M. (1987). Genetic stability of cognitive development from childhood to adulthood. *Developmental Psychology, 23,* 4–12.

DeMeuse, K. P. (1985). The relationship between life events and indices of classroom performance. *Teaching of Psychology, 12,* 146–149.

de Schonen, S., & Mathivet, E. (1989). First come, first served. *European Bulletin of Cognitive Psychology, 9,* 3–44.

Dethier, V. G. (1962). *To know a fly.* San Francisco: Holden-Day.

Deutscher, I. (1964). The quality of postparental life: Definitions of the situation. *Journal of Marriage and the Family, 26,* 52–59.

DeValois, R. L. (1960). Color vision mechanisms in monkey. *Journal of General Physiology, 43,* 115–128.

DeValois, R. L., & DeValois, K. (1980). Vision. *Annual Review of Psychology, 31,* 309–341.

DeVilliers, J. G. (1980). The process of rule learning in child speech: A new look. In K. Nelson (Ed.), *Child Language* (Vol. 2). New York: Gardner Press.

De Vries, R. (1969). Constancy of generic identity in the years three to six. *Monographs of the Society for Research in Child Development, 34*(3, Serial No. 127).

Dewan, M., Haldipur, C., Lane, E., Ispahani, A., Boucher, M., & Mayor, L. (1988). Bipolar affective disorder: I. Comprehensive quantitative computed tomography. *Acta Psychiatrica Scandinavica, 77,* 670–676.

De Witt, K. (1991, August 27). Verbal scores hit new low in scholastic aptitude tests. *New York Times,* pp. A1, A20.

Dews, P. B. (1984). Behavioral effects of caffeine. In P. B. Dews (Ed.), *Caffeine: Perspectives from recent research* (pp. 86–103). New York: Springer-Verlag.

DiCara, L. V., & Miller, N. E. (1968). Instrumental learning of vasomotor responses by rats: Learning to respond differentially in the two ears. *Science, 159,* 1485–1486.

Dickens, C. (1962). *A tale of two cities.* New York: Oxford University Press. (Original work published 1859).

Dickinson, D. (1974). But what happens when you take that reinforcement away? *Psychology in the Schools, 11,* 158–160.

DiClemente, R. J. (1990). The emergence of adolescents as a risk group for human immunodeficiency virus infection. *Journal of Adolescent Research, 5,* 7–17.

Diehl, M., & Stroebe, W. (1987). Productivity loss in brainstorming groups: Toward the solution of a riddle. *Journal of Personality and Social Psychology, 53,* 497–509.

Dienstbier, R. A. (1979). Emotion-attribution theory: Establishing roots and exploring future perspectives. In H. Howe & R. A. Dienstbier (Eds.), *Nebraska Symposium on Motivation, 1978* (pp. 237–306). Lincoln: University of Nebraska Press.

Digman, J. M. (1990). Personality structure: Emergence of the five-factor model. *Annual Review of Psychology, 41,* 417–440.

Dodd, B. (1979). Lipreading in infants: Attention to speech presented in and out of synchrony. *Cognitive Psychology, 11,* 478–484.

Domjan, M. (1993). *The principles of learning and behavior.* Pacific Grove, CA: Brooks/Cole.

Domjan, M., & Galef, B. F. (1983). Biological constraints of instrumental and classical conditioning: Retrospect and prospect. *Animal Learning and Behavior, 11,* 151–161.

Donaldson, M. (1978). *Children's minds.* New York: Norton.

Donovan, J. E., & Jessor, R. (1985). Structure of problem behavior in adolescence and young adulthood. *Journal of Consulting and Clinical Psychology, 53,* 890–904.

Dorn, L. D., Susman, E. J., Nottelmann, E. D., Inoff-Germain, G., & Chrousos, G. P. (1990). Perceptions of puberty: Adolescent, parent, and health care personnel. *Developmental Psychology, 26,* 322–329.

Doty, R. L., Green, P. A., Ram, C., & Yankell, S. L. (1982). Communication of gender from human breath odors: Relationship to perceived intensity and pleasantness. *Hormones and Behavior, 16,* 13–22.

Doty, R. L., Shaman, P., Appelbaum, S. L., Giberson, R., Sikorski, L., & Rosenberg, L. (1984). Smell identification ability: Changes with age. *Science, 226,* 1441–1443.

Douvan, E., & Adelson, J. (1966). *The adolescent experience.* New York: Wiley.

Drachman, D. A., & Arbit, J. (1966). Memory and the hippocampal complex: II. Is memory a multiple process? *Archives of Neurology (Chicago), 15,* 52–61.

Dreistadt, R. (1971). How dreams are used in creative behavior. *Psychology, 8,* 24–50.

DuBois, P. H. (1972). The Scholastic Aptitude Test. In O. K. Buros (Ed.), *The Seventh Mental Measurements Yearbook* (pp. 646–648). Highland Park, NJ: Gryphon Press.

Dudley, R. M. (1991). IQ and heredity. *Science, 46,* 191.

Duke, M. P. (1986). Personality science: A proposal. *Journal of Personality and Social Psychology, 50,* 382–385.

Dulit, E. (1975). Adolescent thinking à la Piaget: The formal stage. In R. E. Grinder (Ed.), *Studies in adolescence* (3rd ed.). New York: Macmillan.

Dunn, A. J. (1980). Neurochemistry of learning and memory: An evaluation of recent data. *Annual Review of Psychology, 31,* 343–390.

Dusek, J. B. (1980). The development of test anxiety in children. In I. Sarason (Ed.), *Test anxiety: Theory, research and applications* (pp. 87–110). Hillsdale, NJ: Erlbaum.

Duyme, M. (1988). School success and social class: An adoption study. *Developmental Psychology, 24,* 203–209.

Dworkin, B. R., & Miller, N. E. (1986). Failure to replicate visceral learning in the acute curarized rat preparation. *Behavioral Neuroscience, 100,* 299–314.

Dyck, D. G., Greenberg, A. H., & Osachuk, T. A. G. (1986). Tolerance to drug-induced (Poly I:C) natural killer cell activation: Congruence with a Pavlovian conditioning model. *Journal of Experimental Psychology: Animal Behavior Processes, 12,* 25–31.

Eagly, A. H. (1987). *Sex differences in social behavior: A social-role interpretation.* Hillsdale, NJ: Erlbaum.

Eagly, A. H., Wood, W., & Chaiken, S. (1978). Causal inferences about communicators and their effect on opinion change. *Journal of Personality and Social Psychology, 36,* 424–435.

East, P. L., & Rook, K. (1992). Compensatory patterns of support among children's peer relationships: A test using school friends, nonschool friends, and siblings. *Developmental Psychology, 28,* 163–172.

Eastwood, M., Sweeney, D., & Piercy, F. (1987). The "no-problem" problem: A family therapy approach for certain first-time adolescent substance abusers. *Family Relations: Journal of Applied Family and Child Studies, 36,* 125–128.

Eaton, S. B., & Konner, M. (1985). Paleolithic nutrition: A consideration of its nature and current implications. *New England Journal of Medicine, 64,* 1111–1114.

Eaton, S. B., Shostak, M., & Konner, M. (1988). *The paleolithic prescription.* New York: Harper & Row.

Eaves, G., & Rush, A. J. (1984). Cognitive patterns in symptomatic and remitted unipolar depression. *Journal of Abnormal Psychology, 93,* 31–40.

Ebbinghaus, H. (1964). Retention of nonsense syllable lists learned by Ebbinghaus as measured by the method of "savings." In *Memory: A contribution to experimental psychology*. New York: Dover. (Original work published in 1885).

Edelson, E. (1987). *Drugs and the brain*. New York: Chelsea House.

Egeland, B., Jacobvitz, D., & Sroufe, L. A. (1988). Breaking the cycle of abuse. *Child Development, 59*, 1080–1088.

Ehrenwald, J. (1976). *The history of psychotherapy: From healing magic to encounter*. New York: Jason Aranson.

Eich, J. E. (1989). Theoretical issues in state-dependent memory. In H. L. Roediger & F. I. M. Craik (Eds.), *Varieties of memory and consciousness: Essays in honor of Endel Tulving* (pp. 331–354). Hillsdale, NJ: Erlbaum.

Eich, J. E., & Metcalfe, J. (1989). Mood dependent memory for internal versus external events. *Journal of Experimental Psychology: Learning, Memory, and Cognition, 15*, 443–455.

Ekman, P. (1972). Universal and cultural differences in facial expressions of emotion. In J. Cole (Ed.), *Nebraska Symposium on Motivation, 1971*. Lincoln: University of Nebraska Press.

Ekman, P., Davidson, R. J., & Friesen, W. V. (1990). The Duchenne smile: Emotional expression and brain physiology: 2. *Journal of Personality and Social Psychology, 58*, 342–353.

Ekman, P., & Friesen, W. V. (1975). *Unmasking the face*. Englewood Cliffs, NJ: Prentice-Hall.

Ekman, P., Friesen, W. V., & Ellsworth, P. (1972). *Emotion in the human face: Guidelines for research and an integration of findings*. New York: Pergamon.

Ekman, P., Friesen, W. V., & O'Sullivan, M. (1988). Smiles when lying. *Journal of Personality and Social Psychology, 54*, 414–420.

Ekman, P., Friesen, W. V., O'Sullivan, M., & Scherer, K. (1980). Relative importance of face, body, and speech in judgments of personality and affect. *Journal of Personality and Social Psychology, 38*, 270–277.

Ekman, P., Levenson, R. W., & Friesen, W. V. (1983). Autonomic nervous system activity distinguishes among emotions. *Science, 221*, 1208–1210.

Elias, J., & Gebhard, P. (1969). Sexuality and sexual learning in children. *Phi Delta Kappan, 50*, 401–406.

Elkind, D. (1967). Egocentrism in adolescence. *Child Development, 38*, 1025–1034.

Elkind, D. (1987). *Miseducation: Preschoolers at risk*. New York: Knopf.

Elliott, C., Jay, S., & Woody, P. (1987). An observation scale for measuring children's distress during medical procedures. *Journal of Pediatric Psychology, 12*, 543–551.

Ellis, A. (1962). *Reason and emotion in psychotherapy*. New York: Lyle Stuart.

Ellis, A., & Grieger, R. (1986). *Handbook of rational-emotive therapy* (Vol. 2). New York: Springer-Verlag.

Ellis, H. C., & Hunt, R. R. (1989). *Fundamentals of human memory and cognition*. Dubuque, IA: W. C. Brown.

Engel, G. L. (1968). A life setting conducive to illness: The giving-up given-up complex. *Bulletin of the Menninger Clinic, 32*, 355–365.

Engel, G. L. (1971). Sudden and rapid death during psychological stress: Folklore or folk wisdom? *Annals of Internal Medicine, 74*, 771–782.

Engel, G. L., & Schmale, A. H. (1972). Conservation-withdrawal: A primary regulatory process for organismic homeostasis. *Ciba Foundation Symposium, 8*.

Engler, J., and Goleman, D. (1992). *The Consumer's Guide to Psychotherapy*. New York: Simon & Schuster.

Epstein, L. H. (1985). Family-based treatment for pre-adolescent obesity. *Advances in Developmental and Behavioral Pediatrics, 6*, 1–39.

Erickson, P. M., Adlaf, E. M., Murray, G. F., & Smart, R. G. (1987). *The steel drug: Cocaine in perspective*. Lexington, MA: Lexington Books.

Erikson, E. H. (1963). *Childhood and society* (2nd ed.). New York: Norton.

Erikson, E. H. (1968). *Identity: Youth and crisis*. New York: Norton.

Eron, L. D. (1987). The development of aggressive behavior from the perspective of a developing behaviorism. *American Psychologist, 42*, 435–442.

Eron, L. D., Huesmann, L. R., Brice, P., Fischer, P., & Mermelstein, R. (1983). Age trends in the development of aggression, sex typing and related television habits. *Developmental Psychology, 19*, 71–77.

Evans, R. B. (1981). Introduction: The historical context. In *William James' principles of psychology* (pp. xli-lxviii). Cambridge, MA: Harvard University Press.

Evans, R. W., Gualtieri, T., & Hicks, R. E. (1986). A neuropathic substrate for stimulant drug effects in hyperactive children. *Clinical Neuropharmacology, 9*, 264–281.

Eysenck, H. J. (1952). The effects of psychotherapy: An evaluation. *Journal of Consulting Psychology, 16*, 319–324.

Eysenck, H. J. (1960). *Behavior therapy and the neuroses*. Oxford: Pergamon Press.

Eysenck, H. J. (1982). *Personality, genetics, and behavior: Selected papers*. New York: Praeger.

Eysenck, H. J. (1983, April-May). The roots of creativity: Cognitive ability or personality trait? *Roeper Review*, pp. 10–12.

Eysenck, H. J. (1991). Dimensions of personality: 16, 5, or 3? Criteria for a taxonomic paradigm. *Personality and Individual Differences, 12*, 773–779.

Eysenck, H. J., & Wilson, G. D. (1973). Comment on Hall and Van de Castle. In H. J. Eysenck, & G. D. Wilson (Eds.), *The experimental study of Freudian theories* (pp. 166–167). London: Methuen.

Ezzell, C. (1991). Memories might be made of this. *Science News, 139*, 328–330.

Fabes, R. A. (1987). Effects of reward contexts on young children's task interest. *Journal of Psychology, 121*, 5–19.

Fagenson, E., & Burke, W. W. (1990a). Organization development practitioners' activities and intervention in organizations during the 1980s [Special issue: Organizational consultation]. *Journal of Applied Behavioral Science, 26*(3), 285–297.

Fagenson, E., & Burke, W. W. (1990b). The activities of organization development practitioners at the turn of the decade of the 1990s: A study of their predictions. *Group and Organization Studies, 15*(4), 366–380.

Fagot, B. I. (1978). The influence of sex of child on parental reactions in toddler children. *Child Development, 49*, 459–465.

Fagot, B. I., & Hagen, R. (1991). Observations of parent reactions to sex-stereotyped behaviors: Age and sex effects. *Child Development, 62*, 617–628.

Fancher, R. E. (1973). *Psychoanalytic psychology: The development of Freud's thought*. New York: Norton.

Fantz, R. L. (1961). The origin of form perception. *Scientific American, 204*(5), 66–72.

Fantz, R. L., & Nevis, S. (1967). Pattern preferences and perceptual-cognitive development in early infancy. *Merrill-Palmer Quarterly, 13*, 88–108.

Faraone, S. V., Kremen, W. S., & Tsuang, M. T. (1990). Genetic transmission of major affective disorders: Quantitative models and linkage analyses. *Psychological Bulletin, 108*, 109–127.

Farkas, T., Wolf, A. P., Jaeger, J., Brodie, J. D., Christman, D. R., & Fowler, J. S. (1984). Regional brain glucose metabolism in chronic schizophrenia: A position emission transaxial tomographic study. *Archives of General Psychiatry, 41*, 293–300.

Farley, J., & Alkon, D. L. (1985). Cellular mechanisms of learning, memory, and information storage. *Annual Review of Psychology, 36*, 419–494.

Fehr, L. (1976). J. Piaget and S. Claus: Psychology makes strange bedfellows. *Psychological Reports, 39*, 740–742.

Fein, A., & Szuts, E. Z. (1982). *Photo-receptors: Their role in vision*. London: Cambridge University Press.

Feingold, A. (1988). Cognitive gender differences are disappearing. *American Psychologist, 43*, 95–103.

Feinsein, J. (1985, August 25). The summer of John McEnroe's content: Winning isn't everything when you can lose and still be happy. *Washington Post*, pp. B1–B2.

Feldman, H., Goldin-Meadow, S., & Gleitman, L. R. (1978). Beyond Herodotus: The creation of language by linguistically deprived children. In A. Lock (Ed.), *Action, gesture, and symbol: The emergence of language*. New York: Academic Press.

Feller, R. (1991). Employment and career development in a world of change: What is ahead for the next twenty-five years? Special Issue: National Employment Counselors Association's twenty-fifth anniversary. *Journal of Employment Counseling, 28*(1), 13–20.

Feltz, D. L., & Landers, D. M. (1983). The effects of mental practice on motor skill learning and performance: A meta-analysis. *Journal of Sport Psychology, 5*, 25–57.

Fernald, L. D. (1984). *The Hans legacy*. Hillsdale, NJ: Erlbaum.

Fernström, M. H., Krowinski, R. L., & Kupfer, D. J. (1987). Appetite and food preferences in depression: Effects of imipramine treatment. *Biological Psychiatry, 22*, 529–539.

Ferri, R., Dequae, P., Colognola, R. M., & Bergonzi, P. (1989). A single electronic and computer system for automatic spindle detection. *Neurophysiology Clinic, 19*, 171–177.

Feshbach, N. D. (1987). Parental empathy and child adjustment/maladjustment. In N. Eisenberg & J. Strayer (Eds.), *Empathy and its development*. New York: Cambridge University Press.

Festinger, L. (1957). *A theory of cognitive dissonance*. Stanford, CA: Stanford University Press.

Festinger, L., & Carlsmith, J. M. (1959). Cognitive consequences of forced compliance. *Journal of Abnormal and Social Psychology, 58*, 203–210.

Fiedler, F. E. (1964). A contingency model of leadership effectiveness. In L. Berkowitz (Ed.), *Advances in Experimental Social Psychology* (Vol. 1). New York: Academic Press.

Fiedler, F. E. (1978). The contingency model and the dynamics of the leadership process. In L. Berkowitz (Ed.), *Advances in Experimental Social Psychology* (Vol. 2). New York: Academic Press.

Field, T. (1991). Quality infant day-care and grade school behavior and performance. *Child Development, 62*, 863–870.

Field, T., Greenwald, P., Morrow, C., Healy, B., Foster, T., Guthertz, M., & Frost, P. (1992). Behavior state matching during interactions of preadolescent friends versus acquaintances. *Developmental Psychology, 28*, 242–250.

Fields, H. L., & Levine, J. D. (1984). Placebo analgesia: A role for endorphins. *Trends in Neuroscience, 7*, 271–273.

Fink, M. (1988). Use of ECT in the United States. *American Journal of Psychiatry, 145*, 133–134.

Finke, R. A. (1986). Mental imagery and the visual system. *Scientific American, 68*, 88–95.

Finke, R. A. (1990). *Creative imagery: Discoveries and invention in visualization*. Hillsdale, NJ: Erlbaum.

Finke, R. A., Ward, T. B., & Smith, S. M. (1992). *Creative cognition: Theory, research, and applications*. Cambridge, MA: MIT Press.

Finkelhor, D. (1979). *Sexually victimized children*. New York: Free Press.

Finkelhor, D., Hotaling, G., Lewis, I. A., & Smith, C. (1990). Sexual abuse in a national survey of adult men and women: Prevalence, characteristics, and risk factors. *Child Abuse and Neglect, 14*, 19–28.

Fischer, K. W. (1983). Commentary: Illuminating the processes of moral development. *Monographs of the Society for Research in Child Development, 48*(1–2, Serial No. 200).

Fischer, K. W., & Silvern, L. (1985). Stages and individual differences in cognitive development. *Annual Review of Psychology, 36*, 613–648.

Fischman, J. (1987, February). Type A on trial. *Psychology Today*, pp. 42–50.

Fisher, D., Cohen, H., Davis, D., Edwards, A., Furman, B., & Ward, K. M. (1980). Increased vaginal blood flow during sleep and waking. *Sleep Research, 9*, 47.

Fisher, R. P., Geiselman, R. E., & Amador, M. (1989). Field test of the cognitive interview: Enhancing the recollection of actual victims and witnesses of crime. *Journal of Applied Psychology, 74*, 722–727.

Flacelière, R. (1960). *Love in ancient Greece* (J. Cleugh, Trans.). New York: Crown.

Floderus-Myrhed, B., Pedersen, N., & Rasmuson, I. (1980). Assessment of heritability for personality, based on a short-form of the Eysenck Personality Inventory: A study of 12,898 twin pairs. *Behavior Genetics, 10*(2), 153–162.

Flynn, J. (1984). The mean IQ of Americans: Massive gains 1932 to 1978. *Psychological Bulletin, 95*, 29–51.

Foa, E. B., Grayson, J. B., Steketee, G. S., Doppelt, H. G., Turner, R. M., & Latimer, P. R. (1983). Success and failure in the behavioral treatment of obsessive-compulsives. *Journal of Consulting and Clinical Psychology, 51*, 287–297.

Fodor, J. A. (1983). *Modularity of mind: Faculty psychology*. Cambridge, MA: MIT Press.

Fodor, J. A., & Pylyshyn, Z. W. (1988). Connectionism and cognitive architecture: A critical analysis. *Cognition, 28*, 3–71.

Fogel, A., Toda, S., & Kawai, M. (1988). Mother-infant face-to-face interaction in Japan and the United States: A laboratory comparison using 3-month-old infants. *Developmental Psychology, 24*, 398–406.

Foley, J. M. (1985). Binocular distance perception: Ergocentric distance tasks. *Journal of Experimental Psychology: Human Perception and Performance, 11*, 133–149.

Foley, M. A., Johnson, M. K., & Raye, C. L. (1983). Age-related changes in confusion between memories for thoughts and memories for speech. *Child Development, 54*, 51–60.

Folkman, S. (1984). Personal control and stress and coping processes: A theoretical analysis. *Journal of Personality and Social Psychology, 46*, 839–852.

Fonagy, P., Steele, H., & Steele, M. (1991). Maternal representations of attachment during pregnancy predict the organization of infant-mother attachment at one year of age. *Child Development, 62*, 891–905.

Food and Drug Administration. (1986). *Drug utilization in the U.S.* (6th ed.). Washington, DC: U.S. Government Printing Office.

Foos, P. W. (1989). Adult age differences in working memory. *Psychology and Aging, 4*, 269–275.

Ford, M. E. (1985). Two perspectives on the validation of developmental constructs: Psychometric and theoretical limitations in research on egocentrism. *Psychological Bulletin, 97*, 497–501.

Forgus, R. H., & Melamed, L. E. (1976). *Perception: A cognitive-stage approach* (2nd ed.). New York: McGraw-Hill.

Forno, L. S. (1978). The locus ceruleus in Alzheimer's disease. *Journal of Neuropathology and Experimental Neurology, 37*, 614.

Fosarelli, P. D. (1984). Latchkey children. *Journal of Developmental and Behavioral Pediatrics, 5*, 173–177.

Fossey, D. (1979). Development of the mountain gorilla: The first 36 months. In D. A. Hamburg & E. R. McCown (Eds.), *The great apes* (pp. 139–186). Menlo Park, CA: Benjamin/Cummings.

Fouts, R. S., & Rigby, R. L. (1977). Man-chimpanzee communication. In T. A. Sebeok (Ed.), *How animals communicate*. Bloomington: Indiana University Press.

Fox, N. A., Kimmerly, N. L., & Schafer, W. D. (1991). Attachment to mother/attachment to father: A meta-analysis. *Child Development, 62*, 210–225.

Fox, R., Aslin, R. N., Shea, S. L., & Dumais, S. T. (1980). Stereopsis in human infants. *Science, 207*, 323–324.

Fox, R., Lehmkuhle, S. W., & Westendorff, D. H. (1976). Falcon visual acuity. *Science, 192*, 263–265.

Foy, D. W., Sipprelle, R. C., Rueger, D. B., & Carroll, E. M. (1984). Etiology of post-traumatic stress disorder in Vietnam veterans: Analysis of premilitary, military, and combat exposure influences. *Journal of Consulting and Clinical Psychology, 52*, 79–87.

Frances, A. J., First, M. B., Widiger, T. A., Miele, G. M., Tilly, S. M., Davis, W. W., & Pincus, H. A. (1991). An A to Z guide to DSM-IV conundrums. *Journal of Abnormal Psychology, 100*, 407–412.

Frankel, F. H. (1976). *Hypnosis: Trance as a coping mechanism.* New York: Plenum.

Frankenburg, W. K., Frandal, A., Sciarillo, W., & Burgess, D. (1981). The newly abbreviated and revised Denver Developmental Screening Test. *Journal of Pediatrics, 99*, 995–999.

Franks, J. J., & Bransford, J. D. (1971). Abstraction of visual patterns. *Journal of Experimental Psychology, 90*, 65–74.

Freedman, J. L. (1986). Television violence and aggression: A rejoinder. *Psychological Bulletin, 100*, 372–378.

Freedman, J. L., Sears, D. O., & Carlsmith, J. M. (1981). *Social psychology.* Englewood Cliffs, NJ: Prentice-Hall.

French, J. R. P., Jr., & Raven, B. (1958). The bases of social power. In D. Cartwright (Ed.), *Studies in Social Power.* Ann Arbor, MI: Institute for Social Research.

French, W. L., & Bell, C. H., Jr. (1990). Organization development (4th ed.). New Jersey: Prentice-Hall, Inc.

Frese, M. (1985). Stress at work and psychosomatic complaints: A causal interpretation. *Journal of Applied Psychology, 70*, 314–328.

Freud, A. (1966). *The writings of Anna Freud: Vol. 2. The ego and the mechanisms of defense* (rev. ed.). New York: International Universities Press.

Freud, S. (1924a). The passing of the Oedipus-complex. In J. Riviere (Trans.), *Collected papers* (Vol. 2). London: Hogarth Press. (Original work published 1916).

Freud, S. (1924b). On the transformation of instincts with special reference to anal eroticism. In E. Grover (Trans.), *Collected papers* (Vol. 2). London: Hogarth Press. (Original work published 1916).

Freud, S. (1949a). Instincts and their vicissitudes. In J. Strachey (Ed. and Trans.), *The standard edition of the complete psychological works of Sigmund Freud* (Vol. 14). London: Hogarth Press. (Original work published 1915).

Freud, S. (1949b). *An outline of psychoanalysis.* (J. Strachey, Trans.). New York: Norton. (Original work published 1940).

Freud, S. (1952). *A general introduction to psychoanalysis* (J. Riviere, Trans.). New York: Washington Square Press. (Original work published 1917).

Freud, S. (1955a). *The interpretation of dreams.* New York: Basic Books. (Original work published 1900).

Freud, S. (1955b). *Beyond the pleasure principle.* In J. Strachey (Ed. and Trans.), *The standard edition of the complete works of Sigmund Freud* (Vol. 18, pp. 3–64). London: Hogarth Press. (Original work published 1920).

Freud, S. (1961). Civilization and its discontents. In J. Strachey (Ed. and Trans.), *The standard edition of the complete works of Sigmund Freud* (Vol. 21). London: Hogarth. (Original work published 1930).

Freud, S. (1962). *Three essays on the theory of sexuality.* (J. Strachey, Trans.). New York: Avon. (Original work published 1905).

Freud, S. (1964). Femininity. In J. Strachey (Trans.), *New introductory lectures on psychoanalysis* (Lecture 33, pp. 112–135). New York: Norton. (Original work published 1933).

Freud, S. (1977a). Analysis of a phobia in a five-year-old boy. In A. Strachey & J. Strachey (Eds. and Trans.), *Cast histories 1: "Dora" and "Little Hans"* (Vol. 8, pp. 165–305). New York: Penguin (Penguin Freud Library). (Original work published 1909).

Freud, S. (1977b). Fragment of an analysis of a case of hysteria. In J. Strachey (Ed. and Trans.), *Case histories 1: "Dora" and "Little Hans"* (Vol. 8, pp. 29–164). New York: Penguin (Pelican Freud Library). (Original work published 1905).

Frick, R. W. (1985). Communicating emotion: The role of prosodic features. *Psychological Bulletin, 97*, 412–429.

Fried, P. A., & Watkinson, B. (1990). 36- and 48-month neurobehavioral follow-up of children prenatally exposed to marijuana, cigarettes, and alcohol. *Journal of Developmental and Behavioral Pediatrics, 11*, 49–58.

Friedman, M., & Rosenman, R. H. (1974). *Type A behavior and your heart.* New York: Knopf.

Friedrich-Cofer, L., & Huston, A. C. (1986). Television violence and aggression. *Psychological Bulletin, 100*, 364–371.

Frisch, R. (1983). In J. Brooks-Gunn & A. C. Petersen (Eds.), *Girls at puberty: Biological and psychosocial perspectives.* New York: Plenum.

Frost, J. M., Hopkins, B. L., & Conrad, R. J. (1982). An analysis of the effects of feedback and reinforcement on machine-paced production. *Journal of Organizational Behavior Management, 3*, 5–17.

Fry, P. S. (1990). A factor analytic investigation of home-bound elderly individuals' concerns about death and dying, and their coping responses. *Journal of Clinical Psychology, 46*, 737–748.

Frye, D., Rawlings, P., Moore, C., & Myers, I. (1983). Object-person discrimination and communication at 3 and 10 months. *Developmental Psychology, 19*, 303–309.

Fuchs, D., Featherstone, N. L., Garwick, D. R., & Fuchs, L. S. (1984). Effects of examiner familiarity and task characteristics on speech and language-impaired children's test performance. *Measurement and Evaluation in Guidance, 16*, 198–204.

Furman, W. (1987). Acquaintanceship in middle childhood. *Developmental Psychology, 23*, 563–570.

Furman, W., & Buhrmester, D. (1992). Age and sex differences in perceptions of networks of personal relationships. *Child Development, 63*, 103–115.

Furnham, A. (1990). Can people accurately estimate their own personality test scores? *European Journal of Personality, 4*, 319–327.

Fuson, K. C., Secada, W. G., & Hall, J. W. (1983). Matching, counting, and conservation of numerical equivalence. *Child Development, 54*, 91–97.

Galton, F. (1966). Francis Galton (1822–1911) on the inheritance of intelligence, 1869. In R. J. Hernstein & E. G. Boring (Eds.), *A sourcebook in the history of psychology* (pp. 414–420). Cambridge, MA: Harvard University Press. (Original work published 1869).

Galton, F. (1978). *Hereditary genius: An inquiry into its laws and consequences.* New York: St. Martin's Press. (Original work published 1869).

Galvin, R. M. (1982, August). Control of dreams may be possible for a resolute few. *Smithsonian*, pp. 110–117.

Galvin, R. M. (1992, March-April). The nature of shyness. *Harvard Magazine*, pp. 41–45.

Ganellen, R. J., & Blaney, P. H. (1984). Hardiness and social support as moderators of the effects of life stress. *Journal of Personality and Social Psychology, 47*, 156–163.

Gangestad, S., & Snyder, M. (1985). "To carve nature at its joints": On the existence of discrete classes in personality. *Psychological Review, 92*, 317–349.

Garcia, J., & Koelling, R. (1966). Relation of cue to consequence in avoidance learning. *Psychonomic Science, 4*, 123–124.

Garcia Coll, C. T. (1990). Developmental outcome of minority infants: A process-oriented look into our beginnings. *Child Development, 61,* 270–289.

Gardner, B. T., & Gardner, R. A. (1971). Two-way communication with an infant chimpanzee. *Behavior of Nonhuman Primates, 4,* 117–184.

Gardner, B. T., & Gardner, R. A. (1980). Two comparative psychologists look at language acquisition. In K. E. Nelson (Ed.), *Children's language.* New York: Halsted.

Gardner, H. (1983). *Frames of mind: The theory of multiple intelligences.* New York: Basic Books.

Gardner, R. A., & Gardner, B. T. (1969). Teaching sign language to a chimpanzee. *Science, 165,* 664–672.

Gardner, R. C., & Desrochers, A. (1981). Second-language acquisition and bilingualism: Research in Canada (1970–1980). *Canadian Psychology, 22,* 146–162.

Garfield, S. L. (1986). Research on client variables in psychotherapy. In S. L. Garfield & A. E. Bergin (Eds.), *Handbook of psychotherapy and behavior change.* New York: Wiley.

Garmon, L. (1985, November). Of hemispheres, handedness, and more. *Psychology Today,* pp. 40–48.

Garrison, E. G. (1987). Psychological maltreatment of children: An emerging focus for inquiry and concern. *American Psychologist, 42,* 157–159.

Garvey, M., Wesner, R., & Godes, M. (1988). Comparison of seasonal and nonseasonal affective disorders. *American Journal of Psychiatry, 145,* 100–102.

Garzino, S. J. (1982). Lunar effects on mental behavior: A defense of the empirical research. *Environment and Behavior, 14,* 395–417.

Gazzaniga, M. S. (1987). Perceptual and attentional processes following callosal selection in humans. *Neuropsychologia, 25,* 119–133.

Geiselman, R. E., Fisher, R. P., MacKinnon, D. P., & Holland, H. L. (1985). Eyewitness memory enhancement in the police interview: Cognitive retrieval mnemonics versus hypnosis. *Journal of Applied Psychology, 70,* 401–412.

Geldard, F. A. (1972). *The human senses* (2nd ed.). New York: Wiley.

Gelfand, S. A. (1981). *Hearing: An introduction to psychological and physiological acoustics.* New York: Dekker.

Gelman, R., & Baillargeon, R. (1983). A review of some Piagetian concepts. In J. H. Flavell & E. M. Markman (Eds.), *Mussen's handbook of child psychology: Vol. 3. Cognitive development* (4th ed.). New York: Wiley.

Gentry, W. D., & Kobasa, S. C. O. (1984). Social and psychological resources mediating stress-illness relationships in humans. In W. D. Gentry (Ed.), *Handbook of behavioral medicine* (pp. 87–116). New York: Guilford Press.

Gerard, H. B. (1983). School desegregation: The social science role. *American Psychologist, 38,* 869–877.

Gerner, R., & Bunney, W., Jr. (1986). Biological hypotheses of affective disorders. In P. A. Berger, K. H. Brodie, & S. Arieti (Eds.), *American handbook of psychiatry: Vol. 8. Biological psychiatry* (2nd ed., pp. 265–301). New York: Basic Books.

Gibran, K. (1923). *The prophet.* New York: Knopf.

Gibson, E. (1988). Exploratory behavior in the development of perceiving, acting, and the acquiring of knowledge. *Annual Review of Psychology, 39,* 1–41.

Gibson, E. J. (1969). *Principles of perceptual learning and development.* New York: Appleton-Century-Crofts.

Gibson, E. J., & Levin, H. (1975). *The psychology of reading.* Cambridge, MA: MIT Press.

Gibson, E. J., & Spelke, E. S. (1983). The development of perception. In J. H. Flavell & E. M. Markman (Eds.), *Mussen's handbook of child psychology: Vol. 3. Cognitive development* (4th ed.). New York: Wiley.

Gibson, E. J., & Walk, R. D. (1960). The "visual cliff." *Scientific American, 202*(4), 64–71.

Gibson, J. J. (1966). *The senses considered as perceptual systems.* Boston: Houghton-Mifflin.

Gibson, J. J. (1968). What gives rise to the perception of motion? *Psychological Review, 75,* 335–346.

Gibson, J. J. (1979). *The ecological approach to visual perception.* Boston: Houghton-Mifflin.

Gibson, J. J., & Gibson, E. J. (1955). Perceptual learning: Differentiation or enrichment? *Psychological Review, 62,* 32–41.

Gilden, N., & Bodewitz, H. (1991). Regulating teratogenicity as a health risk. *Social Science and Medicine, 32,* 1191–1198.

Gilhooly, K. J. (1982). *Thinking: Directed, undirected and creative.* London: Academic Press.

Gilligan, C. (1982). *In a different voice: Psychological theory and women's development.* Cambridge, MA: Harvard University Press.

Ginsburg, D., & Gottman, J. (1986). Conversations of college roommates: Similarities and differences in male and female friendship. In J. M. Gottman & J. G. Parker (Eds.), *Conversations of friends: Speculations on affective development* (pp. 241–291). New York: Cambridge University Press.

Ginzburg, H. M., Fleming, P. L., & Miller, K. D. (1988). Selected public health observations derived from the multicenter AIDS cohort study. *Journal of Acquired Immune Deficiency Syndrome, 1,* 2–7.

Gjerde, P. F. (1986). The interpersonal structure of family interaction settings: Parent-adolescent relations in dyads and triads. *Development Psychology, 22,* 297–304.

Glanzer, M., & Cunitz, A. R. (1966). Two storage mechanisms in free recall. *Journal of Verbal Learning and Verbal Behavior, 5,* 351–360.

Glass, D. C. (1977). *Behavior patterns, stress, and coronary disease.* Hillsdale, NJ: Erlbaum.

Glass, D. C., & Singer, J. E. (1972). *Urban stress.* New York: Academic Press.

Glenberg, A., Smith, S. M., & Green, C. (1977). Type I rehearsal: Maintenance and more. *Journal of Verbal Learning and Verbal Behavior, 16,* 339–352.

Glenberg, A. M., Wilkinson, A. C., and Epstein, W. (1982). The illusion of knowing: Failure in the self-assessment of comprehension. *Memory and Cognition, 10,* 597–602.

Glenn, N. D. (1975). Psychological well-being in the postparental stage: Some evidence from national surveys. *Journal of Marriage and the Family, 37,* 105–110.

Glenn, S. M., & Cunningham, C. C. (1983). What do babies listen to most? A developmental study of auditory preferences in nonhandicapped infants and infants with Down's syndrome. *Developmental Psychology, 19,* 332–337.

Glick, P., Zion, C., & Nelson, C. (1988). What mediates sex discrimination in hiring practices? *Journal of Personality and Social Psychology, 55,* 178–186.

Glynn, S. M. (1990). Token economy approaches for psychiatric patients: Progress and pitfalls over 25 years. *Behavior Modification, 14,* 383–407.

Goldberg, I. R. (1990). An alternative "description of personality": The big-five factor structure. *Journal of Personality and Social Psychology, 59,* 1216–1229.

Goldfried, M. R., Greenberg, L., Marmar, C. (1990). Individual psychotherapy: Process and outcome. *Annual Review of Psychiatry, 41,* 659–688.

Goldman-Rakic, P. S. (1988). Topography of cognition: Parallel distributed networks in primate association cortex. *Annual Review of Neuroscience, 11,* 137–156.

Goldstein, A. P., & Sorcher, M. (1974). *Changing supervisor behavior.* New York: Pergamon.

Goldstein, E. B. (1984). *Sensation and perception* (2nd ed.). Belmont, CA: Wadsworth.

Goldstein, E. B. (1988). *Sensation and perception* (3rd ed.). Belmont, CA: Wadsworth.

Goldstein, E. B. (1989). *Sensation and perception*. Belmont, CA: Wadsworth.

Goldstein, I. L. (1986). *Training in organizations: Needs assessment, development, and evaluation* (2nd ed.). Monterey, CA: Brooks/Cole.

Goleman, S. (1992). New storm brews on whether crime has roots in genes. *The New York Times*, Sept. 15, 1–7.

Gonzales, H. M., Davis, J. M., Loney, G. L., Lokens, C. K., & Junghans, C. M. (1983). Interactional approach to interpersonal attraction. *Journal of Personality and Social Psychology, 44*, 1192–1197.

Goodall, J. (1971). *In the shadow of man*. Boston: Houghton-Mifflin.

Goodall, J. (1987). A plea for the chimpanzees. *American Scientist, 75*, 574–577.

Goodstein, L. D., & Calhoon, J. F. (1982). *Understanding abnormal behavior: Description, explanation, and management*. Reading, MA: Addison-Wesley.

Goossens, F. A., & van Ijzendoorn, M. H. (1990). Quality of infants' attachments to professional caregivers: Relation to infant-parental attachment and day-care characteristics. *Child Development, 61*, 832–837.

Gordon, J., & Abramov, I. (1977). Color vision in the peripheral retina. II. Hue and saturation. *Journal of the Optical Society of America, 67*, 202–207.

Gordon, S., & Gilgun, J. F. (1987). Adolescent sexuality. In V. B. Van Hasselt & M. Hersen (Eds.), *Handbook of adolescent psychology* (pp. 147–167). New York: Pergamon.

Gorlin, R. J. (1977). Classical chromosome disorders. In J. J. Yunis (Ed.), *New chromosome syndromes*. New York: Academic Press.

Gormezano, I. (1972). Investigators of defense and reward conditioning in the rabbit. In A. H. Black & W. F. Prokasy (Eds.), *Classical conditioning II: Current research and theory*. New York: Appleton-Century-Crofts.

Gortmaker, S. L., Dietz, W. H., Sobal, A., & Wehler, C. A. (1987). Increasing pediatric obesity in the United States. *American Journal of Diseases of Children, 141*, 535–540.

Gottfredson, L. S., & Sharf, J. C. (1988). Fairness in employment testing [Special issue]. *Journal of Vocational Behavior, 33*.

Goulart, F. S. (1984). *The caffeine book: A user's and abuser's guide*. New York: Dodd, Mead.

Gould, S. J. (1981). *The mismeasure of man*. New York: Norton.

Gould, J. L. (1986). The ethology of learning. *Annual Review of Psychology, 37*, 163–192.

Graham, C. H., Sperling, H. G., Hsia, Y., & Coulson, A. H. (1961). The determina-tion of some visual functions of a uni-laterally color-blind subject: Methods and results. *Journal of Psychology, 51*, 3–32.

Graham, R. B. (1990). *Physiological psychology*. Belmont, CA: Wadsworth.

Grandjean, P., Olsen, N. B., & Hollnagel, H. (1981). Influence of smoking and alcohol consumption on blood lead levels. *International Archives of Occupational and Environmental Health, 48*, 391–397.

Gray, L., & Stafford, M. (1988). On choice behavior in individual and social situations. *Social Psychology Quarterly, 51*, 58–65.

Gray, W. M., & Hudson, L. M. (1984). Formal operations and the imaginary audience. *Developmental Psychology, 20*, 619–627.

Green, D. M., & Birdsall, T. G. (1978). Detection and recognition. *Psychological Review, 85*, 192–206.

Green, S. K., & Sandos, P. (1983). Perceptions of male and female initiators of relationships. *Sex Roles, 9*, 849–852.

Greenberg, R. R., & Gordon, M. (1983). Examiner's sex and children's Rorschach productivity. *Psychological Reports, 53*, 355–357.

Greene, E. (1986). Forensic hypnosis to life amnesia: The jury is still out. *Behavioral Sciences and the Law, 4*, 65–72.

Greenfield, P. M., & Smith, J. H. (1976). *The structure of communication in early language development*. New York: Academic Press.

Greenwald, D. F. (1990). An external construct validity study of Rorschach personality variables. *Journal of Personality Assessment, 55*, 768–780.

Gretarsson, S., & Gelfand, D. (1988). Mothers' attributions regarding their children's social behavior and personality characteristics. *Developmental Psychology, 24*, 264–269.

Grier, J. W., & Burk, T. (1992). *Biology of animal behavior*. St. Louis, MO: Mosby-Year Book.

Grieser, D., & Kuhl, P. (1988). Maternal speech to infants in a tonal language: Support for universal prosodic features in motherese. *Developmental Psychology, 24*, 14–20.

Grigg, D. N., & Friesen, J. D. (1989). Family patterns associated with anorexia nervosa. *Journal of Marital and Family Therapy, 15*, 29–42.

Grigsby, J. P., & Weatherley, D. (1983). Gender and sex-role differences in intimacy and self-disclosure. *Psychological Reports, 53*, 891–897.

Grinker, J. A. (1982). Physiological and behavioral basis for human obesity. In D. W. Pfaff (Ed.), *The physiological mechanisms of motivation*. New York: Springer-Verlag.

Gross, A. M., & Shapiro, R. (1981). Public posting of photographs: A new class-room reinforcer. *Child Behavior Therapy, 3*, 81–82.

Grossman, H. J. (Ed.). (1983). *Classification in mental retardation*. Washington, DC: American Association on Mental Deficiency.

Grossman, S. (1975). Role of the hypothalamus in the regulation of food and water intake. *Psychological Review, 82*, 200–224.

Grossman, S. R. (1982). Training creativity and creative problem-solving. *Training and Development Journal, 36*, 62–68.

Grotevant, H. D. (1985, April). *Assessment of identity development: Where are we and where do we need to go?* Paper presented at the biennial meeting of the Society for Research in Child Development, Toronto, Canada.

Groth-Marnat, G. (1984). *Handbook of psychological assessment*. New York: Van Nostrand-Reinhold.

Groves, P. M., & Thompson, R. F. (1970). Habituation: A dual process theory. *Psychological Review, 77*, 419–450.

Gualtieri, C. T., & Hicks, R. E. (1985). Neuropharmacology of methylphenidate and a neural substrate for childhood activity. *Psychiatric Clinics of North America, 8*, 875–891.

Guilford, J. P. (1959). Three faces of intellect. *American Psychologist, 14*, 469–479.

Guilford, J. P. (1967). *The nature of human intelligence*. New York: McGraw-Hill.

Guilford, J. P. (1985). The structure of intellect model. In B. B. Wolman (Ed.), *Handbook of intelligence: Theories, measurements, and applications* (pp. 225–266). New York: Wiley.

Guion, R. M. (1983). Recruiting, selection, and job placement. In M. D. Dunnette (Ed.), *Handbook of industrial and organizational psychology* (pp. 777–828). New York: Wiley.

Gur, R. E., Gur, R. C., Skolnick, B. E., Caroff, S., Obrist, W. D., Resnick, S., & Reivich, M. (1985). Brain function in psychiatric disorders. Regional cerebral blood flow in unmedicated schizophrenics. *Archives of General Psychiatry, 42*, 329–334.

Haaga, D. A., Dyck, M. J., & Ernst, D. (1991). Empirical status of cognitive theory of depression. *Psychological Bulletin, 110*, 215–236.

Haber, R. N., & Haber, R. B. (1964). Eidetic imagery: I. Frequency. *Perceptual and Motor Skills, 19*, 131–138.

Hackett, R. D., & Guion, R. M. (1985). A reevaluation of the absenteeism-job satisfaction relationship. *Organizational Behavior and Human Decision Processes, 35*, 340–381.

Haier, R. J., Siegel, B. V., Nuechterlein, K. H., Haslet, E., Wu, J. C., Pack, J., Browning, H. L., & Buchsbaum, M. S. (1988). Cortical glucose metabolic rate correlates of abstract reasoning and attention studied with positron emission tomography. *Intelligence, 12,* 199–217.

Haig, N. D. (1985). How faces differ—a new comparative technique. *Perception, 14,* 601–615.

Haley, W. E. (1985). Social skills deficits and self-evaluation among depressed and nondepressed psychiatric patients. *Journal of Clinical Psychology, 41,* 162–172.

Halford, G. S., & Boyle, F. M. (1985). Do young children understand conservation of number? *Child Development, 56,* 165–176.

Hall, C. S., Lindzey, G., Loehlin, J. C., & Manosevitz, M. (1985). *Introduction to theories of personality* (with V. O. Locke). New York: Wiley.

Hall, C. S., & Van de Castle, R. L. (1973). An empirical investigation of the castration complex in dreams. In H. J. Eysenck & G. D. Wilson (Eds.), *The experimental study of Freudian theories* (pp. 157–169). London: Methuen. (Original work published 1965).

Hall, D. T. (Ed.). (1986). *Career development in organizations.* San Francisco: Jossey-Bass.

Hall, D. T. (1990). Promoting work/family balance: An organization-change approach. *Organizational Dynamics, 18*(3), 5–18.

Hall, G. S. (1904). *Adolescence: Its psychology and its relations to physiology, anthropology, sociology, sex, crime, religion, and education* (Vols. 1 & 2). New York: Appleton.

Hall, J. F. (1989). *Learning and memory.* Boston: Allyn & Bacon.

Hall, W., & Oppenheim, R. (1987). Developmental psychology: Prenatal, perinatal, and early postnatal aspects of behavioral development. *Annual Review of Psychology, 38,* 91–128.

Halmi, K. A. (1978). Anorexia nervosa: Recent investigations. *Annual Review of Medicine, 29,* 137–148.

Halmi, K. A. (1987). Anorexia nervosa and bulimia. *Annual Review of Medicine, 38,* 373–380.

Hamilton, E. W., & Abramson, L. Y. (1983). Cognitive patterns and major depressive disorder: A longitudinal study in a hospital setting. *Journal of Abnormal Psychology, 92,* 173–184.

Hamilton, J. O. (1974). Motivation and risk-taking behavior: A test of Atkinsson's theory. *Journal of Personality and Social Psychology, 29,* 856–864.

Hampton, J. A. (1987). Inheritance of attributes in natural concept conjunctions. *Memory and Cognition, 15,* 55–71.

Hansen, J. E., & Schuldt, J. W. (1982). Physical distance, sex, and intimacy in self-disclosure. *Psychological Reports, 51,* 3–6.

Hansen, S. L. (1977, April). Dating choices of high school students. *Family Coordinator,* pp. 133–318.

Hardy, J. B. (1973). Clinical and developmental aspects of congenital rubella. *Archives of Otolaryngology, 98,* 230–236.

Hargreaves, D. J. (1986). Psychological theories of sex-role stereotyping. In D. J. Hargreaves & A. M. Colley (Eds.), *The psychology of sex roles* (pp. 27–44). London: Harper & Row.

Harlow, H. F., & Zimmerman, R. R. (1959). Affectional responses in the infant monkey. *Science, 130,* 421–432.

Harmon, R. L. (1974). Techniques of Gestalt therapy. *Professional Psychology, 5,* 257–263.

Harper, L. V., & Huie, K. S. (1985). The effects of prior group experience, age, and familiarity on the quality and organization of preschoolers' social relationships. *Child Development, 56,* 704–717.

Harper, R. W., Leake, B., Hoffman, H., Walter, D. O., Hoppenbrouwers, T., Hodgeman, J., & Sternon, M. B. (1990). Periodicity of sleep states is altered in infants at risk for the sudden infant death syndrome. *Science, 213,* 1030–1032.

Harris, E. L., Noyes, R., Jr., Crowe, R. R., & Chaudhry, D. R. (1983). Family study of agoraphobia: Report of a pilot study. *Archives of General Psychiatry, 40,* 1061–1064.

Harrison, A. O., Wilson, M. N., Pine, C. J., Chan, S. Q., & Buriel, R. (1990). Family ecologies of ethnic minority children. *Child Development, 61,* 347–362.

Hart, S. N., & Brassard, M. R. (1987). A major threat to children's mental health: Psychological maltreatment. *American Psychologist, 42,* 160–165.

Hartline, H. K. (1938). The response of single optic nerve fibers of the vertebrate eye to illumination of the retina. *American Journal of Physiology, 121,* 400–415.

Hartmann, E. (1970). A note on the nightmare. In E. Hartmann (Ed.), *Sleep and dreaming* (pp. 192–197). Boston: Little, Brown.

Hartmann, E. (1973). *The functions of sleep.* New Haven, CT: Yale University Press.

Hartmann, E. (1978). *The sleeping pill.* New York: Basic Books.

Hartmann, E. (1981, April). The strangest sleep disorder. *Psychology Today,* pp. 14–18.

Hartmann, E., Baekeland, F., Zwilling, G., & Hoy, P. (1971). Sleep need: How much sleep and what kind? *American Journal of Psychiatry, 127,* 1001–1008.

Harvey, J. H., & Weary, G. (1984). Current issues in attribution theory. *Annual Review of Psychology, 35,* 427–459.

Hasher, L., & Griffin, M. (1978). Reconstruction and reproductive processes in memory. *Journal of Experimental Psychology: Human Learning and Memory, 4,* 318–330.

Haslam, D. R. (1983). The incentive effect and sleep deprivation. *Sleep, 6,* 362–368.

Hatfield, G., & Epstein, W. (1895). The status of the minimum principle in the theoretical analysis of visual perception. *Psychological Bulletin, 97,* 155–186.

Hattie, J. A., Sharpley, C. F., & Rogers, H. J. (1984). Comparative effectiveness of professional and paraprofessional helpers. *Psychological Bulletin, 95,* 534–541.

Hauri, P. (1982). *The sleep disorders* (2nd ed.). Kalamazoo, MI: Upjohn.

Hauri, P., & Fisher, B. (1986). Issues on sleeplessness and insomnia. *Psychophysiology, 15,* 83–90.

Hause, J. S. (1984). Barriers to work stress: I. Social support. In W. D. Gentry, H. Benson, & C. DeWolff (Eds.), *Behavioral medicine: Work, stress, and health.* The Hague: Nijhoff.

Hay, D. (1986). Infancy. *Annual Review of Psychology, 37,* 135–161.

Hayden-Thomson, L., Rubin, K., & Hymel, S. (1987). Sex preferences in sociometric choices. *Developmental Psychology, 23,* 558–562.

Hayes, C. (1951). *The ape in our house.* New York: Harper & Row.

Hayes, J. R. (1978). *Cognitive psychology: Thinking and creating.* Homewood, IL: Dorsey Press.

Hazan, C., & Shaver, P. (1987). Romantic love conceptualized as an attachment process. *Journal of Personality and Social Psychology, 52,* 511–524.

Healy, D., & Williams, J. (1988). Dysrhythmia, dysphoria, and depression: The interaction of learned helplessness and circadian dysrhythmia in the pathogenesis of depression. *Psychological Bulletin, 103,* 163–178.

Hebb, D. O. (1949). *The organization of behavior.* New York: Wiley.

Hebb, D. O. (1980a). *Essay on mind.* Hillsdale, NJ: Erlbaum.

Hebb, D. O. (1980b). The structure of thought. In P. W. Jusczyk & R. M. Klein (Eds.), *The nature of thought: Essays in honor of D. O. Hebb.* Hillsdale, NJ: Erlbaum.

Hebb, D. O. (1982, May). Understanding psychological man. *Psychology Today,* 52–54.

Hécaen, H., & Albert, M. L. (1978). *Human neuropsychology.* New York: Wiley.

Heider, F. (1958). *The psychology of interpersonal relations.* New York: Wiley.

Heinrichs, D., & Buchanan, R. (1988). Significance and meaning of neurological signs in schizophrenia. *American Journal of Psychiatric, 145,* 11–18.

Heinrichs, R. W. (1993). Schizophrenia and the brain: Conditions for a neuropsychology of madness. *American Psychologist, 48,* 221–233.

Hellige, J. B. (1990). Hemispheric asymmetry. *Annual Review of Psychology, 41,* 55–80.

Helson, R., Mitchell, V., & Moane, G. (1984). Personality and patterns of adherence to the social clock. *Journal of Personality and Social Psychology, 46,* 1079–1096.

Hemingway, M. W. (1976). *How it was.* New York: Knopf.

Hendrick, C., & Hendrick, S. S. (1986). A theory and method of love. *Journal of Personality and Social Psychology, 50,* 392–402.

Hendrick, C., & Hendrick, S. S. (1989). Research on love: Does it measure up? *Journal of Personality and Social Psychology, 56,* 784–794.

Hendrick, S. S., Hendrick, C., & Adler, N. (1988). Romantic relationships, love, satisfaction, and staying together. *Journal of Personality and Social Psychology, 54,* 980–988.

Henker, B., & Whalen, C. K. (1989). Hyperactivity and attention deficiency. *American Psychologist, 44,* 216–223.

Henwood, K. L., & Pidgeon, N. F. (1992). Qualitative research and psychological theorizing. *British Journal of Psychology, 83,* 97–111.

Hepburn, C., & Locksley, A. (1983). Subjective awareness of stereotyping: Do we know when our judgments are prejudiced? *Social Psychology Quarterly 46,* 311–318.

Heppner, P. P., & Neal, G. W. (1983). Holding up the minor: Research on the roles and functions of counseling centers in higher education. *Counseling Psychologist, 11,* 81–98.

Heslin, R., Nguyen, T., & Nguyen, M. (1983). Meaning of touch: The case of touch from a stranger or same sex person. *Journal of Nonverbal Behavior, 7,* 147–157.

Hess, E. H. (1970). Ethology and developmental psychology. In P. H. Mussen (Ed.), *Carmichael's manual of child psychology* (3rd ed., pp. 1–38). New York: Wiley.

Hetherington, E. M. (1989). Coping with family transitions: Winners, losers, and survivors. *Child Development, 60,* 1–14.

Hetherington, E. M., Stanley-Hagan, M., & Anderson, E. R. (1989). Marital transitions: A child's perspective. *American Psychologist, 44,* 303–312.

Hilgard, E. R. (1965). *Hypnotic susceptibility.* New York: Harcourt Brace Jovanovich.

Hilgard, E. R. (1977). *Divided consciousness: Multiple controls of human thought and action.* New York: Wiley.

Hindler, C. G., & Norris, D. L. (1986). A case of anorexia nervosa in Klinefelter's syndrome. *British Journal of Psychiatry, 149,* 659–660.

Hirschfeld, R. M. A., & Cross, C. K. (1982). Epidemiology of affective disorders. Psychosocial risk factors. *Archives of General Psychiatry, 38,* 35–46.

Hirst, W. (1988). *The making of cognitive science: Essays in honor of George Miller.* New York: Cambridge University Press.

Hirst, W., Spelke, E. S., Reaves, C. C., Caharack, G., & Neisser, U. (1980). Dividing attention without alternation or automaticity. *Journal of Experimental Psychology: General, 109,* 98–117.

Hobson, J. A., & McCarley, R. W. (1977). The brain as a dream state generator: An activation-synthesis hypothesis of the dream process. *American Journal of Psychiatry, 134,* 1335–1348.

Hochberg, J. E. (1978). *Perception* (2nd ed.). Englewood Cliffs, NJ: Prentice-Hall.

Hockey, G. R. J. (1978). Effects of noise on human work efficiency. In D. N. May (Ed.), *Handbook of noise assessment.* New York: Van Nostrand-Reinhold.

Hodge, B. J., & Anthony, W. P. (1984). *Organization theory.* Newton, MA: Allyn & Bacon.

Hodgson, J. W., & Fischer, J. L. (1981). Pathways of identity development in college women. *Sex Roles, 7,* 681–690.

Hoebel, B. G. (1971). Feeding: Neural control of intake. *Annual Review of Physiology, 33,* 533–568.

Hoffman, J. (1987). Semantic control of selective attention. *Psychological Research, 49,* 123–129.

Hogan, R., & Nicholson, R. A. (1988). The meaning of personality test scores. *American Psychologist, 43,* 621–626.

Holden, N. L. (1990). Is anorexia an obsessive-compulsive disorder? *British Journal of Psychiatry, 157,* 1–5.

Holland, M. R., & Tarlow, G. (1980). *Using psychology: Principles of behavior and your life* (2nd ed.). Boston: Little, Brown.

Hollingshed, A. B., & Redlich, F. C. (1958). *Social class and mental illness: A community study.* New York: Wiley.

Holmes, D. S. (1984). Meditation and somatic arousal reduction: A review of the experimental evidence. *American Psychologist, 39,* 1–10.

Holmes, T. H., & Rahe, R. H. (1967). The social readjustment rating scale. *Journal of Psychosomatic Research, 11,* 213–218.

Holroyd, K. A., & Appel, M. A. (1980). Test anxiety and physiological responding. In I. Sarason (Ed.), *Test anxiety: Theory, research and applications* (pp. 129–141). Hillsdale, NJ: Erlbaum.

Holroyd, K. A., Holm, J. E., Hursey, K. G., Penzien, D. B., Cardingley, G. E., Theofonous, A. G., Richardson, S. C., & Tobin, D. L. (1988). Recurrent vascular headache: Home-based behavioral treatment versus abortive pharmacological treatment. *Journal of Counseling and Clinical Psychology, 56,* 218–223.

Hoon, P. W., Bruce, K., & Kinchloe, B. (1982). Does the menstrual cycle play a role in sexual arousal? *Psychophysiology, 19,* 21–26.

Hope, S. L., & Jackson, H. F. (1988). Helping: The effects of sex differences and locus of causality. *British Journal of Social Psychology, 27,* 209–219.

Hopkins, E. (1990, October 18). Childhood's end: Babies born to crack-addicted mothers. *Rolling Stone,* pp. 66–68, 71, 72, 108, 110.

Hopkins, J. R. (1974). *Curvature as a dimension in infant visual perception.* Unpublished doctoral dissertation, Harvard University, Cambridge, MA.

Hopkins, J. R., Kagan, J., Brachfeld, S., Hans, S., & Linn, S. (1976). Infant responsivity to curvature. *Child Development, 47,* 1166–1171.

Hopson, J. L. (1988). A pleasurable chemistry. *Psychology Today, 22,* 29–33.

Horger, B. A., Giles, M., & Schenk, S. (1992). Preexposure to amphetamine and nicotine preexposes rats to self-administer a low dose of cocaine. *Psychopharmacology, 107,* 271–276.

Horger, B. A., Wellman, P. W., Morien, A., Davies, B. T., & Schenk, S. (1991). Caffeine exposure sensitizes rats to the reinforcing effects of cocaine. *NeuroReport, 2,* 53–56.

Horley, J. (1991). Values and beliefs as personal constructs. *International Journal of Personal Construct Psychology, 4,* 1–14.

Horn, W. F., & O'Donnell, J. P. (1984). Early identification of learning disabilities: A comparison of two methods. *Journal of Educational Psychology, 76,* 1106–1118.

Horne, J. A. (1981). The effects of exercise on sleep: A critical review. *Biological Psychology, 12,* 241–290.

Horner, M. S. (1970). Femininity and successful achievement: A basic inconsistency, In J. M. Bradwick, E. Douvan, M. S. Horner, & D. Gutmann (Eds.), *Feminine personality and conflict.* Belmont, CA: Brooks/Cole.

Horney, K. (1939). *New ways in psychoanalysis.* New York: Norton.

Horney, K. (1967). *Feminine psychology.* New York: Norton. (Original work published in 1926).

Horney, K. (1939). *New ways in psychoanalysis.* New York: Norton.

Hornstein, G. (1986). The structuring of identity among midlife women as a function of their degree of involvement in employment. *Journal of Personality, 54,* 551–575.

Horton, D. L., & Mills, C. B. (1984). Human learning and memory. *Annual Review of Psychology, 35,* 361–394.

Horvath, T. (1986). The psychological presentations of somatic disorders. In P. A. Berger, K. H. Brodie, & S. Arieti (Eds.), *American handbook of psychiatry: Vol. 8. Biological psychiatry* (2nd ed., pp. 900–943). New York: Basic Books.

Hostetler, A. J. (1988, July). Will America respond to the AIDS mailing? *American Psychological Association Monitor,* p. 43.

Houston, J. P. (1981). *Fundamentals of learning and memory* (2nd ed.). New York: Academic Press.

Houston, J. P. (1985). *Motivation.* New York: Macmillan.

Hovland, C. I. (1937). The generalization of conditioned responses. I. The sensory generalization of conditioned responses with varying frequencies of tone. *Journal of General Psychology, 17,* 125–148.

Hovland, C. I. (1958). The role of primacy and recency in persuasive communication. In E. E. Maccoby, T. M. Newcomb, & E. L. Hartley (Eds.), *Readings in social psychology* (3rd ed.). New York: Holt, Rinehart, & Winston.

Hovland, C. I., Lumsdaine, A. A., & Sheffield, F. D. (1949). *Experiments in mass communication.* Princeton, NJ: Princeton University Press.

Howard, A. (1990). *The multiple facets of industrial-organizational psychology.* Chicago, IL: Society for Industrial and Organizational Psychology.

Howard, K. I., Kopta, S. M., Krause, M. S., & Orlinsky, D. E. (1986). The dose effect relationship in psychotherapy. *American Psychologist, 41,* 159–164.

Hoyenga, K. B., & Hoyenga, K. T. (1988). *Psychobiology: The neuron and behavior.* Pacific Grove, CA: Brooks/Cole.

Hubel, D. H., & Wiesel, T. N. (1962). Receptive fields, binocular interaction and functional architecture in the cat's visual cortex. *Journal of Physiology (London), 160,* 106–154.

Hubel, D. H., & Wiesel, T. N. (1963). Shape and arrangement of columns in cat's striate cortex. *Journal of Physiology (London), 165,* 559–568.

Hubel, D. H., & Wiesel, T. N. (1965). Receptive fields and functional architecture in two non-striate visual areas (18 and 19) of the cat. *Journal of Neurophysiology, 28,* 229–289.

Hull, J. G., Van Treuren, R. R., & Vinelli, A. (1988). Hardiness and health: A critique and alternative approach. *Journal of Personality and Social Psychology, 53,* 518–530.

Humphrey, G. K., & Humphrey, D. E. (1986). Pattern perception in infants: Effects of structure and transformation. *Journal of Experimental Child Psychology, 41,* 128–148.

Humphreys, L. G. (1979). The construct of general intelligence. *Intelligence, 3,* 105–120.

Hunt, E. (1982). Towards new ways of assessing intelligence. *Intelligence, 6,* 231–240.

Hunt, M. (1974). *Sexual behavior in the 1970s.* New York: Playboy Press.

Hunter, J. E., & Hunter, R. F. (1984). Validity and utility of alternative predictors of job performance. *Psychological Bulletin, 96,* 72–98.

Hurvich, L. (1981). *Color vision.* Sunderland, MA: Sinauer.

Hurvich, L., & Jameson, D. (1957). An opponent-process theory of color vision. *Psychological Review, 64,* 384–404.

Hurvich, L., & Jameson, D. (1974). Opponent processes as a model of neural organization. *American Psychologist, 29,* 88–102.

Hynd, G. W., Hern, K. L., Voeller, K. K., & Marshall, R. M. (1991). Neurobiological basis of attention-deficit hyperactivity disorder (ADHD). *School Psychology Review, 20,* 174–186.

Iaffaldano, M. T., & Murchinsky, P. M. (1985). Job satisfaction and job performance. *Psychological Bulletin, 97,* 251–273.

Ikels, C., Keith, J., Dickerson-Putnam, J., Draper, P., Fry, C., Glascock, A., & Harpending, H. (1992). Perceptions of the adult life course: A cross-cultural analysis. *Aging and Society, 12,* 49–84.

Inhelder, B., & Piaget, J. (1958). *The growth of logical thinking from childhood to adolescence* (A. Parsons & S. Milgram, Trans.). London: Routledge & Kegan Paul. (Original work published 1955).

Insel, R. R., Gillin, C., Moore, A., Mendelson, W. B., Loewenstein, R. J., & Murphy, D. L. (1982). The sleep of patients with obsessive-compulsive disorder. *Archives of General Psychiatry, 39,* 1372–1377.

Institute for Personality and Ability Testing. (1979). *Administrator's Manual for the 16 PF.* Champaign, IL: Author.

Institute of Medicine. (1979). *Sleeping pills, insomnia, and medical practice.* Washington, DC: National Academy of Sciences.

Izard, C. E. (1971). *The face of emotion.* New York: Appleton-Century-Crofts.

Izard, C. E. (1977). *Human emotions.* New York: Plenum.

Izard, C. E. (1979). Emotions as motivations: An evolutionary-developmental perspective. In H. Howe & R. A. Dienstbier (Eds.), *Nebraska Symposium on Motivation, 1978* (pp. 163–200). Lincoln: University of Nebraska Press.

Jaccard, J. (1981). Attitudes and behavior: Implications of attitudes toward behavioral alternatives. *Journal of Experimental Social Psychology, 17,* 286–307.

Jackson, S. E., & Schuler, R. S. (1990). Human resource planning: Challenges for industrial/organizational psychologists. Special Issue: Organizational psychology. *American Psychologist, 452,* 223-239.

Jacobs, B. L. (1987). How hallucinogenic drugs work. *American Scientist, 75,* 386–392.

Jacobs, J. B., & Zimmer, L. (1991). Drug treatment and workplace drug testing: Politics, symbolism and organizational dilemmas. *Behavioral Sciences and the Law, 9*(3), 345–360.

Jacobsen, R. H., Tamkin, A., & Blount, J. B. (1987). The efficacy of rational-emotive group therapy in psychiatric inpatients. *Journal of Rational-Emotive Therapy, 5,* 22–31.

Jacobson, J. L., Boersma, D. C., Fields, R. B., & Olson, K. L. (1983). Paralinguistic features of adult speech to infants and small children. *Child Development, 54,* 436–442.

Jacobson, M. (1991). *Junk-food ads urge unhealthy eating.* Washington, DC: Center for Science in the Public Interest.

Jacobson, S. W. (1979). Matching behavior in the young infant. *Child Development, 50,* 425–430.

Jacobson, S. W., Fein, G. G., Jacobson, J. L., Schwartz, P. M., & Dowler, J. K. (1985). The effect of intrauterine PCB exposure on visual recognition memory. *Child Development, 56,* 853–860.

Jacobson, S. W., & Frye, K. F. (1991). Effect of maternal social support on attachment: Experimental evidence. *Child Development, 62,* 572–582.

Jacoby, L. L., & Witherspoon, D. (1981). Remembering without awareness. *Canadian Journal of Psychology, 36,* 300–324.

James, L. R., & Sells, S. B. (1981). Psychological climate. In D. Magnusson (Ed.), *Toward a psychology of situations: An interactional perspective.* Hillsdale, NJ: Erlbaum.

James, S. P., Wehr, T. A., Sack, D. A., Parry, B. L., & Rosenthal, N. E. (1985). Treatment of seasonal affective disorder with light in the evening. *British Journal of Psychiatry, 147,* 424–428.

James, W. (1884). What is emotion? *Mind, 19,* 188–205.

James, W. (1890). *The principles of psychology* (2 vols.). New York: Holt.

Jamison, K. (1988). Manic depressive illness and accomplishment: Creativity, leadership, and social class. In F. K. Goodwin & K. R. Jamison (Eds.), *Manic-depressive illness.* New York: Oxford University Press.

Janeway, E. (1974). On female sexuality. In J. Strouse (Ed.), *Women and analysis: Dialogue on psychoanalytic views of femininity.* New York: Dell.

Janis, I. L., & Feshbach, S. (1953). Effects of fear-arousing communications. *Journal of Abnormal and Social Psychology, 48,* 78–92.

Janis, I. L., Mahl, G. F., Kagan, J., & Holt, R. R. (1969). *Personality: Dynamics, development, and assessment.* New York: Harcourt, Brace & World.

Jansson, D. G., & Smith, S. M. (1991). Design fixation. *Design Studies, 12*(1), 3–11.

Jason, L. A. (1987). Reducing children's excessive television viewing and assessing secondary changes. *Journal of Clinical Child Psychology, 16,* 245–250.

Jasper, H. H. (1958). The ten twenty electrode system of the International Federation. *Electroencephalography and Clinical Neurophysiology, 10,* 371–375.

Javid, J., Musa, M., Fischman, M., Schuster, C., & Davis, J. (1983). Kinetics of cocaine in humans after intravenous and intranasal administration. *Biopharmaceutics and Drug Disposition, 4,* 9–18.

Jefferson, J. W., Greist, J. H., & Marcetich, J. R. (1980). Searching the lithium literature. In F. N. Johnson (Ed.), *Handbook of lithium therapy.* Lancaster, England: Falcon House.

Jemmott, J. B., & Locke, S. E. (1984). Psychosocial factors, immunologic mediation, and human susceptibility to infectious diseases: How much do we know? *Psychological Bulletin, 95,* 78–108.

Jenkins, J. G., & Dallenbach, K. M. (1924). Obliviscence during sleep and waking. *American Journal of Psychology, 35,* 605–612.

Jensen, A. R. (1969). How much can we boost IQ and scholastic achievement? *Harvard Educational Review, 39,* 1–123.

John, E. R., Prichep, J., Fridman, J., & Easton, P. (1988). Neurometrics: Computer-assisted differential diagnosis of brain dysfunctions. *Science, 239,* 162–169.

Johnson, L. C. (1969). Psychological and physiological changes following total sleep deprivation. In A. Kales (Ed.), *Sleep: Physiology and pathology* (pp. 206–220). Philadelphia: Lippincott.

Johnston, W. A., & Dark, V. J. (1986). Selective attention. *Annual Review of Psychology, 37,* 43–75.

Jolly, A. (1985). *The evolution of primate behavior* (2nd ed.). New York: Macmillan.

Jones, E. E. (1979). The rocky road from acts to dispositions. *American Psychologist, 34,* 107–117.

Jones, E. F., Forrest, J. D., Goldman, N., Henshaw, S., Lincoln, R., Rosoff, J. I.,

Westoff, C. F., & Wulf, D. (1986). *Teenage pregnancy in industrialized countries: A study by the Alan Guttmacher Institute.* New Haven, CT: Yale University Press.

Jones, J. W., & Terris, W. (1991). Integrity testing for personnel selection: An overview. Special Issue: Integrity testing. *Forensic Reports, 4*(2), 117–140.

Jones, L. V. (1984). Black-white achievement differences: The narrowing gap. *American Psychologist, 39,* 1207–1213.

Jones, M. C. (1924). Elimination of children's fears. *Journal of Experimental Psychology, 7,* 382.

Joseph, L. E. (1990). *Gaia.* New York: St. Martin's Press.

Jouvet, M. (1967). The stages of sleep. *Scientific American, 216*(2), 62–72.

Judd, C., & Park, B. (1988). Out-group homogeneity: Judgments of variability at the individual and group levels. *Journal of Personality and Social Psychology, 54,* 778–788.

Jung, C. G. (1933). *Modern man in search of a soul.* New York: Harcourt, Brace & World.

Jung, C. G. (1953). *Two essays on analytical psychology* (R. F. C. Hull, Trans.). Princeton, NJ: Princeton University Press.

Jung, C. G. (1958). Psychology and religion. In R. F. C. Hull (Trans.), *Collected works* (Vol. 11). Princeton, NJ: Princeton University Press. (Original work published 1939).

Jung, C. G. (1959a). Concerning the archetypes, with special reference to the anima complex. In R. F. C. Hull (Trans.), *Collected works* (Vol. 9, pp. 54–75). Princeton, NJ: Princeton University Press. (Original work published 1936).

Jung, C. G. (1959b). Conscious, unconscious, and individuation. In S. Dell (Trans.), *Collected works* (Vol. 9, pp. 275–384). Princeton, NJ: Princeton University Press. (Original work published 1939).

Jung, C. G. (1961). *Memories, dreams, and reflections.* (R. Winston & C. Winston, Trans.), New York: Pantheon.

Jung, C. G. (1967a). *The collected works of C. G. Jung: Vol. 13. Alchemical studies* (R. F. C. Hull, Trans.). Princeton, NJ: Princeton University Press (Original work published 1942–1957).

Jung, C. G. (1967b). The dual mother. In *Collected works* (Vol. 5, pp. 306–393). Princeton, NJ: Princeton University Press. (Original work published 1952).

Jung, C. G. (1968). *Analytical psychology: Its theory and practice. The Tavistock lectures.* New York: Pantheon.

Just, M. A., & Carpenter, P. A. (1980). A theory of reading: From eye fixations to comprehension. *Psychological Review, 87,* 329–354.

Kaczmarek, M. G., & Backlund, B. A. (1991). Disenfranchised grief: The loss of an adolescent romantic relationship. *Adolescence, 26,* 253–259.

Kagan, J. (1971). *Change and continuity in infancy.* New York: Wiley.

Kagan, J. (1992, April). *The significance of temperament in children's development.* Distinguished lecture, Eastern Psychological Association, Boston.

Kagan, J., Reznick, S., & Snidman, N. (1988). Biological bases of childhood shyness. *Science, 240,* 167–171.

Kahneman, D., & Tversky, A. (1973). On the psychology of prediction. *Psychological Review, 80,* 237–251.

Kahneman, D., & Tversky, A. (1984). Choices, values, and frames. *American Psychologist, 39,* 341–350.

Kaitz, M., Lapidot, P., Bronner, R., & Eidelman, A. I. (1992). Parturient women can recognize their infants by touch. *Developmental Psychology, 28,* 35–39.

Kaitz, M., Meschulach-Sarfaty, O., Auerbach, J., & Eidelman, A. (1988). A reexamination of newborns' ability to imitate facial expressions. *Developmental Psychology, 24,* 3–7.

Kalinowsky, L. B. (1980). The discovery of somatic treatments in psychiatry: Facts and myths. *Comprehensive Psychiatry, 21,* 428.

Kalinowsky, L. B., Hippius, H., & Klein, H. E. (1982). *Biological treatments in psychiatry.* New York: Grune & Stratton.

Kamin, L. J. (1969). Predictability, surprise, attention, and conditioning. In S. A. Campbell & R. M. Church (Eds.), *Punishment and aversive behavior.* New York: Appleton-Century-Crofts.

Kamin, L. J. (1974). *The science and politics of I.Q.* Hillsdale, NJ: Erlbaum.

Kandel, D. B., & Lesser, G. S. (1969). Parental and peer influences on educational plans of adolescents. *American Sociological Review, 34,* 213–223.

Kandel, E. R., Schwartz, J. P., & Jessell, E. (1991). *Principles of Neural Science* (3rd ed.). New York: Elsevier.

Kantrowitz, B., Murr, A., Annin, P., Carroll, G., & Clifton, T. (1993, March 15). The messiah of Waco. *Newsweek,* pp. 56, 57–58.

Kaplan, R. (1985). The controversy related to the use of psychological tests. In B. B. Wolman (Ed.), *Handbook of intelligence: Theories, measurements, and applications* (pp. 465–504). New York: Wiley.

Karno, M., & Golding, J. M. (1991). Obsessive-compulsive disorder. In L. N. Robins & D. A. Regier (Eds.), *Psychiatric disorders in America: The Epidemiologic Catchment Area Study.* New York: Free Press.

Karson, C., Coppola, R., & Daniel, D. (1988). Alpha frequency in schizophrenia: An association with enlarged cerebral ventricles. *American Journal of Psychiatry, 145*, 861–864.

Katchadourian, H. A. (1989). *Fundamentals of human sexuality* (5th ed.). Forth Worth, TX: Holt, Rinehart, & Winston.

Katz, D., & Braly, K. W. (1933). Racial stereotypes of 100 college students. *Journal of Abnormal and Social Psychology, 28*, 280–290.

Katz, D., & Kahn, R. (1966). *The social psychology of organizations.* New York: Wiley.

Katz, S., Lautenschlager, G. J., Blackburn, A. B., & Harris, F. H. (1990). Answering reading comprehension items without passages on the SAT. *Psychological Science, 1*, 122–127.

Kaufman, A. S., Reynolds, C. R., & McLean, J. E. (1989). Age and WAIS-R intelligence in a national sample of adults in the 20- to 74-year age range: A cross-sectional analysis with educational level controlled. *Intelligence, 13*, 235–253.

Kaufman, J., & Cicchetti, D. (1989). Effects of maltreatment on school-age children's socioemotional development: Assessments in a day-camp setting. *Developmental Psychology, 25*, 516–524.

Kay, B. R. (1990). Presidential services. *Journal of Autism and Developmental Disorders, 20*, 309–321.

Kaylor, J., King, G., & King, L. (1987). Psychological effects of military service in Vietnam: A meta-analysis. *Psychological Bulletin, 102*, 257–271.

Kazdin, A. E. (1989). Developmental psychopathology: Current research, issues and directions. *American Psychologist, 44*, 180–187.

Keating, D. P., & Clark, L. V. (1980). Development of physical and social reasoning in adolescence. *Developmental Psychology, 16*, 23–30.

Keesey, R. E., & Powley, T. L. (1986). The regulation of body weight. *Annual Review of Psychology, 37*, 109–134.

Kelley, H. H. (1950). The warm-cold variable in the first impressions of persons. *Journal of Personality, 18*, 431–439.

Kelley, H. H. (1967). Attribution theory in social psychology. In D. Levin (Ed.), *Nebraska Symposium on Motivation* (pp. 192–238). Lincoln: University of Nebraska Press.

Kellogg, W. N., & Kellogg, L. (1933). *The ape and the child.* New York: McGraw-Hill.

Kelly, G. A. (1955). *A theory of personality: The psychology of personal constructs.* New York: Norton.

Kelly, J. E. (1982). *Scientific management, job redesign, and work performance.* New York: Academic Press.

Kemper, T. D. (1978). *A social interactional theory of emotions.* New York: Wiley.

Kendler, K. S. (1980). The nosologic validity of paranoia (simple delusional disor-

der). *Archives of General Psychiatry, 37*, 699–706.

Kendler, K. S. (1988). Indirect vertical cultural transmission: A model for nongenetic parental inferences on the liability to psychiatric illness. *American Journal of Psychiatry, 145*, 657–665.

Kennedy, S. H., McVey, G., & Katz, R. (1990). Personality disorders in anorexia nervosa and bulimia. *Journal of Psychiatric Research, 24*, 259–269.

Kenny, D. A., & Nasby, W. (1980). Splitting the reciprocity correlation. *Journal of Personality and Social Psychology, 38*, 249–256.

Kenshalo, D. R. (1971). The cutaneous senses. In J. W. Kling & L. A. Riggs (Eds.), *Woodworth and Schlosberg's experimental psychology* (3rd ed.). New York: Holt, Rinehart, & Winston.

Kertesz, A., Polk, M., Howell, J., & Black, S. E. (1987). Cerebral dominance, sex, and callosal size in MRI. *Neurology, 37*, 1385–1388.

Kessler, R. C., Price, R. H., & Wortman, C. B. (1985). Social factors in psychopathology: Stress, social support, and coping processes. *Annual Review of Psychology, 36*, 531–572.

Kestenbaum, C. (1981). The child at risk for major psychiatric illness. In S. Arieti & K. H. Brodie (Eds.), *American handbook of psychiatry: Advances and new directions* (2nd ed., Vol. 7, pp. 152–171). New York: Basic Books.

Kiecolt-Glaser, J. K., & Glaser, R. (1986). Psychological influences on immunity. *Psychosomatics, 27*, 621–624.

Kiesler, C. A. (1982a). Mental hospitals and alternative care: Noninstitutionalization as a potential public policy for mental patients. *American Psychologist, 37*, 349–360.

Kiesler, C. A. (1982b). Public and professional myths about mental hospitalization. *American Psychologist, 37*, 1323–1339.

Kiesler, C. A., & Pallak, M. S. (1975). Minority influence: The effect of majority reactionaries and defectors, and minority and majority compromisers, upon majority opinion and attraction. *European Journal of Social Psychology, 5*, 237–256.

Kiggundu, M. N. (1986). Limitations to the application of sociotechnical systems in developing countries. *Journal of Applied Behavioral Science, 22*(3), 341–353.

Kihlström, J. F. (1985). Hypnosis. *Annual Review of Psychology, 36*, 385–418.

Kimelberg, H. K. (1988). *Glial cell receptors.* New York: Raven Press.

Kimelberg, H. K., & Norenberg, M. D. (1989, April). Astrocytes. *Scientific American*, pp. 66–76.

Kimble, D. P. (1988). *Biological psychology.* New York: Holt, Rinehart, & Winston.

Kinsey, A. C., Pomeroy, W. B., & Martin, C. E. (1948). *Sexual behavior in the human male.* Philadelphia: Saunders.

Kinsey, A. C., Pomeroy, W. B., Martin, C. E., & Gebhard, P. H. (1953). *Sexual behavior in the human female.* Philadelphia: Saunders.

Kirkley, B. G., Schneider, J. A., Agras, W. S., & Bachman, J. A. (1985). Comparison of two group treatments for bulimia. *Journal of Consulting and Clinical Psychology, 53*, 43–48.

Kirmayer, L. J. (1983). Paranoia and pronoia: The visionary and the banal. *Social Problems, 31*, 170–179.

Kirsch, B. (1983). Sex roles and language use: Implications for mental health. In V. Franks & E. D. Rothblum (Eds.), *The stereotyping of women: Its effects on mental health* (pp. 59–79). New York: Springer-Verlag.

Kirton, M. J., & Pender, S. (1982). The adaptation-innovation continuum, occupational type, and the course selection. *Psychological Reports, 51*, 883–886.

Kitterle, F. (1989). *Cerebral laterality: Theory and research.* Hillsdale, NJ: Erlbaum.

Klagsbrun, F. (1976). *Youth and suicide: Too young to die.* Boston: Houghton-Mifflin.

Klaus, M. H. (1978). The biology of parent to infant attachment. *Birth and the Family Journal, 5*, 200–203.

Klein, D. N. (1990). Symptom criteria and family history in major depression. *American Journal of Psychiatry, 147*, 850–854.

Klein, S. B., & Mower, R. R. (1991). *Contemporary learning theories: Instrumental conditioning theory and the impact of biological constraints on learning.* Hillsdale, NJ: Erlbaum.

Kobasa, S. C. (1979). Stressful life events, personality, and health: An inquiry into hardiness. *Journal of Personality and Social Psychology, 37*, 1–11.

Kochanska, G., & Radke-Yarrow, M. (1992). Inhibition in toddlerhood and the dynamics of the child's interaction with an unfamiliar peer at age five. *Child Development, 63*, 325–335.

Koehler-Troy, C., Strober, M., & Malenbaum, R. (1986). Methylphenidate-induced mania in a prepubertal child. *Journal of Clinical Psychiatry, 47*, 566–567.

Kohl, R. M., & Roenker, D. L. (1980). Bilateral transfer as a function of mental imagery. *Journal of Motor Behavior, 15*, 179–190.

Kohl, R. M., & Roenker, D. L. (1983). Mechanism involvement during skill imagery. *Journal of Motor Behavior, 15*, 179–190.

Kohlberg, L. (1969). Stage and sequence: The cognitive-developmental approach to socialization. In D. A. Goslin (Ed.), *Handbook of socialization theory and research.* Chicago: Rand McNally.

Kohlberg, L. (1976). Moral stages and moralization: The cognitive-developmental approach. In T. Lickona (Ed.), *Moral development and behavior: Theory, research and social issues*. New York: Holt, Rinehart, & Winston.

Kohlberg, L. (1985). A current statement on some theoretical issues. In S. Modgil & C. Modgil (Eds.), *Lawrence Kohlberg: Consensus and controversy* (pp. 485–546). Philadelphia: Falmer Press.

Köhler, W. (1925). *The mentality of apes*. London: Routledge & Kegan Paul.

Kojima, S., & Goldman-Rakic, P. S. (1984). Fundamental analysis of spatially discriminative neurons in prefrontal cortex of rhesus monkey. *Brain Research, 291*, 229–240.

Kolata, G. (1986). New drug counters alcohol intoxication. *Science, 234*, 1198–1199.

Kolb, B., & Whishaw, I. O. (1990). *Fundamentals of human neuropsychology*. New York: Freeman.

Kolers, P. A. (1972). Experiments in reading. *Scientific American, 227*(1), 84–91.

Kolotkin, R. L., Revis, E. S., Kirkley, B. G., & Janick, L. (1987). Binge eating in obesity: Associated MMPI characteristics. *Journal of Consulting and Clinical Psychology, 55*, 872–876.

Konner, M. (1991). *Childhood*. Boston: Little, Brown.

Konovsky, M. A., & Cropanzano, R. (1991). Perceived fairness of employee drug testing as a predictor of employee attitudes and job performance. *Journal of Applied Psychology, 76*(5), 698–707.

Korchin, S. J., & Schuldberg, D. (1981). The future of clinical assessment. *American Psychologist, 36*, 1147–1158.

Korn, J. H. (1987). Judgments of acceptability of deception in psychological research. *Journal of General Psychology, 114*, 205–216.

Korn, J. H. (1988). Students' roles, rights, and responsibilities as research participants. *Teaching of Psychology, 15*, 74–78.

Kornhauser, A. (1965). *Mental health of the industrial worker*. New York: Wiley.

Kosambi, D. D. (1967). Living prehistory in India. *Scientific American, 216*, 105–114.

Kosslyn, S. M. (1975). Information representation in visual images. *Cognitive Psychology, 7*, 341–370.

Kosslyn, S. M. (1980). *Image and mind*. Cambridge, MA: Harvard University Press.

Kosslyn, S. M. (1981). The medium and the message in mental imagery: A theory. *Psychological Review, 88*, 46–66.

Koulack, D., & Goodenough, D. R. (1976). Dream recall and dream recall failure: An arousal-retrieval model. *Psychological Bulletin, 83*, 975–984.

Kow, L. M., & Pfaff, D. W. (1988). Neuromodulatory actions of peptides. *Annual Review of Pharmacology and Toxicology, 28*, 163, 188.

Krafka, C., & Penrod, S. (1985). Reinstatement of context in a field experiment on eyewitness identification. *Journal of Personality and Social Psychology, 49*, 58–69.

Krantz, D. S., Grunberg, N. E., & Baum, A. (1985). Health psychology. *Annual Review of Psychology, 36*, 349–383.

Kranzler, J. H., & Jensen, A. R. (1991). The nature of psychometric g: Unitary process or a number of independent processes? *Intelligence, 15*, 397–422.

Krauthammer, C. (1985, December 2). When liberty means neglect. *Time*, pp. 103–104.

Kreitner, R. (1982). The feedforward and feedback control of job performance through organizational behavioral management. *Journal of Organizational Behavior Management, 3*, 3–20.

Kretschmer, E. (1921). *Physique and character*. New York: Harcourt.

Kreuz, R. J., & Glucksberg, S. (1989). How to be sarcastic: The echoic reminder theory of verbal irony. *Journal of Experimental Psychology: General, 118*, 374–386.

Kripke, D. F., Simons, R. N., Garfinkle, L., & Hammond, E. C. (1979). Short and long sleep and sleeping pills: Is increased mortality associated? *Archives of General Psychiatry, 36*, 103–116.

Kroening, R. J., & Oleson, T. D. (1985). Rapid narcotic detoxification in chronic pain patients treated with auricular electroacupuncture and naloxone. *International Journal of Addictions, 20*, 1347–1360.

Kuffler, S. W. (1953). Discharge patterns and functional organization of mammalian retina. *Journal of Neurophysiology, 16*, 37–68.

Kurdek, L. A., & Krile, D. (1982). A developmental analysis of the relation between peer acceptance and both interpersonal understanding and perceived social self-competence. *Child Development, 53*, 1485–1491.

Kurtines, W., & Grief, E. B. (1974). The development of moral thought: Review and evaluation of Kohlberg's approach. *Psychological Bulletin, 81*, 453–470.

Kurtz, H. (1987, November 13). Policy of hospitalizing N. Y. homeless set back. *Washington Post*, p. A3.

LaBerge, S. F., Greenleaf, W., & Kedzierski, B. (1983). Physiological responses to dreamed sexual activity during lucid REM sleep. *Psychophysiology, 20*, 454–455.

LaBerge, S. F., Levitan, L., & Dement, W. C. (1986). Lucid dreaming: Physiological correlates of consciousness during REM sleep. *Journal of Mind and Behavior, 7*, 251–258.

LaBerge, S. F., Nagel, L. E., Dement, W. C., & Zarcone, V. P. (1981). Lucid dreaming verified by volitional communication during REM sleep. *Perceptual and Motor Skills, 52*, 727–732.

Labouvie-Vief, G. (1986). Modes of knowledge and the organization of development. In M. Commons, L. Kohlberg, F. Richards, & J. Sinnott (Eds.), *Beyond formal operations: 3. Models and methods in the study of adult and adolescent thought*. New York: Praeger.

Lack, D. (1943). *The life of the robin*. London: Witherby.

Lacks, P., Bertelson, A. D., Sugerman, J., & Kinkel, J. (1983). The treatment of sleep-maintenance insomnia with stimulus-control techniques. *Behavior Research Therapy, 21*, 291–295.

Lacoste-Utamsing, C. M., & Holloway, R. L. (1982). Sexual dimorphism in the human corpus callosum. *Science, 216*, 1431–1432.

Lamberg, L. (1984). *The American Medical Association guide to better sleep*. New York: Random House.

Lambert, M. J., Shapiro, D. A., & Bergin, A. E. (1986). The effectiveness of psychotherapy. In S. L. Garfield & A. E. Bergin (Eds.), *Handbook of psychotherapy and behavior change*. New York: Wiley.

Lambert, W. E. (1981). Bilingualism and language acquisition. *Annals of the New York Academy of Sciences, 379*, 9–22.

Lamborn, S. D., Mounts, N. S., Steinberg, L., & Dornbusch, S. M. (1991). Patterns of competence and adjustment among adolescents from authoritative, authoritarian, indulgent, and neglectful families. *Child Development, 62*, 1049–1065.

Landers, S. (1988, August). Commission, Congress heeds APA on AIDS. *American Psychological Association Monitor*, p. 25.

Landy, F. J., & Becker, W. S. (1987). Motivation theory reconsidered. *Research in Organizational Behavior, 9*, 1–38.

Lang, K. A., Mueller, J. H., & Nelson, R. E. (1983). Test anxiety and self-schemas. *Motivation and Emotion, 7*, 169–178.

Langer, E. J., & Rodin, J. (1976). The effects of choice and enhanced personal responsibility for the aged: A field experiment in an institutional setting. *Journal of Personality and Social Psychology, 34*, 191–198.

Langsdorf, P., Izard, C. E., Rayias, M., & Hembree, E. A. (1983). Interest expression, visual fixation, and heart rate changes in 2- to 8-month-old infants. *Developmental Psychology, 19*, 375–386.

Lanktree, C., Briere, J., & Zaidi, L. (1991). Incidence and impact of sexual abuse in a child outpatient sample: The role of direct inquiry. *Child Abuse and Neglect, 15*, 447–453.

Lantz, J. E. (1987). Emotional motivations for family treatment. *Social Casework, 68*, 284–289.

Lanyon, R. I. (1984). Personality assessment. *Annual Review of Psychology, 35*, 677–701.

LaPiere, R. T. (1934). Attitudes versus action. *Social Forces, 13*, 230–237.

LaPlante, M. N., McCormick, N., & Brannigan, G. G. (1980). Living the sexual script: College students' views of influence in sexual encounters. *Journal of Sex Research, 16*, 338–355.

Lappin, J., & Preble, L. D. (1975). A demonstration of shape constancy. *Perception and Psychophysics, 17*, 439–444.

Larkin, J. H., McDermott, J., Simon, D. P., & Simon, H. A. (1980). Expert and novice performance in solving physics problems. *Science, 208*, 1335–1342.

Lashley, K. (1950). In search of the engram. *Symposia of the Society for Experimental Biology, 4*, 454–482.

Latané, B., & Bidwell, L. D. (1977). Sex and affiliation in college cafeterias. *Personality and Social Psychology Bulletin, 3*, 571–574.

Latané, B., & Darley, J. M. (1970). *The unresponsive bystander: Why doesn't he help?* New York: Appleton-Century-Crofts.

Latham, G. P., Erez, M., & Locke, E. A. (1988). Resolving scientific disputes by the joint design of crucial experiments by the antagonists: Application to the Erez-Latham dispute regarding participation in goal setting. *Journal of Applied Psychology, 73*, 753–772.

Lauber, J. K., & Kayten, P. J. (1988). Sleepiness, circadian dysrhythmia, and fatigue in transportation system accidents. *Sleep, 11*, 503–512.

Laudenslager, M. L., Ryan, S. M., Drugan, R. C., Hyson, R. L., & Maier, S. F. (1983). Coping and immunosuppression: Inescapable but not escapable shock suppresses lymphocyte proliferation. *Science, 221*, 568–570.

Laurent, J., Swerdlik, M., & Ryburn, M. (1992). Review of validity research on the Stanford-Binet Intelligence Scale: Fourth edition. *Psychological Assessment, 4*, 102–112.

Lavey, R. S., & Taylor, C. B. (1985). The nature of relaxation therapy. In S. R. Burchfield (Ed.), *Stress: Psychological and physiological interactions*. Washington, DC: Hemisphere.

Lawler, E. E. (1983). Control systems in organizations. In M. D. Dunnette (Ed.), *Handbook of industrial and organizational psychology* (pp. 1247–1292). New York: Wiley.

Lawrence, P. R., & Lorsch, J. W. (1967). *Organization and environment: Managing differentiation and integration*. Boston: Harvard Graduate School of Business Administration.

Layton, J. R. (1979). *The psychology of learning to read*. New York: Academic Press.

Lazarus, R. S. (1966). *Psychological stress and the coping process*. New York: McGraw-Hill.

Lazarus, R. S. (1981, July). Little hassles can be hazardous to your health. *Psychology Today*, pp. 58–62.

Lazarus, R. S. (1982). Thoughts on the relations between emotion and cognition. *American Psychologist, 37*, 1019–1024.

Lazarus, R. S. (1984). The trivialization of distress. In B. L. Hammonds & C. J. Scheirer (Eds.), *Psychology and health: The Master Lecture Series* (Vol. 3), Washington, DC: American Psychological Association.

Leahey, T. H. (1986). History without the past. *Contemporary Psychology, 31*, 648–649.

Lee, M., Flegel, P., Greden, J., & Cameron, O. (1988). Anxiogenic effects of caffeine on panic and depressed patients. *American Journal of Psychiatry, 145*, 632–635.

Lee, S. (1977). *Kinds of love*. New York: Victory Day.

Lee, V. E., Brooks-Gunn, J., & Schnur, E. (1988). Does Head Start work? A 1-year follow-up comparison of disadvantaged children attending Head Start, no preschool, and other preschool programs. *Developmental Psychology, 24*, 210–222.

Lee, V. E., Brooks-Gunn, J., Schnur, E., & Liaw, F.-R. (1990). Are Head Start effects sustained? A longitudinal follow-up comparison of disadvantaged children attending Head Start, no preschool, and other preschool programs. *Child Development, 61*, 495–507.

Lehman, E. B., & Mellinger, J. C. (1984). Effects of aging on memory for presentation modality. *Developmental Psychology, 20*, 1210–1217.

Leibowitz, H. W. (1985). Grade-crossing accidents and human factors engineering. *American Scientist, 73*, 558–562.

Leibowitz, S. F. (1983). Hypothalamic catecholamine systems controlling eating behavior: A potential model for anorexia nervosa. In P. L. Darby, P. E. Garfinkel, D. M. Graner, & D. V. Coscina (Eds.), *Anorexia nervosa: Recent developments in research*. New York: Alan R. Liss.

Leibowitz, Z. B., Farren, C., & Kaye, B. L. (1986). *Designing career development systems*. San Francisco: Jossey-Bass.

Lemley, B. (1984, June). Synesthesia: Seeing is feeling. *Psychology Today*, p. 65.

Lent, R. H., Aurbach, H. D., & Levin, L. S. (1971). Predictors, criteria, and significant results. *Personnel Psychology, 24*, 519–533.

Lepper, M. R. (1985). Microcomputers in education: Motivational and social issues. *American Psychologist, 40*, 1–18.

Lepper, M. R., & Greene, D. (1978). *The hidden cost of reward: New perspectives on the psychology of human motivation*. New York: Halsted.

Lepper, M. R., Greene, D., & Nisbett, R. E. (1973). Understanding children's intrinsic interest with extrinsic rewards: A test of the "overjustification" hypothesis. *Journal of Personality and Social Psychology, 28*, 129–137.

Lepper, M. R., & Malone, T. W. (1986). Intrinsic motivation and instructional effectiveness in computer-based education. In R. E. Snow & M. C. Farr (Eds.), *The hidden costs of reward*. Hillsdale, NJ: Erlbaum.

Leslie, C., & Rosenberg, D. (1990, November 12). I hear America scratching. *Newsweek*, p. 88.

Lester, B. M., Corwin, M. J., Sepkoski, C., Seifer, R., Peucker, M., McLaughlin, S., & Golub, H. L. (1991). Neurobehavioral syndromes in cocaine-exposed newborn infants. *Child Development, 62*, 694–705.

LeVay, S. (1992, February 24). Born or bred? *Newsweek*, pp. 46–49.

Lever, J. (1976). Sex differences in the games children play. *Social Problems, 23*, 478–487.

Levine, B., Roehrs, T., Zorick, F., & Roth, T. (1988). Daytime sleepiness in young adults. *Sleep, 11*, 39–46.

Levine, E. L., Sistrunk, F., McNutt, K. J., & Gael, S. (1988). Exemplary job analysis systems in selected organizations: A description of process and outcomes. *Journal of Business and Psychology, 3*, 3–21.

Levinson, D. J. (1978). *The seasons of a man's life*. New York: Alfred A. Knopf.

Levinson, D. J. (1986). A conception of adult development. *American Psychologist, 41*, 3–13.

Levis, D. J. (1989). The case for a return to two-factor theory of avoidance: The failure of non-fear interpretations. In S. Klein & R. Mower (Eds.), *Contemporary learning theories*. Hillsdale, NJ: Erlbaum.

Levy, M. B., & Davis, K. E. (1988). Lovestyles and attachment styles compared: Their relations to each other and to various relationship characteristics. *Journal of Social and Personal Relationship, 5*, 439–471.

Lewin, K. (1945). The research center for group dynamics at Massachusetts Institute of Technology. *Sociometry, 8*, 126–136.

Lewin, K. (1948). *Resolving social conflicts*. New York: Harper.

Lewin, R. (1987). Environmental hypothesis for brain diseases strengthened by new data. *Science, 231*, 483–484.

Lewis, D. A., & Bloom, F. E. (1987). Clinical perspectives on neuropeptides. *Annual Review of Medicine, 38,* 143–148.

Lewis, E. R., Everhart, T. E., & Zeevi, Y. Y. (1969). Study of neural organization in Aplysia with the scanning electron microscope. *Science, 165,* 1140–1143.

Lewis, H. B. (1984). Freud and modern psychology: The social nature of humanity. *Psychoanalytic Review, 71,* 7–26.

Lewis, R. J., Gibbons, F. X., & Gerrard, M. (1986). Sexual experience and recall of sexual versus nonsexual information. *Journal of Personality, 54,* 676–693.

Lewkowicz, D. (1988a). Sensory dominance in infants: 1. Six-month-old infants' response to auditory-visual compounds. *Developmental Psychology, 24,* 155–171.

Lewkowicz, D. (1988b). Sensory dominance in infants: 2. Ten-month-old infants' response to auditory-visual compounds. *Developmental Psychology, 24,* 172–182.

Liebert, R. M., Sprafkin, J. N., & Davidson, E. S. (1982). *The early window: Effects of television on children and youth* (2nd ed.). New York: Pergamon.

Lieblich, I. (1979). Eidetic imagery: Do not use ghosts to hunt ghosts of the same species. *Behavioral and Brain Sciences, 2,* 608–609.

Lifton, R. J., & Olson, E. (1976). The human meaning of total disaster. *Psychiatry, 39,* 1–18.

Light, L. L., & Singh, A. (1987). Implicit and explicit memory in young and older adults. *Journal of Experimental Psychology: Learning, Memory, and Cognition, 13,* 531–541.

Lightman, S., & Poser, E. G. (1988). The effects of mood on cognitive functioning. *Exercise and Sport, 16,* 16–23.

Likert, R. (1967). *The human organization.* New York: McGraw-Hill.

Likert, R. (1979). From production and employee-centeredness to Systems 1–4. *Journal of Management, 5,* 147–56.

Lin, C.-Y. C., & Fu, V. R. (1990). A comparison of child-rearing practices among Chinese, immigrant Chinese, and Caucasian-American parents. *Child Development, 61,* 429–433.

Lindley, R., Smith, W., & Thomas, T. (1988). The relationship between speed of information processing as measured by timed paper-and-pencil tests and psychometric intelligence. *Intelligence, 12,* 17–25.

Lindsay, P. H., & Norman, D. A. (1977). *Human information processing* (2nd ed.). New York: Academic Press.

Lipmann, J. J., Cross, K. S., & Young, N. L. (1990). Peak ß-endorphin concentration in cerebrospinal fluid: Reduced in chronic pain patients and increased during the placebo response. *Psychopharmacology, 102,* 112–116.

Locke, E. A., Latham, G. P., & Erez, M. (1988). The determinants of goal commitment. *Academy of Management Review, 13,* 23–39.

Locke, A. E., Shaw, K. N., Saari, L. M., & Latham, G. P. (1981). Goal setting and task performance: 1969–1980. *Psychological Bulletin, 90,* 125–152.

Loehlin, J. C. (1992). Should we do research on race differences in intelligence? *Intelligence, 16,* 1–4.

Loevinger, J., & Knoll, E. (1983). Personality: Stages, traits, and the self. *Annual Review of Psychology, 34,* 195–222.

Loftus, E. F. (1983). Misfortunes of memory. *Philosophical Transactions of the Royal Society of London, 302,* 413–421.

Loftus, E. F. (1984, February). Eyewitness: Essential but unreliable. *Psychology Today,* pp. 22–27.

Loftus, E. F., & Palmer, J. C. (1974). Reconstruction and automobile destruction. An example of the interaction between language and memory. *Journal of Verbal Learning and Verbal Behavior, 13,* 585–589.

Loftus, G. R., & Mackworth, N. H. (1978). Cognitive detriments of fixation location during picture viewing. *Journal of Experimental Psychology: Human Perception and Performance, 4,* 565–572.

Logue, A. W. (1986). *The psychology of eating and drinking.* New York: Freeman.

Loher, B. T., Noe, R. A., Moeller, N. L., & Fitzgerald, M. P. (1985). A meta-analysis of the relation of job characteristics to job satisfaction. *Journal of Applied Psychology, 70,* 280–289.

Long, B. C., & Haney, C. J. (1988). Coping strategies for working women: Aerobic exercise and relaxation interventions. *Behavior Therapy, 19,* 75–83.

Long, G. M., & Beaton, R. J. (1982). The case for peripheral persistence: Effects of target and background luminance on a partial-report task. *Journal of Experimental Psychology: Human Perception and Performance, 8,* 383–391.

Lorenz, K. (1981). *The foundations of ethology.* New York: Springer-Verlag.

Lorsch, J. W., & Lawrence, P. R. (1970). *Studies in organization design.* Homewood, IL: Richard D. Irwin & The Dorsey Press.

Lowe, G. (1987). Combined effects of alcohol and caffeine on human state-dependent learning. *Medical Science Research: Psychology & Psychiatry, 15,* 25–26.

Lubin, A. J. (1972). *Stranger on the earth: A psychological biography of Vincent Van Gogh.* New York: Holt, Rinehart, & Winston.

Lubin, B., Larsen, R. M., Matarazzo, J. D., & Seever, M. (1985). Psychological test usage patterns in five professional settings. *American Psychologist, 40,* 857–861.

Luchins, A. S. (1942). Mechanization in problem-solving: The effect of Einstellung. *Psychological Monographs, 54*(Whole No. 248).

Ludel, J. (1978). *Introduction to sensory processes.* San Francisco: Freeman.

Lunt, P. (1988). The perceived causal structure of examination failure. *British Journal of Social Psychology, 27,* 171–179.

Luria, A. R. (1980). *High cortical functions in man.* New York: Basic Books.

Lustman, P. J., & Sowa, C. J. (1983). Comparative efficacy of biofeedback and stress-inoculation for stress reduction. *Journal of Clinical Psychology, 39,* 191–197.

Luthans, F., Paul, R., & Baker, D. (1981). An experimental analysis of the impact of contingent reinforcement of salespersons performance behavior. *Journal of Applied Psychology, 66,* 314–323.

Lykken, D. T., McGue, M., Tellegen, A., & Bouchard, T. J., Jr. (1992). Emergenesis: Genetic traits that may not run in families. *American Psychologist, 47,* 1565–1577.

Lyles, J. N., Burish, T. G., Krozely, M. G., & Oldham, R. K. (1982). Efficacy of relaxation training and guided imagery in reducing the aversiveness of cancer chemotherapy. *Journal of Consulting and Clinical Psychology, 50,* 509–524.

Lytton, H., & Romney, D. M. (1991). Parents' differential socialization of boys and girls: A meta-analysis. *Psychological Bulletin, 109,* 267–296.

Maccoby, E. E. (1988). Gender as a social category. *Developmental Psychology, 24,* 755–765.

Maccoby, E. E., & Jacklin, C. N. (1974). *The psychology of sex differences.* Stanford, CA: Stanford University Press.

MacCoun, R., & Kerr, N. (1988). Asymmetric influence in mock jury deliberation: Jurors' bias for leniency. *Journal of Personality and Social Psychology, 54,* 21–33.

MacDonald, K., & Parke, R. D. (1984). Bridging the gap: Parent-child play interaction and peer interactive competence. *Child Development, 55,* 1265–1277.

MacKay, D. G. (1981). The problem of rehearsal or mental practice. *Journal of Motor Behavior, 13,* 274–285.

MacKay, M. (1981). Special symptoms of childhood. In S. Arieti & K. H. Brodie (Eds.), *American handbook of psychiatry: Advances and new directions* (Vol. 7, pp. 187–203). New York: Basic Books.

Mackenzie, B. (1984). Explaining race differences in IQ: The logic, the methodology, and the evidence. *American Psychologist, 39,* 1214–1233.

Mackie, D., & Cooper, J. (1984). Attitude polarization: Effects of group membership. *Journal of Personality and Social Psychology, 46,* 575–585.

MacKinnon, D. W. (1970). The personality correlates of creativity: A study of American architects. In P. E. Vernon (Ed.), *Creativity.* London: Penguin.

Mackintosh, N. J. (1975). A theory of attention: Variation of the associability of stimuli with reinforcement. *Psychological Review, 82,* 276–298.

MacLagan, D. (1983). Methodical madness. *Spring,* pp. 3–11.

MacLean, P. D. (1973). New findings on brain function and sociosexual behavior. In J. Zubin & J. Money (Eds.), *Contemporary sexual behavior: Critical issues in the 1970s.* Baltimore: Johns Hopkins University Press.

MacLeod, D. A. (1978). Visual sensitivity. *Annual Review of Psychology, 29,* 613–645.

Madden, D. J. (1983). Aging and distraction by highly familiar stimuli during visual search. *Developmental Psychology, 19,* 499–507.

Maddux, J. E., & Rogers, R. W. (1980). Effects of source expertness, physical attractiveness, and supporting arguments on persuasion: A case of brains over beauty. *Journal of Personality and Social Psychology, 39,* 235–244.

Mahoney, M. J. (1985). Psychotherapy and human change processes. In M. J. Mahoney & A. Freeman (Eds.), *Cognition and psychotherapy.* New York: Plenum.

Main, M., & Cassidy, J. (1988). Categories of response to reunion with the parent at age 6: Predictable from infant attachment classifications and stable over a 1-month period. *Developmental Psychology, 24,* 415–426.

Majors, R. (1992). *Cool pose. The dilemmas of black manhood in America.* New York: Maxwell Macmillan.

Malpass, R. S., & Kravitz, J. (1969). Recognition for faces of own and other race. *Journal of Personality and Social Psychology, 13,* 330–334.

Mangan, G. L., & Golding, J. F. (1984). *The psychopharmacology of smoking.* New York: Cambridge University Press.

Manoach, D., Maher, B., & Manschreck, T. (1988). Left-handedness and thought disorder in the schizophrenias. *Journal of Abnormal Psychology, 97,* 97–99.

Manosevitz, M. (1972). The development of male homosexuality. *Journal of Sex Research, 8,* 31–40.

Manz, C. C., Keating, D. E., & Donnellon, A. (1990). Preparing for organizational change to employee self-management: The managerial transition. *Organizational Dynamics, 19,* 15–26.

Marcia, J. E. (1966). Development and validation of ego-identity status. *Journal of Personality and Social Psychology, 3,* 551–558.

Margulies, N., & Raia, A. P. (1978). *Conceptual foundations of organizational psychology.* New York: McGraw-Hill.

Margulies, N., & Raia, A. P. (1984). The politics of organization development. *Training and Development Journal, 38,* 20–23.

Markesbery, W. R., Ehrmann, W. D., Hossain, T. I., Alauddin, M., & Goodin, D. T. (1981). Instrumental neutron activation analysis of brain aluminum in Alzheimer's disease and aging. *Annals of Neurology, 10,* 511–516.

Markides, K. S., & Mindel, C. H. (1987). *Aging and ethnicity.* Newbury Park, CA: Sage.

Markovits, H., & Vachon, R. (1989). Reasoning with contrary-to-fact propositions. *Journal of Experimental Child Psychology, 47,* 398–412.

Markus, H., Smith, J., & Moreland, R. (1985). Role of the self-concept in the perception of others. *Journal of Personality and Social Psychology, 49,* 1494–1512.

Marlatt, G. A., & Baer, J. S. (1988). Addictive behaviors: Etiology and treatment. *Annual Review of Psychology, 39,* 223–242.

Marmar, C. R., Horowitz, M. J., Weiss, D., Wilner, N. R., et al. (1988). A controlled trial of brief psychotherapy and mutual-help group treatment of conjugal bereavement. *American Journal of Psychiatry, 145,* 203–209.

Mars, D. (1981). Creativity and urban public leadership. *Journal of Creative Behavior, 15,* 199–204.

Marshall, G. D. (1976). The affective consequences of "inadequately explained" physiological arousal (Doctoral dissertation, Stanford University). *Dissertation Abstracts International, 37*(2–B), 1041.

Marshall, W. A., & Tanner, J. M. (1970). Variations in the pattern of pubertal changes in boys. *Archives of Disease in Childhood, 45,* 13–23.

Martin, G. A., McNair, D., & Hight, W. (1988). Contributing factors to early premature termination at a college counseling center. *Journal of Counseling and Development, 66,* 233–236.

Martin, G. A., & Pear, J. (1988). *Behavior modification: What it is and how to do it.* Englewood Cliffs, NJ: Prentice-Hall.

Martin, J. A., & Elmer, E. (1992). Battered children grown up: A follow-up study of individuals severely maltreated as children. *Child Abuse and Neglect, 16,* 75–87.

Masi, D. A., & Friedland, S. J. (1988). EAP: Actions and options. *Personnel Journal, 67,* 60–67.

Maslow, A. H. (1962). *Toward a psychology of being.* Princeton, NJ: Van Nostrand-Reinhold.

Maslow, A. H. (1970). *Motivation and personality* (2nd ed.). New York: Harper & Row.

Massaro, D. W. (1988). Some criticisms of connectionist models of human performance. *Journal of Memory & Language, 27,* 213–234.

Massaro, D. W., Taylor, G. A., Venezky, R. L., Jastrzembski, J. E., & Lucas, P. A. (1980). *Letter and word perception.* New York: North-Holland.

Massey, C., & Gelman, R. (1988). Preschoolers' ability to decide whether a photographed unfamiliar object can move itself. *Developmental Psychology, 24,* 307–317.

Masson, J. (1984). *The assault on truth: Freud's suppression of the seduction theory.* New York: Farrar, Straus, & Giroux.

Masters, J. C., Burish, T. G., Hollon, S. D., & Rimm, D. C. (1987). *Behavior therapy: Techniques and empirical findings.* San Diego: Harcourt Brace Jovanovich.

Masters, W. H., & Johnson, V. E. (1979). *Homosexuality in perspective.* Boston: Little, Brown.

Matarazzo, J. D. (1984). Behavior immunogens and pathogens in health and illness. In B. L. Hammonds & C. J. Scheirer (Eds.), *Psychology and health: The master lecture series* (Vol. 3). Washington, DC: American Psychological Association.

Matlin, A., & Foley, M. A. (1992). *Sensation and perception.* Needham Heights, MA: Allyn & Bacon.

Matlin, M. (1983). *Cognition.* New York: Holt, Rinehart, & Winston.

Matlin, M. (1988). *Sensation and perception* (2nd ed.). Boston: Allyn & Bacon.

Matsumoto, K., & Morita, Y. (1987). Effects of nighttime nap and age on sleep patterns of shift workers. *Sleep, 10,* 580–589.

Matthews, K. A. (1982). Psychological perspectives on the Type A behavior pattern. *Psychological Bulletin, 91,* 293–323.

Matthews, R. W., Paulus, P. B., & Baron, R. A. (1979). Physical aggression after being crowded. *Journal of Nonverbal Behavior, 4,* 5–17.

Mauro, R. R., & Costa, P. T. (1991). The NEO Personality Inventory: Using the five-factor model in counseling. *Journal of Counseling and Development, 69*(4), 367–372.

Mauro, R., Sato, K. & Tucker, J. (1992). The role of appraisal in human emotions: A cross-cultural study. *Journal of Personality and Social Psychology, 62,* 301–317.

May, D. N. (1978). Basic subjective responses to noise. In D. N. May (Ed.), *Handbook of noise assessment.* New York: Van Nostrand-Reinhold.

Mayes, A. R. (1988). *Human organic memory disorders*. New York: Cambridge University Press.

Mazur, J. E. (1990). *Learning and behavior*. Englewood Cliffs, NJ: Prentice-Hall.

McAdams, D. (1988). Biography, narrative, and lives: An introduction. *Journal of Personality, 56,* 1–18.

McBurney, D. H., & Collings, V. B. (1984). *Introduction to sensation and perception*. Englewood Cliffs, NJ: Prentice-Hall.

McCartney, K., Harris, M. J., & Bernieri, F. (1990). Growing up and growing apart: A developmental meta-analysis of twin studies. *Psychological Bulletin, 107,* 226–237.

McClelland, D. C. (1961). *The achieving society*. New York: Van Nostrand-Reinhold.

McClelland, D. C. (1985a). How do motives, skills, and values determine what people do? *American Psychologist, 40,* 812–825.

McClelland, D. C. (1985b). *Human motivation*. Glenview, IL: Scott, Foresman.

McCloskey, M. (1983). Intuitive physics. *Scientific American, 248*(4), 122–130.

McCloskey, M., Wible, C. G., & Cohen, N. J. (1988). Is there a special flashbulb-memory mechanism? *Journal of Experimental Psychology: General, 117,* 171–181.

McCormick, D. A., & Thompson, R. F. (1984). Cerebellum: Essential involvement in classically conditioned eyelid response. *Science, 223,* 296–298.

McCrae, R. R. (1984). Situational determinants of coping responses: Loss, threat, and challenge. *Journal of Personality and Social Psychology, 46,* 919–928.

McCready, D. (1986). Moon illusions redescribed. *Perception and Psychophysics, 39,* 64–72.

McDowd, J. M., & Craik, F. I. M. (1988). Effects of aging and task difficulty on divided attention performance. *Journal of Experimental Psychology: Human Perception and Performance, 14,* 267–280.

McEvoy, G. M., & Beatty, R. W. (1989). Assessment centers and subordinate appraisals of managers: A seven-year examination of predictive validity. *Personnel Psychology, 42,* 37–52.

McEwan, N. H., & Yuille, J. C. (1981). *The effects of training and experience on eyewitness testimony*. Paper presented at the meeting of the Canadian Psychological Association.

McGaugh, J. L. (1989). Involvement of hormonal and neuromodulatory systems in the regulation of memory storage. *Annual Review of Neuroscience, 12,* 255–288.

McGlashan, T. H. (1984). The Chestnut Lodge follow-up study: 2. Long-term outcome of schizophrenia and the affective disorders. *Archives of General Psychiatry, 41,* 586–601.

McGlashan, T. H. (1988). Adolescent versus adult onset of mania. *American Journal of Psychiatry, 145,* 221–223.

McGrath, J. E., & Kravitz, D. A. (1982). Group research. *Annual Review of Psychology, 33,* 195–230.

McGregor, D. (1960). *The human side of enterprise*. New York: McGraw-Hill.

McGuire, W. (Ed.). (1974). *The Freud/Jung letters: The correspondence between Sigmund Freud and C. G. Jung* (R. Manheim & R. F. C. Hull, Trans.), Princeton, NJ: Princeton University Press.

McKim, W. A. (1991). *Drugs and behavior: An introduction to behavioral pharmacology*. Englewood Cliffs, NJ: Prentice-Hall.

McKoon, G., Ratcliffe, R., & Dell, G. S. (1986). A critical evaluation of the semantic-episodic distinction. *Journal of Experimental Psychology: Learning, Memory, and Cognition, 12,* 295–306.

McLoyd, V. C. (1990). The impact of economic hardship on black families and children: Psychological distress, parenting, and socioemotional development. *Child Development, 61,* 311–346.

McLuhan, T. C. (1971). *Touch the earth*. New York: Promontory Press.

McNally, R. J. (1987). Preparedness and phobias: A review. *Psychological Bulletin, 101,* 283–303.

McNally, R. J. (1990). Psychological approaches to panic disorder: A review. *Psychological Bulletin, 108,* 403–419.

McNamara, C. G., Davidson, E. S., and Schenk, S. (1993). A comparison of the motor activating effects of acute and chronic exposure to amphetamine and methylphenidate. *Pharmacology, Biochemistry, & Behavior, 21,* 234–239.

Meacham, J. A., & Santilli, N. R. (1982). Interstage relationships in Erikson's theory: Identity and intimacy. *Child Development, 53,* 1461–1467.

Mead, M. (1974). On Freud's view of female psychology. In J. Strouse (Ed.), *Women and analysis: Dialogues on psychoanalytic views of femininity*. New York: Dell.

Medin, D. L., & Smith, E. E. (1984). Concepts and concept formation. *Annual Review of Psychology, 35,* 113–138.

Mednick, S. A., Gabrielli, W. F., & Hutchings, B. (1984). Genetic influences in criminal convictions: Evidence from an adoption cohort. *Science, 224,* 891–894.

Mednick, S. A., & Mednick, M. T. (1967). *Remote Associates Test*. Boston: Houghton-Mifflin.

Meeker, M. (1985). Toward a psychology of giftedness: A concept in search of measurement. In B. B. Wolman (Ed.), *Handbook of intelligence: Theories, measurements, and applications* (pp. 787–799). New York: Wiley.

Meichenbaum, D. H. (1977). *Cognitive behavior modification: An integrative approach*. New York: Plenum.

Meichenbaum, D. H., & Cameron, R. (1983). Stress inoculation training: Toward a general paradigm for training coping skills. In D. Meichenbaum & M. E. Jaremko (Eds.), *Stress reduction and prevention*. New York: Plenum.

Meichenbaum, D. H., & Novaco, R. (1978). Stress inoculation: A preventive approach. In C. D. Spielberger & I. G. Sarason (Eds.), *Stress and anxiety* (Vol. 5, pp. 317–330). New York: Wiley.

Melton, G. B., & Davidson, H. A. (1987). Child protection and society: When should the state intervene? *American Psychologist, 42,* 172–175.

Melton, G. B., & Garrison, E. (1987). Fear, prejudice, and neglect: Discrimination against mentally disabled persons. *American Psychologist, 42,* 1007–1026.

Melton, G. B., & Wilcox, B. L. (1989). Changes in family law and family life: Challenges for psychology. *American Psychologist, 44,* 1213–1216.

Meltzoff, A. N., & Moore, M. K. (1983). Newborn infants imitate adult facial gestures. *Child Development, 54,* 702–709.

Melzack, R., & Wall, P. D. (1965). Pain mechanisms: A new theory. *Science, 150,* 971–979.

Melzack, R., & Wall, P. D. (1988). *The challenge of pain*. New York: Penguin.

Merikangas, K. R., Leckman, J. F., Prusoff, B. A., Pauls, D., & Weissman, M. M. (1985). Familial transmission of depression and alcoholism. *Archives of General Psychiatry, 42,* 367–372.

Meshberger, F. L. (1990). An interpretation of Michelangelo's creation of Adam based on neuroanatomy. *JAMA, Journal of the American Medical Association, 264,* 1837–1840.

Mesulam, M.-M., Muffson, E. J., Levey, A. I., & Wainer, B. H. (1983). Alzheimer's disease and the cholinergic innervation of neocortex by the nucleus basalis of Meynert. *Banbury Reports, 15,* 79–93.

Metcalfe, J. (1986). Feeling of knowing in memory and problem solving. *Journal of Experimental Psychology: Learning, Memory, and Cognition, 12,* 288–294.

Metcalfe, J., & Wiebe, D. (1987). Intuition in insight and non-insight problem solving. *Memory and Cognition, 15,* 238–246.

Michaels, C. F. (1986). An ecological analysis of binocular vision. *Psychological Research, 48,* 1–22.

Miele, F. (1979). Cultural bias in the WISC. *Intelligence, 3,* 149–164.

Miklowitz, D. J., Strachan, A. M., Goldstein, M. J., Doane, J. A., Snyder, K. S., Hogarty, G. E., & Falloon, I. R. (1986). Expressed emotion and communication deviance in the families of schizophrenics. *Journal of Abnormal Psychology, 95*, 60–66.

Milgram, S. (1974). *Obedience to authority*. New York: Harper & Row.

Millar, J. M., & Whitaker, H. A. (1983). The right hemisphere's contribution to language: A review of the evidence from brain-damaged subjects. In S. Sagalowitz (Ed.), *Language function and brain organization*. New York: Academic Press.

Miller, B. C., McCoy, J. K., Olson, T. D., & Wallace, C. M. (1986). Parental discipline and control attempts in relation to adolescent sexual attitudes and behavior. *Journal of Marriage and the Family, 48*, 503–512.

Miller, B. C., & Moore, K. A. (1990). Adolescent sexual behavior, pregnancy, and parenting: Research through the 1980s. *Journal of Marriage and the Family, 52*, 1025–1044.

Miller, D., & Dröge, C. (1986). Psychological and traditional determinants of structure. *Administrative Science Quarterly, 31*, 539–560.

Miller, G. A. (1956). The magic number seven, plus or minus two: Some limits of our capacity for processing information. *Psychological Review, 63*, 81–97.

Miller, G. A. (1981). *Language and speech*. San Francisco: Freeman.

Miller, G. A., & Gildea, P. M. (1987). How children learn words. *Scientific American, 257*, 94–99.

Miller, J. D., Cisin, I. H., Gardner-Deaton, H., Harrello, A. V., Wirtz, P. W., Abelson, H. I., & Fishburne, P. M. (1982). *National survey on drug abuse: Main findings*. Rockville, MD: National Institute on Drug Abuse.

Miller, L. B., & Dyer, L. J. (1975). Four preschool programs: Their dimensions and effects. *Monographs of the Society for Research in Child Development, 40*(5–6, Serial No. 162).

Miller, L. M. (1978). *Behavior management: The new science of managing people at work*. New York: Wiley.

Miller, M. V. (1990). Toward a psychology of the unknown. *Twelfth Annual Conference on the Theory and Practice of Gestalt Therapy: Gestalt Journal, 13*, 23–41.

Miller, N. E. (1985). The value of behavioral research on animals. *American Psychologist, 40*, 423–440.

Miller, N. E., & Carmona, A. (1967). Modification of a visceral response, salivation in thirsty dogs, by instrumental training with water reward. *Journal of Comparative and Physiological Psychology, 63*, 1–6.

Miller, N. S., Giannini, A. J., Gold, M. S., & Philomena, J. A. (1990). *Journal of Substance Abuse Treatment, 7*(4), 239–244.

Miller, P. A., & Eisenberg, N. (1988). The relation of empathy to aggressive and externalizing/antisocial behavior. *Psychological Bulletin, 103*, 324–344.

Miller, S. (1986). Certainty and necessity in the understanding of Piagetian concepts. *Developmental Psychology, 22*, 3–18.

Miller, T. R., Scott, R., & Searight, H. (1990). Ethics for marital and family therapy and subsequent training issues. *Family Therapy, 17*, 163–171.

Miller-Jones, D. (1989). Culture and testing. *American Psychologist, 44*, 360–366.

Millodot, M. (1982). Accommodation and refraction of the eye. In H. B. Barlow & J. D. Mollon (Eds.), *The senses*. London: Cambridge University Press.

Mindus, P., Bergström, K., Levander, S. E., Noren, G., et al. (1987). Magnetic resonance images related to clinical outcome after psychosurgical intervention in severe anxiety disorder. *Journal of Neurology, Neurosurgery and Psychiatry, 50*, 1288–1293.

Miner, J. B. (1984). The validity and usefulness of theories in an emerging organizational science. *Academy of Management Review, 9*, 296–306.

Mingay, D. J. (1987). The effects of hypnosis on eyewitness memory: Reconciling forensic claims and research findings. *Applied Psychology: An International Review, 36*, 163–183.

Mintzberg, H. (1983). *Power in and around organizations*. Englewood Cliffs, NJ: Prentice-Hall.

Mirande, A. M. (1968). Reference group theory and adolescent sexual behavior. *Journal of Marriage and the Family, 30*, 572–577.

Mischel, W., & Peake, P. K. (1982). Beyond *déjà vu* in the search for cross-situational consistency. *Psychology Review, 89*, 730–755.

Mishkin, M., Malamut, B., & Bechevalier, J. (1984). Memories and habits: Two neural systems. In G. Lynch, J. L. McGaugh, & N. M. Weinberger (Eds.), *Neurobiology of learning and memory*. New York: Guilford Press.

Mishra, S. (1983). Evidence of item bias in the verbal subtests of the WISC-R for Mexican-American children. *Journal of Psychological Assessment, 1*, 321–328.

Misiasek, J., Cork, R. C., Hameroff, S. R., Finley, J., & Weiss, J. L. (1984). The effects of electroconvulsive therapy on plasma ß-endorphin. *Biological Psychiatry, 19*, 451–455.

Moates, D. R., & Schumacher, G. M. (1980). *An introduction to cognitive psychology*. Belmont, CA: Wadsworth.

Mollon, J. D. (1982). Color vision and color blindness. In H. B. Barlow & J. D. Mollon (Eds.), *The senses*. London: Cambridge University Press.

Monahan, J., & Loftus, E. F. (1982). The psychology of law. *Annual Review of Psychology, 33*, 441–475.

Money, J. (1984). Paraphilias: Phenomenology and classification. *American Journal of Psychotherapy, 38*, 164–179.

Money, J. (1987). Sin, sickness, or status? Homosexual gender identity and psychoneuroendocrinology. *American Psychology, 42*, 384–399.

Monk, T. H., Moline, M. L., & Graeber, R. C. (1988). Inducing jet lag in the laboratory: Patterns of adjustment to an acute shift in routine. *Aviation Space and Environmental Medicine, 59*, 703–710.

Monmaney, T. (1987, September). Are we led by the nose? *Discovery*, pp. 48–54, 56.

Montemayor, R. (1982). The relationship between parent-adolescent conflict and the amount of time adolescents spend alone and with parents and peers. *Child Development, 53*, 1512–1519.

Mook, D. G. (1987). *Motivation: The organization of action*. New York: Norton.

Moore, S. M., & Barling, N. R. (1991). Developmental status and AIDS attitudes in adolescence. *Journal of Genetic Psychology, 152*, 5–16.

Moore, T. E. (1982). Subliminal advertising: What you see is what you get. *Journal of Marketing, 46*, 38–47.

Moore, T. E. (1985, July). Subliminal delusion. *Psychology Today*, pp. 10–11.

Moore, T. E. (1988). The case against subliminal manipulation. *Psychology and Marketing, 5*, 118–121.

Moore, V., & Callias, M. (1987). A systematic approach to teaching reading and spelling to a nine-year-old boy with severely impaired literacy skills. *Educational Psychology, 7*, 113–115.

Mor, V., McHorney, C., & Sherwood, S. (1986). Secondary morbidity among the recently bereaved. *American Journal of Psychiatry, 143*, 158–163.

Moran, J., & Desimone, R. (1985). Selective attention gates visual processing in the extrastriate cortex. *Science, 229*, 782–784.

Moray, N. (1969). *Attention: Selective processes in vision and hearing*. London: Hutchinson.

Moreland, K. L. (1990). Some observations on computer-assisted psychological testing. *Journal of Personality Assessment, 55*, 820–823.

Morgan, A. H. (1973). The heritability of hypnotic susceptibility in twins. *Journal of Abnormal Psychology, 82*, 55–61.

Morgan, D. C., & Murray, H. A. (1935). A method for investigating fantasies: The thematic apperception test. *Archives of Neurological Psychiatry, 34,* 289–306.

Morgan, W. P. (1985). Affective beneficence of vigorous physical activity. *Medicine and Science in Sports and Exercise, 17,* 94–100.

Morgan, W. P., and Rachlin, P. (1985). Exercise and psychotherapy. *Journal of Abnormal Psychology, 96,* 321–333.

Morin, S. F. (1988). AIDS: The challenge to psychology. *American Psychologist, 43,* 838–842.

Morison, P., & Masten, A. S. (1991). Peer reputation in middle childhood as a predictor of adaptation in adolescence: A seven-year follow-up. *Child Development, 62,* 991–1007.

Moscovici, S., Lage, E., & Naffrechoux, M. (1969). Influence of a consistent minority on the responses of a majority in a color perception task. *Sociometry, 32,* 365–380.

Moshman, D. (1977). Consolidation and stage formation in the emergence of formal operations. *Developmental Psychology, 13,* 95–100.

Moskowitz, D. (1986). Comparison of self-reports, reports by knowledgeable informants, and behavioral observation data. *Journal of Personality, 54,* 294–317.

Motowidlo, S. J., Packard, J. S., & Manning, M. R. (1986). Occupational stress: Its causes and consequences for job performance. *Journal of Applied Psychology, 71,* 618–629.

Moyer, R. S., & Bayer, R. H. (1976). Mental comparisons and the symbolic distance effects. *Cognitive Psychology, 8,* 228–246.

Muehlenhard, C., & Hollabaugh, L. (1988). Do women sometimes say no when they mean yes? The prevalence and correlates of women's token resistance to sex. *Journal of Personality and Social Psychology, 54,* 872–879.

Muench, G. A. (1963). A clinical psychologist's treatment of labor-management conflicts: A four-year study. *Journal of Humanistic Psychology, 1,* 92–97.

Mungy, G. (1982). *The power of minorities.* New York: Academic Press.

Murphy, K. R., Thornton, G. C., & Prue, K. (1991). Influence of job characteristics on the acceptability of employee drug testing. *Journal of Applied Psychology, 76*(3), 447–453.

Murray, A. M., & Mishra, S. (1983). Item bias in individually administered ability tests: Implications for nondiscrimination assessment. *Journal of Psychological Assessment, 1,* 353–366.

Murray, E. B., & Armstrong, S. L. (1978). Adult nonconservation of numerical

equivalence. *Merrill-Palmer Quarterly, 24,* 255–263.

Murray, G. F. (1984). The cannabis-cocaine connection: A comparative study of use and users. *Journal of Drug Issues, 14,* 665–675.

Murray, H. A. (1938). *Explorations in personality.* New York: Oxford University Press.

Myers, D. G. (1978). Polarizing effects of social comparison. *Journal of Experimental Social Psychology, 14,* 554–563.

Nadi, N. S., Nurnberger, J. I., & Gershon, E. S. (1984). Muscarinic cholinergic receptors on skin fibroblasts in familial affective disorder. *New England Journal of Medicine, 311,* 225–230.

Nairne, J. S., & Pusen, C. (1984). Serial recall of imagined voices. *Journal of Verbal Learning and Verbal Behavior, 23,* 331–342.

Naranjo, C., & Ornstein, R. E. (1977). *On the psychology of meditation.* New York: Penguin.

Nash, M. (1987). What, if anything, is regressed about hypnotic age regression? A review of the empirical literature. *Psychological Bulletin, 102,* 42–52.

Nathan, P. E., & Skinstad, A. H. (1987). Outcomes of treatment for alcohol problems: Current methods, problems, and results. *Journal of Consulting and Clinical Psychology, 55,* 332–340.

Nation, J. R., & Cooney, J. B. (1982). The time-course of extinction-induced aggressive behavior in humans: Evidence for a stage model of extinction. *Learning and Motivation, 13,* 95–112.

Nation, J. R., Grover, C. A., Salinas, J. A., Pugh, C. K., Peltier, R., Horger, B., & Bratton, G. R. (1991). Effects of cadmium on cocaine-induced changes in activity. *Behavioral Neuroscience, 105,* 998–1003.

National Center for Health Statistics. (1993). *Advance report of final mortality statistics, 1990, Monthly Vital Statistics Report No. 41*(7, Suppl.). Hyattsville, MD: Public Health Service.

National Institute of Mental Health (NIMH). (1982). *Television and behavior: Ten years of scientific progress and implications for the eighties: Vol. 1. Summary Report* (DHHS Publication No. ADM 82–1195). Washington, DC: U.S. Government Printing Office.

Natsoulas, T. (1981). Basic problems of consciousness. *Journal of Personality and Social Psychology, 41,* 132–178.

Natsoulas, T. (1983). Concepts of consciousness. *Journal of Mind and Behavior, 4,* 13–59.

Nauta, W. H., & Feirtag, M. (1979). The organization of the brain. *Scientific American, 241,* 88–111.

Nauta, W. H., & Feirtag, M. (1986). *Fundamental neuroanatomy.* New York: Freeman.

Neal, N. D. (1981, December). Mental imagery and relaxation in skill rehearsal. *Scholastic Coach,* pp. 48, 80.

Needleman, H. (1992, March 6, 8). Research on lead poisoning is questioned. *Wall Street Journal,* p. 8.

Neiner, A. G. (1985). Employee attitude surveys: Opinions and experiences of human resource executives. *TIP: The Industrial Psychologist, 22*(3), 44–48.

Neisser, U. (1984). Interpreting Harry Bahrick's discovery: What confers immunity against forgetting? *Journal of Experimental Psychology: General, 113,* 32–35.

Neisser, U. (1987). *Concepts and conceptual development: Ecological and intellectual factors in categorization.* New York: Cambridge University Press.

Neisser, U., & Becklen, R. (1975). Selective looking: Attending to visually significant events. *Cognitive Psychology, 7,* 480–494.

Neisser, U., Winograd, E., & Weldon, M. S. (1992, November). *Remembering the earthquake: "What I experienced" versus "How I heard the news."* Paper presented at the annual convention of the Psychonomic Society, San Francisco.

Nelson, D. L., Bajo, M. T., & Casanova, D. (1985). Prior knowledge and memory: The influence of natural category size as a function of intention and distraction. *Journal of Experimental Psychology: Learning, Memory, and Cognition, 11,* 94–105.

Nelson, D. L., & Friedrich, M. A. (1980). Encoding and cuing sounds and senses. *Journal of Experimental Psychology: Human Learning and Memory, 6,* 717–731.

Nelson, K. (1981). Individual differences in language development: Implications for development and language. *Developmental Psychology, 17,* 170–187.

Nelson, K., & Gruendel, J. (1979). At morning it's lunchtime: A scriptal view of children's dialogues. *Discourse Processes, 2,* 73–94.

Nemeroff, C., & Bissette, G. (1986). Neuropeptides in psychiatric disorders. In P. A. Beyer, K. H. Brodie & S. Arieti (Eds.), *American handbook of psychiatry: Biological psychiatry* (2nd ed., Vol. 8, pp. 64–110). New York: Basic Books.

Nemeth, C. J. (1992). Minority dissent as a stimulant to group performance. In S. Worchel, W. Wood, & J. A. Simpson (Eds.), *Group process and productivity.* Newbury Park, CA: Sage.

Nemeth, C. J., & Wachtler, J. (1974). Creating perceptions of consistency and confidence: A necessary condition for minority influence. *Sociometry, 37,* 529–540.

Nemeth, C. J., Wachtler, J., & Endicott, J. (1977). Increasing the size of a minority: Some gains and some losses. *European Journal of Social Psychology, 7,* 15–27.

Neugarten, B. L., Wood, V., Kraines, R. J., & Loomis, B. (1963). Women's attitudes toward the menopause. *Vita Humana, 6,* 140–151.

Newcomb, M. D., & Bentler, P. M. (1986). Loneliness and social support: A confirmatory hierarchical analysis. *Personality and Social Psychology Bulletin, 12,* 520–535.

Newcomb, T. M. (1966). The general nature of peer-group influence. In T. M. Newcomb & E. K. Wilson (Eds.), *College peer groups: Problems and prospects for research.* Chicago: Aldine.

Newell, A., Shaw, J. C., & Simon, H. A. (1962). The processes of creative thinking. In H. E. Gruber, G. Terrell, & M. Wertheimer (Eds.), *Contemporary approaches to creative thinking.* New York: Atherton.

Newman, J. E., & Beehr, T. A. (1979). Personal and organizational strategies for handling job stress: A review of research and opinion. *Personnel Psychology, 32,* 1–43.

New York Graphic Society. (1959). *The complete letters of Vincent Van Gogh* (Vols. 1–3). Greenwich, CT: Author.

Ninio, A., & Rinott, N. (1988). Fathers' involvement in the care of their infants and their attributions of cognitive competence to infants. *Child Development, 59,* 652–663.

Noble, E. P., & Blum, K. (1992). A controversial alcohol gene. *JAMA, Journal of the American Medical Association, 264,* 811–819.

Nolen-Hoeksema, S. (1987). Sex differences in unipolar depression: Evidence and theory. *Psychological Bulletin, 101,* 259–282.

Norcross, J. C. (1987). A rational and empirical analysis of existential psychotherapy. *Journal of Humanistic Psychology, 27,* 41–68.

Norman, D. A. (1976). *Memory and attention: An introduction to human information processing* (2nd ed.). New York: Wiley.

Norman, W. T. (1963). Toward an adequate taxonomy of personality attributes: Replicated factor structure in peer nomination personality ratings. *Journal of Abnormal and Social Psychology, 66,* 574–583.

Normand, J., Salyards, S. D., & Mahoney, J. J. (1990). An evaluation of preemployment drug-testing. *Journal of Applied Psychology, 75*(6), 629–639.

Notz, W. W. (1975). Work motivation and the negative effects of extrinsic rewards. *American Psychologist, 30,* 884–891.

Novaco, R. (1977). A stress-inoculation approach to anger management in the training of law enforcement officers. *American Journal of Community Psychology, 5,* 327–346.

Oatley, K., & Bolton, W. (1985). A social-cognitive theory of depression in reaction to life events. *Psychological Review, 92,* 372–388.

O'Hara, K., Johnson, C. M., & Beehr, T. A. (1985). Organizational behavioral management: A review of empirical research and recommendations for further investigations. *Academy of Management Review, 10,* 848–864.

O'Leary, E., & Page, R. (1990). An evaluation of a person-centered Gestalt group using the semantic differential. *Counseling Psychology Quarterly, 3,* 13–20.

Oltmanns, T., Neale, J., & Davison, G. (1986). *Case studies in abnormal psychology* (2nd ed.). New York: Wiley.

Olton, R. M. (1979). Experimental studies of incubation: Searching for the elusive. *Journal of Creative Behavior, 13,* 9–22.

Orne, M. T. (1966). Mechanisms of post-hypnotic amnesia. *International Journal of Clinical and Experimental Hypnosis, 14,* 121–134.

Osborn, A. F. (1963). *Applied imagination* (3rd ed.). New York: Scribner's.

Owen, S. R., Halford, J. R., & Gilbert, R. (1986). Kicking the habit. *Life Sciences, 29,* 64–73.

Paikoff, R. L., & Brooks-Gunn, J. (1991). Do parent-child relationships change during puberty? *Psychological Bulletin, 110,* 47–66.

Paivio, A. (1971). *Imagery and verbal processes.* New York: Holt, Rinehart, & Winston.

Paivio, A. (1980). On weighing things in your mind. In P. W. Jusczyk & R. M. Klein (Eds.), *The nature of thought: Essays in honor of D. O. Hebb* (pp. 133–154). Hillsdale, NJ: Erlbaum.

Palmer, S., Schreiber, C., & Fox, C. (1991, November). *Remembering the earthquake: "Flashbulb" memory for experienced versus reported events.* Paper presented at the annual convention of the Psychonomic Society, San Francisco.

Papez, J. W. (1937). A proposed mechanism of emotion. *Archives of Neurology and Psychiatry, 38,* 725–743.

Parry, G., & Brewin, C. R. (1988). Cognitive style and depression: Symptom-related, event-related or independent provoking factor. *British Journal of Clinical Psychology, 27,* 25–35.

Parten, M. B. (1932). Social participation among preschool children. *Journal of Abnormal and Social Psychology, 27,* 243–269.

Paunonen, S. V., Jackson, D. N., Trzebinski, J., & Forsterling, F. (1992). Personality

structure across cultures: A multimethod evaluation. *Journal of Personality and Social Psychology, 62,* 447–456.

Pavlov, I. P. (1927). *Conditioned reflexes.* New York: Oxford University Press.

Peacock, B., Glube, R., Miller, M., & Clune, P. (1983). Police officers' responses to 8- and 12-hour-shift schedules. *Ergonomics, 26,* 479–493.

Pedersen, N. L., Plomin, R., McClearn, G. E., & Friberg, L. (1988). Neuroticism, extraversion, and related traits in adult twins reared apart and reared together. *Journal of Personality and Social Psychology, 55,* 950–957.

Peplau, L. A., Miceli, M., & Morasch, B. (1982). Loneliness and self-evaluation. In L. A. Peplau & D. Perlman (Eds.), *Loneliness: A sourcebook of current theory, research and therapy.* New York: Wiley.

Peplau, L. A., & Perlman, D. (1982). Perspectives on loneliness. In L. A. Peplau & D. Perlman (Eds.), *Loneliness: A sourcebook of current theory, research and therapy* (pp. 1–18). New York: Wiley.

Peplau, L. A., Rubin, Z., & Hill, C. T. (1977). Sexual intimacy in dating relationships. *Journal of Social Issues, 33,* 86–109.

Peplau, L. A., Russell, D., & Heim, M. (1982). An attributional analysis of loneliness. In I. H. Frieze, D. Bar-tal, & J. Carroll (Eds.), *Attributional theory: Applications to social problems.* New York: Jossey-Bass.

Peretz, D. (1970). Reaction to loss. In B. Schoenberg, A. C. Carr, D. Peretz, & A. H. Kutscher (Eds.), *Loss and grief: Psychological management in medical practice.* New York: Columbia University Press.

Perlman, D., & Peplau, L. A. (1981). Toward a social psychology of loneliness. In S. Duck & R. Gilmour (Eds.), *Personal relationships: 3. Personal relationships in disorder.* New York: Academic Press.

Perlman, T., Loper, M., & Tillery, L. (1990). Should psychiatrists administer anesthesia for ECT? *American Journal of Psychiatry, 147,* 1553–1556.

Perls, F. S. (1969). *Gestalt therapy verbatim.* Lafayette, CA: Real People Press.

Pervin, L. A. (1985). Personality: Current controversies, issues, and directions. *Annual Review of Psychology, 36,* 83–114.

Peters, T., & Austin, N. (1985). *A passion for excellence.* New York: Random House.

Petersen, A. (1988). Adolescent development. *Annual Review of Psychology, 39,* 583–607.

Peterson, C. C., & Murphy, L. (1990). Adolescents' thoughts and feelings about AIDS in relation to cognitive maturity. *Journal of Adolescence, 13,* 185–187.

Peterson, C. C., & Seligman, M. E. P. (1984). Causal explanations as a risk factor for depression: Theory and evidence. *Psychological Review, 91,* 347–374.

Peterson, D. I., Price, M. L., & Small, C. S. (1988). Autopsy findings in a patient that had an adrenal-to-brain transplant for Parkinson's disease. *Neurology, 39,* 144.

Peterson, L. R., & Peterson, M. J. (1959). Short-term retention with individual verbal items. *Journal of Experimental Psychology, 58,* 193–198.

Peterson, S. E., Fox, P. T., Posner, M., Mintun, M., & Raichle, M. E. (1988). Positron emission tomographic studies of the cortical anatomy of single-word processing. *Nature (London), 331,* 585–589.

Pettigrew, T. F. (1969). Racially separate or together? *Journal of Social Issues, 25,* 43–69.

Petty, M. M., McGee, G. W., & Cavender, J. W. (1984). A meta-analysis of the relationships between individual job satisfaction and individual performance. *Academy of Management Review, 9,* 712–721.

Petty, R. E., & Cacioppo, J. T. (1981). *Attitudes and persuasion: Classic and contemporary approaches.* Dubuque, IA: W. C. Brown.

Pfefferbaum, A., Rosenbloom, M. Crusan, K., & Jermigan, T. L. (1988). Brain CT changes in alcoholics: Effects of age and alcohol consumption. *Alcoholism: Clinical and Experimental Research, 12,* 81–87.

Piaget, J. (1952). *The origins of intelligence in children* (M. Cook, Trans.). New York: International Universities Press.

Piaget, J. (1965). *The child's conception of the world.* (J. Tomlinson & A. Tomlinson, Trans.). New York: Norton. (Original work published 1929).

Piaget, J. (1967). *Six psychological studies* (A. Tenzer, Trans.). New York: Vintage. (Original work published 1964).

Piaget, J. (1972). Intellectual evolution from adolescence to adulthood. *Human Development, 15,* 1–12.

Piaget, J., & Inhelder, B. (1967). *The child's conception of space.* (F. J. Langdon & J. L. Lunzer, Trans.). New York: Norton. (Original work published 1948).

Piotrowski, C., & Keller, J. W. (1984). Psychodiagnostic testing in APA-approved clinical psychology programs. *Professional Psychology: Research and Practice, 15,* 450–456.

Pittenger, D. J., Pavlik, W. B., Flora, S. R., & Kontos, J. M. (1988). The persistence of learned behaviors in humans as a function of changes in reinforcement schedule and response. *Learning and Motivation, 19,* 300–316.

Plomin, R., McClearn, G. E., Pedersen, N. L., Nesselroade, J. R., & Bergeman, C. S. (1988). Genetic influence on childhood family environment perceived retrospectively from the last half of the life span. *Research on Aging, 10,* 220–234.

Plug, C., & Ross, H. E. (1989). Historical review. In M. Hershenson (Ed.), *The moon illusion* (pp. 5–27). Hillsdale, NJ: Erlbaum.

Pohorecky, L. A. (1991). Stress and alcohol interaction: An update of human research. *Alcoholism: Clinical and Experimental Research, 15,* 438–459.

Pokorny, A. D. (1964). Suicide rates and various psychiatric disorders. *Journal of Nervous and Mental Disease, 139,* 499–506.

Pola, J., & Matin, L. (1977). Eye movements following autokinesis. *Bulletin of the Psychonomic Society, 10,* 397–398.

Pollack, J. R. (1991). Narcolepsy and its determinants. *Journal of Abnormal Psychology, 51,* 456–461.

Pollak, C. P. (1989). Biological rhythms and narcolepsy. *Narcolepsy: Third International Symposium.* Oak Park, IL: Matrix Communications.

Pomerleau, O. R. (1980). Why people smoke: Current psychobiological models. In P. O. Davidson & S. M. Davidson (Eds.), *Behavioral medicine: Changing health life-styles.* New York: Brunner/Mazel.

Pomerleau, O. R., & Rodin, J. (1986). Behavioral medicine and health psychology. In S. L. Garfield & A. E. Bergin (Eds.), *Handbook of psychotherapy and behavior change.* New York: Wiley.

Pool, R. (1989). Illuminating jet lag. *Science News, 244,* 1256–1257.

Popkin, A. J., Schaie, K. W., & Krauss, I. K. (1983). Age-fair assessment of psychometric intelligence. *Educational Gerontology, 9,* 47–55.

Porter, R. H., Balogh, R. D., Cernoch, J. M. & Franchi, C. (1986). Recognition of kin through characteristic body odors. *Chemical Senses, 11,* 389–395.

Posner, M. I. (1973). *Cognition: An introduction.* Glenview, IL: Scott, Foresman.

Powley, T. (1977). The ventromedial hypothalamic syndrome, satiety, and a cephalic phase hypothesis. *Psychological Review, 84,* 89–126.

Poyatos, F. (1983). *New perspectives in nonverbal communication.* New York: Pergamon.

Premack, A. J., & Premack, D. (1972). Teaching language to an ape. *Scientific American, 227*(4), 92–99.

Premack, D. (1962). Reversibility of the reinforcement relation. *Science, 136,* 235–237.

Premack, D., & Premack, A. J. (1983). *The mind of an ape.* New York: Norton.

Press, G. A., Amaral, D. G., & Squire, L. R. (1989). Hippocampal abnormalities in amnesic patients revealed by high resolution MRI. *Nature (London), 341,* 54–57.

Pressley, M., McDaniel, M. A., Turnure, J. E., Wood, E., & Ahmad, M. (1987). Generation and precision of elaboration: Effects on intentional and incidental learning. *Journal of Experimental Psychology: Learning, Memory, and Cognition, 13,* 291–300.

Price, D. L., Whitehouse, P. J., & Struble, R. G. (1985). Alzheimer's disease. *Annual Review of Medicine, 36,* 349–356.

Price, J. L., & Mueller, C. W. (1986). *Handbook of organizational measurement.* Marshfield, MA: Pitman.

Prien, E. P. (1977). The function of job analysis in content validation. *Personnel Psychology, 30,* 167–174.

Prien, R. F. (1980). Predicting lithium responders and nonresponders: Illness indicators. In F. N. Johnson (Ed.), *Handbook of lithium therapy.* Lancaster, England: MTP Press.

Principe, J. C., & Smith, J. R. (1982). Sleep spindle characteristics as a function of age. *Sleep, 5,* 73–84.

Quadagno, J. S., & Hardy, M. (1991). Regulating retirement through the age discrimination in employment act. *Research on Aging, 13,* 470–475.

Quadrel, M. J., Fischoff, B., & Davis, W. (1993). Adolescent (in)vulnerability. *American Psychologist, 48,* 102–116.

Qualls, P. J., & Sheehan, P. W. (1981). Electromyograph biofeedback as a relaxation technique: A critical appraisal and reassessment. *Psychological Bulletin, 90,* 21–42.

Quinn, K. M. (1986). Competency to be a witness: A major child forensic issue. *Bulletin of the American Academy of Psychiatry and the Law, 14,* 311–321.

Rados, R., & Cartwright, R. D. (1982). Where do dreams come from? A comparison of presleep and REM sleep thematic content. *Journal of Abnormal Psychology, 19,* 433–436.

Ragland, D. R., & Brand, R. J. (1988). Type A behavior and mortality from coronary heart disease. *New England Journal of Medicine, 318*(2), 65–69.

Raglin, J. S., & Morgan, W. P. (1985). Influence of vigorous exercise on mood state. *Behavior Therapist, 8,* 179–183.

Rahe, R. H. (1975). Life changes and near-future illness reports. In L. Levi (Ed.), *Emotions—Their parameters and measurement* (pp. 511–529). New York: Raven Press.

Rainville, R. E. (1988). *Dreams across the life span.* Boston: American Press.

Rajecki, D. W. (1982). *Attitudes: Themes and advances.* Sunderland, MA: Sinauer.

Ramachandran, V., & Anstis, S. M. (1986). The perception of apparent motion. *Scientific American, 254,* 102–109.

Randi, J. (1980). *Flim-flam: The truth about unicorns, parapsychology, and other delusions.* New York: Lippincott.

Raps, C. S., Peterson, C., Reinhard, K. E., Abramson, L. Y., & Seligman, M. E. P. (1982). Attributional style among depressed patients. *Journal of Abnormal Psychology, 91*, 102–108.

Ratcliffe, R., & McKoon, G. (1986). More on the distinction between episodic and semantic memories. *Journal of Experimental Psychology: Learning, Memory, and Cognition, 12*, 312–313.

Ratner, H., Schell, D., Crimmins, A., Mittelman, D., & Baldinelli, L. (1987). Changes in adult's prose recall: Aging or cognitive demands. *Developmental Psychology, 23*, 521–525.

Rauschenberg, J. M., & Schmidt, F. L. (1987). Measuring the economic impact of human resource programs. *Journal of Business and Psychology, 2*, 50–59.

Raven, B. H. (1990). Political applications of the psychology of interpersonal influence and social power. *Political Psychology, 11*(3), 493–520.

Ray, O. S., & Ksir, C. (1993). *Drugs, society and human behavior* (6th ed.). St. Louis, MO: Mosby.

Raz, S., & Raz, N. (1990). Structural brain abnormalities in the major psychoses: A quantitative review of the evidence from computerized imaging. *Psychological Bulletin, 108*, 93–108.

Reason, J., & Mycielska, K. (1982). *Absent minded? The psychology of mental lapses and everyday errors.* Englewood Cliffs, NJ: Prentice-Hall.

Rechtschaffen, A., Gilliland, M. A., Bergmann, B. M., & Winter, J. B. (1983). Physiological correlates of prolonged sleep deprivation in rats. *Science, 221*, 182–184.

Rechtschaffen, A., & Kales, A. (Eds.). (1968). *The manual of standardized terminology techniques and scoring system for sleep stages of human subjects.* Washington, DC: National Institute of Mental Health.

Reddy, N., & Reddy, S. (1986). A scale to measure the attitude of rural people towards adoption of poultry farming. *Asian Journal of Psychology and Education, 17*, 12–17.

Redington, N. (1987). *Identifying and helping children with dyslexia.* New York: Macmillan.

Reed, J. G., & Baxter, P. M. (1983). *Library use: A handbook for psychology.* Washington, DC: American Psychological Association.

Regier, D. A., Boyd, J. H., Burke, J. D., Rae, D. S., Myers, J. K., Kramer, M., Robbins, L. N., George, L. K., Karno, M., & Locke, B. Z. (1988). One-month prevalence of mental disorders in the United States. *Archives of General Psychiatry, 45*, 977–986.

Regoli, B., Crank, J. P., & Rivera, G. F. (1990). The construction and imple-

mentation of an alternative measure of police cynicism. *Criminal Justice and Behavior, 17*, 395–409.

Reidy, T. J., Anderegg, T. R., Tracy, R. J., & Cotler, S. (1980). Abused and neglected children: The cognitive, social, and behavioral correlates. In G. J. Williams & J. Money (Eds.), *Traumatic abuse and neglect of children at home.* Baltimore: Johns Hopkins University Press.

Reiman, E. M., Raichle, M. E., Butler, F. K., Herscovitch, P., & Robins, E. (1984). A focal brain abnormality in panic disorder, a severe form of anxiety. *Nature (London), 310*, 683–685.

Reinisch, J. M. (1981). Prenatal exposure to synthetic progestins increases potential for aggression in humans. *Science, 211*, 1171–1173.

Reinsel, R., Wollman, M., & Antrobus, J. S. (1984). Bizarreness: A function of report length in waking, REM and stage-2 reports. *Sleep Research, 13*, 105.

Reisenzein, R. (1983). The Schachter theory of emotion: Two decades later. *Psychological Bulletin, 94*, 239–264.

Reiser, M. (1988). Are psychiatric educators "losing the mind"? *American Journal of Psychiatry, 145*, 148–153.

Rescorla, R. A. (1988). Pavlovian conditioning: It's not what you think. *American Psychologist, 43*, 151–160.

Rescorla, R. A., & Wagner, A. R. (1972). A theory of Pavlovian conditioning: Variations in the effectiveness of reinforcement and non-reinforcement. In A. H. Black & W. F. Prokasy (Eds.), *Classical conditioning II.* New York: Appleton-Century-Crofts.

Reynolds, C., Chastain, R., Kaufman, A., & McLean, J. (1987). Demographic characteristics and IQ among adults: Analysis of the WAIS-R standardization sample as a function of the stratification variables. *Journal of School Psychology, 25*, 323–342.

Reynolds, R. I., & Takooshian, H. (1988). Where were you August 8, 1985? *Bulletin of the Psychonomic Society, 26*, 23–25.

Ricci, L. C., & Wellman, M. M. (1990). Monoamines. Biochemical markers of suicide? *Journal of Clinical Psychiatry, 46*, 106–116.

Riccio, D. C., & Richardson, R. (1984a). Memory retrieval deficits based upon altered contextual cues: A paradox. *Psychological Bulletin, 96*, 152–165.

Riccio, D. C., & Richardson, R. (1984b). The status of memory following experimentally induced amnesias: Gone but not forgotten. *Physiological Psychology, 12*, 59–72.

Rice, B. (1984, May). Imagination to go. *Psychology Today*, pp. 48–56.

Rice, D. M., Buchsbaum, M. S., Hardy, D., & Burgwald, L. (1991). Focal left tempo-

ral slow EEG activity is related to a verbal recent memory deficit in a nondemented elderly population. *Journal of Gerontology (Psychological Sciences), 46*, P144–P151.

Rice, D. M., Buchsbaum, M. S., Starr, A. Auslander, L., Hagman, J., & Evans, W. J. (1990). Abnormal EEG slow activity in left temporal areas in senile dementia of the Alzheimer type. *Journal of Gerontology (Medical Sciences), 45*, M145–M151.

Rich, C. L., Ricketts, J. E., Fowler, R. C., & Young, D. (1988). Some differences between men and women who commit suicide. *American Journal of Psychiatry, 145*, 718–722.

Richards, R. (1981). Relationships between creativity and psychopathology: An evaluation and interpretation of the evidence. *Genetic Psychology Monographs, 103*, 261–324.

Richardson, A., & Harris, L. (1986). Age trends in eidetikers. *Journal of Genetic Psychology, 147*, 303–308.

Richardson, D., Medvin, N., & Hammock, G. (1988). Love styles, relationship experience, and sensation seeking: A test of validity. *Personality and Individual Differences, 9*, 645–651.

Richardson, J. E. T. (1983). Mental imagery in thinking and problem solving. In J. S. T. Evans (Ed.), *Thinking and reasoning: Psychological approaches* (pp. 197–226). London: Routledge & Kegan Paul.

Richardson, L. W. (1981). *The dynamics of sex and gender: A sociological perspective* (2nd ed.). Boston: Houghton-Mifflin.

Richardson, M. A., Craig, T. J., & Haughland, G. (1985). Treatment patterns of young chronic schizophrenic patients in the era of deinstitutionalization. *Psychiatric Quarterly, 57*, 104–110.

Richardson-Klavehn, A., & Bjork, R. A. (1988). Measures of memory. *Annual Review of Psychology, 39*, 415–543.

Riggs, L. A. (1965). Electrophysiology of vision. In C. H. Graham (Ed.), *Vision and visual perception.* New York: Wiley.

Rimmer, S. M., & Myers, J. E. (1982). Testing and older persons: A new challenge for counselors. *Measurement and Evaluation in Guidance, 15*, 182–187.

Robbins, P. R., & Houshi, F. (1983). Some observations on recurrent dreams. *Bulletin of the Menninger Clinic, 47*, 262–265.

Robbins, S. (1990). *Organization theory: Structure, design, and applications.* Englewood Cliffs, NJ: Prentice-Hall.

Roberts, A. H. (1985). Biofeedback: Research, training, and clinical roles. *American Psychologist, 40*, 938–941.

Roberts, B. K., Done, W. B., and Crow, E. M. (1990). Displacement of symptoms following surgical intervention. *Archives of General Psychiatry, 47*, 89–96.

Robertson, C. M., Doran, B. B., Trimble, W. M., and Lees, L. G. (1990). A case history of Tourette syndrome: Surgical intervention. *Annual Review of Psychology, 41*, 123–134.

Rock, I. (1984). *Perception*. New York: Freeman.

Rock, I., & Kaufman, L. (1962). The moon illusion: 2. *Science, 136*, 1023–1031.

Rodin, J. (1981). Current status of the internal-external hypothesis of obesity: What went wrong? *American Psychologist, 36*, 361–372.

Rodin, J. (1986). Aging and health: Effects of the sense of control. *Science, 233*, 1271–1276.

Rodman, H., Pratto, D. J., & Nelson, R. S. (1985). Childcare arrangements and children's functioning: A comparison of self-care and adult-care children. *Developmental Psychology, 21*, 413–418.

Rodman, H., Pratto, D. J., & Nelson, R. (1988). Toward a definition of self-care children: A commentary on Steinberg (1986). *Developmental Psychology, 24*, 292–294.

Roe, A. (1952). A psychologist examines sixty-four eminent scientists. *Scientific American, 187*(5), 21–25.

Rogel, M. (1978). A critical evaluation of the possibility of higher primate reproductive and sexual pheromones. *Psychological Bulletin, 85*, 810–830.

Rogers, C. R. (1959). Toward a theory of creativity. In H. H. Anderson (Ed.), *Creativity and its cultivation*. New York: Harper & Row.

Rogers, C. R. (1961). *On becoming a person*. Boston: Houghton-Mifflin.

Rogers, C. R. (1967). A silent young man. In C. R. Rogers (Ed.), *The therapeutic relationship and its impact*. Madison: University of Wisconsin Press.

Rogers, C. R. (1986). Carl Rogers on the development of the person-centered approach. *Person-Centered Review, 1*, 257–259.

Rogers, R. W., & Deckner, C. W. (1975). Effects of fear appeals and physiological arousal upon emotion, attitudes and cigarette smoking. *Journal of Personality and Social Psychology, 32*, 225–230.

Roitblat, H. L. (1987). *Introduction to comparative cognition*. New York: Freeman.

Rollin, H. R. (1990). The dark before the dawn. *Journal of Psychopharmacology, 4*, 109–114.

Rorer, L. G., & Widiger, T. A. (1983). Personality structure and assessment. *Annual Review of Psychology, 34*, 431–463.

Rosch, E. (1973). On the internal structure of perceptual and semantic categories. In T. E. Moore (Ed.), *Cognitive develop-*

ment and the acquisition of language (pp. 111–144). New York: Academic Press.

Rosch, E., Mervis, C. B., Gray, W. D., Johnson, D. M., & Boyes-Braem, P. (1976). Basic objects in natural categories. *Cognitive Psychology, 8*, 382–439.

Roscoe, B., Diana, M. S., & Brooks, R. H. (1987). Early, middle, and late adolescents' views on dating and factors influencing partner selection. *Adolescence, 22*, 59–68.

Rosenberg, J., & Pettenati, H. M. (1984). Differential memory and unilateral ECT. *American Journal of Psychiatry, 141*, 1071–1074.

Rosenhan, D. L. (1973). On being sane in insane places. *Science, 179*, 250–258.

Rosenhan, D. L., & Seligman, M. E. P. (1989). *Abnormal psychology* (2nd ed.). New York: Norton.

Rosenkrantz, P., Vogel, S., Bee, H., Broverman, I., & Broverman, D. M. (1968). Sex-role stereotypes and self-concepts in college students. *Journal of Consulting and Clinical Psychology, 32*, 287–295.

Rosenthal, N. E., Sack, D. A., Carpenter, C. J., Parry, B. L., Mendelson, W. B., & Wehr, T. A. (1985). Antidepressant effects of light in seasonal affective disorder. *American Journal of Psychiatry, 142*, 163–170.

Rosenthal, R., & Jacobson, L. (1968). *Pygmalion in the classroom: Teacher expectations and pupils' intellectual development*. New York: Holt, Rinehart, & Winston.

Rosenzweig, M. R., & Leiman, A. L. (1982). *Physiological psychology*. Toronto: D. C. Heath.

Ross, L. (1977). The intuitive psychologist and his shortcomings: Distortions in the attribution process. *Advances in Experimental Social Psychology, 10*, 174–220.

Rossi, A., Stratta, P., Gallucci, M., Passariello, R., & Casacchia, M. (1988). Brain morphology in schizophrenia by magnetic resonance imaging. *Acta Psychiatrica Scandinavica, 77*, 741–745.

Rotberg, I. C. (1982). Some legal and research considerations in establishing federal policy in bilingual education. *Harvard Educational Review, 52*, 149–168.

Rothbart, M. (1993). Intergroup perception and social conflict. In S. Worchel & J. A. Simpson (Eds.), *Conflict between people and groups: Causes, processes, and resolutions*. Chicago: Nelson-Hall.

Rothstein, H. R., Schmidt, F. L., Erwin, F. W., Owens, W. A., & Sparks, C. P. (1990). Biographical data in employment selection: Can validities be made

generalizable? *Journal of Applied Psychology, 75*, 175–184.

Rotton, J., & Kelly, I. W. (1985). Much ado about the full moon: A meta-analysis of lunar-lunacy research. *Psychological Bulletin, 97*, 286–306.

Rovee-Collier, C. (1988). The rise and fall of infant classical conditioning research: Its promise for the study of early development. *Advances in Infancy Research, 4*, 139–159.

Rovee-Collier, C., Griesler, P. C., & Earley, L. A. (1985). Contextual determinants of retrieval in three-month-old infants. *Learning and Motivation, 16*, 139–157.

Rowe, C. J. (1980). *An outline of psychiatry*. Dubuque, IA: W. C. Brown.

Rubenstein, C., & Shaver, P. (1982). The experience of loneliness. In L. A. Peplau & D. Perlman (Eds.), *Loneliness: A sourcebook of current theory, research and therapy*. New York: Wiley.

Rubin, W. (1984). Modernist primitivism: An introduction. In W. Rubin (Ed.), *"Primitivism" in 20th century art: Affinity of the tribal and the modern* (Vol. 1). New York: Museum of Modern Art.

Rubin, Z. (1973). *Liking and loving: An invitation to social psychology*. New York: Holt, Rinehart, & Winston.

Rubonis, A. V., & Bickman, L. (1991). Psychological impairment in the wake of disaster-psychopathology relationship. *Psychological Bulletin, 3*, 384–399.

Ruckmick, C. A. (1936). *The psychology of feeling and emotion*. New York: McGraw-Hill.

Ruff, H. A., & Birch, H. G. (1974). Infant visual fixation: The effect of concentricity, curvilinearity, and number of directions. *Journal of Experimental Child Psychology, 17*, 460–473.

Rumelhart, D. E., McClelland, J. L., & The PDP Research Group. (1987). *Parallel distributed processing: Exploration in the microstructure of cognition*. Cambridge, MA: MIT Press.

Rundus, D. (1971). Analysis of rehearsal process in free recall. *Journal of Experimental Psychology, 89*, 63–77.

Runyan, W. M. (1981). Why did Van Gogh cut off his ear? The problem of alternative explanations in psychobiography. *Journal of Personality and Social Psychology, 40*, 1070–1077.

Runyan, W. M. (1988). Progress in psychobiography. *Journal of Personality, 56*, 295–326.

Rushton, W. A. H. (1962). Visual pigments in man. *Scientific American, 207*(5), 120–132.

Rushton, W. A. H., Powell, D. S., & White, K. D. (1973). Exchange thresholds in dichromats. *Vision Research, 13*, 1993–2002.

Russell, C. J., Mettson, J., Devlin, S. E., & Atwater, D. (1990). Predictive validity of biodata items generated from retrospective life experience essays. *Journal of Applied Psychology, 75*, 569–80.

Russell, G., & Russell, A, (1987). Mother-child and father-child relations in middle childhood. *Child Development, 58*, 1573–1585.

Russell, J. A., & Fehr, B., (1987). Relativity in the perception of emotion in facial expressions. *Journal of Experimental Psychology: General, 116*, 223–227.

Russell, W. R., & Nathan, P. W. (1946). Traumatic amnesia. *Brain, 69*, 280–300.

Rust, M. (1987, October 1). New tactics for injured workers. *ABA Journal*, pp. 72–76.

Ryan, A. M., & Sackett, P. R. (1987). Pre-employment honesty testing: Fakability, reactions of test takers, and company image. *Journal of Business and Psychology, 1*, 248–256.

Ryan, M. (1989). Political behavior and management development. Special Issue: Politics and management development. *Management Education and Development, 20*(3), 238–253.

Rymer, R. (1992, April 13). Annals of science: A silent childhood: 1. *New Yorker*, pp. 41–81.

Sacks, O. (1985). *The man who mistook his wife for a hat and other clinical tales.* New York: Summit Books.

Saegert, J. (1987). Why marketing should quit giving subliminal advertising the benefit of the doubt. *Psychology and Marketing, 4*, 107–120.

Sagi, A., van Ijzendoorn, M. H., & Koren-Karie, N. (1991). Primary appraisal of the strange situation: A cross-cultural analysis of preseparation episodes. *Developmental Psychology, 27*, 587–596.

Sagi, D., & Julesz, B. (1985). "Where" and "what" in vision. *Science, 228*, 1217–1219.

Saitoh, T., Ito, B., Shatite, B. R., Covey, S., Hurley, R. T., Griffith, A. B., Matzel, R. J., Dorey, A. B., & Whitney, A. S. (1990). The role of protein kinase C (PKC) in Alzheimer's disease. *Journal of Neuroscience, 10*, 2041–2045.

Sarason, I. G. (1980). Introduction to the study of test anxiety. In I. Sarason (Ed.), *Test anxiety: Theory, research and applications* (pp. 3–14). Hillsdale, NJ: Erlbaum.

Sarason, I. G. (1984). Stress, anxiety, and cognitive interference: Reactions to tests. *Journal of Personality and Social Psychology, 46*, 929–938.

Sarason, I. G., & Sarason, B. R. (1989). *Abnormal psychology.* Englewood Cliffs, NJ: Prentice-Hall.

Sarason, I. G., & Spielberger, C. G. (Eds.). (1979). *Stress and anxiety* (Vol. 6). Washington, DC: Hemisphere.

Sarason, S. B. (1977). *Work, aging, and social change.* New York: Free Press.

Satter, J. M. (1991). How good are federal judges in detecting differences in item difficulty on intelligence tests for ethnic groups? *Psychological Assessment, 3*, 125–129.

Scadden, L. (1969, March, 27). A tactual substitute for sight. *New Scientist*, pp. 677–678.

Schachter, D. L. (1987). Implicit memory: History and current status. *Journal of Experimental Psychology: Learning, Memory, and Cognition, 13*, 501–518.

Schachter, D. L., & Tulving, E. (1982). Memory, amnesia, and the episodic/semantic distinction. In R. L. Isaacson & N. E. Spear (Eds.), *The expression of knowledge.* New York: Plenum.

Schachter, S. (1968). Obesity and eating. *Science, 161*, 751–756.

Schachter, S. (1971). Some extraordinary facts about obese humans and rats. *American Psychologist, 26*, 129–144.

Schachter, S. (1980). Urinary pH and the psychology of nicotine addiction. In P. O. Davidson & S. M. Davidson (Eds.), *Behavioral medicine: Changing health lifestyles.* New York: Brunner/Mazel.

Schachter, S. (1982). Recidivism and self-cure of smoking and obesity. *American Psychologist, 37*, 436–444.

Schachter, S., & Singer, J. E. (1962). Cognitive, social and physiological determinants of emotional state. *Psychological Review, 69*, 379–399.

Schaie, K. W. (1983). The Seattle Longitudinal Study: A 21-year exploration of psychometric intelligence in adulthood. In K. W. Schaie (Ed.), *Longitudinal studies of adult psychological development* (pp. 64–135). New York: Guilford Press.

Schaie, K. W., & Hertzog, C. (1983). Fourteen-year cohort-sequential analyses of adult intellectual development. *Developmental Psychology, 19*, 531–543.

Schaie, K. W., & Willis, S. (1986). Can decline in adult intellectual functioning be reversed? *Developmental Psychology, 22*, 223–232.

Schalin, L. J. (1985). On the normal and pathological middle-age crisis: Erich Maria Remarque, a lost survivor. *Scandinavian Psychoanalytic Review, 8*, 115–139.

Schaller, M., & Cialdini, R. B. (1988). The economics of empathic helping: Support for a mood management motive. *Journal of Experimental Social Psychology, 24*, 163–181.

Schalling, D., & Waller, D. (1980). Psychological effects of tobacco smoking. *Acta Physiologica Scandinavica, Supplementum, 479*, 53–56.

Schaufeli, W. (1988). Perceiving the causes of unemployment. An evaluation of the causal dimensions scale in a real life situation. *Journal of Personality and Social Psychology, 54*, 347–356.

Schechtman, V. L., Harper, R. M., Kluge, K. A., Wilson, A. J., & Southall, D. P. (1990). Correlation between cardiorespiratory measures in normal infants and victims of sudden infant death syndrome. *Sleep, 16*, 304–317.

Schein, E. H. (1985). *Organizational leadership and culture: A dynamic view.* San Francisco: Jossey-Bass.

Schiffman, S. S., Reynolds, M. L., & Young, F. L. (1981). *Introduction to multidimensional scaling.* New York: Academic Press.

Schilling, R. F., & Weaver, G. E. (1983). Effect of extraneous verbal information on memory for telephone numbers. *Journal of Applied Psychology, 68*, 559–564.

Schleiser-Stropp, B. (1984). Bulimia: A review of the literature. *Psychological Bulletin, 95*, 247–257.

Schlingensiepen, K. H., Campell, F. W., Legge, G. E., & Walker, T. D. (1986). The importance of eye movements in the analysis of simple patterns. *Vision Research, 26*, 1111–1117.

Schmidt, F. L., Hunter, J. E., McKenzie, R. C., & Muldrow, T. W. (1979). Impact of valid selection procedures on work force productivity. *Journal of Applied Psychology, 65*, 609–626.

Schmidt, F. L., Hunter, J. E., Outerbridge, A. N., & Trattner, M. H. (1986). The economic impact of job selection methods on size, productivity, and payroll costs of the federal work force: An empirically based demonstration. *Personnel Psychology, 39*, 1–29.

Schmidt, S. R., & Bohanon, J. N. (1988). In defense of the flashbulb-memory hypothesis: A comment on McCloskey, Wible, and Cohen (1988). *Journal of Experimental Psychology: General, 117*, 332–334.

Schmitt, N., Gooding, R. Z., Noe, R. A., & Kirsch, M. (1984). Meta-analyses of validity studies published between 1964 and 1982 and the investigation of study characteristics. *Personnel Psychology, 37*, 257–281.

Schneider, J. W., & Hacker, S. L. (1973). Sex-role imagery and the use of generic "man" in introductory texts. *American Sociologist, 8*, 12–18.

Schneider, W., & Shiffrin, R. M. (1977). Controlled and automatic human information processing: I. Detection, search, and attention. *Psychological Review, 84*, 1–66.

Schooler, J. W., & Engstler-Schooler, T. Y. (1990). Verbal overshadowing of visual memories, some things are better left unsaid. *Cognitive Psychology, 22*, 36–71.

Schretlen, D., Wilkins, S. S., Van Gorp, W. G., & Bobholz, J. H. (1992). Cross-validation of a test battery to detect faked insanity. *Psychological Assessment, 4,* 77–83.

Schuler, R. S. (1980). Definition and conceptualization of stress in organizations. *Organizational Behavior and Human Performance, 25,* 184–215.

Schultz, D. (1985). *The last battle station: The sage of the USS Houston.* New York: St. Martin's Press.

Schultz, D., & Schultz, S. E. (1992). *A history of modern psychology* (5th ed.). San Diego: Harcourt Brace Jovanovich.

Schulz, B., Bohrnstedt, G. W., Borgatta, E. F., & Evans, R. R. (1977). Explaining premarital intercourse among college students: A causal model. *Social Forces, 56,* 148–165.

Schulz, R., & Schlarb, J. (1988). Two decades of research on dying: What do we know about the patient? *Omega, 18,* 299–317.

Schwartz, B. (1981). Control of complex, sequential operants by systematic visual information in pigeons. *Journal of Experimental Psychology: Animal Learning and Behavior, 7,* 31–44.

Schwartz, B. (1982). Reinforcement-induced behavioral stereotype: How not to teach people to discover rules. *Journal of Experimental Psychology: General, 111,* 23–59.

Schwartz, B. (1989). *Psychology of learning and behavior.* New York: Norton.

Schwartz, B., & Reilly, M. (1985). Long-term retention of a complex operant in pigeons. *Journal of Experimental Psychology: Animal Behavior Processes, 11,* 337–356.

Schwartz, B., & Reisberg, D. (1991). *Learning and memory.* New York: Norton.

Schwartz, G. E., & Beatty, J. (1977). *Biofeedback: Theory and research.* New York: Academic Press.

Schwartz, M. A. (1984). Expansionary America tightens its belt: Social scientific perspectives on obesity. *Marriage and Family Review, 7,* 49–63.

Schwartzman, A., Gold, D., Andres, D., Arbuckle, T., & Chaikelson, J. (1987). Stability of intelligence: A 40-year follow-up. *Canadian Journal of Psychology, 41,* 244–256.

Scott, K. D., & Taylor, G. S. (1985). An examination of conflicting findings on the relationship between job satisfaction and absenteeism: A meta-analysis. *Academy of Management Journal, 28,* 599–612.

Scoville, W. B., & Milner, B. (1957). Loss of recent memory after bilateral hippocampal lesions. *Journal of Neurology, Neurosurgery and Psychiatry, 20,* 11–19.

Scrivner, E. (1991). Integrity testing: A new frontier for psychology. Special Issue: Integrity testing. *Forensic Reports, 4(2),* 75–89.

Searles, J. (1988). The role of genetics in the pathogenesis of alcoholism. *Journal of Abnormal Psychology, 97,* 153–167.

Sebald, H., & White, B. (1980). Teenagers' divided reference groups: Uneven alignment with parents and peers. *Adolescence, 15,* 979–984.

Sechenov, I. M. (1965). *Reflexes of the brain: An attempt to establish the physiological basis of psychological processes* (S. Belsky, Trans.). Boston: MIT Press. (Original work published 1863).

Segal, Z. (1988). Appraisal of the self-schemata construct in cognitive models of depression. *Psychological Bulletin, 103,* 147–162.

Segall, M. H. (1979). *Cross-cultural psychology: Human behavior in global perspective.* Monterey, CA: Brooks/Cole.

Sekaran, U., & Hall, D. T. (1989). Asynchronism in dual-career and family linkages. In Arthur, Hall, & Lawrence (Eds.), *Handbook of career theory.* Cambridge, England: Cambridge University Press.

Sekuler, R., & Blake, R. (1985). *Perception.* New York: Knopf.

Selfridge, O. G. (1959). Pandemonium: A paradigm of learning. In S. S. Smith (Ed.). *The mechanization of thought processes.* London: HM Stationery Office.

Seligman, D. (1992, March, 23). Who are the teachers' pets? *Fortune,* p. 132.

Seligman, M. E. P. (1970). On the generalities of the laws of learning. *Psychological Review, 77,* 406–418.

Seligman, M. E. P. (1990). *Learned optimism.* New York: Knopf.

Seligman, M. E. P., & Maier, S. F. (1967). Failure to escape traumatic shock. *Journal of Experimental Psychology, 75,* 1–9.

Seligman, M. E. P., & Rosenhan, D. L. (1983). *Abnormal Psychology.* New York: Norton.

Seligman, M. E. P., & Schulman, P. (1986). Explanatory style as a predictor of productivity and quitting among life insurance sales agents. *Journal of Personality and Social Psychology, 50,* 832–838.

Selye, H. (1956). *The stress of life.* New York: McGraw-Hill.

Senneker, P., & Hendrick, C. (1983). Androgyny and helping behavior. *Journal of Personality and Social Psychology, 45,* 916–925.

Shaffer, L. H. (1975). Multiple attention in continuous verbal tasks. In P. M. Rabbitt & S. Dornic (Eds.), *Attention and performance* (Vol. 5). New York: Academic Press.

Shantz, C. U. (1967). A developmental study of Piaget's theory of logical multiplication. *Merrill-Palmer Quarterly, 13,* 121–137.

Shantz, C. U. (1983). Social cognition. In J. H. Flavell & E. M. Markham (Eds.), *Mussen's handbook of child psychology: Vol. 3. Cognitive development* (4th ed.). New York: Wiley.

Shao, A. T., & Hill, J. S. (1992). Executing transactional advertising campaigns: Do U.S. agencies have the overseas talent? *Journal of Advertising Research, 32(1),* 49–58.

Shapiro, C. M. (1982). Energy expenditure and restorative sleep. *Biological Psychology, 15,* 229–239.

Shapiro, S., Skinner, E. A., Kessler, L. G., Von Korff, M., German, P. S., Tischler, G. L., Leaf, P. J., Benham, L., Cotler, L., & Regier, D. A. (1984). Utilization of health and mental health services. *Archives of General Psychiatry, 41,* 971–978.

Shavit, Y., Terman, G. W., Martin, F. C., Lewis, J. W., Liebeskind, J. C., & Gale, R. P. (1984). Stress, opioid peptides, the immune system and cancer. *Journal of Immunology, 135,* 834–837.

Sheldon, W. H. (1940). *The varieties of human physique: An introduction to constitutional psychology* (with S. S. Stevens & W. B. Tucker). New York: Harper.

Sheldon, W. H. (1942). *The varieties of temperament: A psychology of constitutional differences* (with S. S. Stevens). New York: Harper.

Shelton, R., Karson, C., Doran, A., Pickar, D., Bigelow, L., & Weinberger, D. (1988). Cerebral structural pathology in schizophrenia: Evidence for a selective prefrontal cortical defect. *American Journal of Psychiatry, 145,* 154–163.

Shepard, R. A. (1986). Neurotransmitters, anxiety, and benzodiazepines: A behavioral review. *Neuroscience and Biobehavioral Reviews, 10,* 449–461.

Shepard, R. N., & Cooper, L. A. (1982). *Mental images and their transformations.* Cambridge, MA: MIT Press.

Shepard, S., & Metzger, D. (1988). Mental rotation: Effects of dimensionality of objects and type of task. *Journal of Experimental Psychology: Human Perception and Performance, 14,* 3–11.

Sher, K. J., & Levenson, R. W. (1982). Risk for alcoholism and individual differences in the stress-response-dampening effect of alcohol. *Journal of Abnormal Psychology, 91,* 350–367.

Sherif, M. (1935). A study of some social factors in perception. *Archives in Psychology, 187,* 1–60.

Sherif, M. (1953). The concept of reference groups in human relations. In M. Sherif & M. O. Wilson (Eds.), *Group relations at the crossroads: The University of Oklahoma lectures in social psychology.* New York: Harper & Row.

Sherif, M. (1965). Superordinate goals in the reduction of intergroup conflicts. In H. Proshansky & B. Seidenberg (Eds.), *Basic studies in social psychology*. New York: Holt, Rinehart, & Winston. (Original work published 1958).

Sherman, B., & Dominick, J. R. (1986). Violence and sex in music videos: TV and rock'n'roll. *Journal of Communication, 36*, 79–93.

Sherman, E. (1987, November). The miracle of Maranda. *Ladies Home Journal*, pp. 48–49.

Sherrington, R., Brynjolfsson, J., Petursson, H., Barraclough, B., Wasmuth, J., Dobbs, M., & Gurling, H. (1988). Localization of a susceptibility locus for schizophrenia on chromosome 5. *Nature (London), 336*, 164–167.

Shilts, R. (1987). *And the band played on: Politics, people, and the AIDs epidemic*. New York: St. Martin's Press.

Shorey, H. H. (1977). Pheromones. In T. A. Sebeok (Ed.), *How animals communicate*. Bloomington: Indiana University Press.

Shotland, R., & Craig, J. (1988). Can men and women differentiate between friendly and sexually interested behavior? *Social Psychology Quarterly, 51*, 66–73.

Siegel, S. (1986). Morphine tolerance acquisition as an associative process. In N. A. Marlin (Ed.), *Directed readings for the principles of learning and behavior*. Monterey, CA: Brooks/Cole.

Siegel, S., Krank, M. D., & Hinson, R. E. (1987). Anticipation of pharmacological and nonpharmacological events: Classical conditioning and addictive behavior. *Journal of Drug Issues, 17*, 83–110.

Silfverskiold, P., Rosen, I., & Risberg, J. (1987). Effects of electroconvulsive therapy on EEG and cerebral blood flow in depression. *European Archives of Psychiatry and Neurological Sciences, 236*, 202–208.

Silveira, J. (1971). *Incubation: The effect of interruption timing and length on problem solution and quality of problem processing*. Doctoral dissertation, University of Oregon, Eugene.

Silverstein, A. (1988). An Aristotelian resolution of the idiographic versus nomothetic tension. *American Psychologist, 43*, 425–430.

Silverstein, L. B. (1991). Transforming the debate about child care and maternal employment. *American Psychologist, 46*, 1025–1032.

Simons, A. D., McGowen, C. R., Epstein, L. H., & Kupfer, D. J. (1985). Exercise as a treatment for depression: An update. *Clinical Psychology Review, 5*, 553–568.

Simons, R. L., Whitbeck, L. B., Conger, R. D., & Chyi-In, W. (1991). Intergenerational transmission of harsh parenting. *Developmental Psychology, 27*, 159–171.

Simpson, J. A. (1990). Influence of attachment styles on romantic relationships. *Journal of Personality and Social Psychology, 59*, 971–980.

Simpson, J. A., Rholes, W. S., & Nelligan, J. S. (1992). Support seeking and support giving within couples in an anxiety-provoking situation. *Journal of Personality and Social Psychology, 62*, 434–446.

Singer, S., & Kolligian, J. (1987). Personality: Developments in the study of private experience. *Annual Review of Psychology, 38*, 533–574.

Skinner, B. F. (1948). *Walden two*. New York: Macmillan.

Skinner, B. F. (1953). *Science and human behavior*. New York: Free Press.

Skinner, B. F. (1957). *Verbal behavior*. New York: Appleton-Century-Crofts.

Skinner, B. F. (1969). *Contingencies of reinforcement: A theoretical analysis*. New York: Appleton-Century-Crofts.

Skinner, B. F. (1971). *Beyond freedom and dignity*. New York: Knopf.

Skinner, B. F. (1974). *About behaviorism*. New York: Knopf.

Skinner, B. F. (1976). *Particulars of my life*. New York: McGraw-Hill.

Sklar, L. S., & Anisman, H. (1981a). Stress and cancer. *Psychological Bulletin, 98*, 108–138.

Sklar, L. S., & Anisman, H. (1981b). Stress and cancer. *Psychological Bulletin, 98*, 369–406.

Sladek, J. R., and Shoulson, I. (1988). Neural transplantation: A call for patience rather than patients. *Science, 240*, 1386–1388.

Sloan, L. L., & Wollach, L. (1948). A case of unilateral deuteranopia. *Journal of the Optical Society of America, 38*, 502–509.

Slobin, D. I. (1979). *Psycholinguistics* (2nd ed.). Glenview, IL: Scott, Foresman.

Smith, A. P., & Lee, N. M. (1988). Pharmacology of dynorphin. *Annual Review of Pharmacology and Toxicology, 28*, 123–140.

Smith, C., and Kelly, G. (1988). Paradoxical sleep deprivation. *Physiology and Behavior, 43*, 213–216.

Smith, C., and Lapp, L. (1991). Increases in numbers of REMS and REM density in humans following an intensive learning period. *Association of Professional Sleep Societies, 14*, 325–330.

Smith, D. J. (1986). Do tests and examinations alienate the gifted student? *Gifted Education International, 4*, 101–105.

Smith, G. A., & Stanley, G. (1983). Clocking: Relating intelligence and measures of timed performance. *Intelligence, 7*, 353–368.

Smith, M. J. (1978). *A review of NIOSH psychological stress research—1977*. *Proceedings of the occupational stress conference*. Washington, DC: National Institute of Occupational Safety and Health.

Smith, M. L., & Glass, G. V. (1977). Meta-analysis of psychotherapy outcome studies. *American Psychologist, 32*, 752–760.

Smith, P. C., Kendall, L. M., & Hulin, C. L. (1969). *The measurement of satisfaction in work and retirement*. Chicago: Rand McNally.

Smith, S. M. (1979). Remembering in and out of context. *Journal of Experimental Psychology: Human Learning and Memory, 5*, 460–471.

Smith, S. M. (1986). Environmental context-dependent recognition memory using a short-term memory task for input. *Memory and Cognition, 14*, 347–354.

Smith, S. M. (1988). Environmental context-dependent memory. In G. Davies & D. Thomson (Eds.), *Memory in context: Context in memory* (pp. 13–33). New York: Wiley.

Smith, S. M. (in press). Theoretical principles of context-dependent memory. In P. Morris & M. Gruneberg (Eds.), *Aspects of memory: Theoretical aspects* (2nd ed.). London: Routledge & Kegan Paul.

Smith, S. M., & Blankenship, S. E. (1989). Incubation effects. *Bulletin of the Psychonomic Society, 27*, 311–314.

Smith, S. M., & Blankenship, S. E. (1991). Incubation and the persistence of fixation in problem solving. *American Journal of Psychology, 104*, 61–87.

Smith, S. M., Glenberg, A. M., & Bjork, R. A. (1978). Environmental context and human memory. *Memory and Cognition, 6*, 342–353.

Smith, S. M., & Vela, E. (1988). *Environmental context-dependent eyewitness recognition* (Tech. Rep. No. CSCS-002). College Station: Texas A&M University.

Smith, S. M., & Vela, E. (1992). Environmental context-dependent eyewitness recognition. *Applied Cognitive Psychology, 6*, 125–139.

Snarey, J. R. (1985). Cross-cultural universality of social-moral development: A critical review of Kohlbergian research. *Psychological Bulletin, 97*, 202–232.

Snarey, J. R., Son, L., Kuehne, V., Hauser, S., & Vaillant, G. (1987). The role of parenting in men's psychosocial development: A longitudinal study of early adulthood infertility and midlife generativity. *Developmental Psychology, 23*, 593–603.

Snyder, D. K., and Wills, R. M. (1989). Behavioral versus insight-oriented marital therapy: Effects on individual and interspousal functioning. *Journal of Consulting and Clinical Psychology, 57*, 39–46.

Snyder, D. K., Wills, R. M., & Grady-Fletcher, A. (1991). Long-term effectiveness of behavioral versus insight-oriented marital therapy: A 4-year follow-up. *Journal of Consulting and Clinical Psychology, 59*, 138–141.

Snyder, S. H. (1984). Cholinergic mechanisms in affective disorders. *New England Journal of Medicine, 311*, 254–255.

Snyder, S. S., & Feldman, D. H. (1977). Internal and external influences on cognitive developmental change. *Child Development, 48*, 937–943.

Sochurek, H. (1987). Medicine's new vision. *National Geographic, 171*, 2–41.

Sokal, M. M. (1980). *An education in psychology: James McKeen Cattel's journal and letters from Germany and England, 1880–1888.* Cambridge, MA: MIT Press.

Solano, C. H., Batten, P. G., & Parish, E. A. (1982). Loneliness and patterns of self-disclosure. *Journal of Personality and Social Psychology, 43*, 524–531.

Solas, J. (1991). A constructive alternative to family assessment. *Journal of Family Therapy, 13*(2), 149–169.

Solso, R. L. (1991). *Cognitive psychology* (3rd ed.). Needham Heights, MA: Allyn & Bacon.

Solzhenitsyn, A. I. (1980). *The oak and the calf.* New York: Harper & Row.

Spear, N. E., Miller, J. S., & Jagielo, J. A. (1990). Animal memory and learning. *Annual Review of Psychology, 41*, 43–61.

Spector, P. E., Dwyer, D. J., & Jex, S. M. (1988). Relation of job stressors to affective, health, and performance outcomes: A comparison of multiple data sources. *Journal of Applied Psychology, 73*, 11–19.

Spelke, E., Hirst, W., & Neisser, U. (1976). Skills of divided attention. *Cognition, 4*, 215–230.

Sperling, G. (1960). The information available in brief visual presentations. *Psychological Monographs, 74*(Whole No. 498).

Sperry, R. W. (1974). Lateral specialization in surgically separated hemispheres. In F. O. Schmitt & F. G. Worden (Eds.), *The neurosciences* (Vol. 3). Cambridge, MA: MIT Press.

Spiegel, D. (1987, March/April). The healing trance. *The Sciences*, pp. 35–40.

Spiegel, D., & Cardeña, E. (1991). Disintegrated experience: The dissociative disorders revisited. *Journal of Abnormal Psychology, 100*, 366–378.

Spiegel, R., Koberle, S., & Allen, S. R. (1986). Significance of slow wave sleep: Considerations from a clinical viewpoint. *Sleep, 9*, 66–79.

Spiegler, M. D., & Guevrement, D. C. (1993). *Contemporary behavior therapy.* Pacific Grove, CA: Brooks/Cole.

Spielman, A. J., Saskin, P., & Thorpy, M. J. (1987). Treatment of chronic insomnia by restriction of time in bed. *Sleep, 10*, 45–56.

Spitzer, R. L. (1983). *Psychopathology: A casebook.* New York: McGraw-Hill.

Spitzer, R. L., Skodol, A. E., Gibbon, M., & Williams, J. B. W. (1981). *DSM-III case book: A learning companion to the diagnostic and statistical manual of mental disorders (third edition).* Washington, DC: American Psychiatric Association.

Springer, S. P., & Deutsch, G. (1985). *Left brain, right brain.* San Francisco: Freeman.

Squire, L. R. (1982). The neuropsychology of human memory. *Annual Review of Neuroscience, 5*, 241–273.

Squire, L. R. (1988). Memory: Neural systems and behavior. In F. Plum (Ed.), *Handbook of physiology: Higher functions of the nervous system.* Bethesda, MD: American Physiological Society.

Squire, L. R. (1992). Memory and the hippocampus: A synthesis of findings with rats, monkeys, and humans. *Psychological Review, 2*, 195–231.

Squire, L. R., Amaral, D. G., & Press, G. A. (1990). Magnetic resonance imaging of the hippocampus and mammillary nuclei distinguish medial temporal lobe and diencephalic amnesia. *Journal of Neuroscience, 10*, 3106–3117.

Squire, L. R., & Slater, P. C. (1983). Electroconvulsive therapy and complaints of memory dysfunction: A prospective three-year follow-up study. *British Journal of Psychiatry, 142*, 1–8.

Squire, L. R., & Zola-Morgan, S. (1991). The medial temporal lobe memory system. *Science, 253*, 1380–1386.

Staats, A. W., & Staats, C. K. (1958). Attitudes established by classical conditioning. *Journal of Abnormal and Social Psychology, 57*, 37–40.

Stabell, U., Stabell, B., & Nordby, K. (1986). Dark adaptation of the human rod system: A new hypothesis. *Scandinavian Journal of Psychology, 27*, 175–183.

Stall, R. D., Coates, T. J., & Hoff, C. (1988). Behavioral risk reduction for HIV infection among gay and bisexual men: A review of results from the United States. *American Psychologist, 43*, 878–885.

Stampfl, T. G., & Levis, D. J. (1967). Essentials of implosive therapy: A learning-theory-based psychodynamic behavioral therapy. *Journal of Abnormal Psychology, 72*, 496.

Stapp, J., Fulcher, R., & Wicherski, M. (1984). The employment of 1981 and 1982 doctorate recipients in psychology. *American Psychologist, 39*, 1408–1423.

Staub, E., Tursky, B., & Schwartz, G. E. (1971). Self-control and predictability: Their effects on reactions to aversive stimulation. *Journal of Personality and Social Psychology, 18*, 157–162.

Stein, N., & Sanfilipo, M. (1985). Depression and the wish to be held. *Journal of Clinical Psychology, 41*, 3–9.

Steinberg, L. (1981). Transformations in family relations at puberty. *Developmental Psychology, 17*, 833–840.

Steinberg, L. (1986). Latchkey children and susceptibility to peer pressure: An ecological analysis. *Developmental Psychology, 22*, 433–439.

Steinberg, L. (1987). Impact of puberty on family relations: Effects of pubertal status and pubertal timing. *Developmental Psychology, 23*, 451–460.

Steinberg, L. (1988). Reciprocal relation between parent-child distance and pubertal maturation. *Developmental Psychology, 24*, 122–128.

Steinberg, L. (1989). Pubertal maturation and parent-adolescent distance: An evolutionary perspective. In G. R. Adams, R. Montemayor, & T. P. Gullota (Eds.), *Biology of adolescent behavior and development* (pp. 71–97). Newbury Park, CA: Sage.

Steinberg, L., & Silverberg, S. B. (1986). The vicissitudes of autonomy in early adolescence. *Child Development, 57*, 841–851.

Stelmack, R. M., & Stalikas, A. (1991). Galen and the humor theory of temperament. *Personality and Individual Differences, 12*(3), 255–263.

Stepney, R. (1984). Human smoking behavior and the development of dependence on tobacco smoking. In D. K. Balfour (Ed.), *Nicotine and the smoking habit* (pp. 153–176). New York: Pergamon.

Sternberg, R. J. (1981). Testing and cognitive psychology. *American Psychologist, 36*, 1181–1189.

Sternberg, R. J. (1985). *Beyond IQ: A triarchic theory of human intelligence.* New York: Cambridge University Press.

Sternberg, R. J. (1986). A triangular theory of love. *Psychological Review, 93*, 119–135.

Sternberg, R. J. (1987). Liking versus loving: A comparative evaluation of theories. *Psychological Bulletin, 102*, 331–345.

Sternberg, R. J. (1988). A triarchic view of intelligence in cross-cultural perspective. In S. H. Irvine & J. W. Berry (Eds.). *Human abilities in cultural context* (pp. 60–85). New York: Cambridge University Press.

Sternberg, R. J., & Detterman, D. (1986). *What is intelligence? Contemporary viewpoints on its nature and definition.* Norwood, NJ: Ablex.

Sternberg, R. J., & Powell, J. S. (1982). Theories of intelligence. In R. J. Sternberg (Ed.), *Handbook of human intelligence* (pp. 975–1005). New York: Cambridge University Press.

Stevens, S. S. (1962). The surprising simplicity of sensory metrics. *American Psychologist, 17*, 29–39.

Stewart, R. B. (1983). Sibling attachment relationships: Child-infant interactions in the strange situation. *Developmental Psychology, 19*, 192–199.

Stoffregen, T. A., & Riccio, G. E. (1988). An ecological theory of orientation and the vestibular system. *Psychological Review, 95*, 3–14.

Stone, A. A., & Neale, J. M. (1984). New measures of daily coping: Development and preliminary results. *Journal of Personality and Social Psychology, 46*, 892–906.

Storr, A. (1983). Individuation and the creative process. *Journal of Analytical Psychology, 28*, 329–343.

Straussner, S. L. A. (1988, January/February). Comparison of in-house and contracted-out employee assistance programs. *Social Work*, pp. 53–55.

Streissguth, A. P., Barr, H. M., & Martin, D. C. (1983). Maternal alcohol use and neonatal habituation assessed with the Brazelton scale. *Child Development, 54*, 1109–1118.

Streissguth, A. P., Landesman-Dwyer, S., Martin, J. C., & Smith, D. W. (1980). Teratogenic effects of alcohol in humans and laboratory animals. *Science, 209*, 353–361.

Stricker, E. M., & Verbalis, J. (1987). Biological bases of hunger and satiety. *Annals of Behavioral Medicine, 9*, 3–8.

Stricker, E. M., & Verbalis, J. G. (1988). Hormones and behavior: The biology of thirst and sodium appetite. *American Scientist, 76*, 261–267.

Strodtbeck, F. L., James, R. M., & Hawkins, C. (1958). In E. E. Maccoby, T. M. Newcomb, & E. L. Hartley (Eds.), *Readings in social psychology* (3rd ed.). New York: Holt, Rinehart, & Winston.

Stunkard, A. J., Sorënson, T., Hanis, C., Teasdale, T. W., Chakraborty, R., Schull, W. J., & Schulsinger, F. (1986). An adoption study of human obesity. *New England Journal of Medicine, 314*, 193–198.

Stuss, D. T., & Benson, D. F. (1984). Neuropsychological studies of the frontal lobes. *Psychological Bulletin, 95*, 3–28.

Sue, S. (1977). Community mental health services to minority groups: Some optimism, some pessimism. *American Psychologist, 32*, 616–624.

Sue, S., and Zane, N. (1987). The role of culture and cultural techniques in psychotherapy: A critique and reformulation. *American Psychologist, 42*, 37–45.

Suinn, R. M. (1976, July). Body thinking: Psychology for Olympic champs. *Psychology Today*, pp. 38–43.

Sullivan, M., & O'Leary, S. G. (1990). Maintenance following reward and cost token programs. *Behavior Therapy, 21*, 139–149.

Suomi, S. J., & Harlow, H. F. (1972). Social rehabilitation of isolate-reared monkeys. *Developmental Psychology, 6*, 487–496.

Sutton-Smith, B., & Rosenberg, B. G. (1970). *The sibling*. New York: Holt, Rinehart, & Winston.

Swanson, L. W., & Lind, R. W. (1986). Neural projections subserving the initiation of a specific motivated behavior in the rat: New projections from the subfornical organ. *Brain Research, 379*, 399–403.

Swets, J. A., Tanner, W. P., & Birdsall, T. G. (1961). Decision processes in perception. *Psychological Review, 68*, 301–340.

Symons, D. K., & Moran, G. (1987). The behavioral dynamics of mutual responsiveness in early face-to-face mother-infant interactions. *Child Development, 58*, 1488–1495.

Tabor, B. L., Smith-Wallace, T., & Yonekura, M. L. (1990). Perinatal outcome associated with PCP versus cocaine use. *American Journal of Drug and Alcohol Abuse, 16*, 337–348.

Tajfel, H. (1982). Social psychology of intergroup relations. *Annual Review of Psychology, 33*, 1–39.

Takai, M., Nozoe, S., Tanaka, H., et al. (1989). Clinical features in anorexia nervosa lasting 10 years or more. *Psychotherapy and Psychosomatics, 52*, 140–145.

Takooshian, H. (1982). Bystander indifference to street crime. In L. Savitz & N. Johnston (Eds.), *Contemporary criminology* (pp. 209–215). New York: Wiley.

Tanner, J. M. (1978). *Fetus into man: Physical growth from conception to maturity*. Cambridge, MA: Harvard University Press.

Tartter, V. X. (1986). *Language processes*. New York: Holt, Rinehart, & Winston.

Taulbee, P. (1983). Solving the mystery of anxiety. *Science News, 124*, 45–46.

Taylor, C. W. (Ed.). (1972). *Climate for creativity*. New York: Pergamon.

Taylor, F. W. (1911). *The principles of scientific management*. New York: Harper.

Taylor, M. A., & Abrams, R. (1984). Cognitive impairment in schizophrenia. *American Journal of Psychiatry, 141*, 196–201.

Taylor, S. E. (1976). Developing a cognitive social psychology. In J. S. Carroll & J. W. Payne (Eds.), *Cognition and social behavior*. Hillsdale, NJ: Erlbaum.

Taylor, S. E. (1986). *Health psychology*. New York: Random House.

Taylor, S. E., & Brown, J. D. (1988). Illusion and well-being: A social psychological perspective on mental health. *Psychological Bulletin, 103*, 193–210.

Teasdale, J. D., & Russell, M. L. (1983). Differential effects of induced mood on the recall of positive, negative, and neutral words. *British Journal of Clinical Psychology, 22*, 163–172.

Teicher, M. H, Glod, C. A., & Cole, J. O. (1990). Emergence of intense suicidal preoccupation during fluoxetine treatment. *American Journal of Psychiatry, 147*, 207–210.

Teitelbaum, P., & Epstein, A. N. (1962). The lateral hypothalamic syndrome: Recovery of feeding and drinking after lateral hypothalamic lesions. *Psychological Review, 69*, 74–90.

Tellegen, A., Lykken, D. T., Bouchard, T. J., Wilcox, K. J., Segal, N. L., & Rich, S. (1988). Personality similarity in twins reared apart and together. *Journal of Personality and Social Psychology, 58*, 1031–1039.

Temple, D. E., & Geisinger, K. F. (1990). Response latency to computer-administered inventory items as an indicator of emotional arousal. *Journal of Personality Assessment, 54*, 289–297.

Tennen, H., & Affleck, G. (1990). Blaming others for threatening events. *Psychological Bulletin, 108*(2), 209–232.

Teri, L., Hughes, J. P., & Larson, E. B. (1990). Cognitive deterioration in Alzheimer's disease: Behavioral and health factors. *Journal of Gerontology (Psychological Sciences), 45*, P58–P63.

Terman, L. M., & Merrill, M. A. (1973). *Stanford-Binet Intelligence Scale: 1972 norms edition*. Boston: Houghton-Mifflin.

Terrace, H. S. (1979). Is problem-solving language? *Journal of Experimental Analysis of Behavior, 31*, 161–175.

Terrace, H. S. (1985). In the beginning was the "name." *American Psychologist, 40*, 1011–1028.

Terry, W. S. (1988). Everyday forgetting: Data from a diary study. *Psychological Reports, 62*, 299–303.

Thomann, D., & Weiner, R. (1987). Physical and psychological causality as determinants of culpability in sexual harassment cases. *Sex Roles, 17*, 573–591.

Thomas, A., & Chess, S. (1977). *Temperament and development*. New York: Brunner/Mazel.

Thomas, A., Chess, S., & Birch, H. G. (1970). The origin of personality. *Scientific American, 223*, 102–109.

Thompson, R. F. (1986). The neurobiology of learning and memory. *Science, 223*, 941–947.

Thompson, S. C. (1981). Will it hurt less if I can control it? A complex answer to a simple question. *Psychological Bulletin, 90*, 89–101.

Thoreau, H. D. (1887). Winter. In H. G. O. Blake (Ed.), *From the journal of Henry David Thoreau*. New York: Houghton-Mifflin.

Thorndike, E. L. (1898). Animal intelligence: An experimental study of the associative processes in animals. *Psychological Monographs, 2*(No. 8).

Thorndike, R. L., Hagen, E. P., & Sattler, J. M. (1986). *The Stanford-Binet Intelligence Scale: Guide for administering and scoring* (4th ed.). Chicago: Riverside Publishing.

Tilley, A. J., Wilkinson, R. T., Warren, P. S., Watson, B., & Drud, M. (1982). The sleep and performance of shift workers. *Human Factors, 24,* 629–641.

Tilson, H. A. (1987). Behavioral indices of neurotoxicity: What can be measured? *Neurotoxicity and Teratology, 9,* 427–443.

Tilson, H. A., & Mitchell, C. L. (1984). Neurobehavioral techniques to assess the effects of chemicals on the nervous system. *Annual Review of Pharmacology and Toxicology, 24,* 425–450.

Tinbergen, N. (1948). Social releasers and the experimental method required for their study. *Wilson Bulletin, 60,* 6–52.

Titchener, E. B. (1901–1905). *Experimental psychology* (Vols. 1–4). New York: Macmillan.

Titchener, J. L., & Kapp, F. T. (1976). Family and character change at Buffalo Creek. *American Journal of Psychiatry, 133,* 295–299.

Titone, R. (1980). Psycholinguistic variables of child bilingualism: Cognition and personality development. *International Journal of Psycholinguistics, 7,* 5–19.

Toews, J., & Barnes, G. (1986). The chronic mental patient and community psychiatry: A system in trouble. *Canada's Mental Health, 34,* 2–7.

Tolman, E. C., & Honzik, C. H. (1930). Introduction and removal of reward and maze performance in rats. *University of California, Berkeley, Publications in Psychology, 4,* 257–275.

Tomlinson-Keasey, C., & Keasey, C. B. (1972). Long-term cultural change in cognitive development. *Perceptual and Motor Skills, 35,* 135–139.

Tompkins, R. D. (1981). *Before it's too late . . . The prevention manual on drug abuse for people who care.* Englewood, NJ: Family Information Services.

Torgersen, S. (1983). Genetic factors in anxiety disorders. *Archives of General Psychiatry, 40,* 1085–1989.

Tourangeau, R., & Rasinski, K. (1988). Cognitive processes underlying context effects in attitude measurement. *Psychological Bulletin, 103,* 299–314.

Treisman, A. M. (1986). Features and objects in visual processing. *Scientific American, 255,* 114–125.

Treisman, A. M., & Gormican, S. (1988). Feature analysis in early vision: Evidence from search asymmetries. *Psychological Review, 95,* 15–48.

Trice, H. M., & Beyer, J. M. (1993). *The culture of work organizations.* Englewood Cliffs, NJ: Prentice-Hall.

Trimble, W. S., Linial, M., & Scheller, R. H. (1991). Cellular and molecular biology of the presynaptic nerve terminal. *Annual Review of Neuroscience, 14,* 106–143.

Triplett, N. (1898). The dynamogenic factors in pacemaking and competition. *American Journal of Psychology, 9,* 507–533.

Tryon, R. C. (1940). Genetic differences in maze learning in rats. *Yearbook of the National Society for Studies in Education, 39,* 111–119.

Tulving, E. (1962). Subjective organization in free recall of unrelated words. *Psychological Review, 69,* 344–354.

Tulving, E. (1972). Episodic and semantic memory. In E. Tulving & W. Donaldson (Eds.), *Organization of memory.* New York: Academic Press.

Tulving, E. (1983). *Elements of episodic memory.* New York: Oxford University Press.

Tulving, E. (1985). How many memory systems are there? *American Psychologist, 40,* 385–398.

Tulving, E., & Schachter, D. (1990). Priming and human memory systems. *Science, 247,* 301–306.

Turnbull, W. W. (1979). Intelligence testing in the year 2000. *Intelligence, 3,* 275–282.

Turner, S. M., Beidel, D. C., & Nathan, R. S. (1985). Biological factors in obsessive-compulsive disorders. *Psychological Bulletin, 97,* 430–450.

Turnquist, D. C., Harvey, J. H., & Andersen, B. L. (1988). Attributions and adjustment to life-threatening illness. *British Journal of Clinical Psychology, 27,* 55–65.

Tyler, L. E. (1965). *The psychology of human differences.* New York: Appleton-Century-Crofts.

Tyrer, P., Murphy, S., Kingdom, D., Brothwell, J., Gregory, S., et al. (1988, July 30). The Nottingham study of neurotic disorder: Comparison of drug and psychological treatments. *Lancet,* pp. 231–239.

Udry, R., & Tolbert, L. (1988). Sex hormone effects on personality at puberty. *Journal of Personality and Social Psychology, 54,* 291–295.

Underwood, B. J. (1957). Interference and forgetting. *Psychological Review, 64,* 48–60.

U. S. Bureau of the Census. (1984). *Statistical abstract of the United States: 1985* (105th ed.). Washington, DC: Author.

U. S. Bureau of the Census. (1985). *Current population reports. Population profile of the United States: 1983–1984* (Series P–23, No. 145). Washington, DC: U. S. Government Printing Office.

U. S. Bureau of the Census (1992). *Statistical Abstract of the United States: 1992* (112th ed.). Washington, DC: U. S. Government Printing Office.

U. S. Public Health Service. (1979). *Smoking and health: A report of the Surgeon General* (DHEW Publication No. 79–5006). Washington, DC: U. S. Government Printing Office.

Valenstein, E. S. (1980). *The psychosurgery debate.* San Francisco: Freeman.

Valenstein, E. S. (1986). *Great and desperate cures: The rise and decline of psychosurgery and other radical treatments of mental illness.* New York: Basic Books.

Vander Zanden, J. W. (1989). *Human development* (4th ed.). New York: Knopf.

Van Egeren, L., Haynes, S. N., Franzen, M., & Hamilton, J. (1983). Presleep conditions and attributions in sleep-onset insomnia. *Journal of Behavioral Medicine, 6,* 217–232.

van Ijzendoorn, M. H., & Kroonenberg, P. M. (1988). Cross-cultural patterns of attachment: A meta-analysis of the strange situation. *Child Development, 59,* 147–156.

Van Toller, C., Dodd, G. H., & Billing, A. (1985). *Ageing and the sense of smell.* Springfield, IL: Charles C. Thomas.

Vaughan, E., & Fisher, A. E. (1962). Male sexual behavior induced by intracranial electrical stimulation. *Science, 137,* 758.

Ventura, S. J., Taffel, S. M., Mosher, W. D., & Henshaw, S. (1992). *Trends in pregnancies and pregnancy rates, United States, 1980–1988,* Monthly Vital Statistics Report No. 41(6, Suppl.). Hyattsville, MD: National Center for Health Statistics.

Verhave, T. (1966). The pigeon as a quality control inspector. *American Psychologist, 21,* 109–115.

Verner, A. M., & Krupka, L. R. (1985). Over-the-counter anorexiants: Use and perceptions among young adults. In J. P. Morgan, D. U. Kagen, & J. S. Brody (Eds.), *Phenylpropanolamine: Risks, benefits, and controversies.* New York: Praeger.

Vernon, P. A. (1983). Speed of information processing and general intelligence. *Intelligence, 7,* 53–70.

Vernon, P. A. (1991). Studying intelligence the hard way. *Intelligence, 15,* 389–395.

Vernon, P. A., & Mori, M. (1992). Intelligence, reaction times, and peripheral nerve conduction velocity. *Intelligence, 16,* 273–288.

Vicario, G. B. (1982). Some observations in the auditory field. In J. Beck (Ed.),

Organization and representation in perception (pp. 269–283). Hillsdale, NJ: Erlbaum.

Vidmar, N., & Laird, N. M. (1983). Adversary social roles: Their effects on witness communication of evidence and the assessments of adjudicators. *Journal of Personality and Social Psychology, 44,* 888–898.

Vincent, K. R. (1991). Black/white IQ differences: Does age make the difference? *Journal of Clinical Psychology, 47,* 266–270.

Violato, C., & Wiley, A. J. (1990). Images of adolescence in English literature: The middle ages to the modern period. *Adolescence, 25,* 253–264.

Vogel, J. M. (1980). Getting letters straight. In F. B. Murray (Ed.), *Some perceptual prerequisites for learning.* Newark, DE: International Reading Association.

Vokey, J. R., & Read, J. D. (1985). Subliminal messages: Between the devil and the media. *American Psychologist, 40,* 1231–1239.

von Frisch, K. (1950). *Bees: Their vision, chemical senses, and language.* Ithaca, NY: Cornell University Press.

von Frisch, K. (1962). Dialects in the language of bees. *Scientific American, 207*(2), 78–86.

von Glinow, M. A., & Milliman, J. (1990). Developing human resource strategic management: Prescriptions for multinational company success. *Journal of Management Issues, 2,* 91–104.

Wakefield, J. C. (1992). The concept of mental disorder: On the boundary between biological facts and social values. *American Psychologist, 47,* 373–388.

Wald, G. (1968). The molecular basis of visual excitation. *Science, 162,* 230–239.

Wald, G., & Brown, P. K. (1958). Human rhodopsin. *Science, 127,* 222–226.

Walden, E. L., & Thompson, S. A. (1981). A review of some alternative approaches to drug management of hyperactivity in children. *Journal of Learning Disabilities, 14,* 213–232.

Walk, R. D. (1978). Perceptual learning. In E. C. Carterette & M. P. Friedman (Eds.), *Handbook of perception* (Vol. 9, pp. 257–297). New York: Academic Press.

Walk, R. D., & Gibson, E. J. (1961). A comparative and analytic study of visual depth perception. *Psychological Monographs, 75,* 1–44.

Wallace, B. (1979). *Applied hypnosis: An overview.* Chicago: Nelson Hall.

Wallace, P. (1977). Individual discrimination of humans by odor. *Physiology and Behavior, 19,* 577, 579.

Wallach, H. (1963). The perception of neutral colors. *Scientific American, 208,* 107–116.

Wallas, G. (1926). *The art of thought.* New York: Harcourt, Brace & World.

Walsh, E. (1992, February 4). Psychiatrist says Dahmer has a terrible sickness. *Washington Post,* p. A8.

Walster, E., Walster, G. W., & Berscheid, E. (1978). *Equity: Theory and research.* Boston: Allyn & Bacon.

Ward, T. B. (1991, November). *Structured imagination: The role of category structure in exemplar generation.* Paper presented at the annual meeting of the Psychonomic Society, San Francisco.

Warnath, M. (1987). *Power dynamism* (working paper).

Warren, B. (1990). Psychoanalysis and personal construct theory: An exploration. *Journal of Psychology, 124*(4), 449–463.

Warren, M. (1983). Physical and biological aspects of puberty. In J. Brooks-Gunn & A. C. Petersen (Eds.), *Girls at puberty: Biological and psychosocial perspectives* (pp. 3–28). New York: Plenum.

Warren, R. M. (1982). *Auditory perception: A new synthesis.* New York: Pergamon.

Wasik, B. H., Ramey, C. T., Bryant, D. M., & Sparling, J. J. (1990). A longitudinal study of two early intervention strategies: Project CARE. *Child Development, 61,* 1682–1696.

Wason, P. C., & Johnson-Laird, P. N. (1972). *Psychology of reasoning: Structure and content.* Cambridge, MA: Harvard University Press.

Watson, D. (1991). Drugs and behavior. *Journal of Consulting and Clinical Psychology, 65,* 34–43.

Watson, J. B. (1913). Psychology as the behaviorist views it. *Psychological Review, 20,* 158–177.

Watson, J. B. (1929). *Psychology from the standpoint of a behaviorist* (3rd ed.). Philadelphia: Lippincott.

Watson, J. B., & Rayner, R. (1920). Conditional emotional reactions. *Journal of Experimental Psychology, 3,* 1–14.

Weaver, C. A., III. (1991, November). *Is the "flash" necessary to form a flashbulb memory?* Paper presented at the annual convention of the Psychonomic Society, San Francisco.

Webb, E. J., Campbell, D. T., Schwartz, R. D., & Sechrest, L. (1966). *Unobtrusive measures: Nonreactive research in the social sciences.* Chicago: Rand McNally.

Webb, W. B. (1974). Sleep as an adaptive response. *Perceptual and Motor Skills, 38,* 1023–1027.

Webb, W. B. (1975). *Sleep, the gentle tyrant.* Englewood Cliffs, NJ: Prentice-Hall.

Webb, W. B. (1981a). The return of consciousness. In L. T. Benjamin (Ed.), *The G. Stanley Hall lecture series* (Vol. 1, pp. 133–152). Washington, DC: American Psychological Association.

Webb, W. B. (1981b). Some theories about sleep and their clinical implications. *Psychiatric Annals, 11,* 415–422.

Webb, W. B. (1982). The measurement and characteristics of sleep in older persons. *Neurobiology of Aging, 3,* 311–319.

Webb, W. B. (1985). A further analysis of age and sleep deprivation effects. *Psychophysiology, 22,* 156–161.

Webb, W. B. (1988). An objective behavioral model of sleep. *Sleep, 11,* 488–496.

Webb, W. B. (1992). *Sleep: The gentle tyrant.* Bolton, MA: Anker.

Webb, W. B., & Agnew, H. W., Jr. (1975). Are we chronically sleep-deprived? *Bulletin of the Psychonomic Society, 6,* 47–48.

Weber, M. (1946). *The theory of social and economic organization.* A. H. Henderson & T. Parsons (Eds.). Glencoe, IL: Free Press. (Original work published 1924).

Weber, R., & Crocker, J. (1983). Cognitive processes in the revision of stereotypic beliefs. *Journal of Personality and Social Psychology, 45,* 961–977.

Wegmann, H. M., Conrad, B., & Klein, K. E. (1983). Flight, flight duty and rest times: A comparison between the regulations of different countries. *Aviation, Space and Environmental Medicine, 54,* 212–217.

Wehr, T., Sack, D., Rosenthal, N., & Cowdry, R. (1988). Rapid cycling affective disorder: Contributing factors and treatment responses in 51 patients. *American Journal of Psychiatry, 145,* 179–184.

Weidner, G., Sexton, G., Matarazzo, J. D., Pereira, C., & Friend, R. (1988). Type A behavior in children, adolescents, and their parents. *Developmental Psychology, 24,* 118–121.

Weinberg, R. A., Scarr, S., & Waldman, I. D. (1992). The Minnesota transracial adoption study: A follow-up of IQ test performance at adolescence. *Intelligence, 16,* 117–135.

Weiner, B. (1980). *Human motivation.* New York: Holt, Rinehart, & Winston.

Weiner, E. L. (1977). Controlled flight into terrain accidents: System-induced errors. *Human Factors, 19,* 171–181.

Weisberg, R. W. (1986). *Creativity: Genius and other myths.* New York: Freeman.

Weisberg, R. W. (1992). Metacognition and insight during problem solving: Comment on Metcalfe. *Journal of Experimental Psychology: Learning, Memory, and Cognition, 18,* 426–431.

Weisberg, R. W., & Alba, J. W. (1981). An examination of the alleged role of "fixation" in the solution of several "insight" problems. *Journal of Experimental Psychology: General, 110,* 169–192.

Weisburd, S. (1988, January 16). Water contents hard to swallow. *Science News,* p. 20.

Weiss, D. S. (1981). A multigroup study of personality patterns in creativity. *Perceptual and Motor Skills, 52,* 735–746.

Weiss, R. S. (1973). *Loneliness*. Cambridge, MA: MIT Press.

Wells, G. L., & Murray, D. M. (1984). What can psychology say about the Neil v. Biggers criteria for judging eyewitness accuracy? *Journal of Applied Psychology, 68,* 347–362.

Welsh, G. S. (1975). *Creativity and intelligence: A personality approach*. Chapel Hill: University of North Carolina Press.

Wenzlaff, R., & Grozier, S. (1988). Depression and the magnification of failure. *Journal of Abnormal Psychology, 97,* 90–93.

Wernicke, C. (1874). Der Aphasische Symptomenkomplex. Breslau, Poland: M. Cohn and Weigert.

Wertheimer, M. (1945). *Productive thinking*. New York: Harper.

Wesnes, K., & Warburton, D. M. (1984). Smoking, nicotine, and human performance. In D. K. Balfour (Ed.), *Nicotine and the smoking habit* (pp. 133–152). New York: Pergamon.

West, R. L., & Crook, T. H. (1990). Age differences in everyday memory: Laboratory analogues of telephone number recall. *Psychology and Aging, 5,* 520–529.

Wever, E. G., & Bray, W. C. (1937). The perception of low tones and the resonance-volley theory. *Journal of Psychology, 3,* 101–114.

Wexley, K. N., & Latham, G. P. (1991). *Developing and training human resources in organizations*. New York: Harper-Collins.

White, B. L., Castle, P. W., & Held, R. (1964). Observations on the development of visually-directed reaching. *Child Development, 35,* 349–364.

Whorf, B. L. (1956). *Language, thought and reality*. New York: Wiley.

Wickens, C. D. (1984). *Engineering psychology and human performance*. Columbus, OH: Charles E. Merrill.

Wicker, A. W. (1969). Attitudes versus actions: The relationship of verbal and overt behavioral responses to attitude objects. *Journal of Social Issues, 25,* 41–78.

Widiger, T. A., Frances, A., Spitzer, R., & Williams, J. (1988). The DSM-III-R personality disorder: An overview. *American Journal of Psychiatry, 145,* 786–795.

Widiger, T. A., & Trull, T. J. (1991). Diagnosis and clinical assessment. *Annual Review of Psychology, 42,* 109–133.

Wigginton, E. (1985). *Sometimes a shining moment: The foxfire experience*. New York: Doubleday.

Wilder, D., & Thompson, J. (1988). Assimilation and contrast effects in the judgments of groups. *Journal of Personality and Social Psychology, 54,* 62–73.

Wilding, J. M. (1983). *Perception: From sense to object*. New York: St. Martin's Press.

Willerman, L. (1979). *The psychology of individual and group differences*. San Francisco: Freeman.

Williams, C. D. (1959). The elimination of tantrum behavior by extinction procedures. *Journal of Abnormal and Social Psychology, 59,* 269.

Williams, D. A., & Overmier, J. B. (1988). Backward inhibitory conditioning with signaled and unsignaled unconditioned stimuli: Distribution of trials across days and intertrial interval. *Journal of Experimental Psychology: Animal Behavior Processes, 14,* 26–35.

Williams, R. L., Karacan, I., & Hursch, C. J. (1974). *EEG of human sleep*. New York: Wiley.

Williams, W. L. (1992). *The spirit and the flesh: Sexual diversity in American Indian culture*. Boston: Beacon Pres.

Willmer, E. N. (1982). Anatomy of the visual system. In H. B. Barlow & J. D. Mollon (Eds.), *The senses*. London: Cambridge University Press.

Wilson, E. O. (1975). *Sociobiology: The new synthesis*. Cambridge, MA: Harvard University Press.

Winer, G., Hemphill, J., & Craig, R. (1988). The effect of misleading questions in promoting nonconservation responses in children and adults. *Developmental Psychology, 24,* 197–202.

Winograd, E., & Soloway, R. M. (1986). On forgetting the locations of things stored in special places. *Journal of Experimental Psychology: General, 115,* 366–372.

Witelson, S. F. (1985). The brain connection: The corpus callosum is larger in left-handers. *Science, 229,* 665–667.

Wixted, J. R., Belleck, A. R., and Hersen, D. S. (1990). The role of modeling in treatment of abusive behavior. *Annual Review of Psychology, 23, 34 56.*

Wodarski, J. S., Kurtz, P. D., Gaudin, J. M., & Howing, P. T. (1990). Maltreatment and the school-age child: Major academic, socioemotional and adaptive outcomes. *Social Work, 35,* 506–513.

Wolberg, L. R. (1982). *The practice of psychotherapy*. New York: Brunner/Mazel.

Wolf, M. M., Birnbrauer, J. S., Williams, T., & Lawler, J. (1965). A note on apparent extinction of the vomiting behavior of a retarded child. In L. Ullman & L. Krazner (Eds.), *Case studies in behavior modification*. New York: Holt, Rinehart, & Winston.

Wolfe, J. (1986). Computerized testing technology. *Advances in Reading/Language Research, 4,* 71–78.

Wolfe, J. B. (1936). Effectiveness of token rewards for chimpanzees. *Comparative Psychology Monographs, 12*(Whole No. 60).

Wolkin, A., Angrist, B., Wolf, A., Brodie, J., Wolkin, B., Jaeger, J., Cancro, R., & Rotrosen, J. (1988). Low frontal glucose utilization in chronic schizophrenia: A replication study. *American Journal of Psychiatry, 145,* 251–253.

Wong, P. T. P., & Peacock, E. J. (1986). When does reinforcement induce stereotyping? A test of the differential reinforcement hypothesis. *Learning and Motivation, 17,* 139–161.

Wood, W., Jones, M., & Benjamin, L. T. (1986). Surveying psychology's public image. *American Psychologist, 41,* 947–953.

Woodruffe, C. (1985). Consensual validation of personality traits: Additional evidence and individual differences. *Journal of Personality and Social Psychology, 48,* 1240–1252.

World Health Organization. (1981). *The influence of alcohol and drugs on driving*. Albany, NY: WHO Publication Centre.

Worringham, C. J., & Messick, D. M. (1983). Social facilitation of running: An unobtrusive study. *Journal of Social Psychology, 121,* 23–29.

Wright, A. A., Cook, R. G., Rivera, J. J., Sands, S. F., & Delius, J. D. (1988). Concept learning by pigeons: Matching-to-sample with trial-unique video picture stimuli. *Animal Learning and Behavior, 16,* 436–444.

Wurtman, R. J., & Wurtman, J. J. (1989). Carbohydrates and depression. *Scientific American, 260*(1), 68–75.

Yaniv, I., & Meyer, D. E. (1987). Activation and metacognition of inaccessible stored information: Potential bases for incubation effects in problem solving. *Journal of Experimental Psychology: Learning, Memory, and Cognition, 13,* 187–205.

Yates, F. A. (1966). *The art of memory*. London: Routledge & Kegan Paul.

Yerkes, R. M., & Dodson, J. D. (1908). The relation of strength of stimulus to rapidity of habit formation. *Journal of Comparative Neurology and Psychology, 18,* 459–482.

Yerkes, R. M., & Morgulis, S. (1909). The method of Pavlov in animal psychology. *Psychological Bulletin, 6,* 257–273.

Yost, W. A., & Nielsen, D. W. (1985). *Fundamentals of hearing: An introduction* (2nd ed.). New York: Holt, Rinehart, & Winston.

Young, F. G. (1990). Techniques of psychoanalysis in contemporary society. *Archives of General Psychiatry, 45,* 98–111.

Youniss, J., & Smollar, J. (1985). *Adolescent relations with mothers, fathers, and friends*. Chicago: University of Chicago Press.

Ysseldyke, J. E., Algozzine, B., Shinn, M. R., & McGue, M. (1982). Similarities and differences between low achievers and students classified as learning disabled. *Journal of Special Education, 16,* 73–85.

Yurek, D. M., & Sladek, J. R. (1990). Dopamine cell replacement: Parkinson's disease. *Annual Review of Neuroscience, 13,* 387–402.

Zajonc, R. B. (1965). Social facilitation. *Science, 149,* 269–274.

Zajonc, R. B. (1968). Attitudinal effects of mere exposure. *Journal of Personality and Social Psychology Monograph, 9*(1–29, pt. 2).

Zajonc, R. B. (1985). Emotion and facial efference: A theory reclaimed. *Science, 288,* 15–21.

Zametkin, A. J., Nordahl, T. E., Gross, M., King, A. C., Semple, W. E., Rumsey, J., Hamburger, S., & Cohen, R. M. (1990). Cerebral glucose metabolism in adults with hyperactivity of childhood onset. *New England Journal of Medicine, 323,* 1361–1366.

Zarbatany, L., Hartmann, D. P., & Rankin, D. B. (1990). The psychological functions of preadolescent peer activities. *Child Development, 61,* 1067–1080.

Zedeck, S., & Cascio, W. F. (1984). Psychological issues in personnel decisions. *Annual Review of Psychology, 35,* 461–518.

Zhang, G., & Simon, H. A. (1985). STM capacity for Chinese words and idioms: Chunking and acoustical loop hypotheses. *Memory and Cognition, 13,* 193–201.

Zihl, J., von Cramon, D., & Mai, N. (1983). Selective disturbance of movement vision after bilateral brain damage. *Brain, 106,* 313–340.

Zimbardo, P. G. (1969). The human choice: Individuation, reason and order versus deindividuation, impulse and chaos. In W. J. Arnold & D. Levin (Eds.), *Nebraska Symposium on Motivation, 1969.* Lincoln: University of Nebraska Press.

Zimbardo, P. G. (1970). The human choice: Individuation, reason and order versus individuation, impulse and chaos. Reprinted from the *1969 Nebraska Symposium on Motivation.* Lincoln: University of Nebraska Press.

Zimmerman, D. R. (1983). *The essential guide to nonprescription drugs.* New York: Harper & Row.

Zimmerman, I., & Woo-Sam, J. (1985). Clinical applications. In B. B. Wolman (Ed.), *Handbook of intelligence: Theories, measurements, and applications* (pp. 873–898). New York: Wiley.

Zuckerman, M. (1984). Sensation-seeking: A cooperative approach to a human approach. *Behavioral and Brain Sciences, 7,* 413–471.

Zuckerman, M., & Feldman, L. S. (1984). Actions and occurrences in attribution theory. *Journal of Personality and Social Psychology, 46,* 541–550.

Zwislocki, J. J. (1981). Sound analysis in the ear: A history of discoveries. *American Scientist, 69,* 184–192.

CREDITS

Table and Line Art Credits

Chapter 1: Introduction to Psychology

Table 1–1: Office of Demographic, Employment and Educational Research. APA Education Directorate. © by The American Psychological Association. Reprinted by permission.

Table 1–4: Korn, J. H. (1988). Students' rules, rights and responsibilities as research participants. *Teaching of Psychology*, 15, 74–78. Hillsdale, NJ: Erlbaum. Reprinted by permission of publisher and author.

Chapter 2: Biological Bases of Behavior

Table 2–2: Kow, L. M. & Pfaff, D. W. (1988). Neuromodulatory actions of peptides. *Annual Review of Pharmacology and Toxicology*, Volume 28. © (1988) by Annual Reviews Inc., CA. Used with permission.

Figure 2–17: Adapted from Nauta, W. J. H. & Feirtag, M. (1979). The organization of the brain. *Scientific American*, September 1979. Copyright © (1979) by Scientific American Inc. All rights reserved.

Figure 2–25: Figure adapted from Lindsey, P. H. & Norman, D. A. *Human Information Processing*, 2nd ed. © (1977) Harcourt Brace and Company, Chicago, IL. Reprinted by permission of the publisher.

Table 2–4: Bouchard, J. & Lykken, D. T. Sources of human psychological differences: The Minnesota study of twins reared apart. *Science*, 10/12/90, 223–228. Copyright (1990) by the A.A.A.S.

Chapter 3: Sensory Processes

Figure 3–11: Riggs, L. A. (1965). Visual acuity. In C. H. Graham (Ed.), *Vision and Visual Perception*. New York: Wiley. Reprinted by permission of John Wiley & Sons, Inc.

Figure 3–24: Adapted from Hubool & Woiool. (1961). *Journal of Physiology*. United Kingdom: The Physiological Society.

Figure 3–30: Matlin, M. W. (1983). *Perception*. Copyright © (1983) by Allyn & Bacon, Needham Heights, MA. Reprinted by permission of Simon & Schuster.

Chapter 4: Perception

Figure 4–7: Matlin, M. W. & Foley, H. J. (1992). *Sensation and Perception*, 3rd ed. Copyright © (1992) by Allyn and Bacon, Needham Heights, MA. Reprinted by permission of Simon & Schuster.

Figure 4–9: From Prinzmetal & Banks (1977). *Journal of Perception & Psychophysics*, 21, 389–395. Reprinted by permission of The Psychonomic Society, Inc., Austin, TX.

Figure 4–21: From Goldstein, E. B. (1984). *Sensation and Perception*, 2nd ed. Copyright © (1984) by Wadsworth, Inc. Reprinted by permission of Brooks/Cole Publishing Co., Pacific Grove, CA 93950.

Figure 4–23: Brown & Deffenbacher (1979). *Perception & the Senses*, p. 156. New York: Oxford University Press. Reprinted by permission of Oxford University Press, New York.

Figure 4–24: Figure from Coren, S. & Ward, L. M. (1989). *Sensation & Perception*, 3rd ed. Copyright (1989) by Harcourt Brace and Company. Reprinted by permission of the publishers.

Chapter 5: States of Consciousness

Figure 5–5 and 5–6: From Coleman, R. M. (1986). *Wide Awake at 3:00 AM*. Reprinted with permission of W. H. Freeman & Co.

Figure 5–10: Adapted from Jouvet, M. (1967). The states of sleep. *Scientific American*, 216 (2), 62–72. © February (1967) by Scientific American, Inc. Reprinted by permission of Scientific American, Inc. All rights reserved.

Table 5–1: Adapted from Tompkins, R. D. (1981). *Before It's Too Late: The Preventative Manual on Drug Abuse for People Who Care*. Englewood, NJ: Family Information Services.

Table 5–2: Adapted from Ray, O. S. & Ksir, C. (1993). *Drugs, Society and Human Behavior*, 6th ed. 192. St. Louis, MO: Times Mirror/Mosby College Publishing. Adapted with permission.

Chapter 6: Learning

Figure 6–3: Adapted from Pavlov, I. P. (1927). *Conditioned Reflexes*. New York: Oxford University Press. Adapted by permission of Oxford University Press, New York.

Chapter 7: Memory

Figure 7–8: Adapted from Glanzer, M. & Cunitz, A. R. (1966). Two storage mechanisms in free recall. *Journal of Verbal Learning and Verbal Behavior*, 5, 351–360. Reprinted by permission of Academic Press, Inc., Orlando, FL.

Figure 7–15: Smith, S. M., Glenberg, A. M., & Bjork, R. A. (1978). Environmental context and human memory. *Memory and Cognition*, 6, 342–353. Reprinted by permission of The Psychonomic Society, Inc., Austin, TX.

Figure 7–16: Adapted from Bower, G. H. (1981). Mood and memory. *American Psychology*, 36, 129–148. © (1981) by American Psychological Association. Adapted by permission.

Figure 7–20: From Ellis, H. C. & Hunt, R. (1989). *Fundamentals of Human Memory and Cognition*, 4th ed. © (1989) Wm. C. Brown Publishers, Inc., Dubuque, IA. All rights reserved. Reprinted by permission.

Figure 7–22. From Thompson, R. F., et al. (1986). The neurobiology of learning and memory. *Science*, 223, 941–947. Copyright (1986) by the A.A.A.S.

Chapter 8: Thought and Language

Figure 8–3: Adapted from Shepard, R. H. & Cooper, L. A. (1982). *Mental Images & Their Transformations*. Cambridge, MA: MIT Press. © (1982). Reprinted by permission.

Figure 8–9: Design fixation. Jansson, D. G. & Smith, S. M. (1991). *Design Studies*, 12, 1, 3–11. Reprinted by permission of the publishers, Butterworth-Heinemann Ltd. © (1991).

Figure 8–11: Fink, R. A., Ward, T. B., & Smith, S. M. (1992). *Creative Cognition: Theory, Research & Applications*. Cambridge, MA: MIT Press. © (1992). Reprinted by permission.

Figure 8–12: From Ward, T. B. (1991). Structured imagination: The role of category structure in exemplar generation. Paper presented at Psychonomic Society. Reprinted by permission of the author.

Figure 8–14: Reprinted from Karl von Frisch. (1950) *Bees: Their Vision, Chemical Senses, and Language*, revised edition. Copyright (1950), © (1971) by Cornell University. Used by permission of the publisher, Cornell University Press.

Chapter 9: Motivation and Emotion

Figure 9–2: Adapted from Lack, D. (1943). *The Life of the Robin*. Victor Gollancz Ltd., London. Adapted by permission.

Figure 9–3: Adapted from Tinbergen, N. (1948). Social releasers and the experimental method required for their study. *Wilson Bulletin*, 60, 6–52. Adapted by permission. VA: Virginia Commonwealth University Press.

Figure 9–5: Houston, J. P. (1985). *Motivation*. Reprinted by permission of Macmillan Publishing Company from *Motivation* by John P. Houston. Copyright © (1985) by Macmillan Publishing Company, New York.

Figure 9–9: Calorie Control Council National Consumer Surveys. Atlanta, GA. Reprinted with permission of the Calorie Control Council.

Figure 9–13: Adapted from Anderson, C. A. & Anderson, D. C. (1984). Ambient temperature and violent crime: Tests of the linear and curvilinear hypotheses. Adapted from *Journal of Personality and Social Psychology*, 46, 91–97. Copyright (1985) by the American Psychological Association. Adapted by permission.

Figure 9–14: Hamilton, J. O. (1974). Motivation and risk-taking behavior: A test of Atkinson's theory. Adapted from *Journal of*

Personality and Social Psychology, 29, 856–864. Copyright (1974) by the American Psychological Association. Adapted by permission.

Figure 9–16: Ekman, P., Friesen, W. & Ellsworth, P. (1972). *Emotion in the Human Face: Guidelines for Research and an Integration of Findings*. Elmsford Park, NY: Pergamon Press. Reprinted by permission.

Chapter 10: Personality

Table 10–3: From Lubin, A. J. (1972). *Stranger on Earth: A Psychological Biography of Vincent Van Gogh*. Copyright © (1972) by Albert J. Lubin. Reprinted by permission of Henry Holt & Co., Inc., New York. Also adapted from Runyan, W. M. (1981). Why did Vincent Van Gogh cut off his ear? The problem of alternative explanations in psychobiography. *Journal of Personality & Social Psychology*, 40, 1070–1077. Copyright (1981) by the American Psychological Association. Adapted by permission.

Table 10–4: Adapted from Freud, A. (1966). *The Writings of Anna Freud: Volume 2. The Ego & the Mechanisms of Defense* (rev. ed.) New York: International Universities Press. Also from Fancher, R. E. (1973). *Psychoanalytic Psychology: The Development of Freud's Thoughts*. New York: Norton. Used by permission.

Figure 10–1: Adapted from Hall, C. & Van De Castle, R. L. (1973). An empirical investigation of the castration complex in dreams. In Eysenck, H. J. & Wilson, G. D. (Eds.) *The Experimental Study of Freudian Theories*, 157–169. London: Methuen. Adapted by permission.

Chapter 11: Intelligence and Personality

Table 11–1: From Anastasi, A. (1988). *Psychological Testing*, 6th ed. Copyright © (1988) by Anne Anastasi. Reprinted with permission of Macmillan Publishing Company from *Psychological Testing*, 6th ed. by Anne Anastasi.

Table 11–5: Sternberg, R. J. (1985). *Beyond IQ: A Triarchic Theory of Human Intelligence*, 81. New York: Cambridge University Press. Used with permission.

Table 11–6: Thorndike, R. L., Hagen, E. P., & Sattler, J. M. (1986). *The Stanford-Binet Intelligence Scale*, 4th ed. Reprinted with permission of the publisher, The Riverside Publishing Company, 8420 Bryn Mawr Ave., Chicago, IL 60631. All rights reserved.

Figure 11–5: Adapted from Guilford, J. (1985). The structure of intellect model. In B. B. Wolman (Ed.). *Intelligence: Theories, Measurements and Applications*, 225–266. Copyright © 1985. New York: Wiley. Reprinted by permission of John Wiley & Sons, Inc.

Table 11–8: Reprinted from Costa, P. T. and McCrae, R. R. (1992). Four ways five factors are basic. *Personality and Individual Differences*, 13, p. 654. Copyright (1992). With kind permission from Pergamon Press

Ltd., Headington Hill Hall, Oxford OX3 OBW, UK.

Figure 11–9: Adapted from Popkin, A. J., Schaie, K. W. & Krauss, I. K. (1983). Age-fair assessment of psychometric intelligence. *Educational Gerontology*, 9, 47–55. Washington, DC: Taylor & Francis Publishing Co. Adapted by permission.

Table 11–11: Adapted from Bouchard, T., Jr., & Segal, N. (1985). Environment and IQ, Table 23. In B. B. Wolman (Ed.) *Handbook of Intelligence: Theories, Measurements and Applications*, 453. New York: Wiley. Reprinted by permission of John Wiley & Sons, Inc.

Chapter 12: Physical and Cognitive Development

Table 12–1: From Plomin, R., McClearn, G. E., Pederson, N. L., Nesselroade, J. R., & Bergeman, C. S. (1988). Genetic influence on childhood family environment perceived retrospectively from the last half of the life span. *Research on Aging*, 10, 220–234. Newbury Park, CA: Sage. Reprinted by permission.

Figure 12–1(a) & (b): From Kauffman, A. S., Reynolds, C. R. & McLean, J. E. (1989). Age and WAIS-R Intelligence in a national sample of adults in the 20 to 74-year age range: A cross-sectional analysis with educational level controlled. *Intelligence*, 13, 235–253. Norwood, NJ: Ablex Publishing Co. Reprinted by permission.

Figure 12–3: From Tanner, J. M. (1978). *Fetus Into Man: Physical Growth from Conception to Maturity*. Cambridge, MA: Harvard University Press. Copyright © (1978) by J. M. Tanner. Reprinted by permission of the author.

Figure 12–5(a) & (b): Adapted from Frantz, R. L. & Nevis, S. (1967). Pattern preferences and perceptual cognitive development in early infancy. *Merrill-Palmer Quarterly*, 13, 88–108. © (1967). Adapted by permission of Wayne State University Press, Detroit, MI.

Figure 12–7: Piaget, J. & Inhelder, B. (1967). *The Child's Conception of Space*. F. J. Langdon & J. L. Lunzer, Trans. London: Routledge & Kegan Paul. Reprinted by permission.

Figure 12–9: Piaget, J. & Inhelder, B. (1958). *The Growth of Logical Thinking: From Childhood to Adolescence*. A. Parsons & S. Milgram, Trans. London: Routledge & Kegan Paul. Reprinted by permission.

Figure 12–10: Adapted from Winer, G., Hemphill, J. & Craig, R. (1988). The effect of misleading questions in promoting nonconversational responses in children & adults. *Developmental Psychology*, 24, 197–202. Copyright (1988) by the American Psychological Association. Adapted by permission.

Figure 12–11: Adapted from West, R. L. & Crook, T. H. (1990). Age differences in everyday memory: Laboratory analogues of telephone number recall. *Psychology and Aging*, 5, 520–529. Copyright (1990) by the American Psychological Association. Adapted by permission.

Chapter 13: Social Development

Table 13–2: Thomas, A. & Chess, S. (1977). *Temperament and Development*. New York: Brunner/Mazel. Reprinted with permission of the publisher and the authors.

Table 13–3: Galvin, R. M. (1992). The nature of shyness. *Harvard Magazine*, 94 (4), 41–45. © (1992) Harvard Magazine. Reprinted with permission.

Figure 13–4: Finkelhor, D., Hotaling, G., Lewis, I. A., & Smith, C. (1990). Sexual abuse in a national survey of adult men and women: Prevalence, characteristics, & risk factors. *Child Abuse and Neglect*, 14, 19–28. Reprinted with kind permission from Pergamon Press Ltd., Headington Hall, Oxford, OX3 ONW, UK.

Table 13–7: Erikson, E. H. (1968). *Identity: Youth & Crisis*, Chapter 3. New York: Norton. © (1968). Reprinted by permission.

Figure 13–6: Adapted from Steinberg, L. & Silverberg, S. B. (1986). The vicissitudes of autonomy in early adolescence. *Child Development*, 57, 841–851. © (1986) The Society for Research and Development, Inc., Chicago, IL.

Figure 13–7: From Levinson, D. J. (1978). *The Seasons of a Man's Life*. Copyright © (1978) by Daniel J. Levinson. Reprinted by permission of Alfred A. Knopf, Inc., New York.

Figure 13–8: Glenn, N. D. (1975). Table 2, p. 106 in Psychological well-being in the postparental stage: Some evidence from national surveys. *Journal of Marriage and the Family*, 37 (1), 105–110. Copyright (1975) by The National Council on Family Relations, 3989 Central Ave., NE, Suite 550, Minneapolis, MN 55421. Reprinted by permission.

Chapter 14: Social Psychology

Table 14–1: Adapted from Tourangeau, R. & Rasinski, K. (1988). Cognitive processes underlying context effects in attitude measurement. *Psychological Bulletin*, 103, 200–314. Copyright (1988) by the American Psychological Association. Adapted by permission.

Table 14–3: Adapted from Brown, R. (1986). *Social Psychology*, 2nd ed. © (1986) by The Free Press, New York. Reprinted by permission of Macmillan, Inc.

Table 14–4: Adapted from P. K. Lunt. (1988). The perceived causal structure of examination failure. *British Journal of Social Psychology*, 27, 171–179. Adapted by permission from Fig. 2.

Table 14–6: Adapted from Hendrick, C. & Hendrick, S. (1986). A theory and method of love. *Journal of Personality and Social Psychology*, 50, 392–402. Copyright (1986) by the American Psychological Association. Adapted by permission.

Table 14–7: Rubenstein, C. & Shaver, P. (1982). The experience in loneliness. In L. A. Peplav and D. Perlman (Eds.). *Loneliness: A Sourcebook of Current Theory, Research & Therapy*. New York: Wiley. Reprinted by permission.

Chapter 15: Health, Stress, and Coping

Chart on pp. 613–614: Blake, P., Fry, R., & Pesjack, M. (1984). *Self Assessment & Behavioral Change Manual.* New York: McGraw Hill. Reprinted by permission.
Text: Techniques to alter mental states. *American Psychological Society Observer,* November 1991.
Table 15–1: Matarazzo, J. D. (1984). *Behavioral Heatlh: A Handbook of Health Enhancement and Disease Prevention.* New York: Wiley. Used by permission of the author.
Table 15–4: Adapted from Stone, A. A. & Neale, J. M. (1984). New measurements of daily coping: Development and preliminary results. *Journal of Personality and Social Psychology,* 46, 892–906. Copyright (1984) by the American Psychological Association. Adapted by permission.

Chapter 16: Psychological Disorders

Table 16–1: Adapted from MacKay, M. (1981). Special symptoms of childhood. In S. Ariety & K. H. Brodie (Eds.). *American Handbook of Psychiatry,* 2e. 7, pp. 187–203. Adapted from Advances & New Directions ADA.

Table 16–2: Beck, A. T. & Freeman, A. and Associates. (1990). *Cognitive Therapy of Personality Disorders,* p. 26. NY: Guilford Press. Used with permission.

Chapter 17: Treatment of Psychological Disorders

Text: Rogers, Carl. (1967). A silent young man. *The Therapeutic Relationship and Its Impact.* Westport, Ct: Greenwood Press. Used with permission.
Figure 17–1: Shapiro, S., Skinner, E. A., Kessler, L. G., VonKorff, M., German, P. S., Tischler, G. L., Leaf, P. J., Benham, L., Cottler, L. & Regier, D. A. (1984). Utilization of health and mental health services. *Archives of General Psychiatry,* 41, 971–978. Copyright (1984) by the American Medical Association, Chicago, IL.
Figure 17–4: Adapted from Bassuk, E. L. & Gerson, S. (1978). Deinstitutionalization and mental health services. *Scientific American,* 238 (2), 46–53. Copyright © (1978) by Scientific American, Inc. All rights reserved. Also adapted from Kiesler, C. A. (1982). Public and professional myths about mental hospitalization. *American Psychologist,* 37, 1323–

1339. Copyright (1982) by the American Psychological Association. Adapted with permission. Also adapted from Kiesler, C. A. (1982). Mental hospitals and alternative care: Noninstitutionalization as a potential public policy for mental patients. *American Psychologist,* 37, 349–360. Copyright (1982) by the American Psychological Association. Adapted with permission.
Figure 17–13: William A. McKim. (1991). *Drugs and Behavior: An Introduction to Behavioral Pharmacology,* © (1991), p. 257. Reprinted with permission of Prentice Hall, Englewood Cliffs, NJ.
Figure 17–14: Adapted from Smith, M. L. & Glass, G. V. (1977). Meta-analysis of psychotherapy outcome studies. *American Psychologist,* 32, 752–760. Copyright (1977) by the American Psychological Association. Adapted by permission.

Appendix C: Psychology Resources in the Library

Table C–1: Reed, J. G. & Baxter, P. M. (1992). *Library Use: A Handbook for Psychology,* 2nd ed. Washington, DC: American Psychological Association.

Photo Credits

Chapter 1: Introduction to Psychology

Page 1: Joel Gordon/Joel Gordon Photography; *page 3:* Kindra Clineff/Kindra Clineff; *page 5:* Eugene Richards/Magnum; *page 5:* Courtesy of Colorado State University; *page 7:* Courtesy Dr. Stephen F. Davis; *page 8:* Linda Bartlett; *page 8:* Courtesy Stanley Sue, Ph.D., University of California, Los Angeles; *page 9:* Scala/Art Resource; *page 11:* Brundy Library; *page 11:* National Portrait Gallery, London, Eng.; *page 12:* Melissa Benjamin/Courtesy of Ludy Benjamin; *page 13:* Archives of the History of American Psychology, University of Akron; *page 15:* Courtesy of Harvard University; *page 15:* Culver Pictures, Inc.; *page 20:* Courtesy of NASA's Ames Laboratory; *page 25:* Richard Nowitz/Phototake; *page 28:* Courtesy of Lisa Littlefield, Zoo Atlanta.

Chapter 2: Biological Bases of Behavior

Page 38: Dan McCoy/Rainbow; *page 42:* Hank Morgan/Science Source/Photo Researchers, Inc.; *page 43:* Dr. Michael Lewis, University of CO, EM Laboratory; *page 55:* Dan McCoy/Rainbow; *page 56:* Courtesy of Dr. Alan J. Zametkin/Zametkin et al., 1990; *page 57:* CNRI/Science Photo Library/Photo Researchers; *page 58:* Courtesy Dr. E. R. John, Brain Research Lab, NYU Medical Ctr.; *page 59:* Created for this book by P. Mercurio of Quantitative Morphology Lab, University of CA, San Diego—by kind permission of Dr. Robert Livingston; *page 63:* Courtesy of Dr. L. Squire, Dept. of Psychiatry UCSD School of Medicine; *page 64:* Dr. Richard Haier;

page 65: both photos from Carolina Biological Supply Company; *page 67:* Tetryakov Gallery, Moscow; *page 71:* Created for this book by P. Mercurio of Quantitative Morphology Lab, University of CA, San Diego—by kind permission of Dr. Robert Livingston; *page 83:* Art Resource.

Chapter 3: Sensory Processes

Page 86: Superstock; *page 88:* The Image Bank; *page 93:* Charles Bonnay/Black Star; *page 95:* Courtesy of Bausch & Lomb; *page 97:* OMIKRON/Photo Researchers, Inc.; *page 102:* Georges Seurat, French, 1859–1891, "A Sunday on La Grande Jatte," 1884, oil on canvas, 1884–86, 207.6 x 308 cm. Helen Birch Bartlett Memorial Collection, 1926.224. Photograph © 1993, The Art Institute of Chicago. All Rights Reserved; *page 103:* Georges Seurat, French, 1859–1891, "A Sunday on La Grande Jatte," 1884, oil on canvas, 1884–86, 207.6 x 308 cm. Helen Birch Bartlett Memorial Collection, 1926.224. Detail: view #31. Photograph © 1993, The Art Institute of Chicago. All Rights Reserved; *page 107:* Susanne Pasko/Envision; *page 118:* Prof. A. Motta/Dept. of Anatomy, University "La Sapienza," Rome/ Science Photo Library/ Photo Researchers, Inc.

Chapter 4: Perception

Page 130: Chris Arnesen/Allstock; *page 133:* From "States of Mind," Jonathan Miller, editor, Tony Spaul, artist © 1985 BBC Publications & Pantheon Books; *page 138:* Archive of Children's Art, Courtesy of UNICEF; *page 138:*

Milwaukee Art Museum; *page 139:* John Schultz; *page 140:* William Vandivert; *page 143:* Photo Researchers, Inc.; *page 147:* Dave Schaeffer/The Picture Cube; *page 154:* both photos by Jon Brenneis.

Chapter 5: States of Consciousness

Page 164: David Delossy/Image Bank; *page 166:* The Detroit Institute of Arts; *page 169:* Will & Deni McIntyre/Photo Researchers, Inc.; *page 169:* Stephen Green-Armytage/The Stock Market; *page 170:* Melissa Benjamin; *page 174:* Dominique Aubert/Sygma; *page 185:* Belgium Postal Services; *page 186:* Mary Evans/Freuds Copyrights; *page 189:* Macdonald/Aldus Archive; *page 190:* Western Historical Manuscript Collection, Columbia, MO; *page 192:* Mary Evans Picture Library; *page 193:* Courtesy of Stanford University; *page 200:* Gregory G. Dimijian/Photo Researchers, Inc.

Chapter 6: Learning

Page 210: Dallas & John Heaton/Westlight; *page 225:* Courtesy John N. Coulbourn, Coulbourn Instruments, Inc.; *page 229:* both photos courtesy of Thom Verhave, CUNY Queens College; *page 231:* Yerkes Regional Primate Center of Emory Univ.; *page 232:* © Meyer Liebowitz/NYT Pictures—from Feb. 1, 1958 NY Times; *page 233:* James Marshall/The Stock Market; *page 236:* John Coulbourn/ Coulbourn Instruments, Lehigh Valley, PA; *page 241:* Marian Breland/ Animal Behavior Enterprises.

Chapter 7: Memory

Page 250: © 91 Mug Shots/The Stock Market; *page 258*: Grant Wood, American, 1891–1942, "American Gothic," oil on beaver board, 1930, 76 x 63.3 cm. Friends of American Art Collection, 1930.934. Photograph © 1993, The Art Institute of Chicago. All Rights Reserved; *page 265*: John Schultz/PAR/NYC; *page 269*: Courtesy Caroline Rovee-Collier, Prof. of Psych., Rutgers University; *page 269*: Courtesy Caroline Rovee-Collier, Prof. of Psych., Rutgers University; *page 273*: Seth Resnick; *page 273*: David Welcher/Sygma; *page 275*: both photos froms A/P Wide World; *page 282*: Courtesy of Dr. Suzanne Corkin, Orig. printed in *Neurology*, Vol. 4, No. 2 (June 1984); *page 282*: Courtesy of Dr. Suzanne Corkin, Orig. printed in *Neurology*, Vol. 4, No. 2 (June 1984).

Chapter 8: Thought and Language

Page 290: © Peter Timmermans/Allstock; *page 292*: Philippe Halsman/Magnum Photos; *page 292*: National Library of Medicine; *page 297*: Laura Dwight; *page 314*: Ian Yeomans/Woodfin Camp & Associates; *page 317*: Marc & Evelyn Bernheim/Woodfin Camp & Associates; *page 320*: Courtesy of Donna Coveney/MIT; *page 321*: Kindra Clineff/Allstock; *page 322*: Courtesy of Roger Brown, Harvard University, Dept. of Psychology; *page 327*: Courtesy of Beatrice T. Gardner, Univ. of Nevada, Reno; *page 328*: Courtesy of Dr. Herbert Terrace, Dept. of Psych., Columbia University.

Chapter 9: Motivation and Emotion

Page 332: Tim Davis/Allstock; *page 335*: Bildarchiv Okapia/Photo Researchers, Inc.; *page 335*: The Bettmann Archive; *page 340*: Kindra Clineff/Allstock; *page 345*: Dr. Neal E. Miller, Yale University; *page 351*: Lynn McAfee/Globe Photos, Inc.; *page 353*: David Vance/The Image Bank; *page 354*: Desazo Rapho/Photo Researchers, Inc.; *page 358*: Jim Pickerell/West Light; *page 361*: © Paul Ekman and Consulting Psychologists Press, Inc.; *page 363*: both photos from Human Interaction Lab, University of CA, San Francisco/Psychiatry; *page 364*: Hugo von Lawick; *page 364*: AP/Wide World; *page 369*: Jerry Mesmer/Folio, Inc.

Chapter 10: Personality

Page 374: Vince Streano/Allstock; *page 384*: Diane Weiss/UPI/The Bettmann Archive; *page 380*: Winnie Klotz, Metropolitan Opera Association; *page 380*: Alpha/London/Globe Photos, Inc.; *page 382*: Art Resource; *page 386*: Mary Evans/Freud Copyright/Mary Evans Picture Library, London; *page 388*: Jeffry W. Myers/The Stock Market; *page 390*: Frank Siteman/The Picture Cube; *page 393*: Karsh/Woodfin Camp & Associates; *page 395*: Princeton University Press; *page 395*: Nick Welsh; *page 396*: Musee Barbier-Muller/Geneva, Switzerland; *page 396*: Galerie Beyeler, Switzerland; *page 396*: Coll. of The Salvador Dali Museum/St. Petersburg,

Florida; *page 399*: The Bettmann Archive; *page 401*: Rick Friedman/Black Star; *page 404*: Albert Bandura; *page 410*: Adamsmith Productions/Woodfin Camp & Associates; *page 416*: Louvre/Giraudon/Art Resource.

Chapter 11: Intelligence and Personality

Page 422: Stock Market; *page 425*: Woodfin Camp & Associates; *page 426*: John Schultz/PAR/NYC; *page 427*: Dan McCoy/Rainbow; *page 431*: Pat Benik/Reuters/The Bettmann Archive; *page 438*: Will & Deni McIntyre/Photo Researchers, Inc.; *page 444*: Richard Hutchings/PhotoEdit; *page 446*: Photo by Redneck/Gamma-Liaison; *page 449*: Adapted from Popkin, A. J., Schaie, K. W., & Krauss, I. K. (1983). Age-fair assessment of psychometric intelligence. 9, 47–55. *Education Gerontology*; *page 450*: Cleveland Museum of Art; *page 451*: Mark Antman/The Image Works; *page 453*: Dr. Rose K. Gantner/Comstock.

Chapter 12: Physical and Cognitive Development

Page 462: Janet Century; *page 466*: Dan Heringa/The Image Bank; *page 472*: Lennart Nilsson/Bokforlaget Bonnier Alba; *page 472*: Petit Format/Nestle/Science Source/Photo Researchers, Inc.; *page 472*: Lennart Nilsson/Bokforlaget Bonnier Alba; *page 473*: Ansell Horn/Phototake; *page 474*: Courtesy of Barbara O'Hara/FAS Research/Univ. of Wash., Seattle; *page 476*: Jeff Greenberg/The Picture Cube; *page 476*: Steve Dunwell/The Image Bank; *page 477*: Harold Hoffman/Photo Researchers, Inc.; *page 478*: Stephen Trimble; *page 480*: Julie Markes; *page 485*: Woodfin Camp & Associates; *page 490*: Bob Daemmrich/The Image Works; *page 491*: Anderson/Monkmeyer Photo Service; *page 495*: Bob Daemmrich/The Image Works.

Chapter 13: Social Development

Page 504: Jon Feingersh/The Stock Market; *page 507*: Andrew W. Meltzoff, University of Washington, Seattle; *page 507*: Millard H. Sharp/Black Star; *page 507*: John Schultz/PAR/NYC; *page 507*: Erika Stone/Peter Arnold, Inc.; *page 509*: Rosane Olson/Allstock; *page 510*: L.O.L., Inc./FPG International; *page 510*: Superstock; *page 510*: Art Wolfe/Allstock; *page 512*: both photos courtesy of Harry E. Harlow, Univ. of Wisconsin, Madison/Primate Lab; *page 513*: Myrleen Ferguson/Photo Edit; *page 516*: Ken Fisher/Tony Stone Worldwide; *page 517*: Janet Century; *page 527*: Chris Rainier/Photographers Aspen; *page 529*: E. Bernager/Explorer/Photo Researchers, Inc.; *page 530*: Gary S. Chapman; *page 537*: Gary S. Chapman; *page 538*: Eunice Harris/Photo Researchers, Inc.; *page 539*: Gamma Liaison; *page 539*: Mary Ellen Mark; *page 542*: Ann Chwatsky.

Chapter 14: Social Psychology

Page 549: Robert Frerck/Odyssey/Frerck/Chicago; *page 551*: James Nachiwey/Magnum Photos; *page 558*: Ed Bock/The Stock Market;

page 562: Jim Corwin/Allstock; *page 562*: Janet Century; *page 563*: Hangarter/The Picture Cube; *page 565*: all three photos by P. Robert/Sygma; *page 566*: Bud Freund/Westlight; *page 566*: Lawrence Migdale; *page 568*: Courtesy of Alexandra Milgram; *page 569*: Eric Bouvet/Gamma-Liaison; *page 573*: Tom Kelly; *page 576*: Billy Barnes; *page 581*: Tom McCarthy/Picture Cube; *page 584*: Win McNamee/Reuters/Bettmann; *page 585*: Billy Barnes.

Chapter 15: Health, Stress, and Coping

Page 592: Janet Century; *page 595*: Courtesy of Harvard University, Cambridge, MA; *page 601*: Robert Rathe/Folio, Inc.; *page 602*: Malcolm S. Kirk; *page 606*: Robert Bennett/FPG International; *page 608*: Tim Gibson/Envision; *page 609*: Superstock; *page 610*: Lee Celano/Reuters/Bettmann; *page 612*: Doug Menuez/Picture Group; *page 615*: Allan Tanenbaum/Sygma; *page 617*: Courtesy of American Psychological Association; *page 619*: Les Stone/Sygma; *page 621*: Rob Nelson/Picture Group; *page 625*: Kal Muller/Woodfin Camp & Associates; *page 627*: Carl Frank/Photo Researchers, Inc.; *page 628*: Dr. Alvin E. Lake, III, Ph.D., Senior Behavioral Psychologist, Michigan Headache & Neurological Institute; *page 629*: Bob Daemmrich.

Chapter 16: Psychological Disorders

Page 634: Superstock; *page 637*: Bettmann Archive; *page 640*: Ellis Herwig/The Picture Cube; *page 641*: Andy Caulfield/Image Bank; *page 645*: Robert Brenner/PhotoEdit; *page 645*: Photo Researchers, Inc.; *page 646*: Courtesy of Dr. Eric M. Reiman, Wash. Univ., St. Louis, Missouri; *page 646*: Peter Turnley/Black Star; *page 648*: Andy Sacks/Tony Stone Worldwide; *page 653*: Steve Varnedoe; *page 653*: Elliott Erwitt/Magnum Photos; *page 656*: Miro Vintoniv/Stock Boston; *page 661*: Courtesy Barry M. Cohen, Dir. of Expressive Therapy, Mt. Vernon Hosp., Alexandria, VA; *page 666*: both photos by Andrew Popper/The Picture Group; *page 672*: Tim Kelly/Black Star.

Chapter 17: Treatment of Psychological Disorders

Page 679: Brent Peterson/The Stock Market; *page 683*: both photos by Chip Clark/Smithsonian Institution; *page 684*: Chip Clark/Smithsonian Institution; *page 685*: The Bettmann Archive; *page 689*: Edmund Engelman; *page 696*: Courtesy, Institute for Rational-Emotive Therapy; *page 698*: Dick Luria/FPG International; *page 701*: David Young-Wolfe/PhotoEdit; *page 702*: Erik Leigh Simmons/The Image Bank; *page 706*: Paul Fusco/Magnum Photos, Inc.; *page 713*: Steve Goldberg/Monkmeyer Press.

Appendix B

Page 742: Ken Kerbs/Ken Kerbs Photography; *page 743*: Joseph Nettis/Photo Researchers, Inc.; *page 746*: SIPA; *page 749*: Louie Psihoyos/Matrix; *page 749*: Wallis/SIPA.

Author Index

Lettvin, J. Y., 101
Levander, S. E., 709
LeVay, S., 30
Levenson, R. W., 607
Lever, J., 517
Levey, A. I., 481
Levin, H., 150
Levin, J. D., 47
Levine, B., 179
Levinson, D. J., 535, 543
Levis, D. J., 236, 692, 693
Levitan, L., 188
Levy, M. B., 580
Lewin, K., 358, 748
Lewis, D. A., 45
Lewis, E. R., 43
Lewis, H. B., 392
Lewis, I. A., 523, 659
Lewis, J. W., 48
Lewis, M., 487, 488
Lewis, R. J., 410
Lewkowicz, D., 484
Liaw, F. R., 489
Lieberman, M., 532
Liebert, R. M., 405
Liebeskind, J. C., 48
Lieblich, I., 268
Lifton, R. J., 615
Light, L. L., 281
Lightman, S., 698
Likert, R., 746, 747
Lin, C. Y. C., 477
Lincoln, R., 531
Linden, L., 101
Lindley, R., 436
Lindsay, P. H., 74, 150
Lindzey, G., 397
Linial, M., 42
Linn, S., 485
Lipmann, J. J., 47
Litman, C., 522
Locke, B. Z., 682
Locke, S. E., 622
Lockhart, R. S., 264
Locksley, A., 572
Loehlin, J. C., 397, 456
Loevinger, J., 378
Loewenstein, R. J., 647
Loftus, E. F., 274, 275, 575
Loftus, G. R., 133
Lokens, C. K., 577
Loney, G. L., 577
Long, B. C., 698
Long, G. M., 254
Loomis, B., 481
Loper, M., 707
Lorenz, K., 334, 335
Lorsch, J., 748
Losch, M. E., 571
Lovaas, D. I., 238
Lowe, G., 270
Lubin, A. J., 381, 382, 383
Lubin, B., 441
Lucas, P. A., 160
Luchins, A. S., 305, 306
Lumsdaine, A. A., 554
Lunt, P., 557
Luria, A. R., 67

Lykken, D. T., 80, 81, 412, 413
Lyles, J. N., 626
Lytton, H., 517

Maass, A., 277
Maccoby, E. E., 72, 454, 586, 587, 588
MacCoun, R., 575
MacDonald, K., 451
MacGregor, S., 474
MacKay, M., 669
Mackenzie, B., 455, 457
Mackle, D., 574
Mackintosh, N. J., 222
Mackworth, N. H., 133
MacLagan, D., 418
MacLeod, D. A., 107
MacPhie, D. L., 222
Madden, D. J., 500
Maddux, J. E., 553
Maher, B., 667
Mahl, G. F., 450
Mahoney, J. J., 743
Mai, N., 147
Maier, S. F., 239
Main, M., 513
Major, B., 588
Majors, R., 363
Malamut, B., 285
Malone, T. W., 341
Maloney, A. J. F., 481
Malpass, R. S., 276
Mangan, G. L., 202
Mann, L. M., 607
Manoach, D., 667
Manosevitz, M., 397, 583
Manschreck, T., 667
Manz, C. C., 748
Marcia, J. E., 543
Margande, N. A., 512
Markelbery, W. R., 481
Markides, K. S., 483, 540
Markovits, H., 496
Markus, H., 410
Marlatt, G. A., 605
Marmar, C., 720
Marmar, C. R., 704
Mars, D., 313
Marshall, G. D., 367
Marshall, R. M., 70
Marshall, W. A., 478
Martin, C. E., 582
Martin, D. C., 474
Martin, F. C., 48
Martin, G. A., 680, 693, 694
Martin, J. A., 523
Martin, J. C., 474
Martinez, D., 277
Maslow, A. H., 17, 342, 407, 408
Massaro, D. W., 160, 293
Massey, C., 497
Masten, A. S., 529
Matarazzo, J. D., 441, 595, 603
Mathivet, E., 72
Matin, L., 146
Matlin, A., 106, 107, 116, 121, 123, 135
Matlin, M., 116, 141, 308
Matthews, K. A., 603
Matzel, L., 222

Matzel, R. J., 222
Mauro, R., 380
Mayes, A. R., 283
Mayor, L., 656
Mazur, J. E., 239
McAdams, D., 377
McBurney, D. H., 157
McCarley, R. W., 187
McCartney, K., 466
McClearn, G. E., 412, 465, 466
McClelland, D. C., 356
McClelland, J. L., 246, 293
McCloskey, M., 273, 301
McCormack, W. M., 611
McCormick, D. A., 283
McCoy, J. K., 522
McCrae, R. R., 379, 446, 447, 623
McDaniel, M. A., 265
McDermott, J., 302
McDowd, J. M., 157, 500
McEvoy, G. M., 743
McEwan, N. H., 274
McGaugh, J. L., 286
McGlashan, T. H., 655, 719
McGowen, C. R., 698
McGrath, J. E., 562, 575, 576, 578
McGregor, D., 746, 747
McGue, M., 80, 81, 111, 413
McGuire, W., 393
McHorney, C., 48
McKeon, P., 607
McKim, W. A., 47, 197, 202, 711, 714
McKoon, G., 262
McLaren, R., 296
McLaughlin, S., 474
McLean, J., 454, 455
McLean, J. E., 469
McLoyd, V. C., 478
McLuhan, T. C., 594
McNair, D., 680
McNally, R. J., 644, 645
McNamara, C. G., 56
McNeill, D., 271
McVey, G., 350
Meacham, J. A., 543
Mead, M., 390
Mealey, L., 177
Medin, D. L., 298
Mednick, M. T., 311
Mednick, S. A., 311
Medvin, N., 578, 579
Meeker, M., 436
Meichenbaum, D. H., 616, 696
Melamed, L. E., 144
Melby, C., 582
Mellinger, J. C., 499
Melton, G. B., 520, 674
Meltzoff, A. N., 506
Melzack, R., 87, 122, 124
Mendelson, W. B., 647, 652, 653
Mendenhall, M., 743
Merikangas, K. R., 607
Mermelstein, R., 405
Merrill, M. A., 439
Mervis, C. B., 300
Meschulach-Sarfaty, O., 506
Meshberger, F. L., 83
Messick, D. M., 564

Subject Index

cross-cultural research on, 380
defined, 376
evaluation of genetic approaches to,
    413–414
factors in, 379t
genetics and, 412–414
hardy, 629–630
health and, 602–604
heritability of, 412–413
humanistic models of, 407–409
models of, 608
multiple, 649–650
psychoanalytic models of, 384–400
research methods in, 377–380
socialization of, 402–403
split, 649
theories of, in psychology, 380–383
Type A, 603
Type B, 603
Personality disorders, 668, 670–672
Personality profiles, faking, 447–448
Personalization, 630
Personal unconscious, 394
Person-centered therapy, 698
Personnel selection, 743
Personologists, 376
Person permanence, 514
Perspective
    aerial, 137–138
    linear, 137
Persuasion
    attitude changes and, 553–555
    model of, 555
Pervasiveness, 630
PET (positron emission tomography), 55, 56
Phallic stage, 388–389
Phencyclidine (PCP), 203, 204
Phenothiazines, 711
Pheromones, 119
Phi phenomenon, 146, 147f
Phobias, 643–644
Phobic disorders, factors associated with, 644
Phonemes, 318
Phonological rules, 318
Photographic memory, 268
Phrase structure approach, 319
Physical development, 471–483
Physiological activity, 167
Physiological addiction, 195
Piaget, Jean, 490–499
Pinel, Philippe, 685
Pinna, 113
Pitch of sound, 112
Pituitary, 76–77
PKC (protein kinase C), 222
PL (Public Law) 94–142, 444
Placebo, 21, 47
Place theory of hearing, 114–115
Plato, 8–9
Pleasure principle, 384
Pluralistic ignorance, 571
PMS (premenstrual syndrome), 653
PNS (peripheral nervous system), 51–52, 53f
Polarization, 576
Politics in workplace, 745–747
Pons, 58
Population, 727
Positive correlation, 735

Positively skewed polygon, 728–729
Positive reinforcement, 227–228
Positive reinforcement techniques, 694
Positron emission tomography (PET), 55, 56
Postconventional level, 532
Posthypnotic amnesia, 193
Posthypnotic suggestions, 192–193
Postparenthood, 536–537
Post-traumatic stress disorder, 615, 645–646
Posture and balance, 125
"Pot," 204
Power
    nature of, 746–747
    outcomes of use of, 745–746
    and politics in workplace, 745–747
    sources of, 745
Power tests, 443
Pragma, 579t
Prägnanz, law of, 134
Preattentive processes, 155
Preconscious, 392
Preconventional level, 532
Prediction, 737
Predictive validity, 428–429
Preference technique, 485–486
Prefrontal cortex, 67
Prefrontal lobotomy, 708–709
Pregnancy, phases of, 471–473
Prejudice, 572–574
    racial, 572–573
    reducing, 573–574
Premack principle, 234–235
Premenstrual syndrome (PMS), 653
Premotor cortex, 67
Preoperational thinking, 492–493
Preparedness, 240
Preschool education, 488–489, 490f
Prescientific psychology, 10–11
Prescriptive grammar, 319
Present-day treatment, 685–688
Prevention of mental disorders, 686
Primary appraisal, 619
Primary effect, 259
Primary mental abilities, 433
Primary reinforcers, 229
Primary visual cortex, 67
Privacy, right to, 31
Proactive interference, 279
Problem solving, 301–308
    exercise in, 304t
    hindrances in, 305–308
    stages in, 302–305
Procedural memory, 261
Processes, memory, 252
Productivity, 328
Progressive relaxation, 626
Projective techniques, 448–451
Projective tests, 377
Proof, nature of, 19–20
Prophecy, self-fulfilling, 560–561
Prosocial behavior, 569–571
    sex differences and, 587–588
Prosodic features, 361
Prospective study, 482
Protanopia, 106, 107f
Protein kinase C (PKC), 222
Protocol, 293
Protocol analysis, 293

Prototype-matching theory, 149–150
Proximal stimulus, 141
Proximity, acquaintance process and, 577
Proximity law of grouping, 135, 136f
Proximo-distal development, 472
Prozac, 714–715
Psychedelic drugs, 203–205
Psychoactive drugs, 194–195, 196t
Psychoanalysis, 688
    feminist revisions of, 398–400
Psychoanalytic approach, 17
    evaluation of, 400
Psychoanalytic models of personality,
    384–400, 639
    defined, 384
Psychoanalytic perspective, modern, 690
Psychoanalytic therapy, 688–690
Psychobiography, 377
Psychodynamic psychotherapy, 688
Psychogenic amnesia, 649
Psychoimmunology, 48
Psycholinguistics, 317–318
Psychological Abstracts (PA), 753–754
Psychological addition, 196–197
Psychological assessment
    in different cultures, 457–458
    social issues in, 452–458
Psychological control
    health and, 598–602
    loss of, with aging, 600–602
Psychological disorders
    categorizing, 642–643
    contemporary views of, 638–640
    defined, 637–638
    defining and diagnosing, 636–643
Psychologically hardy individuals, 630
Psychological maltreatment, 522–523
Psychological numbing, 615
Psychological research
    with animals, 27–30
    evaluating, 30–31
Psychological tests
    characteristics of scores, 427–431
    construction and standardization of,
        426–427
    functions and characteristics of, 424–431
    individual differences measured by, 425–426
    issues of interpretation of, 426–431
    research on bias in, 458
Psychology, 1–2
    American, 13–15
    applications of, 35
    clinical, 3
    contemporary approaches to, 15–18
    counseling, 3–4
    definition of, 2–3
    detailed sources on library work in, 755
    developmental. *See* Developmental
        psychology
    diversity of, 3–8
    environmental, 6f
    experimental, 6–7
    Gestalt, 12
    health, 594–595
    history of, 8–15
    human factors, 6, 158
    industrial-organizational. *See* Industrial-
        organizational psychology (I/O)